Street by Str...

BIRMING
WOLVERHAMPTON
DUDLEY, SOLIHULL, STOURBRIDGE, WALSALL, WEST BROMWICH

Aldridge, Alvechurch, Codsall, Coleshill, Dorridge, Halesowen, Knowle, Pelsall, Sutton Coldfield, Wombourne

C000299282

Ist edition May 2001

© Automobile Association Developments Limited 2001

This product includes map data licensed from Ordnance Survey® with the permission of the Controller of Her Majesty's Stationery Office. © Crown copyright 2000. All rights reserved. Licence No: 399221.

Published by AA Publishing (a trading name of Automobile Association Developments Limited, whose registered office is Norfolk House, Priestley Road, Basingstoke, Hampshire, RG24 9NY. Registered number 1878835).

Mapping produced by the Cartographic Department of The Automobile Association.

A CIP Catalogue record for this book is available from the British Library.

Printed by G. Canale & C. S.P.A., Torino, Italy

The contents of this atlas are believed to be correct at the time of the latest revision. However, the publishers cannot be held responsible for loss occasioned to any person acting or refraining from action as a result of any material in this atlas, nor for any errors, omissions or changes in such material. The publishers would welcome information to correct any errors or omissions and to keep this atlas up to date. Please write to Publishing, The Automobile Association, Fanum House, Basing View, Basingstoke, Hampshire, RG21 4EA.

Ref: MD033

Key to map pages ii-iii

Key to map symbols iv-1

Enlarged scale pages 2-7

Street by Street 8-223

Index – towns & villages 224-225

Index – streets 227-301

Index – featured places 301-318

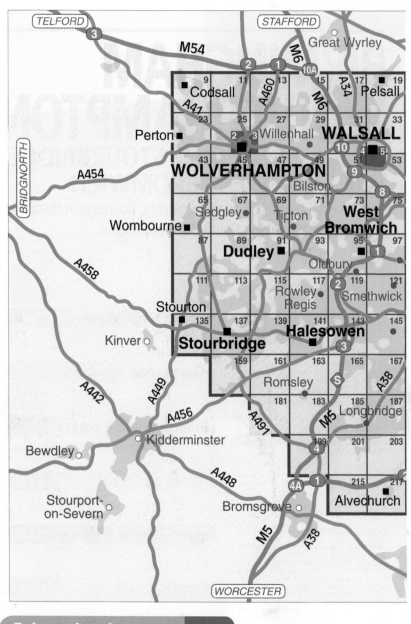

ii

TELFORD

STAFFORD

M54

Great Wyrley

9 · Codsall · 11 · A460 · 13 · M6 · 10A · 15 · A34 · 17 · 19 · Pelsall

A41

23 · 25 · 27 · Willenhall · 29 · 31 · 33

Perton · 2 · 3 · **WALSALL**

BRIDGNORTH

A454

43 · 45 · 47 · 49 · 10 · 4 · 5 · 51 · 53

WOLVERHAMPTON

9

Bilston · 8

65 · 67 · 69 · 71 · 73 · 75

Sedgley · Tipton · **West Bromwich**

Wombourne

87 · 89 · 91 · 93 · 95 · 97

Dudley · Oldbury · 1

111 · 113 · 115 · 117 · 2 · 119 · 121

A458 · Rowley Regis · Smethwick

Stourton · 135 · 137 · 139 · 141 · 143 · 145

Kinver · **Stourbridge** · **Halesowen** · 3

A442 · A449 · 159 · 161 · 163 · 165 · 167

Romsley · S · A38

A456 · 181 · 183 · 185 · 187 · M5 · Longbridge

Bewdley · A491 · 199 · 201 · 203

Kidderminster · 4

4A · 1 · 215 · 217

Stourport-on-Severn · Bromsgrove · **Alvechurch**

M5 · A38 · A448

WORCESTER

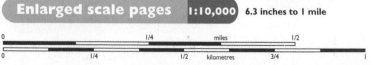

Enlarged scale pages 1:10,000 6.3 inches to 1 mile

0 · 1/4 · miles · 1/2

0 · 1/4 · 1/2 · kilometres · 3/4 · 1

BURTON UPON TRENT

NOTTINGHAM

Brownhills

Tamworth

A461 | 21

A5

A38

Aldridge | 35 | 37 | 39 | 41

A453

Fazeley

A5

10

S

55 | 57 | 59 | 61 | 63

Atherstone

Kingstanding

Sutton Coldfield

M42

77 | 79 | 81 | 83 | 85

Hartshill

7

M6

A452

A38

9

A34

Erdington

99 | 101 | 103 | 105 | 107 | 109

Handsworth

6

5

Castle Bromwich

8

Coleshill

123 | 125 | 127 | 129 | 131 | 133

6 | 7

BIRMINGHAM

7/7A

4

M6

S

3

147 | 149 | 151 | 153 | 155 | 157

Harborne

Sheldon

Birmingham

NEC

169 | 171 | 173 | 175 | 177 | 179

Selly Oak

A435

A41

6

Stonebridge

A45

189 | 191 | 193 | 197

Shirley

Solihull

A34

Knowle

Coventry

205 | 207 | 209 | 211 | 213

Hollywood

4

Dorridge

Balsall Common

A46

219 | 221 | 223

3

3A

Redditch

M42

16

M40

Kenilworth

3.6 inches to 1 mile

Scale of main map pages 1:17,500

0 | 1/2 | miles | 1

0 | 1/2 | 1 | kilometres | 1 1/2

iv

Junction 9	Motorway & junction
Services	Motorway service area
	Primary road single/dual carriageway
Services	Primary road service area
	A road single/dual carriageway
	B road single/dual carriageway
	Other road single/dual carriageway
	Restricted road
	Private road
← ←	One way street
	Pedestrian street
	Track/ footpath
	Road under construction
	Road tunnel
P	Parking

P+	Park & Ride
	Bus/coach station
	Railway & main railway station
	Railway & minor railway station
⊖	Underground station
⊖	Light railway & station
++++++++	Preserved private railway
LC	Level crossing
•—•—•	Tramway
--------	Ferry route
....	Airport runway
—·—·—·	Boundaries- borough/ district
▼▼▼▼▼▼▼	Mounds
93	Page continuation 1:17,500
7	Page continuation to enlarged scale 1:10,000

	River/canal lake, pier		♿	Toilet with disabled facilities
	Aqueduct lock, weir		⛽	Petrol station
465 ▲ Winter Hill	Peak (with height in metres)		PH	Public house
	Beach		PO	Post Office
	Coniferous woodland		📖	Public library
	Broadleaved woodland		ℹ	Tourist Information Centre
	Mixed woodland		♟	Castle
	Park		🏛	Historic house/ building
	Cemetery		Wakehurst Place NT	National Trust property
	Built-up area		Ⓜ	Museum/ art gallery
	Featured building		✝	Church/chapel
	City wall		♈	Country park
A&E	Accident & Emergency hospital		🎭	Theatre/ performing arts
	Toilet			Cinema

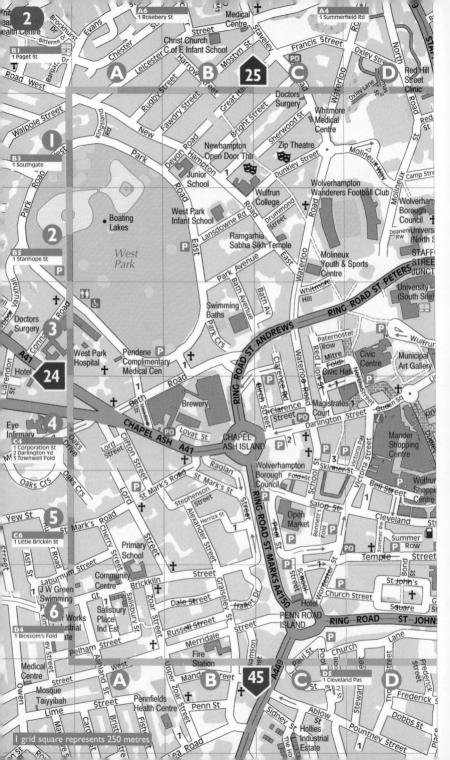

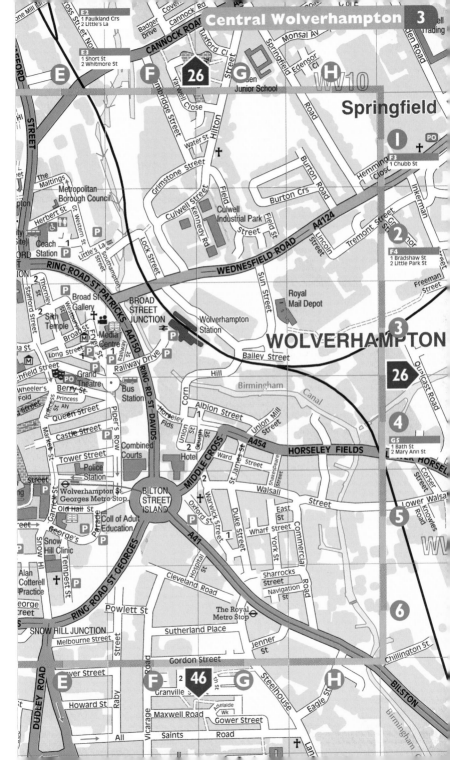

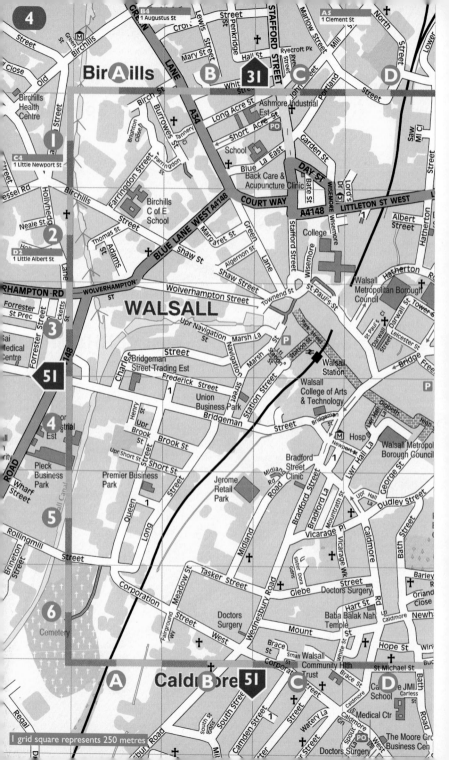

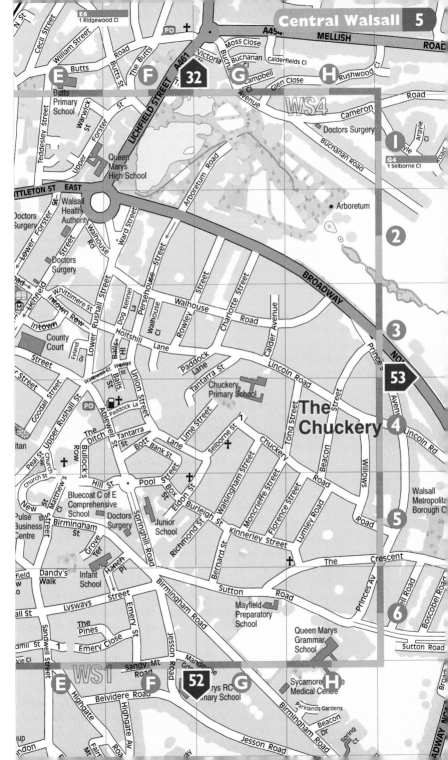

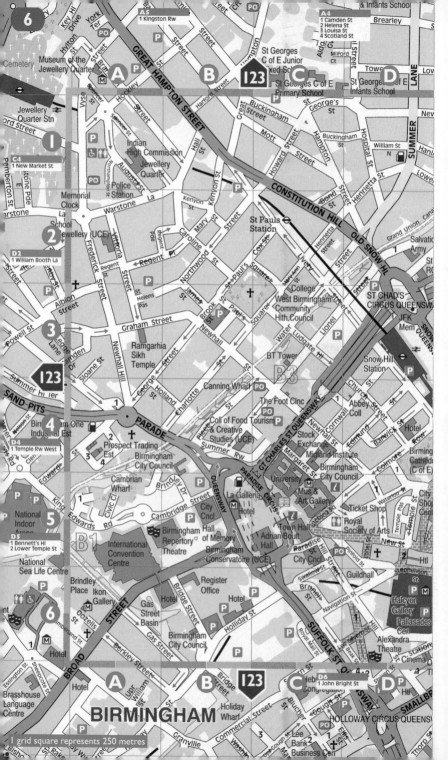

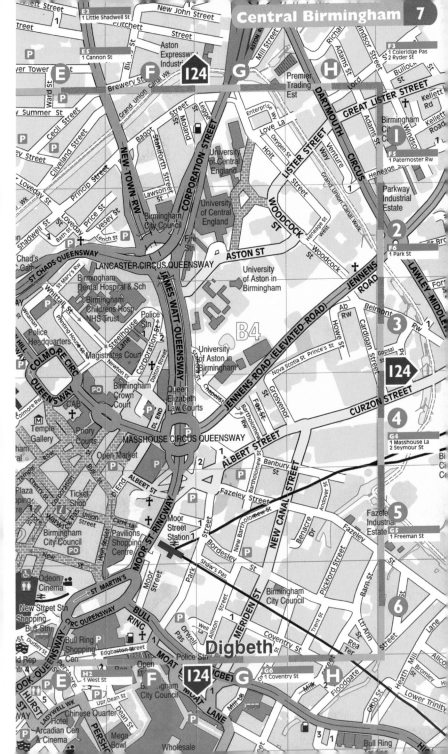

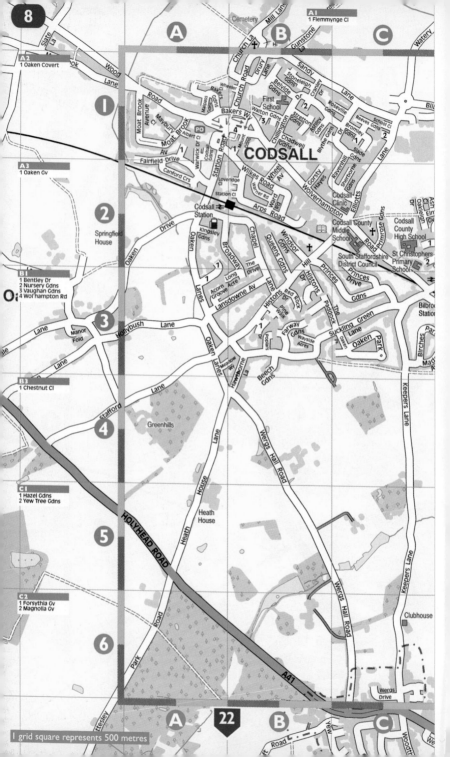

Bilbrook

Lane Green

Dam Mill

Palmers Cross

Claregate

Bilbrook

Lane Green County First School

Manor House Pk

Joeys Lane

Middle School

Homefield Rd

Mill Gv

Pendeford

Withers Rd

Lime Tree Gdns

Cherry Tree La

Bilbrook Medical Centre

Florence Rd

Clifton Gdns

Downie Rd

Brookfield Rd

Ringhills Rd

Green Oak Rd

Wesley Av

Oakfield Rd

Wesley Rd

Lane Green Rd

Orchard

Carter Av

Duck Lane

Birches

Parkes Av

Kynaston

Greenacre Dr

Meadow Vale

South View Close

Palmers Cl

Palmers Wy

Charters Av

Birches First School

Birches Avenue

Eastward Grn

Eastward Cl

Lane Green Avenue

Codsall Road

River Penk

Palmers Cross Primary School

Coniston Road

Buttermere Cl

Windermere Rd

Ennerdale Rd

Thirlmere

Grasmere Road

Derwent Road

Links Av

Staffordshire County

Coppice Lane

Wolverhampton

Cemetery

Mill Lane

Wobaston Rd

Wobaston Lane

Barnhurst Lane

Balliol Business Park

Shropshire Union Canal

Weyhill

Fallow

Middlefield

Torfield

Conifield

Ryefield

Barnwood Rd

The Brackens

Dovecote Junior & Infant Sc

Aldersley High School

Granary Rd

Forge

Ryefield

Fullerton

Eastney

Pendeford Avenue

Macrome Road

Lawnswood Av

Cheam Gdns

Calcot Dr

Green

Crestwood

Aldersley Avenue

Blackburn

PO

Knights Av

Tyninghame Av

Codsall Rd

Tyninghame Avenue

Coppice

Burland

Lynton

Derby Av

Sandford Rise

St Josephs Com Preparatory Sch

Golf Course

23

10

1 1 Cottage Vw

2

3

4

5

6

D E F

D E F

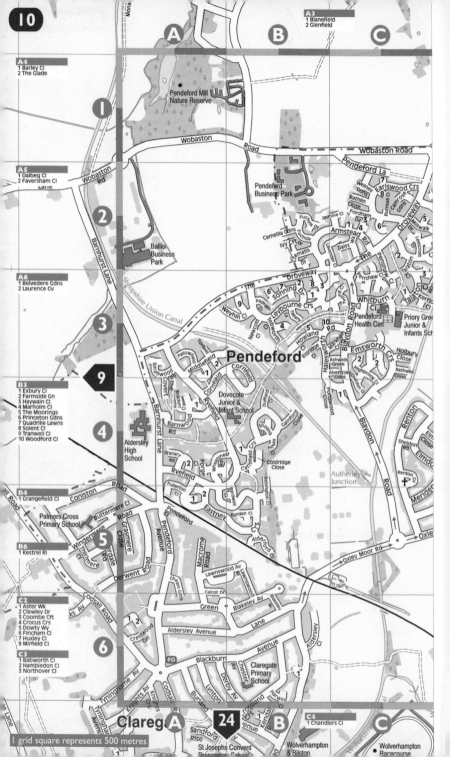

A   B   C

A3
1 Blanefield
2 Glenfield

A4
1 Barley Cl
2 The Glade

1

Pendeford Mill
Nature Reserve

Wobaston   Road   Wobaston Road

Pendeford La

A5
1 Daibeg Cl
2 Faversham Cl

Pendeford
Business Park

Wobaston Rd
Lane

Weiner Gdns   Larlswood Crs
Rathlin Close
Fordham Gv
Camore
Millwalk
Burnsall

Droveway

2

Balliol
Business
Park

Jasmine Cl
Camellia Gdns
Fuchsia
Ivy Cft
ematis

Daisy
Armstead Rd

The Penshaw

Barnhurst Lane
Shropshire Union Canal

A6
1 Belvedere Gdns
2 Laurence Gv

The
Droveway
Sonning Dr

Whitburn
Cl
Talaton
Talaton Cl

3

Pendeford

Weyhill
Newcott

Levbourne Crs

Pendeford
Health Cen

Priory Gree
Junior &
Infants Sch

Howland
Cl

9

B3
1 Exbury Cl
2 Farmside Gn
3 Haywain Cl
4 Marholm Cl
5 The Moorings
6 Princeton Gdns
7 Quadrille Lawns
8 Solent Cl
9 Tranwell Cl
10 Woodford Cl

4

Smallwood
Fallowfield
Middlefield
Cornfield
Cornfield

Dovecote
Junior &
Infant School

Emsworth Crs
Blaydon Rd

Holbury
Close
Rathwell
Close

Ashwells Grove
Highbrook
Alverstoke Close
Cl

Aldersley
High School

Barnwo
Rd
Forge

Gainsford
Close

Coldridge
Close

Blaydon   Road

Renton
Elm
Close
Eimdon

B4
1 Grangefield Cl

Coniston
Road

Ryefield
Granary
Rd

Wrasshear

Fullerton

Eastney

Borden Cl

Autherley
Junction

Oxley

Renton

Merlder

Palmers Cross
Primary School

Buttermere Cl
Grasmere
Close
Windermere
Road

Pendeford
Avenue

B6
1 Kestrel Ri

5

Windermere
Thirlmere
Derwent Rd

Pendeford
Road

Oxley Moor Rd

C2
1 Aster Wk
2 Clewley Dr
3 Coombe Cft
4 Crocus Crs
5 Dowty Wy
6 Fincham Cl
7 Huxley Cl
8 Mirfield Cl

6

Codsall Road
ks Av

Macrome
Road
Lawnswood Av
Calcot Dr

Green   Blakeley Av

Aldersley Avenue

Crestwood Gdn
Cheam Gdns

Lane

Aldersley

C3
1 Babworth Cl
2 Hambledon Cl
3 Northover Cl

PO

Blackburn

Tyninghame Av

Codsall Road
Knights
Av
Knights
Avenue

Burland
Derby Av
Chester
Av

Lynton

Avenue

Claregate
Primary School

Harwin
Crossland
Crs
Kendal

Aldersley

Tyninghame
Lane

Sandford
Rise

St Josephs Convent

C4
1 Chandlers Cl

Wolverhampton
& Bilston

Wolverhampton
Racecourse

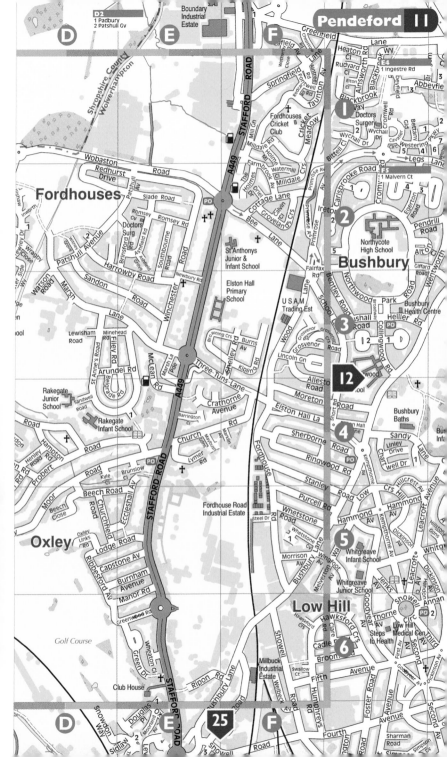

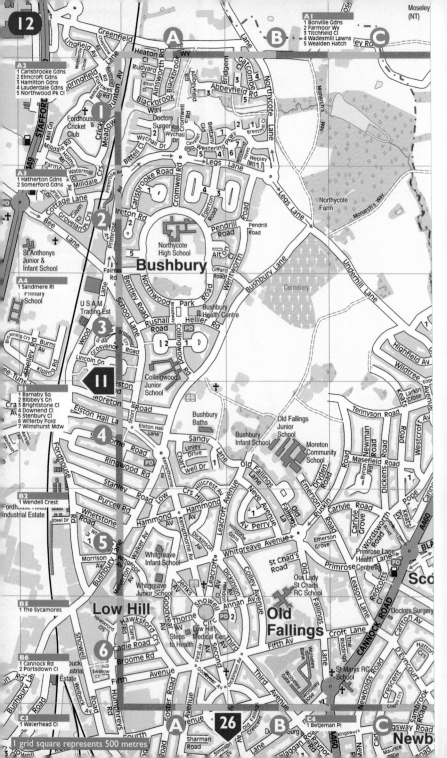

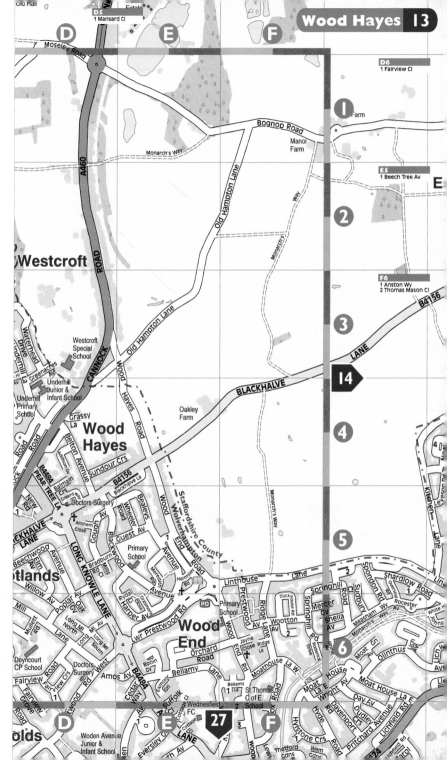

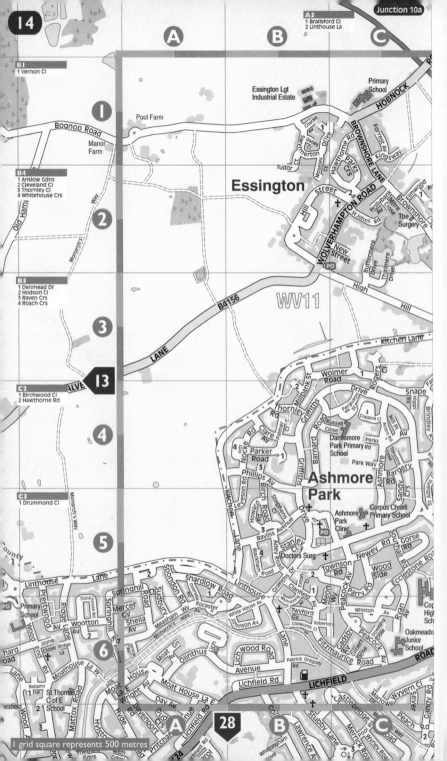

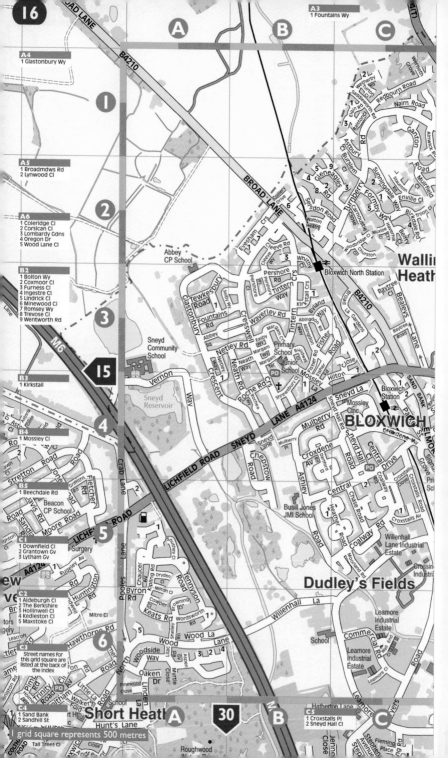

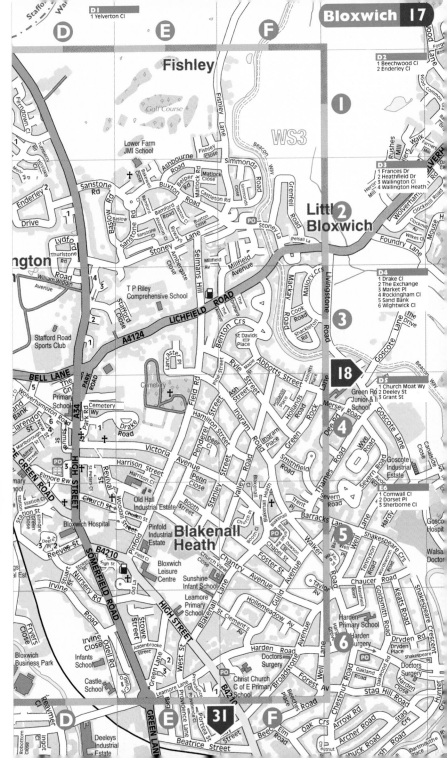

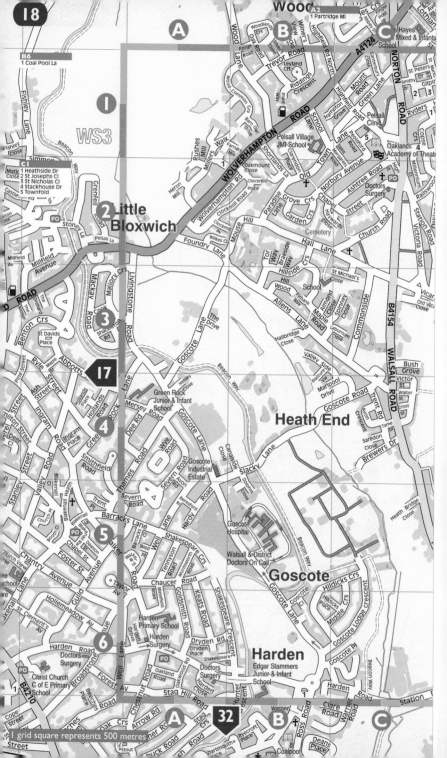

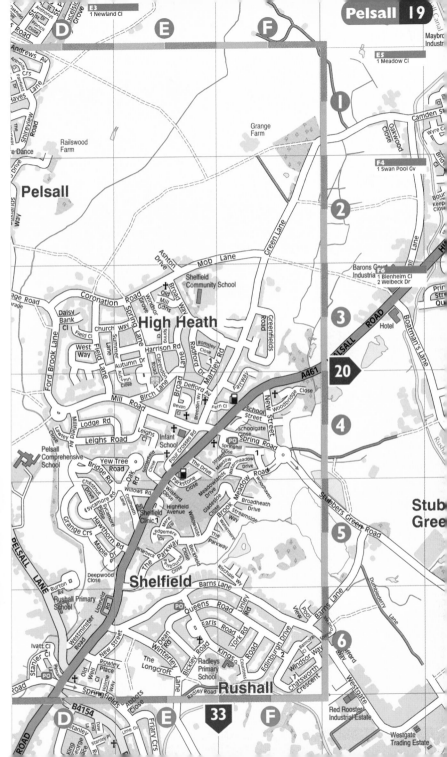

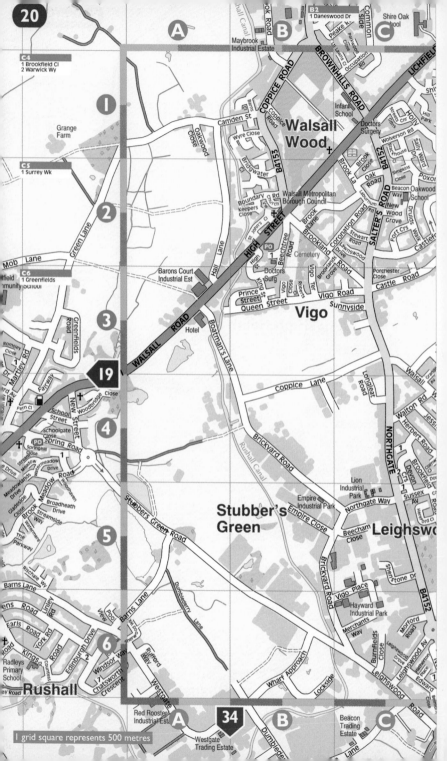

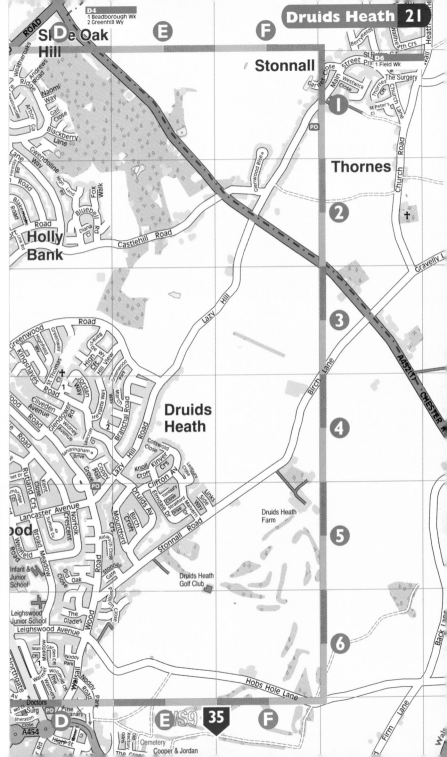

Side Oak Hill

D4
1 Beadborough Wk
2 Greenhill Wy

E

F

D6
1 Field Wk

Stonnall

St Peter's C of E Prim

The Surgery

St Peter's Cl

Thornes

1

Church Road

2

Gravelly L

3

A452(T) · CHESTER R

Holly Bank

Castlehill Road

Lazy Hill

Greenwood Road

Kingshayes Road

Road

Cliveden Avenue

Glendon Avenue

Sandringham Drive

Branchal Road

Lazy Hill Road

Copsy Rake

Druids Heath

Cotswold Close

Knoll Croft

Kinver Crs

Clifton Av

Elmdale Dr

Links Slade

Way

Druids Av

Birch Croft

Mountford Crs

Stonnall Road

Druids Heath Farm

4

Birch Lane

Glenwood Rise

5

Druids Heath Golf Club

Lancaster Avenue

Norfolk Crescent

Rutland Crs

Broad Meadow

Wellfield Road

Infant & Junior School

Leighswood Junior School

Leighswood Avenue

Old Oak

The Glades

Northgate

Walsall Road

Noddy Park

Hobs Hole Lane

6

Back Lane

Firm Lane

D

PO

Doctors Surg

Sheraton Close

A454

High St

E/S9 **35** F

Cooper & Jordan

Cemetery

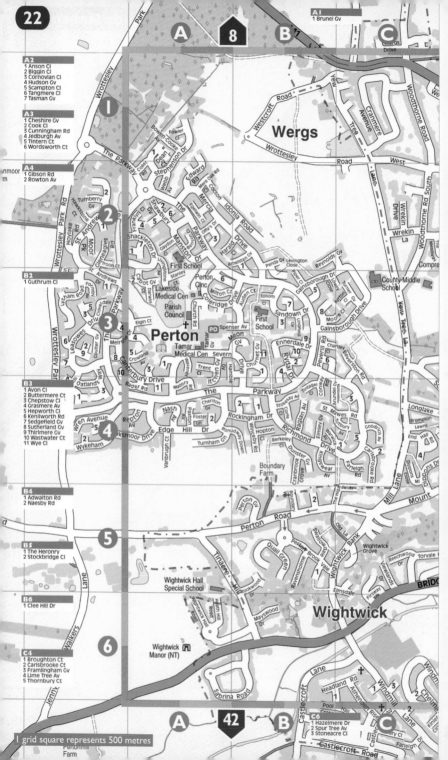

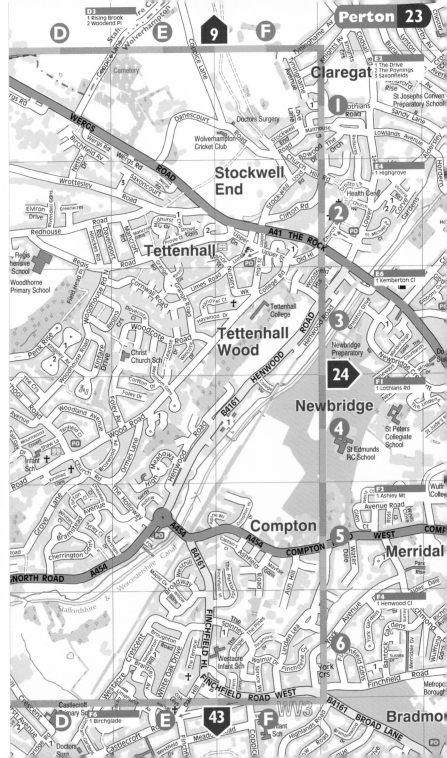

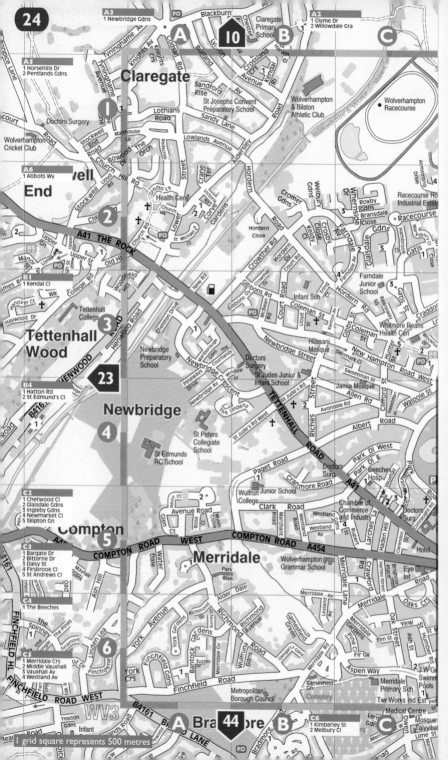

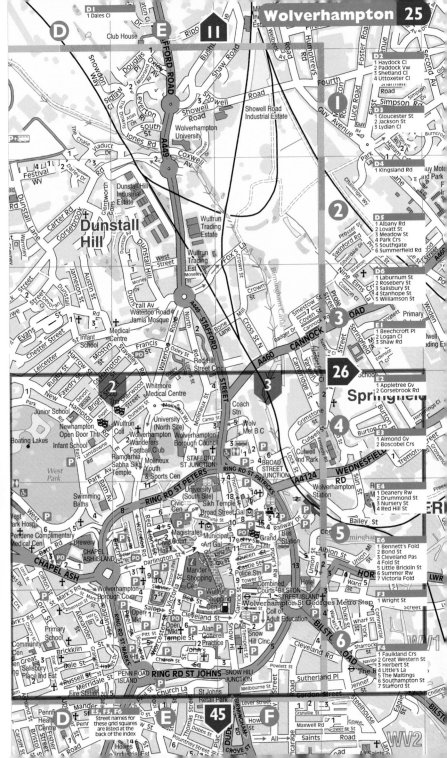

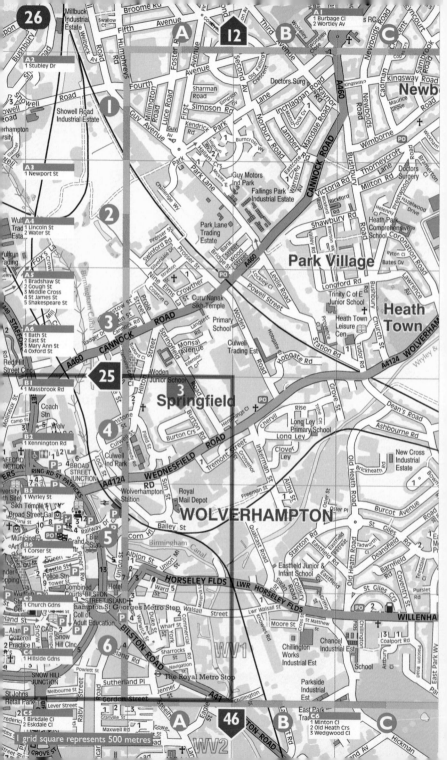

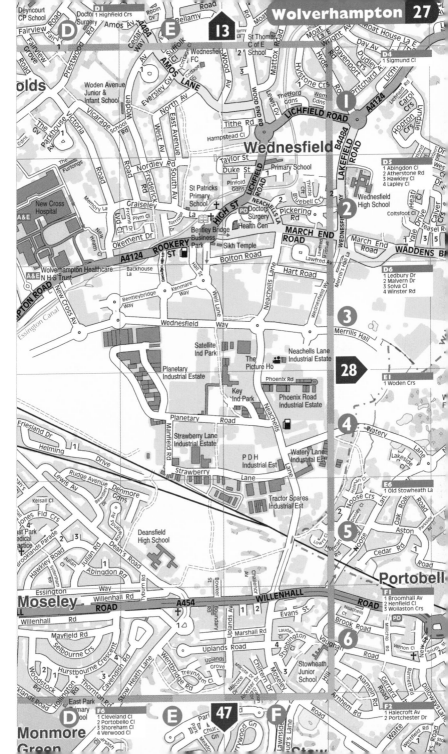

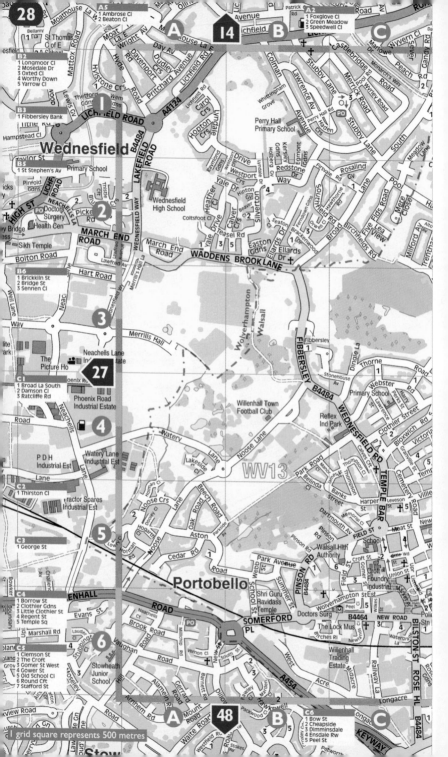

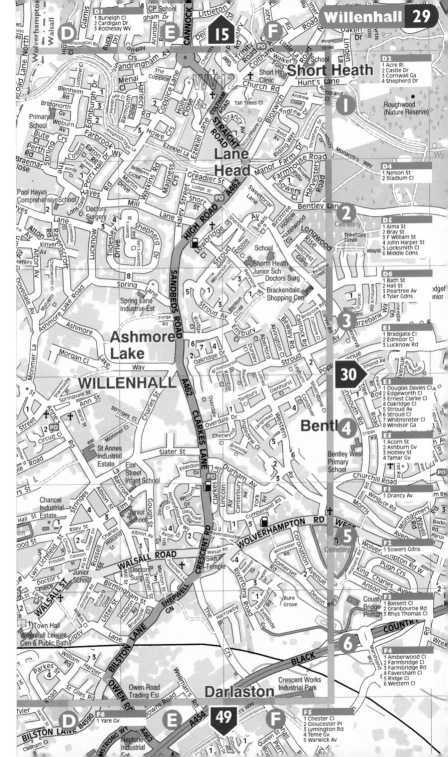

1 grid square represents 500 metres

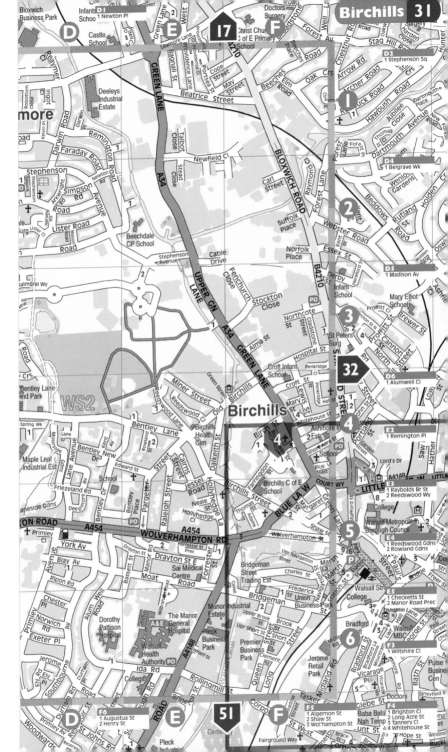

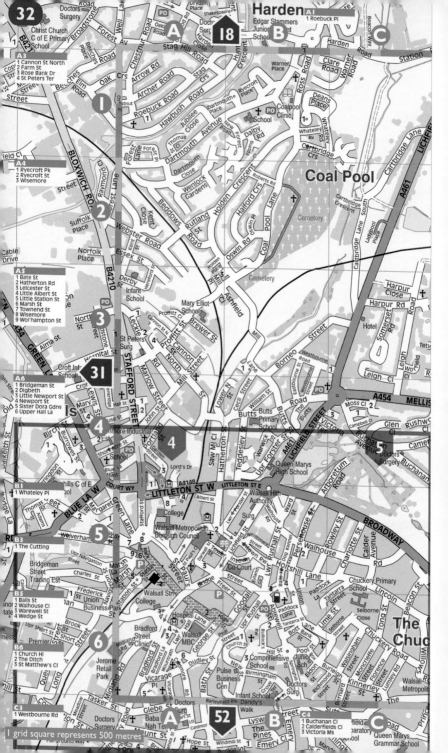

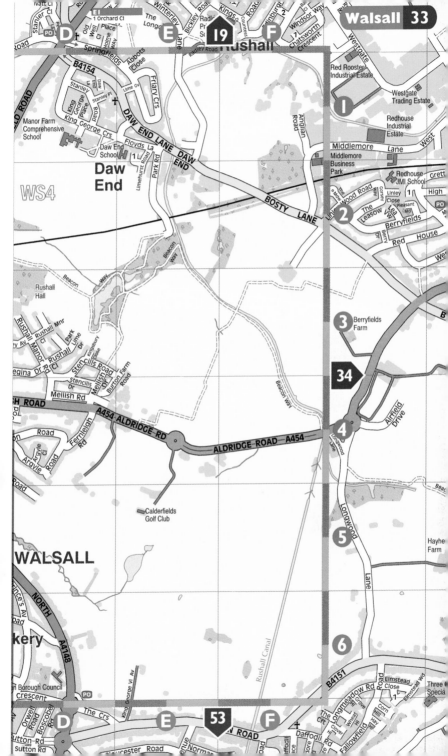

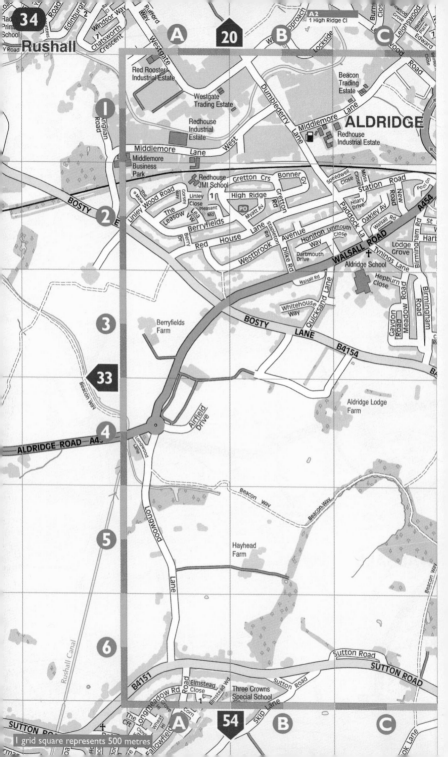

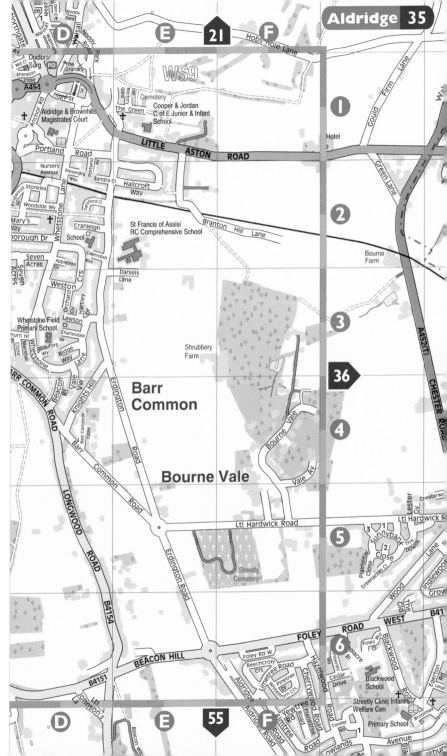

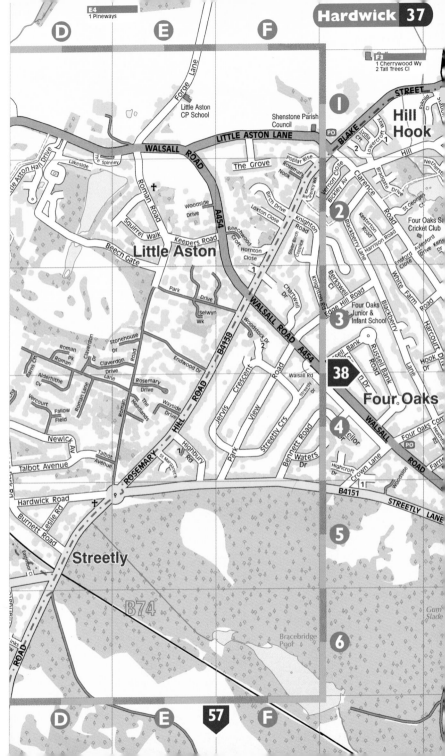

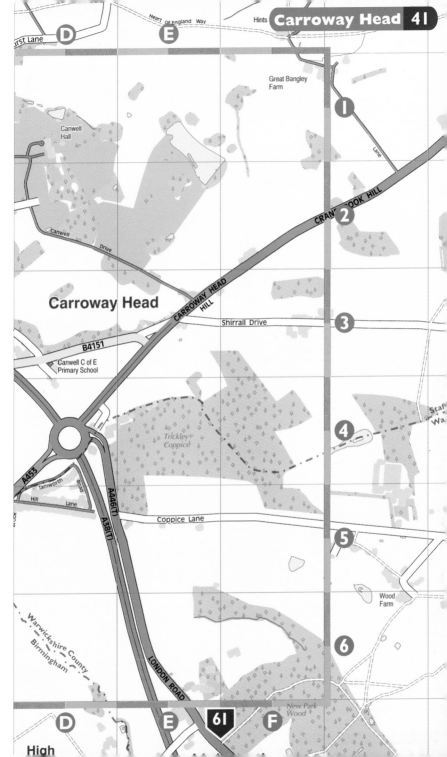

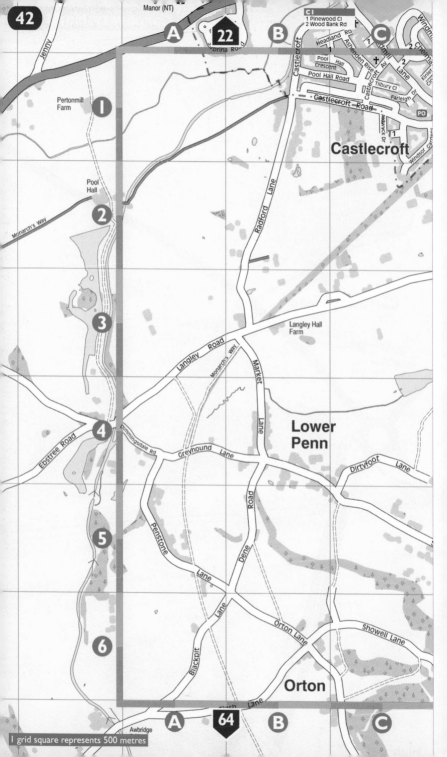

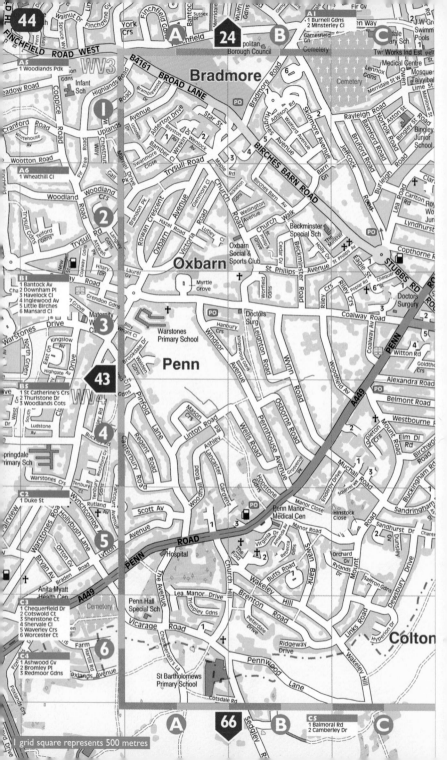

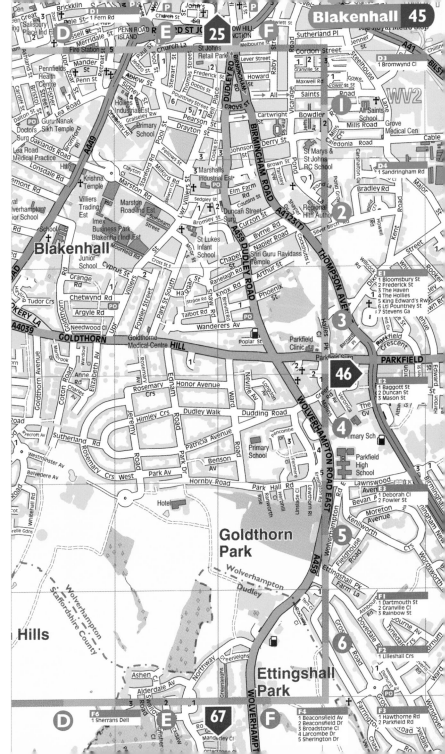

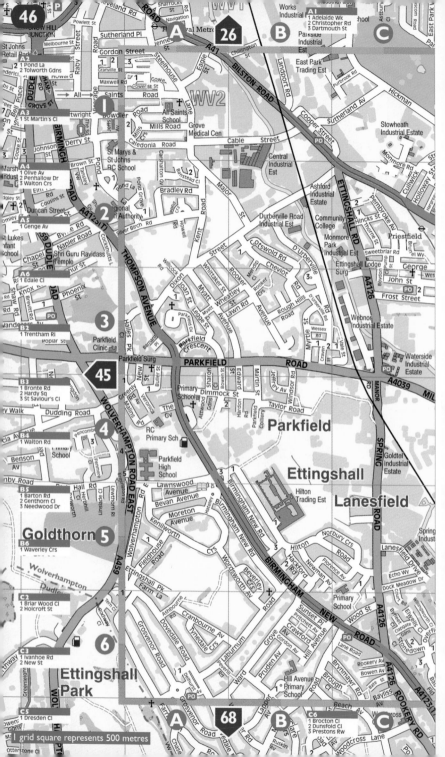

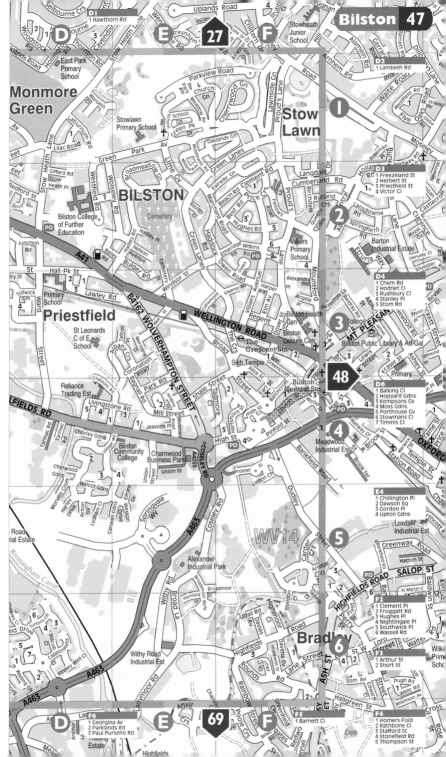

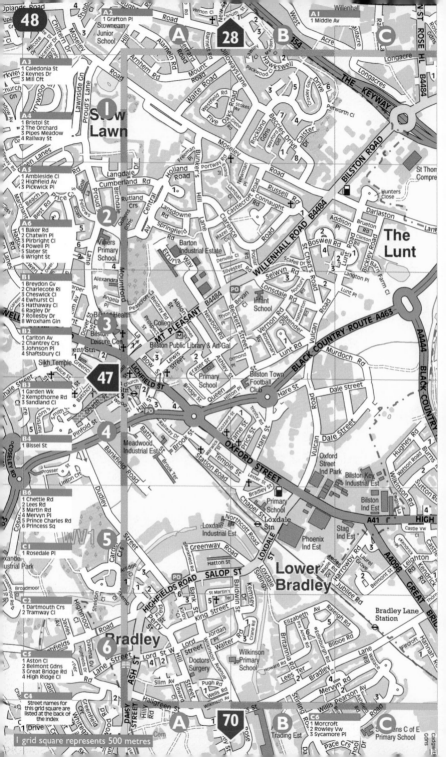

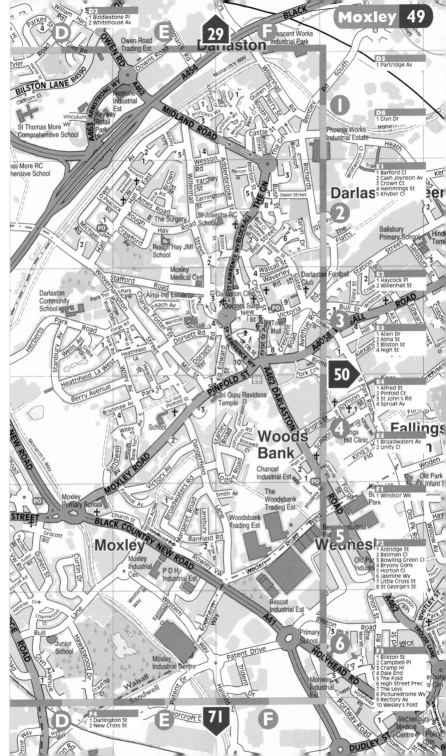

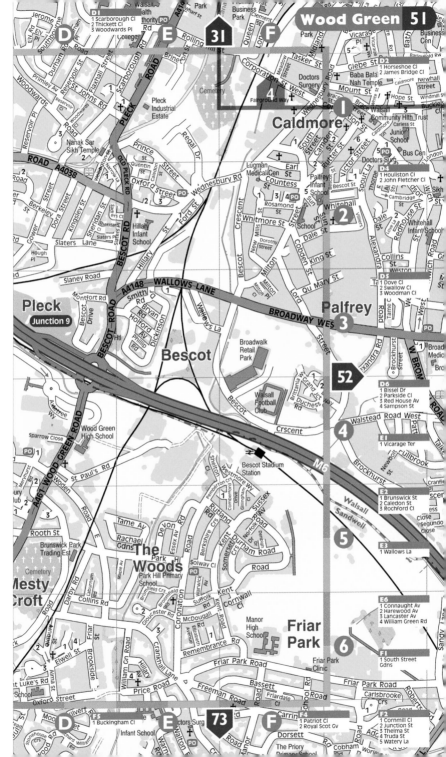

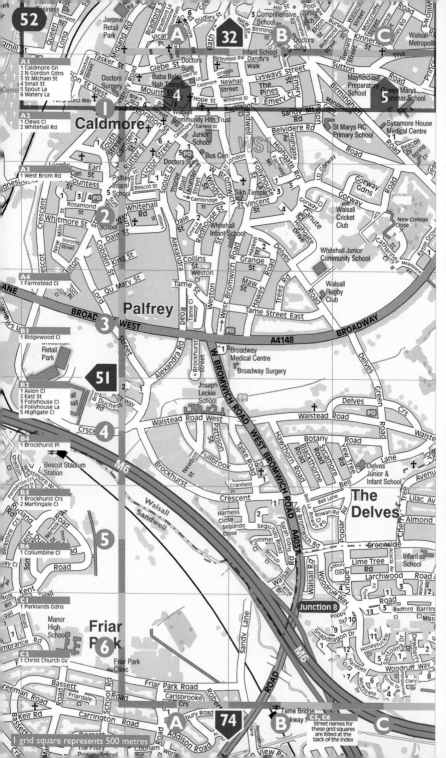

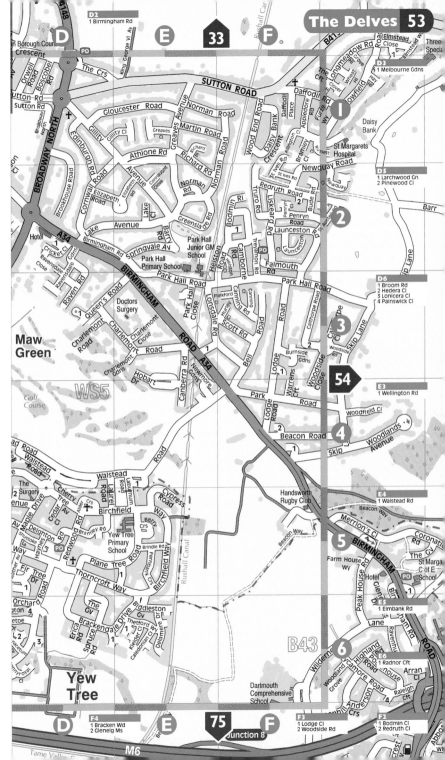

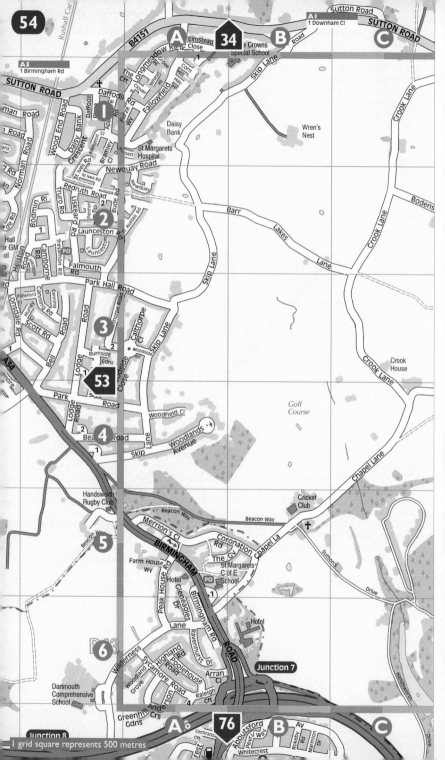

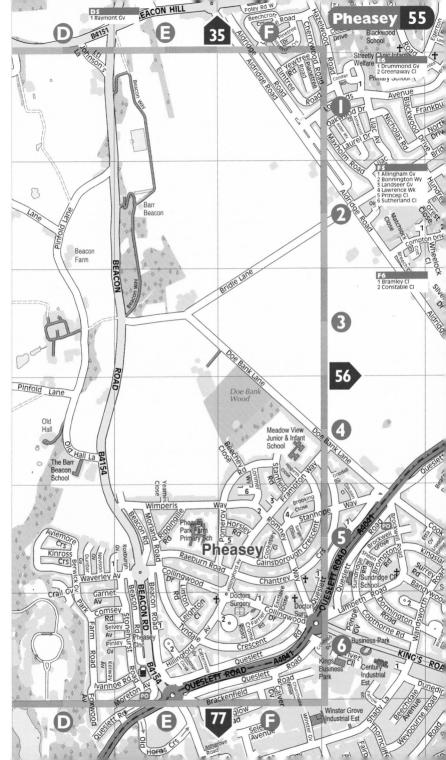

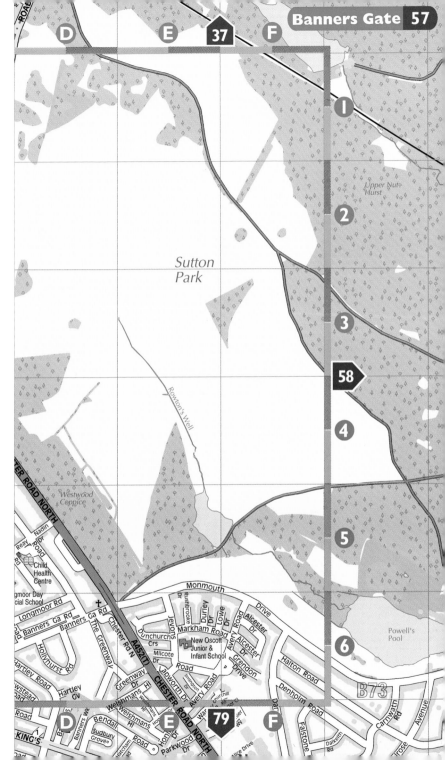

37

D E F

I

Upper Nut
Hurst

2

Sutton
Park

3

58

4

Rowton's Well

5

*Westwood
Coppice*

Child
Health
Centre

Powell's
Pool

6

B73

moor Day
cial School

Longmoor Rd

Monmouth

Reay

Naden

Road

Banners Ga Rd

Banners Ga The Greenway

Hollyhurst Rd

Hartley Road

Hartley GV

Chester Rd N

A452(T)

Greenway Dr

Dunchurch's Crs

Milcote Dr

Jevons

Markham Road

Lapworth Dr

Lowe Dr

Durley Dr

Rushbrooke Dr

New Oscott
Junior &
Infant School

Road

Avery Road

Grendon Drive

Alcester Dr

Alcester Dr

Drive

Halton Road

Denholm Road

Powell's
Pool

stead
oad

Road

Welshmans Hl

Welshmans Hl

Bendall

Sudbury
Grove

Banners Wk

CHESTER ROAD NORTH

Honiton

Parkwood Dr

Churchill Road

War

79

Dalkeith Rd

Falstone

Carnwath Rd

rose Avenue

D E F

KING'S

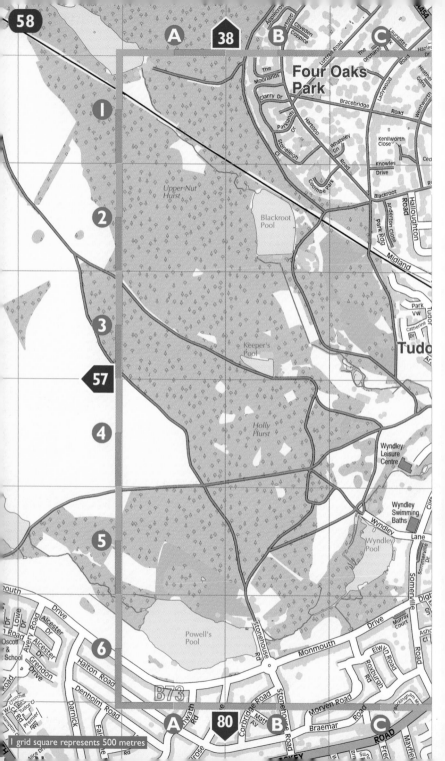

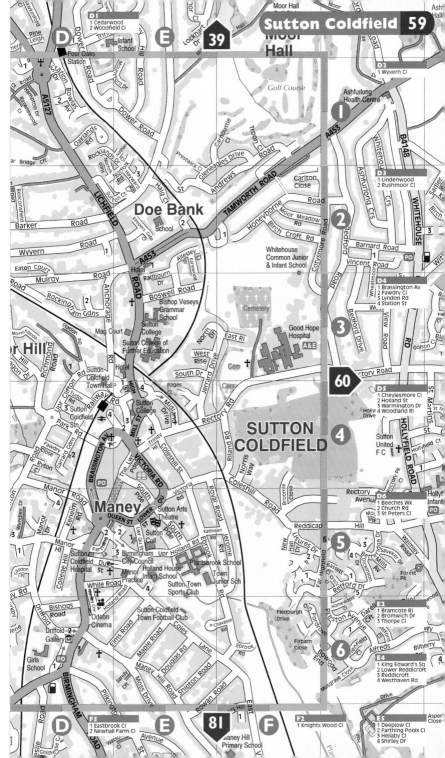

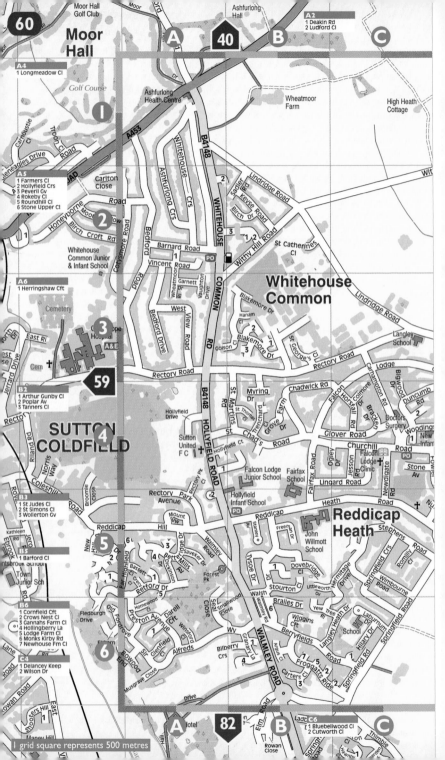

D3
1 Repington Wy

D4
1 The Falcons
2 Goodeve Wk
3 Repington Wy
4 Wilson Dr

**High
Heath**

**Littleworth
End**

New Park
Wood

Withy Hill Road

Withy Hill
Farm

Langley Mill
Farm

LONDON ROAD

LOND ROAD

A38(T)

A446(T)

**Falcon
Lodge**

Lindridge Road

The
Lindridge

Leigh

Wyatt

Crescent Rd

Road

Langley Hall Dr

Newhall Junior
& Infant School

Langley Hall
Rd

Arden Dr

ton Road

Hall Junior &
t School

Cattell
Dr

Holpeche Rd

Springfield Road

Lindridge Rd

Holly Lane

Moxhull
Hall (Hotel)

Holly Lane

thurst

Rd

Ox Leys Road

Langley
Hall

Holly Lane
Farm

Warwickshire County
Birmingham

Grov
Farr

Ox Leys
Farm

Ox Leys Road

Fox Hollies Rd

Langley
Gorse

Bull's Lane

A38(T)

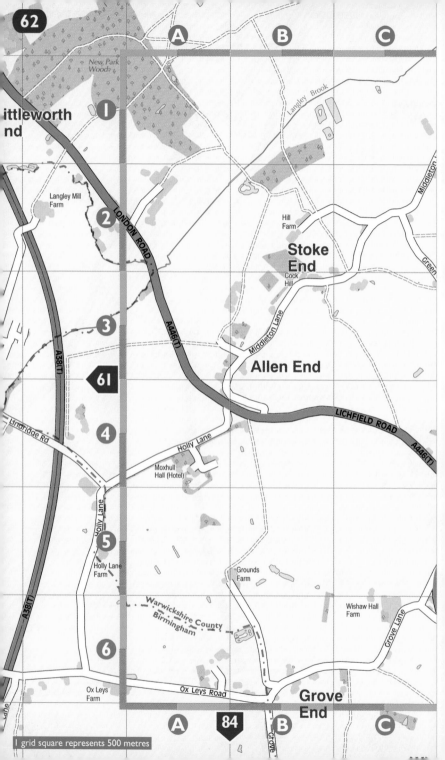

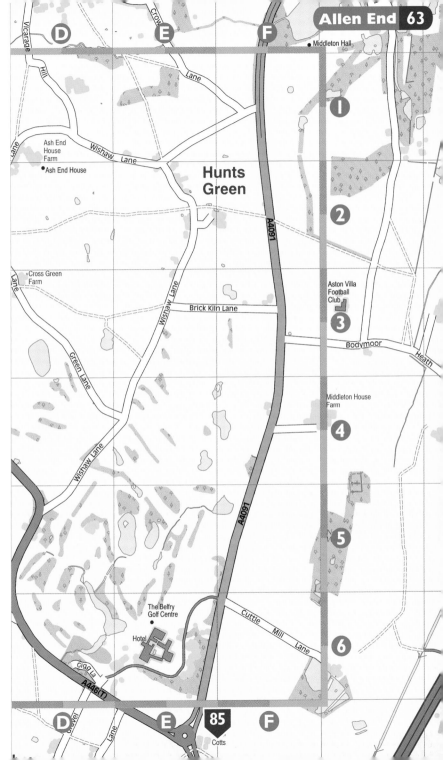

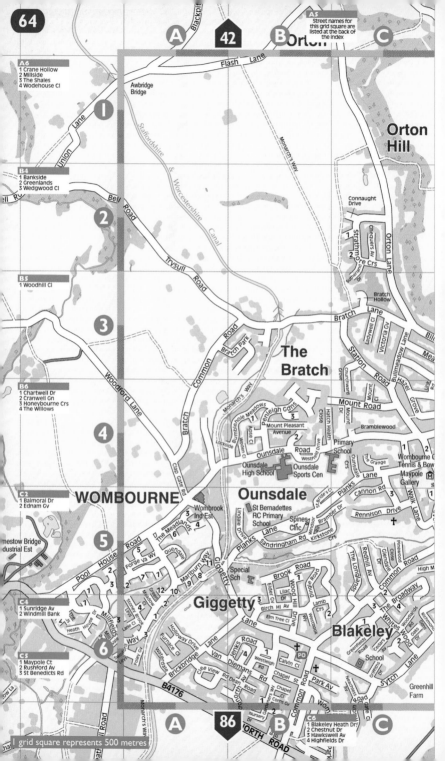

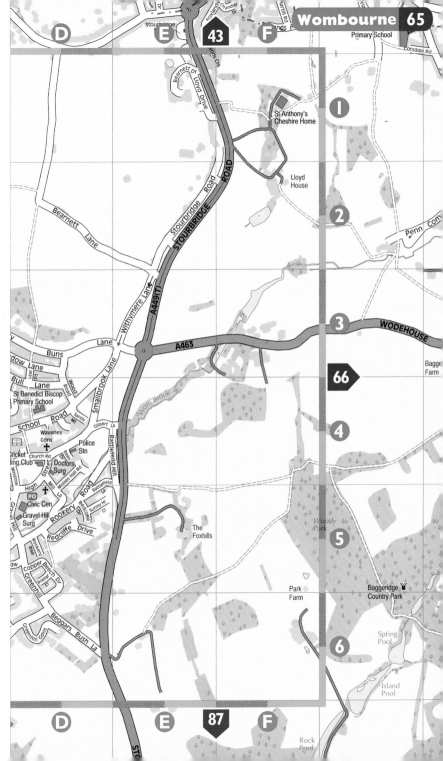

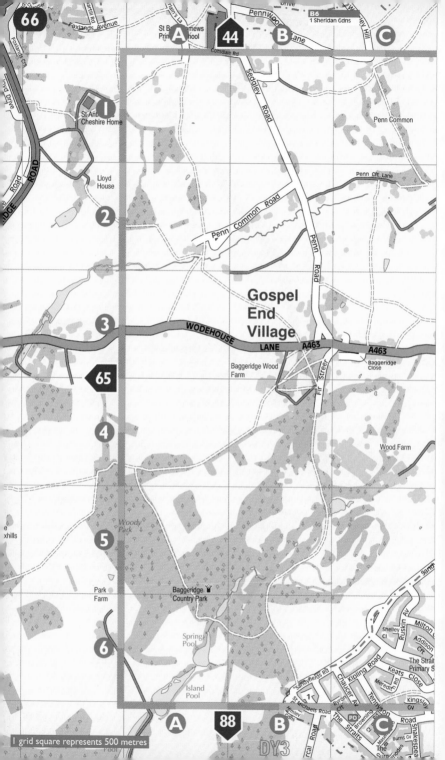

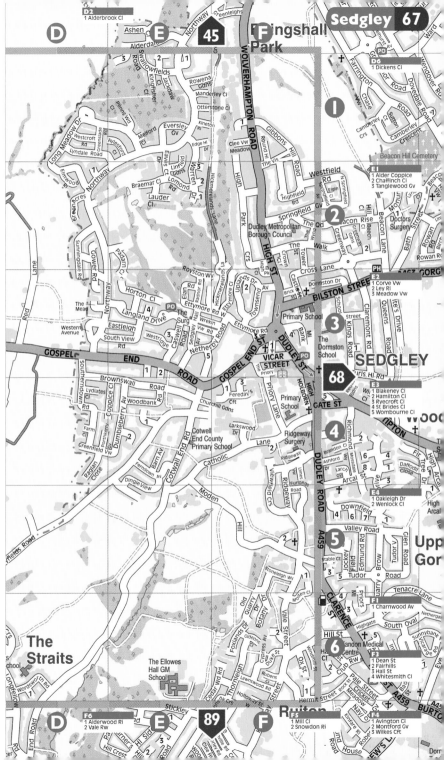

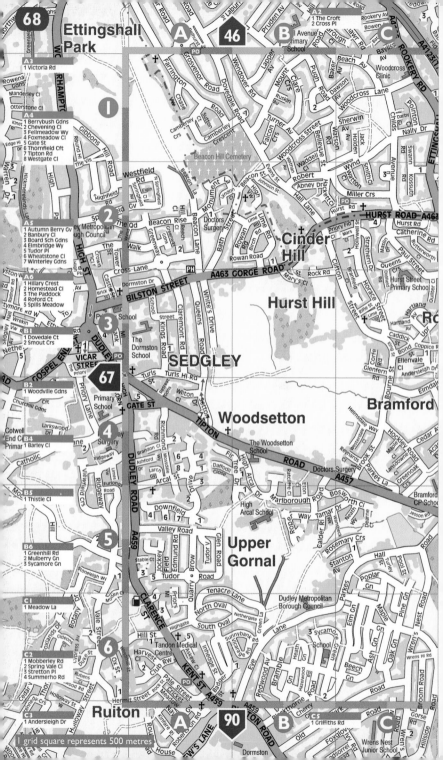

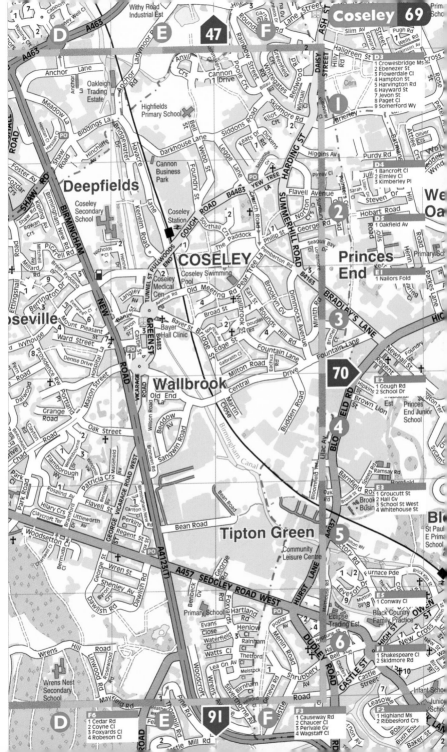

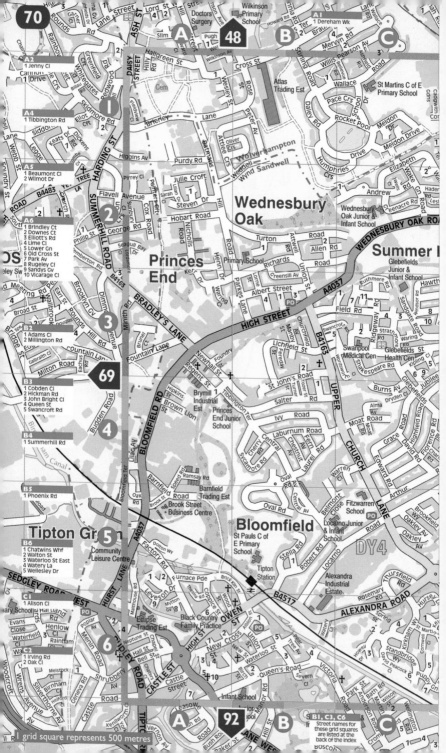

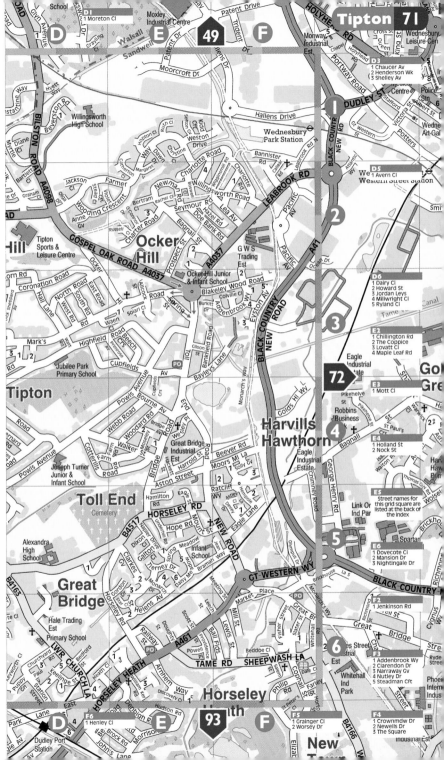

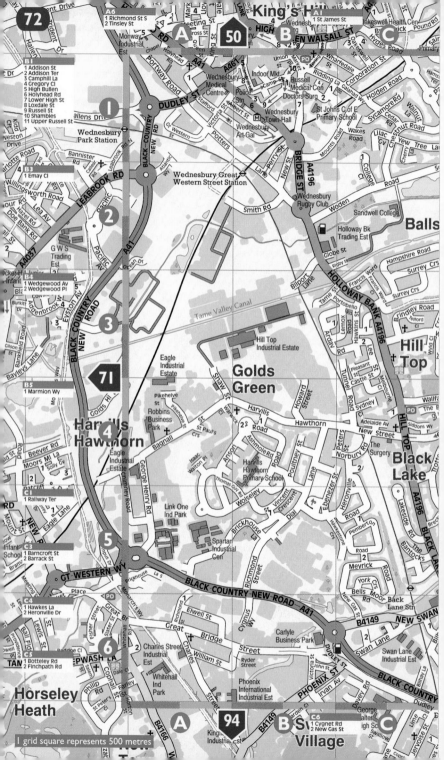

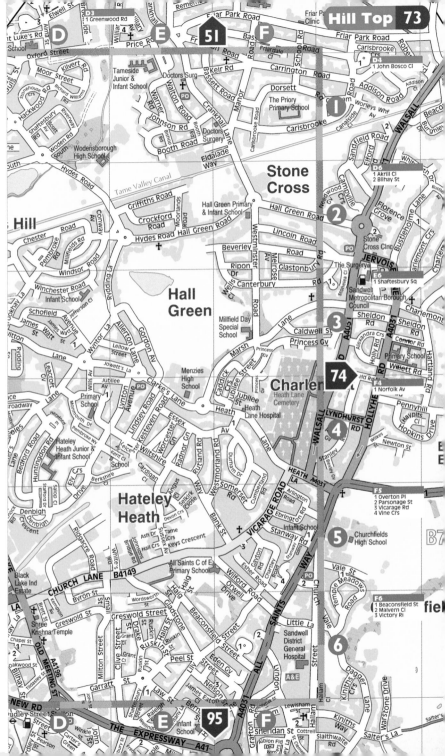

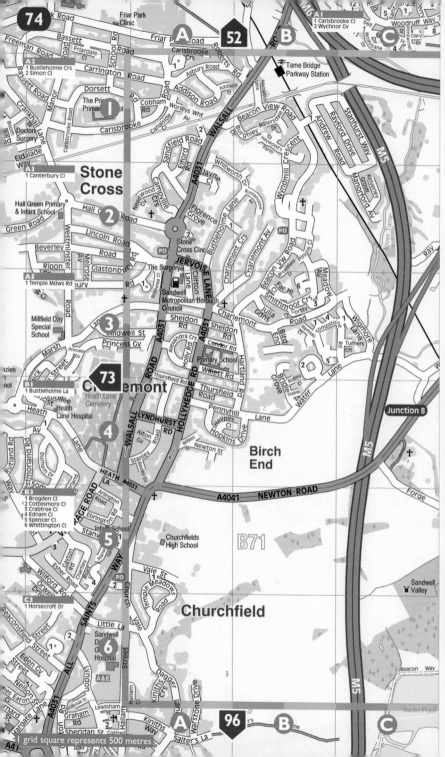

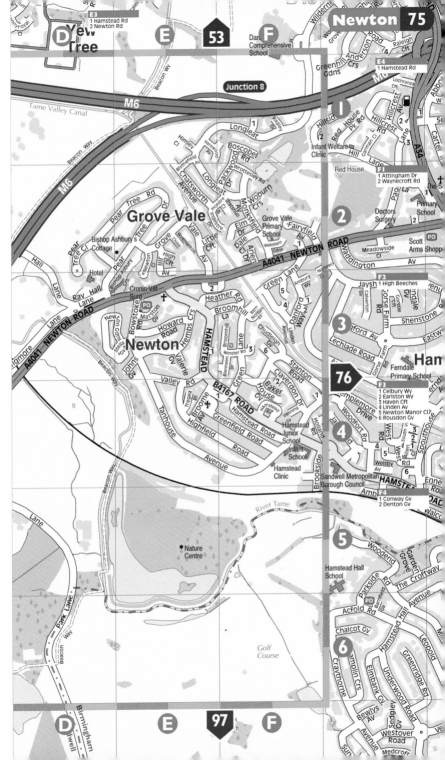

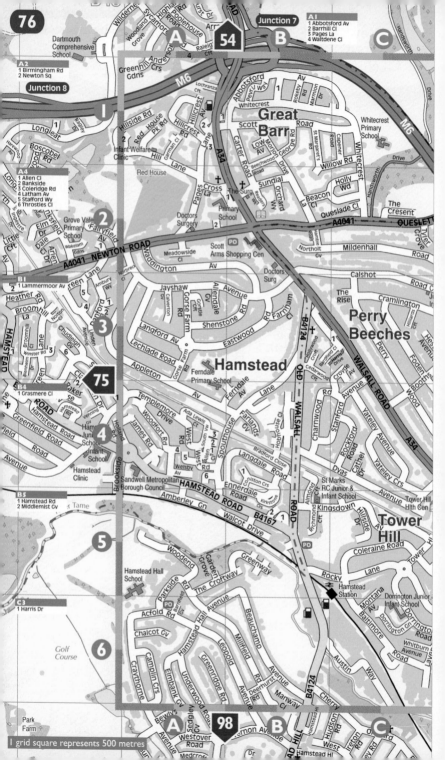

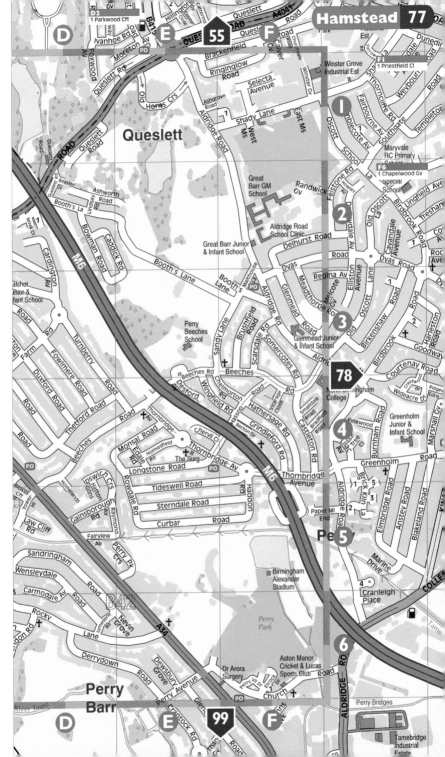

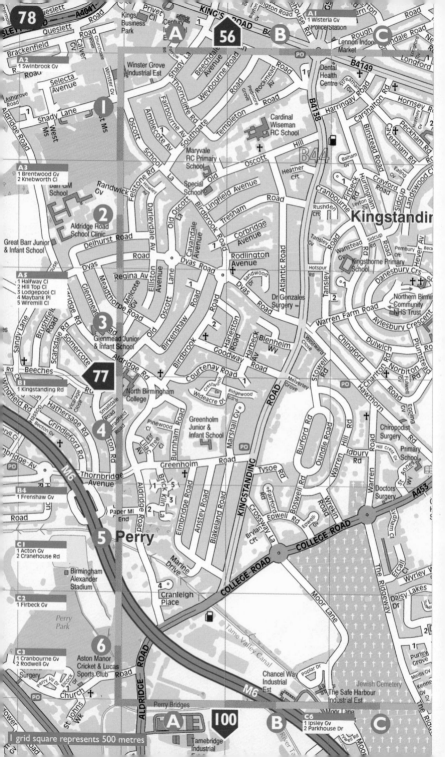

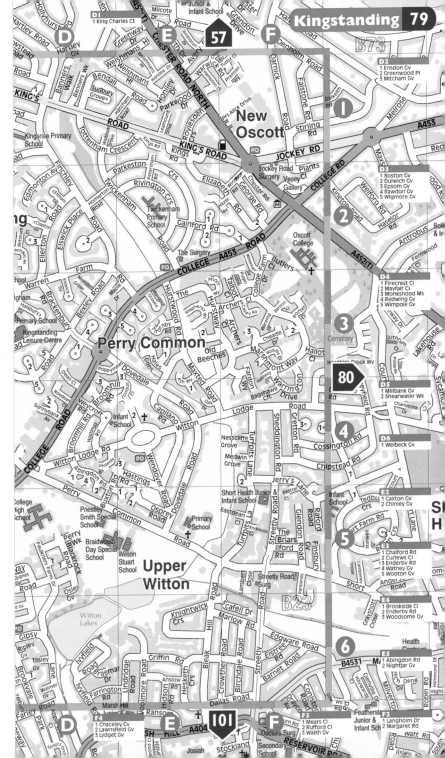

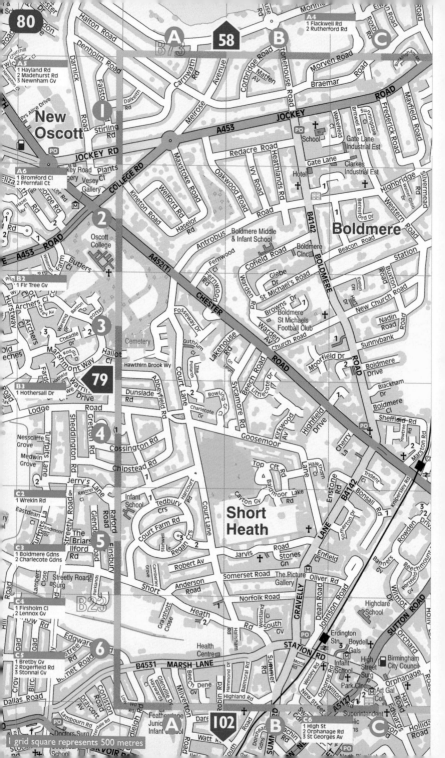

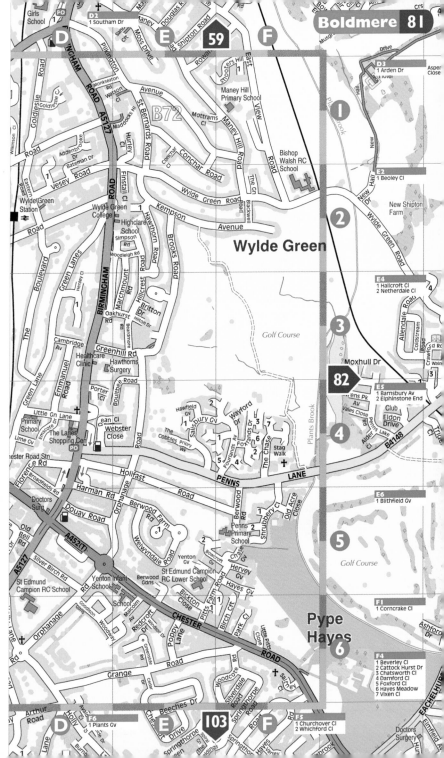

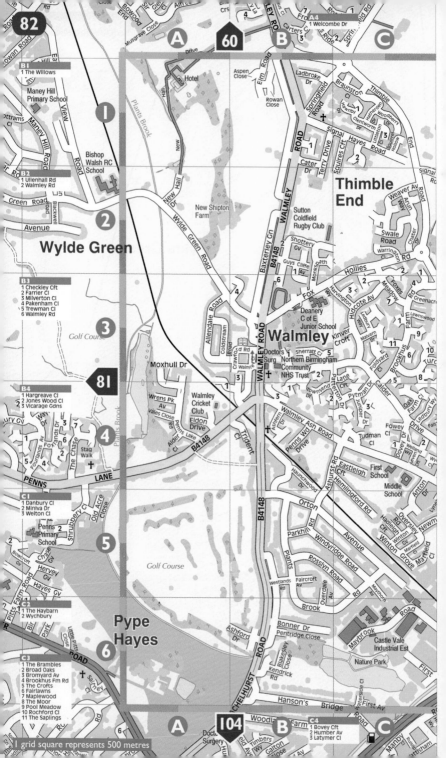

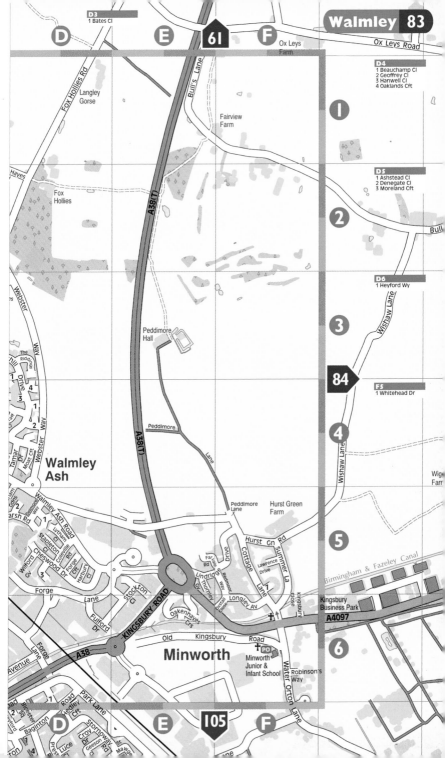

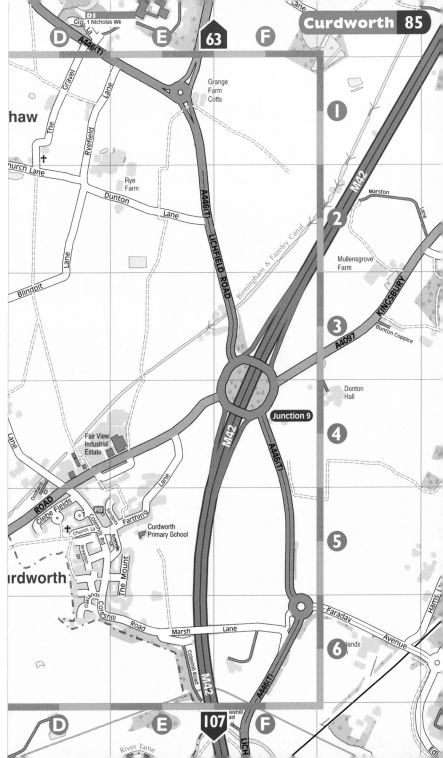

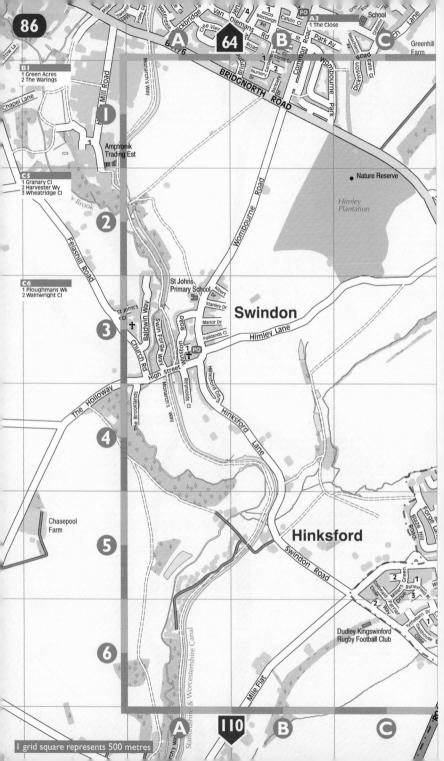

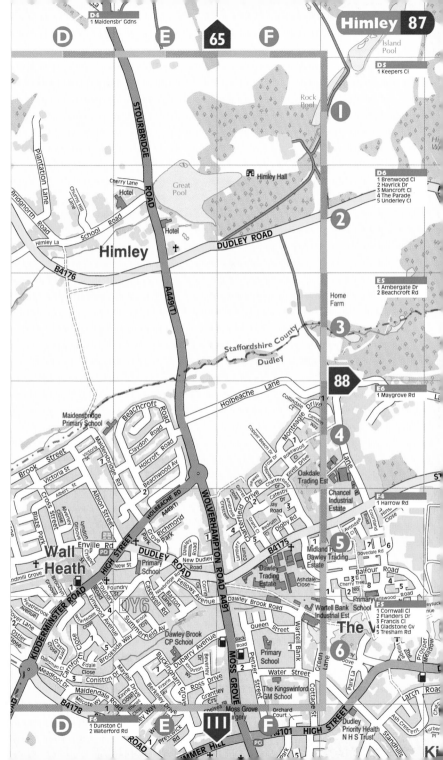

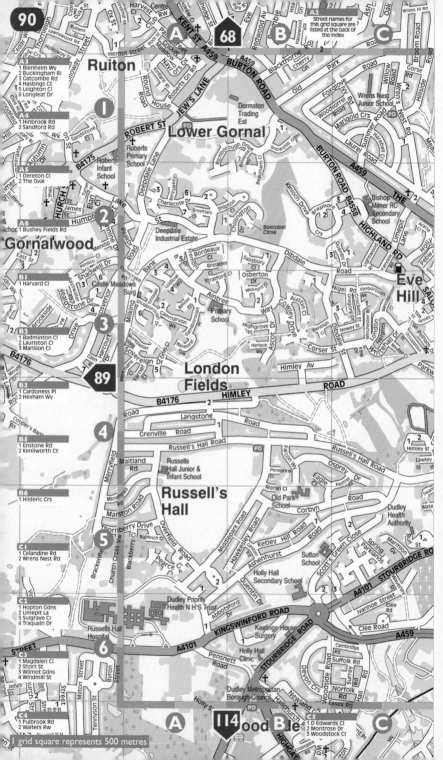

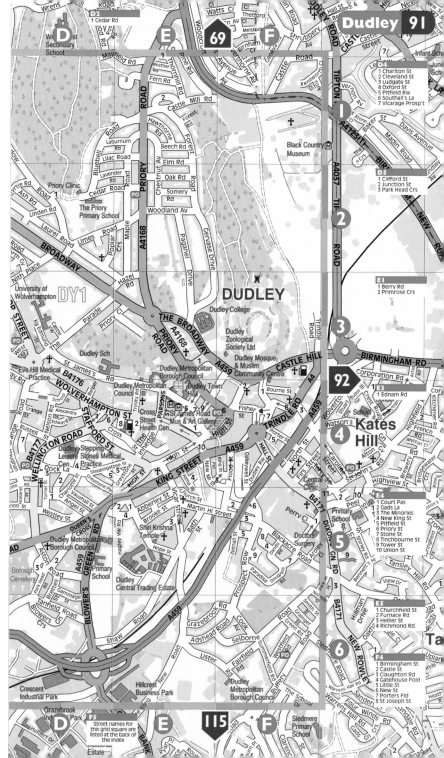

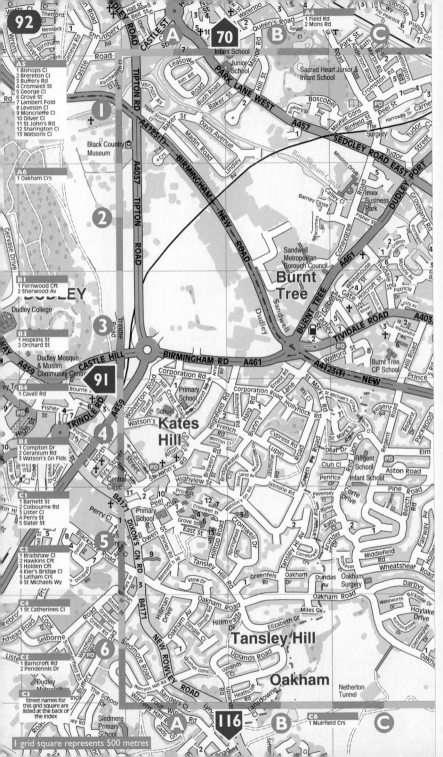

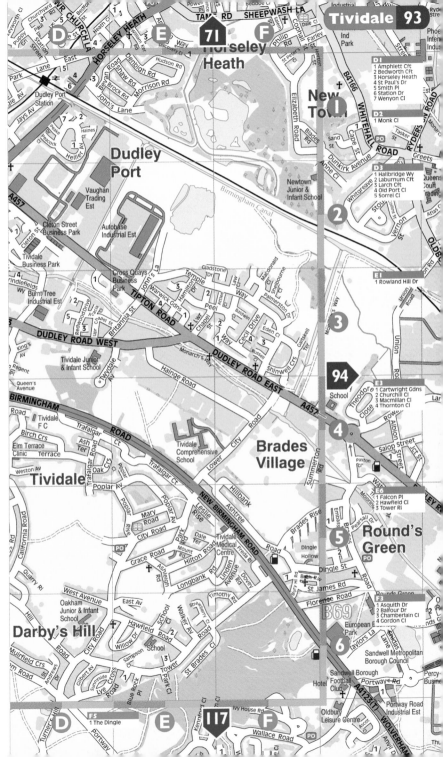

Horseley Heath
Dudley Port
New Town
Tividale
Darby's Hill
Brades Village
Round's Green

71
94
117

D1
1 Amphlett Cft
2 Bedworth Cft
3 Horseley Heath
4 St Paul's Dr
5 Smith Pl
6 Station Dr
7 Wenyon Cl

D2
1 Monk Cl

D3
1 Hallbridge Wy
2 Laburnum Cft
3 Larch Cft
4 Old Port Cl
5 Sorrel Cl

E1
1 Rowland Hill Dr

E3
1 Cartwright Gdns
2 Churchill Cl
3 Macmillan Cl
4 Thornton Cl

E4
1 Falcon Pl
2 Hawfield Cl
3 Tower Ri

F3
1 Asquith Dr
2 Balfour Dr
3 Chamberlain Cl
4 Gordon Cl

F5
1 The Dingle

Birmingham Canal
Newtown Junior & Infant School
Vaughan Trading Est
Cleton Street Business Park
Tividale Business Park
Burnt Tree Industrial Est
Cross Quays Business Park
Autobase Industrial Est
Tividale Junior & Infant School
Queen's Avenue
Tividale F C
Elm Terrace Clinic
Tividale Comprehensive School
Brades Village
Round's Green
Tividale Medical Centre
Oakham Junior & Infant School
Sandwell Metropolitan Borough Council
European Park
Sandwell Borough Football Club
Oldbury Leisure Centre
Portway Road Industrial Est

Dudley Port Station

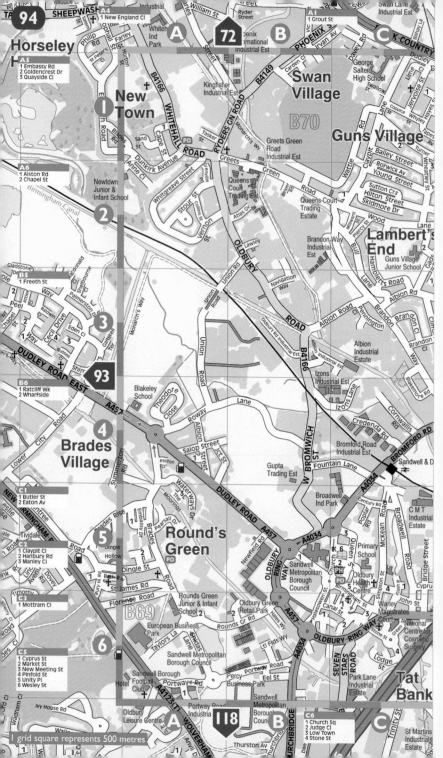

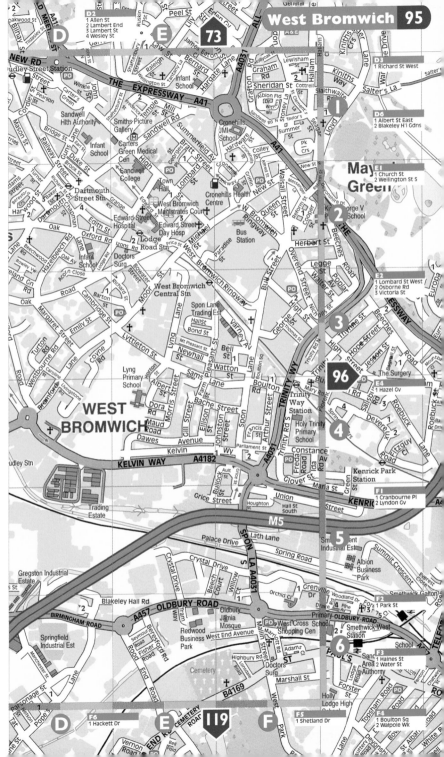

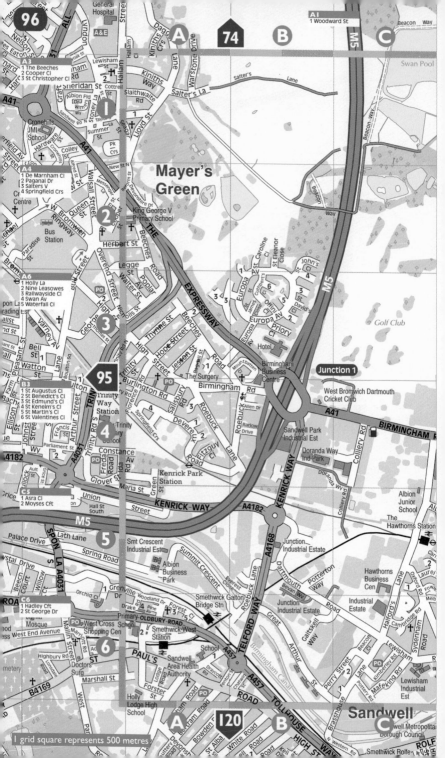

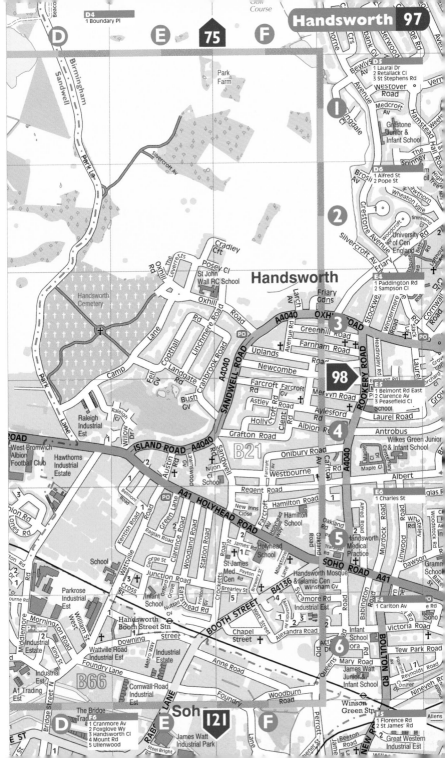

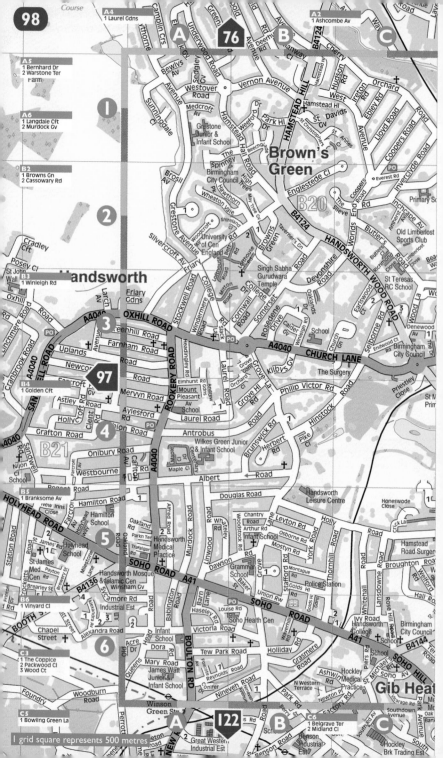

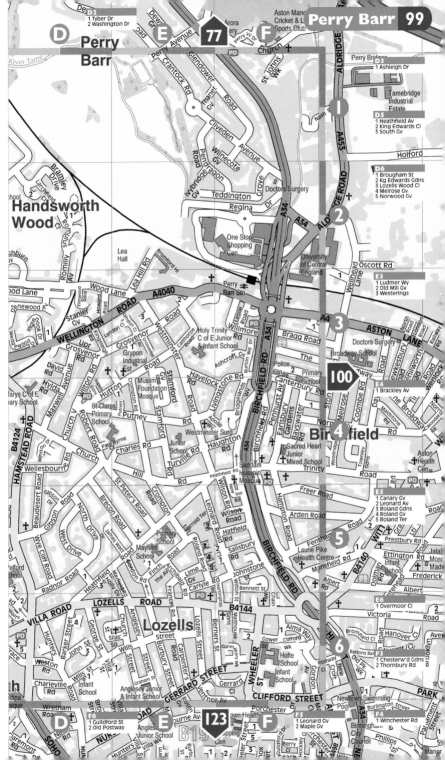

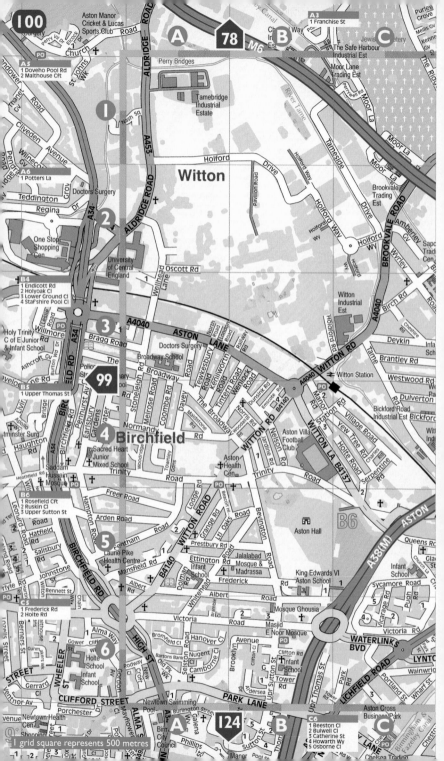

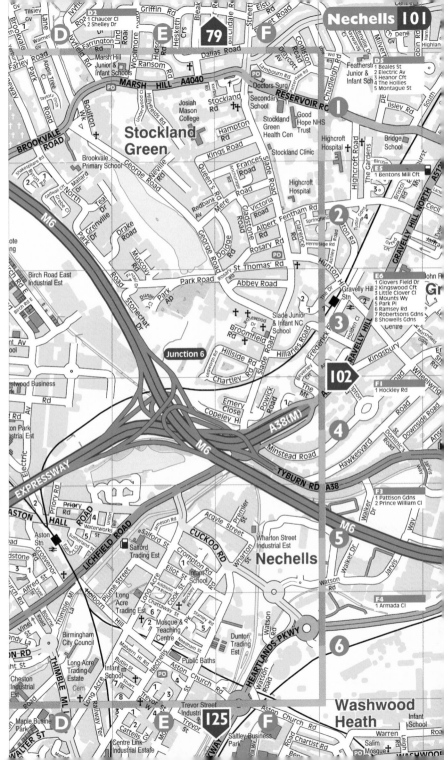

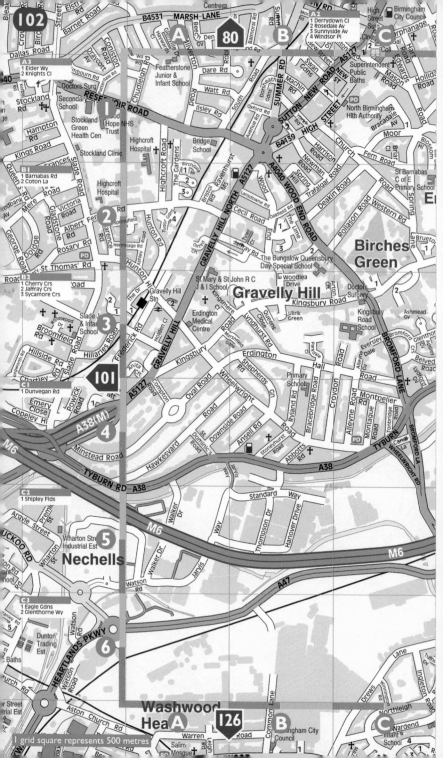

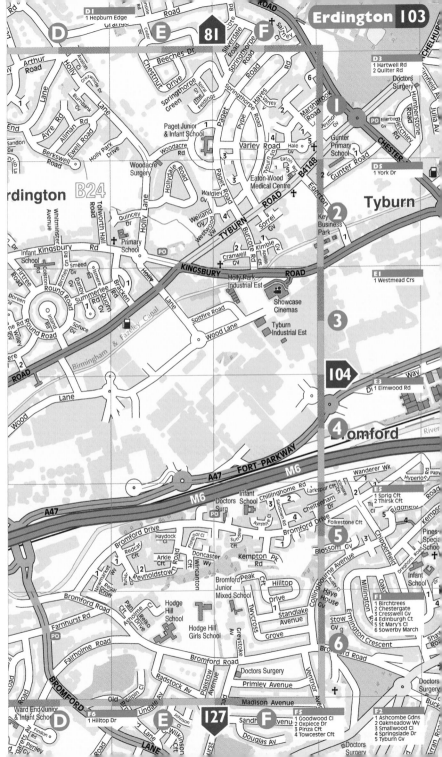

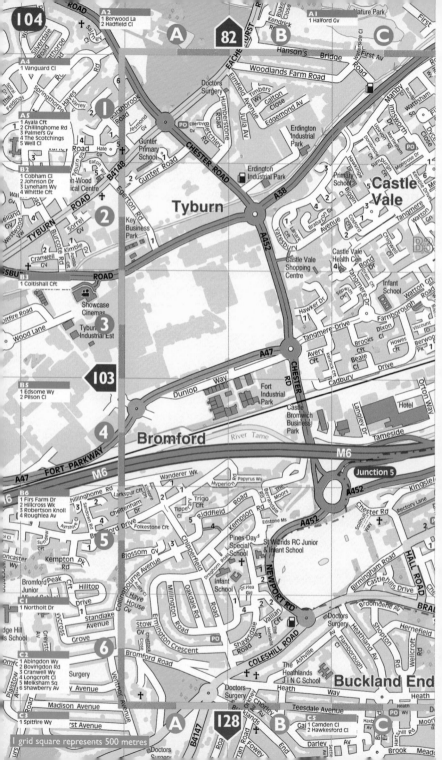

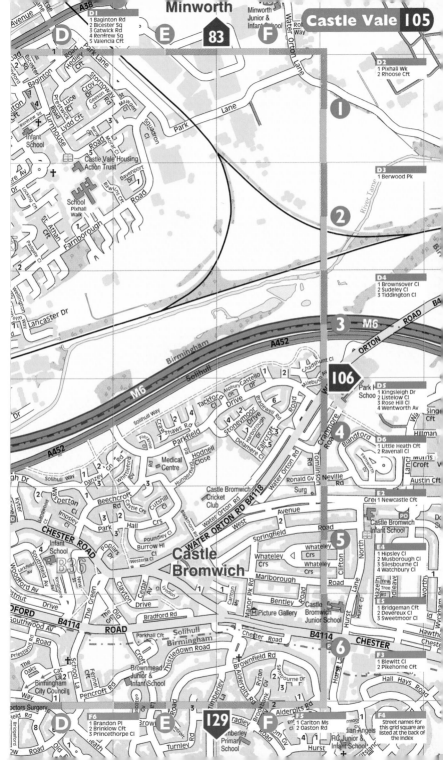

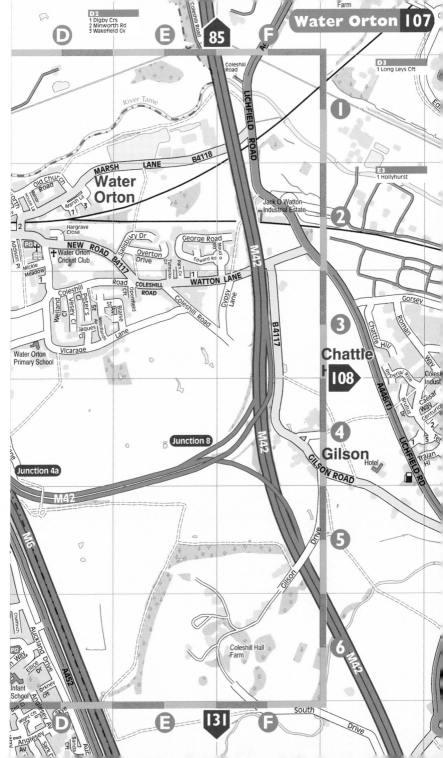

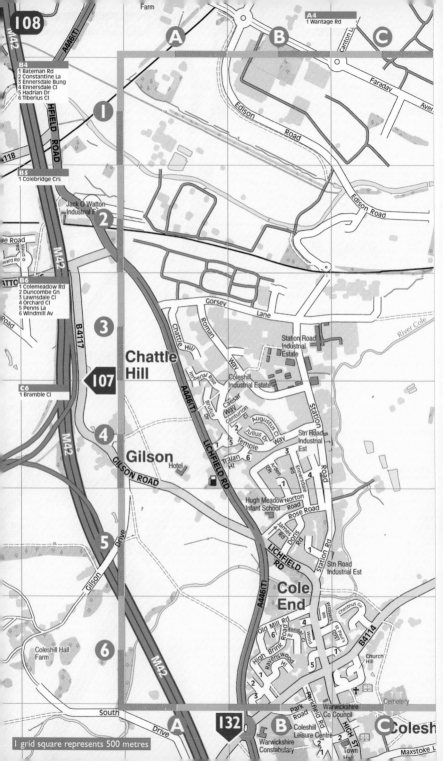

D Hams
Hall

E

F

1

Heart of England Way

River Tame

Station Road

Centenary Way

2

Centenary Way

Watery La

Watery Lane

**Blyth
End**

ROAD

B4114

COLESHILL

3

River Blythe

4

S

BLYTHE ROAD

Blyth Bridge

5

B46

6

Maxstoke
Castle

Golf Course

D

hill

ane

E

133

Castle
Farm

F

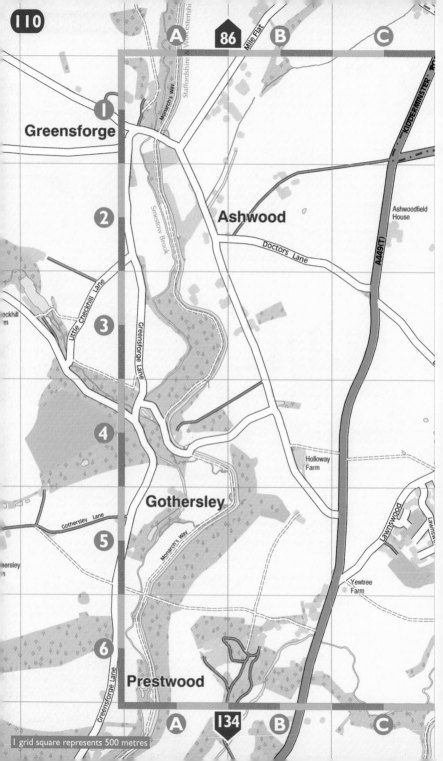

Greensforge

Ashwood

Ashwoodfield House

Gothersley

Holloway Farm

Lawnswood

Yewtree Farm

Prestwood

Monarch's Way

Staffordshire × Worcestershi

Mile Flat

KIDDERMINSTER

A449(T)

Smestow Brook

Greensforge Lane

Little Checkhill Lane

Gothersley Lane

Monarch's Way

Greensforge Lane

Lawnswood

Doctors Lane

86

134

1 grid square represents 500 metres

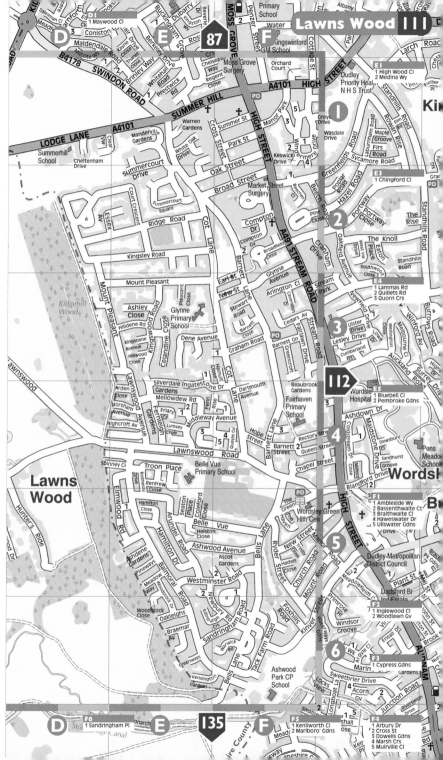

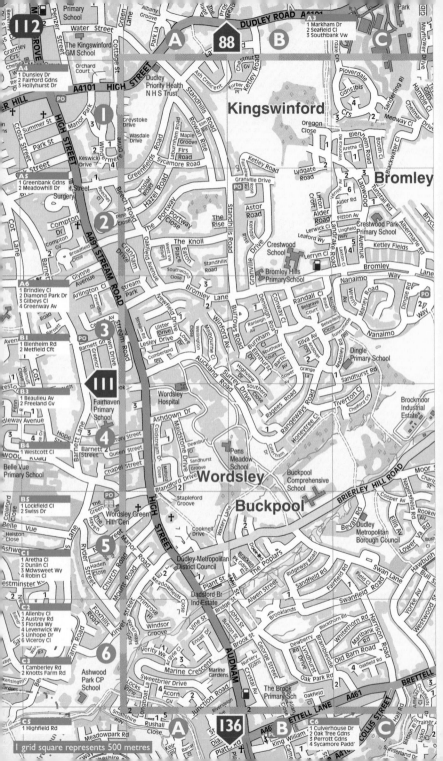

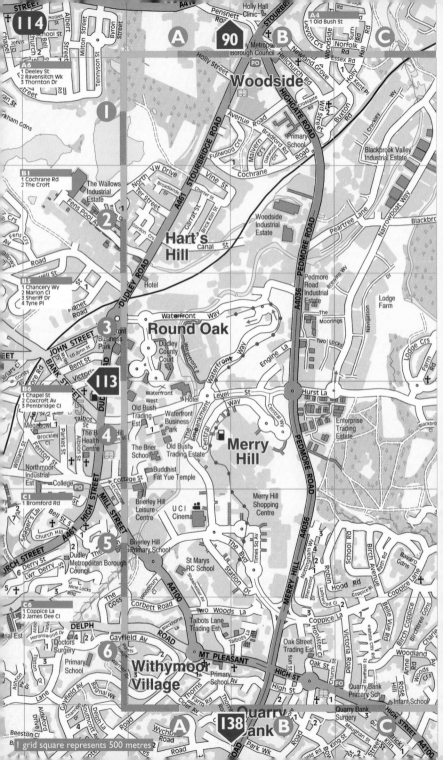

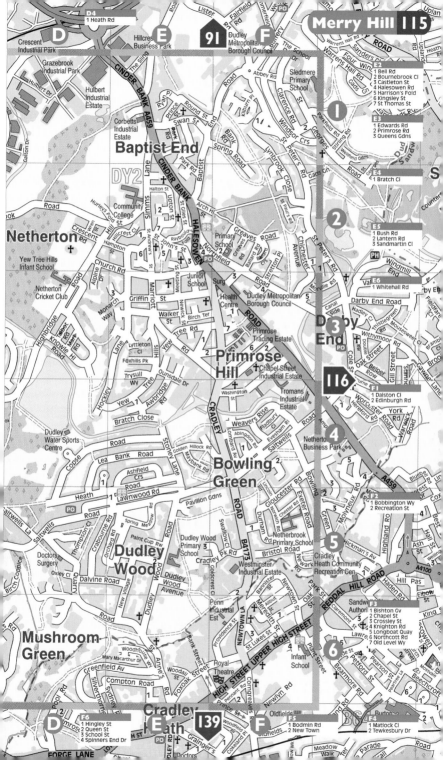

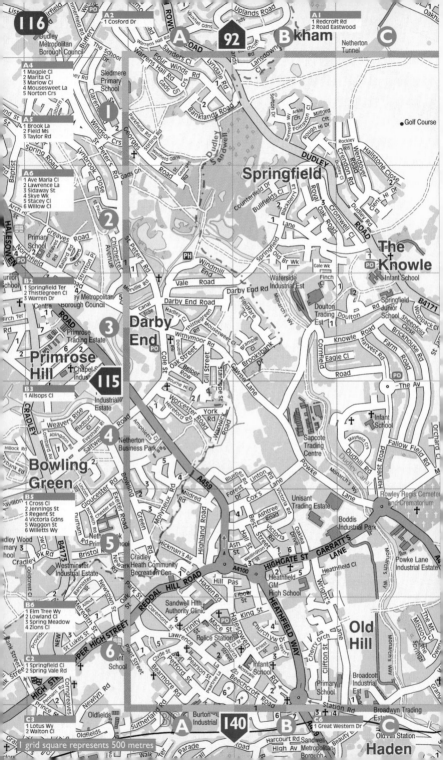

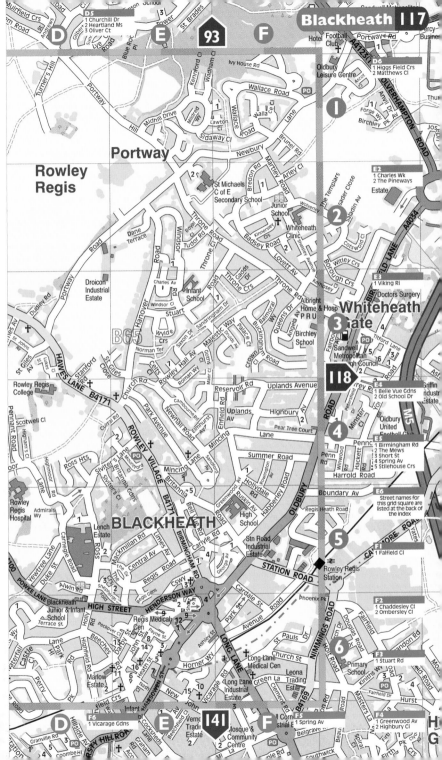

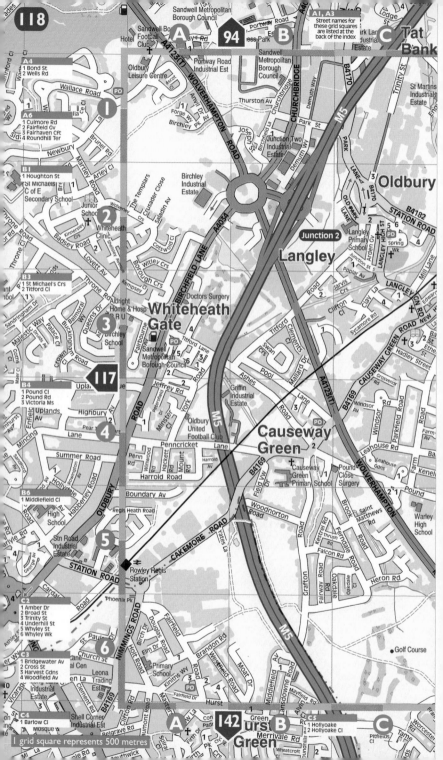

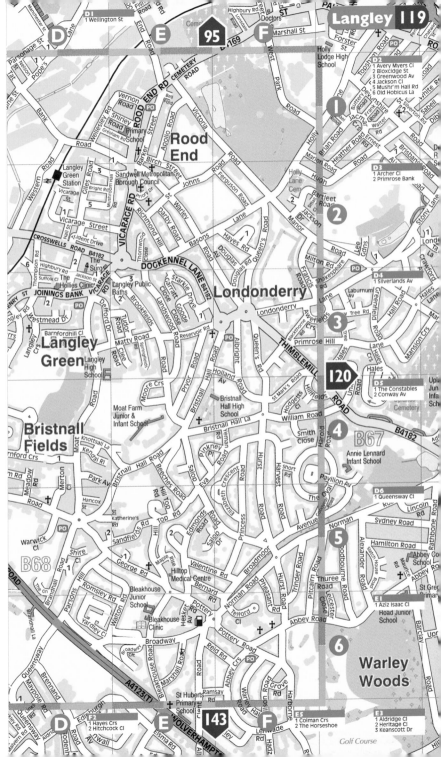

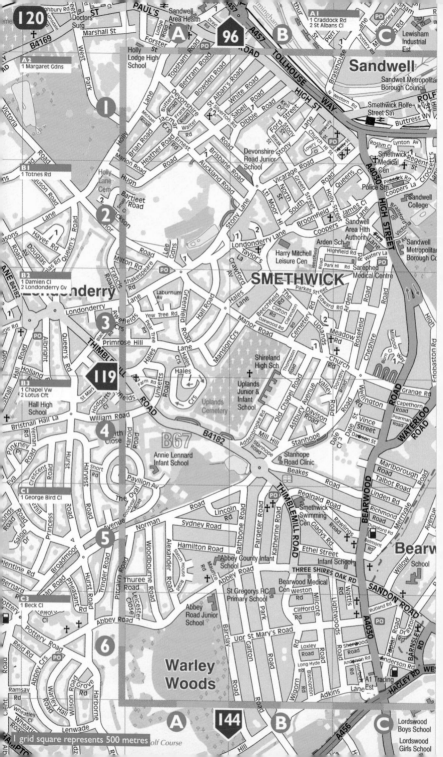

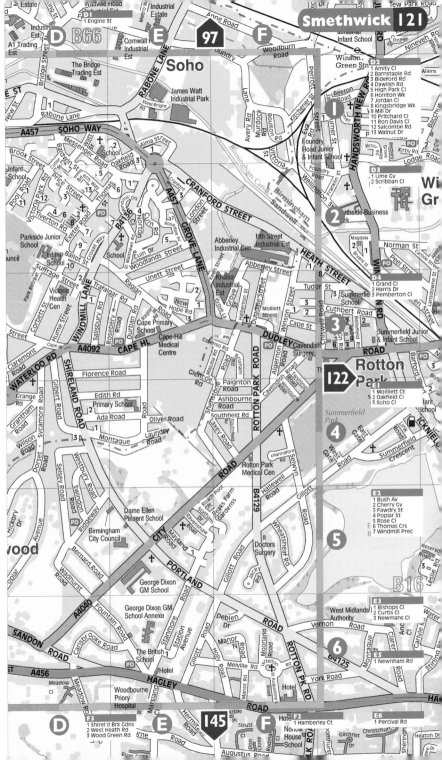

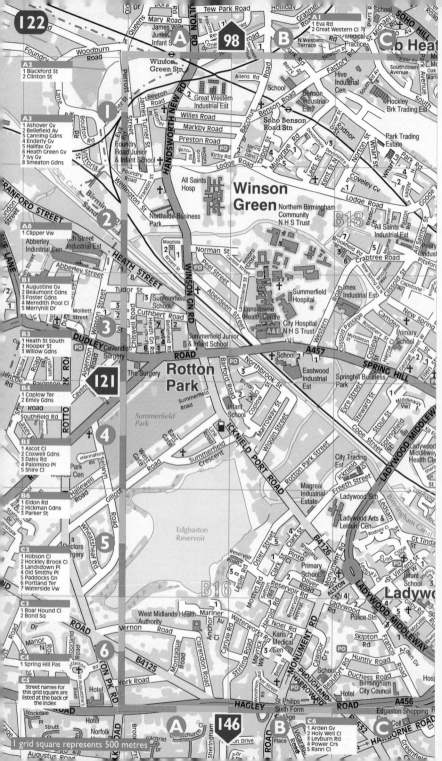

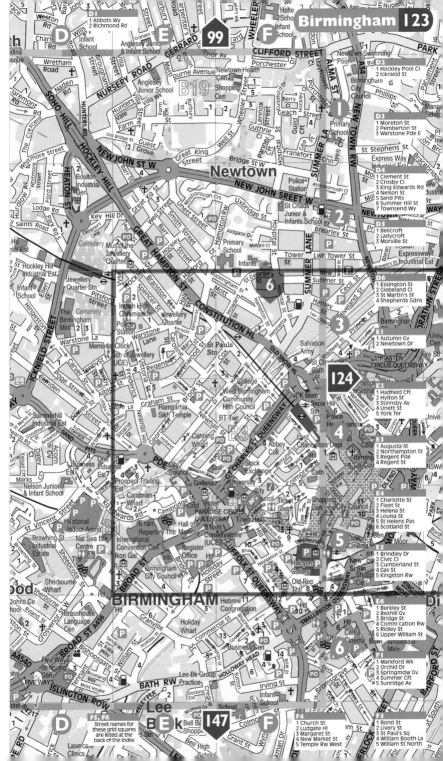

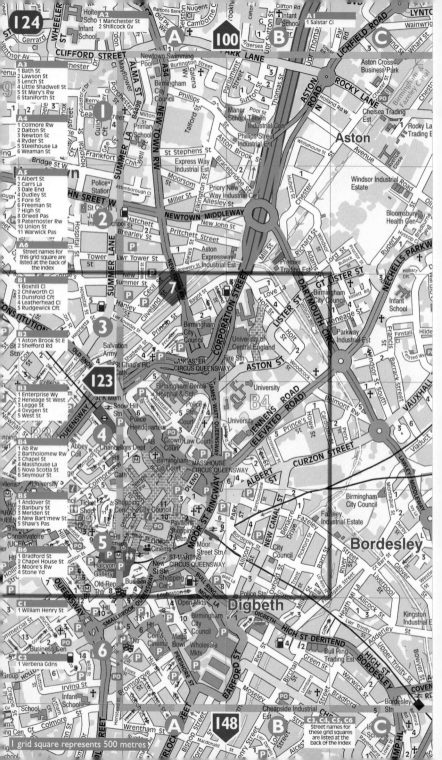

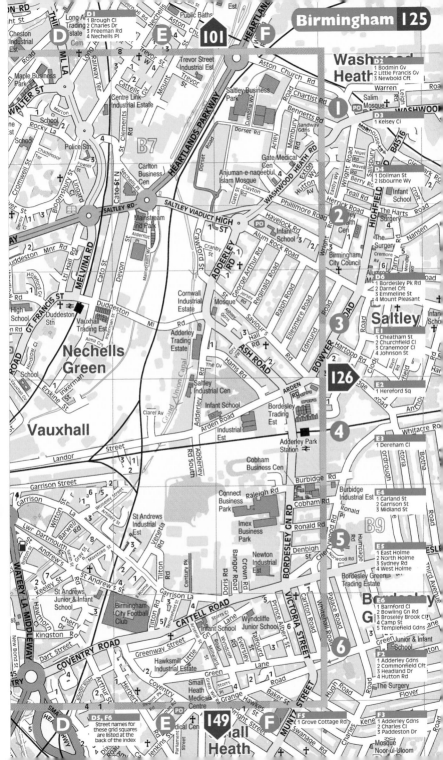

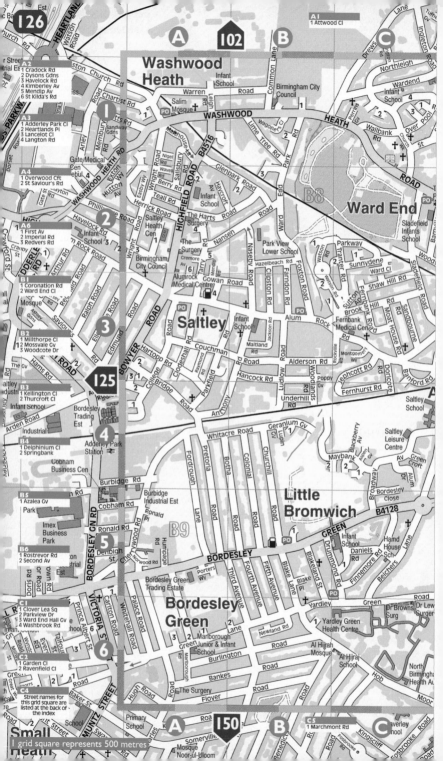

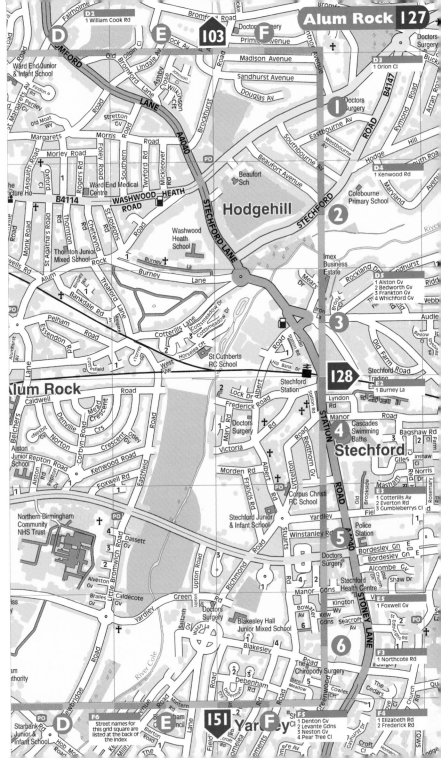

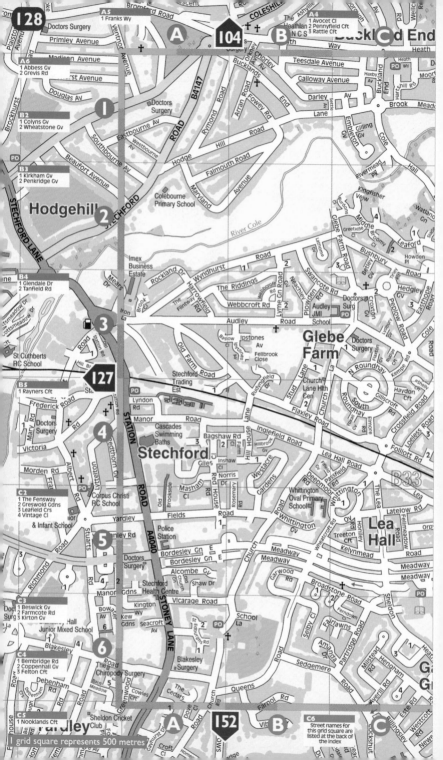

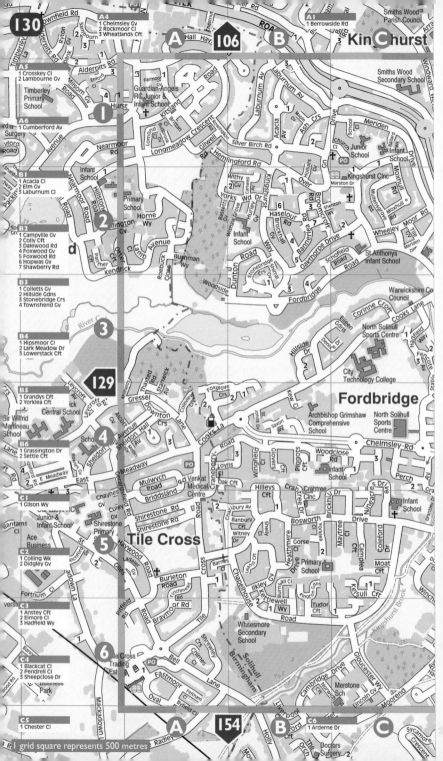

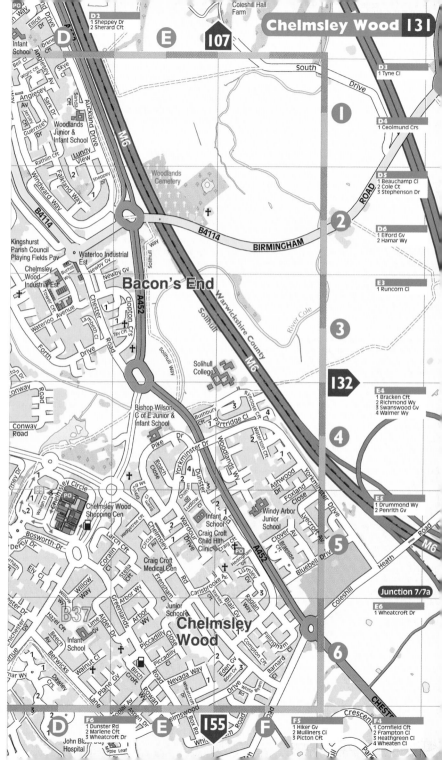

Chelmsley Wood 131

D2
1 Sheppey Dr
2 Sherard Cft

D **E** **107**

South Drive

D3
1 Tyne Cl

Infant School

Bell Ln

Skye Cl

Wight Cft

I

D4
1 Ceolmund Crs

Anglesey Av

Sark Dr

Jersey Dr

Guernsey Dr

Auckland Drive

Sandy

Woodlands Junior & Infant School

Rathlin Cft

Lundy View

Sheppey Dr

M6

Woodlands Cemetery

D5
1 Beauchamp Cl
2 Cole Ct
3 Stephenson Dr

Windward Way

Falkland Way

ROAD

D6
1 Elford Gv
2 Hamar Wy

B4114

B4114

BIRMINGHAM

2

Kingshurst Parish Council Playing Fields Pav

Waterloo Industrial Est

Newby Gv

Newby Gv

E3
1 Runcorn Cl

Chelmsley Wood Industrial Est

Burnill Gv

Tower Cft

Bacon's End

River Cole

Waterloo Avenue

Chester Road

Clopton Crs

A452

Solihull

Warwickshire County

3

Forth Drive

Carpenter Cft

Tay Cft

Solihull Way

M6

132

E4
1 Bracken Cft
2 Richmond Wy
3 Swanswood Gv
4 Walmer Wy

Conway Road

Solihull College

Ryecroft Cl

4

Conway Road

Bishop Wilson C of E Junior & Infant School

Bushbury Cft

Partridge Cl

Waterson Cft

Swanswood Gv

Pike Dr

Yorkminster Dr

Woodlands Wy

Ashwood Dr

Yorkminster Drive

E5
1 Drummond Wy
2 Penrith Gv

Roach Close

Chinn

Dunster

Ludlow

Foxland Close

Lyecroft Av

ROAD

M6

Chelmsley Circle

PO

Chelmsley Wood Shopping Cen

Infant School

Craig Croft Child Hlth Clinic

Windy Arbor Junior School

Clover Av

Beaside

5

Bosworth Dr

Derby Dr

Larch Cft

Circus

Chelmsley Drive

Wardour Drive

Craig Croft

PO

Hedingham Gv

Bluebell Drive

Coleshill

Heath Road

Junction 7/7a

Ely Cl

Coralin Cl

Stella Cft

Craig Croft Medical Cen

Erlebarn Rd

Carisbrooke Rd

Lumley Rd

E6
1 Wheatcroft Dr

B37

Willow Way

Greenlands

Arbor Wy

Junior School

Blair Rd

Raglan Way

6

Hazel Cft

Alder Wy

Lumley Rd

Chelmsley Wood

Fulringham

Barnard Rd

Beech

Piccadilly

Piccadilly Close

Compton Cft

Infant School

Walnut Cl

Plane Av

Birch Croft Road

Piccadilly

Nevada Way

Eden Gv

White Beam

Bewicks

Dawley Cft

Poplar Av

Aspen Cl

Rowan

Wheatcroft Cl

Drive

White

D **E** **155** **F**

F6
1 Dunster Rd
2 Marlene Cft
3 Wheatcroft Dr

Chelmswood

Box Rd

Crescent

F5
1 Hiker Gv
2 Mulliners Cl
3 Picton Cft

F4
1 Cornfield Cft
2 Frampton Cl
3 Heathgreen Cl
4 Wheaten Cl

John Blaze Day Hospital

Apple Leaf

CHEST

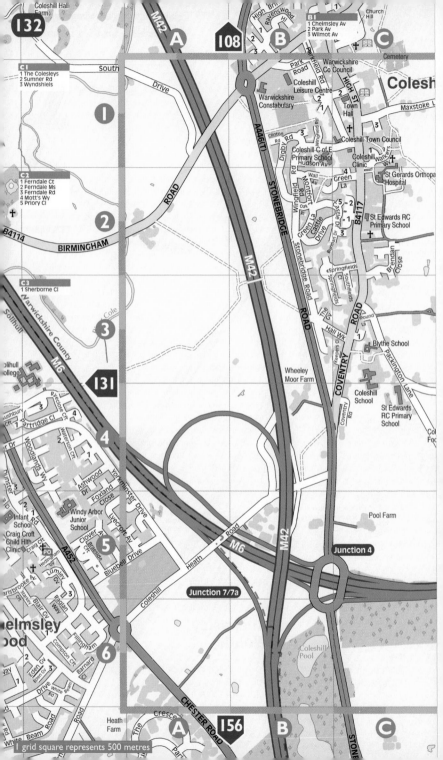

I grid square represents 500 metres

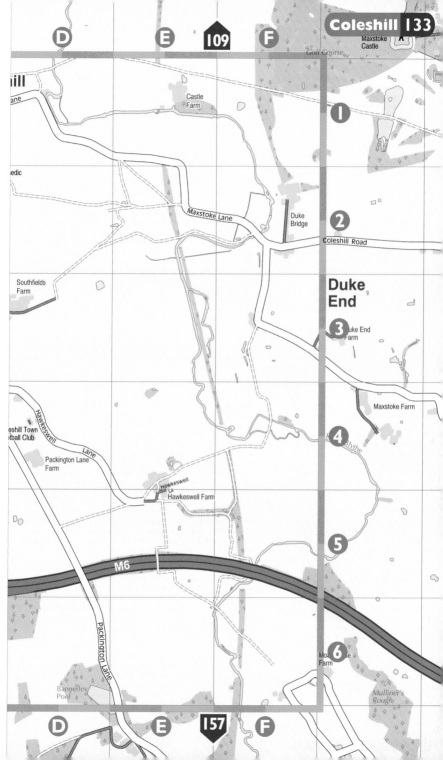

D E **109** F

I

Castle Farm

edic

Maxstoke Lane

Duke Bridge

2

Coleshill Road

Southfields Farm

Duke End

3 uke End Farm

Maxstoke Farm

Hawkeswell Lane

eshill Town tball Club

Packington Lane Farm

4 Blythe

Hawkeswell

Hawkeswell Farm

5

M6

6 Mo se Farm

Bannerley Pool

Packington Lane

Mulliner's Rough

D E **157** F

Golf Course

Maxstoke Castle

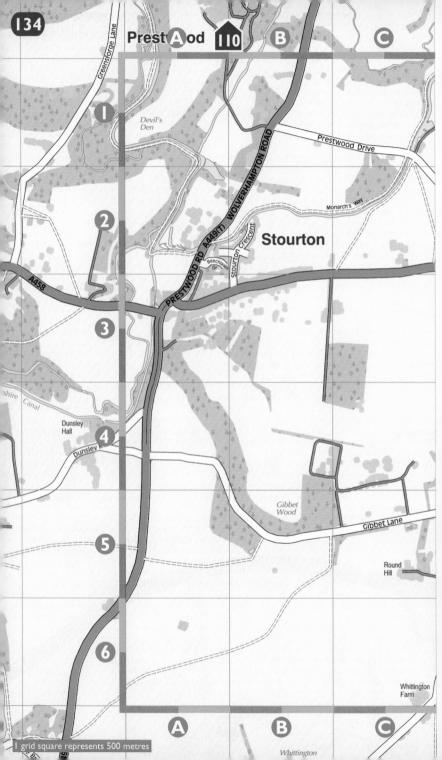

Prest A od 110 B C

Greensforge Lane

1

Devil's Den

Prestwood Drive

WOLVERHAMPTON ROAD

2

Monarch's Way

PRESTWOOD RD A449(T)

Stourton Crescent

Stourton

Beecham Dr

A458

3

...shire Canal

Dunsley Hall

4

Dunsley R...

Gibbet Wood

5

Gibbet Lane

Round Hill

6

Whittington Farm

A B C

Whittington

1 grid square represents 500 metres

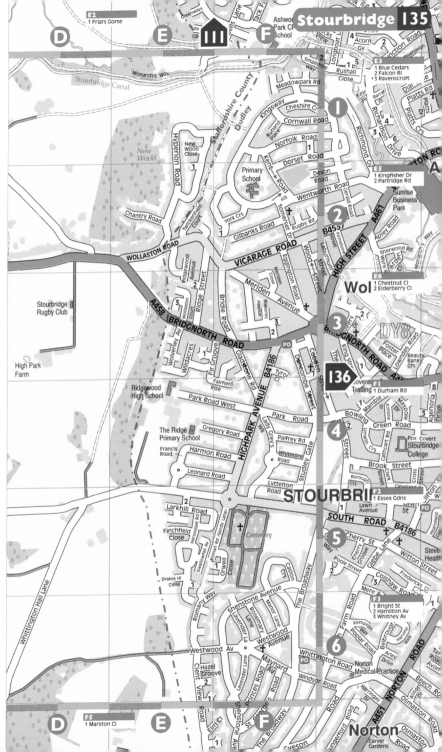

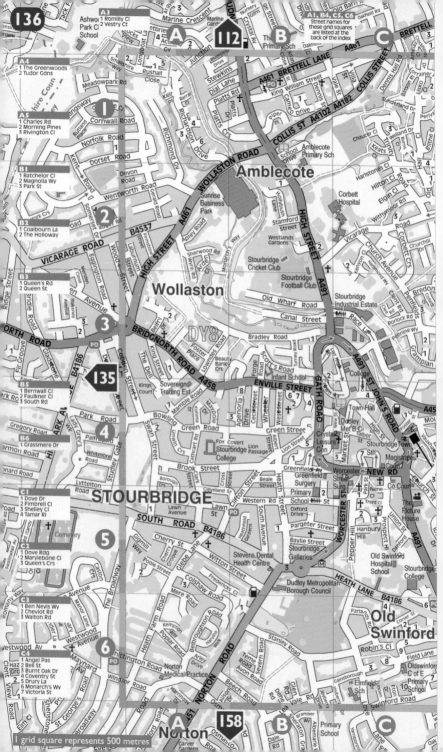

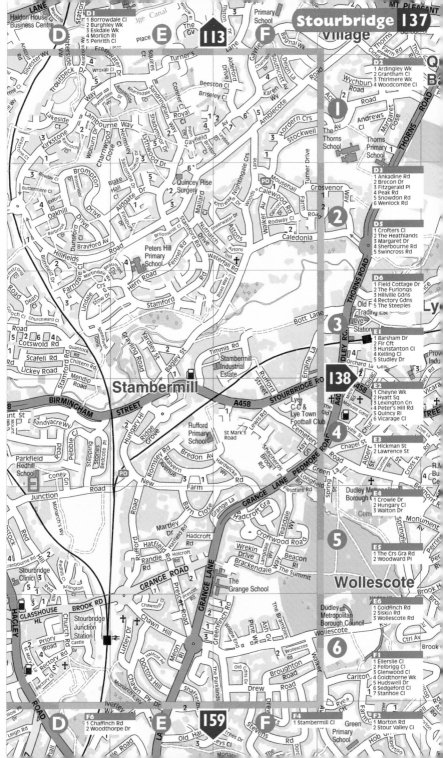

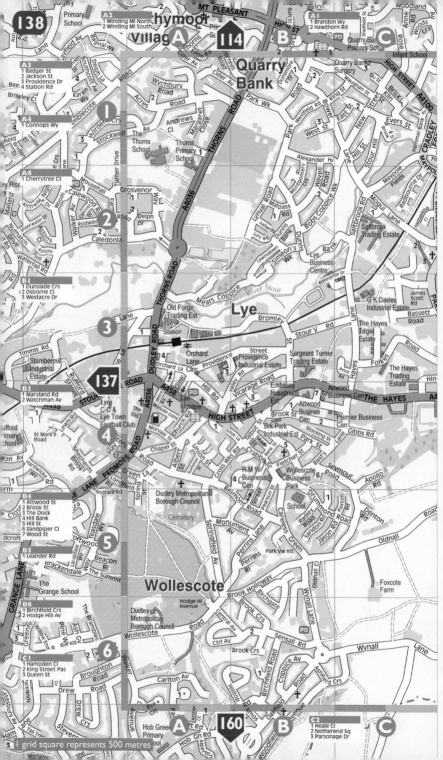

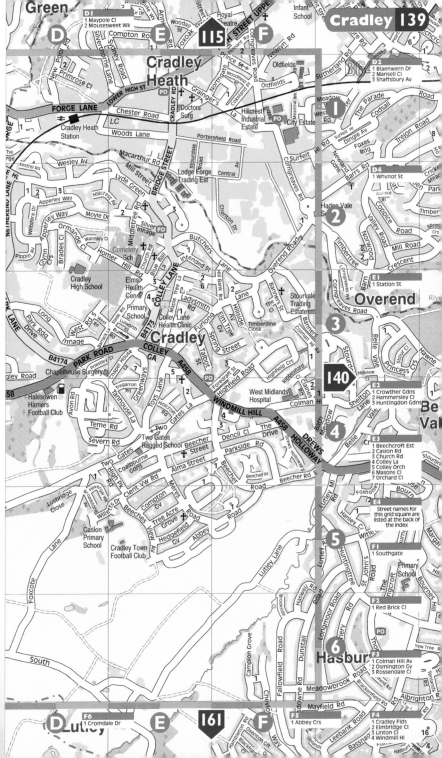

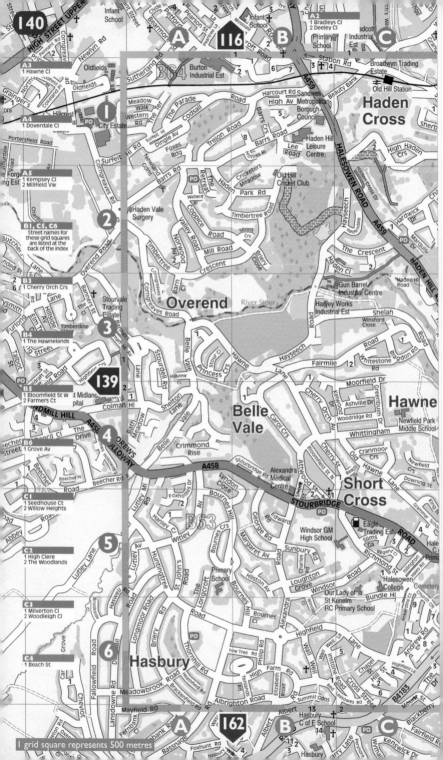

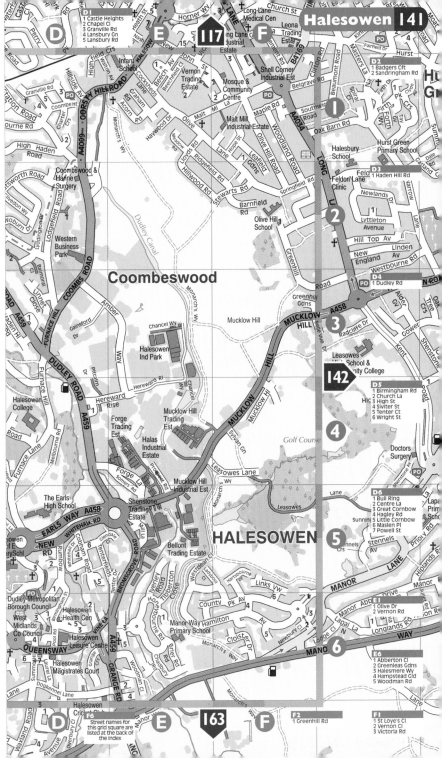

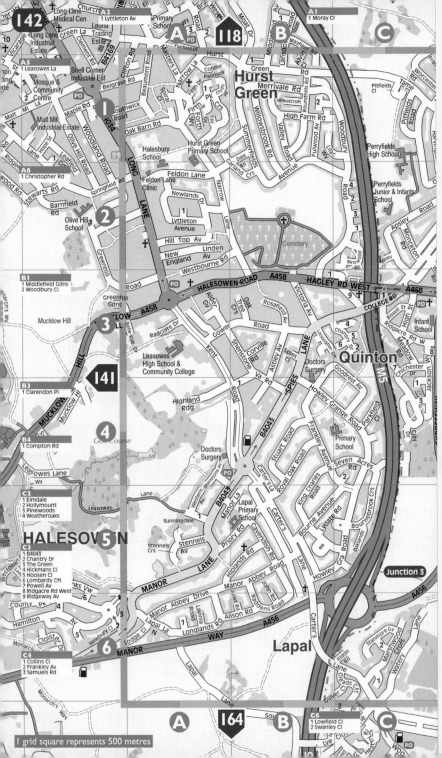

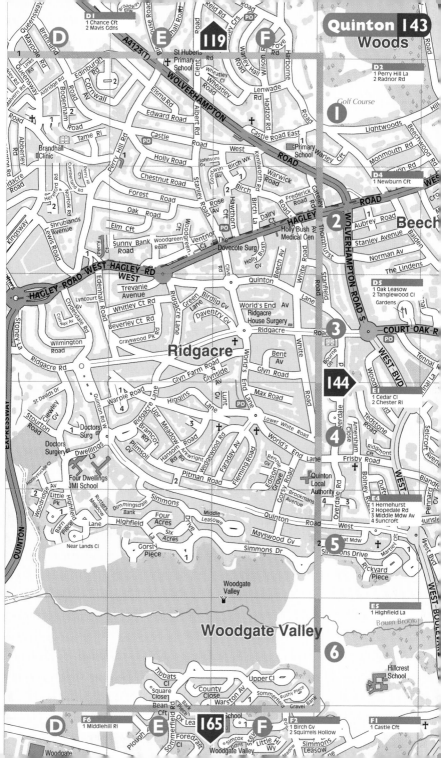

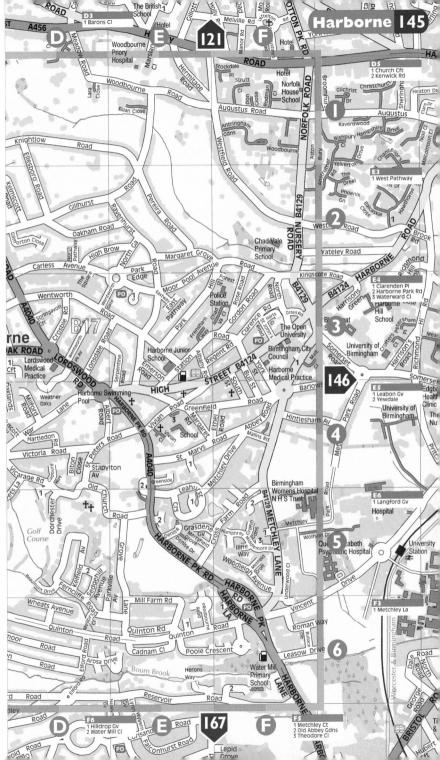

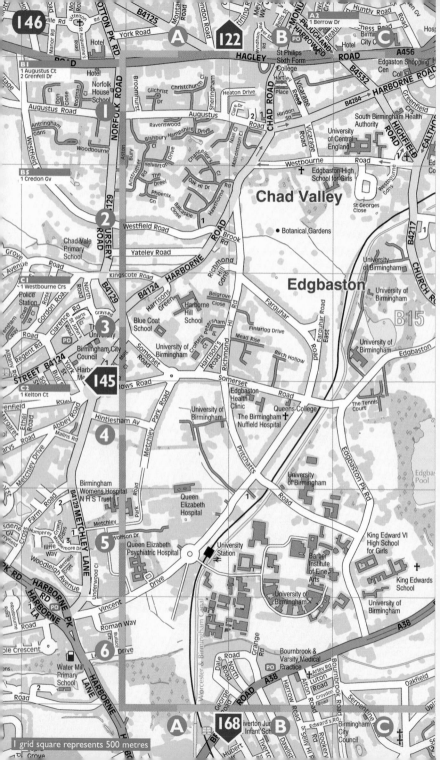

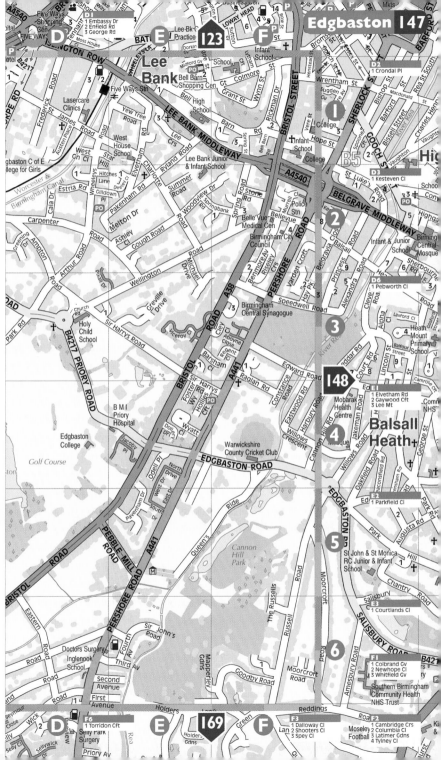

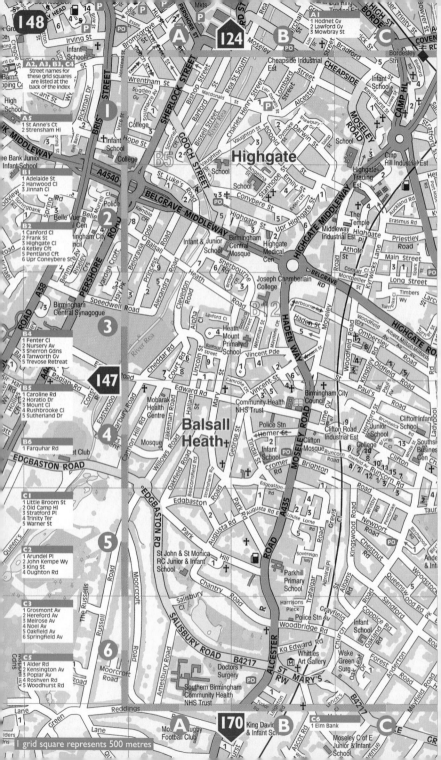

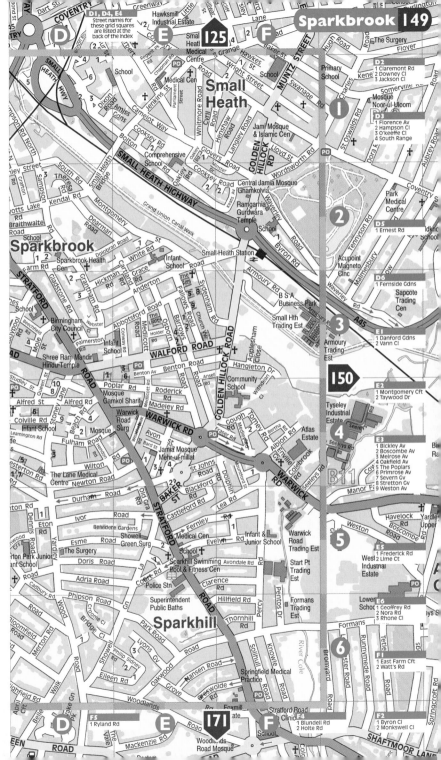

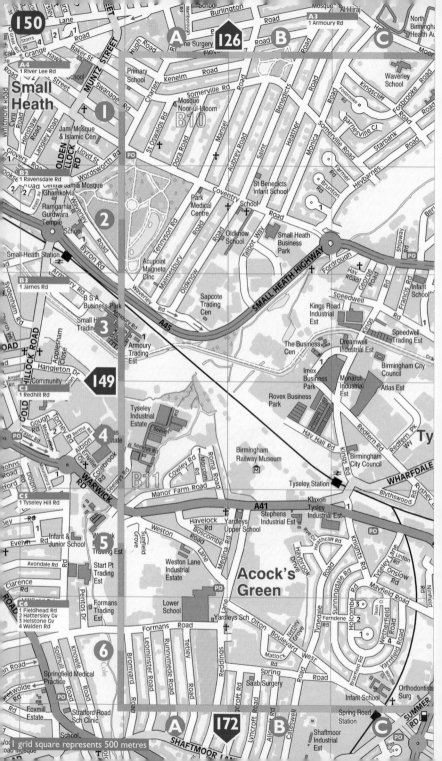

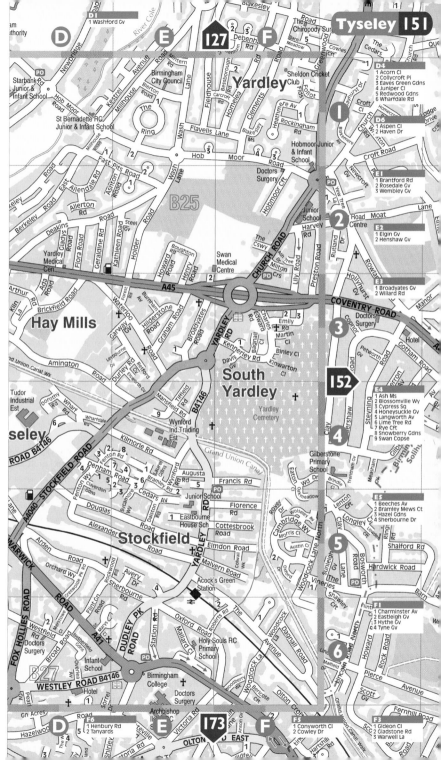

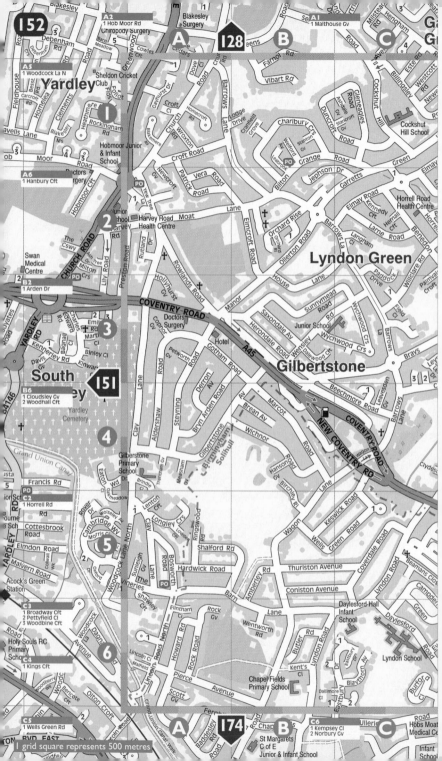

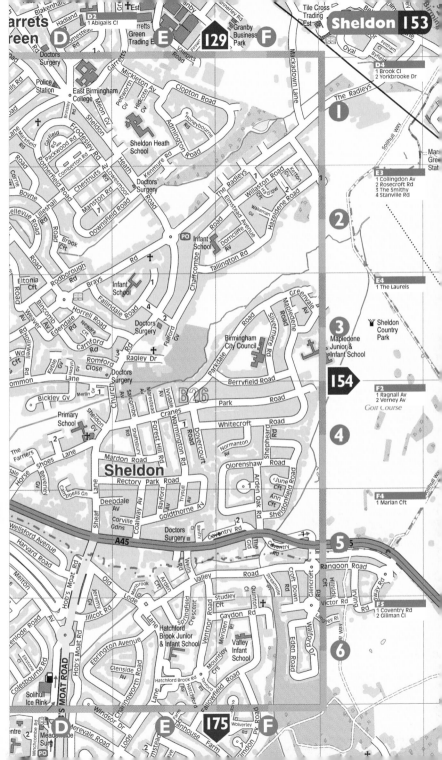

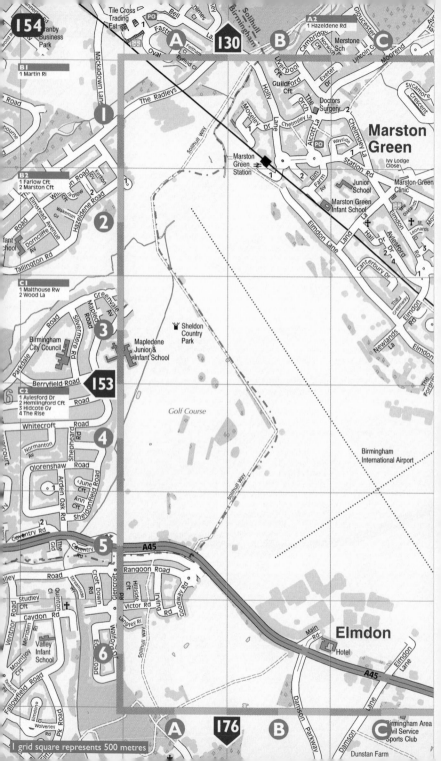

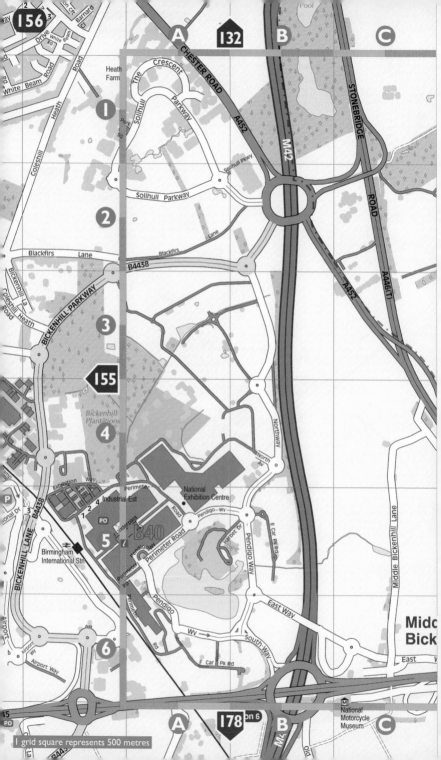

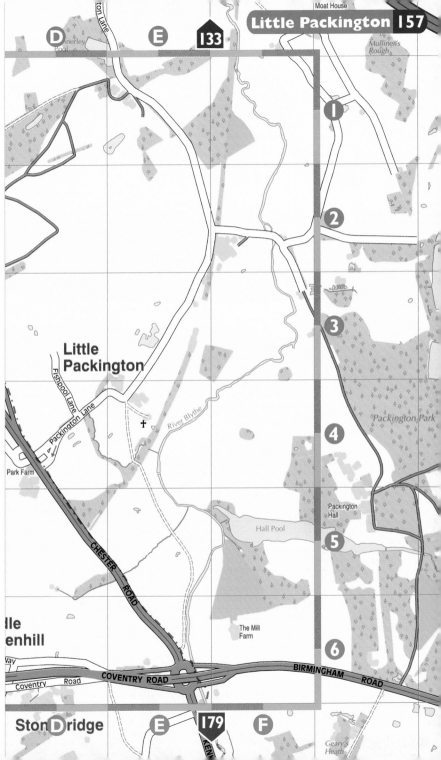

D Dinerley Pool

E

133

Moat House

Mulliner's Rough

1

2

3

Little
Packington

Fishpool Lane

Packington Lane

River Blythe

Packington Park

4

Packington Hall

Hall Pool

5

Park Farm

CHESTER ROAD

lle enhill

Way

Coventry Road

COVENTRY ROAD

The Mill Farm

6

BIRMINGHAM ROAD

Ston D ridge

E

179

KEN

F

Geary's Heath

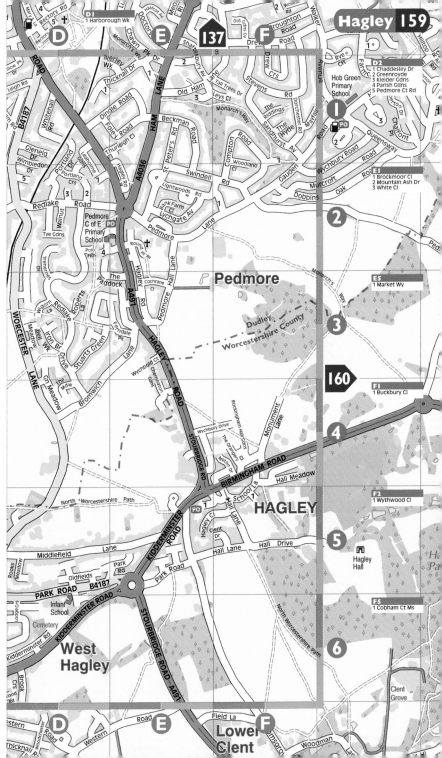

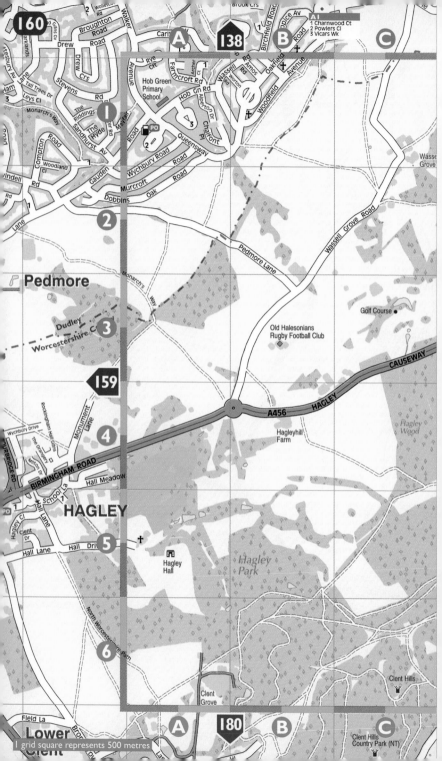

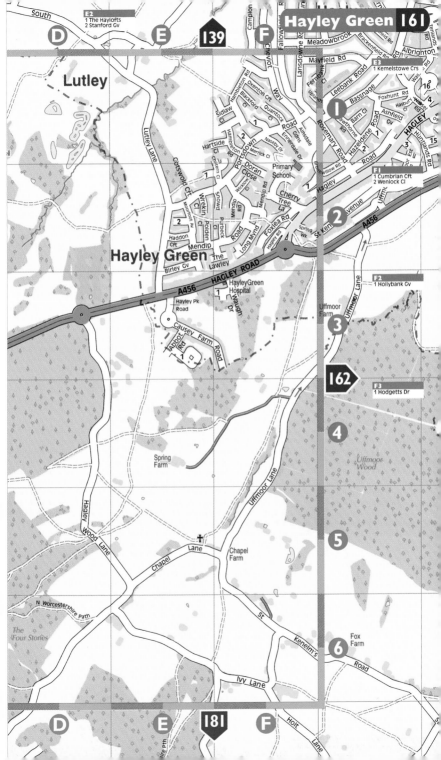

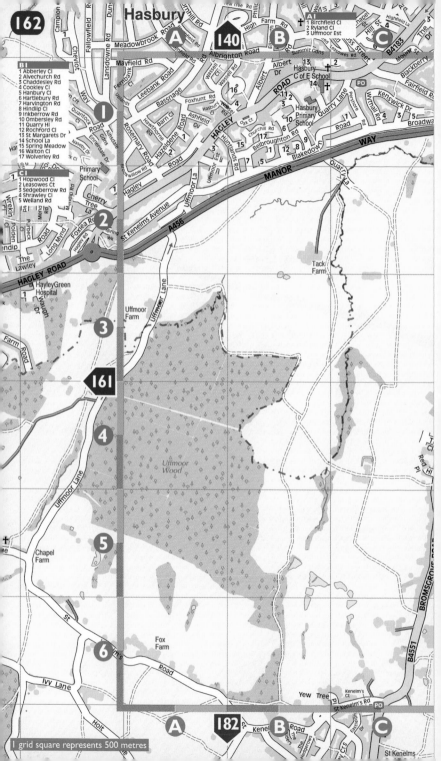

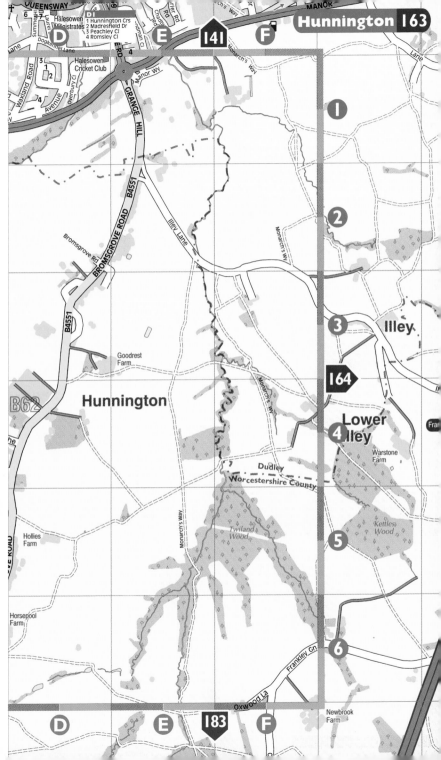

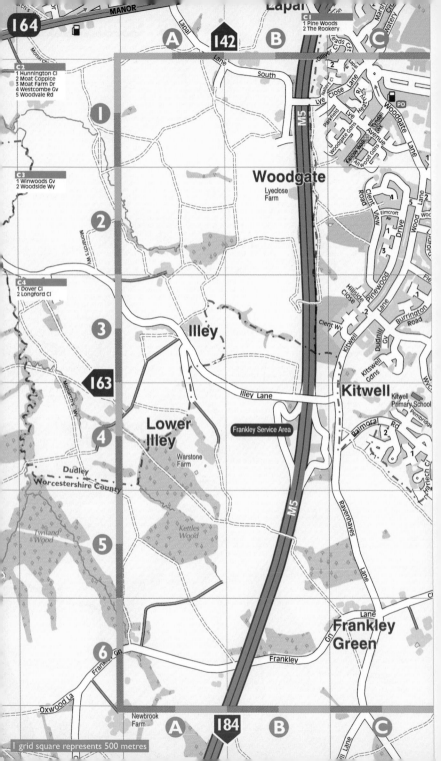

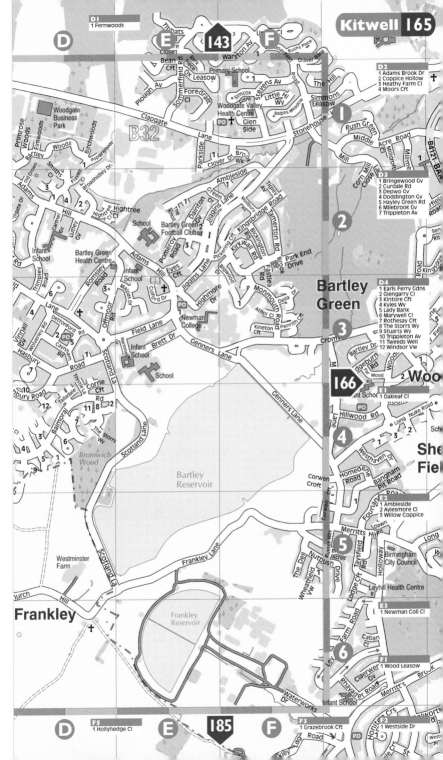

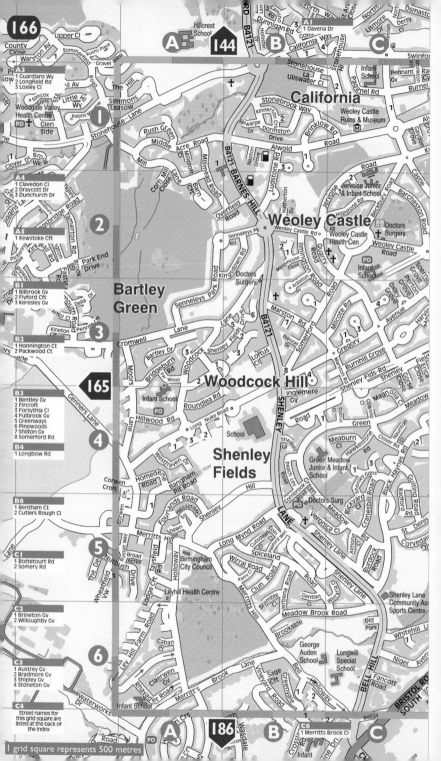

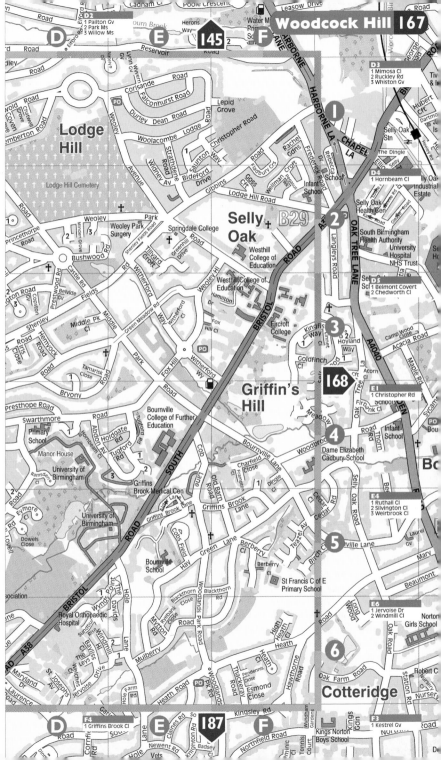

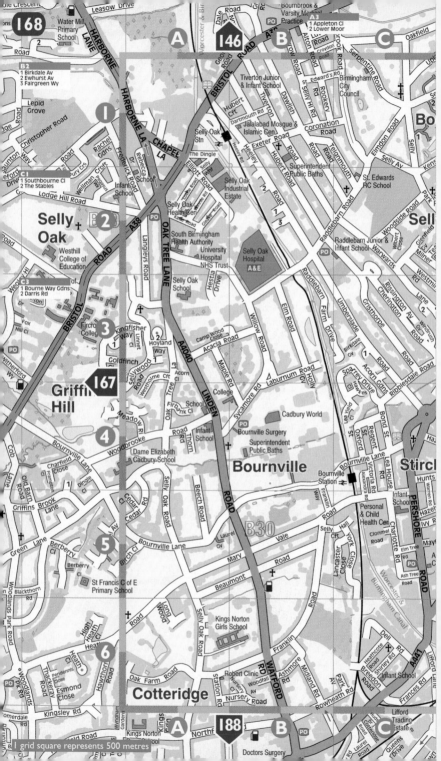

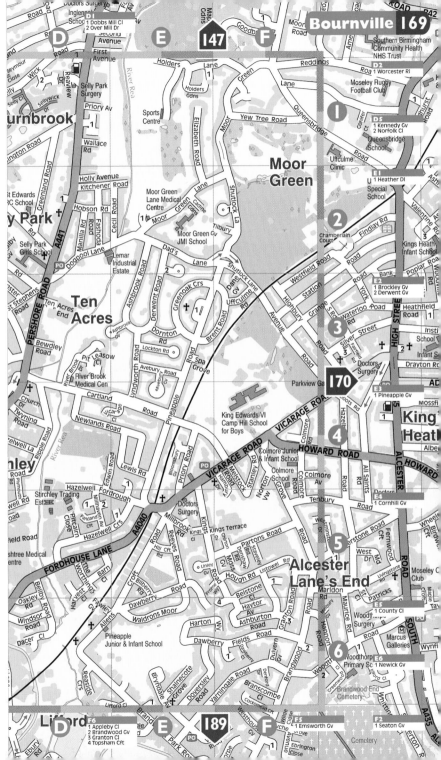

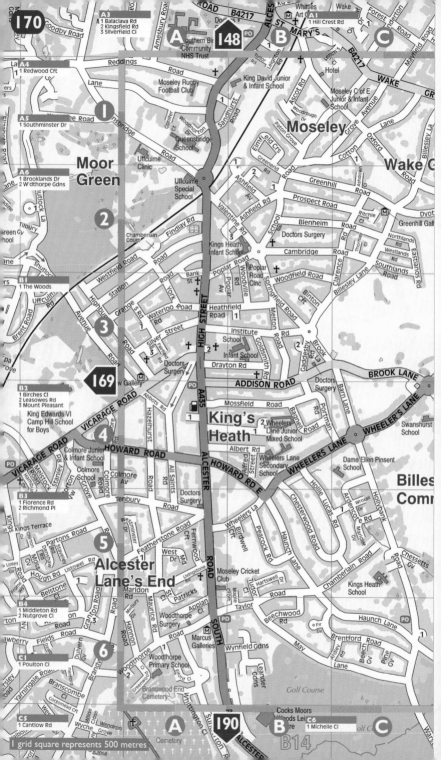

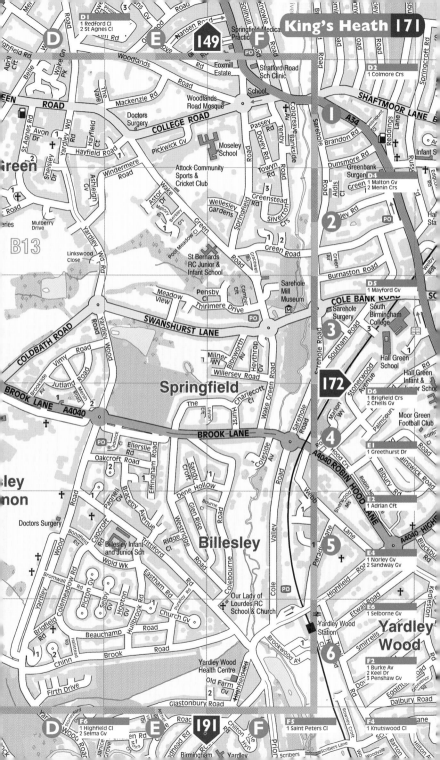

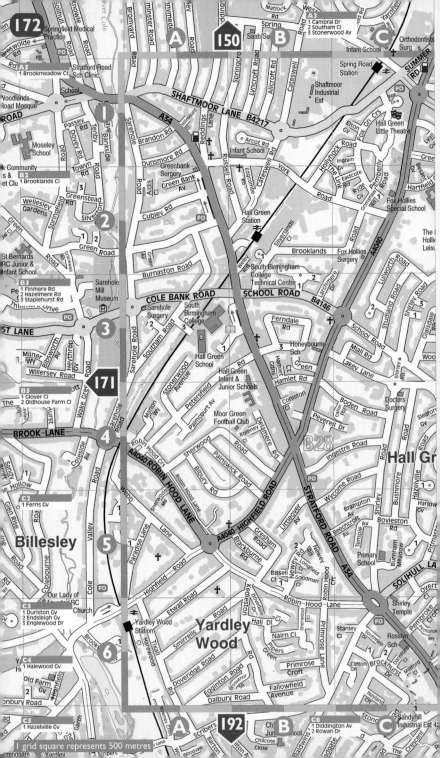

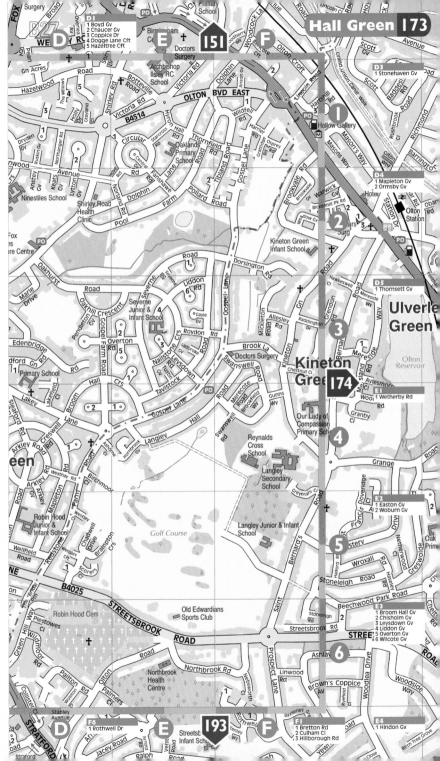

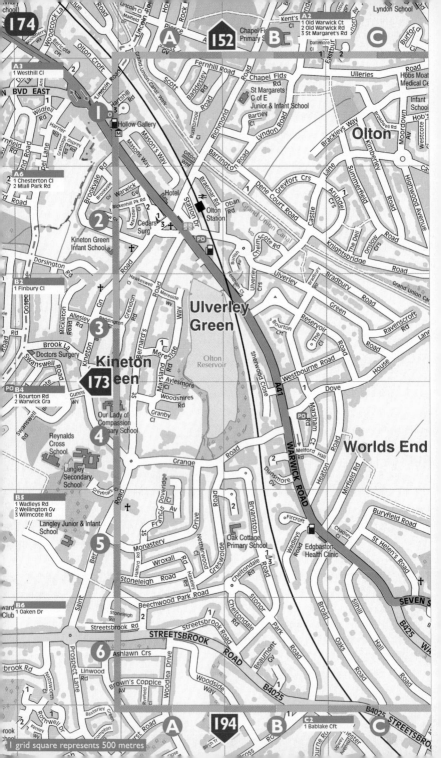

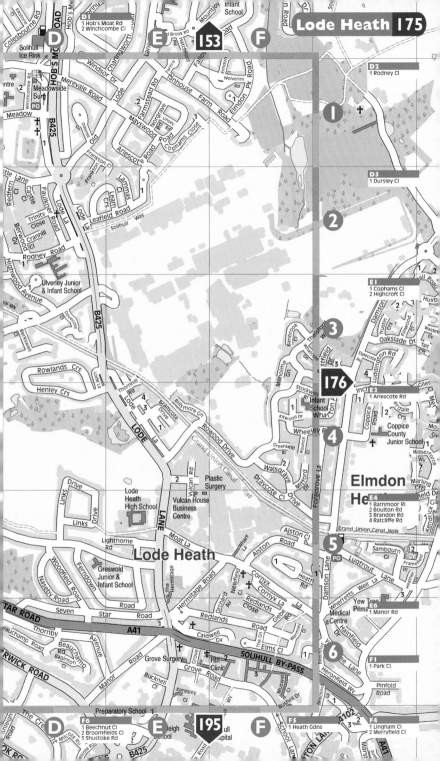

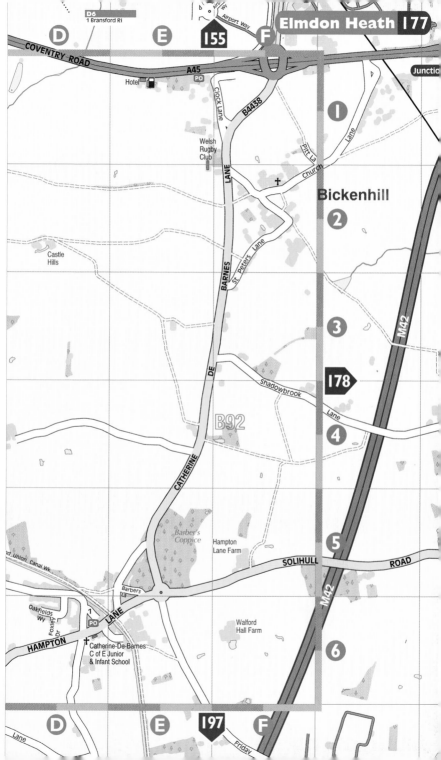

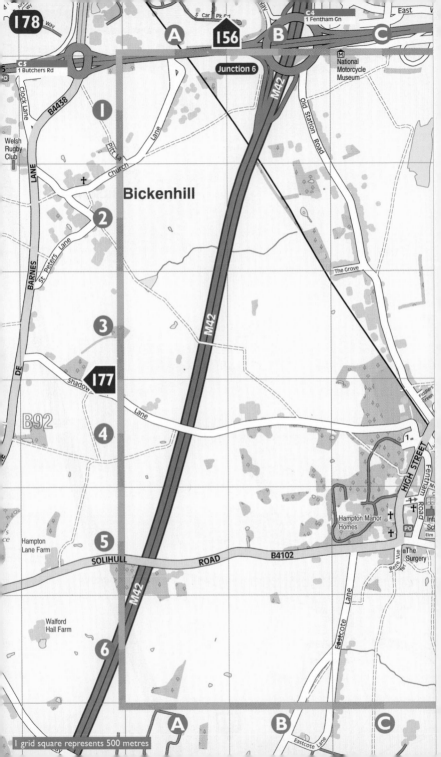

I grid square represents 500 metres

Stonebridge

Pasture Farm

KENILWORTH ROAD

Warwickshire County

Solihull

Geary's

The Som

Molands Bridge

A452

B4102

Diddington Lane

River Blythe

MERIDEN ROAD

Corbett's Close

Lapwing Drive

Hampton in Arden Station

The Crescent

Patrick Bridge

Hornbrook Farm

Corner's End Lane

KENILWORTH ROAD

Hampton in Arden

Peel Close

Bellemere Road

Marsh Lane

Hook End

Arden House

Marsh Lane

Coventry Road

COVENTRY R

157

D · E · F

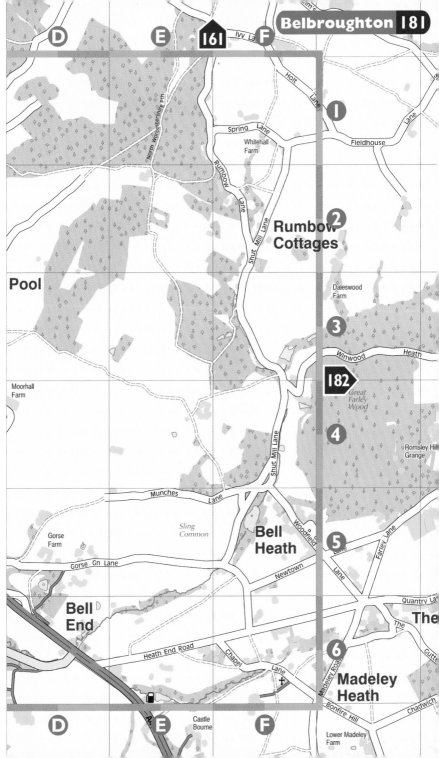

161

Ivy Lane

I

Holt Lane

Spring Lane

Whitehall Farm

Fieldhouse Lane

Rumbow Lane

2

Rumbow Cottages

Shut Mill Lane

Pool

Daleswood Farm

3

Winwood Heath

182

Moorhall Farm

Great Farley Wood

4

Romsley Hill Grange

Shut Mill Lane

Munches Lane

Sling Common

Bell Heath

Woodfield Lane

5

Gorse Farm

Gorse Gn Lane

Newtown

Farley Lane

Lane

Quantry La

The

Bell End

Heath End Road

Chapel Lane

The

Gutt

6

Madeley Road

Madeley Heath

Castle Bourne

Bonfire Hill

Chadwick

Lower Madeley Farm

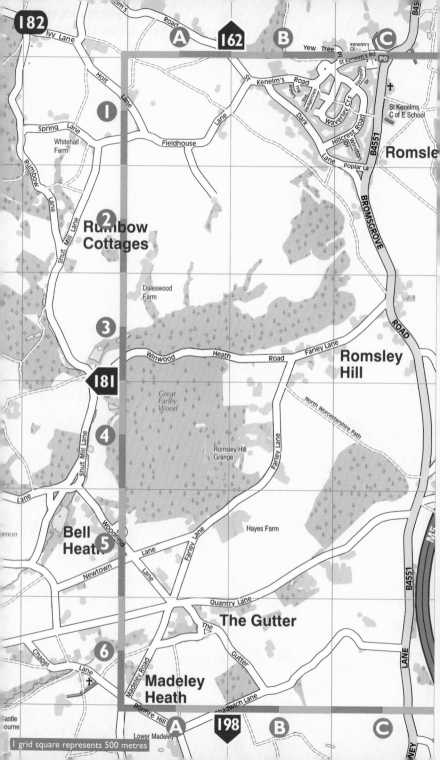

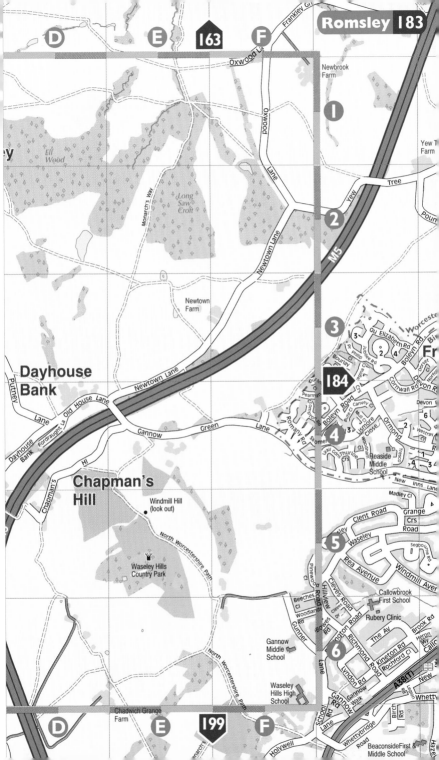

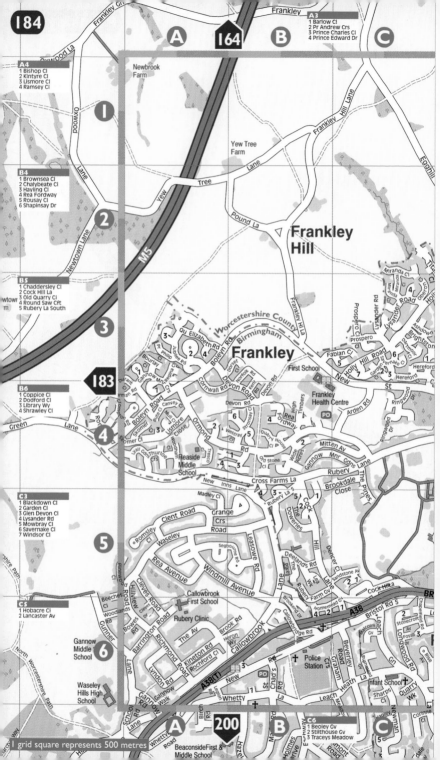

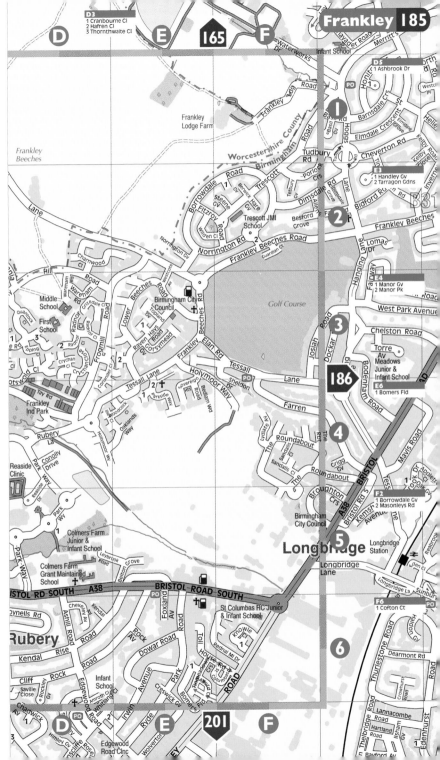

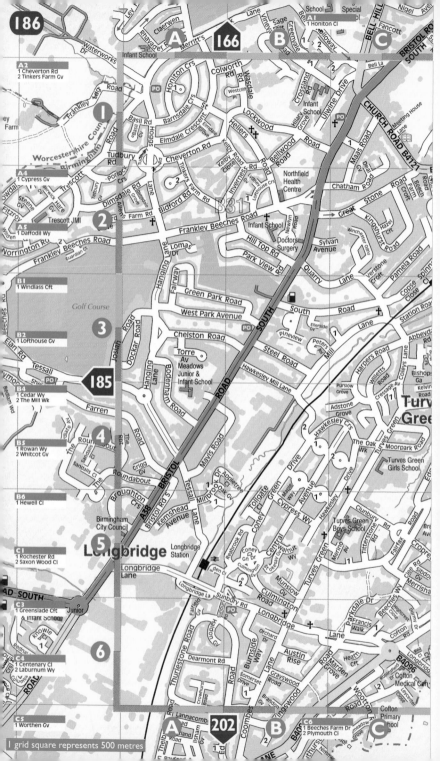

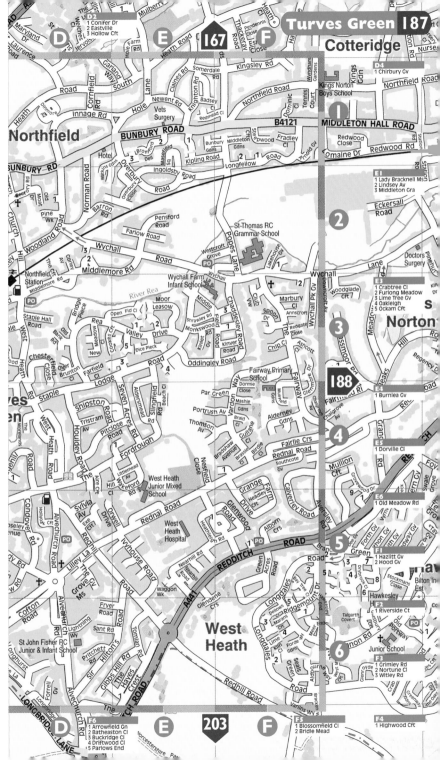

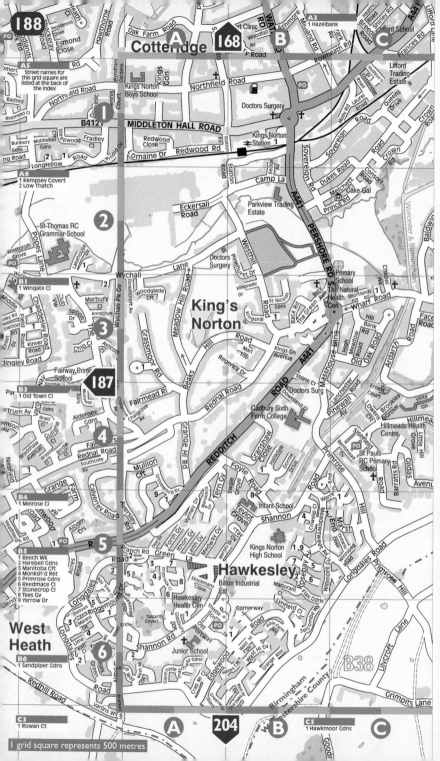

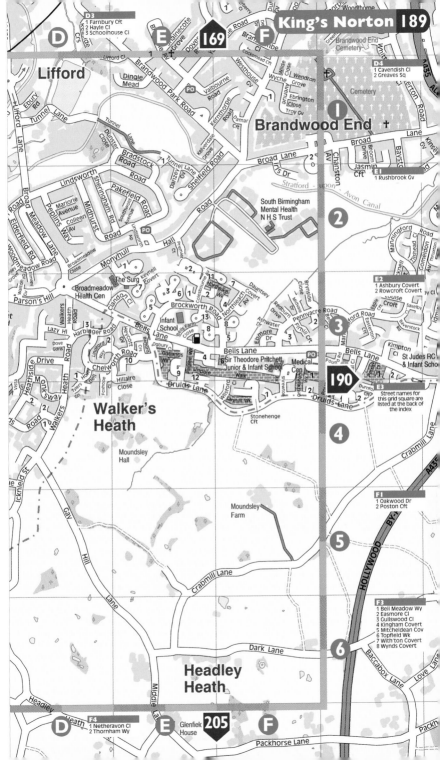

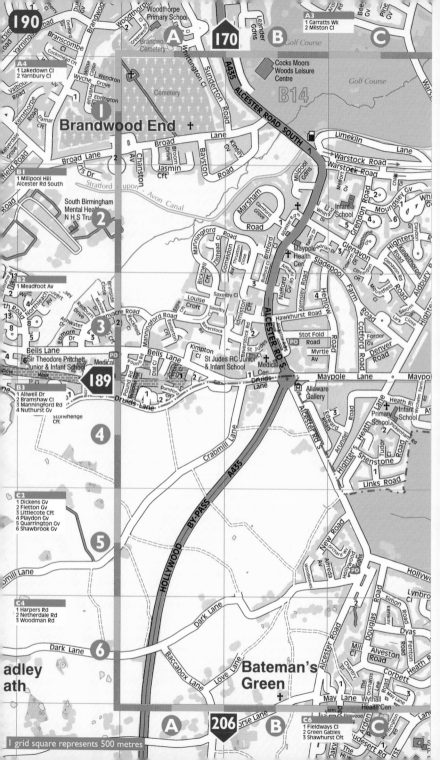

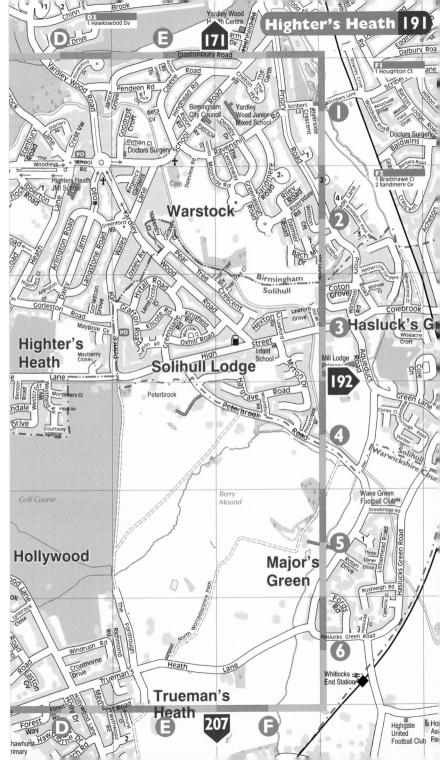

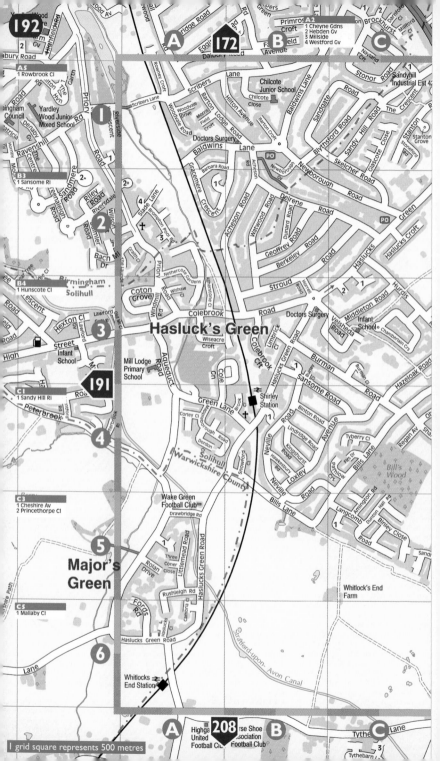

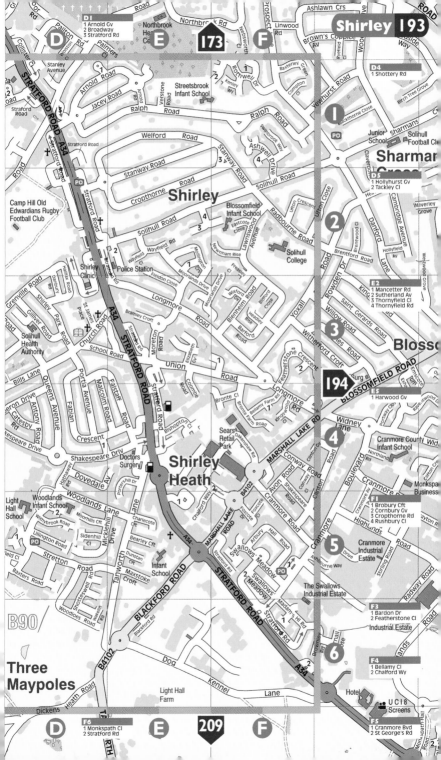

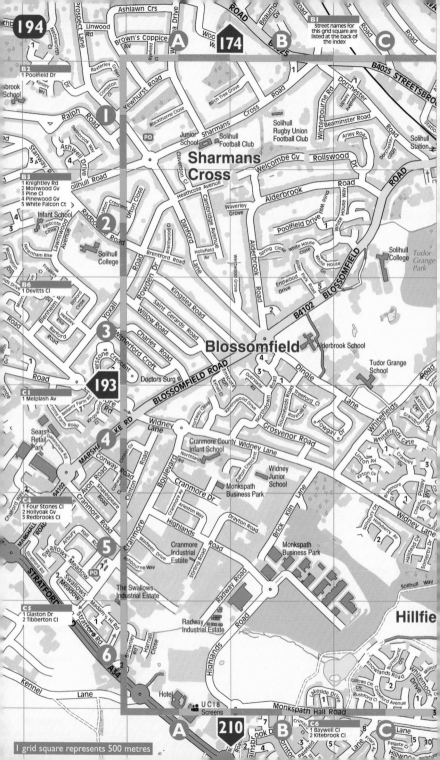

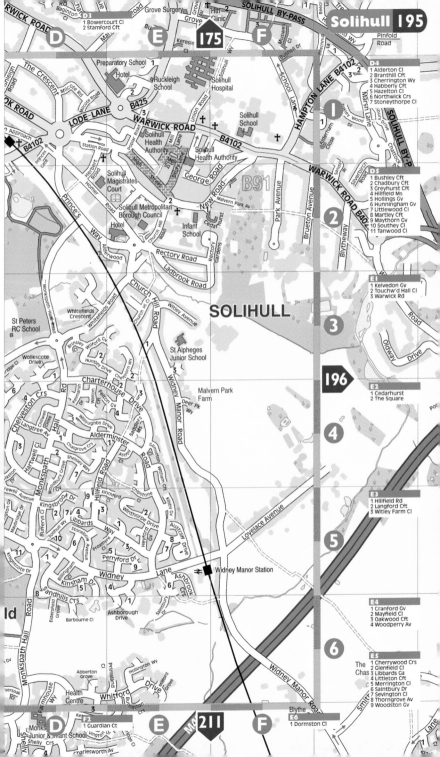

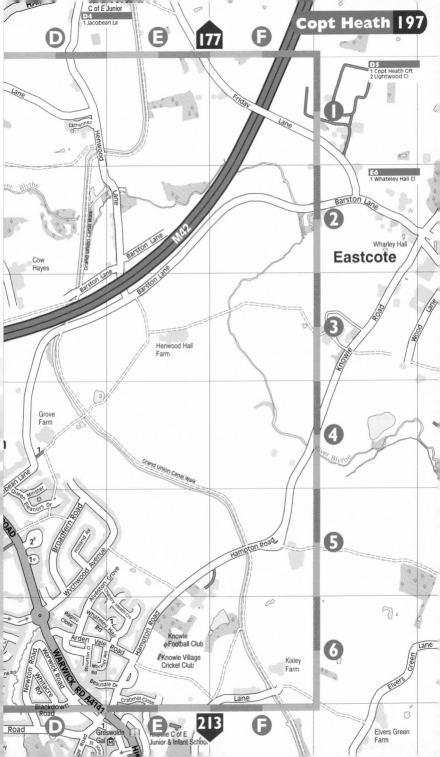

D E **177** F

Eastcote

Wharley Hall

Cow Hayes

Henwood Hall Farm

Grove Farm

Knowle Football Club

Knowle Village Cricket Club

Kixley Farm

Elvers Green Farm

D4
1 Jacobean La

D5
1 Copt Heath Cft
2 Lightwood Cl

E6
1 Whateley Hall Cl

Friday Lane

Barston Lane

M42

Grand Union Canal Walk

Henwood Lane

Knowle Road

Wood Lane

Lane

River Blythe

Hampton Road

Broadfern Road

Wychwood Avenue

Holland Av

Alveston Grove

Cherry Heath Crs

Hampton Road

Queen Eleanor's Dr

Minster Cl

Jacobean Lane

Ragley Close

Whateley Hall Rd

Arden Vale Road

Stourton Cl

Mock's Rd

Warwick Road

Newton Road

Whitacre Rd

Beausale Dr

WARWICK RD A4141

Blackdown Road

Crabmill Close

Greswolde Gal

213

Knowle C of E Junior & Infant School

D E F

Elvers Green Lane

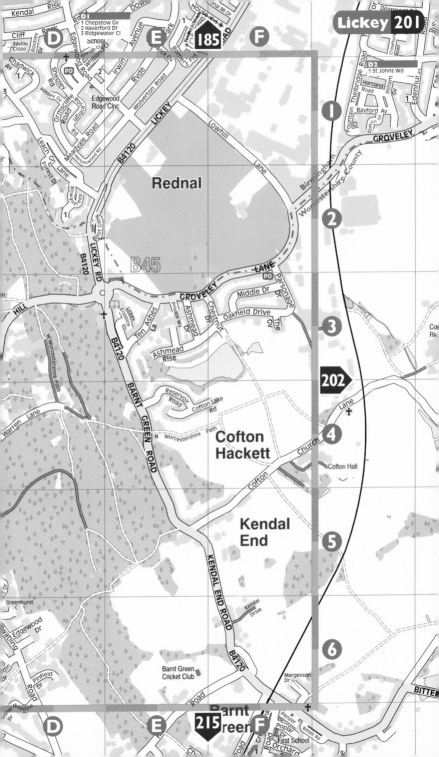

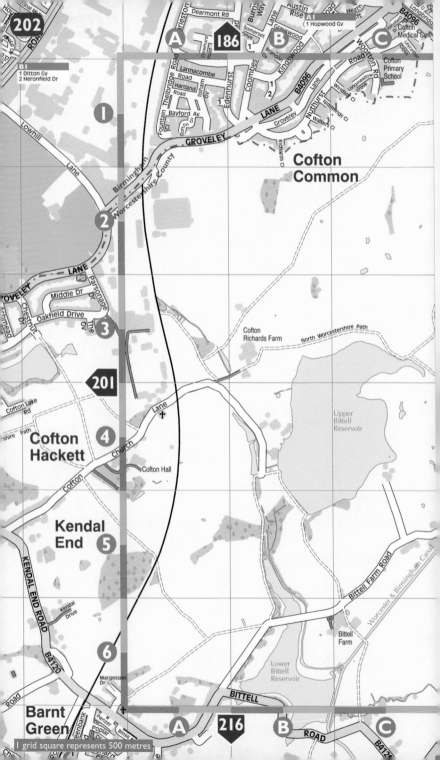

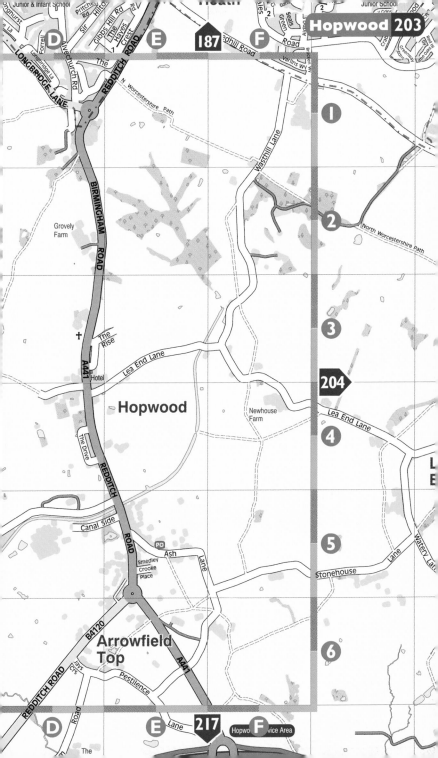

Junior School

Junior & Infant School

LONGBRIDGE LANE

Alvechurch Rd

REDDITCH ROAD

edhill Road

Varlins Wy

N Worcestershire Path

Wasthill Lane

1

2   North Worcestershire Path

BIRMINGHAM ROAD

Grovely Farm

3

The Rise

Lea End Lane

A441   Hotel

204

Lea End Lane

Hopwood

Newhouse Farm

4

L
E

The Drive

REDDITCH ROAD

5

Canal Side

PO

Ash Lane

Stonehouse

Lane

Watery Lan

6

Smedley Crooke Place

B4120

Arrowfield Top

A441

REDDITCH ROAD

Jays Crs

Pestilence

The

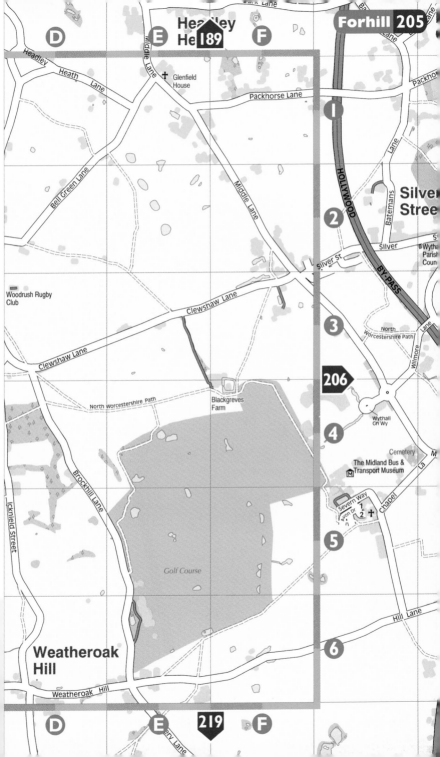

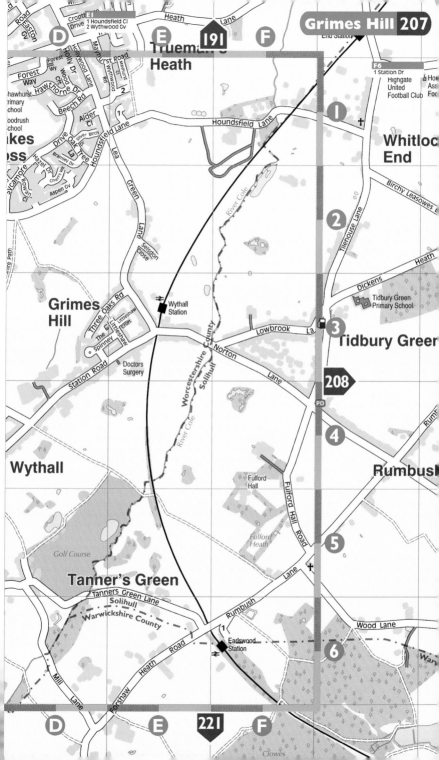

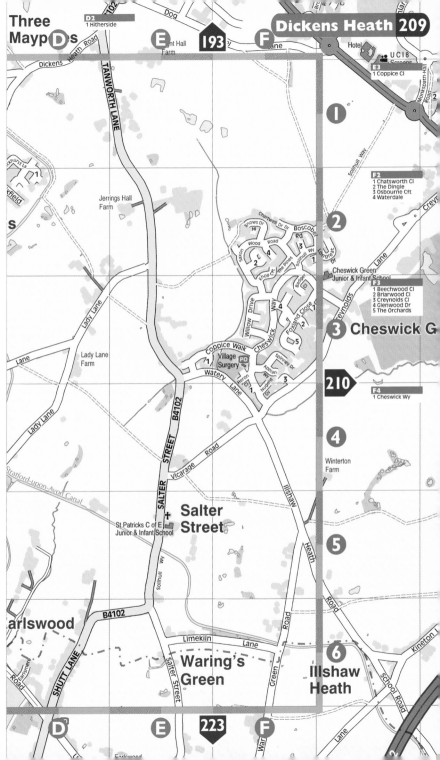

210 ▲ **194** **A** **B** **C**

A34

Knowlands Road

Monkspath Hall Road

UCI 8 Screens

B1
1 Colehurst Cft
2 Dunley Cft
3 Metchley Cft
4 Sandbarn Cl
5 Sherdmore Cft
6 Stonehill Cft
7 Tylers Gv

B2
1 Bretshall Cl

Meerhill Av
Hay Lane
Hillwood
Rainsbrook Dr
Thornton Road
Farnborough Dr
Rushwick Grove
Frankholmes
Stepenhall Road
Stanbrook Road

STRATFORD ROAD

Creynolds Lane

Kemerton Westgrove Av

I

Sollihull Way

C1
1 Bellington Cft
2 Highdown Crs
3 Himbleton Cft
4 Monkspath
5 Oldberrow Cl
6 Rochford Ct
7 Slateley Crs
8 Slimbridge Cl
9 Whitwell Dr
10 Wynbrook Gv

2

Saxon Wood Road
The Fenns
Longfield
Solihull Way

Cheswick Green
Junior & Infant School

C2
1 Barham Cl
2 Bowbrook Av
3 Norcombe Gv

Creynolds Lane

Cheswick Green

Shirley Park Sports Club

River Blythe

Junction 4

3

Coppice Walk
Village Surgery PO
Watery Lane
Cheswick Way
Willow

209

4

Road

Winterton Farm

Sidenhales Farm

Ilshaw

alter reet

5

Heath Road

eklin Lane

aring's reen

Green Road

Kineton Lane

6

Ilshaw Heath

School Road

M42

A **B** **C**

I grid square represents 500 metres

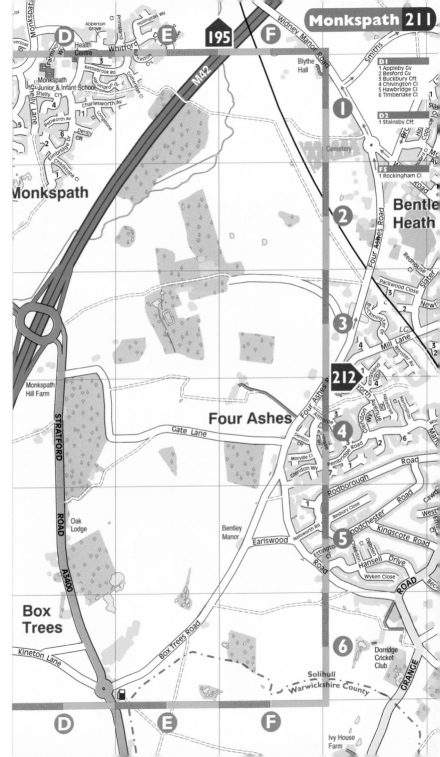

Monkspath

Monkspath Junior & Infant School

Health Centre

Blythe Hall

Smiths

Cemetery

Bentley Heath

Four Ashes

Gate Lane

Monkspath Hill Farm

STRATFORD ROAD A3400

Oak Lodge

Bentley Manor

Earlswood

Box Trees

Kineton Lane

Box Trees Road

Solihull Warwickshire County

Ivy House Farm

Dorridge Cricket Club

Four Ashes Road

Widney Manor Road

Mill Lane

Rodborough Road

Goodchester Road

Kingscote Road

Hansell Drive

ROAD

GRANGE

195

212

D1
1 Appleby Gv
2 Besford Gv
3 Buckbury Cft
4 Chivington Cl
5 Hawbridge Cl
6 Timberlake Cl

D2
1 Stainsby Cft

F1
1 Rockingham Cl

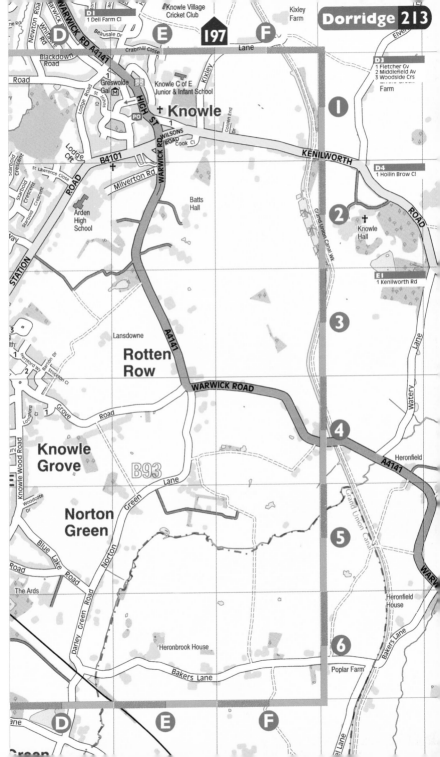

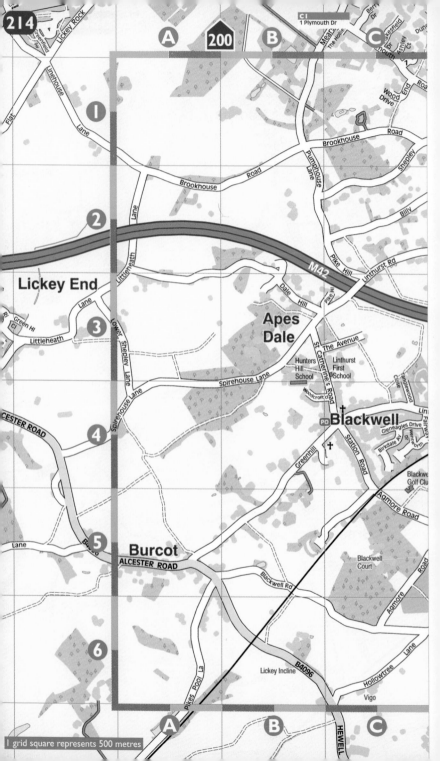

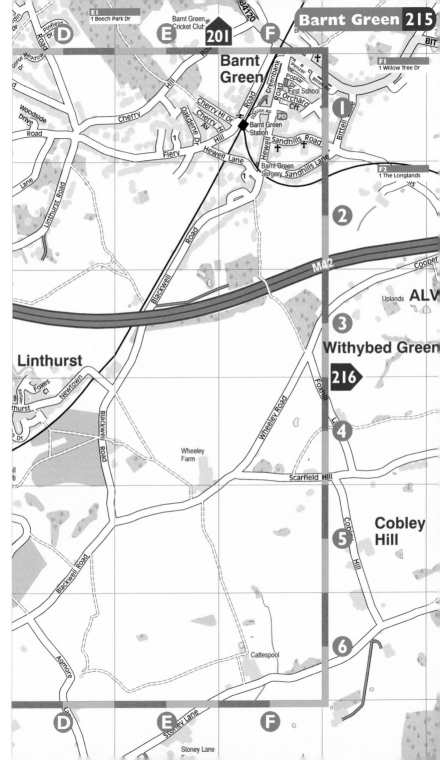

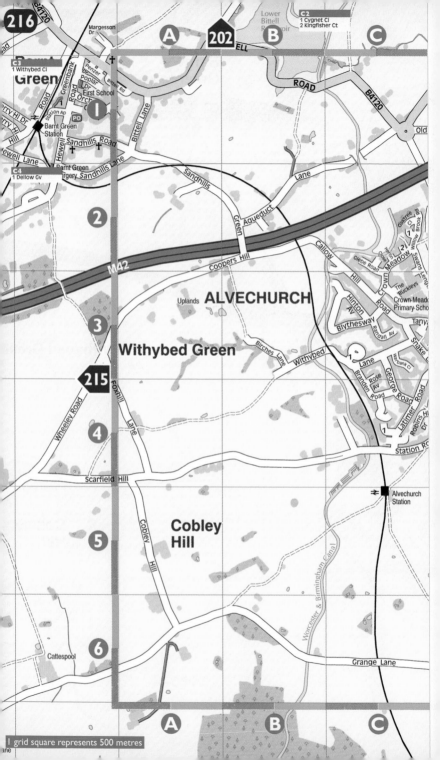

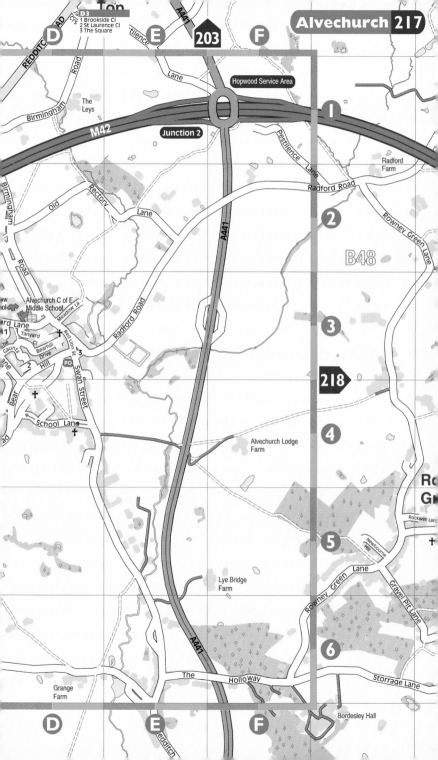

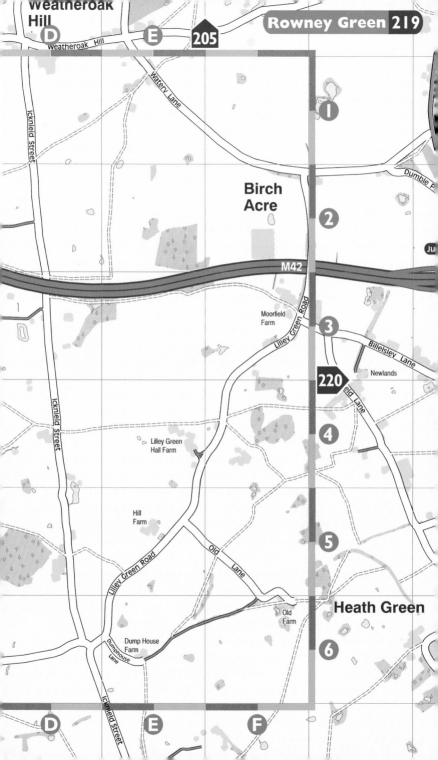

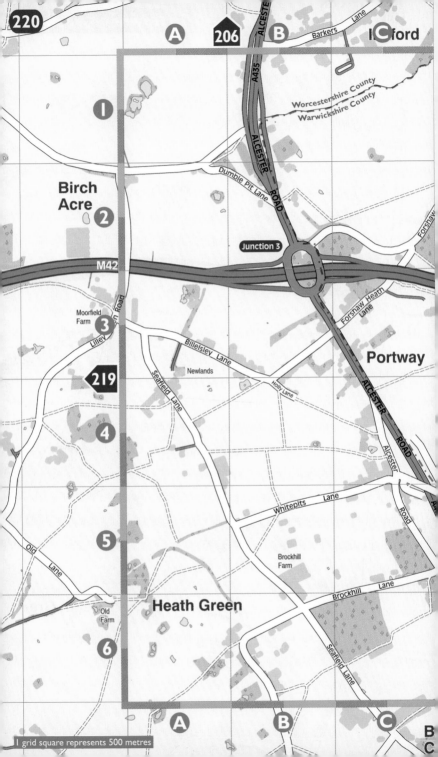

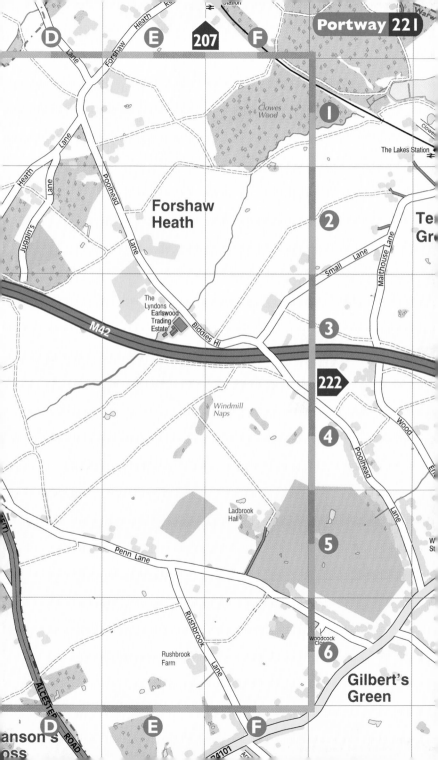

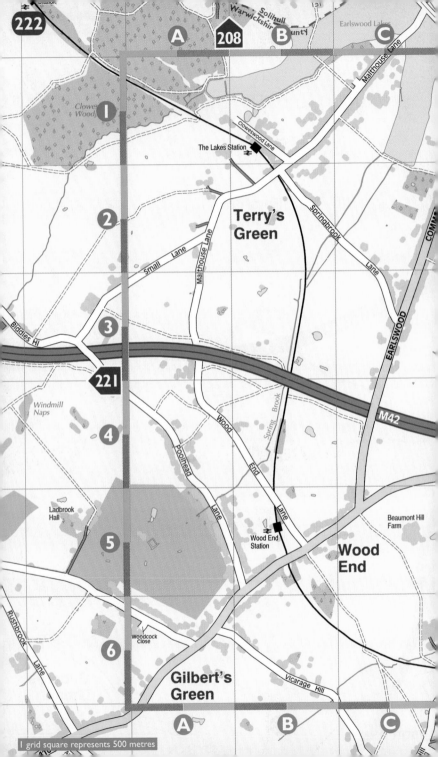

222

208

Solihull
Warwickshire

Earlswood Lakes

Malthouse Lane

Clowes
Wood

I

Clowerwood Lane

The Lakes Station

Springbrook Lane

EARLSWOOD

COMM

Terry's
Green

2

Small Lane

Malthouse Lane

3

Biddles Hl

221

Windmill
Naps

4

Wood End Lane

Spring Brook

M42

5

Ladbrook
Hall

Poolhead Lane

Wood End Station

Beaumont Hill
Farm

Wood
End

6

Woodcock
Close

Rushbrook Lane

Gilbert's
Green

Vicarage Hill

A

B

C

1 grid square represents 500 metres

Waring's
Gr 209

D E F

PO

B4102

Umberslade Road

Earlswood
Court

Cut Throat Lane

Salter Street

Warings

Dyers

Lane

M42

Timkers Lane

I

Cut Throat Lane

Tinkers Lane

Woodlands
Farm

2

Clay Bank
Farm

Tithe Barn Lane

The Beeches

Umberslade Road

Old Grove

Arnold's
Wood

3

Junction 3a

Tithe Barn Lane

M40

4

Umberslade Road

Birchy Cross
Farm

BROAD LANE B4101

5

B4101 POU

Umberslade
Business Centre

Tom Hill

Brown's Green

Brook
House
Farm

6

Umberslade Road

D E F

Acock's Green	150 B5
Alcester Lane's End	169 F5
Aldridge	34 C1
Allen End	62 B3
Alum Rock	126 C4
Alvechurch	216 A3
Amblecote	136 B2
Apes Dale	214 B3
Arrowfield Top	29 D3
Ashmore Lake	29 D3
Ashmore Park	14 B4
Ashwood	110 A2
Aston	124 C1
Bacon's End	131 E3
Balls Hill	72 C2
Balsall Heath	148 A4
Banners Gate	56 C5
Baptist End	115 E1
Barnt Green	215 F1
Barr Common	35 E4
Bartley Green	165 F3
Bateman's Green	190 B6
Bearwood	120 C5
Beech Lanes	144 A2
Belbroughton	180 B6
Bell End	181 D6
Belle Vale	140 B4
Bellevue	199 E5
Bell Heath	181 F5
Bentley	29 F4
Bentley Heath	212 A2
Bescot	51 E3
Bickenhill	177 F2
Bilbrook	9 E1
Billesley	171 E5
Billesley Common	170 C4
Bilston	47 E2
Birch Acre	219 F2
Birch End	74 B4
Birches Green	102 C2
Birchfield	99 F4
Birchills	31 F4
Birmingham	123 D6
Blackheath	117 D5
Black Lake	72 C4
Blackwell	214 C4
Blakeley	64 C6
Blakenall Heath	17 E5
Blakenhall	45 D2
Bloomfield	70 B5
Blossomfield	194 A3
Bloxwich	16 C4
Blyth End	109 E3
Boldmere	80 C2
Bordesley	124 C5
Bordesley Green	126 A6
Bournbrook	168 C1
Bourne Vale	35 E4
Bournville	168 B4
Bowling Green	115 E5
Box Trees	211 D6
Brades Village	93 F4
Bradley	47 F6
Bradmore	44 A1
Bramford	68 C4
Brandwood End	189 F1
The Bratch	64 B3
Brierley Hill	113 E5
Bristnall Fields	119 D4
Brockmoor	113 D3
Bromford	104 A4
Bromley	112 C2
Brown's Green	98 B1
Buckland End	104 C6
Buckpool	112 B5
Burcot	214 A5
Burnt Tree	92 B3
Bushbury	12 A2
Caldmore	51 F1
California	166 B1
Carroway Head	41 D3
Castle Bromwich	105 E5
Castlecroft	42 C1
Castle Vale	104 C2
Catherine-de-Barnes	176 C6
Causeway Green	118 B4
Chad Valley	146 B2
Chapman's Hill	183 D4
Charlemont	73 F4
Chattle Hill	108 A3
Chelmsley Wood	131 E6
Cheswick Green	210 A3
The Chuckery	5 H4
Churchfield	74 A6
Church Hill	50 C5
Cinder Hill	68 B2
Claregate	23 F1
Clent	180 C2
Coal Pool	32 B2
Cobley Hill	216 A5
Codsall	8 B1
Cofton Common	202 B1
Cofton Hackett	201 F4
Cole End	108 B5
Colehall	129 D2
Coleshill	108 B6
Colton Hills	44 C6
Compton	23 C5
Coombeswood	141 D3
Copt Heath	196 C4
Coseley	69 E2
Cotteridge	168 A6
Cradley	139 E3
Cradley Heath	139 E1
Curdworth	84 C5
Dam Mill	9 D4
Darby End	115 F3
Darby's Hill	93 D6
Darlaston	29 E6
Darlaston Green	50 A2
Daw End	33 D2
Dayhouse Bank	183 D3
Deepfields	69 D2
The Delves	52 C5
Dickens Heath	208 C2
Digbeth	7 G6
Doe Bank	59 E2
Dorridge	212 C4
Drakes Cross	206 C1
Druids Heath	21 E4
Dudley	91 F3
Dudley Port	93 E1
Dudley's Fields	16 B5
Dudley Wood	115 E5
Dunstall Hill	25 D2
Eachway	200 B1
Earlswood	208 C6
Edgbaston	146 B3
Elmdon	154 C6
Elmdon Heath	176 A4
Erdington	102 C2
Essington	14 B2
Ettingshall	46 B4
Ettingshall Park	45 F6
Eve Hill	90 C3
Falcon Lodge	61 D3
Fallings Heath	50 A4
Fishley	17 E1
Fordbridge	130 C1
Fordhouses	11 D2
Forhill	204 C3
Forshaw Heath	221 E2
Four Ashes	38 A4
Four Oaks	58 B1
Four Oaks Park	58 B1
Frankley	165 D6
Frankley	184 B3
Frankley Green	164 C6
Frankley Hill	184 B2
Friar Park	51 F6
Garrets Green	128 C6
Gib Heath	98 C6
Giggetty	64 A6
Gilbert's Green	222 A6
Gilbertstone	152 B3
Gilson	108 A4
Glebe Farm	128 B3
Golds Green	72 A3
Goldthorn Park	45 F5
Gornalwood	89 E2
Goscote	18 B5
Gospel End Village	66 B3
Gothersley	110 A5
Gravelly Hill	102 B3
Great Barr	76 B1
Great Bridge	71 D5
Great Wyrley	167 F4
Griffin's Hill	207 D3
Grimes Hill	62 B6
Grove End	75 E2
Grove Vale	94 C1
Guns Village	94 C1
The Gutter	182 A6
Haden Cross	140 C1
Hagley	159 F5
Halesowen	141 E5
Hall Green	73 E3
Hall Green	172 C4
Hampton in Arden	179 D5
Hamstead	76 A3
Handsworth	97 D2
Handsworth Wood	99 D2
Harborne	144 C3
Harden	18 B6
Hardwick	36 B5
Hart's Hill	114 A2
Harvills Hawthorn	71 F4
Hasbury	140 A6
Hasluck's Green	192 A3
Hateley Heath	73 E5
Hawkesley	188 A5
Hawne	140 C4
Hayley Green	161 E2
Hay Mills	151 D3
Headley Heath	189 E6
Heath End	18 B4
Heath Green	220 A6
Heath Town	26 C3
Highgate	148 B1
High Heath	19 E3
High Heath	61 D1
Highter's Heath	191 D3
Hill	38 C3
Hillfield	194 C6
Hill Hook	38 A1
Hill Top	72 C3
Hill Wood	39 E2
Himley	87 D2
Hinksford	86 B5
Hodgehill	127 F2
Holly Bank	21 D2
Hollywood	191 D5
Holy Cross	180 A3
Hook End	179 D6
Hopwood	203 E4
Horseley Heath	71 E6
Hunnington	163 D4
Hunts Green	63 E2
Hurst Green	142 B1
Hurst Hill	68 B3
Illey	164 A3
Illshaw Heath	209 F6
Inkford	206 C6
Kates Hill	92 A4
Kendal End	201 F5
Kineton Green	173 F3
King's Heath	170 A4
King's Hill	50 B6
Kingshurst	106 C6
King's Norton	188 A3
Kingstanding	78 C2
Kingswinford	112 B1
Kitt's Green	129 E3
Kitwell	164 C4
Knowle	213 E1
Knowle Grove	213 D4
The Knowle	116 C2
Ladywood	122 C5
Lambert's End	94 C2
Lane Green	9 E2
Lane Head	29 E1
Lanesfield	46 C5
Langley	118 B2
Langley Green	119 D3
Lapal	142 B6
Lawns Wood	111 D4
Lea End	204 B4
Lea Hall	128 C5
Leamore	30 C1
Lea Bank	147 E1
Leighswood	20 C5
Ley Hill	38 C6
Lickey	200 C4
Lifford	189 D1
Linthurst	215 D3
Little Aston	37 E2
Little Bloxwich	17 E2
Little Bromwich	126 B5
Little Packington	157 D3
Littleworth End	61 E1
Lode Heath	175 E5
Lodge Hill	167 D1
Londonderry	119 E3
London Fields	90 A3
Longbridge	185 F5
Lower Bradley	48 B5
Lower Gornal	90 A1
Lower Illey	164 A4
Lower Penn	42 B4
Low Hill	11 F6
Lozells	99 E6
The Lunt	48 C2
Lutley	161 D1
Lydiate Ash	199 E4
Lye	138 B3
Lyndon Green	152 B2

Madeley Heath	182 A6
Major's Green	191 F5
Maney	59 D5
Marlbrook	199 F6
Marston Green	154 C1
Maw Green	53 D3
Mayer's Green	96 A2
Mere Green	39 D4
Merridale	24 A5
Merry Hill	43 E2
Mesty Croft	50 C5
Middle Bickenhill	156 C6
Minworth	83 E6
Monkspath	210 C2
Monmore Green	46 C1
Moor Green	169 F2
Moor Hall	39 F6
Moseley	26 C6
Moseley	170 B1
Moxley	49 D5
Mushroom Green	115 D6
Nechells	101 F5
Nechells Green	125 D3
Netherton	115 D2
Newbolds	26 C1
Newbridge	23 F4
New Invention	15 E5
New Oscott	79 F1
Newton	75 E3
New Town	93 F1
Newtown	123 E2
Northfield	187 D1
Norton	158 A1
Norton Green	213 D5
Oakham	92 B6
Ocker Hill	71 E2
Oldbury	118 C2
Old Fallings	12 B6
Old Hill	116 C6
Old Swinford	136 C6
Olton	174 C1
Orton	42 B6
Orton Hill	64 C1
Ounsdale	64 B5
Overend	140 A3
Over Green	84 B2
Oxbarn	44 A2
Oxley	11 D5
Packwood Gullet	212 B6
Palfrey	51 F3
Palmers Cross	9 D5
Parkfield	46 B4
Park Village	26 B2
Pedmore	159 F3
Pelsall	19 D2
Pendeford	10 A3
Penn	44 A3
Pensnett	89 D6
Perry	77 F5
Perry Barr	77 D6
Perry Beeches	76 C3
Perry Common	79 D3
Perton	22 A3
Pheasey	55 E5
Pleck	51 D3
Portobello	28 A5
Portway	117 E1
Portway	220 C3
Prestwood	110 A6
Priestfield	47 D3
Primrose Hill	115 F3
Princes End	70 A2
Pype Hayes	81 F6
Quarry Bank	138 B1
Queslett	77 E1
Quinton	142 C3
Reddicap Heath	60 C5
Rednal	201 E2
Ridgacre	143 E3
Romsley	182 C1
Romsley Hill	182 C3
Rood End	119 E1
Roseville	68 C3
Rotten Row	213 E3
Rotton Park	122 A3
Roughley	39 E4
Round Oak	114 A3
Round's Green	94 A5
Rowley Regis	117 D2
Rowney Green	218 B4
Rubery	184 C6
Ruiton	89 F1
Rumbow Cottages	181 F2
Rumbush	208 A4
Rushall	19 E6
Russell's Hall	90 A5
Salter Street	209 E5
Saltley	126 A3
Sandwell	120 C1
Scotlands	12 C5
Sedgley	68 A3
Selly Oak	167 F2
Selly Park	168 C2
Shard End	129 F2
Sharmans Cross	194 A1
Sheldon	153 D4
Shelfield	19 E5
Shenley Fields	166 A4
Shirley	193 E2
Shirley Heath	193 E4
Short Cross	140 C4
Short Heath	29 F1
Short Heath	80 B5
Silver End	113 D6
Silver Street	206 A2
Small Heath	149 E1
Small Heath	150 C2
Smethwick	120 B3
Soho	121 E1
Solihull	195 E3
Solihull Lodge	191 E3
South Yardley	151 F3
Sparkbrook	149 D2
Sparkhill	149 E6
Springfield	3 H1
Springfield	116 B2
Springfield	171 E4
Spring Hill	43 E1
Stambermill	137 E4
Stechford	128 A4
Stirchley	168 C4
Stockfield	151 E5
Stockland Green	101 E1
Stockwell End	23 E2
Stoke End	62 B2
Stonebridge	179 D1
Stone Cross	73 F2
Stonnall	21 F1
Stourbridge	135 F5
Stourton	134 B2
Stow Lawn	47 F1
The Straits	67 D6
Streetly	37 D5
Stubber's Green	20 A5
Summer Hill	70 C2
Sutton Coldfield	60 C2
Swan Village	94 B1
Swindon	86 B3
Tanner's Green	207 D5
Tansley Hill	92 B6
Tat Bank	94 C6
Ten Acres	169 D3
Terry's Green	222 B2
Tettenhall	23 E2
Tettenhall Wood	23 F3
Thimble End	82 B2
Three Maypoles	193 D6
Tidbury Green	208 A3
Tile Cross	130 A5
Tilehouse Green	212 C2
Tipton	70 C4
Tipton Green	69 F5
Tividale	93 D4
Toll End	71 D5
Tower Hill	76 C5
Trueman's Heath	191 E6
Tudor Hill	58 C3
Turves Green	186 C4
Tyburn	104 A2
Tyseley	150 C4
Ulverley Green	174 A3
Upper Catshill	199 D6
Upper Gornal	68 A5
Upper Witton	79 E5
Vauxhall	125 D4
Vigo	20 B3
The Village	88 A6
Wake Green	170 C2
Walker's Heath	189 D4
Wallbrook	69 E4
Wall Heath	87 D5
Wallington Heath	16 C2
Walmley	82 B3
Walmley Ash	83 D4
Walsall	33 D5
Walsall Wood	20 B1
Walton Pool	180 C3
Ward End	126 C4
Waring's Green	209 E6
Warley Woods	120 A6
Warstock	191 E2
Washwood Heath	126 A1
Water Orton	107 D2
Weatheroak Hill	205 D6
Wednesbury	49 F5
Wednesbury Oak	70 B2
Wednesfield	27 F1
Weoley Castle	166 B2
Wergs	22 B1
Westcroft	13 D2
West Hagley	159 D6
West Heath	187 E6
Whiteheath Gate	118 A3
Whitehouse Common	60 B3
Whitlock's End	208 A1
Wightwick	22 B6
Wildmoor	198 B3
Willenhall	29 D4
Winson Green	122 B2
Wishaw	84 C1
Withybed Green	216 A3
Withymoor Village	114 A6
Witton	100 A2
Wollaston	136 A3
Wollescote	138 A5
Wolverhampton	3 G3
Woodcock Hill	166 A3
Wood End	13 E6
Wood End	222 C5
Woodgate	164 B2
Woodgate Valley	143 E6
Wood Green	50 C4
Wood Hayes	13 D4
Woods Bank	49 F4
Woodsetton	68 A4
Woodside	114 B1
The Woods	51 E5
Wordsley	112 A4
Worlds End	174 C4
Wylde Green	81 F2
Wythall	206 A5
Yardley	151 F1
Yardley Wood	172 A6
Yew Tree	53 D6

USING THE STREET INDEX

Street names are listed alphabetically. Each street name is followed by its postal town or area locality, the Postcode District, the page number, and the reference to the square in which the name is found.

Example: **Abberley Cl** *HALE* B63......................**162** B1 1

Some entries are followed by a number in a blue box. This number indicates the location of the street within the referenced grid square. The full street name is listed at the side of the map page.

GENERAL ABBREVIATIONS

ACC	ACCESS
ALY	ALLEY
AP	APPROACH
AR	ARCADE
ASS	ASSOCIATION
AV	AVENUE
BCH	BEACH
BLDS	BUILDINGS
BND	BEND
BNK	BANK
BR	BRIDGE
BRK	BROOK
BTM	BOTTOM
BUS	BUSINESS
BVD	BOULEVARD
BY	BYPASS
CATH	CATHEDRAL
CEM	CEMETERY
CEN	CENTRE
CFT	CROFT
CH	CHURCH
CHA	CHASE
CHYD	CHURCHYARD
CIR	CIRCLE
CIRC	CIRCUS
CL	CLOSE
CLFS	CLIFFS
CMP	CAMP
CNR	CORNER
CO	COUNTY
COLL	COLLEGE
COM	COMMON
COMM	COMMISSION
CON	CONVENT
COT	COTTAGE
COTS	COTTAGES
CP	CAPE
CPS	COPSE
CR	CREEK
CREM	CREMATORIUM
CRS	CRESCENT
CSWY	CAUSEWAY
CT	COURT
CTRL	CENTRAL
CTS	COURTS
CTYD	COURTYARD
CUTT	CUTTINGS
CV	COVE
CYN	CANYON
DEPT	DEPARTMENT
DL	DALE
DM	DAM
DR	DRIVE
DRO	DROVE
DRY	DRIVEWAY
DWGS	DWELLINGS
E	EAST
EMB	EMBANKMENT
EMBY	EMBASSY
ESP	ESPLANADE
EST	ESTATE
EX	EXCHANGE
EXPY	EXPRESSWAY
EXT	EXTENSION
F/O	FLYOVER
FC	FOOTBALL CLUB
FK	FORK
FLD	FIELD
FLDS	FIELDS
FLS	FALLS
FLS	FLATS
FM	FARM
FT	FORT
FWY	FREEWAY
FY	FERRY

GA	GATE
GAL	GALLERY
GDN	GARDEN
GDNS	GARDENS
GLD	GLADE
GLN	GLEN
GN	GREEN
GND	GROUND
GRA	GRANGE
GRG	GARAGE
GT	GREAT
GTWY	GATEWAY
GV	GROVE
HGR	HIGHER
HL	HILL
HLS	HILLS
HO	HOUSE
HOL	HOLLOW
HOSP	HOSPITAL
HRB	HARBOUR
HTH	HEATH
HTS	HEIGHTS
HVN	HAVEN
HWY	HIGHWAY
IMP	IMPERIAL
IN	INLET
IND EST	INDUSTRIAL ESTATE
INF	INFIRMARY
INFO	INFORMATION
INT	INTERCHANGE
IS	ISLAND
JCT	JUNCTION
JTY	JETTY
KG	KING
KNL	KNOLL
L	LAKE
LA	LANE
LDG	LODGE
LGT	LIGHT
LK	LOCK
LKS	LAKES
LNDG	LANDING
LTL	LITTLE
LWR	LOWER
MAG	MAGISTRATE
MAN	MANSIONS
MD	MEAD
MDW	MEADOWS
MEM	MEMORIAL
MKT	MARKET
MKTS	MARKETS
ML	MALL
ML	MILL
MNR	MANOR
MS	MEWS
MSN	MISSION
MT	MOUNT
MTN	MOUNTAIN
MTS	MOUNTAINS
MUS	MUSEUM
MWY	MOTORWAY
N	NORTH
NE	NORTH EAST
NW	NORTH WEST
O/P	OVERPASS
OFF	OFFICE
ORCH	ORCHARD
OV	OVAL
PAL	PALACE
PAS	PASSAGE
PAV	PAVILION
PDE	PARADE
PH	PUBLIC HOUSE
PK	PARK
PKWY	PARKWAY

PL	PLACE
PLN	PLAIN
PLNS	PLAINS
PLZ	PLAZA
POL	POLICE STATION
PR	PRINCE
PREC	PRECINCT
PREP	PREPARATORY
PRIM	PRIMARY
PROM	PROMENADE
PRS	PRINCESS
PRT	PORT
PT	POINT
PTH	PATH
PZ	PIAZZA
QD	QUADRANT
QU	QUEEN
QY	QUAY
R	RIVER
RBT	ROUNDABOUT
RD	ROAD
RDG	RIDGE
REP	REPUBLIC
RES	RESERVOIR
RFC	RUGBY FOOTBALL CLUB
RI	RISE
RP	RAMP
RW	ROW
S	SOUTH
SCH	SCHOOL
SE	SOUTH EAST
SER	SERVICE AREA
SH	SHORE
SHOP	SHOPPING
SKWY	SKYWAY
SMT	SUMMIT
SOC	SOCIETY
SP	SPUR
SPR	SPRING
SQ	SQUARE
ST	STREET
STN	STATION
STR	STREAM
STRD	STRAND
SW	SOUTH WEST
TDG	TRADING
TER	TERRACE
THWY	THROUGHWAY
TNL	TUNNEL
TOLL	TOLLWAY
TPK	TURNPIKE
TR	TRACK
TRL	TRAIL
TWR	TOWER
U/P	UNDERPASS
UNI	UNIVERSITY
UPR	UPPER
V	VALE
VA	VALLEY
VIAD	VIADUCT
VIL	VILLA
VIS	VISTA
VLG	VILLAGE
VLS	VILLAS
VW	VIEW
W	WEST
WD	WOOD
WHF	WHARF
WK	WALK
WKS	WALKS
WLS	WELLS
WY	WAY
YD	YARD
YHA	YOUTH HOSTEL

POSTCODE TOWNS AND AREA ABBREVIATIONS

ACGN	Acock's Green
ALDR	Aldridge
ALE/KHTH/YWD	Alcester Lane's End/King's Heath/Yardley Wood
ALVE	Alvechurch
AST/WIT	Aston/Witton
BDMR/CCFT	Bradmore/Castlecroft
BFLD/HDSWWD	Birchfield/Handsworth Wood
BHAMNEC	Birmingham N.E.C.
BHTH/HG	Balsall Heath/Highgate
BILS/COS	Bilston/Coseley

BKDE/SHDE	Buckland End/Shard End
BKHL/PFLD	Blakenhall/Priestfield
BLKHTH/ROWR	Blackheath/Rowley Regis
BLOX/PEL	Bloxwich/Pelsall
BORD	Bordesley
BRGRVE	Bromsgrove east
BRGRVW	Bromsgrove west
BRLYHL	Brierley Hill
BRWNH	Brownhills
BVILLE	Bournville
CBHAM	Central Birmingham
CBHAMNE	Central Birmingham northeast

CBHAMNW	Central Birmingham northwest
CBHAMW	Central Birmingham west
CBROM	Castle Bromwich
CDSL	Codsall
CDYHTH	Cradley Heath
CHWD/FDBR/MGN	Chelmsley Wood/Fordbridge/Marston Green
COVEN	Coven
CSCFLD/WYGN	Central Sutton Coldfield/Wylde Green
CSHL/WTROR	Coleshill/Water Orton
CVALE	Castle Vale

DARL/WED ....Darlaston/Wednesbury
DIG/EDG ....Digbeth/Edgbaston
DOR/KN ....Dorridge/Knowle
DSYBK/YTR ....Daisy Bank/Yew Tree
DUDN ....Dudley north
DUDS ....Dudley south
DUNHL/THL/PER.................Dunstall Hill/
                                              Tettenhall/Perton
EDG ....Edgbaston
ERDE/BCHGN...Erdington east/Birches Green
ERDW/GRVHL...Erdington west/Gravelly Hill
ETTPK/GDPK/PENN.............Ettingshall Park/
                                         Goldthorn Park/Penn
FOAKS/STRLY ....Four Oaks/Streetly
GTB/HAM ....Great Barr/Hamstead
GTWY ....Great Wyrley
HAG/WOL ....Hagley/Wollescote
HALE ....Halesowen
HDSW ....Handsworth
HHTH/SAND ....Hateley Heath/Sandwell
HIA/OLT ....Hampton in Arden/Olton
HLGN/YWD............Hall Green/Yardley Wood
HLYWD...Hollywood
HOCK/TIA ....Hockley Heath/
                                         Tanworth-in-Arden
HRBN ....Harborne

HWK/WKHTH ....Hawkesley/Walker's Heath
KGSTG ....Kingstanding
KGSWFD ....Kingswinford
KINVER ....Kinver
LDYWD/EDGR...........................Ladywood/
                                         Edgbaston Reservoir
LGLYGN/QTN............Langley Green/Quinton
LGN/SDN/BHAMAIR.............Lyndon Green/
                                 Sheldon/Birmingham Airport
LICHS ....Lichfield south
LOZ/NWT ....Lozells/Newtown
MGN/WHC...............................Mere Green/
                                              Whitehouse Common
MOS/BIL ....Moseley/Billesley
NFLD/LBR................Northfield/Longbridge
OLDBY ....Oldbury
PBAR/PBCH ....Perry Bar/Perry Beeches
POL/KGSB/FAZ..........................Polesworth/
                                             Kingsbury/Fazeley
RBRY ....Rubery
RCOVN/BALC/EX ....Rural Coventry north/
                                     Balsall Common/Exhall
REDE..Redditch east
RIDG/WDGT................Ridgacre/Woodgate
RMSLY ....Romsley
RUSH/SHEL ....Rushall/Shelfield

SCFLD/BOLD........Sutton Coldfield/Boldmere
SEDG ....Sedgley
SHHTH ....Short Heath
SHLY ....Shirley
SLYOAK ....Selly Oak
SMHTH ....Small Heath
SMTHWK..Smethwick
SMTHWKW.........................Smethwick west
SOLH ....Solihull
SPARK ....Sparkhill/Sparkbrook
STETCH..Stetchford
STRBR ....Stourbridge
TPTN/OCK ....Tipton/Ocker Hill
VAUX/NECH............Vauxhall/Nechells
WALM/CURD............Walmley/Curdworth
WASH/WDE ....Washwood Heath/Ward End
WBROM..................................West Bromwich
WLNHL ....Willenhall
WMBN ....Wombourne
WNSFLD ....Wednesfield
WOLV ....Wolverhampton
WOLVN...............Wolverhampton north
WSL ....Walsall
WSLW ....Walsall west
WSNGN...............................Winson Green
YDLY ....Yardley

Index - streets

A

Abb - Alb

Abberley Cl HALE B63 .... 162 B1 ⑪
Abberley Rd LGLYGN/QTN B68 .... 143 D1
    SEDG DY3 .... 89 E1
Abberley St DUDS DY2 .... 91 E5
    SMTHWK B66 .... 121 F2
Abberton Cl HALE B63 .... 141 E6 ⑪
Abberton Gv SOLH B91 .... 195 D6
Abbess Gv YDLY B25 .... 128 A6 ⑪
Abbey Crs HALE B63 .... 139 F5 ⑪
    LGLYGN/QTN B68 .... 119 F6
Abbeydale Rd NFLD/LBR B31 .... 186 C3
Abbeyfield Rd ERDW/GRVHL B23 ... 80 A3
    WOLVN WV10 .... 12 A1
Abbey Rd DUDS DY2 .... 115 F1
    ERDW/GRVHL B23 .... 101 F3
    HALE B63 .... 139 E5
    HRBN B17 .... 145 F4
    SEDG DY3 .... 89 E2
    SMTHWKW B67 .... 119 F6
Abbey Sq BLOX/PEL WS3 .... 16 A3
Abbey St SEDG DY3 .... 89 E2
Abbey St North WSNGN B18 .... 122 C2
Abbot Rd HALE B63........................ 161 E3
Abbots Cl DOR/KN B93 .... 196 C6
    RUSH/SHEL WS4 .... 33 E1
Abbotsford Av GTB/HAM B43 ...... 76 A1 ⑪
Abbotsford Dr DUDN DY1 .... 90 A6
Abbotsford Rd SPARK B11 .... 149 E3
Abbots Ms BRLYHL DY5 .... 115 F6
Abbots Rd ALE/KHTH/YWD B14 ... 170 A4
Abbots St BLOX/PEL WS3 .... 17 F3
Abdon Av SLYOAK B29 .... 167 D4
Aberdeen St WSNGN B18 .... 122 A3
Aberford Cl SHHTH WV12 .... 29 F3
Abigails Cl
    LGN/SDN/BHAMAIR B26 .... 153 D2 ⑪
Abingdon Cl WOLV WV1 .... 27 D5 ⑪
Abingdon Rd BLOX/PEL WS3 .... 16 B3
    DUDS DY2 .... 115 F4
    ERDW/GRVHL B23 .... 79 D3
    WOLV WV1 .... 27 D5
Abingdon Wy BLOX/PEL WS3 ...... 16 B3
    CVALE B35 .... 104 C2 ⑪
Ablewell St WSL WS1 .... 5 E4
Ablow St BKHL/PFLD WV2 .... 45 E1
Abney Dr BILS/COS WV14 .... 68 B2
Aboyne Cl DIG/EDG B5 .... 147 F3
Ab Rw CHBAMNE B4 .... 7 H3
Acacia Av CHWD/FDBR/MGN B37 ... 130 B3
    DSYBK/YTR WS5 .... 52 C5
Acacia Cl
    CHWD/FDBR/MGN B37 .... 130 B3 ⑪
    DUDN DY1 .... 90 C2
    OLDBY B69 .... 93 D3
Acacia Crs CDSL WV8 .... 9 D2
Acacia Dr BILS/COS WV14 .... 68 C4
Acacia Rd BVILLE B30 .... 168 A3

Acfold Rd BFLD/HDSWWD B20 ...... 76 A6
Acheson Rd HLGN/YWD B28 ...... 192 B1
Ackleton Gdns BDMR/CCFT WV3 ... 44 B2
Ackleton Gv SLYOAK B29 .... 166 B3
Acorn Cl ACGN B27 .... 151 D4 ⑪
    BVILLE B30 .... 168 A3
    WBROM B70 .... 95 D3
Acorn Gdns SLYOAK B29............... 168 C3
Acorn Gv CBHAMW B1 .... 123 D4
    CDSL WV8 .... 8 A3
    STRBR DY8 .... 112 A6
Acorn Rd RMSLY B62 .... 141 E1
    WNSFLD WV11 .... 14 C4
Acorn St WLNHL WV13 .... 29 E5 ⑪
    WNSFLD WV11 .... 14 C4
Acre Ri SHHTH WV12 .... 29 D2 ⑪
Acres Rd BRLYHL DY5 .... 138 A1
Acton Dr SEDG DY3 .... 89 D2
Acton Gv BILS/COS WV14 .... 47 D5
    KGSTG B44 .... 78 C1 ⑪
Ada Lewis Ct GTB/HAM B43 .... 76 A4
Adams Brook Dr
    RIDG/WDGT B32 .... 165 D2 ⑪
Adams Cl SMTHWK B66 .... 95 F6
    TPTN/OCK DY4 .... 70 B2 ⑪
Adam's Hl HAG/WOL DY9 .... 180 A1 ⑪
    RIDG/WDGT B32 .... 165 D2
Adams Rd BDMR/CCFT WV3 .... 43 E2
Adams St VAUX/NECH B7 .... 7 H1
    WBROM B70 .... 94 C2
    WSLW WS2 .... 4 A2
Ada Rd SMTHWK B66 .... 121 D4
    VDLY B25 .... 151 D3
Ada Wrighton Cl SHHTH WV12 ... 15 E6 ⑪
Addenbrooke Dr SCFLD/BOLD B73 .. 81 D1
Addenbrooke Rd SMTHWKW B67... 120 B4
    DARL/WED WS10 .... 49 F1
Addenbrooke Wy TPTN/OCK DY4 ... 71 F3 ⑪
Adderley Gdns WASH/WDE B8 ..... 125 F3 ⑪
    WASH/WDE B8 .... 125 F3 ⑪
Adderley Park Cl
    WASH/WDE B8 .... 126 A3 ⑪
Adderley Rd WASH/WDE B8 .... 125 E4
Adderley Rd South
    WASH/WDE B8 .... 125 E4
Adderley St BORD B9 .... 124 C6
Addison Cl DARL/WED WS10 .... 72 B2 ⑪
Addison Cft SEDG DY3 .... 66 C6
Addison Gv WNSFLD WV11 .... 13 D4
Addison Pl BILS/COS WV14 .... 48 B2
    CSHL/WTROR B46............................. 107 D2
Addison Rd ALE/KHTH/YWD B14 ... 170 B4
    BDMR/CCFT WV3 .... 44 B1
    BRLYHL DY5 .... 113 D5
    DARL/WED WS10 .... 74 A1
    VAUX/NECH B7 .... 101 E5
Addison St DARL/WED WS10 .... 72 B1 ⑪
Addison Ter DARL/WED WS10 ..... 72 B1 ⑪
Adelaide Av WBROM B70................. 72 C4
Adelaide St BHTH/HG B12 .... 148 B1 ⑪
    BRLYHL DY5 .... 113 F4
Adelaide Wk BKHL/PFLD WV2 ..... 46 A1 ⑪
Adey Rd WNSFLD WV11 .... 14 B5
Adkins La SMTHWKW B67 .... 120 B6

Admington Rd STETCH B33 .... 153 E1
Admiral Pl MOS/BIL B13................ 148 B5
Admirals Wy BLKHTH/ROWR B65 ... 117 D5
Adrian Cft MOS/BIL B13 .... 171 E2 ⑪
Adria Rd SPARK B11 .... 149 D5
Adshead Rd DUDS DY2 .... 91 E6
Adstone Gv NFLD/LBR B31 .... 186 C4
Adwalton Rd
    DUNHL/THL/PER WV6 .... 22 B4 ⑪
Agenoria Dr STRBR DY8.............. 136 B4
Agmore La BRGRVE B60 .... 215 D6
Agmore Rd BRGRVE B60 .... 214 C5
Ainsdale Cl STRBR DY8 .... 158 B1
Ainsdale Gdns HALE B63 .... 161 F1
Ainsworth Rd WOLVN WV10 .... 12 A1
Aintree Cl BRGRVW B61 .... 198 C6
Aintree Gv BKDE/SHDE B34 .... 129 F1 ⑪
Aintree Rd WOLVN WV10 .... 11 F1
Aintree Wy DUDN DY1 .... 90 A3
Aire Cft NFLD/LBR B31 .... 187 D4
Airfield Dr ALDR WS9 .... 34 A4
Airport Wy BHAMNEC B40............. 155 F6
    HIA/OLT B92 .... 155 F6
    LGN/SDN/BHAMAIR B26 .... 155 E5
Akrill Cl WBROM B70 .... 73 D6 ⑪
Alamein Rd WLNHL WV13 .... 28 A6
Albany Crs BILS/COS WV14 .... 47 E3
Albany Gdns SOLH B91 .... 196 A1 ⑪
Albany Gv KGSWFD DY6 .... 88 A6
    SHHTH WV12 .... 15 E4
Albany Rd HRBN B17 .... 145 E3
Albemarle Rd STRBR DY8.............. 158 B1
Albermarle Rd KGSWFD DY6 ...... 112 C2
Albert Clarke Dr SHHTH WV12 ... 15 E6 ⑪
Albert Cl CDSL WV8 .... 8 A1
Albert Dr HALE B63 .... 162 B1
    SEDG DY5 .... 86 A3
Albert Rd ALE/KHTH/YWD B14 ... 170 B4
    AST/WIT B6 .... 100 A2
    ERDW/GRVHL B23 .... 101 F2
    HALE B63 .... 162 B1
    HDSW B21 .... 98 A4
    HRBN B17 .... 145 D4
    LGLYGN/QTN B68 .... 143 E1
    STETCH B33 .... 127 F4
    WOLV WV1 .... 24 C4
Albert St BRLYHL DY5 .... 89 F6
    CBHAMNE B4 .... 7 F5
    DARL/WED WS10 .... 72 A1
    DIG/EDG B5... 7 G5
    HAG/WOL DY9 .... 138 A4
    KGSWFD DY6 .... 87 D5
    STRBR DY8 .... 136 B4
    TPTN/OCK DY4 .... 70 B3
    WBROM B70 .... 95 E4
    WSL WS1 .... 4 D2
Albert St East OLDBY B69 .... 95 D6 ⑪
Albion Av WLNHL WV13 .... 29 E5
Albion Field Dr HHTH/SAND B71... 95 F1
Albion Industrial Est WBROM B70 ... 94 B3
Albion Rd HDSW B21 .... 97 F4
    HHTH/SAND B71 .... 96 C5
    SPARK B11... 149 F4
    WBROM B70 .... 94 B3
Albion St BILS/COS WV14 .... 48 A3

BRLYHL DY5................................ 113 F4
CBHAMW B1................................. 123 D4
KGSWFD DY6............................... 87 D5
OLDBY B69................................. 94 A4
TPTN/OCK DY4............................. 70 B6
WLNHL WV13.............................. 29 D5
WOLV WV1................................. 3 F4
Alborn Crs *HWK/WKHTH* B38......... 187 F5
Albrighton Rd *HALE* B63................ 140 A6
Albright Rd *LGLYGN/QTN* B68........ 119 F3
Alcester Dr *SCFLD/BOLD* B73.......... 57 F6
WLNHL WV13.............................. 47 F1
Alcester Rd *ALVE* B48.................... 220 C5
HLYWD B47................................ 206 B3
HLYWD B47................................ 220 B1
MOS/BIL B13.............................. 148 B6
Alcester Rd South
ALE/KHTH/YWD B14................... 170 A4
ALE/KHTH/YWD B14................... 190 B3
Alcester St *BRTH/HG* B12............... 148 B1
Alcombe Gv *STECH* B33................. 128 A5
Alcott Cl *DOR/KN* B93.................... 212 B5
Alcott Gv *STECH* B33..................... 129 F4
Alcott La *CHWD/FDBR/MGN* B37.... 154 B1
The Alcove *BLOX/PEL* WS3.............. 17 F3
Aldbourne Rd *HWK/WKHTH* B38..... 187 F6
Aldbury Rd *ALE/KHTH/YWD* B14..... 190 C3
Aldeburgh Cl *BLOX/PEL* WS3.......... 16 C2
Aldeford Dr *BRLYHL* DY5................ 137 F1
Alderbrook Cl *SEDG* DY3................ 67 D2
Alderbrook Rd *SOLH* B91................ 194 B2
Alder Cl *HLYWD* B47...................... 207 D1
WALM/CURD B76.......................... 82 A4
Alder Coppice *SEDG* DY3............... 67 E1
Alder Cl *DSYBK/YTR* WS5............... 53 D5
Alderdale Av *SEDG* DY3................. 45 E6
Alderdale Crs *HIA/OLT* B92............ 176 A4
Alder Dr *CHWD/FDBR/MGN* B37..... 131 D6
Alderflat Pl *WASH/WDE* B8............. 125 D2
Alderford Cl *CDSL* WV8.................. 10 B5
Alder Gv *RMSLY* B62...................... 142 A3
Alderham Cl *SOLH* B91.................. 196 A1
Alderhithe Gv *FOAKS/STRLY* B74.... 37 D4
Alder La *NFLD/LBR* B31................... 167 E5
Alderlea Cl *STRBR* DY8.................. 158 C1
Alderminster Rd *SOLH* B91............ 195 D4
Alderney Gdns *BRLYHL* DY5........... 188 B4
Alder Park Rd *SOLH* B91................ 194 B2
Alderpits Rd *BKDE/SHDE* B34........ 129 F1
Alder Rd *BHTH/HG* B12................... 148 C5
DARL/WED WS10.......................... 50 C3
KGSWFD DY6.............................. 112 B2
Aldersea Dr *AST/WIT* B6................. 100 B6
Aldershaw Rd
LGN/SDN/BHAMAIR B26.............. 152 A4
Aldershaws *SHLY* B90.................... 208 C2
Aldersley Av *DUNHL/THL/PER* WV6.. 10 A6
Aldersley Cl *DUNHL/THL/PER* WV6... 10 B6
Aldersley Rd *DUNHL/THL/PER* WV6.. 24 B2
Aldersmead Rd *NFLD/LBR* B31....... 187 E4
Alderson Rd *WASH/WDE* B8........... 126 B3
The Alders *RMSLY* B62................... 182 B1
Alderton Cl *SOLH* B91.................... 195 D4
Alderton Dr *BDMR/CCFT* WV3........ 44 A1
Alder Wy *FOAKS/STRLY* B74............ 56 A1
Alderwood Pl *SOLH* B91................. 195 D2
Alderwood Ri *SEDG* DY3................. 67 E6
Aldgate Dr *BRLYHL* DY5................. 137 E2
Aldgate Gv *LOZ/NWT* B19............... 123 F2
Aldis Cl *HLGN/YWD* B28.................. 172 A2
Aldis Rd *WSLW* WS2...................... 50 C1
Aldridge Cl *LGLYGN/QTN* B68........ 119 E3 [box]
STRBR DY8................................. 136 A1 [box]
Aldridge Rd *FOAKS/STRLY* B74....... 35 F6
FOAKS/STRLY B74....................... 36 C2
FOAKS/STRLY B74....................... 55 F1
LGLYGN/QTN B68....................... 145 D1
PBAR/PBCH B42.......................... 100 A2
RUSH/SHEL WS4......................... 52 C4
Aldridge St *DARL/WED* WS10......... 49 F2 [box]
Aldwych Cl *ALDR* WS9................... 21 D5
Aldwyck Dr *BDMR/CCFT* WV3......... 42 A1
Alexander Cl *BRGRVW* B61............ 198 C6
Alexander Hl *BRLYHL* DY5.............. 138 B1
Alexander Rd *ACGN* B27................. 151 D5
CDSL WV8................................... 9 E2
SMTHWKW B67.......................... 120 A5
WSLW WS2................................. 30 B5
Alexander St *BDMR/CCFT* WV3....... 2 B5
Alexandra Av *HDSW* B21................ 97 F6
Alexandra Crs *HHTH/SAND* B71...... 74 A3
Alexandra Pl *BILS/COS* WV14......... 47 F3
Alexandra Rd *BVILLE* B30............... 168 C4
DARL/WED WS10......................... 50 A3
DIG/EDG B5................................ 148 A3
ETTPK/GDPK/PENN WV4............. 44 C4
HALE B63.................................... 140 B6
HDSW B21.................................. 97 F6
TPTN/OCK DY4.......................... 70 C6
WSL WS1................................... 52 A4
Alexandra St *DUDN* DY1................ 91 D4
Alexandra Wy *ALDR* WS9.............. 35 D2
TPTN/OCK DY4.......................... 92 C3
Alford Cl *RBRY* B45...................... 185 E6

Alfreda Av *HLYWD* B47.................. 190 B5
Alfred Rd *HDSW* B21...................... 98 A5
SPARK B11................................. 149 D4
Alfred St *ALE/KHTH/YWD* B14....... 170 B4
AST/WIT B6................................ 101 D5
BHTH/HG B12............................. 149 D4
BLOX/PEL WS3........................... 17 D4
DARL/WED WS10........................ 49 E4 [box]
SMTHWK B66.............................. 97 D6 [box]
WBROM B70............................... 95 F1
Algernon Rd *LDYWD/EDGR* B16..... 121 F3
Algernon St *WSLW* WS2................. 4 B2
Alice St *BILS/COS* WV14................. 47 F3
Alison Cl *TPTN/OCK* DY4............... 70 C1 [box]
Alison Dr *STRBR* DY8.................... 158 A1
Alison Rd *RMSLY* B62.................... 142 A6
Allan Cl *STRBR* DY8...................... 112 B6
Allbut St *CDYHTH* B64.................. 115 F6
Allcock St *DIG/EDG* B5.................. 7 G6
Allcroft Rd *SPARK* B11.................. 172 B1
Allenby Cl *KGSWFD* DY6............... 112 C2 [box]
Allen Cl *GTB/HAM* B43.................. 76 A4 [box]
Allendale Gv *GTB/HAM* B43.......... 76 A3
Allendale Rd *WALM/CURD* B76...... 82 A3
YDLY B25.................................... 151 D2
Allen Dr *DARL/WED* WS10............. 49 E3 [box]
WBROM B70............................... 96 B4
Allen Rd *DARL/WED* WS10............ 50 B4
DUNHL/THL/PER WV6.................. 24 C4
TPTN/OCK DY4.......................... 70 B2
Allens Cl *SHHTH* WV12.................. 29 D2
Allens Croft Rd
ALE/KHTH/YWD B14................... 169 D6
Allens Farm Rd *NFLD/LBR* B31...... 185 F2
Allens La *BLOX/PEL* WS3.............. 18 B3
Allen St *WBROM* B70..................... 95 D2 [box]
Allerton La *HHTH/SAND* B71.......... 73 E3
Allerton Rd *YDLY* B25.................... 151 D2
Allesley Cl *MGN/WHC* B75............. 59 E2
Allesley Rd *HIA/OLT* B92............... 173 F3
Allesley St *AST/WIT* B6.................. 124 A2
Alleston Rd *WOLVN* WV10.............. 11 F4
Alleyne Gv *ERDE/BCHGN* B24........ 102 C3
Alleyne Rd *ERDE/BCHGN* B24........ 102 C4
The Alley *SEDG* DY3...................... 89 D2
Allingham Gv *GTB/HAM* B43.......... 55 F5 [box]
Allington Cl *DSYBK/YTR* WS5........ 53 F1
Allison St *DIG/EDG* B5................... 7 G5
Allman Rd *ERDE/BCHGN* B24......... 103 D1
Allmyn Dr *FOAKS/STRLY* B74........ 56 C3
All Saints' Rd *WSNGN* B18............. 122 A2
All Saints Wy *HHTH/SAND* B71...... 73 F6
Allsops Cl *BLKHTH/ROWR* B65...... 116 B3
Allwell Dr *ALE/KHTH/YWD* B14...... 190 B3 [box]
Allwood Gdns *RIDG/WDGT* B32..... 164 C1
Alma Cl *TPTN/OCK* DY4................ 70 C4
Alma Crs *VAUX/NECH* B7............... 125 D3
Alma Pl *DUDS* DY2........................ 91 E4
Alma St *DARL/WED* WS10.............. 49 E3 [box]
DARL/WED WS10.......................... 51 D6
HALE B63.................................. 139 E4
LOZ/NWT B19............................. 124 A1
SMTHWK B66.............................. 121 E1
WLNHL WV13.............................. 29 D5 [box]
WOLVN WV10.............................. 26 B4
WSLW WS2................................. 31 F3
Alma Wy *LOZ/NWT* B19................. 99 F6
Almond Av *DSYBK/YTR* WS5.......... 52 C5
WSLW WS2................................. 30 A3
Almond Cl *BLOX/PEL* WS3............. 18 B3
SLYOAK B29............................... 166 C5
Almond Cft *PBAR/PBCH* B42......... 76 B5
Almond Gv
DUNHL/THL/PER WV6.................. 25 E3 [box]
Almond Rd *KGSWFD* DY6............... 88 A5 [box]
Alnwick Rd *BLOX/PEL* WS3........... 16 C1
Alperton Dr *HAG/WOL* DY9........... 160 A1
Alpha Cl *BHTH/HG* B12................. 148 A3
Alpine Dr *DUDS* DY2..................... 115 D3
Alpine Wy *DUNHL/THL/PER* WV6... 23 E1
Alport Cft *BORD* B9....................... 125 D5 [box]
Alston Cl *FOAKS/STRLY* B74.......... 38 C5
SOLH B91................................... 195 D1
Alston Gv *BORD* B9....................... 127 D5 [box]
Alston Rd *BORD* B9....................... 127 D4
OLDBY B69................................. 94 A6 [box]
SOLH B91................................... 175 F5
Alston St *LDYWD/EDGR* B16......... 122 B1
Althorpe Dr *DOR/KN* B93.............. 211 F4
Alton Av *SHHTH* WV12................... 28 C2
Alton Cl *WOLVN* WV10.................. 12 A2
Alton Gv *DUDS* DY2...................... 92 A4
HHTH/SAND B71......................... 74 A1
Alton Rd *SLYOAK* B29................... 146 B6
Alum Dr *BORD* B9......................... 126 C4
Alumhurst Av *WASH/WDE* B8........ 127 D3
Alum Rock Rd *WASH/WDE* B8....... 125 F2
Alumwell Cl *WSLW* WS2................ 31 D6 [box]

Alum Well Rd *WSLW* WS2............... 31 D6
Alvaston Cl *BLOX/PEL* WS3........... 17 E2
Alvechurch Hwy *BRGRVE* B60....... 199 E4
Alvechurch Rd *HALE* B63.............. 162 B1 [box]
NFLD/LBR B31............................. 187 D5
Alverley Cl *KGSWFD* DY6.............. 87 D5
Alverstoke Cl *COVEN* WV9............. 10 B3
Alveston Gv *BORD* B9................... 127 D5
DOR/KN B93.............................. 197 D6
Alveston Rd *HLYWD* B47............... 190 C6
Alvin Cl *RMSLY* B62..................... 142 B1
Alvington Cl *SHHTH* WV12............. 29 F3
Alwen St *STRBR* DY8.................... 112 B6
Alwin Rd *BLKHTH/ROWR* B65........ 117 D5
Alwold Rd *SLYOAK* B29................. 166 B1
Amanda Av
ETTPK/GDPK/PENN WV4.............. 44 B5
Amanda Dr
LGN/SDN/BHAMAIR B26.............. 128 B6
Amber Dr *OLDBY* B69.................... 118 C2 [box]
Ambergate Cl *BLOX/PEL* WS3........ 17 E2
Ambergate Dr *KGSWFD* DY6......... 87 E5 [box]
Amberley Gn *GTB/HAM* B43.......... 76 A5
Amberley Rd *AST/WIT* B6.............. 100 C2
Amberley Rd *HIA/OLT* B92............. 152 B6
Amberley Wy *FOAKS/STRLY* B74.... 36 A6
Amber Wy *RMSLY* B62.................. 141 D3
Amberwood Cl *WSLW* WS2............ 29 F4 [box]
Amblecote Av *KGSTG* B44............. 78 A1
Amblecote Rd *BRLYHL* DY5............ 137 F1
Ambleside *RIDG/WDGT* B32......... 165 E2 [box]
Ambleside Cl *BILS/COS* WV14........ 48 A5 [box]
Ambleside Dr *BRLYHL* DY5............. 137 E1
Ambleside Wy *KGSWFD* DY6......... 111 F1 [box]
Ambrose Cl *WLNHL* WV13.............. 28 A5 [box]
Ambrose Crs *KGSWFD* DY6........... 87 F5
Ambury Wy *GTB/HAM* B43............ 75 F5
Amelas Cl *STRBR* DY8................... 136 C1
Amersham Cl *RIDG/WDGT* B32...... 144 A4
Amesbury Rd *MOS/BIL* B13........... 148 A6
Ames Rd *DARL/WED* WS10............ 49 E2
Amherst Av *ERDW/HDSWWD* B20.. 98 C2
Amington Cl *MGN/WHC* B75......... 39 F4 [box]
Amington Rd *SHLY* B90................. 192 C5
YDLY B25.................................. 151 D3
Amiss Gdns *SMHTH* B10.............. 149 E1
Amity Cl *SMTHWK* B66................. 121 D2 [box]
Amos Av *WNSFLD* WV11............... 13 D6
Amos La *WNSFLD* WV11............... 27 E1
Amos Rd *HAG/WOL* DY9............... 160 B1
Amphlett Cft *TPTN/OCK* DY4........ 93 D1 [box]
Amphletts Cl *DUDS* DY2................ 116 A4
Ampton Rd *EDG* B15..................... 147 D2
Amroth Cl *RBRY* B45.................... 185 D6
Amwell Gv *ALE/KHTH/YWD* B14.... 190 B2
Anchorage Rd *ERDW/GRVHL* B23.. 101 F2
FOAKS/STRLY B74....................... 59 D3
Anchor Cl *LDYWD/EDGR* B16........ 122 A6
Anchor La *BILS/COS* WV14............ 69 D1
BILS/COS WV14.......................... 69 E1
Andersleigh Dr *BILS/COS* WV14.... 68 C3
Anderson Crs *GTB/HAM* B43......... 76 A1
Anderson Rd *ERDW/GRVHL* B23... 80 A5
SMTHWK B66.............................. 120 C6
SMTHWKW B67.......................... 120 C6
TPTN/OCK DY4.......................... 70 C6
Anderton Cl *FOAKS/STRLY* B74...... 58 C2
Anderton Park Rd *MOS/BIL* B13.... 148 C6
Anderton Rd *SPARK* B11............... 149 E3
Anderton St *CBHAMW* B1.............. 123 D4
Andover Cft *DIG/EDG* B5.............. 7 H5
Andover St *DIG/EDG* B5............... 7 H5
Andrew Cl *SHHTH* WV12............... 29 F1
Andrew Dr *SHHTH* WV12............... 29 F1
Andrew Gdns *HDSW* B21............... 98 A4
Andrew Rd *HALE* B63.................... 139 F5
HHTH/SAND B71......................... 74 B1
TPTN/OCK DY4.......................... 70 C2
Andrews Cl *BRLYHL* DY5.............. 138 A1
Andrews Rd *ALDR* WS9................. 21 D1
Anerley Gv *KGSTG* B44................. 56 B5
Anerley Rd *KGSTG* B44................. 56 B5
Angela Av *BLKHTH/ROWR* B65...... 117 F3
Angela Pl *BILS/COS* WV14............. 47 F3
Angelica Cl *DSYBK/YTR* WS5......... 52 C5 [box]
Angelina St *BHTH/HG* B12............. 148 B3
Angel Pas *STRBR* DY8................... 136 C4 [box]
Angel St *DUDN* DY1...................... 91 D5
Anglesey Av *CBROM* B36.............. 107 D6
CBROM B36.............................. 131 D1
Anglesey St *LOZ/NWT* B19........... 99 E6
Anglian Rd *ALDR* WS9.................. 33 F1
Angus Cl *HHTH/SAND* B71........... 73 E5
Anita Av *TPTN/OCK* DY4............... 92 C3
Anita Cft *ERDW/GRVHL* B23......... 102 A3
Ankadine Rd *STRBR* DY8.............. 137 D3 [box]
Ankerdine Ct *HALE* B63................ 140 C6
Ankermoor Cl *BKDE/SHDE* B34..... 129 D1 [box]
Annan Av *WOLVN* WV10................ 12 A6
Ann Cft *LGN/SDN/BHAMAIR* B26.. 153 F5
Anne Cl *WBROM* B70.................... 94 A2
Anne Gv *TPTN/OCK* DY4.............. 71 D2
Anne Rd *BRLYHL* DY5................... 114 C6
ETTPK/GDPK/PENN WV4............. 45 D4

SMTHWK B66 ... 97 E6
Ann Rd HLYWD B47 ... 206 C4
Annscroft HWK/WKHTH B38 ... 187 F3
Ann St WLNHL WV13 ... 29 D4
Ansbro Cl WSNGN B18 ... 122 B3
Anscufl Rd STRBR DY8 ... 113 D6
Ansell Rd ERDE/BCHGN B24 ... 102 B3
  SPARK B11 ... 149 E3
Anslow Gdns WNSFLD WV11 ... 14 D4 [1]
Anslow Rd ERDW/GRVHL B23 ... 79 E6
Anson Cl DUNHL/THL/PER WV6 ... 22 A2 [1]
Anson Gv ACGN B27 ... 173 F1
Anson Rd WBROM B70 ... 72 A4
  WSLW WS2 ... 30 A5
Anstey Cft
  CHWD/FDBR/MGN B37 ... 130 C3 [1]
Anstey Gv ACGN B27 ... 173 D2
Anstey Rd KGSTG B44 ... 78 A5
Anston Wy WNSFLD WV11 ... 13 F6 [1]
Anstruther Rd EDG B15 ... 146 A4
Anthony Rd WASH/WDE B8 ... 126 A4
Antony Rd SHLY B90 ... 193 D4
Antringham Gdns EDG B15 ... 145 F1
Antrobus Rd HDSW B21 ... 98 A4
  SCFLD/BOLD B73 ... 80 A2
Anvil Crs BILS/COS WV14 ... 69 E1
Anvil Dr OLDBY B69 ... 118 A1
Apley Rd STRBR DY8 ... 136 A2
Apollo Cft ERDE/BCHGN B24 ... 103 F2
Apollo Rd HAG/WOL DY9 ... 138 C4
  LGLYGN/QTN B68 ... 119 E1
Apollo Wy BFLD/HDSWWD B20 ... 99 E4
Apperley Wy HALE B63 ... 139 D2
Appian Cl ALE/KHTH/YWD B14 ... 170 A6
Appian Wy SHLY B90 ... 209 F3
Appleby Cl ALE/KHTH/YWD B14 ... 169 F6 [1]
Appleby Gdns WNSFLD WV11 ... 15 E3
Appleby Gv SHLY B90 ... 211 D1 [1]
Applecross FOAKS/STRLY B74 ... 38 B6
Appledore Rd DSYBK/YTR WS5 ... 53 F1
Appledore Gdns
  BKDE/SHDE B34 ... 129 D1 [2]
Applesham Cl SPARK B11 ... 149 F3
Appleton Av GTB/HAM B43 ... 76 A3
  STRBR DY8 ... 158 C1
Appleton Cl BVILLE B30 ... 168 A3 [1]
Appleton Crs
  ETTPK/GDPK/PENN WV4 ... 44 C4
Apple Tree La ERDW/GRVHL B23 ... 101 D4
Appletree Cl NFLD/LBR B31 ... 186 A4
Appletree Gv ALDR WS9 ... 35 D2
  DUNHL/THL/PER WV6 ... 25 E2 [1]
Applewood Gv CDYHTH B64 ... 140 B1 [1]
April Cft MOS/BIL B13 ... 171 D1
Apse Cl WMBN WV5 ... 64 B4
Apsley Cl LGLYGN/QTN B68 ... 142 C2
Apsley Gv DOR/KN B93 ... 212 B5
  ERDE/BCHGN B24 ... 102 C3
Apsley Rd LGLYGN/QTN B68 ... 142 C2
Aqueduct La ALVE B48 ... 216 B2
Aqueduct Rd SHLY B90 ... 192 A3
Aragon Dr SCFLD/BOLD B73 ... 58 C3
Arboretum Rd WSL WS1 ... 5 F2
Arbor Cl ALDR WS9 ... 21 D1
Arbor Wy CHWD/FDBR/MGN B37 ... 131 E6
Arbury Dr STRBR DY8 ... 111 F4 [1]
Arbury Hall Rd SHLY B90 ... 193 F5
Arcal St SEDG DY3 ... 68 A4
Archer Cl DARL/WED WS10 ... 50 A6 [1]
  LGLYGN/QTN B68 ... 119 D3 [1]
Archer Ct HAG/WOL DY9 ... 160 A1
Archer Rd ALE/KHTH/YWD B14 ... 191 E1
  BLOX/PEL WS3 ... 32 A1
Archers ERDW/GRVHL B23 ... 79 E3
Arch Hill St DUDS DY2 ... 115 E2
Archibald Rd LOZ/NWT B19 ... 99 E3
Arcot Rd HLGN/YWD B28 ... 172 B1
Ardarth Rd HWK/WKHTH B38 ... 188 C3
Ardav Rd WBROM B70 ... 72 B3
Arden Cl STRBR DY8 ... 111 E4
  STRBR DY8 ... 136 A3
Ardencote Rd MOS/BIL B13 ... 170 C5
Arden Cft CSHL/WTROR B46 ... 108 B4
  HIA/OLT B92 ... 153 E5
Arden Dr DOR/KN B93 ... 212 C6
  LGN/SDN/BHAMAIR B26 ... 152 B2 [1]
  MGN/WHC B75 ... 81 D3 [1]
  SCFLD/BOLD B73 ... 61 D3
Arden Gv LDYWD/EDGR B16 ... 122 C6 [1]
  OLDBY B69 ... 118 C2
Arden Oak Rd
  LGN/SDN/BHAMAIR B26 ... 153 F4
Arden Pl DARL/WED WS10 ... 49 D5
Arden Rd ACGN B27 ... 151 D5
  AST/WIT B6 ... 99 F5
  DOR/KN B93 ... 212 B6
  HLYWD B47 ... 206 B2
  RBRY B45 ... 184 C4
  SMTHWKW B67 ... 120 C3
  WASH/WDE B8 ... 125 E4
Arden Vale Rd DOR/KN B93 ... 197 D6
Arderne Dr
  CHWD/FDBR/MGN B37 ... 130 C6 [1]
Ardingley Wk BRLYHL DY5 ... 137 D2 [1]

Ardley Cl DUDS DY2 ... 91 F5
Ardley Rd ALE/KHTH/YWD B14 ... 170 C6
Aretha Cl KGSWFD DY6 ... 112 C1 [1]
Argus Cl WALM/CURD B76 ... 60 B6
Argyle Cl RUSH/SHEL WS4 ... 33 D4
  STRBR DY8 ... 112 A6
Argyle Rd BKHL/PFLD WV2 ... 45 D3
  RUSH/SHEL WS4 ... 33 D4
Argyle St VAUX/NECH B7 ... 101 E3
Arkle Cft BLKHTH/ROWR B65 ... 116 B1
  CBROM B36 ... 103 E5
Arkley Cl HLGN/YWD B28 ... 173 D4
Arkley Rd HLGN/YWD B28 ... 173 D4
Arkwright Rd RIDG/WDGT B32 ... 143 E4
  WSLW WS2 ... 31 D2
Arlen Dr GTB/HAM B43 ... 75 F2
Arlescote Cl WHC/WHC B75 ... 39 E5
Arlescote Rd HIA/OLT B92 ... 175 E2 [1]
Arleston Wy SHLY B90 ... 194 A5
Arley Cl OLDBY B69 ... 117 F2
Arley Dr STRBR DY8 ... 136 A6
Arley Gv ETTPK/GDPK/PENN WV4 ... 43 F4
  SOLH B91 ... 194 C1
Arley Rd SLYOAK B29 ... 146 B6
  SOLH B91 ... 194 C1
  WASH/WDE B8 ... 125 F1
Arlidge Cl BILS/COS WV14 ... 47 F5
Arlington Cl KGSWFD DY6 ... 111 F3
Arlington Ct STRBR DY8 ... 137 D5
Arlington Gv ALE/KHTH/YWD B14 ... 191 D3
Arlington Rd ALE/KHTH/YWD B14 ... 191 D2
  HHTH/SAND B71 ... 73 F5
Armada Cl ERDW/GRVHL B23 ... 101 F4 [1]
Armoury Rd SPARK B11 ... 149 F2
Armside Cl BLOX/PEL WS3 ... 18 C1
Armstead Rd COVEN WV9 ... 10 C2
Armstrong Cl STRBR DY8 ... 137 D5
Armstrong Dr CBROM B36 ... 106 B4
  DUNHL/THL/PER WV6 ... 24 C1
  WSLW WS2 ... 30 C1
Armstrong Wy WLNHL WV13 ... 49 D1
Arnhem Cl WNSFLD WV11 ... 13 D5
Arnhem Rd WLNHL WV13 ... 48 A1
Arnhem Wy TPTN/OCK DY4 ... 71 E6
Arnold Cl WSLW WS2 ... 30 B4
  SHLY B90 ... 193 D1 [1]
Arnold Gv BVILLE B30 ... 187 F1
  SHLY B90 ... 193 D1
Arnold Rd SHLY B90 ... 193 E1
Arnwood Cl WSLW WS2 ... 30 B5
Arosa Dr HRBN B17 ... 145 D6
Arps Rd CDSL WV8 ... 8 B2
Arran Cl GTB/HAM B43 ... 54 A6
Arran Rd BKDE/SHDE B34 ... 128 B1
Arran Wy CBROM B36 ... 106 C6
Arras Rd DUDS DY2 ... 92 A3
Arrow Cl DOR/KN B93 ... 212 C1
Arrowfield Gn
  HWK/WKHTH B38 ... 187 F6 [1]
Arrow Rd BLOX/PEL WS3 ... 32 A1
Arsenal St BORD B9 ... 125 E6
Arthur Gunby Cl MGN/WHC B75 ... 60 B2 [1]
Arthur Pl CBHAMW B1 ... 123 D4
Arthur Rd EDG B15 ... 147 D3
  ERDE/BCHGN B24 ... 103 D1
  HDSW B21 ... 98 B5
  TPTN/OCK DY4 ... 70 C5
  YDLY B25 ... 150 C3
Arthur St BILS/COS WV14 ... 47 F3
  BKHL/PFLD WV2 ... 45 F3
  SMHTH B10 ... 125 D6
  WBROM B70 ... 95 F4
Artillery St BORD B9 ... 125 D5
Arton Cft ERDE/BCHGN B24 ... 102 C4
Arundel Av DARL/WED WS10 ... 50 B6
Arundel Crs HIA/OLT B92 ... 174 C2
Arundel Dr OLDBY B69 ... 92 B5
Arundel Gv DUNHL/THL/PER WV6 ... 22 C4
Arundel Pl SPARK B11 ... 148 C3
Arundel Rd ALE/KHTH/YWD B14 ... 190 C4
  SHHTH WV12 ... 15 E6
  STRBR DY8 ... 111 E5
  WOLVN WV10 ... 11 D3
Arundel St WSL WS1 ... 52 A2
Arun Wy WALM/CURD B76 ... 82 C2
Asbury Rd DARL/WED WS10 ... 74 A1
Ascot Cl LDYWD/EDGR B16 ... 122 B6 [1]
  OLDBY B69 ... 118 A1
Ascot Dr DUDN DY1 ... 90 B3
  ETTPK/GDPK/PENN WV4 ... 44 C5
Ascot Gdns STRBR DY8 ... 111 E5
Ascot Rd MOS/BIL B13 ... 170 B1
Ash Av BRHTH/HG B12 ... 148 C4 [1]
Ashborough Dr SOLH B91 ... 195 E6
Ashbourne Rd BLOX/PEL WS3 ... 17 E2
  ETTPK/GDPK/PENN WV4 ... 46 A6
  LDYWD/EDGR B16 ... 121 F4
  WOLV WV1 ... 26 C4
Ashbourne Wy SHLY B90 ... 193 F5
Ashbrook Crs SOLH B91 ... 195 E5
Ashbrook Dr RBRY B45 ... 185 D5 [1]
Ashbrook Gv BVILLE B30 ... 169 E4
Ashbrook Rd BVILLE B30 ... 169 E4
Ashburn Gv WLNHL WV13 ... 29 E5 [1]
Ashburton Rd
  ALE/KHTH/YWD B14 ... 169 F6
Ashbury Covert BVILLE B30 ... 189 E2 [1]

Ashby Cl CBROM B36 ... 127 E1
Ashby Ct SOLH B91 ... 195 E4
Ash Cl CDSL WV8 ... 8 C2
Ashcombe Av
  BFLD/HDSWWD B20 ... 98 A2 [1]
Ashcombe Gdns
  ERDE/BCHGN B24 ... 103 F2 [1]
Ashcott Cl HWK/WKHTH B38 ... 187 F3
Ashcroft Gv BFLD/HDSWWD B20 ... 99 F3
Ashdale Cl KGSWFD DY6 ... 87 F5
Ashdale Dr ALE/KHTH/YWD B14 ... 190 C4
Ashdale Gv LGN/SDN/BHAMAIR B26.. 152 C1
Ashdene Cl SCFLD/BOLD B73 ... 58 C6
Ashdene Gdns STRBR DY8 ... 111 E5
Ashdown Cl MOS/BIL B13 ... 170 C2
  RBRY B45 ... 184 C3
Ashdown Dr STRBR DY8 ... 112 A4
Ash Dr BRGRVW B61 ... 198 C6
  HHTH/SAND B71 ... 73 E5
Ashen Cl ETTPK/GDPK/PENN WV4 ... 45 E6
Ashenden Ri BDMR/CCFT WV3 ... 22 C6
Ashenhurst Rd DUDN DY1 ... 90 B5
Ashes Rd OLDBY B69 ... 118 B3
Ashfern Dr WALM/CURD B76 ... 82 A4
Ashfield Av ALE/KHTH/YWD B14 ... 170 B2
Ashfield Cl BLOX/PEL WS3 ... 32 A3
Ashfield Crs DUDS DY9 ... 115 E4
  HAG/WOL DY9 ... 138 B6
Ashfield Gv HALE B63 ... 162 A1
  WOLVN WV10 ... 11 F2
Ashfield Rd ALE/KHTH/YWD B14 ... 170 B2
  BDMR/CCFT WV3 ... 23 F5
  BILS/COS WV14 ... 48 C6
  WOLVN WV10 ... 11 F2
Ashford Dr SEDG DY3 ... 68 A4
  WALM/CURD B76 ... 82 A6
Ashfurlong Crs MGN/WHC B75 ... 60 A2
Ash Gn DUDN DY1 ... 68 C6
Ash Gv BHTH/HG B12 ... 149 D4 [1]
  HAG/WOL DY9 ... 137 F6
  SEDG DY3 ... 89 E3
Ashgrove Cl BRGRVE B60 ... 199 F6
Ashgrove Rd KGSTG B44 ... 77 E1
Ash Hl BDMR/CCFT WV3 ... 23 F6
Ashill Rd RBRY B45 ... 185 D6
Ashland St BDMR/CCFT WV3 ... 2 A6
Ashlawn Crs SOLH B91 ... 173 F6
Ashleigh Dr BFLD/HDSWWD B20 ... 99 D3 [1]
Ashleigh Gv MOS/BIL B13 ... 171 D2
Ashleigh Rd OLDBY B69 ... 93 E5
  SOLH B91 ... 195 D1
Ashley Cl EDG B15 ... 147 D2
  KGSWFD DY6 ... 111 E3
Ashley Ct RBRY B45 ... 200 C5
Ashley Gdns CDSL WV8 ... 8 B1
  WASH/WDE B8 ... 125 F3
Ashley Mt DUNHL/THL/PER WV6 ... 23 E2 [1]
Ashley Rd BLOX/PEL WS3 ... 16 B4
  ERDW/GRVHL B23 ... 102 A2
  ETTPK/GDPK/PENN WV4 ... 44 A4
Ashley St BILS/COS WV14 ... 48 A3
  BLKHTH/ROWR B65 ... 117 E6
Ashmead Dr RBRY B45 ... 201 E5
Ashmead Gv ERDE/BCHGN B24 ... 102 C3
Ashmead Ri RBRY B45 ... 201 E5
Ash Ms ACGN B27 ... 151 E4 [1]
Ashmole Rd WBROM B70 ... 72 B4
Ashmore Av WNSFLD WV11 ... 14 C4
Ashmore Lake Rd SHHTH WV12 ... 29 D3
Ashmore Lake Wy SHHTH WV12.. 29 D3
Ashmore Rd BVILLE B30 ... 168 B6
Asholme Cl CBROM B36 ... 105 E6
Ashorne Cl ACGN B27 ... 173 D4
Ash Tree Dr
  LGN/SDN/BHAMAIR B26 ... 151 F2
Ashtree Gv BILS/COS WV14 ... 49 D6
Ash Tree Rd BVILLE B30 ... 168 C5
Ashtree Rd BLOX/PEL WS3 ... 18 C2
  CDYHTH B64 ... 116 B5
  OLDBY B69 ... 93 F5
Ashurst Rd WALM/CURD B76 ... 82 B5
Ashville Av BKDE/SHDE B34 ... 104 B6
Ashville Dr HALE B63 ... 140 C4
Ashwater Dr ALE/KHTH/YWD B14 ... 189 F3
Ash Wy ERDW/GRVHL B23 ... 79 E3
  SPARK B11 ... 149 D4 [2]

Ashwell Dr *SHLY* B90 .... 193 F1
Ashwells Gv *COVEN* WV9 .... 10 B3
Ashwin Rd *HDSW* B21 .... 98 B6
Ashwood Av *STRBR* DY8 .... 111 E5
Ashwood Cl *FOAKS/STRLY* B74 .... 56 A1
Ashwood Dr
CHWD/FDBR/MGN B37 .... 131 F4
Ashwood Gv
ETTPK/GDPK/PENN WV4 .... 44 C4
WALM/CURD B76 .... 82 B1
Aspen B27 .... 151 D6
Aspen Cl *CHWD/FDBR/MGN* B37 .... 155 E1
WALM/CURD B76 .... 82 B1
Aspen Gdns *BFLD/HDSWWD* B20 .... 99 D4
Aspen Gv *BORD* B9 .... 207 D2
HLYWD B47 .... 190 A6
SHHTH WV12 .... 16 A6
Aspen Wy *BDMR/CCFT* WV3 .... 43 C1
Asquith Dr *OLDBY* B69 .... 93 F3
Asquith Rd *WASH/WDE* B8 .... 127 D2
Asra Cl *SMTHWK* B66 .... 96 C5
Aster Wk *COVEN* WV9 .... 10 C2
Astley Av *RMSLY* B62 .... 142 B3
Astley Cl *TPTN/OCK* DY4 .... 71 F5
Astley Rd *HDSW* B21 .... 97 F4
Aston Brook St
AST/WIT B6 .... 124 A1
Aston Brook St East
AST/WIT B6 .... 124 B2
Aston Bury *EDG* B15 .... 145 F1
Aston Church Rd *VAUX/NECH* B7 .... 101 E6
WASH/WDE B8 .... 125 F1
Aston Cl *BILS/COS* WV14 .... 48 C5
Aston Hall Rd *AST/WIT* B6 .... 100 C5
Aston La *BFLD/HDSWWD* B20 .... 100 A3
Aston Rd *DUDS* DY2 .... 91 D5
OLDBY B69 .... 92 C4
WLNHL WV13 .... 28 A5
Aston Rd North *AST/WIT* B6 .... 124 B1
Astons Cl *BRLYHL* DY5 .... 137 F2
Astons Fold *BRLYHL* DY5 .... 137 F2
Aston St *BDMR/CCFT* WV3 .... 44 C1
CBHAMNE B4 .... 7 G2
TPTN/OCK DY4 .... 71 E5
Astor Dr *MOS/BIL* B13 .... 171 E2
Astoria Cl *SHHTH* WV12 .... 15 F4
Astor Rd *FOAKS/STRLY* B74 .... 36 C6
KGSWFD DY6 .... 112 B2
Athelstan Gv *DUNHL/THL/PER* WV6 .... 22 A2
Atherstone Cl *SHLY* B90 .... 192 A3
Atherstone Rd *WOLV* WV1 .... 27 D5
Athlone Cl *WSL* WS4 .... 53 E1
Athol Cl *RIDG/WDGT* B32 .... 144 A2
Athole St *BHTH/HG* B12 .... 148 C2
Atlantic Rd *KGSTG* B44 .... 78 B3
Atlantic Wk *DARL/WED* WS10 .... 72 A2
Attenborough Cl *LOZ/NWT* B19 .... 123 F2
Attingham Dr *GTB/HAM* B43 .... 75 F1
Attleborough La
CSHL/WTROR B46 .... 106 C4
Attlee Cl *OLDBY* B69 .... 93 F3
Attlee Crs *BILS/COS* WV14 .... 70 A1
Attlee Rd *WSL* WS2 .... 30 A4
Attwell Pk *BDMR/CCFT* WV3 .... 43 F2
Attwell Rd *TPTN/OCK* DY4 .... 70 B2
Attwood Cl *WASH/WDE* B8 .... 126 A1
Attwood Gdns
ETTPK/GDPK/PENN WV4 .... 46 A1
HALE B63 .... 140 B4
SMHTH B10 .... 150 B2
Aubrey Rd *RIDG/WDGT* B32 .... 144 A2
Auckland Dr *CBROM* B36 .... 106 B5
Auckland Rd *KGSWFD* DY6 .... 112 A3
SMTHWKW B67 .... 120 A2
SPARK B11 .... 148 C2
Auden Ct *DUNHL/THL/PER* WV6 .... 22 B3
Audley Rd *STETCH* B33 .... 128 A3
Audnam *STRBR* DY8 .... 112 A6
Augusta Rd East *MOS/BIL* B13 .... 148 B5
Augusta Rd *WSNGN* B18 .... 6 A1
Augusta St *WSNGN* B18 .... 122 B1
Augustine Gv *FOAKS/STRLY* B74 .... 38 C2
WSNGN B18 .... 122 B1
Augustus Cl *CSHL/WTROR* B46 .... 108 B4
Augustus Ct *EDG* B15 .... 146 B1
Augustus Rd *EDG* B15 .... 145 F1
Augustus St *WSLW* WS2 .... 4 B4
Aulton Rd *MGN/WHC* B75 .... 40 A5
Ault St *WBROM* B70 .... 95 F4
Austcliff Dr *SOLH* B91 .... 195 E5
Austen Pl *EDG* B15 .... 147 D1
Austin Cl *ACGN* B27 .... 151 F5
DUDN DY1 .... 90 B3
Austin Cft *CBROM* B36 .... 106 A4
Austin Ri *NFLD/LBR* B31 .... 186 B6
Austin Rd *HDSW* B21 .... 97 E4

Austin St *DUNHL/THL/PER* WV6 .... 25 D3
Austin Wy *PBAR/PBCH* B42 .... 76 C6
Austrey Cl *DOR/KN* B93 .... 212 C1
Austrey Gv *SLYOAK* B29 .... 166 C3
Austrey Rd *KGSWFD* DY6 .... 112 C2
Austy Cl *CBROM* B36 .... 104 A5
Autumn Berry Gv *SEDG* DY3 .... 68 A5
Autumn Cl *RUSH/SHEL* WS4 .... 19 E3
Autumn Dr *RUSH/SHEL* WS4 .... 19 E3
SEDG DY3 .... 89 F2
Autumn Gv *LOZ/NWT* B19 .... 123 E1
Avalon Cl *ERDE/BCHGN* B24 .... 103 D1
Avebury Gv *BVILLE* B30 .... 169 E4
Avebury Rd *BVILLE* B30 .... 169 E5
Ave Maria Cl *CDYHTH* B64 .... 116 A6
Avenbury Dr *SOLH* B91 .... 196 A1
Avenue Cl *DOR/KN* B93 .... 212 C4
VAUX/NECH B7 .... 124 C2
Avenue Perry *WOLVN* WV10 .... 12 B5
Avenue Rd *ALE/KHTH/YWD* B14 .... 169 F3
BILS/COS WV14 .... 69 E3
BLKHTH/ROWR B65 .... 117 F6
DARL/WED WS10 .... 49 F3
DOR/KN B93 .... 212 C4
DUDS DY2 .... 114 A1
DUNHL/THL/PER WV6 .... 24 A5
ERDW/GRVHL B23 .... 102 B1
HDSW B21 .... 97 F3
VAUX/NECH B7 .... 124 C1
The Avenue *ACGN* B27 .... 151 F6
BDMR/CCFT WV3 .... 43 D1
BLKHTH/ROWR B65 .... 116 C4
BRGRVE B60 .... 214 B3
ETTPK/GDPK/PENN WV4 .... 44 A5
RBRY B45 .... 184 A6
Averill Rd *LGN/SDN/BHAMAIR* B26 .... 152 C1
Avern Cl *TPTN/OCK* DY4 .... 71 D5
Aversley Rd *HWK/WKHTH* B38 .... 187 F5
Avery Cl *CVALE* B35 .... 104 B3
Avery Dr *ACGN* B27 .... 151 E5
Avery Myers Cl
LGLGYN/QTN B68 .... 119 D2
Avery Rd *SCFLD/BOLD* B73 .... 57 F6
SCFLD/BOLD B73 .... 79 E1
SMTHWK B66 .... 121 F1
Aviemore Crs *GTB/HAM* B43 .... 75 E5
Avington Cl *SEDG* DY3 .... 67 F4
Avion Cl *WSL* WS1 .... 52 B2
Avocet Cl *STETCH* B33 .... 128 A4
Avon Cl *BLOX/PEL* WS3 .... 89 D6
DUNHL/THL/PER WV6 .... 22 A3
Avon Crs *BLOX/PEL* WS3 .... 18 C4
Avondale Cl *KGSWFD* DY6 .... 88 A5
Avondale Rd *DUNHL/THL/PER* WV6 .... 24 A5
SPARK B11 .... 148 C4
Avon Dr *CBROM* B36 .... 106 B6
HLYWD B47 .... 206 A5
MOS/BIL B13 .... 171 D1
WLNHL WV13 .... 29 E5
Avon Rd *BLOX/PEL* WS3 .... 18 A4
HALE B63 .... 139 D4
SHLY B90 .... 193 F5
STRBR DY8 .... 136 B6
Avon St *SPARK* B11 .... 149 E4
Awbridge Rd *WMBN* WV5 .... 64 A1
Awbridge Rd *DUDS* DY2 .... 115 E4
Awefields Crs *SMTHWKW* B67 .... 119 F3
Axletree Wk *DARL/WED* WS10 .... 50 C5
DARL/WED WS10 .... 51 D4
Ayala Cft *CBROM* B36 .... 104 A5
Aylesbury Crs *KGSTG* B44 .... 78 C3
Aylesford Cl *SEDG* DY3 .... 67 D1
Aylesford Dr
CHWD/FDBR/MGN B37 .... 154 C2
FOAKS/STRLY B74 .... 38 A2
Aylesford Rd *HDSW* B21 .... 97 F4
Aylesmore Cl *HIA/OLT* B92 .... 174 A3
RIDG/WDGT B32 .... 165 E2
Ayre Rd *ERDE/BCHGN* B24 .... 103 D1
Ayrshire Cl *CBROM* B36 .... 103 F5
Ayrton Cl *DUNHL/THL/PER* WV6 .... 22 C3
Azalea Cl *CDSL* WV8 .... 9 D1
Azalea Gv *BORD* B9 .... 126 B5
Aziz Isaac Cl *LGLGYN/QTN* B68 .... 119 E1

B

Babington Rd *HDSW* B21 .... 98 A6
Bablake Cft *HIA/OLT* B92 .... 174 C2
Babors Fld *BILS/COS* WV14 .... 46 C6
Babworth Cl *COVEN* WV9 .... 10 C3
Baccabox La *HLYWD* B47 .... 190 A6
Bacchus Rd *WSNGN* B18 .... 122 B1
Bache St *WBROM* B70 .... 95 E4
Bach Mill Dr *ALE/KHTH/YWD* B14 .... 191 F2
Backhouse La *WLNHL* WV13 .... 27 E3
WNSFLD WV11 .... 27 E3
Back Rd *HWK/WKHTH* B38 .... 188 B3
HWK/WKHTH B38 .... 188 B3
KGSWFD DY6 .... 87 F6
Baddesley Rd *HIA/OLT* B92 .... 174 A1

Bader Rd *WSLW* WS2 .... 30 B5
Badger Cl *SHLY* B90 .... 209 F3
Badger Dr *WOLVN* WV10 .... 25 F3
Badgers Bank Rd
FOAKS/STRLY B74 .... 38 B2
Badgers Cft *RMSLY* B62 .... 141 D2
The Badgers *RBRY* B45 .... 200 C5
Badger St *HAG/WOL* DY9 .... 138 A3
SEDG DY3 .... 68 A6
Badger Wy *BRCRVE* B60 .... 215 D4
Badminton Cl *DUDN* DY1 .... 90 B2
Badsey Cl *NFLD/LBR* B31 .... 187 E1
Badsey Rd *OLDBY* B69 .... 117 F2
Baggeridge Cl *SEDG* DY3 .... 66 C3
Baggott St *BKHL/PFLD* WV2 .... 45 E2
Baginton Cl *SOLH* B91 .... 175 D6
Baginton Rd *CVALE* B35 .... 105 D1
Bagley St *HAG/WOL* DY9 .... 137 E3
Bagnall Cl *LGN/SDN/BHAMAIR* B26 .... 151 F3
Bagnall Rd *BILS/COS* WV14 .... 47 E3
Bagnall St *BLOX/PEL* WS3 .... 17 E6
TPTN/OCK DY4 .... 71 E2
TPTN/OCK DY4 .... 72 A4
WBROM B70 .... 96 A3
Bagnall Wk *BRLYHL* DY5 .... 113 F6
Bagnell Rd *ALE/KHTH/YWD* B14 .... 170 B4
Bagot St *CBHAMNE* B4 .... 7 F1
Bagridge Cl *BDMR/CCFT* WV3 .... 43 D1
Bagridge Rd *BDMR/CCFT* WV3 .... 43 D1
Bagshawe Cft *ERDW/GRVHL* B23 .... 79 F4
Bagshaw Rd *STETCH* B33 .... 128 A4
Bailey Rd *BILS/COS* WV14 .... 47 D2
Bailey St *WBROM* B70 .... 94 C1
WOLVN WV10 .... 3 G3
Baker Av *BILS/COS* WV14 .... 68 B1
Baker House Gv *GTB/HAM* B43 .... 75 F4
Baker Rd *BILS/COS* WV14 .... 48 A6
Bakers Gdns *CDSL* WV8 .... 8 A1
Baker's La *ALDR* WS9 .... 35 D1
DOR/KN B93 .... 213 E6
FOAKS/STRLY B74 .... 56 B4
Baker St *BORD* B9 .... 125 F6
HDSW B21 .... 98 B5
SPARK B11 .... 149 E5
TPTN/OCK DY4 .... 92 A1
WBROM B70 .... 95 D2
Bakers Wy *CDSL* WV8 .... 8 A1
Bakewell Cl *BLOX/PEL* WS3 .... 17 E2
Balaclava Rd
ALE/KHTH/YWD B14 .... 170 A1
Balcaskie Cl *EDG* B15 .... 146 A2
Balden Rd *RIDG/WDGT* B32 .... 144 A2
Baldmoor Lake Rd
ERDW/GRVHL B23 .... 80 B4
Bald's La *HAG/WOL* DY9 .... 138 B4
Baldwin Cl *OLDBY* B69 .... 93 F3
Baldwin Rd *BVILLE* B30 .... 188 C2
Baldwins La *HLGN/YWD* B28 .... 192 B3
Baldwin St *BILS/COS* WV14 .... 48 B5
SMTHWK B66 .... 121 D1
Baldwin Wy *SEDG* DY3 .... 86 A3
Balfour Cl *OLDBY* B69 .... 93 F3
Balfour Rd *KGSWFD* DY6 .... 88 A5
Balfour St *BHTH/HG* B12 .... 148 A3
Balham Gv *KGSTG* B44 .... 78 C1
Balking *BILS/COS* WV14 .... 47 D6
Ballarat Wk *STRBR* DY8 .... 136 B4
Ballard Crs *DUDS* DY2 .... 115 F2
Ballard Rd *DUDS* DY2 .... 115 F2
Ballard Wk *CHWD/FDBR/MGN* B37 .... 130 C1
Ball Flds *TPTN/OCK* DY4 .... 71 E6
Ball St *SMTHWK* B66 .... 121 D2
Balls Hi *WSL* WS1 .... 5 F3
Balls St *WSL* WS1 .... 5 F3
Balmain Gv *WNSFLD* WV11 .... 13 D5
Balmoral Cl *RMSLY* B62 .... 141 D2
RUSH/SHEL WS4 .... 19 F6
Balmoral Dr *SHHTH* WV12 .... 15 D6
WMBN WV5 .... 64 C2
Balmoral Rd *CBROM* B36 .... 106 C6
ERDW/GRVHL B23 .... 80 B6
ETTPK/GDPK/PENN WV4 .... 44 C5
FOAKS/STRLY B74 .... 38 B2
RIDG/WDGT B32 .... 164 C4
STRBR DY8 .... 111 E5
Balmoral Vw *DUDN* DY1 .... 90 A3
Balmoral Wy *BLKHTH/ROWR* B65 .... 117 F5
WSLW WS2 .... 30 C3
Balsall Heath Rd *DIG/EDG* B5 .... 148 A3
Baltimore Rd *PBAR/PBCH* B42 .... 76 C6
Balvenie Wy *DUDN* DY1 .... 90 B2
Bamber Cl *BDMR/CCFT* WV3 .... 44 A1
Bamford Cl *BLOX/PEL* WS3 .... 17 E2
Bamford Rd *BDMR/CCFT* WV3 .... 44 C1
BLOX/PEL WS3 .... 17 E2
Bamville Rd *WASH/WDE* B8 .... 126 C2
Banbery Dr *WMBN* WV5 .... 86 B1
Banbrook Cl *HIA/OLT* B92 .... 175 F3
Banbury Cl *SEDG* DY3 .... 68 A5
Banbury Cft
CHWD/FDBR/MGN B37 .... 130 B5
Banbury St *DIG/EDG* B5 .... 7 G4
Bancroft Cl *DUDN* DY1 .... 69 D4
Bandywood Rd *KGSTG* B44 .... 56 A5
Banfield Av *DARL/WED* WS10 .... 49 E2

Banfield Rd *DARL/WED* WS10 .... 49 E5
Banford Rd *WASH/WDE* B8 .... 126 C3
Bangham Pit Rd *NFLD/LBR* B31 .. 166 A4
Bangor Rd *BORD* B9 .... 125 F5
Bankdale Rd *WASH/WDE* B8 .... 127 D3
Bankes Rd *SMHTH* B10 .... 126 A6
Bankfield Rd *BILS/COS* WV14 .... 47 F4
 BILS/COS WV14 .... 48 A5
 TPTN/OCK DY4 .... 71 E3
Banklands Rd *DUDS* DY2 .... 116 A2
Bank Rd *DUDS* DY2 .... 115 F1
 SEDG DY3 .... 89 G2
Bankside *GTB/HAM* B43 .... 76 A4 ⊡
 MOS/BIL B13 .... 171 F1
 WMBN WV5 .... 64 B4 ⊡
Bankside Crs *FOAKS/STRLY* B74 ... 56 B2
Bankside Wy *ALDR* WS9 .... 21 D3
Banks St *WLNHL* WV13 .... 28 C5
Bank St *ALE/KHTH/YWD* B14 .... 170 A3
 BILS/COS WV14 .... 48 A5
 BILS/COS WV14 .... 69 E3
 BRLYHL DY5 .... 113 F3
 CDYHTH B64 .... 115 E6
 HAG/WOL DY9 .... 138 B4
 HHTH/SAND B71 .... 73 E5
 WOLVN WV10 .... 26 A2
 WSL WS1 .... 5 F4
Bankwell St *BRLYHL* DY5 .... 113 F3
Bannerlea Rd
 CHWD/FDBR/MGN B37 .... 130 B2
Bannerley Rd *STECH* B33 .... 129 E5
Banners Gate Rd *SCFLD/BOLD* B73 ... 57 D6
Banners Gv *ERDW/GRVHL* B23 ...... 80 C5
Banners La *HALE* B63 .... 139 F3
Banners St *HALE* B63 .... 139 F3
Banners Wk *KGSTG* B44 .... 79 D1
Bannister Rd *DARL/WED* WS10 ...... 71 F1
Bannister St *CDYHTH* B64 .... 115 F5
Banstead Cl *BKHL/PFLD* WV2 .... 46 A2
Bantams Cl *STECH* B33 .... 129 E5
Bantock Av *BDMR/CCFT* WV3 .... 44 B1 ⊡
Bantock Gdns *BDMR/CCFT* WV3 .... 24 A6
The Bantocks *WBROM* B70 .... 72 C5
Banton Cl *ERDW/GRVHL* B23 .... 79 F3
Bantry Cl *LGN/SDN/BHAMAIR* B26 .. 153 E5
Baptist End Rd *DUDS* DY2 .... 115 F2
Barbara Rd *ALE/KHTH/YWD* B28 .. 192 A2
Barbers La *HIA/OLT* B92 .... 177 E5
Barbourne Cl *SOLH* B91 .... 195 D6
Barbrook Dr *BRLYHL* DY5 .... 137 D2
Barcheston Rd *DOR/KN* B93 .... 212 C2
 SLYOAK B29 .... 166 C2
Barclay Rd *SMTHWKW* B67 .... 120 A6
Barcroft *WLNHL* WV13 .... 29 D4
Bardfield Cl *PBAR/PBCH* B42 .... 76 B3
Bardon Dr *SHLY* B90 .... 193 F5 ⊡
Bard St *SPARK* B11 .... 149 E2
Bardwell Cl *CDSL* WV8 .... 10 B5
Barford Cl *DARL/WED* WS10 .... 49 E1 ⊡
 WALM/CURD B76 .... 60 B5 ⊡
Barford Crs *ALE/KHTH/YWD* B14 .. 189 E3
Barford Rd *SHLY* B90 .... 193 F3
 WSNGN B18 .... 122 A3
Barford St *DIG/EDG* B5 .... 124 B6
 DIG/EDG B5 .... 148 A3
Bargate Dr
 DUNHL/THL/PER WV6 .... 24 C3 ⊡
Bargery Rd *WNSFLD* WV11 .... 14 C4
Barham Cl *SHLY* B90 .... 210 C2 ⊡
Barker Rd *FOAKS/STRLY* B74 .... 59 D2
Barkers La *HLYWD* B47 .... 206 B6
Barker St *LGLYGN/QTN* B68 .... 119 E2
 LOZ/NWT B19 .... 99 D6
Bark Piece *RIDG/WDGT* B32 .... 143 E5
Barlands Cft *BKDE/SHDE* B34 ..... 129 E1 ⊡
Barle Gv *CBROM* B36 .... 106 B6
Barley Cl *ALDR* WS9 .... 36 A5 ⊡
 CDSL WV8 .... 10 A4 ⊡
 SEDG DY3 .... 68 A2
Barleyfield Ri *KGSWFD* DY6 .... 86 C5
Barleyfield Rw *WSL* WS1 .... 4 D6
Barlow Cl *LGLYGN/QTN* B68 .... 118 C2
 RBRY B45 .... 184 A3 ⊡
Barlow Dr *WBROM* B70 .... 96 B4
Barlow Rd *DARL/WED* WS10 .... 50 C4
Barlows Rd *EDG* B15 .... 145 F4
Barmouth Cl *SHHTH* WV12 .... 29 E1
Barnabas Rd *ERDW/GRVHL* B23 .. 102 B3 ⊡
Barnaby Sq *WOLVN* WV10 .... 13 F1
Barnard Cl *CHWD/FDBR/MGN* B37 .. 131 F6
Barnard Pl *BKHL/PFLD* WV2 .... 46 A3
Barnard Rd *MGN/WHC* B75 .... 60 A2
 WNSFLD WV11 .... 14 B4
Barn Av *SEDG* DY3 .... 67 E4
Barnbrook Rd *DOR/KN* B93 .... 196 C6
Barn Cl *BVILLE* B30 .... 169 D5
 CDYHTH B64 .... 140 A3
 HAG/WOL DY9 .... 137 E5
 HALE B63 .... 162 A1
Barn Cft *RIDG/WDGT* B32 .... 166 A2
Barncroft Rd *OLDBY* B69 .... 92 C5 ⊡
Barncroft St *WBROM* B70 .... 72 C3 ⊡
Barnes Cl *STECH* B33 .... 130 A5
Barnes HI *SLYOAK* B29 .... 166 B1

Barnesville Cl *SMHTH* B10 .... 150 C1
Barnet Rd *ERDW/GRVHL* B23 .... 79 F6
Barnett Cl *BILS/COS* WV14 .... 47 F5 ⊡
 KGSWFD DY6 .... 111 F3
Barnett Gn *KGSWFD* DY6 .... 111 F3
Barnett La *KGSWFD* DY6 .... 111 F2
Barnett Rd *WLNHL* WV13 .... 28 A6
Barnett St *STRBR* DY8 .... 111 F4
 TPTN/OCK DY4 .... 92 C1 ⊡
 TPTN/OCK DY4 .... 92 C3 ⊡
Barney Cl *TPTN/OCK* DY4 .... 92 B2
Barn Farm Cl *BILS/COS* WV14 ...... 48 C2
Barnfield Dr *HIA/OLT* B92 .... 176 B5
Barnfield Gv *BFLD/HDSWWD* B20 .. 76 A6
Barnfield Rd *RMSLY* B62 .... 141 F2
 TPTN/OCK DY4 .... 70 A4
 WOLV WV1 .... 26 C5
Barnford Cl *SMTHY* B10 .... 125 E6 ⊡
Barnford Crs *LGLYGN/QTN* B68 ... 118 C4
Barnfordhill Cl *LGLYGN/QTN* B68 .. 119 D3
Barn Gn *BDMR/CCFT* WV3 .... 44 B2
Barnhurst La *CDSL* WV8 .... 9 F2
Barn La *HDSW* B21 .... 98 A6
 HIA/OLT B92 .... 152 A5
 MOS/BIL B13 .... 170 C4
Barn Meadow *YDLY* B25 .... 127 F6
Barnmoor Ri *SOLH* B91 .... 175 E4 ⊡
Barn Owl Dr *BLOX/PEL* WS3 .... 18 B1
Barnpark Covert *BVILLE* B30 ...... 189 E3 ⊡
Barn Piece *RIDG/WDGT* B32 .... 143 D5
Barnsbury Av *CSCFLD/WYGN* B72 .. 81 E5 ⊡
Barns Cl *ALDR* WS9 .... 20 B1
Barns Cft *FOAKS/STRLY* B74 .... 37 D4
Barnsdale Crs *NFLD/LBR* B31 ...... 186 A1
Barns La *RUSH/SHEL* WS4 .... 19 E5
Barnsley Rd *HRBN* B17 .... 120 C6
Barnstaple Rd *SMTHWK* B66 ...... 121 D2 ⊡
Barn St *DIG/EDG* B5 .... 7 H6
Barnt Green Rd *RBRY* B45 .... 201 E4
Barnwood Rd *CDSL* WV8 .... 10 A4
 RIDG/WDGT B32 .... 144 B5
Barons Cl *HRBN* B17 .... 145 D3 ⊡
Barrack La *HALE* B63 .... 139 D3
Barracks Cl *BLOX/PEL* WS3 .... 18 A5
Barracks La *BLOX/PEL* WS3 .... 17 F5
Barrack St *VAUX/NECH* B7 .... 124 C3
 WBROM B70 .... 72 C3 ⊡
Barra Cft *CVALE* B35 .... 105 D1
Barrar Cl *STRBR* DY8 .... 136 A1
Barratts Cft *BRLYHL* DY5 .... 89 E4 ⊡
Barratts Rd *HWK/WKHTH* B38 ..... 188 C5
Barr Common Cl *ALDR* WS9 .... 35 D4
Barr Common Rd *ALDR* WS9 .... 34 C3
Barrhill Cl *GTB/HAM* B43 .... 76 A1 ⊡
Barrington Cl *DSYBK/YTR* WS5 .... 52 C6
 WOLVN WV10 .... 11 E4
Barrington Rd *HIA/OLT* B92 .... 174 A1
 RBRY B45 .... 184 A6
Barr Lakes La *DSYBK/YTR* WS5 .... 54 A2
Barron Rd *NFLD/LBR* B31 .... 187 D2
Barrow Hill Rd *BRLYHL* DY5 .... 89 E4
Barrows La
 LGN/SDN/BHAMAIR B26 .... 152 C3
Barrows Rd *SPARK* B11 .... 149 E3
Barrow Wk *DIG/EDG* B5 .... 148 A2 ⊡
Barrs Crs *CDYHTH* B64 .... 140 B1
Barrs Rd *CDYHTH* B64 .... 140 A2
Barrs St *LGLYGN/QTN* B68 .... 118 C3
Barr St *LOZ/NWT* B19 .... 123 E2
 SEDG DY3 .... 89 E2
Barry Rd *DSYBK/YTR* WS5 .... 53 E2
Barsham Cl *DIG/EDG* B5 .... 147 E3
Barsham Dr *BRLYHL* DY5 .... 137 E1 ⊡
Barston Cl *SOLH* B91 .... 197 D3
Bartholomew Rw *CBHAMNE* B4 ..... 7 G4
Bartholomew St *DIG/EDG* B5 .... 7 H7
Bartic Av *KGSWFD* DY6 .... 112 B3
Bartleet Rd *SMTHWKW* B67 .... 119 F2
Bartlett Cl *TPTN/OCK* DY4 .... 71 D2
Bartley Cl *HIA/OLT* B92 .... 174 B1
Bartley Dr *NFLD/LBR* B31 .... 166 A3
Bartley Woods *RIDG/WDGT* B32 .. 165 D1
Barton Cft *HLGN/YWD* B28 .... 192 B1
Barton Dr *DOR/KN* B93 .... 213 D3
Barton La *KGSWFD* DY6 .... 87 E5
Barton Lodge Rd *HLGN/YWD* B28 .. 192 A1
Barton Rd
 ETTPK/GDPK/PENN WV4 .... 46 B5 ⊡
Bartons Bank *LOZ/NWT* B19 .... 100 A6
Barton St *WBROM* B70 .... 95 D3
Barwell Cl *DOR/KN* B93 .... 212 A5 ⊡
Barwell Rd *BORD* B9 .... 125 D5
Barwick St *CBHAMNW* B3 .... 6 D4
Basalt Cl *WSLW* WS2 .... 30 C3
Basil Gv *NFLD/LBR* B31 .... 186 A1
Basil Rd *NFLD/LBR* B31 .... 186 A1
Baslow Cl *BLOX/PEL* WS3 .... 17 D2
 STECH B33 .... 128 A3
Baslow Rd *BLOX/PEL* WS3 .... 17 D2
Basons La *LGLYGN/QTN* B68 .... 119 E2
Bassano Rd *BLKHTH/ROWR* B65 .. 117 E6 ⊡
Bassenthwaite Ct *KGSWFD* DY6 .. 111 F3 ⊡
Bassett Cl
 ETTPK/GDPK/PENN WV4 .... 43 E3
 SHHTH WV12 .... 29 F3 ⊡

Bassett Cft *SMHTH* B10 .... 149 D1 ⊡
Bassett Rd *DARL/WED* WS10 .... 73 E1
 HALE B63 .... 138 C3
Bassetts Gv
 CHWD/FDBR/MGN B37 .... 130 A2
Bassett St *WSLW* WS2 .... 31 E5
Bassnage Rd *HALE* B63 .... 162 A1
Batchcroft *BILS/COS* WV14 .... 47 F4
 DARL/WED WS10 .... 49 F1
Batchelor Cl *STRBR* DY8 .... 136 B1 ⊡
Bateman Dr *SCFLD/BOLD* B73 ..... 81 D2
Bateman Rd *CSHL/WTROR* B46 .. 108 B4 ⊡
Batemans La *HLYWD* B47 .... 206 A2
Bates Cl *WALM/CURD* B76 .... 83 D3 ⊡
Bates Gv *WNSFLD* WV11 .... 26 C2
Bate St *ETTPK/GDPK/PENN* WV4 .. 46 C6
 WSLW WS2 .... 4 C1
Bath Av *WOLV* WV1 .... 2 B2
Batheaston Cl
 HWK/WKHTH B38 .... 187 F6 ⊡
Bath Meadow *HALE* B63 .... 140 A4
Bath Pas *DIG/EDG* B5 .... 124 A6 ⊡
Bath Rd *BRLYHL* DY5 .... 114 C5
 STRBR DY8 .... 136 B3
 TPTN/OCK DY4 .... 70 C6
 WOLV WV1 .... 2 A4
Bath Rw *EDG* B15 .... 123 E6
 OLDBY B69 .... 93 F5
Bath St *BILS/COS* WV14 .... 48 A4
 CBHAMNE B4 .... 7 E2
 DUDS DY2 .... 91 E5
 SEDG DY3 .... 68 A2
 WLNHL WV13 .... 29 D6 ⊡
 WOLV WV1 .... 3 G5 ⊡
 WSL WS1 .... 4 D5
Batmans Hill Rd *BILS/COS* WV14 .. 70 A1
Batson Ri *STRBR* DY8 .... 136 C1
Battenhall Rd *HRBN* B17 .... 144 C4
Battlefield HI *WMBN* WV5 .... 65 D4
Battlefield La *WMBN* WV5 .... 65 D4
Bavaro Gdns *BRLYHL* DY5 .... 114 C5
Baverstock Rd
 ALE/KHTH/YWD B14 .... 190 A3
Baxterley Gn *SOLH* B91 .... 193 F1
 WALM/CURD B76 .... 82 B2
Baxter Rd *BRLYHL* DY5 .... 113 E5 ⊡
Baxters Rd *SHLY* B90 .... 193 D5
Bayer St *BILS/COS* WV14 .... 69 E4
Bayford Av
 LGN/SDN/BHAMAIR B26 .... 153 E5
 NFLD/LBR B31 .... 202 A1 ⊡
Bayley Crs *DARL/WED* WS10 .... 49 E3
Bayleys La *TPTN/OCK* DY4 .... 71 E4
Baylie St *STRBR* DY8 .... 136 B5
Bayliss Av *BILS/COS* WV14 .... 68 C1
 WNSFLD WV11 .... 14 B5
Bayliss Cl *BILS/COS* WV14 .... 47 F2
 NFLD/LBR B31 .... 167 D6
Baynton Rd *SHHTH* WV12 .... 15 E6
Bayston Av *BDMR/CCFT* WV3 .... 44 A1
Bayston Rd *ALE/KHTH/YWD* B14 .. 190 A1
Bayswater Rd *BFLD/HDSWWD* B20 .. 99 F4
 SEDG DY3 .... 89 F3
Baytree Cl *BLOX/PEL* WS3 .... 16 C3
Bay Tree Cl *HWK/WKHTH* B38 ..... 187 F5
Baytree Rd *BLOX/PEL* WS3 .... 16 C3
Baywell Cl *SHLY* B90 .... 194 C6 ⊡
Beach Av *BHTH/HG* B12 .... 149 D4 ⊡
 BILS/COS WV14 .... 68 C1
Beach Brook Cl *SPARK* B11 .... 149 D4 ⊡
Beachburn Wy
 BFLD/HDSWWD B20 .... 98 C2
Beach Cl *NFLD/LBR* B31 .... 187 E4
Beachcroft Rd *KGSWFD* DY6 .... 87 E5 ⊡
Beach Dr *HALE* B63 .... 140 C4
Beach Rd *BILS/COS* WV14 .... 47 F2
 SPARK B11 .... 149 D4
Beach St *HALE* B63 .... 140 C4 ⊡
Beachwood Av *KGSWFD* DY6 .... 87 E4
Beacon Cl *GTB/HAM* B43 .... 78 B2
 RBRY B45 .... 200 B1
 SMTHWK B66 .... 96 C5
Beacon Dr *WSL* WS1 .... 52 C1
Beacon HI *ALDR* WS9 .... 35 E6
 AST/WIT B6 .... 100 A5
 RBRY B45 .... 200 A2
Beacon La *BRGRVE* B60 .... 199 F4
 SEDG DY3 .... 68 A2
Beacon Ri *ALDR* WS9 .... 35 D4
 HAG/WOL DY9 .... 137 F5
 SEDG DY3 .... 68 A2
Beacon Rd *ALDR* WS9 .... 55 D2
 DSYBK/YTR WS5 .... 53 F4
 GTB/HAM B43 .... 55 E6
 KGSTG B44 .... 56 C5
 SCFLD/BOLD B73 .... 80 C2
 SHHTH WV12 .... 15 E5 ⊡
Beaconsfield Av
 ETTPK/GDPK/PENN WV4 .... 45 F4 ⊡
Beaconsfield Dr
 ETTPK/GDPK/PENN WV4 .... 45 F4 ⊡
Beaconsfield Rd *BHTH/HG* B12 ... 148 A5
 FOAKS/STRLY B74 .... 59 D2
Beacon St *BILS/COS* WV14 .... 68 B2

WSL WS1 .... 5 H5
Beacon Vw *RBRY* B45 .... 200 B1
Beacon View Gv *KGSTG* B44 .... 56 B5
Beacon View Rd *HHTH/SAND* B71 .... 74 B1
Beacon Wy *ALDR* WS9 .... 20 C2
  RUSH/SHEL WS4 .... 33 E2
Beadborough Wk *ALDR* WS9 .... 21 D4
Beakes Rd *SMTHWKW* B67 .... 120 B4
Beaks Farm Gdns
  LDYWD/EDGR B16 .... 121 F5
Beaks Hill Rd *HWK/WKHTH* B38 .... 188 A4
Beak St *CBHAMW* B1 .... 6 D6
Beale Cl *CVALE* B35 .... 104 C3
Beales St *AST/WIT* B6 .... 101 D5 ▪
Beale St *STRBR* DY8 .... 136 B4
Bealeys Av *WNSFLD* WV11 .... 13 E5
Bealeys La *BLOX/PEL* WS3 .... 16 C3
Beamans Cl *HIA/OLT* B92 .... 152 C5
Beaminster Rd *SOLH* B91 .... 194 B1
Bean Cft *RIDG/WDGT* B32 .... 165 E1 ▪
Bean Rd *DUDS* DY2 .... 91 F5 ▪
  TPTN/OCK DY4 .... 69 E5
Beardmore Rd *CSCFLD/WYGN* B72 .. 58 B3 ▪
Bear Hill *ALVE* B48 .... 217 D4
Bearhill Dr *ALVE* B48 .... 217 D3
Bearley Cft *SHLY* B90 .... 193 E5
Bearmore Rd *CDYHTH* B64 .... 116 A6
Bearnett Dr
  ETTPK/GDPK/PENN WV4 .... 65 C1
Bearnett La *WMBN* WV5 .... 65 D2
Bearwood Rd *SMTHWK* B66 .... 120 C5
Beasley Gv *PBAR/PBCH* B42 .... 77 D2
Beaton Cl *WLNHL* WV13 .... 28 A5 ▪
Beaton Rd *FOAKS/STRLY* B74 .... 38 C4
Beatrice St *BLOX/PEL* WS3 .... 31 E1
Beatrice Wk *TPTN/OCK* DY4 .... 92 C3 ▪
Beaubrook Gdns *STRBR* DY8 .... 111 F4
Beauchamp Av
  BFLD/HDSWWD B20 .... 76 B6
Beauchamp Cl
  CHWD/FDBR/MGN B37 .... 131 D5 ▪
  WALM/CURD B76 .... 83 D4 ▪
Beauchamp Rd *MOS/BIL* B13 .... 171 D6
  SOLH B91 .... 174 C6
Beaudesert Cl *HLYWD* B47 .... 206 C1 ▪
Beaudesert Rd
  BFLD/HDSWWD B20 .... 99 D5
  HLYWD B47 .... 206 C1 ▪
Beaufort Av *CBROM* B36 .... 127 E4
Beaufort Rd *LDYWD/EDGR* B16 ..... 122 B6
Beaufort Wy *ALDR* WS9 .... 35 F3
Beaulieu Av *KGSWFD* DY6 .... 112 B3 ▪
Beaumaris Cl *DUDN* DY1 .... 90 B2
Beaumont Cl *TPTN/OCK* DY4 .... 70 A5 ▪
Beaumont Dr *BRLYHL* DY5 .... 137 D2
  HRBN B17 .... 145 D5
Beaumont Gdns *WNSGN* B18 .... 122 B1 ▪
Beaumont Gv *SOLH* B91 .... 174 B6
Beaumont Lawns *BRGRVE* B60 ...... 199 E5
Beaumont Rd *BVILLE* B30 .... 168 A5
  DARL/WED WS10 .... 50 B5
  RMSLY B62 .... 103 E1 ▪
Beausale Dr *DOR/KN* B93 .... 197 D6
Beauty Bank *CDYHTH* B64 .... 140 B1
Beauty Bank Crs *STRBR* DY8 .... 136 A3
Beaver Cl *WNSFLD* WV11 .... 28 B1
Bebington Cl *COVEN* WV9 .... 10 B4
Beccles Dr *WLNHL* WV13 .... 48 B1
Beckbury Av
  ETTPK/GDPK/PENN WV4 .... 43 D3
Beckbury Rd *SLYOAK* B29 .... 166 C2
Beck Cl *SMTHWK* B66 .... 120 C3 ▪
Beckenham Av *KGSTG* B44 .... 78 C2
Becket Cl *MGN/WHC* B75 .... 38 C1
Beckett St *BILS/COS* WV14 .... 48 A3
Beckfield Cl *ALE/KHTH/YWD* B14 .. 190 A3
  RUSH/SHEL WS4 .... 19 E5
Beckford Cft *DOR/KN* B93 .... 212 B4 ▪
Beckman Rd *HAG/WOL* DY9 .... 159 E1
Beckminster Rd *BDMR/CCFT* WV3 .. 44 B3
Beconsfield Cl *DOR/KN* B93 .... 212 B5
Becton Gv *PBAR/PBCH* B42 .... 77 F2
Bedcote Pl *STRBR* DY8 .... 137 D4
Beddoe Cl *TPTN/OCK* DY4 .... 71 F6
Beddow Av *BILS/COS* WV14 .... 69 E5
Beddows Rd *BLOX/PEL* WS3 .... 32 A2
Bedford Dr *MGN/WHC* B75 .... 60 A3
Bedford Rd *HHTH/SAND* B71 .... 73 D4
  MGN/WHC B75 .... 60 A2
  SPARK B11 .... 148 C1
Bedford Ter *TPTN/OCK* DY4 .... 71 D6
  WOLV WV1 .... 46 C2
Bedlam Wood Rd *NFLD/LBR* B31 ... 185 E4
Bedworth Cft *TPTN/OCK* DY4 .... 93 D1 ▪
Bedworth Gv *BORD* B9 .... 127 D5 ▪
Beebee Rd *DARL/WED* WS10 .... 50 B4
Beecham Cl *ALDR* WS9 .... 20 C5
Beech Av *BHTH/HG* B12 .... 148 C4 ▪
  CHWD/FDBR/MGN B37 .... 131 D6
  RIDG/WDGT B32 .... 143 F3
  RMSLY B62 .... 141 E1
Beech Cl *SEDG* DY3 .... 68 A2
  WOLVN WV10 .... 11 D5
Beech Crs *SMTHWK* B66 .... 95 E6
Beech Crs *DARL/WED* WS10 .... 50 B4

TPTN/OCK DY4 .... 71 E3
Beechcroft Av *HLGN/YWD* B28 ...... 172 B5
Beechcroft Crs *FOAKS/STRLY* B74 .. 35 F4
Beechcroft Est *HALE* B63 .... 139 E3 ▪
Beechcroft Pl *WOLVN* WV10 .... 25 E1 ▪
Beechcroft Rd *CBROM* B36 .... 105 D5
  CDYHTH B64 .... 116 A6
Beechdale Av *KGSTG* B44 .... 78 A1
Beech Dene Gv *ERDW/GRVHL* B23 .. 80 A6
Beechdale Rd *BLOX/PEL* WS3 .... 16 B5 ▪
Beecher Pl *HALE* B63 .... 139 E4
Beecher Rd *HALE* B63 .... 139 E4
Beecher Rd East *HALE* B63 .... 139 E4
Beecher St *HALE* B63 .... 139 E4
Beeches Av *ACGN* B27 .... 151 E5 ▪
Beeches Cl *KGSWFD* DY6 .... 111 F2
  RBRY B45 .... 183 F6
Beeches Dr *ERDE/BCHGN* B24 ...... 103 E1
Beeches Farm Dr
  NFLD/LBR B31 .... 186 C6 ▪
Beeches Pl *BLOX/PEL* WS3 .... 17 F6
Beeches Rd *BLKHTH/ROWR* B65 ... 117 D6
  BLOX/PEL WS3 .... 31 F1 ▪
  HHTH/SAND B71 .... 96 A2
  LGLYGN/QTN B68 .... 119 E4
  PBAR/PBCH B42 .... 77 D4
  WBROM B70 .... 96 A3
The Beeches *WBROM* B70 .... 96 A3 ▪
  WOLV WV1 .... 24 C4 ▪
Beeches View Av *HALE* B63 .... 139 E3
Beeches Wk *SCFLD/BOLD* B73 .... 59 D6 ▪
Beeches Wy *NFLD/LBR* B31 .... 186 C6
Beechey Cl *GTB/HAM* B43 .... 55 F4
Beech Farm Cft *NFLD/LBR* B31 ..... 186 C2
Beechfield Cl *RMSLY* B62 .... 141 E1
Beechfield Gv *BILS/COS* WV14 .... 69 D4
Beechfield Rd *SMTHWK* B67 .... 120 B5
  SPARK B11 .... 149 D3 ▪
Beech Gdns *CDSL* WV8 .... 8 B4
Beech Ga *FOAKS/STRLY* B74 .... 37 D2
Beechglade *BFLD/HDSWWD* B20 .... 98 B1
Beech Gn *DUDN* DY1 .... 68 C6
Beech Gv *ALE/KHTH/YWD* B14 ...... 170 C6
Beech Hurst *HWK/WKHTH* B38 ..... 188 A5 ▪
Beechlawn Dr *KINVER* DY7 .... 134 A2 ▪
Beechmore Rd
  LGN/SDN/BHAMAIR B26 .... 152 B4
Beechmount Dr *ERDW/GRVHL* B23 .. 80 C5
Beechnut Cl *SOLH* B91 .... 175 F5 ▪
Beechnut La *SOLH* B91 .... 176 A6
Beech Park Dr *RBRY* B45 .... 215 E1 ▪
Beech Rd *BVILLE* B30 .... 168 A4
  DARL/WED WS10 .... 50 B4
  DUDN DY1 .... 91 E1
  ERDW/GRVHL B23 .... 80 B4
  HLYWD B47 .... 207 D1
  KGSWFD DY6 .... 111 F2
  OLDBY B69 .... 92 C5
  STRBR DY8 .... 136 A6
  WLNHL WV13 .... 28 A5
  WOLVN WV10 .... 11 D5
Beech Tree Av *WNSFLD* WV11 .... 13 E5 ▪
Beech Tree Cl *KGSWFD* DY6 .... 88 A5 ▪
Beechtree Rd *ALDR* WS9 .... 20 B2
Beech Wk *HWK/WKHTH* B38 .... 188 B5 ▪
Beech Wy *SMTHWK* B66 .... 121 D5
Beechwood Av *WNSFLD* WV11 .... 13 D5
  SHLY B90 .... 209 F3 ▪
Beechwood Cft *FOAKS/STRLY* B74 .. 37 F2
Beechwood Dr
  DUNHL/THL/PER WV6 .... 22 C5
Beechwood Park Rd *SOLH* B91 ..... 174 A6
Beechwood Rd
  ALE/KHTH/YWD B14 .... 170 B6
  DUDS DY2 .... 92 A4
  GTB/HAM B43 .... 76 B2
  SMTHWK B67 .... 120 B5
  WBROM B70 .... 95 D2
Beehive Cl *BRGRVW* B61 .... 198 C6
Beehive La *WALM/CURD* B76 .... 85 E5
Bee La *WOLVN* WV10 .... 11 E3
Beeston Cl *AST/WIT* B6 .... 100 C6 ▪
  BRLYHL DY5 .... 137 F1
Beeton Rd *WNSGN* B18 .... 122 A1
Beet St *BLKHTH/ROWR* B65 .... 117 E6 ▪
Beever Rd *TPTN/OCK* DY4 .... 71 F4
Beggars Bush La *WMBN* WV5 .... 65 D6
Beighton Cl *FOAKS/STRLY* B74 .... 38 B1
Beilby Rd *BVILLE* B30 .... 169 D5
Belbroughton Rd *HAG/WOL* DY9 ... 180 A4
  HALE B63 .... 162 B1
  STRBR DY8 .... 136 A3
Belchers La *BORD* B9 .... 126 C5
Beldray Rd *BILS/COS* WV14 .... 48 A3
Belfry Cl *BLOX/PEL* WS3 .... 16 C2
Belfry Dr *STRBR* DY8 .... 136 A5 ▪
Belgrade Rd *WOLVN* WV10 .... 11 D3
Belgrave Middleway *DIG/EDG* B5 .. 148 A2
Belgrave Rd *BHTH/HG* B12 .... 148 B3
  RMSLY B62 .... 141 D4
Belgrave Ter *HDSW* B21 .... 98 C6 ▪
Belgravia Cl *DIG/EDG* B5 .... 148 A2

Belgrove Cl *EDG* B15 .... 146 A3
Belinda Cl *WLNHL* WV13 .... 28 B4
Bellamy Cl *SHLY* B90 .... 193 F4 ▪
Bellamy Farm Rd *SHLY* B90 .... 193 F4
Bellamy La *WNSFLD* WV11 .... 13 E6
Bell Barn Rd *EDG* B15 .... 147 E1
Bell Cl *CBROM* B36 .... 131 D1
  DARL/WED WS10 .... 49 F2
Bellcroft *LDYWD/EDGR* B16 .... 123 D5 ▪
Bell Dr *DSYBK/YTR* WS5 .... 52 C4
Bellefield Av *WSNGN* B18 .... 122 A3 ▪
Bellefield Rd *WSNGN* B18 .... 122 A3
Belle Isle *BRLYHL* DY5 .... 113 E4
Bellemere Rd *HIA/OLT* B92 .... 179 D6
Bellencroft Gdns *BDMR/CCFT* WV3 .. 43 D2
Belle V *HALE* B63 .... 140 A4
Bellevue *DIG/EDG* B5 .... 147 F2
Belle Vue *STRBR* DY8 .... 111 E5
Belle Vue Dr *RMSLY* B62 .... 141 F3
Belle Vue Gdns
  BLKHPN/ROWR B65 .... 117 E4 ▪
Belle Vue Rd *BRLYHL* DY5 .... 114 C6
Bellevue Rd *BILS/COS* WV14 .... 70 B1
  LGN/SDN/BHAMAIR B26 .... 152 C2
Bellevue St *BILS/COS* WV14 .... 68 B1
Belle Vue Ter *HIA/OLT* B92 .... 178 C5
Belle Wk *MOS/BIL* B13 .... 171 D1
Bell Fold *LGLYGN/QTN* B68 .... 119 E1
Bell Green La *HWK/WKHTH* B38 ... 205 D2
Bell Hl *NFLD/LBR* B31 .... 166 C6
Bell Holloway *NFLD/LBR* B31 .... 166 B6
Bellington Cft *SHLY* B90 .... 210 C1 ▪
Bellis St *LDYWD/EDGR* B16 .... 122 B6
Bell La *BLOX/PEL* WS3 .... 17 D4
  DSYBK/YTR WS5 .... 52 C5
  NFLD/LBR B31 .... 186 C1
  STETCH B33 .... 130 A6
Bellman Cl *DARL/WED* WS10 .... 49 F2 ▪
Bell Meadow *HAG/WOL* DY9 .... 159 D3
Bell Meadow Wy
  ALE/KHTH/YWD B14 .... 189 F3 ▪
Bell Pl *BKHL/PFLD* WV2 .... 45 E1
Bell Rd *DSYBK/YTR* WS5 .... 53 F3
  DUDS DY2 .... 115 E2 ▪
Bells Farm Cl *ALE/KHTH/YWD* B14 .. 189 E3
Bells La *HWK/WKHTH* B38 .... 188 E3
  STRBR DY8 .... 111 F6
Bells Moor Rd *WBROM* B70 .... 72 C5
Bell St *BILS/COS* WV14 .... 47 E3
  BILS/COS WV14 .... 69 E1
  BRLYHL DY5 .... 89 F6
  BRLYHL DY5 .... 113 F5
  DARL/WED WS10 .... 49 F2
  STRBR DY8 .... 136 C4 ▪
  TPTN/OCK DY4 .... 70 A6
  WBROM B70 .... 95 F3
  WOLV WV1 .... 2 D5
Bell St South *BRLYHL* DY5 .... 113 F5
Bell Vue Rd *BLKHTH/ROWR* B65 ... 117 E5
Bellwood Rd *NFLD/LBR* B31 .... 186 B1
Belmont Cl *ALDR* WS9 .... 20 C6
  TPTN/OCK DY4 .... 70 B5
Belmont Covert *NFLD/LBR* B31 .... 167 E5 ▪
Belmont Gdns *BILS/COS* WV14 ...... 48 C5 ▪
Belmont Pas *CBHAMNE* B4 .... 124 C5 ▪
Belmont Rd *BRLYHL* DY5 .... 113 F1
  ETTPK/GDPK/PENN WV4 .... 44 C4
  HAG/WOL DY9 .... 138 A5
  HDSW B21 .... 97 E5
  RBRY B45 .... 200 B1
  SMTHWK B66 .... 120 C5
Belmont Rd East *HDSW* B21 .... 97 E5 ▪
Belmont Rw *CBHAMNE* B4 .... 7 H5
Belmont St *BILS/COS* WV14 .... 48 C5
Belper *DUDN* DY1 .... 91 D4
Belper Rd *BLOX/PEL* WS3 .... 17 E2
  WBROM B70 .... 94 B2
Belper Rw *DUDS* DY2 .... 116 A3
Belstone Cl *ALE/KHTH/YWD* B14 ... 169 F6
Belton Av *WNSFLD* WV11 .... 13 D4
Belton Gv *RBRY* B45 .... 185 E5
Belvedere Av
  ETTPK/GDPK/PENN WV4 .... 45 D4
Belvedere Cl *KGSWFD* DY6 .... 112 B3
Belvedere Gdns
  DUNHL/THL/PER WV6 .... 10 A6 ▪
Belvedere Rd *ERDE/BCHGN* B24 ... 102 C3
Belvide Gdns *CDSL* WV8 .... 8 B1
Belvide Gv *SLYOAK* B29 .... 167 D3
Belvidere Gdns *SPARK* B11 .... 149 D5
Belvidere Rd *WSL* WS1 .... 52 B1
Belvoir Cl *DUDN* DY1 .... 90 A3
Belwell Dr *FOAKS/STRLY* B74 .... 38 C5
Belwell La *FOAKS/STRLY* B74 .... 38 C5
Bembridge Cl *WNSFLD* WV11 .... 15 D5
Bembridge Rd *STETCH* B33 .... 128 C4 ▪
Benacre Dr *EDG* B5 .... 7 H5
Benbeck Gv *TPTN/OCK* DY4 .... 69 E5
Bendall Rd *KGSTG* B44 .... 79 D1
Benedon Rd
  LGN/SDN/BHAMAIR B26 .... 152 C2
Benmore Av *DIG/EDG* B5 .... 147 F3
Bennett Av *DUDN* DY1 .... 69 D5
Bennett Rd *FOAKS/STRLY* B74 .... 37 F4
Bennett's Fold *BKHL/PFLD* WV2 ..... 2 C5

Bennett's HI CBHAMNW B3 .... 6 D5 🆔
 DUDS DY2 .... 92 A5
Bennetts Rd WASH/WDE B8 .... 125 F1
Bennett St LOZ/NWT B19 .... 99 F5
Ben Nevis Wy STRBR DY8 .... 136 C3 🆔
Benson Av
 ETTPK/GDPK/PENN WV4 .... 45 E4
Benson Cl DUNHL/THL/PER WV6 ..... 22 A2
Benson Rd ALE/KHTH/YWD B14 .... 191 D4
 WSNGN B18 .... 122 B1
Bent Av RIDG/WDGT B32 .... 143 F3
Bentham Ct NFLD/LBR B31 .... 166 B6 🆔
Bentleybridge Wy WLNHL WV13 ...... 27 E3
Bentley Dr CDSL WV8 .... 8 B1 🆔
 WSLW WS2 .... 31 D5
Bentley Farm Cl DOR/KN B93 .... 212 A3 🆔
Bentley Gv SLYOAK B29 .... 166 B3 🆔
Bentley La SHHTH WV12 .... 29 F2
 WSLW WS2 .... 30 C3
 WSLW WS2 .... 31 E4
Bentley Mill Cl WSLW WS2 .... 30 B6
Bentley Mill La WSLW WS2 .... 30 B6
Bentley Mill Wy WSLW WS2 .... 30 B6
Bentley New Dr WSLW WS2 .... 31 D4
Bentley Pl WSLW WS2 .... 31 E5
Bentley Rd CBROM B36 .... 105 F6
 WOLVN WV10 .... 12 A3
Bentley Rd North WSLW WS2 .... 30 A6
Bentley Rd South DARL/WED WS10 .. 49 F1
Bentmead Gv HWK/WKHTH B38 .... 188 C4
Benton Av SPARK B11 .... 149 E3
Benton Cl SHHTH WV12 .... 29 F3
Benton Crs BLOX/PEL WS3 .... 17 F3
Benton Rd SPARK B11 .... 149 E3
Bentons Mill Cft VAUX/NECH B7 .. 101 E5 🆔
Bent St BRLYHL DY5 .... 113 F3
Ben Willetts Wk
 BLKHTH/ROWR B65 .... 117 E6 🆔
Beoley Cl CSCFLD/WYGN B72 .... 81 E2 🆔
Beoley Gv RBRY B45 .... 184 C6 🆔
Berberry Cl BVILLE B30 .... 167 F5
Beresford Crs WBROM B70 .... 95 D2
Beresford Dr BLOX/PEL WS3 .... 18 A5
Beresford Rd BLOX/PEL WS3 .... 18 A3
 OLDBY B69 .... 95 E6
Bericote Cft ACGN B27 .... 127 F1
Berkeley Cl DUNHL/THL/PER WV6 ... 22 B4
 WSLW WS2 .... 30 B4
Berkeley Dr KGSWFD DY6 .... 87 E6
Berkeley Rd SHLY B90 .... 192 B2
 YDLY B25 .... 150 C2
Berkeley Rd East YDLY B25 .... 150 D2
Berkeley St WSLW WS2 .... 51 D2
Berkley Crs MOS/BIL B13 .... 171 E2
Berkley St CBHAMW B1 .... 6 A6
 CBHAMW B1 .... 123 E6 🆔
Berkshire Cl HHTH/SAND B71 .... 73 D4
Berkshire Crs DARL/WED WS10 .... 51 E5
The Berkshire BLOX/PEL WS3 .... 16 C2 🆔
Berkswell Cl DUDN DY1 .... 90 A2
 FOAKS/STRLY B74 .... 38 A3
 HIA/OLT B92 .... 175 D3
Berkswell Rd ERDE/BCHGN B24 .... 103 D1
Bermuda Cl DUDN DY1 .... 69 D5
Bernard Rd HRBN B17 .... 121 D5
 LGLYGN/QTN B68 .... 119 E5
 TPTN/OCK DY4 .... 70 C4
Bernard St HHTH/SAND B71 .... 95 E1
 WSL WS1 .... 5 G6
Berners St LOZ/NWT B19 .... 99 E6
Bernhard Dr HDSW B21 .... 98 A5 🆔
Bernwall Cl STRBR DY8 .... 136 B5 🆔
Berrandale Rd CBROM B36 .... 104 B5
Berrington Dr BILS/COS WV14 .... 69 D3
Berrington Wk DIG/EDG B5 .... 148 A3 🆔
Berrow Dr EDG B15 .... 146 A2 🆔
Berrowside Rd BKDE/SHDE B34 .... 130 A1 🆔
Berry Av DARL/WED WS10 .... 49 D4
Berrybush Gdns SEDG DY3 .... 68 A4 🆔
Berry Cl LOZ/NWT B19 .... 123 F1
Berry Crs DSYBK/YTR WS5 .... 53 D5
Berry Dr ALDR WS9 .... 34 A2
 RBRY B45 .... 200 C6
Berryfield Rd
 LGN/SDN/BHAMAIR B26 .... 153 F4
Berryfields ALDR WS9 .... 34 A2
Berryfields Rd WALM/CURD B76 ...... 60 B6
Berry Hall La SOLH B91 .... 196 C1
Berry Rd DUDN DY1 .... 91 E1 🆔
 WASH/WDE B8 .... 126 A2
Berry St WOLV WV1 .... 2 E4 🆔
 WSNGN B18 .... 122 B1
Bertha Rd SPARK B11 .... 149 F4
Bertram Cl TPTN/OCK DY4 .... 71 E3
Bertram Rd BORD B9 .... 125 F6 🆔
 SMTHWKW B67 .... 120 A1
Berwick Gv GTB/HAM B43 .... 55 D5
 NFLD/LBR B31 .... 185 F2
Berwicks La
 CHWD/FDBR/MGN B37 .... 131 D6
 CHWD/FDBR/MGN B37 .... 155 D1
Berwood Farm Rd
 CSCFLD/WYGN B72 .... 81 E5
Berwood Gdns ERDE/BCHGN B24 ... 81 E5
Berwood Gv HIA/OLT B92 .... 175 D2

Berwood La ERDE/BCHGN B24 .... 104 A2 🆔
Berwood Rd CSCFLD/WYGN B72..... 81 F5
Besant Gv ACGN B27 .... 172 C1
Besbury Cl DOR/KN B93 .... 212 A5
Bescot Crs DARL/WED WS10 .... 51 F4
 WSL WS1 .... 51 F3
Bescot Cft PBAR/PBCH B42 .... 77 D4
Bescot Dr WSLW WS2 .... 51 D3
Bescot Rd WSLW WS2 .... 51 E2
Bescot St WSL WS1 .... 52 A2
Besford Gv NFLD/LBR B31 .... 185 F2 🆔
 SHLY B90 .... 211 D1 🆔
Bessborough Rd YDLY B25 .... 151 F1
Best Rd BILS/COS WV14 .... 47 F2
Best St CDYHTH B64 .... 116 B5
Beswick Gv STECH B33 .... 128 C3 🆔
Beta Gv ALE/KHTH/YWD B14 .... 191 E1
Betjeman Pl WOLVN WV10 .... 12 C4 🆔
Betley Gv STECH B33 .... 128 C3
Betony Cl DSYBK/YTR WS5 .... 52 C6 🆔
Betsham Cl KGSTG B44 .... 79 D2
Bettany Gld WOLVN WV10 .... 12 A1
Betteridge Dr WALM/CURD B76 ...... 60 A5
Bett Rd BFLD/HDSWWD B20 .... 98 A2
Bevan Av ETTPK/GDPK/PENN WV4 .. 46 A5
Bevan Cl BILS/COS WV14 .... 48 A5
 RUSH/SHEL WS4 .... 19 E4
Bevan Rd BRLYHL DY5 .... 112 C5
 TPTN/OCK DY4 .... 93 D1
Bevan Wy SMTHWK B66 .... 96 B5
Beverley Cl CSCFLD/WYGN B72 .... 81 F4 🆔
Beverley Court Rd
 RIDG/WDGT B32 .... 143 D3
Beverley Crs
 ETTPK/GDPK/PENN WV4 .... 46 B5
Beverley Cft ERDW/GRVHL B23 .... 101 F4
Beverley Dr KGSWFD DY6 .... 87 E6
Beverley Gv
 LGN/SDN/BHAMAIR B26 .... 153 D4
Beverley Rd HHTH/SAND B71 .... 73 F2
 RBRY B45 .... 184 C6
Beverston Rd
 DUNHL/THL/PER WV6 .... 22 C3
 TPTN/OCK DY4 .... 71 D1
Bevington Rd AST/WIT B6 .... 100 A4
Bevin Rd WSLW WS2 .... 30 A4 🆔
Bewdley Dr WOLV WV1 .... 27 E4
Bewdley Rd BVILLE B30 .... 169 D3
Bewlay Cl BRLYHL DY5 .... 137 D2
Bewley Rd SHHTH WV12 .... 29 F3
Bewlys Av BFLD/HDSWWD B20 .... 98 A1
Bexhill Gv EDG B15 .... 123 E6 🆔
Bexley Gv HHTH/SAND B71 .... 74 A4
Bexley Rd KGSTG B44 .... 79 D3
Bhylls Crs BDMR/CCFT WV3 .... 43 E2
Bhylls La BDMR/CCFT WV3 .... 43 D3
Bibbey's Gn WOLVN WV10 .... 12 B1 🆔
Bibsworth Av MOS/BIL B13 .... 171 E4
Bibury Rd HLGN/YWD B28 .... 172 A4
Bicester Sq CVALE B35 .... 105 D1 🆔
Bickenhill La BHAMNEC B40 .... 155 E5
 CHWD/FDBR/MGN B37 .... 155 E5
Bickenhill Park Rd HIA/OLT B92 .... 173 F2
Bickenhill Pkwy
 CHWD/FDBR/MGN B37 .... 155 F3
Bickenhill Rd
 CHWD/FDBR/MGN B37 .... 155 D2
Bickford Rd AST/WIT B6................. 100 C4
 WOLVN WV10 .... 26 B2
Bickington Rd RIDG/WDGT B32 .... 165 F2
Bickley Av BILS/COS WV14 .... 48 C3
 RUSH/SHEL WS4 .... 19 E6
Bicknell Cft ALE/KHTH/YWD B14 .. 190 A3
Bickton Cl ERDE/BCHGN B24 .... 81 E5
Biddings La BILS/COS WV14 .... 69 D1
Biddles HI HOCK/TIA B94 .... 221 E3
Biddlestone Pl DARL/WED WS10 .. 49 D2 🆔
Biddlestone Gv DSYBK/YTR WS5 .... 53 E6
Bideford Dr SLYOAK B29 .... 167 E2
Bideford Rd SMTHWK B66 .... 121 D2 🆔
Bidford Cl SHLY B90 .... 193 F3
Bidford Rd NFLD/LBR B31 .... 186 A2
Bierton Rd YDLY B25 .... 151 E1
Biggin Cl CVALE B35 .... 104 C2
 DUNHL/THL/PER WV6 .... 22 A2 🆔
Bigwood Dr MON/WHC B75 .... 60 C3
 RIDG/WDGT B32 .... 165 E2
Bilberry Crs WALM/CURD B76 .... 60 A6
Bilberry Dr RBRY B45 .... 200 A6
Bilberry Rd ALE/KHTH/YWD B14.... 169 D5
Bilboe Rd BILS/COS WV14 .... 48 B5
Bilbrook Ct CDSL WV8 .... 9 D2 🆔
Bilbrook Gv CDSL WV8 .... 9 D2 🆔
 SLYOAK B29 .... 166 B1 🆔
Bilbrook Rd CDSL WV8 .... 8 C1
Bilhay La WBROM B70 .... 72 C3
Bilhay St WBROM B70 .... 73 D6 🆔
Billau Rd BILS/COS WV14 .... 69 F1
Billesley La ALVE B48 .... 220 A3
Billesley La MOS/BIL B13 .... 170 C5
Billingham Cl SOLH B91 .... 195 D5

Billingsley Rd
 LGN/SDN/BHAMAIR B26 .... 152 C1
Bills La SHLY B90 .... 192 B5
Billsmore Gn HIA/OLT B92 .... 175 E4
Bills St DARL/WED WS10 .... 50 A3
Billy Buns La WMBN WV5 .... 64 C3
Billy La BRGRVE B60 .... 214 C2
Billy Wright Cl
 ETTPK/GDPK/PENN WV4 .... 43 F3
Bilport La DARL/WED WS10 .... 72 B3
Bilston La WLNHL WV13 .... 29 D6
 WLNHL WV13 .... 49 D1
Bilston Rd BKHL/PFLD WV2 .... 46 B1
 DARL/WED WS10 .... 49 F6
 TPTN/OCK DY4 .... 71 D1
 WLNHL WV13 .... 48 C2
 WOLV WV1 .... 3 F5
Bilston St DARL/WED WS10 .... 49 E3 🆔
 DARL/WED WS10 .... 49 F3 🆔
 SEDG DY3 .... 67 F3
 WLNHL WV13 .... 28 C6
Bilton Grange Rd
 LGN/SDN/BHAMAIR B26 .... 152 B2
Bilton Street Island WOLV WV1 .... 3 F5
Binbrook Rd SHHTH WV12 .... 29 F3
Bincomb Av
 LGN/SDN/BHAMAIR B26 .... 153 D3
Binfield St TPTN/OCK DY4 .... 92 C1
Bingley Av WALM/WDE B8 .... 127 D3
Bingley St BDMR/CCFT WV3 .... 44 C1
Biniey Cl LGN/SDN/BHAMAIR B26 .. 151 F3
 SHLY B90 .... 192 C5
Binstead Rd KGSTG B44 .... 78 C1
Binswood Rd RMSLY B62 .... 142 C2
Binton Cft MOS/BIL B13 .... 170 B3
Binton Rd SHLY B90 .... 192 B4
Birbeck Pl BRLYHL DY5 .... 113 D1
Birchall St BHTH/HG B12 .... 124 B6
Birch Av BRLYHL DY5 .... 114 C5
Birch Cl BVILLE B30 .... 167 F5
Birch Coppice BRLYHL DY5 .... 114 C6
 DUDS DY2 .... 115 D5
 WMBN WV5 .... 64 A5 🆔
Birchcoppice Gdns SHHTH WV12 .... 30 A3
Birch Crs OLDBY B69 .... 93 D4
Birch Cft ALDR WS9 .... 21 E5
 CHWD/FDBR/MGN B37 .... 131 E6
 ERDE/BCHGN B24 .... 81 F6
Birch Croft Rd MGN/WHC B75 .... 59 F2
Birchdale BILS/COS WV14 .... 47 F2
Birchdale Rd ERDW/GRVHL B23 ... 102 A2
Birchdale Rd ERDW/GRVHL B23 .... 79 F6
Birch Dr FOAKS/STRLY B74 .... 37 F2
 MGN/WHC B75 .... 60 B2
 RMSLY B62 .... 118 A4
Birches Av CDSL WV8 .... 9 E4
Birches Barn Av BDMR/CCFT WV3 .. 44 B2
Birches Barn Rd BDMR/CCFT WV3 .. 44 B1
Birches Cl MOS/BIL B13 .... 170 B2 🆔
Birches Green Rd
 ERDE/BCHGN B24 .... 103 D3
Birches La ALVE B48 .... 216 A3
Birches Park Rd CDSL WV8 .... 8 C3
Birches Ri WLNHL WV13 .... 28 B6
Birches Rd CDSL WV8 .... 9 D3
Birchfield Av DUNHL/THL/PER WV6.. 23 D1
Birchfield Cl HALE B63 .... 162 A1 🆔
Birchfield Crs HAG/WOL DY9 .... 138 B6 🆔
Birchfield La OLDBY B69 .... 118 A3
Birchfield Rd BFLD/HDSWWD B20 ... 99 D4
 HAG/WOL DY9 .... 138 B6
 LOZ/NWT B19 .... 99 F5
 PBAR/PBCH B42 .... 99 F2
Birchfields Rd SHHTH WV12 .... 28 C2
Birchfield Wy DSYBK/YTR WS5 .... 53 D5
Birchgate HAG/WOL DY9 .... 138 B5
Birchglade BDMR/CCFT WV3 .... 23 F6 🆔
Birch Gv LGLYGN/QTN B68 .... 143 F2 🆔
Birch Hill Av WMBN WV5 .... 64 B6
Birch Hollow EDG B15 .... 146 B3
Birchills St WSLW WS2 .... 31 E5
Birch La ALDR WS9 .... 21 F4
 LGLYGN/QTN B68 .... 143 F2
 RUSH/SHEL WS4 .... 19 E4
Birchley Park Av OLDBY B69 .... 118 A4
Birchley Ri HIA/OLT B92 .... 152 B4
Birchmoor Cl HLGN/YWD B28 .... 173 D4
Birchover Rd WSLW WS2 .... 30 C3
Birch Rd AST/WIT B6...................... 100 C4
 LGLYGN/QTN B68 .... 143 F2
 RBRY B45 .... 200 A1
 SEDG DY3 .... 68 B2
 WNSFLD WV11 .... 14 B4
Birch Rd East AST/WIT B6 .... 100 C2
Birch St LGLYGN/QTN B68 .... 119 E1
 TPTN/OCK DY4 .... 70 B6
 WOLV WV1 .... 2 C4 🆔
 WSLW WS2 .... 4 A1
Birch Ter DUDS DY2 .... 115 E3
Birchtree Gdns BRLYHL DY5 .... 114 C6
Birch Tree Gv SOLH B91 .... 194 A1
Birchtree Hollow SHHTH WV12 .... 29 F2
Birchtrees ERDE/BCHGN B24 .... 103 F1 🆔
Birchtrees Dr STECH B33 .... 129 F5 🆔
Birch Wk LGLYGN/QTN B68 .... 143 F2

Birchwood Cl WNSFLD WV11 .... **14** C2
Birchwood Rd BHTH/HG B12 ...... **148** C5
Birchwood Rd BHTH/HG B12 ...... **148** C5
  ETTPK/GDPK/PENN WV4 .... **44** C4
Birchwoods RIDG/WDGT B32 ...... **165** D1
Birchy Cl SHLY B90 .... **208** B1
Birchy Leasowes La SHLY B90 ...... **208** A2
Birdbrook Rd KGSTG B44 .... **78** A3
Birdie Cl HWK/WKHTH B38 .... **187** F4
Birdlip Gv RIDG/WDGT B32 .... **143** E5
Birds Meadow BRLYHL DY5 .... **89** D6
Bird St SEDG DY3 .... **89** E2
Birdwell Cft MOS/BIL B13 .... **170** B5
Birkdale Av BRGRVE B60 .... **214** C4
  SLYOAK B29 .... **168** B2
Birkdale Cl STRBR DY8 .... **158** B2
  WOLV WV1 .... **26** C5
Birkdale Dr OLDBY B69 .... **92** C6
Birkdale Gv SLYOAK B29 .... **168** C3
Birkdale Rd BLOX/PEL WS3 .... **16** C2
Birkenshaw Rd KGSTG B44 .... **78** A3
Birley Gv HALE B63 .... **161** E3
Birmingham New Rd
  BILS/COS WV14 .... **46** C6
  BILS/COS WV14 .... **60** D2
  DUDN DY1 .... **69** E5
  ETTPK/GDPK/PENN WV4 .... **46** A5
Birmingham Rd ALDR WS9 .... **34** C2
  ALVE B48 .... **203** D3
  ALVE B48 .... **216** C2
  BKHL/PFLD WV2 .... **45** F1
  BLKHTH/ROWR B65 .... **117** E5
  BLKHTH/ROWR B65 .... **117** E6
  BRGRVE B60 .... **199** E5
  BRGRVW B61 .... **199** E3
  CBROM B36 .... **104** C5
  CSCFLD/WYGN B72 .... **81** D3
  CSHL/WTROR B46 .... **106** B3
  CSHL/WTROR B46 .... **131** F2
  DSYBK/YTR WS5 .... **53** D2
  DUDN DY1 .... **91** E2
  GTB/HAM B43 .... **54** A5
  GTB/HAM B43 .... **76** A2
  HAG/WOL DY9 .... **159** F5
  HALE B63 .... **141** D5
  HHTH/SAND B71 .... **96** C4
  HWK/WKHTH B38 .... **203** D2
  OLDBY B69 .... **95** D6
  RCOVN/BALC/EX CV7 .... **157** F6
  WBROM B70 .... **96** A4
  WSL WS1 .... **5** F6
Birmingham St DARL/WED WS10 .... **49** F3
  DUDS DY2 .... **91** F4
  HALE B63 .... **141** D6
  OLDBY B69 .... **94** C5
  STRBR DY8 .... **136** C4
  WLNHL WV13 .... **29** D5
  WSL WS1 .... **5** D5
Birnham Cl TPTN/OCK DY4 .... **69** F6
Bisell Wy BRLYHL DY5 .... **137** F3
Bisbury Cl EDG B15 .... **146** A1
Bishop Asbury Crs GTB/HAM B43 ... **75** D3
Bishop Rd DARL/WED WS10 .... **73** E1
Bishops Cl DUDS DY2 .... **92** A5
  SMTHWK B66 .... **121** E3
Bishops Ga NFLD/LBR B31 .... **186** D3
Bishopsgate St EDG B15 .... **123** D6
Bishops Meadow MGN/WHC B75 .... **40** A4
Bishops Rd SCFLD/BOLD B73 .... **59** D6
Bishops Wy FOAKS/STRLY B74 ...... **38** B1
Bishopton Cl SHLY B90 .... **193** E4
Bishopton Rd SMTHWK B67 .... **120** B6
Bishton Gv DUDS DY2 .... **115** F3
Bissel Br DARL/WED WS10 .... **51** D6
Bissell Cl HLGN/YWD B28 .... **172** B5
Bissell St DIG/EDG B5 .... **148** A1
  RIDG/WDGT B32 .... **142** C3
Bissel St BILS/COS WV14 .... **48** B4
  RIDG/WDGT B32 .... **144** B6
Bitell Cl WOLVN WV10 .... **12** A1
Bittell Farm Rd RBRY B45 .... **202** C6
Bittell La RBRY B45 .... **216** A6
Bittell Rd RBRY B45 .... **202** A6
  RBRY B45 .... **215** F1
Bitterne Dr
  DUNHL/THL/PER WV6 .... **24** C3
Blackacre Rd DUDS DY2 .... **91** F5
Blackberry Av BORD B9 .... **126** C4
Blackberry Cl DUDN DY1 .... **90** A5
Blackberry La ALDR WS9 .... **21** D1
  BLKHTH/ROWR B65 .... **116** B2
  FOAKS/STRLY B74 .... **38** A2
  HALE B63 .... **162** C1
Blackbird Cft CBROM B36 .... **106** C6
Blackbrook Cl DUDS DY2 .... **114** C4
Blackbrook Rd DUDS DY2 .... **114** C2
Blackbrook Wy WOLVN WV10 ...... **12** A1
Blackburn Av
  DUNHL/THL/PER WV6 .... **10** A6
Blackburne Rd HLGN/YWD B28 .... **172** B5
Blackbushe Cl HRBN B17 .... **144** B3

Blackcat Cl
  CHWD/FDBR/MGN B37 .... **130** C4
Black Country New Rd
  BILS/COS WV14 .... **48** C3
Black Country Route
  BILS/COS WV14 .... **48** B3
Blackdown Cl RBRY B45 .... **184** C3
Blackdown Rd DOR/KN B93 .... **213** D1
Blackfirs La
  CHWD/FDBR/MGN B37 .... **155** F2
Blackford Cl HALE B63 .... **161** F1
Blackford Rd SHLY B90 .... **193** E6
  SPARK B11 .... **149** E5
Blackford St WSNGN B18 .... **122** A2
Blackhalve La WNSFLD WV11 ...... **12** C5
Blackham Dr SCFLD/BOLD B73 ...... **80** C4
Blackham Rd WNSFLD WV11 .... **14** B5
Black Haynes Rd SLYOAK B29 ...... **166** C4
Black Lake HHTH/SAND B71 .... **72** C5
Blackmoor Cft STETCH B33 .... **129** F5
Blackpit La WMBN WV5 .... **42** A6
Blackrock Rd ERDW/GRVHL B23 .... **79** D5
Blackroot Dr FOAKS/STRLY B74 .... **58** C2
Blackthorn Cl BVILLE B30 .... **167** E6
Blackthorn Dr BVILLE B30 .... **126** B5
Blackthorne Cl SOLH B91 .... **194** A1
Blackthorne Rd DSYBK/YTR WS5 .... **52** B4
  DUDN DY1 .... **90** B1
  SMTHWK B67 .... **119** F3
Blackthorn Rd BVILLE B30 .... **167** E6
  CBROM B36 .... **105** E5
  STRBR DY8 .... **112** B6
Blackwater Cl BRLYHL DY5 .... **112** C2
Blackwell Rd BRGRVE B60 .... **214** B5
  CSCFLD/WYGN B72 .... **81** F2
  RBRY B45 .... **215** E3
Blackwood Av WNSFLD WV11 ...... **13** D5
Blackwood Dr FOAKS/STRLY B74 .... **56** A1
Blackwood Rd FOAKS/STRLY B74 .... **36** A6
Blades Rd WBROM B70 .... **93** F1
Blaenwern Dr HALE B63 .... **139** D2
Blagdon Rd HALE B63 .... **140** C3
Blair Gv CHWD/FDBR/MGN B37 .... **131** F6
Blakedon Rd DARL/WED WS10 ...... **50** A6
Blakedown Rd HALE B63 .... **162** B1
Blake Hall Cl BRLYHL DY5 .... **137** D2
Blakeland Rd KGSTG B44 .... **78** A5
Blakeland St BORD B9 .... **126** B5
Blakeley Av DUNHL/THL/PER WV6 ... **10** B6
Blakeley Hall Gdns OLDBY B69 ...... **95** D6
Blakeley Hall Rd OLDBY B69 .... **95** D6
Blakeley Heath Dr WMBN WV5 .... **64** C6
Blakeley Ri DUNHL/THL/PER WV6 ... **10** B6
Blakeley Wood Rd TPTN/OCK DY4 .. **71** E3
Blakemere Av YDLY B25 .... **152** A1
Blakemore Cl RIDG/WDGT B32 .... **144** B6
Blakemore Dr MGN/WHC B75 ...... **60** B3
Blakemore Rd ALDR WS9 .... **21** D2
  WBROM B70 .... **92** C3
Blakenall Cl BLOX/PEL WS3 .... **17** F4
Blakenall Heath Rd BLOX/PEL WS3 .. **17** F5
Blakenall La BLOX/PEL WS3 .... **17** F5
Blakenall Rw BLOX/PEL WS3 .... **17** F5
Blakeney Av HRBN B17 .... **144** C2
  STRBR DY8 .... **135** F3
Blakeney Cl SEDG DY3 .... **67** E3
Blakenhale Rd STETCH B33 .... **129** D6
Blake Pl BORD B9 .... **126** B5
Blakesfield Dr RBRY B45 .... **200** C6
Blakesley Cl WALM/CURD B76 ...... **82** B6
Blakesley Ms YDLY B25 .... **151** F1
Blakesley Rd YDLY B25 .... **127** F6
Blake St FOAKS/STRLY B74 .... **38** A1
Blakewood Cl BKDE/SHDE B34 .... **129** E2
Blandford Av CBROM B36 .... **106** A4
Blandford Dr STRBR DY8 .... **112** A5
Blandford Rd RIDG/WDGT B32 .... **144** A4
Blanefield CDSL WV8 .... **10** A3
Blay Av WSLW WS2 .... **31** D5
Blaydon Av MGN/WHC B75 .... **40** A5
Blaydon Rd COVEN WV9 .... **10** C4
Blaythorn Av HIA/OLT B92 .... **152** C6
Blaze Hill Rd KGSWFD DY6 .... **86** C5
Blaze Pk KGSWFD DY6 .... **87** D5
Bleak Hill Rd ERDW/GRVHL B23 .... **79** E6
Bleakhouse Rd OLDBY B68 .... **119** E6
Bleak St SMTHWK B67 .... **107** D4
Blenheim Av RUSH/SHEL WS4 ...... **19** F6
Blenheim Dr GTB/HAM B43 .... **75** F3
Blenheim Rd KGSWFD DY6 .... **112** B1
  MOS/BIL B13 .... **170** B2
  SHHTH WV12 .... **29** D1
  SHLY B90 .... **193** F3
Blenheim Wy CVALE B35 .... **104** C3
  DUDN DY1 .... **90** A3
  KGSTG B44 .... **78** B3
Bletchley Rd ERDE/BCHGN B24 .... **104** A1
Blewitt Cl CBROM B36 .... **105** F3
Blewitt St BRLYHL DY5 .... **113** E1
Blews St AST/WIT B6 .... **124** A2
Blindpit La WALM/CURD B76 .... **85** D3
Blithe Cl STRBR DY8 .... **136** C1
Blithfield Dr BRLYHL DY5 .... **137** D2
Blithfield Gv ERDE/BCHGN B24 .... **81** E6

Blockall DARL/WED WS10 .... **49** F2
Bloomfield Dr SHHTH WV12 .... **15** F4
Bloomfield Rd MOS/BIL B13 .... **148** C5
  TPTN/OCK DY4 .... **70** A4
Bloomfield St North HALE B63 .... **140** B4
Bloomfield St West HALE B63 .... **140** B5
Bloomfield Ter TPTN/OCK DY4 ...... **69** F5
Bloomsbury Gv
  ALE/KHTH/YWD B14 .... **169** E4
Bloomsbury St BKHL/PFLD WV2 ...... **2** C6
  BKHL/PFLD WV2 .... **45** E1
  VAUX/NECH B7 .... **125** D2
Blossomfield Cl
  HWK/WKHTH B38 .... **187** F5
  KGSWFD DY6 .... **88** A5
Blossomfield Rd SOLH B91 .... **194** B3
Blossom Gv CBROM B36 .... **103** F5
Blossom Hl ERDE/BCHGN B24 ...... **102** C1
Blossom's Fold WOLV WV1 .... **2** D4
Blossomville Wy ACGN B27 .... **151** E4
Blowers Green Crs DUDS DY2 ...... **91** D6
Blower's Green Rd DUDS DY2 ...... **91** D6
Bloxcidge St LGLYGN/QTN B68 .... **119** D2
Bloxwich La WSLW WS2 .... **30** C1
Bloxwich Rd BLOX/PEL WS3 .... **17** F6
  WSLW WS2 .... **31** F1
Bloxwich Rd North WNSFLD WV12 .. **29** F1
Bloxwich Rd South WLNHL WV13 .. **28** C3
Blucher St CBHAMW B1 .... **123** F6
Blue Ball La HALE B63 .... **139** E3
Bluebell Cl STRBR DY8 .... **111** E5
Bluebell Crs WNSFLD WV11 .... **27** D1
Bluebell Dr
  CHWD/FDBR/MGN B37 .... **131** F5
Bluebell Rd ALDR WS9 .... **21** D2
  CDYHTH B64 .... **116** A4
  DUDN DY1 .... **91** D2
Bluebellwood Cl
  WALM/CURD B76 .... **60** C6
Blue Cedars STRBR DY8 .... **135** E3
Blue Lake Rd DOR/KN B93 .... **213** D5
Blue La East WSLW WS2 .... **4** B1
Blue La West WSLW WS2 .... **4** A2
Blue Rock Pl OLDBY B69 .... **117** E1
Blundell St SPARK B11 .... **149** F4
Blyth Br CSHL/WTROR B46 .... **109** E5
Blythe Cdns CDSL WV8 .... **8** B1
Blythe Gv KGSTG B44 .... **56** B6
Blythe Rd CSHL/WTROR B46 ...... **109** D5
Blythesway ALVE B48 .... **216** C3
Blytheway SOLH B91 .... **196** A2
Blythewood Cl DOR/KN B93 .... **196** B4
Blythsford Rd HLGN/YWD B28 .... **192** B1
Blythswood Rd SPARK B11 .... **150** C5
Blyton Cl LDYWD/EDGR B16 .... **122** C3
Board School Gdns SEDG DY3 ...... **68** A5
Boar Hound Cl WSNGN B18 .... **122** C3
Boatman's La ALDR WS9 .... **20** A3
Bobbington Wy DUDS DY2 .... **115** F2
Bobs Coppice Wk BRLYHL DY5 .... **138** B2
Bodenham Rd LGLYGN/QTN B68 .. **143** D1
  NFLD/LBR B31 .... **186** A3
Boden Rd HLGN/YWD B28 .... **172** C4
Bodens La ALDR WS9 .... **54** C2
Bodicote Gv MGN/WHC B75 .... **40** A4
Bodington Rd MGN/WHC B75 ...... **39** D4
Bodmin Cl DSYBK/YTR WS5 .... **53** D2
Bodmin Gv VAUX/NECH B7 .... **125** D2
Bodmin Ri DSYBK/YTR WS5 .... **53** F2
Bodmin Rd DUDS DY2 .... **115** F5
Bognop Rd WNSFLD WV11 .... **13** F1
Boldmere Cl SCFLD/BOLD B73 ...... **80** C4
Boldmere St West HALE B63 .... **80** C3
Boldmere Gdns SCFLD/BOLD B73 .. **80** C3
Boldmere Rd SCFLD/BOLD B73 .... **80** B2
Boleyn Rd RBRY B45 .... **184** A4
Bolney Rd RIDG/WDGT B32 .... **144** A4
Bolton Rd SMHTH B10 .... **149** D1
  WNSFLD WV11 .... **27** E2
Bolton St BORD B9 .... **125** D5
Bolton Wy BLOX/PEL WS3 .... **16** B2
Bomers Fold RBRY B45 .... **185** E6
Bond Dr CVALE B35 .... **104** C2
Bondfield Rd MOS/BIL B13 .... **171** D5
Bond Sq WSNGN B18 .... **122** C3
Bond St BILS/COS WV14 .... **68** C3
  BKHL/PFLD WV2 .... **2** D6
  BLKHTH/ROWR B65 .... **118** A4
  BVILLE B30 .... **168** C4
  LOZ/NWT B19 .... **6** C2
  WBROM B70 .... **95** E3
Bone Mill La WOLV WV1 .... **25** E3
Bonfire Hl HAG/WOL DY9 .... **198** A1
Bonham Gv YDLY B25 .... **127** F6
Boningale Wy DOR/KN B93 .... **211** F4
Bonner Dr WALM/CURD B76 .... **82** B6
Bonner Gv ALDR WS9 .... **34** B2
Bonnington Wy GTB/HAM B43 .... **55** F5
Bonsall Rd ERDW/GRVHL B23 ...... **80** C5
Bonville Gdns WOLVN WV10 .... **12** A1
Booth Cl BLOX/PEL WS3 .... **17** F5
  KGSWFD DY6 .... **112** C1
Booth Rd DARL/WED WS10 .... **73** E1
Booths Farm Rd PBAR/PBCH B42 .. **76** C4

Booth's La PBAR/PBCH B42 .... 77 F3
Booth St BLOX/PEL WS3 .... 17 E5
  DARL/WED WS10 .... 49 F1
  HDSW B21 .... 97 E6
Bordeaux Cl DUDN DY1 .... 90 A2
Borden Cl CDSL WV8 .... 10 B3
Bordesley Gn BORD B9 .... 126 C5
Bordesley Gn BORD B9 .... 126 A5
Bordesley Gn East STETCH B33 .... 128 A5
Bordesley Green Rd BORD B9 .... 125 F5
Bordesley Park Rd SMHTH B10 .... 125 D6
Bordesley St DIG/EDG B5 .... 7 C5
Borneo St RUSH/SHEL WS4 .... 32 B3
Borough Crs OLDBY B69 .... 118 A2
  STRBR DY8 .... 136 A4
Borrowdale Cl BRLYHL DY5 .... 137 D1
Borrowdale Gv NFLD/LBR B31 .... 185 F2
Borrowdale Rd NFLD/LBR B31 .... 185 E2
Borrow St WLNHL WV13 .... 28 C4
Borwick Av WBROM B70 .... 94 C2
Boscobel Av TPTN/OCK DY4 .... 90 B2
Boscobel Cl DUDN DY1 .... 90 B2
Boscobel Crs WOLV WV1 .... 25 E3
Boscobel Rd GTB/HAM B43 .... 75 F1
  SHLY B90 .... 209 F2
  WSL WS1 .... 53 D1
Boscombe Av SPARK B11 .... 149 E3
Boscombe Rd SPARK B11 .... 150 A5
Bosty La ALDR WS9 .... 33 F2
Boswell Cl DARL/WED WS10 .... 49 F4
  DARL/WED WS10 .... 71 E2
Boswell Rd BILS/COS WV14 .... 48 B2
  FOAKS/STRLY B74 .... 59 E3
  KGSTG B44 .... 78 B5
Bosworth Cl SEDG DY3 .... 68 B5
Bosworth Dr
  CHWD/FDBR/MGN B37 .... 130 B5
Bosworth Rd
  LGN/SDN/BHAMAIR B26 .... 152 A5
Botany Dr SEDG DY3 .... 67 F6
Botany Rd DSYBK/YTR WS5 .... 52 B4
Botha Rd BORD B9 .... 126 A4
Botteley Rd WBROM B70 .... 72 C5
Bottetourt Rd HRBN B17 .... 144 C6
  SLYOAK B29 .... 166 C1
Botteville Rd ACGN B27 .... 173 E1
Bott La HAG/WOL DY9 .... 137 F3
  WSL WS1 .... 5 F4
Boughton Rd YDLY B25 .... 151 E2
The Boulevard BRLYHL DY5 .... 114 A5
  SCFLD/BOLD B73 .... 81 D3
Boultbee Rd CSCFLD/WYGN B72 .... 81 E4
Boulton Rd HDSW B21 .... 98 A6
  SMTHWK B66 .... 121 F1
  SOLH B91 .... 175 E4
  WBROM B70 .... 95 F4
Boulton Sq WBROM B70 .... 95 F4
Boulton Wk ERDW/GRVHL B23 .... 101 D1
Boundary Av BLKHTH/ROWR B65 .... 118 A5
Boundary Crs SEDG DY3 .... 89 E2
Boundary Hl SEDG DY3 .... 89 E1
Boundary Pl HDSW B21 .... 97 D4
Boundary Rd ALDR WS9 .... 20 B2
  FOAKS/STRLY B74 .... 56 B2
  WLNHL WV13 .... 27 E6
Boundary Wy
  DUNHL/THL/PER WV6 .... 22 B5
  ETTPK/GDPK/PENN WV4 .... 43 E3
Bourlay Cl RBRY B45 .... 184 A3
Bournbrook Rd SLYOAK B29 .... 146 B6
Bourne Av BRGRVW B61 .... 198 B6
  RMSLY B62 .... 142 B5
  TPTN/OCK DY4 .... 71 E4
Bournebrook Cl DUDS DY2 .... 115 E2
Bournebrook Crs RMSLY B62 .... 142 C5
Bourne Cl MOS/BIL B13 .... 171 E5
  SOLH B91 .... 176 A5
Bourne St BILS/COS WV14 .... 91 F4
  DUDS DY2 .... 91 F4
Bourne V ALDR WS9 .... 35 F4
Bourne Way Gdns SLYOAK B29 .... 168 C3
Bournville La BVILLE B30 .... 167 F4
Bourton Cl DSYBK/YTR WS5 .... 52 C6
Bourton Cft HIA/OLT B92 .... 174 B3
Bourton Rd HIA/OLT B92 .... 174 B4
Bovey Cft WALM/CURD B76 .... 82 C4
Bovingdon Rd CVALE B35 .... 104 C2
Bowater Av STETCH B33 .... 127 F6
Bowater St WBROM B70 .... 95 E2
Bowbrook Av SHLY B90 .... 210 C2
Bowcroft Gv ERDE/BCHGN B24 .... 81 E5
Bowden Rd SMTHWK B67 .... 120 A1
Bowdler Rd BKHL/PFLD WV2 .... 45 F1
Bowen Av ETTPK/GDPK/PENN WV4 .... 46 C6
Bowen-Cooke Av CDSL WV8 .... 22 A1
Bowen St ETTPK/GDPK/PENN WV4 .... 46 A4
Bowercourt Cl SOLH B91 .... 195 D3
Bower La BRLYHL DY5 .... 138 B1

Bowes Rd RBRY B45 .... 184 A6
Bowker St WLNHL WV13 .... 27 E5
Bowlas Av MGN/WHC B75 .... 59 D1
Bowling Green Cl
  DARL/WED WS10 .... 49 F2
  ERDW/GRVHL B23 .... 80 A4
Bowling Green La
  BFLD/HDSWWD B20 .... 98 C5
Bowling Green Rd BORD B9 .... 125 E6
  DUDS DY2 .... 115 F4
  STRBR DY8 .... 136 A4
Bowman Rd PBAR/PBCH B42 .... 77 D2
Bowman's Ri WOLV WV1 .... 26 C4
Bowood Crs NFLD/LBR B31 .... 186 C3
Bowood Dr DUNHL/THL/PER WV6 .... 23 F2
Bowood End WALM/CURD B76 .... 59 F6
Bowshot Cl CBROM B36 .... 105 F4
Bowstoke Rd GTB/HAM B43 .... 75 D2
Bow St BILS/COS WV14 .... 48 A3
  CBHAMW B1 .... 123 F6
  WLNHL WV13 .... 28 C6
Bowyer Rd WASH/WDE B8 .... 125 C4
Bowyer St BORD B9 .... 124 C6
Boxhill Cl AST/WIT B6 .... 124 B1
Box Rd CHWD/FDBR/MGN B37 .... 155 E1
Box St WSL WS1 .... 5 F5
Box Trees Rd HOCK/TIA B94 .... 211 E6
Boyd Gv ACGN B27 .... 173 D1
Boydon Cl BKHL/PFLD WV2 .... 46 C3
Boyleston Rd HLGN/YWD B28 .... 172 C5
Boyne Rd LGN/SDN/BHAMAIR B26 .... 153 D2
Boyton Gv KGSTG B44 .... 56 B6
Brabazon Dr CVALE B35 .... 104 B2
Brabham Crs FOAKS/STRLY B74 .... 56 B3
Bracadale Av ERDE/BCHGN B24 .... 102 C1
Bracebridge Rd ERDE/BCHGN B24 .... 102 B4
  FOAKS/STRLY B74 .... 58 C1
Bracebridge St AST/WIT B6 .... 124 A1
Braceby Av MOS/BIL B13 .... 171 E4
Braces La BRGRVE B60 .... 199 D6
Brace St WSL WS1 .... 4 C6
Brackenbury Rd KGSTG B44 .... 79 D3
Bracken Cl CDSL WV8 .... 10 A4
Bracken Cft
  CHWD/FDBR/MGN B37 .... 131 E4
Brackendale Dr DSYBK/YTR WS5 .... 53 D6
Brackendale Wy HAG/WOL DY9 .... 137 F5
Bracken Dr MGN/WHC B75 .... 60 C4
Brackenfield Rd HALE B63 .... 140 A6
  KGSTG B44 .... 77 E1
Brackenfield Vw BRLYHL DY5 .... 89 F5
Bracken Gv BRGRVW B61 .... 198 C6
Bracken Park Gdns STRBR DY8 .... 112 B5
Bracken Rd ERDE/BCHGN B24 .... 103 E3
Bracken Wy FOAKS/STRLY B74 .... 56 B1
  HWK/WKHTH B38 .... 187 F6
Bracken Wd DSYBK/YTR WS5 .... 53 F4
Brackenwood Dr WNSFLD WV11 .... 28 B3
Brackley Av BFLD/HDSWWD B20 .... 99 E4
Brackleys Wy HIA/OLT B92 .... 174 B1
Bradburne Wy VAUX/NECH B7 .... 124 C2
Bradburn Rd WNSFLD WV11 .... 13 D5
Bradbury Rd HIA/OLT B92 .... 174 B3
Braden Rd
  ETTPK/GDPK/PENN WV4 .... 43 F5
Brades Cl HALE B63 .... 139 D2
Brades Ri OLDBY B69 .... 93 F5
Brades Rd OLDBY B69 .... 94 A5
Bradewell Rd CBROM B36 .... 105 F4
Bradfield Rd PBAR/PBCH B42 .... 77 F4
Bradford La WSL WS1 .... 4 C5
Bradford Rd CBROM B36 .... 104 C5
  DUDS DY2 .... 114 B1
Bradford St BHTH/HG B12 .... 124 C6
  DIG/EDG B5 .... 124 B6
  WSL WS1 .... 4 C6
Bradgate Cl SHHTH WV12 .... 29 E1
Bradgate Dr FOAKS/STRLY B74 .... 38 A2
Bradley Av ALDR WS9 .... 21 E4
Bradleymore Rd BRLYHL DY5 .... 113 E4
Bradley Rd BKDE/SHDE B34 .... 129 F1
  BKHL/PFLD WV2 .... 46 A2
  STRBR DY8 .... 136 B3
Bradleys Cl CDYHTH B64 .... 140 A2
Bradley's La BILS/COS WV14 .... 70 A3
Bradley St BILS/COS WV14 .... 48 B5
  BRLYHL DY5 .... 89 D6
  TPTN/OCK DY4 .... 92 B3
Bradmore Cl SOLH B91 .... 194 C5
Bradmore Gv SLYOAK B29 .... 166 C3
Bradmore Rd BDMR/CCFT WV3 .... 44 B1
Bradnock Cl MOS/BIL B13 .... 171 E4
Bradnock's Marsh La
  HIA/OLT B92 .... 187 F4
Bradshaw Av DARL/WED WS10 .... 49 D4
  HWK/WKHTH B38 .... 187 F4
Bradshaw Cl TPTN/OCK DY4 .... 92 C3
Bradshawe Cl
  ALE/KHTH/YWD B14 .... 191 F2
Bradshaw St WOLV WV1 .... 3 F4
Bradstock Rd BVILLE B30 .... 189 E1
Bradwell Cft MGN/WHC B75 .... 40 A4
Braemar Av STRBR DY8 .... 111 E6
Braemar Cl SEDG DY3 .... 67 E2
  SHHTH WV12 .... 28 C1
Braemar Dr ERDW/GRVHL B23 .... 79 D6

Braemar Rd HIA/OLT B92 .... 174 A2
  SCFLD/BOLD B73 .... 80 B1
Braeside Cft
  CHWD/FDBR/MGN B37 .... 131 F5
Braeside Wy BLOX/PEL WS3 .... 18 B2
Bragg Rd BFLD/HDSWWD B20 .... 99 F3
Braggs Farm La SHLY B90 .... 208 C3
Braid Cl HWK/WKHTH B38 .... 187 F4
Brailes Cl HIA/OLT B92 .... 176 A4
Brailes Dr WALM/CURD B76 .... 60 B6
Brailes Gv BORD B9 .... 127 D6
Brailsford Cl WNSFLD WV11 .... 14 A5
Brailsford Dr SMTHWK B66 .... 120 C2
Braithwaite Cl KGSWFD DY6 .... 111 F1
Braithwaite Rd SPARK B11 .... 148 C2
Brake La STRBR DY8 .... 158 A5
Bramah Wy TPTN/OCK DY4 .... 71 E5
Bramber Dr WMBN WV5 .... 64 B5
Bramber Wy STRBR DY8 .... 158 B1
Bramble Cl AST/WIT B6 .... 100 A6
  CDYHTH B64 .... 116 B3
  CSHL/WTROR B46 .... 108 C6
  NFLD/LBR B31 .... 166 B6
  SHHTH WV12 .... 15 E6
Bramble Dell BORD B9 .... 126 C4
Bramble Gn DUDN DY1 .... 68 B6
Brambleside STRBR DY8 .... 112 B6
The Brambles HAG/WOL DY9 .... 137 F6
  WALM/CURD B76 .... 82 C3
Bramblewood WMBN WV5 .... 64 A4
Bramblewood Dr BDMR/CCFT WV3 .... 44 A3
Bramblewoods BKDE/SHDE B34 .... 129 E2
Bramcote Dr HIA/OLT B92 .... 175 D4
Bramcote Ri FOAKS/STRLY B74 .... 59 E2
Bramcote Rd RIDG/WDGT B32 .... 143 E2
Bramerton Cl WNSFLD WV11 .... 26 C1
Bramford Dr DUDN DY1 .... 69 D5
Bramley Cl DSYBK/YTR WS5 .... 53 F1
  GTB/HAM B43 .... 55 F6
Bramley Cft SHLY B90 .... 193 E3
Bramley Dr BFLD/HDSWWD B20 .... 99 D2
  HLYWD B47 .... 207 D1
Bramley Mews Ct ACGN B27 .... 151 E5
Bramley Rd ACGN B27 .... 151 E4
  DSYBK/YTR WS5 .... 53 D5
Brampton Av HLGN/YWD B28 .... 172 C5
Brampton Crs HIA/OLT B92 .... 173 D5
Bramshall Dr DOR/KN B93 .... 212 A4
Bramshaw Cl
  ALE/KHTH/YWD B14 .... 190 B3
Bramstead Av
  DUNHL/THL/PER WV6 .... 23 D5
Branchal Rd ALDR WS9 .... 21 E4
Branch Rd HWK/WKHTH B38 .... 187 F6
Branden Rd ALVE B48 .... 216 C3
Brandhall La LGLYGN/QTN B68 .... 119 D6
Brandhall Rd LGLYGN/QTN B68 .... 119 D6
Brandon Cl FOAKS/STRLY B74 .... 36 B4
  SEDG DY3 .... 68 A4
  WBROM B70 .... 94 C3
Brandon Gv NFLD/LBR B31 .... 186 B6
Brandon Pk BDMR/CCFT WV3 .... 44 A2
Brandon Pl BKDE/SHDE B34 .... 105 F4
Brandon Rd HLGN/YWD B28 .... 172 A1
  RMSLY B62 .... 118 A6
  SOLH B91 .... 175 E4
Brandon Wy BRLYHL DY5 .... 138 A1
  WBROM B70 .... 94 C3
Brandwood Gv
  ALE/KHTH/YWD B14 .... 169 F6
Brandwood Park Rd
  ALE/KHTH/YWD B14 .... 189 C1
Brandwood Rd
  ALE/KHTH/YWD B14 .... 169 F6
Branfield Cl BILS/COS WV14 .... 68 C2
Branksome Av HDSW B21 .... 98 B5
Branscombe Cl
  ALE/KHTH/YWD B14 .... 169 F6
Bransdale Cl DUNHL/THL/PER WV6 .... 24 C2
Bransford Ri SOLH B91 .... 177 D6
Brantford Rd YDLY B25 .... 151 D4
Branthill Cft SOLH B91 .... 195 D4
Brantley Av BDMR/CCFT WV3 .... 23 E6
Brantley Rd AST/WIT B6 .... 100 C3
Branton Hill La ALDR WS9 .... 35 E2
Brasshouse La SMTHWK B66 .... 120 A3
Brassie Cl HWK/WKHTH B38 .... 187 E6
Brassington Av SCFLD/BOLD B73 .... 59 D4
Bratch Cl DUDS DY2 .... 115 E4
Bratch Common Rd WMBN WV5 .... 64 A4
Bratch Hollow WMBN WV5 .... 64 C3
Bratch La WMBN WV5 .... 64 C3
Bratch Pk WMBN WV5 .... 64 C3
Bratt St WBROM B70 .... 95 E1
Braunston Cl WALM/CURD B76 .... 82 C1
Brayford Av BRLYHL DY5 .... 137 D2
Braymoor Rd STETCH B33 .... 130 A6
Brays Rd LGN/SDN/BHAMAIR B26 .... 152 C3
Bray St WLNHL WV13 .... 29 D5
Bream Cl CHWD/FDBR/MGN B37 .... 131 E5
Breamore Dr DUDN DY1 .... 90 B2
Brean Av LGN/SDN/BHAMAIR B26 .... 152 B4
Brearley St HDSW B21 .... 97 F5
  LOZ/NWT B19 .... 123 F2
Brecknock Rd HHTH/SAND B71 .... 72 C5

Brecon Dr *STRBR* DY8 .... **137** D3
Brecon Rd *BFLD/HDSWWD* B20 ...... **99** D5
Bredon Av *HAG/WOL* DY9 .... **137** E4
Bredon Ct *HALE* B63 .... **140** C6
Bredon Cft *WSNGN* B18 .... **122** C2
Bredon Rd *OLDBY* B69 .... **117** F2
_____ *STRBR* DY8 .... **136** C3
Breech Cl *FOAKS/STRLY* B74 .... **56** A2
Breeden Dr *WALM/CURD* B76 .... **85** D5
Breedon Rd *BVILLE* B30 .... **168** C6
Breedon Wy *RUSH/SHEL* WS4 .... **19** E4
Breen Rydding Dr *BILS/COS* WV14 ... **69** D2
Brelades Cl *DUDN* DY1 .... **90** A2
Brendan Cl *CSHL/WTROR* B46 .... **132** C2
Brennand Rd *LGLYGN/QTN* B68 ...... **119** D6
Brentford Rd *ALE/KHTH/YWD* B14 .. **170** B6
_____ *SOLH* B91 .... **194** A2
Brentmill Cl *WOLVN* WV10 .... **12** B1
Brentnall Dr *MGN/WHC* B75 .... **39** D4
Brenton Rd
_____ *ETTPK/GDPK/PENN* WV4 ...... **44** B5
Brett Rd *BVILLE* B30 .... **169** E3
Brentwood Cl *SOLH* B91 .... **194** A2
Brentwood Gv *KGSTG* B44 .... **78** A5
Brenwood Cl *KGSWFD* DY6 .... **87** D6
Brereton Cl *DUDS* DY2 .... **92** A5
Brereton Rd *SHHTH* WV12 .... **15** E6
Bretby Gv *ERDW/GRVHL* B23 .... **80** C5
Bretshall Cl *SHLY* B90 .... **210** B2
Brett Dr *RIDG/WDGT* B32 .... **165** E3
Brettell La *BRLYHL* DY5 .... **113** E6
_____ *STRBR* DY8 .... **112** C6
_____ *STRBR* DY8 .... **136** B1
Brettell St *DUDS* DY2 .... **91** D6
Bretton Rd *ACGN* B27 .... **173** F1
Brett St *HHTH/SAND* B71 .... **73** D6
Brevitt Rd *BKHL/PFLD* WV2 .... **45** F3
Brewers Dr *BLOX/PEL* WS3 .... **18** C4
Brewer St *WSLW* WS2 .... **32** A3
Brewery St *AST/WIT* B6 .... **124** A2
_____ *DUDS* DY2 .... **92** A4
_____ *HDSW* B21 .... **97** F5
_____ *SMTHWKW* B67 .... **120** B1
_____ *TPTN/OCK* DY4 .... **82** B1
Breydon Gv *WLNHL* WV13 .... **48** B1
Brian Rd *SMTHWKW* B67 .... **120** A1
Briar Av *FOAKS/STRLY* B74 .... **36** C6
Briarbeck *RUSH/SHEL* WS4 .... **19** E5
Briar Cl *ERDE/BCHGN* B24 .... **102** C1
Briarfield Rd *SPARK* B11 .... **150** C6
Briars Cl *BRLYHL* DY5 .... **113** E3
The Briars *ERDW/GRVHL* B23 .... **79** F5
Briar Wood Cl *BKHL/PFLD* WV2 ..... **46** C2
Brickbridge La *WMBN* WV5 .... **64** A6
Brickfield Rd *YDLY* B25 .... **151** D3
Brickheath Rd *WOLV* WV1 .... **26** C4
Brickhill Dr
_____ *CHWD/FDBR/MGN* B37 .... **130** C5
Brickhouse La South
_____ *TPTN/OCK* DY4 .... **71** F5
Brickhouse Rd
_____ *BLKHTH/ROWR* B65 .... **116** C3
Brick Kiln La *HLYWD* B47 .... **206** B3
_____ *KGSTG* B44 .... **78** A4
_____ *POL/KGSB/FAZ* B78 .... **63** E3
_____ *SEDG* DY3 .... **88** C2
_____ *SOLH* B91 .... **194** B5
Brick Kiln St *BRLYHL* DY5 .... **114** A2
_____ *BRLYHL* DY5 .... **138** C1
_____ *TPTN/OCK* DY4 .... **70** A5
Brickkiln St *WLNHL* WV13 .... **28** B6
Brick St *SEDG* DY3 .... **67** F3
Brickyard Rd *ALDR* WS9 .... **20** B4
The Bridal Pth *HLGN/YWD* B28 ...... **173** D6
Briddsland Rd *STECH* B33 .... **130** A5
Bridge Av *TPTN/OCK* DY4 .... **71** E4
Bridgeburn Rd *NFLD/LBR* B31 .... **166** A3
Bridge Cl *SPARK* B11 .... **149** D6
Bridge Cft *BHTH/HG* B12 .... **148** A3
Bridgeford Rd *BKDE/SHDE* B34 ...... **129** D1
Bridgelands Wy
_____ *BFLD/HDSWWD* B20 .... **99** F4
Bridgeman Cft *CBROM* B36 .... **105** E5
Bridgeman St *WSLW* WS2 .... **4** B4
Bridgemary Cl *WOLVN* WV10 .... **12** B1
Bridge Meadow Gv *DOR/KN* B93 ... **212** B2
Bridgend Cft *BRLYHL* DY5 .... **113** D1
Bridge Piece *NFLD/LBR* B31 .... **187** D3
Bridge Rd *RUSH/SHEL* WS4 .... **19** D4
_____ *TPTN/OCK* DY4 .... **71** E4
_____ *WASH/WDE* B8 .... **126** A4
Bridge St *BILS/COS* WV14 .... **48** A4
_____ *BILS/COS* WV14 .... **69** E3
_____ *CBHAMW* B1 .... **6** B6
_____ *CBHAMW* B1 .... **123** E6
_____ *DARL/WED* WS10 .... **72** B1
_____ *HALE* B63 .... **139** E2
_____ *OLDBY* B69 .... **94** C5
_____ *STRBR* DY8 .... **112** A6
_____ *WBROM* B70 .... **95** D1
_____ *WLNHL* WV13 .... **28** B6
_____ *WOLVN* WV10 .... **26** A2
_____ *WSL* WS1 .... **4** D3

Bridge St North *SMTHWK* B66 .... **121** D1
Bridge St West *LOZ/NWT* B19 .... **121** F1
Bridgewater Av *OLDBY* B69 .... **118** C3
Bridgwater Crs *DUDS* DY2 .... **92** A4
Bridgewater Dr *BILS/COS* WV14 .... **69** E1
Bridgnorth Av *WMBN* WV5 .... **82** B1
Bridgnorth Gv *SHHTH* WV12 .... **29** D1
Bridgnorth Rd *DUNHL/THL/PER* WV6 **23** D1
_____ *KINVER* DY7 .... **135** E3
_____ *SEDG* DY3 .... **86** C2
_____ *STRBR* DY8 .... **136** A3
Bridgwater Cl *ALDR* WS9 .... **20** B1
Bridle Gv *HHTH/SAND* B71 .... **74** B3
Bridle La *FOAKS/STRLY* B74 .... **55** F3
Bridle Md *WKH/WKHTH* B38 .... **187** F5
Bridle Rd *STRBR* DY8 .... **135** F3
Bridlewood *FOAKS/STRLY* B74 ...... **56** B1
Brierley La *BILS/COS* WV14 .... **70** A1
Brier Road Rd *HALE* B63 .... **141** E6
Briery Cl *CDYHTH* B64 .... **140** B2
Briery Rd *HALE* B63 .... **140** A6
Brigfield Crs *MOS/BIL* B13 .... **171** D6
Brigfield Rd *MOS/BIL* B13 .... **171** D6
Brighton Cl *WSLW* WS2 .... **4** A1
Brighton Pl *BDMR/CCFT* WV3 .... **24** C5
Brighton Rd *BHTH/HG* B12 .... **148** B4
Bright Rd *LGLYGN/QTN* B68 .... **119** D2
Brightstone Cl *WOLVN* WV10 .... **12** B1
Brightstone Rd *RBRY* B45 .... **184** C3
Bright St *DARL/WED* WS10 .... **49** F4
_____ *STRBR* DY8 .... **135** F3
_____ *WOLV* WV1 .... **2** B1
Brightwell Crs *DOR/KN* B93 .... **212** A4
Brindle Cl *LGN/SDN/BHAMAIR* B26 .. **152** A4
Brindlefields Wy *TPTN/OCK* DY4 ... **92** C3
Brindle Rd *DSYBK/YTR* WS5 .... **53** E5
Brindley Av *WNSFLD* WV11 .... **14** C4
Brindley Cl *STRBR* DY8 .... **112** A6
_____ *WSLW* WS2 .... **30** C2
Brindley Ct *TPTN/OCK* DY4 .... **70** A6
Brindley Dr *CBHAMW* B1 .... **6** A5
Brindley Rd *HHTH/SAND* B71 .... **72** C3
Brineton Gv *SLYOAK* B29 .... **166** C2
Brineton St *WSLW* WS2 .... **51** E1
Bringewood Gv
_____ *RIDG/WDGT* B32 .... **165** D3
Brinklow Cft *BKDE/SHDE* B34 .... **105** F6
Brinklow Rd *SLYOAK* B29 .... **166** B1
Brinley Wy *KGSWFD* DY6 .... **111** E1
Brinsford Rd *WOLVN* WV10 .... **11** E2
Brinsley Cl *SOLH* B91 .... **195** D3
Brinsley Rd
_____ *LGN/SDN/BHAMAIR* B26 .... **153** D1
Brisbane Rd *SMTHWKW* B67 .... **120** A1
Briseley Cl *BRLYHL* DY5 .... **137** E1
Bristam Ct *OLDBY* B69 .... **118** A1
Bristnall Hall La *LGLYGN/QTN* B68 .. **119** E4
Bristnall Hall Rd *LGLYGN/QTN* B68 .. **119** E5
Bristol Rd *DIG/EDG* B5 .... **147** E4
_____ *DUDS* DY2 .... **115** F5
_____ *ERDW/GRVHL* B23 .... **102** A2
_____ *SLYOAK* B29 .... **167** F3
Bristol Rd South *NFLD/LBR* B31 ..... **166** C6
_____ *NFLD/LBR* B31 .... **186** A4
_____ *RBRY* B45 .... **184** C6
Briston Cl *BRLYHL* DY5 .... **137** E1
Britannia Gdns
_____ *BLKHTH/ROWR* B65 .... **117** E4
Britannia Rd *BILS/COS* WV14 .... **48** B6
_____ *BLKHTH/ROWR* B65 .... **117** E4
Britannia St *OLDBY* B69 .... **93** E3
Britford Cl *ALE/KHTH/YWD* B14 .... **190** B2
Brittan Cl *BKDE/SHDE* B34 .... **130** A1
Brittania Wy *WSL* WS1 .... **51** F4
Britton Dr *CSCFLD/WYGN* B72 .... **81** F3
Britwell Rd *SCFLD/BOLD* B73 .... **80** C1
Brixfield Wy *SHLY* B90 .... **208** C2
Brixham Rd *LDYWD/EDGR* B16 ...... **121** F3
Broad Acres *NFLD/LBR* B31 .... **166** A5
Broad Cft *TPTN/OCK* DY4 .... **71** E5
Broadfern Rd *DOR/KN* B93 .... **197** D5
Broadfield Cl *HHTH/SAND* B71 ...... **74** B3
_____ *KGSWFD* DY6 .... **111** F2
Broadfields *HAG/WOL* DY9 .... **158** C5
Broadfields Rd *ERDW/GRVHL* B23 .. **81** D4
Broadheath Dr *RUSH/SHEL* WS4 .... **19** F5
Broadhidley Dr *RIDG/WDGT* B32 ... **165** D2
Broadlands Dr *BRLYHL* DY5 .... **114** A2
Broad La *ALE/KHTH/YWD* B14 .... **189** F2
_____ *BDMR/CCFT* WV3 .... **44** A1
_____ *BLOX/PEL* WS3 .... **17** D5
_____ *HOCK/TIA* B94 .... **223** E5
_____ *RUSH/SHEL* WS4 .... **19** F5
Broad Lane Gdns *BLOX/PEL* WS3 ... **16** C3
Broad La North *SHHTH* WV12 .... **29** D1
Broad Lanes *BILS/COS* WV14 .... **47** E5
Broad La South *SHHTH* WV12 .... **28** C1
Broad Meadow *ALDR* WS9 .... **21** D5
Broadmeadow Cl *BVILLE* B30 .... **189** D2
Broadmeadow Gn *BILS/COS* WV14 .. **47** E2
Broad Meadow La *BVILLE* B30 .... **189** D2

Broadmeadows Rd *SHHTH* WV12 .. **16** A5
Broadmoor Av *LGLYGN/QTN* B68 .. **119** F5
Broadmoor Cl *BILS/COS* WV14 ...... **47** E5
Broadmoor Rd *BILS/COS* WV14 ..... **47** E5
Broad Oaks *WALM/CURD* B76 .... **82** C3
Broad Oaks Rd *SOLH* B91 .... **174** B6
Broad Rd *ACGN* B27 .... **151** D6
Broadstone Av *BLOX/PEL* WS3 ...... **17** F5
_____ *HALE* B63 .... **139** D5
Broadstone Cl
_____ *ETTPK/GDPK/PENN* WV4 ...... **45** F4
Broadstone Rd
_____ *LGN/SDN/BHAMAIR* B26 .... **128** B5
Broad St *BILS/COS* WV14 .... **47** E5
_____ *BILS/COS* WV14 .... **69** E3
_____ *BRLYHL* DY5 .... **113** E1
_____ *EDG* B15 .... **123** D6
_____ *KGSWFD* DY6 .... **111** F2
_____ *OLDBY* B69 .... **118** C2
_____ *WOLV* WV1 .... **3** E3
Broad Street Jct *WOLV* WV1 .... **3** F3
Broadwaters Av
_____ *DARL/WED* WS10 .... **49** E5
Broadwaters Rd *DARL/WED* WS10 .. **49** E5
Broad Wy *RUSH/SHEL* WS4 .... **19** E3
Broadway *BDMR/CCFT* WV3 .... **23** E6
_____ *CDSL* WV8 .... **8** A2
_____ *LGLYGN/QTN* B68 .... **119** E6
_____ *SHLY* B90 .... **193** D1
_____ *WOLVN* WV10 .... **12** A3
_____ *WSL* WS1 .... **52** C3
Broadway Av *BORD* B9 .... **126** C5
_____ *HALE* B63 .... **162** C1
Broadway Cft *LGLYGN/QTN* B68 ... **119** E6
_____ *LGN/SDN/BHAMAIR* B26 .... **152** C3
Broadway North *WSL* WS1 .... **5** H2
_____ *WSL* WS1 .... **53** D1
The Broadway *BFLD/HDSWWD* B20 **99** F3
_____ *DUDN* DY1 .... **90** C2
_____ *HHTH/SAND* B71 .... **72** C4
_____ *WMBN* WV5 .... **64** C6
Broadway West *WSL* WS1 .... **51** F3
Broadwell Rd *HIA/OLT* B92 .... **174** C1
_____ *OLDBY* B69 .... **94** C5
Broadyates Gv *YDLY* B25 .... **151** E3
Broadyates Rd *YDLY* B25 .... **151** E3
Brobury Cft *SHLY* B90 .... **193** F1
Brockeridge Cl *SHHTH* WV12 .... **15** E4
Brockhall Gv
_____ *CHWD/FDBR/MGN* B37 .... **130** B2
Brockhill La *ALVE* B48 .... **205** D4
_____ *REDE* B98 .... **220** B6
Brockhurst Dr
_____ *DUNHL/THL/PER* WV6 .... **24** C3
_____ *HLGN/YWD* B28 .... **172** C6
Brockhurst La *MGN/WHC* B75 .... **40** C1
_____ *SHLY* B90 .... **208** C2
Brockhurst Pl *DSYBK/YTR* WS5 ..... **52** B4
Brockhurst Rd *CBROM* B36 .... **127** E3
_____ *MGN/WHC* B75 .... **39** F6
Brockhurst St *DSYBK/YTR* WS5 ..... **52** A3
Brockley Cl *BRLYHL* DY5 .... **113** F4
Brockley Gv *MOS/BIL* B13 .... **169** E2
Brockley Pl *VAUX/NECH* B7 .... **101** E6
Brockmoor Cl *HAG/WOL* DY9 .... **159** E1
Brock Rd *TPTN/OCK* DY4 .... **93** D1
Brockwell Gv *KGSTG* B44 .... **56** A5
Brockwell Rd *KGSTG* B44 .... **56** A5
Brockworth Rd *BVILLE* B30 .... **189** E3

Brocton Cl
_____ *ETTPK/GDPK/PENN* WV4 ...... **46** C5
Brogden Cl *HHTH/SAND* B71 .... **74** B3
Bromfield Cl *AST/WIT* B6 .... **100** A6
Bromfield Crs *DARL/WED* WS10 .... **51** E6
Bromford Cl *ERDW/GRVHL* B23 ..... **80** A6
Bromford Crs *ERDE/BCHGN* B24 ... **102** C3
Bromford Dell *NFLD/LBR* B31 .... **187** E1
Bromford Dr *CBROM* B36 .... **103** E5
Bromford Hl *BFLD/HDSWWD* B20 .. **99** E2
Bromford La *ERDE/BCHGN* B24 ..... **102** C3
_____ *OLDBY* B69 .... **94** C5
_____ *WASH/WDE* B8 .... **103** D6
_____ *WBROM* B70 .... **95** D4
Bromford Ri *BDMR/CCFT* WV3 ...... **45** D1
Bromford Rd *CBROM* B36 .... **103** D6
_____ *DUDS* DY2 .... **114** C1
_____ *WBROM* B70 .... **94** C4
Bromley *BRLYHL* DY5 .... **113** D2
Bromley Gdns *CDSL* WV8 .... **8** C1
Bromley La *KGSWFD* DY6 .... **112** A3
Bromley Pl
_____ *ETTPK/GDPK/PENN* WV4 ...... **44** C4
Bromley St *BKHL/PFLD* WV2 .... **45** E2
_____ *BORD* B9 .... **124** C6
_____ *HAG/WOL* DY9 .... **138** B3
Brompton Dr *BRLYHL* DY5 .... **137** D2
Brompton Lawns
_____ *DUNHL/THL/PER* WV6 .... **22** C4
Brompton Pool Rd
_____ *HLGN/YWD* B28 .... **192** A2
Brompton Rd *KGSTG* B44 .... **56** A5
Bromsgrove Rd *HAG/WOL* DY9 ..... **180** A2
_____ *HALE* B63 .... **141** E6
_____ *RMSLY* B62 .... **162** C6

RMSLY B62 .... 182 C2
Bromsgrove St DIG/EDG B5 .... 123 F6
Bromwall Rd MOS/BIL B13 .... 171 D5
Bromwich Dr MGN/WHC B75 .... 59 E2
Bromwich La HAG/WOL DY9 .... 159 D4
Bromwynd Cl BKHL/PFLD WV2 .... 45 D3
Bromyard Av WALM/CURD B76 .... 82 C3
Bromyard Rd SPARK B11 .... 150 A6
Bronte Cl SHLY B90 .... 193 F4
Bronte Farm Rd SHLY B90 .... 193 F4
Bronte Rd BKHL/PFLD WV2 .... 46 B3
Bronwen Rd BILS/COS WV14 .... 69 E4
Brookbank Av BKDE/SHDE B34 .... 129 F1
Brookbank Gdns SEDG DY3 .... 89 D3
Brookbank Rd SEDG DY3 .... 89 D3
Brook Cl ALDR WS9 .... 20 C2
  LGN/SDN/BHAMAIR B26 .... 153 D4
  SHLY B90 .... 192 B4
  STETCH B33 .... 128 A3
Brook Crs HAG/WOL DY9 .... 138 B6
  HAG/WOL DY9 .... 159 D6
  KGSWFD DY6 .... 87 E6
Brook Cft CHWD/FDBR/MGN B37 .... 155 F2
  LGN/SDN/BHAMAIR B26 .... 153 D2
Brookdale SEDG DY3 .... 89 E2
Brookdale Cl RBRY B45 .... 184 B4
Brookdale Dr
  ETTPK/GDPK/PENN WV4 .... 43 F3
Brook Dr RIDG/WDGT B32 .... 165 F1
Brookend Dr RBRY B45 .... 184 B6
Brooke St DUDS DY2 .... 91 E5
Brookfield Cl ALDR WS9 .... 20 C4
  CDSL WV8 .... 9 D2
  WSNGN B18 .... 122 B2
Brook Fields Cl BRGRVE B60 .... 199 E6
Brookfields Rd LCLYGN/QTN B68 .... 119 E3
Brookfield Wy HIA/OLT B92 .... 173 F4
  TPTN/OCK DY4 .... 70 C5
Brook Gv CDSL WV8 .... 9 D2
Brookhill Cl SHHTH WV12 .... 15 E4
Brook Hill Rd WASH/WDE B8 .... 126 C3
Brook Holloway HAG/WOL DY9 .... 138 A6
  DSYBK/YTR WS5 .... 53 D2
Brookhus Farm Rd
  WALM/CURD B76 .... 82 C3
Brooking Cl GTB/HAM B43 .... 55 F5
Brookland Rd ALDR WS9 .... 20 B2
  HAG/WOL DY9 .... 158 C6
Brooklands Cl STRBR DY8 .... 112 B6
Brooklands Dr
  ALE/KHTH/YWD B14 .... 170 A6
Brooklands Gv BILS/COS WV14 .... 20 B3
Brooklands Pde WOLV WV1 .... 27 D5
Brooklands Rd HLGN/YWD B28 .... 172 B2
The Brooklands SEDG DY3 .... 86 A4
Brook La ALDR WS9 .... 20 B2
  ALE/KHTH/YWD B14 .... 170 B3
  CDYHTH B64 .... 116 A5
  HIA/OLT B92 .... 173 C3
  MOS/BIL B13 .... 170 C3
Brooklea Gv HWK/WKHTH B38 .... 188 C4
Brooklyn Av AST/WIT B6 .... 100 B6
Brooklyn Gv BILS/COS WV14 .... 69 F3
  KGSWFD DY6 .... 87 D5
Brookmans Av RIDG/WDGT B32 .... 143 F5
Brookmeadow Rd
  HLGN/YWD B28 .... 172 A5
Brook Meadow Rd
  BKDE/SHDE B34 .... 128 C1
  RUSH/SHEL WS4 .... 19 F5
Brook Rd EDG B15 .... 146 A2
  LGLYGN/QTN B68 .... 118 C2
  RBRY B45 .... 184 A6
  STRBR DY8 .... 137 D6
  WLNHL WV13 .... 28 A6
  WMBN WV5 .... 64 B5
Brooksbank Dr CDYHTH B64 .... 116 B3
Brooksby Gv DOR/KN B93 .... 212 C5
Brookside DARL/WED WS10 .... 51 D6
  GTB/HAM B43 .... 75 F3
  NFLD/LBR B31 .... 166 B6
  SEDG DY3 .... 89 E3
Brookside Av MOS/BIL B13 .... 171 D4
Brookside Cl ALVE B48 .... 217 D3
  ERDW/GRVHL B23 .... 79 E4
  HALE B63 .... 139 F6
  WMBN WV5 .... 64 A5
Brookside Wy KGSWFD DY6 .... 87 D6
Brooks Cft CVALE B35 .... 104 C3
Brook St BILS/COS WV14 .... 48 A4
  BRLYHL DY5 .... 138 C1
  CBHAMW B3 .... 6 B3
  HAG/WOL DY9 .... 138 B4
  KGSWFD DY6 .... 87 D4
  SEDG DY3 .... 68 C4
  SEDG DY3 .... 89 E2
  SMTHWK B66 .... 121 D1
  STRBR DY8 .... 112 B6
  STRBR DY8 .... 136 A4
  TPTN/OCK DY4 .... 70 A5
  WBROM B70 .... 95 D1

WSLW WS2 .... 4 A4
Brook Ter BILS/COS WV14 .... 48 A4
Brookthorpe Dr SHHTH WV12 .... 29 E3
Brookvale Gv HIA/OLT B92 .... 173 F2
Brookvale Park Rd
  ERDW/GRVHL B23 .... 79 D6
Brookvale Rd AST/WIT B6 .... 100 C2
  HIA/OLT B92 .... 173 F2
Brook Wk RIDG/WDGT B32 .... 165 F1
Brookwillow Rd HALE B63 .... 161 F1
Brookwood Av HLGN/YWD B28 .... 171 F6
Broomcroft Rd
  CHWD/FDBR/MGN B37 .... 130 B2
Broomdene Av BKDE/SHDE B34 .... 104 C6
Broom Dr ALE/KHTH/YWD B14 .... 190 A1
Broome Av GTB/HAM B43 .... 75 E4
Broome Cl HALE B63 .... 140 C6
Broomehill Cl BRLYHL DY5 .... 137 E2
Broome Rd WOLVN WV10 .... 11 F6
Broomfield SMTHWKW B67 .... 120 B2
Broomfield Rd DARL/WED WS10 .... 51 E6
  ERDW/GRVHL B23 .... 101 F3
Broomfields Cl SOLH B91 .... 175 F6
Broomhall Av WNSFLD WV11 .... 27 F1
Broom Hall Crs ACGN B27 .... 173 D4
Broom Hall Gv ACGN B27 .... 173 E3
Broomhill Cl GTB/HAM B43 .... 75 F3
Broomhill La GTB/HAM B43 .... 75 F3
Broomhill Rd ERDW/GRVHL B23 .... 79 D4
Broomhurst EDG B15 .... 146 A1
Broomie Cl MGN/WHC B75 .... 59 F5
Broomlea Cl FOAKS/STRLY B74 .... 56 A1
Broom Rd DSYBK/YTR WS5 .... 53 D6
  DUDN DY1 .... 90 C1
Broomy Cl STETCH B33 .... 128 C2
Broseley Av NFLD/LBR B31 .... 186 C5
Broseley Brook Cl BORD B9 .... 125 E6
Brosil Av BFLD/HDSWWD B20 .... 98 A2
Brougham St LOZ/NWT B19 .... 99 D6
Brough Cl BILS/COS WV14 .... 46 B6
  VAUX/NECH B7 .... 125 D1
Broughton Ct
  DUNHL/THL/PER WV6 .... 22 C4
Broughton Crs NFLD/LBR B31 .... 185 F5
Broughton Rd BDMR/CCFT WV3 .... 23 E6
  BFLD/HDSWWD B20 .... 98 A5
  HAG/WOL DY9 .... 137 F6
Brownfield Rd BKDE/SHDE B34 .... 129 E1
Browning Cl SHHTH WV12 .... 16 A6
Browning Crs WOLVN WV10 .... 11 E3
Browning Rd SEDG DY3 .... 88 C1
Browning St LDYWD/EDGR B16 .... 123 D5
Brownley Rd SHLY B90 .... 194 A6
Brown Lion St TPTN/OCK DY4 .... 70 A4
Brown Rd DARL/WED WS10 .... 49 E2
Brown's Coppice Av SOLH B91 .... 173 F6
Browns Dr SCFLD/BOLD B73 .... 80 B3
Brownsea Cl RBRY B45 .... 184 B4
Brownsea Dr CBHAMW B1 .... 123 F6
Browns Gn BFLD/HDSWWD B20 .... 98 B2
Brownshore La WNSFLD WV11 .... 14 C2
Browns La DOR/KN B93 .... 212 A1
Brownsover Cl CBROM B36 .... 105 D4
Brown St BKHL/PFLD WV2 .... 45 D4
Brownswall Rd SEDG DY3 .... 67 D4
Broxwood Pk
  DUNHL/THL/PER WV6 .... 23 D4
Brueton Av SOLH B91 .... 195 F2
Brueton Dr ERDE/BCHGN B24 .... 102 C2
Brueton Rd BILS/COS WV14 .... 48 C2
Bruford Rd BDMR/CCFT WV3 .... 44 C1
Brunel Cl BHTH/HG B12 .... 148 C4
Brunel Ct BILS/COS WV14 .... 70 A3
Brunel Gv CDSL WV8 .... 22 A1
Brunel Rd OLDBY B69 .... 117 F1
Brunel St CBHAM B2 .... 6 C6
Brunel Wy BKHL/PFLD WV2 .... 46 C2
Brunslow Cl WLNHL WV13 .... 29 E6
  WOLVN WV10 .... 11 E4
Brunswick Ga STRBR DY8 .... 158 C2
Brunswick Park Rd
  DARL/WED WS10 .... 50 C6
  HDSW B21 .... 98 B4
Brunswick St CBHAMW B1 .... 123 D5
  WSLW WS2 .... 51 E2
Brunswick Ter DARL/WED WS10 .... 50 B6
Brunton Rd SMHTH B10 .... 150 B2
Brushfield Rd PBAR/PBCH B42 .... 77 F3
Brutus Dr CSHL/WTROR B46 .... 108 A4
Bryan Av ETTPK/GDPK/PENN WV4 .... 43 F5
Bryan Rd WSLW WS2 .... 51 E3
Bryanston Rd SOLH B91 .... 174 B5
Bryant St WSNGN B18 .... 122 A2
Bryce Rd BRLYHL DY5 .... 112 C2
Brylan Cft KGSTG B44 .... 78 B5
Bryn Arden Rd
  LGN/SDN/BHAMAIR B26 .... 152 A4
Bryndale Av ALE/KHTH/YWD B14 .... 169 E6
Brynmawr Rd BILS/COS WV14 .... 46 B6
Brynside Cl BVILLE B30 .... 189 F5
Bryony Gdns DARL/WED WS10 .... 49 F2
Bryony Rd SLYOAK B29 .... 167 D3
Buchanan Cl RUSH/SHEL WS4 .... 32 C4
Buchanan Rd RUSH/SHEL WS4 .... 5 H1

Buckbury Cl HAG/WOL DY9 .... 159 F1
Buckbury Cft SHLY B90 .... 211 D1
Buckingham Cl DARL/WED WS10 .... 51 F1
Buckingham Dr SHHTH WV12 .... 15 D6
Buckingham Gv KGSWFD DY6 .... 87 E6
Buckingham Ms SCFLD/BOLD B73 .... 80 C1
Buckingham Ri DUDN DY1 .... 90 A3
Buckingham Rd BLKHTH/ROWR B65 .... 117 F3
  CBROM B36 .... 106 B6
  ETTPK/GDPK/PENN WV4 .... 44 C5
Buckingham St LOZ/NWT B19 .... 6 B1
Bucklands End La
  BKDE/SHDE B34 .... 128 B1
Buckle Cl WSL WS1 .... 52 A1
Buckley Rd
  ETTPK/GDPK/PENN WV4 .... 43 F4
The Buckleys ALVE B48 .... 216 C3
Buckminster Dr DOR/KN B93 .... 212 A3
Bucknall Rd WNSFLD WV11 .... 14 C4
Bucknell Cl SOLH B91 .... 175 E6
Buckridge Cl HWK/WKHTH B38 .... 187 F6
Buckton Cl MGN/WHC B75 .... 40 A4
Budbrook Gv BKDE/SHDE B34 .... 130 A1
Budden Rd TPTN/OCK DY4 .... 69 F4
Bude Rd DSYBK/YTR WS5 .... 53 F2
Buffery Rd DUDS DY2 .... 92 A5
Bufferys Cl SOLH B91 .... 195 D5
Buildwas Cl BLOX/PEL WS3 .... 16 B3
Bulford Cl ALE/KHTH/YWD B14 .... 190 B3
Bulger Rd BILS/COS WV14 .... 47 E2
Bullace Cft EDG B15 .... 145 F6
Buller St ETTPK/GDPK/PENN WV4 .... 46 A4
Bullfields Cl BLKHTH/ROWR B65 .... 116 B2
Bullfinch Cl DUDN DY1 .... 90 A5
Bullivents Cl DOR/KN B93 .... 212 B2
Bull La BILS/COS WV14 .... 49 D6
  WBROM B70 .... 94 C2
  WMBN WV5 .... 65 D4
Bullmeadow La WMBN WV5 .... 64 C4
Bullock's Rw WSL WS1 .... 5 E4
Bullock St VAUX/NECH B7 .... 124 C2
  WBROM B70 .... 95 F5
Bull Ring DIG/EDG B5 .... 7 F6
  HALE B63 .... 141 D6
Bull's La WALM/CURD B76 .... 83 E1
Bull St BRLYHL DY5 .... 112 C5
  CBHAM B2 .... 7 E4
  DARL/WED WS10 .... 50 A3
  DUDN DY1 .... 90 C5
  HRBN B17 .... 145 F3
  SEDG DY3 .... 89 E3
  WBROM B70 .... 95 F3
Bulwell Cl AST/WIT B6 .... 100 C6
Bumblehole Mdw WMBN WV5 .... 64 B4
Bunbury Gdns NFLD/LBR B31 .... 187 E1
Bunbury Rd NFLD/LBR B31 .... 187 E1
Bundle HI HALE B63 .... 140 C6
Bunker's Hill La BILS/COS WV14 .... 48 A1
Bunn's La DUDS DY2 .... 92 B4
Burbage Cl WOLVN WV10 .... 26 A1
Burbidge Rd BORD B9 .... 125 F4
Burbury St LOZ/NWT B19 .... 99 E6
  LOZ/NWT B19 .... 123 E1
Burcot Av WOLV WV1 .... 26 C5
Burcote Rd ERDE/BCHGN B24 .... 103 F2
Burdock Cl DSYBK/YTR WS5 .... 52 C6
Burdock Rd SLYOAK B29 .... 166 C5
Burdons Cl STETCH B33 .... 128 C2
Bure Gv WLNHL WV13 .... 29 F6
Burfield Rd HALE B63 .... 139 E3
Burford Cl DSYBK/YTR WS5 .... 52 C5
  HIA/OLT B92 .... 152 C2
Burford Rd HLYWD B47 .... 206 C1
  KGSTG B44 .... 78 B4
Burgess Cft HIA/OLT B92 .... 176 B4
Burghley Dr HHTH/SAND B71 .... 74 B1
Burghley Wk BRLYHL DY5 .... 137 D2
Burgh Wy WSLW WS2 .... 30 C3
Burhill Wy CHWD/FDBR/MGN B37 .... 131 D5
Burke Av MOS/BIL B13 .... 171 F2
Burkitt Dr TPTN/OCK DY4 .... 71 E5
Burland Av DUNHL/THL/PER WV6 .... 10 A6
Burleigh Cl SHHTH WV12 .... 29 D1
Burleigh Rd BDMR/CCFT WV3 .... 44 C2
  WSL WS1 .... 5 F5
Burleton Rd STETCH B33 .... 130 A5
Burley Cl SHLY B90 .... 192 B3
Burlington Rd SMHTH B10 .... 126 A6
  WBROM B70 .... 95 F6
Burlington St AST/WIT B6 .... 124 A1
Burlish Av HIA/OLT B92 .... 174 B2
Burman Cl SHLY B90 .... 192 C3
Burman Dr CSHL/WTROR B46 .... 132 B2
Burman Rd SHLY B90 .... 192 B3
Burmese Wy BLKHTH/ROWR B65 .... 116 B3
Burnaston Crs SHLY B90 .... 195 E6
Burnaston Rd HLGN/YWD B28 .... 172 A3
Burnbank Gv ERDE/BCHGN B24 .... 103 D1
Burn Cl SMTHWKW B67 .... 120 C3
Burncross Wy WOLVN WV10 .... 26 B1
Burnell Gdns BDMR/CCFT WV3 .... 44 A1
Burnel Rd SLYOAK B29 .... 166 C1
Burnett Rd FOAKS/STRLY B74 .... 37 D5
Burney La WASH/WDE B8 .... 127 E2

Burnfields Cl *ALDR* WS9 .... 20 C6
Burnham Av *WOLVN* WV10 .... 11 E5
  YDLY B25 .... 151 E3
Burnham Cl *KGSWFD* DY6 .... 112 B3
Burnham Meadow
  HLGN/YWD B28 .... 172 C5
Burnham Rd *KGSTG* B44 .... 78 A4
Burnhill Gv *SLYOAK* B29 .... 166 C3
Burnlea Gv *NFLD/LBR* B31 .... 187 E4
Burnsall Cl *CHWD/FDBR/MGN* B37 .. 130 B5
  COVEN WV9 .... 10 C2
Burns Av *TPTN/OCK* DY4 .... 70 C4
  WOLVN WV10 .... 11 F3
Burns Cl *STRBR* DY8 .... 135 F1
Burns Gv *SEDG* DY3 .... 88 C1
Burnside Gdns *DSYBK/YTR* WS5 .. 53 F3
Burnside Wy *NFLD/LBR* B31 ...... 186 B6
Burns Pl *DARL/WED* WS10 .... 48 C4
Burns Rd *DARL/WED* WS10 .... 48 C4
Burnthurst Crs *SOLH* B91 .... 194 C6
Burnt Oak Dr *STRBR* DY8 .... 136 C4
Burrington Rd *RIDG/WDGT* B32 .. 164 C3
Burrowes St *WSLW* WS2 .... 4 A1
Burrow Hill Cl *CBROM* B36 .... 105 E5
Burrows Rd *KGSWFD* DY6 .... 112 B3
Burslem Cl *BLOX/PEL* WS3 .... 16 C1
Bursnips Rd *WNSFLD* WV11 .... 15 E1
Burton Av *RUSH/SHEL* WS4 ...... 19 D6
Burton Crs *WOLV* WV1 .... 3 G2
Burton Farm Rd *RUSH/SHEL* WS4 .. 33 D4
Burton Rd *DUDN* DY1 .... 90 C2
  WOLVN WV10 .... 3 H1
Burton Wood Dr
  BFLD/HDSWWD B20 .... 99 F3
Buryfield Rd *SOLH* B91 .... 174 C5
Bury Hill Rd *OLDBY* B69 .... 93 F6
Bush Av *SMTHWK* B66 .... 121 E2
Bushbury Cft
  CHWD/FDBR/MGN B37 .... 131 E4
Bushbury La *WOLVN* WV10 .... 12 B3
Bushbury Rd *STETCH* B33 .... 128 C2
  WOLVN WV10 .... 26 C1
Bushell Dr *SOLH* B91 .... 195 F1
Bushey Cl *FOAKS/STRLY* B74 .... 36 B5
Bushey Fields Rd *DUDN* DY1 .... 90 A6
Bush Gv *BLOX/PEL* WS3 .... 18 C3
  HDSW B21 .... 97 H4
Bushey Cft *SOLH* B91 .... 195 D5
Bushman Wy *BKDE/SHDE* B34 .. 130 A2
Bushmore Rd *HIA/OLT* B92 ...... 172 C5
Bush Rd *DUDS* DY2 .... 115 F5
  TPTN/OCK DY4 .... 92 A1
Bush St *DARL/WED* WS10 .... 49 F2
Bushway Cl *BRLYHL* DY5 .... 112 C5
Bushwood Dr *DOR/KN* B93 ...... 212 C4
Bushwood Rd *SLYOAK* B29 ...... 167 D2
Bustleholme Av *HHTH/SAND* B71 .. 74 B2
Bustleholme Crs
  HHTH/SAND B71 .... 74 A2
Bustleholme La *HHTH/SAND* B71 .. 74 B1
Butchers La *HALE* B63 .... 139 E2
Butchers Rd *HIA/OLT* B92 ...... 178 C5
Butcroft Gdns *DARL/WED* WS10 .. 50 A1
Bute Cl *RBRY* B45 .... 184 A4
  SHHTH WV12 .... 29 D1
Butler Rd *HIA/OLT* B92 .... 178 A3
Butlers Cl *BFLD/HDSWWD* B20 .. 98 C2
  ERDW/GRVHL B23 .... 79 F2
Butlers La *FOAKS/STRLY* B74 ... 38 B4
Butler's Rd *BFLD/HDSWWD* B20 .. 98 C2
Butler St *WBROM* B70 .... 94 C1
Butlin St *VAUX/NECH* B7 .... 101 E6
Buttercup Cl *DSYBK/YTR* WS5 '.. 52 C6
Butterfield Rd *BRLYHL* DY5 ...... 89 D6
Buttermere Cl *BRLYHL* DY5 ...... 137 D2
  DUNHL/THL/PER WV6 .... 9 F5
Buttermere Ct
  DUNHL/THL/PER WV6 .... 22 B3
Buttermere Dr *RIDG/WDGT* B32 .. 144 B6
  WNSFLD WV11 .... 14 C3
Buttermere Gv *WNSFLD* WV11 .. 15 D4
Butterworth Cl *BILS/COS* WV14 .. 68 C2
Buttery Rd *SMTHWKW* B67 ...... 120 A1
Buttons Farm Rd
  ETTPK/GDPK/PENN WV4 .... 43 F6
Buttress Wy *SMTHWK* B66........ 120 C1
Butts Rd *ETTPK/GDPK/PENN* WV4 .. 44 B5
  RUSH/SHEL WS4 .... 32 B4
Butts St *RUSH/SHEL* WS4 .... 32 B4
The Butts *RUSH/SHEL* WS4 .... 32 B4
Buxton Cl *BLOX/PEL* WS3 .... 17 E2
Buxton Rd *BLOX/PEL* WS3 .... 17 E2
  DUDS DY2 .... 114 C1
  ERDW/GRVHL B23 .... 79 D5
  SCFLD/BOLD B73 .... 80 C2
Byfield Cl *STETCH* B33 .... 130 A6
Byfleet Cl *ETTPK/GDPK/PENN* WV4 .. 46 C6
Byland Wy *BLOX/PEL* WS3 .... 16 B3
Byrchen Moor Gdns *BRLYHL* DY5 .. 89 D6
Byrne Rd *BKHL/PFLD* WV2 .... 45 F2
Byron Av *AST/WIT* B6 .... 101 D2
Byron Cl *SMHTH* B10 .... 149 F2
Byron Crs *DUDN* DY1 .... 69 D6
Byron Cft *FOAKS/STRLY* B74 ..... 38 B1

  SEDG DY3 .... 88 C1
Byron Rd *SHHTH* WV12 .... 16 A6
  SMHTH B10 .... 149 F2
  WOLVN WV10 .... 12 C4
Byron St *BRLYHL* DY5 .... 89 F6
  HHTH/SAND B71 .... 73 D6
Byways *BLOX/PEL* WS3 .... 17 E2

C

Caban Cl *NFLD/LBR* B31 .... 166 A6
Cable Dr *WSLW* WS2 .... 31 E2
Cable St *BKHL/PFLD* WV2 .... 46 A1
Cabot Gv *DUNHL/THL/PER* WV6 .. 22 A3
Cadbury Dr *CVALE* B35 .... 104 B4
Cadbury Rd *MOS/BIL* B13 .... 149 D5
Cadbury Wy *HRBN* B17 .... 145 D4
Caddick Crs *HHTH/SAND* B71 .... 73 F4
Caddick Rd *PBAR/PBCH* B42 ..... 77 D2
Caddick St *BILS/COS* WV14 .... 68 C3
Cadgwith Gdns *BILS/COS* WV14 .. 70 C1
Cadine Gdns *MOS/BIL* B13 ...... 169 E2
Cadle Rd *WOLVN* WV10 .... 11 F6
Cadman Crs *WOLVN* WV10 .... 26 C1
Cadnam Cl *HRBN* B17 .... 145 E6
  WLNHL WV13 .... 49 D1
Caernarvon Cl *SHHTH* WV12 ..... 15 E6
Caernarvon Wy *DUDN* DY1 .... 90 A3
Caesar Wy *CSHL/WTROR* B46 .. 108 A4
Cairn Dr *WSLW* WS2 .... 30 B5
Cairns St *WSLW* WS2 .... 31 E4
Caister Dr *WLNHL* WV13 .... 48 B1
Cakemore Rd *RMSLY* B62 .... 118 A5
Cala Dr *EDG* B15 .... 147 D2
Calcot Dr *DUNHL/THL/PER* WV6 .. 10 A6
Calcutt Wy *SHLY* B90 .... 208 C1
Caldecote Cv *BORD* B9 .... 127 E6
Calderfield *SHLY* B90 .... 194 C6
Calder Av *WSL* WS1 .... 5 G3
Calder Dr *WALM/CURD* B76 .... 82 C3
Calderfields Cl *RUSH/SHEL* WS4 .. 32 C4
Calder Gv *BFLD/HDSWWD* B20 .. 98 B3
Calder Ri *DUDN* DY1 .... 68 B5
Caldmore Gn *WSL* WS1 .... 52 A1
Caldmore Rd *WSL* WS1 .... 4 D5
Caldwell Gv *SOLH* B91 .... 175 E6
Caldwell Rd *BORD* B9 .... 127 D4
Caldwell St *HHTH/SAND* B71 ..... 73 F3
Caledonia *BRLYHL* DY5 .... 137 F2
Caledonia Cl *GTB/HAM* B43 .... 53 E6
Caledonian Cl *BKHL/PFLD* WV2 .. 46 A1
Caledonia St *BILS/COS* WV14 ..... 48 A3
Caledon St *WSLW* WS2 .... 51 E2
Calewood Rd *BRLYHL* DY5 .... 137 F2
California *WY RIDG/WDGT* B32 .. 144 B6
California Rd *OLDBY* B69 .... 93 D5
California Wy *RIDG/WDGT* B32 .. 144 A6
Callcott Dr *BRLYHL* DY5 .... 137 F2
Callear Rd *DARL/WED* WS10 .... 71 F2
Caley Cl *TPTN/OCK* DY4 .... 92 B2
Callowbridge Rd *RBRY* B45 ...... 184 B6
Callowbrook La *RBRY* B45 .... 184 B6
Callow Hill Rd *ALVE* B48 .... 216 B2
Calshot Rd *PBAR/PBCH* B42 ...... 76 C3
Calstock Rd *SHHTH* WV12 .... 29 F3
Calthorpe Cl *DSYBK/YTR* WS5 ... 54 A3
Calthorpe Rd *BFLD/HDSWWD* B20 .. 99 E3
  DSYBK/YTR WS5 .... 53 F3
  EDG B15 .... 146 C1
Calver Gv *WNSFLD* WV11 .... 28 B2
Calver Gv *KGSTG* B44 .... 55 F6
Calverley Rd *HWK/WKHTH* B38 .. 187 F4
Calverton Gv *GTB/HAM* B43 .... 76 A3
Calves Cft *WLNHL* WV13 .... 28 C4
Calvin Cft *WMBN* WV5 .... 64 B6
  WOLVN WV10 .... 11 F2
Camberley Crs
  ETTPK/GDPK/PENN WV4 .... 68 A1
  SEDG DY3 .... 68 A1
Camberley Dr
  ETTPK/GDPK/PENN WV4 .... 44 C5
Camberley Rd *KGSWFD* DY6 .... 112 C3
Camborne Cl *AST/WIT* B6 .... 100 A6
Camborne Rd *DSYBK/YTR* WS5 .. 53 F2
Cambourne Rd
  BLKHTH/ROWR B65 .... 117 G4
Cambrai Dr *HLGN/YWD* B28 .... 172 A3
Cambria Cl *SHLY* B90 .... 192 A6
Cambridge Cl *ALDR* WS9 .... 20 C5
Cambridge Crs *EDG* B15 .... 147 F2
Cambridge Dr
  CHWD/FDBR/MGN B37 .... 130 B6
Cambridge Rd *DUDS* DY2 .... 90 C6
  MOS/BIL B13 .... 170 B2
  SMTHWK B66 .... 96 C6
Cambridge St *CBHAMW* B1 .... 6 B5
  WBROM B70 .... 95 D3
  WOLVN WV10 .... 25 F3
  WSL WS1 .... 52 A2
Cambridge Wy *ACGN* B27 .... 151 F5

Camden Cl *CBROM* B36 .... 104 C5
  DSYBK/YTR WS5 .... 52 C5
Camden Dr *CBHAMW* B1 .... 123 D4
Camden St *ALDR* WS9 .... 20 A1
  CBHAMW B1 .... 6 A4
  WSL WS1 .... 51 F1
  WSNGN B18 .... 122 C3
Camden Wy *KGSWFD* DY6 .... 87 F4
Camellia Gdns *COVEN* WV9 ...... 10 B2
Camelot Wy *SMHTH* B10 .... 149 E1
Cameo Dr *STRBR* DY8 .... 136 B1
Cameron Rd *RUSH/SHEL* WS4 ..... 5 H1
Camford Gv *ALE/KHTH/YWD* B14 .. 190 B2
Cam Gdns *BRLYHL* DY5 .... 113 D2
Camino Rd *RIDG/WDGT* B32 .... 144 B6
Camomile Cl *DSYBK/YTR* WS5 .. 52 C6
Campbell Cl *RUSH/SHEL* WS4 ..... 32 C4
Campbell Pl *DARL/WED* WS10 .. 49 F3
Campbells Gn
  LGN/SDN/BHAMAIR B26 .... 153 D4
Campbell St *BRLYHL* DY5 .... 113 E3
  DUDS DY2 .... 91 F5
Campden Cl *HIA/OLT* B92 .... 152 C6
Camp Hl *BHTH/HG* B12 .... 148 C1
Camphill La *DARL/WED* WS10 .... 72 B1
Camphion Cl *DSYBK/YTR* WS5 .. 52 C6
  WMBN WV5 .... 64 A5
Campion Gv *HALE* B63 .... 139 F6
Campion Wy *SHLY* B90 .... 208 C2
Camp La *HDSW* B21 .... 97 D3
  HWK/WKHTH B38 .... 188 B2
Camplea Cft
  CHWD/FDBR/MGN B37 .... 130 C5
Camplin Crs *BFLD/HDSWWD* B20 .. 76 A6
Camp Rd *MGN/WHC* B75 .... 39 F5
Camp St *BORD* B9 .... 125 E6
  DARL/WED WS10 .... 72 B1
  WOLV WV1 .... 2 D1
Campville Crs *HHTH/SAND* B71 .. 74 A3
Campville Gv
  CHWD/FDBR/MGN B37 .... 130 B2
Camp Wood Cl *SLYOAK* B29 .... 168 A3
Camrose Cft *BHTH/HG* B12 ...... 148 A3
  BKDE/SHDE B34 .... 129 D1
Camrose Gdns *COVEN* WV9 ...... 10 C2
Canal La *ERDE/BCHGN* B24 ..... 102 C4
Canal Side *ALVE* B48 .... 205 D5
  DUDS DY2 .... 116 A3
Canalside Cl *BLOX/PEL* WS3 ...... 18 A4
  HHTH/SAND B71 .... 74 A1
Canal St *BRLYHL* DY5 .... 114 A2
  OLDBY B69 .... 94 B6
  STRBR DY8 .... 136 B3
Canary Gv *LOZ/NWT* B19 .... 99 E5
Canberra Rd *DSYBK/YTR* WS5 .. 53 E4
Canford Cl *BHTH/HG* B12 .... 148 B2
Canford Crs *CDSL* WV8 .... 8 A2
Canning Cl *DSYBK/YTR* WS5 ..... 53 F3
Canning Gdns *WSNGN* B18 ..... 122 A3
Canning Rd *DSYBK/YTR* WS5 ..... 53 F3
Cannock Rd *SHHTH* WV12 .... 15 E6
  WOLVN WV10 .... 12 B6
  WOLVN WV10 .... 13 D4
  WOLVN WV10 .... 25 F5
Cannon Dr *BILS/COS* WV14 .... 69 E1
Cannon Hill Rd *BHTH/HG* B12 .. 147 F4
Cannon Rd *WMBN* WV5 .... 64 C5
Cannon St *CBHAM* B2 .... 7 E5
  WLNHL WV13 .... 29 D5
  WSLW WS2 .... 32 A3
Cannon St North *WSLW* WS2 .... 32 A3
Canterbury Av *WLNHL* WV13 .... 29 F5
Canterbury Cl
  BLKHTH/ROWR B65 .... 118 A3
  HHTH/SAND B71 .... 74 A3
Canterbury Dr
  CHWD/FDBR/MGN B37 .... 154 C2
Canterbury Rd *BFLD/HDSWWD* B20 .. 99 F4
  ETTPK/GDPK/PENN WV4 .... 43 F4
  HHTH/SAND B71 .... 73 F3
Cantlow Rd *MOS/BIL* B13 .... 170 C5
Canute Cl *WSL* WS1 .... 52 B2
Canvey Cl *RBRY* B45 .... 184 A4
Canwell Av
  CHWD/FDBR/MGN B37 .... 130 B2
Canwell Dr *MGN/WHC* B75 .... 40 C2
Canwell Gdns *BILS/COS* WV14 ... 47 D5
Capcroft Rd *MOS/BIL* B13 .... 171 D5
Cape Hl *SMTHWK* B66 .... 121 D3
Capener Rd *GTB/HAM* B43 .... 76 C1
Capern Gv *RIDG/WDGT* B32 .... 144 B4
Cape St *WBROM* B70 .... 94 A1
  WSNGN B18 .... 121 F3
Capethorn Rd *SMTHWK* B66 .... 120 C4
Capilano Rd *ERDW/GRVHL* B23 .. 79 E4
Capponfield Cl *BILS/COS* WV14 .. 47 D6
Capstone Av *WOLVN* WV10 .... 11 D5
  WSNGN B18 .... 122 C3
Captain's Cl *BDMR/CCFT* WV3 .. 23 F5
Carcroft Rd *YDLY* B25 .... 151 E1
Cardale St *BLKHTH/ROWR* B65 .. 117 F5
Carden Cl *WBROM* B70 .... 94 B1
Carder Crs *BILS/COS* WV14 .... 47 F5
Carder Dr *BRLYHL* DY5 .... 113 E5
Cardiff St *BDMR/CCFT* WV3 ...... 45 D1

Cardigan Cl *HHTH/SAND* B71 .... 73 E4
Cardigan Dr *SHHTH* WV12 .... 29 D1 ▣
Cardigan St *CBHAMNE* B4 .... 7 H3
Cardington Av *PBAR/PBCH* B42 .... 77 D2
Cardoness Pl *DUDN* DY1 .... 90 B3 ▣
Carehampton Rd *MGN/WHC* B75 .... 60 C3
Careless Gn *HAG/WOL* DY9 .... 138 B5
Carisbrooke Av
  CHWD/FDBR/MGN B37 .... 131 E5
Carisbrooke Cl *DARL/WED* WS10 .. 74 A1 ▣
Carisbrooke Ct
  DUNHL/THL/PER WV6 .... 22 C4 ▣
Carisbrooke Dr *DARL/WED* WS10 .... 52 A6
Carisbrooke Dr *RMSLY* B62 .... 141 F6 ▣
Carisbrooke Gdns *WOLVN* WV10 .. 12 A2 ▣
Carisbrooke Rd *DARL/WED* WS10...... 73 F1
  DUNHL/THL/PER WV6 .... 22 C4
  HRBN B17 .... 121 D6
  WOLVN WV10 .... 12 A2
Carlyle Gv *WOLVN* WV10............... 12 C5
Carlyle Rd *BLKHTH/ROWR* B65 ...... 117 E5
  LDYWD/EDGR B16 .... 122 A6
  LOZ/NWT B19 .... 99 E5
  WOLVN WV10 .... 12 B5
Carmel Gv *RIDG/WDGT* B32 .... 165 D2
Carmodale Av *PBAR/PBCH* B42 .... 77 D5
Carnegie Av *TPTN/OCK* DY4 .... 92 C1
Carnegie Dr *DARL/WED* WS10 ...... 50 C6 ▣
Carnegie Rd *BLKHTH/ROWR* B65 .... 117 D5
Carnford Rd
  LGN/SDN/BHAMAIR B26 .... 153 D3
Carnforth Cl *KGSWFD* DY6 .... 87 D6
Carnoustie Cl *BLOX/PEL* WS3 .... 16 C2
  MGN/WHC B75 .... 59 F1
Carnwath Rd *SCFLD/BOLD* B73........ 80 A1
Carol Crs *HALE* B63 .... 140 B4
  WNSFLD WV11 .... 28 A1
Caroline Rd *MOS/BIL* B13 .... 148 B5 ▣
Caroline St *CBHAMNE* B1................. 6 B2
  DUDS DY2 .... 92 A4
  WBROM B70 .... 90 D3
Carpenter Rd *EDG* B15 .... 147 D2
Carpenter's La *LOZ/NWT* B19 .... 99 E6
Carriers Cl *WSLW* WS2.................... 30 E6
Carrington Rd *DARL/WED* WS10 ...... 73 F1
Carroway Head Hl *MGN/WHC* B75.... 41 E5
Carrs La *CBHAMNE* B4 .... 7 F5
Carshalton Gv *BKHL/PFLD* WV2 ...... 46 A1
Carshalton Rd *KGSTG* B44 .... 78 C1
Cartbridge Cls *BLOX/PEL* WS3 .... 32 B1
Cartbridge La *RUSH/SHEL* WS4 ...... 32 C2
Cartbridge La South
  RUSH/SHEL WS4 .... 32 C2
Carter Av *CDSL* WV8 .... 9 D2
Carter Rd *DUNHL/THL/PER* WV6...... 25 D2
  GTB/HAM B43 .... 76 B1
Carters Cl *WALM/CURD* B76............ 60 B6
Carter's Gn *WBROM* B70 .... 90 D1
Carters Hurst *STETCH* B33 .... 129 D6 ▣
Carter's La *RMSLY* B62 .... 142 B4
Cartland Rd *BVILLE* B30 .... 169 D4
  SPARK B11 .... 149 E2
Cartwright Gdns *OLDBY* B69 .... 93 E3 ▣
Cartwright Rd *MGN/WHC* B75 .... 39 E4
Cartwright St *BKHL/PFLD* WV2 .... 45 F1
Carver Gdns *STRBR* DY8 .... 158 A1
Carver St *CBHAMNE* B1 .... 123 D3
Caswell Rd *KGSWFD* DY6 .... 87 F3
Casey Av *ERDW/GRVHL* B23 .... 79 F3
Cash Joynson Av
  DARL/WED WS10 .... 49 E1 ▣
Caslon Crs *STRBR* DY8 .... 135 F5
Caslon Rd *HALE* B63 .... 139 E3 ▣
Cassandra Cl *BRLYHL* DY5 .... 89 E4 ▣
Cassowary Rd
  BFLD/HDSWWD B20 .... 98 B2 ▣
Castello Dr *CBROM* B36 .... 105 F4
Castlebridge Rd *WNSFLD* WV11 ...... 14 C6
Castle Cl *CDYHTH* B64 .... 117 D6
  HIA/OLT B92 .... 175 D4
Castle Crs *CBROM* B36 .... 105 E5
Castle Cft *LGLYGN/QTN* B68 .... 143 F1 ▣
Castlecroft Av *BDMR/CCFT* WV3 ..... 42 C1
Castlecroft Gdns *BDMR/CCFT* WV3 .. 43 D1
Castlecroft La *BDMR/CCFT* WV3 ..... 42 B1
Castlecroft Rd *BDMR/CCFT* WV3 ..... 42 B1
  BILS/COS WV14 .... 68 A2
Castle Dr *CSHL/WTROR* B46.......... 132 B2
  SHHTH WV12 .... 29 D2 ▣

Castleford Rd *SPARK* B11 .... 149 E5
Castlefort Rd *ALDR* WS9 .... 20 C2
Castle Gv *STRBR* DY8 .... 137 D6
Castle Hts *CDYHTH* B64 .... 141 D1 ▣
Castle Hl *DUDN* DY1 .... 91 E1
Castlehill Rd *ALDR* WS9 .... 21 E2
Castlehills Dr *CBROM* B36 .... 104 C5
Castle La *HIA/OLT* B92 .... 174 B2
Castle Mill Rd *DUDN* DY1 .... 91 E1
Castle Rd *ALDR* WS9 .... 20 C3
  SLYOAK B29 .... 166 C1
  TPTN/OCK DY4 .... 91 F1
Castle Rd East *LGLYGN/QTN* B68... 143 F1
Castle Rd West *LGLYGN/QTN* B68 .. 143 E1
Castle St *BILS/COS* WV14 .... 69 E3
  DARL/WED WS10 .... 49 F1
  DUDN DY1 .... 91 F4 ▣
  SEDG DY3 .... 67 D3
  TPTN/OCK DY4 .... 70 A4
  WBROM B70 .... 72 C4
  WOLV WV1 .... 3 F4
Castleton Rd *BLOX/PEL* WS3 .... 17 E2
  PBAR/PBCH B42 .... 77 F4
Castleton St *DUDS* DY2 .... 115 E2 ▣
Castle Vw *DUDN* DY1 .... 91 D3
Castle View Cl *DARL/WED* WS10 ..... 48 C5
Castle View Rd *DARL/WED* WS10 .... 48 C5
Caswell Rd *SEDG* DY3 .... 67 E3
Cater Dr *WALM/CURD* B76 .... 82 B1
Caterham Dr *STRBR* DY8 .... 112 B4
Catesby Dr *KGSWFD* DY6 .... 87 F5
Catesby Rd *SHLY* B90 .... 193 D4
Cateswell Rd *HLGN/YWD* B28 .... 172 B2
Cathcart Rd *STRBR* DY8 .... 136 A4
Cathel Dr *PBAR/PBCH* B42 .... 76 C4
Catherine de Barnes La
  HIA/OLT B92 .... 177 E5
Catherine Dr *SCFLD/BOLD* B73 ...... 58 C3
Catherine Rd *BILS/COS* WV14 .... 68 C3
Catherines Cl *SOLH* B91 .... 197 D1
Catherine St *AST/WIT* B6 .... 100 C6 ▣
Catherton Cl *TPTN/OCK* DY4 .... 71 E1
Catholic La *SEDG* DY3 .... 67 E4
Catisfield Crs *CDSL* WV8 .... 10 D4
Cat La *BKDE/SHDE* B34................ 105 D6
Caton Gv *HLGN/YWD* B28............. 172 C4
Cato St *VAUX/NECH* B7 .... 125 D3
Cato St North *VAUX/NECH* B7 ...... 125 D3
Cattell Dr *MGN/WHC* B75............... 61 D4
Cattell Rd *BORD* B9 .... 125 E6
Cattells Gv *VAUX/NECH* B7 .... 125 E1
Cattermole Gv *GTB/HAM* B43 .... 55 E6
Cattock Hurst Dr
  CSCFLD/WYGN B72 .... 81 F4 ▣
Causeway *BLKHTH/ROWR* B65 ...... 117 E5
Causeway Green Rd
  LGLYGN/QTN B68 .... 118 C4
Causeway Rd *BILS/COS* WV14 ...... 69 F3 ▣
The Causeway *YDLY* B25 .... 151 F2
Causey Farm Rd *HALE* B63 .... 161 E3
Cavalier Circ *WOLVN* WV10 .... 12 A1
Cavandale Av *KGSTG* B44 .... 78 A2
Cavell Rd *DUDS* DY2 .... 92 B4 ▣
Cavendish Cl *BRGRVE* B60 .... 199 E6 ▣
  HWK/WKHTH B38 .... 189 D4 ▣
  KGSWFD DY6 .... 111 F3
Cavendish Gdns *WSLW* WS2 .... 30 C5 ▣
Cavendish Rd *LDYWD/EDGR* B16 ... 121 F4
  RMSLY B62 .... 142 B5
  WOLV WV1 .... 27 D6
  WSLW WS2 .... 30 C5
Cavendish Wy *ALDR* WS9 .... 35 D2
Caversham Rd *KGSTG* B44 .... 78 C1
Cawdon Gv *DOR/KN* B93 .... 212 A5
Cawdor Crs *LDYWD/EDGR* B16 ..... 122 B6
Caxton Gv *KGSTG* B44 .... 79 E2 ▣
Caynham Rd *RIDG/WDGT* B32 ...... 165 D3
Cayton Gv *ERDW/GRVHL* B23 .... 80 B5
Cecil Dr *OLDBY* B69 .... 93 F3
Cecil Rd *ERDE/BCHGN* B24 .... 102 B2
  SLYOAK B29 .... 169 E2
Cecil St *CBHAMNE* B4 .... 7 E1
  RUSH/SHEL WS4 .... 32 B4
  STRBR DY8 .... 136 B4
Cedar Av *BILS/COS* WV14 .... 68 C4
  CBROM B36 .... 105 E6
Cedar Bridge Cft *FOAKS/STRLY* B74.. 58 C1
Cedar Cl *BVILLE* B30 .... 167 F5
  DSYBK/YTR WS5 .... 53 D5
  LGLYGN/QTN B68 .... 143 E1 ▣
Cedar Dr *ERDE/BCHGN* B24 .... 81 E6
  FOAKS/STRLY B74 .... 36 A6
Cedar Gv *BDMR/CCFT* WV3 .... 42 B2
  CDSL WV8 .... 9 D2 ▣
  HAG/WOL DY9 .... 158 C5 ▣
Cedarhurst *RIDG/WDGT* B32 .... 144 C4
  SOLH B91 .... 195 E2 ▣
Cedar Park Rd *SHHTH* WV12 .... 15 E4
Cedar Rd *BVILLE* B30.................. 168 A5
  DARL/WED WS10 .... 72 C1
  DUDN DY1 .... 91 D2 ▣
  TPTN/OCK DY4 .... 69 F6 ▣
  WLNHL WV13 .... 28 A5
Cedars Av *ACGN* B27 .... 151 E5
  KGSWFD DY6 .... 111 F3

WMBN WV5 .... 64 C6
The Cedars *YDLY* B25 .... 128 A6
Cedar Wy *NFLD/LBR* B31 .... 186 B4 ▣
  WNSFLD WV11 .... 13 E6
Cedarwood *FOAKS/STRLY* B74 ...... 59 D1 ▣
Cedarwood Cft *PBAR/PBCH* B42 .... 76 B3
Cedar Wood Rd *SEDG* DY3 .... 89 E1
Celandine Cl *STRBR* DY8 .... 111 E3
Celandine Rd *DUDN* DY1 .... 90 C1 ▣
The Celandines *WMBN* WV5 .... 64 A5 ▣
Celbury Wy *GTB/HAM* B43 .... 75 F3 ▣
Celts Cl *BLKHTH/ROWR* B65 .... 117 E3
Cemetery La *WSNGN* B18.............. 123 D2
Cemetery Rd *HAG/WOL* DY9 .... 137 F4
  LGLYGN/QTN B68 .... 119 E1
  SMTHWKW B67 .... 120 B3
  WLNHL WV13 .... 28 C4
  WSLW WS2 .... 50 B1
Cemetery St *BILS/COS* WV14 .... 47 E2
Cemetery Wy *BLOX/PEL* WS3 .... 17 D4
Centenary Cl *NFLD/LBR* B31 ...... 186 C4 ▣
Centenary Dr *HDSW* B21 .... 98 A4
Central Av *BILS/COS* WV14 .... 48 A2
  BLKHTH/ROWR B65 .... 117 E5
  HAG/WOL DY9 .... 138 A6
  NFLD/LBR B31 .... 186 B5
  TPTN/OCK DY4 .... 70 B4
Central Cl *BLOX/PEL* WS3............. 16 C4
Central Dr *BILS/COS* WV14 .... 69 F4
  BLOX/PEL WS3 .... 16 B5
  SEDG DY3 .... 89 E3 ▣
Central Gv *ACGN* B27 .... 173 E1
Central Wy *BRLYHL* DY5 .... 114 A3
Centre La *HALE* B63 .... 141 D6 ▣
The Centreway
  ALE/KHTH/YWD B14 .... 191 F1
Centurion Cl *CSHL/WTROR* B46...... 108 A4
Century Pk *BORD* B9 .... 125 E5
Century Rd *OLDBY* B69 .... 94 C5
Ceolmund Crs
  CHWD/FDBR/MGN B37 .... 131 D4 ▣
Chaceley Gv *NFLD/LBR* B23 .... 79 F4 ▣
Chadbury Cft *SOLH* B91 .... 195 D5 ▣
Chadbury Rd *HALE* B63 .... 141 E6
Chadcote Wy *BRGRVW* B61 .... 198 B6
Chaddersley Cl *RBRY* B45 .... 184 B5 ▣
Chaddesley Cl *OLDBY* B69 .... 117 F2 ▣
Chaddesley Dr *HAG/WOL* DY9 ...... 159 D2 ▣
Chaddesley Rd *HALE* B63 .... 162 B1 ▣
  HWK/WKHTH B38 .... 187 F3
Chadley Cl *SOLH* B91.................. 174 C5
Chad Rd *DUDN* DY1...................... 69 D4
  EDG B15 .... 146 B1
Chadshunt Cl *CBROM* B36 .... 105 F3
Chadsmoor Ter *VAUX/NECH* B7 ... 125 D1
Chadstone Cl *SHLY* B90 .... 211 D1
Chad Valley Cl *HRBN* B17 .... 145 F3
Chadwell Dr *HIA/OLT* B92 .... 173 D5
Chadwell Gdns *CDSL* WV8 .... 8 B1
Chadwich La *HAG/WOL* DY9 .... 198 A3
Chadwick Av *RBRY* B45 .... 201 D1
Chadwick Cl
  ETTPK/GDPK/PENN WV4 .... 43 E3
Chadwick Rd *MGN/WHC* B75 .... 60 B4
Chadworth Av *DOR/KN* B93 .... 212 A3
Chaffcombe Rd
  LGN/SDN/BHAMAIR B26 .... 153 D3
Chaffinch Cl *SEDG* DY3 .... 67 E1 ▣
Chaffinch Dr *CBROM* B36 .... 107 F5
Chaffinch Rd *HAG/WOL* DY9 .... 137 F6 ▣
Chainmakers Cl *BILS/COS* WV14 ... 47 E6
Chain Wk *LOZ/NWT* B19 .... 99 F5
Chalcot Gv *BFLD/HDSWWD* B20 ..... 76 A5
Chaldon Cl *COVEN* WV9 .... 10 C3
Chale Gv *ALE/KHTH/YWD* B14 ...... 190 C1
Chalfont Pl *HAG/WOL* DY9 .... 160 A1
Chalford Rd *ERDW/GRVHL* B23 ..... 79 E3 ▣
Chalford Wy *SHLY* B90 .... 193 F4 ▣
Chalgrove Av *HWK/WKHTH* B38 ..... 188 A4
Chalgrove Crs *SOLH* B91 .... 195 D4
Challenor Av *WLNHL* WV13 .... 27 F5
Chalybeate Cl *RBRY* B45 .... 184 B4 ▣
Chamberlain Cl *OLDBY* B69 .... 93 F3 ▣
Chamberlain Crs *MOS/BIL* B13 .... 170 A2
Chamberlain Crs *SHLY* B90 .... 192 C3
Chamberlain Rd *MOS/BIL* B13 .... 170 B5
Chamberlain's La
  ETTPK/GDPK/PENN WV4 .... 44 A6
Chance Cft *LGLYGN/QTN* B68 ..... 143 D1 ▣
Chancellor's Cl *EDG* B15............. 146 A1
Chancel Wy *RMSLY* B62 .... 141 E4
Chancery Wy *BRLYHL* DY5 .... 114 B5 ▣
Chandler Dr
  ETTPK/GDPK/PENN WV4 .... 43 F6
Chandlers Cl *COVEN* WV9 .... 10 C4
Channon Dr *BRLYHL* DY5 .... 137 F1
Chanston Av *ALE/KHTH/YWD* B14 .. 190 C1
Chanterelle Gdns
  ETTPK/GDPK/PENN WV4 .... 44 C5
Chantrey Crs *BILS/COS* WV14 .... 48 B2 ▣
  GTB/HAM B43 .... 55 F5
Chantry Av *BLOX/PEL* WS3 .... 17 F5
Chantry Cl *HLYWD* B47 .... 190 C6
Chantry Dr *RMSLY* B62 .... 142 C3 ▣

Chantry Heath Crs *DOR/KN* B93 ...... **197** D5
Chantry Rd *HDSW* B21 .... **98** B5
  KINVER DY7 .... **135** E2
  MOS/BIL B13 .... **148** A5
Chapel Ash *WOLV* WV1 .... **2** A4
Chapel Ash Island *WOLV* WV1 .... **2** B4
Chapel Cl *CDYHTH* B64 .... **141** D1 🔢
  WMBN WV5 .... **64** B6
Chapel Dr *HLYWD* B47 .... **206** B4
Chapelfield Rd *RBRY* B45 .... **184** C5
Chapel Fields Rd *HIA/OLT* B92 .... **174** B2
Chapel House La *HALE* B63 .... **139** E4
Chapelhouse Rd
  CHWD/FDBR/MGN B37 .... **130** B5
Chapel House St *BHTH/HG* B12 .... **124** B6 🔢
Chapel La *ALVE* B48 .... **218** B5
  CDSL WV8 .... **8** B2
  GTB/HAM B43 .... **54** B5
  HAG/WOL DY9 .... **181** F6
  HLYWD B47 .... **206** A5
  RMSLY B62 .... **161** E5
  SLYOAK B29 .... **168** A1
Chapel St *BKHL/PFLD* WV2 .... **45** F2
  BLOX/PEL WS3 .... **17** F5
  BLOX/PEL WS3 .... **18** B2
  BRLYHL DY5 .... **89** E6
  BRLYHL DY5 .... **113** F5 🔢
  BRLYHL DY5 .... **114** B6 🔢
  CBHAMNE B4 .... **7** G4
  DARL/WED WS10 .... **50** A6
  DUDS DY2 .... **115** F3 🔢
  HAG/WOL DY9 .... **138** A4
  HAG/WOL DY9 .... **158** C5
  HALE B63 .... **140** C6
  HDSW B21 .... **97** F6
  KGSWFD DY6 .... **87** D5
  OLDBY B69 .... **94** A6 🔢
  STRBR DY8 .... **111** F4
  STRBR DY8 .... **136** C5 🔢
  TPTN/OCK DY4 .... **70** A6
  WBROM B70 .... **73** D6
Chapel Vw *SMTHWKW* B67 .... **120** B3 🔢
Chapel Wk *BVILLE* B30 .... **188** C2
  SEDG DY3 .... **89** E3
Chapelwood Gv *PBAR/PBCH* B42 .... **77** F6 🔢
Chapman Rd *SMHTH* B10 .... **149** E1
Chapman's HI *BRGRVW* B61 .... **183** D5
Chapmans Pas *CBHAMW* B1 .... **123** F6 🔢
Chapman St *WBROM* B70 .... **95** D2
Charfield Cl *BVILLE* B30 .... **167** F4
Charingworth Rd *HIA/OLT* B92 ...... **175** E1
Charlbury Av
  CHWD/FDBR/MGN B37 .... **130** B5
Charlbury Crs
  LGN/SDN/BHAMAIR B26 .... **152** B1
Charlecote Cft *SHLY* B90 .... **193** E5
Charlecote Dr *DUDN* DY1 .... **90** A2
  ERDW/GRVHL B23 .... **80** A4
Charlecote Gdns
  SCFLD/BOLD B73 .... **80** C3 🔢
Charlecote Ri *WLNHL* WV13 .... **48** B1 🔢
Charlecott Cl *MOS/BIL* B13 .... **171** F4
Charlemont Av *HHTH/SAND* B71 ...... **74** B3
Charlemont Cl *DSYBK/YTR* WS5 .... **53** E5
Charlemont Crs *HHTH/SAND* B71 ..... **74** A3
Charlemont Gdns *DSYBK/YTR* WS5 ... **53** D5
Charlemont Rd *DSYBK/YTR* WS5 ..... **53** D5
  HHTH/SAND B71 .... **74** A3
Charles Av *BLKHTH/ROWR* B65 ...... **117** E3
  ETTPK/GDPK/PENN WV4 .... **45** D4
  WNSFLD WV11 .... **14** B1
Charles Cl *WASH/WDE* B8 .... **125** F3 🔢
Charlesdale Dr *ALDR* WS9 .... **35** D3
Charles Dr *VAUX/NECH* B7 .... **125** D1 🔢
Charles Edward Rd
  LGN/SDN/BHAMAIR B26 .... **151** F3
Charles Foster St *DARL/WED* WS10 ... **49** E3
Charles Henry St *DIG/EDG* B5 .... **148** A1
Charles Holland St *WLNHL* WV13 ..... **29** D5
Charles Rd *AST/WIT* B6 .... **100** C4
  BFLD/HDSWWD B20 .... **99** E4
  BRLYHL DY5 .... **114** C6
  HALE B63 .... **140** D5
  SMHTH B10 .... **150** A1
  SOLH B91 .... **194** A3
  STRBR DY8 .... **136** A5 🔢
  TPTN/OCK DY4 .... **70** C4
Charles St *SMTHWK* B66 .... **97** E6 🔢
  WBROM B70 .... **72** A6
  WLNHL WV13 .... **29** E4
  WSLW WS2 .... **4** A4
Charles Wk *BLKHTH/ROWR* B65 ... **117** E2 🔢
Charlesworth Av *SHLY* B90 .... **211** D1
Charleville Rd *LOZ/NWT* B19 .... **99** D6
Charlotte Cl *TPTN/OCK* DY4 .... **92** C3 🔢
Charlotte Rd *BVILLE* B30 .... **168** C2
  DARL/WED WS10 .... **71** E2
  EDG B15 .... **147** E1
Charlotte St *CBHAMNW* B3 .... **6** B4
  DUDN DY1 .... **91** D5
  WSL WS1 .... **5** G3
Charlton Rd *KGSTG* B44 .... **78** C4

Charlton St *BRLYHL* DY5 .... **112** C4
  DUDN DY1 .... **91** D4 🔢
Charminster Av *YDLY* B25 .... **151** F1 🔢
Charnley Dr *MCN/WHC* B75 .... **40** A5 🔢
Charnwood Av *SEDG* DY3 .... **67** F1 🔢
Charnwood Cl *BILS/COS* WV14 .... **49** D6
  BRLYHL DY5 .... **137** D2
  RBRY B45 .... **185** D2
Charnwood Ct *HAG/WOL* DY9 .... **160** A1 🔢
Charnwood Rd *DSYBK/YTR* WS5 ..... **52** C5 🔢
  PBAR/PBCH B42 .... **76** B4
Charter Crs *CDYHTH* B64 .... **141** D1
Charterfield Dr *KGSWFD* DY6 .... **87** F5
Charterhouse Dr *SOLH* B91 .... **195** D4
Charter Rd *TPTN/OCK* DY4 .... **71** E2
Charters Av *CDSL* WV8 .... **9** D4
Charter St *BRLYHL* DY5 .... **114** A2
Chartist Rd *WASH/WDE* B8 .... **125** F1
Chartley Cl *DOR/KN* B93 .... **212** A4 🔢
  DUNHL/THL/PER WV6 .... **22** B3
Chartley Rd *ERDW/GRVHL* B23 ...... **101** E4
  HHTH/SAND B71 .... **73** F5
The Chartway *BLOX/PEL* WS3 .... **19** D1
Chartwell Cl *DUDN* DY1 .... **69** D5
Chartwell Dr *FOAKS/STRLY* B74 ..... **37** F3
  SHLY B90 .... **209** F2
  WMBN WV5 .... **64** B6 🔢
  WOLVN WV10 .... **12** A4
Chase Gv *ERDE/BCHGN* B24 .... **81** F5
Chase Rd *BLOX/PEL* WS3 .... **16** C5
  SEDG DY3 .... **89** D4
The Chase *DUNHL/THL/PER* WV6 ..... **25** D1
  WALM/CURD B76 .... **81** H4
Chase Vw *ETTPK/GDPK/PENN* WV4 ... **68** A1
Chater Dr *WALM/CURD* B76 .... **82** C2
Chaters Cl *TPTN/OCK* DY4 .... **70** A6
Chatham Rd *NFLD/LBR* B31 .... **186** C2
Chatsworth Av *GTB/HAM* B43 .... **54** B5
Chatsworth Cl
  CSCFLD/WYGN B72 .... **81** F4 🔢
  SHHTH WV12 .... **29** D2
  SHLY B90 .... **209** F2
Chatsworth Crs *RUSH/SHEL* WS4 ..... **19** F6
Chatsworth Rd *CDYHTH* B64 .... **140** C2
Chattaway St *VAUX/NECH* B7 .... **101** E6
Chattle HI *CSHL/WTROR* B46 .... **108** A3
Chattock Av *SOLH* B91 .... **196** A1
Chattock Cl *CBROM* B36 .... **104** A6
Chatwell Gv *SLYOAK* B29 .... **167** D1
Chatwin Pl *BILS/COS* WV14 .... **48** A6 🔢
Chatwin St *SMTHWK* B66 .... **96** B6
Chatwins Whf *TPTN/OCK* DY4 .... **70** B6 🔢
Chaucer Av *SEDG* DY3 .... **66** C6
  SHHTH WV12 .... **16** A5
  TPTN/OCK DY4 .... **71** D3 🔢
Chaucer Cl *BILS/COS* WV14 .... **69** F3 🔢
  ERDW/GRVHL B23 .... **101** D2 🔢
  STRBR DY8 .... **136** C1
Chaucer Gv *ACGN* B27 .... **173** D1 🔢
Chaucer Rd *BLOX/PEL* WS3 .... **18** A5
Chauson Gv *SOLH* B91 .... **194** C5
Chavasse Rd *CSCFLD/WYGN* B72 .... **59** E6
Chawn HI *HAG/WOL* DY9 .... **137** E6
Chawnhill Cl *HAG/WOL* DY9 .... **137** E6
Chawn Park Dr *HAG/WOL* DY9 .... **137** E6
Chaynes Gv *STECH* B33 .... **129** F5
Cheadle Dr *ERDW/GRVHL* B23 .... **79** F3
Cheam Gdns *DUNHL/THL/PER* WV6 ... **24** A3
Cheapside *BHTH/HG* B12 .... **148** B1
  WLNHL WV13 .... **28** C2 🔢
Cheatham St *VAUX/NECH* B7 .... **125** E1
Checketts St *WSLW* WS2 .... **31** E5 🔢
Checkley Cft *WALM/CURD* B76 .... **82** B3 🔢
Cheddar Rd *BHTH/HG* B12 .... **148** A3
Chedworth Cl *SLYOAK* B29 .... **167** D5 🔢
Cheedon Cl *DOR/KN* B93 .... **212** A5
Chelford Crs *KGSWFD* DY6 .... **112** C4
Chells Gv *MOS/BIL* B13 .... **171** D6 🔢
Chelmar Cl *CBROM* B36 .... **106** A5
Chelmar Dr *BRLYHL* DY5 .... **112** C1
Chelmarsh Av *BDMR/CCFT* WV3 ...... **22** C6
Chelmorton Rd *PBAR/PBCH* B42 ..... **77** E3
Chelmscote Rd *HIA/OLT* B92 .... **174** B2
Chelmsley Av *CSHL/WTROR* B46 .... **132** B1 🔢
Chelmsley Cir
  CHWD/FDBR/MGN B37 .... **131** D5
Chelmsley Gv *STECH* B33 .... **130** A4 🔢
Chelmsley La
  CHWD/FDBR/MGN B37 .... **154** B1
Chelmsley Rd
  CHWD/FDBR/MGN B37 .... **130** C4
Chelsea Cl *RIDG/WDGT* B32 .... **144** B5
Chelsea Dr *FOAKS/STRLY* B74 .... **38** B3
Chelsea Wy *KGSWFD* DY6 .... **111** E1
Chelston Dr *DUNHL/THL/PER* WV6 .... **24** A3
Chelston Rd *NFLD/LBR* B31 .... **186** A3
Cheltenham Dr *CBROM* B36 .... **103** F5
  KGSWFD DY6 .... **111** D1
Chelthorn Wy *SOLH* B91 .... **195** E3
Cheltondale Rd *SOLH* B91 .... **174** B5
Chelveston Crs *SOLH* B91 .... **195** D4
Chelwood Gdns
  ETTPK/GDPK/PENN WV4 .... **47** D3
Chelworth Rd *HWK/WKHTH* B38 .... **189** D3
Chem Rd *BILS/COS* WV14 .... **47** D4 🔢

Cheniston Rd *SHHTH* WV12 .... **29** E1
Chepstow Cl
  DUNHL/THL/PER WV6 .... **22** B3 🔢
Chepstow Gv *RBRY* B45 .... **201** D1 🔢
Chepstow Rd *BLOX/PEL* WS3 .... **16** B4
Chequerfield Dr
  BDMR/CCFT WV3 .... **44** C3 🔢
Chequers Av *WMBN* WV5 .... **64** C2
Chequer St *BDMR/CCFT* WV3 .... **44** C3 🔢
Cherhill Covert *BVILLE* B30 .... **189** E3 🔢
Cherington Rd *SLYOAK* B29 .... **168** C3
Cheriton Gv *DUNHL/THL/PER* WV6 .. **22** A4
Cherrington Gdns
  DUNHL/THL/PER WV6 .... **23** D5
  HAG/WOL DY9 .... **159** E3
Cherrington Wy *SOLH* B91 .... **195** D4 🔢
Cherry Crs *ERDE/BCHGN* B24 .... **102** B2 🔢
Cherry Dr *BORD* B9 .... **125** D6
Cherry Gn *DUDN* DY1 .... **90** B1
Cherry Gv *SMTHWK* B66 .... **121** E2 🔢
  STRBR DY8 .... **136** A5
Cherry Hill Av *RBRY* B45 .... **215** E1
Cherry Hill Dr *RBRY* B45 .... **215** E1
Cherry Hill Rd *RBRY* B45 .... **215** E1
Cherry La *DARL/WED* WS10 .... **72** C1
  SCFLD/BOLD B73 .... **80** C4
  SEDG DY3 .... **87** D2
Cherry Lea *BKDE/SHDE* B34 .... **129** D1
Cherry Orch *CDYHTH* B64 .... **116** B6
Cherry Orchard Av *HALE* B63 .... **140** B4
Cherry Orchard Crs *HALE* B63 .... **140** B3 🔢
Cherry Orchard Rd
  BFLD/HDSWWD B20 .... **76** B6
Cherry Rd *TPTN/OCK* DY4 .... **70** B4
Cherry St *BDMR/CCFT* WV3 .... **2** A5
  CBHAM B2 .... **7** E5
  HALE B63 .... **140** B4
  STRBR DY8 .... **136** A5
Cherry Tree Av *DSYBK/YTR* WS5 ..... **52** C5
Cherrytree Ct *HAG/WOL* DY9 .... **138** A6 🔢
Cherry Tree Gdns *CDSL* WV8 .... **9** D2 🔢
Cherry Tree La *CDSL* WV8 .... **9** D2
  HALE B63 .... **161** F2
Cherry Tree Rd *KGSWFD* DY6 .... **88** A5
Cherry Wk *HLYWD* B47 .... **207** D2
Cherrywood Crs *SOLH* B91 .... **195** E5 🔢
Cherrywood Gn *BILS/COS* WV14 ...... **47** F1
Cherrywood Rd *BORD* B9 .... **125** D5
  FOAKS/STRLY B74 .... **35** F6
Cherrywood Wy
  FOAKS/STRLY B74 .... **37** F3 🔢
Chervil Cl *PBAR/PBCH* B42 .... **77** E4
Chervil Ri *WOLVN* WV10 .... **26** B4
Cherwell Dr *CBROM* B36 .... **106** B5
Cheshire Av *SHLY* B90 .... **192** C3 🔢
Cheshire Cl *STRBR* DY8 .... **135** F1
Cheshire Gv
  DUNHL/THL/PER WV6 .... **22** A3 🔢
Cheshire Rd *AST/WIT* B6 .... **100** C3
  SMTHWKW B67 .... **120** C3
  WSLW WS2 .... **30** B5 🔢
Chessetts Gv *MOS/BIL* B13 .... **170** C5
Chester Av *DUNHL/THL/PER* WV6 .... **10** B6
Chester Cl
  CHWD/FDBR/MGN B37 .... **130** C5
  WLNHL WV13 .... **29** F5 🔢
Chesterfield Cl *NFLD/LBR* B31 ...... **187** D5
Chestergate Croft *ERDE/BCHGN* B24 ... **103** F1 🔢
Chester Pl *WSLW* WS2 .... **31** D6
Chester Ri *LGLYCN/QTN* B68 .... **143** E1 🔢
Chester Rd *CBROM* B36 .... **104** C5
  CBROM B36 .... **106** B6 🔢
  CDYHTH B64 .... **139** E1
  CHWD/FDBR/MGN B37 .... **131** D3
  CSHL/WTROR B46 .... **132** A6
  CVALE B35 .... **104** B2
  DUDS DY2 .... **115** F3
  ERDE/BCHGN B24 .... **104** A1
  ERDW/GRVHL B23 .... **80** A3
  FOAKS/STRLY B74 .... **36** B6
  FOAKS/STRLY B74 .... **56** C1 🔢
  HHTH/SAND B71 .... **73** D2
  RCOVN/BALC/EX CV7 .... **157** D5
  SCFLD/BOLD B73 .... **79** F2
Chester Rd North
  FOAKS/STRLY B74 .... **56** C5
  SCFLD/BOLD B73 .... **56** C5
Chester Rd South
  AST/WIT B6 .... **124** B2
  DUNHL/THL/PER WV6 .... **25** D3
Chesterton Av *BHTH/HG* B12 .... **149** D4 🔢
Chesterton Cl *SOLH* B91 .... **174** A6 🔢
Chesterton Rd *BHTH/HG* B12 .... **148** C4
  WOLVN WV10 .... **12** C5
Chesterwood *ALDR* WS9 .... **34** A5
  HLYWD B47 .... **206** C1
Chesterwood Gdns
  BFLD/HDSWWD B20 .... **99** F3 🔢
Chesterwood Rd *MOS/BIL* B13 .... **170** B5
Chestnut Av *DUDN* DY1 .... **91** E2
  TPTN/OCK DY4 .... **70** B4
Chestnut Cl *CDSL* WV8 .... **8** B3 🔢
  FOAKS/STRLY B74 .... **36** C5
  HIA/OLT B92 .... **173** F5
  STRBR DY8 .... **135** E6 🔢
Chestnut Ct *CBROM* B36 .... **106** A6

Chestnut Dr *CBROM* B36 .... 104 C5
ERDE/BCHGN B24 .... 103 E1
RBRY B45 .... 201 E3
RUSH/SHEL WS4 .... 19 D5
WMBN WV5 .... 64 C6
Chestnut Gv *CSHL/WTROR* B46 .. 108 C6
KGSWFD 112 B1
Chestnut Pl *BLOX/PEL* WS3 .... 31 F1
Chestnut Rd *BLOX/PEL* WS3 .... 32 A1
DARL/WED WS10 .... 72 C1
LGLYGN/QTN B68 .... 143 E2
MOS/BIL B13 .... 148 C5
Chestnuts Av
LGN/SDN/BHAMAIR B26 .... 153 D2
Chestnut Wy *BDMR/CCFT* WV3... 43 F1
Cheston Rd *VAUX/NECH* B7 .... 124 C1
Cheswell Cl *DUNHL/THL/PER* WV6 ... 23 D5
Cheswick Cl *WLNHL* WV13 .... 48 B1
Cheswick Wy *SHLY* B90 .... 209 F4
Cheswood Dr *WALM/CURD* B76 .... 83 D5
Chetland Cft *HIA/OLT* B92 .... 176 B3
Chettle Rd *BILS/COS* WV14 .... 48 B6
Chetwood Cl
DUNHL/THL/PER WV6 .... 24 C2
Chetwynd Cl *WSLW* WS2 .... 29 E4
Chetwynd Rd *BKHL/PFLD* WV2 .... 45 D3
WASH/WDE B8 .... 127 D2
Cheveley Av *RBRY* B45 .... 185 D6
Chevening Cl *SEDG* DY3 .... 68 A4
Cheveridge Cl *SOLH* B91 .... 194 C4
Cheverton Rd *NFLD/LBR* B31 .... 186 A2
Cheviot Gv
CHWD/FDBR/MGN B37 .... 131 D6
Chigwell Cl *CVALE* B35 .... 104 C2
Chilcote Cl *HLGN/YWD* B28 .... 192 B1
Childs Av *BILS/COS* WV14 .... 68 C1
Chilgrove Gdns
DUNHL/THL/PER WV6 .... 23 E2
Chilham Dr
CHWD/FDBR/MGN B37 .... 131 E5
Chillinghome Rd *CBROM* B36 .... 104 A5
Chillington Dr *CDSL* WV8 .... 8 B1
DUDN DY1 .... 90 B2
Chillington Flds *WOLV* WV1 .... 26 C6
Chillington Pl *BILS/COS* WV14 .... 47 E4
Chillington Rd *TPTN/OCK* DY4 .... 71 E2
Chillington St *WOLV* WV1 .... 46 B1
Chiltern Cl *HALE* B63 .... 161 E1
SEDG DY3 .... 89 F2
Chiltern Dr *WLNHL* WV13 .... 27 F6
Chiltern Rd *STRBR* DY8 .... 137 D3
Chilton Rd *ALE/KHTH/YWD* B14 .. 191 F1
Chilwell Cl *SOLH* B91 .... 195 F6
Chilwell Cft *LOZ/NWT* B19 .... 124 A1
Chilworth Av *WNSFLD* WV11 .... 14 B6
Chilworth Cl *AST/WIT* B6 .... 124 B1
Chimes Cl *STETCH* B33 .... 130 A6
Chimney Rd *TPTN/OCK* DY4 .... 71 F4
Chingford Cl *STRBR* DY8 .... 111 E3
Chingford Rd *KGSTG* B44 .... 78 C5
Chinley Gv *KGSTG* B44 .... 79 E2
Chinn Brook Rd *MOS/BIL* B13 .... 171 D6
Chip Cl *HWK/WKHTH* B38 .... 187 F3
Chipperfield Rd *CBROM* B36 .... 104 A5
Chipstead Rd *ERDW/GRVHL* B23... 79 F4
Chipstone Cl *SOLH* B91 .... 195 F6
Chirbury Gv *NFLD/LBR* B31 .... 187 D4
Chirton Gv *ALE/KHTH/YWD* B14 .. 169 F5
Chiseldon Cft *ALE/KHTH/YWD* B14.. 190 C2
Chisholm Gv *ACGN* B27 .... 173 E2
Chiswell Rd *WSNGN* B18 .... 122 A3
Chivington Cl *SHLY* B90 .... 211 D1
Chorley Av *BKDE/SHDE* B34 .... 104 B6
Chorley Gdns *BILS/COS* WV14 .... 47 E5
Christchurch Cl *EDG* B15 .... 146 A1
Christ Church Gv *WSL* WS1 .... 52 C1
Christine Cl *DARL/WED* WS10 .... 71 E1
Christopher Rd *BKHL/PFLD* WV2 ... 46 A1
RMSLY B62 .... 142 A6
SLYOAK B29 .... 167 E3
Chubb St *WOLV* WV1 .... 3 F5
Chuckery Rd *WSL* WS1 .... 5 G4
Chudleigh Gv *GTB/HAM* B43 .... 75 F3
Chudleigh Rd *ERDW/GRVHL* B23 ... 102 A1
Church Av *HAG/WOL* DY9 .... 180 A3
STRBR DY8 .... 136 C2
Churchbridge *OLDBY* B69 .... 118 B1
Church Cl *CHWD/FDBR/MGN* B37... 130 C1
HLYWD B47 .... 206 B3
Church Cft *HALE* B63 .... 140 C5
HRBN B17 .... 145 D5
Church Cross Vw *BRLYHL* DY5 .... 89 F5
Churchdale Rd *KGSTG* B44 .... 55 F5
Church Dr *BVILLE* B30 .... 169 D4

Churchfield Av *TPTN/OCK* DY4 .... 70 B3
Churchfield Cl *VAUX/NECH* B7 .... 125 E1
Churchfield Rd *WOLN* WV10 .... 11 D5
Churchfields Rd *DARL/WED* WS10 .... 50 B6
Churchfield St *DUDS* DY2 .... 91 E5
Church Gdns *WOLN* WV10 .... 26 C3
Church Gn *BFLD/HDSWWD* B20 .... 98 B3
BILS/COS WV14 .... 47 E1
Church Gv *MOS/BIL* B13 .... 171 E5
Church Hi *BRLYHL* DY5 .... 113 F5
Church Hill *BRLYHL* DY5 .... 113 F5
CSHL/WTROR B46 .... 108 C6
DARL/WED WS10 .... 50 B6
ETTPK/GDPK/PENN WV4 .... 44 A5
NFLD/LBR B31 .... 186 C2
RIDG/WDGT B32 .... 164 C6
WSL WS1 .... 5 E4
Church Hill Cl *SOLH* B91 .... 195 E3
Church Hill Rd *BFLD/HDSWWD* B20 .. 99 D3
DUNHL/THL/PER WV6 .... 23 F1
SOLH B91 .... 195 E3
Church Hill St *SMTHWKW* B67 .... 120 B1
Churchill Cl *OLDBY* B69 .... 93 E3
Churchill Dr *BLKHTH/ROWR* B65 .. 117 D5
STRBR DY8 .... 136 C2
Churchill Gdns *SEDG* DY3 .... 67 E4
Churchill Pl *STETCH* B33 .... 129 D6
Churchill Rd *BORD* B9 .... 126 B4
BRGRVW B61 .... 198 C6
HALE B63 .... 162 B1
MGN/WHC B75 .... 60 C4
SCFLD/BOLD B73 .... 79 E1
WSLW WS2 .... 30 A4
Church La *AST/WIT* B6 .... 100 C5
BFLD/HDSWWD B20 .... 98 B3
BKHL/PFLD WV2 .... 2 C6
CDSL WV8 .... 8 B1
HALE B63 .... 141 D5
HHTH/SAND B71 .... 73 E5
HIA/OLT B92 .... 177 F1
STETCH B33 .... 128 B4
WALM/CURD B76 .... 84 B2
WALM/CURD B76 .... 72 B2
Church Moat Wy *BLOX/PEL* WS3 .. 17 D5
Churchover Cl *WALM/CURD* B76 .... 81 F5
Church Pl *BLOX/PEL* WS3 .... 17 F5
Church Rd *AST/WIT* B6 .... 100 C5
BDMR/CCFT WV3 .... 44 A2
BILS/COS WV14 .... 69 F2
BLKHTH/ROWR B65 .... 117 E3
BLOX/PEL WS3 .... 18 C2
CDSL WV8 .... 8 B1
CSCFLD/WYGN B72 .... 59 D6
DUDS DY2 .... 115 D2
DUNHL/THL/PER WV6 .... 22 A3
DUNHL/THL/PER WV6 .... 23 D4
DUNHL/THL/PER WV6 .... 24 A2
EDG B15 .... 146 C2
EDG B15 .... 147 D3
ERDE/BCHGN B24 .... 102 C1
HAG/WOL DY9 .... 138 A4
HALE B63 .... 139 E3
LGN/SDN/BHAMAIR B26 .... 152 A1
LGN/SDN/BHAMAIR B26 .... 153 E4
MOS/BIL B13 .... 148 C6
NFLD/LBR B31 .... 186 C1
PBAR/PBCH B42 .... 77 F6
SCFLD/BOLD B73 .... 80 B3
SEDG DY3 .... 86 A3
SHHTH WV12 .... 29 F1
SHLY B90 .... 193 D3
SMTHWKW B67 .... 120 B3
STETCH B33 .... 128 B5
STRBR DY8 .... 111 F5
STRBR DY8 .... 137 D6
WMBN WV5 .... 65 D4
WOLVN WV10 .... 11 E4
YDLY B25 .... 152 A1
Church Sq *OLDBY* B69 .... 94 C3
Church St *BILS/COS* WV14 .... 47 F4
BKHL/PFLD WV2 .... 2 C6
BLOX/PEL WS3 .... 17 D5
BRLYHL DY5 .... 89 F6
BRLYHL DY5 .... 113 E5
BRLYHL DY5 .... 114 B6
CBHAMNW B3 .... 6 D4
CDYHTH B64 .... 116 A6
DARL/WED WS10 .... 49 D5
DARL/WED WS10 .... 49 F3
DUDS DY2 .... 91 E5
HAG/WOL DY9 .... 158 C6
LOZ/NWT B19 .... 99 E6
OLDBY B69 .... 94 C5
RMSLY B62 .... 117 H6
SEDG DY3 .... 89 F2
STRBR DY8 .... 136 C4
TPTN/OCK DY4 .... 92 C3
WBROM B70 .... 95 E1
WLNHL WV13 .... 29 D5
WOLVN WV10 .... 26 C3
WSL WS1 .... 5 E5
Church V *BFLD/HDSWWD* B20 .... 99 D4
HHTH/SAND B71 .... 73 E1
Church Vw *ALDR* WS9 .... 20 B2
SPARK B11 .... 149 E3
Church View Cl *BLOX/PEL* WS3 .. 17 E5

Church View Dr *CDYHTH* B64 .... 116 B6
Church Wk *BDMR/CCFT* WV3 .... 44 B2
DUNHL/THL/PER WV6 .... 24 A2
WASH/WDE B8 .... 126 C1
Churchward Cl *STRBR* DY8 .... 137 D3
Churchward Gv *WMBN* WV5 .... 64 C3
Church Wy *RUSH/SHEL* WS4 .... 19 D3
Churchyard Rd *TPTN/OCK* DY4 .... 71 D6
Churnet Gv *DUNHL/THL/PER* WV6 ... 22 B3
Churn Hill Rd *ALDR* WS9 .... 34 C3
Churns Hill La *SEDG* DY3 .... 87 D2
Churston Cl *BLOX/PEL* WS3 .... 16 C2
Cider Av *BRLYHL* DY5 .... 114 A6
BRLYHL DY5 .... 138 A1
Cinder Bank *DUDS* DY2 .... 115 E1
Cinder Rd *SEDG* DY3 .... 89 D4
Cinder Wy *DARL/WED* WS10 .... 50 A6
Cinquefoil Leasow
TPTN/OCK DY4 .... 71 E5
Circuit Cl *WLNHL* WV13 .... 29 D4
Circular Rd *ACGN* B27 .... 173 E2
Circus Av *CHWD/FDBR/MGN* B37 ... 131 E5
City Rd *LDYWD/EDGR* B16 .... 121 E5
OLDBY B69 .... 93 D6
City Vw *WASH/WDE* B8 .... 125 F3
Civic Cl *CBHAMW* B1 .... 6 A5
Claerwen Gv *NFLD/LBR* B31 .... 166 A6
Claines Rd *HALE* B63 .... 139 F4
NFLD/LBR B31 .... 187 E1
Clandon Cl *ALE/KHTH/YWD* B14 .. 189 D3
Clanfield Av *WNSFLD* WV11 .... 14 B5
Clapgate Gdns
ETTPK/GDPK/PENN WV4 .... 46 C6
Clap Gate Gv *WMBN* WV5 .... 64 C5
Clapgate La *RIDG/WDGT* B32 .... 165 E1
Clap Gate Rd *WMBN* WV5 .... 64 A4
Clapton Gv *KGSTG* B44 .... 79 D2
Clare Av *WNSFLD* WV11 .... 14 B4
Clare Crs *BILS/COS* WV14 .... 68 B1
Clare Dr *EDG* B15 .... 146 B1
Clarel Av *WASH/WDE* B8 .... 125 E4
Claremont Rd *BDMR/CCFT* WV3 .... 44 C2
SEDG DY3 .... 68 A3
SMTHWK B66 .... 121 D3
SPARK B11 .... 149 D2
WSNGN B18 .... 122 C1
Claremont St *BILS/COS* WV14 .... 47 E3
CDYHTH B64 .... 116 A6
Claremont Wy *HALE* B63 .... 140 C6
Clarence Av *HDSW* B21 .... 99 D2
Clarence Gdns *FOAKS/STRLY* B74 .. 38 B5
Clarence Rd *BILS/COS* WV14 .... 48 A2
DUDS DY2 .... 115 F1
ERDW/GRVHL B23 .... 101 F2
FOAKS/STRLY B74 .... 38 A2
HDSW B21 .... 97 E5
HRBN B17 .... 145 F3
MOS/BIL B13 .... 170 C3
SPARK B11 .... 149 E5
WOLV WV1 .... 2 C3
Clarence St *SEDG* DY3 .... 68 A6
WOLV WV1 .... 2 C4
Clarendon Pl *HRBN* B17 .... 145 E4
Clarendon Dr *TPTN/OCK* DY4 .... 71 F3
Clarendon Pl *BLOX/PEL* WS3 .... 18 B1
RMSLY B62 .... 142 B3
Clarendon Rd *LDYWD/EDGR* B16... 122 A6
MGN/WHC B75 .... 39 F5
RUSH/SHEL WS4 .... 19 D3
SMTHWKW B67 .... 120 B3
Clarendon St *BDMR/CCFT* WV3... 24 C5
BLOX/PEL WS3 .... 17 D4
Clare Rd *BLOX/PEL* WS3 .... 32 B1
WOLVN WV10 .... 12 A6
Clarewell Av *SOLH* B91 .... 194 C4
Clarkes Gv *TPTN/OCK* DY4 .... 71 E5
Clarke's La *HHTH/SAND* B71 .... 73 E4
WLNHL WV13 .... 29 E4
Clark Rd *BDMR/CCFT* WV3 .... 24 B5
Clarkson Rd *DARL/WED* WS10 .... 50 B6
Clark St *LDYWD/EDGR* B16 .... 122 B5
STRBR DY8 .... 136 A4
Clarry Dr *FOAKS/STRLY* B74 .... 58 B1
Clary Gv *DYSBK/YTR* WS5 .... 52 C6
Clatterbach La *HAG/WOL* DY9 .... 180 C3
Claughton Rd *DUDS* DY2 .... 91 F4
Clausen Cl *GTB/HAM* B43 .... 56 A5
Clavedon Cl *NFLD/LBR* B31 .... 166 A4
Claverdon Cl *SOLH* B91 .... 194 A1
Claverdon Dr *FOAKS/STRLY* B74 .... 37 D3
GTB/HAM B43 .... 75 F3
Claverdon Gdns *ACGN* B27 .... 151 D4
Claverley Dr
ETTPK/GDPK/PENN WV4 .... 43 F4
Claybrook St *DIG/EDG* B5 .... 124 A6
Claycroft Ter *DUDN* DY1 .... 69 D5
Claydon Gv *ALE/KHTH/YWD* B14... 190 C2
Claydon Rd *KGSWFD* DY6 .... 87 E4
Clay Dr *RIDG/WDGT* B32 .... 142 C4
Clay La *LGN/SDN/BHAMAIR* B26 .. 152 A5
OLDBY B69 .... 93 D6
Claypit Cl *WBROM* B70 .... 94 C2
Claypit La *BRGRVW* B61 .... 198 A6
WBROM B70 .... 94 C2
Clayton Cl *BKHL/PFLD* WV2 .... 45 E2

Clayton Dr *CBROM* B36 105 E5
Clayton Rd *BILS/COS* WV14 69 D4
WASH/WDE B8 125 F2
Clear Vw *KGSWFD* DY6 111 D1
Clearwell Gdns *DUDN* DY1 90 A2 1
Clee Hill Dr *BDMR/CCFT* WV3 22 B6 1
Clee Hill Rd *SEDG* DY3 89 E1
Clee Rd *DUDS* DY2 90 C6
LGLYGN/QTN B68 119 E3
NFLD/LBR B31 186 C5
STRBR DY8 136 C3
Cleeve Dr *FOAKS/STRLY* B74 38 B1 2
Cleeve Rd *ALE/KHTH/YWD* B14 191 E1
BLOX/PEL WS3 16 B2
Cleeve Wy *BLOX/PEL* WS3 16 B3
Clee View Meadow *SEDG* DY3 67 F1
Clee View Rd *WMBN* WV5 64 A6
Clematis Dr *COVEN* WV9 10 B2
Clement Pl *BILS/COS* WV14 47 F2 1
Clement Rd *BILS/COS* WV14 47 F2
RMSLY B62 117 F6
Clements Cl *OLDBY* B69 118 B3
Clements Rd *YDLY* B25 151 F1
Clement St *CBHAMW* B1 123 D4 1
WSLW WS2 4 A5 1
Clemson St *WLNHL* WV13 28 C5 1
Clent Dr *HAG/WOL* DY9 159 E5
Clent Hill Dr *BLKHTH/ROWR* B65 116 C2
Clent Rd *HDSW* B21 97 F4
LGLYGN/QTN B68 143 E1
RBRY B45 184 A5
STRBR DY8 136 C3
Clent View Rd *HALE* B63 139 E5
RIDG/WDGT B32 164 C2
STRBR DY8 135 E6
Clent Wy *RIDG/WDGT* B32 164 B3
Cleobury La *HOCK/TIA* B94 208 C4
Cleton St *TPTN/OCK* DY4 93 D2
Clevedon Av *CBROM* B36 106 A5 1
Clevedon Rd *BHTH/HG* B12 148 A3
Cleveland Cl *WLNHL* WV13 27 F6 1
WNSFLD WV11 14 B4 2
Cleveland Dr *RBRY* B45 200 C5 1
Cleveland Pas *WOLV* WV1 2 D5 1
Cleveland Rd *BKHL/PFLD* WV2 3 F6
Cleveland St *BKHL/PFLD* WV2 2 D5
DUDN DY1 91 D4 2
STRBR DY8 136 A5
Cleves Dr *RBRY* B45 184 A6
Cleves Rd *RBRY* B45 184 A5
Clewley Dr *COVEN* WV9 10 C2 2
Clewley Gv *RIDG/WDGT* B32 143 D4
Clews Cl *WSL* WS1 52 A2 1
Clewshaw La *HWK/WKHTH* B38 205 D3
Cley Cl *DIG/EDG* B5 147 F3
Cliffe Dr *STETCH* B33 129 D4
Clifford Rd *DOR/KN* B93 212 B3
SMTHWKW B67 120 B6
WBROM B70 94 C3
Clifford St *DUDN* DY1 91 D5 1
DUNHL/THL/PER WV6 24 C4
LOZ/NWT B19 99 F6
Clifford Wk *LOZ/NWT* B19 99 F6
Cliff Rock Rd *RBRY* B45 185 D6
Clift Av *SHHTH* WV12 15 F6
Clift Cl *SHHTH* WV12 29 E1
Clifton Av *ALDR* WS9 21 E5
Clifton Cl *AST/WIT* B6 100 B6
OLDBY B69 118 B3
Clifton Crs *SHLY* B90 194 B4
Clifton Gdns *CDSL* WV8 9 E2
Clifton Gn *HLGN/YWD* B28 172 C6
Clifton La *HHTH/SAND* B71 74 A3
Clifton Rd *AST/WIT* B6 100 B6
BHTH/HG B12 148 C4
CBROM B36 106 A5
DUNHL/THL/PER WV6 23 F2
RMSLY B62 141 F1
SCFLD/BOLD B73 58 C5
SMTHWKW B67 120 B3
Clifton St *BDMR/CCFT* WV3 2 A4
BILS/COS WV14 68 B2
CDYHTH B64 116 B6
STRBR DY8 136 B5
Clinic Dr *HAG/WOL* DY9 138 A4
Clinton Gv *SHLY* B90 193 F4
Clinton Rd *BILS/COS* WV14 48 C2
CSHL/WTROR B46 132 B1
SHLY B90 194 A5
Clinton St *WSNGN* B18 122 A2 2
Clipper Vw *LDYWD/EDGR* B16 122 A6 1
Clipston Rd *WASH/WDE* B8 126 B2
Clissold Cl *DIG/EDG* B5 148 A2 3
Clissold Pas *WSNGN* B18 122 C3
Clissold St *WSNGN* B18 122 C3
Clive Cl *MGN/WHC* B75 39 F5
Cliveden Av *ALDR* WS9 21 D4
PBAR/PBCH B42 99 E1
Cliveden Coppice
FOAKS/STRLY B74 38 B6
Clivedon Wy *CDYHTH* B64 140 C2
Cliveland St *CBHAMNE* B4 7 E1
Clive Rd *RIDG/WDGT* B32 143 F2
Clive St *HHTH/SAND* B71 73 E6
Clockfields Dr *STRBR* DY8 112 C6
Clock La *HIA/OLT* B92 177 F1
Clockmill Av *BLOX/PEL* WS3 18 A2
Clockmill Pl *BLOX/PEL* WS3 18 B2
Clockmill Rd *BLOX/PEL* WS3 18 A2
Clodeshall Rd *WASH/WDE* B8 126 A3
Cloister Dr *RMSLY* B62 141 F6
Clonmel Rd *BVILLE* B30 168 C5
Clopton Crs
CHWD/FDBR/MGN B37 131 E3
Clopton Rd *STETCH* B33 153 E1
The Close *DARL/WED* WS10 50 A6 3
HALE B63 139 F3
HIA/OLT B92 174 B3
HLYWD B47 206 C2
HRBN B17 144 B2
RMSLY B62 162 C4
SEDG DY3 86 A3 1
SEDG DY3 89 E1
Clothier Gdns *WLNHL* WV13 28 C4 2
Clothier St *WLNHL* WV13 28 C4
Cloudbridge Dr *HIA/OLT* B92 176 B4 3
Cloudsley Gv *HIA/OLT* B92 152 B6 1
Clover Av *CHWD/FDBR/MGN* B37 131 F5
Clover Dr *RIDG/WDGT* B32 165 E1
Clover Hl *DSYBK/YTR* WS5 54 A1
Clover La *KGSWFD* DY6 86 C6
Clover Lea Sq *WASH/WDE* B8 126 C1 1
Clover Ley *WOLVN* WV10 26 B4
Clover Piece *TPTN/OCK* DY4 71 E5 3
Clover Rd *SLYOAK* B29 166 C4
Cloweswood La *HOCK/TIA* B94 222 B1
Club Rw *SEDG* DY3 68 A6
Club Vw *HWK/WKHTH* B38 187 F3
Clunbury Cft *BKDE/SHDE* B34 129 D2 1
Clunbury Rd *NFLD/LBR* B31 186 C5
Clun Cl *DUDS* DY2 92 B4
Clun Rd *NFLD/LBR* B31 166 B5
Clyde Av *RMSLY* B62 142 A1
Clyde Ms *BRLYHL* DY5 113 D1
Clyde Rd *DOR/KN* B93 212 C5
Clydesdale
LGN/SDN/BHAMAIR B26 152 C4
Clydesdale Rd *RIDG/WDGT* B32 143 D3
Clyde St *BHTH/HG* B12 124 C6 2
CDYHTH B64 116 A6
Coalbourne Gdns *HALE* B63 139 E4
Coalbourn La *STRBR* DY8 136 B2 1
Coalheath La *RUSH/SHEL* WS4 19 E5
Coal Pool La *BLOX/PEL* WS3 18 B6 1
BLOX/PEL WS3 32 B2
Coalport Rd *WOLV* WV1 26 C6
Coalway Av
ETTPK/GDPK/PENN WV4 44 C3
LGN/SDN/BHAMAIR B26 153 E5
Coalway Gdns *BDMR/CCFT* WV3 43 F3
Coalway Rd *BLOX/PEL* WS3 16 C4
ETTPK/GDPK/PENN WV4 43 F3
The Cobbles *CSCFLD/WYGN* B72 81 E4
Cobden Cl *DARL/WED* WS10 50 B3
TPTN/OCK DY4 70 B3 1
Cobden Gdns *BHTH/HG* B12 148 A3 1
Cobden St *DARL/WED* WS10 50 B3
STRBR DY8 135 F3
WSL WS1 51 F2
Cobham Cl *CVALE* B35 104 B2 1
Cobham Court Ms
HAG/WOL DY9 159 F5 1
Cobham Rd *BORD* B9 125 F5
DARL/WED WS10 74 A1
HALE B63 141 D5
STRBR DY8 158 C1
Cob La *NFLD/LBR* B31 167 E4
Cobley Hl *ALVE* B48 216 A5
Cobnall Rd *BRGRVW* B61 198 C5
Cobs Fld *BVILLE* B30 167 E5
Coburg Cft *TPTN/OCK* DY4 71 E5 4
Coburn Dr *MGN/WHC* B75 39 F5
Cochrane Cl *HAG/WOL* DY9 159 E3
TPTN/OCK DY4 71 E5 5
Cochrane Rd *BRLYHL* DY5 114 B2
DUDS DY2 114 B1 1
Cock Hill La *RBRY* B45 184 B5 2
Cocksheds La *RMSLY* B62 141 E1
Cockshut Hl
LGN/SDN/BHAMAIR B26 152 C1
Cockshutts La *BKHL/PFLD* WV2 45 F2
Cocksmead Cft
ALE/KHTH/YWD B14 169 F6
Cockthorpe Cl *HRBN* B17 144 B2
Cocton Cl *DUNHL/THL/PER* WV6 22 A2
Codsall Gdns *CDSL* WV8 8 A1
Codsall Rd *CDSL* WV8 9 E4
CDYHTH B64 140 A1
DUNHL/THL/PER WV6 10 A6
Cofield Rd *SCFLD/BOLD* B73 80 B2
Cofton Church La *RBRY* B45 201 F5
Cofton Ct *RBRY* B45 185 F6 1
Cofton Gv *NFLD/LBR* B31 202 A1
Cofton Lake Rd *RBRY* B45 201 E4
Cofton Rd *NFLD/LBR* B31 186 C6
Cokeland Pl *CDYHTH* B64 139 F1
Colaton Cl *WOLVN* WV10 26 A3
Colbourne Rd *TPTN/OCK* DY4 92 C1 2
Colbrand Gv *EDG* B15 147 F1 1
Coldbath Rd *MOS/BIL* B13 171 D3
Coldridge Cl *COVEN* WV9 10 B4
Coldstream Dr *STRBR* DY8 112 A4
Coldstream Rd *WALM/CURD* B76 82 A3
Cole Bank Rd *HLGN/YWD* B28 172 A3
Colebourne Rd *MOS/BIL* B13 171 F5
Colebridge Crs
CSHL/WTROR B46 108 B5 1
Colebrook Cft *SHLY* B90 192 B3
Colebrook Rd *SHLY* B90 192 A3
SPARK B11 149 F4
Cole Ct *CHWD/FDBR/MGN* B37 131 D5 2
Coleford Cl *STRBR* DY8 111 E5
Coleford Dr
CHWD/FDBR/MGN B37 130 C5
Cole Gn *SHLY* B90 192 A3
Cole Hall La *BKDE/SHDE* B34 129 D2 2
STETCH B33 128 C3
Colehurst Cft *SHLY* B90 210 B1 1
Coleman Rd *DARL/WED* WS10 50 C4
Coleman St *DUNHL/THL/PER* WV6 24 B3
Colemeadow Rd
CSHL/WTROR B46 108 B6 1
MOS/BIL B13 171 D6
Colenso Rd *SMTHWK* B66 121 E3
Coleraine Rd *PBAR/PBCH* B42 76 C5
Coleridge Cl *SHHTH* WV12 16 A6 1
Coleridge Dr *DUNHL/THL/PER* WV6 22 A3
Coleridge Pas *CBHAMNE* B4 7 F3 1
Coleridge Ri *SEDG* DY3 88 C1
Coleridge Rd *GTB/HAM* B43 76 A4 3
Colesbourne Av *BVILLE* B30 189 E3
Colesbourne Rd *HIA/OLT* B92 153 D6
Coleshill Heath Rd
CHWD/FDBR/MGN B37 155 E3
CSHL/WTROR B46 132 A6
Coleshill Rd *BKDE/SHDE* B34 104 B6
CHWD/FDBR/MGN B37 155 E1
CSHL/WTROR B46 107 E3
CSHL/WTROR B46 109 F3
MGN/WHC B75 59 F4
WALM/CURD B76 85 E6
WALM/CURD B76 107 F1
Coleshill St *CSCFLD/WYGN* B72 59 E4
Coleside Av *MOS/BIL* B13 171 F4
Coles La *CSCFLD/WYGN* B72 59 E6
HHTH/SAND B71 72 C4
The Colesleys *CSHL/WTROR* B46 132 C1 1
Cole St *DUDS* DY2 116 A3
Cole Valley Rd *HLGN/YWD* B28 171 F5
Coleview Crs *STETCH* B33 130 A4
Coleville Rd *WALM/CURD* B76 83 D5
Coleys La *NFLD/LBR* B31 186 C3
Colgreave Av *MOS/BIL* B13 171 F1
Colindale Rd *KGSTG* B44 56 C6
Colleen Av *BVILLE* B30 189 D2
College Cl *DARL/WED* WS10 72 C1
College Dr *BFLD/HDSWWD* B20 98 B3
College Farm Dr *ERDW/GRVHL* B23 79 F3
College Hl *SCFLD/BOLD* B73 59 D5
College Rd *BFLD/HDSWWD* B20 98 A3
DUNHL/THL/PER WV6 23 F3
KGSTG B44 78 A6
MOS/BIL B13 171 E1
RMSLY B62 142 C3
SCFLD/BOLD B73 80 A2
STRBR DY8 136 C5 2
WASH/WDE B8 126 A4
College St *WSNGN* B18 122 C3
College Vw *DUNHL/THL/PER* WV6 23 F4
Collet Rd *CDSL* WV8 22 A2
Collets Brook *MGN/WHC* B75 40 C5
Collett Cl *STRBR* DY8 136 C3
Colletts Gv
CHWD/FDBR/MGN B37 130 B3 1
Colley Av *WOLVN* WV10 12 B5
Colley Ga *HALE* B63 139 E3
Colley La *HALE* B63 139 E3 4
Colley Orch *HALE* B63 139 E3 5
Colley St *WBROM* B70 95 F1
Colliers Cl *SHHTH* WV12 29 D1
Colliery Dr *BLOX/PEL* WS3 16 B2
Colliery Rd *HHTH/SAND* B71 96 C5
WOLV WV1 26 B5
Collindale Ct *KGSWFD* DY6 87 F4
Collingbourne Av *CBROM* B36 103 F6
Collingdon Av
LGN/SDN/BHAMAIR B26 153 E3 1
Colling Wk
CHWD/FDBR/MGN B37 130 C2 1
Collingwood Dr *GTB/HAM* B43 55 E5
Collingwood Rd *WOLVN* WV10 12 A3
Collins Cl *RIDG/WDGT* B32 142 C4 1
Collins Rd *DARL/WED* WS10 51 D6
Collins St *WBROM* B70 94 A2
WSL WS1 52 A2
Collis St *STRBR* DY8 136 B1
Collister Cl *SHLY* B90 173 D6
Collumbine Cl *DSYBK/YTR* WS5 52 B6 1
Colly Cft *CHWD/FDBR/MGN* B37 130 B2 2
Collycroft Pl *ACGN* B27 151 D4 2
Colman Av *WNSFLD* WV11 28 B1
Colman Crs *LGLYGN/QTN* B68 119 E5 1
Colman Hl *HALE* B63 139 F4
Colman Hill Av *HALE* B63 139 F3 1
Colmore Av *ALE/KHTH/YWD* B14 169 F4

Colmore Circus Queensway
CBHAMNE B1 .... **7** E3
Colmore Crs *MOS/BIL* B13 ..... **171** D2 🔲
Colmore Dr *MOS/WHC* B75 .... **60** C4
Colmore Rd *ALE/KHTH/YWD* B14 ... **169** F4
Colmore Rw *CBHAMNW* B3 .... **6** D4
Coln Cl *NFLD/LBR* B31 .... **166** B5
Colonial Rd *BORD* B9 .... **126** B4
Colshaw Rd *STRBR* DY8 .... **136** A5
Colston Rd *ERDE/BCHGN* B24 ...... **103** D2
Colt Cl *FOAKS/STRLY* B74 .... **56** A2
Coltham Rd *SHHTH* WV12 .... **29** E1
Coltishall Cft *CVALE* B35 .... **104** B3 🔲
Coltsfoot Cl *WNSFLD* WV11 .... **28** A2
Columbia Cl *DIG/EDG* B5 .... **147** F2 🔲
Colville Cl *TPTN/OCK* DY4 .... **71** F3
Colville Rd *BHTH/HG* B12 .... **149** D4
Colville Wk *BHTH/HG* B12 .... **149** D4 🔲
Colwall Rd *SEDG* DY3 .... **89** F1
Colwall Wk *ACGN* B27 .... **151** F5
Colworth Rd *NFLD/LBR* B31 ...... **186** A1
Colyns Gv *STETCH* B33 .... **128** D2 🔲
Comber Cft *MOS/BIL* B13 .... **171** F3
Comber Dr *BRLYHL* DY5 .... **113** D1
Comberford Dr *DARL/WED* WS10 ... **51** F5
Comberton Rd
LGN/SDN/BHAMAIR B26 .... **153** D2
Commercial Rd *WOLV* WV1 .... **3** H5
WSLW WS2 .... **16** C6
Commercial St *CBHAMW* B1 .... **123** E6
Commonfield Cft
WASH/WDE B8 .... **125** F2 🔲
Common La
LGN/SDN/BHAMAIR B26 .... **152** C4
WASH/WDE B8 .... **126** B1
Common Rd *WMBN* WV5 .... **86** B1
Commonside *BLOX/PEL* WS3 .... **18** C3
BRLYHL DY5 .... **113** E1
Communication Rw *EDG* B15 .... **123** E6 🔲
Compton Cl *SOLH* B91 .... **193** F1
Compton Cft
CHWD/FDBR/MGN B37 .... **131** F6 🔲
Compton Dr *DUDS* DY2 .... **92** B5 🔲
FOAKS/STRLY B74 .... **56** A2
KGSWFD DY6 .... **111** F2
Compton Gv *HALE* B63 .... **139** E5
KGSWFD DY6 .... **111** F2
Compton Hill Dr
DUNHL/THL/PER WV6 .... **25** F1
Compton Rd *BDMR/CCFT* WV3 ... **24** B5
CDYHTH B64 .... **115** E6
ERDE/BCHGN B24 .... **102** A4
HAG/WOL DY9 .... **159** F2
RMSLY B62 .... **142** B3 🔲
Compton Rd West
BDMR/CCFT WV3 .... **23** F5
Comsey Rd *GTB/HAM* B43 .... **55** D6
Conchar Cl *BLOX/PEL* WS3 ..... **17** E6 🔲
Conchar Cl *CSCFLD/WYGN* B72 ... **81** E1
Conchar Rd *CSCFLD/WYGN* B72 ... **81** E1
Condover Cl *WSLW* WS2 .... **29** F4
Condover Rd *NFLD/LBR* B31 ...... **187** D5
Coneyford Rd *BKDE/SHDE* B34... **129** E1
Coney Gn *STRBR* DY8 .... **137** D4
Coney Green Dr *NFLD/LBR* B31 ... **186** B5
Coneygree Rd *TPTN/OCK* DY4... **92** C2
Conifer Cl *BRLYHL* DY5 .... **137** E1
Conifer Cl *MOS/BIL* B13 .... **170** A1
Conifer Dr *HDSW* B21 .... **88** A6
NFLD/LBR B31 .... **187** D2 🔲
Conifer Paddock *RMSLY* B62 .... **142** A1
Conifer Rd *FOAKS/STRLY* B74 .... **56** A1
Conington Gv *HRBN* B17 .... **144** C4
Coniston Av *HIA/OLT* B92 .... **152** B5
Coniston Cl *HLGN/YWD* B28........ **172** B4
Coniston Crs *GTB/HAM* B43........ **76** B4
Coniston Dr *KGSWFD* DY6 .... **87** D6
Coniston Rd *DUNHL/THL/PER* WV6 ... **9** F5
ERDW/GRVHL B23 .... **79** F6
FOAKS/STRLY B74 .... **56** A2
Connaught Av *DARL/WED* WS10 ... **51** E6 🔲
Connaught Cl *DSYBK/YTR* WS5 .... **53** E2
Connaught Dr *WMBN* WV5 .... **64** C2
Connaught Rd *BILS/COS* WV14 .... **48** B2
WOLV WV1 .... **24** C5
Connops Wy *HAG/WOL* DY9 ...... **138** A4 🔲
Connor Rd *HHTH/SAND* B71 .... **74** A3
Conolly Dr *RBRY* B45 .... **185** D4
Conrad Cl *BHTH/HG* B12............ **148** C2
Consort Crs *BRLYHL* DY5 .... **113** E1 🔲
Consort Dr *DARL/WED* WS10....... **49** E1
Consort Rd *BVILLE* B30................ **188** C2
Constable Cl *GTB/HAM* B43 ...... **55** F6 🔲
The Constables
LGLYGN/QTN B68 .... **119** D5 🔲
Constance Av *WBROM* B70 .... **95** F4
Constance Rd *DIG/EDG* B5 .... **147** F4
Constantine La
CSHL/WTROR B46 .... **108** A4 🔲
Constantine Wy *BILS/COS* WV14 ... **70** C1
Constitution Hill *DUDS* DY2 ... **91** F5 🔲
LOZ/NWT B19 .... **6** C1
Conway Av *HHTH/SAND* B71 .... **73** D2
LGLYGN/QTN B68 .... **119** D5 🔲
RIDG/WDGT B32 .... **143** D3

Conway Cl *DUDN* DY1 .... **69** E5 🔲
KGSWFD DY6 .... **112** B3
SHLY B90 .... **193** H4 🔲
Conway Crs *SHHTH* WV12 .... **15** E6
Conway Gv *GTB/HAM* B43 ..... **75** F4 🔲
Conway Rd
CHWD/FDBR/MGN B37 .... **130** C4
DUNHL/THL/PER WV6 .... **22** B4
SHLY B90 .... **193** F4
SPARK B11 .... **149** E3
Conwy Cl *WSLW* WS2 .... **30** C3 🔲
Conybere St *BHTH/HG* B12 .... **148** B2
Conyworth Cl *ACGN* B27 ...... **151** F5 🔲
Cook Av *DUDS* DY2 .... **91** F6
Cook Cl *DOR/KN* B93 .... **213** E1
DUNHL/THL/PER WV6 .... **22** A3 🔲
Cookes Cft *NFLD/LBR* B31 .... **187** E3
Cookesley Cl *GTB/HAM* B43........ **55** F5
Cooke St *BKHL/PFLD* WV2 .... **45** E2
Cookley Cl *HALE* B63 .... **162** B1 🔲
Cooknell Dr *STRBR* DY8 .... **112** A5
Cook Rd *BLOX/PEL* WS3 .... **17** F3
Cooksey La *KGSTG* B44 .... **56** B5
Cooksey Rd *SMTHK* B10 .... **149** D1 🔲
Cooks La *CHWD/FDBR/MGN* B37 ... **130** C3
STETCH B33 .... **130** A4
Cook St *DARL/WED* WS10............ **50** B3
VAUX/NECH B7 .... **101** E6
Coombe Av *COVEN* WV9 .... **10** C2 🔲
Coombe Hl *CDYHTH* B64 .... **141** D1
Coombe Pk *FOAKS/STRLY* B74...... **58** B2
Coombe Rd *BFLD/HDSWWD* B20 ... **100** A4
SHLY B90 .... **193** E3
Coombes La *NFLD/LBR* B31 ...... **202** B3
Coombs Rd *RMSLY* B62 .... **141** D3
Cooper Av *BRLYHL* DY5 .... **112** C5
Cooper Cl *WBROM* B70 .... **96** A3 🔲
Cooper's Bank Rd *BRLYHL* DY5... **89** E4
SEDG DY3 .... **89** E4
Coopers Hl *ALVE* B48................. **216** A3
Coopers La *SMTHWK* B66 .... **120** C2
SMTHWKW B67 .... **120** B2
Coopers Rd *BFLD/HDSWWD* B20 ... **98** C2
Cooper St *WBROM* B70 .... **95** F2
WOLV WV1 .... **46** B1
Copeley Hl *AST/WIT* B6.............. **101** E4
Copes Crs *WOLVN* WV10 .... **26** C1
Cope St *BLOX/PEL* WS3 .... **31** E1
DARL/WED WS10 .... **50** A3
WSNGN B18 .... **122** C4
Cophall St *TPTN/OCK* DY4 .... **71** F4
Cophams Cl *HIA/OLT* B92 .... **175** E1 🔲
Coplow St *LDYWD/EDGR* B16 ... **122** B4
Coplow Ter *LDYWD/EDGR* B16 ... **122** B4 🔲
Copnor Gv
LGN/SDN/BHAMAIR B26 .... **152** A3
Coppenhall Gv *STETCH* B33 ..... **128** C4 🔲
Copperbeech Cl *RIDG/WDGT* B32 ... **144** B4
Copper Beech Dr *KGSWFD* DY6.... **87** F4
WMBN WV5.. **65** D5
Coppice Av *HAG/WOL* DY9 .... **138** B6
Coppice Cl *RBRY* B45 .... **184** B6 🔲
SEDG DY3 .... **67** E4
SHLY B90 .... **209** E3 🔲
WNSFLD WV11 .... **14** C4
Coppice Dr *ACGN* B27 .... **173** D1 🔲
Coppice Farm Wy *SHHTH* WV12 ... **15** D6
Coppice Hollow
RIDG/WDGT B32 .... **165** D2 🔲
Coppice La *ALDR* WS9 .... **20** B4
BRLYHL DY5 .... **114** C6 🔲
DUNHL/THL/PER WV6 .... **23** D1
POL/KGSB/FAZ B78 .... **41** E5
SHHTH WV12 .... **29** E1
Coppice Ri *BRLYHL* DY5 .... **114** C5
Coppice Rd *ALDR* WS9 .... **20** B1
BDMR/CCFT WV3 .... **43** F1
BILS/COS WV14 .... **68** C3
CDYHTH B64 .... **140** A2
HIA/OLT B92 .... **176** A4
MOS/BIL B13 .... **148** C6
Coppice St *TPTN/OCK* DY4 .... **70** A5
WBROM B70 .... **94** C1
The Coppice *BFLD/HDSWWD* B20 ... **98** C3 🔲
SHHTH WV12 .... **29** E1
TPTN/OCK DY4 .... **71** E2 🔲
Coppice View Rd *SCFLD/BOLD* B73 ... **56** C5
Coppice Wk *SHLY* B90................ **209** E3
Copplestone Cl
BKDE/SHDE B34 .... **129** D1 🔲
Coppy Hall Gv *ALDR* WS9 .... **21** D4
Copse Cl *NFLD/LBR* B31 .... **186** C3
Copse Crs *BLOX/PEL* WS3 .... **18** C1
Copse Rd *DUDS* DY2 .... **115** D4
The Copse *FOAKS/STRLY* B74....... **38** B6
Copstone Dr *DOR/KN* B93 .... **212** B4
Copston Gv *SLYOAK* B29............ **169** D4
Copthall Rd *HDSW* B21 .... **97** E5
Copt Heath Cft *DOR/KN* B93 ... **197** D5 🔲
Copt Heath Dr *DOR/KN* B93 ...... **196** C4
Copthorne Rd *BDMR/CCFT* WV3... **44** C2
KGSTG B44 .... **56** A4
Coralin Cl *CHWD/FDBR/MGN* B37 ... **131** D5
Corbett Crs *STRBR* DY8 .... **136** C2
Corbett Rd *BRLYHL* DY5 .... **114** A6

Corbetts Cl *HIA/OLT* B92........... **179** D4
Corbett Dr *SMTHWK* B66 .... **121** D3
Corbridge Av *KGSTG* B44 .... **78** B2
Corbridge Rd *SCFLD/BOLD* B73... **80** B1
Corbyn Rd *BORD* B9 .... **127** D4
DUDN DY1 .... **90** B5
Corbyns Cl *BRLYHL* DY5 .... **89** D6
Corbyns Hall La *BRLYHL* DY5 ..... **89** D6
Corbyns Hall Rd *BRLYHL* DY5 .... **89** D6
Cordley St *WBROM* B70 .... **95** D1
Corfe Cl *DUNHL/THL/PER* WV6 ... **22** B4
RIDG/WDGT B32 .... **144** B4
Corfe Dr *OLDBY* B69 .... **92** C5
Corfe Rd *BILS/COS* WV14 .... **68** C3
Corfton Dr *DUNHL/THL/PER* WV6... **23** E4
Coriander Cl *NFLD/LBR* B31....... **185** D4
Corinne Cl *RBRY* B45................. **200** C1 🔲
Corinne Cft
CHWD/FDBR/MGN B37 .... **130** C3
Corisande Rd *SLYOAK* B29 .... **167** E1
Corley Av *NFLD/LBR* B31 .... **187** D2
Corley Cl *SHLY* B90 .... **192** A4
Cornbrook Rd *SLYOAK* B29 ...... **166** B5
Cornbury Gv *SHLY* B90 .... **193** F1 🔲
Corncrake Cl *CSCFLD/WYGN* B72 ... **81** F1 🔲
Corncrake Dr *CBROM* B36......... **106** C5
Corncrake Rd *SEDG* DY3 .... **89** F2
Cornel Cl *CHWD/FDBR/MGN* B37 ... **155** E1
Cornerway *HWK/WKHTH* B38 ... **188** B6
Cornfield *CDSL* WV8 .... **10** A4
Cornfield Cl *KGSWFD* DY6.......... **86** C5
Cornfield Cft
CHWD/FDBR/MGN B37 .... **131** F4 🔲
WALM/CURD B76 .... **60** B6 🔲
Cornfield Rd *BLKHTH/ROWR* B65 ... **116** B3
NFLD/LBR B31 .... **187** D1
Cornflower Crs *DUDS* DY2 .... **92** B5
Cornflower Rd *CDYHTH* B64 ...... **115** F6
CDYHTH B64 .... **139** F1
The Corngreaves
BKDE/SHDE B34 .... **129** E1 🔲
Corngreaves Wk *CDYHTH* B64 ... **140** A2
Corn Hl *DSYBK/YTR* WS5............ **54** A1
WOLV WV1 .... **3** F4
Cornhill Gv *BVILLE* B30 .... **169** E4 🔲
Corn Mill Cl *RIDG/WDGT* B32 ... **166** A2
Cornmill Cl *WSL* WS1 .... **51** F2 🔲
Cornovian Cl
DUNHL/THL/PER WV6 .... **22** A2 🔲
Corns Gv *WMBN* WV5 .... **64** B6
Cornwall Av *LGLYGN/QTN* B68... **143** D1
Cornwall Cl *ALDR* WS9 .... **20** C4
DARL/WED WS10 .... **51** F6
KGSWFD DY6 .... **87** F5 🔲
Cornwall Ga *SHHTH* WV12 .... **29** D2 🔲
Cornwallis Rd *WBROM* B70 .... **94** C4
Cornwall Pl *WSLW* WS2 .... **29** F4
Cornwall Rd *BFLD/HDSWWD* B20 ... **98** B3
DSYBK/YTR WS5 .... **53** D2
DUNHL/THL/PER WV6 .... **23** E3
RBRY B45 .... **184** A3
STRBR DY8 .... **135** F1
Cornwall St *CBHAMNW* B3........... **6** C4
Cornwell Cl *TPTN/OCK* DY4 .... **70** C6
Cornyx La *SOLH* B91 .... **175** F5
Coronation Av *WLNHL* WV13 .... **29** F5
Coronation Rd *ALDR* WS9 .... **20** B2
BILS/COS WV14 .... **47** E3
DARL/WED WS10 .... **51** E6
GTB/HAM B43 .... **54** A5
RUSH/SHEL WS4 .... **19** D3
SLYOAK B29 .... **168** B1
TPTN/OCK DY4 .... **71** D3
WASH/WDE B8 .... **126** B1 🔲
WNSFLD WV11 .... **26** C2
Corporation Rd *DUDS* DY2 .... **92** B4
Corporation St *CBHAM* B2 .... **7** E5
CBHAMNE B4 .... **7** F3
DARL/WED WS10 .... **72** C1
WOLV WV1 .... **2** C4 🔲
Corporation St West *WSLW* WS2 ... **4** A6
Corrie Cft *LGN/SDN/BHAMAIR* B26 ... **153** D2
RIDG/WDGT B32 .... **165** D4
Corrin Gv *KGSWFD* DY6 .... **87** E5
Corser St *DUDN* DY1 .... **90** B3
STRBR DY8 .... **136** C6
WOLV WV1 .... **26** B6 🔲
Corsican Cl *SHHTH* WV12 .... **16** A6 🔲
Corvedale Rd *SLYOAK* B29 .... **166** C5
Corve Gdns *DUNHL/THL/PER* WV6 ... **24** B2
Corve Vw *SEDG* DY3 .... **67** E2 🔲
Corville Gdns
LGN/SDN/BHAMAIR B26 .... **153** D5
Corville Rd *RMSLY* B62.............. **142** B3
Corwen Cft *NFLD/LBR* B31 .... **166** A5
Cory Cft *TPTN/OCK* DY4 .... **70** C6 🔲
Coseley Rd *BILS/COS* WV14 .... **47** E5
Cosford Crs *CVALE* B35.............. **104** C2
Cosford Dr *DUDS* DY2 .... **116** A3 🔲
Cossington Rd *ERDW/GRVHL* B23 ... **79** F4
Cotford Rd *ALE/KHTH/YWD* B14 ... **190** C3
Cotheridge Cl *SHLY* B90 .... **211** E1
Cot La *STRBR* DY8 .... **111** F3
Cotleigh Gv *KGSTG* B44 .... **55** F6

Cotman Cl GTB/HAM B43 .... 55 E6
Coton Cv SHLY B90 .... 192 A3
Coton La ERDW/GRVHL B23 ... 102 B1 🟦
Coton Rd ETTPK/GDPK/PENN WV4... 45 D4
Cotsdale Rd
  ETTPK/GDPK/PENN WV4 .... 44 A6
Cotswold Cl ALDR WS9 .... 21 E4
  OLDBY B69 .... 118 A2
  RBRY B45 .... 184 C4
Cotswold Cft BKHL/PFLD WV2 .... 44 C3 🟦
Cotswold Cft HALE B63 .... 161 E1
Cotswold Gv SHHTH WV12 .... 15 D4 🟦
Cotswold Rd BKHL/PFLD WV2 .... 46 B2
  STRBR DY8 .... 137 D3
Cottage Cl WNSFLD WV11 .... 27 E1
Cottage Dr BRGRVE B60 .... 199 E6
Cottage Farm La BRGRVE B60 .. 199 E5 🟦
Cottage Gdns RBRY B45 .... 200 B1
Cottage La BRGRVE B60 .... 199 E5
  WALM/CURD B76 .... 83 F5
  WOLVN WV10 .... 11 F2
Cottage Vw BRLYHL DY5 .... 113 F4
  KGSWFD DY6 .... 87 F6
Cottage Vw CDSL WV8 .... 9 D1 🟦
Cotteridge Rd BVILLE B30 .... 188 C1 🟦
Cotterills Av WASH/WDE B8 ...... 127 E5 🟦
Cotterills La WASH/WDE B8 ...... 127 E3 🟦
Cotterills Rd TPTN/OCK DY4 .... 71 E3 🟦
Cottesbrook Rd ACGN B27 .... 151 F5
Cottesfield Cl WASH/WDE B8 ..... 127 D3
Cottesmore Cl HHTH/SAND B71 .. 74 B3 🟦
Cottle Cl WSLW WS2 .... 30 B4 🟦
Cotton La MOS/BIL B13 .... 170 C1
Cottrell St HHTH/SAND B71 .... 95 F1
Cottsmeadow Dr WASH/WDE B8 .. 127 E3 🟦
Cotwall End Rd SEDG DY3 .... 89 D1
Cotysmore Rd MGN/WHC B75 ...... 59 F2
Couchman Rd WASH/WDE B8 .... 126 A3
Counterfield Dr
  BLKHTH/ROWR B65 .... 116 B2
Countess Dr ALDR/SHEL WS4 .... 19 F6
Countess St WSL WS1 .... 51 F2
County Cl BVILLE B30 .... 169 E5 🟦
  RIDG/WDGT B32 .... 143 F6 🟦
County Park Av RMSLY B62 .... 141 F6 🟦
Courts CL KGSWFD DY6 .... 111 F2
Courtenay Rd KGSTG B44 .... 78 A4
Court Farm Rd ERDW/GRVHL B23 .. 80 A3
Court La ERDW/GRVHL B23 .... 80 A3
Court Oak La RIDG/WDGT B32 ... 144 B3
Court Oak Rd HRBN B17 .... 144 C3
  RIDG/WDGT B32 .... 144 A3
Court Pas DUDN DY1 .... 91 E4 🟦
Court Rd BHTH/HG B12 .... 148 A3
  DUNHL/THL/PER WV6 .... 24 B3
  ETTPK/GDPK/PENN WV4 .... 46 C5
  SPARK B11 .... 149 E5
Court St CDYHTH B64 .... 116 A6
Courtway Av ALE/KHTH/YWD B14 .. 191 D4
Cousins St BKHL/PFLD WV2 .... 45 F2
Coveley Gv WSNGN B18 .... 122 C2
Coven Cl SLYOAK B29 .... 167 D1
Coven St WOLVN WV10 .... 25 F1
Coverdale Rd HIA/OLT B92 .... 152 C5
The Covert CDSL WV8 .... 10 A4
Cowles Cft VDLY B25 .... 128 B4
Cowley Cl CBROM B36 .... 106 B4
Cowley Dr ACGN B27 .... 151 F5 🟦
  DUDN DY1 .... 90 B3
Cowley Rd SPARK B11 .... 150 A4
Cowper Cl SHHTH WV12 .... 16 A4
Cowslip Cl HWK/WKHTH B38 .... 188 B5 🟦
  SLYOAK B29 .... 166 C4
Coxcroft Av BRLYHL DY5 .... 114 B6 🟦
Coxmoor Cl BLOX/PEL WS3 .... 16 B2 🟦
Cox Rd BILS/COS WV14 .... 70 A2
Cox's La CDYHTH B64 .... 116 B5
Cox St CBHAMNW B3 .... 6 C2
Coxwell Av WOLVN WV10 .... 25 E1
Coxwell Gdns
  LDYWD/EDGR B16 .... 122 B5 🟦
Coyne Cl TPTN/OCK DY4 .... 69 F6 🟦
Coyne Rd WBROM B70 .... 95 D3
Crabbe St HAG/WOL DY9 .... 138 B4
Crab La SHHTH WV12 .... 15 F4
Crabmill Cl DOR/KN B93 .... 197 E6
Crab Mill Cl HWK/WKHTH B38 .. 188 A6
Crabmill La HWK/WKHTH B38 ... 189 E5 🟦
Crabourne Rd DUDS DY2 .... 115 D5
Crabtree Cl HHTH/SAND B71 .... 74 B3 🟦
  NFLD/LBR B31 .... 187 E3 🟦

Crabtree Dr
  CHWD/FDBR/MGN B37 .... 130 B4
Crabtree Rd WSNGN B18 .... 122 C2
Craddock Rd SMTHWKW B67 ...... 120 A1 🟦
Craddock St DUNHL/THL/PER WV6 .. 24 C3
Cradley Cft HDSW B21 .... 97 F2
Cradley Flds HALE B63 .... 139 F4 🟦
Cradley Forge HALE B63 .... 138 C1
Cradley Park Rd DUDS DY2 .... 115 E6
Cradley Rd CDYHTH B64 .... 139 E1
  DUDS DY2 .... 115 F4
Cradock Rd WASH/WDE B8 .... 126 A2 🟦
Craig Cft CHWD/FDBR/MGN B37 .. 131 F5 🟦
Crail Gv GTB/HAM B43 .... 55 D6
Cramlington Rd PBAR/PBCH B42 .. 76 C3
Cramnore Cl TPTN/OCK DY4 .... 70 C3 🟦
Cramp HI DARL/WED WS10 .... 49 F3 🟦
Cranbourne Av
  ETTPK/GDPK/PENN WV4 .... 46 A6
Cranbourne Cl RBRY B45 .... 185 D3 🟦
Cranbourne Gv KGSTG B44 .... 78 C3 🟦
Cranbourne Pl HHTH/SAND B71 .. 95 F1 🟦
Cranbourne Rd KGSTG B44 .... 78 B2
  STRBR DY8 .... 136 C5
Cranbrook Av
  DUNHL/THL/PER WV6 .... 22 B4
Cranbrook Rd HDSW B21 .... 97 E4
Cranby St WASH/WDE B8 .... 125 E2
Craneberry Rd STETCH B33 .... 130 A4
Cranebrook HI POL/KGSB/FAZ B78.. 41 F2
Crane Hollow WMBN WV5 .... 64 A6 🟦
Cranehouse Rd KGSTG B44 .... 78 C1 🟦
Cranemoor Cl VAUX/NECH B7 ... 125 E1 🟦
Crane Rd BILS/COS WV14 .... 48 B6
Cranesbill Rd SLYOAK B29 .... 166 C5
Cranes Park Rd
  LGN/SDN/BHAMAIR B26 .... 153 E4
Crane Ter DUNHL/THL/PER WV6 .. 24 A2
Cranfield Gv
  LGN/SDN/BHAMAIR B26 .... 152 B1
Cranfield Pl DSYBK/YTR WS5 .... 52 B5
Cranford Gv SOLH B91 .... 195 E4 🟦
Cranford Rd BDMR/CCFT WV3 ..... 43 E1
Cranford St SMTHWK B66 .... 121 E2
Cranham Dr KGSWFD DY6 .... 111 F2
Cranhill Cl HIA/OLT B92 .... 175 D2
Crankhall La DARL/WED WS10 ..... 51 E6
Cranleigh Cl ALDR WS9 .... 35 D2
  SHHTH WV12 .... 15 E4 🟦
Cranleigh Pl KGSTG B44 .... 78 A6
Cranley Dr CDSL WV8 .... 8 B1
Cranmer Av SHHTH WV12 .... 15 F6
Cranmere Av
  DUNHL/THL/PER WV6 .... 22 C1
Cranmer Rd FOAKS/STRLY B74 ..... 38 B1
Cranmoor Crs HALE B63 .... 140 C4
Cranmore Av HDSW B21 .... 97 F6 🟦
  SHLY B90 .... 194 A5
Cranmore Blvd SHLY B90 .... 193 F5 🟦
Cranmore Cl TPTN/OCK DY4 .... 70 A2
Cranmore Dr SHLY B90 .... 194 A4
Cranmore Rd BDMR/CCFT WV3 .... 24 B4
  CBROM B36 .... 106 A4
  SHLY B90 .... 193 F5
Cransley Gv SOLH B91 .... 194 C4
Crantock Cl SHHTH WV12 .... 15 E4
Crantock Rd PBAR/PBCH B42 ...... 99 E1
Cranwell Gn WMBN WV5 .... 64 B6 🟦
Cranwell Gv ERDE/BCHGN B24 ... 103 C2 🟦
Cranwell Wy CVALE B35 .... 104 C2 🟦
Crathorne Av WOLVN WV10 .... 11 E4
Craufurd Ct STRBR DY8 .... 136 C6 🟦
Craufurd St STRBR DY8 .... 136 C6 🟦
Craven St BKHL/PFLD WV2 .... 46 B3
Crawford Av DARL/WED WS10 ..... 49 E2
  ETTPK/GDPK/PENN WV4 .... 46 B6
  SMTHWKW B67 .... 120 A2
Crawford Rd WASH/WDE B8 ...... 125 E2
  WOLVN WV3 .... 43 D1
Crawford St WASH/WDE B8 .... 125 E2 🟦
  WOLVN CURD B76 .... 82 B3
Crawshays Rd CBROM B36 .... 105 E4
Crayford Rd KGSTG B44 .... 78 C2
Craythorne Av BFLD/HDSWWD B20 .. 76 A6
Crecy Cl WALM/CURD B76 .... 60 A5
Credenda Rd WBROM B70 .... 94 A5
Credon Gv EDG B15 .... 146 B5 🟦
Cregoe St EDG B15 .... 123 E6
Cremore Av WASH/WDE B8 .... 126 A2
Cremore Rd MGN/WHC B75 .... 39 D5
Crendon Rd BLKHTH/ROWR B65 .. 116 C1
Crescent Av BRLYHL DY5 .... 113 E5
The Crescent Grange Rd
  HAG/WOL DY9 .... 137 E5 🟦
Crescent Rd DARL/WED WS10 ..... 49 F3
  DUDS DY2 .... 115 D2
  WLNHL WV13 .... 29 E5
Crescent Stennels RMSLY B62 ... 142 A5 🟦
The Crescent BILS/COS WV14 ...... 47 F3
  BLKHTH/ROWR B65 .... 117 D5
  CDYHTH B64 .... 140 C2
  CSHL/WTROR B46 .... 156 A1
  DARL/WED WS10 .... 50 C5 🟦
  DUDN DY1 .... 92 A1
  DUNHL/THL/PER WV6 .... 23 D4
  GTB/HAM B43 .... 76 C2

HAG/WOL DY9 .... 158 B6
HIA/OLT B92 .... 179 D4
SHLY B90 .... 192 C1
SOLH B91 .... 195 D1
WLNHL WV13 .... 29 E6
WSL WS1 .... 5 H5
WSNGN B18 .... 123 D1
Cressage Av NFLD/LBR B31 .... 186 C4
Cressett Av BRLYHL DY5 .... 113 D3
Cressett La BRLYHL DY5 .... 113 E3
Cressington Dr FOAKS/STRLY B74 .. 38 C6
Cresswell Crs BLOX/PEL WS3 .... 16 B3
Cresswell Gv ERDE/BCHGN B24 . 103 F3 🟦
The Crest NFLD/LBR B31 .... 203 D1
Crest Vw ALE/KHTH/YWD B14 .... 191 D1
  FOAKS/STRLY B74 .... 36 B6
Crestwood Dr KGSTG B44 .... 78 A4
Crestwood Gln
  DUNHL/THL/PER WV6 .... 10 A6
Creswell Rd HLGN/YWD B28 .... 173 D4
Creswick Gv RBRY B45 .... 185 E6
Crew Rd DARL/WED WS10 .... 50 C5
Creynolds Cl SHLY B90 .... 209 F3 🟦
Creynolds La SHLY B90 .... 210 B2
Cricket Cl DSYBK/YTR WS5 .... 53 D2
Cricketers Meadow CDYHTH B64 .. 140 B2
Cricket Meadow SEDG DY3 .... 68 A6
  WOLVN WV10 .... 11 F1
Crick La BFLD/HDSWWD B20 .... 98 C5
Cricklewood Dr RMSLY B62 .... 141 F6 🟦
Crimmond Ri HALE B63 .... 140 A4
Crimscote Gv SHLY B90 .... 210 B1
Cripps Rd WSLW WS2 .... 31 F3
Crockett's La SMTHWK B66 .... 120 C2
Cocketts Rd HDSW B21 .... 97 F6
Crockett St DUDN DY1 .... 90 C3
Crockford Dr MGN/WHC B75 .... 38 C4
Crockford Rd HHTH/SAND B71 ..... 73 E2
Crocus Crs COVEN WV9 .... 10 C2 🟦
Croft Cl YDLY B25 .... 152 A1
Croft Down Rd HIA/OLT B92 .... 153 F5
Croftdown Rd HRBN B17 .... 144 B3
Crofters Cl STRBR DY8 .... 137 D5 🟦
Crofters Ct EDG B15 .... 146 A3
Croft La WOLVN WV10 .... 12 B6
Croft Rd LGN/SDN/BHAMAIR B26 .. 152 A1
The Crofts WALM/CURD B76 .... 82 C3 🟦
Croft St WLNHL WV13 .... 28 C5
  WSLW WS2 .... 31 F4
The Croft DSYBK/YTR WS5 .... 53 F1
  DUDS DY2 .... 114 B1 🟦
  NFLD/LBR B31 .... 187 D2
  SEDG DY3 .... 68 A2 🟦
  WLNHL WV13 .... 28 C5 🟦
The Croftway BFLD/HDSWWD B20 .. 76 A5
Croftwood Rd HAG/WOL DY9 ..... 137 F5
Cromdale Dr HALE B63 .... 139 F4 🟦
Cromer Gdns
  DUNHL/THL/PER WV6 .... 24 B2
Crome Rd GTB/HAM B43 .... 55 F6
Cromer Rd BHTH/HG B12 .... 148 B4
Crompton Cl WSLW WS2 .... 30 C2
Crompton Rd BFLD/HDSWWD B20 .. 99 E5 🟦
  RBRY B45 .... 185 F4
  TPTN/OCK DY4 .... 92 C1
  VAUX/NECH B7 .... 101 E5
Cromwell Cl BLKHTH/ROWR B65... 116 B2
  WSLW WS2 .... 30 A3
Cromwell Dr DUDS DY2 .... 92 B5
Cromwell La RIDG/WDGT B32 .... 165 F3
Cromwell Rd WOLVN WV10 .... 12 B3
Cromwell St DUDS DY2 .... 92 A5 🟦
  VAUX/NECH B7 .... 125 D2
Crondal Pl EDG B15 .... 147 D2 🟦
Cronehills Linkway WBROM B70 ... 95 F2
Cronehills St WBROM B70 .... 95 F2
Crookham Cl HRBN B17 .... 144 B2
Crookhay La HHTH/SAND B71 ...... 72 C3
Crook La ALDR WS9 .... 54 C3
Croome Cl SPARK B11 .... 149 D6
Cropredy Rd NFLD/LBR B31 .... 186 C5
Cropthorne Dr HLYWD B47 .... 191 D6
Cropthorne Rd SHLY B90 .... 193 F1 🟦
Crosbie Rd HRBN B17 .... 145 D3
Crosby Cl CBHAMW B1 .... 123 D3 🟦
  DUNHL/THL/PER WV6 .... 24 B2
Cross Cl CDYHTH B64 .... 116 B5 🟦
Cross Farm Rd HRBN B17 .... 145 F5
Cross Farms La RBRY B45 .... 184 B5
Crossfield Rd STETCH B33 .... 128 C4
Crossgate Rd DUDS DY2 .... 114 B1
Crosskey Cl STETCH B33 .... 130 A3 🟦

Crossland Crs
  DUNHL/THL/PER WV6 .... 24 B1
Crossland Rd NFLD/LBR B31 ...... 186 B1
Cross La GTB/HAM B43 .... 76 A2
  SEDG DY3 .... 67 F3
Crossley St DUDS DY2 .... 115 F3 🟦
Cross Pl SEDG DY3 .... 68 A2 🟦
Cross St BILS/COS WV14 .... 70 B1
  BLKHTH/ROWR B65 .... 117 E6 🟦
  BLOX/PEL WS3 .... 18 C4
  DARL/WED WS10 .... 50 A6
  DUDN DY1 .... 91 D4
  HALE B63 .... 140 C6

HDSW B21 .... 97 E5
KGSWFD DY6 .... 87 D5
KGSWFD DY6 .... 111 E1
LGLYGN/QTN B68 .... 118 C3 🔲
STRBR DY8 .... 111 F4 🔲
STRBR DY8 .... 136 A4
WLNHL WV13 .... 28 C6
WOLV WV1 .... 26 B6
Cross St North *WOLV* WV1 .... 25 F5
Cross St South *BKHL/PFLD* WV2 .... 45 E2
Cross Walks Rd *HAG/WOL* DY9 ..... 138 A4
Crossway La *KGSTG* B44 .... 78 B3
Crosswells Rd *LGLYGN/QTN* B68 ... 119 D2
Crowesbridge Ms
BILS/COS WV14 .... 69 D3 🔲
Crowhurst Rd *NFLD/LBR* B31 .... 186 A6
Crowland Av *DUNHL/THL/PER* WV6.. 22 A3
Crowle Dr *HAG/WOL* DY9 .... 137 E4 🔲
Crown Cl *BLKHTH/ROWR* B65 .... 117 F3
SEDG DY3 .... 67 F2
Crown Ct *DARL/WED* WS10 .... 49 E1 🔲
Crown Gn *FOAKS/STRLY* B74 .... 38 A5
STRBR DY8 .... 136 B3
Crown Meadow *ALVE* B48 .... 216 C3
Crownmeadow Dr
TPTN/OCK DY4 .... 71 F4 🔲
Crown Rd *BORD* B9 .... 125 F5
BVILLE B30 .... 188 C1
Crown St *WOLV* WV1 .... 25 F2
Crown Wk *TPTN/OCK* DY4 .... 92 C3 🔲
Crows Nest Cl *WALM/CURD* B76 .... 60 B6 🔲
Crowther Gdns *HALE* B63 .... 139 E2 🔲
Crowther Rd *DUNHL/THL/PER* WV6.. 24 B3
Crowther St *DUNHL/THL/PER* WV6.. 24 B3
ERDW/GRVHL B23 .... 79 F6
Crowther St *WOLVN* WV10 .... 26 A3
Croxall Wy *SMTHWK* B66 .... 121 D2
Croxdene Av *BLOX/PEL* WS3 .... 16 B4
Croxley Gdns *WLNHL* WV13 .... 48 B1
Croxstalls Av *BLOX/PEL* WS3 .... 16 C5
Croxstalls Cl *BLOX/PEL* WS3 .... 16 C4
Croxstalls Pl *BLOX/PEL* WS3 .... 16 C5 🔲
Croxstalls Rd *BLOX/PEL* WS3 .... 16 C4
Croxton Cv *STETCH* B33 .... 128 C3
Croyde Av *PBAR/PBCH* B42 .... 76 C3
Croydon Rd *ERDE/BCHGN* B24 .... 102 C4
SLYOAK B29 .... 146 B6
Croy Dr *CVALE* B35 .... 105 D1
Crusader Cl *OLDBY* B69 .... 118 A2
Crychan Cl *RBRY* B45 .... 185 D3
Cryersoak Cl *SHLY* B90 .... 194 C6
Crystal Dr *STRBR* DY8 .... 112 B6
Crystal Dr *SMTHWK* B66 .... 95 E5
Cubley Rd *HLGN/YWD* B28 .... 172 A2
Cuckoo Rd *VAUX/NECH* B7 .... 101 E5
Cuin Dr *SMTHWK* B66 .... 121 E1
Cuin Rd *SMTHWK* B66 .... 121 E2
Culey Gv *STETCH* B33 .... 129 F5
Culford Dr *RIDG/WDGT* B32 .... 165 E3
Culham Cl *ACGN* B27 .... 173 F1 🔲
Cullwick St *WOLV* WV1 .... 46 C2
Culmington Rd *NFLD/LBR* B31 .... 186 A6
Culmington Rd *NFLD/LBR* B31 .... 186 B5
Culmore Cl *SHHTH* WV12 .... 29 F3
Culmore Rd *RMSLY* B62 .... 118 A6 🔲
Culverhouse Dr *STRBR* DY8 .... 112 C6 🔲
Culverley Crs *DOR/KN* B93 .... 212 B4
Culwell St *WOLVN* WV10 .... 25 F2
Cumberford Av *STETCH* B33 .... 130 A6 🔲
Cumberland Av *DIG/EDG* B5 .... 148 A2 🔲
Cumberland Cl *KGSWFD* DY6 ..... 112 A3
Cumberland Rd *BILS/COS* WV14 .. 47 F2
HHTH/SAND B71 .... 73 F5
LGLYGN/QTN B68 .... 143 D1
WLNHL WV13 .... 29 F5
Cumbrian Cft *HALE* B63 .... 161 F1 🔲
Cunningham Rd
DUNHL/THL/PER WV6 .... 22 A3
WSLW WS2 .... 30 A5
Cupfields Av *TPTN/OCK* DY4 .... 71 E3
Cupfields Crs *TPTN/OCK* DY4 .... 71 E4
Curbar Rd *PBAR/PBCH* B42 .... 77 E5
Curdale Rd *RIDG/WDGT* B32 .... 165 D3
Curdworth La *WALM/CURD* B76 .... 84 B2
Curlews Cl *ERDW/GRVHL* B23 .... 79 E3 🔲
Curral Rd *BLKHTH/ROWR* B65 ..... 117 D4
Curtin Dr *DARL/WED* WS10 .... 49 D5
Curtis Cl *SMTHWK* B66 .... 121 E3 🔲
Curzon St *BKHL/PFLD* WV2 .... 45 F2
CBHAMNE B4 .... 7 H4
Cuthbert Rd *WSNGN* B18 .... 122 A3
Cutlers Rough Cl *NFLD/LBR* B31 .. 166 B3 🔲
Cutler St *SMTHWK* B66 .... 121 D2
Cutsdean Cl *NFLD/LBR* B31 .... 166 B5
Cutshill Cl *CBROM* B36 .... 105 E5
Cut Throat La *HOCK/TIA* B94 ...... 223 E1
The Cutting *RUSH/SHEL* WS4 .... 32 B3 🔲
Cuttle Mill La *WALM/CURD* B76 .... 63 F6
Cutworth Cl *WALM/CURD* B76 .... 60 A2
Cygnet Cl *ALVE* B48 .... 216 C2 🔲
Cygnet Cv *ERDW/GRVHL* B23 .... 78 C5
Cygnet La *BRLYHL* DY5 .... 89 E6
Cygnet Rd *WBROM* B70 .... 72 C6
Cygnus Wy *WBROM* B70 .... 72 B6
Cypress Av *SEDG* DY3 .... 67 F6

Cypress Gdns *KGSWFD* DY6 .... 111 F3 🔲
Cypress Gv *NFLD/LBR* B31 .... 186 A4 🔲
Cypress Rd *DSYBK/YTR* WS5 .... 53 E5
DUDS DY2 .... 92 B4
Cypress Sq *ACGN* B27 .... 151 E3 🔲
Cypress Wy *NFLD/LBR* B31 .... 186 B5
Cyprus Cl *SLYOAK* B29 .... 166 C4
Cyprus St *BKHL/PFLD* WV2 .... 44 C5 🔲
OLDBY B69 .... 94 C1
Cyril Rd *SMHTH* B10 .... 149 D1

D

Dacer Cl *BVILLE* B30 .... 169 D2
Dadford Vw *BRLYHL* DY5 .... 113 D5
Dad's La *MOS/BIL* B13 .... 169 E2
Daffodil Cl *SEDG* DY3 .... 68 A4
Daffodil Pl *DSYBK/YTR* WS5 .... 53 F1
Daffodil Rd *DSYBK/YTR* WS5 .... 53 F1
Daffodil Wy *NFLD/LBR* B31 .... 186 A5 🔲
Dagger La *HHTH/SAND* B71 .... 74 A6
Dagnall Rd *ACGN* B27 .... 151 E3
Daimler Cl *CBROM* B36 .... 106 B4
Daimler Rd *ALE/KHTH/YWD* B14... 191 F2
Dainton Gv *RIDG/WDGT* B32 .... 165 E2
Dairy Cl *TPTN/OCK* DY4 .... 71 D6 🔲
Dairy Ct *LGLYGN/QTN* B68 .... 143 F2
Daisy Bank *BLOX/PEL* WS3 .... 19 D3
Daisy Bank Crs *DSYBK/YTR* WS5 ... 53 F1
Daisy Dr *ERDW/GRVHL* B23 .... 78 C6
Daisy Farm Rd
ALE/KHTH/YWD B14 .... 191 D3
Daisy Meadow *TPTN/OCK* DY4 ...... 71 E5
Daisy Rd *LDYWD/EDGR* B16 .... 122 B3 🔲
Daisy St *BILS/COS* WV14 .... 70 A1
DUNHL/THL/PER WV6 .... 24 C3 🔲
Daisy Wk *COVEN* WV9 .... 10 C2
Dalbeg Cl *CDSL* WV8 .... 10 A5 🔲
Dalbury Rd *HLGN/YWD* B28 .... 172 A6
Dalby Rd *BLOX/PEL* WS3 .... 32 B1
Dale Cl *GTB/HAM* B43 .... 75 F2
SMTHWK B67 .... 120 C4
TPTN/OCK DY4 .... 71 F6
Dalecote Av *HIA/OLT* B92 .... 176 A3 🔲
Dale End *CBHAMNE* B4 .... 7 F5
DARL/WED WS10 .... 49 F3 🔲
Dale Hl *BRGRVE* B60 .... 214 B3 🔲
Dale Rd *RMSLY* B62 .... 142 B1
SLYOAK B29 .... 146 A6
STRBR DY8 .... 108 C4
Dales Cl *DUNHL/THL/PER* WV6 ..... 25 D1 🔲
Dalesman Cl *KGSWFD* DY6 .... 87 D6
Dale St *BDMR/CCFT* WV3 .... 2 B6
BILS/COS WV14 .... 48 B4
DARL/WED WS10 .... 50 A4
SMTHWK B66 .... 120 C4
WSL WS1 .... 51 F2
Dale Ter *OLDBY* B69 .... 93 E5
Daleview Rd *ALE/KHTH/YWD* B14 . 191 D2
Dalewood Cft
LGN/SDN/BHAMAIR B26 .... 152 B3
Dalewood Rd
CHWD/FDBR/MGN B37 .... 130 B2 🔲
Daley Cl *CBHAMW* B1 .... 123 D4
Daley Rd *BILS/COS* WV14 .... 70 B1
Dalkeith Rd *SCFLD/BOLD* B73 .... 80 A1
Dalkeith St *WSLW* WS2 .... 31 E4
Dallas Rd *ERDW/GRVHL* B23 .... 101 D3
Dallimore Cl *HIA/OLT* B92 .... 152 B6
Dalloway's Cl *DIG/EDG* B5 .... 147 F3 🔲
Dalston Cl *DUDS* DY2 .... 115 F1 🔲
Dalston Rd *ACGN* B27 .... 151 E5
Dalton Rd *WSLW* WS2 .... 30 C4
Dalton St *BDMR/CCFT* WV3 .... 45 D1
CBHAMNE B4 .... 7 F4
Dalvine Rd *DUDS* DY2 .... 115 D5
Dalwood Cl *BILS/COS* WV14 .... 69 D4
Damar Cft *ALE/KHTH/YWD* B14 ... 189 F1
Damien Cl *SMTHWK* B67 .... 120 B2 🔲
Damson Cl *WNSFLD* WV11 .... 28 C1 🔲
Damson Pkwy *HIA/OLT* B92 .... 154 B6
HIA/OLT B92 .... 176 B4
Danbury Cl *WALM/CURD* B76 .... 82 C1 🔲
Danbury Rd *SHLY* B90 .... 193 D2
Danby Gv *ERDE/BCHGN* B24 .... 103 D3
Dando Rd *DUDS* DY2 .... 91 F5
Dandy Bank Rd *KGSWFD* DY6 .... 88 C5
Dandy's Wk *WSL* WS1 .... 5 E6
Dane Gv *MOS/BIL* B13 .... 169 F3
Danesbury Crs *KGSTG* B44 .... 78 C3
Daneswood Rd *WNSFLD* WV11 .... 14 B1
Danescourt Rd
DUNHL/THL/PER WV6 .... 23 E1
Danes Rd *BLKHTH/ROWR* B65 ..... 117 D2
Daneways Cl *FOAKS/STRLY* B74 .... 56 C1
Danford Cl *STRBR* DY8 .... 136 C5
Danford Gdns *SMHTH* B10 .... 149 E1 🔲
Danford La *SOLH* B91 .... 194 A2
Danford Rd *HLYWD* B47 .... 206 B1 🔲
Danford Wy *GTB/HAM* B43 .... 75 F3
Dangerfield La *DARL/WED* WS10 ... 49 E4

Daniels La *ALDR* WS9 .... 35 E3
Daniels Rd *BORD* B9 .... 126 C5
Danks St *TPTN/OCK* DY4 .... 92 C3 🔲
Danzey Green Rd *CBROM* B36 .... 105 D4
Danzey Gv *BVILLE* B30 .... 189 D2
Darby Cl *BILS/COS* WV14 .... 68 C1
Darby End Rd *BLKHTH/ROWR* B65.. 116 A3
DUDS DY2 .... 116 A3
Darby Rd *DARL/WED* WS10 .... 51 D6
LGLYGN/QTN B68 .... 119 E2
Darbys Hill Rd *OLDBY* B69 .... 92 C5
Darby St *BLKHTH/ROWR* B65 .... 117 E6
Darell Cft *WALM/CURD* B76 .... 60 A6
Daren Cl *CBROM* B36 .... 106 B5
Dark La *HAG/WOL* DY9 .... 180 A6
HWK/WKHTH B38 .... 189 F6
RMSLY B62 .... 182 B1
Darlaston La *BILS/COS* WV14 .... 48 C2
Darlaston Rd *DARL/WED* WS10 ..... 49 F4
WSLW WS2 .... 50 C1
Darley Av *BKDE/SHDE* B34 .... 128 B1
Darleydale Av *KGSTG* B44 .... 78 A2
Darley Dr *DUNHL/THL/PER* WV6 .... 25 D2
Darley Green Rd *DOR/KN* B93 ..... 213 D6
Darley Wy *FOAKS/STRLY* B74 .... 56 B2
Darlington St *DARL/WED* WS10 .... 49 F3 🔲
WOLV WV1 .... 2 C4
Darlington Yd *WOLV* WV1 .... 2 C4 🔲
Darnel Cft *SMHTH* B10 .... 125 D6 🔲
Darnel Hurst Rd *MGN/WHC* B75 .... 39 E4
Darnford Cl *CSCFLD/WYGN* B72 ... 81 F4 🔲
HLGN/YWD B28 .... 172 C6
Darnick Rd *SCFLD/BOLD* B73 .... 57 F6
Darnley Rd *LDYWD/EDGR* B16 .... 122 C5 🔲
Darris Rd *SLYOAK* B29 .... 168 C1
Dartford Rd *BLOX/PEL* WS3 .... 16 B4
Dartmoor Cl *RBRY* B45 .... 184 C3
Dartmouth Av *BLOX/PEL* WS3 .... 32 A2
STRBR DY8 .... 111 F4
WLNHL WV13 .... 28 B5
Dartmouth Cl *BLOX/PEL* WS3 .... 32 A2
Dartmouth Crs *BILS/COS* WV14 .... 48 C2 🔲
Dartmouth Dr *ALDR* WS9 .... 34 B2
Dartmouth Pl *BLOX/PEL* WS3 .... 32 A1
Dartmouth Rd *SLYOAK* B29 .... 168 B1
SMTHWK B66 .... 96 B5
Dartmouth St *BKHL/PFLD* WV2 .... 45 F1 🔲
BKHL/PFLD WV2 .... 46 A1 🔲
WBROM B70 .... 95 E1
Dart St *BORD* B9 .... 125 D6
Darvel Rd *SHHTH* WV12 .... 29 F3
Darwall St *WSL* WS1 .... 4 D3
Darwin Ct *DUNHL/THL/PER* WV6 ... 22 A3
Darwin Pl *WSLW* WS2 .... 31 D1
Darwin Rd *WSLW* WS2 .... 31 D1
Darwin St *BHTH/HG* B12 .... 148 B1
Dassett Gv *BORD* B9 .... 127 E5
Dassett Rd *DOR/KN* B93 .... 212 B5
Dauntsey Covert *BVILLE* B30 ..... 189 F3 🔲
Davena Dr *SLYOAK* B29 .... 166 A1 🔲
Davena Gv *BILS/COS* WV14 .... 47 F6
Davenport Dr
DUNHL/THL/PER WV6 .... 23 D2
WNSFLD WV11 .... 28 A1
Daventry Gv *RIDG/WDGT* B32 ..... 143 E3
Davey Rd *BFLD/HDSWWD* B20 .... 100 A4
WBROM B70 .... 94 C1
David Peacock Cl *TPTN/OCK* DY4.. 70 C6
David Rd *BFLD/HDSWWD* B20 ...... 99 D3
TPTN/OCK DY4 .... 70 C4
The Davids *NFLD/LBR* B31 .... 167 E5
Davies Av *BILS/COS* WV14 .... 47 F4 🔲
Davis Av *TPTN/OCK* DY4 .... 92 A1
Davis Gv *LGN/SDN/BHAMAIR* B26.. 151 E3
Davison Rd *SMTHWKW* B67 .... 120 B4
Davis Rd *SHHTH* WV12 .... 15 F5
Davy Rd *WSLW* WS2 .... 30 C2
Dawberry Fields Rd
ALE/KHTH/YWD B14 .... 169 E6
Dawberry Rd *ALE/KHTH/YWD* B14.. 169 E6
Daw End *RUSH/SHEL* WS4 .... 33 E5
Daw End La *RUSH/SHEL* WS4 .... 33 D1
Dawes Av *WBROM* B70 .... 95 E4
Dawley Brook Rd *KGSWFD* DY6 .... 87 F6
Dawley Cft
CHWD/FDBR/MGN B37 .... 131 D5
Dawley Rd *KGSWFD* DY6 .... 87 E5
Dawlish Rd *DUDN* DY1 .... 69 E6
SLYOAK B29 .... 168 B1
SMTHWK B66 .... 121 D2 🔲
Dawn Dr *DARL/WED* WS10 .... 71 E1
Dawney Dr *MGN/WHC* B75 .... 38 C3
Dawn Rd *NFLD/LBR* B31 .... 166 A5
Dawson Av *BILS/COS* WV14 .... 68 B1
Dawson Rd *HDSW* B21 .... 98 A5
Dawson Sq *BILS/COS* WV14 .... 47 E4 🔲
Dawson St *BLOX/PEL* WS3 .... 17 F5
SMTHWK B66 .... 120 C4
Day Av *WNSFLD* WV11 .... 14 A6
Dayhouse Bank *RMSLY* B62 .... 183 D4
Daylesford Rd *HIA/OLT* B92 .... 152 C6

Day St WSLW WS2 .... 4 C1
Deakin Rd ERDE/BCHGN B24.......... 102 B2
  MGN/WHC B75 .... 60 A2 🖪
Deakins Rd YDLY B25 .... 151 D2
Deal Dr DUDS DY2 .... 92 B4
Deal Gv NFLD/LBR B31 .... 186 C1
Deanbrook Cl SHLY B90 .... 210 C1 🖪
Dean Cl CSCFLD/WYGN B72 .... 81 D4
  KGSTG B44... 79 D3
  STRBR DY8 .... 137 D3
Deanery Rw WOLV WV1 .... 2 D2
Dean Rd ERDW/GRVHL B23 .... 80 B6
  RUSH/SHEL WS4 .... 19 E6
  WMBN WV5 .... 64 B6
Deansfield Rd WOLV WV1 .... 26 C5
Deans Pl BLOX/PEL WS3 .... 32 B1
Dean's Rd WOLV WV1 .... 26 C4
Dean St DIG/EDG B5 .... 124 A6 🖪
  SEDG DY3 .... 67 F3 🖪
Dearman Rd SPARK B11...................... 149 D2
Dearmont Rd NFLD/LBR B31................ 186 A6
Dearne Ct SEDG DY3 .... 68 C5
Debden Rd DOR/KN B93 .... 212 A5
Debenham Crs YDLY B25..................... 127 F6
Debenham Rd YDLY B25 .... 127 F6
Deblen Dr LDYWD/EDGR B16 .... 121 F6
Deborah Cl
  ETTPK/GDPK/PENN WV4 .... 45 E3 🖪
Dee Gv HWK/WKHTH B38...................... 188 A5
Deelands Rd RBRY B45 .... 184 B5
Deeley Cl CDYHTH B64 .... 140 C2 🖪
  EDG B15... 147 E2
Deeley Dr TPTN/OCK DY4 .... 71 E5 🖪
Deeley Pl BLOX/PEL WS3 .... 17 D5
Deeley St BLOX/PEL WS3 .... 17 D5 🖪
  BRLYHL DY5 .... 114 A6 🖪
Deepdale Av
  LGN/SDN/BHAMAIR B26 .... 153 D5
Deepdale La DUDN DY1 .... 90 A2
Deepdales WMBN WV5 .... 64 A5 🖪
Deeplow Cl CSCFLD/WYGN B72 .... 59 E5 🖪
Deepmoor Rd STETCH B33 .... 128 B3
Deepmore Av WSLW WS2 .... 31 D5
Deepwood Cl RUSH/SHEL WS4 .... 19 D5
Deer Cl BLOX/PEL WS3 .... 17 E4
Dee Rd BLOX/PEL WS3 .... 18 A4
Deer Park Wy SOLH B91...................... 195 E4
Defford Av RUSH/SHEL WS4 .... 19 E4
Defford Dr LGLYGN/QTN B68............. 119 D3
Deighton Rd DSYBK/YTR WS5............. 53 D5
Delamere Cl CBROM B36 .... 105 F4
Delamere Rd GTB/HAM B43................ 53 E6
  HLGN/YWD B28 .... 172 B4
  SHHTH WV12 .... 15 E6
Delancey Keep MGN/WHC B75 .... 60 C4 🖪
Delhurst Av
  ETTPK/GDPK/PENN WV4 .... 46 A6
Delhurst Rd KGSTG B44 .... 77 F2
Della Dr RIDG/WDGT B32 .... 165 F3
Dell Farm Cl DOR/KN B93 .... 213 D1 🖪
Dellow Gv ALVE B48 .... 216 C4 🖪
Dellows Cl HWK/WKHTH B38.............. 187 E5
Dell Rd BRLYHL DY5 .... 113 D2
  BVILLE B30 .... 168 C6
The Dell HIA/OLT B92 .... 174 C2
  NFLD/LBR B31 .... 165 F1
  STRBR DY8 .... 136 A3
Delmore Wy WALM/CURD B76 .... 83 D5
Delph Dr BRLYHL DY5 .... 138 A2
Delph La BRLYHL DY5 .... 137 F1
Delph Rd BRLYHL DY5 .... 113 D6
Delrene Rd HLGN/YWD B28 .... 192 B2
Delves Crs DSYBK/YTR WS5................. 53 D5
Delves Green Rd DSYBK/YTR WS5 .... 52 C3
Delves Rd WSL WS1 .... 52 B2
Delville Rd DARL/WED WS10 .... 50 B6
De Marnham Cl WBROM B70 .... 96 A4 🖪
De Moram Gv HIA/OLT B92 .... 176 B4
Demuth Wy OLDBY B69 .... 118 B3
Denaby Gv ALE/KHTH/YWD B14 ...... 191 F1
Denbigh Cl DUDN DY1 .... 90 B3
Denbigh Crs HHTH/SAND B71 .... 73 D5
Denbigh Dr DARL/WED WS10 .... 51 F5
  HHTH/SAND B71.................................... 73 D5
Denbigh Rd TPTN/OCK DY4 .... 93 E1
Denbigh St BORD B9 .... 125 F5
Denby Cl VAUX/NECH B7 .... 125 D2
Denby Cft SHLY B90 .... 211 D1
Dencer Cl RBRY B45............................ 184 B5
Dencil Cl HALE B63 .... 139 F4
Dene Av KGSWFD DY6 .... 111 E3
Dene Court Rd HIA/OLT B92 .... 174 B2
Denegate Cl WALM/CURD B76 .... 83 D5 🖪
Denehurst Cl RBRY B45...................... 200 C6
Dene Rd ETTPK/GDPK/PENN WV4 ... 42 B5
  STRBR DY8 .... 136 B6
Denewood Av BFLD/HDSWWD B20 .. 98 C3
Denford Gv ALE/KHTH/YWD B14 ...... 169 F6
Denham Gdns BDMR/CCFT WV3........ 43 D1
Denham Rd ACGN B27.......................... 151 D4
Denholme Gv ALE/KHTH/YWD B14.. 190 C2

Denholm Rd SCFLD/BOLD B73 .... 57 F6
Denise Dr BILS/COS WV14 .... 69 D3
  CHWD/FDBR/MGN B37...................... 130 B3
  HRBN B17 .... 145 E5
Denleigh Rd KGSWFD DY6 .... 112 B3
Denmark Cl DUNHL/THL/PER WV6.... 24 C3
Denmead Dr WNSFLD WV11 .... 14 B5 🖪
Denmore Gdns WOLV WV1 .... 27 D5
Dennis Hall Rd STRBR DY8 .... 136 C1
Dennis Rd BHTH/HG B12 .... 149 D5
Dennis St STRBR DY8 .... 136 B1
Denshaw Rd ALE/KHTH/YWD B14 .. 169 F5
Denton Cft DOR/KN B93 .... 211 F4
Denton Gv GTB/HAM B43 .... 75 F4 🖪
  STETCH B33 .... 127 F5 🖪
Denton Rd HAG/WOL DY9 .... 138 C5
Denver Rd ALE/KHTH/YWD B14 ...... 190 C3
Denville Cl BILS/COS WV14................ 48 A2
Denville Crs BORD B9 .... 127 D4
Depwo Gv RIDG/WDGT B32 .... 165 D3 🖪
Derby Av DUNHL/THL/PER WV6 .... 10 A6
Derby Dr CHWD/FDBR/MGN B37..... 131 D5
Derby St DIG/EDG B5 .... 124 C5
  WSLW WS2 .... 31 F3
Dereham Cl WASH/WDE B8 .... 125 E3 🖪
Dereham Wk BILS/COS WV14 .... 70 A1 🖪
Dereton Cl DUDN DY1 .... 90 A5 🖪
Derron Av
  LGN/SDN/BHAMAIR B26 .... 152 A4
Derry Cl HRBN B17 .... 144 C6
Derrydown Cl
  ERDW/GRVHL B23 .... 102 A2 🖪
Derrydown Rd PBAR/PBCH B42 .... 77 D6
Derry St BKHL/PFLD WV2 .... 45 F1
  BRLYHL DY5 .... 113 E5
Derwent Cl BRLYHL DY5 .... 113 D1
  FOAKS/STRLY B74................................ 36 B5
  WLNHL WV13 .... 28 C3
Derwent Gv ACGN B27 .... 169 E2 🖪
Derwent Rd BVILLE B30 .... 169 E3
  DUNHL/THL/PER WV6 .... 9 F5
Desford Av PBAR/PBCH B42 .... 77 E4
Dettonford Rd RIDG/WDGT B32 ...... 165 D3
Devereux Cl CBROM B36 .... 105 E3 🖪
Devereux Rd MGN/WHC B75................ 39 E6
  WBROM B70 .... 96 A4
Devey Dr TPTN/OCK DY4 .... 71 F5
Devine Cft TPTN/OCK DY4 .... 70 C6 🖪
Devitts Cl SHLY B90 .... 194 B6 🖪
Devon Cl ALDR WS9 .... 20 C4
  DUDS DY2 .... 90 B6
  HHTH/SAND B71 .... 73 E5
Devon Crs ALDR WS9 .... 20 C4
  DARL/WED WS10 .... 51 E5
  RBRY B45... 184 A3
  SMTHWKW B67 .... 144 A2
  STRBR DY8 .... 135 F2
  WLNHL WV13 .... 29 F6
  WOLV WV1 .... 2 B1
Devonshire Av WSNGN B18............... 122 B1
Devonshire Dr HHTH/SAND B71 .... 96 A2
Devonshire Rd BFLD/HDSWWD B20.. 98 B3
  SMTHWKW B67 .... 120 A1
Devonshire St WSNGN B18 .... 122 B1
Devon St VAUX/NECH B7 .... 125 E3
Devoran Cl DUNHL/THL/PER WV6 .... 25 D3
Dewberry Dr DSYBK/YTR WS5 .... 52 C4
Dewberry Rd STRBR DY8 .... 112 B6
Dewhurst Cft STETCH B33 .... 129 D4 🖪
Dewsbury Cl STRBR DY8 .... 112 A4
Dewsbury Dr
  ETTPK/GDPK/PENN WV4 .... 44 C6
Dewsbury Gv PBAR/PBCH B42 .... 77 D3
Deykin Av AST/WIT B6 .... 100 C3
D'eyncourt Rd WNSFLD WV11............ 12 C6
Dial Cl ALE/KHTH/YWD B14 .... 190 A3
Dial La STRBR DY8 .... 136 A1
  WBROM B70 .... 72 B5
Diamond Park Dr STRBR DY8 .... 112 A6 🖪
Diana Cl ALDR WS9 .... 21 D2
Diane Cl TPTN/OCK DY4 .... 71 D1
Dibble Cl SHHTH WV12 .... 29 F2
Dibble Rd SMTHWKW B67 .... 120 B1
Dibdale Rd DUDN DY1 .... 90 B2
Dibdale St DUDN DY1 .... 90 B3
Dice Pleck NFLD/LBR B31 .... 187 E3
Dickens Cl SEDG DY3 .... 67 D6 🖪
Dickens Rd ALE/KHTH/YWD B14 ..... 190 C1
Dickens Heath Rd SHLY B90 .... 208 C1 🖪
  SHLY B90 .... 208 C2 🖪
  SHLY B90 .... 209 D1
Dickens Rd BILS/COS WV14................ 69 D1
  WOLVN WV10 .... 12 C5
Dickinson Av WOLVN WV10 .... 12 A5
Dickinson Dr WALM/CURD B76......... 60 A5
  WSLW WS2 .... 51 E3
Dickinson Rd WMBN WV5 .... 86 C1
Dick Sheppard Av TPTN/OCK DY4 ... 71 D3
Diddington Av HLGN/YWD B28 .... 172 C6 🖪
Diddington La HIA/OLT B92 .... 179 E3 🖪
Didgley Gv
  CHWD/FDBR/MGN B37...................... 130 C2 🖪
Digbeth DIG/EDG B5 .... 124 B6
  WSL WS1 .... 4 D4
Digby Crs CSHL/WTROR B46 .... 107 D2 🖪
Digby Dr CHWD/FDBR/MGN B37 .... 155 D3

Digby Rd CSHL/WTROR B46............. 132 B1
  KGSWFD DY6 .... 87 F5
  SCFLD/BOLD B73 .... 58 C6
Dilke Rd ALDR WS9 .... 34 B2
Dilloways La WLNHL WV13 .... 28 A6
Dimmingsdale Bank
  RIDG/WDGT B32 .... 143 E5
Dimminsdale WLNHL WV13 .... 28 C6 🖪
Dimmocks Av BILS/COS WV14........... 69 F3
Dimmock St
  ETTPK/GDPK/PENN WV4 .... 46 A4
Dimsdale Gv NFLD/LBR B31............. 186 A2
Dimsdale Rd NFLD/LBR B31 .... 185 F2
Dingle Av CDYHTH B64 .... 140 A1
Dingle Cl BVILLE B30 .... 167 F4
  DUDS DY2 .... 92 A6
Dingle Hollow OLDBY B69 .... 93 F5
Dingle La SOLH B91............................ 194 B3
  WLNHL WV13 .... 28 C3
Dingle Md ALE/KHTH/YWD B14 ...... 189 E1
Dingle Rd DUDS DY2 .... 92 A6
  HAG/WOL DY9 .... 159 D1
  KGSWFD DY6 .... 112 C3
  WMBN WV5 .... 64 B6
Dingle St OLDBY B69 .... 93 F5
The Dingle BDMR/CCFT WV3............. 23 F6 🖪
  OLDBY B69 .... 93 F5 🖪
  SHLY B90 .... 209 F2 🖪
  SLYOAK B29 .... 168 A1
Dingle Vw SEDG DY3 .... 67 E4
Dingley Rd DARL/WED WS10.............. 50 C4
Dinham Gdns DUDN DY1 .... 90 A2 🖪
Dinmore Av NFLD/LBR B31................ 187 D1
Dippons Dr DUNHL/THL/PER WV6 .... 22 C4
Dippons Mill Cl
  DUNHL/THL/PER WV6 .... 22 C4
Dirtyfoot La
  ETTPK/GDPK/PENN WV4 .... 42 C4
Discovery Cl TPTN/OCK DY4 .... 71 E6
The Ditch WSL WS1 .... 5 E4
Ditton Gv NFLD/LBR B31 .... 202 B1 🖪
Dixon Cl CVALE B35 .... 104 C3
  TPTN/OCK DY4 .... 71 E5
Dixon Rd SMHTH B10 .... 149 D1
Dixon's Green Rd DUDS DY2 .... 92 A5
Dixon St BKHL/PFLD WV2 .... 46 A3
Dobbins Oak Rd HAG/WOL DY9 ..... 159 F2
Dobbs Mill Cl SLYOAK B29 .... 169 D1 🖪
Dobbs St BKHL/PFLD WV2 .... 45 E1
Dockar Rd NFLD/LBR B31 .... 186 A3
Dock La DUDN DY1 .... 91 D4
Dock Meadow Dr
  ETTPK/GDPK/PENN WV4 .... 46 C5
Dock Rd STRBR DY8 .... 112 B5
The Dock HAG/WOL DY9 .... 138 B4 🖪
Doctors Hill HAG/WOL DY9 .... 137 F6
Doctors La KGSWFD DY6 .... 110 B2
Doctor's Piece WLNHL WV13.............. 29 D5
Doddington Gv
  RIDG/WDGT B32 .... 165 D3 🖪
Dodford Cl RBRY B45.......................... 184 B6 🖪
Doe Bank La ALDR WS9 .... 55 F3
Doe Bank Rd TPTN/OCK DY4 .... 71 E2
Dogge Lane Cft ACGN B27 .... 171 D1 🖪
Dogkennel La HALE B63...................... 141 D6
  LGLYGN/QTN B68 .... 119 D2
Dog Kennel La SHLY B90 .... 193 E6
  WSL WS1 .... 5 F3
Dogpool La BVILLE B30 .... 169 D2
Doidge Rd ERDW/GRVHL B23 .... 101 F2
Dollery Dr DIG/EDG B5 .... 147 E4
Dollis Gv KGSTG B44 .... 56 B5
Dolman St VAUX/NECH B7 .... 125 D4 🖪
Dolman Rd AST/WIT B6 .... 100 A5
Dolobran Rd SPARK B11 .... 149 D2
Dolphin Cl BLOX/PEL WS3 .... 18 B4
Dolphin La ACGN B27 .... 173 E2
Dolphin Rd SPARK B11....................... 149 F4
Dolton Wy TPTN/OCK DY4 .... 70 A5
Dominic Cl BVILLE B30 .... 187 F1
Doncaster Wy CBROM B36................ 103 E5
Don Cl EDG B15................................... 145 F1
Donegal Cl FOAKS/STRLY B74 .... 56 B4
Donibristle Cft CVALE B35 .... 104 C1
Dooley Cl WLNHL WV13 .... 28 A5
Doran Cl HALE B63 .... 161 F2
Doranda Wy HHTH/SAND B71 .... 96 B4
Dora Rd HDSW B21 .... 98 A6
  SMHTH B10 .... 150 A2
  WBROM B70 .... 95 E4
Dora St WSLW WS2 .... 51 D2
Dorchester Cft SHHTH WV12 .... 15 E5 🖪
Dorchester Ct SOLH B91 .... 194 C3
Dorchester Dr HRBN B17 .... 145 D5
Dorchester Rd HAG/WOL DY9 .... 159 F1
  SHHTH WV12 .... 15 E5
  SOLH B91 .... 194 C1
Dordon Cl SHLY B90 .... 192 A4
Doreen Gv ERDE/BCHGN B24 .... 103 D3
Doris Rd BORD B9 .... 125 F6
  CSHL/WTROR B46............................... 108 B5
  SPARK B11 .... 149 D5
Dorking Gv EDG B15 .... 123 E6
Dorlcote Rd WASH/WDE B8............... 126 A3
Dormie Cl HWK/WKHTH B38 .... 187 F4

Dormington Rd *KGSTG* B44 .... 56 A6
Dormston Cl *SOLH* B91 .... 195 E6 🔢
Dormston Dr *SEDG* DY3 .... 67 F3
  SLYOAK B29 .... 166 B1
Dormy Dr *NFLD/LBR* B31 .... 186 C6
Dorncliffe Av *STETCH* B33 .... 153 F2
Dornie Dr *HWK/WKHTH* B38 .... 188 B4
Dornton Rd *BVILLE* B30 .... 169 E3
Dorothy Av *SMTHWKW* B67 .... 120 C4
  SPARK B11 .... 151 D4
Dorothy Gv *WSL* WS1 .... 51 F2
Dorridge Cft *DOR/KN* B93 .... 212 B5
Dorridge Rd *DOR/KN* B93 .... 212 C5
Dorrington Gn *PBAR/PBCH* B42 ...... 76 C6
Dorrington Rd *PBAR/PBCH* B42 ...... 76 C6
Dorset Cl *RBRY* B45...................... 184 B3
Dorset Dr *ALDR* WS9 .... 20 C4
Dorset Pl *BLOX/PEL* WS3 .... 17 E6 🔢
Dorset Rd *HRBN* B17 .... 121 D4
  STRBR DY8 .... 135 F2
  WASH/WDE B8 .... 125 E2
Dorsett Rd *DARL/WED* WS10 .... 49 E3
  DARL/WED WS10 .... 73 F1
Dorsett Road Ter *DARL/WED* WS10 .. 49 E3
Dorsheath Gdns
  ERDW/GRVHL B23 .... 102 B3
Dorsington Rd *ACGN* B27 .... 173 F2
Dorstone Covert *BVILLE* B30 .... 189 E3 🔢
Dorville Cl *HWK/WKHTH* B38 .... 187 E5 🔢
Douay Rd *ERDE/BCHGN* B24 .... 81 D5
Double Rw *DUDS* DY2 .... 116 A3
Doughty St *TPTN/OCK* DY4 .... 71 E6
Douglas Av *CBROM* B36 .... 127 F1
  LGLYGN/QTN B68 .... 119 F2
Douglas Davies Cl *SHHTH* WV12 ..... 29 E3 🔢
Douglas Pl *WOLVN* WV10 .... 25 E1
Douglas Rd *ACGN* B27 .... 151 D5
  BILS/COS WV14.......................... 69 F3
  CSCFLD/WYGN B72....................... 59 E6
  HDSW B21................................... 88 A1
  HLYWD B47 .... 190 C6
  LGLYGN/QTN B68 .... 119 F3
  RMSLY B62 .... 118 A6
Douglass Rd *DUDS* DY2 .... 91 F5
Doulton Cl *RIDG/WDGT* B32.......... 144 B6
Doulton Rd *BLKHTH/ROWR* B65 .... 116 C3
Dovebridge Cl *WALM/CURD* B76 ...... 60 B5
Dove Cl *DARL/WED* WS10 .... 51 D5 🔢
  YDLY B25 .... 152 A1
Dovecote Cl *DUNHL/THL/PER* WV6 .. 23 E3
  SOLH B91 .... 175 D3
  TPTN/OCK DY4 .... 71 F6
The Dovecotes *MGN/WHC* B75 .... 39 D4 🔢
Dovedale Av *SHHTH* WV12 .... 28 C3
  SHLY B90 .... 193 D4
Dovedale Ct
  ETTPK/GDPK/PENN WV4 .... 68 B1 🔢
Dovedale Dr *HLGN/YWD* B28.......... 172 B5
Dovedale Rd *ERDW/GRVHL* B23 ...... 79 E5
  ETTPK/GDPK/PENN WV4 .... 68 A5
  KGSWFD DY6 .... 88 A5
Dove Dr *STRBR* DY8 .... 136 C1 🔢
Dove Gdns *HWK/WKHTH* B38 .... 189 D3
Dove House La *HIA/OLT* B92 .... 174 B4
Dovehouse Pool Rd
  AST/WIT B6 .... 100 A5 🔢
Dover Cl *RIDG/WDGT* B32 .... 164 C4 🔢
Dovercourt Rd
  LGN/SDN/BHAMAIR B26 .... 153 E4
Doverdale Cl *HALE* B63 .... 140 A4 🔢
Dove Rdg *STRBR* DY8 .... 136 C2 🔢
Doveridge Cl *SOLH* B91 .... 174 A5
Doveridge Rd *HLGN/YWD* B28 .... 172 A4
Doversley Rd *ALE/KHTH/YWD* B14.. 169 E6
Dover St *BILS/COS* WV14 .... 47 F3
  WSNGN B18................................ 122 B1
Dove Wy *CBROM* B36 .... 106 B5
Dovey Dr *WALM/CURD* B76 .... 82 C4
Dovey Rd *MOS/BIL* B13 .... 171 F1
  OLDBY B69 .... 93 F5
Dowar Rd *RBRY* B45..................... 185 E6
Dowells Gdns *STRBR* DY8 .... 111 F4 🔢
The Doweries *RBRY* B45 .... 184 B5
Dower Rd *MGN/WHC* B75 .... 39 D6
  MGN/WHC B75............................. 59 E1
Dowles Cl *SLYOAK* B29 .... 167 D5
Downcroft Av *HWK/WKHTH* B38 ... 188 A3
Downend Cl *WOLVN* WV10 .... 12 B1 🔢
Downes Ct *TPTN/OCK* DY4 .... 70 A6 🔢
Downey Cl *SPARK* B11 .... 149 D2 🔢
Downfield Cl *BLOX/PEL* WS3 .... 16 C1 🔢
Downfield Dr *SEDG* DY3................. 66 B6
Downham Cl *DSYBK/YTR* WS5 .... 54 A1 🔢
Downham Pl *BDMR/CCFT* WV3 .... 44 B1 🔢
Downie Rd *CDSL* WV8..................... 9 E2
Downing Cl *BLKHTH/ROWR* B65 .. 117 E6 🔢
  DOR/KN B93 .... 212 C3
  WNSFLD WV11 .... 14 C6
Downing St *HALE* B63 .... 140 C4
  RMSLY B62 .... 97 E6
Dowland Cl *HWK/WKHTH* B38....... 188 A3
Downsfield Rd
  LGN/SDN/BHAMAIR B26 .... 153 D2
Downside Rd *ERDE/BCHGN* B24...... 102 A4
Downs Rd *WLNHL* WV13................. 49 E1

The Downs *FOAKS/STRLY* B74 .... 36 A5
  WOLVN WV10 .... 25 E1
Downton Crs *STECH* B33 .... 130 A4
Dowty Wy *COVEN* WV9 .... 10 C2 🔢
Drake Cl *BLOX/PEL* WS3 .... 17 E4 🔢
Drake Rd *BLOX/PEL* WS3 .... 17 E4
  ERDW/GRVHL B23 .... 101 E2
  SMTHWK B66 .... 95 F6
Drakes Cross Pde *HLYWD* B47 ...... 206 C2 🔢
Drakes Hill Cl *KINVER* DY7 .... 135 E5
Drake St *HHTH/SAND* B71 .... 73 E5
Drancy Av *SHHTH* WV12 .... 29 F1 🔢
Drawbridge Rd *SHLY* B90 .... 192 A5
Draycote Cl *HIA/OLT* B92 .... 175 F4
Draycott Av *ERDW/GRVHL* B23 ...... 79 F3
Draycott Cl
  ETTPK/GDPK/PENN WV4 .... 43 C4
Draycott Dr *NFLD/LBR* B31 .... 166 A4 🔢
Draycott Rd *SMTHWK* B66.............. 96 A6
Drayton Cl *MCN/WHC* B75 .... 39 D4 🔢
Drayton Rd *ALE/KHTH/YWD* B14 ... 170 A3
  SHLY B90 .... 194 A5
  SMTHWK B66 .... 120 C6
Drayton St *BKHL/PFLD* WV2 .... 45 E1
  WSLW WS2 .... 31 E5
Drayton St East *WSLW* WS2 .... 31 E5
Dreadnought Rd *BRLYHL* DY5........ 89 D6
The Dreel *EDG* B15 .... 146 A2
Dreghorn Rd *CBROM* B36 .... 104 A5
Drem Cft *CVALE* B35 .... 104 C2
Dresden Cl
  ETTPK/GDPK/PENN WV4 .... 46 C5 🔢
Drew Crs *HAG/WOL* DY9 .... 137 F6
Drew Rd *HAG/WOL* DY9 .... 137 F6
Drews Holloway *HALE* B63 .... 139 F4
Drews Holloway South *HALE* B63 .. 139 F4
Drews La *WASH/WDE* B8 .... 126 C1
Drews Meadow Cl
  ALE/KHTH/YWD B14 .... 189 E3 🔢
Driffold *SCFLD/BOLD* B73............... 59 D6
Driftwood Cl *HWK/WKHTH* B38 .... 187 F6 🔢
Drive Flds *ETTPK/GDPK/PENN* WV4 .. 43 D1
The Drive *ALVE* B48 .... 203 D4
  BFLD/WBROM B20 .... 98 C3
  BLOX/PEL WS3 .... 18 A3
  BRLYHL DY5................................ 113 E2
  CDSL WV8 .... 8 B1
  DUNHL/THL/PER WV6 .... 23 E2 🔢
  ERDW/GRVHL B23 .... 102 A3
  HALE B63 .... 139 F4
  HALE B63 .... 140 C6
  RUSH/SHEL WS4 .... 19 E4
The Droveway *COVEN* WV9 .... 10 B3
Druid Park Rd *SHHTH* WV12 .... 15 E4
Druids Av *ALDR* WS9 .... 21 E5
  BLKHTH/ROWR B65 .... 117 F3
Druids La *ALE/KHTH/YWD* B14 ..... 190 B4
  HWK/WKHTH B38 .... 188 B6
Druids Wk *ALDR* WS9 .... 20 C2
Drummond Cl *WNSFLD* WV11 .... 14 C3 🔢
Drummond Gv *GTB/HAM* B43 .... 55 E6 🔢
Drummond Rd *BORD* B9 .... 126 B5
  HAG/WOL DY9 .... 138 B5
Drummond St *WOLV* WV1 .... 2 C1
Drummond Wy
  CHWD/FDBR/MGN B37 .... 131 E5 🔢
Drury La *CDSL* WV8 .... 9 D3
  SOLH B91 .... 195 E2
  STRBR DY8 .... 136 C4 🔢
Drybrook Cl *HWK/WKHTH* B38 ..... 188 A5
Dryden Cl *SHHTH* WV12 .... 16 A5
  TPTN/OCK DY4 .... 70 C4
Dryden Gv *ACGN* B27 .... 173 D1
Dryden Pl *BLOX/PEL* WS3............... 18 A6
Dryden Rd *BLOX/PEL* WS3 .... 18 A6
  WOLVN WV10 .... 12 B4
Drylea Gv *CBROM* B36.................. 104 B5
Dubarry Av *KGSWFD* DY6............... 87 E6
Duchess Rd *LDYWD/EDGR* B16 ..... 122 C6
  WSL WS1 .... 51 F4
Duckhouse Rd *WNSFLD* WV11 .... 13 F6
Duck La *CDSL* WV8 .... 9 D5
Duddeston Manor Rd
  VAUX/NECH B7 .... 124 C2
Duddeston Mill Rd *VAUX/NECH* B7.. 125 D3
Dudding Rd
  ETTPK/GDPK/PENN WV4 .... 45 F4
Dudhill Rd *CDYHTH* B64 .... 116 C4
Dudley Cl *BLKHTH/ROWR* B65 ...... 116 B1
Dudley Crs *WNSFLD* WV11 .... 28 A1
Dudley Park Rd *ACGN* B27 .... 151 E6
Dudley Port *TPTN/OCK* DY4........... 92 C2
Dudley Rd *BKHL/PFLD* WV2 .... 45 F2
  BLKHTH/ROWR B65 .... 116 B1
  BRLYHL DY5............................... 113 F3
  HAG/WOL DY9 .... 138 A3
  HALE B63 .... 140 D1
  KGSWFD DY6 .... 87 E5
  OLDBY B69 .... 94 A5
  RMSLY B62 .... 141 D4 🔢
  SEDG DY3 .... 67 F4
  SEDG DY3 .... 87 E2
  TPTN/OCK DY4 .... 69 F6
  WSNGN B18................................ 121 F3
Dudley Rd East *OLDBY* B69 .... 93 E3

Dudley Rd West *OLDBY* B69 .... 93 D3
Dudley Rw *DUDS* DY2 .... 91 F4
Dudley St *BILS/COS* WV14 .... 47 F5
  DARL/WED WS10 .... 72 A1
  DIG/EDG B5................................. 7 E6
  SEDG DY3 .... 67 F3
  WBROM B70 .... 72 C6
  WOLV WV1 .... 2 D4
  WSL WS1 .... 4 D5
Dudley Wk
  ETTPK/GDPK/PENN WV4 .... 45 E4
Dudley Wood Av *DUDS* DY2 .... 115 E5
Dudley Wood Rd *DUDS* DY2 .... 115 E6
Dudmaston Wy *DUDN* DY1 .... 90 A2 🔢
Dudnill Gv *RIDG/WDGT* B32 .... 164 C3
Duffield Cl *CDSL* WV8 .... 10 B4
Dufton Rd *RIDG/WDGT* B32 .... 144 A4
Dugdale Crs *MGN/WHC* B75 .... 39 E4
Dugdale St *WSNGN* B18 .... 121 F3
Dukes Rd *BVILLE* B30 .... 188 B2
Duke St *BDMR/CCFT* WV3 .... 44 C2 🔢
  BLKHTH/ROWR B65 .... 117 E5
  CSCFLD/WYGN B72....................... 59 D5
  SEDG DY3 .... 67 F6
  STRBR DY8 .... 136 C4
  WBROM B70 .... 95 D1
  WNSFLD WV11 .... 27 F2
  WOLV WV1 .... 3 G5
Dulvern Gv *ALE/KHTH/YWD* B14.... 169 F6
Dulverton Rd *AST/WIT* B6 .... 100 C4
Dulwich Gv *KGSTG* B44 .... 79 D3
Dulwich Rd *KGSTG* B44 .... 78 C3
Dumbleberry Av *SEDG* DY3 .... 67 E4
Dumbleberry La *ALDR* WS9 .... 20 A5
  ALDR WS9 .... 34 B1
Dumble Pit La *HLYWD* B47 .... 220 A2
Dumphouse La *ALVE* B48 .... 219 E6
Dunard Rd *SHLY* B90 .... 192 B2
Dunbar Gv *GTB/HAM* B43 .... 55 D5
Duncalfe Dr *MGN/WHC* B75 .... 39 D4
Duncan Edwards Cl *DUDN* DY1 ...... 90 C5 🔢
Duncan St *BKHL/PFLD* WV2 .... 45 E2 🔢
Dunchurch Crs *SCFLD/BOLD* B73 .... 57 E6
Dunchurch Dr *NFLD/LBR* B31 ...... 166 A4 🔢
Duncombe Gn *CSHL/WTROR* B46 .. 108 B6 🔢
Duncombe Gv *HRBN* B17............... 104 B2
Duncombe St *STRBR* DY8 .... 135 F3
Duncroft Rd
  LGN/SDN/BHAMAIR B26 .... 152 B1
Duncumb Rd *MGN/WHC* B75 .... 60 C4
Dundas Av *OLDBY* B69 .... 92 B5
Dunedin Dr *RBRY* B45 .... 200 C6
Dunedin Rd *KGSTG* B44 .... 56 A6
Dunkirk Av *WBROM* B70 .... 94 A1
Dunkley St *WOLV* WV1 .... 2 C1
Dunley Cft *SHLY* B90 .... 210 B1 🔢
Dunlin Cl *ERDW/GRVHL* B23.......... 101 E3
  KGSWFD DY6 .... 112 C1 🔢
Dunlop Wy *ERDE/BCHGN* B24 .... 104 A4
Dunnigan Rd *RIDG/WDGT* B32 ...... 144 B6
Dunns Bank *BRLYHL* DY5 .... 138 B2
Dunsfold Cl
  ETTPK/GDPK/PENN WV4 .... 46 C6 🔢
Dunsfold Cft *AST/WIT* B6 .... 124 B1 🔢
Dunsford Cl *BRLYHL* DY5 .... 137 D2
Dunsford Rd *SMTHWK* B66 .... 120 B5
Dunsink Rd *BFLD/HDSWWD* B20..... 100 B4
Dunslade Crs *BRLYHL* DY5 .... 138 B1 🔢
Dunslade Rd *ERDW/GRVHL* B23 ...... 80 A1
Dunsley Dr *STRBR* DY8 .... 112 A4 🔢
Dunsley Gv
  ETTPK/GDPK/PENN WV4 .... 44 C5
Dunsmore Dr *BRLYHL* DY5 .... 138 B1
Dunsmore Gv *SOLH* B91 .... 174 B4
Dunsmore Rd *HLGN/YWD* B28 ...... 172 A2
Dunstall Av *DUNHL/THL/PER* WV6 .. 25 E2
Dunstall Gv *SLYOAK* B29 .... 166 B3
Dunstall Hl *DUNHL/THL/PER* WV6 .. 25 E2
Dunstall La *DUNHL/THL/PER* WV6 .. 25 D3
Dunstall Rd *DUNHL/THL/PER* WV6 .. 25 D3
  HALE B63 .... 139 F6
Dunstan Cft *SHLY* B90 .... 193 E5
Dunstan Hl *BVILLE* B30 .... 189 D1
Dunster Gv *DUNHL/THL/PER* WV6 .. 22 B4
Dunster Rd
  CHWD/FDBR/MGN B37 .... 131 F6 🔢
Dunston Cl *KGSWFD* DY6 .... 87 F6 🔢
Dunton Cl *MGN/WHC* B75 .... 38 C3
Dunton Hall Rd *SHLY* B90 .... 192 C5
Dunton La *WALM/CURD* B76 .... 85 D2
Dunton Rd *CHWD/FDBR/MGN* B37.. 130 B3
Dunvegan Cl
  ERDE/BCHGN B24 .... 102 C1 🔢
Durant Cl *RBRY* B45 .... 183 F4
Durban Rd *SMTHWK* B66 .... 121 E3
D'urberville Rd *BKHL/PFLD* WV2..... 46 B2
Durham Av *WLNHL* WV13................ 29 E4
Durham Cft
  CHWD/FDBR/MGN B37 .... 130 C5
Durham Dr *HHTH/SAND* B71 .... 73 F4
Durham Pl *WSLW* WS2 .... 31 D6
Durham Rd *BLKHTH/ROWR* B65 .. 118 A3 🔢
  DARL/WED WS10 .... 51 F5
  DUDS DY2 .... 115 F5
  SPARK B11 .... 149 D5

STRBR DY8 .... **135** F1 ◫
WSLW WS2 .... **51** D1
Durley Dean Rd *SLYOAK* B29 .... **167** E1
Durley Dr *SCFLD/BOLD* B73 .... **57** E6
Durley Rd *YDLY* B25 .... **151** E4
Durlston Gv *HLGN/YWD* B28 .... **172** C3 ◫
Durnford Cft *ALE/KHTH/YWD* B14 .. **190** A4
Dursley Cl *HIA/OLT* B92 .... **175** D3 ◫
SHHTH WV12 .... **29** F3
Dutton's La *MGN/WHC* B75 .... **40** A3
Duxford Rd *PBAR/PCHB* B42 .... **77** D3
Dwellings La *RIDG/WDGT* B32 .... **143** D4
Dyas Av *PBAR/PCHB* B42 .... **76** C4
Dyas Rd *HLYWD* B47 .... **190** C6
KGSTG B44 .... **77** F3
Dyce Cl *CVALE* B35 .... **104** C1
Dyers La *HOCK/TIA* B94 .... **223** F1
Dymoke St *BHTH/HG* B12 .... **148** B1
Dyott Rd *MOS/BIL* B13 .... **170** C2
Dyson Cl *WSLW* WS2 .... **30** B4
Dysons Gdns *WASH/WDE* B8 ...... **126** A2 ◫

E

Eachelhurst Rd *ERDE/BCHGN* B24 .. **104** A1
Eachus Rd *BILS/COS* WV14 .... **69** F3
Eachway *RBRY* B45 .... **200** B1
Eachway La *RBRY* B45 .... **200** C1
Eagle Cl *BLKHTH/ROWR* B65 .... **116** B3
DUDN DY1 .... **90** B4
Eagle Cft *ALE/KHTH/YWD* B14 ...... **190** A3
Eagle Gdns *ERDE/BCHGN* B24 ..... **102** C3 ◫
Eagle Gv *CBROM* B36 .... **106** C5
Eagle La *TPTN/OCK* DY4 .... **71** F5
Eagle St *BDMR/CCFT* WV3 .... **44** C2
BKHL/PFLD WV2 .... **46** A1
TPTN/OCK DY4 .... **71** E5
Ealing Gv *KGSTG* B44 .... **78** C2
Earlsbury Gdns
 BFLD/HDSWWD B20 .... **99** F4
Earls Court Rd *HRBN* B17 .... **144** C3
Earlsmead Rd *HDSW* B21 .... **97** F3
Earlsmere *HOCK/TIA* B94 .... **209** D6
Earls Rd *RUSH/SHEL* WS4 .... **19** L6
Earlsmere Rd *GTB/HAM* B43 .... **75** F3 ◫
Earl St *BILS/COS* WV14 .... **47** F1
BILS/COS WV14 .... **69** F3
KGSWFD DY6 .... **111** F3
WBROM B70 .... **95** D1
WSL WS1 .... **51** F2
Earls Wy *HALE* B63 .... **141** D5
Earlswood Common
 HOCK/TIA B94 .... **222** C3
Earlswood Ct *BFLD/HDSWWD* B20... **98** C3
Earlswood Crs *COVEN* WV9 .... **10** C3
Earlswood Dr *MGN/WHC* B75 .... **59** E2
Earlswood Rd *DOR/KN* B93 .... **211** F5
KGSWFD DY6 .... **88** A5 ◫
Easby Wy *BLOX/PEL* WS3 .... **16** B3
WASH/WDE B8 .... **126** A2
Easenhall Cl *DOR/KN* B93 .... **212** A2
Easmore Cl *ALE/KHTH/YWD* B14 .. **189** F3 ◫
East Av *OLDBY* B69 .... **93** E6
WNSFLD WV11 .... **27** E1
Eastbourne Av *BKDE/SHDE* B34 ... **127** F1
Eastbourne St *RUSH/SHEL* WS4 ...... **32** B4
Eastbrook Cl *WALM/CURD* B76 ...... **59** F5 ◫
Eastbury Dr *HIA/OLT* B92 .... **152** C6
 HIA/OLT B92 .... **174** C1
East Car Park Rd *BHAMNEC* B40 .. **156** B5
Eastcote Cl *SHLY* B90 .... **193** F2
Eastcote La *HIA/OLT* B92 .... **178** C5
Eastcote Rd *ACGN* B27 .... **172** C2
 WOLVN WV10 .... **26** B2
East Croft Rd
 ETTPK/GDPK/PENN WV4 .... **43** E5
Eastdean Cl *ERDW/GRVHL* B23 .... **79** E3
East Dr *DIG/EDG* B5 .... **147** E5
Eastern Av *BRLYHL* DY5 .... **113** D5
Eastern Cl *DARL/WED* WS10 .... **49** E6
Eastern Rd *SCFLD/BOLD* B73 .... **81** D2
SLYOAK B29 .... **147** D6
Easterton Cft *ALE/KHTH/YWD* B14.. **190** A3
Eastfield Dr *HIA/OLT* B92 .... **176** A3
Eastfield Gv *WOLV* WV1 .... **26** B5
Eastfield Retreat *WOLV* WV1 .... **26** B5
Eastfield Rd *BORD* B9 .... **127** E5
 TPTN/OCK DY4 .... **70** C3 ◫
 WOLV WV1 .... **26** B5
East Ga *LDYWD/EDGR* B16 .... **122** A4
East Gn *ETTPK/GDPK/PENN* WV4 ... **43** F3
Eastham Rd *MOS/BIL* B13 .... **171** E5
East Holme *BORD* B9 .... **125** E5 ◫
Easthope Rd *STECH* B33 .... **128** C3
Eastlake Cl *GTB/HAM* B43 .... **55** F6
Eastlands Rd *MOS/BIL* B13 .... **170** C5
Eastleigh *SEDG* DY3 .... **67** D3
Eastleigh Cft *WALM/CURD* B76 ...... **82** C4
Eastleigh Dr *RMSLY* B62 .... **182** C1

Eastleigh Gv *YDLY* B25 .... **151** F1 ◫
East Meadway *STECH* B33 .... **129** F4
East Ms *KGSTG* B44 .... **77** H1
Eastmoor Cl *FOAKS/STRLY* B74 ...... **37** D5
Eastney Crs *CDSL* WV8 .... **10** A5
Easton Gdns *WNSFLD* WV11 .... **28** B2
Easton Gv *ACGN* B27 .... **173** E2 ◫
 HLYWD B47 .... **191** D6
East Park Wy *WOLV* WV1 .... **26** C6
East Pathway *HRBN* B17 .... **145** E5
East Ri *MGN/WHC* B75 .... **59** F3
East St *BRLYHL* DY5 .... **138** C1
 DUDS DY2 .... **92** A5
 SEDG DY3 .... **89** E2
 WOLV WV1 .... **3** C5
 WSL WS1 .... **52** B2 ◫
East View Rd *WALM/CURD* B76 ...... **59** F6
Eastville *NFLD/LBR* B31 .... **187** D2 ◫
Eastward Gln *CDSL* WV8 .... **9** E4
East Wy *BHAMNEC* B40 .... **156** B6
 HIA/OLT B92 .... **156** C6
Eastway *HRBN* B17 .... **145** E5
Eastwood Rd *BHTH/HG* B12 .... **147** F4
 GTB/HAM B43 .... **76** A3
Eatesbrook Rd *STECH* B33 .... **129** E4
Eathorpe Cl *BKDE/SHDE* B34 .... **129** F1 ◫
Eaton Av *WBROM* B70 .... **94** C1 ◫
Eaton Ct *FOAKS/STRLY* B74 .... **59** D2
Eaton Crs *SEDG* DY3 .... **89** D2
Eaton Pl *KGSWFD* DY6 .... **112** A2
Eaton Ri *SHHTH* WV12 .... **29** D1
Eaton Wd *ERDE/BCHGN* B24 .... **103** F2
Eaton Wood Dr
 LGN/SDN/BHAMAIR B26 .... **151** F4
Eaves Court Dr *SEDG* DY3 .... **67** F1
Eaves Green Gdns *ACGN* B27 ...... **151** D4 ◫
 WBROM B70 .... **72** B5
Ebenezer St *BILS/COS* WV14 .... **69** D3 ◫
 WBROM B70 .... **72** B5
Ebley Rd *BFLD/HDSWWD* B20 .... **98** C1
Ebmore Dr *ALE/KHTH/YWD* B14 .... **189** F3
Ebrington Av *HIA/OLT* B92 .... **153** D6
Ebrington Cl *ALE/KHTH/YWD* B14 .. **189** F1
Ebrington Rd *WBROM* B71 .... **73** F5
Ebrook Rd *CSCFLD/WYGN* B72 ...... **59** E5
Ebury Rd *BVILLE* B30 .... **189** D1
Eccleshall Av *WOLVN* WV10 .... **11** F5
Ecclestone Rd *WNSFLD* WV11 .... **14** C5
Echo Wy *ETTPK/GDPK/PENN* WV4 .. **46** C5
Eckersall Rd *HWK/WKHTH* B38 ..... **188** A2
Edale Cl *ETTPK/GDPK/PENN* WV4 .. **46** A1 ◫
 KGSWFD DY6 .... **87** D2
Edale Rd *PBAR/PCHB* B42 .... **77** E4
Eddish Rd *STECH* B33 .... **129** D3
Edenbridge Rd *HLGN/YWD* B28 .... **173** D3
Eden Cl *NFLD/LBR* B31 .... **186** A5
 OLDBY B69 .... **93** F3
Edendale Rd
 LGN/SDN/BHAMAIR B26 .... **153** D6
Eden Gv *CHWD/FDBR/MGN* B37 ... **131** F6
 HHTH/SAND B71 .... **72** A5
Edenhall Rd *RIDG/WDGT* B32 .... **143** D5
Edenhurst Rd *NFLD/LBR* B31 .... **202** B1
Eden Rd *HIA/OLT* B92 .... **153** F6
Edensor Cl *WOLVN* WV10 .... **26** A3
Edgbaston Park Rd *EDC* B15 .... **146** C3
Edgbaston Rd *BHTH/HG* B12 .... **148** A5
 DIG/EDG B5 .... **147** E4
 SMTHWK B66 .... **121** D4
Edgbaston St *DIG/EDG* B5 .... **7** E6
 DIG/EDG B5 .... **124** A6
Edgcombe Rd *HLGN/YWD* B28 ..... **172** B2
Edge Hill Av *WOLV* WV10 .... **12** C4
Edge Hill Dr *DUNHL/THL/PER* WV6.. **22** A2
 SEDG DY3 .... **67** E1
Edge Hill Rd *FOAKS/STRLY* B74 ...... **38** C3
Edgehill Rd *NFLD/LBR* B31 .... **186** C4
Edgemond Av *ERDE/BCHGN* B24 .. **104** B1
Edge St *BILS/COS* WV14 .... **69** D3
Edgewood Cl *CDYHTH* B64 .... **140** B1 ◫
Edgewood Dr *RBRY* B45 .... **201** D6
Edgewood Rd *HWK/WKHTH* B38 ... **188** A6
 RBRY B45 .... **185** D6
Edgeworth Cl *SHHTH* WV12 .... **29** E3 ◫
Edgware Rd *ERDW/GRVHL* B23 ...... **79** F6
Edinburgh Av *WSLW* WS2 .... **30** A4
Edinburgh Cl *ERDE/BCHGN* B24 .. **103** F1 ◫
Edinburgh Crs *STRBR* DY8 .... **111** E6
Edinburgh Dr *RUSH/SHEL* WS4 ...... **19** F6
 SHHTH WV12 .... **29** D1
Edinburgh La *WSLW* WS2 .... **30** C3 ◫
Edinburgh Rd *BILS/COS* WV14 .... **48** B6
 DSYBK/YTR WS5 .... **53** D2
 DUDS DY2 .... **115** F1 ◫
 LGLYGN/QTN B68 .... **143** D3
Edison Gv *RIDG/WDGT* B32 .... **143** F4
Edison Rd *WALM/CURD* B76 .... **108** B1
 WSLW WS2 .... **30** C2
Edith Rd *SMTHWK* B66 .... **121** D4
Edith St *WBROM* B70 .... **72** B5
Edmonds Cl *STECH* B33 .... **129** D5 ◫
Edmonds Rd *LGLYGN/QTN* B68 .... **119** E5
Edmonton Av *KGSTG* B44 .... **79** D2
Edmoor Cl *SHHTH* WV12 .... **29** E1 ◫
Edmund Rd *SEDG* DY3 .... **68** A5

WASH/WDE B8 .... **125** F3
Edmund St *CBHAMNW* B3 .... **6** D4
Ednam Cl *HHTH/SAND* B71 .... **74** B3 ◫
Ednam Gv *WMBN* WV5 .... **64** C2 ◫
Ednam Rd *DUDN* DY1 .... **91** E3 ◫
 ETTPK/GDPK/PENN WV4 .... **45** E6
Edsome Wy *CBROM* B36 .... **104** B5 ◫
Edstone Cl *DOR/KN* B93 .... **212** B3
Edstone Ms *CBROM* B36 .... **104** B5
Edward Av *ALDR* WS9 .... **20** C6
Edward Fisher Dr *TPTN/OCK* DY4 .. **70** C6 ◫
Edward Rd *ALE/KHTH/YWD* B14.... **190** B4
 BHTH/HG B12 .... **148** A4
 CSHL/WTROR B46 .... **107** E2
 DIG/EDG B5 .... **147** F3
 DUNHL/THL/PER WV6 .... **22** A2
 HALE B63 .... **140** B5
 LGLYGN/QTN B68 .... **143** E1
 SMTHWK B67 .... **120** B3
 TPTN/OCK DY4 .... **70** C4
Edwards Rd *DUDS* DY2 .... **115** E3 ◫
 ERDE/BCHGN B24 .... **80** C6
 MGN/WHC B75 .... **39** F4
Edward St *CBHAMW* B1 .... **123** D5
 DARL/WED WS10 .... **50** A3
 DUDN DY1 .... **91** D4
 ETTPK/GDPK/PENN WV4 .... **46** B3
 LGLYGN/QTN B68 .... **118** C3
 WBROM B70 .... **95** E2
 WSLW WS2 .... **31** D4
Edwin Rd *BVILLE* B30 .... **169** D4
Eel St *OLDBY* B69 .... **94** B6
Effingham Rd *MOS/BIL* B13 .... **171** E5
Egbert Cl *AST/WIT* B6 .... **101** D5
Egelwin Cl *DUNHL/THL/PER* WV6 .. **22** A2
Egerton Rd *ERDE/BCHGN* B24 ...... **103** F2
 FOAKS/STRLY B74 .... **36** B5
 WOLVN WV10 .... **12** A2
Egghill La *RIDG/WDGT* B32 .... **184** C1
Eggington Rd *STRBR* DY8 .... **135** F2
Egginton Rd *HLGN/YWD* B28 .... **172** A6
Egmont Gdns *WNSFLD* WV11 .... **28** B2
Eileen Gdns
 CHWD/FDBR/MGN B37 .... **130** C3
Eileen Rd *SPARK* B11 .... **149** D6
Elan Cl *SEDG* DY3 .... **89** D2
Elan Rd *NFLD/LBR* B31 .... **185** E3
 SEDG DY3 .... **67** E3
Elbow St *CDYHTH* B64 .... **116** B6
Elbury Cft *DOR/KN* B93 .... **212** B3
Elcock Dr *PBAR/PCHB* B42 .... **77** F6
Eldalade Wy *DARL/WED* WS10 .... **73** D2
Elderberry Cl *STRBR* DY8 .... **135** E6 ◫
Elderfield Rd *BVILLE* B30 .... **189** D2
Elder Gv *WMBN* WV5 .... **64** B5
Eldersfield Gv *SOLH* B91 .... **195** D6
Elder Wy *ERDW/GRVHL* B23 .... **102** A3 ◫
Eldon Dr *WALM/CURD* B76 .... **82** A4
Eldon Rd *LDYWD/EDGR* B16 .... **122** B6 ◫
 RIDG/WDGT B32 .... **142** C3
Eldon St *DARL/WED* WS10 .... **49** F2
 WSL WS1 .... **5** F5
Eldridge Cl *COVEN* WV9 .... **10** B3
Eleanor Rd *BILS/COS* WV14 .... **47** F3
Electric Av *AST/WIT* B6 .... **101** D5 ◫
Elford Cl *ALE/KHTH/YWD* B14 ...... **170** A6
Elford Gv *BILS/COS* WV14 .... **47** F5
 CHWD/FDBR/MGN B37 .... **131** D6 ◫
Elford Rd *HHTH/SAND* B71 .... **74** A2
 HRBN B17 .... **145** D6
 SLYOAK B29 .... **145** D6
Elgar Crs *BRLYHL* DY5 .... **89** F6
Elgin Cl *SEDG* DY3 .... **68** A3
 STRBR DY8 .... **136** C2
Elgin Ct *DUNHL/THL/PER* WV6 ...... **22** A3
Elgin Gv *YDLY* B25 .... **151** E2 ◫
Elgin Rd *BLOX/PEL* WS3 .... **16** C1
Eliot Cft *BILS/COS* WV14 .... **69** F1
Eliot St *VAUX/NECH* B7 .... **101** E5
Elizabeth Av *BILS/COS* WV14 .... **48** B6
 DARL/WED WS10 .... **51** E6
 ETTPK/GDPK/PENN WV4 .... **45** D4
Elizabeth Crs *LGLYGN/QTN* B68 ... **119** F5
Elizabeth Gv *DUDS* DY2 .... **92** B4
 SHLY B90 .... **193** E3
Elizabeth Ms *OLDBY* B69 .... **92** C3 ◫
Elizabeth Rd *DSYBK/YTR* WS5 .... **53** E2
 HALE B63 .... **140** B6
 MOS/BIL B13 .... **169** E1
 SCFLD/BOLD B73 .... **79** E2
 STETCH B33 .... **127** F4 ◫
 TPTN/OCK DY4 .... **93** F1
Elizabeth Wk *TPTN/OCK* DY4....... **70** C2
Elkington Cft *SHLY* B90 .... **210** B2
Elkington St *AST/WIT* B6 .... **124** A2
Elkstone Cl *HIA/OLT* B92 .... **153** D6
Elkstone Covert
 ALE/KHTH/YWD B14 .... **189** E3 ◫
Ellards Dr *WNSFLD* WV11 .... **28** B2
Ellen St *WSNGN* B18 .... **122** C3
Ellenvale Cl *BILS/COS* WV14 .... **68** C3
Ellerby Gv *ERDE/BCHGN* B24 ...... **104** A1
Ellerside Gv *NFLD/LBR* B31 .... **186** B3
Ellerslie Cl *BRLYHL* DY5 .... **137** F1 ◫

Ellerslie Rd *MOS/BIL* B13 .... 171 E4
Ellerton Rd *KGSTG* B44 .... 79 D2
Ellerton Wk *WOLVN* WV10 .... 26 B3
Ellesboro' Rd *HRBN* B17 .... 145 D1
Ellesmere Rd *WASH/WDE* B8 .... 125 F3
Ellice Dr *CBROM* B36 .... 107 D6
Elliot Gdns *RBRY* B45 .... 201 D2
Elliott Rd *SLYOAK* B29 .... 168 A1
Elliotts La *CDSL* WV8 .... 8 C2
Elliott's Rd *TPTN/OCK* DY4 .... 70 A6 🔲
Ellis Av *BRLYHL* DY5 .... 112 C5
Ellison St *WBROM* B70 .... 95 E4
Ellis St *CBHAMW* B1 .... 125 F6 🔲
Elliston Av *KGSTG* B44 .... 78 A3
Ellowes Rd *SEDG* DY3 .... 89 E1
Elm Av *BHTH/HG* B12 .... 148 C4 🔲
  BILS/COS WV14 .... 47 F3
  DARL/WED WS10 .... 50 B5
  WNSFLD WV11 .... 13 D5
Elmay Rd *LGN/SDN/BHAMAIR* B26 ..... 152 C2
Elm Bank *MOS/BIL* B13 .... 148 C6 🔲
Elmbank Gv *BFLD/HDSWWD* B20 .... 76 A6
Elmbank Rd *DSYBK/YTR* WS5 .... 53 E5 🔲
Elmbridge Cl *HALE* B63 .... 139 F4 🔲
Elmbridge Dr *SHLY* B90 .... 211 D1
Elmbridge Rd *KGSTG* B44 .... 78 A5
Elmbridge Wy *SEDG* DY3 .... 68 A5 🔲
Elm Cl *SEDG* DY3 .... 89 D3
Elm Cft *LGLYGN/QTN* B68 .... 143 E2
Elmcroft Av *RIDG/WDGT* B32 .... 164 C2
Elmcroft Gdns *WOLVN* WV10 .... 12 A2 🔲
Elmcroft Rd
  LGN/SDN/BHAMAIR B26 .... 152 B2
Elmdale *RMSLY* B62 .... 142 C2 🔲
Elmdale Crs *NFLD/LBR* B31 .... 186 A1
Elmdale Dr *ALDR* WS9 .... 21 E5
Elmdale Gv *NFLD/LBR* B31 .... 186 A1
Elmdale Rd *BILS/COS* WV14 .... 68 C4 🔲
Elm Dale Rd
  ETTPK/GDPK/PENN WV4 .... 44 C4
  WOLVN WV10 .... 10 C4
Elmdon Coppice *HIA/OLT* B92 .... 176 B4 🔲
Elmdon La *CHWD/FDBR/MGN* B37 .... 154 D2
  LGN/SDN/BHAMAIR B26 .... 154 C6
Elmdon Park Rd *HIA/OLT* B92 .... 175 F1
Elmdon Rd *ACGN* B27 .... 151 E5
  CHWD/FDBR/MGN B37 .... 154 C2
  SLYOAK B29 .... 168 C1
  WOLVN WV10 .... 10 C4
Elm Dr *GTB/HAM* B43 .... 75 F2
  RMSLY B62 .... 118 A6
Elm Farm Av
  CHWD/FDBR/MGN B37 .... 154 B2
Elm Farm Rd *BKHL/PFLD* WV2 .... 45 F2
Elmfield Av *ERDE/BCHGN* B24 .... 104 A1
Elmfield Crs *MOS/BIL* B13 .... 170 B1
Elmfield Rd *CBROM* B36 .... 106 A6
Elm Gn *DUDN* DY1 .... 68 C6
  CHWD/FDBR/MGN B37 .... 130 B1 🔲
Elm Gv *CDSL* WV8 .... 8 C2
Elmhurst Av *BLKHTH/ROWR* B65 ...... 117 F4
Elmhurst Dr *KGSWFD* DY6 .... 112 B3
Elmhurst Rd *HDSW* B21 .... 98 A4
Elmley Cl *DUDN* DY1 .... 69 D4 🔲
Elmley Gv *BVILLE* B30 .... 189 D2
  DUNHL/THL/PER WV6 .... 22 B4
Elmore Cl
  CHWD/FDBR/MGN B37 .... 130 C3 🔲
Elmore Green Cl *BLOX/PEL* WS3 .... 17 D5
Elmore Green Rd *BLOX/PEL* WS3 .... 16 C4
Elmore Rw *STETCH* B33 .... 128 C4
Elmore Rw *BLOX/PEL* WS3 .... 17 D4
Elm Rd *BDLY/PEL* WS3 .... 31 F1
  BVILLE B30 .... 168 B3
  DUDN DY1 .... 91 E2
  KGSWFD DY6 .... 112 A1
  WALM/CURD B76 .... 82 B1
Elms Cl *SOLH* B91 .... 175 F6
Elmsdale *DUNHL/THL/PER* WV6 .... 22 B5
Elms Rd *CSCFLD/WYGN* B72 .... 59 D6
Elmstead Av *STETCH* B33 .... 153 F2
Elmstead Cl *DSYBK/YTR* WS5 .... 34 A6
Elmstead Wd *DSYBK/YTR* WS5 .... 54 A1
Elm St *BDMR/CCFT* WV3 .... 24 C6
  WLNHL WV13 .... 29 D5
Elm Ter *OLDBY* B69 .... 92 C4
Elm Tree Cl *WMBN* WV5 .... 64 B6
Elm Tree Gv *HALE* B63 .... 139 F3
Elm Tree Ri *HIA/OLT* B92 .... 178 C5
Elm Tree Rd *BVILLE* B30 .... 168 C5
  HRBN B17 .... 144 C3
Elmtree Rd *FOAKS/STRLY* B74 .... 55 F1
Elm Tree Wy *CDYHTH* B64 .... 116 B6 🔲
Elmwood Av *WNSFLD* WV11 .... 14 C2
Elmwood Gdns
  BFLD/HDSWWD B20 .... 99 D3
Elmwood Gv *HLYWD* B47 .... 206 C1
Elmwood Ri *SEDG* DY3 .... 67 D2
Elmwood Rd *ERDE/BCHGN* B24 .... 103 D3 🔲
  FOAKS/STRLY B74 .... 56 C3
  STRBR DY8 .... 111 E4
Elmwoods *RIDG/WDGT* B32 .... 165 D1
Elphinstone End
  CSCFLD/WYGN B72 .... 81 E5 🔲

Elsma Rd *LGLYGN/QTN* B68 .... 143 E1
Elston Hall La *WOLVN* WV10 .... 11 F4
Elstree Rd *ERDW/GRVHL* B23 .... 79 F6
Elswick Gv *KGSTG* B44 .... 79 D3
Elswick Pl *KGSTG* B44 .... 79 D2
Elsworth Gv *YDLY* B25 .... 151 E3
Eltham Gv *KGSTG* B44 .... 79 D2
Elton Cl *WOLVN* WV10 .... 12 A1
Elton Cft *DOR/KN* B93 .... 212 B3
Elton Gv *ACGN* B27 .... 172 C1
Eltonia Cft
  LGN/SDN/BHAMAIR B26 .... 153 D3
Elva Cft *CBROM* B36 .... 106 B4
Elvetham Rd *EDG* B15 .... 147 E1 🔲
Environ Dr *DUNHL/THL/PER* WV6 ..... 23 D2
Elwells Cl *ETTPK/GDPK/PENN* WV4 .... 46 C5
Elwell St *DARL/WED* WS10 .... 51 D6
  WBROM B70 .... 72 A6
Elwyn Rd *SCFLD/BOLD* B73 .... 58 C6
Ely Cl *BLKHTH/ROWR* B65 .... 118 A3 🔲
  CHWD/FDBR/MGN B37 .... 131 D5
Ely Crs *HHTH/SAND* B71 .... 73 D5
Ely Gv *RIDG/WDGT* B32 .... 144 B5
Ely Pl *WSLW* WS2 .... 31 D6
Ely Rd *WSLW* WS2 .... 31 D6
Emay Cl *WBROM* B70 .... 72 B3 🔲
The Embankment *BRLYHL* DY5 .... 114 A4
Embassy Dr *EDG* B15 .... 147 D1 🔲
  OLDBY B69 .... 94 A5
Embassy Rd *OLDBY* B69 .... 94 A5 🔲
Embleton Gv *BKDE/SHDE* B34 .... 128 C1
Emerson Cl *SEDG* DY3 .... 88 C1 🔲
Emerson Gv *WOLVN* WV10 .... 12 B5
Emerson Rd *HRBN* B17 .... 145 E3
  WOLVN WV10 .... 12 B4
Emery Cl *ERDW/GRVHL* B23 .... 101 F4
  WSL WS1 .... 5 E6
Emery St *WSL* WS1 .... 5 E6
Emily Gdns *LDYWD/EDGR* B16 .... 122 B4 🔲
Emily Rd *LGN/SDN/BHAMAIR* B26 ... 151 F3
Emily St *BHTH/HG* B12 .... 148 B2 🔲
  WBROM B70 .... 95 D3
Emmanuel Rd *SCFLD/BOLD* B73 ...... 81 D4
Emmeline St *BORD* B9 .... 125 D6 🔲
Empire Cl *ALDR* WS9 .... 20 B5
Empress Wy *DARL/WED* WS10 .... 49 F1
Emscote Dr *SCFLD/BOLD* B73 .... 81 D4
Emscote Gn *SOLH* B91 .... 194 A3
Emscote Rd *AST/WIT* B6 .... 100 B4
Emsworth Crs *COVEN* WV9 .... 10 C3
Emsworth Gv
  ALE/KHTH/YWD B14 .... 169 F5 🔲
Enderby Dr
  ETTPK/GDPK/PENN WV4 .... 44 B5
Enderby Rd *ERDW/GRVHL* B23 .... 79 E3 🔲
  ERDW/GRVHL B23 .... 79 E4 🔲
Enderley Cl *BLOX/PEL* WS3 .... 17 D2 🔲
Enderley Dr *BLOX/PEL* WS3 .... 17 D2
Enderly Gv *WSNGN* B18 .... 122 A3 🔲
End Hall Rd *DUNHL/THL/PER* WV6 ... 22 C4
Endhill Rd *KGSTG* B44 .... 56 C6
Endicott Rd *AST/WIT* B6 .... 100 B4
Endmoor Gv *ERDW/GRVHL* B23 .... 79 F5
Endsleigh Gv *HLGN/YWD* B28 .... 172 C3 🔲
Endwood Court Rd
  BFLD/HDSWWD B20 .... 98 C3
Endwood Dr *FOAKS/STRLY* B74 .... 37 E3
  SOLH B91 .... 194 B3
Enfield Cl *ERDW/GRVHL* B23 .... 80 B5
Enfield Rd *BLKHTH/ROWR* B65 .... 117 F4
  EDG B15 .... 147 D1 🔲
Enford Cl *BKDE/SHDE* B34 .... 129 F1 🔲
Enfield Gv *DARL/WED* WS10 .... 50 B5
Enford Ct *FOAKS/STRLY* B74 .... 38 A3
Enstone Rd *DUDN* DY1 .... 90 B5 🔲
  ERDW/GRVHL B23 .... 80 C5
Enterprise Dr *HAG/WOL* DY9 .... 138 B3
Enterprise Wy *CBHAMNE* B4 .... 7 G1
Enville Cl *BLOX/PEL* WS3 .... 16 B2
Enville Gv *SPARK* B11 .... 149 F4
Enville Pl *STRBR* DY8 .... 136 B4 🔲
Enville Rd *ETTPK/GDPK/PENN* WV4 ... 43 E4
  KGSWFD DY6 .... 87 D5
  SEDG DY3 .... 89 F1

Enville St *STRBR* DY8 .... 136 B4
Epping Cl *BLOX/PEL* WS3 .... 32 B1
  RBRY B45 .... 185 D3
Epping Gv *KGSTG* B44 .... 78 C4
Epsom Cl *DUNHL/THL/PER* WV6 .... 22 B3
Epsom Gv *KGSTG* B44 .... 79 D3 🔲
Epsom Rd *BRGRVW* B61 .... 198 C6
Epwell Gv *KGSTG* B44 .... 78 B5
Epwell Rd *KGSTG* B44 .... 78 B5
Erasmus Rd *SPARK* B11 .... 148 C2
Ercall Cl *ERDW/GRVHL* B23 .... 78 C5
Erdington Hall Rd
  ERDE/BCHGN B24 .... 102 B3
Erdington Rd *ALDR* WS9 .... 35 D4
Erica Cl *SLYOAK* B29 .... 166 C3
Erica Rd *DSYBK/YTR* WS5 .... 53 D5
Ermington Crs *CBROM* B36 .... 104 A6
Ermington Rd
  ETTPK/GDPK/PENN WV4 .... 45 F4
Ernest Clarke Cl *SHHTH* WV12 .... 29 E3 🔲
Ernest Ct *HWK/WKHTH* B38 .... 188 C4
Ernest Rd *BHTH/HG* B12 .... 149 D5 🔲
  DUDS DY2 .... 92 B4
  SMTHWKW B67 .... 120 A1
Ernest St *CBHAMW* B1 .... 123 F6 🔲
Ernsford Cl *DOR/KN* B93 .... 212 B5
Erskine St *VAUX/NECH* B7 .... 125 D4
Esher Rd *HHTH/SAND* B71 .... 73 F5
  KGSTG B44 .... 56 B5
Eskdale Cl *WOLV* WV1 .... 26 C5 🔲
Eskdale Wk *BRLYHL* DY5 .... 137 D1 🔲
Esme Rd *SPARK* B11 .... 149 D5
Esmond Cl *BVILLE* B30 .... 167 F6
Essendon Rd *WASH/WDE* B8 .... 127 F1
Essex Av *DARL/WED* WS10 .... 51 E5
  HHTH/SAND B71 .... 73 E4
  KGSWFD DY6 .... 111 D2
Essex Gdns *STRBR* DY8 .... 135 F2 🔲
Essex Rd *DUDS* DY2 .... 114 B1
  MGN/WHC B75 .... 39 F6
Essex St *DIG/EDG* B5 .... 124 A6
  WSLW WS2 .... 31 F2
Essington Cl *STRBR* DY8 .... 136 A1 🔲
Essington St *SHHTH* WV12 .... 15 D4
Essington St *LDYWD/EDGR* B16 ...... 123 D6 🔲
Essington Wy *WOLV* WV1 .... 27 D6
Este Rd *LGN/SDN/BHAMAIR* B26 ..... 152 C1
Estria Rd *EDG* B15 .... 147 D2
Ethelfleda Ter *DARL/WED* WS10 .... 50 B6
Ethelred Cl *FOAKS/STRLY* B74 .... 38 C4
Ethel Rd *HRBN* B17 .... 145 F4
Ethel St *CBHAM* B2 .... 6 D5
  LGLYGN/QTN B68 .... 118 C3
  SMTHWKW B67 .... 120 B5
Etheridge Rd *BILS/COS* WV14 .... 47 F2
Eton Cl *SEDG* DY3 .... 68 B4
Eton Dr *STRBR* DY8 .... 136 C6
Eton Rd *BHTH/HG* B12 .... 149 D5
Eton Wk *HAG/WOL* DY9 .... 158 C5
Etruria Wy *BILS/COS* WV14 .... 48 A3
Etta Gv *KGSTG* B44 .... 56 A5
Ettingshall Park Farm La
  ETTPK/GDPK/PENN WV4 .... 45 F5
Ettingshall Rd *BILS/COS* WV14 .... 68 C2
  BKHL/PFLD WV2 .... 46 C2
Ettington Cl *DOR/KN* B93 .... 211 F5
Ettington Rd *AST/WIT* B6 .... 100 A5
Ettymore Cl *SEDG* DY3 .... 67 F3
Ettymore Rd *SEDG* DY3 .... 67 F3
Ettymore Rd West *SEDG* DY3 .... 67 E3
Etwall Rd *HLGN/YWD* B28 .... 172 A6
Euan Cl *HRBN* B17 .... 145 E1
Europa Av *WBROM* B70 .... 96 B3
Europa Wy
  LGN/SDN/BHAMAIR B26 .... 155 E5
Evans Cl *TPTN/OCK* DY4 .... 69 E6
Evans Pl *BILS/COS* WV14 .... 48 A2
Evans St *BILS/COS* WV14 .... 68 B2
  DUNHL/THL/PER WV6 .... 25 D3
  WLNHL WV13 .... 27 F6
Eva Rd *LGLYGN/QTN* B68 .... 119 E5
  WSNGN B18 .... 122 A1 🔲
Eve La *DUDN* DY1 .... 68 B6
Evelyn Cft *SCFLD/BOLD* B73 .... 80 C3
Evelyn Rd *SPARK* B11 .... 149 E5
Evenlode Gv *WLNHL* WV13 .... 29 F6
Evenlode Rd *HIA/OLT* B92 .... 152 C5
Everest Cl *SMTHWK* B66 .... 96 A5
Everest Rd *BFLD/HDSWWD* B20 .... 98 C2
  WSLW WS2 .... 30 B3 🔲
Evergreen Cl *BILS/COS* WV14 .... 69 D3
Everitt Dr *DOR/KN* B93 .... 212 C1
Eversley Dl *ERDE/BCHGN* B24 .... 102 C3
Eversley Gv *SEDG* DY3 .... 67 E1
  WNSFLD WV11 .... 27 E1
Eversley Rd *BORD* B9 .... 125 F6 🔲
Evers St *BRLYHL* DY5 .... 138 C1
Everton Rd *WASH/WDE* B8 .... 127 E3 🔲
Eves Cft *RIDG/WDGT* B32 .... 165 E2
Evesham Cars *BLOX/PEL* WS3 .... 16 B2
Evesham Ri *DUDS* DY2 .... 115 F4
Ewart Rd *WSLW* WS2 .... 30 A4
Ewell Rd *ERDE/BCHGN* B24 .... 103 D1
Ewhurst Av *SLYOAK* B29 .... 168 B2 🔲
Ewhurst Cl *WLNHL* WV13 .... 48 B1 🔲

Exbury Cl COVEN WV9 .... 10 B3 🆔
Exchange St BRLYHL DY5 .... 113 F3 🆔
The Exchange BLOX/PEL WS3 ...... 17 D4 🆔
Exe Cft NFLD/LBR B31 .... 187 D5
Exeter Dr CHWD/FDBR/MGN B37 ... 154 B1 🆔
Exeter Pas CBHAMW B1 .... 123 F6 🆔
Exeter Pl WSLW WS2 .... 31 D6
Exeter Rd DUDS DY2 .... 115 F5
   SLYOAK B29 .... 168 B1
   SMTHWK B66 .... 121 D2
Exford Cl BRLYHL DY5 .... 137 D2
Exhall Cl SOLH B91 .... 194 A3
Exhibition Wy BHAMNEC B40 .... 155 F5
Exmoor Gn WNSFLD WV11 .... 13 G6
The Expressway WBROM B70 .... 95 E3
Exton Cl WNSFLD WV11 .... 14 B5
Exton Wy WASH/WDE B8 .... 125 F2
Eyland Gv WSL WS1 .... 5 E3
Eymore Cl SLYOAK B29 .... 167 G6
Eyre St WSNGN B18 .... 122 C4
Eyston Av TPTN/OCK DY4 .... 71 G3
Eyton Cft BHTH/HG B12 .... 148 B2 🆔
Ezekiel La SHHTH WV12 .... 29 E1

F

Fabian Cl RBRY B45 .... 184 B3
Fabian Crs SHLY B90 .... 193 D4
Facet Rd HWK/WKHTH B38 .... 188 C3
Factory Rd TPTN/OCK DY4 .... 70 A5
   WSNGN B18 .... 122 B1
Factory St DARL/WED WS10 .... 49 E3
Fairbourne Av
   BLKHTH/ROWR B65 .... 118 A3
   KGSTG B44 .... 78 A1
Faircroft Av WALM/CURD B76 ...... 82 B5
Faircroft Rd BDMR B36 .... 105 F4
Fairfax Rd MGN/WHC B75 .... 60 D1
   NFLD/LBR B31 .... 186 C5
   WOLVN WV10 .... 11 F2
Fairfield Dr BLOX/PEL WS3 .... 19 D1
   CDSL WV8 .... 8 A2
   RMSLY B62 .... 118 A6
Fairfield Gv RMSLY B62 .... 118 A6 🆔
Fairfield Mt WSL WS1 .... 52 B1
Fairfield Ri STRBR DY8 .... 135 E4
Fairford Gdns STRBR DY8 .... 112 A4 🆔
Fairford Rd KGSTG B44 .... 78 B5
Fairgreen Gdns BRLYHL DY5 .... 113 E2 🆔
Fairgreen Wy FOAKS/STRLY B74 ... 36 C6
   SLYOAK B29 .... 168 B2 🆔
Fairground Wy WSL WS1 .... 4 B6
Fairhaven Cft RMSLY B62 .... 118 A6 🆔
Fairhills SEDG DY3 .... 67 G3
Fairholme Rd CBROM B36 .... 103 D6
Fairlawn Cl SHHTH WV12 .... 15 E4
Fairlawn Dr KGSWFD DY6 .... 117 F3
Fairlawns LGN/SDN/BHAMAIR B26 . 128 C6
   WALM/CURD B76 .... 82 C5 🆔
Fairlie Crs HWK/WKHTH B38 .... 187 F4
Fairlight Dr RBRY B45 .... 200 C6
Fairmead Ri HWK/WKHTH B38 ..... 188 A4
Fairmile Rd HALE B63 .... 164 B1
Fairoak Dr DUNHL/THL/PER WV6 .. 22 C4
Fairview Av PBAR/PBCH B42 .... 77 D5
Fairview Cl WNSFLD WV11 .... 13 D6 🆔
Fairview Crs KGSWFD DY6 .... 112 B1
   WNSFLD WV11 .... 13 D6
Fairview Gv WNSFLD WV11 .... 13 D6
Fairview Rd DUDN DY1 .... 90 C3
   ETTPK/GDPK/PENN WV4 .... 43 E5
   WNSFLD WV11 .... 13 D6
Fairway NFLD/LBR B31 .... 186 A3
   RUSH/SHEL WS4 .... 19 F4
Fairway Av OLDBY B69 .... 92 C5
Fairway Dr RBRY B45 .... 200 B1
Fairway Gn BILS/COS WV14 .... 47 E2
Fairway Rd LGLYGN/QTN B68 ...... 118 B6
Fairways Av STRBR DY8 .... 158 A1
Fairways Cl STRBR DY8 .... 158 A1
Fairways Dr BRGRVE B60 .... 214 C4
The Fairway HWK/WKHTH B38 ..... 187 F3
Fairyfield Av GTB/HAM B43 .... 75 D2
Fakenham Cft HRBN B17 .... 144 B2 🆔
Falcon Crs BILS/COS WV14 .... 68 B1
Falcondale Rd SHHTH WV12 .... 15 E4
Falconhurst Rd SLYOAK B29 .... 167 E1
Falcon Lodge Crs MGN/WHC B75 . 60 C4
Falcon Pl OLDBY B69 .... 93 E6 🆔
Falcon Ri STRBR DY8 .... 135 E3 🆔
Falcon Rd LGLYGN/QTN B68 .... 90 B4
The Falcons MGN/WHC B75 .... 61 D4 🆔
Falcon Wy DUDN DY1 .... 90 A4
Falfield Cl OLDBY B69 .... 117 F1 🆔
Falfield Gv NFLD/LBR B31 .... 186 A6
Falkland Cft BVILLE B30 .... 169 D5
Falklands Cl SEDG DY3 .... 86 A3

Falkland Wy CBROM B36 .... 131 D2
Falkwood Gv DOR/KN B93 .... 212 B1
Fallindale Rd
   LGN/SDN/BHAMAIR B26 .... 153 D3
Fallings Heath Cl DARL/WED WS10 . 50 B2
Fallowfield CDSL WV8 .... 10 A3
Fallow Fld FOAKS/STRLY B74 ...... 37 D4
Fallowfield Av HLGN/YWD B28 ..... 172 B6
Fallow Field Rd
   BLKHTH/ROWR B65 .... 116 C4
Fallowfield Rd DSYBK/YTR WS5 ... 54 A1
   HALE B63 .... 139 F6
   HIA/OLT B92 .... 175 D5
Fallows Rd SPARK B11 .... 149 E3
Fallow Wk RIDG/WDGT B32 .... 164 C1
Falmouth Rd BKDE/SHDE B34 ..... 128 A3
   DSYBK/YTR WS5 .... 53 F2
Falstaff Av HLYWD B47 .... 206 C1
Falstaff Cl WALM/CURD B76 .... 82 C4
Falstaff Rd SHLY B90 .... 193 E5
Falstone Rd SCFLD/BOLD B73 ..... 79 F1
Fancott Rd NFLD/LBR B31 .... 166 C6
Fancourt Av
   ETTPK/GDPK/PENN WV4 .... 43 F4
Fane Rd WNSFLD WV11 .... 14 C2
Fanshawe Rd ACGN B27 .... 173 E2
Faraday Av RIDG/WDGT B32 .... 143 F4
   WALM/CURD B76 .... 108 C1
Faraday Rd WSLW WS2 .... 31 D1
Farbrook Wy SHHTH WV12 .... 29 D1
Farcroft Av HDSW B21 .... 97 F5
Farcroft Gv HDSW B21 .... 97 F5
Farcroft Rd HDSW B21 .... 97 F5
Fardon Wy ERDW/GRVHL B23 ..... 79 F3
Fareham Crs
   ETTPK/GDPK/PENN WV4 .... 43 E3
Farfield Cl NFLD/LBR B31 .... 187 D3
Far Highfield WALM/CURD B76 .... 59 F5
Far Hill Cl HHTH/SAND B71 .... 74 B3
Farlands Dr STRBR DY8 .... 136 C6 🆔
Farlands Gv GTB/HAM B43 .... 76 B4
Farlands Rd STRBR DY8 .... 136 C6
Farleigh Dr BDMR/CCFT WV3 ..... 42 C1
Farleigh Rd DUNHL/THL/PER WV6 . 22 C4
Farley La HAG/WOL DY9 .... 182 A5
Farley Rd ERDW/GRVHL B23 .... 101 D1
Farley St TPTN/OCK DY4 .... 71 F6
Farlow Cft
   CHWD/FDBR/MGN B37 .... 154 B2 🆔
Farlow Rd NFLD/LBR B31 .... 187 E2
Farmacre BORD B9 .... 125 D5 🆔
Farm Cl LGLYGN/QTN B68 .... 118 C4
Farmbridge Cl WSLW WS2 .... 29 F4 🆔
Farmbridge Rd WSLW WS2 .... 29 F4 🆔
Farmbrook Av WOLVN WV10 ...... 11 F2
Farm Cl CDSL WV8 .... 9 D3
   HIA/OLT B92 .... 175 D1
   SEDG DY3 .... 67 D4
   STECH B33 .... 128 B4
Farmcote Rd STECH B33 .... 128 C3 🆔
Farm Cft LOZ/NWT B19 .... 123 E1
Farmcroft Rd HAG/WOL DY9 ...... 160 A1
Farmdale Gv RBRY B45 .... 200 C1
Farmer Rd SMHTH B10 .... 150 C2
Farmers Cl WALM/CURD B76 ...... 60 A5 🆔
Farmers Fold HALE B63 .... 140 B5 🆔
Farmer Wy TPTN/OCK DY4 .... 71 D2
Farmhouse Rd SHHTH WV12 ...... 29 F2
Farm House Wy GTB/HAM B43 .... 54 A5
Farmhouse Wy SHLY B90 .... 211 D1
Farmoor Gv BKDE/SHDE B34 ...... 130 A1
Farmoor Wy WOLVN WV10 .... 12 A1 🆔
Farm Rd BDMR/CCFT WV3 .... 43 E1
   BLKHTH/ROWR B65 .... 116 C3
   BRLYHL DY5 .... 114 A6
   DUDS DY2 .... 114 C3
   LGLYGN/QTN B68 .... 118 C4
   SMTHWKW B67 .... 120 A4
   SPARK B11 .... 149 D3
   TPTN/OCK DY4 .... 71 D4
Farmside Gn COVEN WV9 .... 10 B3 🆔
Farmstead Cl WSL WS1 .... 52 A4 🆔
Farmstead Rd HIA/OLT B92 .... 175 E1
Farm St LOZ/NWT B19 .... 123 E1
   WBROM B70 .... 95 E4
   WSLW WS2 .... 32 A3 🆔
Farnborough Ct MGN/WHC B75 .. 39 E5 🆔
Farnborough Dr SHLY B90 .... 210 B1
Farnborough Rd CVALE B35 .... 104 C3
Fanbury Cft HWK/WKHTH B38 .... 189 D3 🆔
Farncote Dr FOAKS/STRLY B74 .... 38 A3
Farndale Av DUNHL/THL/PER WV6 . 24 C2
Farndale Cl BRLYHL DY5 .... 137 D5
Farndon Av
   CHWD/FDBR/MGN B37 .... 155 D2
Farndon Rd WASH/WDE B8 .... 126 B2
Farnham Cl GTB/HAM B43 .... 76 B3
Farnham Rd HDSW B21 .... 97 F3
Farnhurst Rd CBROM B36 .... 103 D6
Farnol Rd LGN/SDN/BHAMAIR B26 . 152 B3
Farnworth Gv CBROM B36 .... 106 A4
Farquhar Rd EDG B15 .... 122 B6
   MOS/BIL B13 .... 148 B6 🆔
Farquhar Rd East EDG B15 .... 146 B3
Farren Rd NFLD/LBR B31 .... 185 F4

Farrier Cl WALM/CURD B76 .... 82 B3 🆔
Farrier Rd GTB/HAM B43 .... 55 F6
Farriers Ml BLOX/PEL WS3 .... 18 A1
The Farriers
   LGN/SDN/BHAMAIR B26 .... 153 D4
Farrier Wy KGSWFD DY6 .... 86 C6
Farringdon St WSLW WS2 .... 4 A2
Farrington Rd ERDW/GRVHL B23 . 79 D6
   ETTPK/GDPK/PENN WV4 .... 68 A1
Farrow Rd KGSTG B44 .... 56 A6
Farthing La CSCFLD/WYGN B72 ... 59 D5
   WALM/CURD B76 .... 85 E5
Farthing Pools Cl
   CSCFLD/WYGN B72 .... 59 E5 🆔
Farvale Rd WALM/CURD B76 .... 83 E5
Farway Gdns CDSL WV8 .... 8 B3
Far Wood Rd NFLD/LBR B31 .... 166 A3
Fashoda Rd SLYOAK B29 .... 169 D2
Fastlea Rd RIDG/WDGT B32 .... 165 F2
Fastmoor Ov STECH B33 .... 130 A6
Fast Pits Rd YDLY B25 .... 151 D1
Fatherless Barn Crs HALE B63 .... 139 E4 🆔
Faulkland Crs WOLV WV1 .... 3 E2 🆔
Faulkner Cl STRBR DY8 .... 136 B5 🆔
Faulkner Rd HIA/OLT B92 .... 175 D2
Faulkners Farm Dr
   ERDW/GRVHL B23 .... 79 D5
Faulknor Dr BRLYHL DY5 .... 89 D3
Faversham Cl CDSL WV8 .... 10 A5 🆔
   WSLW WS2 .... 29 F4 🆔
Fawdry Cl SCFLD/BOLD B73 .... 59 D4 🆔
Fawdry St DIG/EDG B5 .... 124 C5 🆔
   SMTHWK B66 .... 121 E2 🆔
   WOLV WV1 .... 2 B1
Fawley Cl WLNHL WV13 .... 48 B1
Fawley Gv ALE/KHTH/YWD B14 ... 169 D6
Fazeley St DIG/EDG B5 .... 7 G5
Featherston Cl SHLY B90 .... 193 F3 🆔
Featherstone Crs SHLY B90 .... 193 F4
Featherstone Rd
   ALE/KHTH/YWD B14 .... 170 A5
   FOAKS/STRLY B74 .... 36 C5
Felbrigg Cl BRLYHL DY5 .... 137 F1 🆔
The Feldings ERDE/BCHGN B24 ... 103 E1
Feldon La RMSLY B62 .... 142 A2
Felgate Cl SHLY B90 .... 210 C1
Fellbrook Cl STECH B33 .... 128 B3
Fell Gv HDSW B21 .... 97 E4
Fellmeadow Rd STECH B33 .... 128 C5
Fellmeadow Wy SEDG DY3 .... 68 A4 🆔
Fellows Av KGSWFD DY6 .... 87 E5
Fellows La HRBN B17 .... 144 C3
Fellows Rd BILS/COS WV14 .... 47 F2
Fellows St BKHL/PFLD WV2 .... 45 E1
Felsted Wy VAUX/NECH B7 .... 124 C3
Felstone Rd KGSTG B44 .... 78 A2
Feltham Cl STECH B33 .... 130 A6
Felton Cft STECH B33 .... 128 C4 🆔
Felton Gv SOLH B91 .... 195 D4
Fenbourne Cl RUSH/SHEL WS4 ... 19 E5
Fenchurch Cl WSLW WS2 .... 31 F1
Fencote Av
   CHWD/FDBR/MGN B37 .... 130 C3
Fenmere Cl
   ETTPK/GDPK/PENN WV4 .... 45 F4
Fennel Cl BKDE/SHDE B34 .... 105 D6
Fennel Rd BRLYHL DY5 .... 137 E2
Fennis Cl DOR/KN B93 .... 212 B4
Fenn Ri SHHTH WV12 .... 29 D1
   STRBR DY8 .... 111 E4
Fens Crs BRLYHL DY5 .... 113 E2
Fens Pool Av BRLYHL DY5 .... 113 E2 🆔
The Fensway BKDE/SHDE B34 ..... 128 C2 🆔
Fenter Cl MOS/BIL B13 .... 148 B4 🆔
Fentham Cl HIA/OLT B92 .... 179 D5
Fentham Ct HIA/OLT B92 .... 174 B2
Fentham Gn HIA/OLT B92 .... 178 C4 🆔
Fentham Rd AST/WIT B6 .... 99 F5
   ERDW/GRVHL B23 .... 101 F2
   HIA/OLT B92 .... 178 C4
Fenton Rd ACGN B27 .... 151 D5
   HLYWD B47 .... 190 C6
Fenton St BRLYHL DY5 .... 113 F4
   SMTHWK B66 .... 96 A6
Fenton Wy ACGN B27 .... 151 D5
Fereday Rd ALDR WS9 .... 21 D2
Fereday's Cft SEDG DY3 .... 67 F4
Fereday St TPTN/OCK DY4 .... 70 B3
Ferguson Rd LGLYGN/QTN B68 ... 119 F2
Ferguson St WNSFLD WV11 .... 14 C4
Fern Av TPTN/OCK DY4 .... 70 B4
Fernbank Cl HALE B63 .... 161 F1
Fernbank Crs DSYBK/YTR WS5 .... 53 F5
Fernbank Rd WASH/WDE B8 .... 126 C3
Ferncliffe Rd HRBN B17 .... 145 E3
Fern Cl BILS/COS WV14 .... 69 D3
   RUSH/SHEL WS4 .... 19 E5
Ferndale Av GTB/HAM B43 .... 76 B4
Ferndale Cl BRGRVW B61 .... 198 C6
   HAG/WOL DY9 .... 158 C6 🆔
Ferndale Ct CSHL/WTROR B46 .... 132 C2 🆔
Ferndale Ms CSHL/WTROR B46 ... 132 C2 🆔
Ferndale Pk HAG/WOL DY9 .... 159 E3
Ferndale Rd CSHL/WTROR B46 ... 132 C2 🆔
   FOAKS/STRLY B74 .... 56 B1

HLGN/YWD B28	**172** B3
LGLYGN/QTN D68	**118** C5
WNSFLD WV11	**15** D2
Ferndene Rd SPARK B11	**150** B6
Ferndown Av SEDG DY3	**67** E4
Ferndown CI BLOX/PEL WS3	**17** D1
LGN/SDN/BHAMAIR B26	**128** C6
Ferndown Gdns WNSFLD WV11	**28** B2
Ferndown Rd SOLH B91	**175** D5
Fernhill Gv KGSTG B44	**56** B6
Fernhill Rd HIA/OLT B92	**174** A1
Fernhurst Dr BRLYHL DY5	**89** D6
Fernhurst Rd WASH/WDE B8	**126** C4
Fernleigh Gdns STRBR DY8	**111** E4
Fernleigh Rd RUSH/SHEL WS4	**33** D4
Fernley Rd SPARK B11	**149** E5
Fern Leys BDMR/CCFT WV3	**23** F6
Fern Rd BDMR/CCFT WV3	**45** D1 [2]
DUDN DY1	**91** E1
ERDE/BCHGN B24	**102** C1
Fernside Gdns SPARK B11	**149** D6 [2]
Fernwood CI SCFLD/BOLD B73	**80** A2
Fernwood Cft	
ALE/KHTH/YWD B14	**170** A5
TPTN/OCK DY4	**92** B1 [2]
Fernwood Rd SCFLD/BOLD B73	**80** A3
Fernwoods RIDG/WDGT B32	**165** D1 [3]
Ferrers CI MGN/WHC B75	**39** F5
Ferris Gv ACGN B27	**172** C2 [2]
Festival Av DARL/WED WS10	**49** E5
Festival Wy DUNHL/THL/PER WV6	**25** D2
Ffernfail Ct ERDW/GRVHL B23	**80** A6 [2]
Fibbersley WLNHL WV13	**28** B3
WNSFLD WV11	**28** B3
Fibbersley Bank WLNHL WV13	**28** B3 [3]
Fiddlers CI HIA/OLT B92	**178** C4
Field CI BLOX/PEL WS3	**17** E5
BLOX/PEL WS3	**19** D3
LGN/SDN/BHAMAIR B26	**152** C3
STRBR DY8	**112** C5
Field Cottage Dr STRBR DY8	**137** D6 [2]
Fieldfare CI BLKHTH/ROWR B65	**116** B3
Fieldfare Cft CBROM B36	**106** C3
Fieldfare Rd HAG/WOL DY9	**137** F5
Field Head PI	
DUNHL/THL/PER WV6	**23** D3
Fieldhead Rd SPARK B11	**150** C6 [1]
Fieldhouse La RMSLY B62	**182** A1
Fieldhouse Rd	
ETTPK/GDPK/PENN WV4	**46** A5
YDLY B25	**151** E1
Field La RIDG/WDGT B32	**164** C3
RUSH/SHEL WS4	**19** D3
SOLH B91	**176** C6
STRBR DY8	**136** C6
Field Ms DUDS DY2	**116** A5 [2]
Fieldon CI SHLY B90	**193** E2
Field Rd BLOX/PEL WS3	**17** D2
DUDS DY2	**92** A4 [1]
TPTN/OCK DY4	**70** B3
Field St BILS/COS WV14	**48** A6
WLNHL WV13	**28** C5
WOLVN WV10	**26** A1
Fieldview CI BILS/COS WV14	**69** F1
Field View Dr BLKHTH/ROWR B65	**118** B5
Fieldways HLYWD B47	**190** C6 [2]
Fiery Hill Rd RBRY B45	**215** E1
Fifield Gv STETCH B33	**128** B4
Fifth Av BORD B9	**126** B5
WOLVN WV10	**11** F6
Filey Rd WOLVN WV10	**11** D3
Fillingham CI	
CHWD/FDBR/MGN B37	**131** F6
Filton Cft CVALE B35	**104** C1
Fimbrell CI STRBR DY8	**136** C1 [2]
Finbury CI HIA/OLT B92	**174** B2 [2]
Finchall Cft HIA/OLT B92	**176** A4 [2]
Fincham CI COVEN WV9	**10** C2 [3]
Finch CI BLKHTH/ROWR B65	**116** B3
Finchdene Gv BDMR/CCFT WV3	**23** F6
Finch Dr FOAKS/STRLY B74	**56** C4
Finches End BRDE/SHDE B34	**129** E2
Finchfield CI STRBR DY8	**135** E5
Finchfield Gdns BDMR/CCFT WV3	**24** A6
Finchfield HI BDMR/CCFT WV3	**23** F5
Finchfield La BDMR/CCFT WV3	**43** E1
Finchfield Rd BDMR/CCFT WV3	**24** A6
Finchfield Rd West	
BDMR/CCFT WV3	**23** E6
Finchley CI SEDG DY3	**89** F3 [1]
Finchley Rd KGSTG B44	**79** D1
Finchmead Rd STETCH B33	**130** A5
Finchpath Rd WBROM B70	**72** C5 [3]
Finch Rd LOZ/NWT B19	**99** E5
Findlay Rd ALE/KHTH/YWD B14	**170** A2
Findon Rd WASH/WDE B8	**127** D1
Finlarigg Dr EDG B15	**146** B3
Finmere Rd HLGN/YWD B28	**172** B3
Finnemore Rd BORD B9	**126** C5
Finney Well CI BILS/COS WV14	**47** D6
Finnsbury Dr BRLYHL DY5	**137** E2 [2]
Finsbury Gv ERDW/GRVHL B23	**79** F5
Finstall CI CSCFLD/WYGN B72	**81** E2
VAUX/NECH B7	**124** C3
Finwood CI HIA/OLT B92	**176** A3
Fir Av BHTH/HG B12	**148** C4 [2]
Firbank CI BVILLE B30	**168** A4
Firbank Wy BLOX/PEL WS3	**18** B3
Firbarn CI WALM/CURD B76	**59** F6
Firbeck Gv KGSTG B44	**78** C2 [2]
Firbeck Rd KGSTG B44	**78** C2
Fir Cft BRLYHL DY5	**137** E1 [2]
Fircroft BILS/COS WV14	**48** C6
NFLD/LBR B31	**166** B3 [2]
SOLH B91	**174** B5
Firecrest CI ERDW/GRVHL B23	**79** D4 [2]
Fir Gv ALE/KHTH/YWD B14	**170** B6
BDMR/CCFT WV3	**24** C6
STRBR DY8	**135** E3
Firhill Cft ALE/KHTH/YWD B14	**189** F3
Firmstone St STRBR DY8	**136** A2
Firsbrook CI	
DUNHL/THL/PER WV6	**24** C3 [2]
Firs Dr SHLY B90	**192** C4
Firs Farm Dr CBROM B36	**104** B6 [3]
Firsholm CI SCFLD/BOLD B73	**80** C4 [3]
Firs La SMTHWKW B67	**120** C2
Firs Rd KGSWFD DY6	**112** A1
Firs St DUDS DY2	**91** F4
First Av BORD B9	**126** A6 [1]
KGSWFD DY6	**88** C5
SLYOAK B29	**147** D6
WALM/CURD B76	**82** C6
WOLVN WV10	**12** A6
WOLVN WV10	**26** A1
First Exhibition Av	
BHAMNEC B40	**155** F5 [1]
The Firs SPARK B11	**149** E3
First Meadow Piece	
RIDG/WDGT B32	**144** A5 [3]
Fir St SEDG DY3	**66** B4
Firsvale Rd WNSFLD WV11	**28** B2
Firsway DUNHL/THL/PER WV6	**23** F2
Firswood Rd STETCH B33	**129** E6
Firth Dr ALE/KHTH/YWD B14	**171** D6
RMSLY B62	**142** A1
Firth Park Crs RMSLY B62	**142** A1
Fir Tree CI KGSTG B44	**78** A4
Fir Tree Dr DSYBK/YTR WS5	**53** D5
SEDG DY3	**68** A4
Fir Tree Gv SCFLD/BOLD B73	**80** B2 [1]
Fir Tree Rd BDMR/CCFT WV3	**43** F2
Firtree Rd ERDE/BCHGN B24	**103** D3
Fisher Rd BLOX/PEL WS3	**16** B3
OLDBY B69	**95** E6
Fishers Dr SHLY B90	**208** B3
Fisher St BDMR/CCFT WV3	**45** D1
BRLYHL DY5	**113** D4
DUDS DY2	**91** F4
TPTN/OCK DY4	**71** F6
TPTN/OCK DY4	**92** C2
WLNHL WV13	**29** E5
Fishley CI BLOX/PEL WS3	**17** E1
Fishley La BLOX/PEL WS3	**17** E1
Fishpool CI CBROM B36	**103** E5
Fishpool La RCOVN/BALC/EX CV7	**157** D3
Fitters Mill CI DIG/EDG B5	**148** A3 [2]
Fitton Av KGSWFD DY6	**112** C2
Fitzgerald PI BRLYHL DY5	**137** D3 [3]
Fitzguy CI WBROM B70	**96** A4
Fitzmaurice Rd WNSFLD WV11	**14** B6
Fitz Roy Av HRBN B17	**144** B2
Fitzroy Rd NFLD/LBR B31	**185** E2
Five Fields Rd SHHTH WV12	**28** C2
Five Oaks Rd WLNHL WV13	**48** A1
Five Ways LDYWD/EDGR B16	**123** D6
Flackwell Rd ERDW/GRVHL B23	**80** A3 [2]
Fladbury CI DUDS DY2	**115** F4
Fladbury Crs SLYOAK B29	**167** F1
Flamborough CI BKDE/SHDE B34	**104** C6
Flamborough Wy DUDN DY1	**69** D3 [4]
Flanders Dr KGSWFD DY6	**87** F5 [3]
Flash La WMBN WV5	**64** A1
Flash Rd OLDBY B69	**96** A1
The Flatts DARL/WED WS10	**50** A4
Flavel Av BILS/COS WV14	**69** F2
Flavell CI RIDG/WDGT B32	**165** D2 [2]
Flavells La SEDG DY3	**89** D3
YDLY B25	**151** E1
Flavell St DUDN DY1	**69** D5
Flax CI HLYWD B47	**206** C2
Flax Gdns HWK/WKHTH B38	**188** B5
Flaxhall St WSLW WS2	**51** D1
Flaxley Rd STETCH B33	**128** A4
Flaxton Gv STETCH B33	**128** C3
Flecknoe CI CBROM B36	**105** D4
Fledburgh Dr WALM/CURD B76	**59** F6
Fleet St CBHAMNW B3	**6** D3
Fleetwood Gv	
LGN/SDN/BHAMAIR B26	**128** C6 [1]
Fleming PI WSLW WS2	**30** C1
Fleming Rd RIDG/WDGT B32	**143** F4
WSLW WS2	**30** C1
Flemmynge Ct CDSL WV8	**8** A1 [3]
Fletcher Gv DOR/KN B93	**213** D3 [2]
Fletcher Rd SHHTH WV12	**15** F4
Fletcher's La WLNHL WV13	**29** E5
Fletcher St HAG/WOL DY9	**138** B4
Fletton Gv ALE/KHTH/YWD B14	**190** C2 [2]
Flinkford CI DSYBK/YTR WS5	**53** E3
Flint Green Rd ACGN B27	**151** D6
Flintham CI ACGN B27	**152** A6
The Flintway STETCH B33	**128** A3
Floodgate St DIG/EDG B5	**124** B6
Flood St DUDS DY2	**91** F4
Flora Rd YDLY B25	**151** D2
Florence Av	
ETTPK/GDPK/PENN WV4	**46** B5
SPARK B11	**149** D3 [3]
Florence Gv HHTH/SAND B71	**74** A2
Florence Rd ACGN B27	**151** F5
ALE/KHTH/YWD B14	**170** B3 [1]
CDSL WV8	**9** E2
ERDW/GRVHL B23	**81** D4
HDSW B21	**97** F5 [1]
OLDBY B69	**93** F6
SMTHWK B66	**121** D3
TPTN/OCK DY4	**70** C4
WBROM B70	**96** A4
Florence St CBHAMWG B1	**123** F6
WSL WS1	**5** G5
Florian Gv DARL/WED WS10	**50** A2
Florida Wy KGSWFD DY6	**112** C2 [3]
Flowerdale CI BILS/COS WV14	**69** D3 [3]
Floyds La RUSH/SHEL WS4	**33** E1
Floyer Rd SMTH B10	**126** A6
Flyford Cft SLYOAK B29	**166** B1 [3]
Foden Rd PBAR/PBCH B42	**76** C3
Foinavon CI BLKHTH/ROWR B65	**116** B1
Fold St WOLV WV1	**2** C5
The Fold DARL/WED WS10	**49** F3 [3]
ETTPK/GDPK/PENN WV4	**44** B5
Foldyard CI WALM/CURD B76	**82** C3
Foley Av DUNHL/THL/PER WV6	**23** D4
Foley Church CI FOAKS/STRLY B74	**36** C5
Foley Dr DUNHL/THL/PER WV6	**23** E4
Foley Gv WMBN WV5	**64** A6
Foley Rd HAG/WOL DY9	**159** D1 [3]
WASH/WDE D8	**127** D1
Foley Rd East FOAKS/STRLY B74	**36** B6
Foley Rd West FOAKS/STRLY B74	**35** F6
Foley St DARL/WED WS10	**50** C6
Foley Wood CI FOAKS/STRLY B74	**36** A6
Foliot Flds YDLY B25	**151** F1
Folkes Rd HAG/WOL DY9	**138** C2
Folkestone Cft CBROM B36	**104** A5
Folliott Rd STETCH B33	**128** C4
Follyhouse CI WSL WS1	**52** B2 [3]
Follyhouse La WSL WS1	**52** B2 [3]
Fontley CI	
LGN/SDN/BHAMAIR B26	**128** C6 [2]
Fontwell Rd WOLVN WV10	**11** F1
Fordbridge Rd	
CHWD/FDBR/MGN B37	**130** B3
Ford Brook La BLOX/PEL WS3	**19** D4
Forder Gv ALE/KHTH/YWD B14	**190** C3
Forde Way Gdns	
HWK/WKHTH B38	**187** F6
Fordfield Rd STETCH B33	**129** E3
Fordham Gv COVEN WV9	**10** C2
Fordhouse La BVILLE B30	**169** D5
Fordhouse Rd WOLVN WV10	**11** F5
Fordraught La RMSLY B62	**183** D4
The Fordrift	
CHWD/FDBR/MGN B37	**154** C4
Fordrough YDLY B25	**150** B2
Fordrough La WASH/WDE B8	**126** A4
The Fordrough FOAKS/STRLY B74	**38** C6
NFLD/LBR B31	**187** D4
SHLY B90	**191** E6
Fords Rd SHLY B90	**192** A6
Ford St SMTHWKW B67	**120** B1
WSLW WS2	**51** E2
WSNGN B18	**123** D2
Fordwater Rd FOAKS/STRLY B74	**56** B3
Foredraft CI RIDG/WDGT B32	**165** E1 [3]
Foredraft St HALE B63	**139** F4
Foredrove La HIA/OLT B92	**176** A5
Forest Av BLOX/PEL WS3	**17** F6
Forest CI FOAKS/STRLY B74	**56** A2
SMTHWK B66	**96** A5
Forest DI RBRY B45	**201** D1
Forest Dr CDYHTH B64	**116** A5
HRBN B17	**121** E3
Forest Ga SHHTH WV12	**15** F5 [1]
Forest Hill Rd	
LGN/SDN/BHAMAIR B26	**153** E4
Forest La BLOX/PEL WS3	**32** A2
Forest Pk WALM/CURD B76	**60** C5
Forest PI BLOX/PEL WS3	**32** A1
Fore St CBHAM B2	**7** E5
Forest Rd DOR/KN B93	**212** C4 [3]
DUDN DY1	**91** E1
LGLYGN/QTN D68	**143** E2
MOS/BIL B13	**148** C6
YDLY B25	**151** E3
Forest Wy HLYWD B47	**207** D1
Forge CI CDSL WV8	**10** A4
Forge Cft WALM/CURD B76	**83** D5
Forge La ALDR WS9	**36** B1
CDYHTH B64	**139** D1
FOAKS/STRLY B74	**37** E1
HHTH/SAND B71	**74** C5

KGSWFD DY6 .... 86 C5
RMSLY B62 .... 141 E4
WALM/CURD B76 .... 83 D6
Forge Levs *WMBN* WV5 .... 64 A5 🔟
Forge Rd *DARL/WED* WS10 .... 49 D3
SHHTH WV12 .... 29 E3
STRBR DY8 .... 136 E3
Forge St *DARL/WED* WS10 .... 50 A5
The Forge *HALE* B63 .... 138 C1
Forge Valley Wy *WMBN* WV5 .... 64 A5
Formans Rd *SPARK* B11 .... 150 A6
Formby Wy *BLOX/PEL* WS3 .... 16 C2
Forrell Gv *NFLD/LBR* B31 .... 187 D6
Forrest Av *WNSFLD* WV11 .... 14 C1
Forrester St *WSLW* WS2 .... 31 E5
Forrester Street Prec *WSLW* WS2 .... 31 E5
Forshaw Heath La *HOCK/TIA* B94 .... 220 C3
Forshaw Heath Rd *HOCK/TIA* B94 .... 221 E1
Forster St *SMTHWKW* B67 .... 96 A6
VAUX/NECH B7 .... 124 C1 🔟
Forsythia Cl *NFLD/LBR* B31 .... 166 B3 🔟
Forsythia Gv *CDSL* WV8 .... 8 C2 🔟
Fort Crs *ALDR* WS9 .... 20 C2
Forth Dr *CHWD/FDBR/MGN* B37 .... 131 D3
Forth Gv *HWK/WKHTH* B38 .... 188 D5
Forth Wy *RMSLY* B62 .... 142 A1
Fortnum Cl *STECH* B33 .... 129 E5
Forton Cl *DUNHL/THL/PER* WV6 .... 23 D5
Fort Pkwy *ERDW/GRVHL* B23 .... 103 D3
Fosbrooke Rd *SMHTH* B10 .... 150 C1
Fosseway Dr *ERDW/GRVHL* B23 .... 80 A3
Fossil Dr *RBRY* B45 .... 184 C6
Foster Av *BILS/COS* WV14 .... 69 D2
Foster Gdns *WSNGN* B18 .... 122 B1 🔟
Foster Pl *WOLVN* WV10 .... 26 A1
Foster St *BLOX/PEL* WS3 .... 17 F5
DARL/WED WS10 .... 49 F2
Foster St East *STRBR* DY8 .... 136 C4
Foster Wy *DIG/EDG* B5 .... 147 E4
Fotherley Brook Rd *ALDR* WS9 .... 36 B2
Foundry La *BLOX/PEL* WS3 .... 17 E6
SMTHWK B66 .... 97 F6
Foundry Rd *KGSWFD* DY6 .... 87 D5
WSNGN B18 .... 121 F5
Foundry St *BILS/COS* WV14 .... 69 D2
KGSWFD DY6 .... 87 D5
TPTN/OCK DY4 .... 70 A3
Fountain Cl *NFLD/LBR* B31 .... 202 A1
Fountain La *BILS/COS* WV14 .... 69 E4
OLDBY B69 .... 94 B4
Fountains Rd *BLOX/PEL* WS3 .... 16 A3
Fountains Wy *BLOX/PEL* WS3 .... 16 A3 🔟
Four Acres *RIDG/WDGT* B32 .... 143 E5
Four Ashes Rd *DOR/KN* B93 .... 211 F4
Four Crosses Rd *RUSH/SHEL* WS4 .... 19 E4
Fourlands Av *CSCFLD/WYGN* B72 .... 81 F4
Fourlands Rd *NFLD/LBR* B31 .... 166 B3
Four Oaks Common Rd
FOAKS/STRLY B74 .... 38 A4
Four Oaks Rd *FOAKS/STRLY* B74 .... 38 B5
Four Stones Cl *SOLH* B91 .... 194 C4 🔟
Four Stones Gv *DIG/EDG* B5 .... 148 A3 🔟
Fourth Av *BORD* B9 .... 126 B5
SLYOAK B29 .... 147 E6
WOLVN WV10 .... 25 F1
Four Winds Dr *DUDS* DY2 .... 92 A6
Fowey Cl *WALM/CURD* B76 .... 82 C4
Fowey Rd *BKDE/SHDE* B34 .... 128 B1
Fowgay Dr *SOLH* B91 .... 194 B4
Fowler Cl *CDSL* WV8 .... 22 A1
SMTHWK B66 .... 96 C5
Fowler Rd *MGN/WHC* B75 .... 60 C4
Fowler St *BKHL/PFLD* WV2 .... 45 E3 🔟
VAUX/NECH B7 .... 125 D2
Fowlmere Rd *PBAR/PBCH* B42 .... 77 D3
Foxbury Dr *DOR/KN* B93 .... 212 C4
Foxcote Av *HDSW* B21 .... 98 A6
Foxcote Cl *SOLH* B90 .... 193 F5
Foxcote Dr *SHLY* B90 .... 193 F5
Foxcote La *HAG/WOL* DY9 .... 139 D6
Foxdale Dr *BRLYHL* DY5 .... 113 D4
Foxdale Gv *STECH* B33 .... 129 E4 🔟
Foxes Cl *BRGRVE* B60 .... 215 D4
Foxes Meadow *WALM/CURD* B76 .... 82 C3
Foxes Rdg *CDYHTH* B64 .... 146 A1
Foxfield Dr *STRBR* DY8 .... 136 C6 🔟
Fox Foot Dr *BRLYHL* DY5 .... 113 E3
Foxford Cl *CBROM* B36 .... 105 F4 🔟
CSCFLD/WYGN B72 .... 81 F4 🔟
Foxglove Cl *WNSFLD* WV11 .... 28 A2 🔟
Foxglove Crs
CHWD/FDBR/MGN B37 .... 130 A4
Foxglove Rd *DUDN* DY1 .... 90 B1
Foxglove Wy *HDSW* B21 .... 97 F6 🔟
Fox Green Crs *ACGN* B27 .... 172 C1
Fox Gv *ACGN* B27 .... 172 C1
Fox Hi *SLYOAK* B29 .... 167 E3
Fox Hill Cl *SLYOAK* B29 .... 167 E3
Foxhill La *ALVE* B48 .... 215 F4
Fox Hill Rd *MGN/WHC* B75 .... 40 B5

Foxhills Pk *DUDS* DY2 .... 115 E3
Foxhills Rd
ETTPG/GDPK/PENN WV4 .... 43 E6
STRBR DY8 .... 111 F6
Foxholies Dr *HALE* B63 .... 140 A5
Fox Hollies Rd *ACGN* B27 .... 151 D6
WALM/CURD B76 .... 82 B3
Fox Hollow *DUNHL/THL/PER* WV6 .... 23 E5
Foxhope Cl *HWK/WKHTH* B38 .... 189 D4
Foxhunt Rd *HALE* B63 .... 162 A1
Foxland Av *RBRY* B45 .... 185 E6
Foxland Cl *CHWD/FDBR/MGN* B37 .... 131 F5
SHLY B90 .... 209 F3
Foxlands Av
ETTPG/GDPK/PENN WV4 .... 43 E6
Foxlands Crs
ETTPG/GDPK/PENN WV4 .... 43 E6
Foxlands Dr *CSCFLD/WYGN* B72 .... 81 F4
ETTPG/GDPK/PENN WV4 .... 43 E6
SEDG DY3 .... 67 F6
Foxlea Rd *HALE* B63 .... 161 F2
Foxley Dr *SOLH* B91 .... 177 D6
Foxmeadow Cl *SEDG* DY3 .... 68 A4 🔟
Foxoak St *CDYHTH* B64 .... 115 E6
Fox's La *WOLV* WV1 .... 25 F2
Fox St *CBHAMNE* B4 .... 7 G4
DUDN DY1 .... 69 E5
Foxton Rd *WASH/WDE* B8 .... 126 B2
Fox Wk *ALDR* WS9 .... 21 D2
Foxwell Gv *BORD* B9 .... 127 E5 🔟
Foxwell Rd *BORD* B9 .... 127 D5
Foxwood Av *GTB/HAM* B43 .... 55 D6
Foxwood Gv
CHWD/FDBR/MGN B37 .... 130 B2 🔟
Foxwood Rd
CHWD/FDBR/MGN B37 .... 130 B2 🔟
Foxyards Cl *TPTN/OCK* DY4 .... 69 F6 🔟
Foxyards Rd *TPTN/OCK* DY4 .... 69 F6
Foyle Rd *HWK/WKHTH* B38 .... 188 B4
Fozdar Crs *BILS/COS* WV14 .... 68 C2
Fradley Cl *BVILLE* B30 .... 187 F1
Framefield Dr *SOLH* B91 .... 176 A5 🔟
Framingham Gv
DUNHL/THL/PER WV6 .... 22 C4 🔟
Frampton Cl *BVILLE* B30 .... 167 F4
CHWD/FDBR/MGN B37 .... 131 F4 🔟
Frampton Wy *GTB/HAM* B43 .... 55 F5
Frances Dr *BLOX/PEL* WS3 .... 17 D3 🔟
Frances Rd *BVILLE* B30 .... 168 C6
ERDW/GRVHL B23 .... 101 F2
LOZ/NWT B19 .... 99 E5
Franchise Gdns *DARL/WED* WS10 .... 50 A3 🔟
Franchise St *DARL/WED* WS10 .... 50 A4
PBAR/PBCH B42 .... 100 A3 🔟
Francis Cl *FOAKS/STRLY* B74 .... 56 B1
KGSWFD DY6 .... 87 F5 🔟
Francis Rd *ACGN* B27 .... 151 D6
LDYWD/EDGR B16 .... 122 C6
SMTHWKW B67 .... 119 F2
STECH B33 .... 127 F4
STRBR DY8 .... 135 E4
YDLY B25 .... 150 C3
Francis St *VAUX/NECH* B7 .... 124 C3
WBROM B70 .... 95 F4
WOLV WV1 .... 25 F3
Francis Wk *NFLD/LBR* B31 .... 186 C6
Francis Ward Cl *HHTH/SAND* B71 .... 72 C3
Frankburn Rd *FOAKS/STRLY* B74 .... 56 A1
Frankfort St *LOZ/NWT* B19 .... 123 F1
Frankholmes Dr *SHLY* B90 .... 210 A1
Frankley Av *RMSLY* B62 .... 142 C4 🔟
Frankley Beeches Rd
NFLD/LBR B31 .... 185 F2
Frankley Gn *RMSLY* B62 .... 163 F6
Frankley Green La
RIDG/WDGT B32 .... 164 B6
Frankley Hill La *RBRY* B45 .... 184 B3
RIDG/WDGT B32 .... 184 B1
Frankley La *NFLD/LBR* B31 .... 185 F1
Frankley Lodge Rd *NFLD/LBR* B31 .... 185 F1
Frankley Rd *LGLYGN/QTN* B68 .... 142 C1
Franklin Rd *BVILLE* B30 .... 168 B4
Franklin St *WSNGN* B18 .... 122 A2
Franklin Wy *BVILLE* B30 .... 168 A4
Franklyn Cl *DUNHL/THL/PER* WV6 .... 22 A2
Frank Rd *SMTHWKW* B67 .... 120 A1
Frank St *BHTH/HG* B12 .... 148 B2 🔟
Franks Wy *STECH* B33 .... 128 A5 🔟
Frank Tommey Cl
BLKHTH/ROWR B65 .... 117 E6 🔟
Frankton Cl *HIA/OLT* B92 .... 175 D2
Frankton Gv *BORD* B9 .... 127 D5 🔟
Fraser Gv *SPARK* B11 .... 149 E4
Fraser St *BILS/COS* WV14 .... 48 A3
Frayne Av *KGSWFD* DY6 .... 87 E6
Freasley Cl *SHLY* B90 .... 193 F2
Freasley Rd *BKDE/SHDE* B34 .... 129 F2 🔟
Freda Rd *OLDBY* B69 .... 93 F5
Freda Rd *WBROM* B70 .... 95 F4
Fredas Gv *HRBN* B17 .... 144 C5
Frederick Rd *AST/WIT* B6 .... 100 C5 🔟
EDG B15 .... 147 D1
ERDW/GRVHL B23 .... 101 F3
LGLYGN/QTN B68 .... 143 F2
SCFLD/BOLD B73 .... 80 C1

Slyoak B29 .... 167 F1
Spark B11 .... 149 E5 🔟
Stetch B33 .... 127 F4 🔟
WNSFLD WV11 .... 27 E2
Fredericks Cl *STRBR* DY8 .... 136 A5
Frederick St *BKHL/PFLD* WV2 .... 45 E1 🔟
CBHAMW B1 .... 6 A2
WBROM B70 .... 95 E1
WSLW WS2 .... 4 A4
Frederick William St
WLNHL WV13 .... 29 D5 🔟
Freeland Gv *KGSWFD* DY6 .... 112 B3 🔟
Freeman Dr *WALM/CURD* B76 .... 60 B5
Freeman Pl *BILS/COS* WV14 .... 48 A1
Freeman Rd *DARL/WED* WS10 .... 51 E6
VAUX/NECH B7 .... 125 D1 🔟
Freeman St *DIG/EDG* B5 .... 7 G5 🔟
WOLVN WV10 .... 26 B5
Freer Rd *AST/WIT* B6 .... 99 F5
Freer St *WSL* WS1 .... 4 D3
Freeth St *LDYWD/EDGR* B16 .... 122 C5
OLDBY B69 .... 94 B5 🔟
Freezeland St *BILS/COS* WV14 .... 47 D3 🔟
Fremont Dr *DUDN* DY1 .... 90 A2
French Rd *DUDS* DY2 .... 92 A4
Frensham Cl
CHWD/FDBR/MGN B37 .... 131 E5
Frensham Wy *HRBN* B17 .... 145 E3
Frenshaw Gv *KGSTG* B44 .... 78 B4 🔟
Freshwater Dr *BRLYHL* DY5 .... 113 D6
Friardale Cl *DARL/WED* WS10 .... 51 F6
Friar Park Rd *DARL/WED* WS10 .... 51 E6
Friars Cl *STRBR* DY8 .... 111 E4
Friars Gorse *KINVER* DY7 .... 135 E2 🔟
Friar St *DARL/WED* WS10 .... 51 D6
Friary Av *SHLY* B90 .... 210 C1
Friary Crs *RUSH/SHEL* WS4 .... 33 E1
Friary Gdns *HDSW* B21 .... 97 F3
Friary Rd *HDSW* B21 .... 98 A3
Friday La *HIA/OLT* B92 .... 197 F1
Friar Wy *WOLV* WV1 .... 27 D4
Friezeland La *WSLW* WS2 .... 31 D5
Friezeland Rd *WSLW* WS2 .... 31 D5
Frinton Gv *HDSW* B21 .... 97 E6
Frisby Rd *RIDG/WDGT* B32 .... 144 A4
Friston Av *LDYWD/EDGR* B16 .... 123 D6
Frodesley Rd
LGN/SDN/BHAMAIR B26 .... 153 D1
Froggatt Rd *BILS/COS* WV14 .... 47 F2 🔟
Froggatts Ride *WALM/CURD* B76 .... 60 B6
Frogmill Rd *NFLD/LBR* B31 .... 185 D3
Frome Dr *WNSFLD* WV11 .... 27 E3
Frome Wy *ALE/KHTH/YWD* B14 .... 169 E5
Frost St *BKHL/PFLD* WV2 .... 46 A3
Froxmere Cl *SOLH* B91 .... 195 D5
Froyle Cl *DUNHL/THL/PER* WV6 .... 23 E2
Froysell St *WLNHL* WV13 .... 29 D5
Fryer Rd *NFLD/LBR* B31 .... 187 D6
Fryers Cl *BLOX/PEL* WS3 .... 17 D6
Fryers Rd *WSLW* WS2 .... 30 C1
Fryer St *WOLV* WV1 .... 3 E3
Fuchsia Dr *COVEN* WV9 .... 10 B2
Fugelmere Cl *HRBN* B17 .... 144 B2
Fulbrook Gv *SLYOAK* B29 .... 166 B3 🔟
Fulbrook Rd *DUDN* DY1 .... 90 C4 🔟
Fulford Dr *WALM/CURD* B76 .... 83 D6
Fulford Gv
LGN/SDN/BHAMAIR B26 .... 153 E3
Fulford Hall Rd *HOCK/TIA* B94 .... 207 F4
Fulham Rd *SPARK* B11 .... 149 D4
Fullbrook Cl *SHLY* B90 .... 210 C2
Fullbrook Rd *DSYBK/YTR* WS5 .... 52 A4
Fullerton Cl *CDSL* WV8 .... 10 A4
Fullwood Crs *DUDS* DY2 .... 114 A1
Fullwoods End *BILS/COS* WV14 .... 69 E4
Fulwell Gv *KGSTG* B44 .... 78 C3
Fulwood Av *RMSLY* B62 .... 142 B1
Furber Pl *KGSWFD* DY6 .... 112 B1
Furlong La *HALE* B63 .... 139 E3
Furlong Meadow
NFLD/LBR B31 .... 187 E3 🔟
Furlongs Rd *SEDG* DY3 .... 67 F5
The Furlongs *STRBR* DY8 .... 137 D6 🔟
WOLVN WV10 .... 27 D2
The Furlongs *DARL/WED* WS10 .... 50 A4
Furlong Wk *SEDG* DY3 .... 89 F1
Furnace Cl *WMBN* WV5 .... 64 A6
Furnace Hl *HALE* B63 .... 141 D4
RMSLY B62 .... 141 D3
Furnace La *HALE* B63 .... 141 D4
Furnace Pde *TPTN/OCK* DY4 .... 70 A5
Furnace Rd *DUDS* DY2 .... 91 E5 🔟
Furness Cl *BLOX/PEL* WS3 .... 16 B2 🔟
Furzebank Wy *SHHTH* WV12 .... 30 A3
Furze Wy *DSYBK/YTR* WS5 .... 53 F1

G

Gaddesby Rd *ALE/KHTH/YWD* B14 .... 170 B3
Gadds Dr *BLKHTH/ROWR* B65 .... 117 F3
Gadsby Av *WNSFLD* WV11 .... 14 C6
Gads Gn *DUDS* DY2 .... 115 D2
Gads Green Crs *DUDS* DY2 .... 116 A1
Gads La *DUDN* DY1 .... 91 E4 🔟

WBROM B70 .... **94** C2
Gadwall Cft *ERDW/GRVHL* B23 ..... **101** D2
Gail Cl *ALDR* WS9 .... **21** D1
Gailey Cft *KGSTG* B44 .... **56** A6
Gail Pk *BDMR/CCFT* WV3 .... **43** F2
Gainford Cl *COVEN* WV9 .... **10** B4
Gainford Rd *KGSTG* B44 .... **79** E2
Gainsborough Crs *DOR/KN* B93 .... **212** C1
    GTB/HAM B43 .... **55** F5
Gainsborough Dr
    DUNHL/THL/PER WV6 .... **22** B3
Gainsborough Hl *STRBR* DY8 .... **136** C6
Gainsborough Pl *DUDN* DY1 .... **90** A3
Gainsborough Rd *PBAR/PBCH* B42 . **77** D5
Gairloch Rd *WNSFLD* WV11 .... **15** D4
Gaitskell Ter *OLDBY* B69 .... **93** F3
Gaitskell Wy *SMTHWK* B66 .... **96** B6
Galahad Wy *DARL/WED* WS10 .... **72** C1
Galbraith Cl *BILS/COS* WV14 .... **69** F3
Galena Wy *AST/WIT* B6 .... **124** A1
Gale Wk *BLKHTH/ROWR* B65 .... **116** B2
Galloway Av *BKDE/SHDE* B34 .... **128** B1
Galton Cl *ERDE/BCHGN* B24 .... **104** B1
    TPTN/OCK DY4 .... **71** E5
Galton Rd *SMTHWKW* B67 .... **120** B6
Galtons La *HAG/WOL* DY9 .... **108** C6
Gamesfield Rd *BDMR/CCFT* WV3 ..... **24** B6
Gammage St *DUDS* DY2 .... **91** D5
Gandy Rd *SHHTH* WV12 .... **28** C1
Gannahs Farm Cl
    WALM/CURD B76 .... **60** B6
Gannow Green La *RBRY* B45 .... **183** E4
Gannow Manor Crs *RBRY* B45 .... **184** A3
Gannow Manor Gdns *RBRY* B45 .... **184** B4
Gannow Rd *RBRY* B45 .... **184** A6
Gannow Wk *RBRY* B45 .... **184** A6
Ganton Rd *BLOX/PEL* WS3 .... **16** C1
Garden Cl *DOR/KN* B93 .... **212** B1
    RBRY B45 .... **184** C3
    WASH/WDE B8 .... **126** C2
Garden Crs *BLOX/PEL* WS3 .... **18** B2
Garden Cft *ALDR* WS9 .... **21** D6
Gardeners Wy *WMBN* WV5 .... **86** B1
Garden Gv *BFLD/HDSWWD* B20 ...... **76** A5
The Gardens *ERDW/GRVHL* B23 .... **102** A2
Garden St *WSLW* WS2 .... **4** C1
Garden Wk *BILS/COS* WV14 .... **48** B5
    SEDG DY3 .... **89** E3
Garfield Rd
    LGN/SDN/BHAMAIR B26 .... **153** D3
Garland Cl *RMSLY* B62 .... **142** A1
Garland St *BORD* B9 .... **125** E4
Garland Wy *NFLD/LBR* B31 .... **187** D1
Garman Cl *GTB/HAM* B43 .... **76** A1
Garner Cl *BILS/COS* WV14 .... **47** F6
Garnet Av *GTB/HAM* B43 .... **55** D6
Garnet Cl *ALDR* WS9 .... **21** F1
Garnett Dr *MGN/WHC* B75 .... **60** A3
Garrard Gdns *SCFLD/BOLD* B73 ..... **59** D4
Garrat St *BRLYHL* DY5 .... **114** A2
Garratt Cl *LGLYGN/QTN* B68 .... **119** E3
Garratt's La *CDYHTH* B64 .... **116** B5
Garratt St *HHTH/SAND* B71 .... **73** F6
Garratts Wk
    ALE/KHTH/YWD B14 .... **190** A3
Garret Cl *KGSWFD* DY6 .... **87** F4
Garretts Green La
    LGN/SDN/BHAMAIR B26 .... **152** C2
    STETCH B33 .... **153** D1
Garrick Cl *WOLV* WV1 .... **3** E5
Garrington St *DARL/WED* WS10 ...... **49** E2
Garrison La *BORD* B9 .... **125** E5
Garrison St *BORD* B9 .... **125** E4
The Garth *ALE/KHTH/YWD* B14 .... **191** F1
Garway Gv *YDLY* B25 .... **151** D2
Garwood Rd
    LGN/SDN/BHAMAIR B26 .... **128** B5
Gas St *CBHAMW* B1 .... **6** A6
Gatacre St *SEDG* DY3 .... **89** E2
Gatcombe Cl *WOLVN* WV10 .... **12** B1
Gatcombe Rd *DUDN* DY1 .... **90** A3
Gate Cl *WMBN* WV5 .... **64** C6
Gatehouse Fold *DUDS* DY2 .... **91** F4
Gate La *HOCK/TIA* B94 .... **211** E4
    SCFLD/BOLD B73 .... **80** B1
Gateley Rd *LGLYGN/QTN* B68 .... **143** F2
Gate St *SEDG* DY3 .... **68** A4
    TPTN/OCK DY4 .... **92** C5
    WASH/WDE B8 .... **125** F2
Gatis St *DUNHL/THL/PER* WV6 .... **24** C2
Gatwick Rd *CVALE* B35 .... **105** D1
Gauden Rd *HAG/WOL* DY9 .... **159** F2
The Gaunts *ALVE* B48 .... **217** D3
Gawne La *DUDS* DY2 .... **116** A3
Gaydon Cl *DUNHL/THL/PER* WV6 ... **22** A2
Gaydon Gv *SLYOAK* B29 .... **166** C1
Gaydon Pl *SCFLD/BOLD* B73 .... **59** D5
Gaydon Rd *ALDR* WS9 .... **34** C3
    HIA/OLT B92 .... **153** F6
Gayfield Av *BRLYHL* DY5 .... **113** F6
    BRLYHL DY5 .... **137** E1
Gay Hill La *HWK/WKHTH* B38 ...... **189** D5
Gayhurst Dr *YDLY* B25 .... **152** A1
Gayle Gv *ACGN* B27 .... **173** E3
Gayton Rd *HHTH/SAND* B71 .... **73** F5

Gaywood Cft *EDG* B15 .... **147** E1
Geach St *LOZ/NWT* B19 .... **123** F1
Gedney Cl *ALE/KHTH/YWD* B14 .... **191** E2
Geeson Cl *CVALE* B35 .... **105** D1
Gee St *LOZ/NWT* B19 .... **123** F1
Geneva Rd *TPTN/OCK* DY4 .... **91** F1
Genge Av
    ETTPK/GDPK/PENN WV4 .... **46** A5
Genners La *RIDG/WDGT* B32 .... **165** E3
Genthorn Cl
    ETTPK/GDPK/PENN WV4 .... **46** B5
Gentian Cl *NFLD/LBR* B31 .... **166** B5
Geoffrey Cl *WALM/CURD* B76 .... **83** D4
Geoffrey Rd *SHLY* B90 .... **192** B2
    SPARK B11 .... **149** E6
George Arthur Rd *WASH/WDE* B8 .. **125** F3
George Av *BLKHTH/ROWR* B65 ...... **117** F5
George Bird Cl *SMTHWK* B66 .... **120** C1
George Cl *DUDS* DY2 .... **92** A5
George Frederick Rd
    SCFLD/BOLD B73 .... **56** C5
George Henry Rd *TPTN/OCK* DY4 ... **72** A4
George Rd *ALVE* B48 .... **216** C3
    BILS/COS WV14 .... **69** F2
    CSHL/WTROR B46 .... **107** E2
    EDG B15 .... **147** E1
    ERDW/GRVHL B23 .... **101** E2
    GTB/HAM B43 .... **76** B1
    HALE B63 .... **140** B5
    LGLYGN/QTN B68 .... **119** E5
    SCFLD/BOLD B73 .... **79** F2
    SLYOAK B29 .... **168** A1
    SOLH B91 .... **195** E2
    TPTN/OCK DY4 .... **69** F5
    YDLY B25 .... **150** C3
George Rose Gdns
    DARL/WED WS10 .... **49** D3
George's Pde *BKHL/PFLD* WV2 .... **3** E5
George St *BHTH/HG* B12 .... **148** B4
    BKHL/PFLD WV2 .... **2** D1
    BKHL/PFLD WV2 .... **46** C2
    CBHAMNW B3 .... **6** A4
    DUDN DY1 .... **69** D5
    HDSW B21 .... **97** E5
    LOZ/NWT B19 .... **99** D6
    STRBR DY8 .... **112** B6
    WBROM B70 .... **95** F3
    WLNHL WV13 .... **28** C3
    WSL WS1 .... **4** D5
George St West *WSNGN* B18 .... **122** C3
Georgina Av *BILS/COS* WV14 .... **47** F6
Geraldine Rd *YDLY* B25 .... **151** D2
Gerald Rd *STRBR* DY8 .... **136** A2
Geranium Gv *BORD* B9 .... **126** B4
Geranium Rd *DUDS* DY2 .... **92** B5
Gerardsfield Rd *STETCH* B33 .... **129** F4
Germander Dr *DSYBK/YTR* WS5 ..... **52** C6
Gerrard Cl *LOZ/NWT* B19 .... **99** F5
Gerrard Rd *WLNHL* WV13 .... **28** A6
Gerrard St *LOZ/NWT* B19 .... **123** C1
Gervase Dr *DUDN* DY1 .... **91** E2
Geston Rd *DUDN* DY1 .... **90** B5
Gibbet La *KINVER* DY7 .... **134** C5
Gibbins Rd *SLYOAK* B29 .... **167** E2
Gibbons Gv *DUNHL/THL/PER* WV6 .. **24** A3
Gibbons Hill Rd *SEDG* DY3 .... **67** F1
Gibbons La *BRLYHL* DY5 .... **88** C6
Gibbons Rd *DUNHL/THL/PER* WV6 .. **24** A3
    MGN/WHC B75 .... **39** D4
Gibbs Hill Rd *NFLD/LBR* B31 .... **187** D6
Gibbs Rd *HAG/WOL* DY9 .... **138** C4
Gibbs St *DUNHL/THL/PER* WV6 ...... **24** C3
Gibb St *BORD* B9 .... **124** B6
Gibson Dr *BFLD/HDSWWD* B20 .... **99** D5
Gibson Rd *BFLD/HDSWWD* B20 ...... **99** D5
    DUNHL/THL/PER WV6 .... **22** A4
Gideon Cl
    LGN/SDN/BHAMAIR B26 .... **151** F3
Gideons Cl *SEDG* DY3 .... **67** F6
Giffard Rd *WOLV* WV1 .... **12** A2
    WOLVN WV10 .... **12** A2
Giggetty La *WMBN* WV5 .... **64** A5
Gigg La *WALM/CURD* B76 .... **63** D6
Gigmill Wy *STRBR* DY8 .... **136** A5
Gilbanks Rd *STRBR* DY8 .... **135** F2
Gilberry Cl *DOR/KN* B93 .... **212** C2
Gilbert Av *OLDBY* B69 .... **93** D6
Gilbert Cl *WNSFLD* WV11 .... **14** C6
Gilbert La *WMBN* WV5 .... **65** D4
Gilbert Rd *SMTHWK* B66 .... **121** D3
Gilbertstone Av
    LGN/SDN/BHAMAIR B26 .... **152** A4
Gilbert St *TPTN/OCK* DY4 .... **92** B3
Gilbeys Cl *STRBR* DY8 .... **112** A6
Gilby Rd *LDYWD/EDGR* B16 .... **122** C6
Gilchrist Dr *EDG* B15 .... **146** A1
Gildas Av *HWK/WKHTH* B38 .... **188** C4
Giles Cl *HIA/OLT* B92 .... **176** B4
    STETCH B33 .... **129** E4
Giles Rd *LGLYGN/QTN* B68 .... **119** D2
Gilldown Pl *EDG* B15 .... **147** D2
Gillespie Cft *AST/WIT* B6 .... **100** B6
Gillhurst Rd *HRBN* B17 .... **105** D2
Gilling Gv *BKDE/SHDE* B34 .... **128** C1
Gillingham Cl *DARL/WED* WS10 .... **51** F5

Gilllity Av *DSYBK/YTR* WS5 .... **53** D1
Gillity Cl *DSYBK/YTR* WS5 .... **53** D1
Gilliver Rd *SHLY* B90 .... **193** D1
Gillman Cl
    LGN/SDN/BHAMAIR B26 .... **153** F5
Gillott Cl *SOLH* B91 .... **196** A2
Gillott Rd *LDYWD/EDGR* B16 .... **121** E6
Gillows Cft *SHLY* B90 .... **194** C6
Gillscroft Rd *STETCH* B33 .... **128** C4
Gill St *DUDS* DY2 .... **116** A4
    WBROM B70 .... **95** E4
Gilmorton Cl *HRBN* B17 .... **145** D2
    SOLH B91 .... **195** E4
Gilpin Cl *CBROM* B36 .... **127** E1
Gilpin Crs *BLOX/PEL* WS3 .... **18** C1
Gilson Dr *CSHL/WTROR* B46 .... **107** F5
Gilson Rd *CSHL/WTROR* B46 .... **107** F4
Gilson St *TPTN/OCK* DY4 .... **71** E3
Gilson Wy
    CHWD/FDBR/MGN B37 .... **130** C1
Gilwell Rd *BKDE/SHDE* B34 .... **130** A1
Gipsy La *ERDW/GRVHL* B23 .... **79** D6
    WLNHL WV13 .... **29** D6
Gisborn Cl *SMHTH* B10 .... **149** D1
Gladeside Cl *RUSH/SHEL* WS4 .... **19** E5
The Glades *ALDR* WS9 .... **21** D6
The Glade *CDSL* WV8 .... **10** A4
    FOAKS/STRLY B74 .... **36** A6
    HAG/WOL DY9 .... **138** A4
    LGN/SDN/BHAMAIR B26 .... **153** F5
Gladstone Dr *OLDBY* B69 .... **93** E2
Gladstone Gv *KGSWFD* DY6 .... **87** F5
Gladstone Rd *DOR/KN* B93 .... **212** C5
    ERDW/GRVHL B23 .... **101** F2
    LGN/SDN/BHAMAIR B26 .... **151** F3
    SPARK B11 .... **149** D3
    STRBR DY8 .... **135** F3
Gladstone St *AST/WIT* B6 .... **100** C5
    DARL/WED WS10 .... **50** A3
    HHTH/SAND B71 .... **73** E6
    WSLW WS2 .... **31** F3
Gladys Rd *SMTHWKW* B67 .... **120** B5
    YDLY B25 .... **151** D2
Glaisdale Gdns
    DUNHL/THL/PER WV6 .... **24** C2
Glaisdale Rd *HLGN/YWD* B28 .... **172** C3
Glaisedale Gv *WLNHL* WV13 .... **29** E5
Glaisher Dr *WOLVN* WV10 .... **11** D6
Glamis Rd *SHHTH* WV12 .... **15** D6
Glanville Dr *MGN/WHC* B75 .... **38** C3
Glasbury Cft *HWK/WKHTH* B38 .... **188** A6
Glascote Cl *SHLY* B90 .... **192** C2
Glascote Gv *BKDE/SHDE* B34 .... **129** E1
Glasshouse Hl *STRBR* DY8 .... **137** D3
Glastonbury Crs *BLOX/PEL* WS3 .... **16** A3
Glastonbury Rd
    ALE/KHTH/YWD B14 .... **171** E6
    HHTH/SAND B71 .... **73** F1
Glastonbury Wy *BLOX/PEL* WS3 .... **16** A4
Glaston Dr *SOLH* B91 .... **194** C5
Gleads Cft *RIDG/WDGT* B32 .... **142** C6
Gleave Rd *SLYOAK* B29 .... **168** A2
Glebe Dr *SCFLD/BOLD* B73 .... **80** B3
Glebe Farm Rd *STETCH* B33 .... **128** C2
Glebe Flds *WALM/CURD* B76 .... **85** D5
Glebefields Rd *TPTN/OCK* DY4 .... **70** C5
Glebeland Cl *LDYWD/EDGR* B16 ... **123** D6
Glebe La *STRBR* DY8 .... **136** A5
Glebe Pl *DARL/WED* WS10 .... **49** D3
Glebe Rd *ALVE* B48 .... **216** C2
    SOLH B91 .... **175** F6
    WLNHL WV13 .... **48** B1
Glebe St *WSL* WS1 .... **4** D6
Glenavon Rd *ALE/KHTH/YWD* B14 . **190** C2
Glen Cl *RUSH/SHEL* WS4 .... **32** C4
Glencoe Rd *SMTHWK* B66 .... **121** E3
Glen Ct *DUNHL/THL/PER* WV6 .... **24** A5
Glencroft Rd *HIA/OLT* B92 .... **153** F6
Glendale Cl *BDMR/CCFT* WV3 .... **43** E1
    HALE B63 .... **141** D5
Glendale Dr *STETCH* B33 .... **128** B4
    WMBN WV5 .... **64** C5
Glendene Crs *HWK/WKHTH* B38 ... **187** E6
Glen Devon Cl *RBRY* B45 .... **184** C3
Glendon Rd *ERDW/GRVHL* B23 ...... **79** D5
Glendon Wy *DOR/KN* B93 .... **211** F4
Glendower Rd *ALDR* WS9 .... **21** D4
    PBAR/PBCH B42 .... **77** E6
Gleneagles Dr *BRGRVE* B60 .... **214** C4
    GTB/HAM B43 .... **54** A5
    MGN/WHC B75 .... **59** E2
    OLDBY B69 .... **92** C6
Gleneagles Rd *BLOX/PEL* WS3 .... **16** B2
    LGN/SDN/BHAMAIR B26 .... **152** C1
Glenelg Dr *STRBR* DY8 .... **159** D1
Glenelg Ms *DSYBK/YTR* WS5 .... **53** F4
Glenfern Rd *BILS/COS* WV14 .... **68** C3
Glenfield *CDSL* WV8 .... **10** A3
Glenfield Cl *SOLH* B91 .... **195** E5
    WALM/CURD B76 .... **60** A6
Glenfield Gv *SLYOAK* B29 .... **168** C2
Glengarry Cl *RIDG/WDGT* B32 ...... **165** D4
Glengarry Gdns *BDMR/CCFT* WV3 .. **24** B6
Glenhurst Cl *WSLW* WS2 .... **29** F4
Glenmead Cl *KGSTG* B44 .... **77** F3

Glenmore Cl *BDMR/CCFT* WV3 ..... **44** A2
Glenmore Dr *HWK/WKHTH* B38 ..... **187** F4
Glen Park Rd *SEDG* DY5 ..... **89** F3
Glenpark Rd *WASH/WDE* B8 ..... **126** A2
Glen Ri *MOS/BIL* B13 ..... **171** E5
Glen Rd *SEDG* DY3 ..... **68** A5
  STRBR DY8 ..... **136** B6
Glenroyde *HWK/WKHTH* B38 ..... **188** A6
Glen Side *RIDG/WDGT* B32 ..... **165** F1
Glenside Av *HIA/OLT* B92 ..... **153** D6
Glenthorne Rd *ERDE/BCHGN* B24 ..... **102** C3
Glenthorne Wy
  ERDE/BCHGN B24 ..... **102** C3 ▣
Glentworth Dr *WALM/CURD* B76 ..... **82** C1
Glentworth Gdns
  DUNHL/THL/PER WV6 ..... **25** D2
Glenville Dr *ERDW/GRVHL* B23 ..... **80** A6
Glenwood Cl *BRLYHL* DY5 ..... **137** F1 ▣
Glenwood Dr *SHLY* B90 ..... **209** F3
Glenwood Ri *ALDR* WS9 ..... **21** F2
Glenwood Rd *HWK/WKHTH* B38 ..... **187** F5
Globe St *DARL/WED* WS10 ..... **72** B3
Gloucester Pl *WLNHL* WV13 ..... **29** F5 ▣
Gloucester Rd *DARL/WED* WS10 ..... **51** E6
  DSYBK/YTR WS5 ..... **53** D1
  DUDS DY2 ..... **115** F5
Gloucester St *DIG/EDG* B5 ..... **124** A6 ▣
  DUNHL/THL/PER WV6 ..... **25** D3 ▣
Gloucester Wy
  CHWD/FDBR/MGN B37 ..... **130** C6
Clover Cl *HLGN/YWD* B28 ..... **172** B5 ▣
Glover Rd *MGN/WHC* B75 ..... **60** B4
Glovers Cft
  CHWD/FDBR/MGN B37 ..... **130** B4
Glovers Field Dr *VAUX/NECH* B7 ..... **101** E6 ▣
Glovers Rd *SMHTH* B10 ..... **149** E1
Glover St *BORD* B9 ..... **124** C5
  WBROM B70 ..... **95** F4
Glyne Dr *DUNHL/THL/PER* WV6 ..... **24** A2 ▣
Glyn Av *BILS/COS* WV14 ..... **49** D6
Glyn Dr *BILS/COS* WV14 ..... **49** D6 ▣
Glyn Farm Rd *RIDG/WDGT* B32 ..... **143** E4
Glynn Crs *HALE* B63 ..... **139** D2
Glynne Av *KGSWFD* DY6 ..... **111** F3
Glyn Rd *RIDG/WDGT* B32 ..... **143** F3
Glynside Av *RIDG/WDGT* B32 ..... **143** E4
Goffs Cl *RIDG/WDGT* B32 ..... **144** B6
Goldcrest Cl *DUDS* DY2 ..... **115** F5
Goldcrest Cft *CBROM* B36 ..... **106** C5
Goldencrest Dr *OLDBY* B69 ..... **94** A5 ▣
Golden Cft *BFLD/HDSWWD* B20 ..... **98** B4 ▣
Golden End Dr *DOR/KN* B93 ..... **213** F2
Golden Hillock Rd *DUDS* DY2 ..... **115** E4
  SMHTH B10 ..... **149** F2
  SPARK B11 ..... **149** F4
Goldfinch Cl *SLYOAK* B29 ..... **167** F3
Goldfinch Rd *HAG/WOL* DY9 ..... **137** E6 ▣
Goldicroft Rd *DARL/WED* WS10 ..... **50** C5
Goldieslie Cl *SCFLD/BOLD* B73 ..... **81** D1
Goldieslie Rd *SFCLD/BOLD* B73 ..... **81** D1
Golds Hill Gdns *HDSW* B21 ..... **98** B6
Golds Hill Rd *HDSW* B21 ..... **98** B5
Golds Hill Wy *TPTN/OCK* DY4 ..... **71** F4
Goldsmith Rd *ALE/KHTH/YWD* B14 ..... **170** D5
  BLOX/PEL WS3 ..... **18** A5
Goldstar Wy *STECH* B33 ..... **129** E5
Goldthorn Av
  ETTPK/GDPK/PENN WV4 ..... **45** D4
Goldthorn Crs
  ETTPK/GDPK/PENN WV4 ..... **44** C3
Goldthorne Av
  LGN/SDN/BHAMAIR B26 ..... **153** F3
Goldthorne Wk *BRLYHL* DY5 ..... **137** F1 ▣
Goldthorn Hl
  ETTPK/GDPK/PENN WV6 ..... **45** D3
Goldthorn Rd
  ETTPK/GDPK/PENN WV4 ..... **45** D3
Golf La *BILS/COS* WV14 ..... **47** F2
Golson Cl *MGN/WHC* B75 ..... **60** A3
Gomeldon Av *ALE/KHTH/YWD* B14 ..... **190** B2
Gomer St *WLNHL* WV13 ..... **28** C5 ▣
Gomer St West *WLNHL* WV13 ..... **28** C5 ▣
Gooch Cl *STRBR* DY8 ..... **136** C3
Gooch St *DIG/EDG* B5 ..... **148** A1
Gooch St North *DIG/EDG* B5 ..... **124** A6
Goodall Gv *GTB/HAM* B43 ..... **56** A4
Goodall St *WSL* WS1 ..... **5** E4
Goodby Rd *MOS/BIL* B13 ..... **147** F6
Goode Av *WSNGN* B18 ..... **122** C4
Goode Cl *LGLYGN/QTN* B68 ..... **119** E3
Goodeve Wk *MGN/WHC* B75 ..... **61** D4 ▣
Goodison Gdns *ERDE/BCHGN* B24 ..... **81** D6
Goodman Cl *HLGN/YWD* B28 ..... **172** B5
Goodman St *CBHAMW* B1 ..... **123** D4
Goodrest Av *RMSLY* B62 ..... **142** C3
Goodrest Cft *ALE/KHTH/YWD* B14 ..... **191** E1
Goodrest La *HWK/WKHTH* B38 ..... **204** B1
Goodrich Av *DUNHL/THL/PER* WV6 ..... **22** C4
Goodrich Covert *BRLYHL* B30 ..... **189** E3 ▣
Goodway Rd *HIA/OLT* B92 ..... **154** A6
  KGSTG B44 ..... **78** A3
Goodwood Cl *CBROM* B36 ..... **103** F5 ▣
Goodwood Dr *FOAKS/STRLY* B74 ..... **56** B3
Goodwyn Av *LGLYGN/QTN* B68 ..... **143** F2
Goodyear Av *WOLVN* WV10 ..... **12** A5

Goodyear Rd *SMTHWKW* B67 ..... **119** F5
Goosemoor La *ERDW/GRVHL* B23 ..... **80** B4
Gopsal St *CBHAMNE* B4 ..... **124** C4 ▣
Gordon Av
  ETTPK/GDPK/PENN WV4 ..... **46** B6
  HHTH/SAND B71 ..... **73** E3
  LOZ/NWT B19 ..... **99** F6
Gordon Cl *OLDBY* B69 ..... **73** F3 ▣
Gordon Crs *BRLYHL* DY5 ..... **114** A5
Gordon Dr *TPTN/OCK* DY4 ..... **71** F6
Gordon Pl *BILS/COS* WV14 ..... **47** E6 ▣
Gordon Rd *HRBN* B17 ..... **121** E5
  LOZ/NWT B19 ..... **99** E5
Gordon St *BKHL/PFLD* WV2 ..... **45** F1
  DARL/WED WS10 ..... **49** F3
Gorey La *WNSFLD* WV11 ..... **15** D5
Gorge Rd *SEDG* DY3 ..... **66** C5
Gorleston Gv *ALE/KHTH/YWD* B14 ..... **191** D5
Gorleston Rd *ALE/KHTH/YWD* B14 ..... **191** D5
Gorsebrook Rd
  DUNHL/THL/PER WV6 ..... **25** E2 ▣
Gorse Cl *CHWD/FDBR/MGN* B37 ..... **130** B5
  SLYOAK B29 ..... **166** C3
Gorse Farm Rd *GTB/HAM* B43 ..... **76** A3
Gorsefield Rd *BKDE/SHDE* B34 ..... **129** E2
Gorse Green La *HAG/WOL* DY9 ..... **181** D5
Gorse Meadow Dr *RBRY* B45 ..... **215** D1
Gorsemoor Wy *WNSFLD* WV11 ..... **15** D2 ▣
Gorse Rd *DUDN* DY1 ..... **90** C1
  WNSFLD WV11 ..... **14** C5
Gorsey La *CSHL/WTROR* B46 ..... **108** A3
  HLYWD B47 ..... **206** C5
Gorsey Wy *ALDR* WS9 ..... **34** A2
Gorsly Piece *RIDG/WDGT* B32 ..... **145** E5
Gorstie Cft *GTB/HAM* B43 ..... **76** A3
Gorsty Av *BRLYHL* DY5 ..... **113** E3
Gorsty Cl *HHTH/SAND* B71 ..... **74** B3
Gorsty Hayes *CDSL* WV8 ..... **8** B2
Gorsty Hill Rd *RMSLY* B62 ..... **141** D1
Gorsymead Gv *NFLD/LBR* B31 ..... **185** E3
Gorsy Rd *RIDG/WDGT* B32 ..... **143** F5
Gorway Cl *WSL* WS1 ..... **52** B2
Gorway Gdns *WSL* WS1 ..... **52** C2
Gorway Rd *WSL* WS1 ..... **52** C2
Goscote Cl *BLOX/PEL* WS3 ..... **18** B6
Goscote La *BLOX/PEL* WS3 ..... **18** A4
Goscote Lodge Crs *BLOX/PEL* WS3 ..... **18** C6
Goscote Pl *BLOX/PEL* WS3 ..... **18** C6
Goscote Rd *BLOX/PEL* WS3 ..... **18** B4
Gosford St *BHTH/HG* B12 ..... **148** B3
Gospel End Rd *SEDG* DY3 ..... **66** C3
Gospel End St *SEDG* DY3 ..... **67** F4
Gospel Farm Rd *ACGN* B27 ..... **173** D5
Gospel La *ACGN* B27 ..... **173** E4
Gospel Oak Rd *TPTN/OCK* DY4 ..... **71** D2
Gosport Cl *WOLV* WV1 ..... **47** D2
Goss The *WOLV* WV1 ..... **167** F2
Gossey La *STECH* B33 ..... **129** E5
The Goss *BRLYHL* DY5 ..... **113** F6
Gotham Rd
  LGN/SDN/BHAMAIR B26 ..... **152** A3
Goths Cl *BLKHTH/ROWR* B65 ..... **117** E3
Gough Av *WNSFLD* WV11 ..... **13** D5
Gough Rd *BILS/COS* WV14 ..... **69** E2 ▣
  EDG B15 ..... **147** E2
  SPARK B11 ..... **149** E4
Gough St *WLNHL* WV13 ..... **29** E5 ▣
  WOLV WV1 ..... **3** D1
Gould Firm La *ALDR* WS9 ..... **36** A1
Gowan Rd *WASH/WDE* B8 ..... **126** A3
Gower Av *WOLVN* WV10 ..... **12** B3
Gower Rd *KGSWFD* DY6 ..... **112** B3
  SEDG DY3 ..... **66** A1
Gower St *BKHL/PFLD* WV2 ..... **45** F1 ▣
  LOZ/NWT B19 ..... **99** F6
  WLNHL WV13 ..... **28** C5 ▣
  WSLW WS2 ..... **51** D2
Gozzard St *BILS/COS* WV14 ..... **48** A4
Gracemere Crs *HLGN/YWD* B28 ..... **192** A1
Grace Rd *OLDBY* B69 ..... **93** E5
  SPARK B11 ..... **149** E3
  TPTN/OCK DY4 ..... **70** C4
Gracewell Rd *MOS/BIL* B13 ..... **171** F2
Grafton Dr *WLNHL* WV13 ..... **27** F6
Grafton Gdns *SEDG* DY3 ..... **89** D3
Grafton Pl *BILS/COS* WV14 ..... **48** A2 ▣
Grafton Rd *HDSW* B21 ..... **97** F4
  HHTH/SAND B71 ..... **95** F1
  LGLYGN/QTN B68 ..... **118** B5
  SHLY B90 ..... **191** E3
  SPARK B11 ..... **149** D2
Graham Cl *TPTN/OCK* DY4 ..... **71** D2
Graham Crs *RBRY* B45 ..... **184** B6
Graham Rd *HHTH/SAND* B71 ..... **95** F1
  RMSLY B62 ..... **141** E1
  STRBR DY8 ..... **111** F3
  YDLY B25 ..... **151** E3
Graham St *CBHAMW* B1 ..... **6** A3
  LOZ/NWT B19 ..... **99** E6
Grainger Cl *TPTN/OCK* DY4 ..... **71** F5 ▣
Grainger's La *CDYHTH* B64 ..... **139** E1
Grainger St *DUDS* DY2 ..... **91** F6
Graiseley HI *BKHL/PFLD* WV2 ..... **45** D1
Graiseley La *WNSFLD* WV11 ..... **27** E1
Graiseley Rw *BKHL/PFLD* WV2 ..... **45** E1

Graiseley St *BDMR/CCFT* WV3 ..... **2** B6
Graith Cl *ALE/KHTH/YWD* B14 ..... **192** A2
Grammar School La *HALE* B63 ..... **140** C5
Grampian Rd *STRBR* DY8 ..... **136** C3
Granary Cl *KGSWFD* DY6 ..... **86** C5 ▣
Granary La *WALM/CURD* B76 ..... **60** B6
Granary Rd *CDSL* WV8 ..... **10** A4
The Granary *ALDR* WS9 ..... **35** D1
Granbourne Rd *WSLW* WS2 ..... **29** F3 ▣
Granby Av *STECH* B33 ..... **129** E6
Granby Cl *HIA/OLT* B92 ..... **174** A4
Grandborough Dr *SOLH* B91 ..... **194** C4
Grand Cl *SMTHWK* B66 ..... **121** D4 ▣
Grand Junction Wy *WSL* WS1 ..... **51** F4
Grand Union Canal Wk
  CBHAMNE B4 ..... **6** D2
  DOR/KN B93 ..... **213** F2
  SOLH B91 ..... **197** D2
  SPARK B11 ..... **149** E2
  YDLY B25 ..... **150** C3
Grandys Cft
  CHWD/FDBR/MGN B37 ..... **130** B5 ▣
Grange Av *ALDR* WS9 ..... **20** C4
  MGN/WHC B75 ..... **39** E4 ▣
Grange Crs *HALE* B63 ..... **141** D6
  RBRY B45 ..... **184** A5
  RUSH/SHEL WS4 ..... **19** D5
Grange Farm Dr
  HWK/WKHTH B38 ..... **187** F5
Grangefield Cl *CDSL* WV8 ..... **10** B4 ▣
Grange HI *RMSLY* B62 ..... **163** E1
Grange Hill Rd *HWK/WKHTH* B38 ..... **188** A4
Grange La *BRGRVE* B60 ..... **216** C5 ▣
  HAG/WOL DY9 ..... **137** F5
  KGSWFD DY6 ..... **112** B3
  MGN/WHC B75 ..... **39** E4
Grange Ri *HWK/WKHTH* B38 ..... **188** B6
Grange Rd *ALE/KHTH/YWD* B14 ..... **169** F3
  AST/WIT B6 ..... **100** A5
  BILS/COS WV14 ..... **69** D4
  BKHL/PFLD WV2 ..... **45** D3
  BORD B9 ..... **149** F1
  CDYHTH B64 ..... **116** C5
  CDYHTH B64 ..... **141** D1
  DOR/KN B93 ..... **212** A6
  DUDN DY1 ..... **91** D4
  DUNHL/THL/PER WV6 ..... **23** E2
  ERDE/BCHGN B24 ..... **81** D6
  HAG/WOL DY9 ..... **137** C5
  HALE B63 ..... **141** D6
  HIA/OLT B92 ..... **174** A4
  SLYOAK B29 ..... **146** B6
  SMTHWK B66 ..... **120** C4
  WBROM B70 ..... **95** D2
Grange St *DUDN* DY1 ..... **91** D4
  WSL WS1 ..... **52** B2
The Grange *WMBN* WV5 ..... **64** C4
Granshaw Cl *HWK/WKHTH* B38 ..... **188** B4
Grant Cl *HHTH/SAND* B71 ..... **73** E6
  KGSWFD DY6 ..... **87** F5
Grantham Cl *BRLYHL* DY5 ..... **137** D2 ▣
Grantham Rd *SMTHWK* B66 ..... **121** D4
  SPARK B11 ..... **149** D3
Grantley Crs *KGSWFD* DY6 ..... **87** E6
Grantley Dr
  CHWD/FDBR/MGN B37 ..... **130** C4
Granton Cl *ALE/KHTH/YWD* B14 ..... **169** F6 ▣
Granton Rd *ALE/KHTH/YWD* B14 ..... **169** F6
Grantown Gv *GTWY* WS6 ..... **16** C1 ▣
Grant St *BLOX/PEL* WS3 ..... **17** D5 ▣
  EDG B15 ..... **147** F1
Granville Cl *BKHL/PFLD* WV2 ..... **45** F1 ▣
Granville Dr *KGSWFD* DY6 ..... **112** B3
Granville Rd *CDYHTH* B64 ..... **141** D1 ▣
  DOR/KN B93 ..... **212** C5
Granville St *BKHL/PFLD* WV2 ..... **45** F1
  CBHAMW B1 ..... **123** E6
  WLNHL WV13 ..... **28** C4
Grasdene Gv *HRBN* B17 ..... **145** E5
Grasmere Av
  DUNHL/THL/PER WV6 ..... **22** B3 ▣
  FOAKS/STRLY B74 ..... **36** C4
Grasmere Cl
  DUNHL/THL/PER WV6 ..... **9** F5
  GTB/HAM B43 ..... **76** B4 ▣
  KGSWFD DY6 ..... **87** D6
  WNSFLD WV11 ..... **13** E6
Grasmere Rd *HDSW* B21 ..... **98** B6
Grassington Dr
  CHWD/FDBR/MGN B37 ..... **130** B6 ▣
Grasmere Dr *STRBR* DY8 ..... **136** B6 ▣
Grassmoor Rd *HWK/WKHTH* B38 ..... **188** A3
Grassy La *WOLVN* WV10 ..... **13** D4
Graston Cl *LDYWD/EDGR* B16 ..... **122** C5 ▣
Grattidge Rd *HIA/OLT* B92 ..... **173** F1
Gravel Bank *RIDG/WDGT* B32 ..... **165** F1
Gravel HI *WMBN* WV5 ..... **65** D5
Gravelly HI *ERDE/BCHGN* B24 ..... **102** A3
Gravelly HI North
  ERDE/BCHGN B24 ..... **102** A2
Gravelly La *ERDW/GRVHL* B23 ..... **80** B2
Gravel Pit La *ALVE* B48 ..... **218** A5
The Gravel *WALM/CURD* B76 ..... **85** D1
Grayfield Av *MOS/BIL* B13 ..... **148** B6
Grayland Cl *ACGN* B27 ..... **173** D1

Grayling Cl *DARL/WED* WS10 ...... 49 D6
Grayling Rd *BRLYHL* DY5 .... 137 E3
Grayling Wk
 CHWD/FDBR/MGN B37 .... 131 E5
Grayshott Cl *ERDW/GRVHL* B23 ...... 80 A3
Grays Rd *HRBN* B17 .... 145 F3
Gray St *BORD* B9 .... 125 D5
Grayswood Park Rd
 RIDG/WDGT B32 .... 143 E3
Grayswood Rd *NFLD/LBR* B31 ...... 186 B6
Grazebrook Cft
 RIDG/WDGT B32 .... 165 F3 ◨
Grazebrook Rd *DUDS* DY2 .... 91 E6
Grazewood Cl *SHHTH* WV12 ...... 15 D6 ◨
Greadier St *SHHTH* WV12 .... 29 E2
Great Arthur St *SMTHWK* B66 ...... 96 B6
Great Barr St *BORD* B9 .... 124 C5
Great Brickkiln St *BDMR/CCFT* WV3 .... 2 A6
Great Br *TPTN/OCK* DY4 .... 71 F6
Great Bridge Rd *BILS/COS* WV14 ... 48 C5 ◨
Great Bridge St *WBROM* B70 ...... 72 A6
Great Brook St *VAUX/NECH* B7 .... 124 C3 ◨
Great Charles Street Queensway
 CBHAMNW B3 .... 6 C4
Great Colmore St *EDG* B15 .... 147 F1
Great Cornbow *HALE* B63 .... 141 D6 ◨
Great Croft St *DARL/WED* WS10 ...... 49 F3
Great Francis St *VAUX/NECH* B7 .... 125 D3
Great Hampton Rw *LOZ/NWT* B19 .... 6 B1
Great Hampton St *WOLV* WV1 .... 2 B1
 WSNGN B18 .... 123 E2
Great King St *LOZ/NWT* B19 ...... 123 E1
Great Lister St *VAUX/NECH* B7 .... 7 H1
Great Stone Rd *NFLD/LBR* B31 ... 186 C2
Great Tindal St *LDYWD/EDGR* B16 .. 122 C5
Great Western Cl *WSNGN* B18 .... 122 A1 ◨
Great Western Dr *CDYHTH* B64 ... 116 C6 ◨
Great Western St *DARL/WED* WS10 .. 72 A1
 WOLV WV1 .... 3 E2
Great Western Wy *TPTN/OCK* DY4 ... 71 F5
Great Wood Rd *BORD* B9 .... 125 E6
Greaves Av *DSYBK/YTR* WS5 ...... 53 E1
Greaves Cl *DSYBK/YTR* WS5 ...... 53 E1
Greaves Crs *SHHTH* WV12 .... 15 E5
Greaves Rd *DUDS* DY2 .... 115 F2
Greaves Sq *HWK/WKHTH* B38 ... 189 D4 ◨
Grebe Cl *ERDW/GRVHL* B23 ...... 101 D2
Greenacre Dr *CDSL* WV8 .... 9 D3
Greenacre Rd *TPTN/OCK* DY4 .... 70 C2
Green Acres *ACGN* B27 .... 173 D1
 WMBN WV5 .... 86 B1 ◨
Greenacres *DUNHL/THL/PER* WV6 .. 23 D2
 SEDG DY3 .... 67 D2
 WALM/CURD B76 .... 82 C3
Greenacres Av *WOLVN* WV10 .... 13 D4
Greenacres Cl *FOAKS/STRLY* B74.. 36 A5
Green Acres Rd *HWK/WKHTH* B38 .. 187 F5
Greenaleigh Rd
 ALE/KHTH/YWD B14 .... 191 F2
Green Av *HLGN/YWD* B28 .... 172 A2
Greenaway Cl *GTB/HAM* B43 ...... 55 E6 ◨
Greenbank *RBRY* B45 .... 215 F1
Green Bank Av *HLGN/YWD* B28 .... 172 A2
Greenbank Gdns *STRBR* DY8 ...... 112 A5 ◨
Greenbush Dr *HALE* B63 .... 140 C4
Green Cl *HLYWD* B47 .... 206 C4
Green Ct *HLGN/YWD* B28 .... 172 B3
Green Cft *BORD* B9 .... 126 C4
Greencroft *BILS/COS* WV14 ...... 47 F5
 KGSWFD DY6 .... 111 F3
Green Dr *RIDG/WDGT* B32 .... 165 E2
 WOLVN WV10 .... 11 E6
Greenend Rd *MOS/BIL* B13 .... 170 B1
Greenfels Ri *DUDS* DY2 .... 92 B5
Greenfield Av *BRGRVE* B60 ...... 199 F6
 CDYHTH B64 .... 115 D6
 STRBR DY8 .... 136 B4
Greenfield Crs *EDG* B15 .... 146 C1
Greenfield Cft *BILS/COS* WV14 .... 47 F5
Greenfield Rd *GTB/HAM* B43 ...... 75 E4
 HRBN B17 .... 145 E4
 SMTHWK B67 .... 120 A3
Greenfields *WS9 .... 20 C6 ◨
Greenfields Rd *KGSWFD* DY6 .... 112 A2
 RUSH/SHEL WS4 .... 19 F5
 WMBN WV5 .... 64 C6
Greenfield Vw *SEDG* DY3 .... 67 D4
Greenfinch Rd *CBROM* B36 ...... 106 C5
 HAG/WOL DY9 .... 137 F6
Greenford Rd
 ALE/KHTH/YWD B14 .... 191 D2
Green Gables *HLYWD* B47 .... 190 C6 ◨
Greenhill *BRGRVE* B60 .... 214 B4
 WMBN WV5 .... 65 D5
Greenhill Cl *SHHTH* WV12 .... 29 D2
Greenhill Dr *SLYOAK* B29 .... 167 E2
Greenhill Gdns *GTB/HAM* B43 ...... 75 F1
 RMSLY B62 .... 141 F3
 WMBN WV5 .... 65 D6
Greenhill Rd *CSCFLD/WYGN* B72 .. 81 D3
 HDSW B21 .... 97 F3
 MOS/BIL B13 .... 170 B2
 RMSLY B62 .... 141 F2 ◨
 SEDG DY3 .... 68 B6 ◨
Greenhill Wy *ALDR* WS9 .... 21 D4 ◨

Green Hill Wy *SHLY* B90 .... 173 D6
Greenholm Rd *KGSTG* B44 .... 78 A4
Greenhurst *RBRY* B45 .... 201 D6
Greening Dr *EDG* B15 .... 147 D2
Greenland Cl *KGSWFD* DY6 ...... 88 A5 ◨
Greenland Dr *HIA/OLT* B92 ...... 175 F4
Greenland Rd *SLYOAK* B29 ...... 169 D2
Greenlands *WMBN* WV5 .... 64 B3 ◨
Greenlands Rd
 CHWD/FDBR/MGN B37 .... 131 E5
Green La *ALDR* WS9 .... 36 A2
 BLOX/PEL WS3 .... 17 E6
 BORD B9 .... 125 E6
 BRGRVW B61 .... 198 C6
 CBROM B36 .... 106 A5
 CSHL/WTROR B46 .... 132 B2
 DUDN DY1 .... 68 B6
 DUNHL/THL/PER WV6 .... 10 A6
 GTB/HAM B43 .... 75 F4
 HAG/WOL DY9 .... 137 F4
 HDSW B21 .... 97 E5
 HWK/WKHTH B38 .... 188 A5
 POL/KGSB/FAZ B78 .... 62 C2
 RIDG/WDGT B32 .... 143 E3
 RMSLY B62 .... 117 F6
 RUSH/SHEL WS4 .... 19 F2
 SHLY B90 .... 192 A4
 WSLW WS2 .... 4 B2
 BILS/COS WV14 .... 47 E2
 SCFLD/BOLD B73 .... 81 D4
Greenleas Gdns *HALE* B63 ...... 141 E6 ◨
Green Leigh *ERDW/GRVHL* B23 .... 80 B3
Greenleighs *SEDG* DY3 .... 45 F6
Greenoak Crs *BVILLE* B30 .... 169 E3
 SEDG DY3 .... 68 C4
Green Oak Rd *CDSL* WV8 .... 9 D3
Green Park Av *BILS/COS* WV14 ... 47 D1
Green Park Dr *BILS/COS* WV14 ... 47 E1
Green Park Rd *DUDS* DY2 .... 92 B4
 NFLD/LBR B31 .... 186 A3
Greenridge Rd *BFLD/HDSWWD* B20 .. 76 A6
Green Rd *DUDS* DY2 .... 91 F6
 MOS/BIL B13 .... 171 F2
Green Rock La *BLOX/PEL* WS3 .... 17 F4
Greenroyde *HAG/WOL* DY9 ...... 159 D2 ◨
Greenside *HRBN* B17 .... 145 E4
Greenside Rd *ERDE/BCHGN* B24.. 81 E6
Greenside Wy *DSYBK/YTR* WS5... 52 C5
Greensill Av *TPTN/OCK* DY4 ...... 70 B3
Green Slade Crs *BRGRVE* B60 .... 199 E6
Greenslade Cft *NFLD/LBR* B31 .. 186 C3 ◨
Greenslade Rd *DSYBK/YTR* WS5 .. 53 E2
 SEDG DY3 .... 67 D1
 SHLY B90 .... 191 E3
Greensleeves *FOAKS/STRLY* B74.. 38 B5
Greenstead Rd *MOS/BIL* B13 .... 171 F2
Green St *BHTH/HG* B12 .... 124 B6
 BILS/COS WV14 .... 69 E3
 OLDBY B69 .... 94 C6
 SMTHWK B67 .... 120 B2
 STRBR DY8 .... 136 B4
 WBROM B70 .... 96 A5
 WSLW WS2 .... 31 E4
Greensway *WNSFLD* WV11 .... 13 D5
The Green *ALDR* WS9 .... 35 E1
 BLOX/PEL WS3 .... 17 D4
 CBROM B36 .... 105 D6
 CSCFLD/WYGN B72 .... 81 F2
 DARL/WED WS10 .... 49 F2
 HWK/WKHTH B38 .... 188 B3
 LGLYGN/QTN B68 .... 119 D5
 RIDG/WDGT B32 .... 142 C3 ◨
 SOLH B91 .... 175 F6
 STRBR DY8 .... 111 F5
Greenvale *NFLD/LBR* B31 .... 166 B6
Greenvale Av
 LGN/SDN/BHAMAIR B26 .... 153 F3
Greenway *ALDR* WS9 .... 21 D3
 BFLD/HDSWWD B20 .... 76 B5
 SEDG DY3 .... 68 A2
Greenway Av *STRBR* DY8 .... 112 A6 ◨
Greenway Dr *SCFLD/BOLD* B73... 57 E6
 SEDG DY3 .... 68 A2
Greenway Gdns *HWK/WKHTH* B38.. 188 A6
 SEDG DY3 .... 68 A2
Greenway Rd *BILS/COS* WV14 .... 48 A5
Greenways *HALE* B63 .... 139 E4
 NFLD/LBR B31 .... 166 B3 ◨
 STRBR DY8 .... 111 E5
Greenway St *BORD* B9 .... 125 E6
The Greenway
 CHWD/FDBR/MGN B37 .... 131 E5
 HAG/WOL DY9 .... 158 B6
 SCFLD/BOLD B73 .... 57 D6
Greenwood *YDLY* B25 .... 151 F1
Greenwood Av *ACGN* B27 .... 172 C1
 BLKHTH/ROWR B65 .... 117 F4 ◨
 LGLYGN/QTN B68 .... 119 D2 ◨

Greenwood Cl
 ALE/KHTH/YWD B14 .... 170 A6
Greenwood Pk *ALDR* WS9 .... 21 E4
Greenwood Pl *KGSTG* B44 .... 79 D2 ◨
Greenwood Rd *ALDR* WS9 .... 21 D3
 HHTH/SAND B71 .... 73 D5 ◨
 WOLVN WV10 .... 11 E6
The Greenwoods *STRBR* DY8 .... 136 A4 ◨
Greethurst Dr *MOS/BIL* B13 ...... 171 E1 ◨
Greets Green Rd *WBROM* B70.... 94 A1
Greetville Ct *STETCH* B33 .... 128 C2 ◨
Gregory Av *SLYOAK* B29 .... 166 C3
Gregory Cl *DARL/WED* WS10 .... 72 B1 ◨
Gregory Dr *DUDN* DY1 .... 90 C3
Gregory Rd *STRBR* DY8 .... 135 E4
Grendon Dr *SCFLD/BOLD* B73 .... 57 F6
Grendon Gdns
 ETTPK/GDPK/PENN WV4 .... 43 F3
Grendon Rd *ALE/KHTH/YWD* B14 .. 190 C2
 HIA/OLT B92 .... 174 A3
Grenfell Dr *EDG* B15 .... 146 B1 ◨
Grenfell Rd *BLOX/PEL* WS3 ...... 17 F2
Grenville Cl *WSLW* WS2 .... 29 F4
Grenville Dr *ERDW/GRVHL* B23 .. 101 D2
 SMTHWK B66 .... 95 F5
Grenville Pl *WBROM* B70 .... 94 A2
Grenville Rd *DUDN* DY1 .... 90 A4
 SHLY B90 .... 193 D2
Gresham Rd *HLGN/YWD* B28 .... 172 B5
 LGLYGN/QTN B68 .... 119 D1
Gresley Cl *MGN/WHC* B75 .... 38 C3
Gressel La *STETCH* B33 .... 129 E4
Grestone Av *BFLD/HDSWWD* B20 .. 98 A2
Greswolde Dr *ERDE/BCHGN* B24.. 103 D1
Greswolde Park Rd *ACGN* B27 .. 151 D6
Greswolde Rd *SOLH* B91 .... 174 A5
 SPARK B11 .... 149 E6
Greswold Gdns *STETCH* B33 .... 128 C2 ◨
Greswold St *HHTH/SAND* B71.... 73 D6
Gretton Crs *ALDR* WS9 .... 34 B2
Gretton Rd *ALDR* WS9 .... 34 B2
 ERDW/GRVHL B23 .... 79 F4
Greville Dr *EDG* B15 .... 147 E3
Grevis Cl *MOS/BIL* B13 .... 148 B5
Grevis Dr *YDLY* B25 .... 128 A6 ◨
Greyfort Crs *HIA/OLT* B92 .... 174 B2
Greyfriars Cl *DUDN* DY1 .... 90 A2
 HIA/OLT B92 .... 173 F4
Greyhound La
 ETTPK/GDPK/PENN WV4 .... 42 A4
Greyhurst Cft *SOLH* B91 .... 195 D5 ◨
Grey Mill Cl *SHLY* B90 .... 210 B1
Greystoke Av *CBROM* B36 .... 103 F6
Greystoke Dr *KGSWFD* DY6 ...... 111 F1
Greystone Pas *DUDN* DY1 .... 91 D4
Greystone St *DUDS* DY2 .... 91 E4
Grey Tree Crs *DOR/KN* B93 ...... 212 A4
Grice St *WBROM* B70 .... 95 E5
Griffin Gdns *HRBN* B17 .... 145 F5
Griffin Rd *ERDW/GRVHL* B23 .... 79 E6
Griffins Brook Cl *BVILLE* B30 .... 167 F4 ◨
Griffins Brook La *BVILLE* B30.... 167 E5
 NFLD/LBR B31 .... 167 E5
Griffin St *DUDS* DY2 .... 115 E3
 WBROM B70 .... 95 F2
 WOLV WV1 .... 26 B6
Griffiths Dr *WMBN* WV5 .... 64 C6
 WNSFLD WV11 .... 14 B4
Griffiths Rd *DUDN* DY1 .... 68 C5 ◨
 HHTH/SAND B71 .... 73 E2
 SHHTH WV12 .... 15 F5
Grigg Gv *NFLD/LBR* B31 .... 186 A4
Grimley La *HWK/WKHTH* B38 .... 188 C5
Grimpitts La *HWK/WKHTH* B38 .. 188 C5
Grimshaw Rd *HLGN/YWD* B28 .. 172 A4
Grimstone St *WOLVN* WV10 .... 3 F2
Grindleford Rd *PBAR/PBCH* B42 .. 77 F1
Gristhorpe Rd *SLYOAK* B29 ...... 168 C3
Grizedale Cl *RBRY* B45 .... 185 D3
Grocott Rd *DARL/WED* WS10..... 49 D5
Grosmont Av *BHTH/HG* B12 .... 148 C3
Grosvenor Av *AST/WIT* B6 .... 101 D5
 BFLD/HDSWWD B20 .... 99 E3
 ETTPK/GDPK/PENN WV4 .... 46 A6
 HRBN B17 .... 144 C5
 LGLYGN/QTN B68 .... 118 C3
 SEDG DY3 .... 89 F3
 SOLH B91 .... 194 B4
 WOLVN WV10 .... 11 F3
Grosvenor Sq *HLGN/YWD* B28 .. 172 A6
Grosvenor St *CBHAMNE* B4 .... 7 G4
 WOLVN WV10 .... 26 B4
Grosvenor St West
 LDYWD/EDGR B16 .... 123 D6
Grosvenor Wy *BRLYHL* DY5 ...... 137 E3
Grotto La *DUNHL/THL/PER* WV6.... 24 A2
Groucutt St *BILS/COS* WV14 ...... 69 E3 ◨
Grounds Dr *FOAKS/STRLY* B74 .. 38 B4 ◨

Grounds Rd FOAKS/STRLY B74 .... 38 B4
Grout St WBROM B70 .... 94 A1 🛈
Grove Av HALE B63 .... 140 B6 🛈
  MOS/BIL B13 .... 170 C1
  SOLH B91 .... 175 E6
Grove Cottage Rd BORD B9 .... 125 F5 🛈
  BRLYHL DY5 .... 113 E2
Grove Gdns HDSW B21 .... 98 B3
Grove Hl DSYBK/YTR WS5 .... 54 A1
Grove Hill Rd HDSW B21 .... 98 B4
Groveland Rd TPTN/OCK DY4 .... 92 C2
Grovelands St WOLVN WV10 .... 11 F2
Grove La BFLD/HDSWWD B20 .... 98 B3
  DUNHL/THL/PER WV6 .... 23 D5
  HDSW B21 .... 98 B3
  HRBN B17 .... 145 E5
  SMTHWK B66 .... 121 E2
  WALM/CURD B76 .... 62 C6
  WALM/CURD B76 .... 84 B1
  WSNGN B18 .... 121 F3
Groveley La NFLD/LBR B31 .... 202 B1
  RBRY B45 .... 201 E3
Grove Ms NFLD/LBR B31 .... 187 D5
Grove Pk KGSWFD DY6 .... 87 E5
Grove Rd ALE/KHTH/YWD B14 ...... 169 F4
  DOR/KN B93 .... 212 C3
  LGLYGN/QTN B68 .... 119 F6
  SOLH B91 .... 175 E6
  SPARK B11 .... 149 E6
Grove St BKHL/PFLD WV2 .... 45 F1
  DUDS DY2 .... 92 A5 🛈
  WOLVN WV10 .... 26 B4
  WSNGN B18 .... 121 F3
Grove Ter WSL WS1 .... 5 E5
The Grove BLKHTH/ROWR B65 ..... 117 E5
  BRLYHL DY5 .... 113 E6
  CSHL/WTROR B46 .... 53 D6
  DSYBK/YTR WS5 .... 54 A5
  ETTPK/GDPK/PENN WV4 .... 46 A4
  FOAKS/STRLY B74 .... 37 F2
  GTB/HAM B43 .... 54 A5
  HIA/OLT B92 .... 178 C3
  NFLD/LBR B31 .... 187 D5
  RBRY B45 .... 201 F3
  WASH/WDE B8 .... 125 E3
  WSNGN WV11 .... 27 D1
Grove Vale Av GTB/HAM B43 .... 75 E2
Grove Wy FOAKS/STRLY B74 .... 56 B2
Grovewood Dr HWK/WKHTH B38 .. 188 A4
Guardian Ct NFLD/LBR B31 .... 186 C2
  SOLH B91 .... 195 F2 🛈
Guardians Wy NFLD/LBR B31 ...... 166 A3 🛈
Guernsey Dr CBROM B36 .... 131 D1
Guest Av WNSFLD WV11 .... 13 E5
Guest Gv LOZ/NWT B19 .... 123 E1
Guild Av WALM/CURD WS3 .... 7 F6
Guild La LDYWD/EDGR B16 .... 122 C5
Guild Cft LOZ/NWT B19 .... 123 F1
Guildford Cft
  CHWD/FDBR/MGN B37 .... 154 B1
Guildford Dr LOZ/NWT B19 .... 123 F1
Guildford Dr LOZ/NWT B19 .... 99 F5
Guiting Rd SLYOAK B29 .... 166 C4
Gullane Cl HWK/WKHTH B38 .... 187 F3
Gullswood Cl
  ALE/KHTH/YWD B14 .... 189 F3 🛈
Gumbleberrys Cl
  WASH/WDE B8 .... 127 E3 🛈
Gunmakers Wy LOZ/NWT B19 .... 99 F6
Gunner La RBRY B45 .... 183 E5
Gunns Wy HIA/OLT B92 .... 173 F4
Guns La WBROM B70 .... 95 D1
Gunstock Cl FOAKS/STRLY B74 ..... 56 A2 🛈
Gunter Rd ERDE/BCHGN B24 .... 104 A3
Gurnard Cl WNSFLD WV11 .... 15 D4
Gurney Pl WSLW WS2 .... 30 C2
Gurney Rd WSLW WS2 .... 30 C2
Guthrie Cl LOZ/NWT B19 .... 123 F1
Gutrium Cl
  DUNHL/THL/PER WV6 .... 22 B2 🛈
  ERDW/GRVHL B23 .... 80 A3
The Gutter HAG/WOL DY9 .... 182 A6
Guy Av WOLVN WV10 .... 25 F1
Guys Cliffe Av WALM/CURD B76 ..... 82 B1
Guy's La SEDG DY3 .... 89 D3
Gwendoline Wy ALDR WS9 .... 21 D1
Gypsy La CSHL/WTROR B46 .... 107 F3

H

Habberley Rd BLKHTH/ROWR B65 .. 117 F5
Habberly Cft SOLH B91 .... 195 D4 🛈
Hackett Cl BILS/COS WV14 .... 68 C3
Hackett Dr SMTHWK B66 .... 95 F6 🛈
Hackett Rd BLKHTH/ROWR B65 .... 118 A4
Hackett St TPTN/OCK DY4 .... 71 E4
Hackford Rd
  ETTPK/GDPK/PENN WV4 .... 46 B5
Hack St BORD B9 .... 124 C6 🛈
Hackwood Rd DARL/WED WS10 ..... 73 D1

Hadcroft Gra HAG/WOL DY9 .... 137 F5
Hadcroft Rd HAG/WOL DY9 .... 137 F5
Haddock Rd BILS/COS WV14 .... 47 F2
Haddon Crs SHHTH WV12 .... 15 F6
Haddon Cft HALE B63 .... 161 E2
Haddon Rd PBAR/PBCH B42 .... 77 F4
Haden Cl CDYHTH B64 .... 140 B2
  STRBR DY8 .... 111 F5
Haden Cross Dr CDYHTH B64 ...... 140 C2
Hadendale CDYHTH B64 .... 140 C2
Haden Hl BDMR/CCFT WV3 .... 24 C5
Haden Hill Rd CDYHTH B64 .... 140 C2
  RMSLY B62 .... 141 D5 🛈
Haden Park Rd CDYHTH B64 .... 140 A2
Haden Rd CDYHTH B64 .... 116 A5
  TPTN/OCK DY4 .... 70 C2
Haden St BHTH/HG B12 .... 148 B3
Hadfield Cl ERDE/BCHGN B24 ...... 104 A2 🛈
Hadfield Cft LOZ/NWT B19 .... 123 D3
Hadfield Wy
  CHWD/FDBR/MGN B37 .... 130 C3 🛈
Hadland Rd STETCH B33 .... 129 D6
Hadleigh Cft WALM/CURD B76 .... 82 C5
Hadley Cl DUDS DY2 .... 116 A3
  HLYWD B47 .... 206 C2
Hadley Cft SMTHWK B66 .... 96 C6 🛈
Hadley Pl BILS/COS WV14 .... 47 E1
Hadley Rd BILS/COS WV14 .... 47 E2
  WSLW WS2 .... 🛈
Hadley St LGLYGN/QTN B68 .... 118 C3
Hadlow Cft STETCH B33 .... 153 F2
Hadrian Dr CSHL/WTROR B46 ...... 108 A3 🛈
Hadyn Gv LGN/SDN/BHAMAIR B26 . 153 D3
Hadzor Rd LGLYGN/QTN B68 .... 143 F1
Hafren Cl RBRY B45 .... 185 D3 🛈
Hafton Gv BORD B9 .... 125 F6 🛈
Haggar St BKHL/PFLD WV2 .... 45 E3
Hagley Cswy HAG/WOL DY9 .... 160 B4
Hagley Cl HAG/WOL DY9 .... 159 E5
Hagley Park Dr RBRY B45 .... 200 C3
Hagley Rd HALE B63 .... 141 D6 🛈
  HALE B63 .... 161 F2
  HRBN B17 .... 121 E6
  LDYWD/EDGR B16 .... 146 B1
  STRBR DY8 .... 137 D6
Hagley Rd West HRBN B17 .... 120 C6
  LGLYGN/QTN B68 .... 143 E2
  RIDG/WDGT B32 .... 142 A3
  RMSLY B62 .... 142 B3
Hagley View Rd DUDS DY2 .... 91 E5
Hagley Wood La HAG/WOL DY9 ... 161 D5
Haig Cl MGN/WHC B75 .... 59 D4
Haig Rd DUDS DY2 .... 92 B4
Haig St WBROM B70 .... 95 F3 🛈
Hainfield Dr SOLH B91 .... 176 A6
Hainge Rd OLDBY B69 .... 93 E3
Hainult Cl STRBR DY8 .... 111 F3
Halberton St WSNGN B18 .... 121 F3
Haldon Gv NFLD/LBR B31 .... 186 A6
Halecroft Av WNSFLD WV11 .... 27 F2 🛈
Hale Gv ERDE/BCHGN B24 .... 103 F1
Hales Crs SMTHWK B67 .... 120 A3
Halescroft Sq NFLD/LBR B31 ...... 166 A5
Hales Gdns ERDW/GRVHL B23 .... 79 E3
Hales La SMTHWK B67 .... 120 A3
Halesmere Wy HALE B63 .... 141 E6 🛈
Halesowen Rd BRGRVW B61 .... 199 E5
  CDYHTH B64 .... 116 A6
  CDYHTH B64 .... 140 B1
  DUDS DY2 .... 115 E2 🛈
  RMSLY B62 .... 142 A3
Halesowen St OLDBY B69 .... 94 B6
  RMSLY B62 .... 141 E1
Hales Rd DARL/WED WS10 .... 50 C3
  HALE B63 .... 140 C5
Hales Wy OLDBY B69 .... 94 B6
Halesworth Rd COVEN WV9 .... 10 B3
Halewood Dr HLGN/YWD B28 ...... 172 C4 🛈
Haley St SHHTH WV12 .... 29 E2
Halfcot Av HAG/WOL DY9 .... 137 E6
Halford Crs BLOX/PEL WS3 .... 32 B2
Halford Gv ERDE/BCHGN B24 ...... 104 A1 🛈
Halford Rd SOLH B91 .... 96 C6
Halford's La SMTHWK B66 .... 78 A5 🛈
Halfway Cl KGSTG B44 .... 78 A1
Halifax Gv WSNGN B18 .... 122 A3 🛈
Halladale HWK/WKHTH B38 .... 188 B4
Hallam Cl HHTH/SAND B71 .... 96 A1
Hallam Crs WOLVN WV10 .... 26 A1
Hallam St BHTH/HG B12 .... 148 A3
  HHTH/SAND B71 .... 95 F1
Hallbridge Cl BLOX/PEL WS3 .... 18 B3
Hallbridge Wy OLDBY B69 .... 93 D3 🛈
Hallchurch Rd DUDS DY2 .... 90 B6
Hall Crs HHTH/SAND B71 .... 73 E5

Hallcroft Cl CSCFLD/WYGN B72 ..... 81 E4 🛈
Hallcroft Wy ALDR WS9 .... 35 E2
  DOR/KN B93 .... 212 C1
Hall Dale Cl HLGN/YWD B28 .... 172 B6
Hall Dr CHWD/FDBR/MGN B37 .... 154 C2
  HAG/WOL DY9 .... 159 F5
Hall End DARL/WED WS10 .... 50 B6
Hallens Dr DARL/WED WS10 .... 49 F6
  DARL/WED WS10 .... 71 F1
Hallet Dr BDMR/CCFT WV3 .... 2 B6
Hallewell Rd LDYWD/EDGR B16 ... 121 F5
Hall Green Rd HHTH/SAND B71 ..... 73 F2
Hallgreen St BILS/COS WV14 .... 48 A6
Hall Hays Rd BKDE/SHDE B34 ...... 106 A6
Hall La ALDR WS9 .... 20 A3
  BILS/COS WV14 .... 68 B2
  BLOX/PEL WS3 .... 18 B2
  HAG/WOL DY9 .... 159 F5
  TPTN/OCK DY4 .... 71 D3
Hall Meadow HAG/WOL DY9 .... 159 F4
Hallmoor Rd STETCH B33 .... 129 D4
Hallot Cl ERDW/GRVHL B23 .... 79 F3
Halloughton Rd FOAKS/STRLY B74 . 58 C2
Hall Park St BILS/COS WV14 .... 47 D3
Hall Rd BFLD/HDSWWD B20 .... 98 C6
  CBROM B36 .... 104 C5
  SMTHWK B67 .... 120 A3
  WASH/WDE B8 .... 125 F3
Hallstead Rd MOS/BIL B13 .... 171 D6
Hall St BILS/COS WV14 .... 48 A4
  CDYHTH B64 .... 116 B5
  DARL/WED WS10 .... 49 D2
  DUDS DY2 .... 91 F4
  LGLYGN/QTN B68 .... 119 D2
  SEDG DY3 .... 67 F3 🛈
  STRBR DY8 .... 136 C6 🛈
  TPTN/OCK DY4 .... 70 A4
  WBROM B70 .... 95 E3
  WLNHL WV13 .... 29 D6
  WNSFLD WV11 .... 27 E2
  WSLW WS2 .... 31 F4
  WSNGN B18 .... 6 B1
Hall St East DARL/WED WS10 .... 49 E2
Hall St South WBROM B70 .... 95 F5
Hall Wk CSHL/WTROR B46 .... 132 B3
Halsbury Gv KGSTG B44 .... 79 D3
Halstead Gv SOLH B91 .... 194 C5
Halswelle Gv GTB/HAM B43 .... 56 A5 🛈
Halton Rd SCFLD/BOLD B73 .... 57 F6
Halton St DUDS DY2 .... 115 E2
Hamar Wy
  CHWD/FDBR/MGN B37 .... 131 D6 🛈
Hamberley Ct WSNGN B18 .... 121 F2 🛈
Hamble Cl BRLYHL DY5 .... 112 C1
Hambledon Cl COVEN WV9 .... 10 C3 🛈
Hamble Gv DUNHL/THL/PER WV6 . 22 A3
Hamble Rd
  ETTPK/GDPK/PENN WV4 .... 43 E3
  PBAR/PBCH B42 .... 76 B2
Hambleton Rd HALE B63 .... 161 F1
Hambletts Rd WBROM B70 .... 94 C2
Hambrook Cl
  DUNHL/THL/PER WV6 .... 24 C2
Hambury Dr ALE/KHTH/YWD B14 . 169 F4
  RMSLY B62 .... 141 E6
  STRBR DY8 .... 135 F3 🛈
Hamilton Av HRBN B17 .... 144 C1
  HAG/WOL DY9 .... 159 F5
Hamilton Cl SEDG DY3 .... 67 E3 🛈
  STRBR DY8 .... 111 E5
Hamilton Dr OLDBY B69 .... 93 E2
  STRBR DY8 .... 111 E5
Hamilton Gdns WOLVN WV10 .... 12 A2 🛈
Hamilton Rd HDSW B21 .... 97 F5
  SMTHWK B67 .... 120 A5
  TPTN/OCK DY4 .... 71 E5
Hamilton St BLOX/PEL WS3 .... 17 E4
Ham La HAG/WOL DY9 .... 159 E1
  KGSWFD DY6 .... 88 A4
Hamlet Gdns HLGN/YWD B28 ...... 172 B3
Hamlet Rd HLGN/YWD B28 .... 172 B3
Hammer Bank HALE B63 .... 138 C1
Hammersmith Cl HALE B63 .... 139 E2 🛈
Hammond Av WOLVN WV10 .... 12 A5
Hammond Dr ERDW/GRVHL B23 ... 80 B6
Hammond Wy STRBR DY8 .... 136 C2
Hampden Retreat
  BHTH/HG B12 .... 148 A3 🛈
Hampshire Dr EDG B15 .... 146 A1
Hampshire Rd HHTH/SAND B71 .... 72 C2
Hampson Cl SPARK B11 .... 149 D3 🛈
Hampstead Cl WNSFLD WV11 .... 27 E1
Hampstead Gld HALE B63 .... 141 E6 🛈
Hampton Cl SCFLD/BOLD B73 .... 79 E1
Hampton Court Rd HRBN B17 ..... 144 B5
Hampton Dr FOAKS/STRLY B74 ..... 59 D1
Hampton Gv BLOX/PEL WS3 .... 18 B1
Hampton La SOLH B91 .... 177 D6
  SOLH B91 .... 195 F1
  SOLH B91 .... 196 A1 🛈
Hampton Rd AST/WIT B6 .... 99 F5
  DOR/KN B93 .... 197 E6
  ERDW/GRVHL B23 .... 101 F1
  WOLVN WV10 .... 11 D4

Hampton St *BILS/COS* WV14 .... 69 D3
DUDS DY2 .... 115 D2
LOZ/NWT B19 .... 6 C1
Hams Rd *WASH/WDE* B8 .... 125 F3
Hamstead Hall Av
BFLD/HDSWWD B20 .... 76 A6
Hamstead Hall Rd
BFLD/HDSWWD B20 .... 98 A1
Hamstead Hl *BFLD/HDSWWD* B20 .... 98 B1
Hamstead Rd *BFLD/HDSWWD* B20 .... 99 D4
GTB/HAM B43 .... 75 E3
GTB/HAM B43 .... 75 E4
GTB/HAM B43 .... 76 B5
Hamstead Ter *DARL/WED* WS10 .... 72 C1
Hanam Cl *MGN/WHC* B75 .... 60 D3
Hanbury Cl *HALE* B63 .... 162 B1
Hanbury Crs
ETTPK/GDPK/PENN WV4 .... 44 A3
Hanbury Cft *ACGN* B27 .... 152 A6
Hanbury Hl *STRBR* DY8 .... 136 C5
Hanbury Rd *DOR/KN* B93 .... 212 B4
WBROM B70 .... 94 C2
Hanch Pl *WSL* WS1 .... 5 F6
Hancock Rd *WASH/WDE* B8 .... 126 B3
Hancox St *LGLYGN/QTN* B68 .... 119 D5
Handley Gv *NFLD/LBR* B31 .... 185 E3
Handley St *DARL/WED* WS10 .... 50 C5
Handsworth Cl *HDSW* B21 .... 97 F6
Handsworth Dr *GTB/HAM* B43 .... 76 C2
Handsworth New Rd *WSNGN* B18 .... 122 A2
Handsworth Wood Rd
BFLD/HDSWWD B20 .... 98 B2
Hanging La *NFLD/LBR* B31 .... 186 A3
Hangleton Dr *SPARK* B11 .... 149 F3
Hanley Cl *HALE* B63 .... 140 A5
Hanley St *LOZ/NWT* B19 .... 6 D1
Hannafore Rd *LDYWD/EDGR* B16 .... 121 F4
Hannah Rd *BILS/COS* WV14 .... 48 C5
Hannon Rd *ALE/KHTH/YWD* B14 .... 170 A6
Hanover Cl *AST/WIT* B6 .... 100 A6
Hanover Ct *DUNHL/THL/PER* WV6 .... 23 D1
WSLW WS2 .... 30 A6
Hanover Dr *VAUX/NECH* B7 .... 102 B3
Hanover Rd *BLKHTH/ROWR* B65 .... 117 E3
Hansell Dr *DOR/KN* B93 .... 212 A5
Hansom Rd *RIDG/WDGT* B32 .... 143 E4
Hanson Gv *HIA/OLT* B92 .... 152 B4
Hanson's Bridge Rd
ERDE/BCHGN B24 .... 82 B6
Hanwell Cl *WALM/CURD* B76 .... 83 D4
Hanwood Cl *BHTH/HG* B12 .... 148 B1
Harald Cl *DUNHL/THL/PER* WV6 .... 22 A2
Harbeck Av *KGSTG* B44 .... 78 B3
Harberrow Cl *HAG/WOL* DY9 .... 158 C5
Harbet Dr *BHAMNEC* B40 .... 156 A5
Harbinger Rd *HWK/WKHTH* B38 .... 189 D3
Harborne La *HRBN* B17 .... 145 F5
SLYOAK B29 .... 145 F6
SLYOAK B29 .... 161 F1
Harborne Park Rd *HRBN* B17 .... 145 E3
Harborne Rd *EDG* B15 .... 146 A3
SMTHWK B67 .... 119 F6
Harborough Dr *ALDR* WS9 .... 34 C2
CBROM B36 .... 105 F4
Harborough Rd *HAG/WOL* DY9 .... 159 D1
Harbours Hl *HAG/WOL* DY9 .... 198 A6
Harbury Cl *WALM/CURD* B76 .... 83 D5
Harbury Rd *BHTH/HG* B12 .... 147 F4
Harcourt Dr *DUDN* DY1 .... 89 F3
FOAKS/STRLY B74 .... 38 A3
Harcourt Rd *CDYHTH* B64 .... 140 B1
DARL/WED WS10 .... 50 B5
ERDW/GRVHL B23 .... 80 A5
Harden Cl *BLOX/PEL* WS3 .... 18 A6
Harden Gv *BLOX/PEL* WS3 .... 18 A6
Harden Rd *BLOX/PEL* WS3 .... 17 F6
Harding St *BILS/COS* WV14 .... 69 F2
Hardon Rd
ETTPK/GDPK/PENN WV4 .... 46 B3
Hardware St *WBROM* B70 .... 95 F1
Hardwick Dr *CDYHTH* B64 .... 140 C2
Hardwicke Wy *HAG/WOL* DY9 .... 137 F4
Hardwick Rd *FOAKS/STRLY* B74 .... 36 B5
LGN/SDN/BHAMAIR B26 .... 152 A5
Hardwick Wk *BVILLE* B30 .... 189 E3
Hardy Rd *BLOX/PEL* WS3 .... 18 A5
DARL/WED WS10 .... 50 C6
Hardy Sq *BKHL/PFLD* WV2 .... 46 B3
Harebell Cl *DSYBK/YTR* WS5 .... 52 C6
Harebell Crs *DUDN* DY1 .... 90 C1
Harebell Gdns
HWK/WKHTH B38 .... 188 B3
Hare Ov *NFLD/LBR* B31 .... 185 F2
Hare St *BILS/COS* WV14 .... 48 B4
Harewell Dr *MGN/WHC* B75 .... 39 E6
Harewood Av *DARL/WED* WS10 .... 51 E6
GTB/HAM B43 .... 75 E1
Harewood Rd *HLGN/YWD* B28 .... 172 A6
Harford St *LOZ/NWT* B19 .... 6 B1
Hargate La *HHTH/SAND* B71 .... 95 E1
Hargrave Cl *CSHL/WTROR* B46 .... 107 D2
Hargrave Rd *SHLY* B90 .... 191 F3
Hargreaves St *BKHL/PFLD* WV2 .... 46 C2
Harland Rd *FOAKS/STRLY* B74 .... 38 C4

Harlech Cl *OLDBY* B69 .... 92 C4
RIDG/WDGT B32 .... 164 C5
Harlech Rd *SHHTH* WV12 .... 29 E1
Harlech Wy *DUDN* DY1 .... 90 B3
Harleston Rd *KGSTG* B44 .... 78 B3
Harley Dr *BILS/COS* WV14 .... 47 D5
Harlstones Cl *STRBR* DY8 .... 136 C2
Harlow Gv *HLGN/YWD* B28 .... 172 C5
Harman Rd *WSNGN* B18 .... 122 C2
Harmer St *WSNGN* B18 .... 122 C2
Harmon Rd *STRBR* DY8 .... 135 E4
Harnall Cl *SHLY* B90 .... 194 A6
Harness Cl *DSYBK/YTR* WS5 .... 52 A5
Harold Rd *LDYWD/EDGR* B16 .... 122 B6
SMTHWKW B67 .... 120 A4
Harper Av *WNSFLD* WV11 .... 15 E6
Harper Rd *BILS/COS* WV14 .... 47 F3
Harpers Rd *HLYWD* B47 .... 190 C4
NFLD/LBR ....

C5
Harpur Cl *RUSH/SHEL* WS4 .... 32 C3
Harpur Rd *RUSH/SHEL* WS4 .... 32 C3
Harrier Rd *ACGN* B27 .... 173 F1
Harriet Cl *BRLYHL* DY5 .... 113 D2
Harringay Dr *STRBR* DY8 .... 136 A6
Harringay Rd *KGSTG* B44 .... 78 B1
Harris Dr *PBAR/PBCH* B42 .... 76 C3
SMTHWK B66 .... 121 D4
Harrison Cl *BLOX/PEL* WS3 .... 17 E4
Harrison Rd *ERDE/BCHGN* B24 .... 102 B1
FOAKS/STRLY B74 .... 38 A2
RUSH/SHEL WS4 .... 19 E3
STRBR DY8 .... 112 C6
Harrison's Fold *DUDS* DY2 .... 115 E2
Harrisons Cn *EDG* B15 .... 146 A3
Harrisons Pleck *MOS/BIL* B13 .... 148 B6
Harrison's Rd *EDG* B15 .... 146 A3
Harrison St *BLOX/PEL* WS3 .... 17 E4
Harrold Av *BLKHTH/ROWR* B65 .... 118 A4
Harrold Rd *BLKHTH/ROWR* B65 .... 118 A4
Harrold St *TPTN/OCK* DY4 .... 71 E4
Harrold Ter *LOZ/NWT* B19 .... 99 E5
Harrop Wy *STRBR* DY8 .... 136 A1
Harrowby Dr *TPTN/OCK* DY4 .... 92 C1
Harrowby Pl *WLNHL* WV13 .... 29 E6
Harrowby Rd *BILS/COS* WV14 .... 48 C5
WOLVN WV10 .... 11 D2
Harrow Cl *HAG/WOL* DY9 .... 158 C5
Harrowfield Rd *STECH* B33 .... 128 A3
Harrow Rd *KGSWFD* DY6 .... 87 F4
SLYOAK B29 .... 146 B6
Harrow St *WLNHL* WV13 .... 25 D3
Harry Perks St *WLNHL* WV13 .... 28 C4
Hart Dr *SCFLD/BOLD* B73 .... 80 C5
Hartfield Crs *ACGN* B27 .... 172 C2
Hartford Cl *HRBN* B17 .... 144 C2
Hartill Rd *ETTPK/GDPK/PENN* WV4 .... 43 F5
Hartill St *WLNHL* WV13 .... 49 D1
Hartington Cl *DOR/KN* B93 .... 212 A4
Hartington Rd *LOZ/NWT* B19 .... 99 F5
Hartland Av *BILS/COS* WV14 .... 68 C3
Hartland Rd *HHTH/SAND* B71 .... 74 B3
NFLD/LBR B31 .... 202 A1
TPTN/OCK DY4 .... 69 F6
Hartland St *BRLYHL* DY5 .... 89 F6
Hartlebury Cl *DOR/KN* B93 .... 212 B4
Hartlebury Rd *HALE* B63 .... 162 B1
Hartledon Rd *HRBN* B17 .... 145 D4
Hartley Dr *ALDR* WS9 .... 35 D3
Hartley Gv *KGSTG* B44 .... 57 D6
Hartley Pl *EDG* B15 .... 146 B1
Hartley Rd *KGSTG* B44 .... 56 C6
Hartley St *BDMR/CCFT* WV3 .... 24 C5
Harton Wy *ALE/KHTH/YWD* B14 .... 169 E6
Hartop Rd *FOAKS/STRLY* B74 .... 38 B6
WASH/WDE B8 .... 113 E3
Hart Rd *ERDE/BCHGN* B24 .... 80 C6
WNSFLD WV11 .... 27 F3
Hartsbourne Dr *RMSLY* B62 .... 141 F5
Harts Cl *HRBN* B17 .... 145 F3
Harts Green Rd *HRBN* B17 .... 144 C5
Hartshill Rd *BKDE/SHDE* B34 .... 128 C1
HIA/OLT B92 .... 173 F1
Hartshorn St *BILS/COS* WV14 .... 47 F4
Hartside Cl *HALE* B63 .... 139 E1
Harts Rd *WASH/WDE* B8 .... 126 A2
Hart St *WSL* WS1 .... 4 D6
Hartswell Dr *MOS/BIL* B13 .... 170 B5
Hartwell Cl *SOLH* B91 .... 195 D4
Hartwell Rd *ERDE/BCHGN* B24 .... 103 D3
Harvard Cl *DUDN* DY1 .... 90 A1
Harvard Rd *HIA/OLT* B92 .... 153 D5
Harvest Cl *BVILLE* B30 .... 169 D6
SEDG DY3 .... 66 C3
Harvesters Cl *FOAKS/STRLY* B74 .... 36 A5
Harvesters Rd *SHHTH* WV12 .... 29 F2
Harvester Wy *KGSWFD* DY6 .... 86 C5
Harvest Gdns *LGLYGN/QTN* B68 .... 118 C3
Harvest Rd *BLKHTH/ROWR* B65 .... 116 C4
SMTHWKW B67 .... 119 F4
Harvey Dr *MGN/WHC* B75 .... 39 E5
Harvey Rd
LGN/SDN/BHAMAIR B26 .... 151 F2
WSLW WS2 .... 31 D2
Harvills Hawthorn *WBROM* B70 .... 72 B4

Harvine Wk *STRBR* DY8 .... 136 A6
Harvington Dr *SHLY* B90 .... 211 D1
Harvington Rd *BILS/COS* WV14 .... 69 D3
HALE B63 .... 162 B1
LGLYGN/QTN B68 .... 142 C1
SLYOAK B29 .... 166 C3
Harvington Wy *WALM/CURD* B76 .... 82 B3
Harwin Cl *DUNHL/THL/PER* WV6 .... 10 B6
Harwood Cl *SHLY* B90 .... 193 E5
Harwood St *WBROM* B70 .... 95 D2
Hasbury Cl *HALE* B63 .... 162 A1
Hasbury Rd *RIDG/WDGT* B32 .... 165 D3
Haseley Rd *HDSW* B21 .... 98 A6
SOLH B91 .... 174 A5
Haselor Rd *SCFLD/BOLD* B73 .... 80 A2
Haselour Rd
CHWD/FDBR/MGN B37 .... 130 B2
Haskell St *WSL* WS1 .... 52 B2
Haslucks Cl *SHLY* B90 .... 192 A6
Haslucks Cft *SHLY* B90 .... 192 C2
Haslucks Green Rd *SHLY* B90 .... 192 C2
Hassop Rd *PBAR/PBCH* B42 .... 77 F4
Hastings Cl *DUDN* DY1 .... 90 A3
Hastings Rd *ERDW/GRVHL* B23 .... 79 E4
Haswell Rd *HALE* B63 .... 139 F6
Hatcham Rd *KGSTG* B44 .... 79 E1
Hatchett St *LOZ/NWT* B19 .... 124 A2
Hatchford Av *HIA/OLT* B92 .... 153 E6
Hatchford Brook Rd *HIA/OLT* B92 .... 153 E6
Hatch Heath Cl *WMBN* WV5 .... 64 B4
Hateley Dr
ETTPK/GDPK/PENN WV4 .... 46 A5
Hatfield Cl *ERDW/GRVHL* B23 .... 79 F4
Hatfield Rd *HAG/WOL* DY9 .... 137 E5
LOZ/NWT B19 .... 99 F5
Hathaway Cl *WLNHL* WV13 .... 48 B1
Hathaway Rd *MGN/WHC* B75 .... 38 C5
SHLY B90 .... 193 D4
Hatherden Dr *WALM/CURD* B76 .... 82 C1
Hathersage Rd *PBAR/PBCH* B42 .... 77 F4
Hatherton Gdns *WOLVN* WV10 .... 12 A3
Hatherton Gv *SLYOAK* B29 .... 166 B2
Hatherton Pl *ALDR* WS9 .... 20 C6
Hatherton Rd *BILS/COS* WV14 .... 48 B3
WSL WS1 .... 4 D2
Hatherton St *WSL* WS1 .... 4 D2
Hattersley Gv *SPARK* B11 .... 150 C6
Hatton Crs *WNSFLD* WV11 .... 12 C6
Hatton Gdns *PBAR/PBCH* B42 .... 77 D4
Hatton Rd *BDMR/CCFT* WV3 .... 24 B4
Hattons Gv *CDSL* WV8 .... 9 D3
Hatton St *BILS/COS* WV14 .... 48 A5
Haughton Rd *BFLD/HDSWWD* B20 .... 99 E4
Haunch La *MOS/BIL* B13 .... 170 B5
Haunchwood Dr *WALM/CURD* B76 .... 82 B4
Havacre La *BILS/COS* WV14 .... 69 E1
Havelock Cl *BDMR/CCFT* WV3 .... 44 B1
Havelock Rd *BFLD/HDSWWD* B20 .... 99 E3
SPARK B11 .... 150 A5
WASH/WDE B8 .... 126 A3
Haven Cft *GTB/HAM* B43 .... 75 F3
Haven Dr *ACGN* B27 .... 151 D6
The Haven *ALE/KHTH/YWD* B14 .... 191 F1
BKHL/PFLD WV2 .... 45 F3
STRBR DY8 .... 111 F5
Haverford Dr *RBRY* B45 .... 201 D1
Havergal Wk *HALE* B63 .... 139 D5
Haverhill Cl *BLOX/PEL* WS3 .... 16 C1
Hawbridge Cl *SHLY* B90 .... 211 D1
Hawbush Rd *BLOX/PEL* WS3 .... 32 A1
BRLYHL DY5 .... 112 C5
Hawcroft Dr *BKDE/SHDE* B34 .... 129 E1
Hawes La *BLKHTH/ROWR* B65 .... 117 D3
Hawes Rd *WSL* WS1 .... 52 B3
Haweswater Dr *KGSWFD* DY6 .... 111 F1
Hawfield Cl *OLDBY* B69 .... 93 E6
Hawfield Gv *CSCFLD/WYGN* B72 .... 81 E4
Hawfield Rd *OLDBY* B69 .... 93 E6
Hawker Dr *CVALE* B35 .... 104 B3
Hawkesbury Rd *SHLY* B90 .... 192 B4
Hawkes Cl *SLYOAK* B29 .... 168 C3
Hawkesford Cl *CBROM* B36 .... 104 C5
FOAKS/STRLY B74 .... 39 D6
Hawkesford Rd *STECH* B33 .... 129 F4
Hawkes La *MOS/BIL* B13 ....
Hawkes La *HHTH/SAND* B71 .... 72 C4
Hawkesley Crs *NFLD/LBR* B31 .... 186 A4
Hawkesley Dr *NFLD/LBR* B31 .... 186 B5
Hawkesley End *HWK/WKHTH* B38 .... 187 F5
Hawkesley Mill La *NFLD/LBR* B31 .... 186 B3
Hawkesley Rd *DUDN* DY1 .... 90 B5
Hawkes St *BORD* B9 .... 125 F6
Hawkestone Crs *WBROM* B70 .... 72 B5
Hawkestone Rd *SLYOAK* B29 .... 166 C4
Hawkeswell Cl *HIA/OLT* B92 .... 174 A3
Hawkeswell La *CSHL/WTROR* B46 .... 133 C4
Hawkesyard Rd
ERDE/BCHGN B24 .... 102 A4
Hawkhurst Rd
ALE/KHTH/YWD B14 .... 190 B3
Hawkinge Dr *CVALE* B35 .... 104 C1
Hawkins Cl *DIG/EDG* B5 .... 148 A3
Hawkins Cft *TPTN/OCK* DY4 .... 92 C2
Hawkins St *WBROM* B70 .... 72 C3
Hawkley Cl *WOLV* WV1 .... 27 D5
Hawkley Rd *WOLV* WV1 .... 27 D5

Hawkmoor Gdns
  HWK/WKHTH B38 .... **188** C5 🔲
Hawksford Crs *WOLVN* WV10 ...... **11** F6
Hawkshead Dr *DOR/KN* B93 ...... **212** B1
Hawkswell Av *WMBN* WV5 ...... **64** C6 🔲
Hawkswell Dr *WLNHL* WV13 ...... **49** D6
Hawkswood Gv
  ALE/KHTH/YWD B14 ...... **191** D2 🔲
Hawnby Gv *WALM/CURD* B76 ...... **82** C1
Hawne Cl *HALE* B63 ...... **140** A3 🔲
The Hawnelands *HALE* B63 ...... **140** B4 🔲
Hawne La *HALE* B63 ...... **140** A3
Hawskford Crs *WOLVN* WV10 ...... **11** F6
Hawthorn Brook Wy
  ERDW/GRVHL B23 ...... **80** A3
Hawthorn Cl *BORD* B9 ...... **125** D6
  ERDW/GRVHL B23 ...... **80** B4
Hawthorn Coppice *HAG/WOL* DY9.. **158** C6 🔲
Hawthorn Cft *LGLYGN/QTN* B68 .... **143** F2
Hawthorne Dr *HLYWD* B47 ...... **207** D1
Hawthorne Gv *SEDG* DY3 ...... **89** F3 🔲
Hawthorne La *CDSL* WV8 ...... **8** B4
Hawthorne Rd *BKHL/PFLD* WV2 .. **167** F6
  BVILLE B30 ...... **167** F6
  CBROM B36 ...... **106** A6
  DUDN DY1 ...... **91** E1
  EDG B15 ...... **146** A2
  HALE B63 ...... **162** A1
  SHHTH WV12 ...... **15** F6
  WNSFLD WV11 ...... **14** C2 🔲
  WNSFLD WV11 ...... **28** B2
Hawthorn Pk *BFLD/HDSWWD* B20.. **98** A2
Hawthorn Pl *WSLW* WS2 ...... **30** A4
Hawthorn Rd *BRLYHL* DY5 ...... **138** A1 🔲
  CSCFLD/WYGN B72 ...... **81** E2
  DARL/WED WS10 ...... **50** B5
  DSYBK/YTR WS5 ...... **52** B4
  FOAKS/STRLY B74 ...... **36** C6
  KGSTG B44 ...... **78** C4
  RUSH/SHEL WS4 ...... **19** D5
  TPTN/OCK DY4 ...... **70** C3
  WOLV WV1 ...... **47** D1 🔲
Hawthorn Ter *DARL/WED* WS10 ...... **50** B5
Haxby Av *BKDE/SHDE* B34 ...... **128** C1
The Haybarn *WALM/CURD* B76 ...... **82** C2 🔲
Haybridge Av *STRBR* DY8 ...... **158** B6
Haybrook Dr *SPARK* B11 ...... **150** B5
Haycock Pl *DARL/WED* WS10 ...... **49** E2 🔲
Haycroft Av *BKHL/PFLD* WV2 .. **126** A2
Haycroft Dr *MGN/WHC* B75 ...... **38** C3
Haydock Cl *CBROM* B36 ...... **105** E5
  DUNHL/THL/PER WV6 ...... **25** D2 🔲
Haydon Cl *DOR/KN* B93 ...... **212** B5
Haydon St *STETCH* B33 ...... **128** C4
Haye House Gv *CBROM* B36 ...... **104** A6
Hayes Crs *LGLYGN/QTN* B68 .. **119** F2 🔲
Hayes Cft *HWK/WKHTH* B38 ...... **188** A6
Hayes Gv *ERDE/BCHGN* B24 ...... **81** F5
Hayes La *HAG/WOL* DY9 ...... **138** C3
Hayes Meadow
  CSCFLD/WYGN B72 ...... **81** F4 🔲
Hayes Rd *LGLYGN/QTN* B68 .. **119** F2
The Hayes *WBROM* B70 ...... **94** C1
The Hayes *HAG/WOL* DY9 ...... **158** C4
  NFLD/LBR B31 ...... **187** E6
  SHHTH WV12 ...... **29** D1
Hayfield Ct *MOS/BIL* B13 ...... **171** E1
Hayfield Rd *MOS/BIL* B13 ...... **171** D1
Hay Gn *HAG/WOL* DY9 ...... **137** F4
Hay Green La *BVILLE* B30 ...... **167** E5
Hay Hall Rd *SPARK* B11 ...... **150** B3
Hay Hl *DSYBK/YTR* WS5 ...... **54** A1
Hayland Rd *ERDW/GRVHL* B23 ...... **80** A5 🔲
Hay La *SHLY* B90 ...... **195** E3
Hayle Cl *HWK/WKHTH* B38 .. **189** D3 🔲
Hayley Green Rd
  RIDG/WDGT B32 ...... **165** D3 🔲
Hayley Park Rd *HALE* B63 ...... **161** E3
Hayling Cl *RBRY* B45 ...... **184** B4 🔲
Hayling Gv *BKHL/PFLD* WV2 .. **45** E2
The Haylofts *HALE* B63 ...... **161** E2 🔲
Haynes Cl *DSYBK/YTR* WS5 ...... **53** D5
Haynes La *DSYBK/YTR* WS5 ...... **53** D4
Hay Pk *DIG/EDG* B5 ...... **5** D4
Haypits Cl *HHTH/SAND* B71 ...... **74** A4
Hayrick Dr *KGSWFD* DY6 ...... **87** D6 🔲
Hay Rd *YDLY* B25 ...... **150** C2
Hayseech *CDYHTH* B64 ...... **140** C2
Hayseech Rd *HALE* B63 ...... **140** B3
The Hays Kent's Moat
  LGN/SDN/BHAMAIR B26 .. **128** C6 🔲
Haytor Av *ALE/KHTH/YWD* B14.. **169** F6
Hawwain Cl *COVEN* WV9 ...... **10** B3
Hayward Rd *MGN/WHC* B75 ...... **59** E2
Haywards Cl *BLOX/PEL* WS3 ...... **18** B2
  ERDW/GRVHL B23 ...... **80** A6
Hayward St *BILS/COS* WV14 ...... **69** D3 🔲
Haywharf Rd *BRLYHL* DY5 ...... **113** D2
Haywood Dr *DUNHL/THL/PER* WV6.. **23** E3
  RMSLY B62 ...... **141** E1
Haywood Rd *STETCH* B33 ...... **129** E3
Haywood's Farm *HHTH/SAND* B71 .. **74** B1
Hazel Av *DARL/WED* WS10 ...... **50** C5
  SCFLD/BOLD B73 ...... **79** E2
Hazelbank *HWK/WKHTH* B38 .. **188** A3 🔲

Hazelbeach Rd *WASH/WDE* B8 .. **126** B2
Hazelbeech Rd *WBROM* B70 ...... **95** D5
Hazel Cft *CHWD/FDBR/MGN* B37 .. **131** D6
  NFLD/LBR B31 ...... **186** C2
Hazeldene Rd *HALE* B63 ...... **162** A1
  STETCH B33 ...... **154** A2 🔲
Hazel Dr *HLYWD* B47 ...... **207** D1
Hazeley Cl *HRBN* B17 ...... **144** B2
Hazel Gdns *ACGN* B27 ...... **151** E5 🔲
  CDSL WV8 ...... **8** C1 🔲
Hazel Gv *BILS/COS* WV14 ...... **48** A2 🔲
  STRBR DY8 ...... **135** E6
  WBROM B70 ...... **95** E4 🔲
  WMBN WV5 ...... **64** C4
Hazelhurst Rd
  ALE/KHTH/YWD B14 ...... **170** A4
  CBROM B36 ...... **106** A6
Hazelmere Dr *BDMR/CCFT* WV3 .... **22** C6 🔲
Hazelmere Rd *HLGN/YWD* B28 .. **172** B3 🔲
Hazeloak Rd *SHLY* B90 ...... **192** C4
Hazel Rd *BDMR/CCFT* WV3 ...... **44** A2
  DUDN DY1 ...... **91** E3
  KGSWFD DY6 ...... **112** A2
  RBRY B45 ...... **200** B1
  TPTN/OCK DY4 ...... **71** E2
Hazelton Cl *SOLH* B91 ...... **195** D4 🔲
Hazeltree Cft *ACGN* B27 ...... **173** D1 🔲
Hazeltree Gv *DOR/KN* B93 ...... **212** A4
Hazelville Gv *HLGN/YWD* B28 .... **172** C5 🔲
Hazelville Rd *HLGN/YWD* B28 .... **172** C5
Hazelwell Crs *BVILLE* B30 ...... **169** D5
Hazelwell Fordrough *BVILLE* B30.. **169** D4
Hazelwell La *BVILLE* B30 ...... **168** C4
Hazelwell Rd *BVILLE* B30 ...... **168** C5
Hazelwood Dr *WNSFLD* WV11 ...... **26** C2
Hazelwood Gv *SHHTH* WV12 ...... **29** F2
Hazelwood Rd *ACGN* B27 ...... **173** D1
  DUDN DY1 ...... **68** B6
  FOAKS/STRLY B74 ...... **35** F6
Hazlemere Dr *FOAKS/STRLY* B74.... **38** C6
Hazlitt Gv *BVILLE* B30 ...... **187** F1 🔲
Headingley Rd *HDSW* B21 ...... **98** A3
Headland Dr *WASH/WDE* B8 .. **125** F2 🔲
Headland Rd *BDMR/CCFT* WV3 ...... **22** B6
The Headlands *FOAKS/STRLY* B74.. **37** E4
Headley Cft *HWK/WKHTH* B38 .. **187** F5
Headley Heath La
  HWK/WKHTH B38 ...... **189** D6
Headley Ri *SHLY* B90 ...... **193** F3
Heale Cl *HALE* B63 ...... **138** C2 🔲
Heanor Cft *AST/WIT* B6 ...... **101** D5 🔲
Heartlands Ms
  BLKHTH/ROWR B65 ...... **117** D5 🔲
Heartlands Pkwy *VAUX/NECH* B7 .. **125** A2 🔲
Heartlands Pl *WASH/WDE* B8 .. **126** A3 🔲
Heath Acres *DARL/WED* WS10 ...... **49** E5
Heath Bridge Cl *BLOX/PEL* WS3 .... **18** C5
Heathbrook Av *KGSWFD* DY6 ...... **87** D6
Heathcliff Rd *DUDS* DY2 ...... **92** B6
  SPARK B11 ...... **150** B5
Heath Cl *BVILLE* B30 ...... **167** F6
  TPTN/OCK DY4 ...... **71** D4
Heathcote Av *SOLH* B91 ...... **194** A2
Heathcote Rd *BVILLE* B30 ...... **168** C5
Heath Cft *NFLD/LBR* B31 ...... **186** C6
Heath Croft Rd *MGN/WHC* B75 ...... **39** E5
Heath End Rd *HAG/WOL* DY9 ...... **181** E6
Heather Av *DSYBK/YTR* WS5 ...... **53** D5
Heather Cl *CBROM* B36 ...... **106** C5
  WNSFLD WV11 ...... **28** A2
Heather Court Gdns
  FOAKS/STRLY B74 ...... **58** C1
Heather Cft *KGSTG* B44 ...... **78** C1
Heather Dl *MOS/BIL* B13 ...... **169** E1 🔲
Heather Dr *RBRY* B45 ...... **200** B1
Heather Gv *SHHTH* WV12 ...... **30** A3
  SOLH B91 ...... **176** A5
Heatherleigh Rd *CBROM* B36 .. **106** B5 🔲
Heather Rd *BLOX/PEL* WS3 ...... **16** B5
  DUDN DY1 ...... **91** E1
  GTB/HAM B43 ...... **77** E5
  SMTHK B10 ...... **150** D1
  SMTHKWW B67 ...... **120** A2
Heath Farm Rd *CDSL* WV8 ...... **9** D3 🔲
  STRBR DY8 ...... **136** A6
Heathfield Av
  BFLD/HDSWWD B20 ...... **99** D5 🔲
Heathfield Cl *CDYHTH* B64 ...... **116** B5
  DOR/KN B93 ...... **212** C2 🔲
Heathfield Dr *BLOX/PEL* WS3 ...... **17** D3 🔲
Heathfield Gdns *STRBR* DY8 ...... **136** B5
Heathfield La *DARL/WED* WS10 ...... **49** D6
Heathfield La West
  DARL/WED WS10 ...... **49** D4
Heathfield Rd
  ALE/KHTH/YWD B14 ...... **170** A3
  BFLD/HDSWWD B20 ...... **99** E4
  FOAKS/STRLY B74 ...... **38** B4
  HALE B63 ...... **140** A6
  LOZ/NWT B19 ...... **99** D6
Heathfield Wy *CDYHTH* B64 ...... **116** B5
Heath Gdns *SOLH* B91 ...... **175** F5 🔲
Heath Gn *DUDN* DY1 ...... **68** B6
Heathgreen Cl
  CHWD/FDBR/MGN B37 ...... **131** F4 🔲

Heath Green Gv *WSNGN* B18 ...... **122** A3 🔲
Heath Green Rd *WSNGN* B18 ...... **122** A3
Heath Gv *CDSL* WV8 ...... **9** D2 🔲
Heath Hill Rd
  DUNHL/THL/PER WV6 ...... **22** A6
Heath House La *CDSL* WV8 ...... **8** A5
Heathland Av *BKDE/SHDE* B34 .. **104** C6
Heathlands Cl *KGSWFD* DY6 ...... **88** A5 🔲
Heathlands Rd *SCFLD/BOLD* B73 ...... **80** B1
The Heathlands
  BLKHTH/ROWR B65 ...... **117** E6 🔲
  STRBR DY8 ...... **73** F4
Heath La *HHTH/SAND* B71 ...... **73** F4
  STRBR DY8 ...... **136** C6 🔲
Heathleigh Rd *HWK/WKHTH* B38 .. **187** E5
Heathmere Av *YDLY* B25 ...... **151** F1
Heathmere Dr
  CHWD/FDBR/MGN B37 ...... **130** B5
Heath Mill La *BORD* B9 ...... **124** C6
Heath Ri *ALE/KHTH/YWD* B14 ...... **190** C4
Heath Rd *BVILLE* B30 ...... **167** F6
  BVILLE B30 ...... **187** E1
  DARL/WED WS10 ...... **50** A1
  DUDS DY2 ...... **115** D4 🔲
  HLYWD B47 ...... **190** C6
  SHHTH WV12 ...... **15** F5
  SOLH B91 ...... **175** F5
Heath Rd South *NFLD/LBR* B31 ...... **187** D1
Heathside Dr *BLOX/PEL* WS3 ...... **18** C1 🔲
  HWK/WKHTH B38 ...... **189** D4
Heath St *BLKHTH/ROWR* B65 ...... **117** E6
  STRBR DY8 ...... **136** B4
  WSNGN B18 ...... **121** F2 🔲
Heath St South *WSNGN* B18 ...... **122** B3 🔲
Heath Wy *BKDE/SHDE* B34 ...... **104** B6
Heathy Farm Cl
  RIDG/WDGT B32 ...... **165** D2 🔲
Heathy Ri *RIDG/WDGT* B32 ...... **164** C1
Heaton Dr *EDG* B15 ...... **146** A1
Heaton Rd *SOLH* B91 ...... **174** B4
Heaton St *WSNGN* B18 ...... **123** D2
Hebden Gv *HLGN/YWD* B28 .. **192** A2 🔲
  WNSFLD WV11 ...... **15** D4
Hedera Cl *DSYBK/YTR* WS5 ...... **53** D6 🔲
Hedgefield Gv *HALE* B63 ...... **139** E5
Hedgerow Dr *KGSWFD* DY6 ...... **87** F4
The Hedgerows *RMSLY* B62 ...... **182** B1
The Hedges *WMBN* WV5 ...... **64** A5 🔲
Hedgetree Cft
  CHWD/FDBR/MGN B37 ...... **131** E5
Hedgley Gv *STETCH* B33 ...... **128** C3
Hedingham Gv
  CHWD/FDBR/MGN B37 ...... **131** F5
Hedley Cft *CVALE* B35 ...... **105** D4
Heeley Rd *SLYOAK* B29 ...... **168** B1
Helena Cl *CBHAMW* B1 ...... **6** A4 🔲
Helena St *CBHAMW* B1 ...... **26** C2
Helford Cl *TPTN/OCK* DY4 ...... **91** F1
Hellaby Cl *CSCFLD/WYGN* B72 .. **59** E5 🔲
Hellier Av *TPTN/OCK* DY4 ...... **93** D1
Hellier Rd *WOLVN* WV10 ...... **12** A3
Hellier St *DUDS* DY2 ...... **91** E5 🔲
Helming Dr *WOLV* WV1 ...... **27** D4
Helmsdale Wy *SEDG* DY3 ...... **68** C4
Helmsley Cl *BRLYHL* DY5 ...... **137** E1
Helmsley Rd *WNSFLD* WV11 ...... **13** E5
Helmswood Dr
  CHWD/FDBR/MGN B37 ...... **155** E1
Helston Cl *DSYBK/YTR* WS5 ...... **53** F2
  STRBR DY8 ...... **111** E5
Helston Gv *SPARK* B11 ...... **150** C6 🔲
Helston Rd *DSYBK/YTR* WS5 ...... **53** E5
Hembs Crs *GTB/HAM* B43 ...... **77** E5
Hemlingford Cft
  CHWD/FDBR/MGN B37 ...... **154** C2 🔲
Hemlingford Rd
  CHWD/FDBR/MGN B37 ...... **130** A1
  WALM/CURD B76 ...... **82** B4
Hemmings Cl *STRBR* DY8 ...... **136** B4 🔲
  WOLVN WV10 ...... **3** H1
Hemmings St *DARL/WED* WS10 ...... **49** E1 🔲
Hemplands Rd *STRBR* DY8 ...... **136** B4 🔲
Hempole La *TPTN/OCK* DY4 ...... **71** F5
Hemyock Rd *SLYOAK* B29 ...... **167** D3
Henbury Rd *ACGN* B27 ...... **151** F6 🔲
Henderson Wk *TPTN/OCK* DY4 ...... **71** D3
Henderson Wy
  BLKHTH/ROWR B65 ...... **117** E6
  SEDG DY3 ...... **89** F3 🔲
  WOLVN WV10 ...... **12** A5
Hendon Rd *SPARK* B11 ...... **149** D3
Heneage St *VAUX/NECH* B7 ...... **7** H1
Heneage St West *VAUX/NECH* B7 .. **7** H2
Henfield Cl *WNSFLD* WV11 ...... **27** F1 🔲
Hengham Rd
  LGN/SDN/BHAMAIR B26 .. **128** C6
Henley Cl *BLOX/PEL* WS3 ...... **18** A4
  SCFLD/BOLD B73 ...... **81** D3
  TPTN/OCK DY4 ...... **71** F6 🔲
Henley Crs *SOLH* B91 ...... **175** D4
Henley Dr *MGN/WHC* B75 ...... **38** C4 🔲
Henley Rd *WOLVN* WV10 ...... **11** D4
Henley St *SPARK* B11 ...... **148** C2
Henlow Cl *TPTN/OCK* DY4 ...... **69** F6
Henlow Rd *ALE/KHTH/YWD* B14 .. **190** B3

Hillary Crest *SEDG* DY3 .... **68** A6 🔟
Hillary St *WSLW* WS2 .... **51** E3
Hill Av *ETTPK/GDPK/PENN* WV4 .... **46** B6
Hill Bank *HALE* B63 .... **139** F2
Hill Bank Rd *HALE* B63 .... **139** F2
   HWK/WKHTH B38 .... **188** C3
Hillbank *OLDBY* B69 .... **93** F5
Hill Bank Rd *STETCH* B33 .... **127** F3
Hillbrook Gv *STETCH* B33 .... **128** B4
Hillbury Dr *SHHTH* WV12 .... **15** D5
Hill Cl *NFLD/LBR* B31 .... **187** D4
   SEDG DY3 .... **68** A2
Hill Crest *SEDG* DY3 .... **89** D1
Hill Crest Av *BRLYHL* DY5 .... **113** E6
Hillcrest Av *GTB/HAM* B43 .... **76** A1
   HALE B63 .... **139** D2
   WOLVN WV10 .... **12** A5
Hillcrest Cl *DUDN* DY1 .... **115** E2
Hill Crest Gdns *SHHTH* WV12 .... **29** F2
Hill Crest Gv *KGSTG* B44 .... **78** C4
Hillcrest Rd *DUDS* DY2 .... **92** A4
   MOS/BIL B13 .... **170** A1
Hillcrest Rd *CSCFLD/WYGN* B72..... **81** E3
   GTB/HAM B43 .... **76** A1
   RMSLY B62 .... **182** B1
Hill Croft Rd *ALE/KHTH/YWD* B14... **169** E5
Hillcroft Rd *KGSWFD* DY6 .... **88** A6
Hillcross Wk *CBROM* B36 .... **104** B6 🔟
Hilldrop Gv *HRBN* B17 .... **145** F6
Hilleys Cft *CHWD/FDBR/MGN* B37 ... **130** B4
Hillfield Ms *SOLH* B91 .... **195** D5 🔟
Hillfield Rd *SOLH* B91 .... **195** E3
   SPARK B11 .... **149** F6
Hillfields *SMTHWKW* B67 .... **119** F4
Hillfields Rd *BRLYHL* DY5 .... **137** D2
Hill Hook Rd *FOAKS/STRLY* B74 ..... **38** A1
Hill House La *STETCH* B33 .... **128** B4
Hillhurst Gv *CBROM* B36 .... **105** F4 🔟
Hilliards Cft *PBAR/PBCH* B42 .... **76** C3
Hillingford Av *GTB/HAM* B43 .... **55** F5
Hill La *GTB/HAM* B43 .... **76** A1
   HAG/WOL DY9 .... **180** A1
   HLYWD B47 .... **206** A6
   MGN/WHC B75 .... **41** D5
Hillman Dr *DUDS* DY2 .... **92** A4
Hillman Gv *CBROM* B36 .... **106** A4
Hillmeads Dr *DUDS* DY2 .... **92** A4
Hillmeads Rd *HWK/WKHTH* B38 ..... **188** C4
Hillmorton Rd *DOR/KN* B93 .... **212** C2 🔟
   FOAKS/STRLY B74 .... **38** B3
Hillmount Cl *HLGN/YWD* B28 .... **172** A1
Hill Pas *CDYHTH* B64 .... **116** A5
Hill Pl *WNSFLD* WV11 .... **14** C4
Hill Rd *HAG/WOL* DY9 .... **138** A4
   OLDBY B69 .... **92** C3
   WLNHL WV13 .... **27** F6
Hill Side *SEDG* DY3 .... **89** E1
Hillside *BLKHTH/ROWR* B65 .... **141** D1
   BRLYHL DY5 .... **138** C1
   HALE B63 .... **139** F3
Hillside Cl *RIDG/WDGT* B32 .... **164** C3
Hillside Crs *BLOX/PEL* WS3 .... **18** B3
Hillside Cft *HIA/OLT* B92 .... **154** A5
Hillside Dr *CHWD/FDBR/MGN* B37 ... **130** B3 🔟
   FOAKS/STRLY B74 .... **56** B2 🔟
   PBAR/PBCH B42 .... **76** C5
Hillside Gdns
   CHWD/FDBR/MGN B37 .... **130** B3 🔟
   WOLV WV1 .... **26** C4 🔟
Hillside Rd *DUDN* DY1 .... **90** C1
   ERDW/GRVHL B23 .... **101** F3
   FOAKS/STRLY B74 .... **38** B3
   GTB/HAM B43 .... **75** F1
Hillstone Gdns *WOLVN* WV10 .... **12** B5
Hillstone Rd *BKDE/SHDE* B34 .... **129** F2
Hill St *BILS/COS* WV14 .... **48** A6
   BRLYHL DY5 .... **113** F5 🔟
   BRLYHL DY5 .... **138** C1
   CBHAM B2 .... **6** D6
   DARL/WED WS10 .... **50** A3
   DUDS DY2 .... **115** D2
   HAG/WOL DY9 .... **138** B4 🔟
   HALE B63 .... **140** C6
   SEDG DY3 .... **68** A6
   SMTHWK B66 .... **120** C1
   STRBR DY8 .... **136** B1
   TPTN/OCK DY4 .... **92** B1
   WNSFLD WV11 .... **14** C1
   WSL WS1 .... **5** E5
The Hill *RIDG/WDGT* B32 .... **165** F1
Hilltop *HHTH/SAND* B71 .... **72** C4
Hill Top *RMSLY* B62 .... **142** A2
Hill Top Cl *KGSTG* B44 .... **78** A5 🔟
Hilltop Dr *CBROM* B36 .... **103** F6 🔟
Hilltop Rd *DUDS* DY2 .... **92** A5
Hill Top Rd *LGLYGN/QTN* B68 .... **119** C6
   NFLD/LBR B31 .... **186** B2
Hill Vw *ALDR* WS9 .... **21** D3
Hillview Cl *HALE* B63 .... **140** A3
Hillview Rd *RBRY* B45 .... **184** A5
Hill Village Rd *MGN/WHC* B75 .... **38** C3

Hillville Gdns *STRBR* DY8 .... **137** D6 🔟
Hill Wd *BLOX/PEL* WS3 .... **18** B3
Hillwood Av *SHLY* B90 .... **210** C1
Hillwood Cl *STRBR* DY8 .... **111** E3
Hillwood Common Rd
   MGN/WHC B75 .... **39** D2
Hill Wood Rd *MGN/WHC* B75 .... **39** E2
Hillyfields Rd *ERDW/GRVHL* B23 .... **101** E1
Hilly Rd *BILS/COS* WV14 .... **70** A1
Hilsea Cl *COVEN* WV9 .... **10** B4
Hilston Av *ETTPK/GDPK/PENN* WV4 .. **43** E5
   HALE B63 .... **140** B5
Hilton Av *HLGN/YWD* B28 .... **192** A1
Hilton Cl *BLOX/PEL* WS3 .... **16** B4
   STRBR DY8 .... **136** C2
Hilton Dr *CSCFLD/WYGN* B72 .... **81** E3
Hilton Pl *BILS/COS* WV14 .... **48** A4
Hilton Rd *ETTPK/GDPK/PENN* WV4 .. **46** B5
   OLDBY B69 .... **93** E5
   SHHTH WV12 .... **15** E5
Hilton St *WBROM* B70 .... **94** C2
   WOLVN WV10 .... **3** G1
Himbleton Cft *SHLY* B90 .... **210** C1 🔟
Himley Av *DUDN* DY1 .... **90** B3
Himley Cl *GTB/HAM* B43 .... **75** E1
   SHHTH WV12 .... **28** C2
Himley Crs
   ETTPK/GDPK/PENN WV4 .... **45** E4
Himley Gdns *SEDG* DY3 .... **88** B1
Himley Gv *RBRY* B45 .... **201** D1
Himley La *SEDG* DY3 .... **86** B3
Himley Rd *DUDN* DY1 .... **90** A4
   SEDG DY3 .... **88** A2
Himley St *DUDN* DY1 .... **90** A4 🔟
Hinbrook Rd *DUDN* DY1 .... **90** A4 🔟
Hinckes Rd *DUNHL/THL/PER* WV6 .. **23** D2
Hinckley Cft *FOAKS/STRLY* B74 ..... **36** B4 🔟
Hinckley St *DIG/EDG* B5 .... **123** F6 🔟
Hincks St *BKHL/PFLD* WV2 .... **46** C2
Hindhead Rd *ALE/KHTH/YWD* B14 .. **191** E1
Hindlip Cl *HALE* B63 .... **162** B1 🔟
Hindlow Cl *VAUX/NECH* B7 .... **125** D3
Hindon Gv *ACGN* B27 .... **173** E4 🔟
Hindon Sq *EDG* B15 .... **146** B1
Hingeston St *WSNGN* B18 .... **123** D3
Hingley Cft *FOAKS/STRLY* B74 ...... **36** B4 🔟
Hingley Rd *HALE* B63 .... **138** C3
Hingley St *CDYHTH* B64 .... **115** F6 🔟
Hinksford Gdns *SEDG* DY3 .... **86** A3
Hinksford La *SEDG* DY3 .... **86** A4
Hinsford Cl *KGSWFD* DY6 .... **88** A5
Hinstock Cl
   ETTPK/GDPK/PENN WV4 .... **44** C5
Hinstock Rd *BFLD/HDSWWD* B20 ... **98** A3
Hintlesham Av *EDG* B15 .... **145** F4
Hinton Av *ALVE* B48 .... **216** C5
Hinton Gv *WNSFLD* WV11 .... **28** B2
Hintons Coppice *DOR/KN* B93 ...... **212** A1 🔟
Hipkins St *TPTN/OCK* DY4 .... **70** A4
Hiplands Rd *RMSLY* B62 .... **142** A3
Hipsley Cl *CBROM* B36 .... **105** E4 🔟
Hipsmoor Cl
   CHWD/FDBR/MGN B37 .... **130** B4 🔟
Hirdemonsfield *SHLY* B90 .... **208** C2 🔟
Hirdemonsway *SHLY* B90 .... **208** B3
Histons Dr *CDSL* WV8 .... **8** B3
Histons HI *CDSL* WV8 .... **8** B3
Hitchcock Cl *SMTHWKW* B67 .... **119** F2 🔟
Hitches La *EDG* B15 .... **147** D2
Hitherside *SHLY* B90 .... **209** D2 🔟
Hoarstone *STRBR* DY8 .... **158** B6 🔟
Hobacre Cl *RBRY* B45 .... **184** C5 🔟
Hobart Cft *VAUX/NECH* B7 .... **124** C3
Hobart Dr *DSYBK/YTR* WS5 .... **53** E3
Hobart Rd *TPTN/OCK* DY4 .... **70** A2
Hobgate Cl *WOLVN* WV10 .... **26** B3
Hobgate Rd *WOLVN* WV10 .... **26** B3
Hob Green Rd *HAG/WOL* DY9 .... **160** A1
Hobhouse Cl *GTB/HAM* B43 .... **76** A1
Hobley St *WLNHL* WV13 .... **29** E5 🔟
Hobmoor Cft *YDLY* B25 .... **151** F2
Hob Moor Rd
   LGN/SDN/BHAMAIR B26 .... **152** A2 🔟
   SMHTH B10 .... **126** C6
   SMHTH B10 .... **151** D1
   YDLY B25 .... **151** E1
Hobnock Rd *WNSFLD* WV11 .... **14** C1
Hobs Hole La *ALDR* WS9 .... **21** F6
Hob's Meadow *HIA/OLT* B92 .... **174** C1
Hob's Moat Rd *HIA/OLT* B92 .... **153** D6
   HIA/OLT B92 .... **175** D1 🔟
Hobson Rd *WSNGN* B18 .... **122** C2 🔟
Hobson Rd *SLYOAK* B29 .... **169** D2
Hobs Rd *DARL/WED* WS10 .... **50** C5
Hockley Brook Cl *WSNGN* B18 ...... **122** C2 🔟
Hockley HI *WSNGN* B18 .... **123** D1
Hockley La *DUDS* DY2 .... **115** D4
Hockley Pool Cl *WSNGN* B18 .... **123** D2 🔟
Hockley Rd *BILS/COS* WV14 .... **68** C4
   ERDW/GRVHL B23 .... **101** F1 🔟
Hockley St *LOZ/NWT* B19 .... **123** E2
   WSNGN B18 .... **6** A1

Hodge Hill Av *HAG/WOL* DY9 .... **138** B6 🔟
Hodge Hill Rd *BKDE/SHDE* B34 ...... **128** A2
Hodgetts Cl *SMTHWKW* B67 .... **119** E3
Hodgetts Dr *HALE* B63 .... **161** F3 🔟
Hodnell Cl *CBROM* B36 .... **105** E4
Hodnet Dr *BRLYHL* DY5 .... **113** E1
Hodnet Gv *DIG/EDG* B5 .... **148** A1 🔟
Hodson Av *WLNHL* WV13 .... **29** E6
Hodson Cl *WNSFLD* WV11 .... **14** B5 🔟
Hoff Beck Court Ct *BORD* B9 .... **125** D5 🔟
Hogarth Cl *GTB/HAM* B43 .... **55** F4
   WLNHL WV13 .... **28** A5
Hoggs La *NFLD/LBR* B31 .... **186** A1
Holbeache La *KGSWFD* DY6 .... **87** F4
Holbeache Rd *KGSWFD* DY6 .... **87** E5
   KINVER DY7 .... **110** C3
Holbeach La *STETCH* B33 .... **129** D5
Holbeche Rd *DOR/KN* B93 .... **196** C6
   MGN/WHC B75 .... **61** D5
Holberg Gv *WNSFLD* WV11 .... **28** B1
Holborn HI *VAUX/NECH* B7 .... **101** D5
Holbury Cl *COVEN* WV9 .... **10** C3
Holcombe Rd *SPARK* B11 .... **150** C6
Holcroft Rd *HAG/WOL* DY9 .... **137** E5
   HALE B63 .... **139** E4
   KGSWFD DY6 .... **87** E4
Holcroft St *BKHL/PFLD* WV2 .... **46** C2
   TPTN/OCK DY4 .... **92** C3
Holden Cl *ERDW/GRVHL* B23 .... **102** A3
Holden Crs *BLOX/PEL* WS3 .... **32** A2
Holden Cft *TPTN/OCK* DY4 .... **92** C3 🔟
Holden Pl *BLOX/PEL* WS3 .... **32** A3
Holden Rd *DARL/WED* WS10 .... **72** C1
   ETTPK/GDPK/PENN WV4 .... **43** F6
Holder Rd *SPARK* B11 .... **149** E3
   YDLY B25 .... **151** E2
Holders Gdns *MOS/BIL* B13 .... **169** E1
Holders La *MOS/BIL* B13 .... **169** E1
Holdford Rd *AST/WIT* B6 .... **100** D3
Holdgate Rd *SLYOAK* B29 .... **167** D4
Hole Farm La *NFLD/LBR* B31 .... **167** E6
Hole Farm Wy *HWK/WKHTH* B38 ... **188** B6
Hole La *NFLD/LBR* B31 .... **167** E5
   NFLD/LBR B31 .... **187** E1
Holford Av *WSLW* WS2 .... **51** E3
Holford Dr *PBAR/PBCH* B42 .... **100** A1
Holford Wy *AST/WIT* B6 .... **100** C2
   PBAR/PBCH B42 .... **100** B2
Holifast Rd *CSCFLD/WYGN* B72 ..... **81** E4
Holland Av *DOR/KN* B93 .... **197** D5
   LGLYGN/QTN B68 .... **119** E3
Holland Rd *BILS/COS* WV14 .... **48** A2
   CSCFLD/WYGN B72 .... **59** D6
   GTB/HAM B43 .... **75** F4
Holland Rd West *AST/WIT* B6 .... **124** B1
Hollands Pl *BLOX/PEL* WS3 .... **17** F4
Hollands Rd *BLOX/PEL* WS3 .... **17** F4
Holland St *CBHAMNW* B3 .... **6** A4
   CSCFLD/WYGN B72 .... **59** D5 🔟
   DUDN DY1 .... **91** D5
   TPTN/OCK DY4 .... **71** E4 🔟
Hollemeadow Av *BLOX/PEL* WS3 ... **17** F6
Holliars Gv *CHWD/FDBR/MGN* B37 .. **130** B2
Holliday Rd *ERDE/BCHGN* B24 .... **102** C1
   HDSW B21 .... **98** B6
Holliday St *CBHAMW* B1 .... **6** B6
   EDG B15 .... **123** E6
Hollie Lucas Rd *MOS/BIL* B13 .... **170** B4
Hollies Cft *DIG/EDG* B5 .... **147** E4
Hollies Dr *DARL/WED* WS10 .... **50** B6 🔟
Hollies Ri *CDYHTH* B64 .... **140** B1
Hollies Rd *OLDBY* B69 .... **92** C5
Hollies St *BRLYHL* DY5 .... **89** F6
The Hollies *AST/WIT* B6 .... **101** D5 🔟
   BKHL/PFLD WV2 .... **45** E1 🔟
   RBRY B45 .... **200** C5
Hollin Brow Cl *DOR/KN* B93 .... **213** D4 🔟
Hollingberry La
   WALM/CURD B76 .... **60** B6 🔟
Hollings Gv *SOLH* B91 .... **195** D5 🔟
Hollington Wy *SOLH* B91 .... **47** D1
Hollington Wy *SOLH* B91 .... **195** E6
Hollinwell Cl *BLOX/PEL* WS3 .... **16** C2 🔟
Hollister Dr *RIDG/WDGT* B32 .... **144** B6
Holloway *NFLD/LBR* B31 .... **166** A5
Holloway Bank *DARL/WED* WS10 ... **72** B3
Holloway Dr *WMBN* WV5 .... **64** A6
Holloway Head *EDG* B15 .... **123** F6
Holloway St *SEDG* DY3 .... **89** F1
   WOLV WV1 .... **46** C2
Holloway St West *SEDG* DY3 .... **67** F6
The Holloway *ALVE* B48 .... **217** E6
   DUNHL/THL/PER WV6 .... **23** D1
   STRBR DY8 .... **136** B2 🔟
Hollow Cft *NFLD/LBR* B31 .... **187** D2 🔟
Hollow Croft Rd *SHHTH* WV12 ..... **15** D6
Hollowtree La *BRGRVE* B60 .... **214** C6
Holly Av *BHTH/HG* B12 .... **148** C4 🔟
   SLYOAK B29 .... **169** D2
Hollybank Av *WNSFLD* WV11 .... **14** C2
Hollybank Cl *BLOX/PEL* WS3 .... **16** C3 🔟
Hollybank Gv *HALE* B63 .... **161** F2 🔟
Hollybank Rd *MOS/BIL* B13 .... **170** C5
Hollyberry Av *SOLH* B91 .... **194** C5

Hollyberry Cft *BKDE/SHDE* B34 .... 129 E1 🔲
Holly Bush Gv *RIDG/WDGT* B32 ..... 143 F2
Hollybush La
　ETTPK/GDPK/PENN WV4............. 43 F5
　STRBR DY8 .... 136 B2
Holly Cl *SHHTH* WV12 .... 29 E1
Hollycot Gdns *BKHTH/HG* B12 .... 148 B3 🔲
Hollycroft Rd *HDSW* B21 .... 97 F4
Hollydale Rd *BLKHTH/ROWR* B65 .... 117 F4
　ERDE/BCHGN B24 .... 103 E2
Holly Dell *HWK/WKHTH* B38............ 189 D3
Holly Dr *ACGN* B27.......................... 173 D1
　HLYWD B47 .... 191 D6
Hollyfaste Rd *STECH* B33 .... 129 D6 🔲
Hollyfield Av *SOLH* B91 .... 194 A3
Hollyfield Ct *MGN/WHC* B75 .... 60 A4
Hollyfield Crs *MGN/WHC* B75 .... 60 A5 🔲
Hollyfield Dr *MGN/WHC* B75.......... 60 A4
　RBRY B45 .... 200 C6
Hollyfield Rd *MGN/WHC* B75........... 60 A4
Holly Gv *BDMR/CCFT* WV3 .... 44 B2
　BVILLE B30 .... 168 B3
　LOZ/NWT B19 .... 99 D5
　STRBR DY8 .... 136 A4 🔲
Holly Hall Rd *DUDS* DY2 .... 114 C1
Hollyhedge Cl *NFLD/LBR* B31 .... 165 F5 🔲
　WSLW WS2 .... 31 E5
Hollyhedge La *WSLW* WS2 .... 31 E4
Hollyhedge Rd *HHTH/SAND* B71.... 74 C1
Holly Hill Rd *RBRY* B45 .... 184 C3
Hollyhock Rd *ACGN* B27 .... 172 B2
　DUDS DY2 .... 92 B4
Hollyhurst *CSHL/WTROR* B46 .... 107 E3 🔲
Hollyhurst Dr *STRBR* DY8 .... 112 A4 🔲
Hollyhurst Gv
　LGN/SDN/BHAMAIR B26 .... 152 A3
　SHLY B90 .... 193 D5 🔲
Hollyhurst Rd *SCFLD/BOLD* B73 .... 57 D6 🔲
Holly La *ALDR* WS9 .... 20 C1
　ALVE B48 .... 220 B4
　CHWD/FDBR/MGN B37 .... 154 D1
　ERDE/BCHGN B24 .... 80 C6
　ERDE/BCHGN B24 .... 103 D1
　MGN/WHC B75 .... 38 C4
　SMTHWK B66 .... 96 A6
　SMTHWKW B67 .... 119 F1
　WALM/CURD B76 .... 61 F5
Hollymoor Wy *NFLD/LBR* B31 .... 185 D4
Hollymount *RMSLY* B62 .... 142 C2 🔲
Hollyoak Cft *NFLD/LBR* B31 .... 187 D5
Hollyoake *LGLYGN/QTN* B68 .... 118 C5 🔲
Hollyoake Cl *LGLYGN/QTN* B68 ..... 118 C5 🔲
Hollyoak Gv *SOLH* B91 .... 194 C4 🔲
Hollyoak St *HHTH/SAND* B71.......... 95 F1
Holly Park Dr *ERDE/BCHGN* B24 .... 103 D2
Holly Rd *BLKHTH/ROWR* B65 .... 117 D6
　BVILLE B30 .... 188 B1
　DARL/WED WS10 .... 50 B4
　DUDN DY1 .... 90 C2
　HDSW B21 .... 98 B5
　HHTH/SAND B71 .... 74 A3
　LDYWD/EDGR B16 .... 121 E6
　LGLYGN/QTN B68 .... 143 E1
Holly St *DUDN* DY1 .... 90 A6
　SMTHWKW B67 .... 120 B2
Hollywell Rd *DOR/KN* B93 .... 212 C2
　LGN/SDN/BHAMAIR B26 .... 153 D3
Hollywell St *BILS/COS* WV14 .... 68 C1
Holly Wd *GTB/HAM* B43 .... 76 C2
Hollywood By-Pass *HLYWD* B47 ..... 190 B4
　HLYWD B47 .... 206 A2
Hollywood Cft *PBAR/PBCH* B42 ..... 76 B3
Hollywood Gdns *HLYWD* B47 .... 190 C5
Hollywood La *HLYWD* B47 .... 190 C5
Holman Cl *WLNHL* WV13 .... 28 A5
Holman Rd *WLNHL* WV13................ 27 F5
Holme Mil *WOLVN* WV10 .... 11 F1
Holmes Dr *RBRY* B45 .... 200 B1
Holmesfield Rd *PBAR/PBCH* B42 .... 77 E4
Holmes St *SHHTH* WV12 .... 15 F6
The Holmes *WOLVN* WV10 .... 11 F2
Holme Wy *RUSH/SHEL* WS4 .... 19 D6
Holmwood Rd *BORD* B9 .... 125 F6 🔲
Holte Dr *MGN/WHC* B75.................. 60 A3
Holte Rd *AST/WIT* B6 .... 100 C5 🔲
　SPARK B11 .... 149 F4 🔲
Holt La *RMSLY* B62 .... 181 F1
Holt Rd *RMSLY* B62 .... 118 A6
Holtshill La *WSL* WS1 .... 5 F1
Holt St *VAUX/NECH* B7 .... 7 C1
Holy Cross Gn *HAG/WOL* DY9 .... 180 A3
Holy Cross La *HAG/WOL* DY9 .... 180 A5
Holyhead Rd *CDSL* WV8 .... 8 B6
　DARL/WED WS10 .... 49 E5
　DARL/WED WS10 .... 72 B3 🔲
　HDSW B21 .... 97 E5
Holyhead Wy *HDSW* B21 .... 97 F5
Holymoor Wy *NFLD/LBR* B31 .... 185 E3
Holyoak Cl *AST/WIT* B6 .... 100 B4 🔲
Holy Well Ln *LDYWD/EDGR* B16 .... 122 C6 🔲
Holywell La *RBRY* B45 .... 199 F1
Homecroft Rd *YDLY* B25 .... 152 A1
Homedene Rd *NFLD/LBR* B31 .... 166 A4
Homefield Rd *CDSL* WV8 .... 9 D2

Homelands *PBAR/PBCH* B42............ 77 D4
Homelea Rd *YDLY* B25 .... 151 F1
Homemead Gv *RBRY* B45 .... 184 B6
Homer Hill Rd *HALE* B63................. 139 D2
Homer Rd *MGN/WHC* B75 .... 39 E5
　SOLH B91 .... 195 D2
Homers Fold *BILS/COS* WV14 .... 47 F4 🔲
Homer St *BHTH/HG* B12 .... 148 B4
Homerton Rd *KGSTG* B44............... 79 D2
Homestead Cl *SEDG* DY3 .... 68 A6 🔲
Homestead Dr *MGN/WHC* B75 .... 39 E4
Homestead Rd *STETCH* B33............ 129 D6
Homewood Cl *WALM/CURD* B76 ..... 60 A6
Honeswode Cl *BFLD/HDSWWD* B20 ... 98 C5
Honeyborne Rd *MGN/WHC* B75 ...... 59 F2
Honeybourne Cl *HALE* B63 .... 140 C6 🔲
Honeybourne Crs *WMBN* WV5 .... 64 B6 🔲
Honeybourne Rd *HALE* B63............. 141 E6
　STETCH B33 .... 153 E1
Honeybourne Wy *WLNHL* WV13...... 29 E5
Honeysuckle Av *KGSWFD* DY6........ 88 A6
Honeysuckle Cl *RIDG/WDGT* B32.... 143 D4
Honeysuckle Dr *DSYBK/YTR* WS5 ... 52 C6
Honeysuckle Gv *ACGN* B27 .... 151 E4 🔲
Honeytree Cl *KGSWFD* DY6 .... 112 B4
Honiley Dr *SCFLD/BOLD* B73 .... 79 E1
Honiley Rd *STETCH* B33 .... 128 C5
Honister Cl *BRLYHL* DY5 .... 114 B6
Honiton Cl *NFLD/LBR* B31 .... 186 A1 🔲
Honiton Crs *NFLD/LBR* B31............. 186 A1
Honiton Wk *SMTHWK* B66 .... 121 D2 🔲
Honiton Wy *ALDR* WS9 .... 34 B2
Honnington Ct *SLYOAK* B29 .... 166 B2 🔲
Honor Av *ETTPK/GDPK/PENN* WV4 ... 45 E4
Hood Gv *BVILLE* B30 .... 187 F2 🔲
Hook Dr *FOAKS/STRLY* B74............. 38 A3
Hooper St *WSNGN* B18 .... 122 B3 🔲
Hoosen Cl *RMSLY* B62 .... 142 C3 🔲
Hopedale Rd *RIDG/WDGT* B32 .... 143 E4 🔲
Hope Rd *TPTN/OCK* DY4 .... 71 E5
Hope St *DIG/EDG* B5 .... 147 F1 🔲
　DUDS DY2 .... 91 G5
　RMSLY B62 .... 141 F1
　STRBR DY8 .... 111 F4
　WBROM B70 .... 96 A3
　WSL WS1 .... 4 D6
Hopkins Dr *HHTH/SAND* B71.......... 74 A4
Hopkins St *DUDN* DY1 .... 92 B3 🔲
Hopstone Gdns
　ETTPK/GDPK/PENN WV4............ 44 B4
Hopstone Rd *SLYOAK* B29 .... 166 C2
Hopton Cl *DUNHL/THL/PER* WV6 .... 22 B4
　TPTN/OCK DY4 .... 71 E1
Hopton Crs *WNSFLD* WV11 .... 28 A1
Hopton Gdns *DUDN* DY1 .... 90 C2 🔲
Hopton Gv *MOS/BIL* B13 .... 171 E6
Hopwas Gv
　CHWD/FDBR/MGN B37 .... 130 B2 🔲
Hopwood Cl *HALE* B63 .... 162 C1 🔲
Hopwood Gv *NFLD/LBR* B31 .... 202 A1 🔲
Hopyard Cl *SEDG* DY3 .... 89 D2 🔲
Hopyard Gdns *BILS/COS* WV14 ...... 47 D6 🔲
Hopyard La *SEDG* DY3 .... 89 D2
Hopyard Rd *WSLW* WS2 .... 30 A5
Horace Partridge Rd
　DARL/WED WS10 .... 48 C4 🔲
Horace St *BILS/COS* WV14 .... 68 C3
Horatio Dr *MOS/BIL* B13 .... 148 B5 🔲
Hordern Cl *DUNHL/THL/PER* WV6 ... 24 B2
Hordern Crs *BRLYHL* DY5 .... 137 F1
Hordern Gv *DUNHL/THL/PER* WV6 ... 24 B2
Hordern Rd *DUNHL/THL/PER* WV6 ... 24 B2
Hornbeam Cl *SLYOAK* B29 .... 167 D4 🔲
Hornbrook Gv *HIA/OLT* B92............ 173 E4
Hornby Gv *ALE/KHTH/YWD* B14 ..... 191 E1
Hornby Rd
　ETTPK/GDPK/PENN WV4............ 45 E5
Horner Wy *BLKHTH/ROWR* B65...... 117 E6
Horne Wy *BKDE/SHDE* B34 .... 130 A2
Horning Dr *BILS/COS* WV14 .... 47 E6
Hornsey Cv *KGSTG* B44................... 78 C1
Hornsey Rd *KGSTG* B44................... 78 C1
Hornton Cl *FOAKS/STRLY* B74......... 37 F2
Horrell Rd
　LGN/SDN/BHAMAIR B26 .... 152 C2 🔲
　SHLY B90 .... 192 B5
Horsecroft Dr *HHTH/SAND* B71...... 74 C3 🔲
Horsehills Dr *BDMR/CCFT* WV3 ...... 24 A5 🔲
Horselea Cft *WASH/WDE* B8 .... 127 E3
Horseley Flds *WOLV* WV1 .... 3 F4
Horseley Heath *TPTN/OCK* DY4 ..... 93 D1 🔲
Horseshoe Cl *WSLW* WS2 .... 51 D2 🔲
Horse Shoes La
　LGN/SDN/BHAMAIR B26 .... 153 D4
The Horseshoe
　LGLYGN/QTN B68 .... 119 E5 🔲
Horsfall Rd *MGN/WHC* B75 .... 60 C4
Horsham Av *STRBR* DY8................. 111 E4
Horsley Rd *GTB/HAM* B43 .... 55 F5
Horton Cl *DARL/WED* WS10 .... 49 F2 🔲
　SEDC DY3 .... 67 E3
Horton Gv *SHLY* B90 .... 210 C2
Horton Pl *DARL/WED* WS10............ 49 F2
Horton Sq *BHTH/HG* B12 .... 148 A2 🔲

Horton St *DARL/WED* WS10 .... 49 F2
　TPTN/OCK DY4 .... 71 F6
　WBROM B70 .... 95 F4
Hospital La *BILS/COS* WV14 .... 69 D4
Hospital St *LOZ/NWT* B19 .... 6 D1
　LOZ/NWT B19 .... 123 F2 🔲
　WOLV WV1 .... 3 F5
　WSLW WS2 .... 31 F3
Hothersall Dr *SCFLD/BOLD* B73 ..... 80 B3 🔲
Hotspur Rd *KGSTG* B44................... 78 B2
Hough Pl *WSLW* WS2 .... 51 D2
Hough Rd *ALE/KHTH/YWD* B14...... 169 F5
　WSLW WS2 .... 50 C2
Houghton Ct *HLGN/YWD* B28 .... 191 F1 🔲
Houghton St *OLDBY* B69 .... 118 B1 🔲
　WBROM B70 .... 95 F5
Houldey Rd *NFLD/LBR* B31 .... 187 D4
Houliston Cl *DARL/WED* WS10 .... 51 D4 🔲
Houndsfield Cl *HLYWD* B47 .... 207 E1 🔲
Houndsfield Gv *HLYWD* B47 .... 206 C2 🔲
Houndsfield La *HLYWD* B47 .... 206 C2
The Houx *STRBR* DY8 .... 136 A1 🔲
Hove Rd *ACGN* B27 .... 173 D2
Howard Rd *ALE/KHTH/YWD* B14.... 169 F4
　BFLD/HDSWWD B20 .... 99 D3
　BILS/COS WV14 .... 48 B6
　GTB/HAM B43 .... 75 E3
　HIA/OLT B92 .... 152 A6
　WNSFLD WV11 .... 14 B5
　SOLH B91 .... 151 E3
Howard Rd East
　ALE/KHTH/YWD B14 .... 170 A4
Howard St *BKHL/PFLD* WV2 .... 45 F1
　LOZ/NWT B19 .... 6 C1
　TPTN/OCK DY4 .... 71 D6 🔲
　WBROM B70 .... 72 B4
Howarth Wy *AST/WIT* B6 .... 100 C6 🔲
Howden Pl *STETCH* B33 .... 128 C2 🔲
Howe Crs *SHHTH* WV12 .... 29 E1
Howell Dr *TPTN/OCK* DY4 .... 70 C6
Howell Rd *BKHL/PFLD* WV2 .... 46 A2
Howes Cft *CVALE* B35 .... 104 C3
Howes St *CBHAMNE* B4 .... 7 H3
Howford Gv *VAUX/NECH* B7 .... 125 D3
Howland Cl *COVEN* WV9................ 10 B3
Howley Av *KGSTG* B44................... 78 A2
Howley Grange Rd *RMSLY* B62 ...... 142 B5
Hoylake Cl *BLOX/PEL* WS3 .... 17 D2
Hoylake Dr *OLDBY* B69.................. 92 C6
Hoyland Wy *BVILLE* B30 .... 168 A3
Hubert Cft *SLYOAK* B29 .... 168 A1
Hubert Rd *SLYOAK* B29 .... 168 B3
Hubert St *AST/WIT* B6................... 124 B2
Hucker Cl *WSLW* WS2 .... 50 C2
Hucker Rd *WSLW* WS2 .... 50 C2
Hudson Av
　DUNHL/THL/PER WV6 .... 22 A2 🔲
Hudson Rd *BFLD/HDSWWD* B20 ..... 98 C1
　TPTN/OCK DY4 .... 93 E1
Hudson's Dr *BVILLE* B30 .... 188 C1
Hudswell Dr *BRLYHL* DY5 .... 137 F1 🔲
Hughes Av *BDMR/CCFT* WV3......... 44 B1
Hughes Pl *BILS/COS* WV14 .... 47 F2 🔲
Hughes Rd *BILS/COS* WV14............ 47 F2
　DARL/WED WS10 .... 48 C4
Hugh Rd *SMTHW* B10 .... 126 A6
　SMTHWKW B67 .... 119 F2
Hulland Pl *BRLYHL* DY5 .... 113 E4 🔲
Hullbrook Rd *MOS/BIL* B13 .... 171 E6
Humber Av *WALM/CURD* B76 .... 82 C4 🔲
Humber Cv *CBROM* B36 .... 106 B4
Humber Rd *BDMR/CCFT* WV3......... 24 C6
Humberstone Rd
　ERDE/BCHGN B24 .... 104 C3
Hume St *SMTHWK* B66 .... 121 D3
Humpage Rd *BORD* B9 .... 126 A5
Humphrey Middlemore Dr
　HRBN B17 .... 145 F3
Humphreys Rd *WOLVN* WV10 .... 11 F6
Humphrey St *SEDG* DY3................. 89 F2
Humphries Crs *BILS/COS* WV14...... 70 B1
Hundred Acre Rd
　FOAKS/STRLY B74..................... 56 B2
Hungary Cl *HAG/WOL* DY9 .... 137 E4 🔲
Hungary Hl *HAG/WOL* DY9 .... 137 E4
Hungerfield Rd *CBROM* B36 .... 105 E4
Hungerford Gv *STRBR* DY8 .... 158 A1
Hunningham Gv *SOLH* B91 .... 195 D5 🔲
Huntcote Rd *BILS/COS* WV14 .... 6 B3
Huntingdon Gdns *HALE* B63 .... 139 E2 🔲
Huntington Rd *HHTH/SAND* B71 .... 73 D4
Huntington Rd *SHHTH* WV12 .... 15 F6

Huntingtree Rd *HALE* B63 .... **140** A5
Huntlands Rd *HALE* B62 .... **162** A1
Huntley Dr *SOLH* B91 .... **195** D3
Hunton HI *ERDW/GRVHL* B23 .... **101** F2
Hunton Rd *ERDW/GRVHL* B23 .... **102** A3
Hunt's La *SHHTH* WV12 .... **29** F1
Hunts Mill Dr *BRLYHL* DY5 .... **89** E4
Hunts Rd *BVILLE* B30 .... **168** C4
Hurdis Rd *SHLY* B90 .... **192** C3
Hurdlow Av *WSNGN* B18 .... **123** D2
Hurley Cl *CSCFLG/WYGN* B72 .... **81** E1
   DSYBK/YTR WS5 .... **53** F3
Hurley Gv *CHWD/FDBR/MGN* B37 .... **130** D2
Hurleys Fold *DUDS* DY2 .... **115** D2
Hursey Dr *TPTN/OCK* DY4 .... **70** C6
Hurstbourne Crs *WOLV* WV1 .... **27** D6
Hurst Cl *CBROM* B36 .... **106** A6
Hurstcroft Rd *STECH* B33 .... **129** D4
Hurst Green Rd *DOR/KN* B93 .... **212** B3
   RMSLY B62 .... **142** A1
   BRLYHL DY5 .... **83** F5
Hurst La *BKDE/SHDE* B34 .... **106** A6
   BRLYHL DY5 .... **114** B4
   TPTN/OCK DY4 .... **69** F6
Hurst La North *BKDE/SHDE* B34 .... **106** A6
   CBROM B36 .... **106** A6
Hurst Rd *BILS/COS* WV14 .... **68** C2
   SMTHWKW B67 .... **119** F5
The Hurst *HLYWD* B47 .... **206** C1
   MOS/BIL B13 .... **171** E4
The Hurstway *ERDW/GRVHL* B23 .... **79** E3
Hurstway Rd *KGSTG* B44 .... **79** E3
Hutton Av *WASH/WDE* B8 .... **125** F2
Hutton Rd *BFLD/HDSWWD* B20 .... **99** D4
   WASH/WDE B8 .... **125** F2 🄲
Huxbey Dr *HIA/OLT* B92 .... **176** B3
Huxley Cl *COVEN* WV9 .... **10** C2 🄱
Hyatt Sq *BRLYHL* DY5 .... **137** E2 🄱
Hyde Rd *WNSFLD* WV11 .... **27** F1
Hydes Rd *DARL/WED* WS10 .... **50** C6
   DARL/WED WS10 .... **73** D2
   HHTH/SAND B71 .... **73** D2
The Hyde *HAG/WOL* DY9 .... **159** F1
Hyett Wy *TPTN/OCK* DY4 .... **71** D1
Hylda Rd *BFLD/HDSWWD* B20 .... **99** D4
Hylstone Crs *WNSFLD* WV11 .... **27** E1
Hylton St *WSNGN* B18 .... **123** E2 🄱
Hyperion Dr
   ETTPK/GDPK/PENN WV4 .... **44** C6
Hyperion Rd *CBROM* B36 .... **104** A4
   KINVER DY7 .... **135** E1
Hyron Hall Rd *ACGN* B27 .... **173** E1
Hyssop Cl *VAUX/NECH* B7 .... **124** C2
Hytall Rd *SHLY* B90 .... **191** E3
Hythe Gv *YDLY* B25 .... **151** F1 🄱

I

Ibberton Rd *ALE/KHTH/YWD* B14 .... **191** D2
Ibis Gdns *KGSWFD* DY6 .... **112** C1
Ibstock Dr *STRBR* DY8 .... **136** C5
Icknield Cl *FOAKS/STRLY* B74 .... **36** C6
Icknield Port Rd
   LDYWD/EDGR B16 .... **122** A4
Icknield Sq *LDYWD/EDGR* B16 .... **122** C4
Icknield St *ALVE* B48 .... **205** D5
   ALVE B48 .... **219** D6
   CBHAMNE B1 .... **123** D4
   HWK/WKHTH B38 .... **189** D5
   WSNGN B18 .... **123** D2 🄱
Ida Rd *WBROM* B70 .... **95** F4
   WSLW WS2 .... **31** E6
Idbury Rd *KGSTG* B44 .... **78** C4
Idmiston Cft *ALE/KHTH/YWD* B14 .... **190** B3
Idonia Rd *DUNHL/THL/PER* WV6 .... **22** A2
Ilford Rd *ERDW/GRVHL* B23 .... **79** F5
Iliffe Wy *HRBN* B17 .... **145** F5
Ilkley Gv *CHWD/FDBR/MGN* B37 .... **130** B3
Illey Cl *NFLD/LBR* B31 .... **185** D4
Illey La *RMSLY* B62 .... **163** E2
Illshaw *COVEN* WV9 .... **10** C2
Illshaw Heath Rd *HOCK/TIA* B94 .... **209** F4
Ilmington Dr *SCFLD/BOLD* B73 .... **57** E6
Ilmington Rd *SLYOAK* B29 .... **166** B2
Ilsham Gv *NFLD/LBR* B31 .... **202** A1
Ilsley Rd *ERDW/GRVHL* B23 .... **102** A1
Imperial Ri *CSHL/WTROR* B46 .... **108** A3
Imperial Rd *BORD* B9 .... **126** A6 🄱
Impsley Cl *CBROM* B36 .... **105** D5
Ince Rd *DARL/WED* WS10 .... **49** E2
Incestre Dr *GTB/HAM* B43 .... **75** E2
Inchcape Av *BFLD/HDSWWD* B20 .... **75** E2
Inchford Rd *HIA/OLT* B92 .... **176** A4
Inchlaggan Rd *WOLV* WV10 .... **26** B1
Ingatestone Dr *STRBR* DY8 .... **111** E4
Ingestre Cl *BLOX/PEL* WS3 .... **16** B2 🄱
Ingestre Dr *GTB/HAM* B43 .... **75** D2
Inge St *DIG/EDG* B5 .... **123** F6
Ingestre Rd *HLGN/YWD* B28 .... **172** B4

Ingham Wy *HRBN* B17 .... **144** B2
Ingleby Gdns
   DUNHL/THL/PER WV6 .... **24** C2 🄱
Ingledew Cl *WSLW* WS2 .... **29** F4
Inglefield Rd *STECH* B33 .... **128** B4
Inglemere Gv *SLYOAK* B29 .... **166** B4
Inglenook Dr *BFLD/HDSWWD* B20 .... **99** D3
Ingleton Rd *WASH/WDE* B8 .... **102** C6
Inglewood Av *BDMR/CCFT* WV3 .... **44** B1 🄱
Inglewood Cl *KGSWFD* DY6 .... **111** F2 🄱
Inglewood Gv *FOAKS/STRLY* B74 .... **36** B5
Inglewood Rd *SPARK* B11 .... **149** E4 🄱
Ingoldsby Rd *NFLD/LBR* B31 .... **187** E2
Ingot Cl *WSLW* WS2 .... **31** D1
Ingram Gv *ACGN* B27 .... **172** C5
Ingram Pl *BLOX/PEL* WS3 .... **17** F4
Ingram Rd *BLOX/PEL* WS3 .... **17** F4
Inhedge St *SEDG* DY3 .... **68** A6
The Inhedge *DUDN* DY1 .... **91** E4
Inkberrow Rd *HALE* B63 .... **162** B1 🄱
Inkerman St *VAUX/NECH* B7 .... **125** D3
   WOLV WV10 .... **26** B4
Inland Rd *ERDE/BCHGN* B24 .... **103** D3
Innage Rd *NFLD/LBR* B31 .... **187** D1
Innsworth Dr *CVALE* B35 .... **104** C1
Inshaw Cl *STECH* B33 .... **128** A4
Institute Rd *ALE/KHTH/YWD* B14 .... **170** D3
Instone Rd *HALE* B63 .... **140** C6 🄱
Instow Cl *WNSFLD* WV11 .... **15** D5
Insull Av *ALE/KHTH/YWD* B14 .... **191** D4
Intended Cl *HALE* B63 .... **139** E2
International Dr
   LGN/SDN/BHAMAIR B26 .... **155** E5
Intown *WSL* WS1 .... **5** E4
Intown Rw *WSL* WS1 .... **5** E4
Inverclyde Rd *BFLD/HDSWWD* B20 .... **98** C2
Inverness Rd *NFLD/LBR* B31 .... **186** B2
Inworth *COVEN* WV9 .... **11** D2
Ipsley Gv *ERDW/GRVHL* B23 .... **78** D3
Ipstones Av *STECH* B33 .... **128** B3
Ipswich Crs *PBAR/PBCH* B42 .... **77** D4
Ireland Green Rd *WBROM* B70 .... **94** C2
Iretonр Rd *BFLD/HDSWWD* B20 .... **98** C1
   WOLV WV10 .... **11** F2
Iris Cl *DUDS* DY2 .... **92** B4
   SLYOAK B29 .... **167** D3
Iris Dr *ALE/KHTH/YWD* B14 .... **189** F1
Irnham Rd *FOAKS/STRLY* B74 .... **38** C5
Iron Bridge Wk *HAG/WOL* DY9 .... **159** D3
Iron La *STECH* B33 .... **127** F3
Irvan Av *WBROM* B70 .... **72** B6
Irvine Cl *BLOX/PEL* WS3 .... **17** D6
Irvine Rd *BLOX/PEL* WS3 .... **17** D5
Irving Cl *SEDG* DY3 .... **88** C1
Irving Rd *HIA/OLT* B92 .... **154** A5
   TPTN/OCK DY4 .... **70** C2 🄱
Irving St *DIG/EDG* B15 .... **123** F6
Irwin Av *RBRY* B45 .... **201** E1
Isaac Walton Pl *WBROM* B70 .... **72** A4
Isbourne Wy *BORD* B9 .... **125** D4 🄱
Isis Cc *CBROM* B36 .... **106** B5
   WLNHL WV13 .... **29** E5
Island Rd *HDSW* B21 .... **97** E4
Islington *HALE* B63 .... **140** C5
Islington Rw *EDG* B15 .... **123** D6
Ismere Rd *ERDE/BCHGN* B24 .... **103** D3
Itchen Gv *DUNHL/THL/PER* WV6 .... **22** A4
Ithon Gv *HWK/WKHTH* B38 .... **188** A1
Ivanhoe Av *BKHL/PFLD* WV2 .... **46** C3 🄱
   GTB/HAM B43 .... **55** D6
Ivanhoe St *DUDS* DY2 .... **90** C6
Ivatt Cl *RUSH/SHEL* WS4 .... **19** D6
Iverley Rd *HALE* B63 .... **141** E6
Iverley Wk *HAG/WOL* DY9 .... **159** D1
Ivor Rd *SPARK* B11 .... **149** D5
Ivy Av *BHTH/HG* B12 .... **148** C4 🄱
   BHTH/HG B12 .... **149** D4 🄱
Ivybridge Gv *PBAR/PBCH* B42 .... **99** C2
Ivy Cft *COVEN* WV9 .... **10** B2
Ivydale Av
   LGN/SDN/BHAMAIR B26 .... **153** E4
Ivyfield Rd *ERDW/GRVHL* B23 .... **79** D6
Ivy Gv *WSNGN* B18 .... **122** A3 🄱
Ivyhouse La *BILS/COS* WV14 .... **69** D3
Ivyhouse Rd *HWK/WKHTH* B38 .... **187** E5
Ivy House Rd *OLDBY* B69 .... **117** F1
Ivy La *CBHAMNE* B4 .... **124** C5
   RMSLY B62 .... **161** F5
Ivy Lodge Cl
   CHWD/FDBR/MGN B37 .... **154** C1
Ivy Rd *BVILLE* B30 .... **168** C5
   DUDN DY1 .... **90** C1
   HDSW B21 .... **98** C6
   SCFLD/BOLD B73 .... **80** B2
   TPTN/OCK DY4 .... **70** B4
Ivy Wy *SHLY* B90 .... **208** C1 🄱
Izons La *WBROM* B70 .... **94** C4
Izons Rd *WBROM* B70 .... **95** D2

J

Jacey Rd *LDYWD/EDGR* B16 .... **121** F5
   SHLY B90 .... **193** D1
Jackdaw Cl *SEDG* DY3 .... **67** E1
Jackdaw Dr *CBROM* B36 .... **106** C5
Jack Holden Av *BILS/COS* WV14 .... **68** C1
Jackson Cl *LCLGCN/QTN* B68 .... **119** D2 🄱
   SPARK B11 .... **149** D2 🄱
   TPTN/OCK DY4 .... **71** D2
Jackson Dr *SMTHWKW* B67 .... **119** F2
Jackson Rd *WASH/WDE* B8 .... **126** B3
Jackson St
   DUNHL/THL/PER WV6 .... **25** D3 🄲
   HAG/WOL DY9 .... **138** A3 🄲
   LGLGCN/QTN B68 .... **119** D3
Jackson Wy *RIDG/WDGT* B32 .... **142** C4
Jacmar Crs *SMTHWKW* B67 .... **120** A1
Jacobean La *DOR/KN* B93 .... **197** D4 🄱
Jacoby Pl *EDG* B15 .... **147** E4
Jaffray Crs *ERDE/BCHGN* B24 .... **102** B2 🄱
Jaffray Rd *ERDE/BCHGN* B24 .... **102** B2
Jakeman Rd *BHTH/HG* B12 .... **148** A4
James Bridge Cl *WSLW* WS2 .... **51** D2 🄱
   SMTHWKW B67 .... **120** C2
James Dee Cl *BRLYHL* DY5 .... **114** C6 🄱
James Eaton Cl *HHTH/SAND* B71 .... **73** E6
Jameson Rd *AST/WIT* B6 .... **101** E5
Jameson St *DUNHL/THL/PER* WV6 .... **25** D3
James Rd *CSHL/WTROR* B46 .... **108** B5
   GTB/HAM B43 .... **76** A4
   SPARK B11 .... **150** B3 🄱
James Scott Rd *HALE* B63 .... **138** C3
James St *BILS/COS* WV14 .... **48** A3
   CBHAMNE B1 .... **6** B3
   WLNHL WV13 .... **28** C5
James Turner St *WSNGN* B18 .... **122** A1
James Watt Dr *BFLD/HDSWWD* B20 .... **99** D5
James Watt Queensway
   CBHAMNE B4 .... **7** F2
James Watt St *HHTH/SAND* B71 .... **73** D3
Jane Lane Cl *WSLW* WS2 .... **30** B3
Janice Gv *ALE/KHTH/YWD* B14 .... **191** D1
Janine Av *WNSFLD* WV11 .... **14** A6
Jaques Cl *CSHL/WTROR* B46 .... **107** D3
Jardine Rd *AST/WIT* B6 .... **100** B4
Jarvis Rd *ERDW/GRVHL* B23 .... **80** B5
Jarvis Rd *OLDBY* B69 .... **118** C3
Jarvis Wy *ERDE/BCHGN* B24 .... **102** A3
   VAUX/NECH B7 .... **102** A5
Jasmin Cft *ALE/KHTH/YWD* B14 .... **190** A2
Jasmine Cl *COVEN* WV9 .... **10** B2
Jasmine Gv *CDSL* WV8 .... **9** D2 🄱
Jasmine Rd *DUDS* DY2 .... **92** B4
Jasmine Wy *DARL/WED* WS10 .... **49** F2 🄱
Jason Rd *HAG/WOL* DY9 .... **138** B5
Jayne Cl *HHTH/SAND* B71 .... **74** A2
   WNSFLD WV11 .... **13** F6
Jay Rd *KGSWFD* DY6 .... **87** F5
Jays Av *TPTN/OCK* DY4 .... **93** D1
Jays Crs *ALVE* B48 .... **203** D6
Jayshaw Av *GTB/HAM* B43 .... **76** A3
Jean Dr *TPTN/OCK* DY4 .... **71** F5
Jeavons Pl *BILS/COS* WV14 .... **47** E4
Jedburgh Av
   DUNHL/THL/PER WV6 .... **22** A3 🄱
Jeddo St *BKHL/PFLD* WV2 .... **45** E1
Jeffcock Rd *BDMR/CCFT* WV3 .... **44** C1
Jefferson Cl *HHTH/SAND* B71 .... **73** D3
Jeffrey Av *ETTPK/GDPK/PENN* WV4 .... **46** B3
Jeffrey Rd *BLKHTH/ROWR* B65 .... **118** A4
Jeffs Av *BKHL/PFLD* WV2 .... **45** F1
Jenkins Cl *BILS/COS* WV14 .... **47** E4
Jenkinson Rd *DARL/WED* WS10 .... **71** F2 🄱
Jenkins St *SMHTH* B10 .... **149** E1
Jenks Av *WOLV* WV10 .... **12** A5
Jenks Rd *WMBN* WV5 .... **64** B6
Jennens Rd (Elevated Road)
   CBHAMNE B4 .... **7** H3
Jennens Rd
   CBHAMNE B4 .... **7** G4
Jenner Cl *WSLW* WS2 .... **30** B1
Jenner Rd *WSLW* WS2 .... **30** B1
Jennet St *BKHL/PFLD* WV2 .... **3** C6
Jennings St *CDYHTH* B64 .... **116** B5 🄱
Jenny Cl *BILS/COS* WV14 .... **70** A1
Jephcott Rd *WASH/WDE* B8 .... **126** C4
Jephson Dr
   LGN/SDN/BHAMAIR B26 .... **152** B2
Jeremy Gv *HIA/OLT* B92 .... **153** D5
Jeremy Rd
   ETTPK/GDPK/PENN WV4 .... **45** E4
Jerome Rd *CSCFLD/WYGN* B72 .... **59** F5
   WSLW WS2 .... **31** D6
Jerrard Dr *MGN/WHC* B75 .... **59** E4
Jerry's La *ERDW/GRVHL* B23 .... **79** F4
Jersey Cft *CBROM* B36 .... **131** D1
Jersey Rd *WASH/WDE* B8 .... **125** F3
Jervis Cl *BRLYHL* DY5 .... **89** E6
Jervis Crs *FOAKS/STRLY* B74 .... **37** F4
Jervoise Dr *NFLD/LBR* B31 .... **167** E6 🄱
Jervoise La *HHTH/SAND* B71 .... **74** A2
Jervoise Rd *SLYOAK* B29 .... **166** B2

Jervoise St *WBROM* B70.............. **94** C1
Jesmond Gv *ERDE/BCHGN* B24 .... **104** A1
Jessel Rd *WSLW* WS2................... **31** E5
Jessie Rd *ALDR* WS9 .... **20** C4
Jesson Cl *WSL* WS1 .... **52** C2
Jesson Rd *MGN/WHC* B75 .... **60** C4
    SEDG DY3 .... **68** C5
    WSL WS1 .... **5** F6
Jesson St *WBROM* B70................. **96** A3
Jevons Rd *SCFLD/BOLD* B73 .... **57** E6
Jevon St *BILS/COS* WV14 .... **69** C5 ▢
Jew's La *DUDN* DY1....................... **90** A1
Jiggins La *RIDG/WDGT* B32 ...... **165** E3
Jill Av *GTB/HAM* B43 .... **75** E2
Jillcot Rd *HIA/OLT* B92 .... **153** D6
Jinnah Cl *BHTH/HG* B12 .... **148** B1 ▢
Joan St *BKHL/PFLD* WV2 .... **46** A3
Jockey Fld *SEDG* DY3 .... **68** A3
Jockey La *DARL/WED* WS10......... **50** C5
Jockey Rd *SCFLD/BOLD* B73 .... **79** F1
Joeys La *CDSL* WV8 .... **9** E2
John Bosco Cl *HHTH/SAND* B71 ... **73** C4 ▢
John Bright Cl *TPTN/OCK* DY4 .... **70** B3 ▢
John Bright St *CBHAM* B2 .... **6** D1 ▢
    CBHAMW B1 .... **123** F6 ▢
John Fletcher Cl
    DARL/WED WS10 .... **51** D4 ▢
John Harper St *WLNHL* WV13 ..... **29** D5 ▢
John Kempe Wy *BHTH/HG* B12 .. **148** C2 ▢
John Riley Dr *SHTH* WV12 .... **15** E5
John Rd *RMSLY* B62 .... **142** B5
Johns Gv *GTB/HAM* B43 .... **75** E3
John's La *OLDBY* B69 .... **93** E5
    TPTN/OCK DY4 .... **93** D1
Johnson Av *WNSFLD* WV11 .... **14** B6
Johnson Cl *CBROM* B36 .... **127** E1
    DARL/WED WS10 .... **49** F4
    SPARK B11 .... **149** E4 ▢
Johnson Dr *CVALE* B35 .... **104** D2 ▢
Johnson Pl *BILS/COS* WV14 .... **48** D3 ▢
Johnson Rd *DARL/WED* WS10 ..... **49** F4
    DARL/WED WS10 .... **73** E1
    ERDW/GRVHL B23 .... **80** B6
    SHHTH WV12 .... **15** F6
Johnsons Bridge Rd
    HHTH/SAND B71........................ **73** E3
Johnsons Gv *LGLYGN/QTN* B68 ... **143** E1
Johnson St *BILS/COS* WV14 .... **68** B2
    BKHL/PFLD WV2 .... **45** F1
    VAUX/NECH B7 .... **125** E1 ▢
Johnstone St *LOZ/NWT* B19 .... **99** F5
Johnston St *WBROM* B70............. **95** F4
John St *BKHL/PFLD* WV2 .... **44** E6
    BLKHTH/ROWR B65 .... **117** E6
    BRLYHL DY5............................. **113** F3
    LOZ/NWT B19 .... **99** D6
    OLDBY B69 .... **94** C6
    STRBR DY8 .... **112** B6
    WBROM B70............................. **72** B6
    WBROM B70............................. **95** D1
    WLNHL WV13 .... **28** C6
    WSLW WS2 .... **4** C1
John St North *HHTH/SAND* B71 ... **73** D6
Joiners Cft *HIA/OLT* B92 .... **176** A3 ▢
Joinings Bank *LGLYGN/QTN* B68 ... **119** D3
Jones Field Crs *WOLV* WV1 .... **27** D3
Jones Rd *SHHTH* WV12 .... **15** F4
    WOLV WV10 .... **25** E1
Jones Wood Cl *WALM/CURD* B76 ... **82** B4 ▢
Jonquil Cl *ERDW/GRVHL* B23 ...... **79** F4
Jordan Cl *MGN/WHC* B75 .... **39** D6
    SMTHWK B66 .... **121** D2
Jordan Leys *TPTN/OCK* DY4 .... **71** D6 ▢
Jordan Pl *BILS/COS* WV14 .... **48** A6
Jordan Rd *MGN/WHC* B75 .... **39** D6
Jordan Wy *ALDR* WS9 .... **21** D4
Joseph St *OLDBY* B69 .... **118** B1
Josiah Rd *NFLD/LBR* B31 .... **185** F3
Jowett's La *HHTH/SAND* B71........ **73** D3
Joyberry Dr *STRBR* DY8 .... **136** B6
Joynson St *DARL/WED* WS10......... **50** A4
Jubilee Av *HHTH/SAND* B71 .... **73** D4
Jubilee Cl *BLOX/PEL* WS3 .... **32** A1
Jubilee Rd *BILS/COS* WV14 .... **48** C5
    RBRY B45 .... **184** A3
    TPTN/OCK DY4 .... **70** C4
Jubilee St *HHTH/SAND* B71 .... **73** F4
Judge Cl *OLDBY* B69 .... **94** C6 ▢
Judge Rd *BRLYHL* DY5................ **138** B2
Juggin's La *HOCK/TIA* B94 .... **221** D2
Julia Av *ERDE/BCHGN* B24 .... **104** A1
Julia Gdns *HHTH/SAND* B71 .... **74** B3
Julian Cl *WOLV* WV1.................... **27** D5
Julie Cft *BILS/COS* WV14 .... **70** A2
Juliet Rd *RMSLY* B62 .... **142** B5
Julius Dr *CSHL/WTROR* B46 ...... **108** B4
Junction Rd *BKHL/PFLD* WV2 ...... **47** D2
    HDSW B21 .... **97** E5
    STRBR DY8 .... **136** A1
    STRBR DY8 .... **137** D5
Junction St *DUDS* DY2 .... **91** D5 ▢
    OLDBY B69 .... **94** A4
    WSL WS1 .... **51** F2 ▢
Junction St South *OLDBY* B69 ... **118** C2

The Junction *STRBR* DY8 .... **136** A1 ▢
June Cft *LGN/SDN/BHAMAIR* B26 ... **153** F4
Juniper Cl *ACGN* B27 .... **151** D4 ▢
Juniper Dr *WALM/CURD* B76......... **82** C4
Juniper Ri *HALE* B63 .... **139** E4 ▢
Jury Rd *BRLYHL* DY5 .... **138** B2
Jutland Rd *MOS/BIL* B13 .... **171** D4

K

Karen Rd *BRLYHL* DY5 .... **137** F1
Katherine Rd *SMTHWKW* B67 .... **120** B5
Kathleen Rd *CSCFLD/WYGN* B72 ... **59** E5
    YDLY B25 .... **151** E2
Katie Rd *SLYOAK* B29 .... **168** A2
Kayne Cl *KGSWFD* DY6 .... **87** E6
Keanscott Dr *LGLYGN/QTN* B68 ... **119** E3 ▢
Keasdon Gv *WLNHL* WV13 .... **29** E4
Keating Gdns *MGN/WHC* B75 ...... **38** C3
Keats Av *SMHTH* B10 .... **149** F2
Keats Cl *FOAKS/STRLY* B74 .... **38** B1 ▢
    SEDG DY3 .... **66** C6
    STRBR DY8 .... **136** C1
Keats Dr *BILS/COS* WV14 .... **69** C5 ▢
Keats Gv *ACGN* B27 .... **173** D2
    WOLV WV10 .... **12** C5
Keats Rd *BLOX/PEL* WS3 .... **18** A6
    SHHTH WV12 .... **16** A6
    WOLV WV10 .... **12** C4
Keble Gv *LGN/SDN/BHAMAIR* B26 ... **153** D3
    WSL WS1 .... **52** C2
Kedleston Cl *BLOX/PEL* WS3 ...... **16** C2 ▢
Kedleston Rd *HLGN/YWD* B28 ... **172** B5
Keel Dr *MOS/BIL* B13 .... **171** F2 ▢
Keeley St *BORD* B9 .... **125** D5
Keelinge St *TPTN/OCK* DY4 .... **71** D6
Keen St *SMTHWK* B66 .... **121** E3
Keepers Cl *ALDR* WS9 .... **20** B2
    CSHL/WTROR B46 .... **132** C3
    KGSWFD DY6 .... **87** D5 ▢
Keepers Gate Cl *MGN/WHC* B75 ... **59** E2
Keepers La *CDSL* WV8 .... **8** C5
Keepers Rd *FOAKS/STRLY* B74 ..... **37** E2
Kegworth Rd *ERDW/GRVHL* B23 ... **101** E4
Keir Pl *STRBR* DY8 .... **136** A1
Keir Rd *DARL/WED* WS10 .... **73** E1
Kelby Cl *NFLD/LBR* B31 .... **186** A3
Kelby Rd *NFLD/LBR* B31 .... **186** A1
Keldy Cl *DUNHL/THL/PER* WV6 .... **24** B2
Keifield Av *HRBN* B17 .... **145** D5
Kelia Dr *SMTHWKW* B67 .... **120** B1
Kellett Rd *VAUX/NECH* B7 .... **124** C3
Kelling Cl *BRLYHL* DY5 .... **137** E1 ▢
Kellington Cl *WASH/WDE* B8 ..... **126** B3 ▢
Kelmarsh Dr *SOLH* **195** D4
Kelmscott Rd *HRBN* B17 .... **145** D2
Kelsall Cl *WOLV* WV1 .... **27** D5
Kelsall Cft *CBHAMW* B1 .... **123** D4
Kelsey Cl *VAUX/NECH* B7 .... **125** D3 ▢
Kelsull Cft *CHWD/FDBR/MGN* B37 . **130** C5
Kelton Ct *EDG* B15 .... **146** C2 ▢
Kelvedon Gv *SOLH* B91 .... **195** E1 ▢
Kelverdale Gv
    ALE/KHTH/YWD B14 .... **189** E1
Kelverley Gv *HHTH/SAND* B71...... **74** C2
Kelvin Pl *WSLW* WS2 .... **31** D1
Kelvin Rd *NFLD/LBR* B31 .... **186** C4
    WSLW WS2.................................. **30** C1
Kelvin Wy *WBROM* B70 .... **95** E4
Kelway Av *GTB/HAM* B43 .... **55** D4
Kelwood Dr *HALE* B63 .... **140** B4
Kelynmead Rd *STECH* B33 .... **128** C5
Kemberton Cl *BDMR/CCFT* WV3 ... **23** E6 ▢
Kemberton Rd *BDMR/CCFT* WV3 .. **23** E6
    SLYOAK B29 .... **166** C1
Kemble Cl *SHHTH* WV12 .... **29** F3
Kemble Cft *DIG/EDG* B5 .... **148** A2
Kemble Dr *CVALE* B35 .... **104** C2
Kemelstowe Crs *HALE* B63 .... **161** E3 ▢
Kemerton Wy *SHLY* B90 .... **210** B2
Kemerton St *STECH* B33 .... **128** C3
Kempsey Cl *HALE* B63 .... **140** A5 ▢
    HIA/OLT B92 .... **152** C6 ▢
    OLDBY B69 .... **117** F3
Kempsey Covert
    HWK/WKHTH B38 .... **188** A6 ▢
Kempson Av *CSCFLD/WYGN* B72 ... **81** C2
    HHTH/SAND B71........................ **73** D6
Kempson Rd *CBROM* B36 .... **104** B5
Kempsons Gv *BILS/COS* WV14 ..... **47** D6 ▢
Kempthorne Av *WOLV* WV10 ...... **12** A5
Kempthorne Gdns
    BLOX/PEL WS3 .... **16** C3 ▢
Kempthorne Rd *BILS/COS* WV14 ... **48** B3 ▢
Kempton Ct *BRGRVW* B61 .... **198** C6 ▢
Kempton Park Rd *CBROM* B36..... **103** F5
Kempton Wy *STRBR* DY8 .... **136** A6
Kemsey Dr *BILS/COS* WV14 .... **48** B5
Kemshead Av *NFLD/LBR* B31 ..... **186** A5
Kemsley Rd *ALE/KHTH/YWD* B14 ... **190** B3
Kendal Av *CSHL/WTROR* B46 ..... **108** B6
    RBRY B45 .... **185** D6
Kendal Dr *DUNHL/THL/PER* WV6 ... **24** B1 ▢

Kendal Dr *RBRY* B45 .... **201** F6
Kendal End Rd *RBRY* B45 .... **201** E5
Kendal Gv *HIA/OLT* B92 .... **176** B3
Kendall Ri *KGSWFD* DY6 .... **112** B2
Kendal Rise Rd *RBRY* B45 .... **185** D6
Kendal Rd *SPARK* B11................. **149** D2
Kendrick Av *BKDE/SHDE* B34 .... **129** F3
Kendrick Cl *HIA/OLT* B92 .... **176** B5
Kendrick Pl *BILS/COS* WV14 .... **48** C5
Kendrick Rd *BILS/COS* WV14 ...... **48** C5
    ERDE/BCHGN B24 .... **82** B6
    WOLV WV10 .... **26** A1
Kendricks Rd *DARL/WED* WS10 .... **50** B2
Kenelm Rd *BILS/COS* WV14 .... **69** E2
    LGLYGN/QTN B68 .... **118** C4
    SCFLD/BOLD B73 .... **59** D5
    SMHTH B10 .... **150** A1
Kenelm's Ct *RMSLY* B62 .... **182** C1
Kenilworth Cl *FOAKS/STRLY* B74... **58** C1
    STRBR DY8 .... **111** F5 ▢
    TPTN/OCK DY4 .... **91** F1
Kenilworth Ct *DUDN* DY1 .... **90** B5 ▢
Kenilworth Crs
    ETTPK/GDPK/PENN WV4 .... **46** A5
    WSLW WS2.................................. **30** C3
Kenilworth Rd
    BFLD/HDSWWD B20................. **100** A4
    DOR/KN B93 .... **213** E1 ▢
    DUNHL/THL/PER WV6 .... **22** B3 ▢
    LGLYGN/QTN B68 .... **143** F1
    RCOVN/BALC/EX CV7 .... **179** E1
Kenley Gv *BVILLE* B30 .... **188** C3
Kenley Wy *SHLY* B90 .... **193** F1
Kenmare Wy *WNSFLD* WV11 .... **27** E3
Kenmure Rd *STECH* B33 .... **153** E2
Kennedy Crs *DARL/WED* WS10 .... **49** E2
    SEDG DY3 .... **89** F1
Kennedy Cft
    LGN/SDN/BHAMAIR B26 .... **152** C2
Kennedy Gv *BVILLE* B30 .... **169** D5 ▢
Kennedy Rd *WOLV* WV10.............. **3** F2
Kennerley Rd
    LGN/SDN/BHAMAIR B26 .... **151** F3
Kennet Gv *CBROM* B36 .... **106** B5
Kenneth Gv *ERDW/GRVHL* B23 ... **78** C6
Kennford Cl *OLDBY* B69 .... **117** E1
Kennington Rd *WOLV* WV10 .... **26** B2 ▢
Kenrick Cft *CVALE* B35 .... **104** B3
Kenrick Wy *SMTHWK* B66 .... **95** A5
    WBROM B70 .... **96** A5
Kensington Av *BHTH/HG* B12 .... **148** C5 ▢
Kensington Dr *FOAKS/STRLY* B74 ... **38** B2
Kensington Gdns *STRBR* DY8 .... **111** E6
Kensington Rd *SHHTH* WV12........ **15** D6
    SLYOAK B29 .... **168** C2
Kenswick Dr *HALE* B63 .... **162** C1
Kent Av *WSLW* WS2 .... **31** D4
Kent Cl *ALDR* WS9 .... **21** D4
    BLOX/PEL WS3 .... **32** A1
    HHTH/SAND B71........................ **73** D4
Kentish Rd *HDSW* B21 .... **97** E5
Kenton Av *DUNHL/THL/PER* WV6 ... **24** B3
Kent Pl *DUDS* DY2 .... **114** C1
Kent Rd *BKHL/PFLD* WV2 .... **46** A2
    DARL/WED WS10 .... **51** E6
    RBRY B45 .... **184** B4
    RMSLY B62 .... **142** A3
    STRBR DY8 .... **135** F1
Kent's Cl *HIA/OLT* B92 .... **152** B6
Kent St *DIG/EDG* B5 .... **148** A1 ▢
    SEDG DY3 .... **68** A6
    WSLW WS2.................................. **32** A2
Kent St North *WSNGN* B18 .... **122** B2
Kenward Cft *HRBN* B17 .... **144** B2
Kenway *HLYWD* B47 .... **190** C6
Kenwick Rd *HRBN* B17 .... **145** D3 ▢
Kenwood Rd *BORD* B9 .... **127** D4 ▢
Kenyon Cl *STRBR* DY8 .... **136** C3
Kenyon St *CBHAMNW* B3............. **6** B2
Kerby Rd *ERDW/GRVHL* B23 ...... **101** D3
Keresley Cl *SOLH* B91 .... **175** E6
Keresley Gv *SLYOAK* B29 .... **166** B1 ▢
Kernthorpe Rd
    ALE/KHTH/YWD B14 .... **189** E1
Kerr Dr *TPTN/OCK* DY4 .... **70** A3
Kerridge Cl *COVEN* WV9 .... **10** C3
Kerry Cl *BRLYHL* DY5 .... **113** E3
    NFLD/LBR B31 .... **186** B5
Kersley Gdns *WNSFLD* WV11 .... **28** D1
Kerswell Dr *SHLY* B90 .... **210** C2
Kesterton Rd *FOAKS/STRLY* B74... **38** A2
Kesteven Cl *EDG* B15 .... **147** D3 ▢
Kesteven Rd *HHTH/SAND* B71 ..... **73** E4
Keston Rd *KGSTG* B44.................. **56** B5
Kestrel Av *YDLY* B25 .... **151** D1
Kestrel Cl *ERDW/GRVHL* B23 ...... **79** F5
Kestrel Dr *FOAKS/STRLY* B74 ..... **38** B3 ▢
Kestrel Gv *SHHTH* WV12 .... **15** E5
    SLYOAK B29 .... **167** F1 ▢
Kestrel Ri *DUNHL/THL/PER* WV6 ... **10** B6 ▢
Kestrel Rd *DUDN* DY1 .... **90** C1
    HALE B63 .... **139** D2

LGLYGN/QTN B68 .... 118 B5
Keswick Dr KGSWFD DY6 ...... 111 F1
Keswick Gv FOAKS/STRLY B74... 36 B5
Keswick Rd HIA/OLT B92 .... 152 B5
Ketley Cft BHTH/HG B12 .... 148 B2
Ketley Flds KGSWFD DY6 .... 112 C2
Ketley Hill Rd DUDN DY1 .... 90 C5
Ketley Rd KGSWFD DY6 .... 112 B1
Kettlebrook Rd SHLY B90 .... 211 D1
Kettlehouse Rd KGSTG B44 .... 56 B6
Kettlesands Rd SEDG DY3 .... 89 D3
Kettlewell Wy
  CHWD/FDBR/MGN B37 .... 130 B5
Ketton Gv STECH B33 .... 153 F2
Kew Cl CHWD/FDBR/MGN B37 ... 130 B4
Kew Dr DUDN DY1 .... 90 C3
Kew Gdns STRBR DY8 .... 127 F6
Kewstoke Cl WNSFLD WV11 ...... 15 D4
Kewstoke Cft NFLD/LBR B31 ..... 166 A5
Kewstoke Rd SHHTH WV12 .... 15 E4
Keyes Dr KGSWFD DY6 .... 87 F4
Key HI WSNGN B18 .... 123 D2
Key Hill Dr WSNGN B18 .... 123 E2
Keynell Covert BVILLE B30 ...... 189 E3
Keynes Dr BILS/COS WV14 .... 48 A3
Keys Crs HHTH/SAND B71 .... 73 C5
Keyse Rd MGN/WHC B75 .... 47 G6
Keyte Cl TPTN/OCK DY4 .... 70 C6
The Keyway WLNHL WV13 .... 68 C1
Keyworth Cl TPTN/OCK DY4 ...... 71 D6
Khyber Cl WED/WED WS10 .... 49 E5
Kidd Cft DARL/WED WS10 .... 71 E1
Kidderminster Rd HAG/WOL DY9 . 159 D6
  KGSWFD DY6 .... 87 D6
  KGSWFD DY6 .... 110 C1
Kielder Cl DSYBK/YTR WS5 .... 53 E6
Kielder Gdns HAG/WOL DY9 ..... 159 D2
Kier's Bridge Cl TPTN/OCK DY4 ... 92 C2
Kilburn Dr KGSWFD DY6 .... 88 A4
Kilburn Gv KGSTG B44 .... 56 B6
Kilburn Pl DUDS DY2 .... 115 E2
Kilburn Rd KGSTG B44 .... 56 B6
Kilby Av LDYWD/EDGR B16 ...... 122 C5
Kilbys Gv BFLD/HDSWWD B20 ... 98 B3
Kilcote Rd SHLY B90 .... 191 E3
Kilmore Cft CBROM B36 .... 104 A4
Kilmorie Rd ACGN B27 .... 145 E1
Kiln La SHLY B90 .... 208 B3
  YDLY B25 .... 151 D3
Kilsby Gv SOLH B91 .... 195 E5
Kilvert Rd DARL/WED WS10 ..... 73 D1
Kimberley Cl FOAKS/STRLY B74 . 36 C5
Kimberley Pl DUDN DY1 .... 69 D3
Kimberley Rd HIA/OLT B92 ...... 174 C1
  SMTHWK B66 .... 96 C5
Kimberley St BDMR/CCFT WV3 ... 24 C6
Kimble Gv ERDE/BCHGN B24 .... 103 F2
Kimpton Cl ALE/KHTH/YWD B14 . 190 A5
Kimsan Cft FOAKS/STRLY B74 .... 56 C2
Kinchford Cl SOLH B91 .... 195 E5
Kineton Cft RIDG/WDGT B32 .... 165 F3
Kineton Green Rd HIA/OLT B92 .. 173 D6
Kineton La HOCK/TIA B94 .... 210 A6
Kineton Ri SEDG DY3 .... 67 E1
Kineton Rd RBRY B45 .... 184 A6
  SCFLD/BOLD B73 .... 80 A2
Kinfare Dr PER/WV6 .... 23 D3
Kinfare Ri SEDG DY3 .... 90 A1
King Charles Av WSLW WS2 ..... 30 A5
King Charles Cl KGSTG B44 ...... 79 D1
King Charles Rd RMSLY B62 ..... 142 B3
King Edmund St DUDN DY1 ..... 91 D3
King Edward Rd CBHAMW B1 .... 122 C4
  CBHAMW B1 .... 123 D4
King Edwards Cl
  BFLD/HDSWWD B20 .... 99 D5
King Edwards Gdns
  BFLD/HDSWWD B20 .... 99 D6
King Edwards Rd CBHAMW B1 ... 122 C4
  CBHAMW B1 .... 123 D4
King Edward's Rw
  BKHL/PFLD WV2 .... 45 E1
King Edward's Sq
  SCFLD/BOLD B73 .... 59 E4
King Edward St DARL/WED WS10 . 49 F4
Kingfield Rd SHLY B90 .... 191 E3
Kingfisher Cl SEDG DY3 .... 67 E1
Kingfisher Ct ALVE B48 .... 218 C2
Kingfisher Dr CBROM B36 ...... 106 C5
  STRBR DY8 .... 135 E5
Kingfisher Gv SHHTH WV12 ..... 15 D5
Kingfisher Veiw STECH B33 ..... 128 C2
Kingfisher Wy SLYOAK B29 ..... 167 F3
King George Crs RUSH/SHEL WS4 33 D1
King George Pl RUSH/SHEL WS4 . 33 D1
King George VI Av DSYBK/YTR WS5 53 E1
Kingham Cl SEDG DY3 .... 89 D3
Kingham Covert BVILLE B30 ... 189 F3
King's Av OLDBY B69 .... 93 D3
Kingsbridge Rd WDGT B32 ...... 165 F2
Kingsbridge Wk SMTHWK B66 .. 121 E5
Kingsbrook Dr SOLH B91 .... 195 D5
Kingsbury Cl RUSH/SHEL WS4 .. 33 D1
  WALM/CURD B76 .... 83 E5

Kingsbury Rd TPTN/OCK DY4 .... 70 C3
  WALM/CURD B76 .... 83 E6
Kingsclere Wk
  ETTPK/GDPK/PENN WV4 ...... 43 E2
Kingscliff Rd SMTH B10 .... 150 C1
Kings Cl ALE/KHTH/YWD B14 ... 169 E5
Kingscote Rd DOR/KN B93 ...... 212 A5
  EDC B15 .... 145 F3
Kings Ct STRBR DY8 .... 136 A4
Kings Cft CBROM B36 .... 106 B6
  LGN/SDN/BHAMAIR B26 .... 152 C4
Kingscroft Cl FOAKS/STRLY B74 . 56 C1
Kingscroft Rd FOAKS/STRLY B74 56 C2
Kingsdene Av STRBR DY8 .... 111 E3
Kingsdown Av PBAR/PBCH B42 . 76 B5
Kingsdown Rd NFLD/LBR B31 ... 166 A2
Kingsfield Rd
  ALE/KHTH/YWD B14 .... 170 A3
Kingsford Cl CBROM B36 .... 105 F4
Kingsford Nouveau
  KGSWFD DY6 .... 113 D2
Kings Gdn BVILLE B30 .... 188 A1
Kings Green Av HWK/WKHTH B38 188 B3
Kingshayes Rd ALDR WS9 ...... 21 D5
Kingshill Dr HWK/WKHTH B38 . 188 B3
King's Hill Fld DARL/WED WS10 . 50 A4
Kingshurst Rd NFLD/LBR B31 ... 186 C2
  SHLY B90 .... 192 B4
Kingshurst Wy
  CHWD/FDBR/MGN B37 .... 130 B2
Kingsland Dr DOR/KN B93 ...... 212 A4
Kingsland Rd KGSTG B44 .... 56 A5
  WOLV WV1 .... 2 A1
Kingslea Rd SOLH B91 .... 194 A3
Kingsleigh Dr CBROM B36 ...... 105 D5
Kingsleigh Rd BFLD/HDSWWD B20 99 D3
Kingsley Av DUNHL/THL/PER WV6 23 D3
Kingsley Gdns CDSL WV8 .... 8 A2
Kingsley Gv SEDG DY3 .... 66 C6
Kingsley Rd BHTH/HG B12 ..... 148 C4
  BVILLE B30 .... 187 F1
  KGSWFD DY6 .... 111 E2
Kingsley St DUDS DY2 .... 115 E2
  WSLW WS2 .... 51 D2
Kingslow Av
  ETTPK/GDPK/PENN WV4 ...... 43 F3
King's Meadow HAG/WOL DY9 . 180 A3
Kingsmere Cl ERDE/BCHGN B24 . 102 A3
Kings Mill Cl DARL/WED WS10 .. 50 A4
Kings Rd ALE/KHTH/YWD B14 ... 169 E5
  ERDW/GRVHL B23 .... 101 E1
  KGSTG B44 .... 56 A6
  KGSTG B44 .... 78 C1
  KGSTG B44 .... 79 D1
  RUSH/SHEL WS4 .... 19 E6
  SEDG DY3 .... 68 A3
  SPARK B11 .... 150 C4
Kings Street Prec DARL/WED WS10 49 F3
Kingstanding Rd KGSTG B44 .... 78 B1
Kings Ter ALE/KHTH/YWD B14 .. 169 E5
Kingsthorpe Rd ALE/KHTH/YWD B14 190 C2
Kingston Rw CBHAMW B1 .... 6 A5
Kingston Rd SMHTW DY6 .... 87 E6
Kingston Wy KGSWFD DY6 ..... 87 E6
King St ALDR WS9 .... 20 B3
  BILS/COS WV14 .... 68 A6
  BILS/COS WV14 .... 48 B4
  BRLYHL DY5 .... 138 B1
  CDYHTH B64 .... 116 B6
  DARL/WED WS10 .... 72 A1
  DUDS DY2 .... 91 E4
  HAG/WOL DY9 .... 138 B5
  HALE B63 .... 140 C5
  SMTHWK B66 .... 97 D4
  SPARK B11 .... 148 C2
  STRBR DY8 .... 136 A3
  WLNHL WV13 .... 29 D5
  WOLV WV1 .... 2 D3
  WSL WS1 .... 51 F2
King Street Pas BRLYHL DY5 ... 138 C1
  DUDS DY2 .... 91 F4
Kingsway LGLYGN/QTN B68 .... 143 D2
  STRBR DY8 .... 135 F1
  WNSFLD WV11 .... 14 C1
  WOLV WV10 .... 26 C1
Kingsway Av TPTN/OCK DY4 .... 70 C3
Kingsway Dr HWK/WKHTH B38 . 188 B3
Kingsway Rd WOLV WV10 ...... 26 C1
Kingswear Av
  DUNHL/THL/PER WV6 .... 22 B4
Kingswinford Rd BRLYHL DY5 ... 90 A6
  DUDN DY1 .... 90 A6
Kingswood Cl SHLY B90 .... 193 F4
Kingswood Cft VAUX/NECH B7 . 101 E6
Kingswood Dr FOAKS/STRLY B74 56 B5
Kingswood Gdns
  ETTPK/GDPK/PENN WV4 ...... 44 B3
Kingswood Rd MOS/BIL B13 .... 148 C5
  NFLD/LBR B31 .... 202 B1
  STRBR DY8 .... 111 E3
Kington Cl SHHTH WV12 .... 15 D5
Kington Gdns
  CHWD/FDBR/MGN B37 .... 130 B5
Kington Wy STECH B33 .... 128 A6

King William St STRBR DY8 .... 136 B1
Kiniths Crs HHTH/SAND B71 .... 96 A1
Kiniths Wy HHTH/SAND B71 .... 96 A1
  RMSLY B62 .... 118 A6
Kinlet Cl BDMR/CCFT WV3 ...... 42 C1
Kinlet Gv NFLD/LBR B31 .... 187 E5
Kinloch Dr DUDN DY1 .... 90 B2
Kinnerley St WSL WS1 .... 5 G5
Kinnersley Crs OLDBY B69 ...... 117 F2
Kinnerton Crs SLYOAK B29 ..... 166 B1
Kinross Crs GTB/HAM B43 .... 55 D5
Kinsey Av ALE/KHTH/YWD B14 . 190 B1
Kinsham Dr SOLH B91 .... 195 D5
Kintore Cft RIDG/WDGT B32 ... 165 D4
Kintyre Cl RBRY B45 .... 184 A4
Kinver Av SHHTH WV12 .... 29 D2
Kinver Crs ALDR WS9 .... 21 E4
Kinver Cft BHTH/HG B12 .... 148 A2
  WALM/CURD B76 .... 82 B3
Kinver Dr ETTPK/GDPK/PENN WV4 43 E4
Kinver Rd NFLD/LBR B31 .... 187 F3
Kinver St STRBR DY8 .... 111 F6
Kinwarton Cl
  LGN/SDN/BHAMAIR B26 ..... 151 F3
Kipling Av BILS/COS WV14 ..... 69 D2
Kipling Cl TPTN/OCK DY4 ...... 70 C3
Kipling Rd NFLD/LBR B31 ...... 187 E1
  SEDG DY3 .... 66 C6
  SHHTH WV12 .... 16 A6
  WOLV WV10 .... 11 F3
Kirby Cl BILS/COS WV14 .... 48 A6
Kirby Rd WSNGN B18 .... 122 A1
Kirkby Gn SCFLD/BOLD B73 .... 58 C6
Kirkham Gdns BRLYHL DY5 ..... 113 C1
Kirkham Gv STECH B33 .... 128 B3
Kirkham Wy TPTN/OCK DY4 .... 70 C6
Kirkstall Cl BLOX/PEL WS3 ..... 16 B3
Kirkstall Crs BLOX/PEL WS3 .... 16 B3
Kirkstone Ct BRLYHL DY5 .... 137 D1
Kirkstone Crs GTB/HAM B43 ... 76 B5
  WMBN WV5 .... 64 B5
Kirkstone Wy BRLYHL DY5 ..... 137 D1
Kirkwall Rd RIDG/WDGT B32 ... 165 F2
Kirkwood Av ERDW/GRVHL B23 . 80 B4
Kirstead Gdns
  DUNHL/THL/PER WV6 .... 23 D4
Kirton Gv DUNHL/THL/PER WV6 . 23 E3
  SOLH B91 .... 194 C3
  STECH B33 .... 128 C3
Kitchener Rd DUDS DY2 .... 92 B4
  SLYOAK B29 .... 169 D2
Kitchener St SMTHWK B66 .... 121 F1
Kitchen La WNSFLD WV11 ..... 14 A5
Kitebrook Cl SHLY B90 .... 194 C6
Kitsland Rd BKDE/SHDE B34 ... 130 A1
Kitswell Gdns RIDG/WDGT B32 . 164 C3
Kittiwake Dr BRLYHL DY5 ...... 137 E2
Kittoe Rd FOAKS/STRLY B74 .... 38 B4
Kitt's Green Rd STECH B33 .... 129 D4
  STECH B33 .... 129 E4
Kitwell La RIDG/WDGT B32 .... 164 C3
Kitwood Dr HIA/OLT B92 .... 175 F4
Kixley La DOR/KN B93 .... 213 E1
Knaresdale Cl BRLYHL DY5 ..... 137 E1
Knebworth Cl KGSTG B44 ...... 78 C3
Knightcote Dr SOLH B91 ...... 195 D5
Knightley Rd SOLH B91 .... 194 B5
Knightlow Rd HRBN B17 .... 145 D1
Knighton Cl FOAKS/STRLY B74 . 38 B4
Knighton Dr FOAKS/STRLY B74 . 38 B5
Knighton Rd DUDS DY2 .... 115 F3
  FOAKS/STRLY B74 .... 37 F2
  NFLD/LBR B31 .... 187 E1
Knights Av DUNHL/THL/PER WV6 24 A1
Knightsbridge Cl FOAKS/STRLY B74 38 B5
Knightsbridge La SHHTH WV12 . 29 D1
Knightsbridge Rd HIA/OLT B92 . 174 B2
Knights Cl ERDW/GRVHL B23 ... 102 A3
Knights Crs DUNHL/THL/PER WV6 10 A6
Knights HI ALDR WS9 .... 35 D4
Knights Rd SPARK B11 .... 150 C5
Knightstone Av WSNGN B18 ... 122 C3
Knights Wood Cl MGN/WHC B75 59 F2
Knightwick Crs ERDW/GRVHL B23 79 E6
Knipersley Rd ERDW/GRVHL B23 80 C5
Knoll Cft ALDR WS9 .... 21 E4
  SHLY B90 .... 209 F3
The Knoll KGSWFD DY6 .... 112 A2
  RIDG/WDGT B32 .... 165 E2
Knottsall La LGLYGN/QTN B68 . 119 D3
Knotts Farm Rd KGSWFD DY6 .. 112 C3
Knowlands Rd SOLH B91 .... 194 C6
Knowle Cl RBRY B45 .... 185 F6
Knowle Hill Rd DUDS DY2 ..... 115 D3
Knowle Rd BLKHTH/ROWR B65 . 116 B3
  SPARK B11 .... 149 F6
Knowles Dr FOAKS/STRLY B74 . 58 C2
Knowles Rd WOLV WV1 .... 26 B6
Knowles St DARL/WED WS10 .. 50 C6
Knowle Wood Rd DOR/KN B93 . 213 D5
Knox Rd BKHL/PFLD WV2 ...... 45 E3
Knutswood Cl MOS/BIL B13 ... 171 F4
Kohima Dr STRBR DY8 .... 136 A4
Kossuth Rd BILS/COS WV14 .... 68 C2
Kyle Cl WOLV WV10 .... 11 D4

Kyles Wy *RIDG/WDGT* B32 ...... **165** D4 🔲
Kynaston Crs *CDSL* WV8 .... **9** D3
Kyngsford Rd *STECH* B33 .... **129** F4
Kyotts Lake Rd *SPARK* B11 ...... **148** C2
Kyrwicks La *SPARK* B11 .... **148** C3
Kyter La *CBROM* B36 .... **105** D5

L

Laburnham Rd *KGSWFD* DY6...... **112** A1
Laburnum Av
  CHWD/FDBR/MGN B37 ...... **130** B1
  SMTHWKW B67.......................... **120** A3
Laburnum Cl *BLOX/PEL* WS3 ...... **18** B3
  CHWD/FDBR/MGN B37 ...... **130** B1 🔲
  HLYWD B47 .... **206** C2
Laburnum Cft *OLDBY* B69 .... **93** D3 🔲
Laburnum Dr *WALM/CURD* B76...... **60** C6
Laburnum Gv *WSLW* WS2............... **30** B4
Laburnum Rd *ALDR* WS9 .... **20** C2
  BVILLE B30 .... **168** B4
  DARL/WED WS10 .... **51** D6
  DSYBK/YTR WS5 .... **53** E4
  DUDN DY1 .... **91** D1
  ETTPK/GDPK/PENN WV4 ...... **46** A1
  TPTN/OCK DY4 .... **70** B4
  WOLV WV1 .... **47** D1
Laburnum St *STRBR* DY8 .... **136** A2
Laburnum Wy *NFLD/LBR* B31 ...... **186** C4 🔲
Ladbroke Dr *WALM/CURD* B76...... **82** B1
Ladbrooke Gv *ACGN* B27 .... **173** E3
Ladbrook Gv *SEDG* DY3 .... **88** C2
Ladbrook Rd *SOLH* B91 .... **195** E2
Ladbury Gv *DSYBK/YTR* WS5 ...... **52** C5
Ladbury Rd *DSYBK/YTR* WS5 ...... **52** C5
Ladeler Gv *STECH* B33 .... **129** F5
Lady Bank *RIDG/WDGT* B32 ...... **165** D4 🔲
Lady Bracknell Ms
  NFLD/LBR B31 .... **187** E1 🔲
Lady Byron La *DOR/KN* B93 ...... **196** B6
Ladycroft *LDYWD/EDGR* B16 ...... **123** D5 🔲
Lady Grey's Wk *STRBR* DY8 ...... **135** F4
Lady La *HOCK/TIA* B94 .... **208** C5
Ladymoor Rd *BILS/COS* WV14...... **69** E1
Ladypool Cl *RMSLY* B62 .... **141** E5
Ladypool Rd *RUSH/SHEL* WS4 ...... **32** C2
Ladypool Rd *BHTH/HG* B12 ...... **148** C4
  SPARK B11 .... **149** D3
Ladysmith Rd *HALE* B63 .... **139** E3
Ladywell Cl *WMBN* WV5 .... **64** C3
Ladywell Wk *DIG/EDG* B5 .... **124** A6 🔲
Ladywood Cl *BRLYHL* DY5 .... **114** B5
Ladywood Middleway
  LDYWD/EDGR B16 .... **122** C5
Ladywood Rd *FOAKS/STRLY* B74 ...... **58** C1
  LDYWD/EDGR B16 .... **122** B6
Lake Av *DSYBK/YTR* WS5 .... **53** D2
Lake Cl *DSYBK/YTR* WS5 .... **53** E2
Lakedown Cl
  ALE/KHTH/YWD B14 .... **190** A4 🔲
Lakefield Cl *HLGN/YWD* B28 ...... **173** D4
Lakefield Rd *WNSFLD* WV11 ...... **28** A3
Lakehouse Gv *HWK/WKHTH* B38...... **187** F2
Lakehouse Rd *ERDW/GRVHL* B23...... **80** A3
Lakeside *FOAKS/STRLY* B74 .... **37** D2
Lakeside Cl *WLNHL* WV13 .... **28** A4
Lakeside Ct *BRLYHL* DY5 .... **137** D1
Lakeside Dr *SHLY* B90 .... **194** B6
Lakeside Rd *WBROM* B70............... **72** C5
Lake St *SEDG* DY3 .... **89** F2
Lakey La *HLGN/YWD* B28 .... **172** C3
Lambah Cl *BILS/COS* WV14............ **48** A2
Lamb Cl *BKDE/SHDE* B34 .... **130** A2
Lamb Crs *WMBN* WV5 .... **64** B6
Lambert Cl *KGSWFD* DY6 .... **87** F5
Lambert End *WBROM* B70 .... **95** D2 🔲
Lambert Fold *DUDS* DY2 .... **92** A5 🔲
Lambert Rd *WOLV* WV10 .... **26** B1
Lambert St *WBROM* B70 .... **95** D2 🔲
Lambeth Cl
  CHWD/FDBR/MGN B37 .... **131** D3
Lambeth Rd *BILS/COS* WV14 ...... **47** D2 🔲
  KGSTG B44................................. **56** A6
Lambourne Cl *STECH* B33 .... **130** A5 🔲
Lambourne Wy *BRLYHL* DY5 ...... **137** D1
Lambourn Rd *ERDW/GRVHL* B23...... **101** F1
  WLNHL WV13 .... **29** F3
Lambscote Cl *SHLY* B90 .... **191** E3
Lammas Cl *HIA/OLT* B92 .... **175** D2
Lammas Rd *STRBR* DY8 .... **111** E4 🔲
Lammermoor Av *GTB/HAM* B43 ...... **76** B1 🔲
Lamont Av *RIDG/WDGT* B32 ...... **144** B6
Lanark Cft *CVALE* B35.................. **104** B2
Lancaster Av *ALDR* WS9 .... **21** D5
  DARL/WED WS10 .... **51** E6 🔲
  RBRY B45................................. **184** C3 🔲
Lancaster Circus Queensway
  CBHAMNE B4 .... **7** E2
Lancaster Cl *BVILLE* B30 .... **168** C5
Lancaster Dr *CVALE* B35 .... **105** D3

Lancaster Gdns
  ETTPK/GDPK/PENN WV4 ...... **44** A4
Lancaster Pl *BLOX/PEL* WS3 ...... **17** E3
Lancaster Rd *BRLYHL* DY5 .... **113** E5 🔲
Lancelot Cl *WASH/WDE* B8 .... **126** A3 🔲
Lanchester Rd *HWK/WKHTH* B38...... **188** C4
Lanchester Wy *CBROM* B36 ...... **106** B4
Lander Cl *RBRY* B45 .... **200** C1
Landgate Rd *HDSW* B21................ **97** E3
Land La *CHWD/FDBR/MGN* B37 ...... **154** C2
Landor Rd *DOR/KN* B93 .... **212** C1
Landor St *WASH/WDE* B8 .... **125** D4
Landport Rd *WOLV* WV1.............. **46** B1
Landrake Rd *KGSWFD* DY6.......... **112** B2
Landsdown Pl *WSNGN* B18 ...... **122** C2 🔲
Landseer Gv *GTB/HAM* B43 ...... **55** F5 🔲
Landsgate *STRBR* DY8 .... **158** C2
Landswood Cl *KGSTG* B44 .... **78** C2
Landswood Rd *LGLYGN/QTN* B68 ...... **119** E3
Lane Av *WSLW* WS2...................... **31** D4
Lane Cl *WALM/CURD* B76 .... **82** C3
Lane Cft *WALM/CURD* B76 .... **82** C3
Lane Green Av *CDSL* WV8............... **9** E4
Lane Green Rd *CDSL* WV8............. **9** E3
Lane Rd *ETTPK/GDPK/PENN* WV4...... **46** C6
Lanesfield Dr
  ETTPK/GDPK/PENN WV4 ...... **46** C5
Laneside Av *FOAKS/STRLY* B74 ...... **56** B2
Laneside Gdns *WSLW* WS2 .... **30** C5
Lane St *BILS/COS* WV14 .... **47** F6
Langcomb Rd *SHLY* B90 .... **192** C5 🔲
Langdale Cft *HDSW* B21............... **98** A6 🔲
Langdale Dr *BILS/COS* WV14 ...... **47** F2
Langdale Rd *GTB/HAM* B43 .... **76** B4
Langdale Wy *HAG/WOL* DY9 ...... **137** F5
Langdon St *BORD* B9 .... **125** D5 🔲
Langfield Rd *DOR/KN* B93 .... **196** C6
Langford Av *GTB/HAM* B43 .... **76** A3
Langford Cft *SOLH* B91 .... **195** E3 🔲
Langford Gv *HRBN* B17 .... **145** E6 🔲
Langham Cl
  LGN/SDN/BHAMAIR B26 ...... **152** C2
Langham Gn *SCFLD/BOLD* B73 ...... **79** F2 🔲
Langland Dr *SEDG* DY3 .... **67** E3
Langley Av *BILS/COS* WV14 .... **68** A1
Langley Crs *LGLYGN/QTN* B68 ...... **119** D3
Langley Dr *CVALE* B35................ **104** C3
Langley Gdns *BDMR/CCFT* WV3 ...... **43** F2
Langley Green Rd *OLDBY* B69 ...... **118** C3
Langley Hall Dr *MGN/WHC* B75...... **61** D3
Langley Hall Rd *HIA/OLT* B92...... **173** E4
  MGN/WHC B75............................ **61** D3
Langley Heath Dr *WALM/CURD* B76...... **60** B6
Langley High St *OLDBY* B69 ...... **118** C2
Langley Ri *HIA/OLT* B92 .... **153** F6
Langley Rd
  ETTPK/GDPK/PENN WV4 ...... **42** A3
  LGLYGN/QTN B68 .... **118** C3
  SMHTH B10.............................. **149** F1
Langleys Rd *SLYOAK* B29 .... **168** A2
Langmead Cl *WSLW* WS2 .... **29** F4
Langsett Rd *WOLV* WV10............. **26** A3
Langstone Rd
  ALE/KHTH/YWD B14 .... **191** D3
  DUDN DY1 .... **90** A4
Langton Pl *BILS/COS* WV14 .... **48** C3
Langton Rd *WASH/WDE* B8 ...... **126** A3 🔲
Langtree Av *SOLH* B91 .... **195** D4
Langwood Ct *CBROM* B36 .... **105** D5
Langworth Av *ACGN* B27 .... **151** E3 🔲
Lannacombe Rd *NFLD/LBR* B31...... **202** A4 🔲
Lansbury Av *DARL/WED* WS10 ...... **49** E5
Lansbury Gn *CDYHTH* B64 .... **141** D1 🔲
Lansbury Rd *CDYHTH* B64 .... **141** D1 🔲
Lansdale Av *HIA/OLT* B92 .... **176** B3
Lansdowne Cl *BILS/COS* WV14 ...... **68** C4
  DUDS DY2 .... **116** B1
Lansdowne Rd *BILS/COS* WV14...... **48** A2
  ERDE/BCHGN B24 .... **102** B2
  HALE B63 .... **161** F1
  HDSW B21 .... **98** C6
  RMSLY B62 .... **142** B1
  WOLV WV1 .... **2** B2
Lansdowne St *WSNGN* B18 ...... **122** B3
Lantern Rd *DUDS* DY2 .... **115** E5 🔲
Lapal La *RIDG/WDGT* B32 .... **164** C1
Lapal La North *RMSLY* B62 ...... **142** A6
Lapal La South *RMSLY* B62 ...... **142** A6
Lapley Cl *WOLV* WV1 .... **27** D5 🔲
Lapper Av *ETTPK/GDPK/PENN* WV4...... **68** B1
Lapwing Dr *HIA/OLT* B92 .... **179** D4
Lapwood Av *KGSWFD* DY6.......... **112** C2
Lapworth Dr *SCFLD/BOLD* B73 ...... **57** E6
Lapworth Gv *BHTH/HG* B12 ...... **148** B3 🔲
Lara Cl *HRBN* B17 .... **145** D1
Lara Gv *TPTN/OCK* DY4 .... **92** C3 🔲
Larch Av *HDSW* B21 .... **97** F3
Larch Cft *CHWD/FDBR/MGN* B37 ...... **131** D5
  OLDBY B69 .... **93** D3 🔲
Larches La *BDMR/CCFT* WV3 ...... **24** C5
Larches St *SPARK* B11................ **148** C4
Larchfield Cl *BFLD/HDSWWD* B20...... **99** D2
Larch Gv *SEDG* DY3 .... **68** A4

Larchmere Dr *HLGN/YWD* B28 ...... **172** B3
  WNSFLD WV11 .... **14** C2
Larch Rd *KGSWFD* DY6 .... **88** A6
Larchwood Crs
  FOAKS/STRLY B74 .... **56** A1 🔲
Larchwood Gn *DSYBK/YTR* WS5 ...... **53** D5
Larchwood Rd *DSYBK/YTR* WS5 ...... **52** C5
Larcombe Dr
  ETTPK/GDPK/PENN WV4 ...... **45** F4 🔲
Large Av *DARL/WED* WS10........... **49** E5
Lark Cl *ALE/KHTH/YWD* B14...... **190** C3
Larkfield Av *CBROM* B36 .... **105** D5
Larkhill Rd *STRBR* DY8 .... **135** E5
Larkhill Wk *ALE/KHTH/YWD* B14...... **189** F4
Larkin Cl *WOLVN* WV10 .... **12** C4
Lark Meadow Dr
  CHWD/FDBR/MGN B37 .... **130** B4 🔲
Larkspur Cft *CBROM* B36............ **103** F5
Larkspur Rd *DUDS* DY2.............. **92** B5
Larkswood Dr
  ETTPK/GDPK/PENN WV4 ...... **43** E6
  SEDG DY3 .... **67** F4
Larne Rd *LGN/SDN/BHAMAIR* B26...... **152** C2
Latches Cl *DARL/WED* WS10 .... **50** A3 🔲
Latelow Rd *STECH* B33 .... **128** C5
Latham Av *GTB/HAM* B43 .... **76** A4 🔲
Latham Crs *TPTN/OCK* DY4 .... **92** C2 🔲
Lath La *SMTHWK* B66 .... **95** F5
Lathom Gv *STECH* B33 .... **128** B3
Latimer Gdns *EDG* B15 .... **147** F2 🔲
Latimer Pl *WSNGN* B18............... **122** A1
Latimer Rd *ALVE* B48 .... **216** C4
Latimer St *WLNHL* WV13 .... **28** C4
Latymer Cl *WALM/CURD* B76 ...... **82** C4 🔲
Lauder Cl *SEDG* DY3 .... **67** E2
  WLNHL WV13 .... **27** F6
Lauderdale Gdns *WOLVN* WV10 ...... **12** A2 🔲
Launceston Cl *DSYBK/YTR* WS5 ...... **53** F2
Launceston Rd *DSYBK/YTR* WS5...... **53** F2
The Launde *ALE/KHTH/YWD* B14...... **191** F2
Laundry Rd *SMTHWK* B66 .... **121** E4
Laural Dr *SMTHWK* B66 .... **97** D5 🔲
Laureates Wk *FOAKS/STRLY* B74 ...... **38** C6
Laurel Av *BHTH/HG* B12 .... **148** C4 🔲
Laurel Dr *FOAKS/STRLY* B74 .... **56** A1
  SMTHWK B66 .... **96** C5
Laurel Gdns *ACGN* B27 .... **151** E4 🔲
  HDSW B21 .... **98** A4 🔲
Laurel Gv *BDMR/CCFT* WV3 .... **44** A3
  BILS/COS WV14........................ **48** C5
  BVILLE B30 .... **168** A5
Laurel La *HALE* B63 .... **141** D6
Laurel Rd *BVILLE* B30 .... **188** C1
  DSYBK/YTR WS5 .... **53** D4
  DUDN DY1 .... **90** C1
  HDSW B21 .... **98** A3
  TPTN/OCK DY4 .... **70** B4
The Laurels
  LGN/SDN/BHAMAIR B26 ...... **153** E4 🔲
Laurence Gv
  DUNHL/THL/PER WV6 .... **10** A6 🔲
Lauriston Cl *DUDN* DY1 .... **90** B2 🔲
Lavender Cl *COVEN* WV9 .... **10** B2
Lavender Gv *BILS/COS* WV14........ **48** B3
Lavender La *STRBR* DY8 .... **135** F6
Lavender Rd *DUDN* DY1 .... **91** D2
Lavendon Rd *PBAR/PBCH* B42 ...... **76** C3
Lavinia Rd *RMSLY* B62 .... **142** A6
Law Cliff Rd *PBAR/PBCH* B42 ...... **77** D5
Law Cl *OLDBY* B69 .... **93** F3
Lawden Rd *SPARK* B11 .... **149** D1 🔲
Lawford Cl *VAUX/NECH* B7 ...... **124** C4 🔲
Lawford Gv *DIG/EDG* B5 .... **148** A1 🔲
  SHLY B90 .... **191** F5
Lawfred Av *WNSFLD* WV11 .... **27** F3
Lawley Cl *RUSH/SHEL* WS4.......... **19** D4
Lawley Middleway *CBHAMNE* B4...... **124** C1
Lawley Rd *BILS/COS* WV14 .... **47** D3
Lawley St *DUDN* DY1 .... **90** C4
  WBROM B70 .... **94** B2
The Lawley *HALE* B63 .... **161** E2
Lawn Av *STRBR* DY8 .... **135** D1
Lawn Rd *BKHL/PFLD* WV2 .... **46** A3
Lawnsdale Cl *CSHL/WTROR* B46 ...... **108** B6 🔲
Lawnsdown Rd *BRLYHL* DY5....... **138** B2
Lawnside Gn *BILS/COS* WV14 ...... **47** F1
Lawn St *STRBR* DY8................... **136** A5
Lawnswood *KINVER* DY7 .... **110** C3
  WALM/CURD B76 .... **82** C3
Lawnswood Av
  DUNHL/THL/PER WV6 .... **10** A5
  ETTPK/GDPK/PENN WV4 ...... **46** A5
  SHLY B90 .... **193** F5
  STRBR DY8 .... **111** E3
Lawnswood Dr *ALDR* WS9 .... **20** C2
  KINVER DY7 .... **110** C5
Lawnswood Gv *HDSW* B21 .... **97** E4
Lawnswood Ri
  DUNHL/THL/PER WV6 .... **10** B5
Lawnswood Rd *SEDG* DY3........... **67** F6
  STRBR DY8 .... **111** E4
Lawnwood Rd *DUDS* DY2 .... **115** E5
Lawrence Av *WNSFLD* WV11 ...... **28** B1
  WOLVN WV10 .... **26** C3

Lawrence Dr WALM/CURD B76 .... 83 F5
Lawrence La CDYHTH B64 .... 116 A6 ⊡
Lawrence St HAG/WOL DY9 .... 137 E3 ⊡
 WLNHL WV13 .... 28 C4
Lawrence Wk GTB/HAM B43 .... 55 F5 ⊡
Lawson Cl ALDR WS9 .... 35 D3
Lawson St CBHAMNE B4 .... 7 F2
Law St HHTH/SAND B71 .... 73 E6
Lawton Cl OLDBY B69 .... 117 E1
Laxey Rd LDYWD/EDGR B16 .... 121 E4
Laxford Cl BHTH/HG B12 .... 148 A3
Laxton Cl KGSWFD DY6 .... 112 C2
Laxton Gv YDLY B25 .... 127 F6 ⊡
Lazy Hi ALDR WS9 .... 21 E3
 HWK/WKHTH B38 .... 189 D3
Lazy Hill Rd ALDR WS9 .... 21 E4
Lea Av DARL/WED WS10 .... 71 F2
Lea Bank Rd DUDS DY2 .... 115 D4
Leabon Gv HRBN B17 .... 145 E5 ⊡
Leabrook LGN/SDN/BHAMAIR B26 .. 152 B3
Leabrook Rd DARL/WED WS10 .... 71 F2
Leabrook Rd North
 DARL/WED WS10 .... 71 F2
Leach Green La RBRY B45 .... 184 C6
 RBRY B45 .... 201 D2
Leach Heath La RBRY B45 .... 184 B6
Leacliffe Wy FOAKS/STRLY B74 ...... 36 B4
Leacote Dr DUNHL/THL/PER WV6 .. 23 E3
Leacroft SHHTH WV12 .... 15 E6
Leacroft Av WOLVN WV10 .... 12 A5
Leacroft Cl ALDR WS9 .... 21 D4
Leacroft Gv HHTH/SAND B71 .... 73 D3
Leacroft Rd KGSWFD DY6 .... 88 A5 ⊡
Lea Dr LGN/SDN/BHAMAIR B26 .... 152 C3
Lea End La ALVE B48 .... 203 E3
Leafield Crs STETCH B33 .... 128 C2 ⊡
Leafield Gdns RMSLY B62 .... 141 E4
Leafield Rd HIA/OLT B92 .... 175 D2
Lea Ford Rd STETCH B33 .... 129 E3
Leaford Wy KGSWFD DY6 .... 112 B2
Leafy Gld FOAKS/STRLY B74 .... 36 C4
Leafy Ri SEDG DY3 .... 89 E1
Lea Green La HLYWD B47 .... 207 E1
Lea Hall Rd STETCH B33 .... 128 B4
Leahill Cft CHWD/FDBR/MGN B37 .. 130 B5
Lea Hill Rd BFLD/HDSWWD B20 ...... 99 E3
Leaholme Gdns HAG/WOL DY9 .... 159 D1
Lea House Rd BVILLE B30 .... 168 C4
Leahouse Gdns LGLYGN/QTN B68 .. 118 C3
Leahurst Crs HRBN B17 .... 145 E5
Lea Manor Dr
 ETTPK/GDPK/PENN WV4 .... 44 A6
Leam Crs HIA/OLT B92 .... 175 E2
Leamington Rd BHTH/HG B12 .... 149 D4
Leamore Cl WSLW WS2 .... 16 C6
Leamore La BLOX/PEL WS3 .... 17 E6
 WSLW WS2 .... 16 C6
Leamount Dr KGSTG B44 .... 79 E1
Leander Gdns
 ALE/KHTH/YWD B14 .... 170 B6
Leander Rd HAG/WOL DY9 .... 138 D5 ⊡
Lea Rd BDMR/CCFT WV3 .... 44 C2
 SPARK B11 .... 149 F5
Lear Rd WMBN WV5 .... 65 D4
Leason La WOLVN WV10 .... 12 C5
Leasow Dr EDG B15 .... 145 F6
Leasowe Rd RBRY B45 .... 184 B5
 TPTN/OCK DY4 .... 92 A1
Leasowes Ct HALE B63 .... 162 C1 ⊡
Leasowes Dr
 ETTPK/GDPK/PENN WV4 .... 43 F3
Leasowes La RMSLY B62 .... 141 E4
 RMSLY B62 .... 142 A5 ⊡
Leasowes Rd
 ALE/KHTH/YWD B14 .... 170 B2 ⊡
The Leasow ALDR WS9 .... 34 A2
Lea Vw WSLW WS9 .... 34 A2
 SHHTH WV12 .... 28 C2
Lea Village STETCH B33 .... 129 E4
Lea Wk RBRY B45 .... 184 B5
Lea Yield Cl SLYOAK B29 .... 168 C4
Lechlade Rd GTB/HAM B43 .... 76 A3
Leckie Rd WSLW WS2 .... 32 A3
Ledbury Cl ALDR WS9 .... 21 E4
 LDYWD/EDGR B16 .... 122 C5
Ledbury Dr WOLV WV1 .... 27 D6 ⊡
Ledbury Wy WALM/CURD B76 ...... 82 C3
Ledsam Gv HRDG/WDGT B32 ...... 144 B3
Ledsam St LDYWD/EDGR B16 ...... 122 C5
Lee Bank Middleway EDG B15 .... 147 E1
Leebank Rd HALE B63 .... 162 A1
Leech St TPTN/OCK DY4 .... 71 E6
Lee Crs EDG B15 .... 147 E1
Lee Gdns SMTHWK B67 .... 120 A2
Lee Mt EDG B15 .... 147 E1 ⊡
Lee Rd CDYHTH B64 .... 140 B1
 HLYWD B47 .... 190 C6
Lees Rd BILS/COS WV14 .... 48 B6 ⊡

Lees St WSNGN B18 .... 122 B2
Lees Ter BILS/COS WV14 .... 48 B6
Lee St WBROM B70 .... 72 C3
Legge La BILS/COS WV14 .... 69 F1
 CBHAMW B1 .... 123 D4
Legge St AST/WIT B6 .... 7 G1
 BKHL/PFLD WV2 .... 46 A3
 WBROM B70 .... 95 F2
Legion Rd RBRY B45 .... 184 A6
Legs La WOLVN WV10 .... 12 B2
Leicester Cl SMTHWKW B67 .... 120 A6
Leicester Pl HHTH/SAND B71 .... 73 E4
Leicester St DUNHL/THL/PER WV6 .. 25 D3
 WSL WS1 .... 4 D5
Leigham Dr HRBN B17 .... 144 B2
Leigh Cl RUSH/SHEL WS4 .... 32 C3
Leigh Rd MGN/WHC B75 .... 61 D3
 RUSH/SHEL WS4 .... 32 C3
 WASH/WDE B8 .... 126 A1
Leighs Cl RUSH/SHEL WS4 .... 19 E4
Leighs Rd RUSH/SHEL WS4 .... 19 D4
Leighswood Av ALDR WS9 .... 20 C6
Leighswood Gv ALDR WS9 .... 20 C6
Leighswood Rd ALDR WS9 .... 20 C6
 ALDR WS9 .... 35 D1
Leighton Cl DUDN DY1 .... 90 A3 ⊡
 GTB/HAM B43 .... 55 E6
Leighton Rd BILS/COS WV14 .... 48 C5
 ETTPK/GDPK/PENN WV4 .... 44 B3
 MOS/BIL B13 .... 170 B1
Leith Gv HWK/WKHTH B38 .... 188 A5
Lelant Gv HRBN B17 .... 144 C4
Lellow St HHTH/SAND B71 .... 73 E3
Le More FOAKS/STRLY B74 .... 38 C5
Lenox Rd WBROM B70 .... 72 C3
Lench Cl RMSLY B62 .... 117 E6 ⊡⊡
Lench's Cl MOS/BIL B13 .... 170 B1
Lench St CBHAMNE B4 .... 7 E2
Len Davies Rd SHHTH WV12 .... 14 C6
Lennox Gdns BDMR/CCFT WV3 .... 44 C1
Lennox Gv SCFLD/BOLD B73 .... 80 C3 ⊡
Lennox St LOZ/NWT B19 .... 123 F1
Lenton Cft
 LGN/SDN/BHAMAIR B26 .... 152 A5
Lenwade Rd LGLYGN/QTN B68 .... 143 F1
Leominster Rd SPARK B11 .... 150 A6
Leonard Gv LOZ/NWT B19 .... 99 F5 ⊡
Leonard Rd LOZ/NWT B19 .... 99 F5 ⊡
Leonard Rd LOZ/NWT B19 .... 99 E5
 STRBR DY8 .... 135 E4
Leopold Gv BFLD/HDSWWD B20 .... 76 A6
Leopold St BHTH/HG B12 .... 148 B1
Lepid Gv SLYOAK B29 .... 167 F1
Lerryn Cl KGSWFD DY6 .... 112 B2
Lerwick Cl KGSWFD DY6 .... 112 B2
Lesley Dr KGSWFD DY6 .... 112 A3
Leslie Dr TPTN/OCK DY4 .... 70 C2
Leslie Ri OLDBY B69 .... 93 E5
Leslie Rd BFLD/HDSWWD B20 ...... 99 F3
 FOAKS/STRLY B74 .... 37 D5
 LDYWD/EDGR B16 .... 122 B5
 WOLVN WV10 .... 26 B3
Lesscroft Cl COVEN WV9 .... 10 C2
Lester Gv ALDR WS9 .... 36 A5
Lester St BILS/COS WV14 .... 48 B4
Levante Gdns STETCH B33 .... 127 F5 ⊡
Leve La WLNHL WV13 .... 29 D6
Level St BRLYHL DY5 .... 114 A4
Leven Cft WALM/CURD B76 .... 82 C4
Leven Dr WNSFLD WV11 .... 15 D4
Levenwick Wy KGSWFD DY6 ...... 112 C2 ⊡
Leverton Ri WOLVN WV10 .... 25 E1
Leveson Cl DUDS DY2 .... 92 A5 ⊡
Leveson Dr TPTN/OCK DY4 .... 70 A5
Leveson Rd WNSFLD WV11 .... 14 B5
Leveson St WLNHL WV13 .... 28 C5
Levington Cl
 DUNHL/THL/PER WV6 .... 22 B3
Lewis Av WOLV WV1 .... 27 D4
Lewis Cl SHHTH WV12 .... 29 F2
Lewis Gv WNSFLD WV11 .... 27 F1
Lewisham Rd SMTHWK B66 .... 96 C6
 WOLVN WV10 .... 11 D3
Lewisham St HHTH/SAND B71 ...... 95 F1
Lewis Rd BVILLE B30 .... 169 E4
 HAG/WOL DY9 .... 137 F4
 LGLYGN/QTN B68 .... 143 D2
Lewis St BILS/COS WV14 .... 48 A3
 TPTN/OCK DY4 .... 71 F6
 WSLW WS2 .... 31 F4
Lewthorn Ri
 ETTPK/GDPK/PENN WV4 .... 45 F5
Lexington Gn BRLYHL DY5 .... 137 E2 ⊡
Leybourne Crs COVEN WV9 .... 10 B3
Leybourne Gv YDLY B25 .... 151 D3
Leybrook Rd RBRY B45 .... 185 D5
Leyburn Cl SHHTH WV12 .... 29 F2
Leyburn Rd LDYWD/EDGR B16 .... 122 C6 ⊡
Leycester Cl NFLD/LBR B31 .... 186 C6
Leycroft Av STETCH B33 .... 129 F4
Ley Hill Farm Rd NFLD/LBR B31 .. 166 A6
Ley Hill Rd MGN/WHC B75 .... 39 E6
Leylan Cft MOS/BIL B13 .... 171 F4

Leyland Av BDMR/CCFT WV3 .... 24 B6
Leyland Cft BLOX/PEL WS3 .... 18 B1
Leyman Cl ALE/KHTH/YWD B14 .. 191 E1
Ley Ri SEDG DY3 .... 67 E2 ⊡
Leys Crs BRLYHL DY5 .... 113 D4
Leysdown Gv ACGN B27 .... 173 E3 ⊡
Leysdown Rd ACGN B27 .... 173 E3
Leys Rd BRLYHL DY5 .... 113 D4
The Leys DARL/WED WS10 .... 49 F3 ⊡
 NFLD/LBR B31 .... 167 D6
Leys Wood Cft
 LGN/SDN/BHAMAIR B26 .... 152 C3
Leyton Cl BRLYHL DY5 .... 137 F1
Leyton Gv KGSTG B44 .... 78 C2
Leyton Rd HDSW B21 .... 98 B5
Libbards Ga SOLH B91 .... 195 E5 ⊡
Libbards Wy SOLH B91 .... 195 D5
Library Wy RBRY B45 .... 184 B6 ⊡
Lich Av WNSFLD WV11 .... 14 A6
Lichfield Rd ALDR WS9 .... 20 C1
 AST/WIT B6 .... 101 D5
 AST/WIT B6 .... 124 C1
 BLOX/PEL WS3 .... 17 E3
 CSHL/WTROR B46 .... 108 B5
 FOAKS/STRLY B74 .... 38 B2 ⊡
 MGN/WHC B75 .... 38 C2
 MGN/WHC B75 .... 59 D2
 POL/KGSB/FAZ B78 .... 62 C4
 RUSH/SHEL WS4 .... 19 D6
 RUSH/SHEL WS4 .... 32 C1
 SHHTH WV12 .... 15 D6
 WALM/CURD B76 .... 85 F6
 WALM/CURD B76 .... 107 F1
 WNSFLD WV11 .... 14 B6
 WNSFLD WV11 .... 27 F1
Lichfield St BILS/COS WV14 .... 48 A3
 RUSH/SHEL WS4 .... 5 F1
 TPTN/OCK DY4 .... 70 B3
 WOLV WV1 .... 2 D4
 WSL WS1 .... 5 E3
Lichwood Rd WNSFLD WV11 .... 14 B6
Lickey Coppice RBRY B45 .... 201 E5
Lickey Grange Dr BRGRVE B60 .... 200 A6
Lickey Rd RBRY B45 .... 201 D2
 STRBR DY8 .... 137 D3
Lickey Rock BRGRVE B60 .... 199 F6
Lickey Sq RBRY B45 .... 200 B5
Liddon Gv ACGN B27 .... 173 E3 ⊡
Liddon Rd ACGN B27 .... 173 E3
Lifford Cl ALE/KHTH/YWD B14 .... 189 D1
Lifford La BVILLE B30 .... 168 C6
 BVILLE B30 .... 189 D1
Lifton Cft KGSWFD DY6 .... 112 B2
Lighthorne Av LDYWD/EDGR B16 .. 122 C4
Lighthorne Rd SOLH B91 .... 175 D5
Lightning Wy NFLD/LBR B31 ...... 187 D6
Lightwood Cl DOR/KN B93 .... 197 D5 ⊡
Lightwood Rd DUDN DY1 .... 90 C2
Lightwoods Hl SMTHWKW B67 .... 144 A1
Lightwoods Rd HAG/WOL DY9 .... 159 E2
 SMTHWK B67 .... 120 B6
Lilac Av BHTH/HG B12 .... 148 C4 ⊡
 DSYBK/YTR WS5 .... 52 C5
 FOAKS/STRLY B74 .... 56 A2
 KGSTG B44 .... 78 A2
 TPTN/OCK DY4 .... 70 A4
Lilac Dr WMBN WV5 .... 64 B5
Lilac Gv DARL/WED WS10 .... 72 C1
 WSLW WS2 .... 30 A4
Lilac Rd DUDN DY1 .... 91 D1
 SHHTH WV12 .... 16 A6
 WOLV WV1 .... 47 D1
Lilac Wy RMSLY B62 .... 142 B1
Lilian Gv BILS/COS WV14 .... 70 A2
Lilleshall Crs BKHL/PFLD WV2 ...... 45 F2 ⊡
Lilleshall Rd
 LGN/SDN/BHAMAIR B26 .... 153 D2
Lilley Green La ALVE B48 .... 219 E6 ⊡
Lilley La NFLD/LBR B31 .... 187 D5
Lillington Gv BKDE/SHDE B34 .... 129 F2
Lillington Rd SHLY B90 .... 193 D5
Lilycroft La HWK/WKHTH B38 .... 188 C5
Lily Rd LGN/SDN/BHAMAIR B26 .. 151 F3
Lily St HHTH/SAND B71 .... 73 E6
Limberlost Cl BFLD/HDSWWD B20 .. 98 C2
Limbrick Cl SHLY B90 .... 192 B3
Limbury Gv HIA/OLT B92 .... 176 B3 ⊡
Lime Av HLYWD B47 .... 206 C2
 TPTN/OCK DY4 .... 70 A6 ⊡
 WBROM B70 .... 94 C1
 WSLW WS2 .... 30 A4
Lime Ct SPARK B11 .... 149 E5 ⊡
Lime Gv BHTH/HG B12 .... 148 B4
 BILS/COS WV14 .... 47 E1
 CHWD/FDBR/MGN B37 .... 131 D6
 LOZ/NWT B19 .... 99 E5
 RUSH/SHEL WS4 .... 33 E1
 SCFLD/BOLD B73 .... 81 D4
 SMTHWK B66 .... 121 D3 ⊡
Limehurst Av BDMR/CCFT WV3 .... 23 E6
Limehurst Rd RUSH/SHEL WS4 .... 33 E2
Lime Kiln Cl HWK/WKHTH B38 .... 187 F6
Limekiln La ALE/KHTH/YWD B14 .. 190 C1

HOCK/TIA B94 .... 209 E6
Limepit La DUDN DY1 .... 90 C2 🔳
Lime Rd BILS/COS WV14 .... 68 E2
  DARL/WED WS10 .... 50 B5
  SEDG DY3 .... 68 B2
Limes Av BLKHTH/ROWR B65 .... 117 E5
  BRLYHL DY5 .... 113 E2
Limes Rd DUDN DY1 .... 91 D2
  DUNHL/THL/PER WV6 .... 23 F2
The Limes ERDE/BCHGN B24 .... 102 B2
  SPARK B11 .... 149 E3
Lime St BDMR/CCFT WV3 .... 44 C1
  BILS/COS WV14 .... 68 C3
  WSL WS1 .... 5 F4
Limes Vw SEDG DY3 .... 67 F4
Lime Tree Av
  DUNHL/THL/PER WV6 .... 22 C4 🔳
Lime Tree Gdns CDSL WV8 .... 9 D2
Lime Tree Gv NFLD/LBR B31 ...... 187 E3 🔳
Lime Tree Rd ACGN B27 .... 151 E4 🔳
  CDSL WV8 .... 52 C5
  DSYBK/YTR WS5 .... 52 C5
  WASH/WDE B8 .... 126 B1
Limetree Rd FOAKS/STRLY B74 .... 35 F6
Linchmere Rd HDSW B21 .... 97 E3
Lincoln Cl ACGN B27 .... 152 A6
Lincoln Gv WOLVN WV10 .... 11 F3
Lincoln Gv CHWD/FDBR/MGN B37 .. 154 C1
Lincoln Rd DUDS DY2 .... 115 F4
  HHTH/SAND B71 .... 73 F2
  HIA/OLT B92 .... 173 F1
  SMTHWKW B67 .... 120 A5
  WSL WS1 .... 5 C3
Lincoln Rd North HIA/OLT B92 .... 152 A6
Lincoln St BHTH/HG B12 .... 148 A3
  WOLVN WV10 .... 3 H2
Lindale Av CBROM B36 .... 127 E1
Lindale Crs BRLYHL DY5 .... 137 D3
Lindale Dr WMBN WV5 .... 64 B5
Linden Av GTB/HAM B43 .... 73 D3
  OLDBY B69 .... 93 F5
  RMSLY B62 .... 142 A2
Linden Dr STRBR DY8 .... 136 C6
Linden La SHHTH WV12 .... 16 A6
Linden Lea BDMR/CCFT WV3 ...... 23 F6
Linden Rd BVILLE B30 .... 168 A4
  DUDN DY1 .... 91 D2
  SMTHWK B66 .... 120 C5
Lindens Dr FOAKS/STRLY B74 ...... 56 B4
The Lindens DUNHL/THL/PER WV6 .. 24 A4
  RIDG/WDGT B32 .... 144 D2
Lindenwood SCFLD/BOLD B73 .... 59 D3 🔳
Lindford Wy HWK/WKHTH B38 .. 189 D3
Lindley Av TPTN/OCK DY4 .... 92 B2
Lindrick Cl BLOX/PEL WS3 .... 16 B2 🔳
Lindridge Dr WALM/CURD B76 .... 83 E5
Lindridge Rd ERDW/GRVHL B23 .. 79 E6
  MGN/WHC B75 .... 60 B2
  SHLY B90 .... 192 B4
Lindrosa Rd FOAKS/STRLY B74 .... 36 B4
Lindsay Rd PBAR/PBCH B42 .... 77 D2
Lindsey Av NFLD/LBR B31 .... 187 E1 🔳
Lindsey Pl BRLYHL DY5 .... 113 E4
Lindsey Rd HHTH/SAND B71 .... 73 E4
Lindsworth Ap BVILLE B30 .... 189 E2
Lindsworth Rd BVILLE B30 .... 189 D2
Linfield Gdns SEDG DY3 .... 67 E3
Linford Gv YDLY B25 .... 127 F6 🔳
Linforth Dr FOAKS/STRLY B74 .... 56 C2
Lingard Cl VAUX/NECH B7 .... 125 D2
Lingard Rd MGN/WHC B75 .... 60 B4
Lingfield Av KGSTG B44 .... 78 A2
Lingfield Gdns BKDE/SHDE B34 .. 129 D1 🔳
Lingfield Gv DUNHL/THL/PER WV6 .. 22 B3
Lingfield Wy KGSWFD DY6 .... 112 C2
Lingham Cl HIA/OLT B92 .... 175 F4 🔳
Linhope Dr KGSWFD DY6 .... 112 C2 🔳
Link Rd ALDR WS9 .... 21 D2
  LDYWD/EDGR B16 .... 122 A4
  WMBN WV5 .... 64 C4
Links Av DUNHL/THL/PER WV6 ...... 9 F6
Links Dr RBRY B45 .... 200 C1
  SOLH B91 .... 175 D5
  STRBR DY8 .... 158 A1
Links Rd ETTPK/GDPK/PENN WV4 .. 44 C6
  HLYWD B47 .... 190 C4
  LGLYGN/QTN B68 .... 143 D1
Links Side Wy ALDR WS9 .... 21 E5
Links Vw FOAKS/STRLY B74 .... 36 C5
  RMSLY B62 .... 141 F5
Linkswood Cl MOS/BIL B13 ...... 171 D2
The Link ACGN B27 .... 172 B2
Linley Cl ALDR WS9 .... 34 C1
Linley Dr WOLVN WV10 .... 12 A4
Linley Gv ALE/KHTH/YWD B14 .. 169 E5
  SEDG DY3 .... 89 D3 🔳
Linley Rd RUSH/SHEL WS4 .... 19 F6
Linley Wood Rd ALDR WS9 .... 34 A2
Linnet Cl RMSLY B62 .... 141 D3
  SLYOAK B29 .... 168 A3
Linnet Gv SHHTH WV12 .... 15 E5
Linpole Wk ALE/KHTH/YWD B14 .. 189 E3
Linsey Rd HIA/OLT B92 .... 175 E1

Linslade Cl
  ETTPK/GDPK/PENN WV4 .... 45 F5
Linthouse La WNSFLD WV11 .... 14 A5 🔳
Linthurst Newtown BRGRVE B60 .. 214 C4
Linthurst Rd BRGRVE B60 .... 214 C3
Linton Av SOLH B91 .... 194 C3
Linton Cl HALE B63 .... 139 F4 🔳
Linton Cft BILS/COS WV14 .... 47 F5
Linton Rd CDYHTH B64 .... 116 B4
  ETTPK/GDPK/PENN WV4 .... 44 A4
  GTB/HAM B43 .... 55 E5
  SPARK B11 .... 150 C5
Linwood Rd DUDN DY1 .... 69 D6
  HDSW B21 .... 98 A5
  SOLH B91 .... 173 F6
Lionel St CBHAMNW B3 .... 6 C3
Lion Pas STRBR DY8 .... 136 B4
Lion St STRBR DY8 .... 136 B4
Liskeard Rd DSYBK/YTR WS5 .... 53 F2
Lisko Cl STRBR DY8 .... 136 C1
Lismore Cl RBRY B45 .... 184 A4 🔳
Lismore Dr HRBN B17 .... 144 C6
Lisson Gv KGSTG B44 .... 56 B5
Listelow Cl CBROM B36 .... 105 D5 🔳
Lister Cl TPTN/OCK DY4 .... 92 C1 🔳
  WSLW WS2 .... 31 D2
Lister Rd DUDS DY2 .... 91 E6
  WSLW WS2 .... 31 D2
Lister St VAUX/NECH B7 .... 7 G1
  WLNHL WV13 .... 29 D6
Listowel Rd ALE/KHTH/YWD B14 .. 169 F5 🔳
Lisures Dr WALM/CURD B76 .... 59 F5
Little Albert St WSL WS1 .... 4 D2 🔳
Little Ann St DIG/EDG B5 .... 7 H6
Little Aston Hall Dr
  FOAKS/STRLY B74 .... 36 C2
Little Aston La FOAKS/STRLY B74 .. 37 F1
Little Aston Park Rd
  FOAKS/STRLY B74 .... 36 C4
Little Aston Rd ALDR WS9 .... 35 E1
Little Barr St BORD B9 .... 124 C5
Little Birches BDMR/CCFT WV3 .... 44 A2
Little Bricklin St BKHL/PFLD WV2 .. 2 C6 🔳
Little Bromwich Rd BORD B9 .... 127 D6
Little Broom St BHTH/HG B12 .... 148 C1 🔳
Little Caldmore WSL WS1 .... 4 D6
Little Clothier St WLNHL WV13 ...... 28 C4 🔳
Little Clover Cl VAUX/NECH B7 .. 101 E6 🔳
Little Cornbow HALE B63 .... 141 D6 🔳
Littlecote
  ALE/KHTH/YWD B14 .... 190 C2 🔳
Littlecote Dr ERDW/GRVHL B23 .... 80 B4
Little Cottage St BRLYHL DY5 .... 113 F4
Little Cft GTB/HAM B43 .... 75 E2
Little Cross St DARL/WED WS10 .. 49 F2 🔳
Little Edward St BORD B9 .... 124 C5 🔳
Little Fields Wy OLDBY B69 .... 94 B6
Little Francis Gv VAUX/NECH B7 .. 125 D2 🔳
Little Gorway WSL WS1 .... 52 B2
Little Green La BORD B9 .... 125 F6 🔳
  SCFLD/BOLD B73 .... 81 D4
Little Hall Rd VAUX/NECH B7 .... 125 D3
Little Hardwick Rd ALDR WS9 ...... 35 F5
Little Heath Cft
  BKDE/SHDE B34 .... 105 D6 🔳
Littleheath La BRGRVE B60 ...... 214 A3
Little Hi DARL/WED WS10 .... 50 B6 🔳
Little Hill Gv HWK/WKHTH B38 .. 188 C4
Little Hill Wy RIDG/WDGT B32 .. 165 F1 🔳
Little Johnson's La ALDR WS9 ...... 35 D6
Little John St BRLYHL DY5 .... 113 F3
Little La HHTH/SAND B71 .... 73 F6
  SHHTH WV12 .... 15 F6
Little London WSL WS1 .... 52 A2
Littlemead Av NFLD/LBR B31 .... 187 E4
Littlemead Rd SHLY B90 .... 192 A5
Little Moor Hl SMTHWKW B67 .. 120 B2
Little Newport St WSL WS1 .... 4 C4 🔳
Little Oaks Rd AST/WIT B6 .... 100 A5
Littleover Av HLGN/YWD B28 .... 172 B5
Little Pk RIDG/WDGT B32 .... 145 D5
Little Park St WOLV WV1 .... 3 G4 🔳
Little Pitts Cl ERDE/BCHGN B24 .. 81 F6
Little Potter St BRLYHL DY5 ...... 113 F5 🔳
Little Pountney St
  BKHL/PFLD WV2 .... 45 E1 🔳
Little Shadwell St CBHAMNE B4 .... 7 E2 🔳
Littleshaw Cft HLYWD B47 .... 207 E3
Littleshaw La HLYWD B47 .... 207 E3
Little's La WOLV WV1 .... 3 E2 🔳
Little Station St WSL WS1 .... 4 C4 🔳
Little St DUDS DY2 .... 91 F4 🔳
Little Sutton La MGN/WHC B75 .... 39 E6
Little Sutton Rd MGN/WHC B75 .... 39 E5
Littleton Cft SOLH B91 .... 195 E5 🔳
Littleton Rd SHHTH WV12 .... 15 E6
Littleton St East WSL WS1 .... 4 D2
Littleton St West WSL WS2 .... 4 D1
Littlewood Cl SOLH B91 .... 195 D5 🔳
Little Wood St WLNHL WV13 .... 28 C5
Littleworth Av DUDN DY1 .... 69 D5
Littleworth Gv WALM/CURD B76 .. 60 B5
Liveridge Cl DOR/KN B93 .... 212 B1

Liverpool Cft
  CHWD/FDBR/MGN B37 .... 130 B6
Liverpool St BORD B9 .... 124 C5
Livery St CBHAMNW B3 .... 6 C2
Livingstone Av
  DUNHL/THL/PER WV6 .... 22 A2
Livingstone Rd
  ALE/KHTH/YWD B14 .... 170 A5
  BFLD/HDSWWD B20 .... 99 E4
  BILS/COS WV14 .... 47 D3
  BLOX/PEL WS3 .... 18 A3
  WBROM B70 .... 95 D4
Lloyd Dr ETTPK/GDPK/PENN WV4 .. 65 E1
Lloyd Rd BFLD/HDSWWD B20 ...... 98 C1
  DUNHL/THL/PER WV6 .... 23 F2
Lloyds Rd RMSLY B62 .... 141 E2
Lloyd St DARL/WED WS10 .... 50 A6
  DUDS DY2 .... 91 F5 🔳
  DUNHL/THL/PER WV6 .... 24 B3
  HHTH/SAND B71 .... 96 A1
  SMHTH B10 .... 149 F1
Locarno Rd TPTN/OCK DY4 .... 70 B5
Lochalsh Gv WNSFLD WV11 ...... 15 D4
Lochranza Cft GTB/HAM B43 ...... 76 A1
Lock Dr STECH B33 .... 127 F4
Locket Cl WSLW WS2 .... 30 B1
Lockfield Cl STRBR DY8 .... 112 B5 🔳
Lockhart Dr MGN/WHC B75 .... 39 E6
Locking Cft CVALE B35 .... 105 D2
Lockington Cft RMSLY B62 .... 142 B3
Lockley Cl WOLVN WV10 .... 26 B3
Lockside ALDR WS9 .... 20 B6
  WMBN WV5 .... 64 A4
Locksmith Cl WLNHL WV13 .... 29 D5 🔳
Lock St WOLV WV1 .... 3 F2
Locks Vw STRBR DY8 .... 111 F6
Lockton Rd BVILLE B30 .... 169 E3
Lockwood Rd NFLD/LBR B31 .... 186 B1
Lode La HIA/OLT B92 .... 175 D2
  SOLH B91 .... 175 E4
  SOLH B91 .... 195 D1
Lodge Cl DSYBK/YTR WS5 .... 53 F5 🔳
  RMSLY B62 .... 141 F6
Lodge Crs DUDS DY2 .... 114 C3
  HAG/WOL DY9 .... 159 D6
Lodge Cft DOR/KN B93 .... 213 D1
  NFLD/LBR B31 .... 186 A6
Lodge Dr LGN/SDN/BHAMAIR B26 .. 152 A1
Lodge Farm Cl WALM/CURD B76 .. 60 B6 🔳
Lodgefield Rd RMSLY B62 .... 141 D2
Lodge Gv ALDR WS9 .... 34 C2
Lodge Hill Rd SLYOAK B29 .... 167 F2
Lodge La KGSWFD DY6 .... 111 D1
Lodgepool Cl KGSTG B44 .... 78 A5 🔳
Lodge Rd AST/WIT B6 .... 100 A5
  BILS/COS WV14 .... 48 B5
  DARL/WED WS10 .... 49 F4
  DOR/KN B93 .... 213 D1
  DSYBK/YTR WS5 .... 53 F4
  RUSH/SHEL WS4 .... 19 D4
  SMTHWKW B67 .... 96 A6
  WBROM B70 .... 95 D2
  WOLVN WV10 .... 11 D5
  WSNGN B18 .... 122 A2
Lodge St OLDBY B69 .... 94 C6
  SHHTH WV12 .... 29 E2
Loeless Rd STETCH B33 .... 128 C4
Lofthouse Crs NFLD/LBR B31 .... 186 B2
Lofthouse Gv NFLD/LBR B31 .... 186 B2 🔳
Lofthouse Rd BFLD/HDSWWD B20 .. 98 A3
Loftus Cl NFLD/LBR B31 .... 166 B3
Logan Cl WOLVN WV10 .... 25 E1 🔳
Lomaine Dr BVILLE B30 .... 188 A1
Lomas Dr NFLD/LBR B31 .... 186 A2
Lomas St WOLV WV1 .... 25 E3
Lombard Av DUDS DY2 .... 115 F4
Lombard St BHTH/HG B12 .... 124 B6
  BHTH/HG B12 .... 148 B1
  WBROM B70 .... 95 E2
Lombard St West WBROM B70 .... 95 E2 🔳
Lombardy Cft RMSLY B62 .... 142 C3 🔳
Lombardy Gdns SHHTH WV12 .... 16 A6 🔳
Lomond Cl BKDE/SHDE B34 ...... 130 A1
Lomond Rd SEDG DY3 .... 67 E2
Londonderry Gv
  SMTHWKW B67 .... 120 B2 🔳
Londonderry La SMTHWKW B67 .. 119 F3
London Hts DUDN DY1 .... 90 C3
London Rd BFLD/HDSWWD B20 .. 100 A3
  MGN/WHC B75 .... 40 C3
London St SMTHWK B66 .... 121 E2
Lones Rd HHTH/SAND B71 .... 97 D5
Long Acre CDSL WV8 .... 8 A3
  VAUX/NECH B7 .... 125 D1
Longacre WLNHL WV13 .... 48 C1
Longacres WLNHL WV13 .... 48 C1 🔳
Long Acre St WSLW WS2 .... 4 B1
Longbank Rd OLDBY B69 .... 93 E5
Longboat La STRBR DY8 .... 136 A1
Longboat Qy DUDS DY2 .... 115 F3 🔳
Longbow Rd SLYOAK B29 .... 166 B4 🔳
Longbridge La NFLD/LBR B31 .... 186 C5
Long Compton Dr HAG/WOL DY9 .. 158 C5
Longcroft Cl CVALE B35 .... 104 C2 🔳
The Longcroft HALE B63 .... 140 A5

RUSH/SHEL WS4 .... 19 E6
Longdales Rd HWK/WKHTH B38 .. 187 F6
HWK/WKHTH B38 .... 188 A5 🔲
Longdon Av
ETTPK/GDPK/PENN WV4 .... 45 F4
Longdon Dr FOAKS/STRLY B74 ...... 38 A3
Longdon Rd BVILLE B30 .... 187 F2
SEDG DY3 .... 🔲
Longfield Cl HLGN/YWD B28 .... 172 B5
Longfield Rd HAG/WOL DY9 .... 137 F4
NFLD/LBR B31 .... 166 C3
Longford Cl DOR/KN B93 .... 213 D4
RIDG/WDGT B32 .... 164 C4 🔲
Longford Gv KGSTG B44 .... 56 C6
Longford Rd KGSTG B44 .... 78 C1
WOLVN WV10 .... 26 B3
Longham Cft RIDG/WDGT B32 .... 144 B5
Longhurst Cft NFLD/LBR B31 .... 186 C6
Long Hyde Rd SMTHWKW B67 ...... 120 B6
Long Innage Rd HALE B63 .... 139 D3
Long Knowle La WNSFLD WV11 ..... 13 D5
Longlake Av DUNHL/THL/PER WV6 .. 22 C4
Longlands Rd RMSLY B62 .... 142 A6
The Longlands RBRY B45 .... 215 F2 🔲
WMBN WV5 .... 64 C5
Long La BLKHTH/ROWR B65 .... 117 F6
RMSLY B62 .... 142 A1
Longleat GTB/HAM B43 .... 75 E2
Longleat Dr DUDN DY1 .... 90 A3 🔲
SHLY B90 .... 210 A2
Longleat Rd ALDR WS9 .... 20 C3
Long Ley WOLVN WV10 .... 26 B4
Longley Crs
LGN/SDN/BHAMAIR B26 .... 152 A5
Long Leys Cft
CSHL/WTROR B46 .... 107 D3 🔲
Longmeadow Cl MGN/WHC B75 .... 60 A4 🔲
Longmeadow Crs
BKDE/SHDE B34 .... 130 A1
Long Meadow Dr SEDG DY3 .... 67 D2
Longmeadow Rd DSYBK/YTR WS5... 54 A1
Longmoor Cl WNSFLD WV11 .... 28 B2
Longmoor Rd HALE B63 .... 140 A6
SCFLD/BOLD B73 .... 57 D6
Longmore Av WSLW WS2 .... 30 B6 🔲
Longmore Rd SHLY B90 .... 193 F4
Longmore St BHTH/HG B12 .... 148 A2 🔲
DARL/WED WED 50 B6
Long Mynd HALE B63 .... 161 F2
Long Mynd Cl WNSFLD WV11 .... 15 D4 🔲
Long Mynd Rd NFLD/LBR B31 ...... 166 A5
Long Nuke Rd NFLD/LBR B31 .... 166 A4
Longshaw Gv BKDE/SHDE B34 ... 129 F1 🔲
Longstone Cl SHLY B90 .... 211 D1
Longstone Rd PBAR/PBCH B42 ..... 77 E4
Long St SPARK B11 .... 148 C3
WOLV WV1 .... 3 E3
WSLW WS2 .... 4 A5
Long Wd BVILLE B30 .... 168 A6
Longwood La RUSH/SHEL WS4 ..... 34 A5
Longwood Ri SHHTH WV12 .... 29 F2
Longwood Rd ALDR WS9 .... 35 D5
RBRY B45 .... 184 C6
Lonicera Cl DSYBK/YTR WS5 .... 53 D6 🔲
Lonsdale Cl SHHTH WV12 .... 29 D2
Lonsdale Rd BDMR/CCFT WV3 ..... 45 D2
BILS/COS WV14 .... 48 C5
DSYBK/YTR WS5 .... 53 E3
HRBN B17 .... 145 D3
SMTHWK B66 .... 95 F6
Lord Austin Dr BRGRVE B60 ...... 200 A6
Lord's Dr WSLW WS2 .... 4 D1
Lordsmore Cl BILS/COS WV14 ...... 69 F2
Lord St BDMR/CCFT WV3 .... 2 A5
BILS/COS WV14 .... 48 A6
VAUX/NECH B7 .... 7 H1
VAUX/NECH B7 .... 124 B2
WSL WS1 .... 51 F3
Lord St West BILS/COS WV14 .... 48 A6
Lordswood Rd HRBN B17 .... 144 C1
Lorimer Wy GTB/HAM B43 .... 55 F4
Lorne St TPTN/OCK DY4 .... 70 B3
Lorrainer Av STRBR DY8 .... 136 C1
Lothians Rd
DUNHL/THL/PER WV6 .... 23 F1 🔲
Lottie Rd SLYOAK B29 .... 168 A2
Lotus Cft SMTHWKW B67 .... 120 B3 🔲
Lotus Wy BLKHTH/ROWR B65 ..... 116 C5 🔲
Loughton Gv HALE B63 .... 140 B5
Louisa St CBHAMW B1 .... 6 A4 🔲
Louise Cft ALE/KHTH/YWD B14 ... 190 A3
Louise Lorne Rd MOS/BIL B13 .... 148 B5
Louise Rd HDSW B21 .... 98 B6
Louise St SEDG DY3 .... 89 D2
Lovat Gv WOLV WV1 .... 1 E2 🔲
Lovatt Cl TPTN/OCK DY4 .... 71 E3 🔲
Loveday St CBHAMNE B4 .... 7 E2
Lovelace Av SOLH B91 .... 195 F5
Love La DUNHL/THL/PER WV6 ..... 23 F1

HAG/WOL DY9 .... 138 A4
HLYWD B47 .... 190 A6
STRBR DY8 .... 136 C6
VAUX/NECH B7 .... 7 G1
WSL WS1 .... 52 A2
Lovell Cl SLYOAK B29 .... 166 C5
Loveridge Cl CDSL WV8 .... 8 A2
Lovett Av OLDBY B69 .... 117 F2
Low Av GTB/HAM B43 .... 76 B1
Lowbridge Cl SHHTH WV12 .... 29 E2
Lowbrook La SHLY B90 .... 207 F3
Lowden Cft
LGN/SDN/BHAMAIR B26 .... 152 A5
Lowe Av DARL/WED WS10 .... 49 D2
Lowe Dr KGSWFD DY6 .... 112 A3
SCFLD/BOLD B73 .... 57 F6
Lower Beeches Rd NFLD/LBR B31 . 185 E3
Lower Chapel St OLDBY B69 .... 93 E3
Lower Church La TPTN/OCK DY4 .. 70 C5
Lower City Rd OLDBY B69 .... 93 E4
Lowercroft Wy FOAKS/STRLY B74 .. 38 A1
Lower Dartmouth St BORD B9 .... 125 D5
Lower Darwin St BHTH/HG B12 ... 148 B1
Lower Derry St BRLYHL DY5 .... 113 F5
Lower Essex St DIG/EDG B5 .... 124 A6
Lower Forster St WSL WS1 .... 5 E2
Lower Gn TPTN/OCK DY4 .... 70 A6 🔲
Lower Ground Cl AST/WIT B6 .... 100 A4 🔲
Lower Hall La WSL WS1 .... 4 D4
Lower High St CDYHTH B64 .... 139 E1
DARL/WED WS10 .... 72 B1 🔲
STRBR DY8 .... 136 B3
Lower Higley Cl RIDG/WDGT B32 . 144 A5 🔲
Lower Horseley Flds WOLV WV1 ... 26 B5
Lower Lichfield St WLNHL WV13 ... 29 D5
Lower Loveday St LOZ/NWT B19 .... 6 D1
Lower Moor SLYOAK B29 .... 168 A3 🔲
Lower North St RUSH/SHEL WS4 .. 32 A4
The Lower Pde CSCFLD/WYGN B72 . 59 E4
Lower Prestwood Rd
WNSFLD WV11 .... 13 E6
Lower Queen St
CSCFLD/WYGN B72 .... 59 E5
Lower Reddicroft
SCFLD/BOLD B73 .... 59 E4 🔲
Lower Rushall St WSL WS1 .... 5 E3
Lower Severn St CBHAMW B1 .... 6 C6
Lowerstack Cft
CHWD/FDBR/MGN B37 .... 130 A4 🔲
Lower St DUNHL/THL/PER WV6 ... 24 A2
Lower Temple St CBHAM B2 .... 6 D5 🔲
Lower Tower St LOZ/NWT B19 .... 123 F2
Lower Trinity St BORD B9 .... 124 C6
Lower Valley Rd BRLYHL DY5 ..... 112 C5
Lower Vauxhall WOLV WV1 .... 24 C5
Lower Villiers St BKHL/PFLD WV2 .. 45 E2
Lower Walsall St WOLV WV1 .... 26 B6
Lower White Rd RIDG/WDGT B32 . 143 F5
Lowesmoor Rd
LGN/SDN/BHAMAIR B26 .... 153 D2
Lowe St BHTH/HG B12 .... 148 C1
DUNHL/THL/PER WV6 .... 24 C3
Lowfield Cl RIDG/WDGT B32 ...... 142 C6 🔲
Low Hill Crs WOLVN WV10 .... 12 A5
Lowhill La RBRY B45 .... 201 E1
Lowland Rd CDYHTH B64 .... 116 B6 🔲
Lowlands Av DUNHL/THL/PER WV6 .. 24 A1
FOAKS/STRLY B74 .... 56 A1
Lowndes Rd STRBR DY8 .... 136 A3
Lowry Cl DUNHL/THL/PER WV6 .... 22 D3
SMTHWKW B67 .... 119 F5
WLNHL WV13 .... 27 F5
Low Thatch HWK/WKHTH B38 ... 188 A5 🔲
Low Town OLDBY B69 .... 94 C6 🔲
Low Wood Rd ERDW/GRVHL B23 . 80 A6
Loxdale Sidings BILS/COS WV14 . 48 B5
Loxdale St BILS/COS WV14 .... 48 B5
DARL/WED WS10 .... 72 B1 🔲
Loxley Av ALE/KHTH/YWD B14 ... 191 E3
SHLY B90 .... 192 B4
Loxley Cl NFLD/LBR B31 .... 166 A3 🔲
Loxley Rd MGN/WHC B75 .... 39 F4
SMTHWKW B67 .... 120 B6
Loxton Cl FOAKS/STRLY B74 ...... 37 F2
Loynells Rd RBRY B45 .... 184 C6
Loyns Cl CHWD/FDBR/MGN B37 . 130 A4
Lozells Rd LOZ/NWT B19 .... 99 D6
Lozells St LOZ/NWT B19 .... 99 D6
Lozells Wood Cl LOZ/NWT B19 .... 99 D6 🔲
Luce Cl CVALE B35 .... 105 D1
Luce Rd WOLVN WV10 .... 26 A1
Lucknow Rd SHHTH WV12 .... 29 E1 🔲
Luddington Rd HIA/OLT B92 .... 174 A4
Ludford Cl MGN/WHC B75 .... 60 A2 🔲
Ludford Rd RIDG/WDGT B32 ...... 158 A2
Ludgate Cl CSHL/WTROR B46 .... 106 C2 🔲
Ludgate Hl CBHAMNW B3 .... 6 C3
Ludgate St DUDN DY1 .... 91 D4 🔲
Ludlow Cl CHWD/FDBR/MGN B37. 131 E5
SHHTH WV12 .... 29 D1
Ludlow La WSLW WS2 .... 30 C3 🔲
Ludlow Rd WASH/WDE B8 .... 126 A4
Ludlow Wy DUDN DY1 .... 90 A3
Ludmer Wy BFLD/HDSWWD B20 .. 99 D3 🔲

Ludstone Av
ETTPK/GDPK/PENN WV4 .... 43 F4
Ludstone Rd SLYOAK B29 .... 166 B2
Lugtrout La SOLH B91 .... 176 A5
Lulworth Cl HALE B63 .... 139 E3
Lulworth Rd HLGN/YWD B28 ...... 172 C3
Lumley Gv CHWD/FDBR/MGN B37 . 131 F5
Lumley Rd WSL WS1 .... 5 H5
Lundy Vw CBROM B36 .... 131 D1
Lunt Gv RIDG/WDGT B32 .... 143 F4
Lunt Pl BILS/COS WV14 .... 48 C3
Lunt Rd BILS/COS WV14 .... 48 B3
Lupin Gv BORD B9 .... 126 B4
Lupin Rd DUDS DY2 .... 92 B4
Lusbridge Cl HALE B63 .... 139 D5
Lutley Av HALE B63 .... 140 A5
Lutley Cl BDMR/CCFT WV3 .... 44 A2
Lutley Dr HAG/WOL DY9 .... 137 E6
Lutley Gv RIDG/WDGT B32 .... 165 D2
Lutley La HALE B63 .... 139 F5
HALE B63 .... 161 E1
Lutley Mill Rd HALE B63 .... 140 A5
Luton Rd SLYOAK B29 .... 146 B6
Luttrell Rd FOAKS/STRLY B74 ..... 58 B1
Lyall Gdns RBRY B45 .... 184 A4
Lyall Gv ACGN B27 .... 172 C1
Lychgate Av HAG/WOL DY9 .... 159 E2
Lydate Rd RMSLY B62 .... 142 B5
Lydbrook Covert
HWK/WKHTH B38 .... 188 A5 🔲
Lydbury Gv STETCH B33 .... 128 C3
Lyd Cl WNSFLD WV11 .... 27 D2
Lydd Cft CVALE B35 .... 105 D1
Lyddington Dr RMSLY B62 .... 141 D2
Lyde Gn HALE B63 .... 139 E2
Lydford Gv ERDE/BCHGN B24 .... 102 C3
Lydford Rd BLOX/PEL WS3 .... 17 D3
Lydgate Rd KGSWFD DY6 .... 112 B2
Lydget Gv ERDW/GRVHL B23 ...... 79 D3
Lydham Cl BILS/COS WV14 .... 47 D5
ERDW/GRVHL B23 .... 78 C5
Lydia Cft FOAKS/STRLY B74 .... 38 A1
Lydian Cl DUNHL/THL/PER WV6 ... 25 D3 🔲
Lydiate Ash Rd BRGRVW B61 ..... 199 E4
Lydiate Av NFLD/LBR B31 .... 185 F4
Lydiates Cl SEDG DY3 .... 67 D4
Lydney Cl SHHTH WV12 .... 29 F3
Lydney Gv NFLD/LBR B31 .... 186 B2
Lye Av RIDG/WDGT B32 .... 164 C1
Lye Close La RIDG/WDGT B32 .... 164 B1
Lyecroft Av
CHWD/FDBR/MGN B37 .... 131 F5
Lye Cross Rd OLDBY B69 .... 93 D6
Lygon Gv RIDG/WDGT B32 .... 144 A5 🔲
Lymedene Rd PBAR/PBCH B42 ... 77 D6
Lyme Green Rd STETCH B33 ..... 128 B3
Lymer Rd WOLVN WV10 .... 11 E4
Lymington Rd WLNHL WV13 ...... 29 F5 🔲
Lymsey Cft STRBR DY8 .... 111 E4
Lynbrook Cl DUDS DY2 .... 115 F1
HLYWD B47 .... 190 C5
Lyncourt Gv RIDG/WDGT B32 .... 143 D3
Lyncroft Rd SPARK B11 .... 172 B1
Lyndale Dr WNSFLD WV11 .... 28 A1
Lyndale Rd DUDS DY2 .... 116 A1
SEDG DY3 .... 67 D1
Lyndhurst Dr STRBR DY8 .... 112 B6
Lyndhurst Rd BDMR/CCFT WV3 ... 44 C2
ERDE/BCHGN B24 .... 102 B3
HHTH/SAND B71 .... 74 A4
Lyndon HHTH/SAND B71 .... 73 F6
Lyndon Cl BFLD/HDSWWD B20 ... 99 D3
CBROM B36 .... 105 E5
HALE B63 .... 140 A4
SEDG DY3 .... 68 A2
Lyndon Cft
CHWD/FDBR/MGN B37 .... 155 D2
Lyndon Gv HHTH/SAND B71 .... 95 F1 🔲
KGSWFD DY6 .... 87 D5
Lyndon Rd HIA/OLT B92 .... 174 B1
RBRY B45 .... 184 A6
SCFLD/BOLD B73 .... 59 D4 🔲
STETCH B33 .... 128 A4
Lyndworth Rd BVILLE B30 .... 169 E4
Lyneham Gdns WALM/CURD B76 . 82 C5
Lyneham Wy CVALE B35 .... 104 B2 🔲
Lynfield Cl HWK/WKHTH B38 ..... 188 B5
Lyng La WBROM B70 .... 95 E3
Lynmouth Cl ALDR WS9 .... 34 B2
Lynn Gv SLYOAK B29 .... 168 A3
Lynton Av DUNHL/THL/PER WV6 . 10 A6
HHTH/SAND B71 .... 73 E4
SMTHWK B66 .... 120 C1
Lynton Rd AST/WIT B6 .... 100 C6
Lynval Rd BRLYHL DY5 .... 138 B2
Lynwood Av KGSWFD DY6 .... 87 D5
Lynwood Cl SHHTH WV12 .... 16 A5 🔲
Lyons Gv SPARK B11 .... 149 E6
Lysander Rd RBRY B45 .... 184 C3 🔲
Lysways St WSL WS1 .... 5 E6
Lytham Cl STRBR DY8 .... 158 C1
WALM/CURD B76 .... 83 D5
Lytham Cft EDG B15 .... 123 F6
Lytham Gv BLOX/PEL WS3 .... 16 C1 🔲
Lythwood Dr BRLYHL DY5 .... 137 E1

Lyttelton Rd *LDYWD/EDGR* B16 ...... **121** F6
　　STETCH B33 .... **127** F5
　　STRBR DY8 .... **135** F4
Lyttleton Av *RMSLY* B62 .... **142** A2
Lyttleton Cl *DUDS* DY2 .... **115** E3
Lyttleton St *WBROM* B70 .... **95** E3
Lytton Av *ETTPK/GDPK/PENN* WV4 .. **43** F1
Lytton Gv *ACGN* B27 .... **173** D2
Lytton La *RIDG/WDGT* B32 .... **144** B6

M

Maas Rd *NFLD/LBR* B31 .... **186** C1
Macarthur Rd *CDYHTH* B64 .... **139** E1
Macdonald Cl *OLDBY* B69 .... **93** F3
Macdonald St *DIG/EDG* B5 .... **148** A1
Mace St *CDYHTH* B64 .... **116** A6
Machin Rd *ERDW/GRVHL* B23 .... **102** B1
Mackadown La *STETCH* B33 .... **129** F5
Mackay Rd *BLOX/PEL* WS3 .... **17** F3
Mackenzie Rd *SPARK* B11 .... **171** E1
Mackmillan Rd
　　BLKHTH/ROWR B65 .... **117** E5
Macmillan Cl *OLDBY* B69 .... **93** E3
Macrome Rd *DUNHL/THL/PER* WV6.. **10** A5
Madam's Hill Rd *SHLY* B90 .... **193** F6
Maddocks HI *CSCFLD/WYGN* B72 .... **81** E1
Madehurst Rd *ERDW/GRVHL* B23 .. **80** A5
Madeira Av *CDSL* WV8 .... **8** C3
Madeley Rd *HAG/WOL* DY9 .... **182** A6
　　KGSWFD DY6 .... **112** C3
　　SPARK B11 .... **149** E4
Madin Rd *TPTN/OCK* DY4 .... **92** A1
Madison Av *CBROM* B36 .... **127** F1
　　WSLW WS2 .... **31** D5
Madley Cl *RBRY* B45 .... **184** A5
Madresfield Dr *HALE* B63 .... **163** D1
Maer Cl *BLKHTH/ROWR* B65 .... **117** E4
Mafeking Rd *SMTHWK* B66 .... **96** C6
Magdala St *WSNGN* B18 .... **122** A2
Magdalen Cl *DUDN* DY1 .... **90** C3
Magdalene Rd *WSL* WS1 .... **52** C2
Magnolia Cl *SLYOAK* B29 .... **166** C4
Magnolia Gv *CDSL* WV8 .... **8** C2
Magnolia Wy *STRBR* DY8 .... **136** B1
Magnum Cl *DUDS* DY2 .... **116** A4
Magpie Cl *DUDS* DY2 .... **116** A4
Maidendale Rd *KGSWFD* DY6 .... **87** D6
Maidensbridge Gdns
　　KGSWFD DY6 .... **87** D4
Maidensbridge Rd *KGSWFD* DY6.. **87** D4
Maidstone Dr *STRBR* DY8 .... **112** A4
Maidstone Rd
　　BFLD/HDSWWD B20 .... **100** A4
Maidwell Dr *SHLY* B90 .... **194** A5
Main Av *LGN/SDN/BHAMAIR* B26 .. **155** A5
Main Rd *LGN/SDN/BHAMAIR* B26 .. **154** B6
Mainstream Wy *VAUX/NECH* B7 ... **114** A1
Main St *SPARK* B11 .... **148** C2
Mainwaring Dr *MGN/WHC* B75 .... **40** A5
Maitland Rd *DUDN* DY1 .... **89** F4
　　WASH/WDE B8 .... **126** B3
Majestic Wy *BLKHTH/ROWR* B65 .. **117** E5
Major St *BKHL/PFLD* WV2 .... **46** A2
Majuba Rd *LDYWD/EDGR* B16 .... **121** F3
Malcolm Av *ERDE/BCHGN* B24 ...... **81** E6
Malcolm Rd *SHLY* B90 .... **193** D3
Malcolmson Cl *EDG* B15 .... **146** B2
Malfield Dr *ACGN* B27 .... **152** A6
Malins Rd *ETTPK/GDPK/PENN* WV4 .. **45** F4
　　HRBN B17 .... **145** F4
Malkit Cl *WSLW* WS2 .... **30** A3
Mallaby Cl *SHLY* B90 .... **192** C5
Mallard Cl *ACGN* B27 .... **151** E6
　　BRLYHL DY5 .... **137** E2
Mallard Dr *ERDW/GRVHL* B23 ...... **101** D2
　　OLDBY B69 .... **118** B4
Mallender Dr *DOR/KN* B93 .... **196** B6
Mallin St *SMTHWK* B66 .... **95** F6
Mallory Crs *BLOX/PEL* WS3 .... **17** F3
Mallory Ri *MOS/BIL* B13 .... **171** E2
Mallory Rd *DUNHL/THL/PER* WV6 .. **22** A4
Mallow Cl *DSYBK/YTR* WS5 .... **52** C6
Malmesbury Rd *SMHTH* B10 .... **150** A3
Malpas Dr *RIDG/WDGT* B32 .... **165** E3
Malpass Gdns *CDSL* WV8 .... **8** A1
Malpass Rd *BRLYHL* DY5 .... **138** B2
Malt Cl *EDG* B15 .... **145** F3
Malthouse Cft *AST/WIT* B6 .... **100** A5
Malthouse Gdns *LOZ/NWT* B19 .... **99** F6
Malthouse Gv *YDLY* B25 .... **152** A1
Malthouse La
　　DUNHL/THL/PER WV6 .... **23** F1
　　HOCK/TIA B94 .... **222** A3
　　PBAR/PBCH B42 .... **77** F3
　　WASH/WDE B8 .... **126** A1
Malthouse Rd *TPTN/OCK* DY4 ...... **70** A6
Malthouse Rw
　　CHWD/FDBR/MGN B37 .... **154** C1
　The Maltings *WOLVN* WV1 .... **3** E1
Malt Mill La *RMSLY* B62 .... **141** E1

Malton Gv *MOS/BIL* B13 .... **171** D4
Malvern Av *HAG/WOL* DY9 .... **182** B4
Malvern Cl *HHTH/SAND* B71 .... **73** F6
　　SHHTH WV12 .... **29** D3
Malvern Ct *WOLVN* WV10 .... **11** F5
Malvern Crs *DUDS* DY2 .... **114** B1
Malvern Dr *ALDR* WS9 .... **21** E5
　　WALM/CURD B76 .... **82** C3
　　WOLV WV1 .... **27** D6
Malvern Hill Rd *VAUX/NECH* B7 ... **101** E6
Malvern Park Av *SOLH* B91 .... **195** F2
Malvern Rd *ACGN* B27 .... **151** E5
　　LGLYGN/QTN B68 .... **143** D1
　　RBRY B45 .... **200** C5
Malvern St *BHTH/HG* B12 .... **148** C4
Malvern View Rd *SEDG* DY3 .... **89** F1
Mamble Rd *STRBR* DY8 .... **136** A4
Manby Rd *CVALE* B35 .... **104** C5
Manby St *TPTN/OCK* DY4 .... **70** B3
Mancetter Rd *SHLY* B90 .... **193** E2
Manchester St *AST/WIT* B6 .... **124** A2
　　OLDBY B69 .... **95** D6
Mancroft Cl *KGSWFD* DY6 .... **87** D6
Mancroft Gdns
　　DUNHL/THL/PER WV6 .... **23** E2
Mancroft Rd *DUNHL/THL/PER* WV6 .. **23** E2
Mandale Rd *WOLVN* WV10 .... **26** B1
Manderley Cl *SEDG* DY3 .... **67** E1
Mander St *BDMR/CCFT* WV3 .... **45** D1
Mandeville Gdns *WSL* WS1 .... **5** F6
Maney Cnr *CSCFLD/WYGN* B72 ..... **59** D5
Maney Hill Rd *CSCFLD/WYGN* B72 .. **59** E6
Manfield Rd *WLNHL* WV13 .... **27** E4
Manilla Rd *SLYOAK* B29 .... **169** D2
Manitoba Cft *HWK/WKHTH* B38 .. **188** B5
Manley Cl *WBROM* B70 .... **94** C2
Manlove St *BDMR/CCFT* WV3 .... **44** C1
Manningford Rd
　　ALE/KHTH/YWD B14 .... **190** B3
Manor Abbey Dr *RMSLY* B62 .... **142** A6
Manor Abbey Rd *RMSLY* B62 .... **142** A6
Manor Cl *CDSL* WV8 .... **9** D2
　　ETTPK/GDPK/PENN WV4 .... **44** B5
　　WLNHL WV13 .... **28** A3
Manor Dr *SCFLD/BOLD* B73 .... **59** D5
　　SEDG DY3 .... **86** A3
　　SEDG DY3 .... **89** D2
Manor Farm Dr *SHHTH* WV12 ...... **29** E2
Manor Farm Rd *SPARK* B11 .... **150** A5
Manorford Av *HHTH/SAND* B71 ... **74** C2
Manor Gdns *STETCH* B33 .... **127** F6
Manor Gv *NFLD/LBR* B31 .... **185** E4
Manor Hl *SCFLD/BOLD* B73 .... **59** D5
Manor House La
　　CSHL/WTROR B46 .... **107** D2
　　LGN/SDN/BHAMAIR B26 .... **152** A3
Manor House Pk *CDSL* WV8 .... **9** D1
Manor House Rd *DARL/WED* WS10 .. **50** B5
Manor La *BRGRVW* B61 .... **199** E2
　　RMSLY B62 .... **142** A5
　　STRBR DY8 .... **135** F6
Manor Pk *KGSWFD* DY6 .... **111** F1
　　NFLD/LBR B31 .... **185** E4
Manor Park Rd *CBROM* B36 .... **105** F5
Manor Rd *AST/WIT* B6 .... **100** B4
　　DARL/WED WS10 .... **73** F1
　　DOR/KN B93 .... **212** B4
　　ETTPK/GDPK/PENN WV4 .... **44** B5
　　ETTPK/GDPK/PENN WV4 .... **66** C4
　　FOAKS/STRLY B74 .... **56** B2
　　HLYWD B47 .... **206** C4
　　LDYWD/EDGR B16 .... **121** F6
　　SCFLD/BOLD B73 .... **59** D4
　　SMTHWKW B67 .... **119** F2
　　SOLH B91 .... **175** E6
　　STETCH B33 .... **128** A4
　　STRBR DY8 .... **111** F5
　　TPTN/OCK DY4 .... **92** B1
　　WOLVN WV10 .... **11** E5
　　WSLW WS2 .... **31** E5
Manor Rd North
　　LDYWD/EDGR B16 .... **121** F6
Manor Road Prec *WSLW* WS2 ...... **31** E5
Manor St *DUNHL/THL/PER* WV6 ... **23** E2
Manor Wy *HALE* B63 .... **162** B2
　　RMSLY B62 .... **161** E1
　　RMSLY B62 .... **163** E1
Mansard Cl *BDMR/CCFT* WV3 ...... **44** B1
　　WNSFLD WV11 .... **13** D5
Mansell Cl *HALE* B63 .... **139** D2
Mansell Rd *TPTN/OCK* DY4 .... **70** C3
Mansel Rd *SMHTH* B10 .... **150** A1
Mansfield Rd *AST/WIT* B6 .... **99** F5
　　YDLY B25 .... **151** E4
Mansion Cl *DUDN* DY1 .... **90** B2
Mansion Crs *SMTHWKW* B67 ...... **120** A3
Mansion Dr *TPTN/OCK* DY4 .... **71** E6
Manston Dr *DUNHL/THL/PER* WV6.. **22** A2
Manston Rd
　　LGN/SDN/BHAMAIR B26 .... **153** D2
Manton Cft *DOR/KN* B93 .... **212** A4
Manway Cl *BFLD/HDSWWD* B20 ... **76** B6
Maple Av *DARL/WED* WS10 .... **51** E5

Maple Cl *BILS/COS* WV14 .... **68** C4
　　HDSW B21 .... **98** A4
Maple Cft *ALE/KHTH/YWD* B14 .... **170** B5
Mapledene Rd
　　LGN/SDN/BHAMAIR B26 .... **153** F3
Maple Dr *DSYBK/YTR* WS5 .... **53** D5
　　KGSTG B44 .... **79** D3
　　RUSH/SHEL WS4 .... **19** D5
　　SEDG DY3 .... **89** D3
Maple Gn *DUDN* DY1 .... **68** C6
Maple Gv *BDMR/CCFT* WV3 .... **23** E5
　　BILS/COS WV14 .... **48** B5
　　CHWD/FDBR/MGN B37 .... **130** B1
　　KGSWFD DY6 .... **112** A1
　　LOZ/NWT B19 .... **99** F5
Maple Leaf Dr
　　CHWD/FDBR/MGN B37 .... **155** D1
Maple Leaf Rd *DARL/WED* WS10 .. **71** E2
Maple Ri *LGLYGN/QTN* B68 .... **119** E5
Maple Rd *BDMR/CCFT* WV3 .... **44** A1
　　BLOX/PEL WS3 .... **18** B3
　　BVILLE B30 .... **168** A3
　　CSCFLD/WYGN B72 .... **59** E6
　　DUDN DY1 .... **91** E2
　　RBRY B45 .... **200** B1
　　RMSLY B62 .... **141** F1
Maple St *BLOX/PEL* WS3 .... **17** F5
Mapleton Gv *HLGN/YWD* B28 ...... **173** D4
Mapleton Rd *HLGN/YWD* B28 ...... **173** D5
Maple Tree La *HALE* B63 .... **139** E3
Maple Wy *NFLD/LBR* B31 .... **186** B5
Maplewood *WALM/CURD* B76 ...... **82** C3
Mapperley Gdns *MOS/BIL* B13 .... **147** E6
Mappleborough Rd *SHLY* B90 ...... **192** A4
Marans Cft *HWK/WKHTH* B38 ...... **187** F6
Marbury Cl *HWK/WKHTH* B38 ...... **187** F6
Marbury Ms *BRLYHL* DY5 .... **113** F6
Marchant Rd *BDMR/CCFT* WV3.... **24** B5
　　BILS/COS WV14 .... **47** E2
March End Rd *WNSFLD* WV11 ...... **27** F2
Marchmont Rd *BORD* B9 .... **126** C5
Marchmount Rd
　　CSCFLD/WYGN B72 .... **81** E3
March Wy *ALDR* WS9 .... **21** E4
Marcliff Crs *SHLY* B90 .... **191** E5
Marcos Dr *CBROM* B36 .... **106** B4
Marcot Rd *HIA/OLT* B92 .... **152** B4
Marden Cl *WLNHL* WV13 .... **28** B6
Marden Gv *NFLD/LBR* B31 .... **186** C6
Mardon Rd
　　LGN/SDN/BHAMAIR B26 .... **153** D4
Maree Gv *WNSFLD* WV11 .... **15** D4
Marfield Cl *WALM/CURD* B76 ...... **82** C5
Margam Crs *BLOX/PEL* WS3 .... **16** B3
Margam Ter *BLOX/PEL* WS3 .... **16** B3
Margam Wy *BLOX/PEL* WS3 .... **16** B3
Margaret Av *HALE* B63 .... **140** B5
Margaret Dr *STRBR* DY8 .... **137** D5
Margaret Gdns *SMTHWKW* B67 .. **120** A2
Margaret Gv *HRBN* B17 .... **145** E2
Margaret Rd *DARL/WED* WS10 .... **49** E5
　　HRBN B17 .... **145** E4
　　SCFLD/BOLD B73 .... **79** D3
　　WSLW WS2 .... **30** A4
Margaret St *CBHAMNW* B3 .... **6** C4
　　WBROM B70 .... **95** D3
　　WSLW WS2 .... **4** B2
Margaret V *TPTN/OCK* DY4 .... **71** E2
Margesson Dr *RBRY* B45 .... **201** E5
Marholm Cl *COVEN* WV9 .... **10** B5
Marian Cft
　　LGN/SDN/BHAMAIR B26 .... **153** F4
Maria St *WBROM* B70 .... **95** F5
Marie Dr *ACGN* B27 .... **173** D2
Marigold Crs *DUDN* DY1 .... **90** C1
Marine Crs *STRBR* DY8 .... **112** A6
Marine Dr *KGSTG* B44 .... **78** A5
Marine Gdns *STRBR* DY8 .... **112** A6
Mariner Av *LDYWD/EDGR* B16...... **122** A6
Marion Cl *BRLYHL* DY5 .... **114** B3
Marion Rd *SMTHWKW* B67 .... **119** F1
Marion Wy *HLGN/YWD* B28 .... **172** A4
Marita Cl *DUDS* DY2 .... **116** A4
Marjoram Cl *HWK/WKHTH* B38 ... **188** B5
Marjorie Av *BVILLE* B30 .... **189** D2
Mark Av *DARL/WED* WS10 .... **50** A6
Markby Rd *WSNGN* B18 .... **122** A1
Market La *ETTPK/GDPK/PENN* WV4 .. **42** B5
Market Pl *BLOX/PEL* WS3 .... **17** D4
　　DARL/WED WS10 .... **72** B1
　　TPTN/OCK DY4 .... **71** F6
　　WLNHL WV13 .... **28** C5
Market St *OLDBY* B69 .... **94** C3
　　STRBR DY8 .... **136** C4
　　WOLV WV1 .... **3** E4
Market Wy *HAG/WOL* DY9 .... **159** E5
Markfield Rd
　　LGN/SDN/BHAMAIR B26 .... **153** D1
Markford Wk *LOZ/NWT* B19 .... **123** F1
Markham Crs *HIA/OLT* B92 .... **176** B2
Markham Dr *KGSWFD* DY6 .... **112** A3
Markham Rd *SCFLD/BOLD* B73 .... **57** E6
Markham Rd *SCFLD/BOLD* B73 .... **57** E6
Marklin Av *WOLVN* WV10 .... **11** F4

Mark Rd *DARL/WED* WS10 ...... **50** A6
Marksbury Cl
  DUNHL/THL/PER WV6 ...... **24** C2
Marlbank Rd *STRBR* DY8 ...... **112** C6
Marlborough Cl
  FOAKS/STRLY B74 ...... **38** A1 🔟
Marlborough Dr *STRBR* DY8 ...... **136** C6 🔟
Marlborough Gdns
  DUNHL/THL/PER WV6 ...... **24** A3
  STRBR DY8 ...... **111** F5 🔟
Marlborough Gv *YDLY* B25 ...... **127** F6 🔟
Marlborough Rd *BORD* B9 ...... **126** A6
  CBROM B36 ...... **105** F5
  SEDG DY3 ...... **68** B5
  SMTHWK B66 ...... **120** C4
Marlbrook Cl *BLOX/PEL* WS3 ...... **17** D4
Marlbrook Cl *HIA/OLT* B92 ...... **153** E5
Marlbrook Dr
  ETTPK/GDPK/PENN WV4 ...... **45** D3
Marlbrook La *BRGRVE* B60 ...... **199** F6
Marlburn Wy *WMBN* WV5 ...... **64** A5
Marlcliff Gv *MOS/BIL* B13 ...... **170** C5
Marldon Rd *ALE/KHTH/YWD* B14 ...... **169** F5
Marlene Cft
  CHWD/FDBR/MGN B37 ...... **131** F6 🔟
Marley Rd *KGSWFD* DY6 ...... **112** C3
Marling Cft *HIA/OLT* B92 ...... **176** A4
Marlow Cl *DUDS* DY2 ...... **116** A4 🔟
Marlowe Dr *WLNHL* WV12 ...... **14** C6
Marlow Rd *ERDW/GRVHL* B23 ...... **79** E6
Marlow St *BLKHTH/ROWR* B65 ...... **117** E6 🔟
  WSLW WS2 ...... **32** A3
Marlpit La *WMC/WHC* B75 ...... **39** F4
Marlpool Dr *BLOX/PEL* WS3 ...... **18** B4
Marl Rd *DUDS* DY2 ...... **115** D5
Marl Top *HWK/WKHTH* B38 ...... **188** B3
Marmion Dr *GTB/HAM* B43 ...... **76** B1
Marmion Gv *DUDN* DY1 ...... **90** C5
Marmion Wy *WBROM* B70 ...... **72** B5 🔟
Marnel Dr *BDMR/CCFT* WV3 ...... **43** F1
Marquis Dr *CDYHTH* B64 ...... **140** C2
Marriott Rd *DUDS* DY2 ...... **115** E3
  SMTHWK B66 ...... **95** F6
Marroway St *LDYWD/EDGR* B16 ...... **122** B4
Mars Cl *BILS/COS* WV14 ...... **68** C2
Marsden Cl *HIA/OLT* B92 ...... **174** A2
Marshall Cl *ALDR* WS9 ...... **35** D3
Marshall Gv *KGSTG* B44 ...... **78** B4
Marshall Lake Rd *SHLY* B90 ...... **193** F4
Marshall Rd *LGLYGN/QTN* B68 ...... **119** E6
  WLNHL WV13 ...... **27** F6
Marshall St *CBHAMW* B1 ...... **123** F6 🔟
  SMTHWK B67 ...... **95** F6
Marsham Court Rd *SOLH* B91 ...... **174** B4
Marsham Rd *ALE/KHTH/YWD* B14 ...... **190** B2
Marshbrook Rd *ERDE/BCHGN* B24 ...... **103** F1
Marsh Crs *STRBR* DY8 ...... **111** F4 🔟
Marsh End *HWK/WKHTH* B38 ...... **188** C5
Marshfield Gdns
  ERDE/BCHGN B24 ...... **102** A3
Marsh Hl *ERDW/GRVHL* B23 ...... **101** E1
Marshland Wy *WSLW* WS2 ...... **30** A4
Marsh La *CSHL/WTROR* B46 ...... **107** D2
  ERDW/GRVHL B23 ...... **80** A6
  HHTH/SAND B71 ...... **73** F3
  HIA/OLT B92 ...... **179** F6
  SOLH B91 ...... **196** A2
  WALM/CURD B76 ...... **85** E6
  WOLVN WV10 ...... **11** D3
  WSLW WS2 ...... **4** B3
Marsh Lane Pde *WOLVN* WV10 ...... **11** E4
Marshmont Wy *ERDW/GRVHL* B23 ...... **79** F3
Marsh St *WSLW* WS2 ...... **4** B3
The Marsh *DARL/WED* WS10 ...... **50** A6
Marsh St *BRGRVW* B61 ...... **198** B6
Marshwood Cft *RIDG/WDGT* B32 ...... **142** C6
Marsland Cl *HRBN* B17 ...... **145** E1
Marsland Rd *HIA/OLT* B92 ...... **174** A4
Marston Av *DARL/WED* WS10 ...... **49** E3
Marston Cl *STRBR* DY8 ...... **135** F5 🔟
Marston Cft
  CHWD/FDBR/MGN B37 ...... **154** B2 🔟
Marston Dr
  CHWD/FDBR/MGN B37 ...... **130** C2
Marston Gv *GTB/HAM* B43 ...... **75** E3
Marston Rd *BKHL/PFLD* WV2 ...... **45** E2
  DUDN DY1 ...... **89** F5
  SCFLD/BOLD B73 ...... **80** C4
  SLYOAK B29 ...... **166** B3
Marston St *WLNHL* WV13 ...... **29** E5
Martham Dr *DUNHL/THL/PER* WV6 ...... **23** D5
Martin Cl *BILS/COS* WV14 ...... **69** F4
  LGN/SDN/BHAMAIR B26 ...... **151** F3
Martindale Wk *BRLYHL* DY5 ...... **137** D3
Martin Dr *SHHTH* WV12 ...... **29** E2
Martingale Cl *DSYBK/YTR* WS5 ...... **52** B5 🔟
Martin Hill St *DUDS* DY2 ...... **91** E5
Martin Ri
  CHWD/FDBR/MGN B37 ...... **154** B1 🔟
Martin Rd *BILS/COS* WV14 ...... **48** B6 🔟
  DSYBK/YTR WS5 ...... **53** E1
  TPTN/OCK DY4 ...... **70** C6
Martin St *ETTPK/GDPK/PENN* WV4 ...... **46** B5 🔟
Martlesham Sq *CVALE* B35 ...... **104** C1
Martley Cft *RIDG/WDGT* B32 ...... **144** A5

SOLH B91 ...... **195** D5 🔟
Martley Dr *HAG/WOL* DY9 ...... **137** E5
Martley Rd *OLDBY* B69 ...... **117** F1
  RUSH/SHEL WS4 ...... **19** E4
Marton Cl *VAUX/NECH* B7 ...... **125** D1
Marwood Cft *FOAKS/STRLY* B74 ...... **36** C5
Mary Ann St *CBHAMNW* B3 ...... **6** C3
  WOLV WV1 ...... **3** G5 🔟
Maryland Av *BKDE/SHDE* B34 ...... **128** A2
Maryland Dr *NFLD/LBR* B31 ...... **160** D6
Maryland Rd *BRLYHL* DY5 ...... **138** B2 🔟
Marylebone Cl *STRBR* DY8 ...... **136** C2 🔟
Mary Macarthur Dr *CDYHTH* B64 ...... **115** D6
Mary Rd *HDSW* B21 ...... **98** A6
  OLDBY B69 ...... **85** E5
  STETCH B33 ...... **127** F4
  WBROM B70 ...... **95** F4
Mary St *BHTH/HG* B12 ...... **148** A4
  CBHAMNW B3 ...... **6** B2
  WSLW WS2 ...... **31** F4
Mary Vale Rd *BVILLE* B30 ...... **168** A5
Marywell Cl *RIDG/WDGT* B32 ...... **165** D4 🔟
Masefield Av *DUDN* DY1 ...... **69** E4
Masefield Cl *BILS/COS* WV14 ...... **70** B1
Masefield Ri *RMSLY* B62 ...... **141** F6 🔟
Masefield Rd *BLOX/PEL* WS3 ...... **18** A5
  SEDG DY3 ...... **88** C1
  WOLVN WV10 ...... **12** C4
Masefield Sq *NFLD/LBR* B31 ...... **187** E1
Masham Cl *STETCH* B33 ...... **128** A5
Mashie Gdns *HWK/WKHTH* B38 ...... **187** F4
Maslen Pl *HALE* B63 ...... **141** D6 🔟
Maslin Dr *BILS/COS* WV14 ...... **68** C2
Mason Crs *ETTPK/GDPK/PENN* WV4 ...... **44** A4
Mason La *HOCK/TIA B94 ...... **208** B6
Masonleys Rd *NFLD/LBR* B31 ...... **185** F2 🔟
Mason Rd *ERDE/BCHGN* B24 ...... **102** C1
  WSLW WS2 ...... **31** D2
Masons Cl *HALE* B63 ...... **139** E3 🔟
Mason St *BILS/COS* WV14 ...... **69** D4
  BKHL/PFLD WV2 ...... **45** E2 🔟
  WBROM B70 ...... **95** D1
Masons Wy *HIA/OLT* B92 ...... **174** A1
  HIA/OLT B92 ...... **174** A1
Massbrook Gv *WOLVN* WV10 ...... **26** B1
Massbrook Rd *WOLVN* WV10 ...... **26** B1 🔟
Masshouse Circus Queensway
  CBHAMNE B4 ...... **7** F4
Masshouse La *DIG/EDG* B5 ...... **7** G4 🔟
  HWK/WKHTH B38 ...... **188** B4
Masters La *RMSLY* B62 ...... **118** A6
Matchlock Cl *FOAKS/STRLY* B74 ...... **56** A2
Matfen Av *SCFLD/BOLD* B73 ...... **80** B1
Math Meadow *RIDG/WDGT* B32 ...... **144** B4
Matlock Cl *BLOX/PEL* WS3 ...... **17** E2
  DUDS DY2 ...... **115** F4 🔟
Matlock Rd *BLOX/PEL* WS3 ...... **17** E2
  SPARK B11 ...... **150** B6
Matthews Cl
  BLKHTH/ROWR B65 ...... **117** D6 🔟
Mattox Rd *WNSFLD* WV11 ...... **27** F1
Matty Rd *LGLYGN/QTN* B68 ...... **119** E3
Maud Rd *CSHL/WTROR* B46 ...... **107** F2
  WBROM B70 ...... **95** D4
Maughan St *BRLYHL* DY5 ...... **138** C1
  DUDN DY1 ...... **90** C4
Maurice Gv *WOLVN* WV10 ...... **26** C1
Maurice Rd *ALE/KHTH/YWD* B14 ...... **170** A5
  SMTHWK B67 ...... **122** A5
Mavis Gdns *LGLYGN/QTN* B68 ...... **143** D1 🔟
Mavis Rd *NFLD/LBR* B31 ...... **186** A4
Maw St *WLS1* WS1 ...... **52** B3
Maxholm Rd *FOAKS/STRLY* B74 ...... **56** A1
Max Rd *RIDG/WDGT* B32 ...... **143** F4
Maxstoke Cl *BLOX/PEL* WS3 ...... **16** C2 🔟
Maxstoke Cft *SHLY* B90 ...... **193** F5
Maxstoke La *CSHL/WTROR* B46 ...... **132** C1
Maxstoke St *SCFLD/BOLD* B73 ...... **80** A1
Maxted Rd *ERDW/GRVHL* B23 ...... **79** E3
Maxwell Av *BFLD/HDSWWD* B20 ...... **99** D4
Maxwell Rd *BKHL/PFLD* WV2 ...... **45** F1
Mayall Dr *MGN/WHC* B75 ...... **39** E3
May Av *BHTH/HG* B12 ...... **148** C4 🔟
Maybank *BORD* B9 ...... **126** B4
Maybank Pl *KGSTG* B44 ...... **78** A5 🔟
Maybank Rd *DUDS* DY2 ...... **115** E4
Mayberry Cl *ALE/KHTH/YWD* B14 ...... **191** D3
Maybridge Dr *SOLH* B91 ...... **195** D5
Maybrook Rd *WALM/CURD* B76 ...... **82** C6
Maybury Cl *CDSL* WV8 ...... **8** A1
Maybush Gdns *WOLVN* WV10 ...... **11** E4
Maydene Cft *BHTH/HG* B12 ...... **148** B5
Mayfair *HAG/WOL* DY9 ...... **159** F1
Mayfair Cl *DUDN* DY1 ...... **90** C3
  KGSTG B44 ...... **79** D4 🔟
Mayfair Gdns *BDMR/CCFT* WV3 ...... **23** F5
  TPTN/OCK DY4 ...... **92** C1
May Farm Cl *HLYWD* B47 ...... **206** B1
Mayfield Cl *BRGRVW* B61 ...... **198** B6
  SOLH B91 ...... **195** E4 🔟
Mayfield Crs *BLKHTH/ROWR* B65 ...... **116** C4
Mayfield Rd *BVILLE* B30 ...... **168** C5
  DUDN DY1 ...... **91** D1

FOAKS/STRLY B74 ...... **56** B1
  HALE B63 ...... **161** F1
  LOZ/NWT B19 ...... **99** D5
  MOS/BIL B13 ...... **170** C1
  RMSLY B62 ...... **118** B6
  SCFLD/BOLD B73 ...... **80** C1
  SPARK B11 ...... **150** C5
  WOLV WV1 ...... **27** D6
Mayflower Cl *LOZ/NWT* B19 ...... **123** F1
Mayflower Dr *BRLYHL* DY5 ...... **88** C6
Mayford Gv *MOS/BIL* B13 ...... **171** D5 🔟
Maygrove Rd *KGSWFD* DY6 ...... **87** E6 🔟
Mayhurst Cl *HLYWD* B47 ...... **207** E1
  TPTN/OCK DY4 ...... **70** C3 🔟
Mayhurst Rd *HLYWD* B47 ...... **191** D6
Mayland Dr *FOAKS/STRLY* B74 ...... **56** B4
Mayland Rd *LDYWD/EDGR* B16 ...... **121** E5
May La *ALE/KHTH/YWD* B14 ...... **170** B6
  HLYWD B47 ...... **190** B6
Maynard Av *STRBR* DY8 ...... **135** F6
Maypole Cl *CDYHTH* B64 ...... **139** D1 🔟
Maypole Ct *WMBN* WV5 ...... **64** C5 🔟
Maypole Dr *STRBR* DY8 ...... **136** A4
Maypole Flds *HALE* B63 ...... **138** C2
Maypole Gv *ALE/KHTH/YWD* B14 ...... **191** D3
Maypole Hl *HALE* B63 ...... **138** C1
Maypole La *ALE/KHTH/YWD* B14 ...... **190** C3
Maypole Rd *LGLYGN/QTN* B68 ...... **119** D6
Maypole St *WMBN* WV5 ...... **65** D4
May St *BLOX/PEL* WS3 ...... **31** F1
Mayswood Dr
  DUNHL/THL/PER WV6 ...... **22** B6
Mayswood Gv *RIDG/WDGT* B32 ...... **143** F5
Mayswood Rd *HIA/OLT* B92 ...... **175** E1
Maythorn Av *WALM/CURD* B76 ...... **82** C5
Maythorn Gdns
  DUNHL/THL/PER WV6 ...... **23** D3
Maythorn Gv *SOLH* B91 ...... **195** D5 🔟
Maytree Cl *CHWD/FDBR/MGN* B37 ...... **130** C5
May Tree Gv *BFLD/HDSWWD* B20 ...... **98** B2
Maywell Dr *HIA/OLT* B92 ...... **176** B3
Maywood Cl *KGSWFD* DY6 ...... **111** D1 🔟
Mcbean Rd *DUNHL/THL/PER* WV6 ...... **24** B3
Mcdougall Rd *DARL/WED* WS10 ...... **51** E6
Mc Kean Rd *OLDBY* B69 ...... **94** C5
Mclean Rd *WOLVN* WV10 ...... **11** E3
Meaburn Cl *SLYOAK* B29 ...... **166** C4
Mead Cl *ALDR* WS9 ...... **35** D1
Mead Crs *BORD* B9 ...... **127** D4
Meadfoot Av
  ALE/KHTH/YWD B14 ...... **190** B2 🔟
Meadfoot Dr *KGSWFD* DY6 ...... **87** D6
The Meadlands *WMBN* WV5 ...... **64** A5
Meadow Av *HHTH/SAND* B71 ...... **74** B2
Meadowbrook Rd *HALE* B63 ...... **139** F6
Meadow Brook Rd *NFLD/LBR* B31 ...... **166** B6
Meadow Cl *FOAKS/STRLY* B74 ...... **36** B6
  HRBN B17 ...... **121** D5
  RUSH/SHEL WS4 ...... **19** E5
Meadow Cft *HLYWD* B47 ...... **206** C4 🔟
Meadow Dr *HIA/OLT* B92 ...... **178** C5
Meadowfield Rd *RBRY* B45 ...... **184** C5
Meadowfields Cl *STRBR* DY8 ...... **112** A5
Meadow Grange Dr
  SHHTH WV12 ...... **15** D6 🔟
Meadow Gv *HIA/OLT* B92 ...... **173** F2
Meadowhill Dr *STRBR* DY8 ...... **112** A5 🔟
Meadow Hill Rd *HWK/WKHTH* B38 ...... **188** A3
Meadowlands Dr *RUSH/SHEL* WS4 ...... **19** E5
Meadow La *ALVE* B48 ...... **217** D3
  BILS/COS WV14 ...... **68** C1 🔟
  SHHTH WV12 ...... **28** C2
  WMBN WV5 ...... **64** C5
Meadowpark Rd *STRBR* DY8 ...... **135** F1
Meadow Ri *BVILLE* B30 ...... **167** F4
Meadow Rd *ALDR* WS9 ...... **34** C3
  BDMR/CCFT WV3 ...... **43** E1
  DUDN DY1 ...... **90** C1
  HLYWD B47 ...... **206** C4
  HRBN B17 ...... **121** D6
  LGLYGN/QTN B68 ...... **119** D5
  RIDG/WDGT B32 ...... **142** C3
  RMSLY B62 ...... **141** E1
  SMTHWK B67 ...... **120** B3
Meadowside Cl *GTB/HAM* B43 ...... **76** A2
Meadowside Rd *FOAKS/STRLY* B74 ...... **38** B3
The Meadows *ALDR* WS9 ...... **34** A2
  HAG/WOL DY9 ...... **159** D4
Meadow St *CDYHTH* B64 ...... **140** B1 🔟
  WOLV WV1 ...... **2** A4
  WSL WS1 ...... **4** B6
Meadowsweet Av
  HWK/WKHTH B38 ...... **188** B5
Meadowsweet Wy
  KGSWFD DY6 ...... **112** C1 🔟
Meadow V *CDSL* WV8 ...... **9** D4
Meadow Vw *MOS/BIL* B13 ...... **171** E3
  SEDG DY3 ...... **67** E2 🔟
Meadow Wk *ALE/KHTH/YWD* B14 ...... **190** A4
  CDYHTH B64 ...... **139** F1
Meadow Wy *CDSL* WV8 ...... **8** A3
  STRBR DY8 ...... **111** E5
Mead Ri *EDG* B15 ...... **146** B3
The Mead *SEDG* DY3 ...... **67** D3
Meadthorpe Rd *KGSTG* B44 ...... **77** F3

Meadvale Rd *RBRY* B45 .... 201 D1
Meadway *STETCH* B33 .... 128 B5
The Meadway
DUNHL/THL/PER WV6 .... 22 C2
Mears Cl *ERDW/GRVHL* B23 .... 79 F3
Mears Coppice *BRLYHL* DY5 .... 138 A3
Mears Dr *STETCH* B33 .... 127 F3
Mearse Cl *WSNGN* B18 .... 122 C2
Mearse La *RBRY* B45 .... 200 B6
Mease Cft *BORD* B9 .... 125 D5 🖪
Measham Gv
LGN/SDN/BHAMAIR B26 .... 152 A4
Measham Wy *WNSFLD* WV11 .... 14 A6
Medcroft Av *BFLD/HDSWWD* B20... 98 A1
Medina Cl *SPARK* B11 .... 150 A5
Medina Wy *KGSWFD* DY6 .... 111 E1 🖪
Medley Rd *SPARK* B11 .... 149 E4
Medlicott Rd *SPARK* B11 .... 149 E4
Medway Cl *BRLYHL* DY5 .... 112 C1
Medway Cft *CBROM* B36 .... 106 B6 🖪
Medway Gv *HWK/WKHTH* B38 .... 188 A5
Medwin Gv *ERDW/GRVHL* B23 ...... 79 F4
Meer End *HWK/WKHTH* B38 .... 187 F6
Meerhill Av *SHLY* B90 .... 210 B5
Meeting House La *NFLD/LBR* B31 .. 186 C1
Meeting La *BRLYHL* DY5 .... 113 D6
Meeting St *DARL/WED* WS10 .... 50 A4
DUDS DY2 .... 115 E3
TPTN/OCK DY4 .... 71 E5
Melbourne Av *LOZ/NWT* B19 .... 123 E1
Melbourne Cl *KGSWFD* DY6 .... 112 A3
WBROM B70 .... 72 C3
Melbourne Gdns
DSYBK/YTR WS5 .... 53 D3 🖪
Melbourne Rd *HALE* B63 .... 141 D4
SMTHWK B66 .... 96 C6
Melbury Cl *BDMR/CCFT* WV3 .... 24 C6 🖪
Melbury Gv *ALE/KHTH/YWD* B14 ... 170 A4
Melchett Rd *BVILLE* B30 .... 188 B2
Melcote Gv *KGSTG* B44 .... 78 A3
Meldon Dr *BILS/COS* WV14.......... 70 C1
Melford Hall Rd *SOLH* B91 .... 174 B4
Melford St *SEDG* DY3 .... 67 E3
Melfort Gv *ALE/KHTH/YWD* B14 ... 190 C2
Melksham Sq *CVALE* B35 .... 104 C2 🖪
Mellis Gv *ERDW/GRVHL* B23 .... 78 C6
Mellish Dr *RUSH/SHEL* WS4 .... 33 D4
Mellish Rd *RUSH/SHEL* WS4 .... 32 C4
Mellor Dr *FOAKS/STRLY* B74 .... 38 A4
Mellors Rd *HRBN* B17 .... 145 D6
Mellowdew Rd *STRBR* DY8 .... 111 E4
Mell Sq *SOLH* B91 .... 195 E1
Melplash Av *SOLH* B91 .... 194 C1 🖪
Melrose Av *BHTH/HG* B12 .... 148 C3 🖪
HHTH/SAND B71 .... 73 F2
SCFLD/BOLD B73 .... 80 A1
SPARK B11 .... 149 E3 🖪
STRBR DY8 .... 158 B1
Melrose Av *HWK/WKHTH* B38 .... 188 B4 🖪
Melrose Gv *LOZ/NWT* B19 .... 99 D6 🖪
Melrose Rd *BFLD/HDSWWD* B20 .. 100 A4
Melstock Cl *TPTN/OCK* DY4 .... 69 F6
Melstock Rd *ALE/KHTH/YWD* B14.. 169 F4
Melton Av *HIA/OLT* B92 .... 153 D5
Melton Dr *EDG* B15 .... 147 D5
Melton Rd *ALE/KHTH/YWD* B14 ... 170 B3
Melverley Gv *KGSTG* B44 .... 78 B4
Melverton Av *WOLVN* WV10 .... 11 F5
Melville Rd *LDYWD/EDGR* B16....... 121 F6
Melvina Rd *VAUX/NECH* B7 .... 125 D3
Membury Rd *WASH/WDE* B8 .... 125 F1
Memorial Cl *WLNHL* WV13 .... 28 C5
Memory La *DARL/WED* WS10 .... 49 F1
WOLVN WV10 .... 27 D2
Menai Cl *SHHTH* WV12 .... 29 E1
Mendip Av *WASH/WDE* B8 .... 126 A2 🖪
Mendip Cl *BKHL/PFLD* WV2 .... 46 B3
SEDG DY3 .... 89 D2
Mendip Rd *HALE* B63 .... 161 F2
STRBR DY8 .... 137 D3
WASH/WDE B8 .... 126 A2
Menin Crs *MOS/BIL* B13 .... 171 D4 🖪
Menin Rd *MOS/BIL* B13 .... 171 D4
TPTN/OCK DY4 .... 69 F6
Meon Gv *DUNHL/THL/PER* WV6 .... 22 A3
STETCH B33 .... 153 D1
Meon Ri *HAG/WOL* DY9 .... 137 E6
Meon Wy *WNSFLD* WV11 .... 14 B6
Meranti Cl *SHHTH* WV12 .... 15 E5
Mercer Av *CSHL/WTROR* B46 .... 106 C2
Mercer Gv *WNSFLD* WV11 .... 13 F6
Merchants Wy *ALDR* WS9 .... 20 C6
Mercia Dr *DUNHL/THL/PER* WV6 ... 22 A2
Mere Av *CVALE* B35 .... 104 C2
Mere Cl *SHHTH* WV12 .... 28 C2
Merecote Rd *HIA/OLT* B92 .... 173 F4
Meredith Pool Cl *WSNGN* B18 ...... 122 B1 🖪
Meredith Rd *SEDG* DY3 .... 66 C6
WNSFLD WV11 .... 13 F5
Meredith St *CDYHTH* B64 .... 115 F6
Mere Dr *MGN/WHC* B75 .... 39 D5
Mere Green Cl *MGN/WHC* B75 ...... 39 E5
Mere Green Rd *MGN/WHC* B75...... 39 E5
Mere Oak Rd *DUNHL/THL/PER* WV6.. 22 A2

Mere Pool Rd *MGN/WHC* B75 .... 39 F5
Mere Rd *ERDW/GRVHL* B23 .... 101 F2
STRBR DY8 .... 136 A5
Mereside Wy *HIA/OLT* B92 .... 174 A3
Meres Rd *HALE* B63 .... 139 E4
Merevale Rd *HIA/OLT* B92 .... 175 D1
Mere Vw *RUSH/SHEL* WS4 .... 19 E5
Meriden Av *STRBR* DY8 .... 135 F3
Meriden Cl *STRBR* DY8 .... 135 F2
Meriden Dr
CHWD/FDBR/MGN B37 .... 130 C1
Meriden Ri *HIA/OLT* B92 .... 153 F6
Meriden Rd *HIA/OLT* B92 .... 179 E4
WOLVN WV10 .... 10 C5
Meriden St *DIG/EDG* B5 .... 7 C6
Merino Av *NFLD/LBR* B31 .... 186 C5
Merlin Cl *DUDN* DY1 .... 90 B5
Merlin Gv *LGN/SDN/BHAMAIR* B26 .. 153 D4
Merrick Cl *HALE* B63 .... 161 F1
Merrick Rd *WNSFLD* WV11 .... 28 C1
Merridale Av *BDMR/CCFT* WV3 .... 24 B5
Merridale Crs *BDMR/CCFT* WV3 ... 24 C5 🖪
Merridale Gdns *BDMR/CCFT* WV3.. 24 C6
Merridale La *BDMR/CCFT* WV3 ..... 24 A6
Merridale Rd *BDMR/CCFT* WV3 .... 24 B6
Merridale St *BDMR/CCFT* WV3 ..... 2 B6
Merridale St West
BDMR/CCFT WV3 .... 44 A5
Merriemont Dr *RBRY* B45 .... 200 C6
Merrill Gdns *BRGRVE* B60 .... 199 F6 🖪
Merrills Hall *WLNHL* WV13 .... 28 A3
Merrill's Hall La *WNSFLD* WV11 .... 28 A3
Merrington Cl *SOLH* B91 .... 195 E5 🖪
Merrion's Cl *GTB/HAM* B43 .... 54 A5
Merrishaw Rd *NFLD/LBR* B31 .... 186 C5
Merritts Brook Cl *SLYOAK* B29 ..... 166 C6 🖪
Merritt's Brook La *NFLD/LBR* B31 .. 166 A6
Merritts Hl *NFLD/LBR* B31 .... 166 A6
Merrivale Rd *RMSLY* B62 .... 142 B1
SMTHWK B66 .... 120 C5
Merryfield Cl *HIA/OLT* B92 .... 175 F4 🖪
Merryfield Gv *HRBN* B17 .... 145 E5
Merryfield Rd *DUDN* DY1 .... 89 F4
Merry Hl *BRLYHL* DY5 .... 114 B6
Merryhill Dr *WSNGN* B18 .... 122 B1 🖪
Mersey Gv *HWK/WKHTH* B38 .... 188 A5
Mersey Rd *BLOX/PEL* WS3 .... 18 A4
Merstal Dr *HIA/OLT* B92 .... 176 B3
Merstone Cl *BILS/COS* WV14 .... 47 E3
Merstowe Cl *ACGN* B27 .... 151 D2
Merton Cl *LGLYGN/QTN* B68 .... 119 D5
Merton Rd *MOS/BIL* B13 .... 149 D6
Mervyn Pl *BILS/COS* WV14 .... 48 B6 🖪
Mervyn Rd *BILS/COS* WV14 .... 48 B6
HDSW B21 .... 97 F4
Meryhurst Rd *DARL/WED* WS10.... 51 D5
Messenger La *WBROM* B70 .... 95 F2
Messenger Rd *SMTHWK* B66 .... 121 D1
Metchley Cl *HRBN* B17 .... 145 F5 🖪
Metchley Cft *SHLY* B90 .... 210 B5 🖪
Metchley Dr *HRBN* B17 .... 145 E4
Metchley La *EDG* B15 .... 145 F3 🖪
HRBN B17
Metchley Park Rd *EDG* B15 .... 146 A4
Metfield Cft *HRBN* B17................. 145 F5
KGSWFD DY6 .... 112 B1 🖪
Metlin Gv *STETCH* B33 .... 130 A4
Metro Wy *SMTHWK* B66 .... 97 E6
The Mews *BLKHTH/ROWR* B65 ... 117 E5 🖪
Meyrick Rd *WBROM* B70 .... 72 C5
Meyrick Wk *LDYWD/EDGR* B16 .... 122 B6
Miall Park Rd *SOLH* B91 .... 174 A6 🖪
Miall Rd *HLGN/YWD* B28 .... 172 C3
Michael Dr *EDG* B15 .... 147 E2
Michael Rd *DARL/WED* WS10....... 49 D2
SMTHWK B67 .... 120 A5
Michelle Cl *MOS/BIL* B13 .... 170 C6 🖪
Micklehill Dr *SHLY* B90 .... 193 D5
Mickle Meadow *CSHL/WTROR* B46.. 107 D2
Mickleover Rd *WASH/WDE* B8 ...... 127 E2
Mickleton Av *STETCH* B33 .... 153 E1
Mickleton Rd *HIA/OLT* B92 .... 173 F3
Mickley Av *WOLVN* WV10 .... 26 A2
Midacre *WLNHL* WV13 .... 28 C6
Middle Acre Rd *RIDG/WDGT* B32 .. 166 A4
Middle Av *WLNHL* WV13 .... 48 A1 🖪
Middle Bickenhill La *HIA/OLT* B92... 156 C5
Middle Crs *BLOX/PEL* WS3 .... 18 B6
Middle Cross *WOLV* WV1 .... 3 F5
Middle Dr *RBRY* B45 .... 201 F3
Middlefield *CDSL* WV8 .... 10 A3
Middlefield Av *DOR/KN* B93 .... 213 D3 🖪
RMSLY B62 .... 142 B1
Middlefield Cl *RMSLY* B62 .... 118 B6 🖪
Middlefield Gdns *RMSLY* B62 .... 142 B1 🖪
Middlefield La *HAG/WOL* DY9 ...... 159 D5
Middle Field Rd *NFLD/LBR* B31 .... 187 D5
Middlefield Rd *OLDBY* B69 .... 92 C5
Middle Gdns *WLNHL* WV13 .... 29 D5 🖪
Middlehill Ri *RIDG/WDGT* B32 ...... 143 F6 🖪
Middle House Dr *BRGRVE* B60 ...... 199 F6 🖪
Middle La *HLYWD* B47 .... 206 B4
HWK/WKHTH B38 .... 189 E6
Middle Leaford *STETCH* B33 .... 128 C2

Middle Leasowe *RIDG/WDGT* B32... 143 E5
Middle Meadow Av
RIDG/WDGT B32 .... 143 E4 🖪
Middlemist Gv *GTB/HAM* B43 .... 76 B5 🖪
Middlemore La *ALDR* WS9 .... 34 B1
Middlemore La West *ALDR* WS9 .... 34 A1
Middlemore Rd *NFLD/LBR* B31 ..... 187 D3
SMTHWK B66 .... 97 D6
Middle Park Cl *SLYOAK* B29 .... 167 D3
Middlepark Rd *DUDN* DY1 .... 90 A5
Middle Park Rd *SLYOAK* B29 .... 167 D3
Middle Rd *BRCRVW* B61 .... 198 B3
Middleton Gdns *BVILLE* B30 .... 187 F1
Middleton Gra *NFLD/LBR* B31 ...... 187 E1 🖪
Middleton Hall Rd *BVILLE* B30 ...... 188 A1
Middleton La *POL/KGSB/FAZ* B78.. 62 B3
Middleton Rd
ALE/KHTH/YWD B14 .... 170 B4 🖪
FOAKS/STRLY B74 .... 36 C6
SHLY B90 .... 192 C5
Middletree Rd *HALE* B63 .... 139 E2
Middle Vauxhall *WOLV* WV1 .... 24 C5 🖪
Middleway Av *STRBR* DY8 .... 111 E4
Middleway Rd *BILS/COS* WV14 ..... 47 E1
Middleway Rd *BILS/COS* WV14 ..... 47 E1
Middleway Vw *WSNGN* B18 .... 122 C4
Midford Gv *EDG* B15 .... 147 E1
Midgley Dr *FOAKS/STRLY* B74 ..... 38 C5
Midhill Dr *OLDBY* B69 .... 117 E1
Midhurst Gv *DUNHL/THL/PER* WV6 .. 23 D2
Midhurst Rd *BVILLE* B30 .... 189 D2
Midland Cl *HDSW* B21 .... 98 C6 🖪
Midland Dr *CSCFLD/WYGN* B72 .... 59 E4
Midland Rd *BVILLE* B30 .... 168 B6
DARL/WED WS10 .... 49 E1
FOAKS/STRLY B74 .... 4 C5
WSL WS1
Midland St *BORD* B9 .... 125 E4 🖪
Midvale Dr *ALE/KHTH/YWD* B14 ... 189 E1
Milburn Rd *KGSTG* B44 .... 56 C6
Milcote Dr *SCFLD/BOLD* B73 .... 57 E6
WLNHL WV13 .... 27 F6
Milcote Rd *SLYOAK* B29 .... 166 C3
SMTHWK B67 .... 120 B5
SOLH B91 .... 195 D1
Milcote Wy *KGSWFD* DY6 .... 87 D6
Mildenhall Rd *PBAR/PCH* B42 ...... 76 C2
Mildred Rd *CDYHTH* B64 .... 116 A5
Mildred Wy *OLDBY* B69 .... 117 E1
Milebrook Gv *RIDG/WDGT* B32 ..... 165 D3 🖪
Milebush Av *CBROM* B36 .... 105 F4
Mile Flat *KGSWFD* DY6 .... 86 B6
Miles Gv *DUDS* DY2 .... 92 B6
Miles Meadow Cl *SHHTH* WV12 .... 15 E5
Milestone La *HDSW* B21 .... 97 F5
Milestone Wy *SHHTH* WV12 .... 15 D5
Milford Av *SHHTH* WV12.............. 28 C2
Milford Cl *STRBR* DY8 .... 112 A3
Milford Ct *LOZ/NWT* B19 .... 123 F2
Milford Cft *BLKHTH/ROWR* B65 ... 116 B1
Milford Gv *SHLY* B90 .... 195 E6
Milford Rd *BKHL/PFLD* WV2 .... 45 E2
HRBN B17 .... 145 D4
Milholme Gn *HIA/OLT* B92 .... 175 F4
Milking Bank *DUDN* DY1 .... 90 A3
Milk St *DIG/EDG* B5 .... 124 D5
Millard Rd *BILS/COS* WV14 .... 69 D2
Mill Bank *SEDG* DY3 .... 67 F3
Millbank Gv *ERDW/GRVHL* B23 .... 79 D3 🖪
Millbank St *WNSFLD* WV11 .... 14 B4
Millbrook Dr *NFLD/LBR* B31 .... 186 A5
Millbrook Rd *ALE/KHTH/YWD* B14 .. 169 E5
Millbrook Wy *BRLYHL* DY5 .... 137 D1
Mill Burn Wy *BORD* B9 .... 125 D5 🖪
Mill Cl *HLYWD* B47 .... 190 C6
SEDG DY3 .... 67 F5 🖪
Mill Cft *BILS/COS* WV14 .... 48 A3 🖪
Millcroft Cl *RIDG/WDGT* B32 .... 166 A1
Millcroft Rd *FOAKS/STRLY* B74 .... 56 C1
Milldale Crs *WOLVN* WV10 .... 11 F2
Milldale Rd *WOLVN* WV10 .... 11 F1
Mill Dr *SMTHWK* B66 .... 121 D2 🖪
Millennium Cl *BLOX/PEL* WS3 ...... 18 C1
Millennium Wy *CDSL* WV8 .... 9 D1
Miller Crs *BILS/COS* WV14 .... 68 C2
Millers Cl *WSLW* WS2 .... 30 B6
Millersdale Dr *HHTH/SAND* B71 ... 74 B1
Millers Green Dr *KGSWFD* DY6 .... 86 C5
Miller St *AST/WIT* B6 .... 124 A2
Millers Wk *BLOX/PEL* WS3 .... 18 A2
Mill Farm Rd *HRBN* B17 .... 145 E6
Millfield Av *BLOX/PEL* WS3 .... 17 F5
RUSH/SHEL WS4 .... 19 D4
Millfield Rd *BFLD/HDSWWD* B20 .. 76 B6
Millfields *STETCH* B33 .... 130 A4
Millfields Rd *BKHL/PFLD* WV2 ...... 46 C4
HHTH/SAND B71 .... 73 E5
Millfield Vw *HALE* B63 .... 140 A5 🖪
Milford Cl *HLGN/YWD* B28............ 172 C6
Mill Gn *WOLVN* WV10 .... 11 F1
Mill Gv *CDSL* WV8 .... 9 E2
Millhaven Av *BVILLE* B30 .... 169 D5
Mill Hl *SMTHWK* B67 .... 120 B4
Millhouse Rd *YDLY* B25 .... 151 D1
Millichip Rd *WLNHL* WV13 .... 28 A6

Millington Rd CBROM B36 .... 104 A5
TPTN/OCK DY4 .... 70 B2 🔟
WOLVN WV10 .... 26 A1
Millison Gv SOLH B91 .... 194 C6
Mill La ALDR WS9 .... 36 C1
BRGRVW B61 .... 198 B4
DIG/EDG B5 .... 124 B6
DOR/KN B93 .... 212 A3
DUNHL/THL/PER WV6 .... 22 C5
HOCK/TIA B94 .... 207 D6
NFLD/LBR B31 .... 186 B3
OLDBY B69 .... 118 C3
RIDG/WDGT B32 .... 166 A1
RMSLY B62 .... 141 E5
RUSH/SHEL WS4 .... 32 B3
SHHTH WV12 .... 29 E2
SOLH B91 .... 195 E1
WMBN WV5 .... 65 D4
WNSFLD WV11 .... 13 D6
Millmead Rd SLYOAK B29 ...... 166 A1
Mill Pl BLOX/PEL WS3 .... 28 A1
Millpool Gdns ALE/KHTH/YWD B14.. 190 B2
Millpool Hill Alcester Rd South
ALE/KHTH/YWD B14 .... 190 B1 🔟
Millpool Wy SMTHWKW B67 ...... 120 C3
Mill Race La STRBR DY8 .... 136 C3
Mill Rd CDYHTH B64 .... 140 A2
RUSH/SHEL WS4 .... 19 D4
Mills Av WALM/CURD B76 .... 60 A5
Mills Cl WNSFLD WV11 .... 13 D5
Mills Crs ALE/KHTH/YWD B14 .... 46 A1
Millside HLGN/YWD B28 .... 192 A2 🔟
WMBN WV5 .... 64 A6 🔟
Mills Rd BKHL/PFLD WV2 ...... 46 A1
Mill St AST/WIT B6 .... 124 B2
BILS/COS WV14 .... 69 E5
BRLYHL DY5 .... 113 F5
CDYHTH B64 .... 139 E2
CSCFLD/WYGN B72 .... 59 E4
DARL/WED WS10 .... 49 E3
STRBR DY8 .... 112 A5
TPTN/OCK DY4 .... 71 F6
WBROM B70 .... 95 E1
WLNHL WV13 .... 29 E5
WSLW WS2 .... 32 A4
Millthorpe Cl WASH/WDE B8 .... 126 B2 🔟
Mill Vw STECH B33 .... 129 E3
Millwalk Dr COVEN WV9 .... 10 C2
The Mill Wk NFLD/LBR B31 ..... 186 B4 🔟
Millward St BORD B9 .... 125 E6
WBROM B70 .... 94 C2
Millwright Cl TPTN/OCK DY4 ... 71 D6 🔟
Milner Rd SLYOAK B29 .... 168 C2
Milner Wy MOS/BIL B13 .... 171 F3
Milsom Gv BKDE/SHDE B34 ..... 129 F1
Milstead Rd
LGN/SDN/BHAMAIR B26 ..... 128 C6
Milston Cl ALE/KHTH/YWD B14 .. 190 A3
SHHTH WV12 .... 16 A6
WSL WS1 .... 51 F3
Milton Ct DUNHL/THL/PER WV6 ... 22 A3
Milton Crs SEDG DY3 .... 66 C6
YDLY B25 .... 151 F2
Milton Dr HAG/WOL DY9 ...... 159 F4
Milton Pl WSL WS1 .... 51 F3
Milton Rd BILS/COS WV14 ..... 69 F4
DOR/KN B93 .... 212 B3
SMTHWKW B67 .... 119 F2
WOLVN WV10 .... 26 C2
Milton St BRLYHL DY5 .... 89 F6
HHTH/SAND B71 .... 73 D6
LOZ/NWT B19 .... 124 A1
WSL WS1 .... 51 F3
Milverton Cl WALM/CURD B76 ... 82 B5 🔟
Milverton Rd DOR/KN B93 ...... 213 E2
ERDW/GRVHL B23 .... 90 A6
Mimosa Cl SLYOAK B29 .... 167 D3 🔟
Mimosa Wk KGSWFD DY6 .... 88 A5 🔟
Mincing La BLKHTH/ROWR B65 .. 117 E4
Minden Gv SLYOAK B29 .... 167 D2
Minehead Rd DUDN DY1 .... 89 F5
WOLVN WV10 .... 11 D3
Miner St WSLW WS2 .... 31 E4
Minerva Cl SHHTH WV12 ...... 30 A3
Minewood Cl BLOX/PEL WS3 ... 16 B2 🔟
Minith Rd BILS/COS WV14 .... 69 F3
Miniva Dr WALM/CURD B76 .... 82 C1 🔟
Minivet Dr BHTH/HG B12 ..... 148 A3 🔟
Minley Av HRBN B17 .... 144 B2
The Minories DUDS DY2 ...... 91 E4 🔟
Minstead Rd ERDE/BCHGN B24 .. 101 F4
Minster Cl BLKHTH/ROWR B65 .. 118 A4
DOR/KN B93 .... 197 D5
Minster Dr SMHTH B10 .... 149 F2
Minsterley Cl BDMR/CCFT WV3 . 44 A1 🔟
The Minster BDMR/CCFT WV3 ... 44 B2
Mintern Rd YDLY B25 .... 127 E6
Minton Cl WOLV WV1 .... 26 C6 🔟
Minton Rd RIDG/WDGT B32 .... 144 B5
Minworth Rd CSHL/WTROR B46 . 107 D2 🔟
Miranda Cl RBRY B45 .... 188 A2
Mirfield Cl COVEN WV9 ...... 10 C2 🔟
Mirfield Rd SOLH B91 .... 174 C5

STETCH B33 .... 129 D5
Mission Cl CDYHTH B64 ...... 116 C6
Mission Dr TPTN/OCK DY4 .... 92 C1
Mistletoe Dr DSYBK/YTR WS5 .. 52 C6
Mitcham Gv KGSTG B44 ...... 79 D2 🔟
Mitcheldean Covert
ALE/KHTH/YWD B14 .... 189 F3 🔟
Mitchell Av BILS/COS WV14 .... 69 D2
Mitchel Rd KGSWFD DY6 ...... 112 B3
Mitford Dr HIA/OLT B92 ...... 175 F4
Mitre Cl SHHTH WV12 .... 15 F6
WNSFLD WV11 .... 14 C2
Mitre Fold WOLV WV1 .... 2 C3
Mitre Rd HAG/WOL DY9 ...... 138 A4
Mitten Av RBRY B45 .... 184 B4
Mitton Rd BFLD/HDSWWD B20 .. 98 A3
Moat Brook Av CDSL WV8 .... 8 A1
Moat Coppice RIDG/WDGT B32 . 164 C2 🔟
Moat Cft CHWD/FDBR/MGN B37 . 130 C5
WALM/CURD B76 .... 83 D4
Moat Dr RMSLY B62 .... 118 B6
Moat Farm Dr RIDG/WDGT B32 . 164 C3 🔟
TPTN/OCK DY4 .... 70 C4
WSLW WS2 .... 31 E5
Moat Green Av WNSFLD WV11 .. 14 A6
Moat House La East WNSFLD WV11.. 13 F6
Moathouse La West WNSFLD WV11. 13 F6
Moat House Rd WASH/WDE B8 .. 126 C3
Moat La LGN/SDN/BHAMAIR B26 . 152 A2
SOLH B91 .... 175 E5
Moat Mdw CHWD/FDBR/MGN B37. 131 E1
Moat Rd LGLYGN/QTN B68 ..... 119 D4
TPTN/OCK DY4 .... 70 C4
WSLW WS2 .... 31 E5
Moat St WLNHL WV13 .... 28 C5
Mobberley Rd BILS/COS WV14 .. 68 C2 🔟
Mob La RUSH/SHEL WS4 ...... 20 A4
Mockley Wood Rd DOR/KN B93 . 197 D6
Modbury Av RIDG/WDGT B32 .. 165 F2
Moden Cl SEDG DY3 .... 67 F6
Moden Hl SEDG DY3 .... 67 E5
Mogul La HALE B63 .... 138 C2
Moilliett Ct SMTHWK B66 .... 121 E1 🔟
Moilliett St WSNGN B18 ...... 121 F1
Moira Crs ALE/KHTH/YWD B14 .. 191 E1
Moises Hall Rd WMBN WV5 .... 65 D5
Moland St AST/WIT B6 ...... 7 F1
Mole St SPARK B11 .... 149 D3
Molineux St WOLV WV1 ...... 2 D2
Molineux Wy WOLV WV1 ...... 2 D1
Mollington Crs SHLY B90 ..... 193 E2
Molyneux Rd DUDS DY2 ...... 116 A5
Monarch Dr TPTN/OCK DY4 .... 71 E5
Monarch's Wy
BLKHTH/ROWR B65 .... 116 B3
HAG/WOL DY9 .... 137 E6
KGSWFD DY6 .... 110 A1
OLDBY B69 .... 93 E5 🔟
STRBR DY8 .... 136 C4 🔟
WNSFLD WV11 .... 13 F2
WSLW WS2 .... 30 C3
Monarch Wy DUDS DY2 ...... 115 D3
Mona Rd ERDW/GRVHL B23 .... 80 B6
Monastery Dr SOLH B91 ...... 174 A5
Monckton Rd LGLYGN/QTN B68 . 142 C2
Moncrieffe Cl DUDS DY2 ..... 92 A5 🔟
Moncrieffe St WSL WS1 ...... 5 C5
Money La BRGRVW B61 .... 198 C5
Monica Rd SMHTH B10 .... 150 B1
Monins Av TPTN/OCK DY4 .... 92 C2
Monk Cl TPTN/OCK DY4 ...... 93 D2 🔟
Monk Rd WASH/WDE B8 ...... 127 D2
Monks Cl WMBN WV5 .... 64 A5 🔟
Monkseaton Rd CSCFLD/WYGN B72.. 81 D1
Monksfield Av GTB/HAM B43 ... 75 F2
Monkshood Ms ERDW/GRVHL B23 79 D4 🔟
Monkshood Retreat
HWK/WKHTH B38 .... 188 B5 🔟
Monks Kirby Rd
WALM/CURD B76 .... 60 B6 🔟
Monkspath SHLY B90 .... 210 C1 🔟
WALM/CURD B76 .... 82 B3
Monkspath Cl SHLY B90 ...... 193 F6 🔟
Monkspath Hall Rd SHLY B90 .. 194 B6
SHLY B90 .... 210 B1
SOLH B91 .... 195 D5
Monksway HWK/WKHTH B38 ... 189 D3
SMHTH B10 .... 149 F2 🔟
Monkswood Rd NFLD/LBR B31 .. 187 E3
Monkton Rd SLYOAK B29 ..... 144 C6
Monmer La WLNHL WV13 ..... 29 D4
Monmore Rd WOLV WV1 ...... 46 C1
Monmouth Dr HHTH/SAND B71 . 73 D4
SCFLD/BOLD B73 .... 57 E5
Monmouth Rd RIDG/WDGT B32 . 165 F3
SMTHWKW B67 .... 144 A1
WSLW WS2 .... 30 A4
Monsal Av WOLVN WV10 ..... 26 A3
Monsal Rd PBAR/PBCH B42 ... 77 F4
Mons Rd DUDS DY2 .... 92 A4 🔟
Montague Rd ERDE/BCHGN B24 . 102 C4
HDSW B21 .... 98 B5
LDYWD/EDGR B16 .... 122 A6
SMTHWK B66 .... 121 D4
Montague St AST/WIT B6 ..... 101 D5 🔟

CBHAMNE B4 .... 124 C4
Montana Av PBAR/PBCH B42 ... 76 C6
Monteagle Dr KGSWFD DY6 .... 87 F4
Montford Gv SEDG DY3 ...... 67 F4 🔟
Montfort Rd CSHL/WTROR B46 . 132 B2
WSLW WS2 .... 51 E2
Montgomery Cl BRGRVW B61 ... 198 C6
Montgomery Crs BRLYHL DY5 .. 138 B2
Montgomery Cft SPARK B11 ... 149 E2 🔟
Montgomery Rd WSLW WS2 ... 30 A5
Montgomery St SPARK B11 .... 149 D2
Montgomery Wy WASH/WDE B8 . 126 C3
Montpelier Rd ERDE/BCHGN B24 . 102 C4
Montpelier Gdns DUDN DY1 ... 90 A3
Montpelier St BHTH/HG B12 ... 148 C5
Montrose Dr CVALE B35 ...... 104 C2
DUDN DY1 .... 90 C5 🔟
Montsford Cl DOR/KN B93 .... 212 B1
Monument Av HAG/WOL DY9 ... 138 A5
Monument La HAG/WOL DY9 ... 159 F4
RBRY B45 .... 200 B3
SEDG DY3 .... 68 A2
Monument Rd LDYWD/EDGR B16 . 122 B6
Monway Ter DARL/WED WS10 .. 50 A6 🔟
Monwood Gv SOLH B91 .... 194 B3 🔟
Monyhull Hall Rd BVILLE B30 .. 189 D2
Moodyscroft Rd STECH B33 ... 129 E4
Moorcroft Rd MOS/BIL B13 .... 148 A5
Moordown Av HIA/OLT B92 ... 174 C1
Moore Cl DUNHL/THL/PER WV6 . 22 B3
FOAKS/STRLY B74 .... 38 D1 🔟
Moore Crs LGLYGN/QTN B68 ... 119 E4
Moorend Av
CHWD/FDBR/MGN B37 ..... 154 C1
Moor End La ERDE/BCHGN B24 . 102 C1
Moore Rd SHHTH WV12 ...... 15 F5
Moore's Rw DIG/EDG B5 ..... 124 B6 🔟
Moore St WOLV WV1 .... 26 B6
Moorfield Av DOR/KN B93 .... 212 B1
Moorfield Dr HALE B63 ...... 140 C4
SCFLD/BOLD B73 .... 80 B3
Moorfield Rd BKDE/SHDE B34 . 128 C1
BKHL/PFLD WV2 .... 45 D2
Moorfoot Av HALE B63 ...... 161 E2
Moor Green La MOS/BIL B13 .. 168 C4
Moor Hall Dr HAG/WOL DY9 ... 180 C4
MGN/WHC B75 .... 40 A6
Moorhills Cft SHLY B90 ..... 193 D5
The Moorings COVEN WV9 .... 10 B3 🔟
OLDBY B69 .... 94 A5
Moorland Av WOLVN WV10 .... 25 E1
Moorland Rd BLOX/PEL WS3 .. 16 C5
LDYWD/EDGR B16 .... 121 F6
Moorlands Rd HHTH/SAND B71 . 73 E2
The Moorlands FOAKS/STRLY B74 . 58 B1
Moor La AST/WIT B6 .... 100 C2
BLKHTH/ROWR B65 .... 116 C4
Moor Leasow NFLD/LBR B31 .. 187 E3
Moor Meadow Rd MGN/WHC B75 . 59 F2
Moorpark Rd NFLD/LBR B31 ... 186 C4
Moors Cft RIDG/WDGT B32 ... 165 D2 🔟
Moorside Gdns WSLW WS2 ... 31 D4
Moorside Rd ALE/KHTH/YWD B14 . 191 E1
Moors La NFLD/LBR B31 ..... 166 A3
Moors Mill La TPTN/OCK DY4 .. 71 E4
Moorsom St AST/WIT B6 ..... 124 A2
The Moors CBROM B36 ...... 104 B5
Moor St BRLYHL DY5 .... 112 C4
DARL/WED WS10 .... 73 D1
DIG/EDG B5 .... 7 F6
WBROM B70 .... 95 E3
Moor Street Ringway CBHAMNE B4 . 7 F6
Moor St South BKHL/PFLD WV2 . 45 E2
The Moor WALM/CURD B76 ... 82 C3 🔟
Morar Cl CVALE B35 .... 105 D1
Moray Cl RMSLY B62 .... 142 A1 🔟
Morcom Rd SPARK B11 ...... 150 A4
Morcroft BILS/COS WV14 .... 48 C6 🔟
Mordaunt Dr MGN/WHC B75 .. 40 A5 🔟
Morden Rd STECH B33 ...... 127 F4
Moreland Cft WALM/CURD B76 . 83 D5 🔟
The Morelands NFLD/LBR B31 . 187 D4
Morestead Av
LGN/SDN/BHAMAIR B26 .... 153 E4
Moreton Av
ETTPK/GDPK/PENN WV4 .... 46 A5
GTB/HAM B43 .... 77 E1
Moreton Cl RIDG/WDGT B32 ... 144 B6 🔟
TPTN/OCK DY4 .... 71 D1 🔟
Moreton Rd SHLY B90 ...... 193 E3
WOLVN WV10 .... 11 F4
Moreton St CBHAMW B1 ..... 123 D3 🔟
Morford Rd ALDR WS9 ...... 20 C6
Morgan Cl WLNHL WV13 ..... 29 D5
Morgan Gv CBROM B36 ..... 106 B4
Morgrove Av DOR/KN B93 .... 212 B1
Morjon Dr GTB/HAM B43 .... 76 B1
Morland Rd GTB/HAM B43 .... 55 E5
Morley Gv DUNHL/THL/PER WV6 . 25 E3
Morley Rd WASH/WDE B8 .... 127 D1
Morlich Ri BRLYHL DY5 ..... 137 D1 🔟

Morning Pines *STRBR* DY8 .... 136 A5 🄳
Morningside *SCFLD/BOLD* B73 ...... 59 D3
Mornington Rd *SMTHWK* B66 .... 97 D6
Morris Av *WSLW* WS2 .... 30 A5
Morris Cl *ACCN* B27 .... 151 F5
Morris Cft *CBROM* B36 .... 106 A4
Morris Field Cft *HLGN/YWD* B28 .... 192 A1
Morrison Rd *WOLVN* WV10 .... 11 F5
Morrison Rd *TPTN/OCK* DY4 .... 93 E1
Morris Rd *WASH/WDE* B8 .... 127 D1
Morris St *WBROM* B70 .... 95 E4
Mortimers Cl *ALE/KHTH/YWD* B14 .. 191 D4
Morton Rd *BRLYHL* DY5 .... 137 F2 🄳
Morvale Gdns *HAG/WOL* DY9 .... 138 A4
Morvale St *HAG/WOL* DY9 .... 138 A4
Morven Rd *SCFLD/BOLD* B73 .... 80 B1
Morville Cl *DOR/KN* B93 .... 211 F4
Morville Cft
   ETTPK/GDPK/PENN WV4 .... 47 D5
Morville Rd *DUDS* DY2 .... 115 F3
Morville St *LDYWD/EDGR* B16 .... 123 D5 🄳
Mosborough Crs *LOZ/NWT* B19 ...... 123 E2
Mosedale Dr *WNSFLD* WV11 .... 28 B2
Moseley Ct *WNSFLD* WV11 .... 14 B2
Moseley Dr
   CHWD/FDBR/MGN B37 .... 154 B1
Moseley Rd *BHTH/HG* B12 .... 148 C1
   WLNHL WV13 .... 27 F6
   WLNHL WV13 .... 48 B1
Moseley St *DIG/EDG* B5 .... 124 B6
   DUNHL/THL/PER WV6 .... 25 E3
   TPTN/OCK DY4 .... 71 E4
Moss Cl *ALDR* WS9 .... 34 C2
   RUSH/SHEL WS4 .... 32 C4
Mossdale *SEDG* DY3 .... 68 A4
Mossdale Cl *WGN* B72 .... 59 E6
Mossfield Rd *ALE/KHTH/YWD* B14 . 170 A4
Moss Gdns *BILS/COS* WV14 .... 47 D6 🄳
Moss Gv *ALE/KHTH/YWD* B14 .... 169 F5
   KGSWFD DY6 .... 92 C2
Moss House Cl *EDG* B15 .... 123 D6
Mossley Cl *BLOX/PEL* WS3 .... 16 B4 🄳
Mossley La *BLOX/PEL* WS3 .... 16 B3
Mossvale Cl *CDYHTH* B64 .... 116 B3
Mossvale Gv *WASH/WDE* B8 .... 126 B2 🄳
Moss Wy *FOAKS/STRLY* B74 .... 56 B2
Mostyn Crs *HHTH/SAND* B71 .... 72 C4
Mostyn Rd *HDSW* B21 .... 98 C3
   LDYWD/EDGR B16 .... 122 B6
Mostyn St *WOLV* WV1 .... 25 D3
Mott Cl *TPTN/OCK* DY4 .... 71 E3
Mottram Cl *WBROM* B70 .... 94 C3 🄳
Mottrams Cl *CSCFLD/WYGN* B72 ...... 81 E1
Mott St *LOZ/NWT* B19 .... 6 C1
Mott's Wy *CSHL/WTROR* B46 .... 132 C2 🄳
Moundsley Gv
   ALE/KHTH/YWD B14 .... 190 C2
Mountain Ash Dr *HAG/WOL* DY9 .. 159 E1 🄳
Mount Av *BRLYHL* DY5 .... 113 F3
Mountbatten Cl *WBROM* B70 .... 96 B3
Mountbatten Rd *WSLW* WS2 .... 30 A5
Mount Cl *MOS/BIL* B13 .... 148 B5 🄳
   SEDG DY3 .... 89 D3
   WMBN WV5 .... 64 C4
Mount Dr *WMBN* WV5 .... 64 C4
Mountfield Cl *ALE/KHTH/YWD* B14. 190 C3
Mountford Cl *BLKHTH/ROWR* B65 . 117 E4
Mountford Crs *ALDR* WS9 .... 21 D5
Mountford Dr *MGN/WHC* B75 .... 59 E1
Mountford La *BILS/COS* WV14 .... 47 F2
Mountford Rd *SHLY* B90 .... 191 F4
Mountford St *SPARK* B11 .... 149 F4
Mount Gdns *CDSL* WV8 .... 8 B3
Mountjoy Crs *HIA/OLT* B92 .... 153 E6
Mount La *HAG/WOL* DY9 .... 180 A1
   SEDG DY3 .... 89 D3
Mount Pleasant
   ALE/KHTH/YWD B14 .... 170 B2 🄳
   BILS/COS WV14 .... 48 A3
   BRLYHL DY5 .... 114 A6
   KGSWFD DY6 .... 111 E3
   SMTHWK B10 .... 125 D6 🄳
Mount Pleasant Av *HDSW* B21 .... 98 A4
   WMBN WV5 .... 64 C4
Mount Pleasant St *BILS/COS* WV14 . 69 D3
   WBROM B70 .... 95 E3
Mountrath St *WSL* WS1 .... 4 C5
Mount St *HALE* B63 .... 162 C1
   STRBR DY8 .... 136 C4
   TPTN/OCK DY4 .... 71 E5
   VAUX/NECH B7 .... 125 E1
   WSL WS1 .... 4 C6
Mounts Wy *VAUX/NECH* B7 .... 101 E6 🄳

The Mount *CDYHTH* B64 .... 116 C6
   ERDW/GRVHL B23 .... 101 F4
   WALM/CURD B76 .... 85 E6
Mount Vw *MGN/WHC* B75 .... 60 A5
Mountwood Covert
   DUNHL/THL/PER WV6 .... 23 D4
Mousehall Farm Rd *BRLYHL* DY5 ... 137 F2
Mouse Hl *BLOX/PEL* WS3 .... 18 B2
Mousesweet Cl *DUDS* DY2 .... 116 A3
Mousesweet La *DUDS* DY2 .... 116 A4 🄳
Mousesweet Wk *CDYHTH* B64 ...... 139 D1 🄳
Mowbray Cl *RBRY* B45 .... 184 C3 🄳
Mowbray St *DIG/EDG* B5 .... 148 A1 🄳
Mowe Cft *CHWD/FDBR/MGN* B37 . 154 C2
Moxhull Cl *SHHTH* WV12 .... 15 E4
Moxhull Dr *WALM/CURD* B76 .... 82 A3
Moxhull Gdns *SHHTH* WV12 .... 15 E4 🄳
Moxhull Rd
   CHWD/FDBR/MGN B37 .... 130 C1
Moxley Rd *DARL/WED* WS10 .... 49 D5
Moyle Dr *HALE* B63 .... 139 D2
Moyses Cft *SMTHWK* B66 .... 96 C5 🄳
Muchall Rd
   ETTPK/GDPK/PENN WV4 .... 44 C4
Mucklow Hl *RMSLY* B62 .... 141 F4
Muirfield Cl *BLOX/PEL* WS3 .... 16 C2
Muirfield Crs *OLDBY* B69 .... 92 C6 🄳
Muirfield Gdns *HWK/WKHTH* B38 . 187 F4
Muirville Cl *STRBR* DY8 .... 111 F4 🄳
Mulberry Dr *MOS/BIL* B13 .... 171 D2
Mulberry Gn *DUDN* DY1 .... 68 B6 🄳
Mulberry Pl *BLOX/PEL* WS3 .... 16 B4
Mulberry Rd *BLOX/PEL* WS3 .... 16 B4
   NFLD/LBR B31 .... 167 E6
Mull Cl *RBRY* B45 .... 184 A4
Mull Cft *CBROM* B36 .... 106 C6 🄳
Mullensgrove Rd
   CHWD/FDBR/MGN B37 .... 130 C2
Mullett Rd *WNSFLD* WV11 .... 13 D6
Mullett St *BRLYHL* DY5 .... 113 D2
Mulliners Cl
   CHWD/FDBR/MGN B37 .... 131 F5 🄳
Mullion Cft *HWK/WKHTH* B38 .... 188 A4
Mulroy Rd *FOAKS/STRLY* B74 .... 59 A4
Mulwych Rd *STETCH* B33 .... 130 A4
Munches La *HAG/WOL* DY9 .... 181 E5
Munslow Gv *NFLD/LBR* B31 .... 186 B5
Muntz St *SMHTH* B10 .... 149 F1
Murcroft Rd *HAG/WOL* DY9 .... 159 F2
Murdock Gv *HDSW* B21 .... 98 A6 🄳
Murdock Rd *HDSW* B21 .... 98 A5
   SMTHWK B66 .... 121 F1
Murdock Wy *WSLW* WS2 .... 30 A5
Murray Ct *SCFLD/BOLD* B73 .... 58 C6
Murrell Cl *DIG/EDG* B5 .... 147 F2
Musborough Cl *CBROM* B36 .... 105 E4 🄳
Muscott Gv *HRBN* B17 .... 144 C4
Muscovy Rd *ERDW/GRVHL* B23 .... 101 E2
Musgrave Cl *WALM/CURD* B76 .... 60 A6
Musgrave Rd *WSNGN* B18 .... 122 C2
Mushroom Hall Rd
   LGLYGN/QTN B68 .... 119 D2 🄳
Musk La *SEDG* DY3 .... 89 D2
Musk La West *SEDG* DY3 .... 89 D2
Muswell Cl *SOLH* B91 .... 175 F6
Muxloe Cl *BLOX/PEL* WS3 .... 16 C2
Myatt Av *ALDR* WS9 .... 34 B2
   BKHL/PFLD WV2 .... 46 A3
Myatt Cl *BKHL/PFLD* WV2 .... 46 A3
Myddleton St *WSNGN* B18 .... 122 C3
Myles Ct *BRLYHL* DY5 .... 113 F3
Mynors Crs *HLYWD* B47 .... 206 C2 🄳
Myring Dr *MGN/WHC* B75 .... 60 B4
Myrtle Av *ALE/KHTH/YWD* B14 ..... 190 B3
   BHTH/HG B12 .... 148 C4 🄳🄳
Myrtle Cl *SHHTH* WV12 .... 16 A6
Myrtle Gv *BDMR/CCFT* WV3 .... 44 A3
Myrtle Rd *DUDN* DY1 .... 90 C2
Myrtle St *BKHL/PFLD* WV2 .... 46 B3
Myrtle Ter *TPTN/OCK* DY4 .... 71 D1
Myton Dr *SHLY* B90 .... 191 F3
Mytton Cl *DUDS* DY2 .... 95 D4
Mytton Gv *TPTN/OCK* DY4 .... 70 A6
Mytton Rd *BVILLE* B30 .... 167 E6
   CSHL/WTROR B46 .... 106 B2
Myvod Rd *DARL/WED* WS10 .... 50 C4

N

Naden Rd *LOZ/NWT* B19 .... 123 D1
Nadin Rd *SCFLD/BOLD* B73 .... 80 C1
Naesby Rd *DUNHL/THL/PER* WV6 .. 22 B4 🄳
Nafford Gv *ALE/KHTH/YWD* B14 ... 190 B3
Nagersfield Rd *BRLYHL* DY5 .... 112 C4
Nailers Cl *RIDG/WDGT* B32 .... 164 B1
Nailors Fold *BILS/COS* WV14 .... 69 E1 🄳
Nailstone Crs *ACGN* B27 .... 173 E3 🄳
Nailsworth Rd *DOR/KN* B93 .... 211 F5 🄳
Nairn Cl *HLGN/YWD* B28 .... 172 B6
Nairn Rd *BLOX/PEL* WS3 .... 16 C1
Nally Dr *BILS/COS* WV14 .... 68 C1
Nanaimo Wy *KGSWFD* DY6 .... 112 C3

Nansen Rd *SPARK* B11 .... 149 E6
   WASH/WDE B8 .... 126 A2
Nantmel Gv *RIDG/WDGT* B32 .... 165 E3 🄳
Naomi Wy *ALDR* WS9 .... 21 D1
Napier Dr *TPTN/OCK* DY4 .... 71 E5
Napier Rd *BKHL/PFLD* WV2 .... 45 F2
   WSLW WS2 .... 30 C2
Napton Gv *SLYOAK* B29 .... 166 B1
Narraway Gv *TPTN/OCK* DY4 .... 71 F3 🄳
Narrowboat Wy *DUDS* DY2 .... 114 C2 🄳
Narrow La *RMSLY* B62 .... 142 A1
   WSLW WS2 .... 51 D2
Naseby Dr *HALE* B63 .... 161 F1
Naseby Rd *SOLH* B91 .... 175 D5
   WASH/WDE B8 .... 126 B2
Nash Av *DUNHL/THL/PER* WV6 ...... 22 A4
Nash Cl *BLKHTH/ROWR* B65 .... 117 E6
Nash Sq *PBAR/PBCH* B42 .... 99 F1
Nately Gv *SLYOAK* B29 .... 145 D6
Nathan Cl *MGN/WHC* B75 .... 59 E1
Naunton Cl *SLYOAK* B29 .... 166 C4
Naunton Rd *WSLW* WS2 .... 30 C4
Navenby Cl *ALE/KHTH/YWD* B14 .. 191 D2
Navigation La *DARL/WED* WS10 .... 74 B1
Navigation St *CBHAMW* B1 .... 6 C6
   WOLV WV1 .... 3 G6
   WSLW WS2 .... 4 B3
Navigation Wy *WBROM* B70 .... 94 B3
Nayland Cft *HLGN/YWD* B28 .... 172 C6
Naylors Gv *SEDG* DY3 .... 90 A1
Neachells Ct *WLNHL* WV13 .... 28 A6
Neachells La *WLNHL* WV13 .... 27 F3
   WNSFLD WV11 .... 27 F3
Neachless Av *WMBN* WV5 .... 64 C6
Neachley Gv *STETCH* B33 .... 128 B3
Neale St *WSLW* WS2 .... 31 E5
Nearhill Rd *HWK/WKHTH* B38 ...... 187 D5
Near Lands Cl *RIDG/WDGT* B32 ... 143 D5
Nearmoor Rd *BKDE/SHDE* B34 .... 129 F2
Neasden Gv *KGSTG* B44 .... 79 D3
Neath Rd *BLOX/PEL* WS3 .... 16 B3
Neath Wy *BLOX/PEL* WS3 .... 16 B3
   SEDG DY3 .... 68 C5
Nebsworth Ct *SHLY* B90 .... 173 F6
Nechells Park Rd *VAUX/NECH* B7 . 101 E6
Nechells Pkwy *VAUX/NECH* B7 .... 124 C3
Nechells Pl *VAUX/NECH* B7 .... 125 D1 🄳
Needham St *VAUX/NECH* B7 .... 101 E6
Needhill Cl *DOR/KN* B93 .... 211 D2
Needwood Cl *BKHL/PFLD* WV2 ...... 45 D3
Needwood Dr
   ETTPK/GDPK/PENN WV4 .... 46 B5 🄳
Needwood Gv *HHTH/SAND* B71 .... 74 A2
Nelson Av *BILS/COS* WV14 .... 47 E2
Nelson Rd *AST/WIT* B6 .... 100 B4
   DUDN DY1 .... 91 D4
Nelson St *CBHAMW* B1 .... 123 D4 🄳
   HHTH/SAND B71 .... 73 E6
   OLDBY B69 .... 119 D1
   WLNHL WV13 .... 29 D4 🄳
Nene Cl *STRBR* DY8 .... 136 C5
Nene Wy *CBROM* B36 .... 106 B5
Neptune St *TPTN/OCK* DY4 .... 69 F6
Nesbit Gv *BORD* B9 .... 127 D4
Nesfield Cl *HWK/WKHTH* B38 ...... 187 E4
Nesfield Gv *HIA/OLT* B92 .... 179 D4
Nesscliffe Gv *ERDW/GRVHL* B23 ... 79 F4
Neston Gv *STETCH* B33 .... 127 F5 🄳
Netheravon Cl
   ALE/KHTH/YWD B14 .... 189 F4 🄳
Netherby Rd *SEDG* DY3 .... 67 E3
Nethercote Gdns *SHLY* B90 .... 192 A2 🄳
Netherdale Cl *CSCFLD/WYGN* B72 . 81 E4 🄳
Netherdale Rd
   ALE/KHTH/YWD B14 .... 190 C4 🄳
Netherend Cl *HALE* B63 .... 138 C2
Netherend La *HALE* B63 .... 139 D2
Netherend Sq *HALE* B63 .... 138 C2 🄳
Netherfield Gdns *ACGN* B27 .... 151 D6
Nethergate *SEDG* DY3 .... 68 B6
Netherstone Gv *FOAKS/STRLY* B74. 38 B2
Netherton Gv *STETCH* B33 .... 129 F4 🄳
Netherwood Cl *SOLH* B91 .... 174 A5
Nethy Dr *DUNHL/THL/PER* WV6 .... 23 D2
Netley Gv *SPARK* B11 .... 150 B6
Netley Rd *BLOX/PEL* WS3 .... 16 A3
Netley Wy *BLOX/PEL* WS3 .... 16 A3
Nevada Wy
   CHWD/FDBR/MGN B37 .... 131 E6
Neve Av *WOLVN* WV10 .... 12 B4
Neville Av *ETTPK/GDPK/PENN* WV4 . 45 F3
Neville Rd *CBROM* B36 .... 106 A4
   ERDW/GRVHL B23 .... 101 E2
   SHLY B90 .... 192 B4
Nevin Gv *PBAR/PBCH* B42 .... 77 E6
Nevis Cl *DUNHL/THL/PER* WV6 ..... 24 A5
Nevis Gv *SHHTH* WV12 .... 15 D4
Nevison Gv *GTB/HAM* B43 .... 55 D5
Newark Cft
   LGN/SDN/BHAMAIR B26 .... 153 D3
Newark Rd *DUDS* DY2 .... 115 F5
   SHHTH WV12 .... 15 E6 🄳
Newbank Gv *BORD* B9 .... 126 C4 🄳
New Bartholomew St *DIG/EDG* B5 ... 7 G5
New Birmingham Rd *OLDBY* B69 ... 92 C4

Newbold Cl *DOR/KN* B93 .... 212 B2
Newbold Cft *VAUX/NECH* B7 ...... 125 D2 🔢
Newbolds Rd *WOLVN* WV10 .... 26 C1
Newbolt Rd *BILS/COS* WV14 .... 48 A3
Newbolt St *DSYBK/YTR* WS5 .... 52 A4
New Bond St *BORD* B9 .... 125 D6
   DUDS DY2 .... 91 F5 🔢
Newborough Gv *HLGN/YWD* B28 .... 192 B3
Newborough Rd *HLGN/YWD* B28 .... 192 B1
Newbourne Hl *ALVE* B48 .... 218 A5
Newbridge Av
   DUNHL/THL/PER WV6 .... 24 A4
Newbridge Crs
   DUNHL/THL/PER WV6 .... 24 A3
Newbridge Gdns
   DUNHL/THL/PER WV6 .... 24 A3 🔢
Newbridge Rd *BORD* B9 .... 151 D1
   KGSWFD DY6 .... 87 E5
Newbridge St
   DUNHL/THL/PER WV6 .... 24 B3
Newburn Cft *RIDG/WDGT* B32 ...... 143 D4 🔢
Newbury Cl *RMSLY* B62 .... 141 F6
Newbury La *OLDBY* B69 .... 117 F1
Newbury Rd *STRBR* DY8 .... 111 E3
   WOLVN WV10 .... 11 E3
Newby Gv *CHWD/FDBR/MGN* B37 .. 131 D3
New Canal St *DIG/EDG* B5 .... 7 G5
Newcastle Cft *CVALE* B35 .... 105 E2 🔢
New Church Rd *SCFLD/BOLD* B73 .. 80 C5
New College Cl *WSL* WS1 .... 52 C2
Newcombe Rd *HDSW* B21 .... 97 F3
Newcomen Dr *TPTN/OCK* DY4 .... 92 B2
Newcott Cl *COVEN* WV9 .... 10 B3
New Coventry Rd
   LGN/SDN/BHAMAIR B26 .... 152 B4
New Cft *LOZ/NWT* B19 .... 100 A6
Newcroft Gv
   LGN/SDN/BHAMAIR B26 .... 152 A2
New Cross Av *WOLVN* WV10 .... 27 D3
New Cross St *DARL/WED* WS10 .... 49 F4 🔢
   TPTN/OCK DY4 .... 70 A6
Newdigate Rd *MGN/WHC* B75 .... 60 C5
New Dudley Rd *KGSWFD* DY6 .... 87 E5 🔢
Newells Dr *TPTN/OCK* DY4 .... 71 F4 🔢
Newells Rd
   LGN/SDN/BHAMAIR B26 .... 152 C1
New England *RMSLY* B62 .... 142 A2
New England Cl *OLDBY* B69 .... 94 A4 🔢
Newent Cl *SHHTH* WV12 .... 29 F3
Newent Rd *NFLD/LBR* B31 .... 187 E1
Newey Cl *RBRY* B45 .... 200 C1 🔢
Newey Rd *HLGN/YWD* B28 .... 172 B5
   WNSFLD WV11 .... 14 C5
Newey St *DUDN* DY1 .... 90 C3
New Farm Rd *KGSWFD* DY9 .... 137 E4
Newfield Cl *SOLH* B91 .... 175 F5
   WSLW WS2 .... 31 E2
Newfield Crs *HALE* B63 .... 140 C4
Newfield Dr *KGSWFD* DY6 .... 112 A3
Newfield La *HALE* B63 .... 140 C4
Newfield Rd *OLDBY* B69 .... 94 B5
New Forest Rd *BLOX/PEL* WS3 ..... 32 A1
New Gas St *WBROM* B70 .... 72 C6 🔢
New Hall Dr *WALM/CURD* B76 .... 59 F5
   WALM/CURD B76 .... 60 A3
Newhall Farm Cl
   WALM/CURD B76 .... 59 F5 🔢
Newhall Hl *BKHL/PFLD* WV2 .... 6 A3
New Hall Pl *DARL/WED* WS10 .... 50 C6 🔢
Newhall Rd *BLKHTH/ROWR* B65 ... 117 E4
New Hall St *WLNHL* WV13 .... 28 C5
Newhall St *CBHAMNW* B3 .... 6 B3
   TPTN/OCK DY4 .... 70 A3
   WBROM B70 .... 95 E3
   WSL WS1 .... 4 D6
New Hampton Rd East *WOLV* WV1 .. 2 A1
New Hampton Rd West
   DUNHL/THL/PER WV6 .... 24 A4
Newhaven Cl *VAUX/NECH* B7 .... 124 C3 🔢
New Henry St *LGLYGN/QTN* B68 .... 118 C3
Newhope Cl *EDG* B15 .... 147 F1 🔢
New Hope Rd *SMTHWK* B66 .... 121 E3
Newhouse Farm Cl
   WALM/CURD B76 .... 60 B6 🔢
Newick Av *FOAKS/STRLY* B74 .... 37 D4
New Ick Av *ALE/KHTH/YWD* B14 .. 169 E6 🔢
Newick St *DUDS* DY2 .... 115 E3
Newington Rd
   CHWD/FDBR/MGN B37 .... 155 D1 🔢
New Inn Rd *LOZ/NWT* B19 .... 99 F4
New Inns Cl *HDSW* B21 .... 97 F5
New Inns La *RBRY* B45 .... 184 A4
New John St *AST/WIT* B6 .... 124 A2
   RMSLY B62 .... 117 E6
John John St West *LOZ/NWT* B19 .. 123 D1
New King St *DUDS* DY2 .... 91 E4 🔢
Newland Cl *RUSH/SHEL* WS4 .... 19 E3 🔢
Newland Gdns *CDYHTH* B64 .... 140 A4
Newland Gv *DUDS* DY2 .... 90 B6
Newland Rd *SMHTH* B10 .... 126 B6
New Landings *WLNHL* WV13 .... 28 C6
Newlands Dr *RMSLY* B62 .... 142 A2
Newlands La
   CHWD/FDBR/MGN B37 .... 154 C3
Newlands Rd *BVILLE* B30 .... 169 D4

DOR/KN B93 .... 212 A3
Newlyn Rd *CDYHTH* B64 .... 139 F1
   NFLD/LBR B31 .... 186 B2
Newman Av
   ETTPK/GDPK/PENN WV4 .... 46 B5
Newman College Cl
   RIDG/WDGT B32 .... 165 E3 🔢
Newman Pl *BILS/COS* WV14 .... 48 B2
Newman Rd *ERDE/BCHGN* B24 .. 102 B1
   TPTN/OCK DY4 .... 71 E2
   WOLVN WV10 .... 12 C4
Newmans Cl *SMTHWK* B66 .... 121 E3 🔢
Newman Wy *RBRY* B45 .... 184 C6
Newmarket Cl
   DUNHL/THL/PER WV6 .... 24 C2 🔢
New Market Wy *CBROM* B36 .... 103 D6
Newmarsh Rd *WALM/CURD* B76 .. 82 C5
New Meadow Cl *NFLD/LBR* B31 .. 187 D3
New Meeting St *OLDBY* B69 .... 94 C5 🔢
New Mills St *WSL* WS1 .... 52 C3
New Mill St *DUDS* DY2 .... 91 E4
Newmore Gdns *DSYBK/YTR* WS5 .. 53 E3
Newnham Gv *ERDW/GRVHL* B23 .. 80 A5 🔢
Newnham Ri *SHLY* B90 .... 193 F2
Newnham Rd
   LDYWD/EDGR B16 .... 121 E5 🔢
New Pool Rd *CDYHTH* B64 .... 139 D1
Newport Cl *BHTH/HG* B12 .... 148 C5
   CBROM B36 .... 104 B5
Newport St *WOLVN* WV10 .... 26 A3 🔢
   WSL WS1 .... 4 C4
Newquay Cl *DSYBK/YTR* WS5 ...... 54 A2
Newquay Rd *DSYBK/YTR* WS5 ..... 53 F2
New Rd *ALDR* WS9 .... 34 C2
   BRGRVW B61 .... 198 A5
   CSHL/WTROR B46 .... 107 D2
   DUDS DY2 .... 91 E6
   DUNHL/THL/PER WV6 .... 24 A3
   HALE B63 .... 141 D5
   HLYWD B47 .... 190 B5
   RBRY B45 .... 184 A6
   SOLH B91 .... 195 E2
   STRBR DY8 .... 136 C4
   TPTN/OCK DY4 .... 71 F5
   WLNHL WV13 .... 28 C6
   WNSFLD WV11 .... 13 D5
New Rowley Rd *DUDS* DY2 .... 92 A6
New Spring St *WSNGN* B18 .... 122 C3
New Spring St North *WSNGN* B18 .. 122 C2
Newstead Rd *KGSTG* B44 .... 56 C6
New St *BDMR/CCFT* WV3 .... 43 F3
   BKHL/PFLD WV2 .... 46 C3 🔢
   BLOX/PEL WS3 .... 17 D4
   BRLYHL DY5 .... 138 C1
   CBHAM B2 .... 6 D5
   CBROM B36 .... 105 D5
   DARL/WED WS10 .... 49 F3
   DARL/WED WS10 .... 72 B2
   DUDS DY2 .... 80 B6
   ERDW/GRVHL B23 .... 102 C1
   ETTPK/GDPK/PENN WV4 .... 46 A4
   KGSWFD DY6 .... 87 E3
   KGSWFD DY6 .... 111 F5
   RBRY B45 .... 184 C5
   RUSH/SHEL WS4 .... 19 F4
   SEDG DY3 .... 89 E2
   SMTHWK B66 .... 121 D1
   STRBR DY8 .... 111 F5
   STRBR DY8 .... 136 C4
   TPTN/OCK DY4 .... 70 A6
   WBROM B70 .... 72 C4
   WBROM B70 .... 95 F2
   WLNHL WV13 .... 28 A6
   WNSFLD WV11 .... 14 C2
   WSL WS1 .... 5 E5
New St North *HHTH/SAND* B71 .... 95 F2
New Summer St *LOZ/NWT* B19 .... 6 D1
New Swan La *WBROM* B70 .... 72 C6
Newton Cl *GTB/HAM* B43 .... 75 E3
Newton Gdns *GTB/HAM* B43 .... 75 D3
Newton Manor Cl *GTB/HAM* B43 .. 75 F4
Newton Pl *WSLW* WS2 .... 31 D1 🔢
   WSNGN B18 .... 98 B6
Newton Rd *DOR/KN* B93 .... 197 D6
   GTB/HAM B43 .... 75 E3 🔢
   HHTH/SAND B71 .... 74 B3
   SPARK B11 .... 149 D4
   WSLW WS2 .... 31 D2
Newton Sq *GTB/HAM* B43 .... 76 A2 🔢
Newton St *CBHAMNE* B4 .... 7 F3
   HHTH/SAND B71 .... 74 A4
New Town *BRLYHL* DY5 .... 113 D5
   DUDS DY2 .... 115 F5 🔢
Newtown Dr *LOZ/NWT* B19 .... 123 E1 🔢
Newtown La *CDYHTH* B64 .... 115 F6
   HAG/WOL DY9 .... 181 F5
   RBRY B45 .... 183 E4
Newtown Middleway *AST/WIT* B6.. 124 A2
New Town Rw *CBHAMNE* B4 .... 7 F1
   LOZ/NWT B19 .... 124 A2
Newtown St *CDYHTH* B64 .... 115 F5
New Village *DUDS* DY2 .... 115 E6
New Wood Cl *KINVER* DY7 .... 135 E1

New Wood Gv *ALDR* WS9 .... 20 C2
Niall Cl *EDG* B15 .... 146 B1
Nicholas Rd *FOAKS/STRLY* B74 .... 56 A1
Nicholas Wk *WALM/CURD* B76 ...... 85 D5 🔢
Nicholds Cl *BILS/COS* WV14 .... 69 D2
Nicholls Rd *TPTN/OCK* DY4 .... 70 A2
Nicholls St *WBROM* B70 .... 95 F3
Nichols Cl *HIA/OLT* B92 .... 176 B4 🔢
Nigel Av *NFLD/LBR* B31 .... 166 C6
Nigel Rd *DUDN* DY1 .... 90 B3
   WASH/WDE B8 .... 126 A1
Nightingale Av *CBROM* B36 .... 106 C5
Nightingale Crs *BRLYHL* DY5 ..... 137 F2
   SHHTH WV12 .... 15 D5
Nightingale Dr *TPTN/OCK* DY4 .... 71 E6 🔢
Nightingale Pl *BILS/COS* WV14 .... 47 F2 🔢
Nightjar Gv *ERDW/GRVHL* B23 ... 79 E5 🔢
Nighwood Dr *FOAKS/STRLY* B74 .. 56 B2
Nijon Cl *HDSW* B21 .... 97 E4
Nimmings Cl *NFLD/LBR* B31 .... 202 B1
Nimmings Rd *RMSLY* B62 .... 117 F6
Nineacres Dr
   CHWD/FDBR/MGN B37 .... 130 C5
Nine Elms La *WOLVN* WV10 .... 26 A3
Nine Leasowes *SMTHWK* B66 ...... 96 A6 🔢
Nine Locks Rdg *BRLYHL* DY5 ..... 113 F5
Nineveh Av *HDSW* B21 .... 98 B6
Nineveh Rd *HDSW* B21 .... 98 B6
Ninfield Rd *ACGN* B27 .... 150 C5
Nith Pl *DUDN* DY1 .... 91 D3
Nocke Rd *WNSFLD* WV11 .... 14 B4
Nock St *TPTN/OCK* DY4 .... 71 E4 🔢
Noddy Pk *ALDR* WS9 .... 21 D6
Noddy Park Rd *ALDR* WS9 .... 21 D6
Noel Av *BHTH/HG* B12 .... 148 C3 🔢
Noele Gordon Gdns *WSL* WS1 ...... 52 A1 🔢
Noel Rd *LDYWD/EDGR* B16 .... 122 B6
Nolton Cl *GTB/HAM* B43 .... 75 D5
Nooklands Cft *STETCH* B33 .... 128 C5 🔢
The Nook *BRLYHL* DY5 .... 113 D2 🔢
Noose Crs *WLNHL* WV13 .... 28 A5
Noose La *WLNHL* WV13 .... 28 A5
Nora Rd *SPARK* B11 .... 149 E6 🔢
Norbiton Rd *KGSTG* B44 .... 78 C3
Norbreck Cl *GTB/HAM* B43 .... 75 F3
Norbury Av *BLOX/PEL* WS3 .... 18 B2
Norbury Crs
   ETTPK/GDPK/PENN WV4 .... 46 B5
Norbury Dr *BRLYHL* DY5 .... 113 F6 🔢
Norbury Gv *HIA/OLT* B92 .... 152 C6 🔢
Norbury Rd *BILS/COS* WV14 .... 48 B3
   KGSTG B44 .... 56 B5
   WBROM B70 .... 72 B4
   WOLVN WV10 .... 26 B1
Norcombe Gv *SHLY* B90 .... 210 C2 🔢
Nordley Rd *WNSFLD* WV11 .... 27 E2
Norfolk Av *HHTH/SAND* B71 .... 73 F4 🔢
Norfolk Cl *BVILLE* B30 .... 169 D5
Norfolk Crs *ALDR* WS9 .... 21 D5
Norfolk Dr *DARL/WED* WS10 .... 51 F5
Norfolk Gdns *MGN/WHC* B75 .... 59 D1
Norfolk New Rd *WSLW* WS2 .... 30 C3
Norfolk Pl *WSLW* WS2 .... 31 F2
Norfolk Rd *BDMR/CCFT* WV3 .... 44 C1
   DUDS DY2 .... 90 C6
   EDG B15 .... 145 F1
   ERDW/GRVHL B23 .... 80 B6
   LGLYGN/QTN B68 .... 143 D2
   MGN/WHC B75 .... 59 E2
   RBRY B45 .... 184 B4
   STRBR DY8 .... 135 F1
Norgrave Rd *HIA/OLT* B92 .... 175 E1
Norlan Dr *ALE/KHTH/YWD* B14 .. 190 B2
Norland Rd *ACGN* B27 .... 173 E2
Norley Gv *MOS/BIL* B13 .... 171 E4 🔢
Norman Av *RIDG/WDGT* B32 .... 144 A2
Normandy Rd *BFLD/HDSWWD* B20 .. 99 F4
Norman Rd *DSYBK/YTR* WS5 .... 53 E2
   NFLD/LBR B31 .... 187 D2
   SMTHWK B67 .... 119 F6
Norman St *DUDS* DY2 .... 91 F5
   WSNGN B18 .... 122 A2
Norman Ter *BLKHTH/ROWR* B65 .. 117 E3
Normanton Av
   LGN/SDN/BHAMAIR B26 .... 153 F4
Norrington Gv *NFLD/LBR* B31 .... 185 E2
Norrington Rd *NFLD/LBR* B31 .... 185 E2
Norris Dr *STETCH* B33 .... 128 A4
Norris Rd *BFLD/HDSWWD* B20 ... 100 B4
Norris Wy *MGN/WHC* B75 .... 59 F4
Northampton St *WSNGN* B18 .... 6 A1
Northanger Rd *ACGN* B27 .... 173 D1
North Av *BHAMNEC* B40 .... 156 B4
   WNSFLD WV11 .... 27 E1
Northbrook Rd *SHLY* B90 .... 173 E6
Northbrook St *LDYWD/EDGR* B16 .. 122 B3
Northcote Rd *STETCH* B33 .... 127 F3 🔢
Northcote St *WSLW* WS2 .... 31 F1
Northcott Rd *BILS/COS* WV14 ...... 48 A5
   DUDS DY2 .... 115 F3 🔢
Northdown Rd *SOLH* B91 .... 194 B4
North Dr *BFLD/HDSWWD* B20 ...... 99 D5
   DIG/EDG B5 .... 147 E4
   MGN/WHC B75 .... 59 E3
Northfield Gv *BDMR/CCFT* WV3 .. 43 E2

Northfield Rd BVILLE B30 ... 187 F1
  DUDS DY2 ... 115 E2
  HRBN B17 ... 144 C5 [1]
Northgate ALDR WS9 ... 20 C6
  CDYHTH B64 ... 139 F1
North Ga HRBN B17 ... 145 E2
Northgate Wy ALDR WS9 ... 20 C5
North Gn ETTPK/GDPK/PENN WV4 ... 43 F3
North Holme BORD B9 ... 125 E5 [1]
Northland Rd SHLY B90 ... 194 A4
Northlands Rd MOS/BIL B13 ... 170 C2
Northleach Av BVILLE B30 ... 189 F3
Northleigh Rd WASH/WDE B8 ... 126 C1
Northolt Dr CVALE B35 ... 104 C1 [1]
Northolt Gv PBAR/PBCH B42 ... 76 B2
North Ov SEDG DY3 ... 68 A6
Northover Cl COVEN WV9 ... 10 C3 [1]
North Park Rd ERDW/GRVHL B23 ... 101 D2
North Pathway HRBN B17 ... 145 D2
North Rd BFLD/HDSWWD B20 ... 100 A3
  HRBN B17 ... 145 F3
  SLYOAK B29 ... 146 A6
  TPTN/OCK DY4 ... 71 D3
  WOLV WV1 ... 25 E3
North Roundhay STECH B33 ... 128 C3
Northside Dr FOAKS/STRLY B74 ... 56 B1
North Springfield SEDG DY3 ... 68 A2
North St BRLYHL DY5 ... 113 E5
  DARL/WED WS10 ... 50 B6 [1]
  DUDS DY2 ... 91 F4
  SMTHWKW B67 ... 120 B2
  WOLV WV1 ... 2 D3
  WSLW WS2 ... 32 A3
Northumberland St
  VAUX/NECH B7 ... 124 C4 [1]
North View Dr BRLYHL DY5 ... 114 A2
North Warwick St BORD B9 ... 125 F6 [1]
Northway BHAMNEC B40 ... 156 B4
  SEDG DY3 ... 67 E3
North Western Rd SMTHWK B66 ... 120 B1
North Western Ter WSNGN B18 ... 98 B6
Northwick Crs SOLH B91 ... 195 D4 [1]
Northwood Park Cl
  WOLVN WV10 ... 12 A2 [1]
Northwood Park Rd WOLVN WV10 ... 12 A3
Northwood St CBHAMW B1 ... 6 B3
North Worcestershire Pth
  HAG/WOL DY9 ... 159 D5
  HAG/WOL DY9 ... 181 E1
  RBRY B45 ... 201 E4
Northycote La WOLVN WV10 ... 12 B1
Norton Cl
  ETTPK/GDPK/PENN WV4 ... 43 E6
  SMTHWK B66 ... 121 E2
Norton Crs BILS/COS WV14 ... 69 F2
  BORD B9 ... 127 D4
  DUDS DY2 ... 116 A4 [1]
Norton Green La DOR/KN B93 ... 213 D5
Norton La SHLY B90 ... 207 F3
Norton Rd CSHL/WTROR B46 ... 108 B5
Norton St WSNGN B18 ... 122 C1
Norton Vw ALE/KHTH/YWD B14 ... 169 F5
Nortune Cl HWK/WKHTH B38 ... 187 F3 [1]
Norwich Cft
  CHWD/FDBR/MGN B37 ... 130 B6
Norwich Dr HRBN B17 ... 144 B1
Norwich Rd DUDS DY2 ... 115 F5
  WSLW WS2 ... 31 D6
Norwood Av CDYHTH B64 ... 140 B5
Norwood Gv LOZ/NWT B19 ... 99 D6 [1]
Norwood Rd BORD B9 ... 126 A5
  BRLYHL DY5 ... 113 E4
Nottingham Dr SHHTH WV12 ... 15 E6
Nottingham Wy BRLYHL DY5 ... 114 B5
Nova Ct PBAR/PBCH B42 ... 77 D2
Nova Scotia St CBHAMNE B4 ... 7 G4
Nowell St DARL/WED WS10 ... 50 A4
Nugent Cl AST/WIT B6 ... 100 A6
Nugent Gv SHLY B90 ... 209 F4
Nursery Av ALDR WS9 ... 36 A5 [1]
  BHTH/HG B12 ... 148 D4 [1]
Nursery Cl BVILLE B30 ... 168 B6
  HAG/WOL DY9 ... 158 C6 [1]
Nursery Dr WMBN WV5 ... 86 B1
Nursery Gdns CDSL WV8 ... 8 B1 [1]
  STRBR DY8 ... 112 B6
Nursery Rd BLOX/PEL WS3 ... 17 D5
  BVILLE B30 ... 168 A6
  EDG B15 ... 145 F2
  LOZ/NWT B19 ... 123 D1
Nursery View Cl ALDR WS9 ... 36 A5 [1]
Nursery Wk DUNHL/THL/PER WV6 ... 23 F2
Nutbush Dr NFLD/LBR B31 ... 165 F5
Nutgrove Cl
  ALE/KHTH/YWD B14 ... 170 B4 [1]
Nuthatch Dr BRLYHL DY5 ... 137 E2
Nuthurst MCN/WHC B75 ... 60 C5
Nuthurst Gv
  ALE/KHTH/YWD B14 ... 190 B3 [1]
  DOR/KN B93 ... 212 C3 [1]
Nuthurst Rd NFLD/LBR B31 ... 202 B1 [1]
Nutley Dr TPTN/OCK DY4 ... 71 F3 [1]
Nuttall Gv HDSW B21 ... 97 E6

O

Oak Av BHTH/HG B12 ... 148 C4 [1][2]
  WBROM B70 ... 95 D2
  WSLW WS2 ... 30 A4
Oak Bank WSNGN B18 ... 122 C1
Oak Barn Rd RMSLY B62 ... 141 F1
Oak Cl HRBN B17 ... 144 C3
  TPTN/OCK DY4 ... 70 C2 [1]
Oak Ct HALE B63 ... 162 B1
Oak Crs BLOX/PEL WS3 ... 31 F1
  OLDBY B69 ... 93 D4
Oak Cft CHWD/FDBR/MGN B37 ... 130 A4
Oakcroft Rd MOS/BIL B13 ... 171 D4
Oakdale Cl BRLYHL DY5 ... 89 D6 [1]
  LGLYCN/QTN B68 ... 118 C5
Oakdale Rd CBROM B36 ... 104 A5
  LGLYCN/QTN B68 ... 118 B5
Oakdene Dr RBRY B45 ... 215 E1
Oak Dr ERDW/GRVHL B23 ... 79 E4
Oaken Covert CDSL WV8 ... 8 A2 [1]
Oaken Dr CDSL WV8 ... 8 A2
  SHHTH WV12 ... 16 A6
  SOLH B91 ... 174 B6 [1]
Oaken Gv CDSL WV8 ... 8 A3 [1]
Oakenhayes Crs WALM/CURD B76 ... 83 E6
Oaken La CDSL WV8 ... 8 A2
Oaken Pk CDSL WV8 ... 8 C3
Oakenshaw Rd SHLY B90 ... 193 F4
Oakeswell St DARL/WED WS10 ... 50 C6
Oakeywell St DUDS DY2 ... 91 F5 [1]
Oak Farm Cl WALM/CURD B76 ... 82 C4
Oak Farm Rd BVILLE B30 ... 168 A6
Oakfield Av BHTH/HG B12 ... 148 C5 [1]
  DUDN DY1 ... 69 D5 [1]
  KGSWFD DY6 ... 112 A2
  SPARK B11 ... 149 E3 [1]
Oakfield Cl SMTHWK B66 ... 121 E1 [1]
  STRBR DY8 ... 112 B6
Oakfield Dr RBRY B45 ... 201 F3
Oakfield Rd BHTH/HG B12 ... 148 A5
  CDSL WV8 ... 9 D5
  ERDE/BCHGN B24 ... 102 B2
  HAG/WOL DY9 ... 160 B1
  SLYOAK B29 ... 146 C6
  SMTHWK B66 ... 121 E2
  STRBR DY8 ... 112 C6
Oakfields Wy SOLH B91 ... 177 D6
Oak Gn DUDN DY1 ... 68 C6
  DUNHL/THL/PER WV6 ... 23 D4
Oak Gv NFLD/LBR B31 ... 186 A4
  WNSFLD WV11 ... 13 D6
Oakhall Dr DOR/KN B93 ... 212 B3 [1]
Oakham Av DUDS DY2 ... 92 A4
Oakham Crs DUDS DY2 ... 92 A6 [1]
Oakham Dr DUDS DY2 ... 92 B5
Oakham Rd DUDS DY2 ... 92 A6
  HRBN B17 ... 145 D2
Oak Hl BDMR/CCFT WV3 ... 43 E1
Oakhill Crs ACGN B27 ... 173 D3
Oakhill Dr BRLYHL DY5 ... 137 D2
Oak Hill Dr EDG B15 ... 146 A2
Oakhurst Rd ACGN B27 ... 173 D2
  CSCFLD/WYGN B72 ... 81 D3
Oakland Cl SOLH B91 ... 196 A1 [1]
Oakland Dr SEDG DY3 ... 89 D3
Oakland Rd BLOX/PEL WS3 ... 18 A6
  HDSW B21 ... 97 F5
  MOS/BIL B13 ... 148 C5
Oaklands RMSLY B62 ... 142 C5
  WALM/CURD B76 ... 85 D6
Oaklands Av HRBN B17 ... 144 C4 [1]
Oaklands Cft WALM/CURD B76 ... 83 D4 [1]
Oaklands Dr BFLD/HDSWWD B20 ... 98 B3
Oaklands Gn BILS/COS WV14 ... 47 E1
Oaklands Rd BDMR/CCFT WV3 ... 45 D1
  FOAKS/STRLY B74 ... 59 D1
The Oaklands
  CHWD/FDBR/MGN B37 ... 154 C2
Oaklands Wy BLOX/PEL WS3 ... 19 D2
  NFLD/LBR B31 ... 185 E4
Oak La KGSWFD DY6 ... 88 A4
  WBROM B70 ... 95 D2
Oaklea Dr CDYHTH B64 ... 116 B5
Oakleaf Cl RIDG/WDGT B32 ... 165 E1 [1]
Oak Leaf Dr MOS/BIL B13 ... 148 C6
Oak Leasow RIDG/WDGT B32 ... 143 D5 [1]
Oakleigh NFLD/LBR B31 ... 187 E3 [1]
Oakleigh Dr CDSL WV8 ... 8 C2
  SEDG DY3 ... 67 E4 [1]
Oak Leigh Rd STRBR DY8 ... 158 C1
Oakleighs STRBR DY8 ... 111 E6
Oakley Av ALDR WS9 ... 34 C2
  TPTN/OCK DY4 ... 70 C5
Oakley Gv ETTPK/GDPK/PENN WV4 ... 43 F4
Oakley Rd BVILLE B30 ... 169 D6
  ETTPK/GDPK/PENN WV4 ... 43 F4
  SMHTH B10 ... 149 E2
Oak Leys BDMR/CCFT WV3 ... 23 E6
Oakley Wood Dr SOLH B91 ... 196 A1
Oakmeadow Cl
  LGN/SDN/BHAMAIR B26 ... 151 E2
  STECH B33 ... 129 F5 [1]

Oakmeadow Wy
  ERDE/BCHGN B24 ... 103 F2 [1]
Oakmount Cl BLOX/PEL WS3 ... 18 B2
Oakmount Rd FOAKS/STRLY B74 ... 56 C2
Oak Park Rd STRBR DY8 ... 112 B6
Oakridge Cl SHHTH WV12 ... 29 E3 [1]
Oakridge Dr SHHTH WV12 ... 29 E3
Oak Ri CSHL/WTROR B46 ... 132 B2
Oak Rd ALDR WS9 ... 20 C2
  DUDN DY1 ... 91 E2
  LGLYCN/QTN B68 ... 143 E2
  RUSH/SHEL WS4 ... 19 E5
  TPTN/OCK DY4 ... 70 C5
  WBROM B70 ... 95 D3
  WLNHL WV13 ... 28 A5
Oaks Crs BDMR/CCFT WV3 ... 24 C6
Oaks Dr BDMR/CCFT WV3 ... 24 C5
  WMBN WV5 ... 64 C1
Oakslade Dr HIA/OLT B92 ... 176 A3
The Oaks BKDE/SHDE B34 ... 105 D6
  HWK/WKHTH B38 ... 204 B1
Oak St BDMR/CCFT WV3 ... 24 C5
  BILS/COS WV14 ... 69 D4
  BRLYHL DY5 ... 114 B6
  CDYHTH B64 ... 115 F6
  DUDS DY2 ... 116 A3
  KGSWFD DY6 ... 111 E2
Oakthorpe Dr
  CHWD/FDBR/MGN B37 ... 130 B2
Oakthorpe Gdns OLDBY B69 ... 92 C3 [1]
Oaktree Cl ALVE B48 ... 216 C1
Oak Tree Cl DOR/KN B93 ... 212 A3 [1]
Oak Tree Crs RMSLY B62 ... 142 B5
Oak Tree Gdns STRBR DY8 ... 112 C6 [1]
Oak Tree La BVILLE B30 ... 168 A4
  HLYWD B47 ... 207 D1
  SLYOAK B29 ... 168 A3
The Oak Wk NFLD/LBR B31 ... 186 C4
Oakwood Cl ALDR WS9 ... 20 A1
  WNSFLD WV11 ... 15 D2 [1]
Oakwood Crs DUDS DY2 ... 114 B1
Oakwood Cft SOLH B91 ... 195 E4 [1]
Oakwood Dr
  ALE/KHTH/YWD B14 ... 189 F1 [1]
  FOAKS/STRLY B74 ... 56 A1
Oakwood Rd BLOX/PEL WS3 ... 18 A6
  HLYWD B47 ... 206 C1
  SCFLD/BOLD B73 ... 80 A2
  SMTHWKW B67 ... 120 B3
  SPARK B11 ... 149 E6
Oakwood St WBROM B70 ... 73 D6
Oasthouse Cl KGSWFD DY6 ... 86 C5
Oaston Rd CBROM B36 ... 105 F3 [1]
Oatlands Wk ALE/KHTH/YWD B14 ... 189 F3 [1]
Oatmill Cl DARL/WED WS10 ... 50 A4 [1]
Oban Rd HIA/OLT B92 ... 174 B2
Oberon Cl RBRY B45 ... 184 C3
Oberon Dr SHLY B90 ... 192 C4
Occupation Rd BRWNH WS8 ... 20 C1
Occupation St DUDN DY1 ... 90 C3
Ocean Dr DARL/WED WS10 ... 71 F2
Ockam Cft NFLD/LBR B31 ... 187 E3 [1]
Ocker Hill Rd TPTN/OCK DY4 ... 71 D2
O'connor Dr TPTN/OCK DY4 ... 71 E2
Oddingley Rd NFLD/LBR B31 ... 187 E3
Odell Crs BLOX/PEL WS3 ... 17 F5
Odell Pl DIG/EDG B5 ... 147 E4
Odell Rd BLOX/PEL WS3 ... 17 D6
Odensil Gn HIA/OLT B92 ... 175 D1
Odnall La HAG/WOL DY9 ... 180 A1
Offa's Dr DUNHL/THL/PER WV6 ... 22 A2
Offenham Covert
  HWK/WKHTH B38 ... 188 A5 [1]
Offini Cl WBROM B70 ... 96 B3
Offmoor Rd RIDG/WDGT B32 ... 165 D3
Ogbury Cl ALE/KHTH/YWD B14 ... 189 E3
Ogley Dr MGN/WHC B75 ... 60 C4
O'keeffe Cl SPARK B11 ... 149 D3 [1]
Okement Gr WNSFLD WV11 ... 27 D2
Old Abbey Gdns HRBN B17 ... 145 F5 [1]
Old Acre Cl WALM/CURD B76 ... 81 F5
Old Acre Dr HDSW B21 ... 98 A6
Oldacre Rd LGLYCN/QTN B68 ... 142 C2
Old Bank Rd NFLD/LBR B31 ... 187 D3
Old Barn Rd BVILLE B30 ... 168 A6
  STRBR DY8 ... 112 C6
Old Beeches ERDW/GRVHL B23 ... 79 E3
Old Bell Rd ERDW/GRVHL B23 ... 81 D5
Oldberrow Cl SHLY B90 ... 210 C1 [1]
Old Birchills WSLW WS2 ... 31 E4
Old Birmingham Rd ALVE B48 ... 216 C1
Old Bridge St LOZ/NWT B19 ... 123 D1
Old Bridge Wk
  BLKHTH/ROWR B65 ... 116 B2
Old Bromford La CBROM B36 ... 127 D1
Old Brookside STETCH B33 ... 128 A5
Oldbury Ring Wy OLDBY B69 ... 94 B5
Oldbury Rd BLKHTH/ROWR B65 ... 117 F5
  OLDBY B69 ... 95 E6
  WBROM B70 ... 94 B2
Oldbury Road Industrial Est
  WBROM B70 ... 94 B3
Oldbury St DARL/WED WS10 ... 51 E6
Old Bush St BRLYHL DY5 ... 114 A4 [1]
Old Camp Hl SPARK B11 ... 148 C1 [1]

Old Chapel Rd *SMTHWKW* B67 ...... **120** B4
Old Church Gn *STETCH* B33 .... **128** A5
Old Church Rd *CSHL/WTROR* B46 .... **107** D2
  HRBN B17 .... **145** D4
Old Croft La *CBROM* B36 .... **105** D6
Old Cross St *TPTN/OCK* DY4 ..... **70** A6 🖪
Old Crown Cl *RIDG/WDGT* B32 ...... **165** D2
Old Damson La *HIA/OLT* B92 .... **176** B1
Old Dickens Heath Rd *SHLY* B90.... **208** C2
Old End La *BILS/COS* WV14 .... **69** E4
Old Fallings Crs *WOLVN* WV10 .... **26** B1
Old Fallings La *WOLVN* WV10 .... **12** B4
Old Farm Dr *A LKHTH/YWD* B14.... **171** E6
Old Farm Meadow
  BDMR/CCFT WV3 .... **43** E3
Old Farm Rd *STETCH* B33 .... **128** A3
Oldfield Dr *STRBR* DY8 .... **136** C6 🖪
Oldfield Rd *BHTH/HG* B12 .... **148** C3
  BILS/COS WV14 .... **68** C3
Oldfields *CDYHTH* B64 .... **139** F1
  HAG/WOL DY9 .... **159** D5
Old Fordrove *WALM/CURD* B76 ...... **59** F6
Old Forest Wy *BKDE/SHDE* B34 .... **129** D1
Old Grange Dr *SPARK* B11 .... **149** E5
Old Grove Gdns *HAG/WOL* DY9 ...... **157** F6
Old Hall Cl *STRBR* DY8 .... **136** C2
Old Hall La *ALDR* WS9 .... **55** D4
Old Hall St *WOLV* WV1 .... **3** E5
Old Ham La *HAG/WOL* DY9 .... **159** E1
Old Hampton La *WNSFLD* WV11 ...... **13** E3
Old Hawne La *HALE* B63 .... **140** C4
Old Heath Crs *WOLV* WV1 .... **26** C6 🖪
Old Heath Rd *WOLV* WV1 .... **26** C5
Old Hobicus La
  LGLYGN/QTN B68 .... **119** D2 🖪
Old Horns Crs *PBAR/PBCH* B42 ...... **77** E1
Oldhouse Farm Cl
  HLGN/YWD B28 .... **172** B5 🖪
Old House La *RMSLY* B62 .... **183** D4
Oldington Gv *SOLH* B91 .... **194** C5
Old Kingsbury Rd *WALM/CURD* B76... **83** E6
Oldknow Rd *SMTHK* B10 .... **150** A3
Old La *ALVE* B48 .... **219** F5
  BLOX/PEL WS3 .... **17** E6
  DUNHL/THL/PER WV6 .... **22** B5
Old Level Wy *DUDS* DY2 .... **115** F3 🖪
Old Lime Gdns
  HWK/WKHTH B38 .... **188** A5 🖪
Old Lindens Cl *FOAKS/STRLY* B74 ... **56** A2
Old Lode La *HIA/OLT* B92 .... **175** D1
Old Meadow Rd *NFLD/LBR* B31 .. **187** E6 🖪
Old Meeting Rd *BILS/COS* WV14 ...... **69** E3
Old Meeting St *HHTH/SAND* B71 ..... **73** D6
Old Mill Cl *SHLY* B90 .... **191** F3
Old Mill Gdns *RUSH/SHEL* WS4 ...... **19** E3
Old Mill Gv *BFLD/HDSWWD* B20 ... **99** E3 🖪
Old Mill Rd *CSHL/WTROR* B46 .... **108** B6
Old Moat Dr *NFLD/LBR* B31 .... **187** D2
Old Moat Wy *WASH/WDE* B8 .... **127** D1
Oldnall Cl *HAG/WOL* DY9 .... **138** B5
Oldnall Rd *HAG/WOL* DY9 .... **138** C5
Old Oak Cl *ALDR* WS9 .... **21** D5
Old Oak Rd *HWK/WKHTH* B38 .... **188** A5
Old Oscott Hl *KGSTG* B44 .... **78** A2
Old Oscott La *KGSTG* B44 .... **78** A3
Old Pk *SLYOAK* B29 .... **166** C6
Old Park La *OLDBY* B69 .... **118** C2
Old Park Rd *DARL/WED* WS10 .... **50** B5
  DUDN DY1 .... **90** B1
Old Park Wk *WSLW* WS2 .... **51** E1
Old Port Cl *TPTN/OCK* DY4 .... **93** D3 🖪
Old Portway *HWK/WKHTH* B38 ...... **188** A6
Old Postway *LOZ/NWT* B19 .... **99** F6 🖪
Old Quarry Cl *RBRY* B45 .... **184** B5 🖪
Old Quarry Dr *SEDG* DY3 .... **67** F6
Old Rectory Gdns *ALDR* WS9 .... **35** E1
Old Rectory La *ALVE* B48 .... **217** D2
Old School Cl *WLNHL* WV13 .... **28** C5 🖪
Old School Dr
  BLKHTH/ROWR B65 .... **117** E4 🖪
Old Scott Cl *STETCH* B33 .... **129** E5
Old Smithy Pl *WSNGN* B18 .... **122** C2 🖪
Old Snow Hl *CBHAMNW* B4 .... **6** D1
Old Station Rd *HIA/OLT* B92 .... **178** B1
  STETCH B33 .... **127** F3
Old Stone Cl *RBRY* B45 .... **184** B4
Old Stowheath La *WLNHL* WV13 ...... **27** E6 🖪
Old Town Cl *HWK/WKHTH* B38 ..... **188** B5 🖪
Old Town La *BLOX/PEL* WS3 .... **18** B2
Old Vicarage Cl *BLOX/PEL* WS3 .... **18** C3
Old Walsall Rd *GTB/HAM* B43 .... **76** B3
Old Warwick Ct *HIA/OLT* B92 .... **174** A2 🖪
Old Warwick Rd *HIA/OLT* B92 .... **174** A2 🖪
Oldway Dr *SOLH* B91 .... **196** A3
Old Well Cl *RUSH/SHEL* WS4 .... **19** D6
Old Wharf Rd *STRBR* DY8 .... **136** B3
Olga Dr *TPTN/OCK* DY4 .... **71** D2
Olinthus Av *WNSFLD* WV11 .... **14** A6
Olive Av *ETTPK/GDPK/PENN* WV4 ... **44** B4
Olive Dr *RMSLY* B62 .... **141** E1
Olive Hill Rd *RMSLY* B62 .... **141** F1
Olive La *RMSLY* B62 .... **141** E1
Oliver Cl *DUDS* DY2 .... **92** A5 🔟

Oliver Ct *BLKHTH/ROWR* B65 ...... **117** D5 🖪
Oliver Crs *BILS/COS* WV14 .... **69** F1
Oliver Rd *ERDW/GRVHL* B23 .... **80** A1
  LDYWD/EDGR B16 .... **122** B5
  SMTHWK B66 .... **121** E4
Oliver St *VAUX/NECH* B7 .... **124** C2
Ollerton Rd
  LGN/SDN/BHAMAIR B26 .... **152** B2
Ollison Dr *FOAKS/STRLY* B74 .... **36** B5
Olliver Cl *RIDG/WDGT* B32 .... **164** B1
Olorenshaw Rd
  LGN/SDN/BHAMAIR B26 .... **153** F4
Olton Bvd East *ACGN* B27 .... **173** E1
Olton Bvd West *SPARK* B11 .... **150** B6
Olton Cft *ACGN* B27 .... **151** F6
Olton Rd *SHLY* B90 .... **173** D6
Olton Whf *HIA/OLT* B92 .... **174** A1
Olympus Dr *TPTN/OCK* DY4 .... **71** F5
Ombersley Cl *OLDBY* B69 .... **117** F2 🖪
Ombersley Rd *BHTH/HG* B12 .... **148** C3
  HALE B63 .... **162** B1 🔟
Onibury Rd *HDSW* B21 .... **97** F4
Onslow Crs *HIA/OLT* B92 .... **174** C3
Onslow Rd *SPARK* B11 .... **150** C5
Ontario Cl *HWK/WKHTH* B38 .... **188** C5
Oozells St *CBHAMW* B1 .... **6** A6
Open Field Cl *NFLD/LBR* B31 .... **187** D3
Openfield Cft *CSHL/WTROR* B46 .... **107** D5
The Orangery *HAG/WOL* DY9 .... **175** F6
Orchard Av *SOLH* B91 .... **175** F5
Orchard Cl *BLKHTH/ROWR* B65 .... **116** C4
  CSHL/WTROR B46 .... **108** B6 🖪
  HALE B63 .... **139** E3 🖪
  HDSW B21 .... **98** B4
  RUSH/SHEL WS4 .... **33** E1 🖪
  WALM/CURD B76 .... **85** D5
  WLNHL WV13 .... **29** D6
Orchard Cft *BDMR/CCFT* WV3 .... **43** D2
  KGSWFD DY6 .... **111** F1
Orchard Dr *ALDR* WS9 .... **35** D3
  ETTPK/GDPK/PENN WV4 .... **44** C5
  FOAKS/STRLY B74 .... **38** B4
  SEDG DY3 .... **89** D2
Orchard Gv *ALDR* WS9 .... **35** D3
  ETTPK/GDPK/PENN WV4 .... **44** C5
Orchard Ri
  LGN/SDN/BHAMAIR B26 .... **152** B2
Orchard Rd *DSYBK/YTR* WS5 .... **53** D6
  DUDS DY2 .... **115** E5
  ERDE/BCHGN B24 .... **80** C6
  WLNHL WV11 .... **29** D6
  WNSFLD WV11 .... **13** E6
The Orchards *FOAKS/STRLY* B74 ..... **38** C6
  SHLY B90 .... **209** F5 🖪
Orchard St *BRLYHL* DY5 .... **113** F3
  OLDBY B69 .... **92** B5 🖪
The Orchard *BILS/COS* WV14 .... **48** A4 🖪
  BLOX/PEL WS3 .... **17** F3
  CHWD/FDBR/MGN B37 .... **154** B1
  DUNHL/THL/PER WV6 .... **24** A1
Orchard Wy *ACGN* B27 .... **151** D5
  GTB/HAM B43 .... **76** B2
  HLYWD B47 .... **190** C5
Orcheston Wk
  ALE/KHTH/YWD B14 .... **189** F4
Orchid Cl *SMTHWK* B66 .... **95** F6
Orchid Dr *LOZ/NWT* B19 .... **123** F1 🖪
Oregon Cl *KGSWFD* DY6 .... **112** B1
Oregon Dr *SHHTH* WV12 .... **16** A6 🖪
Orford Gv *HDSW* B21 .... **97** E6
Oriel Cl *DUDN* DY1 .... **90** A3
Oriel Dr *WOLVN* WV10 .... **11** F2
Orion Cl *WASH/WDE* B8 .... **127** D3 🖪
Orkney Av *WASH/WDE* B8 .... **128** B1
Orkney Cft *CBROM* B36 .... **107** D6
Orlando Cl *WSL* WS1 .... **4** D6
Ormande Cl *HALE* B63 .... **139** D2
Orme Cl *STRBR* DY8 .... **136** C1
Ormes La *DUNHL/THL/PER* WV6 ..... **23** E4
Ormond Pl *BILS/COS* WV14 .... **48** A3
Ormond Rd *RBRY* B45 .... **184** A4
Ormsby Gv *ACGN* B27 .... **173** D4 🖪
Ormscliffe Rd *RBRY* B45 .... **201** D1
Orphanage Rd
  CSCFLD/WYGN B72 .... **81** E5
  ERDE/BCHGN B24 .... **80** C6 🖪
Orpington Rd *KGSTG* B44 .... **56** A6 🖪
Orpwood Rd *STETCH* B33 .... **128** C5
Orton Av *WALM/CURD* B76 .... **82** B5
Orton Cl *CSHL/WTROR* B46 .... **106** C2
Orton Gv *ETTPK/GDPK/PENN* WV4 ... **43** F5
Orton La *ETTPK/GDPK/PENN* WV4 ... **42** B6
Orton Wy *CVALE* B35 .... **104** C3
Orwell Cl *STRBR* DY8 .... **135** F5
  WNSFLD WV11 .... **28** B2
Orwell Dr *HHTH/SAND* B71 .... **73** D5
  NFLD/LBR B31 .... **187** D5
Orwell Pas *DIG/EDG* B5 .... **7** F6
Orwell Rd *WSL* WS1 .... **53** D1
Osberton Dr *DUDN* DY1 .... **90** B3
Osborne Cl *AST/WIT* B6 .... **100** C6 🖪
  BRLYHL DY5 .... **138** B1
Osborne Dr *DARL/WED* WS10 .... **49** F1

Osborne Rd *ERDW/GRVHL* B23 .... **80** B6
  ETTPK/GDPK/PENN WV4 .... **44** B4
  HDSW B21 .... **98** B5
  WBROM B70 .... **95** E2 🖪
Osborn Rd *SPARK* B11 .... **149** E3
Oscott Rd *PBAR/PBCH* B42 .... **100** A2
Oscott School La *KGSTG* B44 .... **78** A1
Osier Gv *ERDW/GRVHL* B23 .... **79** D5
Osier Pl *WOLV* WV1 .... **26** B5
Osier St *WOLV* WV1 .... **26** B5
Osler St *LDYWD/EDGR* B16 .... **122** B5
Osmaston Rd *HRBN* B17 .... **144** C6
  STRBR DY8 .... **136** A6
  STRBR DY8 .... **158** A1
Osmington Gv *HALE* B63 .... **139** F3 🖪
Osprey Dr *DUDN* DY1 .... **90** A3
Osprey Rd *ERDW/GRVHL* B23 .... **79** E5
  HIA/OLT B92 .... **173** F1
Ostler Cl *KGSWFD* DY6 .... **87** D6
Oswin Pl *BLOX/PEL* WS3 .... **32** B2
Oswin Rd *BLOX/PEL* WS3 .... **32** B2
Otley Gv *WASH/WDE* B8 .... **127** E4
Otter Cft *BKDE/SHDE* B34 .... **129** F2
Otterstone Cl *SEDG* DY3 .... **67** E1
Oughton Rd *BHTH/HG* B12 .... **148** C2 🖪
Oundle Rd *KGSTG* B44 .... **78** B4
Ounsdale Crs *WMBN* WV5 .... **64** C4
Ounsdale Dr *DUDS* DY2 .... **115** E3
Ounsdale Rd *WMBN* WV5 .... **64** B4
Ounty John La *STRBR* DY8 .... **158** C3
Outmore Rd *STETCH* B33 .... **129** D6
Oval Rd *ERDE/BCHGN* B24 .... **102** A4
  TPTN/OCK DY4 .... **70** B4
The Oval *DARL/WED* WS10 .... **50** B5
  DUDN DY1 .... **90** A5 🖪
  SMTHWKW B67 .... **119** F5
Overbrook Cl *SEDG* DY3 .... **89** E3 🖪
Over Brunton Cl *NFLD/LBR* B31 .. **187** D3
Overbury Cl *NFLD/LBR* B31 .... **187** E2
  RMSLY B62 .... **163** F3
Overbury Rd *NFLD/LBR* B31 .... **187** E1
Overdale Av *WALM/CURD* B76 .... **82** B6
Overdale Cl *SHHTH* WV12 .... **29** E4
Overdale Dr *WSLW* WS2 .... **29** E4
Overdale Rd *RIDG/WDGT* B32 ...... **144** A5
Overend Rd *HALE* B63 .... **139** D3
Overend St *WBROM* B70 .... **95** F2
Overfield Dr
  ETTPK/GDPK/PENN WV4 .... **46** C6
Overfield Rd *DUDN* DY1 .... **90** A5
  RIDG/WDGT B32 .... **166** A2
Over Green Dr
  CHWD/FDBR/MGN B37 .... **130** B2
Overlea Av *ERDE/BCHGN* B24 .... **102** B5
Over Mill Dr *SLYOAK* B29 .... **169** D1 🖪
Overmoor Cl *LOZ/NWT* B19 .... **99** E6 🖪
Over Pool Rd *WASH/WDE* B8 .... **126** C1
Overseal Rd *WNSFLD* WV11 .... **14** A5
Overslade Rd *SOLH* B91 .... **194** B3
Oversley Rd *WALM/CURD* B76 .... **82** C5
Overton Cl *HLGN/YWD* B28 .... **172** C5
Overton Dr *CSHL/WTROR* B46 ...... **107** F2
Overton Gv *ACGN* B27 .... **173** E3 🖪
Overton Pl *HHTH/SAND* B71 .... **73** F4
Overton Rd *ACGN* B27 .... **173** D5
Overwood Cft *WASH/WDE* B8 ...... **126** A4 🖪
Owen Pl *BILS/COS* WV14 .... **47** F3
Owen Rd *BDMR/CCFT* WV3 .... **44** C1
  BILS/COS WV14 .... **47** F3
  WLNHL WV13 .... **29** D6
Owens Cft *HWK/WKHTH* B38 .... **188** C4
Owen St *DARL/WED* WS10 .... **49** F2
  DUDS DY2 .... **92** A5
  TPTN/OCK DY4 .... **70** A6
Owens Wy *CDYHTH* B64 .... **116** C6
Ownall Rd *BKDE/SHDE* B34 .... **129** E1
Oxbarn Av *BDMR/CCFT* WV3 .... **44** A2
Oxenton Cft *HALE* B63 .... **161** F1
Oxford Cl *WASH/WDE* B8 .... **127** D2
Oxford Dr *ACGN* B27 .... **151** F5
  STRBR DY8 .... **136** B5
Oxford Rd *ACGN* B27 .... **151** E6
  ERDW/GRVHL B23 .... **102** B1
  MOS/BIL B13 .... **170** C1
  SMTHWK B66 .... **96** C5
  WBROM B70 .... **95** D2
Oxford St *BILS/COS* WV14 .... **48** A4
  BVILLE B30 .... **168** C4
  DARL/WED WS10 .... **73** D1
  DUDN DY1 .... **91** D4 🔟
  WOLV WV1 .... **3** F5
  WSLW WS2 .... **51** E2
Oxhill Rd *HDSW* B21 .... **97** E2
  SHLY B90 .... **191** E5
Ox Leasow *RIDG/WDGT* B32 .... **165** E1
Oxley Av *WOLVN* WV10 .... **25** E1
Oxley Cl *DUDS* DY2 .... **115** D5
Oxley Gv *SLYOAK* B29 .... **166** D3
Oxley La *WOLV* WV1 .... **2** D1
Oxley Links Rd *WOLVN* WV10 .... **11** D5
Oxley Moor Rd *COVEN* WV9 .... **10** C5
  WOLVN WV10 .... **10** C5
Ox Leys Rd *MGN/WHC* B75 .... **61** D5
Oxley St *WOLV* WV1 .... **25** E3

Oxlip Cl *DSYBK/YTR* WS5 .... 52 C6 🔟
Oxpiece Dr *CBROM* B36 .... 103 F5 🔟
Oxstall Cl *WALM/CURD* B76 .... 83 F6
Ox St *SEDG* DV3 .... 67 F6
Oxted Cl *WNSFLD* WV11 .... 28 B2 🔟
Oxted Cft *EDR/GRVHL* B23 .... 102 A2
Oxwood La *RMSLY* B62 .... 183 F1
Oxygen St *VAUX/NECH* B7 .... 7 G1

P

Pace Crs *BILS/COS* WV14 .... 70 B1
Pacific Av *DARL/WED* WS10 .... 71 F2
Packhorse La *HWK/WKHTH* B38 .... 205 F1
Packington Av *BKDE/SHDE* B34 .... 129 E2
Packington La *CSHL/WTROR* B46 .... 132 C3
Packwood Cl
  BFLD/HDSWWD B20 .... 98 C3 🔟
  DOR/KN B93 .... 212 A3
  WLNHL WV13 .... 48 B1
Packwood Ct *SLYOAK* B29 .... 166 B2 🔟
Packwood Dr *GTB/HAM* B43 .... 75 F2
Packwood Rd
  LGN/SDN/BHAMAIR B26 .... 153 D1
  OLDBY B69 .... 92 C4
Padarn Cl *SEDG* DV3 .... 67 E2
Padbury *COVEN* WV9 .... 11 D2 🔟
Paddeston Dr *WASH/WDE* B8 .... 125 F3 🔟
Paddington Rd *HDSW* B21 .... 97 E4 🔟
Paddock Dr *DOR/KN* B93 .... 212 C5
Paddock La *LGN/SDN/BHAMAIR* B26 .... 152 C2
Paddock La *ALDR* WS9 .... 34 C2
  WSL WS1 .... 5 F4
Paddocks Gn *WSNGN* B18 .... 122 C2 🔟
Paddocks Rd *HLYWD* B47 .... 206 B1
The Paddocks *BILS/COS* WV14 .... 69 F2
  CDSL WV8 .... 8 C3
  HAG/WOL DY9 .... 159 D3
  SEDG DV3 .... 68 A6 🔟
  WMBN WV5 .... 64 A5 🔟
Paddock Vw
  DUNHL/THL/PER WV6 .... 25 D2 🔟
Padgate Cl *CVALE* B35 .... 105 D2
Paganal Dr *WBROM* B70 .... 96 A4 🔟
Paganal Dr *DUDN* DY1 .... 91 E2
Paganel Rd *SLYOAK* B29 .... 166 C1
Pages Cl *MGN/WHC* B75 .... 59 E4
Pages La *GTB/HAM* B43 .... 76 A1 🔟
Paget Rd *DUNHL/THL/PER* WV6 .... 24 B4
  ERDE/BCHGN B24 .... 103 F2
Paget St *WOLV* WV1 .... 2 B1 🔟
Pagham Cl *COVEN* WV9 .... 10 B3
Pagnell Gv *MOS/BIL* B13 .... 171 E5
Paignton Rd *LDYWD/EDGR* B16 .... 121 F4
Pailton Gv *SLYOAK* B29 .... 167 D2 🔟
Pailton Rd *SHLY* B90 .... 173 D6
Painswick Cl *DSYBK/YTR* WS5 .... 53 D6 🔟
Painswick Rd *HLGN/YWD* B28 .... 172 A4
Paint Cup Rw *DUDS* DY2 .... 115 E5
Painters Cft *BILS/COS* WV14 .... 70 A2
Pakefield Rd *BVILLE* B30 .... 189 D2
Pakenham Cl *WALM/CURD* B76 .... 82 B3 🔟
Pakenham Rd *EDG* B15 .... 147 E2
Palace Cl *BLKHTH/ROWR* B65 .... 117 F3
Palace Dr *SMTHWK* B66 .... 95 E5
Palace Rd *BORD* B9 .... 126 A6
Palefield Rd *SHLY* B90 .... 210 B1
Pale La *HRBN* B17 .... 144 B1
Palethorpe Rd *TPTN/OCK* DY4 .... 70 C3 🔟
Palfrey Rd *STRBR* DY8 .... 135 F4
Palmcourt Av *HLGN/YWD* B28 .... 172 A4
Palm Cft *BRLYHL* DY5 .... 137 E1
Palmer Cl *WNSFLD* WV11 .... 14 B4
Palmers Cl *CDSL* WV8 .... 9 E4
  SHLY B90 .... 173 D6
Palmers Gv *CBROM* B36 .... 104 A5 🔟
Palmerston Dr *OLDBY* B69 .... 93 F3
Palmerston Rd *SPARK* B11 .... 149 D3
Palmer St *BORD* B9 .... 124 C5
Palmers Wy *CDSL* WV8 .... 9 E4
Palmvale Cft
  LGN/SDN/BHAMAIR B26 .... 152 D1
Palomino Pl *LDYWD/EDGR* B16 .... 122 B5 🔟
Pamela Rd *NFLD/LBR* B31 .... 186 C3
Pan Cft *CBROM* B36 .... 103 E6
Pannel Cft *LOZ/NWT* B19 .... 123 F1
Panther Cft *BKDE/SHDE* B34 .... 129 F2
Paper Mill End *PBAR/PBCH* B42 .... 77 F5
Papyrus Wy *CBROM* B36 .... 104 B4
Parade *CBHAMNW* B3 .... 6 A4
The Parade *CDYHTH* B64 .... 140 A1
  DUDN DY1 .... 91 D3
  KGSWFD DY6 .... 87 D6 🔟
Paradise *DUDS* DY2 .... 91 F5
Paradise Circus Queensway
  CBHAMNW B3 .... 6 B4
  CBHAMW B1 .... 6 B5
Paradise La *BLOX/PEL* WS3 .... 18 B2
  HLGN/YWD B28 .... 172 A5
Paradise St *CBHAM* B2 .... 6 C5
  WBROM B70 .... 95 F2

Pardington Cl *HIA/OLT* B92 .... 176 A3 🔟
Pargeter Rd *SMTHWK* B67 .... 120 B5
Pargeter St *STRBR* DY8 .... 136 B5
  WSLW WS2 .... 31 E5
Par Gn *NFLD/LBR* B31 .... 187 E4
Parish Gdns *HAG/WOL* DY9 .... 159 D2 🔟
Park Ap *ERDW/GRVHL* B23 .... 101 E3
Park Av *BLKHTH/ROWR* B65 .... 117 E4
  BVILLE B30 .... 168 C6
  CSHL/WTROR B46 .... 132 B1 🔟
  ETTPK/GDPK/PENN WV4 .... 45 E4
  LGLYGN/QTN B68 .... 119 D4
  SOLH B91 .... 195 F2
  TPTN/OCK DY4 .... 70 A6 🔟
  WLNHL WV13 .... 28 B5
  WMBN WV5 .... 64 B6
  WOLV WV1 .... 2 B3
  WSNGN B18 .... 98 C6
Park Cft *HLYWD* B47 .... 206 C2
Park Cft Av *DARL/WED* WS10 .... 50 C5
Parkdale Cl *ERDE/BCHGN* B24 .... 102 B3
Parkdale Dr *NFLD/LBR* B31 .... 186 C6
Parkdale East *WOLV* WV1 .... 24 C4
Parkdale
  LGN/SDN/BHAMAIR B26 .... 153 E3
Park Dl West *WOLV* WV1 .... 24 C4
Park Dr *ETTPK/GDPK/PENN* WV4 .... 45 E4
  FOAKS/STRLY B74 .... 37 E3
  FOAKS/STRLY B74 .... 38 B5 🔟
Park Edge *HRBN* B17 .... 145 E2
Park End *NFLD/LBR* B31 .... 186 C6
Parker Rd *WNSFLD* WV11 .... 14 B4
Parker St *BLOX/PEL* WS3 .... 16 C4
  LDYWD/EDGR B16 .... 122 B6 🔟
Parkes Av *CDSL* WV8 .... 9 E4
Parkes Hall Rd *DUDN* DY1 .... 68 C6
Parkes La *SEDG* DV3 .... 68 C4
  TPTN/OCK DY4 .... 70 B3
Parkes St *BRLYHL* DY5 .... 113 F4
  SMTHWK B67 .... 120 B3
  WLNHL WV13 .... 29 D6
Parkeston Crs *KGSTG* B44 .... 79 D2
Park Farm Rd *GTB/HAM* B43 .... 55 D6
Park Gv *CSHL/WTROR* B46 .... 107 E2
Park Hall Cl *DSYBK/YTR* WS5 .... 53 E3
Park Hall Crs *CBROM* B36 .... 105 D5
Parkhall Cft *CBROM* B36 .... 105 E6
Park Hall Rd *DSYBK/YTR* WS5 .... 53 E3
  ETTPK/GDPK/PENN WV4 .... 45 F5
Park Head Crs *DUDS* DY2 .... 91 D5 🔟
Park Head Rd *DUDS* DY2 .... 91 D4
Park Hi *BLKHTH/ROWR* B65 .... 117 D6
  DARL/WED WS10 .... 51 D5
  MOS/BIL B13 .... 148 A5
Park Hill Dr *BFLD/HDSWWD* B20 .... 98 B1
Park Hill Rd *HRBN* B17 .... 145 E3
  SMTHWK B67 .... 120 B2
Parkhill Rd *WALM/CURD* B76 .... 82 B5
Park Hill St *DUDS* DY2 .... 92 A5
Parkhouse Av *WNSFLD* WV11 .... 27 D1
Parkhouse Dr *ERDW/GRVHL* B23 .... 78 C3 🔟
Parkhouse Gdns *SEDG* DV3 .... 89 E1 🔟
Parklands Dr *FOAKS/STRLY* B74 .... 58 B1
Parklands Gdns *WSL* WS1 .... 52 C1 🔟
Parklands Rd *BILS/COS* WV14 .... 47 F5 🔟
  DARL/WED WS10 .... 50 A4
  WOLV WV1 .... 26 C6
The Parklands *BDMR/CCFT* WV3 .... 23 F5
  ERDW/GRVHL B23 .... 79 F5
  HAG/WOL DY9 .... 137 E6
Park La *AST/WIT* B6 .... 100 A6
  CVALE B35 .... 83 D1
  CVALE B35 .... 105 E1
  DARL/WED WS10 .... 50 B1
  HALE B63 .... 138 C3
  HDSW B21 .... 97 D3
  KGSWFD DY6 .... 88 A6
  LGN/SDN/BHAMAIR B26 .... 155 D5
  OLDBY B69 .... 118 C3
  WOLVN WV10 .... 26 A1
Park La East *TPTN/OCK* DY4 .... 93 D1
Park La West *TPTN/OCK* DY4 .... 92 A1
Park Lime Dr *RUSH/SHEL* WS4 .... 33 E3
Park Meadow Av *BILS/COS* WV14 .... 47 E1 🔟
Park Ms *SLYOAK* B29 .... 167 D2 🔟

Park Pl *VAUX/NECH* B7 .... 101 E6 🔟
Park Retreat *SMTHWK* B66 .... 121 D3
Park Rdg *FOAKS/STRLY* B74 .... 58 C2
Park Ridge Dr *HALE* B63 .... 139 D3
Park Ri *BDMR/CCFT* WV3 .... 24 A5
Park Rd *AST/WIT* B6 .... 100 C6
  BILS/COS WV14 .... 47 E4
  BLOX/PEL WS3 .... 17 D4
  BRLYHL DY5 .... 138 B1
  CSHL/WTROR B46 .... 132 B1 🔟
  DARL/WED WS10 .... 49 D3
  DSYBK/YTR WS5 .... 53 F4
  DUDN DY1 .... 69 D5
  DUDS DY2 .... 115 E1
  ERDW/GRVHL B23 .... 101 E3
  HAG/WOL DY9 .... 159 E5
  HALE B63 .... 139 D3
  MOS/BIL B13 .... 148 B5
  OLDBY B69 .... 93 E5
  RUSH/SHEL WS4 .... 33 E2
  SCFLD/BOLD B73 .... 59 D4
  SEDG DV3 .... 89 D1
  SMTHWK B67 .... 120 B6
  SPARK B11 .... 149 E6
  STRBR DY8 .... 135 F4
  WLNHL WV13 .... 28 B4
  WSNGN B18 .... 98 B6
Park Rd East *WOLV* WV1 .... 2 A1
Park Rd South *WSNGN* B18 .... 123 D2
Park Rd West *STRBR* DY8 .... 135 E4
  WOLV WV1 .... 24 C4
Parks Crs *WNSFLD* WV11 .... 14 C1
Parkside *RIDG/WDGT* B32 .... 165 E3
Parkside Av *WLNHL* WV13 .... 28 A5
Parkside Cl *DARL/WED* WS10 .... 51 D6 🔟
Parkside Rd *BFLD/HDSWWD* B20 .... 76 A6
  HALE B63 .... 139 F4
Parkside Wy *FOAKS/STRLY* B74 .... 56 C1 🔟
  NFLD/LBR B31 .... 185 E3
Park Sq *CSHL/WTROR* B46 .... 155 F1
Parkstone Cl *RUSH/SHEL* WS4 .... 19 E1
Park St *AST/WIT* B6 .... 100 C6
  BLKHTH/ROWR B65 .... 117 F6
  CDYHTH B64 .... 115 F5
  DARL/WED WS10 .... 49 E4
  DIG/EDG B5 .... 7 F6 🔟
  HAG/WOL DY9 .... 138 B4
  KGSWFD DY6 .... 111 F1
  OLDBY B69 .... 118 B1
  STRBR DY8 .... 136 B1 🔟
  STRBR DY8 .... 136 C5
  TPTN/OCK DY4 .... 70 C6
  WBROM B70 .... 95 F2 🔟
  WSL WS1 .... 4 C3
Park St South *BKHL/PFLD* WV2 .... 45 E3
Park Ter *DARL/WED* WS10 .... 49 E3
  HDSW B21 .... 98 A5
Park Vw *DARL/WED* WS10 .... 49 E3
  SCFLD/BOLD B73 .... 58 C3
Parkview Crs *WSLW* WS2 .... 30 C3
Parkview Dr *WASH/WDE* B8 .... 126 C1 🔟
Parkview Rd *BILS/COS* WV14 .... 47 F5
Park View Rd *FOAKS/STRLY* B74 .... 37 F4
  HAG/WOL DY9 .... 138 B5
  NFLD/LBR B31 .... 186 B2
Parkville Av *HRBN* B17 .... 145 D6
Parkville Cl *BRLYHL* DY5 .... 138 B1
Park Wk *RBRY* B45 .... 185 D4
  WNSFLD WV11 .... 14 C4
Parkway *WASH/WDE* B8 .... 126 C2
Parkway Rd *DUDN* DY1 .... 90 C3
The Parkway
  DUNHL/THL/PER WV6 .... 22 A2
  RUSH/SHEL WS4 .... 19 E5
Parkwood Cft *PBAR/PBCH* B42 .... 77 D2 🔟
Parkwood Dr *SCFLD/BOLD* B73 .... 79 E1
Parliament St *AST/WIT* B6 .... 124 C1
  SMHTH B10 .... 149 E1
  WBROM B70 .... 95 E1
Parlows End *HWK/WKHTH* B38 .... 187 F6 🔟
Parry Rd *WNSFLD* WV11 .... 14 C5
Parsonage Dr *HALE* B63 .... 138 C2 🔟
  RBRY B45 .... 201 F3
Parsonage St *HHTH/SAND* B71 .... 73 F5 🔟
  OLDBY B69 .... 119 D1
Parson's Hl *BVILLE* B30 .... 189 D3
  HWK/WKHTH B38 .... 189 D3
  LGLYGN/QTN B68 .... 119 D6
Parsons St *DUDN* DY1 .... 91 E4
Partons Rd *ALE/KHTH/YWD* B14 .... 169 F5
Partridge Av *DARL/WED* WS10 .... 49 D3 🔟
Partridge Cl
  CHWD/FDBR/MGN B37 .... 131 E4
Partridge Ml *BLOX/PEL* WS3 .... 18 A2 🔟
Partridge Rd
  LGN/SDN/BHAMAIR B26 .... 128 C6
  STRBR DY8 .... 135 E5 🔟
Passey Rd *MOS/BIL* B13 .... 171 F1
Passfield Rd *STETCH* B33 .... 128 B4
Pasture Vw *BLOX/PEL* WS3 .... 18 B4
Patent Dr *DARL/WED* WS10 .... 49 F6
  DARL/WED WS10 .... 71 C1
Paternoster Rw *DIG/EDG* B5 .... 7 F5 🔟
  WOLV WV1 .... 2 C3
Pathlow Crs *SHLY* B90 .... 192 C4

Paton Gv *MOS/BIL* B13.....170 B1
Patricia Av *ALE/KHTH/YWD* B14..191 E1
  ETTPK/GDPK/PENN WV4.....45 E4
Patricia Crs *DUDN* DY1.....69 D5
Patricia Dr *TPTN/OCK* DY4.....92 C3
Patrick Gregory Rd *WNSFLD* WV11 ..14 B6
Patrick Rd
  LGN/SDN/BHAMAIR B26.....152 A2
Patriot Gv *WSL* WS1.....51 F4 🔲
Patshull Av *WOLVN* WV10.....11 E2
Patshull Cl *GTB/HAM* B43.....75 F2
Patshull Gv *WOLVN* WV10 ..11 D2 🔲
Patterdale Rd *ERDW/GRVHL* B23 ..101 F1
Patterdale Wy *BRLYHL* DY5.....137 D1
Patterton Dr *WALM/CURD* B76.....82 B3
Pattison Gdns
  ERDW/GRVHL B23.....101 F3 🔲
Pattison St *DSYBK/YTR* WS5.....52 A4
Paul Byrne Ct *BFLD/HDSWWD* B20 ..99 D3
Paul Pursehouse Rd
  BILS/COS WV14.....47 F6 🔲
Paul St *BILS/COS* WV14.....68 C2
  BKHL/PFLD WV2.....45 E1
  DARL/WED WS10.....72 C1
Paul V *TPTN/OCK* DY4.....71 D6
Pavenham Dr *DIG/EDG* B5.....147 E5
Pavilion Av *SMTHWKW* B67.....120 A4
Pavilion Gdns *DUDS* DY2.....115 E5
Pavilion Rd *PBAR/PBCH* B42.....100 B2
Pavillion Cl *ALDR* WS9.....21 D5
Paxford Wy *NFLD/LBR* B31.....166 B5
Paxton Av *DUNHL/THL/PER* WV6.....22 A4
Paxton Rd *HAG/WOL* DY9.....138 C5
  WSNGN B18.....122 C2
Payne St *BLKHTH/ROWR* B65 ..117 E6 🔲
Payton Cl *OLDBY* B69.....94 A4
Payton Rd *HDSW* B21.....97 F5
Peach Av *DARL/WED* WS10.....49 E3
Peachley Cl *HALE* B63.....163 D1 🔲
Peach Ley Rd *SLYOAK* B29.....166 B4
Peach Rd *SHHTH* WV12.....28 C1
Peacock Av *WNSFLD* WV11.....14 C6
Peacock Cl *TPTN/OCK* DY4.....93 D1
Peacock Rd *DARL/WED* WS10.....49 D5
  MOS/BIL B13.....170 B5
Peak Cft *CBROM* B36.....103 F5
Peak Dr *SEDG* DY3.....89 F2
Peake Dr *TPTN/OCK* DY4.....93 D1
Peak House Rd *GTB/HAM* B43.....54 A6
Peakman Cl *RBRY* B45.....200 C1 🔲
Peak Rd *STRBR* DY8.....137 D3 🔲
Peal St *WSL* WS1.....5 E4
Pearce Cl *DUDN* DY1.....90 A5
Pearl Gv *ACGN* B27.....151 D6
Pearman Rd *RBRY* B45.....183 F4
  SMTHWK B66.....120 C4
Pearmans Cft *SHLY* B47.....206 C1
Pearsall Dr *OLDBY* B69.....94 A5
Pearson St *BKHL/PFLD* WV2.....45 E1
  BRLYHL DY5.....113 F4
  CDYHTH B64.....116 A4
  HAG/WOL DY9.....138 B5
  WBROM B70.....95 D1
Pear Tree Av *TPTN/OCK* DY4.....70 B6
Peartree Av *WLNHL* WV13.....29 D6 🔲
Pear Tree Cl *GTB/HAM* B43.....75 D2
  SHLY B90.....191 F3
  STETCH B33.....127 F5 🔲
Pear Tree Crs *SHLY* B90.....191 E2
Pear Tree Dr *GTB/HAM* B43.....75 E2
Peartree Dr *STRBR* DY8.....158 C1
Pear Tree Gv *SHLY* B90.....191 F3
Pear Tree La *BILS/COS* WV14.....69 F3
  WNSFLD WV11.....13 D4
Peartree La *CDYHTH* B64.....116 A6
  DUDS DY2.....114 B2
Pear Tree Rd *BKDE/SHDE* B34 ..129 E1 🔲
  GTB/HAM B43.....75 D2
  SMTHWK B66.....120 A3
Peascroft La *BILS/COS* WV14...48 A3
Peasefield Cl *HDSW* B21.....97 E5 🔲
Pebble Cl *STRBR* DY8.....137 D4
Pebble Mill Rd *DIG/EDG* B5.....147 D5
Pebworth Av *SHLY* B90.....211 D1
Pebworth Cl *SLYOAK* B29.....147 D6 🔲
Pebworth Gv *DUDN* DY1.....90 C2
  STETCH B33.....153 E1
Peckham Rd *KGSTG* B44.....78 C1
Peckover Cl *BLKHTH/ROWR* B65..117 D6
Peddimore La *WALM/CURD* B76...85 F5
Pedmore Court Rd *STRBR* DY8 ..159 D2 🔲
Pedmore Gv *KGSTG* B44.....78 B1
Pedmore Hall La *HAG/WOL* DY9 ..159 E5
Pedmore La *HAG/WOL* DY9.....159 E2
Pedmore Rd *BRLYHL* DY5.....114 B3
  HAG/WOL DY9.....137 F4
Peel Cl *DARL/WED* WS10.....49 F1
  HIA/OLT B92.....179 D3
  WLNHL WV13.....28 C6
Peel St *BDMR/CCFT* WV3.....2 C5
  DUDS DY2.....92 A5
  HHTH/SAND B71.....73 E6
  TPTN/OCK DY4.....92 C1
  WLNHL WV13.....28 C6 🔲

WSNGN B18.....122 A2
Peel Wy *OLDBY* B69.....93 E3
Pegasus Wk *SLYOAK* B29.....167 F2
Peglee Wk *ALE/KHTH/YWD* B14 ..189 E1
Pelham Dr *DUDN* DY1.....90 C3
Pelham Rd *WALM/WDE* B8.....127 D3
Pelham St *BDMR/CCFT* WV3.....24 C6
Pelsall La *BLOX/PEL* WS3.....17 F2
  RUSH/SHEL WS4.....18 C5
Pemberly Rd *ACGN* B27.....172 C2
Pemberton Cl *SMTHWK* B66.....121 D4 🔲
Pemberton Crs *DARL/WED* WS10 ..51 E5
Pemberton Rd *BILS/COS* WV14.....69 F2
  WBROM B70.....72 C5
Pemberton St *WSNGN* B18.....123 D3 🔲
Pembridge Cl *BRLYHL* DY5.....114 B6 🔲
  RIDG/WDGT B32.....164 C4
Pembridge Rd *DOR/KN* B93.....212 A4
Pembroke Av *BKHL/PFLD* WV2.....46 C2
Pembroke Cl *SHHTH* WV12.....29 D1
Pembroke Cft *HLGN/YWD* B28 ..172 C6
Pembroke Gdns *STRBR* DY8.....111 E5 🔲
Pembroke Rd *BHTH/HG* B12.....148 C5
  HHTH/SAND B71.....73 D2
Pembroke Wy *HHTH/SAND* B71.....73 D4
  HLGN/YWD B28.....172 C6
Pembury Cl *FOAKS/STRLY* B74 ..56 B3 🔲
Pembury Cft *KGSTG* B44.....78 C2
Pencombe Dr
  ETTPK/GDPK/PENN WV4.....45 F4
Pencroft Rd *BKDE/SHDE* B34.....105 D6
Penda Gv *DUNHL/THL/PER* WV6...22 B2
Pendeen Rd *ALE/KHTH/YWD* B14 ..191 E1
Pendeford Av
  DUNHL/THL/PER WV6.....10 A5
Pendeford Cl
  DUNHL/THL/PER WV6.....10 A5
Pendeford La *COVEN* WV9.....10 C1
Pendeford Mill La *CDSL* WV8.....9 E2
Pendennis Cl *BVILLE* B30.....167 F6
Pendennis Dr *OLDBY* B69.....92 C5 🔲
Penderel St *BLOX/PEL* WS3.....17 E4
Pendigo Wy *BHAMNEC* B40.....156 A5
Pendinas Dr *CDSL* WV8.....9 D2 🔲
Pendleton Gv *ACGN* B27.....173 D3
Pendragon Rd *PBAR/PBCH* B42 ..99 E1
Pendrell Cl
  CHWD/FDBR/MGN B37.....130 C4 🔲
Pendrill Gv *WOLVN* WV10.....12 B2
Penfields Rd *STRBR* DY8.....136 C3
Penge Gv *KGSTG* B44.....56 A6
Penhallow Dr
  ETTPK/GDPK/PENN WV4.....46 A4 🔲
Penhurst Av *BFLD/HDSWWD* B20...99 F4
Penkridge Cl *WSLW* WS2.....31 F3
Penkridge Gv *STETCH* B33.....128 B3 🔲
Penkridge St *WSLW* WS2.....31 F4
Penk Ri *DUNHL/THL/PER* WV6.....23 D3
Penleigh Gdns *WMBN* WV5.....64 B4
Penley Gv *WASH/WDE* B8.....127 D1
Pennant Gv *SLYOAK* B29.....166 C1
Pennant Rd *BLKHTH/ROWR* B65.....117 D4
  CDYHTH B64.....115 F6
Pennard Gv *RIDG/WDGT* B32.....144 B5
Penn Cl *BLOX/PEL* WS3.....17 E4
Penn Common Rd
  ETTPK/GDPK/PENN WV4.....66 A2
Penncricket La
  BLKHTH/ROWR B65.....118 A4
Penn Croft La
  ETTPK/GDPK/PENN WV4.....66 C2
Pennhouse Av
  ETTPK/GDPK/PENN WV4.....44 B4
Pennine Dr *SEDG* DY3.....89 F2
Pennine Wy *SHHTH* WV12.....29 F3
  STRBR DY8.....136 C3
Pennington Cl *WBROM* B70.....94 C3
Penn La *HOCK/TIA B94.....221 E5
Penn Rd *BKHL/PFLD* WV2.....45 D1
  BLKHTH/ROWR B65.....118 A4
  ETTPK/GDPK/PENN WV4.....44 A5
  SEDG DY3.....66 B2
Penn Road Island *BDMR/CCFT* WV3 ..2 C6
Penns Lake Rd *WALM/CURD* B76...82 A4
Penns La *CSCFLD/WYGN* B72.....81 F4
  CSHL/WTROR B46.....108 B3 🔲
Penn St *BDMR/CCFT* WV3.....45 D1
  CBHAMNE B4.....124 C4
  CDYHTH B64.....140 B1 🔲
Penns Wood Cl *SEDG* DY3.....67 E1
Penns Wood Dr *WALM/CURD* B76...82 B4
Penwood La *ETTPK/GDPK/PENN* WV4 44 B6
Pennyacre Rd
  ALE/KHTH/YWD B14.....189 F3
Pennyfield Cft *STETCH* B33.....128 A2 🔲
Pennyhill La *HHTH/SAND* B71.....74 A4
Pennyroyal Cl *DSYBK/YTR* WS5...52 C6
Penny Royal Cl *SEDG* DY3.....89 F3 🔲
Penrice Dr *DUDS* DY2.....92 B4
Penrith Cl *BRLYHL* DY5.....137 D1 🔲
Penrith Cft *RIDG/WDGT* B32.....165 F3
Penrith Gv
  CHWD/FDBR/MGN B37.....131 E5 🔲
Penryn Cl *DSYBK/YTR* WS5.....53 F2

Penryn Rd *DSYBK/YTR* WS5.....53 F2
Pensby Cl *MOS/BIL* B13.....171 E3
Pensford Rd *NFLD/LBR* B31.....187 D2
Pensham Cft *SHLY* B90.....210 C1 🔲
Penshaw Cl *COVEN* WV9.....10 C2
Penshaw Gv *MOS/BIL* B13.....171 F2 🔲
Pensnett Rd *BRLYHL* DY5.....113 E5
  DUDN DY1.....90 A6
Penstone La
  ETTPK/GDPK/PENN WV4.....42 A5
Pentland Cft *BHTH/HG* B12.....148 B2 🔲
Pentlands Gdns
  DUNHL/THL/PER WV6.....24 A5 🔲
Pentos Dr *SPARK* B11.....149 F5
Pentridge Cl *WALM/CURD* B76...82 B6
Penzer Dr *RBRY* B45.....215 F1
Penzer St *KGSWFD* DY6.....87 F6
Peolsford Rd *BLOX/PEL* WS3.....18 C1
Peplins Wy *BVILLE* B30.....189 D3
Peplow Rd *STETCH* B33.....128 C3
Pepperbox Dr *TPTN/OCK* DY4 ..70 C6 🔲
Pepper HI *STRBR* DY8.....136 C5
Perch Av *CHWD/FDBR/MGN* B37 ..130 C4
Perch Rd *WSLW* WS2.....30 C5 🔲
Percival Rd *LDYWD/EDGR* B16 ..121 E6 🔲
Percy Rd *SPARK* B11.....149 E5
Peregrine Cl *DUDN* DY1.....90 B4
Pereira Rd *HRBN* B17.....145 E2
Perimeter Rd *BHAMNEC* B40.....155 F5
Perivale Gv *BILS/COS* WV14.....69 F3 🔲
Perivale Wy *STRBR* DY8.....136 C1
Perkins Cl *DUDN* DY1.....69 E5
Perks Rd *WNSFLD* WV11.....14 C4
Perott Dr *MGN/WHC* B75.....39 F5
Perrins Gv *WASH/WDE* B8.....126 C1
Perrins La *HAG/WOL* DY9.....138 B5
Perrins Ri *HAG/WOL* DY9.....138 B5
Perrott Gdns *STRBR* DY8.....112 C6 🔲
Perrott St *WSNGN* B18.....121 F5
Perry Av *PBAR/PBCH* B42.....99 E1
Perry Cl *DUDS* DY2.....91 F5
Perry Common Rd
  ERDW/GRVHL B23.....79 D5
Perry Ct *LGLYGN/QTN* B68.....143 D2 🔲
Perryford Dr *SOLH* B91.....195 D5
Perry Hall Dr *SHHTH* WV12.....29 D2
Perry Hall Rd *WNSFLD* WV11.....28 B1
Perry Hill Crs *LGLYGN/QTN* B68 ..143 D2 🔲
Perry Hill La *LGLYGN/QTN* B68.....143 E2
Perry Hill Rd *LGLYGN/QTN* B68 ..143 D2 🔲
Perry Park Crs *PBAR/PBCH* B42.....77 D5
Perry Park Rd *CDYHTH* B64.....117 D6
Perry St *BILS/COS* WV14.....48 A6
  DARL/WED WS10.....49 F1
  DARL/WED WS10.....72 B2
  SMTHWK B66.....96 B6
  TPTN/OCK DY4.....92 C1 🔲
Perry Villa Dr *PBAR/PBCH* B42.....77 F6
Perry Wk *ERDW/GRVHL* B23.....79 D5
Perrywell Rd *AST/WIT* B6.....100 C1
  PBAR/PBCH B42.....100 B1
Perry Wood Rd *PBAR/PBCH* B42 ..76 C3
Persehouse St *WSL* WS1.....5 F3
Pershore Cl *BLOX/PEL* WS3.....16 B3
Pershore Rd *BLOX/PEL* WS3.....16 B3
  BVILLE B30.....168 C5
  DIG/EDG B5.....147 F3
  HALE B63.....162 C1
Pershore Rd South *BVILLE* B30.....188 B2
Pershore St *DIG/EDG* B5.....124 A6
Pershore Wy *BLOX/PEL* WS3.....16 B3
Perth Rd *SHHTH* WV12.....29 D1
Perton Brook V
  DUNHL/THL/PER WV6.....22 B5
Perton Gv *DUNHL/THL/PER* WV6...22 B5
  SLYOAK B29.....166 C2
Perton Rd *DUNHL/THL/PER* WV6...22 B5
Pestilence La *ALVE* B48.....203 E6
  ALVE B48.....217 F1
Peter Av *BILS/COS* WV14.....70 B1
Peterbrook Ri *SHLY* B90.....191 F4
Peterbrook Rd *SHLY* B90.....191 F4
Peterdale Dr
  ETTPK/GDPK/PENN WV4.....44 B6
Peters Av *NFLD/LBR* B31.....186 B3
Petersfield Dr *BLKHTH/ROWR* B65 ..118 A4
Petersfield Rd *HLGN/YWD* B28.....172 A4
Petersham Pl *DIG/EDG* B15.....146 A3
Petersham Rd *KGSTG* B44.....79 E2
Peter's Hill Rd *BRLYHL* DY5.....137 E2 🔲
Petershouse Dr
  FOAKS/STRLY B74.....38 B2 🔲
Peters St *WBROM* B70.....72 C4
Petford St *CDYHTH* B64.....116 A6
Pettitt Cl *ALE/KHTH/YWD* B14.....190 A3
Pettyfield Cl
  LGN/SDN/BHAMAIR B26.....152 C3 🔲
Pettyfields Cl *DOR/KN* B93.....212 A4
Petworth Cl *WLNHL* WV13.....48 B1
Petworth Gv
  LGN/SDN/BHAMAIR B26.....152 A3
Pevensey Cl *DUDS* DY2.....92 B5
Peverell Dr *HLGN/YWD* B28.....172 B4
Peveril Gv *WALM/CURD* B76.....60 A5 🔲
Peverill Rd *DUNHL/THL/PER* WV6...22 B3

ETTPK/GDPK/PENN WV4.............. 46 A6
Pevrill Wy CTB/HAM B43.............. 76 B1
Pheasant Cft CBROM B36 .... 106 C5
Pheasant Rd SMTHWKW B67 ...... 119 F5
Pheasant St BRLYHL DY5 .... 113 E4
Philip Rd HALE B63..................... 140 B6
TPTN/OCK DY4 .... 71 F6
Philip Sidney Rd SPARK B11 ...... 149 D6
Philip St BILS/COS WV14............. 69 F2
Philip Victor Rd
BFLD/HDSWWD B20................. 98 B4
Phillimore Rd WASH/WDE B8 ...... 125 C3
Phillip Rd WSLW WS2 .... 51 E3
Phillips Av WNSFLD WV11 .... 14 A6
Phillips St AST/WIT B6................ 124 A1
Phipson Rd SPARK B11................ 149 D6
Phoenix Gn EDG B15 .... 146 A2
Phoenix Pk BLKHTH/ROWR B65 .. 117 F6
Phoenix Ri DARL/WED WS10........ 49 F5
ERDW/GRVHL B23.................... 79 D4
Phoenix St TPTN/OCK DY4 .... 70 B5 🔢
WLNHL WV13 .... 27 F4
Phoenix St BKHL/PFLD WV2 .... 45 F3
WBROM B70 .... 72 B6
Piccadilly Cl
CHWD/FDBR/MGN B37........... 131 E6
Pickenham Rd
ALE/KHTH/YWD B14 .... 190 C4
Pickering Cft RIDG/WDGT B32 ... 165 E2
Pickering Rd WNSFLD WV11 .... 27 F2
Pickersleigh Cl HALE B63 .... 140 C6 🔢
Pickford St DIG/EDG B5............... 7 H6
Pickrell Rd BILS/COS WV14 .... 69 D2
Pickwick Gv MOS/BIL B13 .... 171 E1
Pickwick Pl BILS/COS WV14 .... 48 A5 🔢
Picton Cft
CHWD/FDBR/MGN B37........... 131 F5 🔢
Picton Gv MOS/BIL B13 .... 171 D6
Picturedrome Wy
DARL/WED WS10 .... 49 F3 🔢
Piddock Rd SMTHWK B66 .... 120 C1
Pierce Av HIA/OLT B92 .... 152 A6
Piercy St WBROM B70 .... 94 C2
Piers Rd WSNGN B18.................. 98 C6
Piggots Cft
CHWD/FDBR/MGN B37........... 130 B4
Pike Cl BFLD/HDSWWD B20 .... 98 B4
Pike Dr CHWD/FDBR/MGN B37 ... 131 E4
Pikehelve St TPTN/OCK DY4 .... 72 A4
WBROM B70 .... 72 A4
Pike Hl BRGRVE B60 .... 214 C2
Pikehorne Cft CBROM B36 .... 105 F3 🔢
Pike Rd WSLW WS2 .... 30 C3
The Pikes RBRY B45 .... 184 B5
Pilkington Av CSCFLD/WYGN B72..... 59 D6
Pilson Cl CBROM B36 .... 104 B5 🔢
Pimbury Rd SHHTH WV12 .... 15 F6
Pimlico Ct SEDG DY3 .... 89 F2
Pimpernel Dr DSYBK/YTR WS5 .... 52 C6
Pinbury Cft
CHWD/FDBR/MGN B37........... 155 D1 🔢
Pinchers Cl HAG/WOL DY9 .... 180 A6
Pineapple Gv BVILLE B30 .... 169 E3 🔢
Pineapple Rd BVILLE B30 .... 169 E4
Pine Av DARL/WED WS10 .... 50 B4
SMTHWK B66 .... 96 A6
Pine Cl BDMR/CCFT WV3 .... 24 C5
KGSWFD DY6 .... 111 F2
SOLH B91 .... 194 B3 🔢
Pine Gn DUDN DY1 .... 68 C6
Pine Gv ALE/KHTH/YWD B14 ...... 170 C6
RBRY B45 .... 200 B5
Pinehurst Dr HWK/WKHTH B38 .. 188 B2
Pine Leigh FOAKS/STRLY B74 ...... 39 D6
Pineneedle Cft SHHTH WV12........ 30 A3
Pine Rd DUDN DY1 .... 69 E6
OLDBY B69 .... 92 C5
The Pines BDMR/CCFT WV3 .... 23 F6
RBRY B45 .... 184 C4
SHLY B90 .... 209 F2
WSL WS1 .... 5 E6
Pine St BLOX/PEL WS3 .... 17 E4
Pinetree Dr FOAKS/STRLY B74..... 35 F6
Pineview NFLD/LBR B31 .... 186 B3
Pine Wk CDSL WV8 .... 8 B3
HAG/WOL DY9 .... 137 F6
NFLD/LBR B31 .... 187 D2
Pinewall Av HWK/WKHTH B38 .... 188 B4
Pineways FOAKS/STRLY B74 .... 37 E4 🔢
STRBR DY8 .... 111 E5
Pineways Dr DUNHL/THL/PER WV6.. 24 A4
The Pineways OLDBY B69 .... 117 E2 🔢
Pinewood Cl BDMR/CCFT WV3 .... 42 C1 🔢
DSYBK/YTR WS5 .... 53 D5 🔢
KGSTG B44 .... 78 A4
RBRY B45 .... 183 F5
SHHTH WV12 .... 15 F6
WMBN WV5 .... 64 C5
Pinewood Gv SOLH B91 .... 194 B3 🔢
Pinewoods NFLD/LBR B31 .... 166 B3 🔢
Pine Woods RIDG/WDGT B32 .... 164 C1 🔢
Pinewoods RMSLY B62 .... 142 C2 🔢
Pinfield Dr RBRY B45 .... 201 D6
Pinfold BLOX/PEL WS3 .... 17 E5

Pinfold Ct DARL/WED WS10 .... 49 E4 🔢
Pinfold Crs
ETTPK/GDPK/PENN WV4 .... 43 F3
Pinfold Gdns WNSFLD WV11 ...... 27 F2
Pinfold Gv ETTPK/GDPK/PENN WV4.. 43 F3
Pinfold La ALDR WS9 .... 55 D2
ETTPK/GDPK/PENN WV4 .... 44 A4
Pinfold Rd SOLH B91 .... 176 A6
Pinfold St BILS/COS WV14 .... 47 F4
CBHAM B2 .... 6 D5
DARL/WED WS10 .... 49 E4
OLDBY B69 .... 94 C5 🔢
Pingle Cl HHTH/SAND B71 .... 74 B2
Pinkney Pl LGLYGN/QTN B68 ..... 119 E4
Pinley Gv CTB/HAM B43.............. 55 D6
Pinley Wy SOLH B91 .... 194 C5
Pinner Gv RIDG/WDGT B32 .... 144 A5 🔢
Pinson Rd WLNHL WV13.............. 28 B6
Pintail Dr ERDW/GRVHL B23 ...... 101 E3
Pinto Cl LDYWD/EDGR B16 .... 122 B5
Pinza Cft CBROM B36 .... 105 F5 🔢
Piper Cl DUNHL/THL/PER WV6 .... 22 B3
Piper Pl STRBR DY8..................... 136 B1
Piper Rd BDMR/CCFT WV3 .... 43 D1
Pipers Gn HLGN/YWD B28 .... 172 B6
Piper's Rw WOLV WV1 .... 3 F4
Pipes Meadow BILS/COS WV14 ... 48 A4 🔢
Pipit Ct BILS/COS WV14 .... 48 A6 🔢
Pirrey Cl BILS/COS WV14 .... 68 A6 🔢
Pitcairn Cl BVILLE B30............... 169 D5
Pitcairn Dr RMSLY B62 .... 141 D3
Pitcairn Rd SMTHWKW B67 ...... 119 F5
Pitclose Rd NFLD/LBR B31......... 187 D4
Pitfield Dr STETCH B33 .... 129 F5
Pitfield Rw DUDN DY1 .... 91 D4 🔢
Pitfields Cl LGLYGN/QTN B68 .... 142 C1
Pitfields Rd LGLYGN/QTN B68 ... 142 C1
Pitfield St DUDN DY1 .... 91 E4 🔢
Pithall Rd BKDE/SHDE B34 .... 129 F2
Pit Leasow Cl BVILLE B30 .... 169 D3
Pitman Rd RIDG/WDGT B32 ...... 143 E4
Pitmaston Rd HLGN/YWD B28 ... 172 C5
Pitsford St WSNGN B18 .... 122 C2
Pitt La HIA/OLT B92 .... 177 F1
Pitts Farm Rd ERDE/BCHGN B24 .. 81 E6
Pitt St VAUX/NECH B7 .... 124 C4 🔢
Pixall Dr EDG B15 .... 147 D2
Pixhall Wk CVALE B35 .... 105 D2 🔢
Plainview Cl FOAKS/STRLY B74 .... 36 A5
Plaistow Av CBROM B36 .... 105 E6
Plane Gv CHWD/FDBR/MGN B37 . 131 D6
Planetary Rd WLNHL WV13 .... 27 D4
Plane Tree Rd DSYBK/YTR WS5 .... 53 D5
Planetree Rd FOAKS/STRLY B74 .. 55 F1
Planet Rd BRLYHL DY5 .... 113 F2
Plank La CSHL/WTROR B46 ...... 106 C3
Planks La WMBN WV5 .... 64 B5
Plantation La SEDG DY3............. 87 D1
Plantation Rd DSYBK/YTR WS5 ... 52 C5 🔢
The Plantation BRLYHL DY5 .... 89 D6
Plants Brook Rd WALM/CURD B76... 82 B5
Plants Cl SCFLD/BOLD B73........... 79 F2
Plants Gv ERDE/BCHGN B24 .... 81 E6 🔢
Plants Hollow BRLYHL DY5 .... 113 F6
Plant St COYHTH B64 .... 115 F6
STRBR DY8 .... 113 A5
Plant Wy BLOX/PEL WS3 .... 18 B1
Plascom Rd WOLV WV1............... 26 C6
Platts Crs STRBR DY8 .... 136 A1
Platts Dr STRBR DY8.................. 136 B1
Platts Rd STRBR DY8 .... 136 A1
Platt St DARL/WED WS10 .... 49 F4
Playdon Gv
ALE/KHTH/YWD B14 .... 190 C2 🔢
Pleasant Cl KGSWFD DY6 .... 111 E3
Pleasant Md ALDR WS9 .... 34 A3
Pleasant St WBROM B70 .... 72 C3
WBROM B70 .... 95 E4
Pleasant Vw SEDG DY3 .... 89 F3
Pleck Rd WSLW WS2 .... 51 E1
Plestowes Cl SHLY B90 .... 173 D6
Plimsoll Gv RIDG/WDGT B32 ..... 143 E4
Plough & Harrow Rd
LDYWD/EDGR B16 .... 122 B6
Plough Av RIDG/WDGT B32 .... 165 E1
Ploughmans Wk KGSWFD DY6 .... 86 C6 🔢
Ploverdale Crs KGSWFD DY6 ...... 88 C6
KGSWFD DY6 .... 112 C1
Plowden Rd STETCH B33 .... 128 B3
Plume St VAUX/NECH B7 .... 101 D6
Plumstead Rd KGSTG B44 .... 78 C3
Plym Cl WNSFLD WV11 .... 27 E2
Plymouth Cl NFLD/LBR B31 ...... 186 C6 🔢
Plymouth Dr RBRY B45 .... 214 C1 🔢
Plymouth Rd BVILLE B30 .... 169 E4
RBRY B45 .... 200 C6
Pointon Cl BILS/COS WV14 .... 68 C1
Polden Cl HALE B63................... 161 E2
Polesworth Gv BKDE/SHDE B34 .. 129 D1 🔢
Pollard Rd ACGN B27 .... 173 E2
The Pollards ERDW/GRVHL B23 ... 80 A3
Polo Flds HAG/WOL DY9 .... 159 D2
Pomeroy Rd CTB/HAM B43.......... 55 F5
RIDG/WDGT B32 .... 165 E2

Pommel Cl DSYBK/YTR WS5 .... 52 B5
Pond Crs BKHL/PFLD WV2 .... 46 A2
Pond Gv BKHL/PFLD WV2 .... 46 A2
Pond La BKHL/PFLD WV2 .... 46 A2 🔢
Poole Crs BILS/COS WV14 .... 69 F1
HRBN B17 .... 145 E6
Poolehouse Rd CTB/HAM B43 ..... 54 A6
Pool End Cl DOR/KN B93 .... 212 B1
Pooles La SHHTH WV12 .... 16 A2
Poole St STRBR DY8 .... 136 A5
Pool Farm Rd ACGN B27 .... 173 E2
Poolfield Dr SOLH B91 .... 194 B2 🔢
Pool Furlong HAG/WOL DY9 ...... 180 A4
Pool Gn ALDR WS9..................... 34 C2
Pool Hall Crs BDMR/CCFT WV3 .... 42 B1
Pool Hall Rd BDMR/CCFT WV3 .... 42 B1
Pool Hayes La SHHTH WV12 .... 28 C2
Poolhead La HOCK/TIA B94 .... 221 D2
Pool La OLDBY B69 .... 118 B3
Pool Meadow WALM/CURD B76 ... 82 C3 🔢
Pool Meadow Cl MOS/BIL B13 .... 171 E2
SOLH B91................................ 196 B4
Pool Rd HALE B63 .... 141 D6
SMTHWK B66 .... 121 D2
WNSFLD WV11 .... 28 C1
Pool St AST/WIT B6 .... 124 B1
BKHL/PFLD WV2 .... 2 C6
BKHL/PFLD WV2 .... 45 E1
DUDN DY1 .... 68 C5
WSL WS1 .... 5 F5
Pool Vw RUSH/SHEL WS4............ 19 F6
Pope Rd WOLVN WV10 .... 12 C5
Popes La HWK/WKHTH B38 .... 187 F2
OLDBY B69 .... 119 D1
Pope St CBHAMW B1 .... 123 D3
SMTHWK B66 .... 97 D6 🔢
Poplar Av ALE/KHTH/YWD B14 ... 170 A3
BHTH/HG B12 .... 148 C3 🔢
CHWD/FDBR/MGN B37........... 155 E1
DSYBK/YTR WS5 .... 52 C5
HRBN B17 .... 121 D5
MGN/WHC B75 .... 60 B2 🔢
OLDBY B69 .... 93 D6
OLDBY B69 .... 118 C2
TPTN/OCK DY4 .... 69 F6
WBROM B70 .... 96 A3
WNSFLD WV11 .... 13 D6
WSLW WS2 .... 29 F3
Poplar Cl OLDBY B69.................. 93 E4
WMBN WV5 .... 65 D5
WSLW WS2 .... 30 A3
Poplar Crs DUDN DY1 .... 91 D2
Poplar Dr AST/WIT B6 .... 78 B6
RBRY B45 .... 215 F1
Poplar Gn DUDN DY1 .... 68 C5
Poplar La RMSLY B62 .... 182 C2
Poplar Ri FOAKS/STRLY B74 .... 37 F2
OLDBY B69 .... 93 E5
Poplar Rd ALE/KHTH/YWD B14 ... 170 A3
BDMR/CCFT WV3 .... 44 A3
BILS/COS WV14 .... 48 B2
DARL/WED WS10 .... 50 C3
DOR/KN B93 .... 212 B4
KGSWFD DY6 .... 112 A2
OLDBY B69 .... 94 C5
SMTHWK B66 .... 120 C6
SOLH B91............................... 195 E1
SPARK B11 .... 149 D4
STRBR DY8 .... 136 A6
Poplars Dr CBROM B36 .... 105 D5
CDSL WV8 .... 8 B3
The Poplars SPARK B11 .... 149 E5 🔢
STRBR DY8 .... 112 B5
Poplar St BKHL/PFLD WV2 .... 45 F3
SMTHWK B66 .... 121 D2
Poplarwoods RIDG/WDGT B32 ... 165 D1
Poppy Dr DSYBK/YTR WS5 .... 52 B6
Poppy Gv WASH/WDE B8 .... 126 B3
Poppy La ERDE/BCHGN B24 .... 81 E6
Poppymead ERDW/GRVHL B23 ... 79 D3
Porchester Cl ALDR WS9 .... 20 C3
Porchester Dr LOZ/NWT B19 ..... 123 F1
Porchester St LOZ/NWT B19 ...... 123 F1
Porlock Crs NFLD/LBR B31 .... 185 F2
Porlock Rd STRBR DY8 .... 136 C3
Portal Rd WSLW WS2 .... 30 B5
Portchester Dr WNSFLD WV11 .... 27 F2 🔢
Porter Cl CSCFLD/WYGN B72 .... 81 D4
Porters Cft HRBN B17 .... 144 C1
Porters Fld DUDS DY2 .... 91 E4
Portershill Dr SHLY B90 .... 193 C5 🔢
Porter St DUDS DY2 .... 91 F4
Porters Wy BORD B9 .... 126 A5
Portfield Gv TPTN/OCK DY4......... 92 C3
Portfield Gv ERDW/GRVHL B23 .... 80 C5
Porthkerry Gv SEDG DY3 .... 67 D4
Port Hope Rd SPARK B11 .... 148 C2
Porthouse Gv BILS/COS WV14 .... 47 D6 🔢
Portia Av SHLY B90 .... 193 D3
Portland Av ALDR WS9 .... 35 D2
Portland Crs HAG/WOL DY9....... 159 D2
Portland Dr HAG/WOL DY9 .... 159 D2
Portland Pl BILS/COS WV14 .... 69 D4
Portland Rd ALDR WS9................ 35 D1
LDYWD/EDGR B16 .... 121 F5

Portland St *AST/WIT* B6 .... 100 C6
  WSLW WS2 .... 4 C1
Portland Ter *WSNGN* B18 .... 122 C2 ⬚
Portman Rd *ALE/KHTH/YWD* B14 .. 170 B4
Portobello Cl *WLNHL* WV13 .... 27 F6 ⬚
Portobello Rd *WBROM* B70 .... 72 B3
Portrush Av *NFLD/LBR* B31 .... 187 C4
Portsdown Cl *WOLVN* WV10 .... 12 B6 ⬚
Portsdown Rd *HAG* B63 .... 161 F2
Portsea St *BLOX/PEL* WS3 .... 31 E1
Portswood Cl *COVEN* WV9 .... 10 E4
Portway Cl *KGSWFD* DY6 .... 112 A2
  SOLH B91 .... 194 A4
Portway HI *OLDBY* B69 .... 117 D1
Portway Rd *BILS/COS* WV14 .... 48 A2
  BLKHTH/ROWR B65 .... 117 D3
  DARL/WED WS10 .... 72 A1
  OLDBY B69 .... 94 B6
The Portway *KGSWFD* DY6 .... 112 A2
Posey La *HDSW* B21 .... 97 C2
Poston Cft *ALE/KHTH/YWD* B14 .... 189 F1 ⬚
Potter Cl *ERDW/GRVHL* B23 .... 79 F3
Potters La *AST/WIT* B6 .... 100 A6 ⬚
  DARL/WED WS10 .... 72 A1
Potterton Wy *WBROM* B66 .... 96 B5
Pottery Rd *LGLYGN/QTN* B68 .... 119 E6
  SMTHWK B66 .... 96 C6
Pouk Hill Cl *WSLW* WS2 .... 30 C4
Poultney St *WBROM* B70 .... 72 B4
Poulton Cl *MOS/BIL* B13 .... 170 C1 ⬚
Pound Cl *LGLYGN/QTN* B68 .... 118 B4 ⬚
Pound La *CSHL/WTROR* B46 .... 132 C3
  RIDG/WDGT B32 .... 184 B2
Poundley Cl *CBROM* B36 .... 105 E5
Pound Rd *ALE/KHTH/YWD* B14 .... 190 A3
  DARL/WED WS10 .... 50 C6
  LGLYGN/QTN B68 .... 118 C5
  OLDBY B69 .... 118 B4 ⬚
Pountney St *WBROM* B70 .... 72 A4
Powell Av *RIDG/WDGT* B32 .... 142 C3 ⬚
Powell Pl *BILS/COS* WV14 .... 48 A6 ⬚
  TPTN/OCK DY4 .... 71 E6
Powell St *CBHAMW* B1 .... 123 D4
  HALE B63 .... 141 D6 ⬚
  WOLVN WV10 .... 26 B3
Power Crs *LDYWD/EDGR* B16 .... 122 C6 ⬚
Powick Rd *ERDW/GRVHL* B23 ..... 101 F4
Powis Av *TPTN/OCK* DY4 .... 71 D4
Powke La *BLKHTH/ROWR* B65 .... 116 C5
  CDYHTH B64 .... 116 B4
Powlers Cft *HAG/WOL* DY9 .... 160 A1 ⬚
Powlett St *BKHL/PFLD* WV2 .... 3 E6
Poxon Rd *ALDR* WS9 .... 20 C2
The Poynings
  DUNHL/THL/PER WV6 .... 23 E2 ⬚
Premier Av *BVILLE* B30 .... 189 E2
Premier St *VAUX/NECH* B7 .... 101 F5
Premier Wy *SCFLD/BOLD* B73 .... 79 F1
Prescot Rd *HAG/WOL* DY9 .... 137 E5
Prestbury Rd *AST/WIT* B6 .... 100 A5
Presthope Rd *SLYOAK* B29 .... 167 D4
Preston Rd
  LGN/SDN/BHAMAIR B26 .... 151 F3
  WSNGN B18 .... 122 A1
Prestons Rw
  ETTPK/GDPK/PENN WV4 .... 46 C6 ⬚
Prestwick Cl *MGN/WHC* B75 ..... 59 E4
Prestwick Rd *CVALE* B35 .... 105 D1
  KGSWFD DY6 .... 111 E1
Prestwood Av *WNSFLD* WV11 .... 13 F5
Prestwood Dr *KINVER* DY7 .... 134 B6
Prestwood Rd *KINVER* DY7 .... 134 A3
  SLYOAK B29 .... 167 D3
  WNSFLD WV11 .... 26 C2
Prestwood Rd West *WNSFLD* WV11.. 27 D1
Pretoria Rd *BORD* B9 .... 126 A4
Price Crs *BILS/COS* WV14 .... 47 F2
Price Rd *DARL/WED* WS10 .... 51 E6
  HAG/WOL DY9 .... 138 C3
Prices Rd *SEDG* DY3 .... 89 E2 ⬚
Price St *BILS/COS* WV14 .... 48 B4
  CBHAMNE B4 .... 7 E2
  DUDS DY2 .... 92 A5
  SMTHWK B66 .... 121 D2
  WBROM B70 .... 95 E2
Priestfield Cl *KGSTG* B44 .... 77 F1 ⬚
Priestfield St *BILS/COS* WV14 .... 47 D3 ⬚
Priestland Rd *BKDE/SHDE* B34 .. 105 D6
Priestley Cl *BFLD/HDSWWD* B20 .. 98 C4
  HALE B63 .... 139 D3
Priestley Rd *SPARK* B11 .... 148 C2
  WSLW WS2 .... 31 E3
Priest St *CDYHTH* B64 .... 116 B6
Primley Av *CBROM* B36 .... 103 F6
  WSLW WS2 .... 31 D6
Primley Cl *WSLW* WS2 .... 31 D5
Primrose Av *SPARK* B11 .... 149 E3 ⬚
  TPTN/OCK DY4 .... 71 E3
  WOLVN WV10 .... 11 F2
Primrose Bank
  LGLYGN/QTN B68 .... 119 D3 ⬚
Primrose Cl *CDYHTH* B64 .... 139 D1
Primrose Crs *DUDN* DY1 .... 91 E1 ⬚
Primrose Cft *HLGN/YWD* B28 .... 172 B6

Primrose Gdns *CDSL* WV8 .... 8 C2
  HWK/WKHTH B38 .... 188 B5 ⬚
Primrose HI *HWK/WKHTH* B38 ... 188 C5
  SMTHWK B67 .... 119 F3
  STRBR DY8 .... 112 A5
Primrose La *HLGN/YWD* B28 ..... 172 B6
  WOLVN WV10 .... 12 B5
Primrose Pk *DUDS* DY2 .... 89 E6
Primrose Woods *RIDG/WDGT* B32 .. 165 D1
Primsland Cl *SOLH* B91 .... 195 E6
Prince Albert St *BORD* B9 .... 125 F6
Prince Andrew Crs *RBRY* B45 ... 184 A3 ⬚
Prince Charles Cl *RBRY* B45 ..... 184 A3 ⬚
Prince Charles Rd
  BILS/COS WV14 .... 48 B6 ⬚
Prince Edward Dr *RBRY* B45 ..... 184 A3 ⬚
Prince George Rd *DARL/WED* WS10.. 50 C4
Prince of Wales La *SHLY* B90 .... 191 E3
Princep Cl *GTB/HAM* B43 .... 55 F5 ⬚
Prince Philip Cl *RBRY* B45 .... 184 A3
Prince Rd *BVILLE* B30 .... 188 B2
Princes Av *WSL* WS1 .... 5 H6
  WSL WS1 .... 5 H3
Princes Dr *CDSL* WV8 .... 8 C2
Princes Gdns *CDSL* WV8 .... 8 B2
Princes Ga *SOLH* B91 .... 195 D1
Prince's Rd *OLDBY* B69 .... 92 C3
Princess Alice Dr *SCFLD/BOLD* B73 .. 79 F1
Princess Aly *WOLV* WV1 .... 3 E4
Princess Anne Rd *BILS/COS* WV14 .. 48 B6
  WSLW WS2 .... 30 A2
Princess Crs *HALE* B63 .... 140 A3
Princess Gv *HHTH/SAND* B71 ... 73 F3
Princess Rd *DIG/EDG* B5 .... 148 A3
  LGLYGN/QTN B68 .... 119 D1
Princess Sq *BILS/COS* WV14 .... 48 B6 ⬚
Princess St *WOLV* WV1 .... 3 E4
Prince's St *CBHAMNE* B4 .... 7 H3
Princess Wy *DARL/WED* WS10 .. 49 E1
Prince St *ALDR* WS9 .... 20 B3
  CDYHTH B64 .... 115 F6
  DUDS DY2 .... 115 E1
  WSLW WS2 .... 51 E1
Prince's Wy *SOLH* B91 .... 195 D2
Princethorpe Cl
  BKDE/SHDE B34 .... 105 F6 ⬚
  SHLY B90 .... 192 C5 ⬚
Princethorpe Rd *SLYOAK* B29 .. 167 D2
Princeton Gdns *COVEN* WV9 .... 10 B3 ⬚
Prince William Cl
  ERDW/GRVHL B23 .... 101 F3 ⬚
Princip Cl *CBHAMNE* B4 .... 7 E2
Princip St *CBHAMNE* B4 .... 7 E2
Printing House St *CBHAMNE* B4 .. 7 E5
Priors MI *SEDG* DY3 .... 68 A5
Priors Wy *ERDW/GRVHL* B23 .... 79 E3
Priory Av *SLYOAK* B29 .... 169 D1
Priory Cl *CSHL/WTROR* B46 ..... 132 C2 ⬚
  DUDN DY1 .... 91 D3
  WBROM B70 .... 96 B3
Priory Dr *LGLYGN/QTN* B68 ..... 119 E2
Priory Field Cl *BILS/COS* WV14 .. 68 B2
Priory La *SEDG* DY3 .... 67 F4
Priory Rd *ALE/KHTH/YWD* B14 .. 169 E4
  ALE/KHTH/YWD B14 .... 191 F1
  AST/WIT B6 .... 101 D5
  DUDN DY1 .... 91 E3
  EDG B15 .... 147 D3
  RMSLY B62 .... 142 A5
  SHLY B90 .... 192 A2
  STRBR DY8 .... 137 D6
Priory St *DUDN* DY1 .... 91 E4 ⬚
The Priory *SEDG* DY3 .... 67 F3
Priory Wk *CSCFLD/WYGN* B72 ... 81 E4
Pritchard Av *WNSFLD* WV11 ..... 28 A1
Pritchard Cl *SMTHWK* B66 ..... 121 D2 ⬚
Pritchard St *BRLYHL* DY5 .... 113 D4
  DARL/WED WS10 .... 50 B6
Pritchatts Rd *EDG* B15 .... 146 B4
Pritchett Av
  ETTPK/GDPK/PENN WV4 ...... 46 B6
Pritchett Rd *NFLD/LBR* B31 ..... 187 D6
Pritchett St *AST/WIT* B6 .... 124 A2
Private Wy *RBRY* B45 .... 201 E3
Privet Cl *KGSTG* B44 .... 56 A6
Probert Rd *WOLVN* WV10 .... 11 D4
Proctor St *VAUX/NECH* B7 .... 124 C2
Proffitt Cl *WSLW* WS2 .... 32 A3
Proffitt St *WSLW* WS2 .... 32 A3
Prole St *WOLVN* WV10 .... 26 A3
The Promenade *BRLYHL* DY5 ... 113 F5
Prospect Gdns *STRBR* DY8 .... 136 C5 ⬚
Prospect HI *STRBR* DY8 .... 136 C5
Prospect La *SOLH* B91 .... 173 F6
Prospect Rd *MOS/BIL* B13 .... 170 B2
  RMSLY B62 .... 141 E4
  SEDG DY3 .... 89 D3
Prospect Rw *DUDS* DY2 .... 91 F6
  STRBR DY8 .... 136 C6 ⬚
Prospect St *BILS/COS* WV14 .... 48 A3
  TPTN/OCK DY4 .... 71 E3
Prosper Meadow *KGSWFD* DY6 .. 88 A6
Prospero Cl *RBRY* B45 .... 184 C3
Prosser St *BILS/COS* WV14 ..... 47 F4
  WOLVN WV10 .... 26 A2

Prossers Wk *CSHL/WTROR* B46.. 108 B6
Proud's La *BILS/COS* WV14 ...... 47 F1
Provence Cl *WOLVN* WV10 .... 26 B3
Providence Cl *BLOX/PEL* WS3 .. 17 E6
Providence Dr *HAG/WOL* DY9 .. 138 A3 ⬚
Providence La *BLOX/PEL* WS3 .. 17 E6
Providence Rw *BILS/COS* WV14 .. 69 D3
Providence St *CDYHTH* B64 ..... 115 F6
  HAG/WOL DY9 .... 138 A3
  TPTN/OCK DY4 .... 71 E6
Pruden Av
  ETTPK/GDPK/PENN WV4 ...... 46 B6
Pryor Rd *LGLYGN/QTN* B68 ..... 119 E4
Pudsey Dr *MGN/WHC* B75 .... 39 E4
Pugh Crs *WSLW* WS2 .... 30 A5
Pugh Rd *AST/WIT* B6 .... 100 C6
  BILS/COS WV14 .... 48 A6
  BILS/COS WV14 .... 68 A3
Pugin Gdns *ERDW/GRVHL* B23 .. 79 F3
Pumphouse La *BRGRVE* B60 ... 214 B1 ⬚
Pump St *BKHL/PFLD* WV2 .... 46 A2
Puppy Gn *TPTN/OCK* DY4 .... 70 C6
Purbeck Cl *HALE* B63 .... 161 F2
Purbeck Cft *RIDG/WDGT* B32 .. 144 B4 ⬚
Purbrook Rd *WOLV* WV1 .... 46 C1
Purcell Rd *WOLVN* WV10 .... 11 F5
Purdy Rd *BILS/COS* WV14 .... 70 A2
Purefoy Rd *MOS/BIL* B13 .... 171 E6
Purley Gv *ERDW/GRVHL* B23 ... 78 C6
Purnells Wy *DOR/KN* B93 .... 212 C2
Purslet Rd *WOLV* WV1 .... 26 C5
Purslow Gv *NFLD/LBR* B31 ..... 186 C4
Putney Av *BFLD/HDSWWD* B20 .. 99 E4
Putney La *RMSLY* B62 .... 183 D3
Putney Rd *BFLD/HDSWWD* B20 .. 99 E4
Pype Hayes Rd *ERDE/BCHGN* B24 .. 103 F1
Pytman Dr *WALM/CURD* B76 ... 82 C4

The Quadrant *SEDG* DY3 .... 67 F2
Quadrille Lawns *COVEN* WV9 ... 10 B3 ⬚
Quail Gn *DUNHL/THL/PER* WV6 .. 22 B5
Qualcast Rd *WOLVN* WV10 ...... 26 B5
Quantock Cl *HALE* B63 .... 161 F1
  RBRY B45 .... 185 D3
Quantock Rd *STRBR* DY8 .... 137 D3
Quantry La *HAG/WOL* DY9 ...... 182 A6
Quarrington Gv
  ALE/KHTH/YWD B14 .... 190 C2 ⬚
Quarry Brow *SEDG* DY3 .... 68 A6
Quarry HI *HALE* B63 .... 162 B1 ⬚
Quarry House Cl *RBRY* B45 ..... 184 A4
Quarry La *HALE* B63 .... 162 B1
  NFLD/LBR B31 .... 186 B2
  RMSLY B62 .... 162 B1
Quarry Park Rd *STRBR* DY8 .... 158 C3
Quarry Ri *OLDBY* B69 .... 93 D5
Quarry Rd *DUDS* DY2 .... 115 D5
  SLYOAK B29 .... 166 B2
Quarry Wk *RBRY* B45 .... 184 C6
Quayle Gv *STRBR* DY8 .... 111 F4 ⬚
Quayside *OLDBY* B69 .... 94 A5 ⬚
Queen Eleanors Dr *DOR/KN* B93.. 197 D3
Queen Elizabeth Av *WSLW* WS2 .. 30 B5
Queen Elizabeth Rd *RBRY* B45 .. 184 A3
Queen Mary St *WSL* WS1 .... 51 F3
Queen's Av *OLDBY* B69 .... 93 D4
  SHLY B90 .... 193 D5
Queensbridge Rd *MOS/BIL* B13 .. 169 F1
Queens Cl *ERDE/BCHGN* B24 .. 102 B3
  SMTHWK B67 .... 120 C2
Queens Crs *BILS/COS* WV14 .... 68 C2
  STRBR DY8 .... 136 C2 ⬚
Queen's Cross *DUDS* DY2 .... 91 D5
Queens Dr *BLKHTH/ROWR* B65 .. 117 E5
  BVILLE B30 .... 188 C1
Queens Gdns *BILS/COS* WV14 .. 47 F2
  CDSL WV8 .... 8 B2
  DUDS DY2 .... 115 E3 ⬚
Queens Head Rd *HDSW* B21 .... 98 A6
Queen's Lea *SHHTH* WV12 ...... 29 E2
Queen's Park Rd *HRBN* B17 .... 144 B3
Queen Sq *WOLV* WV1 .... 2 D4
Queen's Ride *MOS/BIL* B13 ...... 147 E5
Queens Rd *AST/WIT* B6 .... 100 C5
  DSYBK/YTR WS5 .... 53 D3
  ERDW/GRVHL B23 .... 101 E2
  LGLYGN/QTN B68 .... 119 F2
  LGN/SDN/BHAMAIR B26 .... 128 B6
  RUSH/SHEL WS4 .... 19 E6
  SEDG DY3 .... 68 A3
  SMTHWK B67 .... 119 F3
  STRBR DY8 .... 136 B3 ⬚
  TPTN/OCK DY4 .... 70 B6
Queen St *ALDR* WS9 .... 20 B3
  BHTH/HG B12 .... 149 D4
  BILS/COS WV14 .... 48 A4
  BRLYHL DY5 .... 89 F6 ⬚
  BRLYHL DY5 .... 113 F1 ⬚
  BRLYHL DY5 .... 138 C1 ⬚
  CDYHTH B64 .... 115 F6 ⬚
  CSCFLD/WYGN B72 .... 59 D5

R

Red Lion St *ALVE* B48 .... 217 D3
  WOLV WV1 .... 2 C3
Redmead Cl *NFLD/LBR* B31 .... 187 E1
Redmoor Cft
  ETTPK/GDPK/PENN WV4 .... 44 C4
Redmoor Wy *WALM/CURD* B76 ...... 83 F5
Rednall Dr *MGN/WHC* B75 .... 39 E4
Rednall Mill Dr *RBRY* B45 .... 185 E6
Rednal Rd *HWK/WKHTH* B38 ..... 187 E5
Redpine Crest *SHHTH* WV12 .... 29 F3
Red River Rd *WSLW* WS2 .... 30 C2
Red Rock Dr *CDSL* WV8 .... 8 B3
Redruth Cl *DSYBK/YTR* WS5 .... 53 F2
  KGSWFD DY6 .... 87 F5
Redruth Rd *DSYBK/YTR* WS5 .... 53 F2
Redstone Dr *WNSFLD* WV11 .... 28 B2
Redstone Farm Rd
  HLGN/YWD B28 .... 173 D5
Redthorn Gv *STETCH* B33 .... 127 F4
Redvers Rd *BORD* B9 .... 126 A6
Redwing Gv *ERDW/GRVHL* B23 .. 79 D3
Redwood Av *DUDN* DY1 .... 68 B6
Redwood Cl *BVILLE* B30 .... 188 A1
  FOAKS/STRLY B74 .... 36 B5
Redwood Cft
  ALE/KHTH/YWD B14 .... 170 A4
Redwood Dr *OLDBY* B69 .... 93 D3
Redwood Gdns *ACGN* B27 .... 151 D4
Redwood Rd *BILS/COS* WV14 ...... 69 F1
  BVILLE B30 .... 188 A1
  DSYBK/YTR WS5 .... 53 D5
Redwood Wy *WNSFLD* WV11 ...... 15 D5
Reedham Gdns
  ETTPK/GDPK/PENN WV4 .... 43 E3
Reedly Rd *SHHTH* WV12 .... 15 E4
Reedmace Cl *HWK/WKHTH* B38 . 188 B5
Reedswood Cl *WSLW* WS2 .... 31 E4
Reedswood Gdns *WSLW* WS2 .... 31 E4
  WSLW WS2 .... 31 E4
Reedswood La *WSLW* WS2 .... 31 E4
Reedswood Wy *WSLW* WS2 .... 31 E3
Rees Dr *WMBN* WV5 .... 65 D4
Reeves Gdns *CDSL* WV8 .... 8 C1
Reeves Rd *ALE/KHTH/YWD* B14 . 169 E5
Reeves St *BLOX/PEL* WS3 .... 17 D5
Reform St *HHTH/SAND* B71 .... 95 F2
  WBROM B70 .... 95 F2
Regal Cft *CBHAMW* B1 .... 6 A2
Regal Dr *WSLW* WS2 .... 51 E1
Regan Av *SHLY* B90 .... 192 C4
Regan Crs *ERDW/GRVHL* B23 ...... 80 A5
Regency Dr *HWK/WKHTH* B38 .... 188 A3
Regency Gdns
  ALE/KHTH/YWD B14 .... 191 E2
Regency Wk *FOAKS/STRLY* B74 .... 37 F2
Regent Av *OLDBY* B69 .... 92 C4
Regent Cl *DIG/EDG* B5 .... 147 F3
  HALE B63 .... 140 C5
  KGSWFD DY6 .... 111 E1
  OLDBY B69 .... 92 C5
Regent Dr *OLDBY* B69 .... 92 C4
Regent Pde *CBHAMW* B1 .... 6 A2
Regent Park Rd *SMTHWK* B10 .... 149 E1
Regent Pl *CBHAMW* B1 .... 6 A2
  OLDBY B69 .... 93 D3
Regent Rd
  ETTPK/GDPK/PENN WV4 .... 44 A4
  HDSW B21 .... 97 F5
  HRBN B17 .... 145 E3
  OLDBY B69 .... 92 C4
Regent St *BILS/COS* WV14 .... 47 F3
  BVILLE B30 .... 168 C4
  CBHAMW B1 .... 6 A2
  CDYHTH B64 .... 116 B5
  DUDN DY1 .... 69 E5
  SMTHWK B66 .... 120 C1
  TPTN/OCK DY4 .... 70 A3
  WLNH WV13 .... 28 C4
Regina Av *KGSTG* B44 .... 77 F3
Regina Cl *RBRY* B45 .... 184 A4
Regina Crs *DUNHL/THL/PER* WV6 ... 23 D3
Regina Dr *PBAR/PBCH* B42 .... 99 F2
  RUSH/SHEL WS4 .... 32 C3
Reginald Rd *SMTHWKW* B67 ... 120 B5
  WASH/WDE B8 .... 125 F3
Regis Gdns *BLKHTH/ROWR* B65 . 117 E6
Regis Heath Rd
  BLKHTH/ROWR B65 .... 117 F5
Regis Rd *BLKHTH/ROWR* B65 .... 117 E5
  DUNHL/THL/PER WV6 .... 23 D2
Reid Av *SHHTH* WV12 .... 29 F1
Reid Rd *LGLYGN/QTN* B68 .... 119 D3
Reigate Av *WASH/WDE* B8 .... 127 E3
Reiko Dr *CBROM* B36 .... 103 E6
Remembrance Rd
  DARL/WED WS10 .... 51 E6
Remington Pl *WSLW* WS2 .... 31 E2
Remington Rd *WSLW* WS2 .... 31 D1
Renfrew Cl *STRBR* DY8 .... 111 E4
Renfrew Sq *CVALE* B35 .... 105 D1
Rennie Gv *RIDG/WDGT* B32 ...... 143 F4
Renown Cl *BRLYHL* DY5 .... 89 D6
Renton Gv *WOLVN* WV10 .... 10 C4

Renton Rd *WOLVN* WV10 .... 10 C4
Repington Wy *SLYOAK/WHC* B75 . 61 D3
  MGN/WHC B75 .... 61 D4
Repton Gv *BORD* B9 .... 127 D4
Repton Rd *BORD* B9 .... 127 D4
Reservoir Cl *WSLW* WS2 .... 51 D1
Reservoir Pas *DARL/WED* WS10 ... 50 B6
Reservoir Pl *WSLW* WS2 .... 51 D1
Reservoir Retreat
  LDYWD/EDGR B16 .... 122 B6
Reservoir Rd *BLKHTH/ROWR* B65 . 117 F4
  ERDW/GRVHL B23 .... 101 F1
  HIA/OLT B92 .... 174 B3
  LDYWD/EDGR B16 .... 122 B5
  LGLYGN/QTN B68 .... 119 E3
  RBRY B45 .... 201 E4
  SLYOAK B29 .... 143 D2
Reservoir St *WSLW* WS2 .... 51 D1
Retallack Cl *SMTHWK* B66 .... 97 D5
Retford Dr *WALM/CURD* B76 .... 60 A5
Retford Gv *YDLY* B25 .... 151 E3
Retreat Gdns *SEDG* DY3 .... 68 A4
Retreat St *BDMR/CCFT* WV3 .... 45 D1
The Retreat *CDYHTH* B64 .... 140 A2
Revival St *BLOX/PEL* WS3 .... 17 D4
Reynards Cft *SEDG* DY3 .... 68 C4
Reynolds Cl *SEDG* DY3 .... 86 A3
Reynolds Gv *DUNHL/THL/PER* WV6 . 22 B2
Reynolds Rd *HDSW* B21 .... 98 A6
Reynoldstown Rd *CBROM* B36 ... 103 E5
Reynolds Wk *WNSFLD* WV11 ...... 14 C5
Rhayader Rd *NFLD/LBR* B31 ...... 166 A6
Rhodes Cl *SEDG* DY3 .... 88 C1
Rhone Cl *SPARK* B11 .... 149 E6
Rhoose Cft *CVALE* B35 .... 105 D2
Rhys Thomas Cl *SHMTH* WV12 .. 29 F3
Ribbesford Av *WOLVN* WV10 ...... 11 D5
Ribbesford Cl *HALE* B63 .... 139 F4
Ribbesford Crs *BILS/COS* WV14 .. 69 F2
Ribblesdale Rd *BVILLE* B30 .... 168 C4
Richard Pl *DSYBK/YTR* WS5 .... 53 E1
Richard Rd *TPTN/OCK* DY4 .... 70 B2
Richards Cl *NFLD/LBR* B31 .... 202 B1
  OLDBY B69 .... 118 A3
Richardson Dr *STRBR* DY8 .... 136 A1
Richards Rd *TPTN/OCK* DY4 .... 70 B2
Richards St *DARL/WED* WS10 ...... 49 F1
Richard St *VAUX/NECH* B7 .... 124 B2
  WBROM B70 .... 95 D2
Richard St South *WBROM* B70 .... 95 E3
Richard St West *WBROM* B70 .... 95 D3
Richard Williams Rd
  DARL/WED WS10 .... 73 D1
Richborough Dr *DUDN* DY1 .... 90 A2
Riches St *DUNHL/THL/PER* WV6 . 36 A5
Richford Gv *STETCH* B33 .... 129 F5
Richmond Aston Dr
  TPTN/OCK DY4 .... 70 C6
Richmond Av *BDMR/CCFT* WV3 .. 24 B6
Richmond Cl *BFLD/HDSWWD* B20 . 98 C3
Richmond Cft *PBAR/PBCH* B42 .. 76 B5
Richmond Dr *BDMR/CCFT* WV3 .. 24 A6
  DUNHL/THL/PER WV6 .... 22 B4
Richmond Gdns *WMBN* WV5 ...... 64 C6
Richmond Gv *STRBR* DY8 .... 135 D3
Richmond Hl *LGLYGN/QTN* B68 . 119 E2
Richmond Hill Gdns *EDG* B15 ... 146 A3
Richmond Hill Rd *EDG* B15 ...... 146 A3
Richmond Pk *KGSWFD* DY6 .... 87 E5
Richmond Pl
  ALE/KHTH/YWD B14 .... 170 B3
Richmond Rd *HALE* B63 .... 140 C5
  WBROM B70 .... 72 A6
  WSL WS1 .... 5 F5
Richmond St South *WBROM* B70 . 72 A6
Richmond Wy
  CHWD/FDBR/MGN B37 .... 131 E4
Rickard Cl *DOR/KN* B93 .... 212 A2
Rickman Dr *EDG* B15 .... 147 F1
Rickyard Cl *SLYOAK* B29 .... 166 C5
  YDLY B25 .... 127 F6
Rickyard Piece *RIDG/WDGT* B32 . 144 A5
Riddfield Rd *CBROM* B36 .... 104 A5
Ridding La *DARL/WED* WS10 ...... 72 B1
Riddings Crs *BLOX/PEL* WS3 .... 18 B1
The Riddings *HAG/WOL* DY9 .... 159 F1
  STETCH B33 .... 128 A3
  WALM/CURD B76 .... 83 D3
  WOLVN WV10 .... 11 F4
Ridgacre La *RIDG/WDGT* B32 ... 143 E4
Ridgacre Rd *HHTH/SAND* B71 .... 73 D5
  RIDG/WDGT B32 .... 143 D3
Ridgacre Rd West
  RIDG/WDGT B32 .... 142 C3
Ridge Cl *MOS/BIL* B13 .... 171 E5

  WSLW WS2 .... 29 F4
Ridgefield Rd *RMSLY* B62 .... 141 E1
Ridge Gv *HAG/WOL* DY9 .... 137 E4
Ridge La *WNSFLD* WV11 .... 13 F6
Ridgemount Dr *HWK/WKHTH* B38 . 187 F6
Ridge Rd *KGSWFD* DY6 .... 111 E2
Ridge St *STRBR* DY8 .... 135 E3
Ridgewater Cl *RBRY* B45 .... 201 D1
Ridge Wy *ALDR* WS9 .... 35 D3
Ridgeway *HRBN* B17 .... 121 D5
  SEDG DY3 .... 67 F4
Ridgeway Av *RMSLY* B62 .... 142 C3
Ridgeway Ct *WSLW* WS2 .... 30 B6
Ridgeway Dr
  ETTPK/GDPK/PENN WV4 .... 44 B6
Ridgeway Rd *STRBR* DY8 .... 112 B5
  TPTN/OCK DY4 .... 70 C3
The Ridgeway *ERDW/GRVHL* B23 . 78 C5
Ridgewood *BKDE/SHDE* B34 ... 129 D1
Ridgewood Av *STRBR* DY8 .... 135 E3
Ridgewood Cl *WSL* WS1 .... 5 E6
Ridgewood Dr *MGN/WHC* B75 .... 39 D6
Ridgewood Gdns *KGSTG* B44 .... 78 B4
Ridgmont Cft *RIDG/WDGT* B32 . 144 A4
Riding Cl *HHTH/SAND* B71 .... 74 B4
Riding Wy *SHHTH* WV12 .... 29 F1
Ridley St *CBHAMW* B1 .... 125 E6
Ridpool Rd *STETCH* B33 .... 129 E2
Rifle St *BILS/COS* WV14 .... 68 C3
Rigby St *DARL/WED* WS10 .... 72 B2
Riland Rd *MGN/WHC* B75 .... 59 F4
Riley Crs *BDMR/CCFT* WV3 .... 44 B3
Riley Dr *CBROM* B36 .... 106 C4
Riley Rd *ALE/KHTH/YWD* B14 ... 191 F2
Riley St *WLNH* WV13 .... 29 D5
Rilstone Rd *RIDG/WDGT* B32 ... 144 B4
Rindleford Av
  ETTPK/GDPK/PENN WV4 .... 43 E3
Ringhills Rd *CDSL* WV8 .... 9 D3
Ringinglow Rd *KGSTG* B44 .... 77 E1
Ringmere Av *CBROM* B36 .... 105 D5
Ring Road St Andrews *WOLV* WV1 . 2 B4
Ring Road St Davids *WOLV* WV1 ... 3 F3
Ring Road St Georges
  BKHL/PFLD WV2 .... 3 E6
Ring Road St Johns *BKHL/PFLD* WV2 . 2 C6
Ring Road St Marks
  BDMR/CCFT WV3 .... 2 B5
Ring Road St Patricks *WOLV* WV1 . 3 E2
Ring Road St Peters *WOLV* WV1 ... 2 C5
Ringswood Rd *HIA/OLT* B92 ...... 152 B1
The Ring *YDLY* B25 .... 151 E1
Ringwood Av *ALDR* WS9 .... 35 D2
Ringwood Dr *RBRY* B45 .... 184 C4
Ringwood Rd *WOLVN* WV10 ...... 11 F4
Ripley Cl *DUDS* DY2 .... 92 B5
Ripley Gv *ERDW/GRVHL* B23 ...... 79 D6
Ripon Dr *HHTH/SAND* B71 .... 73 F2
Ripon Rd *ALE/KHTH/YWD* B14 .. 191 E1
  WOLVN WV10 .... 11 E6
  WSLW WS2 .... 31 E5
Rippingille Rd *GTB/HAM* B43 ...... 55 E5
Ripple Rd *BVILLE* B30 .... 169 D4
Rischale Wy *RUSH/SHEL* WS4 ...... 19 E5
Rise Av *RBRY* B45 .... 184 C6
Riseley Crs *DIG/EDG* B5 .... 147 F3
The Rise *ALVE* B48 .... 203 D3
  CHWD/FDBR/MGN B37 .... 154 C2
  KGSWFD DY6 .... 112 A2
  PBAR/PBCH B42 .... 76 C3
Rising Brook
  DUNHL/THL/PER WV6 .... 23 D3
Rissington Av *SLYOAK* B29 .... 168 C3
Ritchie Cl *MOS/BIL* B13 .... 170 C2
Rivendell Gdns
  DUNHL/THL/PER WV6 .... 23 D2
Riverbank Rd *WLNH* WV13 .... 29 F5
River Brook Dr *BVILLE* B30 .... 169 D4
River Lee Rd *SPARK* B11 .... 150 A4
Rivermead Pk *BKDE/SHDE* B34 . 128 C2
Riversdale
  ALE/KHTH/YWD B14 .... 191 F2
Riverside Crt *HWK/WKHTH* B38 . 187 F2
Riverside Crs *HLGN/YWD* B28 ... 191 F1
Riverside Dr *SOLH* B91 .... 196 A3
Riversleigh Dr *STRBR* DY8 .... 136 A1
River St *DIG/EDG* B5 .... 124 C5
Riverway *DARL/WED* WS10 .... 73 D1
Rivington Cl *STRBR* DY8 .... 136 A5
Rivington Crs *KGSTG* B44 .... 79 E2
Roach *BRLYHL* DY5 .... 113 F2
  CHWD/FDBR/MGN B37 .... 131 E4
Roach Crs *WNSFLD* WV11 .... 14 B5
Roach Pool Cft *LDYWD/EDGR* B16 . 121 E5
Road Eastwood *DUDS* DY2 ...... 116 A1
Robert Av *ERDW/GRVHL* B23 ...... 80 A5
Robert Rd *BFLD/HDSWWD* B20 .. 99 D4
  TPTN/OCK DY4 .... 70 B5
Roberts Cl *ALDR* WS9 .... 20 B3
Roberts Green Rd *SEDG* DY3 ...... 90 A1
Roberts La *HAG/WOL* DY9 .... 159 D3
Robertson Knoll *CBROM* B36 ... 104 B3
Robertsons Gdns
  VAUX/NECH B7 .... 101 E6
Roberts Rd *ACGN* B27 .... 151 E6

BLOX/PEL WS3 .... **32** B2
DARL/WED WS10 .... **52** A6
Robert St *SEDG* DY3 .... **90** A1
Robert Wynd *BILS/COS* WV14 .... **68** A4
Robeson Cl *TPTN/OCK* DY4 .... **69** F6 🔟
Robin Cl *CBROM* B36 .... **106** C5
KGSWFD DY6 .... **112** C1 🔟
Robin Gv *WNSFLD* WV11 .... **13** E6
Robin Hood Crs *HLGN/YWD* B28 ... **172** A4
Robin Hood Cft *HLGN/YWD* B28 ... **172** B6
Robin Hood La *HLGN/YWD* B28 ... **172** A4
Robin Hood Rd *BRLYHL* DY5 .... **14** B5
Robin Rd *ERDW/GRVHL* B23 .... **102** A1
Robin's Cl *STRBR* DY8 .... **136** C6
Robinsfield Dr *NFLD/LBR* B31 ...... **186** C6
Robinson's Wy *WALM/CURD* B76 ... **83** F6
Robottom Cl *WSLW* WS2 .... **31** D1
Rocester Av *WNSFLD* WV11 .... **14** A6
Rochester Cft *WSLW* WS2 .... **30** C3 🔞
Rochester Rd *NFLD/LBR* B31 .... **186** C11
Roche Wy *BLOX/PEL* WS3 .... **16** B1
Rochford Cl *HALE* B63 .... **162** B1 🔞🔟
RBRY B45 .... **184** A6
WALM/CURD B76 .... **82** C3 🔟
WSLW WS3 .... **51** E2 🔞
Rochford Ct *SHLY* B90 .... **210** C1 🔟
Rochford Ct
ETTPK/GDPK/PENN WV4 .... **43** F4
Rock Av *RBRY* B45 .... **185** E6
Rocket Pool Dr *BILS/COS* WV14 ... **70** C1
Rockford Rd *PBAR/PBCH* B42 ...... **76** C4
Rock Gv *HIA/OLT* B92 .... **152** A6
Rockingham Cl *BLOX/PEL* WS3 ... **17** D4 🔟
DOR/KN B93 .... **211** F5 🔟
SEDG DY3 .... **89** D2 🔞
Rockingham Dr
DUNHL/THL/PER WV6 .... **22** A4
Rockingham Gdns
FOAKS/STRLY B74 .... **59** D3
Rockingham Hall Gdns
HAG/WOL DY9 .... **159** F4
Rockingham Rd *YDLY* B25 .... **151** F1
Rockland Dr *STECH* B33 .... **128** A3
Rockland Gdns *WLNHL* WV13 ..... **48** B1
Rocklands Dr *MGN/WHC* B75 ...... **59** D1
Rockley Gv *RBRY* B45 .... **185** D6
Rockley Rd *BLKHTH/ROWR* B65 ... **116** C3
Rockmead Av *KGSTG* B44 .... **78** B1
Rockmoor Cl *STECH* B33 .... **130** A4 🔟
Rock Rd *BILS/COS* WV14 .... **68** B3
HIA/OLT B92 .... **152** A6
Rock St *SEDG* DY3 .... **68** A6
The Rock *DUNHL/THL/PER* WV6 ... **23** F2
Rockville Rd *WASH/WDE* B8 ...... **126** C3
Rockwell La *ALVE* B48 .... **218** A5
Rockwood Rd *ACGN* B27 .... **151** D5
Rocky La *AST/WIT* B6 .... **124** C1
PBAR/PBCH B42 .... **76** B5
VAUX/NECH B7 .... **125** D1
Rodborough Rd *DOR/KN* B93 ... **212** A5 🔟
LGN/SDN/BHAMAIR B26 .... **153** D3
Rodbourne Rd *HRBN* B17 .... **145** E6
Roddis Cl *ERDW/GRVHL* B23 ...... **79** F3
Roderick Dr *WNSFLD* WV11 .... **13** F6
Roderick Rd *SPARK* B11 .... **149** E4
Rodlington Av *KGSTG* B44 .... **78** B2
Rodman Cl *EDG* B15 .... **121** F3
Rodney Cl *HIA/OLT* B92 .... **175** D2 🔟
LDYWD/EDGR B16 .... **122** C5
Rodney Rd *HIA/OLT* B92 .... **175** D2
Rodway Cl *BRLYHL* DY5 .... **137** F2
ETTPK/GDPK/PENN WV4 .... **45** F4
LOZ/NWT B19 .... **99** F6
Rodwell Gv *KGSTG* B44 .... **78** C3 🔟
Roebuck Cl *BKDE/SHDE* B34 ...... **130** A3
Roebuck Gld *SHHTH* WV12 .... **30** A3
Roebuck La *SMTHWK* B66 .... **96** B6
WBROM B70 .... **96** A4
Roebuck Pl *BLOX/PEL* WS3 .... **32** A1 🔟
Roebuck Rd *BLOX/PEL* WS3 .... **32** A1
Roebuck St *WBROM* B70 .... **96** B4
Roedean Cl *KGSTG* B44 .... **79** D4
Roford Ct *SEDG* DY3 .... **68** A6 🔟
Rogerfield Rd *ERDW/GRVHL* B23 .. **80** C5 🔞
Rogers Cl *WNSFLD* WV11 .... **14** C4
Rogers Rd *WASH/WDE* B8 .... **127** D2
Rokeby Cl *WALM/CURD* B76 ...... **60** A5 🔟
Rokeby Rd *GTB/HAM* B43 .... **76** B1
Rokewood Cl *KGSWFD* DY6 .... **87** F4
Roland Gdns *LOZ/NWT* B19 ...... **99** E5 🔞
Roland Cv *LOZ/NWT* B19 .... **99** E5 🔞
Rolan Dr *SHLY* B90 .... **192** A6 🔞
Roland Rd *LOZ/NWT* B19 .... **99** E5
Roland Ter *LOZ/NWT* B19 .... **99** E5 🔞
Rolfe St *SMTHWK* B66 .... **120** C1
Rollason Rd *DUDS* DY2 .... **91** F5 🔞
ERDE/BCHGN B24 .... **102** C2 🔞
Rollesby Dr *WLNHL* WV13 .... **48** B1 🔞
Rolling Mill Cl *DIG/EDG* B5 ...... **148** A2 🔞
Rollingmill St *WSLW* WS2 .... **31** E6
Rollswood Dr *SOLH* B91 .... **194** B1
Roman La *FOAKS/STRLY* B74 ..... **37** D3
Roman Pk *FOAKS/STRLY* B74 ..... **37** D3

Roman Rd *FOAKS/STRLY* B74 ..... **37** E2
Roman Rd (Sandy La) *STRBR* DY8 . **135** C5 🔞
Roman Wy *BLKHTH/ROWR* B65 ... **117** E4
CSHL/WTROR B46 .... **108** A3
EDG B15 .... **145** E4
Romany Rd *RBRY* B45 .... **183** F4
Romany Wy *STRBR* DY8 .... **135** C6
Roma Rd *SPARK* B11 .... **150** A4
Romford Cl
LGN/SDN/BHAMAIR B26 .... **153** D3
Romilly Av *BFLD/HDSWWD* B20 ... **99** D3
Romilly Cl *STRBR* DY8 .... **136** A3 🔞
WALM/CURD B76 .... **60** C5
Romney Cl *HLGN/YWD* B28 .... **172** B4
Romney Wy *GTB/HAM* B43 .... **55** F5
Romsey Rd *WOLVN* WV10 .... **11** E2
Romsey Wy *BLOX/PEL* WS3 ...... **16** B2 🔞
Romsley Cl *HALE* B63 .... **163** D1 🔞
RBRY B45 .... **184** A5
RUSH/SHEL WS4 .... **19** E3
Romsley Rd *HAG/WOL* DY9 ...... **137** F6
LGLYGN/QTN B68 .... **119** D5
RIDG/WDGT B32 .... **165** D3
Romulus Cl *BFLD/HDSWWD* B20 . **99** D2
Ronald Gv *CBROM* B36 .... **105** F4
Ronald Pl *BORD* B9 .... **126** A5
Ronald Rd *BORD* B9 .... **125** F5
Ron Davis Cl *SMTHWK* B66 .... **121** D3 🔞
OLDBY B69 .... **95** E6
Rooker Av *BKHL/PFLD* WV2 ...... **46** B3
Rooker Crs *BKHL/PFLD* WV2 ..... **46** A3
Rookery Av *BRLYHL* DY5 .... **112** C5
ETTPK/GDPK/PENN WV4 .... **46** C6
Rookery La *BKHL/PFLD* WV2 ..... **44** C3
Rookery Pk *BRLYHL* DY5 .... **113** D2
Rookery Ri *WMBN* WV5 .... **65** D5
Rookery Rd
ETTPK/GDPK/PENN WV4 .... **46** C6
HDSW B21 .... **98** A4
SLYOAK B29 .... **168** B1
WMBN WV5 .... **65** D5
Rookery St *WNSFLD* WV11 .... **27** E2
The Rookery *RIDG/WDGT* B32 ... **164** C3 🔞
Rooks Meadow *HAG/WOL* DY9 ... **159** D5
Rookwood Dr
DUNHL/THL/PER WV6 .... **22** B6
Rooth St *DARL/WED* WS10 .... **51** D5
Roper Wy *SEDG* DY3 .... **68** B5
Rosafield Av *RMSLY* B62 .... **142** B3
Rosalind Av *DUDN* DY1 .... **69** D5
Rosalind Gv *WNSFLD* WV11 ...... **28** C2
Rosamond St *WSL* WS1 .... **51** F2
Rosary Rd *ERDW/GRVHL* B23 ... **101** F3
Rose Av *ALVE* B48 .... **216** C4
KGSWFD DY6 .... **112** B2
LGLYGN/QTN B68 .... **143** E2
Rose Bank Dr *BLOX/PEL* WS3 ... **32** A3 🔞
Rosebay Av *HWK/WKHTH* B38 ... **188** B5
Roseberry Rd *SMTHWK* B66 ...... **121** E3
Rosebery St *BDMR/CCFT* WV3 ... **2** A6 🔟
WSNGN B18 .... **122** C3
Rosebury Gv *WMBN* WV5 .... **64** A5 🔞🔟
Rose Cl *SMTHWK* B66 .... **121** E2 🔞
Rosecroft Rd
LGN/SDN/BHAMAIR B26 .... **153** E3
Rosedale Av *ERDW/GRVHL* B23 .. **102** A2 🔞
SMTHWK B66 .... **121** E2
Rosedale Gv *YDLY* B25 .... **151** E3
Rosedale Pl *WLNHL* WV13 .... **48** C1 🔞
Rosedene Dr *BFLD/HDSWWD* B20 . **98** B3
Rosefield Cft *AST/WIT* B6 .... **100** B6 🔞
Rosefield Rd *SMTHWK* B67 ...... **120** C3
Rosehall Cl *SOLH* B91 .... **194** B4 🔞
Rose HI *BRLYHL* DY5 .... **114** C6
RBRY B45 .... **200** C3
WLNHL WV13 .... **28** C6
Rose Hill Cl *CBROM* B36 .... **105** D5 🔞
Rose Hill Gdns *WLNHL* WV13 ... **28** C6
Rose Hill Rd *BFLD/HDSWWD* B20 . **98** C6
Rosehip Cl *DSYBK/YTR* WS5 ...... **52** C5 🔞
Roseland Av *DUDS* DY2 .... **92** B4
Roseland Wy *EDG* B15 .... **123** D6
Roseleigh Rd *RBRY* B45 .... **201** D1
Rosemary Av *BILS/COS* WV14 ... **48** B3 🔞
ETTPK/GDPK/PENN WV4 .... **45** E3
Rosemary Crs *DUDN* DY1 .... **68** C5 🔞
ETTPK/GDPK/PENN WV4 .... **45** E4
Rosemary Crs West
ETTPK/GDPK/PENN WV4 .... **45** D4
Rosemary Dr *FOAKS/STRLY* B74 . **37** E4
Rosemary Hill Rd
FOAKS/STRLY B74 .... **37** E5
Rosemary La *STRBR* DY8 .... **135** F6
Rosemary Nook *FOAKS/STRLY* B74 . **37** F2
Rosemary Rd *HALE* B63 .... **161** F1 🔞
STECH B33 .... **128** B3
TPTN/OCK DY4 .... **70** C6
Rosemoor Dr *BRLYHL* DY5 ...... **137** D2
Rose Rd *CSHL/WTROR* B46 .... **108** B5
HRBN B17 .... **145** F3
Rose St *BILS/COS* WV14 .... **70** B1
Roseville Gdns *CDSL* WV8 .... **8** B1
Rosewood Dr *ERDW/GRVHL* B23 . **101** F3

SHHTH *WV12* .... **15** D5 🔞
Rosewood Gdns *WNSFLD* WV11 . **15** D2
Rosewood Rd *DUDN* DY1 .... **69** D6
Roshven Rd *BHTH/HG* B12 .... **148** C5 🔞
Roslin Gv *LOZ/NWT* B19 .... **99** E6
Roslyn Cl *SMTHWK* B66 .... **120** C1
Ross *BLKHTH/ROWR* B65 .... **117** D5
Ross Dr *KGSWFD* DY6 .... **87** F4
Rosse Ct *HIA/OLT* B92 .... **176** B3 🔞
Rossendale Cl *HALE* B63 .... **139** F3 🔞
Ross Hts *BLKHTH/ROWR* B65 ... **117** D4
Rosslyn Rd *WALM/CURD* B76 ... **82** B5
Ross Rd *BLOX/PEL* WS3 .... **32** B1
Rostrevor Rd *BORD* B9 .... **126** B6 🔞
Rotherby Gv
CHWD/FDBR/MGN B37 .... **155** D2 🔞
Rotherfield Rd
LGN/SDN/BHAMAIR B26 .... **153** D1
Rothesay Cft *RIDG/WDGT* B32 ... **165** D4 🔞
Rothesay Dr *STRBR* DY8 .... **111** E4
Rothesay Wy *SHHTH* WV12 ...... **29** D1 🔞
Rothwell Dr *SHLY* B90 .... **173** F6 🔞
Rotton Park Rd
LDYWD/EDGR B16 .... **121** F5
Rotton Park St *LDYWD/EDGR* B16 . **122** B4
Rough Hay Rd *DARL/WED* WS10 .. **49** E2
Rough Hill Dr *BLKHTH/ROWR* B65 . **116** B3
Rough Hills Rd *BKHL/PFLD* WV2 .. **46** B3
Roughlea Av *CBROM* B36 .... **104** B6 🔞
Roughley Dr *MGN/WHC* B75 ..... **39** E5
Rough Rd *KGSTG* B44 .... **56** C6
Rouncil La *HIA/OLT* B92 .... **175** F4
The Roundabout *NFLD/LBR* B31 . **185** F4
Round Cft *WLNHL* WV13 .... **28** C5 🔞
Round HI *SEDG* DY3 .... **67** F1
Round Hill Av *HAG/WOL* DY9 ... **159** F4
Roundhill Cl *WALM/CURD* B76 .. **60** A5 🔞
Roundhills Rd *RMSLY* B62 .... **142** B1
Roundhill Ter *RMSLY* B62 .... **118** A6 🔞
Round House Rd *SEDG* DY3 ..... **90** A1
Roundlea Cl *SHHTH* WV12 ...... **15** D6 🔞
Roundlea Rd *NFLD/LBR* B31 .... **166** A4
Round Rd *ERDE/BCHGN* B24 ... **103** D3
Round Saw Cft *RBRY* B45 .... **184** B5 🔞
Rounds Green Rd *OLDBY* B69 ... **94** A6
Rounds Hill Rd *BILS/COS* WV14 . **69** E5
Rounds Rd *BILS/COS* WV14 ...... **47** F6
Round St *DUDS* DY2 .... **115** E1
Roundway Down
DUNHL/THL/PER WV6 .... **22** A4
Rousay Cl *RBRY* B45 .... **184** B4 🔞
Rousdon Gv *GTB/HAM* B43 ..... **75** F3 🔞
Rover Dr *ACGN* B27 .... **151** F5 🔞
CBROM B36 .... **106** B4
Rowallan Rd *MGN/WHC* B75 ... **39** E5
Rowan Cl *HLYWD* B47 .... **207** D2 🔞
WALM/CURD B76 .... **82** B1
Rowan Ct *BVILLE* B30 .... **188** C3 🔞
Rowan Crs *BDMR/CCFT* WV3 ... **44** A2
BILS/COS WV14 .... **69** D2
Rowan Dr *HLGN/YWD* B28 ...... **172** C6 🔞
WNSFLD WV11 .... **15** D2
Rowan Ri *KGSWFD* DY6 .... **112** A1
Rowan Rd *CSCFLD/WYGN* B72 ... **81** E1
DSYBK/YTR WS5 .... **52** B5
SEDG DY3 .... **68** A2
Rowantrees *RBRY* B45 .... **201** D2
Rowan Wy *CHWD/FDBR/MGN* B37 . **131** E6
NFLD/LBR B31 .... **186** B5 🔞
Roway La *OLDBY* B69 .... **94** A4
Rowbrook Cl *SHLY* B90 .... **192** A5 🔞
Rowcroft Covert *BVILLE* B30 ... **189** E2 🔞
Rowdale Rd *PBAR/PBCH* B42 ... **77** E4
Rowden Dr *ERDW/GRVHL* B23 ... **80** C5
SOLH B91 .... **194** A3
Rowena Gdns *SEDG* DY3 .... **67** E1
Rowheath Rd *BVILLE* B30 .... **188** B1
Rowington Av
BLKHTH/ROWR B65 .... **117** E4
Rowington Rd *BKDE/SHDE* B34 ... **130** A1
Rowland Gdns *WSLW* WS2 ...... **31** E4 🔞
Rowland Hill Dr *TPTN/OCK* DY4 . **93** E1 🔞
Rowlands Av *WOLV* WV1 .... **27** D5
WSLW WS2 .... **30** A4
Rowlands Cl *WSLW* WS2 .... **30** A3
Rowlands Crs *SOLH* B91 .... **175** D3
Rowlands Rd
LGN/SDN/BHAMAIR B26 .... **152** A2
Rowland St *WSLW* WS2 .... **31** E4
Rowley Gv *STECH* B33 .... **129** F4
Rowley Hall Av
BLKHTH/ROWR B65 .... **117** E4
Rowley Hill Vw *CDYHTH* B64 ... **140** B3 🔞
Rowley Pl *RUSH/SHEL* WS4 ...... **19** D6
Rowley St *WSL* WS1 .... **5** F3
Rowley Vw *BILS/COS* WV14 ...... **48** C6 🔞
DARL/WED WS10 .... **49** E5
WBROM B70 .... **95** D2
Rowley Village
BLKHTH/ROWR B65 .... **117** E4
Rowney Cft *HLGN/YWD* B28 .... **192** A1
Rowney Green La *ALVE* B48 ..... **217** F6
Rowood Dr *HIA/OLT* B92 .... **176** A3 🔞
Rowthorn Cl *FOAKS/STRLY* B74 . **56** C2

Rowthorn Dr SHLY B90 .... 210 C1
Rowton Av
  DUNHL/THL/PER WV6 .... 22 A4 🔟
Rowton Dr FOAKS/STRLY B74 .... 56 B4
Roxburgh Gv GTB/HAM B43 .... 55 E5
Roxburgh Rd SCFLD/BOLD B73...... 58 C6
Roxby Gdns DUNHL/THL/PER WV6 .. 24 C2
Royal Cl BLKHTH/ROWR B65 .... 117 E2
  BRLYHL DY5..................... 137 E1
Royal Mail St CBHAMW B1 .... 6 C6
Royal Oak Rd BLKHTH/ROWR B65 .. 116 B2
  RMSLY B62 .... 142 B5
Royal Rd CSCFLD/WYGN B72 .... 59 F4
Royal Scot Gv WSL WS1 .... 51 F4 🔟
Royal Star Cl STETCH B33 .... 129 E5 🔟
Royal Wy TPTN/OCK DY4 .... 92 C3
Roydon Rd ACGN B27 .... 173 E3
Roylesden Crs SCFLD/BOLD B73 ..... 79 E1
Royston Cha FOAKS/STRLY B74 ..... 36 C4
Royston Cft BHTH/HG B12 .... 148 B3 🔟
Royston Wy SEDG DY3............... 67 E3
Rubens Cl SEDG DY3............... 67 F6
Rubery Farm Gv RBRY B45 .... 184 B5
Rubery La RBRY B45.............. 184 B4
Rubery La South RBRY B45 .... 184 B5 🔟
Rubery St DARL/WED WS10 .... 49 F1
Ruckley Rd SLYOAK B29 .... 167 D3 🔟
Rudge Av WOLV WV1 .... 27 D4
Rudge Cl SHHTH WV12 .... 29 E3
Rudge Cft STETCH B33 .... 128 C3
Rudgewick Cft AST/WIT B6 .... 124 D1 🔟
Rudyard Cl WOLVN WV10............ 12 A1
Rudyard Gv STETCH B33 .... 129 D4 🔟
Rudyngfield Dr STETCH B33 .... 128 B4
Rufford Cl ERDW/GRVHL B23 .... 79 F3
Rufford Rd HAG/WOL DY9 .... 137 E5
Rufford St HAG/WOL DY9 .... 137 F3
Rufford Wy ALDR WS9 .... 20 A6
Rugby Rd STRBR DY8 .... 135 F2
Rugby St WOLV WV1 .... 2 A1
Rugeley Av SHHTH WV12 .... 15 F5
Rugeley Cl TPTN/OCK DY4 .... 70 A6 🔟
Ruislip Cl CVALE B35 .... 104 C1
Ruiton St SEDG DY3 .... 89 F1
Rumbow HALE B63 .... 141 D5
Rumbow La RMSLY B62 .... 181 F1
Rumbush La HOCK/TIA B94 .... 207 F6
  SHLY B90 .... 208 B3
Runcorn Cl
  CHWD/FDBR/MGN B37 .... 131 E3 🔟
Runcorn Rd BHTH/HG B12 .... 148 B4
Runnymede Rd SPARK B11 .... 150 A6
Rupert St BDMR/CCFT WV3 .... 24 C5
  VAUX/NECH B7 .... 124 C2
Rushall Cl RUSH/SHEL WS4 .... 33 D3
  STRBR DY8 .... 136 A1
Rushall Manor Cl RUSH/SHEL WS4 .. 33 D3
Rushall Manor Rd RUSH/SHEL WS4 . 33 D3
Rushall Rd WOLVN WV10 .... 12 A3
Rushbrook Cl HIA/OLT B92 .... 174 A1
Rushbrooke Cl MOS/BIL B13 .... 148 B5 🔟
Rushbrooke Dr SCFLD/BOLD B73 .... 57 E5
Rushbrook Gv
  ALE/KHTH/YWD B14 .... 189 E1 🔟
Rushbrook La HOCK/TIA B94....... 221 E6
Rushbury Cl BILS/COS WV14 .... 47 D4 🔟
  SHLY B90 .... 193 F1
Rushden Cft KGSTG B44............. 78 B2
Rushes Mi BLOX/PEL WS3 .... 18 A2
Rushey La SPARK B11 .... 150 C4
Rushford Av WMBN WV5 .... 64 C5 🔟
Rushford Cl SHLY B90............ 194 C6
Rush Gn RIDG/WDGT B32 .... 166 A1
Rushleigh Rd SHLY B90 .... 192 A5
Rushmead Gv RBRY B45 .... 184 C6
Rushmere Rd TPTN/OCK DY4 .... 70 C3
Rushmoor Cl FOAKS/STRLY B74 .... 59 D3
Rushwater Cl WMBN WV5 .... 64 A5 🔟
Rushwick Gv SHLY B90............. 210 C1
Rushwood Cl RUSH/SHEL WS4 .... 32 C4
Rushy Piece RIDG/WDGT B32 ...... 143 F6
Ruskin Av BLKHTH/ROWR B65 ...... 117 F5
  ETTPK/GDPK/PENN WV4 .... 68 B3
  SEDG DY3 .... 66 C6
Ruskin Cl AST/WIT B6 .... 100 B6 🔟
Ruskin Gv ACGN B27 .... 173 D1
Ruskin Rd WOLVN WV10 .... 12 B5
Ruskin St HHTH/SAND B71 .... 73 E6
Russell Bank Rd FOAKS/STRLY B74.. 38 A3
Russell Cl OLDBY B69 .... 93 F3
  TPTN/OCK DY4 .... 71 E2
  WNSFLD WV11 .... 14 B4
Russell Rd BILS/COS WV14 .... 48 B2
  HLGN/YWD B28 .... 172 A1
  MOS/BIL B13 .... 147 F6
Russell's Hall Rd DUDN DY1....... 90 A4
The Russells MOS/BIL B13 .... 147 F6
Russell St BDMR/CCFT WV3 .... 2 B6
  DARL/WED WS10 .... 72 B1 🔟
  DUDN DY1 .... 91 D4
  WLNHL WV13 .... 29 D5
Russett Cl DSYBK/YTR WS5 .... 53 F1
Russett Wy BRLYHL DY5 .... 89 D6 🔟
Russet Wy NFLD/LBR B31 .... 166 A5
Ruston St LDYWD/EDGR B16......... 122 C6

Ruthall Cl SLYOAK B29 .... 167 E4 🔟
Ruth Cl DARL/WED WS10 .... 71 E1
Rutherford Rd
  ERDW/GRVHL B23 .... 80 A4 🔟
  WSLW WS2...................... 30 C1
Rutland Av
  ETTPK/GDPK/PENN WV4 .... 43 F5
Rutland Crs ALDR WS9 .... 21 D4
  BILS/COS WV14 .... 47 F2
Rutland Dr
  LGN/SDN/BHAMAIR B26 .... 152 A2
Rutland Pl STRBR DY8 .... 135 F1
Rutland Rd DARL/WED WS10 .... 51 E5
  HHTH/SAND B71 .... 73 E4
  SMTHWK B66 .... 120 C6
Rutland St BLOX/PEL WS3 .... 32 A2
Rutley Gv RIDG/WDGT B32 .... 144 B5
Rutters Meadow RIDG/WDGT B32 .. 143 D5
Rutter St WSL WS1 .... 52 A2
Ryan Av WNSFLD WV11 .... 14 C6
Ryan Pl DUDS DY2................ 115 E1
Rycroft Gv STETCH B33 .... 129 E5 🔟
Rydal Cl FOAKS/STRLY B74 .... 36 B5
  WNSFLD WV11 .... 13 E6
Rydal Dr DUNHL/THL/PER WV6...... 22 B3
Rydding La HHTH/SAND B71 .... 73 E3
Rydding Sq HHTH/SAND B71 .... 73 D3
Ryde Gv ACGN B27 .... 172 C2
Ryde Park Rd RBRY B45 .... 201 E1
Ryders Green Rd WBROM B70 .... 94 B1
Ryders Hayes La BLOX/PEL WS3..... 19 F3
Ryder St CBHAMNE B4 .... 7 F3 🔟
  STRBR DY8 .... 111 F5
  WBROM B70 .... 72 B6
Ryebank Rd BVILLE B30 .... 167 E6
Ryeclose Cft
  CHWD/FDBR/MGN B37 .... 131 F4
Rye Cft ACGN B27 .... 151 E4 🔟
  HAG/WOL DY9.................. 160 A1
  HLYWD B47 .... 206 C2
Ryecroft Av
  ETTPK/GDPK/PENN WV4 .... 45 D4
Ryecroft Pk WSLW WS2 .... 32 A4 🔟
Ryecroft Pl BLOX/PEL WS3 .... 32 B1
Ryecroft St WSLW WS2 .... 32 A4 🔟
Ryefield CDSL WV8 .... 10 A4
Ryefield Cl SOLH B91 .... 174 A6
Ryefield La WALM/CURD B76 .... 85 D1
Rye Gv SPARK B11................ 150 B5
Ryknild Cl FOAKS/STRLY B74 .... 38 B1
Ryland Cl HALE B63 .... 162 A1 🔟
  TPTN/OCK DY4 .... 71 D6 🔟
Ryland Rd EDG B15 .... 147 E2
  ERDE/BCHGN B24 .... 102 B4
  SPARK B11 .... 149 F5 🔟
Rylands Dr
  ETTPK/GDPK/PENN WV4.......... 44 C5
Ryland St LDYWD/EDGR B16 .... 123 D6
Ryle St BLOX/PEL WS3 .... 17 F5
Rymond Rd BKDE/SHDE B34......... 128 A1
Ryton Cl SCFLD/BOLD B73 .... 59 D4
  WNSFLD WV11 .... 26 C2
Ryton Gv BKDE/SHDE B34.......... 105 F6

Sabell Rd SMTHWK B67 .... 120 B1
Sabrina Rd DUNHL/THL/PER WV6 .. 22 A6
Saddlers Ms SOLH B91 .... 195 E4
Saddleworth Rd GTWY WS6 .... 16 C1
Sadler Rd MGN/WHC B75............ 60 B2
Sadlers Ct WSLW WS2.............. 51 D2
Sadlers Wk LDYWD/EDGR B16 ..... 122 C5 🔟
Saffron Gdns
  ETTPK/GDPK/PENN WV4 .... 44 C5
Sage Cft NFLD/LBR B31 .... 166 B6
St Agatha's Rd WASH/WDE B8 .... 127 D2
St Agnes Cl MOS/BIL B13 .... 171 D1 🔟
St Agnes Rd MOS/BIL B13 .... 171 D1
St Albans Cl SMTHWK B67 .... 120 A1 🔟
  WNSFLD WV11 .... 14 C5
St Albans Rd MOS/BIL B13........ 148 C5
  SMTHWK B67 .... 120 A1
St Andrews Cl
  DUNHL/THL/PER WV6 .... 24 C5 🔟
  HRBN B17 .... 144 C6
  SEDG DY3 .... 88 C2
  STRBR DY8 .... 158 B1
St Andrews Dr OLDBY B69.......... 93 D6
St Andrew's Rd BORD B9 .... 125 D5
  MGN/WHC B75 .... 59 E2
St Andrew's St BORD B9 .... 125 D2
  DUDS DY2 .... 115 E2
St Annes Cl BFLD/HDSWWD B20..... 98 B1
St Anne's Ct MOS/BIL B13 .... 148 A5 🔟
St Annes Gv DOR/KN B93.......... 212 C1
St Anne's Rd CDYHTH B64 .... 115 E6
  WLNHL WV13 .... 29 D4
  WOLVN WV10 .... 11 D4
St Annes Wy KGSTG B44........... 78 C4
St Athan Cft CVALE B35 .... 105 D2

St Augustine's Rd LDYWD/EDGR B16 121 F6
St Augustus Cl HHTH/SAND B71 ... 96 B3 🔟
St Austell Rd DSYBK/YTR WS5...... 53 F2
St Bartholomew Ter
  DARL/WED WS10 .... 50 B6 🔟
St Benedict's Cl WBROM B70 ...... 96 B3 🔟
St Benedicts Rd SMHTH B10...... 150 B1
  WMBN WV5 .... 64 C5 🔟
St Bernards Rd CSCFLD/WYGN B72 .. 81 E1 🔟
  HIA/OLT B92 .... 174 A4
  SOLH B91 .... 173 F6
St Blaise Av CSHL/WTROR B46 .... 107 D3
St Blaise Rd MGN/WHC B75........ 39 F4
St Brades Cl OLDBY B69 .... 93 E6
St Brides Cl SEDG DY3 .... 67 E3 🔟
  WMBN WV5 .... 64 B5
Saintbury Dr SOLH B91 .... 195 E5 🔟
St Caroline Cl WBROM B70 .... 96 B2
St Catharines Cl WSL WS1 .... 52 C2 🔟
St Catherines Cl DUDS DY2 .... 92 C4 🔟
  MGN/WHC B75 .... 60 B2
St Catherine's Crs
  ETTPK/GDPK/PENN WV4 .... 44 B5 🔟
St Catherine's Rd BRGRVE B60 ... 214 B3 🔟
St Chad's Circus Queensway
  CBHAMNW B3 .... 6 D3
St Chad's Cl SEDG DY3 .... 89 D2
St Chads Queensway CBHAMNE B4... 7 E2
St Chad's Rd BILS/COS WV14...... 48 B2
  MGN/WHC B75 .... 60 A4
  RBRY B45 .... 184 B6
  WOLVN WV10 .... 12 B5
St Christopher Cl
  HHTH/SAND B71 .... 96 A3 🔟
St Christophers
  BFLD/HDSWWD B20............... 98 B1
St Clement's Av BLOX/PEL WS3 .... 17 E6
St Clement's La HHTH/SAND B71 ... 95 F1
St Clements Rd VAUX/NECH B7 .... 125 E1
St Columbas Dr RBRY B45 .... 185 F6
St Cuthbert's Cl WBROM B70 ...... 96 B3
St David's Cl WBROM B70 .... 96 B3
St Davids Dr RIDG/WDGT B32 ..... 143 D4
St Davids Gv BFLD/HDSWWD B20... 98 B1
St Davids Pl BLOX/PEL WS3 .... 17 F5
St Denis Rd SLYOAK B29 .... 166 C5
St Dominic's Rd ERDE/BCHGN B24.. 102 A4
St Edburghs Rd STETCH B33 ...... 128 A6
St Edmund's Cl
  DUNHL/THL/PER WV6 .... 24 B3 🔟
  WBROM B70 .... 96 B3 🔟
St Edward's Rd SLYOAK B29 ...... 168 B1
St Eleanor Cl WBROM B70 .... 96 B2
St Francis Av SOLH B91 .... 174 A5
St George Dr SMTHWK B66 .... 96 C6 🔟
St Georges Av ERDW/GRVHL B23 .. 80 C6 🔟
St Georges Cl EDG B15 .... 146 C2
  MGN/WHC B75 .... 60 B3
St Georges Pl DUDS DY2.......... 115 F1
  SHLY B90 .... 193 F5 🔟
St George's St DARL/WED WS10 ... 49 F2 🔟
  LOZ/NWT B19 .... 6 C1
St Gerards Rd SOLH B91 .... 194 B3 🔟
St Giles Av BLKHTH/ROWR B65 .... 117 D3
St Giles Cl BLKHTH/ROWR B65 .... 117 D3
St Giles Crs WOLV WV1 .... 26 C5
St Giles Rd STETCH B33 .... 129 F5
  WLNHL WV13 .... 29 D6
  WOLV WV1...................... 26 C5
St Giles St DUDS DY2............ 115 E2
St Helens Av TPTN/OCK DY4 .... 71 E6
St Helens Pas CBHAMW B1 .... 6 A3
St Helen's Rd SOLH B91 .... 174 C5
St Heliers Rd NFLD/LBR B31 ..... 186 A1
St Ives Rd DSYBK/YTR WS5 .... 53 F2
St James Av BLKHTH/ROWR B65.... 116 C3
St James Cl WBROM B70 .... 96 B3
St James Pl SHLY B90 .... 193 F5 🔟
  VAUX/NECH B7 .... 124 C4 🔟
St James Rd EDG B15 .... 147 D1
  HDSW B21 .... 97 F5 🔟
  MGN/WHC B75 .... 39 E5
  OLDBY B69 .... 93 F5
St James's Rd DUDN DY1.......... 91 D3
St James's Ter DUDN DY1.......... 90 C3
St James St DARL/WED WS10 ...... 72 A1 🔟
  SEDG DY3 .... 89 F2
  WOLV WV1....................... 3 G5
St John Cl MGN/WHC B75.......... 39 F3
St Johns Av BLKHTH/ROWR B65 ... 117 D3
St John's Cl ALDR WS9 .... 20 B2
  DOR/KN B93 .... 213 D1
  WBROM B70 .... 96 B3
St Johns Gv
  CHWD/FDBR/MGN B37 .... 130 B4
St John's Rd DARL/WED WS10 ..... 49 E4 🔟
  DUDS DY2 .... 92 A5 🔟
  HALE B63 .... 140 A5
  HRBN B17 .... 145 F3
  LGLYGN/QTN B68 .... 119 E2
  SPARK B11 .... 149 E4
  STRBR DY8 .... 136 C3

TPTN/OCK DY4	**70** B4
WNSFLD WV11	**14** C2
WSLW WS2	**51** D1
St John's Sq BKHL/PFLD WV2	**2** D6
St John's St DUDS DY2	**115** D2
St Johns Wk PBAR/PBCH B42	**99** F1
St Johns Wd RBRY B45	**201** D2
St Josephs Av NFLD/LBR B31	**167** D6
St Josephs Cl BLOX/PEL WS3	**18** C1
St Josephs Rd WASH/WDE B8	**127** D2
St Joseph St DUDS DY2	**91** F4
St Judes Cl ALE/KHTH/YWD B14	**190** B3
MGN/WHC B75	**60** B3
St Jude's Pas DIG/EDG B5	**123** F6
St Jude's Rd DUNHL/THL/PER WV6	**24** B4
St Jude's Rd West	
DUNHL/THL/PER WV6	**24** B4
St Katherine's Rd	
LGLYGN/QTN B68	**119** E5
St Kenelms Av HALE B63	**161** F2
St Kenelm's Cl WBROM B70	**96** B3
St Kenelm's Rd RMSLY B62	**161** F6
St Kilda's Rd WASH/WDE B8	**126** A2
St Laurence Cl ALVE B48	**217** D3
St Laurence Rd NFLD/LBR B31	**166** C6
St Lawrence Cl DOR/KN B93	**213** D2
St Lawrence Wy DARL/WED WS10	**49** F3
St Leonards Cl	
CHWD/FDBR/MGN B37	**154** C2
St Loye's Cl RMSLY B62	**141** F1
St Lukes Cl BLKHTH/ROWR B65	**117** D3
St Luke's Rd DARL/WED WS10	**50** C6
DIG/EDG B5	**148** A2
St Lukes St CDYHTH B64	**115** F6
St Margaret's FOAKS/STRLY B74	**37** E4
St Margarets Rd WASH/WDE B8	**127** D1
St Margarets Dr HALE B63	**162** B1
St Margarets Rd BLOX/PEL WS3	**18** C1
CTB/HAM B43	**76** B1
HIA/OLT B92	**174** A2
WASH/WDE B8	**126** C1
St Marks Crs CBHAMW B1	**122** C4
St Mark's Rd BDMR/CCFT WV3	**2** A5
BLOX/PEL WS3	**18** C1
DUDS DY2	**92** B3
HAG/WOL DY9	**137** F4
SMTHWKW B67	**119** F4
TPTN/OCK DY4	**70** C3
St Mark's St BDMR/CCFT WV3	**2** B5
CBHAMW B1	**123** D4
St Martin's Circus Queensway	
CBHAM B2	**7** E6
St Martin's Cl BKHL/PFLD WV2	**46** A3
WBROM B70	**96** B3
St Martin's Dr TPTN/OCK DY4	**70** C6
St Martins Rd MGN/WHC B75	**60** B1
St Martin's St EDG B15	**123** D6
St Martin's Ter BILS/COS WV14	**48** A6
St Marys Cl ACGN B27	**151** D6
BILS/COS WV14	**68** B3
ERDE/BCHGN B24	**103** F1
St Mary's La STRBR DY8	**137** D6
St Mary's Rd DARL/WED WS10	**50** B6
HRBN B17	**145** E4
St Mary's Rw CBHAMNW B4	**7** E3
MOS/BIL B13	**148** B6
St Mary's Wy ALDR WS9	**34** C2
St Matthew's Cl WSL WS1	**5** E5
St Matthews Rd LGLYGN/QTN B68	**118** C5
SMTHWK B66	**121** E2
St Matthew St WOLV WV1	**26** B6
St Mawes Rd DUNHL/THL/PER WV6	**22** B4
St Mawgen Cl CVALE B35	**105** E1
St Michael's Cl BLOX/PEL WS3	**18** B3
St Michael's Ct	
DUNHL/THL/PER WV6	**24** A2
St Michael's Crs OLDBY B69	**118** B3
St Michael's Gv DUDS DY2	**92** B4
St Michael's Rd SCFLD/BOLD B73	**80** B3
SEDG DY3	**66** B6
WSNGN B18	**98** C6
St Michael St WBROM B70	**95** E2
WSL WS1	**52** A1
St Michaels Wy TPTN/OCK DY4	**92** C2
St Nicholas Cl BLOX/PEL WS3	**18** C1
St Nicolas Gdns HWK/WKHTH B38	**188** B3
St Oswalds Rd SMHTH B10	**150** A1
St Patricks Cl ALE/KHTH/YWD B14	**170** A5
St Paul's Av BHTH/HG B12	**148** C4
St Paul's Cl WSL WS1	**4** D3
St Paul's Crs CSHL/WTROR B46	**108** C6
WBROM B70	**72** A4
St Pauls Dr RMSLY B62	**117** F6
St Paul's Rd BHTH/HG B12	**148** B3
TPTN/OCK DY4	**93** D1
DARL/WED WS10	**51** D4
DUDS DY2	**115** F2
SMTHWK B66	**95** F6
St Paul's Sq CBHAMNW B3	**6** B3
St Paul's St WSL WS1	**4** D3
St Peters Cl CSCFLD/WYGN B72	**59** D6
CSHL/WTROR B46	**107** D3
HLGN/YWD B28	**171** F5
TPTN/OCK DY4	**93** F1
St Peters Ct BLOX/PEL WS3	**17** D4

St Peters Dr BLOX/PEL WS3	**18** C1
St Peters La HIA/OLT B92	**177** F3
St Peter's Rd BFLD/HDSWWD B20	**99** E5
DUDS DY2	**115** F1
HAG/WOL DY9	**159** E2
HRBN B17	**145** D4
St Peters Ter WSLW WS2	**32** A3
St Philips Av BDMR/CCFT WV3	**44** B2
St Philip's Gv BDMR/CCFT WV3	**44** B2
St Quentin St WSLW WS2	**51** F1
St Saviour's Cl BKHL/PFLD WV2	**46** B3
St Saviour's Rd WASH/WDE B8	**126** A4
St Silas' Sq LOZ/NWT B19	**99** D6
St Simons Cl MGN/WHC B75	**60** B3
St Stephen's Av WLNHL WV13	**28** B5
St Stephens St HHTH/SAND B71	**97** D5
SLYOAK B29	**169** D3
St Stephens St AST/WIT B6	**124** A1
St Thomas' Cl ALDR WS9	**21** D4
BLOX/PEL WS3	**32** A1
MGN/WHC B75	**60** B4
St Thomas' Rd ERDW/GRVHL B23	**101** F3
St Thomas St DUDS DY2	**115** E2
St Valentines Cl WBROM B70	**96** B3
St Vincent Crs WBROM B70	**72** B5
St Vincent St LDYWD/EDGR B16	**123** D5
St Vincent St West	
LDYWD/EDGR B16	**122** C5
Saladin Av OLDBY B69	**118** A2
Salcombe Av	
LGN/SDN/BHAMAIR B26	**153** E4
Salcombe Dr BRLYHL DY5	**137** E1
Salcombe Gv BILS/COS WV14	**69** F2
Salcombe Rd SMTHWK B66	**121** D2
Salem St TPTN/OCK DY4	**71** F4
Salford St AST/WIT B6	**101** E5
Salisbury Cl DUDN DY1	**90** B2
MOS/BIL B13	**148** A6
Salisbury Dr CSHL/WTROR B46	**107** E2
Salisbury Gv CSCFLD/WYGN B72	**81** E4
Salisbury Rd LOZ/NWT B19	**99** F5
MOS/BIL B13	**148** A6
SMTHWK B66	**121** D3
WASH/WDE B8	**126** A2
WBROM B70	**96** A4
Salisbury St BDMR/CCFT WV3	**2** A6
DARL/WED WS10	**50** A2
Sally Ward Dr ALDR WS9	**20** C1
Salop Cl HHTH/SAND B71	**73** D4
Salop Dr LGLYGN/QTN B68	**119** E5
Salop Rd LGLYGN/QTN B68	**119** E4
St BHTH/HG B12	**148** B1
BILS/COS WV14	**48** A5
BKHL/PFLD WV2	**2** C5
DUDN DY1	**90** C3
OLDBY B69	**94** A4
Salstar Cl AST/WIT B6	**124** A1
Saltash Gv YDLY B25	**127** E4
Saltbrook Rd HAG/WOL DY9	**138** C2
Salter La TPTN/OCK DY4	**70** B4
Salter's La HHTH/SAND B71	**96** A1
Salter's Rd ALDR WS9	**20** C2
Salter St HOCK/TIA B94	**209** E5
Salters V WBROM B70	**96** A4
Saltley Rd VAUX/NECH B7	**125** D2
Saltley Viad VAUX/NECH B7	**125** E2
Saltney Cl ERDE/BCHGN B24	**81** F6
Saltwells La DUDS DY2	**114** C5
Saltwells Rd DUDS DY2	**115** F4
Salwarpe Gv SLYOAK B29	**166** B1
Sambourn Cl SOLH B91	**176** A5
Sambourne Dr BKDE/SHDE B34	**105** F6
Sambrook Rd WOLVN WV10	**26** C1
Sampson Cl HDSW B21	**97** E4
OLDBY B69	**93** E6
Sampson Rd SPARK B11	**149** D2
Sampson Rd North SPARK B11	**148** C1
Sampson St DARL/WED WS10	**51** D6
Sam La WBROM B70	**95** E3
Samuels Rd RIDG/WDGT B32	**142** C4
Samuel St BLOX/PEL WS3	**17** D4
Sanda Cft CBROM B36	**131** D1
Sandalls Cl NFLD/LBR B31	**185** F4
Sandal Ri SOLH B91	**196** A2
Sandals Ri RMSLY B62	**141** F6
Sandalwood Cl SHHTH WV12	**15** D5
Sand Bank BLOX/PEL WS3	**16** C4
BLOX/PEL WS3	**17** D4
Sandbarn Cl SHLY B90	**210** B1
Sandbeds Rd SHHTH WV12	**29** E4
Sandbourne Rd WASH/WDE B8	**126** C3
Sanderling Ri BRLYHL DY5	**112** C1
Sanders Cl DUDS DY2	**92** A6
Sandfield Cl SHLY B90	**192** B5
Sandfield Gv SEDG DY3	**89** D3
Sandfield Rd HHTH/SAND B71	**74** A2
STRBR DY8	**112** B5
Sandfields Av SMHTH B10	**149** D1
Sandfields Rd LGLYGN/QTN B68	**119** F5
Sandford Av BLKHTH/ROWR B65	**117** E4
Sandford Ri DUNHL/THL/PER WV6	**24** A1
Sandford Rd DUDN DY1	**90** A4
MOS/BIL B13	**148** C6
Sandgate Rd HLGN/YWD B28	**192** B1
TPTN/OCK DY4	**70** C3

Sandhills Crs SOLH B91	**195** D5
Sandhills Gn RBRY B45	**216** A2
Sandhills La RBRY B45	**215** F2
Sandhills Rd RBRY B45	**215** F1
Sandhurst St BLOX/PEL WS3	**16** C4
Sandhurst Rd CBROM B36	**127** F1
HAG/WOL DY9	**159** F1
Sandhurst Dr	
ETTPK/GDPK/PENN WV4	**44** C5
Sandhurst Gv STRBR DY8	**112** A4
Sandhurst Rd FOAKS/STRLY B74	**38** B2
KGSWFD DY6	**112** C3
MOS/BIL B13	**170** A1
Sandmartin Cl DUDS DY2	**115** E5
Sandmere Gv	
ALE/KHTH/YWD B14	**191** F2
Sandmere Ri WOLVN WV10	**12** A4
Sandmere Rd ALE/KHTH/YWD B14	**191** F2
Sandon Gv ERDE/BCHGN B24	**102** C1
Sandon Rd HAG/WOL DY9	**138** B5
HRBN B17	**121** D6
SMTHWK B66	**120** C5
WOLVN WV10	**11** D3
Sandown Dr DUNHL/THL/PER WV6	**22** B3
Sandown Rd CBROM B36	**103** F5
Sandpiper Cl HAG/WOL DY9	**138** B4
Sandpiper Gdns	
HWK/WKHTH B38	**188** B6
Sand Pits CBHAMW B1	**123** D4
Sandpits Cl WALM/CURD B76	**85** D5
Sandra Cl ALDR WS9	**35** D2
Sandringham Av SHHTH WV12	**29** D1
Sandringham Dr ALDR WS9	**21** D4
BLKHTH/ROWR B65	**117** E3
Sandringham Pl STRBR DY8	**111** F6
Sandringham Rd	
ETTPK/GDPK/PENN WV4	**45** D4
PBAR/PBCH B42	**77** D5
RMSLY B62	**141** D2
STRBR DY8	**111** E6
WMBN WV5	**64** B5
Sandringham Wy BRLYHL DY5	**137** E1
Sandstone Av RBRY B45	**184** C5
Sandstone Cl SEDG DY3	**89** F1
Sand St WBROM B70	**94** A1
Sandway Gdns WASH/WDE B8	**125** F1
Sandway Gv MOS/BIL B13	**171** E4
Sandwell Av DARL/WED WS10	**49** D4
Sandwell Pl SHHTH WV12	**15** F6
Sandwell Rd HDSW B21	**97** E4
WBROM B70	**95** E1
WOLVN WV10	**11** D4
Sandwell Rd North	
HHTH/SAND B71	**95** F1
Sandwell St WSL WS1	**5** E6
Sandwood Dr KGSTG B44	**78** B3
Sandyacre Wy STRBR DY8	**137** D4
Sangy Crs WNSFLD WV11	**14** C5
Sansome Ri SHLY B90	**192** B5
Sansome Rd SHLY B90	**192** B5
Santone Cl BLOX/PEL WS3	**17** E2
Santone Rd BLOX/PEL WS3	**17** D2
Santolina Dr DSYBK/YTR WS5	**52** C6
Sant Rd NFLD/LBR B31	**187** D6
The Saplings WALM/CURD B76	**82** C3
Sara Cl FOAKS/STRLY B74	**38** C4
Sarah Cl BILS/COS WV14	**70** A4
Sarah Gdns DSYBK/YTR WS5	**52** B5
Sarah St BORD B9	**125** D3
Saredon Cl BLOX/PEL WS3	**18** C4
Sarehole Rd HLGN/YWD B28	**172** A3
Sargent Cl GTB/HAM B43	**55** F5
Sark Dr CBROM B36	**131** D1
Saunton Wy SLYOAK B29	**167** E2
Saveker Dr WALM/CURD B76	**60** A5
Savernake Cl RBRY B45	**184** C3
Saville Cl RBRY B45	**185** D6
Savoy Cl RIDG/WDGT B32	**144** B4
Saw Mill Cl RUSH/SHEL WS4	**4** D1
Saxelby Cl ALE/KHTH/YWD B14	**190** A3
Saxoncourt DUNHL/THL/PER WV6	**23** D2
Saxondale Av	
LGN/SDN/BHAMAIR B26	**152** D3
Saxon Dr BLKHTH/ROWR B65	**117** E3

Saxonfields *DUNHL/THL/PER* WV6 .. **23** E2 🔳
Saxons Wy *ALE/KHTH/YWD* B14 ...... **190** C3
Saxon Wy *CHWD/FDBR/MGN* B37 .. **130** B4
Saxon Wood Cl *NFLD/LBR* B31 ...... **186** C1 🔳
Saxon Wood Rd *SHLY* B90 .... **209** F2
Saxton Dr *FOAKS/STRLY* B74 .... **38** B1
Scafell Dr *BILS/COS* WV14 .... **48** B2
  ERDW/GRVHL B23 .... **79** E6
Scafell Rd *STRBR* DY8 .... **137** D3
Scampton Cl
  DUNHL/THL/PER WV6 .... **22** A2 🔳
Scarborough Cl *WSLW* WS2 .... **51** D1 🔳
Scarborough Rd *WSLW* WS2 .... **51** E1
Scarfield Hl *ALVE* B48 .... **215** F4
Scarsdale Rd *PBAR/PBCH* B42 .... **77** F3
Schofield Av *HHTH/SAND* B71 .... **73** D3
Schofield Rd
  CHWD/FDBR/MGN B37 .... **130** B2
Scholars Ga *STETCH* B33 .... **129** D5 🔳
Schoolacre Ri *FOAKS/STRLY* B74.... **36** A6
Schoolacre Rd *BKDE/SHDE* B34 .. **129** D1 🔳
School Cl *BDMR/CCFT* WV3 .... **43** D2
  CDSL WV8 .... **8** C1
  CHWD/FDBR/MGN B37 .... **130** C1
  OLDBY B69 .... **93** E6
School Dr *BILS/COS* WV14 .... **69** E2 🔳
  BILS/COS WV14 .... **70** C1
  HLYWD B47 .... **206** C4
  STRBR DY8 .... **136** B1
The School Dr *DUDS* DY2 .... **91** F6
Schoolgate Cl *RUSH/SHEL* WS4 .... **19** F4
School Gn *BILS/COS* WV14 .... **47** E1
Schoolhouse Cl
  HWK/WKHTH B38 .... **189** D3 🔳
School La *ALVE* B48 .... **217** D4
  BKDE/SHDE B34 .... **105** D6
  BLOX/PEL WS3 .... **18** B1
  BRLYHL DY5 .... **113** D3
  HAG/WOL DY9 .... **159** F5
  HALE B63 .... **162** B1 🔳
  SOLH B91 .... **195** F4
  STETCH B33 .... **128** B6
  WOLVN WV10 .... **11** F3
School Rd *ALE/KHTH/YWD* B14 .... **170** B2
  ALE/KHTH/YWD B14 .... **191** E1
  BRLYHL DY5 .... **114** C5
  DARL/WED WS10 .... **73** F1
  DUNHL/THL/PER WV6 .... **22** C4
  HLGN/YWD B28 .... **172** C3
  HOCK/TIA B94 .... **210** A6
  RBRY B45 .... **200** A1
  SEDG DY3 .... **87** D2
  SHLY B90 .... **193** D3
  WMBN WV5 .... **65** D4
  WNSFLD WV11 .... **27** D1
School St *BKHL/PFLD* WV2 .... **2** C6
  BRLYHL DY5 .... **89** F6
  CDYHTH B64 .... **115** F6 🔳
  DARL/WED WS10 .... **49** E3
  DUDN DY1 .... **91** D4
  RUSH/SHEL WS4 .... **19** F4
  SEDG DY3 .... **68** C3
  STRBR DY8 .... **136** B4 🔳
  WLNHL WV13 .... **28** B5
  WOLV WV1 .... **2** C5
School St West *BILS/COS* WV14 .... **69** C3 🔳
School Wk *BILS/COS* WV14 .... **47** E1
Scorers Cl *HIA/OLT* B92 .... **173** D5
The Scotchings *CBROM* B36 .... **104** A5 🔳
Scotland La *RIDG/WDGT* B32 ...... **165** D3
Scotland St *CBHAMW* B1 .... **6** A4 🔳
Scott Av *DARL/WED* WS10 .... **73** D1
  ETTPK/GDPK/PENN WV4 .... **44** A5
Scott Gv *HIA/OLT* B92 .... **152** A6
  GTB/HAM B43 .... **76** B1
  HIA/OLT B92 .... **174** A1
Scott's Green Cl *DUDN* DY1 .... **90** B5
Scott's Rd *STRBR* DY8 .... **136** B3
Scott St *TPTN/OCK* DY4 .... **71** E6
Scotwell Cl *BLKHTH/ROWR* B65 .. **117** D4
Scout Cl *STETCH* B33 .... **129** E5
Scribban Cl *SMTHWK* B66 .... **121** D3 🔳
Scribers La *HLGN/YWD* B28 .... **191** F1
Seacroft Av *STETCH* B33 .... **128** A6
Seafield Cl *KGSWFD* DY6 .... **112** A3 🔳
Seafield La *ALVE* B48 .... **220** A3
Seaforth Gv *WNSFLD* WV11 .... **15** D4 🔳
Seagar St *HHTH/SAND* B71 .... **95** F1
Seager's La *BRLYHL* DY5 .... **113** F5
Seagull Bay Dr *BILS/COS* WV14 .... **69** F2
Seal Cl *WALM/CURD* B76 .... **60** A6
Seals Gn *HWK/WKHTH* B38 .... **187** F6
Seaton Cl *WNSFLD* WV11 .... **28** B2
Seaton Gv *MOS/BIL* B13 .... **169** F2 🔳
Seaton Pl *STRBR* DY8 .... **111** E5
Second Av *BORD* B9 .... **126** B6 🔳
  KGSWFD DY6 .... **88** D3
  SLYOAK B29 .... **147** D6
  WOLVN WV10 .... **12** A6
Second Exhibition Av
  BHAMNEC B40 .... **155** F5 🔳
Sedge Av *HWK/WKHTH* B38 .... **188** B2
Sedgeberrow Covert
  HWK/WKHTH B38 .... **188** A5 🔳

Sedgeberrow Rd *HALE* B63 .... **162** C1 🔳
Sedgefield Cl *DUDN* DY1 .... **90** A2 🔳
Sedgefield Gv
  DUNHL/THL/PER WV6 .... **22** B3 🔳
Sedgeford Cl *BRLYHL* DY5 .... **137** F1 🔳
Sedgehill Av *HRBN* B17 .... **145** D5
Sedgemere Gv *RUSH/SHEL* WS4 .... **19** E5
Sedgemere Rd
  LGN/SDN/BHAMAIR B26 .... **128** B6
Sedgley Gv *BFLD/HDSWWD* B20 .... **98** A1
Sedgley Hall Av *SEDG* DY3 .... **67** E3
Sedgley Rd
  ETTPK/GDPK/PENN WV4 .... **66** B1
Sedgley Rd East *TPTN/OCK* DY4 .... **92** C1
Sedgley Rd West *TPTN/OCK* DY4 .. **69** E5
Sedgley St *BKHL/PFLD* WV2 .... **45** E2
Seedhouse Ct *CDYHTH* B64 .... **140** C1 🔳
Seeleys Rd *SPARK* B11 .... **149** F5
Sefton Dr *BLKHTH/ROWR* B65 .... **116** B1
Sefton Gv *DARL/WED* WS10 .... **71** C1
Sefton Rd *LDYWD/EDGR* B16 ...... **122** B6
Segbourne Rd *RBRY* B45 .... **184** A5
Segundo Cl *DSYBK/YTR* WS5 .... **52** A5
Segundo Rd *DSYBK/YTR* WS5 ...... **52** B5
Selborne Cl *WSL* WS1 .... **5** G4 🔳
Selborne Gv *MOS/BIL* B13 .... **171** E6 🔳
Selborne Rd *BFLD/HDSWWD* B20 .. **98** C3
Selborne St *WSL* WS1 .... **5** G4
Selbourne Crs *WOLV* WV1 .... **27** D6
Selby Cl *LGN/SDN/BHAMAIR* B26.. **128** B6
Selby Gv *MOS/BIL* B13 .... **171** E6
Selby Wy *BLOX/PEL* WS3 .... **16** A3
Selcombe Wy *HWK/WKHTH* B38 .. **188** B6
Selcroft Av *RIDG/WDGT* B32 ...... **144** B3
Selecta Av *KGSTG* B44 .... **77** F1
Selkirk Cl *HHTH/SAND* B71 .... **73** E5
Selly Av *SLYOAK* B29 .... **168** C1
Selly Cl *SLYOAK* B29 .... **169** D1
Selly Hall Cft *BVILLE* B30 .... **168** B5
Selly Hill Rd *SLYOAK* B29 .... **168** B1
Selly Oak Rd *BVILLE* B30 .... **168** A4
Selly Park Rd *SLYOAK* B29 .... **168** C1
Selly Wht *SLYOAK* B29 .... **168** A2
Sellywick Dr *SLYOAK* B29 .... **168** C1
Selly Wick Rd *SLYOAK* B29 .... **168** C1
Sellywood Rd *BVILLE* B30 .... **168** A4
Selma Gv *ALE/KHTH/YWD* B14 .... **171** F6 🔳
Selmans Hill *BLOX/PEL* WS3 .... **17** E2
Selsdon Cl *HLYWD* B47 .... **207** F1
Selsdon Rd *BLOX/PEL* WS3 .... **16** B2
Selsey Rd *HRBN* B17 .... **121** D4
Selston Rd *AST/WIT* B6 .... **100** A6
Selvey Av *GTB/HAM* B43 .... **55** D6
Selworthy Rd *CBROM* B36 .... **106** B6
Selwyn Cl *BKHL/PFLD* WV2 .... **45** E2
Selwyn Rd *BILS/COS* WV14 .... **48** B3
  LDYWD/EDGR B16 .... **121** F4
Selwyn Wk *FOAKS/STRLY* B74 ...... **37** E3
Senneleys Park Rd *NFLD/LBR* B31 .. **166** B2
Sennen Cl *WLNHL* WV13 .... **28** B6 🔳
Sensall Rd *HAG/WOL* DY9 .... **138** B6
Serpentine Rd *AST/WIT* B6 .... **100** C4
  HRBN B17 .... **145** E4
  SLYOAK B29 .... **146** C6
Settle Av *BKDE/SHDE* B34 .... **128** B1
Settle Cft
  CHWD/FDBR/MGN B37 .... **130** B6 🔳
Setton Dr *SEDG* DY3 .... **68** A4
Seven Acres *ALDR* WS9 .... **35** D2
Seven Acres Rd *NFLD/LBR* B31 .... **187** E4
  RMSLY B62 .... **142** C4
Seven Star Rd *SOLH* B91 .... **174** C6
Seven Stars Rd *OLDBY* B69 .... **94** C6
Severn Cl *CBROM* B36 .... **106** B6
  SHHTH WV12 .... **14** C0
  TPTN/OCK DY4 .... **70** B6
Severn Dr *BRLYHL* DY5 .... **89** D6
  DUNHL/THL/PER WV6 .... **22** A3
Severne Gv *ACGN* B27 .... **173** E2
Severne Rd *ACGN* B27 .... **173** E3
Severn Gv *SPARK* B11 .... **149** E3 🔳
  HALE B63 .... **139** D4
  STRBR DY8 .... **136** B6
Severn St *CBHAMW* B1 .... **123** F6 🔳
Severn Wy *HLYWD* B47 .... **206** A3
Sevington Cl *SOLH* B91 .... **195** E5 🔳
Seymour Cl *SLYOAK* B29 .... **169** D1
Seymour Gdns *FOAKS/STRLY* B74 .. **38** A5 🔳
Seymour Rd *HAG/WOL* DY9 .... **138** B4
  OLDBY B69 .... **95** E6
  TPTN/OCK DY4 .... **71** E2
Seymour St *DIG/EDG* B5 .... **7** G4 🔳
Shackleton Dr *BLOX/PEL* WS3 .... **17** F3
Shadowbrook La *HIA/OLT* B92 .... **177** F4
Shadwell Dr *SEDG* DY3 .... **89** F3
Shadwell St *CBHAMNE* B4 .... **7** E2
Shady La *KGSTG* B44 .... **77** F1
Shadymoor Dr *BRLYHL* DY5 .... **137** E1
Shaftesbury Av *HAG/WOL* DY9 .... **137** E6
Shaftesbury Rd *DARL/WED* WS10 .. **73** D1
Shaftesbury Sq *HHTH/SAND* B71 .. **73** E6 🔳
Shaftesbury St *HHTH/SAND* B71 .... **95** E1
  WBROM B70 .... **95** D1

Shaftmoor La *HLGN/YWD* B28 .... **172** A1
Shaftsbury Av *HALE* B63 .... **139** D2 🔳
Shaftsbury Cl *BILS/COS* WV14 ...... **48** B2 🔳
Shaftsbury Rd
  LGN/SDN/BHAMAIR B26 .... **153** C4
Shakespeare La *BILS/COS* WV14 .... **69** F1 🔳
Shakespeare Crs *BLOX/PEL* WS3 .... **18** A5
Shakespeare Dr *SHLY* B90 .... **192** C4
Shakespeare Pl *BLOX/PEL* WS3 ...... **18** A6
Shakespeare St *AST/WIT* B6 ...... **101** D2
  SEDG DY3 .... **88** C1
  SHLY B90 .... **193** F4
  SMTHWKW B67 .... **119** F3
  TPTN/OCK DY4 .... **70** C3
Shakespeare St *SPARK* B11 .... **149** E4 🔳
  WOLV WV1 .... **3** C5
The Shales *WMBN* WV5 .... **64** A6 🔳
Shale St *BILS/COS* WV14 .... **47** E4
Shalford Rd *HIA/OLT* B92 .... **152** A5
Shallcross La *SEDG* DY3 .... **89** F2
Shalnecote Gv
  ALE/KHTH/YWD B14 .... **169** E6
Shambles *DARL/WED* WS10 .... **72** B1 🔳
Shandon Cl *RIDG/WDGT* B32 ...... **144** B6 🔳
Shannon Rd *HWK/WKHTH* B38 .... **188** A6
Shapinsay Dr *RBRY* B45 .... **184** B4 🔳
Shard End Crs *BKDE/SHDE* B34 .. **129** E2
Shardlow Rd *WNSFLD* WV11 .... **14** A5
The Shardway *BKDE/SHDE* B34 .. **129** E2
Sharesacre St *WLNHL* WV13 .... **29** D4
Sharington Cl *DUDS* DY2 .... **92** A5 🔳🔳
Sharman Rd *WOLVN* WV10 .... **26** A1
Sharmans Cross Rd *SOLH* B91 .... **194** B5 🔳
Sharon Cl *ETTPK/GDPK/PENN* WV4 .. **46** A4
Sharps Cl *RBRY* B45 .... **184** C5
Sharrat Fld *MGN/WHC* B75 .... **39** F5
Sharrocks St *WOLV* WV1 .... **3** G6
Shawberry Av *CVALE* B35 .... **104** C2 🔳
Shawberry Rd
  CHWD/FDBR/MGN B37 .... **130** B3
Shawbrook Gv
  ALE/KHTH/YWD B14 .... **190** C2 🔳
Shawbury Cl *BHTH/HG* B12 .... **148** B1
  DUNHL/THL/PER WV6 .... **22** A2
Shawbury Rd *WOLVN* WV10 .... **26** B2
Shaw Dr *STETCH* B33 .... **128** A5
Shawfield *HLYWD* B47 .... **206** C2
Shawhellier Av *BRLYHL* DY5 ...... **114** A5
Shaw Hill Rd *WASH/WDE* B8 ...... **126** C3
Shawhurst Cft *HLYWD* B47 .... **190** C6 🔳
Shawhurst La *HLYWD* B47 .... **206** C1
Shaw La *DUNHL/THL/PER* WV6 .... **23** D4
Shawley Cft *ACGN* B27 .... **152** A5
Shaw Rd *BILS/COS* WV14 .... **69** D2
  BKHL/PFLD WV2 .... **45** E3
  DUDS DY2 .... **91** D6
  TPTN/OCK DY4 .... **93** E1
  WOLVN WV10 .... **25** D3 🔳
Shawsdale Rd *CBROM* B36 .... **104** B6
Shaw's Pas *DIG/EDG* B5 .... **7** G5
Shaw St *WBROM* B70 .... **72** A3
  WSLW WS2 .... **4** B1
Shayler Gv *BKHL/PFLD* WV2 .... **45** F2
Sheaf La *LGN/SDN/BHAMAIR* B26.. **153** D5
Shearwater Cl *RBRY* B45 .... **200** B1
Shearwater Wk
  ERDW/GRVHL B23 .... **79** D3
Sheaves Cl
  ETTPK/GDPK/PENN WV4 .... **46** C6
Shedden St *DUDS* DY2 .... **91** F5 🔳
Sheddington Rd *ERDW/GRVHL* B23 .. **79** F4
Sheen Rd *KGSTG* B44 .... **56** A5
Sheepclose Dr
  CHWD/FDBR/MGN B37 .... **130** C4 🔳
Sheepcote St *LDYWD/EDGR* B16 .. **123** D3
Sheepfold Cl *BLKHTH/ROWR* B65 .. **116** C3
Sheepmoor Cl *HRBN* B17 .... **144** B1
Sheepwash La *TPTN/OCK* DY4 ...... **71** F6
Sheerwater Dr *BRLYHL* DY5 ...... **137** E2
Sheffield Cl *SCFLD/BOLD* B73 ...... **80** C4
Sheffield Rd *BRLYHL* DY5 .... **114** C6
Shefford Rd *AST/WIT* B6 .... **124** B2 🔳
Sheila Av *WNSFLD* WV11 .... **14** A6
Shelah Rd *HALE* B63 .... **140** C3
Shelbourne Cl *OLDBY* B69 .... **93** F5
Sheldon Av *DARL/WED* WS10 .... **50** C5
Sheldon Cl *BILS/COS* WV14 .... **47** F6
Sheldon Dr *NFLD/LBR* B31 .... **185** F4
Sheldonfield Rd
  LGN/SDN/BHAMAIR B26 .... **153** F5
Sheldon Gv
  LGN/SDN/BHAMAIR B26 .... **153** C6
Sheldon Hall Av *STETCH* B33 ...... **129** F4
Sheldon Heath Rd
  LGN/SDN/BHAMAIR B26 .... **153** D1
  STETCH B33 .... **128** C5
Sheldon Rd *HHTH/SAND* B71 .... **74** A3
  WOLVN WV10 .... **10** C4
Shelfield Rd *ALE/KHTH/YWD* B14 .. **189** E2
Shelley Av *TPTN/OCK* DY4 .... **71** C3
Shelley Cl *SEDG* DY3 .... **66** C6
  STRBR DY8 .... **136** C1 🔳
Shelley Dr *AST/WIT* B6 .... **101** D2 🔳
  FOAKS/STRLY B74 .... **38** B1
Shelley Rd *SHHTH* WV12 .... **16** A6

WOLVN WV10 .... 11 F3
Shelly Cl CHWD/FDBR/MGN B37 ..... 130 B5
Shelly Crs SHLY B90 .... 211 D1
Shelly Cft STETCH B33 .... 128 C4
Shelly La SHLY B90 .... 211 D1
Shelsley Av OLDBY B69 .... 117 F2
Shelsley Dr MOS/BIL B13 .... 171 D2
Shelsley Wy SOLH B91 .... 195 D4
Shelton Cl DARL/WED WS10 .... 51 E4
Shelton La HALE B63 .... 140 A4
Shelwick Gv DOR/KN B93 .... 212 B3 🗓
Shenley Av DUDN DY1 .... 69 D5
Shenley Fields Dr NFLD/LBR B31 .... 166 A4
Shenley Fields Rd SLYOAK B29 .... 166 B4
Shenley Gdns SLYOAK B29 .... 166 C4
Shenley Hl NFLD/LBR B31 .... 166 B4
Shenley La SLYOAK B29 .... 166 B4
Shenstone Av RMSLY B62 .... 142 A5
STRBR DY8 .... 135 F6
Shenstone Cl FOAKS/STRLY B74 .... 38 A1 🗓
Shenstone Cl BDMR/CCFT WV3 ..... 44 C5 🗓
Shenstone Dr ALDR WS9 .... 20 C5
Shenstone Rd
  ALE/KHTH/YWD B14 .... 190 C4
  GTB/HAM B43 .... 76 A3
  LDYWD/EDGR B16 .... 121 E4
Shenstone Valley Rd RMSLY B62 .... 142 A5
Shenton Wk
  CHWD/FDBR/MGN B37 .... 130 B2
Shepheard Rd
  LGN/SDN/BHAMAIR B26 .... 153 F4
Shepherd Dr SHHTH WV12 .... 29 D2 🗓
Shepherds Brook Rd
  HAG/WOL DY9 .... 137 F4
Shepherds Fold
  BLKHTH/ROWR B65 .... 117 D5
Shepherds Green Rd
  ERDE/BCHGN B24 .... 102 B3
Shepherds Pool Rd MGN/WHC B75 .. 40 A5
Shepherds Standing
  BKDE/SHDE B34 .... 129 D1 🗓
Shepherds Wy ERDW/GRVHL B23 .... 79 E3
Shepley Rd BRGRVE B60 .... 214 C2
  RBRY B45 .... 201 D1
Sheppey Dr CBROM B36 .... 131 D2 🗓
Shepwell Gn WLNHL WV13 .... 29 E6
Sherard Cft CBROM B36 .... 131 D2 🗓
Sheraton Cl ALDR WS9 .... 35 D1
Sheraton Gra STRBR DY8 .... 158 B1
Sherborne Cl BLOX/PEL WS3 .... 17 E6 🗓
  CSHL/WTROR B46 .... 132 C3 🗓
Sherborne Gdns CDSL WV8 .... 8 C2
Sherborne Gv CBHAMW B1 .... 122 C4
Sherborne Rd WOLVN WV10 .... 11 F4
  LDYWD/EDGR B16 .... 123 D5
Sherborne Dr ACGN B27 .... 151 E5 🗓
  BHTH/HG B12 .... 148 B3
  CDYHTH B64 .... 140 C1
  STRBR DY8 .... 137 D5 🗓
Sherdmore Cft SHLY B90 .... 210 B1 🗓
Sheridan Cl WSLW WS2 .... 51 D2
Sheridan Gdns SEDG DY3 .... 66 B6 🗓
Sheridan St HHTH/SAND B71 .... 95 F1
  WSLW WS2 .... 51 D2
Sheriff Dr BRLYHL DY5 .... 114 B5 🗓
Sherifoot La MGN/WHC B75 .... 39 D4 🗓
Sheringham EDG B15 .... 146 A1
Sheringham Rd BVILLE B30 .... 189 D2
Sherington Dr
  ETTPK/GDPK/PENN WV4 .... 45 F4 🗓
Sherlock Cl SHHTH WV12 .... 29 F1
Sherlock St DIG/EDG B5 .... 148 A1
Sherrans Dell
  ETTPK/GDPK/PENN WV4 .... 45 F6 🗓
Sherratt Cl WALM/CURD B76 .... 82 B3
Sherringham Dr SHHTH WV12 .... 15 E4
Sherron Gdns BHTH/HG B12 .... 148 B4 🗓
Sherston Covert BVILLE B30 .... 189 E3 🗓
Shervale Cl
  ETTPK/GDPK/PENN WV4 .... 44 C3 🗓
Sherwin Av BILS/COS WV14 .... 68 C1
Sherwood Av TPTN/OCK DY4 .... 92 B4
Sherwood Cl HIA/OLT B92 .... 174 B3
  HLGN/YWD B28 .... 172 B6
Sherwood Dr BRLYHL DY5 .... 114 B6
Sherwood Ms HLGN/YWD B28 .... 172 A5
Sherwood Rd HLGN/YWD B28 .... 172 A4
  SMTHWK B67 .... 120 C6
  STRBR DY8 .... 136 A2
Sherwood St WOLV WV1 .... 2 C1
Sherwood Wk RUSH/SHEL WS4 .... 19 F6
Shetland Cl
  DUNHL/THL/PER WV6 .... 25 D2 🗓
  LDYWD/EDGR B16 .... 122 B5
Shetland Dr SMTHWK B66 .... 95 F5 🗓
Shidas La OLDBY B69 .... 94 A6
Shillcock Gv LOZ/NWT B19 .... 124 A2 🗓
Shilton Cl SHLY B90 .... 210 B1
Shilton Gv SLYOAK B29 .... 166 C3 🗓
Shinwell Crs OLDBY B69 .... 95 F3
Shipbourne Cl RIDG/WDGT B32 .... 144 B4
Shipley Flds ERDE/BCHGN B24 .... 102 C2 🗓
Shipley Gv SLYOAK B29 .... 166 C3 🗓

Shipston Rd NFLD/LBR B31 .... 187 D4
Shipton Cl DUDN DY1 .... 90 A2
Shipton Rd CSCFLD/WYGN B72 ..... 59 E6
Shipway Rd YDLY B25 .... 150 C2
Shire Cl LDYWD/EDGR B16 .... 122 B5 🗓
  LGLGN/QTN B68 .... 119 D5
Shireland Brook Gdns
  WSNGN B18 .... 121 F5 🗓
Shireland Cl BFLD/HDSWWD B20 .... 98 A2
Shireland Rd SMTHWK B66 .... 121 D5
Shire Rdg ALDR WS9 .... 20 C1
Shirestone Rd STETCH B33 .... 130 A5
Shireview Rd BLOX/PEL WS3........... 19 D1
Shirley Dr CSCFLD/WYGN B72 .... 59 E5 🗓
Shirley Park Rd SHLY B90 .... 193 D3
  BVILLE B30 .... 168 C6
  DUDS DY2 .... 92 A5
  HLGN/YWD B28 .... 172 C3
  LGLGN/QTN B68 .... 119 E1
Shirral Gv CHWD/FDBR/MGN B37 .. 130 B2
Shirrall Dr POL/KGSB/FAZ B78....... 41 F3
Sholing Cl CDSL WV8 .... 10 D4
Shooters Cl DIG/EDG B5 .... 147 F3 🗓
Shooters Hl CSCFLD/WYGN B72 .... 81 F1
Shopton Rd BKDE/SHDE B34 .... 104 C6
Shoreham Cl WLNHL WV13 .... 27 F6 🗓
Short Acre St WSLW WS2 .... 4 B1
Shorters Av ALE/KHTH/YWD B14 .. 191 D1
Short Heath Rd ERDW/GRVHL B23.. 80 A5
Shortland Cl DOR/KN B93 .... 212 C1 🗓
Shortlands Cl BVILLE B30 .... 188 C3
Shortlands La BLOX/PEL WS3 .... 18 B3
Short Rd SMTHWK B67 .... 119 F4
  WOLVN WV10 .... 12 A4
Short St BILS/COS WV14 .... 47 F3 🗓
  BLKHTH/ROWR B65 .... 117 E5 🗓
  DARL/WED WS10 .... 50 A6
  DARL/WED WS10 .... 50 A6
  DUDN DY1 .... 90 C3 🗓
  HALE B63 .... 140 B5
  SHHTH WV12 .... 29 E2
  STRBR DY8 .... 136 B4 🗓
  WOLV WV1 .... 3 E3 🗓
  WSLW WS2 .... 4 A4
Shorwell Pl BRLYHL DY5 .... 113 E4
Shottery Gv WALM/CURD B76 .... 82 B2
Shottery Rd SHLY B90 .... 193 D4 🗓
Shotteswell Rd SHLY B90 .... 193 D6
Showell Circ WOLVN WV10 .... 12 A6
Showell Green La SPARK B11 .... 149 D6
Showell La
  ETTPK/GDPK/PENN WV4 .... 42 C6
Showell Rd WOLVN WV10 .... 11 F5
Showells Gdns VAUX/NECH B7 ..... 101 E6 🗓
Shrawley Cl HALE B63 .... 162 C1 🗓
  RBRY B45 .... 184 B6 🗓
Shrawley Rd NFLD/LBR B31 .... 187 D3
Shrewley Crs STETCH B33 .... 130 A6
Shrewsbury Cl BLOX/PEL WS3 .... 16 B4
Shrewton Av ALE/KHTH/YWD B14 . 189 F3
Shrubbery Av TPTN/OCK DY4 .... 69 F6
Shrubbery Cl WALM/CURD B76....... 81 F5
Shrubbery Rd DIG/EDG B5 .... 148 A1
  BVILLE B30 .... 168 C3
Shrublands Av LGLGN/QTN B68 .... 143 D2
Shrub La ERDE/BCHGN B24 .... 102 C1
Shugborough Dr DUDN DY1 .... 90 A3
Shustoke La DSYBK/YTR WS5 .... 53 D5
Shustoke Rd BKDE/SHDE B34......... 129 E1 🗓
  SOLH B91 .... 175 F6 🗓
Shutlock La MOS/BIL B13 .... 169 F2 🗓
Shut Mill La RMSLY B62 .... 181 F4
Shutt La HOCK/TIA B94................. 209 D6
Shyltons Cft LDYWD/EDGR B16 .... 122 C5
Sibdon Gv NFLD/LBR B31 .... 186 C5
Sidaway Cl OLDBY B69 .... 117 E1
Sidaway St CDYHTH B64 .... 116 A6 🗓
Sidbury Gv DOR/KN B93 .... 212 A4 🗓
Sidcup Cl BILS/COS WV14 .... 47 D6
Sidcup Rd KGSTG B44 .... 78 C2
Siddons Rd BILS/COS WV14 .... 69 F1
Siddons Wy HHTH/SAND B71 .... 72 C4
Sidenhill Cl SHLY B90 .... 193 D5
Sidlaw Cl HALE B63 .... 161 F1 🗓
  WOLVN WV10 .... 25 D1
Sidney St BKHL/PFLD WV2 .... 45 E1
Sidwick Crs BKHL/PFLD WV2 .... 47 D5
Sigmund Cl WOLV WV1 .... 27 D4 🗓
Signal Gv BLOX/PEL WS3 .... 16 C4
Signal Hayes Rd WALM/CURD B76 .. 82 B1
Silesbourne Cl CBROM B36 .... 105 E4 🗓
Silhill Hall Rd SOLH B91 .... 174 C6
Silva Av KGSWFD DY6 .... 112 B3

Silverfield Cl
  ALE/KHTH/YWD B14 .... 170 A3 🗓
Silver Innage HALE B63 .... 139 E2
Silverlands Av LGLYGN/QTN B68 .. 119 D4 🗓
Silverlands Cl HLGN/YWD B28 .... 172 B2
Silvermead Rd SCFLD/BOLD B73 .... 80 C2
Silvermere Rd
  LGN/SDN/BHAMAIR B26 .... 153 F3
Silverstone Cl WSLW WS2 .... 29 F4
Silverstone Dr FOAKS/STRLY B74 .. 56 B3
Silver St ALE/KHTH/YWD B14 .... 170 A3
  BRLYHL DY5 .... 113 D5
  HLYWD B47 .... 206 A2
  HWK/WKHTH B38 .... 206 A2
Silverthorne Av TPTN/OCK DY4 ..... 69 F6
Silverthorne La CDYHTH B64......... 115 D6
Silverton Crs MOS/BIL B13 .... 171 F2
Silverton Rd SMTHWK B67 .... 120 A1
Silverton Wy WNSFLD WV11 .... 28 B2
Silvester Rd BILS/COS WV14 .... 48 A3
Silvester Wy STRBR DY5................. 137 D1
Silvington Cl NFLD/LBR B31 .... 167 E4 🗓
Simcox Gdns RIDG/WDGT B32 .... 165 F1
Simcox Rd DARL/WED WS10 .... 50 B4
Simeon Bissell Cl TPTN/OCK DY4 .. 70 C6 🗓
Simeon's Wk BRLYHL DY5 .... 138 B2
Simmonds Cl BLOX/PEL WS3 .... 17 F2
Simmonds Pl DARL/WED WS10 ..... 50 B2 🗓
Simmonds Rd BLOX/PEL WS3 .... 17 F2
Simmons Dr RIDG/WDGT B32 ...... 143 F5
Simmons Leasow
  RIDG/WDGT B32 .... 165 F1 🗓
Simmons Rd WNSFLD WV11 .... 15 D4
Simms La DUDS DY2 .... 115 E2
  HLYWD B47 .... 206 C2
Simon Cl HHTH/SAND B71 .... 74 A2 🗓
Simon Rd HLYWD B47 .... 190 C6
Simpkins Cl ALDR WS9 .... 20 C2
Simpson Gv WOLVN WV10 .... 26 A1
Simpson Rd CSCFLD/WYGN B72 ... 81 E2
  WOLVN WV10 .... 26 A1
  WSLW WS2 .... 31 D2
Simpson St OLDBY B69.................... 94 C6
Singer Cft CBROM B36 .... 106 B4
Sir Alfreds Wy WALM/CURD B76..... 60 A6
Sir Harrys Rd DIG/EDG B5 .... 147 E3
  EDG B15....................................... 147 D3
Sir Hilton's Rd NFLD/LBR B31 ...... 187 D6
Sir John's Rd SLYOAK B29 .... 147 E6
Sir Richards Dr HRBN B17 .... 144 B2
Sisefield Rd HWK/WKHTH B38....... 184 C4
Siskin Dr BHTH/HG B12 .... 148 A3 🗓
Siskin Rd HAG/WOL DY9 .... 137 E6 🗓
Sister Dora Gdns WSL WS1 .... 4 C5
Siviter's Cl BLKHTH/ROWR B65 .... 117 D4
Siviter's La BLKHTH/ROWR B65 .... 117 D4
Siviter St HALE B63 .... 141 D5 🗓
Six Acres RIDG/WDGT B32 .... 143 E5
Skelcher Rd SHLY B90 .... 192 C1
Skemp Cl BILS/COS WV14 .... 47 F4
Skidmore Av BDMR/CCFT WV3 ...... 44 B1
Skidmore Dr WBROM B70 .... 94 C2
Skidmore Rd BILS/COS WV14 ...... 69 F1 🗓
Skinner La DIG/EDG B5 .... 124 A6 🗓
Skinner St WOLV WV1 .... 2 C4
Skip La DSYBK/YTR WS5 .... 54 A4
Skipton Gn
  DUNHL/THL/PER WV6 .... 24 C2 🗓
Skipton Rd LDYWD/EDGR B16....... 122 C6
Skomer Cl RBRY B45 .... 183 F4
Skye Cl CBROM B36...................... 131 D1
Skye Wk CDYHTH B64 .... 116 A6 🗓
Skylark Cl BRLYHL DY5 .... 89 E4 🗓
Slack La BLOX/PEL WS3 .... 18 B4
Slacky La BLOX/PEL WS3 .... 18 A3
Sladefield Rd WASH/WDE B8 .... 126 C2
Slade Gdns CDSL WV8 .... 8 C1
Slade Gv DOR/KN B93 .... 212 B1
Slade La HLGN/YWD B28 .... 192 A2
  MGN/WHC B75 .... 40 C4
Slade Lanker BKDE/SHDE B34....... 128 C2
Sladepool Farm Rd
  ALE/KHTH/YWD B14 .... 190 B2
Slade Rd ERDW/GRVHL B23 .... 101 F3
  HALE B63 .... 139 E3
  MGN/WHC B75 .... 40 A4
  WOLVN WV10 .... 11 E2
Slaithwaite Rd HHTH/SAND B71 ..... 95 F1
Slaney Rd WSLW WS2 .... 51 D3
Slatch House Rd SMTHWK B67 .... 120 A5
Slateley Crs SHLY B90 .... 210 C1 🗓
Slater Rd DOR/KN B93 .... 212 A3
Slaters La WSLW WS2 .... 51 D2
Slaters Pl WSLW WS2 .... 51 E2
Slater St BILS/COS WV14 .... 48 A6 🗓
  DARL/WED WS10 .... 49 F3
  TPTN/OCK DY4 .... 71 F6
  TPTN/OCK DY4 .... 92 C1 🗓
  WLNHL WV13 .... 29 E4
Sleaford Gv HLGN/YWD B28 .... 172 C4
Sleaford Rd HLGN/YWD B28 .... 172 C4
Sledmore Rd DUDS DY2 .... 91 F6
The Slieve BFLD/HDSWWD B20..... 98 C2
Slim Av BILS/COS WV14 .... 48 A6
Slimbridge Cl SHLY B90 .... 210 C1 🗓

Slim Rd WSLW WS2 .... 30 A5
Slims Ga HALE B63 .... 140 C5
Slingfield Rd NFLD/LBR B31 .... 187 F4
The Sling DUDS DY2 .... 115 E1
Sloane St CBHAMW B1 .... 6 A4
Smallbrook La WMBN WV5 .... 65 D4
Smallbrook Queensway
    DIG/EDG B5 .... 123 F6
Small Av DARL/WED WS10 .... 119 F2
Smalldale Rd PBAR/PBCH B42 .... 77 F4
Small Heath Br SPARK B11 .... 148 D1
Small Heath Hwy SMTHK B10 .... 149 D1
    YDLY B25 .... 150 B3
Small La HOCK/TIA B94 .... 222 A3
Smallshire Wy STRBR DY8 .... 135 F1
Small St HHTH/SAND B71 .... 73 D6
    WSL WS1 .... 4 C6
Smallwood Cl
    ERDE/BCHGN B24 .... 103 F2
    WALM/CURD B76 .... 60 A6
Smallwood Rd CDSL WV8 .... 10 A3
Smeaton Gdns WSNGN B18 .... 122 A3
Smedley Crooke Pl ALVE B48 .... 203 E5
Smeed Gv ERDE/BCHGN B24 .... 103 D2
Smestow St WOLVN WV10 .... 25 F3
Smirrells Rd HLGN/YWD B28 .... 172 A6
Smith Av DARL/WED WS10 .... 49 F5
Smith Cl BILS/COS WV14 .... 68 C2
    SMTHKWK B67 .... 119 F4
Smithfield Pas DIG/EDG B5 .... 124 A6
Smithfield Rd BLOX/PEL WS3 .... 17 F4
Smithmoor Crs HHTH/SAND B71 .... 74 B3
Smith Pl TPTN/OCK DY4 .... 93 F3
Smith Rd DARL/WED WS10 .... 72 B2
    WSLW WS2 .... 51 E3
Smiths Cl RIDG/WDGT B32 .... 165 D1
Smiths La DOR/KN B93 .... 212 A1
Smith St BILS/COS WV14 .... 47 F4
    DUDS DY2 .... 91 F6
    LOZ/NWT B19 .... 123 E2
Smiths Wy CSHL/WTROR B46 .... 106 C2
Smithy Dr BLOX/PEL WS3 .... 18 C1
Smitny La BRLYHL DY5 .... 89 D5
The Smithy
    LGN/SDN/BHAMAIR B26 .... 153 E3
Smout Crs BILS/COS WV14 .... 68 B1
Snake La ALVE B48 .... 216 C3
Snapdragon Dr DSYBK/YTR WS5 .... 52 B6
Snape Rd WOLVN WV11 .... 14 C4
Sneyd Hall Cl BLOX/PEL WS3 .... 16 C3
Sneyd Hall Rd BLOX/PEL WS3 .... 16 C4
Sneyd La BLOX/PEL WS3 .... 16 B4
    WNSFLD WV11 .... 15 E4
Snowberry Dr BRLYHL DY5 .... 89 E4
Snowberry Gdns ACGN B27 .... 151 E4
Snowdon Gv HALE B63 .... 161 F2
Snowdon Ri SEDG DY3 .... 67 F5
Snowdon Rd STRBR DY8 .... 137 D3
Snowdon Wy SHHTH WV12 .... 15 D4
    WOLVN WV10 .... 25 D1
Snowford Cl SHLY B90 .... 192 B4
Snow Hl BKHL/PFLD WV2 .... 3 E5
Snow Hill Jct BKHL/PFLD WV2 .... 3 E6
Snow Hill Queensway
    CBHAMNE B4 .... 6 D3
Snows Drive Hl SHLY B90 .... 209 F2
Snowshill Gdns DUDN DY1 .... 90 B1
Soberton Cl WNSFLD WV11 .... 14 B6
Soho Av WSNGN B18 .... 98 C6
Soho Cl SMTHWK B66 .... 121 E1
Soho Hl WSNGN B18 .... 98 C6
Soho Rd HDSW B21 .... 98 B6
Soho Wy SMTHWK B66 .... 121 D1
Solari Gv TPTN/OCK DY4 .... 71 E3
Solent Cl COVEN WV9 .... 10 B3
Solihull By-pass SOLH B91 .... 175 F6
Solihull La HLGN/YWD B28 .... 172 C5
Solihull Pkwy
    CHWD/FDBR/MGN B37 .... 156 A2
    CSHL/WTROR B46 .... 156 A2
    SHLY B90 .... 193 E2
    SPARK B11 .... 149 F6
Solihull Wy CBROM B36 .... 105 D4
    HIA/OLT B92 .... 175 E2
    HOCK/TIA B94 .... 209 E5
Solly Gv TPTN/OCK DY4 .... 71 F4
Solva Cl WOLV WV1 .... 27 D6
Solway Cl DARL/WED WS10 .... 51 E5
Somerby Dr SOLH B91 .... 194 C5
Somercotes Rd PBAR/PBCH B42 .... 77 F3
Somerdale Rd NFLD/LBR B31 .... 187 E1
Somerfield Cl RUSH/SHEL WS4 .... 19 E4
Somerfield Rd BLOX/PEL WS3 .... 17 D5
Somerford Gdns WOLVN WV10 .... 12 A3
Somerford Pl WLNHL WV13 .... 28 B6
Somerford Rd SLYOAK B29 .... 166 B3
Somerford Wy BILS/COS WV14 .... 69 D3
Somerland Rd
    LGN/SDN/BHAMAIR B26 .... 128 C6
Somerset Crs DARL/WED WS10 .... 51 F5
Somerset Dr NFLD/LBR B31 .... 186 B6
    STRBR DY8 .... 135 F2
Somerset Rd BFLD/HDSWWD B20 ..... 98 B3
    EDG B15 .... 146 A3

ERDW/GRVHL B23 .... 80 A5
HHTH/SAND B71 .... 73 F5
RUSH/SHEL WS4 .... 32 C3
WLNHL WV13 .... 29 F5
Somers Rd RMSLY B62 .... 141 E4
    WSLW WS2 .... 50 C2
Somerton Dr
    CHWD/FDBR/MGN B37 .... 155 D2
    ERDW/GRVHL B23 .... 80 C5
Somerville Rd SCFLD/BOLD B73 ...... 58 C5
    SMTH B30 .... 150 A1
Somery Rd DUDN DY1 .... 91 E2
    SLYOAK B29 .... 166 C1
Sommerfield Rd RIDG/WDGT B32 ... 165 E1
Sommerville Dr SCFLD/BOLD B73 ..... 58 C5
Sonning Dr COVEN WV9 .... 10 B3
Sopwith Cft CVALE B35 .... 104 C3
Sorrel Cl OLDBY B69 .... 93 D3
Sorrel Dr ACGN B27 .... 173 D1
    DSYBK/YTR WS5 .... 52 C6
Sorrel Gv ERDE/BCHGN B24 .... 103 F2
Southacre Av DIG/EDG B5 .... 148 A1
Southall Crs BILS/COS WV14 .... 69 E2
Southall Rd WNSFLD WV11 .... 14 C5
Southall's La DUDN DY1 .... 91 D2
Southam Cl HLGN/YWD B28 .... 172 A3
Southam Dr SCFLD/BOLD B73 .... 81 D2
Southampton St WOLV WV1 .... 3 E2
South Av STRBR DY8 .... 136 B5
    WNSFLD WV11 .... 27 E2
South Bank Rd CDYHTH B64 .... 140 B1
Southbank Vw KGSWFD DY6 .... 112 A3
Southbourne Av BKDE/SHDE B34 ... 127 F1
    WSLW WS2 .... 31 D6
Southbourne Cl SLYOAK B29 .... 168 C1
Southbourne Pl WOLVN WV10 .... 11 E2
South Car Park Rd BHAMNEC B40 .. 156 A6
Southcott Av BRLYHL DY5 .... 137 F1
Southdown Av WSNGN B18 .... 122 C1
South Dr CSHL/WTROR B46 .... 131 F1
    DIG/EDG B5 .... 147 E5
    MGN/WHC B75 .... 59 E3
Southern Cl KGSWFD DY6 .... 112 B4
Southerndown Rd SEDG DY3 .... 67 D3
Southern Rd WASH/WDE B8 .... 127 E2
Southern Wy DARL/WED WS10 .... 49 E6
Southey Cl SHHTH WV12 .... 15 F6
    SOLH B91 .... 195 D5
Southfield Av CBROM B36 .... 105 D5
    LDYWD/EDGR B16 .... 121 F4
Southfield Dr HLGN/YWD B28 .... 172 C6
Southfield Gv WOLV WV3 .... 35 D3
Southfield Rd LDYWD/EDGR B16 .... 121 F4
    WNSFLD WV11 .... 28 B2
Southfields Cl CSHL/WTROR B46 ... 132 C2
Southfields Rd SOLH B91 .... 194 B4
Southgate CDYHTH B64 .... 139 F1
    WOLV WV1 .... 2 B1
Southgate Rd KGSTG B44 .... 78 A1
South Gn ETTPK/GDPK/PENN WV4 .. 35 F6
South Gv ERDW/GRVHL B23 .... 80 B6
    LOZ/NWT B19 .... 99 D5
South Holme BORD B9 .... 125 E6
Southlands Rd MOS/BIL B13 .... 170 C2
Southminster Dr
    ALE/KHTH/YWD B14 .... 170 A5
South Ov SEDG DY3 .... 68 A6
South Pde CSCFLD/WYGN B72 .... 59 E5
South Park Ms BRLYHL DY5 .... 113 E5
South Range SPARK B11 .... 148 B2
South Rd ALE/KHTH/YWD B14 .... 170 A3
    ERDW/GRVHL B23 .... 102 B1
    NFLD/LBR B31 .... 186 B3
    SMTHKWK B67 .... 120 B2
    SPARK B11 .... 149 D2
    STRBR DY8 .... 136 B5
    TPTN/OCK DY4 .... 71 D3
    WSNGN B18 .... 122 C1
South Road Av WSNGN B18 .... 122 C1
South Roundhay STETCH B33 .... 128 C4
South St BRLYHL DY5 .... 113 E5
    HRBN B17 .... 145 F3
    WLNHL WV13 .... 28 A6
    WOLVN WV10 .... 25 E1
    WSL WS1 .... 51 F1
South Street Gdns WSL WS1 .... 51 F1
South Vw GTB/HAM B43 .... 76 A4
South View Rd CDSL WV8 .... 9 D3
South View Rd SEDG DY3 .... 67 D3
South Wy BHAMNEC B40 .... 156 B6
Southway Ct KGSWFD DY6 .... 112 B3
Southwick Pl BILS/COS WV14 .... 47 F2
Southwick Rd RMSLY B62 .... 141 F1
Southwold Av BVILLE B30 .... 189 E2
Southwood Av BKDE/SHDE B34 ..... 104 C6
Southwood Cl KGSWFD DY6 .... 112 A2
Southwood Covert
    ALE/KHTH/YWD B14 .... 189 E3
Sovereign Dr DUDN DY1 .... 89 F3
Sovereign Hts NFLD/LBR B31 .... 185 E4
Sovereign Rd BVILLE B30 .... 188 B1
Sovereign Wy MOS/BIL B13 .... 148 B5

Sowerby March
    ERDE/BCHGN B24 .... 103 F1
Sowers Cl SHHTH WV12 .... 29 F2
Sowers Gdns SHHTH WV12 .... 29 F2
Spa Gv BVILLE B30 .... 169 E3
Spark St SPARK B11 .... 148 C3
Sparrey Dr SLYOAK B29 .... 168 C3
Sparrow Cl DARL/WED WS10 .... 51 D4
Speed Rd TPTN/OCK DY4 .... 70 A5
Speedwell Cl ALDR WS9 .... 34 B2
    WNSFLD WV11 .... 28 A2
Speedwell Gdns BRLYHL DY5 .... 137 D3
Speedwell Rd DIG/EDG B5 .... 147 F3
    YDLY B25 .... 150 C3
Spencer Av BILS/COS WV14 .... 69 E3
Spencer Cl HHTH/SAND B71 .... 74 B3
    SEDG DY3 .... 88 C1
Spencer St WSNGN B18 .... 6 A1
Spenser Av DUNHL/THL/PER WV4 ..... 22 A3
Spernall Gv SLYOAK B29 .... 166 C2
Spey Cl DIG/EDG B5 .... 147 F3
Spiceland Rd NFLD/LBR B31 .... 166 B5
Spiers Cft DOR/KN B93 .... 212 C1
Spies Cl RMSLY B62 .... 142 B3
Spies La RMSLY B62 .... 142 B4
Spills Meadow SEDG DY3 .... 68 A6
Spilsbury Cft SOLH B91 .... 194 C5
Spindle La SHLY B90 .... 208 C1
Spinners End Dr CDYHTH B64 .... 115 F6
Spinney Cl BLOX/PEL WS3 .... 18 C3
    NFLD/LBR B31 .... 186 C3
    STRBR DY8 .... 111 D4
Spinney Dr SHLY B90 .... 209 E3
The Spinney BDMR/CCFT WV3 .... 23 F6
    BFLD/HDSWWD B20 .... 98 A1
    FOAKS/STRLY B74 .... 37 D1
    HLYWD B47 .... 207 D3
    SEDG DY3 .... 89 E3
Spiral Cl RMSLY B62 .... 142 A1
Spiral Gn ERDE/BCHGN B24 .... 103 E1
Spitfire Rd ERDE/BCHGN B24 .... 103 E3
Spitfire Wy CVALE B35 .... 104 C3
Spondon Gv BKDE/SHDE B34 .... 129 E2
Spondon Rd WNSFLD WV11 .... 14 A5
Spon La WBROM B70 .... 95 F4
Spon La South SMTHWK B66 .... 95 F5
Spoon Dr HWK/WKHTH B38 .... 187 F3
Spooner Cft DIG/EDG B5 .... 148 A1
Spooners Cl HIA/OLT B92 .... 176 B4
Spouthouse La GTB/HAM B43 .... 76 A4
Spout La WSL WS1 .... 52 A1
Spreadbury Cl HRBN B17 .... 144 B1
Sprig Cft CBROM B36 .... 105 E5
Spring Av BLKHTH/ROWR B65 .... 117 E5
    BLKHTH/ROWR B65 .... 117 F5
Springavon Cft HRBN B17 .... 145 D3
Springbank BORD B9 .... 126 B4
Springbank Rd EDG B15 .... 147 E2
Springbrook Cl CBROM B36 .... 105 F4
Springbrook La HOCK/TIA B94 ...... 222 B2
Spring Cl HLGN/SHEL WS4 .... 19 E3
    SOLH B91 .... 194 B2
Spring Coppice Dr DOR/KN B93 .... 212 C4
Spring Ct WSL WS1 .... 52 C1
Spring Crs CDYHTH B64 .... 140 B2
Springcroft Rd SPARK B11 .... 172 B1
Springfield ERDW/GRVHL B23 .... 101 F2
Springfield Av BHTH/HG B12 .... 148 C3
    HAG/WOL DY9 .... 138 A5
    SEDG DY3 .... 68 A2
Springfield Cl
    BLKHTH/ROWR B65 .... 116 C2
Springfield Crs DUDS DY2 .... 92 B5
    HIA/OLT B92 .... 153 E6
    WALM/CURD B76 .... 60 C5
    WBROM B70 .... 96 A4
Springfield La BLKHTH/ROWR B65 .. 116 B2
    WOLVN WV10 .... 11 F1
Springfield Rd
    ALE/KHTH/YWD B14 .... 170 B3
    BILS/COS WV14 .... 48 A2
    CBROM B36 .... 105 F5
    MOS/BIL B13 .... 171 F2
    RMSLY B62 .... 142 C4
    WALM/CURD B76 .... 60 C6
    WOLVN WV10 .... 26 A3
Springfield Ter
    BLKHTH/ROWR B65 .... 116 B2
Spring Gdns DUDS DY2 .... 91 F5
Spring Grove Gdns WSNGN B18 .... 122 B1
Spring Head DARL/WED WS10 .... 72 B1
Spring Hl ERDE/BCHGN B24 .... 102 B2
    WSNGN B18 .... 122 C3
Springhill Av
    ETTPK/GDPK/PENN WV4 .... 43 E6
Springhill Cl RUSH/SHEL WS4 .... 19 F4
    SHHTH WV12 .... 15 F6
Springhill Gv
    ETTPK/GDPK/PENN WV4 .... 43 E5

Spring Hill La
ETTPK/GDPK/PENN WV4 .... 42 C5
Springhill Pk
ETTPK/GDPK/PENN WV4 .... 43 D6
Spring Hill Pas WSNGN B18 .... 122 C4 🔢
Springhill Rd WNSFLD WV11 .... 13 F5
WSL WS1 .... 5 F5
Spring La ERDE/BCHGN B24 .... 102 C2
RMSLY B62 .... 181 F1
RUSH/SHEL WS4 .... 19 E3
SHHTH WV12 .... 29 D3
Spring Meadow CDYHTH B64 .... 116 B6 🔢
HALE B63 .... 162 B1 🔢
TPTN/OCK DY4 .... 71 E5
Springmeadow Gv
LOZ/NWT B19 .... 123 F1 🔢
Spring Meadow Rd DUDS DY2 .... 115 E5
Spring Parklands DUDN DY1 .... 90 C5
Spring Rd DUDS DY2 .... 115 F1
EDG B15 .... 147 F2
ETTPK/GDPK/PENN WV4 .... 46 C4
RUSH/SHEL WS4 .... 19 F4
SMTHWK B66 .... 95 F5
SPARK B11 .... 150 B6
Springs Av BRGRVW B61 .... 198 B6
Springslade Dr
ERDE/BCHGN B24 .... 103 F2 🔢
The Springs CDYHTH B64 .... 116 C6
Spring St EDG B15 .... 147 F5
HAG/WOL DY9 .... 138 A5
HALE B63 .... 139 E3
TPTN/OCK DY4 .... 70 C6
TPTN/OCK DY4 .... 71 E5
Springthorpe Gn
ERDE/BCHGN B24 .... 103 E1
Springthorpe Rd
ERDE/BCHGN B24 .... 103 F1
Springvale Av DSYBK/YTR WS5 ...... 53 E2
Spring Vale Cl BILS/COS WV14 ...... 68 C2 🔢
Spring Vale Rd
BLKHTH/ROWR B65 .... 116 C2 🔢
Springvale St WLNHL WV13 .... 29 D4
Springvale Wy BILS/COS WV14 ...... 47 E5
Spring Wk HALE B63 .... 161 F2
OLDBY B69 .... 118 C2
WSLW WS2 .... 31 D4
Sproat Av WALM/CURD B76 .... 49 E4 🔢
Spruce Gv ERDE/BCHGN B24 .... 103 E1
Spruce Rd DSYBK/YTR WS5 .... 53 C6
Spruce Wy BDMR/CCFT WV3 .... 23 F6
Spur Tree Av BDMR/CCFT WV3 ...... 22 C6 🔢
Squadron Cl CVALE B35 .... 105 C4
Square Cl RIDG/WDGT B32 .... 143 E6
The Square ALVE B48 .... 217 H3 🔢
BKHL/PFLD WV2 .... 45 F1
HRBN B17 .... 145 D1
SOLH B91 .... 195 E2 🔢
TPTN/OCK DY4 .... 71 F4 🔢
Squires Cft BRLYHL DY5 .... 113 E6
Squires Cft WALM/CURD B76 .... 82 C2
Squirrel Hollow WALM/CURD B76 .. 82 C2
Squirrels Hollow
LGLCYGN/QTN B68 .... 143 F2 🔢
Squirrel Wk
ETTPK/GDPK/PENN WV4 .... 44 C5
FOAKS/STRLY B74 .... 37 E2
Stable Ct SEDG DY3 .... 68 A5
Stable Cft HHTH/SAND B71 .... 74 B4
Stableford Cl RIDG/WDGT B32 ...... 144 B6 🔢
The Stables SLYOAK B29 .... 168 C1 🔢
Stacey Cl CDYHTH B64 .... 116 A6 🔢
Stacey Grange Gdns RBRY B45 .... 200 C1 🔢
Stackhouse Cl ALDR WS9 .... 20 C1
Stackhouse Dr BLOX/PEL WS3 ...... 18 C1 🔢
Stadium Cl WLNHL WV13 .... 29 D4 🔢
Stafford Cl BLOX/PEL WS3 .... 17 E3
Stafford Dr DARL/WED WS10 .... 49 D3
Stafford Dr HHTH/SAND B71 .... 73 D4
HDSW B21 .... 98 B5
WOLVN WV10 .... 11 E5
Staffordshire Pool Cl
AST/WIT B6 .... 100 B4 🔢
Stafford St BILS/COS WV14 .... 47 F3
CBHAMNE B4 .... 7 F3
DARL/WED WS10 .... 72 A1
DUDN DY1 .... 91 D4
WLNHL WV13 .... 28 C5 🔢
WOLV WV1 .... 3 F5
WSLW WS2 .... 4 C2
Stafford Street Jct WOLV WV1 ...... 2 D2
Stafford Wy GTB/HAM B43 .... 76 A4 🔢
Stag Crs BLOX/PEL WS3 .... 32 A1
Stag Hill Rd BLOX/PEL WS3 .... 18 A6
Stag Wk WALM/CURD B76 .... 81 F4
Stainsby Av LOZ/NWT B19 .... 123 E2 🔢
Stainsby Cft SHLY B90 .... 211 D2 🔢
Stalling's La KGSWFD DY6 .... 87 F5
Stambermill La HAG/WOL DY9 .... 137 F4 🔢
Stamford Cft SOLH B91 .... 195 D3 🔢
Stamford Gv BFLD/HDSWWD B20 .. 99 E3
Stamford Rd BFLD/HDSWWD B20 .. 99 E4
BRLYHL DY5 .... 137 E3
STRBR DY8 .... 137 D2
Stamford St STRBR DY8 .... 136 B2

Stanbrook Rd SHLY B90 .... 210 C2
Stanbury Av DARL/WED WS10 ...... 49 D3
Stanbury Rd ALE/KHTH/YWD B14 .. 191 D1
Stancroft Gv
LGN/SDN/BHAMAIR B26 .... 152 C1
Standard Wy VAUX/NECH B7 .... 102 B5
Standbridge Wy TPTN/OCK DY4 .... 70 C6
Standhills Rd KGSWFD DY6 .... 112 A1
Standlake Av CBROM B36 .... 103 F6
Stanfield Rd GTB/HAM B43 .... 55 F4
RIDG/WDGT B32 .... 144 A2
Stanford Av PBAR/PBCH B42 .... 76 C4
Stanford Gv HALE B63 .... 161 E2 🔢
Stanford Rd BKHL/PFLD WV2 ...... 45 E2
BLKHTH/ROWR B65 .... 117 D4
Stanhoe Cl BRLYHL DY5 .... 137 F1 🔢
Stanhope Rd SMTHWKW B67 ...... 120 B4
Stanhope St BDMR/CCFT WV3 ...... 2 B5 🔢
BHTH/HG B12 .... 148 B2
DUDS DY2 .... 116 A3
Stanhope Wy GTB/HAM B43 .... 55 F5
Stanhurst Wy HHTH/SAND B71 .... 74 C1
Stanier Cl RUSH/SHEL WS4 .... 19 D6
Stanier Gv BFLD/HDSWWD B20 .... 99 D3
Staniforth St AST/WIT B6 .... 7 F1
Stanley Av RIDG/WDGT B32 .... 144 A2
SHLY B90 .... 193 D1
WALM/CURD B76 .... 60 B5
Stanley Cl HLGN/YWD B28 .... 172 C6
WNSFLD WV11 .... 14 B5
Stanley Ct SEDG DY3 .... 86 A3
Stanley Dr SEDG DY3 .... 86 A3
Stanley Pl BILS/COS WV14 .... 47 D3 🔢
RUSH/SHEL WS4 .... 33 D1
Stanley Rd ALE/KHTH/YWD B14 .... 169 E1
DARL/WED WS10 .... 49 F4
HHTH/SAND B71 .... 74 A4
LGLCYGN/QTN B68 .... 143 E2
RUSH/SHEL WS4 .... 33 D1
STRBR DY8 .... 136 B6
VAUX/NECH B7 .... 101 E4
WOLVN WV10 .... 11 F4
Stanley St BLOX/PEL WS3 .... 17 E5
Stanmore Gv RIDG/WDGT B32 .... 142 C6
Stanmore Rd LDYWD/EDGR B16 .. 121 D6
Stanton Av DUDN DY1 .... 68 B5
Stanton Rd GTB/HAM B43 .... 75 F3
SHLY B90 .... 192 C1
WOLV WV1 .... 26 B5
Stanville Rd
LGN/SDN/BHAMAIR B26 .... 153 E3 🔢
Stanway Gdns HHTH/SAND B71 .. 73 F5
Stanway Gv KGSTG B44 .... 56 B6
Stanway Rd HHTH/SAND B71 ...... 73 F5
SHLY B90 .... 193 F1
Stanwell Gv ERDW/GRVHL B23 .... 80 A5
Stanwick Av STETCH B33 .... 130 A4
Stapenhall Rd SHLY B90 .... 210 C2
Stapleford Cft
ALE/KHTH/YWD B14 .... 189 E3 🔢
Stapleford Gv STRBR DY8 .... 112 A5
Staple Hall Rd NFLD/LBR B31 ...... 187 D3
Staplehurst Rd HLGN/YWD B28 .. 172 B3 🔢
Staple Lodge Rd NFLD/LBR B31 .. 187 D4
Stapleton Cl WALM/CURD B76 .... 83 D5
Stapleton Dr
CHWD/FDBR/MGN B37 .... 130 C4
Stapleton Rd ALDR WS9 .... 34 B2
Stapylton Av HRBN B17 .... 145 D4
Starbank Rd SMHTH B10 .... 150 C1
Starbold Crs DOR/KN B93 .... 213 D2
Star Cl TPTN/OCK DY4 .... 71 E6
WSLW WS2 .... 30 B3
Starcross Rd ACGN B27 .... 173 E1
Star HI EDG B15 .... 147 D3
Starkey Cft
CHWD/FDBR/MGN B37 .... 131 E5
Starkie Dr LGLCYGN/QTN B68 ...... 119 E3
Starley Wy CHWD/FDBR/MGN B37 .. 155 E5
Star St BDMR/CCFT WV3 .... 44 A1
HAG/WOL DY9 .... 138 A5
Statham Dr LDYWD/EDGR B16 .... 121 E5
Station Ap DOR/KN B93 .... 212 B5 🔢
FOAKS/STRLY B74 .... 38 B1
RBRY B45 .... 215 F1
SCFLD/BOLD B73 .... 59 D3
SOLH B91 .... 194 C1
Station Av LDYWD/EDGR B16 ...... 121 E6
Station Cl BLOX/PEL WS3 .... 17 D5
CDSL WV8 .... 8 A2
Station Dr BRLYHL DY5 .... 113 D6
FOAKS/STRLY B74 .... 59 D1
HAG/WOL DY9 .... 158 C6
HIA/OLT B92 .... 174 A2
HOCK/TIA B94 .... 207 F6 🔢
TPTN/OCK DY4 .... 93 D1 🔢
Station PI BLOX/PEL WS3 .... 17 D5
Station Rd ACGN B27 .... 151 E6
ALDR WS9 .... 20 C2
ALE/KHTH/YWD B14 .... 169 F3
ALVE B48 .... 216 C4

AST/WIT B6 .... 100 B4
BILS/COS WV14 .... 48 A4
BLKHTH/ROWR B65 .... 117 F5
BLOX/PEL WS3 .... 18 C2
BRGRVE B60 .... 214 C4
BRLYHL DY5 .... 113 E3
BVILLE B30 .... 168 A6
CDSL WV8 .... 8 A2
CDYHTH B64 .... 140 B1
CHWD/FDBR/MGN B37 .... 154 C1
CSHL/WTROR B46 .... 108 B5
CSHL/WTROR B46 .... 109 F2
DOR/KN B93 .... 212 C4
ERDW/GRVHL B23 .... 80 B6
HAG/WOL DY9 .... 138 A3 🔢
HAG/WOL DY9 .... 158 C5
HDSW B21 .... 97 E5
HIA/OLT B92 .... 178 C4
HLYWD B47 .... 206 C4
HRBN B17 .... 145 E3
HWK/WKHTH B38 .... 188 B1
NFLD/LBR B31 .... 186 C5
OLDBY B69 .... 118 C2
RUSH/SHEL WS4 .... 32 C1
SCFLD/BOLD B73 .... 80 C2
SOLH B91 .... 195 D1
STETCH B33 .... 127 F4
WMBN WV5 .... 64 C3
WOLVN WV10 .... 26 B3
Station St BLOX/PEL WS3 .... 17 D5
CDYHTH B64 .... 139 E1 🔢
DARL/WED WS10 .... 50 A3
DIG/EDG B5 .... 6 D6
SCFLD/BOLD B73 .... 59 D4 🔢
TPTN/OCK DY4 .... 71 D6
WSL WS1 .... 4 C3
WSLW WS2 .... 4 B4
Station Wy
CHWD/FDBR/MGN B37 .... 155 F5 🔢
Staunton Rd BLOX/PEL WS3 .... 16 C2
Staveley Rd ALE/KHTH/YWD B14 .. 169 F5
WOLV WV1 .... 25 E3
Stead Cl TPTN/OCK DY4 .... 71 D2
WSLW WS2 .... 31 E2
Steadman Cft TPTN/OCK DY4 ...... 71 F3 🔢
Stechford La WASH/WDE B8 .... 127 E2
Stechford Rd BKDE/SHDE B34 .... 127 E2
Steel Bright Rd SMTHWK B66 ...... 121 E1
Steel Cl WOLVN WV10 .... 11 F5
Steel Gv YDLY B25 .... 151 E2
Steelhouse La BKHL/PFLD WV2 .... 46 A1
CBHAMNE B4 .... 7 F3
Steel Rd NFLD/LBR B31 .... 186 B5
Steene Gv NFLD/LBR B31 .... 185 F2
The Steeples STRBR DY8 .... 137 D6 🔢
Steepwood Cft BVILLE B30 .... 187 F1
Stella Cft CHWD/FDBR/MGN B37 .. 131 E5
Stella Gv GTB/HAM B43 .... 75 E3
Stella Rd TPTN/OCK DY4 .... 70 B5
Stenbury Cl WOLVN WV10 .... 12 B1 🔢
Stencills Dr RUSH/SHEL WS4 ...... 33 D4
Stencills Rd RUSH/SHEL WS4 ...... 33 D3
Stennels Av RMSLY B62 .... 142 A5
Stephens Cl
CHWD/FDBR/MGN B37 .... 131 D5 🔢
DUNHL/THL/PER WV6 .... 22 B5 🔢
Stephenson Sq WSLW WS2 .... 31 D2 🔢
Stephenson St BDMR/CCFT WV3 .. 2 B5
CBHAM 🔢 6 D6
Stephens Rd WALM/CURD B76 .... 60 C5
Stepping Stone Cl WSLW WS2 ...... 30 B3
Stepping Stones STRBR DY8 ...... 137 D4
Steppingstone St DUDN DY1 ...... 91 D4
Sterndale Rd PBAR/PBCH B42 .... 77 E5
Steven Dr BILS/COS WV14 .... 70 A2
Stevens Av RIDG/WDGT B32 ...... 165 F1
Stevens Ga BKHL/PFLD WV2 ...... 45 E1 🔢
Stevens Rd HAG/WOL DY9 .... 159 F1
Steward St WSNGN B18 .... 122 C4
Stewart Rd ALDR WS9 .... 20 C2
KGSWFD DY6 .... 111 F3
Stewarts Rd RMSLY B62 .... 141 F2
Stewart St BKHL/PFLD WV2 .... 45 E1
Stewkins STRBR DY8 .... 136 A1
Steyning Rd
LGN/SDN/BHAMAIR B26 .... 152 A4
Stickley La SEDG DY3 .... 89 E1
Stilehouse Crs
BLKHTH/ROWR B65 .... 117 E5 🔢
Stilthouse Gv RBRY B45 .... 184 C6 🔢
Stirling Crs SHHTH WV12 .... 29 D3
Stirling Rd BILS/COS WV14 .... 48 B6
DUDS DY2 .... 116 A1
LDYWD/EDGR B16 .... 122 B6
SCFLD/BOLD B73 .... 79 F1
SHLY B90 .... 194 A5
Stirrup Cl DSYBK/YTR WS5 .... 52 B5
Stockbridge Cl
DUNHL/THL/PER WV6 .... 22 B5 🔢
Stockdale PI EDG B15 .... 145 F1
Stockfield Rd ACGN B27 .... 151 D5
Stockhill Dr RBRY B45 .... 200 B5

Stocking St *HAG/WOL* DY9 ..... **138** B4
Stockland Rd *ERDW/GRVHL* B23 ..... **101** E1
Stockmans Rd *HWK/WKHTH* B38 ..... **188** B5
Stockton Cl *DOR/KN* B93 ..... **213** D3
  WALM/CURD B76 ..... **83** E6
  WSLW WS2 ..... **31** F3
Stockton Gv *STECH* B33 ..... **129** F6 🖪
Stockwell Rd *BRLYHL* DY5 ..... **137** F1
Stockwell End
  DUNHL/THL/PER WV6 ..... **23** F1
Stockwell Ri *HIA/OLT* B92 ..... **175** F4
Stockwell Rd
  DUNHL/THL/PER WV6 ..... **23** F2
  HDSW B21 ..... **98** A3
Stokes Av *TPTN/OCK* DY4 ..... **70** C3 🖫
  WLNHL WV13 ..... **48** B1
Stokesay Av *DUNHL/THL/PER* WV6 .. **22** B4
Stokesay Cl *OLDBY* B69 ..... **92** C5
Stokesay Gv *NFLD/LBR* B31 ..... **186** B5
Stokesay Ri *DUDN* DY1 ..... **90** A2 🖫
Stokes St *BLOX/PEL* WS3 ..... **17** D5
Stom Rd *BILS/COS* WV14 ..... **47** D4 🖫
Stoneacre Cl *BDMR/CCFT* WV3 ..... **22** C6 🖫
Stonebow Av *SOLH* B91 ..... **195** D5
Stonebridge Crs
  CHWD/FDBR/MGN B37 ..... **130** B3 🖫
Stonebridge Rd *CSHL/WTROR* B46.. **132** B2
  CSHL/WTROR B46 ..... **156** C1
Stonebrook Wy *RIDG/WDGT* B32 .. **166** B3
Stonechat Dr *ERDW/GRVHL* B23 ..... **101** E3
Stoneford Rd *SHLY* B90 ..... **192** C1
Stonehaven Gv *HLGN/YWD* B28 .. **173** D3 🖫
Stonehenge Cft *HWK/WKHTH* B38.. **189** F4
Stonehill Cft *SHLY* B90 ..... **210** B1 🖫
Stonehouse Av *WLNHL* WV13 ..... **28** B4
Stonehouse Crs *DARL/WED* WS10 .. **73** D1
Stonehouse Dr *FOAKS/STRLY* B74 .. **37** D3
Stonehouse Hl *SLYOAK* B29 ..... **166** C1
  RIDG/WDGT B32 ..... **165** F1
Stonehouse La *ALVE* B48 ..... **204** A5
  RIDG/WDGT B32 ..... **165** F1
Stonehurst Rd *GTB/HAM* B43 ..... **55** E6
Stonelea *ALDR* WS9 ..... **35** D2
Stonelea Cl *HHTH/SAND* B71 ..... **74** A3
Stoneleigh Cl *FOAKS/STRLY* B74 .. **58** B1
Stoneleigh Gdns *CDSL* WV8 ..... **8** B1
Stoneleigh Rd
  BFLD/HDSWWD B20 ..... **100** A4
  SOLH B91 ..... **173** F5
Stoneleigh Wy *SEDG* DY3 ..... **67** F2
Stone Rd *EDG* B15 ..... **147** F2
Stoneton Gv *SLYOAK* B29 ..... **166** C3 🖫
Stone Upper Cl *WALM/CURD* B76 .. **60** A5 🖫
Stonnal Gv *ERDW/GRVHL* B23 ..... **80** C5 🖫
Stonnall Ga *ALDR* WS9 ..... **21** D5
Stonnall Rd *ALDR* WS9 ..... **21** E5
Stonor Park Rd *SOLH* B91 ..... **174** B5
Stonor Rd *HLGN/YWD* B28 ..... **192** C1
Stony La *SMTHWK* B67 ..... **120** A2
Stony St *SMTHWK* B67 ..... **120** B1
Stornoway Rd *CVALE* B35 ..... **105** D1
Storrage La *ALVE* B48 ..... **218** A6
Storrs Cl *BORD* B9 ..... **125** E6
Storrs Pl *BORD* B9 ..... **125** E6
The Storrs Wy *RIDG/WDGT* B32 .. **165** D4 🖫
Stot Fold Rd *ALE/KHTH/YWD* B14 .. **190** B3
Stourbridge Rd *BRGRVW* B61 ..... **198** A5
  BRLYHL DY5 ..... **114** A2
  DUDN DY1 ..... **90** B6
  DUDS DY2 ..... **90** C5
  ETTPK/GDPK/PENN WV4 ..... **43** E6
  HAG/WOL DY9 ..... **137** F4
  HAG/WOL DY9 ..... **159** E3
  HALE B63 ..... **140** B4
  SEDG DY3 ..... **87** C1
  WMBN WV5 ..... **65** D2
Stour Cl *HALE* B63 ..... **140** A3
Stourdell Rd *HALE* B63 ..... **140** A3
Stour Hl *BRLYHL* DY5 ..... **138** C2

Stourmore Cl *SHHTH* WV12 ..... **29** F1
Stour St *WBROM* B70 ..... **94** A2
  WSNGN B18 ..... **122** C4
Stourton Cl *DOR/KN* B93 ..... **197** D6
  WALM/CURD B76 ..... **60** D5
Stourton Crs *KINVER* DY7 ..... **134** B3
Stourton Dr
  ETTPK/GDPK/PENN WV4 ..... **43** E4
Stourton Rd *RIDG/WDGT* B32 ..... **143** D4
Stour Vale Rd *HAG/WOL* DY9 ..... **138** B3
Stour Valley Cl *BRLYHL* DY5 ..... **137** F2 🖫
Stow Dr *BRLYHL* DY5 ..... **137** D3
Stowell Rd *KGSTG* B44 ..... **78** B4
Stowe St *BLOX/PEL* WS3 ..... **17** E6
Stow Gv *CBROM* B36 ..... **104** A6
Stow Heath La *WOLV* WV1 ..... **47** D2
Stow Heath Pl *WOLV* WV1 ..... **47** D2
Stowmans Cl *BILS/COS* WV14 ..... **47** D6 🖫
Straight Rd *SHHTH* WV12 ..... **29** E1
Straits Gn *SEDG* DY3 ..... **89** D1
Straits Rd *SEDG* DY3 ..... **89** D2
The Straits *SEDG* DY3 ..... **88** C1
Stratford Cl *DUDN* DY1 ..... **90** A3
Stratford Dr *ALDR* WS9 ..... **21** E5
Stratford Pl *BHTH/HG* B12 ..... **148** C1 🖫
Stratford Rd *HLGN/YWD* B28 ..... **172** A1
  HOCK/TIA B94 ..... **211** D4
  SHLY B90 ..... **193** D1 🖫
  SHLY B90 ..... **193** F6 🖫
  SHLY B90 ..... **210** B2
  SPARK B11 ..... **149** D3
Stratford St *SPARK* B11 ..... **149** E4 🖫
Stratford St North *SPARK* B11 ..... **148** C1
Strathdene Rd *SLYOAK* B29 ..... **167** E1
Strathern Dr *BILS/COS* WV14 ..... **68** C1
Strathmore Crs *WMBN* WV5 ..... **64** C2
Strathmore Rd *TPTN/OCK* DY4 ..... **70** C3
Stratton St *WOLN* WV10 ..... **26** A3
Strawberry Cl *OLDBY* B69 ..... **93** E6
Strawberry La *WLNHL* WV13 ..... **27** E4
Stream Meadow *RUSH/SHEL* WS4 .. **19** E5
Stream Pk *KGSWFD* DY6 ..... **111** F3
Stream Rd *KGSWFD* DY6 ..... **111** F3
Streamside Wy *HIA/OLT* B92 ..... **153** F5
  RUSH/SHEL WS4 ..... **19** F5
Streatham Gv *KGSTG* B44 ..... **78** C1
Streather Rd *MGN/WHC* B75 ..... **39** E6
Streetly Crs *FOAKS/STRLY* B74 ..... **37** F4
Streetly La *FOAKS/STRLY* B74 ..... **38** A5
Streetly Rd *ERDW/GRVHL* B23 ..... **79** F5
Streetly Wd *FOAKS/STRLY* B74 ..... **36** C5
Streetsbrook Rd *SHLY* B90 ..... **173** D6
  SOLH B91 ..... **173** F6
Streets Corner Gdns *ALDR* WS9 .. **20** C1
Strensham Hl *MOS/BIL* B13 ..... **148** A5 🖫
Strensham Rd *MOS/BIL* B13 ..... **148** A4
Stretton Dr *RBRY* B45 ..... **200** C5
Stretton Gdns *CDSL* WV8 ..... **8** B1
Stretton Pl *BILS/COS* WV14 ..... **68** C2 🖫
  DUDS DY2 ..... **115** F3
Stretton Rd *SHHTH* WV12 ..... **15** E5
  SHLY B90 ..... **193** D5
Stringer Cl *MGN/WHC* B75 ..... **38** C3 🖫
Stringes La *WLNHL* WV13 ..... **29** D5
Strode Rd *BKHL/PFLD* WV2 ..... **45** E3
Stronsay Cl *RBRY* B45 ..... **184** B4
Stroud Av *SHHTH* WV12 ..... **29** E3
Stroud Cl *SHHTH* WV12 ..... **29** E3
Stroud Rd *SHLY* B90 ..... **192** B3
Strutt Cl *EDG* B15 ..... **145** F1
Stuart Crs *DUDS* DY2 ..... **92** A4
Stuart Rd *BLKHTH/ROWR* B65 ..... **117** F3 🖫
  RMSLY B62 ..... **138** A6
Stuart's Cl *STECH* B33 ..... **127** F6 🖫
Stuarts Gn *HAG/WOL* DY9 ..... **159** D3
Stuarts Rd *STECH* B33 ..... **127** F5
Stuart St *BLOX/PEL* WS3 ..... **17** D5
  VAUX/NECH B7 ..... **101** E6
Stuarts Wy *RIDG/WDGT* B32 ..... **165** D4 🖫
Stubbers Green Rd *ALDR* WS9 ..... **19** F5
Stubbington Cl *WLNHL* WV13 ..... **27** F6
Stubbs Rd *BDMR/CCFT* WV3 ..... **44** C2
Stubby La *WNSFLD* WV11 ..... **28** B1
Stubley Dr *WOLN* WV10 ..... **26** A2 🖫
Studland Rd *HLGN/YWD* B28 ..... **172** C3
Stud La *STECH* B33 ..... **128** B4
Studley Cft *HIA/OLT* B92 ..... **153** F5
Studley Dr *BRLYHL* DY5 ..... **137** E1 🖫
Studley Ga *STRBR* DY8 ..... **135** F4
Studley Rd *BDMR/CCFT* WV3 ..... **43** E1
Sturman Dr *BHTH/HG* B12 ..... **148** C3
  BLKHTH/ROWR B65 ..... **117** E6 🖫🖫
Suckling Green La *CDSL* WV8 ..... **8** B3
Sudbury Cl *WNSFLD* WV11 ..... **14** A5
Sudbury Gv *KGSTG* B44 ..... **79** D1
Sudeley Cl *CBROM* B36 ..... **105** D4 🖫
Suffield Gv *ERDW/GRVHL* B23 ..... **78** C6
Suffolk Cl *LGLYGN/QTN* B68 ..... **119** D3
  WNSFLD WV11 ..... **27** E1
Suffolk Dr *BRLYHL* DY5 ..... **137** E2
Suffolk Gv *ALDR* WS9 ..... **21** D5

Suffolk Pl *CBHAMW* B1 ..... **123** F6 🖫🖫
  WSLW WS2 ..... **31** F2
Suffolk Rd *DARL/WED* WS10 ..... **51** E6
  DUDS DY2 ..... **90** C6
Suffolk Street Queensway
  CBHAMW B1 ..... **6** C6
  DIG/EDG B5 ..... **123** F6
Suffrage St *SMTHWK* B66 ..... **121** D2
Sugden Gv *DIG/EDG* B5 ..... **148** A1
Sulgrave Cl *DUDN* DY1 ..... **90** C2 🖫
Sumburb Cft *CVALE* B35 ..... **104** C2
Summercourt Dr *KGSWFD* DY6... **111** E2
Summercourt Sq *KGSWFD* DY6... **111** E2
Summer Dr *SEDG* DY3 ..... **89** E2
Summerfield Av *KGSWFD* DY6 ..... **87** E6
  WBROM B70 ..... **95** E1
Summerfield Crs
  LDYWD/EDGR B16 ..... **122** A4
Summerfield Dr *SLYOAK* B29 ..... **166** C4 🖫
Summerfield Rd *DUDS* DY2 ..... **91** F6
  HAG/WOL DY9 ..... **180** A3
  HIA/OLT B92 ..... **174** C2
  LDYWD/EDGR B16 ..... **122** A4
  WOLV WV1 ..... **2** A4 🖫
Summerfields Av *RMSLY* B62 ..... **142** B1
Summergate *SEDG* DY3 ..... **89** F2
Summer Hl *HALE* B63 ..... **141** D6
  KGSWFD DY6 ..... **111** F1
Summerhill Rd *BILS/COS* WV14... **69** F2
Summer Hill Rd *CBHAMW* B1 ..... **123** D4
Summerhill Rd *TPTN/OCK* DY4 ..... **70** B4 🖫
Summer Hill St *CBHAMW* B1 ..... **123** D4 🖫
Summer Hill Ter *CBHAMW* B1 ..... **123** D4
Summerhouse Rd
  BILS/COS WV14 ..... **68** C2 🖫
Summer La *LOZ/NWT* B19 ..... **6** D1
  RUSH/SHEL WS4 ..... **19** D3
  SEDG DY3 ..... **89** E2
  WALM/CURD B76 ..... **83** F5
Summerlee Rd *ERDE/BCHGN* B24 .. **103** D3
Summer Rd *ACGN* B27 ..... **172** C1
  BLKHTH/ROWR B65 ..... **117** F4
  DUDN DY1 ..... **90** C1
  EDG B15 ..... **147** E2
  ERDW/GRVHL B23 ..... **80** B6
Summer Rw *BKHL/PFLD* WV2 ..... **2** D5
  CBHAMW B3 ..... **6** B4
Summer St *HAG/WOL* DY9 ..... **138** A4
  HHTH/SAND B71 ..... **95** F1
  KGSWFD DY6 ..... **111** F1
  STRBR DY8 ..... **136** B4 🖫
  WLNHL WV13 ..... **28** B5
Summerton Rd *OLDBY* B69 ..... **93** F5
Summervale Cl *HAG/WOL* DY9 .. **158** C6 🖫
Summervale Rd *HAG/WOL* DY9 .. **158** C6
Summit Crs *SMTHWK* B66 ..... **96** A5
Summit Gdns *HALE* B63 ..... **140** B6
Summit Pl *SEDG* DY3 ..... **89** D3
The Summit *HAG/WOL* DY9 ..... **137** F5
Sumner Rd *CSHL/WTROR* B46 .. **132** C1 🖫
Sunbeam Cl *CBROM* B36 ..... **106** B4
Sunbeam St *BKHL/PFLD* WV2 ..... **45** E2
Sunbeam Wy *STECH* B33 ..... **129** E5 🖫
Sunbury Cl *BILS/COS* WV14 ..... **69** F2
Sunbury Rd *HALE* B63 ..... **140** B5
  NFLD/LBR B31 ..... **186** A5
Suncroft *RIDG/WDGT* B32 ..... **143** E4 🖫
Sundbury Ri *NFLD/LBR* B31 ..... **167** D6
Sunderland Dr *STRBR* DY8 ..... **136** C1
Sunderton Rd
  ALE/KHTH/YWD B14 ..... **190** A1
Sundew Cft *CBROM* B36 ..... **103** F5
Sundial La *GTB/HAM* B43 ..... **76** B2
Sundour Crs *WNSFLD* WV11 ..... **13** D3
Sundridge Rd *KGSTG* B44 ..... **56** A5
Sunfield Gv *SPARK* B11 ..... **150** A5
Sunleigh Gv *ACGN* B27 ..... **152** A5
Sunningdale *RMSLY* B62 ..... **142** A5
Sunningdale Cl
  BFLD/HDSWWD B20 ..... **98** A1
  SCFLD/BOLD B73 ..... **80** C1
  STRBR DY8 ..... **158** B1
Sunningdale Dr *OLDBY* B69 ..... **92** C6
Sunningdale Rd *SEDG* DY3 ..... **67** D2
  SPARK B11 ..... **150** C6
Sunningdale Wy *BLOX/PEL* WS3... **16** C2
Sunny Av *BHTH/HG* B12 ..... **148** C4 🖫
Sunnybank Av *KGSTG* B44 ..... **79** D4
Sunnybank Cl *FOAKS/STRLY* B74... **36** A5
Sunny Bank Rd *LGLYGN/QTN* B68... **143** F2
Sunnybank Rd *SCFLD/BOLD* B73 ..... **80** C3
  SEDG DY3 ..... **68** A6
Sunnydene *WASH/WDE* B8 ..... **126** C2
Sunny Hill Cl *WMBN* WV5 ..... **65** D5
Sunnymead Rd
  LGN/SDN/BHAMAIR B26 ..... **152** B3
Sunnymead Wy
  FOAKS/STRLY B74 ..... **56** B2 🖫
Sunnymede Rd *KGSWFD* DY6 ..... **112** C3
Sunnyside *ALDR* WS9 ..... **20** B3
  OLDBY B69 ..... **93** D6
Sunnyside Av
  ERDW/GRVHL B23 ..... **102** A2 🖫
Sunridge Av *LOZ/NWT* B19 ..... **123** F1 🖫

WMBN WV5 .... 64 C4 🔲
Sunset Pl ETTPK/GDPK/PENN WV4.. 46 B6
Sun St BRLYHL DY5 .... 114 B6
  WOLVN WV10 .... 3 C2
  WSL WS1 .... 51 F2
Surfeit Hl CDYHTH B64 .... 140 A1
Surfeit Hill Rd CDYHTH B64 .... 139 F1
Surrey Crs HHTH/SAND B71 .... 72 C3
Surrey Dr BDMR/CCFT WV3 .... 24 A6
  STRBR DY8 .... 112 A3
Surrey Rd DUDS DY2 .... 90 C6
  KGSTG B44 .... 56 A5
Surrey Wk ALDR WS9 .... 20 C5 🔲
Sussex Av ALDR WS9 .... 20 A5
  DARL/WED WS10 .... 51 F5
  HHTH/SAND B71 .... 73 E5
Sussex Dr BDMR/CCFT WV3 .... 24 A6
Sutherland Av SHLY B90 .... 193 E2 🔲
  WOLV WV1 .... 46 B1
Sutherland Cl GTB/HAM B43 .... 55 F5 🔲
Sutherland Dr MOS/BIL B13 .... 148 B5 🔲
  WMBN WV5 .... 64 C3
Sutherland Gv
  DUNHL/THL/PER WV6 .... 22 B3
Sutherland Pl BKHL/PFLD WV2 .... 3 F6
Sutherland Rd CDYHTH B64 .... 140 A1
  ETTPK/GDPK/PENN WV4 .... 45 D4
Sutherland St AST/WIT B6 .... 101 D5
Sutton Ap WASH/WDE B8 .... 126 C3
Sutton Cl ETTPK/GDPK/PENN WV4 .. 68 A1
  MGN/WHC B75 .... 59 D2
Sutton Crs WBROM B70 .... 94 C2
Sutton New Rd ERDW/GRVHL B23.. 102 B1
Sutton Oak Rd SCFLD/BOLD B73 .. 56 C4 🔲
Sutton Rd ALDR WS9 .... 34 B6
  DARL/WED WS10 .... 48 C4
  DSYBK/YTR WS5 .... 34 B6
  DSYBK/YTR WS5 .... 53 E1
  ERDE/BCHGN B24 .... 80 C6
  WSL WS1 .... 5 G6
Sutton St AST/WIT B6 .... 124 C1
  EDG B15 .... 123 F6
  STRBR DY8 .... 112 A6
Swains Gv KGSTG B44 .... 56 B5
Swale Gv HWK/WKHTH B38 .... 188 B5
  WLNHL WV13 .... 29 F5
Swale Rd WALM/CURD B76 .... 82 C2
Swallow Av CBROM B36 .... 106 C2
Swallow Cl BHTH/HG B12 .... 149 D4 🔲
  DARL/WED WS10 .... 51 D5
  DUDS DY2 .... 115 F5
Swallow Ct WOLVN WV10 .... 11 F6
Swallowdale ALDR WS9 .... 20 C1
  DUNHL/THL/PER WV6 .... 22 B5
Swallowfall Av STRBR DY8 .... 135 E5
Swallowfields Rd SEDG DY3 .... 45 E6
Swallows' Meadow SHLY B90 .... 193 F5
Swallow St CBHAM B2 .... 6 C6
Swanage Rd SMHTH B10 .... 149 F1
Swan Av SMHTWK B66 .... 96 A6 🔲
Swan Bank
  ETTPK/GDPK/PENN WV4 .... 44 B5
Swan Copse YDLY B25 .... 151 E4 🔲
Swancote Dr
  ETTPK/GDPK/PENN WV4 .... 43 E4
Swancote Rd DUDN DY1 .... 90 C5
  STETCH B33 .... 128 B2
Swan Crs OLDBY B69 .... 118 B3
Swanfield Rd STRBR DY8 .... 112 C6
Swan Gdns ERDW/GRVHL B23 .... 102 B3
Swan La STRBR DY8 .... 112 C5
  WBROM B70 .... 72 C6
Swanley Cl RIDG/WDGT B32 .... 142 C6 🔲
Swanmore Cl BDMR/CCFT WV3 .... 44 A2
Swann Rd BILS/COS WV14 .... 68 C1
Swan Pool Gv RUSH/SHEL WS4 .. 19 F4 🔲
Swansbrook Gdns
  HWK/WKHTH B38 .... 189 E3 🔲
Swanshurst La MOS/BIL B13 .... 171 E3
Swans Length ALVE B48 .... 216 C2
Swan St ALVE B48 .... 217 D3
  BRLYHL DY5 .... 89 E6
  DUDS DY2 .... 115 E1
  STRBR DY8 .... 136 A4
  WOLV WV1 .... 26 B5
Swanswell Rd ACGN B27 .... 173 F3
  HIA/OLT B92 .... 173 F4
Swanswood Gv
  CHWD/FDBR/MGN B37 .... 131 E4 🔲
Swarthmore Rd SLYOAK B29 .... 167 D4
Sweetbriar La SHHTH WV12 .... 29 F2
Sweetbriar Rd BKHL/PFLD WV2 ...... 46 C2
Sweetbriar Dr STRBR DY8 .... 112 A6
Sweetman Pl
  DUNHL/THL/PER WV6 .... 24 C4
Sweetman St
  DUNHL/THL/PER WV6 .... 24 C3
Sweetmoor Cl CBROM B36 .... 105 E5 🔲
Sweetpool La HAG/WOL DY9 .... 158 B6
Swift Cl CBROM B36 .... 106 C5
Swinbrook Gv KGSTG B44 .... 78 A2 🔲
Swinbrook Wy SHLY B90 .... 193 F1
Swincross Rd STRBR DY8 .... 137 D5 🔲
Swindell Rd HAG/WOL DY9 .... 159 E2

Swindon Rd HRBN B17 .... 121 D4
  KGSWFD DY6 .... 86 B5
Swinford Gv DOR/KN B93 .... 212 A4 🔲
Swinford Rd SLYOAK B29 .... 144 C6
  STRBR DY8 .... 158 C1
  WOLVN WV10 .... 26 A2
Swin Forge Wy SEDG DY3 .... 86 A3
Swiss Dr STRBR DY8 .... 112 B5 🔲
Swynnerton Dr WNSFLD WV11 .... 14 B1
Sycamore Av BHTH/HG B12 .... 148 C4 🔲
Sycamore Cl RUSH/SHEL WS4 ...... 19 D5
Sycamore Crs
  CHWD/FDBR/MGN B37 .... 154 C1
  ERDE/BCHGN B24 .... 102 B2 🔲
Sycamore Dr BDMR/CCFT WV3 ...... 23 F6
  HLYWD B47 .... 207 D2
Sycamore Gn DUDN DY1 .... 68 B6 🔲
Sycamore Paddock STRBR DY8 .. 112 C6 🔲
Sycamore Pl BILS/COS WV14 .... 48 C6 🔲
  BVILLE B30 .... 168 B4
  DARL/WED WS10 .... 72 C1
  DSYBK/YTR WS5 .... 52 B4
  ERDW/GRVHL B23 .... 80 B4
  GTB/HAM B43 .... 54 A6
  HDSW B21 .... 97 F5
  KGSWFD DY6 .... 112 A1
  OLDBY B69 .... 118 C3
  RUSH/SHEL WS4 .... 19 D5
  SMTHWK B66 .... 121 D4
  TPTN/OCK DY4 .... 70 B4
The Sycamores WOLVN WV10 .... 12 B5 🔲
Sydenham Rd SMTHWK B66 .... 96 C6
  SPARK B11 .... 149 E3
  WOLV WV1 .... 27 D5
Sydney Cl WBROM B70 .... 72 C4
Sydney Rd BORD B9 .... 125 E5 🔲
  CDYHTH B64 .... 115 D6
  SMTHWKW B67 .... 120 A5
Sylvan Av NFLD/LBR B31 .... 186 B2
Sylvan Gn RMSLY B62 .... 141 F4
Sylvia Cl NFLD/LBR B31 .... 187 D3
Sytch La WMBN WV5 .... 64 C6

T

Tack Farm Rd STRBR DY8 .... 111 F3
Tackford Cl CBROM B36 .... 105 E4
Tackley Cl SHLY B90 .... 193 D5 🔲
Tadmore Cl BILS/COS WV14 .... 47 E4
Tadworth Cl WOLV WV1 .... 26 C5
Tait Cft HIA/OLT B92 .... 176 B3
Talaton Cl COVEN WV9 .... 10 C3
Talbot Av FOAKS/STRLY B74 .... 36 C4
Talbot Cl ERDW/GRVHL B23 .... 79 F3
  WSLW WS2 .... 31 E1
Talbot Pl BILS/COS WV14 .... 47 E3
Talbot Rd BKHL/PFLD WV2 .... 45 E3
  DUDS DY2 .... 115 D3
  SMTHWK B66 .... 120 C4
Talbots La BRLYHL DY5 .... 114 A6
Talbot St BRLYHL DY5 .... 113 F4 🔲
  HAG/WOL DY9 .... 138 B4
  HALE B63 .... 139 E3
  STRBR DY8 .... 136 C4
  WSNGN B18 .... 122 B1
Talbot Wy SMTH B10 .... 150 B2
Talford St AST/WIT B6 .... 124 A1
Talfourd St BORD B9 .... 125 F4
Talgarth Covert HWK/WKHTH B38 .. 188 A6
Talke Rd RMSLY B62 .... 142 A1
Talladale RIDG/WDGT B32 .... 165 D4
Tallington Rd
  LGN/SDN/BHAMAIR B26 .... 153 E2
Tall Trees Cl FOAKS/STRLY B74 ... 37 F3 🔲
  SHHTH WV12 .... 29 F1
Tall Trees Dr HAG/WOL DY9 .... 159 F1
Talton Cl SHLY B90 .... 210 C3
Tamar Cl CBROM B36 .... 106 B5
  SEDG DY3 .... 68 B5
  WALM/CURD B76 .... 83 D4
Tamar Gv DUNHL/THL/PER WV6 .. 22 A3
  WLNHL WV13 .... 29 E5 🔲
Tamarisk Cl SLYOAK B29 .... 167 D3
Tamar Ri STRBR DY8 .... 136 C1 🔲
Tame Av DARL/WED WS10 .... 51 E5
Tame Br DSYBK/YTR WS5 .... 52 B5
Tame Cl WSL WS1 .... 52 A3
Tame Crs HHTH/SAND B71 .... 73 E5
Tame Dr BLOX/PEL WS3 .... 18 C4
Tame Ri LGLYGN/QTN B68 .... 143 D1
Tame Rd AST/WIT B6 .... 100 C3
  LGLYGN/QTN B68 .... 142 C1
  TPTN/OCK DY4 .... 71 F6
Tamerton Rd RIDG/WDGT B32 ...... 165 F2
Tameside Dr CVALE B35 .... 104 C4
  PBAR/PBCH B42 .... 100 B1
Tame St BILS/COS WV14 .... 48 B4
  WBROM B70 .... 72 B5
  WSL WS1 .... 52 A3
Tame St East WSL WS1 .... 52 B5
Tamworth Rd FOAKS/STRLY B74.. 59 E2

MGN/WHC B75 .... 41 D5
MGN/WHC B75 .... 59 F2
Tanacetum Dr DSYBK/YTR WS5 ..... 52 C6
Tandy Dr ALE/KHTH/YWD B14 .... 190 B2
Tanfield Cl DUNHL/THL/PER WV6 .. 23 D4
Tanfield Rd DUDS DY2 .... 91 D6
  STETCH B33 .... 128 B4 🔲
Tanford Rd HIA/OLT B92 .... 153 E6
Tanglewood Cl BKDE/SHDE B34 .. 129 E2 🔲
  BRORVE B60 .... 214 C3
  RIDG/WDGT B32 .... 143 D5 🔲
Tanglewood Gv SEDG DY3 .... 67 E1 🔲
Tangmere Cl
  DUNHL/THL/PER WV6 .... 22 A2 🔲
Tangmere Dr CVALE B35 .... 104 C2
Tanhouse Av GTB/HAM B43 .... 75 D4
Tanhouse Farm Rd HIA/OLT B92 .. 175 E1
Tanhouse La HALE B63 .... 139 E4
Tanners Cl MGN/WHC B75 .... 60 B2 🔲
Tanners Green La HLYWD B47 ...... 206 C5
Tannery Cl WSLW WS2 .... 4 B1
Tansey Green Rd BRLYHL DY5 ...... 89 D5
Tansley Cl DOR/KN B93 .... 212 B3
Tansley Gv KGSTG B44 .... 78 B2
Tansley Hill Av DUDS DY2 .... 92 B5
Tansley Hill Rd DUDS DY2 .... 92 A5
Tansley Rd KGSTG B44 .... 78 B3
Tansley Vw BKHL/PFLD WV2 .... 45 F2
Tantany La HHTH/SAND B71 .... 95 E1
Tantarra St WSL WS1 .... 5 F4
Tanwood Cl SOLH B91 .... 195 D5 🔲
Tanworth Gv BHTH/HG B12 .... 148 B4 🔲
Tanworth La SHLY B90 .... 193 C5
Tanyard Cl ALVE B48 .... 217 D3
Tanyard Gv RIDG/WDGT B32 .... 144 B3
Tanyards ACGN B27 .... 151 F6 🔲
Tapestries Av WBROM B70 .... 94 C1
Tapton Cl BLOX/PEL WS3 .... 17 E2
Tarmac Rd
  ETTPK/GDPK/PENN WV4 .... 47 D4
Tarragon Gdns NFLD/LBR B31 ...... 185 E3 🔲
Tarrant Gv RIDG/WDGT B32 .... 144 B3
Tarrington Covert
  HWK/WKHTH B38 .... 188 A5 🔲
Tarry Hollow Rd BRLYHL DY5 .... 89 D5
Tarry Rd WASH/WDE B8 .... 126 A3
Tarvin Ms BRLYHL DY5 .... 113 F6
Taryn Dr DARL/WED WS10 .... 49 F2
Tasker St WBROM B70 .... 94 A1
  WSL WS1 .... 4 B6
Tasman Gv
  DUNHL/THL/PER WV6 .... 22 A2 🔲
Tat Bank Rd OLDBY B69 .... 119 D1
Taunton Av WOLVN WV10 .... 11 F1
Taunton Rd BHTH/HG B12 .... 148 C5
Taverners Cl SHHTH WV12 .... 15 E4 🔲
Taverner's Gn BFLD/HDSWWD B20 .. 98 B2
Tavistock Rd ACGN B27 .... 173 E4
Taw Cl CBROM B36 .... 106 B6
Tay Cft CHWD/FDBR/MGN B37 ..... 131 E3
Tay Gv HWK/WKHTH B38 .... 188 B5
  RMSLY B62 .... 142 A1
Taylor Av BLOX/PEL WS3 .... 17 F5
Taylor Rd ALE/KHTH/YWD B14 ..... 170 B6
  DUDS DY2 .... 116 A3 🔲
  ETTPK/GDPK/PENN WV4 .... 46 B4
Taylor's La HHTH/SAND B71 .... 95 F1
  OLDBY B69 .... 94 A6
  SMTHWK B67 .... 120 B2
Taylors Orch ERDW/GRVHL B23 ... 101 D1
Taylor St WNSFLD WV11 .... 27 F2
Tay Rd RBRY B45 .... 185 D4
Taysfield Rd NFLD/LBR B31 .... 166 A5
Taywood Dr SMHTH B10 .... 149 E2 🔲
Tealby Gv SLYOAK B29 .... 168 C2
Teal Dr ERDW/GRVHL B23 .... 101 D2
Teall Rd WASH/WDE B8 .... 126 A5
Tean Cl SPARK B11 .... 150 C6
Teasdale Wy HAG/WOL DY9 .... 137 F5
Teasel Rd WNSFLD WV11 .... 28 A2
Teazel Av BVILLE B30 .... 167 F5
Tebworth Cl COVEN WV9 .... 10 B3
Tedbury Crs ERDW/GRVHL B23 .... 80 A5
Tedder Rd WSLW WS2 .... 30 B5 🔲
Teddesley Gv STETCH B33 .... 129 E3
Teddesley St RUSH/SHEL WS4 ...... 5 E1
Teddington Gv PBAR/PBCH B42 ... 99 E2
Tedstone Rd RIDG/WDGT B32 ...... 144 A4
Teesdale Av BKDE/SHDE B34 .... 128 B1
Teesdale Cl WOLV WV1 .... 26 C5
Tees Gv HWK/WKHTH B38 .... 188 B1
Teignmouth Rd SLYOAK B29 .... 168 B1
Telford Cl HHTH/SAND B71 .... 72 C5
  SMTHWKW B67 .... 119 F6
  WSLW WS2 .... 30 C2 🔲
Telford Gdns BDMR/CCFT WV3 ..... 43 F2
Telford Rd WSLW WS2 .... 30 C2
Telford St SMTHWK B66 .... 96 B6
Teme Gv WLNHL WV13 .... 29 F5 🔲
Teme Rd HALE B63 .... 139 D4
  STRBR DY8 .... 136 B6
Tempest St BKHL/PFLD WV2 .... 3 E5
The Templars OLDBY B69 .... 118 A2
Temple Av HLGN/YWD B28 .... 172 C5
Temple Bar WLNHL WV13 .... 28 C4

Templefield Gdns *BORD* B9 .... 125 E6 🔲
Templefield St *BORD* B9 .... 125 E6
Temple Meadows Rd
  HHTH/SAND B71 .... 74 A5 🔲
Templemore Dr *GTB/HAM* B43 ... 76 A4
Temple Pas *CBHAM* B2 .... 6 D5
Temple Rd *DOR/KN* B93 .... 212 C4
  WLNHL WV13 .... 28 C4
Temple Rw *CBHAM* B2 .... 7 E5
Temple Rw West *CBHAMNW* B3 .. 6 D4 🔲
Temple Sq *WLNHL* WV13 .... 28 C4 🔲
Temple St *BILS/COS* WV14 .... 48 A4
  BKHL/PFLD WV2 .... 2 D5
  CBHAM B2 .... 6 D5
  SEDG DY3 .... 89 F2
  WBROM B70 .... 95 E1
Templeton Cl *DOR/KN* B93 .... 212 C4
Templeton Rd *KGSTG* B44 .... 78 A1
Temple Wy *CSHL/WTROR* B46 ... 108 B4
  OLDBY B69 .... 93 E3
Tenacre La *SEDG* DY3 .... 68 A6
Ten Acres End *BVILLE* B30 .... 169 D3
Ten Ashes La *RBRY* B45 .... 201 E3
Tenbury Cl *ALDR* WS9 .... 21 E5
  WSLW WS2 .... 29 F4
Tenbury Ct
  ETTPK/GDPK/PENN WV4 ...... 43 F4
Tenbury Gdns
  ETTPK/GDPK/PENN WV4 ...... 43 F4
Tenbury Rd *ALE/KHTH/YWD* B14 ... 169 F5
Tenby St *MOS/BIL* B13 .... 171 F1
Tenby St *CBHAMW* B1 .... 123 D3
Tenby St North *CBHAMW* B1 ...... 123 D3
Tenlands Rd *HALE* B63 .... 140 B6
Tennal Dr *RIDG/WDGT* B32 .... 144 A3
Tennal La *RIDG/WDGT* B32 .... 144 A4
Tennal Rd *RIDG/WDGT* B32 .... 144 A3
Tennant St *EDG* B15 .... 123 D6
Tennis Ct *BVILLE* B30 .... 187 F1
The Tennis *EDG* B15 .... 146 C4
Tennyson Av *FOAKS/STRLY* B74 ... 38 B1
Tennyson Rd *BLOX/PEL* WS3 ...... 18 A5
  SEDG DY3 .... 66 C6
  SHHTH WV12 .... 16 A5
  SMHTH B10 .... 150 A2
  WOLVN WV10 .... 12 C4
Tennyson St *BRLYHL* DY5 .... 113 F1
Tenter Ct *HALE* B63 .... 141 D5 🔲
Tenter Dr *HALE* B63 .... 141 E6
Tenterfields *HALE* B63 .... 141 D5
Tern Cl *ETTPK/GDPK/PENN* WV4 ... 45 F6
Tern Gv *HWK/WKHTH* B38 .... 188 A5
Terrace Rd *LOZ/NWT* B19 .... 98 C6
Terrace St *BLKHTH/ROWR* B65 ... 117 D6
  BRLYHL DY5 .... 114 A2
  DARL/WED WS10 .... 50 B6
The Terrace *BDMR/CCFT* WV3 ... 23 E6
  CDYHTH B64 .... 140 A1
Terry Dr *WALM/CURD* B76 .... 82 D2
Terry St *DUDS* DY2 .... 91 F4
Tessall La *NFLD/LBR* B31 .... 185 E5
Tetbury Gv *NFLD/LBR* B31 .... 185 F2
Tetley Av *RUSH/SHEL* WS4 .... 32 C5
Tetley Rd *SPARK* B11 .... 150 A6
Tetnall St *DUDS* DY2 .... 91 F5
Tettenhall Rd
  DUNHL/THL/PER WV6 .... 24 B4
  WOLV WV1 .... 24 C4
Teviot Gdns *BRLYHL* DY5 .... 112 C1
Teviot Gv *HWK/WKHTH* B38 ...... 188 B5
Tewkesbury Dr *DUDS* DY2 .... 115 F4 🔲
Tewkesbury Rd
  BFLD/HDSWWD B20 .... 100 A4
  BLOX/PEL WS3 .... 16 A3
Tew Park Rd *HDSW* B21 .... 98 A6
Thackeray Rd *BVILLE* B30 .... 167 F6
Thame Ct *HLYWD* B47 .... 206 A5 🔲
Thames Cl *BRLYHL* DY5 .... 89 D6 🔲
Thames Rd *BLOX/PEL* WS3 .... 17 F5
Thanet Cl *KGSWFD* DY6 .... 111 E3
Thanet Gv *PBAR/PBCH* B42 .... 99 E1
Thatchway Gdns
  HWK/WKHTH B38 .... 188 A5
Thaxted Rd *STECH* B33 .... 130 A4
Theatre Ap *DIG/EDG* B5 .... 124 A6 🔲
Thelbridge Rd *NFLD/LBR* B31 ... 202 A1
Thelma Rd *TPTN/OCK* DY4 .... 70 A5
Thelma St *WSL* WS1 .... 51 F2 🔲
Thelsford Wy *HIA/OLT* B92 .... 175 F3
Theodore Cl *HRBN* B17 .... 145 F5 🔲
  OLDBY B69 .... 94 A4
Theresa Rd *SPARK* B11 .... 149 D2
Thetford Cl *TPTN/OCK* DY4 .... 69 F6
Thetford Gdns *WNSFLD* WV11 ... 27 F1
Thetford Rd *PBAR/PBCH* B42 ..... 77 D4
Thetford Wy *DSYBK/YTR* WS5 ... 53 E6
Thickett Cl *WSLW* WS2 .... 51 D1 🔲
Thicknall Dr *HAG/WOL* DY9 .... 159 D1
Thimble End Rd *WALM/CURD* B76 ... 82 C1
Thimble Mill La *AST/WIT* B6 .... 101 D6
Thimble Mill Rd *SMTHWK* B67 ... 119 F3
Third Av *BORD* B9 .... 126 B5
  SLYOAK B29 .... 147 E6

WOLVN WV10 .... 12 A6
Third Exhibition Av
  BHAMNEC B40 .... 155 F5 🔲
Third Rd *BRGRVW* B61 .... 198 B3
Thirlmere Cl *DUNHL/THL/PER* WV6 ... 9 F5
Thirlmere Dr *MOS/BIL* B13 .... 171 E3
  WNSFLD WV11 .... 14 C3
Thirlmere Gv
  DUNHL/THL/PER WV6 .... 22 B3
Thirlmere Wk *BRLYHL* DY5 .... 137 D2 🔲
Thirsk Cft *CBROM* B36 .... 103 E5 🔲
Thirston Cl *WNSFLD* WV11 .... 28 C2 🔲
Thistle Cl *SEDG* DY3 .... 68 B5 🔲
Thistle Cft *WNSFLD* WV11 .... 27 F2
Thistle Down Cl
  FOAKS/STRLY B74 .... 36 C5 🔲
Thistledown Rd *BKDE/SHDE* B34 ... 105 E6
Thistle Gn *HWK/WKHTH* B38 ..... 188 A6
Thistlegreen Cl
  BLKHTH/ROWR B65 .... 116 B2 🔲
Thistlegreen Rd *DUDS* DY2 .... 116 A3
Thistle La *RIDG/WDGT* B32 .... 165 D3
Thomas Crs *SMTHWK* B66 .... 121 E2 🔲
Thomas Guy Rd *WBROM* B70 ..... 72 A4
Thomas Mason Cl *WNSFLD* WV11 ... 13 F6 🔲
Thomas St *BILS/COS* WV14 .... 47 F4 🔲
  BKHL/PFLD WV2 .... 45 E1
  SMTHWK B66 .... 121 D2
  WBROM B70 .... 95 F3
  WSLW WS2 .... 4 A2
Thompson Av *BKHL/PFLD* WV2 ... 45 F2
Thompson Cl *DUDS* DY2 .... 115 D5
  WLNHL WV13 .... 28 C4
Thompson Dr *VAUX/NECH* B7 ... 102 B5
Thompson Rd *LGLYGN/QTN* B68 ... 119 D5
  SMTHWK B67 .... 120 B3
Thompson St *BILS/COS* WV14 ... 47 F4 🔲
  WLNHL WV13 .... 28 C4
Thomson Av *NFLD/LBR* B31 ...... 187 E4
Thornberry Dr *DUDN* DY1 .... 89 F5
Thornbridge Av *PBAR/PBCH* B42 ... 77 E4
Thornbury Ct
  DUNHL/THL/PER WV6 .... 22 C4 🔲
Thornbury Rd
  BFLD/HDSWWD B20 .... 99 F3 🔲
Thornby Av *SOLH* B91 .... 175 D6
Thornby Rd *ERDW/GRVHL* B23 ... 79 D3
Thorncliffe Rd *KGSTG* B44 .... 78 A1
Thorn Cl *DARL/WED* WS10 .... 50 B5
Thorncroft Wy *DSYBK/YTR* WS5 ... 53 D5
Thorne Av *WOLVN* WV10 .... 12 A6
Thorne Rd *WLNHL* WV13 .... 28 C3
Thorne St *BKHL/PFLD* WV2 .... 46 C2
Thorneycroft La *WOLVN* WV10 ... 26 C2
Thorneycroft Rd *BILS/COS* WV14 ... 48 C6
Thorney Rd *FOAKS/STRLY* B74 ... 36 B6
Thornfield Cft *SEDG* DY3 .... 68 A4 🔲
Thornfield Rd *ACGN* B27 .... 147 D3
Thorngrove Av *SOLH* B91 .... 195 E5 🔲
Thornham Wy
  ALE/KHTH/YWD B14 .... 189 F4 🔲
Thornhill Pk *FOAKS/STRLY* B74 ... 56 C1
Thornhill Rd *BRLYHL* DY5 .... 114 A6
  DUDN DY1 .... 91 E1
  FOAKS/STRLY B74 .... 56 C1
  HALE B63 .... 140 A6
  HDSW B21 .... 98 B5
  SOLH B91 .... 175 E4
  SPARK B11 .... 149 F6
Thornhurst Av *RIDG/WDGT* B32 ... 144 A2
Thornleigh *SEDG* DY3 .... 67 F6
Thornley Cl *MOS/BIL* B13 .... 170 C2
  WNSFLD WV11 .... 14 B4 🔲
Thornley Gv *WALM/CURD* B76 ... 83 E5
Thornley Rd *WNSFLD* WV11 ...... 14 B4
Thornley St *WOLV* WV1 .... 3 E2
Thorn Rd *BVILLE* B30 .... 168 A4
Thornsett Gv *HIA/OLT* B92 .... 173 D5 🔲
Thorns Rd *BRLYHL* DY5 .... 138 A1
  HAG/WOL DY9 .... 138 A3
Thornthwaite Av *RBRY* B45 ...... 185 D3 🔲
Thornton Cl *OLDBY* B69 .... 93 E3 🔲
Thornton Dr *BRLYHL* DY5 .... 114 A6 🔲
Thornton Rd *SHLY* B90 .... 210 B1
  WASH/WDE B8 .... 127 D2
  WOLV WV1 .... 27 D6
Thornwood Cl *LGLYGN/QTN* B68 ... 119 E2
Thornyfield Cl *SHLY* B90 .... 193 E3 🔲
Thornyfield Rd *SHLY* B90 .... 193 E2 🔲
Thorpe Cl *MGN/WHC* B75 .... 59 E2 🔲
Thorpe Rd *WSL* WS1 .... 52 A2
Thorp St *DIG/EDG* B5 .... 123 F6
Three Corner Cl *SHLY* B90 .... 192 A5
Three Oaks Rd *HLYWD* B47 ...... 207 D3
Three Shires Oak Rd
  SMTHWK B67 .... 120 B5
Three Tuns La *WOLVN* WV10 ..... 11 E3
Threshers Dr *SHHTH* WV12 .... 29 F1
Throne Cl *BLKHTH/ROWR* B65 ... 117 E3
Throne Crs *BLKHTH/ROWR* B65 ... 117 F3
Throne Rd *BLKHTH/ROWR* B65 ... 117 E2
Throstles Cl *GTB/HAM* B43 .... 76 A4 🔲
Thrush Rd *LGLYGN/QTN* B68 ..... 118 D5
Thruxton Cl *ALE/KHTH/YWD* B14 ... 190 B1

Thurcroft Cl *WASH/WDE* B8 ...... 126 B3 🔲
Thuree Rd *SMTHWK* B67 .... 119 F5
Thurleigh Cl *HAG/WOL* DY9 ...... 159 D1
Thurlestone Rd *HLGL/LBR* B31 ... 186 A6
Thurloe Crs *RBRY* B45 .... 184 A4
Thurlston Av *HIA/OLT* B92 .... 152 B5
Thurlstone Dr
  ETTPK/GDPK/PENN WV4 ...... 44 B5 🔲
Thurlstone Rd *BLOX/PEL* WS3 ... 17 D2
Thursfield Rd *HHTH/SAND* B71 ... 74 A4
  TPTN/OCK DY4 .... 70 C5
Thurston Av *OLDBY* B69 .... 118 B1
Thynne St *WBROM* B70 .... 96 A3
Tibbats Cl *RIDG/WDGT* B32 ...... 143 E6
Tibberton Cl *BDMR/CCFT* WV3 ... 43 F2 🔲
  HALE B63 .... 141 E6
  SOLH B91 .... 194 C5 🔲
Tibbets La *HRBN* B17 .... 144 C5
Tibbington Rd *TPTN/OCK* DY4 ... 70 A4 🔲
Tibbington Ter *TPTN/OCK* DY4 ... 70 A4
Tiberius Cl *CSHL/WTROR* B46 .... 108 B2 🔲
Tibland Rd *ACGN* B27 .... 173 F2
Tiddington Cl *CBROM* B36 .... 105 D4 🔲
Tideswell Rd *PBAR/PBCH* B42 ... 77 E5
Tidworth Cft *ALE/KHTH/YWD* B14 ... 190 C2
Tierney Dr *TPTN/OCK* DY4 .... 71 E5
Tiffany La *COVEN* WV9 .... 10 B3
Tiffield Rd *SPARK* B11 .... 151 E4
Tigley Av *RIDG/WDGT* B32 .... 165 F2
Tilbury Cl *BDMR/CCFT* WV3 ...... 42 C2
Tilbury Gv *MOS/BIL* B13 .... 169 E2
Tildasley St *WBROM* B70 .... 73 D6
Tildesley Dr *SHHTH* WV12 .... 29 D2
Tile Cross Rd *STECH* B33 .... 130 A6
Tiled House La *BRLYHL* DY5 ...... 113 D1
Tile Gv *CHWD/FDBR/MGN* B37 ... 130 C2
Tilehouse Green La *DOR/KN* B93 ... 196 B6
Tilehouse La *SHLY* B90 .... 208 A2
Tilesford Cft *SHLY* B90 .... 210 C2
Tilley St *DARL/WED* WS10 .... 50 A3
Tillyard Cft *SLYOAK* B29 .... 167 E2
Tilshead Cl *ALE/KHTH/YWD* B14 ... 190 A2
Tilsley Gv *ERDW/GRVHL* B23 .... 79 D6
Tilston Dr *BRLYHL* DY5 .... 113 F6
Tilton Rd *BORD* B9 .... 125 E6
Timberdine Cl *HALE* B63 .... 139 F3
Timberlake Cl *SHLY* B90 .... 211 D1 🔲
Timberley La *BKDE/SHDE* B34 ... 129 E1
Timbers Wy *ERDE/BCHGN* B24 ... 104 B1
  SPARK B11 .... 148 C5
Timbertree Crs *CDYHTH* B64 .... 140 A2
Timbertree Rd *CDYHTH* B64 ..... 140 A2
Times Square Av *BRLYHL* DY5 ... 114 B5
Timmins Cl *SOLH* B91 .... 176 A5 🔲
Timmis Cl *BILS/COS* WV14 .... 47 D6 🔲
Timmis Rd *HAG/WOL* DY9 .... 137 E3
Timothy Rd *OLDBY* B69 .... 93 E6
Tinacre Hl *DUNHL/THL/PER* WV6 ... 22 A1
Tinchbourne St *DUDN* DY1 .... 91 E4 🔲
Tindal St *BHTH/HG* B12 .... 148 B4
Tinkers Farm Gv *NFLD/LBR* B31 ... 186 A2 🔲
Tinkers Farm Rd *NFLD/LBR* B31 ... 186 A1
Tinkers La *HOCK/TIA* B94 .... 223 F2
Tinmeadow Crs *RBRY* B45 .... 185 E6
Tinsley St *TPTN/OCK* DY4 .... 72 A6 🔲
Tintagel Cl *DUNHL/THL/PER* WV6 ... 22 B4
Tintagel Dr *DUDN* DY1 .... 90 A3
Tintern Cl *FOAKS/STRLY* B74 ..... 56 C2
Tintern Ct *DUNHL/THL/PER* WV6 ... 22 A3 🔲
Tintern Crs *BLOX/PEL* WS3 .... 16 B3
Tintern Rd *BFLD/HDSWWD* B20 ... 100 A4
Tintern Wy *BLOX/PEL* WS3 .... 16 B3
Tipperary Cl *CBROM* B36 .... 104 A5
Tipps Stone Cl *TPTN/OCK* DY4 ... 92 A1
Tipton Rd *DUDN* DY1 .... 92 A2
  OLDBY B69 .... 93 E3
  SEDG DY3 .... 68 A4 🔲
  TPTN/OCK DY4 .... 92 A1
Tirley Rd *STETCH* B33 .... 128 C3
Titania Cl *RBRY* B45 .... 184 C2
Titchfield Cl *WOLVN* WV10 .... 12 A1 🔲
Titford Cl *OLDBY* B69 .... 118 B3 🔲
Titford La *OLDBY* B69 .... 118 A3
Titford Rd *OLDBY* B69 .... 118 C2
Tithe Barn La *HOCK/TIA* B94 ... 223 D4
Tithe Cft *WOLVN* WV10 .... 26 B4
Tithe Rd *WNSFLD* WV11 .... 27 F1
Titterstone Rd *NFLD/LBR* B31 ... 186 C5
Tiverton Cl *KGSWFD* DY6 .... 112 C4
Tiverton Rd *SLYOAK* B29 .... 168 D1
  SMTHWK B66 .... 121 D2
Tividale Rd *OLDBY* B69 .... 92 C3
Tividale St *TPTN/OCK* DY4 .... 92 C2
Tixall Rd *HLGN/YWD* B28 .... 172 A6
Toll End Rd *TPTN/OCK* DY4 ...... 71 E3
Tollgate Cl *NFLD/LBR* B31 .... 186 B5
Tollgate Dr *BFLD/HDSWWD* B20 ... 98 C6
Toll House Rd *RBRY* B45 .... 185 E6
Tollhouse Wy *SMTHWK* B66 ..... 96 B6
Tolworth Gdns *BKHL/PFLD* WV2 ... 46 A2 🔲
Tolworth Hall Rd
  ERDE/BCHGN B24 .... 103 D2
Tomey Rd *SPARK* B11 .... 149 F4
Tomlan Rd *NFLD/LBR* B31 .... 187 E3
Tomlinson Rd *CBROM* B36 .... 105 F4

Tompstone Rd HHTH/SAND B71 .... 74 B3
Tonadine Cl WNSFLD WV11 .... 14 C4
Tonbridge Rd ERDE/BCHGN B24.... 102 C4
Tong St WSL WS1 .... 5 H4
Top Croft Rd ERDW/GRVHL B23 .... 80 B4
Topfield Wk
  ALE/KHTH/YWD B14 .... 189 F3
Topland Gv NFLD/LBR B31 .... 185 E3
Top Rd BRGRVW B61 .... 198 C3
Topsham Cft
  ALE/KHTH/YWD B14 .... 169 F6
Torfield CDSL WV8 .... 10 A3
Toronto Gdns RIDG/WDGT B32 ...... 144 A3
Torre Av NFLD/LBR B31 .... 186 A3
Torrey Gv WASH/WDE B8 .... 127 E3
Torridge Dr WNSFLD WV11 .... 27 E2
Torridon Rd MOS/BIL B13 .... 147 F6
Torridon Rd WNSFLD WV11 .... 15 D4
Torvale Rd DUNHL/THL/PER WV6.... 22 B4
Tor Wy BLOX/PEL WS3 .... 18 B2
Totnes Rd SMTHWKW B67 .... 120 B1
Tottenham Crs KSGTG B44 .... 79 D1
Touchwood Hall Cl SOLH B91 .... 195 E1
Towcester Cft CBROM B36 .... 103 F5
Tower Cft CHWD/FDBR/MGN B37 .. 131 D3
Tower HI PBAR/PBCH B42 .... 76 C5
Tower Ri OLDBY B69 .... 93 E6
Tower Rd AST/WIT B6 .... 100 B6
  MGN/WHC B75 .... 39 D4
  OLDBY B69 .... 93 E6
Tower St DUDN DY1 .... 91 E4
  LOZ/NWT B19 .... 123 F2
  SEDG DY3 .... 67 F2
  WOLV WV1 .... 3 E4
  WSL WS1 .... 4 D3
Townend St WSLW WS2 .... 4 C3
Townfold BLOX/PEL WS3 .... 18 C1
Townley Gdns
  BFLD/HDSWWD B20.................... 100 A4
Townsend Av SEDG DY3 .... 67 F3
Townsend Dr WALM/CURD B76........ 82 B4
Townsend Wy CBHAMW B1 .... 123 D4
Townshend Gv
  CHWD/FDBR/MGN B37 .... 130 B3
Townson Rd WNSFLD WV11 .... 14 B5
Townwell Fold WOLV WV1 .... 2 C4
Towpath Cl BORD B9 .... 125 D5
Towyn Rd MOS/BIL B13 .... 171 F2
Toys La HALE B63 .... 139 E5
Tozer St TPTN/OCK DY4 .... 70 B4
Traceys Meadow RBRY B45 .... 184 C6
Trafalgar Ct OLDBY B69 .... 93 D4
Trafalgar Rd ERDE/BCHGN B24....... 102 B3
  HDSW B21 .... 98 A5
  MOS/BIL B13 .... 148 A5
  OLDBY B69 .... 93 D4
  SMTHWK B66 .... 121 D3
Trajan HI CSHL/WTROR B46 .... 108 A4
Tram Wy SMTHWK B66 .... 95 E6
Tramway Cl BILS/COS WV14 .... 48 C2
  DARL/WED WS10 .... 50 A2
Tranter Rd WASH/WDE B8 .... 126 C2
Tranwell Cl COVEN WV9 .... 10 B3
Traquain Dr DUDN DY1 .... 90 C2
Treaford La WASH/WDE B8 .... 127 E3
Tredington Cl SLYOAK B29 .... 166 C4
Tree Acre Gv HALE B63 .... 139 E5
Treeford Cl SOLH B91 .... 194 B4
Trees Rd WSL WS1 .... 5 J3
Treeton Cft STETCH B33 .... 128 C5
Treetops Dr SHHTH WV12 .... 30 A2
Trefoil Cl SLYOAK B29 .... 166 C3
Tregarron Rd HALE B63 .... 139 E4
Tregea Ri GTB/HAM B43 .... 75 E4
Trehern Cl DOR/KN B93 .... 212 C2
Treheurnes Dr HAG/WOL DY9 .... 159 D2
Trejon Rd CDYHTH B64 .... 140 A1
Tremaine Gdns WOLVN WV10 .... 25 F3
Tremont St WOLVN WV10............... 3 H2
Trenchard Cl MGN/WHC B75 .... 60 B4
Trent Dr DUNHL/THL/PER WV6.... 22 A3
  STRBR DY8 .... 136 C3
Trent Crs HLYWD B47 .... 206 A5
Trent Dr CBROM B36 .... 106 A5
Trentham Gv
  LGN/SDN/BHAMAIR B26........... 152 A4
Trentham Rd BKHL/PFLD WV2 .... 46 B2
Trent Pl BLOX/PEL WS3 .... 17 F5
Trent Rd BLOX/PEL WS3 .... 18 C4
Trent St DIG/EDG B5 .... 7 H6
Trenville Av SPARK B11 .... 149 D4
Tresco Cl RBRY B45 .... 184 A4
Trescott Rd NFLD/LBR B31 .... 185 F2
Tresham Rd KSGTG B44 .... 78 A2
  KGSWFD DY6 .... 87 F5
Trevanie Av RIDG/WDGT B32 .... 143 E3
Trevorne Cl BHTH/HG B12 .... 148 B3
Tregea Ri GTB/HAM B43
Trevor Rd BLOX/PEL WS3 .... 18 B1
Trevor St VAUX/NECH B7 .... 125 E1
Trevor St West VAUX/NECH B7 ... 101 E6
Trevose Cl BLOX/PEL WS3 .... 16 B2
Trevose Retreat BHTH/HG B12 .... 148 B3
Trewman Cl WALM/CURD B76 .... 82 B3

Treyamon Rd DSYBK/YTR WS5 ...... 53 F2
Treynham Cl WLNHL WV13 .... 27 E6
Trident Cl ERDW/GRVHL B23 .... 80 C3
  WALM/CURD B76 .... 82 B4
Trident Dr DARL/WED WS10 .... 49 F6
  LGLYGN/QTN B68 .... 119 D2
Trigo Cft CBROM B36 .... 104 A5
Trimpley Cl DOR/KN B93 .... 212 A4
Trimpley Gdns
  ETTPK/GDPK/PENN WV4............ 44 A6
Trimpley Rd RIDG/WDGT B32 .... 165 D3
Trinder Rd SMTHWKW B67 .... 119 F6
Trindle Rd DUDN DY1 .... 91 F3
Tring Ct DUNHL/THL/PER WV6 ...... 24 B3
Trinity Av HIA/OLT B92 .... 175 D2
  STRBR DY8 .... 111 F5
Trinity Gv DARL/WED WS10 .... 50 C6
Trinity HI CSCFLD/WYGN B72 .... 59 E4
Trinity Rd AST/WIT B6 .... 99 F4
  BILS/COS WV14 .... 48 A3
  DUDN DY1 .... 91 F4
  MGN/WHC B75 .... 39 D6
  SHHTH WV12 .... 29 F1
  STRBR DY8 .... 136 C1
Trinity Rd North WBROM B70 .... 95 F4
Trinity Rd South WBROM B70 .... 95 F4
Trinity St BRLYHL DY5 .... 113 F4
  CDYHTH B64 .... 116 A6
  OLDBY B69 .... 118 C2
  SMTHWK B66 .... 120 C1
  WBROM B70 .... 95 F4
Trinity Ter SPARK B11 .... 148 C1
Trinity Wy WBROM B70 .... 95 F4
Trippleton Av RIDG/WDGT B32 ..... 165 D3
  RIDG/WDGT B32 .... 165 D4
Tristram Av NFLD/LBR B31 .... 187 D3
Trittiford Rd MOS/BIL B13 .... 171 E5
Troon Cl BLOX/PEL WS3 .... 16 C2
  MGN/WHC B75 .... 59 F1
Troon Pl STRBR DY8 .... 111 E4
Trotter's La HHTH/SAND B71 .... 72 C4
Trouse La DARL/WED WS10 .... 50 A6
Troutbeck Dr BRLYHL DY5 .... 137 D1
Troy Gv ALE/KHTH/YWD B14 .... 189 F1
Truda St WSL WS1 .... 51 F2
Truemans Heath La HLYWD B47 ... 191 D6
Truro Cft BLKHTH/ROWR B65 ...... 118 A3
Truro Rd DSYBK/YTR WS5 .... 53 F2
Trustin Crs HIA/OLT B92 .... 176 A3
Tryon Pl BILS/COS WV14 .... 48 A3
Trysull Av LGN/SDN/BHAMAIR B26 .. 153 E5
Trysull Gdns BDMR/CCFT WV3 ...... 43 F2
Trysull Rd BDMR/CCFT WV3 .... 43 F2
  WMBN WV5 .... 64 A2
Trysull Wy DUDS DY2 .... 115 E3
Tudbury Rd NFLD/LBR B31 .... 185 F1
Tudman Cl WALM/CURD B76 .... 82 C4
Tudor Cl HLYWD B47 .... 190 C4
  MOS/BIL B13 .... 170 B5
  SCFLD/BOLD B73 .... 79 F1
Tudor Ct TPTN/OCK DY4 .... 92 C1
  WNSFLD WV11 .... 14 B2
Tudor Crs BKHL/PFLD WV2 .... 45 D3
Tudor Cft CHWD/FDBR/MGN B37 .. 130 B6
Tudor Gdns ERDW/GRVHL B23 .... 102 A2
  STRBR DY8 .... 136 A4
Tudor Gv FOAKS/STRLY B74 .... 56 C1
Tudor Rd HI SCFLD/BOLD B73 .... 58 C3
Tudor Pl SEDG DY3 .... 68 A5
Tudor Rd BLKHTH/ROWR B65 ...... 117 E2
  DARL/WED WS10 .... 49 D5
  LGLYGN/QTN B68 .... 119 E3
  MOS/BIL B13 .... 148 B6
  SCFLD/BOLD B73 .... 59 D4
  SEDG DY3 .... 68 A5
  WOLVN WV10 .... 26 C1
Tudor St TPTN/OCK DY4 .... 92 C1
  WSNGN B18................................. 121 F3
Tudor Ter DUDS DY2 .... 92 A4
Tudor V SEDG DY3 .... 68 A5
Tufnell Gv WASH/WDE B8 .... 102 C6
Tugford Rd NFLD/LBR B31 .... 167 E4
  SLYOAK B29 .... 167 E4
Tulyar Cl CBROM B36 .... 103 F5
Tunnel La ALE/KHTH/YWD B14 ... 189 D1
  BVILLE B30 .... 189 D1
Tunnel Rd WBROM B70 .... 72 C4
Tunnel St BILS/COS WV14 .... 69 E3
Tunstall Rd KGSWFD DY6 .... 108 C1
Turchill Dr WALM/CURD B76 .... 82 C5
Turfpits La ERDW/GRVHL B23 .... 79 F5
Turf Pitts La MGN/WHC B75 .... 40 B2
Turley St DUDN DY1 .... 68 C5
Turls Hill Rd SEDG DY3 .... 68 A3
Turls St SEDG DY3 .... 68 A4
Turnberry Rd BLOX/PEL WS3 .... 16 C2
  PBAR/PBCH B42 .... 77 D3
Turner Av BILS/COS WV14 .... 68 B3
Turner Dr BRLYHL DY5 .... 137 F2
Turner Gv DUNHL/THL/PER WV6.... 22 C3
Turners Cft HHTH/SAND B71 .... 74 C3
Turner's Gv SEDG DY3 .... 89 E1
Turner's HI BLKHTH/ROWR B65 ... 117 D1
Turner's Hill Rd SEDG DY3 .... 89 E1

Turner's La BRLYHL DY5 .... 137 E1
Turner St DUDN DY1 .... 91 D5
  SEDG DY3 .... 89 F2
  SPARK B11 .... 148 C3
  TPTN/OCK DY4 .... 70 B4
  WBROM B70 .... 94 C1
Turney Rd STRBR DY8 .... 136 B3
Turnham Gn DUNHL/THL/PER WV6 .. 22 A4
Turnhouse Rd CVALE B35.............. 105 F1
Turnley Rd BKDE/SHDE B34 .... 129 E1
Turnpike Cl SPARK B11 .... 148 C3
Turnpike Dr CSHL/WTROR B46 ..... 107 E2
Turton Cl BLOX/PEL WS3 .... 16 C1
Turton Rd TPTN/OCK DY4 .... 70 B2
  WBROM B70 .... 95 D3
Turtons Cft BILS/COS WV14 .... 47 D6
Turves Gn NFLD/LBR B31 .... 186 B5
Turville Rd BFLD/HDSWWD B20 .... 99 E4
Tustin Gv ACGN B27 .... 173 E3
Tutbury Av DUNHL/THL/PER WV6 .. 22 B4
Tuxford Cl WOLVN WV10 .... 26 A3
Twatling Rd RBRY B45 .... 200 C3
Tweeds Well RIDG/WDGT B32 ..... 165 D4
Twickenham Ct STRBR DY8 .... 135 E2
Twickenham Rd KSGTG B44 .... 79 D2
Two Gates HALE B63 .... 139 D4
Two Gates La HALE B63 .... 139 E4
Two Woods La BRLYHL DY5 .... 114 A6
Twycross Gv CBROM B36 .... 103 F6
Twydale Av OLDBY B69 .... 93 D4
Twyford Cl ALDR WS9 .... 35 D2
Twyford Gv WNSFLD WV11 .... 14 B6
Twyford Rd WASH/WDE B8 .... 127 E2
Twynning Rd BVILLE B30 .... 169 D4
  LDYWD/EDGR B16 .... 121 F3
Tyber Dr BFLD/HDSWWD B20 .... 99 D2
Tyberry Cl SHLY B90 .... 192 C4
Tyburn Gv ERDE/BCHGN B24 .... 103 F2
Tyburn Rd ERDE/BCHGN B24........ 101 F4
  WOLV WV1 .... 27 E6
Tyburn Sq ERDE/BCHGN B24........ 103 F2
Tyebeams BKDE/SHDE B34 .... 129 E2
Tye Gdns HAG/WOL DY9 .... 159 D2
Tyler Ct ERDE/BCHGN B24 .... 102 B2
Tyler Gdns WLNHL WV13 .... 29 D6
Tyler Gv PBAR/PBCH B42 .... 76 C2
Tyler Rd WLNHL WV13 .... 48 C1
Tylers Gn HWK/WKHTH B38.......... 189 D4
Tylers Gv SHLY B90 .... 210 B1
Tylney Cl DIG/EDG B5 .... 147 F2
Tyndale Crs GTB/HAM B43.............. 55 E6
Tyndall Wk RIDG/WDGT B32 .... 164 C1
Tyne Cl CHWD/FDBR/MGN B37 ... 131 D1
Tynedale Crs
  DUNHL/THL/PER WV6 .... 23 F1
Tynedale Rd SPARK B11 .... 150 B6
Tyne Gv YDLY B25 .... 151 F1
Tyne Pl BRLYHL DY5 .... 114 B5
Tyning Cl COVEN WV9 .... 10 C3
Tyningham Av
  DUNHL/THL/PER WV6 .... 23 F1
Tynings La ALDR WS9 .... 34 C2
Tyrley Cl DUNHL/THL/PER WV6..... 23 D5
Tyrol Cl STRBR DY8 .... 135 F3
Tyseley Hill Rd SPARK B11 .... 150 C5
Tyseley La SPARK B11 .... 150 C5
Tysoe Dr WALM/CURD B76............. 60 B5
Tysoe Rd KSGTG B44 .... 78 B4
Tythebarn Dr KGSWFD DY6 .... 86 C6
Tythebarn La SHLY B90 .... 208 D1
Tyzack Cl BRLYHL DY5 .... 113 E5

U

Udall Rd BILS/COS WV14 .... 47 F6
Uffculme Rd BVILLE B30 .... 169 F3
Uffmoor Est HALE B63 .... 162 A1
Uffmoor La HALE B63 .... 162 A2
  RMSLY B62 .... 161 F5
Ufton Cl SHLY B90 .... 194 A3
Ufton Crs SHLY B90 .... 193 F2
Ullenhall Rd DOR/KN B93............... 212 C1
  WALM/CURD B76 .... 82 B2
Ullenwood HDSW B21 .... 97 F6
Ulleries Rd HIA/OLT B92 .... 174 C1
Ullrik Gn ERDE/BCHGN B24 .... 102 B3
Ullswater Gdns KGSWFD DY6 ...... 111 F1
Ullswater Ri BRLYHL DY5 .... 113 F2
Ullswater Rd WNSFLD WV11 .... 15 D4
Ulster Dr KGSWFD DY6 .... 112 A3
Ulverley Crs HIA/OLT B92 .... 174 A3
Ulverley Green Rd HIA/OLT B92 ... 174 A3
Ulwine Dr NFLD/LBR B31 .... 186 B1
Umberslade Rd HOCK/TIA B94 ..... 223 D4
  SLYOAK B29 .... 168 C3
The Underpass BHAMNEC B40 ..... 155 F5
Underhill La WOLVN WV10 .... 12 C2
Underhill Rd TPTN/OCK DY4 .... 71 E5
  WASH/WDE B8 .... 126 B4
Underhill St OLDBY B69 .... 118 C2
Underley Cl KGSWFD DY6 .... 87 D6
The Underwood HDSW B21
Underwood Cl EDG B15 .... 145 F6

ERDW/GRVHL B23 .... 101 E1
Underwood Rd
 BFLD/HDSWWD B20 .... 76 A6
Unett St LOZ/NWT B19 ...... 123 E2 🔢
 SMTHWK B66 .... 121 E3
Union Mill St WOLV WV1 .... 3 G4
Union Rd AST/WIT B6 .... 101 D5
 OLDBY B69 .... 94 A3
 SHLY B90 .... 193 E3
 SOLH B91 .... 195 E1
 WBROM B70 .... 94 A3
Union Rw HDSW B21 .... 98 B5
Union St BILS/COS WV14 ...... 47 E4
 BLKHTH/ROWR B65 .... 117 E6 🔢
 CBHAM B2 .... 7 E5
 DARL/WED WS10 .... 72 B1
 DUDS DY2 .... 91 E4 🔟
 HAG/WOL DY9 .... 138 A4
 STRBR DY8 .... 136 C5
 TPTN/OCK DY4 .... 70 B6
 WBROM B70 .... 95 F5
 WLNHL WV13 .... 28 C5
 WOLV WV1 .... 3 F4
 WSL WS1 .... 5 F3
Unity Cl DARL/WED WS10 .... 49 E5 🔢
Unity Pl OLDBY B69 .... 94 C5 🔢
Unketts Rd SMTHWKW B67 ... 104 B5
Unwin Crs STRBR DY8 .... 136 A4
Upavon Cl CVALE B35 .... 104 C1
Upland Rd SLYOAK B29 .... 168 C1
Uplands HALE B63 .... 161 F1
Uplands Av BDMR/CCFT WV3 ... 43 F1
 BLKHTH/ROWR B65 .... 117 F4
 WLNHL WV13 .... 27 F6
Uplands Cl DUDS DY2 .... 92 A6
 SEDG DY3 .... 67 F3
Uplands Gv WLNHL WV13 .... 27 F6
Uplands Dr BDMR/CCFT WV3 .. 44 A1
 SEDG DY3 .... 67 F3
Uplands Rd DUDS DY2 .... 92 A6
 HDSW B21 .... 97 F3
 WLNHL WV13 .... 27 F6
The Uplands SMTHWKW B67 ... 120 B3
Upper Ashley St RMSLY B62 .. 117 E6 🔢
 BHTH/HG B12 .... 148 B3 🔢
Upper Balsall Heath Rd
 BHTH/HG B12 .... 148 B3 🔢
Upper Brook St WSLW WS2 ...... 4 A4
Upper Chapel St OLDBY B69 ... 93 D3
Upper Church La TPTN/OCK DY4 ... 70 B4
Upper Clifton Rd SCFLD/BOLD B73 .. 59 D4
Upper Cl RIDG/WDGT B32 ..... 143 F6
Upper Coneybere St
 BHTH/HG B12 .... 148 B2 🔢
Upper Dean St DIG/EDG B5 .... 124 A6 🔟
Upper Ettingshall Rd
 BILS/COS WV14 .... 68 C3
Upper Forster St RUSH/SHEL WS4 .... 5 E1
Upper Gough St CBHAMW B1 ... 123 F6
Upper Gn DUNHL/THL/PER WV6 ... 23 F2
Upper Green La WSLW WS2 ..... 31 E3
Upper Grosvenor Rd
 BFLD/HDSWWD B20 .... 99 D3
Upper Hall La WSL WS1 .... 4 A4
Upper Highgate St BHTH/HG B12 .. 148 B3
Upper High St CDYHTH B64 ... 115 F6
 DARL/WED WS10 .... 50 B6 🔢
Upper Holland Rd
 CSCFLD/WYGN B72 .... 59 E5
Upper Lichfield St WLNHL WV13 .. 28 C5
Upper Marshall St
 CBHAMW B1 .... 123 F6 🔢
Upper Meadow Rd
 RIDG/WDGT B32 .... 143 E4
Upper Navigation St WSLW WS2 ... 4 B3
Upper Rushall St WSL WS1 .... 5 F2
Upper Russell St
 DARL/WED WS10 .... 72 B1 🔢
Upper St Mary's Rd
 SMTHWK B67 .... 120 B3
Upper Short St WSLW WS2 ...... 4 A4
Upper Sneyd Rd WNSFLD WV11 ... 15 D3
Upper St DUNHL/THL/PER WV6 .. 23 F2
Upper Sutton St AST/WIT B6 .. 100 B6 🔢
Upper Thomas St AST/WIT B6 .. 100 B5 🔟
Upper Trinity St BORD B9 ..... 124 C4
Upper Vauxhall WOLV WV1 ...... 24 C5
Upper Villiers St
 ETTPK/GDPK/PENN WV4 ... 45 D3
Upper William St CBHAMW B1 .. 123 E6 🔢
Upper Zoar St BDMR/CCFT WV3 ... 45 D1
Upton Gdns BILS/COS WV14 .... 47 E4 🔢
Upton Rd STETCH B33 .... 127 E5
Upton St DUDS DY2 .... 115 E2
Upwey Av SOLH B91 .... 194 C1
Usk Wy CBROM B36 .... 106 C5
Uttoxeter Cl
 DUNHL/THL/PER WV6 .... 25 D2 🔢
Uxbridge Cl SEDG DY3 .... 89 F3 🔢
Uxbridge St LOZ/NWT B19 .... 123 F2

V

Valbourne Rd ALE/KHTH/YWD B14 ... 189 E1
Vale Av ALDR WS9 .... 35 F5
Vale Cl RIDG/WDGT B32 ...... 144 B6
Valencia Cft CVALE B35 .... 105 D1 🔢
Valentine Cl FOAKS/STRLY B74 ... 56 B2
Valentine Rd ALE/KHTH/YWD B14 .. 170 A2
 LGLYGN/QTN B68 .... 119 E5
Valepits Rd STETCH B33 ...... 129 E6
Valerie Gv GTB/HAM B43 ...... 75 E3
Vale Rd DUDS DY2 .... 116 A3
Vale Rw SEDG DY3 .... 67 F6 🔢
Vales Cl WALM/CURD B76 ...... 82 A4
Vale St BKHL/PFLD WV2 .... 46 C3
 HHTH/SAND B71 .... 74 A5
 SEDG DY3 .... 67 F6
 STRBR DY8 .... 136 B1
The Vale SPARK B11 .... 171 D1
Vale Vw ALDR WS9 .... 35 D4
Valley Farm Rd RBRY B45 .... 200 B3
Valley Rd BLOX/PEL WS3 .... 17 F5
 CDYHTH B64 .... 140 A2
 FOAKS/STRLY B74 .... 56 B2
 GTB/HAM B43 .... 75 E3
 HAG/WOL DY9 .... 138 B4
 HIA/OLT B92 .... 153 E5
 HOCK/TIA B94 .... 208 C6
 RMSLY B62 .... 142 B1
 SEDG DY3 .... 68 A5
 SMTHWKW B67 .... 120 B4
 WOLV WV10 .... 26 B2
Valley Side BLOX/PEL WS3 ..... 18 B3
Vallian Cft CBROM B36 .... 104 B6
Vanborough Wk DUDN DY1 ...... 90 C3
Vanbrugh Ct DUNHL/THL/PER WV6 .. 22 A4
Van Diemans Rd WMBN WV5 .... 64 A6
Vanguard Cl CBROM B36 ...... 104 A4 🔢
Vann Cl SMITH B10 .... 149 E1 🔢
Varden Cft DIG/EDG B5 .... 147 F5
Vardon Wy HWK/WKHTH B38 .. 187 F4
Varley Rd ERDE/BCHGN B24 .. 103 F1
Varley V ERDE/BCHGN B24 .... 103 F1
Varlins Wy HWK/WKHTH B38 .. 203 F1
Varney Av WBROM B70 .... 95 F3
Vaughan Cl FOAKS/STRLY B74 ... 38 B1
Vaughan Gdns CDSL WV8 .... 8 B1 🔢
Vaughan Rd WLNHL WV13 ...... 27 F6
Vaughton Dr MGN/WHC B75 .... 60 A3
Vaughton St BHTH/HG B12 .... 148 B1
Vaughton St South DIG/EDG B5 .. 148 A2
Vauxhall Av WOLV WV1 .... 24 C5 🔢
Vauxhall Crs CBROM B36 ...... 106 B4
Vauxhall Gdns DUDS DY2 .... 92 A6
Vauxhall Gv VAUX/NECH B7 ... 125 D4
Vauxhall Rd STRBR DY8 .... 136 C4
 VAUX/NECH B7 .... 124 C4
Vauxhall St DUDN DY1 .... 91 D5
Velsheda Rd SHLY B90 .... 192 C5
Venetia Rd BORD B9 .... 125 E5
Venning Gv GTB/HAM B43 ...... 75 E4
Ventnor Av CBROM B36 .... 103 F6
 LOZ/NWT B19 .... 99 E6
Ventnor Cl LGLYGN/QTN B68 .. 119 E2
Ventnor Rd HIA/OLT B92 .... 155 E6
Venture Wy VAUX/NECH B7 ...... 7 H1
Vera Rd LGN/SDN/BHAMAIR B26 .. 152 A1
Verbena Gdns VAUX/NECH B7 .. 124 C2 🔢
Vercourt FOAKS/STRLY B74 .... 37 D4
Vere St DIG/EDG B5 .... 147 F1
Verity Wk STRBR DY8 .... 112 A6
Verney Av STETCH B33 .... 153 F2 🔢
Vernier Av KGSWFD DY6 .... 112 C2
Vernon Av BFLD/HDSWWD B20 .. 98 B3
 TPTN/OCK DY4 .... 92 A1
Vernon Cl FOAKS/STRLY B74 ... 38 A2
 RMSLY B62 .... 141 F1 🔢
 WLNHL WV13 .... 28 A6
 WNSFLD WV11 .... 14 B1 🔢
Vernon Rd BILS/COS WV14 ..... 48 B3
 LDYWD/EDGR B16 .... 121 F6
 LGLYGN/QTN B68 .... 119 E1
 RMSLY B62 .... 141 E1 🔢
Vernon St WBROM B70 .... 94 A2
Vernon Wy BLOX/PEL WS3 ..... 16 A4
Veronica Av
 ETTPK/GDPK/PENN WV4 ... 46 A4
Veronica Cl SLYOAK B29 ...... 166 B5
Veronica Rd KGSWFD DY6 ..... 112 C1
Verstone Cft NFLD/LBR B31 ... 186 C3
Verstone Rd SHLY B90 .... 193 E1
Verwood Cl WLNHL WV13 ...... 27 F6 🔢
Vesey Cl CSHL/WTROR B46 .... 107 D3
 FOAKS/STRLY B74 .... 38 B5
Vesey Rd SCFLD/BOLD B73 .... 81 D2
Vesey St CBHAMNE B4 .... 7 E2
Vestry Cl CDYHTH B64 .... 116 B6
Vestry Ct STRBR DY8 .... 136 A3 🔢
Viaduct Dr DUNHL/THL/PER WV6 .. 25 D1
Viaduct St VAUX/NECH B7 ..... 124 C4
Vibart Rd LGN/SDN/BHAMAIR B26 .. 152 B1

Vicarage Cl BRLYHL DY5 .... 137 E2 🔢
 BVILLE B30 .... 169 D4
 PBAR/PBCH B42 .... 77 F4
 TPTN/OCK DY4 .... 70 A6 🔟
Vicarage Gdns RMSLY B62 .... 117 F6 🔢
 WALM/CURD B76 .... 82 B4 🔢
Vicarage Hl HOCK/TIA B94 .... 222 B6
Vicarage La BRLYHL DY5 .... 89 F5
 CSHL/WTROR B46 .... 107 D3
Vicarage Pl WSL WS1 .... 5 F4
Vicarage Prospect DUDN DY1 .. 91 D4 🔢
Vicarage Rd ALE/KHTH/YWD B14 .. 169 E4
 AST/WIT B6 .... 100 C6
 BILS/COS WV14 .... 69 E4
 BKHL/PFLD WV2 .... 45 F1
 BLOX/PEL WS3 .... 18 C3
 DARL/WED WS10 .... 50 B6
 EDG B15 .... 121 H8
 ETTPK/GDPK/PENN WV4 ... 44 A6
 HAG/WOL DY9 .... 138 B4
 HHTH/SAND B71 .... 73 F5 🔢
 HOCK/TIA B94 .... 209 E4
 HRBN B17 .... 145 D4
 LGLYGN/QTN B68 .... 119 D3
 RMSLY B62 .... 141 E1 🔢
 SEDG DY3 .... 68 A6
 SMTHWKW B67 .... 120 B2
 STETCH B33 .... 128 A6
 STRBR DY8 .... 135 F2
 STRBR DY8 .... 136 C2
 WNSFLD WV11 .... 27 D1
 WSNGN B18 .... 98 C6
Vicarage Rd West DUDN DY1 ... 69 E5
Vicarage St LGLYGN/QTN B68 .. 119 D2
 OLDBY B69 .... 119 D2
Vicarage Ter WSLW WS2 .... 51 E1 🔢
Vicarage Wk WSL WS1 .... 4 C5
Vicar St DARL/WED WS10 ...... 50 C6
 DUDS DY2 .... 91 E5
 SEDG DY3 .... 67 F3
Vicars Wk HAG/WOL DY9 .... 160 A1 🔢
Viceroy Cl EDG B15 .... 147 E3
 KGSWFD DY6 .... 112 C2 🔢
Victor Cl BKHL/PFLD WV2 ...... 47 D3 🔢
Victoria Av BLOX/PEL WS3 ...... 17 E4
 RMSLY B62 .... 142 B3
Victoria Gdns CDYHTH B64 ... 116 B5 🔢
Victoria Gv WMBN WV5 .... 64 C3
Victoria Ms OLDBY B69 .... 118 B3 🔢
 RUSH/SHEL WS4 .... 32 C4 🔢
Victoria Park Rd SMTHWK B66 .. 121 D2
Victoria Pas WOLV WV1 .... 2 D4
Victoria Rd ACGN B27 .... 173 E1
 AST/WIT B6 .... 100 A6
 BDMR/CCFT WV3 .... 44 A4
 BLOX/PEL WS3 .... 18 C2
 BRLYHL DY5 .... 114 C6
 BVILLE B30 .... 168 C4
 CDYHTH B64 .... 116 B5
 CSCFLD/WYGN B72 .... 59 E4
 DARL/WED WS10 .... 49 F3
 DUNHL/THL/PER WV6 .... 24 C1
 ERDW/GRVHL B23 .... 101 F2
 HDSW B21 .... 98 A5
 HRBN B17 .... 145 D4
 LGLYGN/QTN B68 .... 119 E1
 RMSLY B62 .... 141 F1 🔢
 SEDG DY3 .... 68 A3 🔢
 STETCH B33 .... 127 F4
 TPTN/OCK DY4 .... 70 B6
 WNSFLD WV11 .... 27 D1
 WOLV WV10 .... 26 B2
Victoria Sq CBHAMNW B3 .... 6 C5
Victoria St BORD B9 .... 125 F5
 BRLYHL DY5 .... 89 E6
 BRLYHL DY5 .... 113 F4
 DARL/WED WS10 .... 72 A1
 HALE B63 .... 140 C5 🔢
 KGSWFD DY6 .... 87 D4
 STRBR DY8 .... 136 C4 🔢
 WBROM B70 .... 72 B6
 WBROM B70 .... 95 E2 🔢
 WLNHL WV13 .... 28 C4
 WOLV WV1 .... 2 D5
Victoria Ter RUSH/SHEL WS4 .. 32 A4
Victor Rd HIA/OLT B92 .... 154 A6
 WSNGN B18 .... 122 A1
Victor St BLOX/PEL WS3 .... 18 C4
 WSL WS1 .... 52 A2
Victory Av DARL/WED WS10 .... 49 E5
Victory La WSLW WS2 .... 30 C3
Victory Ri HHTH/SAND B71 .... 73 F6 🔢
View Dr DUDS DY2 .... 92 A5
Viewfield Crs SEDG DY3 .... 67 F4
Viewlands Dr
 DUNHL/THL/PER WV6 .... 22 C5
Vigo Cl ALDR WS9 .... 20 B3
Vigo Pl ALDR WS9 .... 20 C6
Vigo Rd ALDR WS9 .... 20 B3
Vigo Ter ALDR WS9 .... 20 B2
Viking Ri BLKHTH/ROWR B65 .. 117 E3 🔢
Village Rd AST/WIT B6 .... 100 C4
The Village KGSWFD DY6 .... 88 A6
Village Wy BILS/COS WV14 ..... 47 D4
Villa Rd LOZ/NWT B19 .... 99 D6

Villa St *LOZ/NWT* B19 .... 99 E6
　STRBR DY8 .... 136 C1
Villa Wk *LOZ/NWT* B19 .... 123 E5
Villette Gv *ALE/KHTH/YWD* B14 ... 191 E1
Villiers Av *BILS/COS* WV14 .... 47 F3
Villiers St *WLNHL* WV13 .... 28 C5
　WSL WS1 .... 52 A2
Vimy Rd *DARL/WED* WS10 .... 50 C5
　MOS/BIL B13 .... 171 D3
Vincent Cl *BHTH/HG* B12 .... 148 B5 ⑥
Vincent Dr *EDG* B15 .... 145 F6
Vincent Pde *BHTH/HG* B12 .... 148 B5
Vincent Rd *MGN/WHC* B75 .... 60 A2
Vincent St *BHTH/HG* B12 .... 148 B4
　WSL WS1 .... 52 B2
Vince St *SMTHWK* B66 .... 120 C4
Vinculum Wy *WLNHL* WV13 .... 49 D1
Vine Av *BHTH/HG* B12 .... 148 C4 ⑬
Vine Crs *HHTH/SAND* B71 .... 73 F5 ⑪
Vine La *HAG/WOL* DY9 .... 180 B2
　HALE B63 .... 141 D6
The Vineries *ACGN* B27 .... 152 A5
Vine St *AST/WIT* B6 .... 101 D6
　BRLYHL DY5 .... 114 A2
　STRBR DY8 .... 112 A6
Vineyard Rd *NFLD/LBR* B31 .... 166 B6
Vinnall Gv *RIDG/WDGT* B32 .... 116 B5 ⑧
Vintage Cl *STETCH* B33 .... 128 C2 ⑥
Vinyard Cl *WSNGN* B18 .... 98 B6 ⑤
Violet Cft *TPTN/OCK* DY4 .... 71 D2
Violet La *HAG/WOL* DY9 .... 180 A1
Virginia Dr
　ETTPK/GDPK/PENN WV4 .... 44 B5
Viscount Cl *CVALE* B35 .... 104 C3
Vista Gn *HWK/WKHTH* B38 .... 188 C4
The Vista *SEDG* DY3 .... 67 F2
Vittoria St *CBHAMW* B1 .... 6 A2
　SMTHWK B66 .... 121 F1
Vivian Cl *HRBN* B17 .... 145 E3
Vivian Rd *HRBN* B17 .... 145 E4
Vixen Cl *WALM/CURD* B76 .... 81 F4 ⑦
Vulcan Rd *BILS/COS* WV14 .... 48 B4
　SOLH B91 .... 175 E5
Vyrnwy Gv *HWK/WKHTH* B38 ...... 188 A5
Vyse St *AST/WIT* B6 .... 101 D5
　WSNGN B18 .... 6 A1

W

Waddell Cl *BILS/COS* WV14 .... 68 B2
Waddens Brook La *WNSFLD* WV11... 28 A2
Waddington Av *GTB/HAM* B43 .... 76 A2
Wadesmill Lawns *WOLVN* WV10 ... 12 A1 ②
Wadham Cl *OLDBY* B69 .... 117 E1
Wadhurst Rd *HRBN* B17 .... 121 D5
Wadleys Rd *SOLH* B91 .... 174 B5 ②
Waen Cl *TPTN/OCK* DY4 .... 71 D3
Waggon St *CDYHTH* B64 .... 116 B5 ⑥
Waggon Wk *HWK/WKHTH* B38 .... 187 E5
Wagoners Cl *WASH/WDE* B8 .... 126 B1
Wagon La *HIA/OLT* B92 .... 152 B5
　LGN/SDN/BHAMAIR B26 .... 152 C4
Wagstaff Cl *BILS/COS* WV14 .... 69 F3 ③
Wainwright Cl *KGSWFD* DY6 .... 86 C6 ②
Wainwright St *AST/WIT* B6 .... 100 C3
Waite Rd *WLNHL* WV13 .... 48 A1
Wakefield Cl *SCFLD/BOLD* B73 ...... 80 B3
Wakeford Rd *NFLD/LBR* B31 .... 187 E4
Wake Green Pk *MOS/BIL* B13 ...... 171 D1
Wake Green Rd *MOS/BIL* B13 ...... 170 C1
　TPTN/OCK DY4 .... 70 C2
Wakelam Gdns *GTB/HAM* B43 .... 75 F2
Wakeley Hl
　ETTPK/GDPK/PENN WV4 .... 44 B5
Wakelin Rd *SHLY* B90 .... 193 D6
Wakeman Gv *STETCH* B33 .... 153 F2
Wakes Cl *WLNHL* WV13 .... 29 D6
Wakes Rd *DARL/WED* WS10 .... 72 C1
Walcot Cl *MGN/WHC* B75 .... 39 D4 ②
Walcot Dr *GTB/HAM* B43 .... 76 A5
Walcot Gdns *BILS/COS* WV14 .... 47 D4
Walcot Gn *DOR/KN* B93 .... 212 C5
Waldale Cl *SHHTH* WV12 .... 15 E4
Walden Gdns
　ETTPK/GDPK/PENN WV4 .... 44 A3
Walden Rd *SPARK* B11 .... 150 C6 ⑥
Waldeve Gv *HIA/OLT* B92 .... 176 B3
Waldley Cv *ERDE/BCHGN* B24 ..... 103 E2
Waldron Av *BRLYHL* DY5 .... 113 D5
Waldron Cl *DARL/WED* WS10 .... 50 B3
Waldrons Moor
　ALE/KHTH/YWD B14 .... 169 E6
Walford Av *BDMR/CCFT* WV3 .... 44 B1
Walford Dr *HIA/OLT* B92 .... 153 F1
Walford Gv *SHLY* B90 .... 149 E3
Walford Rd *SPARK* B11 .... 149 E3
Walford St *OLDBY* B69 .... 92 B5
Walhouse Cl *WSL* WS1 .... 5 F3
Walhouse Rd *WSL* WS1 .... 5 F3
Walker Av *BRLYHL* DY5 .... 137 F2 ④
　HAG/WOL DY9 .... 137 F6
　OLDBY B69 .... 93 E6
　WOLVN WV10 .... 12 A5

Walker Dr *VAUX/NECH* B7 .... 102 A5
Walker Pl *BLOX/PEL* WS3 .... 18 A5
Walker Rd *BLOX/PEL* WS3 .... 17 F5
Walkers Fold *SHHTH* WV12 .... 29 F1
Walkers Heath Rd
　HWK/WKHTH B38 .... 189 D4
Walker St *DUDS* DY2 .... 115 E3
　TPTN/OCK DY4 .... 71 E4
Walkers Wy *CSHL/WTROR* B46 .... 132 C1
Walk La *WMBN* WV5 .... 64 C5
Wallace Cl *OLDBY* B69 .... 117 F1
Wallace Ri *CDYHTH* B64 .... 140 A2
Wallace Rd *BILS/COS* WV14 .... 48 C6
　OLDBY B69 .... 117 F1
　SLYOAK B29 .... 169 D1
Wall Av *CSHL/WTROR* B46 .... 132 B2
Wallbank Rd *WASH/WDE* B8 .... 126 C1
Wallbrook St *BILS/COS* WV14 .... 69 F3
Wall Cft *ALDR* WS9 .... 21 D6
Wall Dr *FOAKS/STRLY* B74 .... 38 B3
Wall End Cl *WSLW* WS2 .... 16 C6
Wallface *HHTH/SAND* B71 .... 72 C4
Walling Cft *BILS/COS* WV14 .... 47 D6
Wallington Cl *BLOX/PEL* WS3 .... 17 D3 ③
Wallington Heath
　BLOX/PEL WS3 .... 17 D3 ④
　WSLW WS2 .... 17 D3 ⑤
Wallows La *WSL* WS1 .... 51 E3
　WSLW WS2 .... 51 E3 ⑪
Wallows Pl *BRLYHL* DY5 .... 113 E2
Wallows Rd *BRLYHL* DY5 .... 113 E3
Wallows Wd *SEDG* DY3 .... 88 C1
Wall St *WOLV* WV1 .... 26 C5
Wall Well La *HALE* B63 .... 140 B6
Wall Well Ri *HALE* B63 .... 140 B6
Walmead Cft *HRBN* B17 .... 144 B2 ⑥
Walmer Gv *ERDW/GRVHL* B23 .... 79 D6
Walmer Meadow *ALDR* WS9 .... 21 D6
The Walmers *ALDR* WS9 .... 21 D6
Walmer Wy
　CHWD/FDBR/MGN B37 .... 131 E4 ④
Walmley Ash Rd *WALM/CURD* B76.. 82 B4
Walmley Cl *HALE* B63 .... 139 D2
Walmley Rd *WALM/CURD* B76 .... 66 B6
　WALM/CURD B76 .... 82 B2 ②
　WALM/CURD B76 .... 82 B3 ⑥
Walnut Av *CDSL* WV8 .... 9 D2 ①
Walnut Cl *CHWD/FDBR/MGN* B37.. 131 D6
　HAG/WOL DY9 .... 159 D2
Walnut Dr *BDMR/CCFT* WV3 .... 23 F6
　SMTHWK B66 .... 121 D2 ⑬
Walnut La *DARL/WED* WS10 .... 72 C1
Walnut Rd *DSYBK/YTR* WS5 .... 52 C6
Walnut Wy *NFLD/LBR* B31 .... 186 B5
Walpole St *DUNHL/THL/PER* WV6.. 24 C4
Walpole Wk *WBROM* B70 .... 95 F4 ⑥
Walsall Rd *ALDR* WS9 .... 20 A3
　BLOX/PEL WS3 .... 18 C3
　DARL/WED WS10 .... 50 A3
　DSYBK/YTR WS5 .... 53 E2
　FOAKS/STRLY B74 .... 37 E1
　HHTH/SAND B71 .... 74 A4
　PBAR/PBCH B42 .... 76 C3
　WLNHL WV13 .... 29 D5
Walsall St *BILS/COS* WV14 .... 47 F4
　DARL/WED WS10 .... 49 F3
　DARL/WED WS10 .... 50 B6
　WBROM B70 .... 95 F2
　WLNHL WV13 .... 29 D6
　WOLV WV1 .... 3 G5
Walsall Wood Rd *ALDR* WS9 .... 20 C5
Walsgrave Dr *HIA/OLT* B92 .... 175 F4
Walsham Cft *BKDE/SHDE* B34 ..... 129 E2
Walsh Dr *WALM/CURD* B76 .... 66 B5
Walsh Gv *ERDW/GRVHL* B23 .... 79 F3 ⑥
Walsingham St *WSL* WS1 .... 5 G5
Walstead Rd *DSYBK/YTR* WS5 .... 52 B4
　DSYBK/YTR WS5 .... 53 E4 ⑪
Walstead Rd West *DSYBK/YTR* WS5.. 52 A4
Waltdene Cl *GTB/HAM* B43 .... 76 A1 ⑥
Walter Cobb Dr *SCFLD/BOLD* B73.. 80 C2
Walter Rd *BILS/COS* WV14 .... 48 A6
　SMTHWK B67 .... 120 A1
Walters Cl *NFLD/LBR* B31 .... 202 B3
Walters Rd *LGLYGN/QTN* B68 ...... 142 C2
Walters Rw *DUDN* DY1 .... 90 C4 ②
Walter St *BLOX/PEL* WS3 .... 18 C4
　VAUX/NECH B7 .... 125 D1
　WBROM B70 .... 95 F3
Waltham Gv *KGSTG* B44 .... 79 D1
Walthamstow Ct *BRLYHL* DY5 ... 113 F6 ⑤
Walton Av *BLKHTH/ROWR* B65 ... 141 D1
Walton Cl *BLKHTH/ROWR* B65 ... 116 C3 ②
　HALE B63 .... 162 B1 ⑪
Walton Crs
　ETTPK/GDPK/PENN WV4 .... 46 A4 ①
Walton Cft *SOLH* B91 .... 195 D4
Walton Dr *HAG/WOL* DY9 .... 137 E4 ②
Walton Gdns *CDSL* WV8 .... 8 B1
Walton Gv *BVILLE* B30 .... 189 D3
Walton Heath *BLOX/PEL* WS3 .... 16 B3
Walton Pool La *HAG/WOL* DY9 .... 180 B3
Walton Ri *HAG/WOL* DY9 .... 180 B3
Walton Rd *ALDR* WS9 .... 20 C4

　DARL/WED WS10 .... 73 E1
　ETTPK/GDPK/PENN WV4 .... 46 B4 ②
　LGLYGN/QTN B68 .... 119 E6
　STRBR DY8 .... 136 C3 ⑥
Walton St *TPTN/OCK* DY4 .... 70 B6 ⑦
Wanderers Av *BKHL/PFLD* WV2 ..... 45 E3
Wanderer Wk *ERDE/BCHGN* B24 . 104 A4
Wandle Gv *SPARK* B11 .... 150 C6
Wandsworth Rd *KGSTG* B44 .... 56 A6
Wansbeck Gv *HWK/WKHTH* B38 . 188 A5
Wansbeck Wk *SEDG* DY3 .... 68 B5
Wanstead Gv *KGSTG* B44 .... 78 C2
Wantage Rd *CSHL/WTROR* B46 ... 108 A4 ①
Warbank Cl *ALVE* B48 .... 216 C3
Ward Cl *WASH/WDE* B8 .... 126 C2
Warden Av *SCFLD/BOLD* B73 .... 80 B3
Ward End Cl *WASH/WDE* B8 .... 126 B1 ②
Ward End Hall Gv
　WASH/WDE B8 .... 126 C1 ①
Ward End Park Rd *WASH/WDE* B8.. 126 B2
Wardend Rd *WASH/WDE* B8 .... 126 C1
Warden Rd *SCFLD/BOLD* B73 .... 80 B3
Ward Gv *ETTPK/GDPK/PENN* WV4.. 46 B6
Wardle Cl *MGN/WHC* B75 .... 38 C3 ②
Wardlow Cl
　ETTPK/GDPK/PENN WV4 .... 45 D3
Wardlow Rd *VAUX/NECH* B7 .... 124 C2
Wardour Dr
　CHWD/FDBR/MGN B37 .... 131 E5
Wardour Gv *KGSTG* B44 .... 79 E3
Ward Rd *CDSL* WV8 .... 8 B2
　ETTPK/GDPK/PENN WV4 .... 45 F4
Ward St *BILS/COS* WV14 .... 69 D3
　BKHL/PFLD WV2 .... 47 D3
　LOZ/NWT B19 .... 72 E1
　WOLV WV1 .... 3 G4
　WSL WS1 .... 5 F2
Wareham Rd *RBRY* B45 .... 185 D3
Wareing Dr *ERDW/GRVHL* B23 ..... 79 F3
Warewell St *WSL* WS1 .... 5 E4
Waring Cl *TPTN/OCK* DY4 .... 70 A3
Waring Rd *TPTN/OCK* DY4 .... 70 C3
Warings Green Rd *HOCK/TIA* B94.. 223 F1
The Warings *WMBN* WV5 .... 86 B1 ②
War La *HRBN* B17 .... 145 D4
Warley Cft *LGLYGN/QTN* B68 ...... 143 F1
Warley Hall Rd *LGLYGN/QTN* B68.. 119 F6
Warley Rd *LGLYGN/QTN* B68 ...... 119 E2
Warmington Dr
　SCFLD/BOLD B73 .... 59 D5 ③
Warmington Rd *HLYWD* B47 .... 206 C1
　LGN/SDN/BHAMAIR B26 .... 153 E4
Warmley Cl *DUNHL/THL/PER* WV6.. 25 D2
　SOLH B91 .... 175 F6
Warner Dr *BRLYHL* DY5 .... 113 F6
Warner Pl *BLOX/PEL* WS3 .... 32 B1
Warner Rd *BLOX/PEL* WS3 .... 32 C1
　CDSL WV8 .... 8 B2
　DARL/WED WS10 .... 73 E1
Warner St *BHTH/HG* B12 .... 148 C1 ⑨
Warple Rd *RIDG/WDGT* B32 .... 143 E4
Warren Av *WOLVN* WV10 .... 26 B2
Warren Cl *TPTN/OCK* DY4 .... 70 B4
Warren Dr *BLKHTH/ROWR* B65 ... 116 B2 ②
　DOR/KN B93 .... 212 C4
　SEDG DY3 .... 67 E1
Warren Farm Rd *KGSTG* B44 .... 78 B3
Warren Gdns *KGSWFD* DY6 .... 111 E1
Warren Hill Rd *KGSTG* B44 .... 78 C4
Warren La *RBRY* B45 .... 201 D4
Warren Rd *BVILLE* B30 .... 168 C4
　KGSTG B44 .... 78 C5
　WASH/WDE B8 .... 126 A1
Warrens Cft *DSYBK/YTR* WS5 ...... 53 F4
Warrens End *HWK/WKHTH* B38 .. 188 B5
Warrens Hall Rd *DUDS* DY2 .... 92 A6
Warrington Cl *WALM/CURD* B76 .... 82 C2
Warrington Dr *ERDW/GRVHL* B23.. 79 F4
Warsash Cl *WOLV* WV1 .... 47 D1
Warstock Cl *ALE/KHTH/YWD* B14.. 190 C1
Warstock Rd *ALE/KHTH/YWD* B14.. 190 B1
Warston Av *RIDG/WDGT* B32 ...... 143 F6
Warstone Dr *HHTH/SAND* B71 ...... 96 A1
Warstone La *CBHAMW* B1 .... 6 A2
Warstone Pde East
　WSNGN B18 .... 123 D3 ③
Warstones Crs
　ETTPK/GDPK/PENN WV4 .... 43 F4
Warstones Dr
　ETTPK/GDPK/PENN WV4 .... 43 E4
Warstones Gdns
　ETTPK/GDPK/PENN WV4 .... 43 E3
Warstones Rd
　ETTPK/GDPK/PENN WV4 .... 43 F5
Warstone Ter *HDSW* B21 .... 98 A5 ②
Wartell Bank *KGSWFD* DY6 .... 87 F6
Warwards La *SLYOAK* B29 .... 168 C2
Warwell La
　LGN/SDN/BHAMAIR B26 .... 151 F3 ⑧
Warwick Av *DARL/WED* WS10 .... 51 E6
　DUNHL/THL/PER WV6 .... 22 B4
　WLNHL WV13 .... 29 F5 ⑥
Warwick Cl *LGLYGN/QTN* B68 ..... 119 D5
　WBROM B70 .... 72 A4

Warwick Dr CDSL WV8 .... 8 A2
Warwick Gdns OLDBY B69 .... 93 E3
Warwick Gra SLYOAK B29 .... 174 B6 ⑥
Warwick Pas CBHAM B2 .... 173 F2 ⑦
Warwick Rd ACGN B27 .... 150 C5
　DOR/KN B93 .... 196 C4
　DOR/KN B93 .... 213 E4
　DUDS DY2 .... 116 A4
　LGLYCGN/QTN B68 .... 143 F2
　SCFLD/BOLD B73 .... 79 E1
　SOLH B91 .... 174 C6
　SOLH B91 .... 195 E1 ③
　SPARK B11 .... 149 E4
　STRBR DY8 .... 111 F6
Warwick St BHTH/HG B12 .... 124 C6
　BILS/COS WV14 .... 48 A4
　RUSH/SHEL WS4 .... 5 E1
　WOLV WV1 .... 3 C5
Warwick Wy ALDR WS9 .... 20 C4 ②
Wasdale Dr KGSWFD DY6 .... 112 A1
Wasdale Rd NFLD/LBR B31 .... 186 B1
Waseley Rd RBRY B45 .... 184 B5
Washbrook Rd WASH/WDE B8 .. 126 C1 ④
Washford Gv YDLY B25 .... 151 D1 ⑪
Washington Dr
　BFLD/HDSWWD B20 .... 99 D2 ②
Washington St CBHAMW B1 .... 123 E6
　DUDS DY2 .... 115 F4
Wash La YDLY B25 .... 127 E6
　YDLY B25 .... 151 E2
Washwood Heath Rd
　WASH/WDE B8 .... 126 A1
　WASH/WDE B8 .... 127 E2
Wasperton Cl CBROM B36 .... 105 D5
Wassell Ct HALE B63 .... 162 A1
Wassell Grove Rd HAG/WOL DY9 .. 160 B2
Wasseil Rd BILS/COS WV14 .... 47 F2 ③
　HAG/WOL DY9 .... 160 A1
　HALE B63 .... 162 A1
Wast Hill Gv HWK/WKHTH B38 .. 188 B6
Wasthill La HWK/WKHTH B38 .. 203 F2
Wastwater Dr
　DUNHL/THL/PER WV6 ...... 22 B3 ⑩
Watchbury Cl CBROM B36 .... 105 E4 ②
Watchman Av BRLYHL DY5 ...... 138 B2 ③
Water Dr BDMR/CCFT WV3 ...... 24 A5
Waterdale SHLY B90 .... 209 F2 ⑥
　WMBN WV5 .... 64 A6
Waterfall Cl SMTHWK B66 .... 96 A6 ③
Waterfall La ALE/KHTH/YWD B14 .. 170 A3
Waterfall Rd BRLYHL DY5 .... 137 E2
Waterfield Cl TPTN/OCK DY4 .... 69 E6
Waterford Pl STETCH B33 .... 129 F4 ⑪
Waterford Rd KGSWFD DY6 .... 87 F6 ②
Waterfront East BRLYHL DY5 .. 114 A3
Waterfront Wy BRLYHL DY5 .. 114 A3
Waterfront West BRLYHL DY5 .. 114 A4
Waterglade La WLNHL WV13 .... 28 C6
Waterhaynes Cl RBRY B45 .... 200 C1 ③
Waterhead Cl WOLVN WV10 .... 12 C5 ③
Waterhead Dr WOLVN WV10 .... 13 D3
Water La HHTH/SAND B71 .... 74 B4
Waterlinks Bvd AST/WIT B6 .... 100 C6
Waterloo Pl
　CHWD/FDBR/MGN B37 .... 131 D3
Waterloo Rd ALE/KHTH/YWD B14 .. 170 A3
　SMTHWK B66 .... 120 C4
　WOLV WV1 .... 2 C3
　YDLY B25 .... 151 D1
Waterloo St CBHAM B2 .... 6 D5
　DUDN DY1 .... 90 C5
　TPTN/OCK DY4 .... 70 B6
Waterloo St East TPTN/OCK DY4 .. 70 B6 ④
Watermeadow Dr RUSH/SHEL WS4 .. 19 F4
Watermere RUSH/SHEL WS4 .... 19 F5
Water Mill Cl SLYOAK B29 ...... 145 F6 ③
Watermill Cl WOLVN WV10 ...... 11 F2
Water Orton La WALM/CURD B76 ... 83 F6
Water Orton Rd CBROM B36 .... 105 D3
Water Rd SEDG DY3 .... 89 E3
Waters Dr FOAKS/STRLY B74 .... 37 F4
Waterside Cl ERDE/BCHGN B24 .. 104 C1
Waterside Vw BRLYHL DY5 .... 113 D6
　WSNGN B18 .... 122 C2 ⑧
Water Side Wy COVEN WV9 .... 10 C3
Waterson Cft
　CHWD/FDBR/MGN B37 .... 131 F4
Water St CBHAMNW B3 .... 6 C3
　KGSWFD DY6 .... 87 F6
　WBROM B70 .... 95 F3 ⑥
　WOLVN WV10 .... 3 F1
Waterward Cl HRBN B17 .... 145 E4 ⑪
Waterways Dr OLDBY B69 .... 94 A4
Waterways Gdns STRBR DY8 .... 112 A6
Waterworks Dr NFLD/LBR B31 .. 165 F6
Waterworks Rd
　LDYWD/EDGR B16 .... 122 B6
Waterworks St AST/WIT B6 .... 101 D5
Watery La ALVE B48 .... 204 A5 ④
　CSHL/WTROR B46 .... 109 F3
　RIDG/WDGT B32 .... 142 C6
　SHLY B90 .... 209 E3
　SMTHWK B67 .... 120 C2
　STRBR DY8 .... 112 A3

Watery Lane Middleway
　BORD B9 .... 125 D5
Watford Rd BVILLE B30 .... 168 B6
Wathan Av BILS/COS WV14 .... 68 D1
Watkins Gdns NFLD/LBR B31 .. 187 D2
Watkins Rd SHHTH WV12 .... 29 E2
Watland Gn BKDE/SHDE B34 .. 128 C2
Watney Gv KGSTG B44 .... 79 E3 ④
Watson Cl CSCFLD/WYGN B72 .. 81 D1
Watson Rd BILS/COS WV14 .... 68 B1
　DARL/WED WS10 .... 48 C4
　VAUX/NECH B7 .... 102 A5
　WASH/WDE B8 .... 126 B2
　WOLVN WV10 .... 11 D3
Watsons Cl DUDS DY2 .... 92 A5 ⑬
Watson's Green Flds DUDS DY2 .. 92 B5 ③
Watson's Green Rd DUDS DY2 .. 92 A5
Wattisham Sq CVALE B35 .... 104 C1
Wattis Rd SMTHWKW B67 .... 120 C5
Wattle Rd WBROM B70 .... 94 C2
Watton Cl BILS/COS WV14 ...... 68 C2
Watton Gn CVALE B35 .... 104 C3
Watton La CSHL/WTROR B46 .. 107 E3
Watton St WBROM B70 .... 95 E3
Watt Rd ERDW/GRVHL B23 .... 102 A1
　TPTN/OCK DY4 .... 71 D3
Watts Cl TPTN/OCK DY4 .... 69 E6
Watt's Rd SMTH B10 .... 149 F1 ②
Watt St HDSW B21 .... 97 F6
　SMTHWK B66 .... 121 D1
Wattville Rd HDSW B21 .... 97 E5
Watwood Rd SHLY B90 .... 192 B2
Waugh Cl CHWD/FDBR/MGN B37 .. 131 D5
Waugh Dr HALE B63 .... 161 F3
Wavell Rd BRLYHL DY5 .... 138 B2
　WASH/WDE B8 .... 126 A2
　WSLW WS2 .... 30 A5
Waveney Av DUNHL/THL/PER WV6 .. 22 A3
Waveney Crt CBROM B36 .... 106 B5
Waverhill Rd HDSW B21 .... 98 B6
Waverley Av BTR/HAM B43 .... 55 D5
Waverley Crs
　ETTPK/GDPK/PENN WV4 .... 44 C3 ⑧
　ETTPK/GDPK/PENN WV4 .... 46 B1 ⑪
　RMSLY B62 .... 182 A1
Waverley Gv WMBN WV5 .... 65 D4
Waverley Gv SOLH B91 .... 194 A2
Waverley Rd BLOX/PEL WS3 .... 16 B3
　DARL/WED WS10 .... 49 D3
　SMHTH B10 .... 150 A3
Waverley St DUDS DY2 .... 90 C5
Waxland Rd HALE B63 .... 163 D1
Wayfield Cl SHLY B90 .... 193 E2
Wayfield Rd SHLY B90 .... 193 E2
Wayford Dr CSCFLD/WYGN B72 .. 81 F4
Wayford Gld WLNHL WV13 .... 48 B1
Waynecroft Rd GTB/HAM B43 .. 75 F1 ④
Wayside CHWD/FDBR/MGN B37 .. 154 C1
Wayside Acres CDSL WV8 .... 8 B3
Wayside Dr FOAKS/STRLY B74 .. 37 E4
Wayside Gdns SHHTH WV12 .... 30 A2
Wayside Wk WSLW WS2 .... 30 C4
Wealden Hatch WOLVN WV10 .. 12 A1 ⑨
Wealdstone Dr SEDG DY3 .... 89 F3
Weaman St CBHAMNE B4 .... 7 E3
Weatheroak Hl ALVE B48 .... 205 D6
Weatheroak Rd SPARK B11 .... 149 E4
Weatheroaks ALDR WS9 .... 21 D1
Weather Oaks HRBN B17 .... 145 D4
Weatheroaks RMSLY B62 .... 142 C2 ④
Weaver Av
　LGN/SDN/BHAMAIR B26 .. 153 D3
　WALM/CURD B76 .... 82 C2
Weaver Cl BRLYHL DY5 .... 113 D1
Weaver Gv WLNHL WV13 .... 29 F5
Weavers Ri DUDS DY2 .... 115 F4
Webb Av DUNHL/THL/PER WV6 .. 22 A2
Webbcroft Rd STETCH B33 .... 128 A3
Webb La HLGN/YWD B28 ...... 172 A5
Webb Rd TPTN/OCK DY4 .... 71 E4
Webb St BILS/COS WV14 .... 69 E1
　WLNHL WV13 .... 28 B5
Webley Ri WOLVN WV10 .... 12 B1
Webster Cl CSCFLD/WYGN B72 .. 81 D4
　SPARK B11 .... 149 D5
Webster Rd WLNHL WV13 .... 28 C4
　WSLW WS2 .... 31 F2
Webster Wy WALM/CURD B76 .. 83 D4
Wedge St WSL WS1 .... 5 F3
Wedgewood Av WBROM B70 .. 72 B4 ⑪
Wedgewood Cl
　BFLD/HDSWWD B20 .... 99 D3
Wedgewood Pl WBROM B70 .... 72 B4 ②
Wedgwood Rd RIDG/WDGT B32 .. 143 E4
Wedgwood Cl WMBN WV5 ...... 64 B3 ⑥
　WOLV WV1 .... 26 C6 ⑪
Wednesbury Oak Rd
　TPTN/OCK DY4 .... 70 C2
Wednesbury Rd WSLW WS2 ...... 51 E2
Wednesfield Rd WLNHL WV13 .. 28 C4

WOLVN WV10 .... 3 H2
Wednesfield Wy WLNHL WV13 .. 27 F3
　WNSFLD WV11 .... 28 A2
Weeford Dr BFLD/HDSWWD B20 .. 98 B1
Weeford Rd MGN/WHC B75 ...... 40 A6
Weirbrook Cl SLYOAK B29 ...... 167 E4 ③
Welbeck Av WOLVN WV10 .... 11 F6
Welbeck Dr RUSH/SHEL WS4 .... 19 F6 ②
Welbeck Gv ERDW/GRVHL B23 .. 79 D6 ⑪
Welbury Gdns
　DUNHL/THL/PER WV6 .... 24 B2
Welby Rd HLGN/YWD B28 ...... 172 B2
Welches Cl NFLD/LBR B31 ...... 167 D6
Welcombe Dr WALM/CURD B76 .. 82 A4 ⑪
Welcombe Gv SOLH B91 .... 194 B2
Welcome Dr BRGRVW B61 ...... 198 C2 ③
Welford Av
　LGN/SDN/BHAMAIR B26 .. 152 B1
Welford Gv FOAKS/STRLY B74 .. 38 B4
Welford Rd BFLD/HDSWWD B20 .. 98 C5
　SCFLD/BOLD B73 .... 80 A2
　SHLY B90 .... 193 E1
Welham Cft SHLY B90 .... 210 C1
Welland Cl CSHL/WTROR B46 .. 107 F3
Welland Dr STRBR DY8 .... 136 C1
Welland Gv ERDE/BCHGN B24 .. 103 E2
　WLNHL WV13 .... 29 E5
Welland Rd HALE B63 .... 162 C1 ③
Welland Wy WALM/CURD B76 .. 82 C4
Well Cl CBROM B36 .... 104 A5 ⑥
Wellcroft Rd BKDE/SHDE B34 .. 104 C6
Wellcroft St DARL/WED WS10 .. 50 B6
Wellesbourne Cl
　BDMR/CCFT WV3 .... 43 D1 ②
Wellesbourne Dr DUDN DY1 .... 69 D4
Wellesbourne Rd
　BFLD/HDSWWD B20 .... 99 D4
Wellesley Dr TPTN/OCK DY4 .. 70 B6 ⑥
Wellesley Gdns MOS/BIL B13 .. 171 F2
Wellesley Rd LGLYGN/QTN B68 .. 119 D1
Wellfield Gdns DUDS DY2 .... 116 A1
Wellfield Rd ALDR WS9 .... 21 D5
　HLGN/YWD B28 .... 173 D3
Wellhead La PBAR/PBCH B42 .. 100 A3
Wellington Av BDMR/CCFT WV3 .. 44 A3
Wellington Cl KGSWFD DY6 .... 112 A3
Wellington Gv SOLH B91 ...... 174 B5 ②
Wellington Pl WLNHL WV13 .... 28 B4
Wellington Rd BFLD/HDSWWD B20 .. 99 D3
　BILS/COS WV14 .... 47 E3
　DYSBK/YTR WS5 .... 53 E3 ⑪
　DUDN DY1 .... 91 D4
　EDG B15 .... 147 D5
　SMTHWKW B67 .... 120 C4
　TPTN/OCK DY4 .... 70 C6
Wellington St CDYHTH B64 .... 116 B5
　HHTH/SAND B71 .... 95 E1
　OLDBY B69 .... 119 D1 ③
　WSLW WS2 .... 51 D2
　WSNGN B18 .... 121 F2
Wellington St South
　WBROM B70 .... 95 E1 ②
Wellington Wy CVALE B35 .... 105 D3
Well La BLOX/PEL WS3 .... 17 F6
　DIG/EDG B5 .... 7 G6
　WNSFLD WV11 .... 27 E3
Wellman Cft SLYOAK B29 ...... 167 F2 ②
Wellman's Rd WLNHL WV13 .... 29 E6
Well Meadow RBRY B45 .... 200 C1 ⑥
Well Pl BLOX/PEL WS3 .... 18 A5
Wells Av DARL/WED WS10 ...... 49 D3
Wells Cl HHTH/SAND B71 .... 73 F3
　TPTN/OCK DY4 .... 70 C2
Wellsford Av HIA/OLT B92 ...... 152 C5
Wells Green Rd HIA/OLT B92 .. 152 C5 ⑪
Wells Rd BILS/COS WV14 .... 48 A6
　BLKHTH/ROWR B65 ...... 118 A4 ②
　BRLYHL DY5 .... 113 D4
　ETTPK/GDPK/PENN WV4 .... 44 B4
　LGN/SDN/BHAMAIR B26 .. 153 E5
Well St DARL/WED WS10 .... 50 A3 ⑪
　LOZ/NWT B19 .... 123 F1
Welney Gdns COVEN WV9 ...... 10 C2
Welsby Av GTB/HAM B43 .... 76 A4
Welsh House Farm Rd
　RIDG/WDGT B32 .... 144 B5
Welshmans Hl SCFLD/BOLD B73 .. 57 F6 ③
Welton Cl WALM/CURD B76 .... 82 C1 ③
Welwyndale Rd CSCFLD/WYGN B72 .. 81 E5
Wembley Gv YDLY B25 .... 151 E1 ③
Wem Gdns WNSFLD WV11 .... 27 F1
Wendell Crest WOLVN WV10 .. 12 B2 ⑥
Wendover Rd BLKHTH/ROWR B65 .. 116 C1
　ERDW/GRVHL B23 .... 79 E4
　ETTPK/GDPK/PENN WV4 .... 68 A1
Wendron Gv ALE/KHTH/YWD B14 .. 189 F1
Wenlock Av BDMR/CCFT WV3 .. 44 A1
Wenlock Cl HALE B63 .... 161 F1 ②
　SEDG DY3 .... 89 D1
Wenlock Gdns BLOX/PEL WS3 .. 32 A2
Wenlock Rd BFLD/HDSWWD B20 .. 100 B4
　STRBR DY8 .... 137 D3 ③
Wenman St BHTH/HG B12 ...... 148 B3
Wensley Cft HIA/OLT B92 ...... 173 D3 ⑪
Wensleydale Rd PBAR/PBCH B42 .. 77 D5

Wensley Rd
LGN/SDN/BHAMAIR B26 .... **152** B3
Wentbridge Rd WLNHL WV13 .... **27** E6
Wentworth Av CBROM B36 .... **105** D5 ⬚
Wentworth Dr BRGRVE B60 .... **214** C4
  OLDBY B69 .... **92** C6
Wentworth Ga HRBN B17 .... **145** D3
Wentworth Park Av HRBN B17 .. **145** D3
Wentworth Ri RMSLY B62 .... **141** F6 ⬚
Wentworth Rd BLOX/PEL WS3 .... **16** B2 ⬚
  FOAKS/STRLY B74 .... **58** C1
  HIA/OLT B92 .... **152** B6
  HRBN B17 .... **145** D3
  STRBR DY8 .... **135** F2
  WOLVN WV10 .... **12** B3
Wentworth Wy RIDG/WDGT B32 .. **144** B6
Wenyon Cl TPTN/OCK DY4 .... **93** D1 ⬚
Weoley Av SLYOAK B29 .... **167** E1
Weoley Castle Rd SLYOAK B29 .. **166** B2
Weoley Hl SLYOAK B29 .... **167** E3
Weoley Park Rd SLYOAK B29 .... **167** D2
Wergs Dr DUNHL/THL/PER WV6 .... **8** C5
Wergs Hall Rd CDSL WV8 .... **8** B4
Wergs Rd DUNHL/THL/PER WV6 .. **22** C1
Werneth Gv BLOX/PEL WS3 .... **16** C1
Wesley Av CDSL WV8 .... **139** D2
  HALE B63 .... **139** D2
Wesley Gv DARL/WED WS10 .... **50** A6
Wesley Pl TPTN/OCK DY4 .... **71** E4
Wesley Rd BRLYHL DY5 .... **113** D2 ⬚
  CDSL WV8 .... **9** D3
  ERDW/GRVHL B23 .... **80** B6
Wesley's Fold DARL/WED WS10 .. **49** F3 ⬚
Wesley St BILS/COS WV14 .... **70** A1
  BKHL/PFLD WV2 .... **46** C3
  OLDBY B69 .... **94** C5 ⬚
  WBROM B70 .... **95** D2 ⬚
Wessex Rd BKHL/PFLD WV2 .... **46** B3
Wesson Gdns HALE B63 .... **140** C6 ⬚
West Acre WLNHL WV13 .... **28** B6
Westacre Crs BDMR/CCFT WV3 .. **43** D1
Westacre Dr BRLYHL DY5 .... **138** B1 ⬚
West Av BKHL/HDSWWD B20 .... **98** B1
  CBROM B36 .... **105** F5
  OLDBY B69 .... **93** D5
  WNSFLD WV11 .... **27** E1
Westbook Av WMBN WV5 .... **64** B6
West Bvd RIDG/WDGT B32 .... **144** B5
Westbourne Av BKDE/SHDE B34 .. **128** A1
Westbourne Crs EDG B15 .... **146** C1 ⬚
Westbourne Gdns EDG B15 ...... **146** C2
Westbourne Rd
  DARL/WED WS10 .... **50** B2 ⬚
  EDG B15 .... **146** B2
  ETTPG/GDPK/PENN WV4 .... **44** C4
  HDSW B21 .... **97** F4
  HIA/OLT B92 .... **174** B4
  RMSLY B62 .... **142** A3
  RUSH/SHEL WS4 .... **32** C5 ⬚
  WBROM B70 .... **95** D4
Westbourne St RUSH/SHEL WS4 .. **32** B4
West Bromwich Ringway
  WBROM B70 .... **95** E2
West Bromwich Rd
  DSYBK/YTR WS5 .... **52** A3 ⬚
West Bromwich St OLDBY B69 .... **94** B4
  WSL WS1 .... **52** A2
Westbrook Av ALDR WS9 .... **34** B2
Westbury Av DARL/WED WS10 ...... **50** B3
Westbury Rd DARL/WED WS10 ..... **50** B3
  HRBN B17 .... **121** D4
Westbury St WOLV WV1 .... **3** E3
Westcliff Pl NFLD/LBR B31 .... **186** B1
Westcombe Gv RIDG/WDGT B32 . **164** C2 ⬚
Westcote Av NFLD/LBR B31 .... **185** E3
Westcote Cl HIA/OLT B92 .... **174** C1
Westcott Cl STRBR DY8 .... **112** B4 ⬚
Westcott Rd
  LGN/SDN/BHAMAIR B26 .... **152** C1
Westcroft Av WOLVN WV10 .... **12** A1
Westcroft Gv NFLD/LBR B31 ...... **187** E2
Westcroft Rd CDSL WV8 .... **22** B1
  SEDG DY3 .... **67** D1
Westcroft Wy
  ALE/KHTH/YWD B14 .... **191** D4
Westdean Cl RMSLY B62 .... **141** E5
West Dr BFLD/HDSWWD B20 .... **99** D5
  DIG/EDG B5 .... **147** E5
West End Av SMTHWK B66 .... **95** E6
Westerdale Cl SEDG DY3 .... **68** C4
Westerham Cl DOR/KN B93 .... **212** B1 ⬚
Westeria Cl CBROM B36 .... **105** E5
Westering Pkwy WOLVN WV10 ..... **12** A1
Westerings BFLD/HDSWWD B20 .. **99** E3 ⬚
Western Av BRLYHL DY5 .... **113** D5
  RMSLY B62 .... **142** A5
  SEDG DY3 .... **67** D3
  WSLW WS2 .... **29** F4
Western Cl WSLW WS2 .... **29** F4 ⬚
Western Rd CDYHTH B64 .... **139** F1
  ERDE/BCHGN B24 .... **102** C2
  OLDBY B69 .... **119** D2
  SCFLD/BOLD B73 .... **80** C2

Western Wy DARL/WED WS10 ...... **49** E6
Westfield Av ALE/KHTH/YWD B14 . **191** D3
Westfield Cl DOR/KN B93 .... **212** A5
Westfield Dr WMBN WV5 .... **64** B4
Westfield Gv BDMR/CCFT WV3 ..... **43** E1
Westfield Mnr MGN/WHC B75 ..... **38** C3 ⬚
Westfield Rd ACGN B27 .... **151** D6
  ALE/KHTH/YWD B14 .... **169** F5
  BILS/COS WV14 .... **47** D2
  BRLYHL DY5 .... **138** B1
  DUDS DY2 .... **91** F6
  EDG B15 .... **145** F1
  RMSLY B62 .... **118** A6
  SEDG DY3 .... **67** F2
  SMTHWK B67 .... **120** B2
  WLNHL WV13 .... **48** B1
Westford Gv HLGN/YWD B28 ...... **192** A2 ⬚
Westgate ALDR WS9 .... **20** A6
West Ga LDYWD/EDGR B16 .... **122** A4
Westgate Cl SEDG DY3 .... **68** A4 ⬚
West Gn ETTPG/GDPK/PENN WV4 . **43** E4
Westgrove Av SHLY B90 .... **210** B1
Westhaven Dr NFLD/LBR B31 ..... **166** A4
Westhaven Rd
  CSCFLD/WYGN B72 .... **59** E4 ⬚
Westhay Rd HLGN/YWD B28 .... **173** D1
West Heath Rd NFLD/LBR B31 .... **187** D4
  WSNGN B18 .... **121** F3 ⬚
Westhill BDMR/CCFT WV3 .... **23** E5
Westhill Rd HWK/WKHTH B38 .... **188** B2
West Holme BORD B9 .... **125** D5 ⬚
Westholme Cft BVILLE B30 .... **168** A4
Westhouse Gv
  ALE/KHTH/YWD B14 .... **189** F1
Westland Av BDMR/CCFT WV3 ..... **24** C5
Westland Cl ERDW/GRVHL B23 ... **80** B6
Westland Gdns BDMR/CCFT WV3 . **24** B5
  STRBR DY8 .... **136** B2
Westland Rd BDMR/CCFT WV3 .... **24** B5
Westlands Rd MOS/BIL B13 .... **170** C2
  WALM/CURD B76 .... **82** B5
Westleigh Rd WMBN WV5 .... **64** B6
Westley Cl HLGN/YWD B28 .... **173** D5
Westley Rd ACGN B27 .... **151** D6
Westley St BORD B9 .... **124** C5
  DUDN DY1 .... **91** D5
Westmead Crs
  ERDE/BCHGN B24 .... **103** E1 ⬚
West Mead Dr
  ALE/KHTH/YWD B14 .... **170** A5
Westmead Dr LGLYGN/QTN B68 . **119** D3
West Ms KGSTG B44 .... **77** F1
West Mill Cft HWK/WKHTH B38 .. **188** A6
Westminster Av
  ETTPG/GDPK/PENN WV4 .... **45** D4
Westminster Cl DUDN DY1 .... **90** C3
Westminster Dr
  ALE/KHTH/YWD B14 .... **169** F5
Westminster Rd
  BFLD/HDSWWD B20 .... **99** E3
  HHTH/SAND B71 .... **73** F2
  RUSH/SHEL WS4 .... **19** D6
  SLYOAK B29 .... **167** D5
  STRBR DY8 .... **111** E5
Westmore Wy DARL/WED WS10 ... **51** F4
Westmorland Rd HHTH/SAND B71 . **73** E5
Weston Av OLDBY B69 .... **93** D4
  SPARK B11 .... **149** E5 ⬚
Weston Cl DOR/KN B93 .... **212** C5
  WSL WS1 .... **52** A3
Weston Crs ALDR WS9 .... **35** D3
Weston Dr BILS/COS WV14 .... **47** E5
  DARL/WED WS10 .... **71** D1
Weston La SPARK B11 .... **150** A5
Weston Rd LOZ/NWT B19 .... **99** D6
  SMTHWK B67 .... **120** B5
Weston St WSL WS1 .... **52** A3
Westover Rd BFLD/HDSWWD B20 . **98** A1
West Park Av NFLD/LBR B31 ...... **186** A3
West Park Rd SMTHWK B67 .... **95** F6
West Pathway HRBN B17 .... **145** E3 ⬚
Westport Crs WNSFLD WV11 .... **28** B2
Westray Cl RBRY B45 .... **184** A4 ⬚
Westridge SEDG DY3 .... **67** E3
Westridge Rd MOS/BIL B13 .... **171** E5
West Ri MGN/WHC B75 .... **59** E3
West Rd GTB/HAM B43 .... **76** A4
  HALE B63 .... **139** D3
  TPTN/OCK DY4 .... **71** D3
West Rd South HALE B63 .... **139** D3
Westside RIDG/WDGT B32 .... **165** F2 ⬚
West St BLKHTH/ROWR B65 .... **117** E6 ⬚
  BLOX/PEL WS3 .... **17** E6
  BRLYHL DY5 .... **138** B1
  DUDN DY1 .... **91** D3
  DUNHL/THL/PER WV6 .... **25** E2
  STRBR DY8 .... **136** B4
  VAUX/NECH B7 .... **7** H2 ⬚
West Vw WASH/WDE B8 .... **127** E3
West View Dr KGSWFD DY6 .... **112** A2
West View Rd MGN/WHC B75 .... **60** A3

Westville Rd WSLW WS2 .... **30** C4
Westward Cl KGSTG B44 .... **78** B3
West Wy RUSH/SHEL WS4 .... **19** D3
Westwood Av STRBR DY8 .... **135** E6
Westwood Rd AST/WIT B6 .... **100** C3
  SCFLD/BOLD B73 .... **56** C5
Westwood St BRLYHL DY5 .... **112** C6
Westwood Vw ERDE/BCHGN B24 . **103** E2 ⬚
Wetherby Cl WOLVN WV10 .... **11** F1
Wetherby Rd ACGN B27 .... **173** D1 ⬚
  BLOX/PEL WS3 .... **16** C1
Wetherfield Rd SPARK B11 .... **150** C6
Wexford Cl DUDN DY1 .... **90** B5
Weybourne Rd KGSTG B44 .... **78** A1
Weycroft Rd ERDW/GRVHL B23 ... **79** D4
Weyhill Cl COVEN WV9 .... **10** A3
Weymoor Rd HRBN B17 .... **144** C6
Weymouth Dr FOAKS/STRLY B74 .. **38** B3
Wharf Ap ALDR WS9 .... **20** B6
Wharfdale Rd SPARK B11 .... **151** D4 ⬚
  YDLY B25 .... **151** D4
Wharfedale Cl KGSWFD DY6 .... **87** D6
Wharfedale St DARL/WED WS10 .. **72** M1
Wharf La SOLH B91 .... **175** F5
  WSNGN B18 .... **122** C2
Wharf Rd BVILLE B30 .... **188** C3
  YDLY B25 .... **151** D4
Wharfside OLDBY B69 .... **94** B6 ⬚
  WOLV WV1 .... **3** G5
  WSLW WS3 .... **31** E6
  WSNGN B18 .... **122** C1
Whar Hall Rd HIA/OLT B92 .... **176** A3
Wharton Rd HIA/OLT B92 .... **176** A4
Wharton St VAUX/NECH B7 .... **101** F5
Whatcote Gn HIA/OLT B92 .... **175** F3
Whateley Av BLOX/PEL WS3 .... **32** B1
Whateley Crs CBROM B36 .... **105** F5
Whateley Gn FOAKS/STRLY B74 .. **58** C1
Whateley Hall Cl DOR/KN B93 .. **197** D6
Whateley Hall Rd DOR/KN B93 . **197** D6
Whateley Pl BLOX/PEL WS3 .... **32** B1
Whateley Rd BLOX/PEL WS3 .... **32** B1
  HDSW B21 .... **98** A5
Wheatcroft Cl RMSLY B62 .... **142** B1
Wheatcroft Dr
  CHWD/FDBR/MGN B37 .... **131** E6 ⬚
  CHWD/FDBR/MGN B37 .... **131** F6 ⬚
Wheatcroft Gv DUDS DY2 .... **92** B4
Wheatcroft Rd STETCH B33 ...... **128** B5
Wheaten Cl
  CHWD/FDBR/MGN B37 .... **131** F4 ⬚
Wheatfield Cl CBROM B36 .... **106** C6 ⬚
Wheatfield Vw NFLD/LBR B31 .... **165** F6 ⬚
Wheat Hl DSYBK/YTR WS5 .... **54** A1
Wheathill Cl
  ETTPG/GDPK/PENN WV4 .... **44** A6 ⬚
Wheatlands Cft STETCH B33 ..... **130** A4 ⬚
Wheatley Cl HIA/OLT B92 .... **176** A3 ⬚
  LGLYGN/QTN B68 .... **143** E1
  MGN/WHC B75 .... **39** E4 ⬚
Wheatley Rd LGLYGN/QTN B68 . **143** E1
Wheatley St BKHL/PFLD WV2 ...... **46** A3
  WBROM B70 .... **94** C1
Wheatmoor Ri MGN/WHC B75 .... **60** A3
Wheaton Cl WOLVN WV10 .... **11** E6
Wheaton V BFLD/HDSWWD B20 .. **98** A2
Wheatridge Cl KGSWFD DY6 .... **86** C5 ⬚
Wheats Av HRBN B17 .... **145** D6
Wheatsheaf Rd CDSL WV8 .... **10** A4
  LDYWD/EDGR B16 .... **121** F5
  OLDBY B69 .... **92** C5
Wheatstone Cl SEDG DY3 .... **68** A5 ⬚
Wheatstone Gv STETCH B33 ...... **128** B2 ⬚
Wheel Av CDSL WV8 .... **8** B2
Wheeler Cl CDSL WV8 .... **8** A1
Wheeler Rd WNSFLD WV11 .... **13** C5
Wheeler's Fold WOLV WV1 .... **3** E4
Wheelers La MOS/BIL B13 .... **170** A5
  MOS/BIL B13 .... **170** A4
Wheeler St LOZ/NWT B19 .... **99** F6
  STRBR DY8 .... **136** B4
Wheeley Moor Rd
  CHWD/FDBR/MGN B37 .... **130** C2
Wheeley Rd ALVE B48 .... **215** F4 ⬚
  HIA/OLT B92 .... **175** F4
Wheeleys La EDG B15 .... **147** E1
Wheeleys Rd EDG B15 .... **147** D2
Wheelock Cl FOAKS/STRLY B74 ... **56** B2
Wheelwright Rd
  ERDE/BCHGN B24 .... **102** A3
Wheldrake Av BKDE/SHDE B34 .. **129** E2
Whernside Dr
  DUNHL/THL/PER WV6 .... **24** C2
Wherretts Well La SOLH B91 .... **176** A6
Whetstone Gv WOLVN WV10 .... **11** F5
Whetstone La ALDR WS9 .... **35** D2
Whetstone Rd WOLVN WV10 .... **11** F5
Whettybridge Rd RBRY B45 ...... **200** A1
Whetty La RBRY B45 .... **184** A6
Whichford Cl WALM/CURD B76 ... **81** F5 ⬚
Whichford Gv BORD B9 .... **127** D5 ⬚
While Rd CSCFLD/WYGN B72 .... **59** D5
Whinberry Ri BRLYHL DY5 .... **89** E4 ⬚

Whiston Av WNSFLD WV11 .... 14 C6
Whiston Gv SLYOAK B29 .... 167 D3 ⑤
Whitacre Rd BORD B9 .... 126 A4
   DOR/KN B93 .... 197 D6
Whitbourne Cl BHTH/HG B12 .. 149 D4 ⑩
Whitburn Av PBAR/PBCH B42........ 76 C6
Whitburn Cl COVEN WV9 .... 10 C3
Whitby Cl BLOX/PEL WS3 .... 16 B2
Whitby Rd BHTH/HG B12 .... 148 C5
Whitcot Gv NFLD/LBR B31 .... 186 B5 ⑤
Whitebeam Cft
   HWK/WKHTH B38 .... 188 A5 ⑥
White Beam Rd
   CHWD/FDBR/MGN B37 .... 131 F6
Whitebeams Cl SEDG DY3 .... 89 E1 ⑤
White City Rd BRLYHL DY5 .... 114 C6
White Cl HAG/WOL DY9 .... 159 E1 ⑥
Whitecrest CBHAMNE B43 .... 76 C1
Whitecroft Rd
   LGN/SDN/BHAMAIR B26 .... 153 F4
White Falcon Ct SOLH B91 ...... 194 B5 ⑤
White Farm Rd FOAKS/STRLY B74... 38 A3
White Field Av HRBN B17 .... 144 C3 ⑤
Whitefield Cl CDSL WV8 .... 9 D3
Whitefields Crs SOLH B91 .... 195 D3
Whitefields Ga SOLH B91 .... 194 C4
Whitefields Rd SOLH B91 .... 194 C4
Whitefriars Dr HALE B63 .... 140 C5 ⑥
Whitegates Rd BILS/COS WV14.... 69 F1
Whitehall Dr DUDN DY1 .... 90 C3
   HALE B63 .... 141 D5
Whitehall Rd BORD B9 .... 126 A6
   CDYHTH B64 .... 115 E6 ⑥
   ETTPK/GDPK/PENN WV4 .... 45 D5
   HALE B63 .... 98 C6
   HDSW B21 .... 111 E1
   KGSWFD DY6 .... 111 E1
   STRBR DY8 .... 159 D1
   TPTN/OCK DY4 .... 71 F6
   WBROM B70 .... 94 A1
   WSL WS1 .... 52 A2 ②
Whitehead Dr WALM/CURD B76 ... 83 F5 ⑥
Whitehead Rd AST/WIT B6 .... 100 A6
Whitehill La SLYOAK B29 .... 166 B6
Whitehouse Av BDMR/CCFT WV3.. 43 E1
   DARL/WED WS10 .... 49 D2 ②
   DARL/WED WS10 .... 50 B6
White House Av WNSFLD WV11 .... 14 B6
White House Cl RBRY B45 .... 200 C6
   SOLH B91 .... 194 B2
Whitehouse Common Rd
   MGN/WHC B75 .... 60 A2
Whitehouse Crs MGN/WHC B75 .... 60 A1
   WNSFLD WV11 .... 14 B4
White House Gn SOLH B91 .... 194 B2
Whitehouse Pl RBRY B45 .... 200 B1 ⑤
Whitehouse St AST/WIT B6 .... 124 B1
   BILS/COS WV14 .... 69 E3 ⑥
   TPTN/OCK DY4 .... 92 C3
   WSLW WS2 .... 31 F4 ②
Whitehouse Wy ALDR WS9 .... 34 B3
White House Wy SOLH B91 .... 194 C3
Whitemoor Dr SOLH B91 .... 194 C6
White Oak Dr BDMR/CCFT WV3 .... 23 E6
   KGSWFD DY6 .... 111 E1
Whitepits La ALVE B48 .... 220 B5
White Rd RIDG/WDGT B32 .... 143 F3
   SMTHWK B67 .... 120 B1
   SPARK B11 .... 149 E2
White's Dr SEDG DY3 .... 68 A3
Whiteslade Cl DOR/KN B93 ...... 196 C6 ⑥
Whitesmith Cl SEDG DY3 .... 67 F4 ⑨
White's Rd HHTH/SAND B71 .... 73 E5
Whitestone Rd HALE B63 .... 140 C3
White St BHTH/HG B12 .... 148 C4 ⑥
   WSL WS1 .... 5 H4
Whites Wd WMBN WV5 .... 64 C6
Whitethorn Crs FOAKS/STRLY B74 .. 35 F6
Whitethorn Rd STRBR DY8 .... 112 C6
Whitewood Gld SHHTH WV12 ...... 30 A3 ⑥
Whitfield Gv EDG B15 .... 147 F1 ⑥
Whitford Dr SHLY B90 .... 195 D6
Whitgreave Av WOLVN WV10 .... 12 A5
Whitgreave St WBROM B70 .... 94 A2
Whitland Cl RBRY B45 .... 201 D1
Whitland Dr ALE/KHTH/YWD B14.. 190 B2
Whitley Cl DUNHL/THL/PER WV6 .. 23 D5
Whitley Court Rd RIDG/WDGT B32.. 143 E3
Whitley Dr FOAKS/STRLY B74 ...... 56 C1
Whitley St DARL/WED WS10 .... 50 A6
Whitlock Gv ALE/KHTH/YWD B14.. 190 C1
Whitminster Av ERDE/BCHGN B24.. 103 D2
Whitminster Cl SHHTH WV12 ...... 29 E5 ⑥
Whitmore HI WOLV WV1 .... 2 C3
Whitmore Rd SMHTH B10 .... 148 E1
   STRBR DY8 .... 3 E3 ②
Whitmore St WOLV WV1 .... 51 F2
   WSL WS1 .... 51 F2
   WSNGN B18 .... 123 D2
Whitney Av STRBR DY8 .... 135 F3 ⑧
Whittaker St WSL WS5 5
Whittall St CBHAMNE B4 .... 7 E3
Whittimere St WSL WS1 5
Whittingham Gv WNSFLD WV11.... 28 B1
Whittingham Rd HALE B63 .... 140 C4

Whittington Cl
   ALE/KHTH/YWD B14 .... 170 A6
   HHTH/SAND B71 .... 74 B3 ⑥
Whittington Gv STETCH B33 .... 128 B5
Whittington Ov STETCH B33 .... 128 C5
Whittle Cft CVALE B35 .... 104 B2 ⑥
Whittleford Gv CBROM B36 .... 105 E4
Whitton St DARL/WED WS10 .... 50 A5
Whitwell Dr SHLY B90 .... 210 C1 ⑥
Whitworth Cl DARL/WED WS10 .... 50 A2
Whitworth Dr HHTH/SAND B71 .... 74 A2
Whyley St OLDBY B69 .... 118 C2 ③
   WBROM B70 .... 94 C1
Whyley Wk OLDBY B69 .... 118 C2 ⑥
Whynot St HALE B63 .... 139 D4 ⑨
Wibert Cl SLYOAK B29 .... 168 C2
Wichnor Rd HIA/OLT B92 .... 152 B4
Wickham Gdns WNSFLD WV11 .... 26 C1
Wicklow Cl HALE B63 .... 161 F2
Wideacre Dr KGSTG B44 .... 78 A4
Wide Acres RBRY B45 .... 184 B4
Widney Av ALDR WS9 .... 21 D4
   SLYOAK B29 .... 167 E1
Widney Cl DOR/KN B93 .... 212 B2 ⑥
Widney La SOLH B91 .... 194 A4
   SOLH B91 .... 195 D5
Widney Manor Rd SOLH B91 ...... 195 E3
Widney Rd DOR/KN B93 .... 212 A2
Wiggins Cft WALM/CURD B76 ...... 60 B6
Wiggins Hill Rd WALM/CURD B76 .. 84 B5
Wigginstall Rd DARL/WED WS10 .. 71 F2
Wiggin St LDYWD/EDGR B16...... 122 B4
Wight Cft CBROM B36 .... 131 D1
Wightwick Bank
   DUNHL/THL/PER WV6 .... 22 B5
Wightwick Cl BLOX/PEL WS3 .... 17 D4 ⑥
Wightwick Gv
   DUNHL/THL/PER WV6 .... 22 C5
Wightwick Hall Rd
   DUNHL/THL/PER WV6 .... 22 A6
Wigmore Cv KGSTG B44 .... 79 D3 ⑧
Wigmore La HHTH/SAND B71 .... 74 C3
Wigorn La HAG/WOL DY9 .... 159 D3
Wigorn Rd SMTHWKW B67 .... 120 B6
Wilberforce Wy HIA/OLT B92 .... 176 A4
Wilbraham Rd WSLW WS2 .... 31 E6
Wilcote Gv ACGN B27 .... 173 E3 ⑥
Wildacres STRBR DY8 .... 135 E3
Wilde Cl ALE/KHTH/YWD B14...... 189 F2
Wilden Cl NFLD/LBR B31 .... 185 E6
Wilderness La GTB/HAM B43 ...... 53 F6
Wildfell Rd ACGN B27 .... 173 F1
Wildmoor La BRGRVW B61 .... 198 C6
Wildmoor Rd SHLY B90 .... 173 D6
Wildtree Av WOLVN WV10 .... 12 C3
Wiley Av DARL/WED WS10 .... 49 E3
Wiley Av South DARL/WED WS10 .. 49 E4
Wilford Gv SOLH B91 .... 195 D3
   WALM/CURD B76 .... 83 D5
Wilford Rd HHTH/SAND B71 ...... 73 F5
Wilkes Av WSLW WS2 .... 30 A5
Wilkes Cl BLOX/PEL WS3 .... 18 A2
Wilkes Cft SEDG DY3 .... 67 F4 ⑧
Wilkes Rd CDSL WV8 .... 8 B2
Wilkes St HHTH/SAND B71 .... 74 B4
   WLNHL WV13 .... 28 C6
Wilkinson Av BILS/COS WV14 .... 48 A6
Wilkinson Cl SCFLD/BOLD B73.... 81 D1
Wilkinson Cft CBROM B36 .... 122 B1
Wilkinson Rd DARL/WED WS10 .... 48 C4
Wilkins Rd BILS/COS WV14........ 47 F2
Willard Rd YDLY B25 .... 151 E3 ⑥
Willaston Rd STETCH B33 .... 153 F2
Willclare Rd
   LGN/SDN/BHAMAIR B26 .... 152 C3
Willcock Rd BKHL/PFLD WV2 ...... 46 A2
Willenhall La WSLW WS2 .... 16 B6
Willenhall Rd BILS/COS WV14 .... 48 B3
   DARL/WED WS10 .... 49 F1
   WLNHL WV13 .... 27 F6
   WOLV WV1 .... 26 C6
Willenhall St DARL/WED WS10 .... 49 E2 ②
Willerby Fold WOLVN WV10 .... 12 B1 ⑥
Willersey Rd MOS/BIL B13 .... 171 F3
Willes Rd WSNGN B18 .... 122 A1
Willett Rd HHTH/SAND B71 .... 74 A3
Willetts Dr HALE B63 .... 139 D5
Willetts Rd NFLD/LBR B31 .... 186 C4
Willetts Wy CDYHTH B64 .... 116 B5 ⑥
Willey Gv ERDE/BCHGN B24 ...... 103 D3
William Booth La CBHAMNE B4 .... 6 D2 ⑩
William Cook Rd WASH/WDE B8 .. 127 D2 ⑥
William Green Rd
   DARL/WED WS10 .... 51 E6 ⑨
William Harper Rd WLNHL WV13 .. 29 D6
William Henry St
   VAUX/NECH B7 .... 124 C1 ⑨
William Ker Rd TPTN/OCK DY4 .... 71 E6
William Rd SMTHWKW B67 .... 119 F4
Williams Cl SHHTH WV12 .... 29 E2
William St BRLYHL DY5 .... 113 E4
   EDG B15 .... 123 E6
   RUSH/SHEL WS4 .... 32 B4
   WBROM B70 .... 72 B4

William St North LOZ/NWT B19...... 6 D1
William St West SMTHWK B66...... 97 D6
William Wiggin Av BLOX/PEL WS3 .. 17 D3
Willingsworth Rd DARL/WED WS10 .. 71 E2
Willingworth Cl
   ETTPK/GDPK/PENN WV4 .... 46 C6
Willis Pearson Av BILS/COS WV14 .... 70 B1
Willmore Gv HWK/WKHTH B38 .... 188 B5
Willmore Rd BFLD/HDSWWD B20.. 99 F3
Willmott Cl MGN/WHC B75 .... 39 F4
Willmott Rd MGN/WHC B75 .... 39 F4
Willoughby Dr SOLH B91 .... 195 D4
Willoughby Gv SLYOAK B29 ...... 166 C2 ②
Willow Av DARL/WED WS10........ 50 B5
   HRBN B17 .... 120 C5
   WNSFLD WV11 .... 13 D5
Willow Bank BDMR/CCFT WV3 .... 23 E6
Willow Bank Rd DOR/KN B93 .... 212 B1
Willow Brook Rd ALVE B48 .... 216 C2
Willow Cl CDYHTH B64 .... 116 A6 ⑥
   HAG/WOL DY9 .... 158 B6
Willow Coppice
   RIDG/WDGT B32 .... 165 E2 ⑤
Willow Ct SMTHWK B66 .... 95 F5
Willowdale Gra DUNHL/THL/PER WV6 .. 24 A2 ⑥
Willow Dr CDSL WV8 .... 9 D2 ⑩
   HDSW B21 .... 97 E4
   OLDBY B69 .... 93 E6
   SHLY B90 .... 209 F3
Willow End HAG/WOL DY9 .... 137 F6
Willow Gdns LDYWD/EDGR B16 .. 122 B3 ⑤
Willow Gv WNSFLD WV11 .... 15 D2
Willow Hts CDYHTH B64 .... 140 C1 ②
Willowherb Cl DSYBK/YTR WS5 .. 52 C5 ⑫
Willowherb Wy SHLY B90 .... 208 C2 ⑥
Willow Ms SLYOAK B29 .... 167 D2 ⑤
Willow Park Dr STRBR DY8 .... 158 C1
Willow Ri BRLYHL DY5 .... 113 E6
Willow Rd BDMR/CCFT WV3 ...... 43 F1
   BVILLE B30 .... 168 B3
   DUDN DY1 .... 90 C1
   GTB/HAM B43 .... 88 B1
   SOLH B91 .... 194 A5
Willowsbrook Rd RMSLY B62 ...... 142 B1
Willows Crs BHTH/HG B12 .... 147 F4
Willowside PUSH/SHEL WS4 ...... 19 E5
Willows Rd BHTH/HG B12 .... 148 A4
   RUSH/SHEL WS4 .... 19 E5
   WSL WS1 .... 5 H4
The Willows ACGN B27 .... 173 D1
   HLYWD B47 .... 206 C1
   WALM/CURD B76 .... 82 B1 ⑥
   WMBN WV5 .... 64 B6 ⑥
Willow Tree Dr RBRY B45 .... 215 F1 ⑥
Willow Wy CHWD/FDBR/MGN B37 .. 131 D5
Wills Av HHTH/SAND B71 .... 73 D4
Willsbridge Covert BVILLE B30 .. 189 E3 ⑩
Wilson Cft ALE/KHTH/YWD B14 .... 191 F2
Wills St LOZ/NWT B19 .... 99 E3
Wilmcote Cl BHTH/HG B12 .... 148 A3 ⑥
Wilmcote Dr MGN/WHC B75 .... 39 D4
Wilmcote Rd SOLH B91 .... 174 B5 ⑤
Wilmington Rd RIDG/WDGT B32.... 143 D3
Wilmore La HLYWD B47 .... 206 A3
Wilmot Av ERDW/GRVHL B23 .... 132 B1 ⑥
Wilmot Dr ERDW/GRVHL B23 .... 80 C5
   TPTN/OCK DY4 .... 70 A5 ②
Wilmot Gdns DUDN DY1 .... 90 C3 ⑧
Wilnecote Gv PBAR/PBCH B42 .... 99 E1
Wilsford Cl ALE/KHTH/YWD B14 .. 189 F4
   RUSH/SHEL WS4 .... 19 E5
Wilson Dr MGN/WHC B75 .... 60 C4 ⑥
   MGN/WHC B75 .... 61 D4 ⑤
Wilson Rd BILS/COS WV14 .... 69 E4
   BRLYHL DY5 .... 113 E3
   LGLYGN/QTN B68 .... 143 F1
   LOZ/NWT B19 .... 99 F5
   SMTHWK B66 .... 121 D4
Wilsons Rd DOR/KN B93 .... 213 E1
Wilson St TPTN/OCK DY4 .... 70 C5
Wilton Cl SEDG DY3 .... 68 A4
Wilton Rd ACGN B27 .... 173 D1 ⑤
   BFLD/HDSWWD B20 .... 99 D4
   ERDW/GRVHL B23 .... 80 B6
   SPARK B11 .... 149 D4
Wilton St LOZ/NWT B19 .... 99 F5
Wiltshire Cl WSLW WS2 .... 31 F3 ⑥
Wiltshire Dr HALE B63 .... 139 D2
Wiltshire Wy HHTH/SAND B71 .... 73 E4
Wimbledon Dr STRBR DY8 .... 159 D1
Wimborne Rd WOLVN WV10 ...... 26 C1
Wimbourne Rd LDYWD/EDGR B16.. 121 F4
   WALM/CURD B76 .... 60 C5
Wimperis Wy GTB/HAM B43 ...... 55 E5
Wimpole Gv KGSTG B44 .... 79 D4 ⑥
Wimshurst Meadow
   WOLVN WV10 .... 12 B1 ⑦
Wincanton Cft CBROM B36 .... 103 D5
Winceby Rd DUNHL/THL/PER WV6 .. 22 B4
Winchcombe Cl DUDN DY1 .... 90 A2 ②
   HIA/OLT B92 .... 175 D1 ⑧
Winchcombe Rd HIA/OLT B92...... 175 D1
Winchester Cl
   BLKHTH/ROWR B65 .... 118 A3 ⑥
   HAG/WOL DY9 .... 158 C4

Winchester Dr
CHWD/FDBR/MGN B37 .... **130** C5
STRBR DY8 .... **136** C6 🔟
Winchester Gdns NFLD/LBR B31 .. **186** C2
Winchester Ri DUDN DY1 .... **90** C3
Winchester Rd
BFLD/HDSWWD B20 .... **99** F4 🔟
HHTH/SAND B71 .... **73** D3
WOLVN WV10 .... **11** E3
Winchfield Dr HRBN B17 .... **144** B3
Wincote Dr DUNHL/THL/PER WV6 ... **23** E3
Wincrest Wy BKDE/SHDE B34 .... **129** E2
Windermere Dr FOAKS/STRLY B74 ... **36** B4
KGSWFD DY6 .... **111** F1
Windermere Rd
DUNHL/THL/PER WV6 .... **9** E3
HDSW B21 .... **98** A3
MOS/BIL B13 .... **171** D2
Winding Ml North BRLYHL DY5 .... **138** A2 🔟
Winding Ml South BRLYHL DY5 .... **138** A2 🔟
Windlass Cft NFLD/LBR B31 .... **186** B1 🔟
Windleaves Rd CBROM B36 .... **106** A6
Windmill Av CSHL/WTROR B46 ..... **108** B6 🔟
RBRY B45 .... **184** A5
Windmill Bank WMBN WV5 .... **64** C4 🔟
Windmill Cl NFLD/LBR B31 .... **167** E6 🔟
Windmill Crs BDMR/CCFT WV3 .... **22** C6
SMTHWK B66 .... **121** E2
Windmill End DUDS DY2 .... **116** A2
Windmill Gv KGSWFD DY6 .... **86** C5
Windmill Hl HALE B63 .... **139** F4 🔟
NFLD/LBR B31 .... **167** D6
Windmill La BDMR/CCFT WV3 .... **22** C6
DOR/KN B93 .... **212** B6
SMTHWK B66 .... **121** D3
Windmill Prec SMTHWK B66 .... **121** E2 🔟
Windmill Rd SHLY B90 .... **192** A3
Windmill St CBHAMW B1 .... **123** F6 🔟
DARL/WED WS10 .... **50** B6
DUDN DY1 .... **90** C3 🔟
SEDG DY3 .... **67** F6
WSL WS1 .... **4** D6
Windmill Vw DUDN DY1 .... **69** D4
Windridge Crs HIA/OLT B92 .... **176** B5 🔟
Windrush Gv SLYOAK B29 .... **168** C3
Windrush Rd HLYWD B47 .... **191** D6

Windsor Av
ETTPK/GDPK/PENN WV4 .... **44** A3
LGLYGN/QTN B68 .... **118** C4
Windsor Ct SEDG DY3 .... **89** D4
Windsor Crs DUDS DY2 .... **115** F1
Windsor Dr ERDE/BCHGN B24 .... **81** E6
HIA/OLT B92 .... **175** D1
Windsor Gdns BDMR/CCFT WV3 ..... **42** C2
CDSL WV8 .... **8** B2
Windsor Ga SHHTH WV12 .... **29** E3 🔟
Windsor Gv RUSH/SHEL WS4 .... **19** E3
STRBR DY8 .... **112** A6
Windsor Pl ERDW/GRVHL B23 .... **102** A2 🔟
Windsor Rd BLKHTH/ROWR B65 .... **117** E2
BVILLE B30 .... **168** D6
CBROM B36 .... **169** D6
ETTPK/GDPK/PENN WV4 .... **46** A3
HALE B63 .... **140** B5
HHTH/SAND B71 .... **73** D3
LGLYGN/QTN B68 .... **118** C4
SCFLD/BOLD B73 .... **79** F2
STRBR DY8 .... **135** F6
TPTN/OCK DY4 .... **70** C3
WMBN WV5 .... **64** B5
Windsor St BILS/COS WV14 .... **47** E3
VAUX/NECH B7 .... **124** C3 🔟
WSL WS1 .... **52** A2
Windsor St South VAUX/NECH B7 .. **124** C4
Windsor Vw RIDG/WDGT B32 .... **165** D4 🔟
Windsor Wk DARL/WED WS10 ...... **49** F1 🔟
Windsor Wy RUSH/SHEL WS4 .... **19** F6
Windward Wy CBROM B36 .... **106** B6 🔟
Windyridge Rd WALM/CURD B76 ... **82** B5
Winford Av KGSWFD DY6 .... **112** A3
Wingate Cl BVILLE B30 .... **188** B1 🔟
Wingate Rd WSLW WS2 .... **30** A5
Wing Cl WSLW WS2 .... **30** B3
Wingfield Cl
CHWD/FDBR/MGN B37 .... **130** B4
Wingfield Rd CSHL/WTROR B46 ..... **132** B2
PBAR/PBCH B42 .... **77** E4
Wingfoot Av WOLVN WV10 .... **11** F5
Winkle St WBROM B70 .... **95** D1
Winleigh Rd BFLD/HDSWWD B20 ... **98** B3 🔟
Winnall Cl BILS/COS WV14 .... **69** F1
Winnie Rd SLYOAK B29 .... **168** A3
Winnington Rd WASH/WDE B8 ...... **102** C6
Winnipeg Rd HWK/WKHTH B38 .... **188** C5
Winsford Cl HALE B63 .... **140** C5
WALM/CURD B76 .... **60** A6
Winslade Gv HDSW B21 .... **97** F5
Winslow Dr DUNHL/THL/PER WV6 .. **24** A3
Winson Green Rd WSNGN B18 ...... **122** A4
Winson St WSNGN B18 .... **121** F3

Winstanley Rd STETCH B33 .... **127** F5
Winster Av DOR/KN B93 .... **212** A3
Winster Gr KGSTG B44 .... **77** F1
Winster Rd GTB/HAM B43 .... **75** F5
WOLV WV1 .... **27** D6 🔟
Winston Dr BFLD/HDSWWD B20 ..... **99** D4
RMSLY B62 .... **182** C1
Winston Rd SEDG DY3 .... **86** A3
Winterbourne Cft
ALE/KHTH/YWD B14 .... **189** E3 🔟 🔟
Winterbourne Rd SOLH B91 .... **194** B1
Winterley Gdns SEDG DY3 .... **68** A3 🔟
Winterley La RUSH/SHEL WS4 .... **19** E6
Winterton Rd KGSTG B44 .... **56** C6
Winthorpe Dr SOLH B91 .... **195** E5
Wintney Cl HRBN B17 .... **144** C2
Winton Gv WALM/CURD B76 .... **82** C5
Winwood Heath Rd RMSLY B62 .... **182** A3
Winwood Rd BLKHTH/ROWR B65 .. **118** A4
Winwoods Gv RIDG/WDGT B32 .... **164** C3 🔟
Wiremill Cl KGSTG B44 .... **78** A5 🔟
Wirral Rd NFLD/LBR B31 .... **166** B5
Wiseacre Cft SHLY B90 .... **192** A3
Wiseman Gv ERDW/GRVHL B23 ...... **79** F2
Wisemore WSL WS1 .... **4** C2
WSLW WS2 .... **4** C2
Wishaw Cl SHLY B90 .... **192** A3
Wishaw Gv
CHWD/FDBR/MGN B37 .... **130** B3
Wishaw La POL/KGSB/FAZ B78 ...... **63** D4
WALM/CURD B76 .... **84** A4
Wisley Wy RIDG/WDGT B32 .... **144** B4 🔟
Wistaria Cl NFLD/LBR B31 .... **166** C5
Wisteria Gv KGSTG B44 .... **78** A1 🔟
Wistmans Cft DUDN DY1 .... **89** F4
Wistwood Hayes WOLVN WV10 .... **12** B1
Witham Cft SOLH B91 .... **195** E4
Withdean Cl SPARK B11 .... **149** F4
Witherford Cft SLYOAK B29 .... **167** E3
Witherford Cft SHLY B90 .... **193** F3
Witherford Wy SLYOAK B29 .... **167** E2
Withern Wy SEDG DY3 .... **89** F2 🔟
Withers Rd CDSL WV8 .... **9** D2
Withers Wy HHTH/SAND B71 .... **95** F1
Withington Covert BVILLE B30 ..... **189** F3 🔟
Withington Gv DOR/KN B93 .... **212** A3 🔟
Withybed Cl ALVE B48 .... **216** B3
Withybed La ALVE B48 .... **216** B3
Withybrook Rd SHLY B90 .... **193** D5
Withy Gv CHWD/FDBR/MGN B37 ... **130** A2
Withy Hill Rd MGN/WHC B75 .... **60** B2
Withymere La WMBN WV5 .... **65** E3
Withymoor Rd DUDS DY2 .... **116** A3
STRBR DY8 .... **136** C2
Withy Rd BILS/COS WV14 .... **47** E6
Withywood Cl SHHTH WV12 .... **15** D4
Witley Av HALE B63 .... **140** A5
SOLH B91 .... **195** E5
Witley Crs OLDBY B69 .... **118** A2
Witley Farm Cl SOLH B91 .... **195** E5 🔟
Witley Rd NFLD/LBR B31 .... **187** F3 🔟
Witney Dr CHWD/FDBR/MGN B37 .. **130** B5
Witney Gv WOLVN WV10 .... **11** D2
Witton La AST/WIT B6 .... **100** B4
WBROM B71 .... **72** C3
Witton Lodge Rd
ERDW/GRVHL B23 .... **79** D4
Witton Rd AST/WIT B6 .... **100** A5
ETTPK/GDPK/PENN WV4 .... **44** C3
Witton St BORD B9 .... **125** D5
STRBR DY8 .... **136** A5
Wixford Gv SHLY B90 .... **193** F5
Wobaston Rd CDSL WV8 .... **9** F2
COVEN WV9 .... **10** A1
WOLVN WV10 .... **10** D1
Woburn Av SHHTH WV12 .... **29** D1
Woburn Crs GTB/HAM B43 .... **75** F2
Woburn Dr BRLYHL DY5 .... **137** D1
CDYHTH B64 .... **140** C2
Woburn Gv ACGN B27 .... **173** E2 🔟
Wodehouse Cl WMBN WV5 .... **64** A6 🔟
Wodehouse La SEDG DY3 .... **66** A3
Woden Av WNSFLD WV11 .... **27** E1 🔟
Woden Cl WMBN WV5 .... **64** B4
Woden Crs WNSFLD WV11 .... **27** E1 🔟
Woden Rd WOLVN WV10 .... **26** B3
Woden Rd East DARL/WED WS10 ... **51** D4
Woden Rd North DARL/WED WS10 . **50** A4
Woden Rd South DARL/WED WS10 . **72** B2
Woden Rd West DARL/WED WS10 .. **49** F5
Wold Wk MOS/BIL B13 .... **171** D5
Wolfsbane Dr DSYBK/YTR WS5 ..... **52** C6
Wolfson Dr EDG B15 .... **145** F5
Wollaston Ct STRBR DY8 .... **135** E3
Wollaston Crs WNSFLD WV11 .... **27** E1 🔟
Wollaston Rd KINVER DY7 .... **135** E2
STRBR DY8 .... **136** A2
Wollerton Gv MGN/WHC B75 .... **60** B3 🔟
Wollescote Dr SOLH B91 .... **195** D3
Wollescote Rd HAG/WOL DY9 ...... **137** E6 🔟
Wolmer Rd WNSFLD WV11 .... **14** B3
Wolseley Av ACGN B27 .... **151** F5
Wolseley Bank WOLVN WV10 .... **12** B6
Wolseley Cl CBROM B36 .... **106** C4
WOLVN WV10 .... **12** B6

Wolseley Ga WOLVN WV10 .... **12** B6
Wolseley Rd BILS/COS WV14 .... **47** D2
WBROM B70 .... **72** B5
Wolseley St BORD B9 .... **125** D5
Wolston Cl SHLY B90 .... **173** D6
Wolverhampton Rd
BLOX/PEL WS3 .... **17** D4
CDSL WV8 .... **8** B1 🔟
KGSWFD DY6 .... **87** E5
KINVER DY7 .... **134** B2
LGLYGN/QTN B68 .... **118** C4
SEDG DY3 .... **45** F6
WNSFLD WV11 .... **14** B2
WOLVN WV10 .... **26** C3
WSLW WS2 .... **30** C5
WSLW WS2 .... **31** E5
Wolverhampton Rd East
ETTPK/GDPK/PENN WV4 .... **45** F5
Wolverhampton Rd South
LGLYGN/QTN B68 .... **144** A2
Wolverhampton Rd West
WSLW WS2 .... **30** A5
Wolverhampton St BILS/COS WV14 .. **47** E3
DARL/WED WS10 .... **49** D3
DUDN DY1 .... **91** D4
WLNHL WV13 .... **28** B6
WSLW WS2 .... **4** B3
Wolverley Av
ETTPK/GDPK/PENN WV4 .... **43** F4
STRBR DY8 .... **135** E3
Wolverley Crs OLDBY B69 .... **117** F2
Wolverley Rd HALE B63 .... **162** B1 🔟
HIA/OLT B92 .... **13** F1
RIDG/WDGT B32 .... **165** D3
Wolverson Cl SHHTH WV12 .... **29** E3
Wolverson Rd ALDR WS9 .... **20** C1
Wolverton Rd
CHWD/FDBR/MGN B37 .... **155** D2
DUDS DY2 .... **92** A4
RBRY B45 .... **201** E1
Wombourne Cl SEDG DY3 .... **67** E3 🔟
Wombourne Pk WMBN WV5 .... **86** B3
Wombourne Rd SEDG DY3 .... **86** B2
Woodacre Rd ERDE/BCHGN B24 .... **103** E1
Woodall Rd BFLD/HDSWWD B20 .... **100** B4
Woodall St BLOX/PEL WS3 .... **17** E5
CDYHTH B64 .... **115** E6
Woodard Rd TPTN/OCK DY4 .... **71** E4
WNSFLD WV11 .... **27** E1
Woodbank Rd SEDG DY3 .... **67** E4
Woodberry Dr WALM/CURD B76 ..... **82** C1
Woodberry Wk ACGN B27 .... **151** F6
Woodbine Cft
LGN/SDN/BHAMAIR B26 .... **152** C3 🔟
Woodbourne EDG B15 .... **145** F1
Woodbourne Rd HRBN B17 .... **145** D1
SMTHWK B66 .... **120** A5
Woodbridge Cl BLOX/PEL WS3 ...... **16** C2
RUSH/SHEL WS4 .... **19** F4
Woodbridge Rd MOS/BIL B13 .... **148** B6
Woodbrooke Rd BVILLE B30 .... **167** F4
Woodburn Rd SMTHWK B66 .... **97** F6
Woodbury Cl BRLYHL DY5 .... **114** A6
RMSLY B62 .... **142** B1 🔟
Woodbury Gv SOLH B91 .... **195** D5
Woodbury Rd RMSLY B62 .... **142** C1
Woodchester Rd DOR/KN B93 ...... **212** A1
Woodclose Rd CSHL/WTROR B46 ... **108** B6
Woodcock Cl HOCK/TIA B94 .... **222** A6
NFLD/LBR B31 .... **185** D4
Woodcock La ACGN B27 .... **151** F6
NFLD/LBR B31 .... **166** A3
Woodcock La North ACGN B27 ..... **151** F5
LGN/SDN/BHAMAIR B26 .... **152** A5 🔟
Woodcock St VAUX/NECH B7 .... **7** H2
Woodcombe Cl BRLYHL DY5 .... **137** D2 🔟
Woodcote Dr DOR/KN B93 .... **213** D5
WASH/WDE B8 .... **126** A2 🔟
Woodcote Rd
DUNHL/THL/PER WV6 .... **23** E3
ERDE/BCHGN B24 .... **86** A5 🔟
Woodcote Wy FOAKS/STRLY B74 ... **56** B3
WSNGN B18 .... **122** C3
Woodcroft Av BFLD/HDSWWD B20 . **98** A2
TPTN/OCK DY4 .... **69** E6
Woodcroft Cl BRGRVE B60 .... **214** B4
CDYHTH B64 .... **140** B1 🔟
Woodcross La BILS/COS WV14 ...... **68** C3
Woodcross St BILS/COS WV14 ...... **68** B1
Woodend BFLD/HDSWWD B20 .... **76** A5
Wood End Dr RBRY B45 .... **214** C1
Wood End La ERDE/BCHGN B24 .... **102** B2
HOCK/TIA B94 .... **222** A4
Woodend Pl
DUNHL/THL/PER WV6 .... **23** D3 🔟
Wood End Rd DSYBK/YTR WS5 ...... **53** F1 🔟
ERDE/BCHGN B24 .... **102** B2
WNSFLD WV11 .... **13** E5

Woodfall Av *BVILLE* B30 .... **168** B6
Woodfield Av *BRLYHL* DY5 .... **89** D6
  CDYHTH B64 .... **139** F1
  ETTPK/GDPK/PENN WV4 .... **44** B3
  HAG/WOL DY9 .... **160** B1
  OLDBY B69 .... **118** C3 ⓘ
Woodfield Cl *DSYBK/YTR* WS5 .... **54** A4
  MGN/WHC B75 .... **59** D1 ⓘ
Woodfield Crs *BHTH/HG* B12 .... **148** C3
Woodfield Hts
  DUNHL/THL/PER WV6 .... **23** F3
Woodfield La *RMSLY* B62 .... **181** F5
Woodfield Rd
  ALE/KHTH/YWD B14 .... **170** B3
  BHTH/HG B12 .... **148** C3
  SEDG DY3 .... **89** E1
  SOLH B91 .... **175** D5
Woodford Cft *ALDR* WS9 .... **21** D6
Woodford Av *CBROM* B36 .... **104** C5
Woodford Cl *COVEN* WV9 .... **10** B3 ⓘ
Woodford Green Rd
  HLGN/YWD B28 .... **172** C3
Woodfort Rd *GTB/HAM* B43 .... **76** A4
Woodgate Dr *RIDG/WDGT* B32 ..... **164** C2
Woodgate Gdns *RIDG/WDGT* B32 .. **164** C1
Woodgate La *RIDG/WDGT* B32 ...... **164** C1
Woodgate Wy *HAG/WOL* DY9 .... **180** A6
Woodglade Cft *HWK/WKHTH* B38 .. **188** A3
Woodgreen Cft *LGLYGN/QTN* B68 .. **143** E2
Wood Green Rd
  DARL/WED WS10 .... **50** B6 ⓘ
  DARL/WED WS10 .... **51** D5
Woodgreen Rd *LGLYGN/QTN* B68 .. **143** E2
Wood Green Rd *WSNGN* B18 .... **121** F3 ⓘ
Woodhall Cl *TPTN/OCK* DY4 .... **70** C5 ⓘ
Woodhall Cft *HIA/OLT* B92 .... **152** B6 ⓘ
Woodhall Rd
  ETTPK/GDPK/PENN WV4 .... **44** A5
Woodham Cl *RBRY* B45 .... **184** A4
Woodhaven *RUSH/SHEL* WS4 .... **19** F4
Wood Hayes Rd *WOLVN* WV10 .... **13** D3
Woodhill Cl *WMBN* WV5 .... **64** B5 ⓘ
Wood Hill Dr *WMBN* WV5 .... **64** B5
Woodhouse Orch
  HAG/WOL DY9 .... **180** A6 ⓘ
Woodhouse Rd
  DUNHL/THL/PER WV6 .... **23** D4
  RIDG/WDGT B32 .... **144** A3
Woodhouse Rd North
  DUNHL/THL/PER WV6 .... **23** D3
Woodhurst Rd *MOS/BIL* B13 .... **148** C5 ⓘ
Wooding Crs *TPTN/OCK* DY4 .... **71** D2
Woodington Rd *MGN/WHC* B75 ..... **60** C4
Woodland Av *BRLYHL* DY5 .... **114** C6
  DUDN DY1 .... **91** E2
  DUNHL/THL/PER WV6 .... **23** D4
  STRBR DY8 .... **158** B6
Woodland Cl *HAG/WOL* DY9 .... **159** F2
  SHHTH WV12 .... **29** F1
Woodland Crs *BDMR/CCFT* WV3 ..... **43** F2
Woodland Dr *SMTHWK* B66 .... **96** A6
Woodland Gv *GTB/HAM* B43 .... **54** A6
  SEDG DY3 .... **89** D2 ⓘ
Woodland Ri *CDYHTH* B64 .... **140** B1 ⓘ
  SCFLD/BOLD B73 .... **59** D5 ⓘ
Woodland Rd *BDMR/CCFT* WV3 ..... **43** F2
  HDSW B21 .... **97** E5
  NFLD/LBR B31 .... **187** D2
  RMSLY B62 .... **141** F1
Woodlands Av *CSHL/WTROR* B46 ... **107** D3
  DSYBK/YTR WS5 .... **54** A4
Woodlands Cottages
  ETTPK/GDPK/PENN WV4 .... **44** B5 ⓘ
Woodlands Farm Rd
  ERDE/BCHGN B24 .... **104** B1
Woodlands La *SHLY* B90 .... **193** D5
Woodlands Paddock
  ETTPK/GDPK/PENN WV4 .... **44** A5 ⓘ
Woodlands Park Rd *BVILLE* B30 ... **167** E5
Woodlands Rd *RBRY* B45 .... **183** F6
  SPARK B11 .... **149** E6
  WASH/WDE B8 .... **126** B3
  WMBN WV5 .... **64** C6
Woodlands St *SMTHWK* B66 .... **121** E2
The Woodlands *CDYHTH* B64 ...... **140** C2 ⓘ
  STRBR DY8 .... **158** C1
Woodlands Wy
  CHWD/FDBR/MGN B37 .... **131** F4
Wood La *BFLD/HDSWWD* B20 .... **98** C3
  CHWD/FDBR/MGN B37 .... **154** C1 ⓘ
  ERDE/BCHGN B24 .... **103** E3
  FOAKS/STRLY B74 .... **36** A6
  HOCK/TIA B94 .... **208** A6
  HRBN B17 .... **144** C3
  RIDG/WDGT B32 .... **164** C2
  SHHTH WV12 .... **94** C2
  WOLVN WV10 .... **11** F3
Wood Lane Cl *SHHTH* WV12 .... **16** A6 ⓘ
Woodlawn Gv *KGSWFD* DY6 .... **111** F2 ⓘ
Woodlea Dr *ERDE/BCHGN* B24 ...... **102** B3
  SOLH B91 .... **174** A6
Wood Leasow *RIDG/WDGT* B32 .... **165** F1 ⓘ
Woodleaves *HLYWD* B47 .... **190** B5

Woodleigh Av *HRBN* B17 .... **145** F5
Woodleigh Cl *HALE* B63 .... **140** C3 ⓘ
Woodleigh Rd *CSCFLD/WYGN* B72 .. **81** D2
The Woodleys
  ALE/KHTH/YWD B14 .... **191** D1
Woodloes Rd *SHLY* B90 .... **193** D6
Woodman Cl *DARL/WED* WS10 ...... **51** D5 ⓘ
  HALE B63 .... **141** E6
Woodman Rd
  ALE/KHTH/YWD B14 .... **190** C4 ⓘ
  HALE B63 .... **141** E6 ⓘ
Woodmeadow Rd *BVILLE* B30 ...... **188** C2
Woodnorton Dr *MOS/BIL* B13 ...... **170** A1
Woodnorton Rd
  BLKHTH/ROWR B65 .... **118** B5
Woodpecker Gv *CBROM* B36 .... **106** C6
Woodperry Av *SLYOAK* B29 .... **195** E4 ⓘ
Woodridge *BFLD/HDSWWD* B20 ... **100** A4
Woodridge Av *RIDG/WDGT* B32 ... **143** D5
Woodridge Rd *HALE* B63 .... **140** C4
Wood Rd *DUNHL/THL/PER* WV6 .... **23** D4
  SEDG DY3 .... **89** E2
  WMBN WV5 .... **65** D4
Woodrough Dr *MOS/BIL* B13 .... **170** B1
Woodrow Cl *BRGRVW* B61 .... **198** B6
Woodrow Crs *DOR/KN* B93 .... **212** C2
Woodrow La *BRGRVW* B61 .... **198** C6
Woodruff Wy *DSYBK/YTR* WS5 ...... **52** B5
Woodrush Dr *HLYWD* B47 .... **206** C2 ⓘ
Woods Bank Ter *DARL/WED* WS10 ... **49** E4
Woods Crs *BRLYHL* DY5 .... **114** C6
Woodsetton Cl *DUDN* DY1 .... **69** D5
Woodshill Av *RBRY* B45 .... **200** C5
Woodshires Rd *HIA/OLT* B92 ...... **174** A4
Woodside *CHWD/FDBR/MGN* B37 .. **130** A3
  FOAKS/STRLY B74 .... **38** A5
Wood Side *WNSFLD* WV11 .... **14** C5
Woodside Cl *DSYBK/YTR* WS5 .... **53** F4
Woodside Crs *DOR/KN* B93 .... **213** D3 ⓘ
Woodside Dr *FOAKS/STRLY* B74 ..... **37** E2
  RBRY B45 .... **215** D1
Woodside Gv *CDSL* WV8 .... **9** D3 ⓘ
Woodside Rd *DSYBK/YTR* WS5 .... **53** F3 ⓘ
  DUDS DY2 .... **114** B1
  SLYOAK B29 .... **168** C2
Woodside Wy *ALDR* WS9 .... **35** D2
  RIDG/WDGT B32 .... **164** C3 ⓘ
  SHHTH WV12 .... **16** A6
  SOLH B91 .... **174** A6
Woods La *BRLYHL* DY5 .... **137** F2
  CDYHTH B64 .... **139** E1
Woodsome Gv
  ERDW/GRVHL B23 .... **79** E4 ⓘ
Woodsorrel Rd *DUDN* DY1 .... **90** B1
The Woods *MOS/BIL* B13 .... **170** B1 ⓘ
Woodstile *BKDE/SHDE* B34 .... **129** D1
Woodstile Cl *MGN/WHC* B75 .... **39** F4 ⓘ
Woodstock Cl *DSYBK/YTR* WS5 ...... **52** C6 ⓘ
  DUDN DY1 .... **90** C5 ⓘ
  STRBR DY8 .... **111** E6
Woodstock Crs *DOR/KN* B93 .... **212** B4
Woodstock Dr *FOAKS/STRLY* B74 ... **37** F3
  STRBR DY8 .... **111** E5
Woodstock Rd *HDSW* B21 .... **98** B5
  MOS/BIL B13 .... **148** C5
  WOLV WV1 .... **27** D6
Woodston Gv *SOLH* B91 .... **195** E5 ⓘ
Wood St *BILS/COS* WV14 .... **47** F4
  DARL/WED WS10 .... **50** B3
  DUDS DY2 .... **114** B1
  ETTPK/GDPK/PENN WV4 .... **44** C6
  HAG/WOL DY9 .... **138** B4 ⓘ
  STRBR DY8 .... **70** A6
  TPTN/OCK DY4 .... **28** C5
  WLNHL WV13 .... **26** A2
  WOLVN WV10 .... **26** A2
Woodthorne Cl *SEDG* DY3 .... **89** F3 ⓘ
Woodthorne Rd
  DUNHL/THL/PER WV6 .... **22** C1
Woodthorne Rd South
  DUNHL/THL/PER WV6 .... **22** C2
Woodthorpe Dr *HAG/WOL* DY9 .... **137** F6 ⓘ
Woodthorpe Gdns
  ALE/KHTH/YWD B14 .... **170** A6 ⓘ
Woodthorpe Rd
  ALE/KHTH/YWD B14 .... **169** F6
Woodvale Dr *HLGN/YWD* B28 .... **192** A1
Woodvale Rd *HLGN/YWD* B28 .... **192** A1
  RIDG/WDGT B32 .... **164** C2 ⓘ
Woodview Dr *EDG* B15 .... **147** E2
Woodville Gdns *SEDG* DY3 .... **68** B2 ⓘ
Woodville Rd *ALE/KHTH/YWD* B14 .. **170** B2
  HRBN B17 .... **144** C3
Woodward Pl *HAG/WOL* DY9 .... **137** E5 ⓘ
Woodwards Cl *WSLW* WS2 .... **51** D1
Woodwards Pl *WSLW* WS2 .... **51** D1
Woodwards Rd *WSLW* WS2 .... **51** D1
Woodward St *HHTH/SAND* B71 ..... **96** A1 ⓘ
Woodway *ERDE/BCHGN* B24 .... **81** D6
Woodwells Rd *WASH/WDE* B8 ...... **126** C2
Woolacombe Lodge Rd
  SLYOAK B29 .... **167** E1
Woolmore Rd *ERDW/GRVHL* B23 .. **101** E1
Woolpack Cl *BLKHTH/ROWR* B65 .. **116** C3
Wooton Gv *KGSTG* B44 .... **79** E3 ⓘ

Wootton Av *WNSFLD* WV11 .... **13** F6
Wootton Rd *BDMR/CCFT* WV3 .... **43** E2
  NFLD/LBR B31 .... **186** C6
Worcester Gv *WOLVN* WV10 .... **18** C6
  MGN/WHC B75 .... **39** F4
Worcester Ct *BDMR/CCFT* WV3 ..... **44** C3 ⓘ
Worcester Gv *HHTH/SAND* B71 ..... **73** E4
Worcester La *HAG/WOL* DY9 .... **159** D3
  MGN/WHC B75 .... **39** F4
  STRBR DY8 .... **159** D1
Worcester Ri *SLYOAK* B29 .... **169** D2 ⓘ
Worcester Rd *DUDS* DY2 .... **116** A4
  HAG/WOL DY9 .... **158** C6
  LGLYGN/QTN B68 .... **142** C1
  WLNHL WV13 .... **29** F5
Worcester St *BKHL/PFLD* WV2 .... **2** C1
  STRBR DY8 .... **136** C5
Word Hl *HRBN* B17 .... **144** B2
Wordsworth Av
  ETTPK/GDPK/PENN WV4 .... **46** A5
Wordsworth Cl *TPTN/OCK* DY4 ...... **70** B3
Wordsworth Ct
  DUNHL/THL/PER WV6 .... **22** A3 ⓘ
Wordsworth Rd *BLOX/PEL* WS3 ...... **18** A5
  SEDG DY3 .... **67** D6
  SHHTH WV12 .... **16** A6
  SMHTH B10 .... **149** F2
  WOLVN WV10 .... **12** C5
Wordsworth St *HHTH/SAND* B71 ... **73** E6
Worfield Cl *RUSH/SHEL* WS4 .... **32** C3
Worfield Gdns *BDMR/CCFT* WV3 ... **44** B3
World's End Av *RIDG/WDGT* B32 .. **143** F3
World's End La *RIDG/WDGT* B32 ... **143** F4
Worlds End Rd *BFLD/HDSWWD* B20 .. **98** C2
Worleys Wharf Av
  DARL/WED WS10 .... **74** A1
Worsey Dr *TPTN/OCK* DY4 .... **71** F5 ⓘ
Worthen Gv *NFLD/LBR* B31 .... **186** C5 ⓘ
The Worthings *BVILLE* B30 .... **169** D5
Worthy Down *WNSFLD* WV11 .... **28** A2 ⓘ
Wortley Av *WOLVN* WV10 .... **160** A1
Worton Rd *HAG/WOL* DY9 .... **160** A1
Wragby Cl *COVEN* WV9 .... **11** D2
Wrekin Cl *HALE* B63 .... **161** E2
Wrekin Dr *BDMR/CCFT* WV3 .... **44** A1
  DUNHL/THL/PER WV6 .... **22** C1
  HAG/WOL DY9 .... **157** F5
Wrekin Gv *SHHTH* WV12 .... **15** D4 ⓘ
Wrekin La *DUNHL/THL/PER* WV6 .... **22** C2
Wrekin Rd *KGSTG* B44 .... **78** B5
  SCFLD/BOLD B73 .... **80** C2 ⓘ
Wrekin View Rd *SEDG* DY3 .... **67** E3
Wrens Av *KGSWFD* DY6 .... **112** C3
  TPTN/OCK DY4 .... **69** E6
Wrens Hill Rd *DUDN* DY1 .... **68** C5
Wren's Nest Rd *DUDN* DY1 .... **68** C5
  DUDN DY1 .... **90** C1 ⓘ
Wrens Park Av *WALM/CURD* B76 .. **82** A4
Wren St *DUDN* DY1 .... **69** D5
  DUDS DY2 .... **115** D2
Wrentham St *DIG/EDG* B5 .... **148** A1
Wretham Rd *LOZ/NWT* B19 .... **123** D1
Wrexham Av *WSLW* WS2 .... **30** B6
Wright Av *WNSFLD* WV11 .... **13** F6
Wrighton Cl *SHHTH* WV12 .... **15** E5
Wrighton Dr *SEDG* DY3 .... **89** E4
Wright La *CDYHTH* B64 .... **116** B5
Wright St *BILS/COS* WV14 .... **48** A6 ⓘ
  HALE B63 .... **141** D5 ⓘ
  SMHTH B10 .... **149** F1
  WOLVN WV10 .... **25** F3 ⓘ
Wrottesley Rd
  DUNHL/THL/PER WV6 .... **23** D2
  GTB/HAM B43 .... **75** F2
Wrottesley Rd West
  DUNHL/THL/PER WV6 .... **22** B1
Wrottesley St *DIG/EDG* B5 .... **124** A6 ⓘ
Wroxall Cl *BRLYHL* DY5 .... **137** D1
Wroxall Gv *MOS/BIL* B13 .... **170** C5
Wroxall Rd *SOLH* B91 .... **174** A5
Wroxham Gln *WLNHL* WV13 .... **48** B1 ⓘ
Wroxton Dr *YDLY* B25 .... **152** A1
Wulfruna Gdns *BDMR/CCFT* WV3 .. **24** B6
  DUDS DY2 .... **2** D5
Wulfruna St *WOLV* WV1 .... **147** D4
Wyatt Cl *DIG/EDG* B5 .... **147** E4
Wyatt Rd *MGN/WHC* B75 .... **61** D3
Wychall Dr *WOLVN* WV10 .... **12** A1
Wychall La *HWK/WKHTH* B38 ...... **187** F3
  NFLD/LBR B31 .... **187** E3
Wychall Park Gv
  HWK/WKHTH B38 .... **187** F3
Wychall Rd *NFLD/LBR* B31 .... **187** D2
Wychbold Cl *SHHTH* WV12 .... **15** F1
Wychbold Ct *HAG/WOL* DY9 .... **159** E3
Wychbold Crs *STETCH* B33 .... **129** E4
Wychbury *WALM/CURD* B76 .... **82** C2 ⓘ
Wychbury Ct *HALE* B63 .... **140** C6 ⓘ
Wychbury Dr *HAG/WOL* DY9 .... **159** E4
Wychbury Rd *BDMR/CCFT* WV3 ..... **43** E2
  BRLYHL DY5 .... **138** A1
  HAG/WOL DY9 .... **160** A2
  RIDG/WDGT B32 .... **164** C3
Wyche Av *ALE/KHTH/YWD* B14 .... **189** F1

Wychelm Farm Rd
 ALE/KHTH/YWD B14 ...... 190 C4
Wychnor Gv HHTH/SAND B71 .... 74 A1 🗓
Wychwood Av DOR/KN B93 ...... 197 D5
Wychwood Crs
 LGN/SDN/BHAMAIR B26 ...... 152 C3
Wyckham Cl HRBN B17 ...... 144 C5
Wyckham Rd CBROM B36 ...... 106 B6
Wycome Rd HLGN/YWD B28 ...... 172 B5
Wye Cliff Rd BFLD/HDSWWD B20 ... 99 D5
Wye Cl DUNHL/THL/PER WV6 ... 22 B3 🗓
 WALM/CURD B76 ...... 82 C4
Wyemanton Cl GTB/HAM B43 ...... 75 E2
Wye Rd BLOX/PEL WS3 ...... 18 A4
Wyken Cl DOR/KN B93 ...... 212 A5
Wyld Cl HHTH/SAND B71 ...... 72 C3
Wylde Crs BLKHTH/ROWR B65 ... 117 E3
Wylde Green Rd
 CSCFLD/WYGN B72 ...... 81 C2
Wymering Av WNSFLD WV11 ...... 14 B6
Wynall La HAG/WOL DY9 ...... 138 B5
Wynall La South HAG/WOL DY9 ... 138 C6
Wynbrook Gv SHLY B90 ...... 210 C1 🗓
Wynchcombe Av
 ETTPK/GDPK/PENN WV4 ...... 43 F5
Wyndcliff Rd BORD B9 ...... 125 F3
Wyndham Gdns BVILLE B30 ...... 187 F1
Wyndham Rd LDYWD/EDGR B16 ... 122 B6
Wyndhurst Rd STETCH B33 ...... 128 A3
Wyndley Dr SCFLD/BOLD B73 ...... 59 D5
Wyndley La SCFLD/BOLD B73 ...... 58 C5
Wyndmill Crs HHTH/SAND B71 ... 74 B2
Wynds Covert BVILLE B30 ...... 189 F3 🗓
Wyndshiels CSHL/WTROR B46 ... 132 C1 🗓
Wynds Point NFLD/LBR B31 ...... 167 D6
The Wynd SEDG DY3 ...... 67 F2
Wynfield Gdns
 ALE/KHTH/YWD B14 ...... 170 A6
Wynford Rd ACGN B27 ...... 151 E4
Wyn-griffith Dr TPTN/OCK DY4 ... 92 C2
Wynne Crs
 ETTPK/GDPK/PENN WV4 ...... 43 E6
Wynn Rd ETTPK/GDPK/PENN WV4 ... 44 B3
Wynn St EDG B15 ...... 147 F1
Wynstead Covert BVILLE B30 .... 189 E3 🗓🗓
Wyntor La HHTH/SAND B71 ...... 73 D3
Wyre Cl ALDR WS9 ...... 20 B1
Wyre Rd STRBR DY8 ...... 136 A2
Wyrley Cl SHHTH WV12 ...... 15 E6
Wyrley Rd AST/WIT B6 ...... 100 C2
 MGN/WHC B75 ...... 39 F6
 WNSFLD WV11 ...... 28 C1
Wyrley St WOLVN WV10 ...... 26 B5 🗓
Wyrley Wy ERDW/GRVHL B23 ... 78 C5
Wythall Green Wy HLYWD B47 ... 206 A4
Wythall Rd HALE B63 ...... 162 C1
Wythwood Cl HAG/WOL DY9 ... 159 F2 🗓
Wythwood Gv HLYWD B47 ...... 207 E1 🗓
 TPTN/OCK DY4 ...... 70 C3 🗓
Wythwood Rd HLYWD B47 ...... 207 D1
Wyvern Cl FOAKS/STRLY B74 ... 59 D1 🗓

 SHHTH WV12 ...... 14 C6
Wyvern Gv SLYOAK B29 ...... 167 E1
Wyvern Rd FOAKS/STRLY B74 ... 59 D2
Wyvis Cl DUNHL/THL/PER WV6 ... 24 A5

Y

Yale Dr WNSFLD WV11 ...... 28 A3
Yardley Cl LGLGYGN/QTN B68 ... 119 D6
Yardley Fields Rd STETCH B33 ... 127 F5
Yardley Green Rd BORD B9 ...... 126 B6
Yardley Rd ACGN B27 ...... 151 E5
 YDLY B25 ...... 151 F3
Yardley St BRLYHL DY5 ...... 137 E3
 DARL/WED WS10 ...... 49 E2
Yardley Wood Rd
 ALE/KHTH/YWD B14 ...... 191 D2
 MOS/BIL B13 ...... 171 D2
Yare Gv WLNHL WV13 ...... 29 F6 🗓
Yarnborough HI STRBR DY8 ...... 158 C1
Yarnbury Cl
 ALE/KHTH/YWD B14 ...... 190 A4 🗓
Yarn Cl HLYWD B47 ...... 206 C2
Yarner Cl DUDN DY1 ...... 90 A4
Yarnfield Rd SPARK B11 ...... 150 C6
Yarningale Rd
 ALE/KHTH/YWD B14 ...... 169 E6
Yarrow Cl WNSFLD WV11 ...... 28 B2 🗓
Yarrow Dr HWK/WKHTH B38 ... 188 B5 🗓
Yarwell Cl WOLVN WV10 ...... 25 F3
Yateley Av PBAR/PBCH B42 ...... 76 C4
Yateley Crs PBAR/PBCH B42 ...... 76 C3
Yateley Rd EDG B15 ...... 146 A2
Yatesbury Av CVALE B35 ...... 104 B2
Yates Cft FOAKS/STRLY B74 ...... 38 B1
Yates La RMSLY B62 ...... 118 A5
Yeadon Gdns BDMR/CCFT WV3 ... 43 F1 🗓
Yeames Cl GTB/HAM B43 ...... 55 E4
Yelverton Cl BLOX/PEL WS3 ... 17 D1 🗓
Yelverton Dr EDG B15 ...... 146 A2
Yeman Rd LGLYGN/QTN B68 ...... 119 F4
Yenton Gv CSCFLD/WYGN B72 ... 81 E5
Yeovil Ct ERDW/GRVHL B23 ...... 78 C6
Yewdale HRBN B17 ...... 145 E5 🗓
Yew Croft Av HRBN B17 ...... 144 C3
Yewhurst Rd SOLH B91 ...... 193 F1
Yew St BDMR/CCFT WV3 ...... 24 C6
Yew Tree Gdns CDSL WV8 ...... 8 C1 🗓
Yew Tree Hills DUDS DY2 ...... 115 E4
Yew Tree La BILS/COS WV14 ...... 69 F2
 DARL/WED WS10 ...... 72 C1
 DUNHL/THL/PER WV6 ...... 22 B1
 LGN/SDN/BHAMAIR B26 ...... 152 A2
 RMSLY B62 ...... 184 A2
 SOLH B91 ...... 176 A6
Yewtree La BLKHTH/ROWR B65 ... 117 D5
Yew Tree Pl RMSLY B62 ...... 162 B5
Yew Tree Ri WALM/CURD B76 ... 60 B6

Yew Tree Rd AST/WIT B6 ...... 100 C4
 CBROM B36 ...... 106 A5
 DSYBK/YTR WS5 ...... 52 C4
 DUDS DY2 ...... 115 E3
 EDG B15 ...... 147 E1
 HALE B63 ...... 140 A6
 MOS/BIL B13 ...... 169 F1
 RUSH/SHEL WS4 ...... 19 D4
 SMTHWKW B67 ...... 120 A3
Yewtree Rd FOAKS/STRLY B74 ... 55 F1
 SCFLD/BOLD B73 ...... 80 C4
Yockleton Rd STETCH B33 ...... 129 E4
York Av BDMR/CCFT WV3 ...... 24 A6
 WLNHL WV13 ...... 29 F5
 WSLW WS2 ...... 31 D5
Yorkbrooke Dr
 LGN/SDN/BHAMAIR B26 ...... 153 D4 🗓
York Cl BVILLE B30 ...... 168 C5
 TPTN/OCK DY4 ...... 91 F1
York Crs BDMR/CCFT WV3 ...... 23 F6
 DARL/WED WS10 ...... 49 F3
 STRBR DY8 ...... 135 F2
 WBROM B70 ...... 72 C5
Yorkdale Cl SEDG DY3 ...... 89 F2 🗓
York Dr CBROM B36 ...... 103 D5 🗓
Yorke Av BRLYHL DY5 ...... 112 C4
York Gdns BDMR/CCFT WV3 ... 24 A6
Yorklea Cl CHWD/FDBR/MGN B37 ... 130 B5
Yorklea Cft
 CHWD/FDBR/MGN B37 ...... 130 B5 🗓
Yorkminster Dr
 CHWD/FDBR/MGN B37 ...... 131 E4
York Rd ALE/KHTH/YWD B14 ... 170 A3
 BDMR/CCFT WV3 ...... 43 D1
 BLKHTH/ROWR B65 ...... 118 A4
 DUDS DY2 ...... 116 A4
 ERDW/GRVHL B23 ...... 102 B1
 HDSW B21 ...... 98 B5
 HLGN/YWD B28 ...... 172 B2
 LDYWD/EDGR B16 ...... 121 F6
 RUSH/SHEL WS4 ...... 19 F6
York St HRBN B17 ...... 145 F3
 WOLV WV1 ...... 3 G5
Yorks Wood Dr
 CHWD/FDBR/MGN B37 ...... 130 A2
York Ter WSNGN B18 ...... 123 E2 🗓
Young St WBROM B70 ...... 94 C2
Yoxall Gv STETCH B33 ...... 128 C4
Yoxall Rd SHLY B90 ...... 193 F3

Z

Zions Cl CDYHTH B64 ...... 116 B6 🗓
Zoar St BDMR/CCFT WV3 ...... 2 A6
 SEDG DY3 ...... 89 E2
Zouche Cl STRBR DY8 ...... 136 A1 🗓

Index - featured places

A1 Trading Estate
 SMTHWK B66 ...... 97 D6
A1 Trading Estate
 SMTHWKW B67 ...... 120 C6
Abberley Industrial Centre
 SMTHWK B66 ...... 121 F2
Abbey College
 CBHAMNW B3 ...... 6 D4
Abbey County Infant School
 SMTHWKW B67 ...... 120 A5
Abbey CP School
 BLOX/PEL WS3 ...... 16 A2
Abbey Road Junior School
 SMTHWKW B67 ...... 120 A6
Abbey Tutorial College
 CBHAMNW B3 ...... 6 C3
Ace Business Park
 STETCH B33 ...... 129 F5
Acocks Green Junior & Infant School
 ACGN B27 ...... 151 D6
Acupoint Magneto Clinic
 SMHTH B10 ...... 150 A2
Adderley Junior & Infant School
 WASH/WDE B8 ...... 125 E4
Adderley Trading Estate
 WASH/WDE B8 ...... 125 E3
Adrian Boult Hall
 CBHAMNW B3 ...... 6 C5
Alan Cotterell Practice
 BKHL/PFLD WV2 ...... 3 E6

Albert Bradford School
 SMTHWK B66 ...... 96 A6
Albert Pritchard Infant School
 DARL/WED WS10 ...... 50 C4
Albion Business Park
 SMTHWK B66 ...... 96 A5
Albion Industrial Estate
 WBROM B70 ...... 94 C3
Albion Junior School
 HHTH/SAND B71 ...... 96 C5
Albion Road Junior School
 WLNHL WV13 ...... 29 E5
Albright Home & Hospital P R U
 BLKHTH/ROWR B65 ...... 117 F3
Alcott Hall Junior & Infant School
 CHWD/FDBR/MGN B37 ...... 131 D6
Alderbrook School
 SOLH B91 ...... 194 B3
Aldersley High School
 CDSL WV8 ...... 10 A4
Aldridge & Brownhills Magistrates Court
 ALDR WS9 ...... 35 D1
Aldridge Road School Clinic
 KGSTG B44 ...... 77 F2
Aldridge School
 ALDR WS9 ...... 34 C2
Alexander Industrial Park
 BILS/COS WV14 ...... 47 E5
Alexandra High School
 TPTN/OCK DY4 ...... 71 D5

Alexandra Industrial Estate
 TPTN/OCK DY4 ...... 70 B5
Alexandra Medical Centre
 HALE B63 ...... 140 B4
Alexandra Theatre
 CBHAMW B1 ...... 6 D6
Al Hijrah Mosque
 SMHTH B10 ...... 126 B6
Al Hijraj School
 SMHTH B10 ...... 126 C6
Allaware Gallery
 ALE/KHTH/YWD B14 ...... 190 B4
Allens Rough Community Primary School
 SHHTH WV12 ...... 15 E4
All Saints C of E Primary School
 HHTH/SAND B71 ...... 73 E5
All Saints Hospital
 WSNGN B18 ...... 122 A2
All Saints Industrial Estate
 WSNGN B18 ...... 122 C2
All Saints School
 BKHL/PFLD WV2 ...... 46 A1
Alma Industrial Estate
 DARL/WED WS10 ...... 49 E3
Alston Junior School
 BORD B9 ...... 127 D4
Alumrock Medical Centre
 WASH/WDE B8 ...... 126 A3
The Alumwell School
 WSLW WS2 ...... 30 C6

Alvechurch C of E Middle School
ALVE B48 .... 216 C3
Amblecote Primary School
STRBR DY8 .... 136 B1
Anderton Park Junior &
Infant School
BHTH/HG B12 .... 148 C5
Anglesey Junior & Infant School
LOZ/NWT B19 .... 99 E6
Anglesey Junior School
LOZ/NWT B19 .... 123 E1
Anita Myatt Health Centre
ETTPK/GDPK/PENN WV4 .... 43 F5
Anjuman-e-naqeebul
Islam Mosque
WASH/WDE B8 .... 125 F2
Annie Lennard Infant School
SMTHWKW B67 .... 120 A4
Archbishop Grimshaw
Comprehensive School
CHWD/FDBR/MGN B37 .... 130 B4
Archbishop Ilsley RC School
ACGN B27 .... 173 E1
Arden High School
DOR/KN B93 .... 213 D2
Arden School
BORD B9 .... 125 F5
Arden School
SMTHWKW B67 .... 120 B2
Armoury Trading Estate
SPARK B11 .... 149 F3
Arran Medical Centre
CBROM B36 .... 106 C6
Arthur Terry School
FOAKS/STRLY B74 .... 38 C4
Ashford Industrial Estate
BKHL/PFLD WV2 .... 46 B2
Ashfurlong Health Centre
MGN/WHC B75 .... 60 A1
Ashmore Industrial Estate
WSLW WS2 .... 4 C1
Ashmore Park Clinic
WNSFLD WV11 .... 14 C5
Ashtree Medical Centre
BVILLE B30 .... 168 C5
Ashwood Park CP School
STRBR DY8 .... 111 F6
Aston Cross Business Park
AST/WIT B6 .... 124 C1
Aston Expressway
Industrial Estate
AST/WIT B6 .... 124 A2
Aston Health Centre
BFLD/HDSWWD B20 .... 100 A4
Aston Manor Cricket &
Lucas Sports Club
PBAR/PBCH B42 .... 77 F4
Aston Manor School
AST/WIT B6 .... 124 B1
Aston Tower Junior &
Infant School
AST/WIT B6 .... 100 B6
Aston Villa Football Club
AST/WIT B6 .... 100 B4
Atlas Estate
SPARK B11 .... 149 F4
Atlas Estate
SPARK B11 .... 150 C4
Atlas Trading Estate
BILS/COS WV14 .... 70 B1
Attock Community Sports &
Cricket Club
MOS/BIL B13 .... 171 E2
Attwood Business Centre
HAG/WOL DY9 .... 138 B4
Audley JMI School
STECH B33 .... 128 B3
Autobase Industrial Estate
OLDBY B69 .... 93 D2
Baba Balak Nah Temple
WSL WS1 .... 4 C6
Back Care & Acupuncture Clinic
WSLW WS2 .... 4 B1
Balliol Business Park
COVEN WV9 .... 10 A1
Banners Gate Infant &
Junior School
SCFLD/BOLD B73 .... 56 C5
Barber Institute of Fine Arts
EDG B15 .... 146 B5
Barford Junior & Infant School
LDYWD/EDGR B16 .... 122 A4

Barnfield Trading Estate
TPTN/OCK DY4 .... 70 A5
Barnt Green Cricket Club
RBRY B45 .... 201 E6
Barnt Green Surgery
RBRY B45 .... 215 F2
Barons Court Industrial Estate
ALDR WS9 .... 20 A3
The Barr Beacon School
ALDR WS9 .... 55 D4
Bartley Green Football Club
RIDG/WDGT B32 .... 165 E2
Bartley Green Health Centre
RIDG/WDGT B32 .... 165 D2
Bartley Green School
RIDG/WDGT B32 .... 165 E2
Barton Industrial Estate
BILS/COS WV14 .... 48 A2
The Baskerville School
HRBN B17 .... 144 C4
Batmans Hill County
Primary School
TPTN/OCK DY4 .... 70 A2
Bayer Hall Clinic
BILS/COS WV14 .... 69 E3
Beacon CP School
SHHTH WV12 .... 15 F5
Beaconside First & Middle School
RBRY B45 .... 200 A1
Beacon Trading Estate
ALDR WS9 .... 34 C1
Bearwood Medical Centre
SMTHWKW B67 .... 120 B5
Bearwood Road Junior &
Infant School
SMTHWKW B67 .... 120 B5
Beaufort School
CBROM B36 .... 127 F2
Beauty Bank County Primary
Junior & Infant School
STRBR DY8 .... 136 B3
Beckminster Special School
BDMR/CCFT WV3 .... 44 B2
Beechdale Centre Surgery
WSLW WS2 .... 30 C2
Beechdale CP School
WSLW WS2 .... 31 E2
Beeches First School
RBRY B45 .... 185 D3
Beeches Hospital
WOLV WV1 .... 24 C4
Belfont Trading Estate
HALE B63 .... 141 E5
The Belfry Golf Centre
WALM/CURD B76 .... 63 E6
Bell Barn Shopping Centre
EDG B15 .... 147 E1
Belle Vue Medical Centre
EDG B15 .... 147 F2
Belle Vue Primary School
STRBR DY8 .... 111 E4
Bellfield Junior & Infant School
NFLD/LBR B31 .... 186 B1
Bells Farm Junior &
Infant School
ALE/KHTH/YWD B14 .... 189 E3
Bennetts Well Junior &
Infant School
CHWD/FDBR/MGN B37 .... 130 B4
Benson Industrial Estate
WSNGN B18 .... 122 B1
Benson Junior Mixed School
WSNGN B18 .... 122 B1
Bentley Bridge Business Park
WNSFLD WV11 .... 27 E2
Bentley Drive Jmi School
WSLW WS2 .... 31 D4
Bentley Heath C of E
Primary School
DOR/KN B93 .... 212 B2
Bentley Lane Industrial Park
WSLW WS2 .... 31 D4
Bentley Mill Industrial Estate
WSLW WS2 .... 30 B6
Bentley West Primary School
WSLW WS2 .... 30 A4
Bescot Industrial Estate
DARL/WED WS10 .... 49 F6
Bescot Industrial Estate
DARL/WED WS10 .... 50 A5
Bhylls Acre County
Primary School
BDMR/CCFT WV3 .... 43 D2

Bickford Road Industrial Estate
AST/WIT B6 .... 100 C4
Bilbrook C of E Middle School
CDSL WV8 .... 9 D2
Bilbrook Medical Centre
CDSL WV8 .... 9 D2
Billesley Infant and
Junior School
MOS/BIL B13 .... 171 E5
Bilston College of Further
Education
BILS/COS WV14 .... 47 D2
Bilston Community College
BILS/COS WV14 .... 47 E4
Bilston Community College
BKHL/PFLD WV2 .... 46 B2
Bilston Health Centre
BILS/COS WV14 .... 47 F3
Bilston Industrial Estate
BILS/COS WV14 .... 48 C5
Bilston Key Industrial Estate
BILS/COS WV14 .... 48 C1
Bilston Leisure Centre
BILS/COS WV14 .... 47 F3
Bilston Public Library &
Art Gallery
BILS/COS WV14 .... 48 A3
Bilston Town Football Club
BILS/COS WV14 .... 48 B3
Bilton Industrial Estate
HWK/WKHTH B38 .... 188 A5
Bingley Junior School
BDMR/CCFT WV3 .... 44 C1
Birches First School
CDSL WV8 .... 9 D4
Birches Green Junior &
Infant School
ERDE/BCHGN B24 .... 103 D2
Birchills C of E School
WSLW WS2 .... 4 A2
Birchills Health Centre
WSLW WS2 .... 31 E4
Birchley Industrial Estate
OLDBY B69 .... 118 A2
Birchley School
BLKHTH/ROWR B65 .... 117 F3
Birch Road East Industrial Estate
AST/WIT B6 .... 101 D3
Birmingham Alexander Stadium
PBAR/PBCH B42 .... 77 F5
Birmingham Area Civil
Service Sports Club
HIA/OLT B92 .... 176 C1
Birmingham Business Centre
WBROM B70 .... 96 B3
Birmingham 1 Business Estate
CBHAMW B1 .... 123 D4
Birmingham Cathedral
CBHAMNW B3 .... 6 D4
Birmingham Central Mosque
BHTH/HG B12 .... 148 A2
Birmingham Central Synagogue
DIG/EDG B5 .... 147 F3
Birmingham Childrens
Hospital NHS Trust
CBHAMNE B4 .... 7 E3
Birmingham City Council
ALE/KHTH/YWD B14 .... 191 E1
Birmingham City Council
AST/WIT B6 .... 101 D6
Birmingham City Council
BFLD/HDSWWD B20 .... 98 A2
Birmingham City Council
BFLD/HDSWWD B20 .... 98 C3
Birmingham City Council
BHTH/HG B12 .... 148 B4
Birmingham City Council
BKDE/SHDE B34 .... 105 D6
Birmingham City Council
CBHAM B2 .... 7 E5
Birmingham City Council
CBHAMNE B4 .... 7 F2
Birmingham City Council
CBHAMNE B4 .... 124 C5
Birmingham City Council
CBHAMNW B3 .... 6 C4
Birmingham City Council
CBHAMW B1 .... 6 A4
Birmingham City Council
CBHAMW B1 .... 6 B5
Birmingham City Council
CSCFLD/WYGN B72 .... 59 E5
Birmingham City Council
DIG/EDG B5 .... 7 G6

Birmingham City Council
DIG/EDG B5............................ **124** A6

Birmingham City Council
DIG/EDG B5............................ **147** F2

Birmingham City Council
ERDE/BCHGN B24 .... **80** C6

Birmingham City Council
HDSW B21 .... **98** C6

Birmingham City Council
HRBN B17 .... **121** D5

Birmingham City Council
HRBN B17 .... **144** B3

Birmingham City Council
HRBN B17 .... **145** F3

Birmingham City Council
LDYWD/EDGR B16 .... **122** C6

Birmingham City Council
LGN/SDN/BHAMAIR B26 .... **153** F3

Birmingham City Council
LOZ/NWT B19 .... **124** A1

Birmingham City Council
NFLD/LBR B31 .... **166** A5

Birmingham City Council
NFLD/LBR B31 .... **185** E3

Birmingham City Council
NFLD/LBR B31 .... **185** F5

Birmingham City Council
SLYOAK B29 .... **168** C3

Birmingham City Council
SPARK B11 .... **149** D3

Birmingham City Council
SPARK B11 .... **150** C3

Birmingham City Council
WASH/WDE B8 .... **126** A2

Birmingham City Council
WASH/WDE B8 .... **126** B1

Birmingham City Council
YDLY B25 .... **151** E1

Birmingham City Football Club
BORD B9 .... **125** E6

Birmingham College
ACGN B27 .... **151** E6

Birmingham Conservatoire
CBHAMW B1 .... **6** B5

Birmingham Crown Court
CBHAMNE B4 .... **7** F4

Birmingham Dental
Hospital & School
CBHAMNE B4 .... **7** E2

Birmingham
International Airport
LGN/SDN/BHAMAIR B26 .... **155** E4

The Birmingham Mint
WSNGN B18 .... **123** D3

The Birmingham
Nuffield Hospital
EDG B15 .... **146** B4

Birmingham One
Industrial Estate
CBHAMW B1 .... **123** D4

Birmingham Railway Museum
SPARK B11 .... **150** B4

Birmingham Repertory Theatre
CBHAMW B1 .... **6** B5

Birmingham Womens
Hospital NHS Trust
EDG B15 .... **145** F4

Bishop Challoner RC School
ALE/KHTH/YWD B14 .... **170** A3

Bishop Milner RC
Secondary School
DUDN DY1 .... **90** C2

Bishop Veseys Grammar School
FOAKS/STRLY B74 .... **59** E3

Bishop Walsh RC School
WALM/CURD B76 .... **81** F1

Bishop Wilson C of E
Junior & Infant School
CHWD/FDBR/MGN B37 .... **131** E4

Blackbrook Valley
Industrial Estate
DUDS DY2 .... **114** C1

Black Country Family Practice
TPTN/OCK DY4 .... **70** A6

Black Country Museum
DUDN DY1 .... **91** F1

Blackheath Junior &
Infant School
BLKHTH/ROWR B65 .... **117** D6

Black Lake Industrial Estate
HHTH/SAND B71 .... **73** D5

Blackwell Golf Club
BRGRVE B60 .... **214** C4

Blackwood School
FOAKS/STRLY B74 .... **36** A6

Blakeley Heath CP School
WMBN WV5 .... **64** C6

Blakeley School
OLDBY B69 .... **94** A4

Blakenhale Infant School
STECH B33............................ **129** D6

Blakenhale Junior Mixed School
STECH B33............................ **129** D6

Blakenhall Industrial Estate
BKHL/PFLD WV2 .... **45** D2

Blakesley Hall Junior
Mixed School
YDLY B25 .... **127** D6

Blakesley Surgery
YDLY B25 .... **128** A6

Blandford Mere Primary School
KGSWFD DY6 .... **88** A6

Bleakhouse Clinic
LGLYGN/QTN B68 .... **119** E6

Bleakhouse Junior School
LGLYGN/QTN B68 .... **119** E5

Bloomsbury Health Centre
VAUX/NECH B7 .... **124** C2

Blossomfield Infant School
SHLY B90 .... **193** F2

Blowers Green Primary School
DUDS DY2 .... **91** D5

Bloxwich Business Park
WSLW WS2 .... **17** D6

Bloxwich C of E Primary School
BLOX/PEL WS3 .... **17** D4

Bloxwich Hospital
BLOX/PEL WS3 .... **17** D5

Bloxwich Lane Industrial Estate
WSLW WS2 .... **30** C1

Bloxwich Leisure Centre
BLOX/PEL WS3 .... **17** E5

Blue Coat C of E (Aided)
Infant School
WSL WS1 .... **5** E6

Blue Coat C of E (Aided)
Junior School
WSL WS1 .... **5** F5

Bluecoat C of E
Comprehensive School
WSL WS1 .... **5** E5

Blue Coat School
EDG B15 .... **146** A3

Blythe School
CSHL/WTROR B46................... **132** C3

B M I Priory Hospital
EDG B15 .... **147** E4

Boddis Industrial Park
CDYHTH B64 .... **116** C5

Boldmere Clinic
SCFLD/BOLD B73 .... **80** B2

Boldmere Middle & Infant School
SCFLD/BOLD B73 .... **80** B2

Boldmere St Michaels
Football Club
SCFLD/BOLD B73 .... **80** B3

Bordesley Green Junior &
Infant School
BORD B9 .... **126** C5

Bordesley Green Trading Estate
BORD B9 .... **126** A5

Bordesley Trading Estate
WASH/WDE B8 .... **125** F4

Bosworth Wood Junior &
Infant School
CBROM B36........................... **106** B4

Boulton Industrial Centre
WSNGN B18 .... **123** D2

Boulton Junior & Infant School
HDSW B21 .... **98** A6

Bournbrook & Varsity
Medical Practice
SLYOAK B29 .... **146** B6

Bournbrook Surgery
BVILLE B30 .... **168** B4

Bournville College of
Further Education
BVILLE B30 .... **168** A4

Bournville College of
Further Education
NFLD/LBR B31 .... **167** E4

Bournville Junior & Infant School
BVILLE B30 .... **168** A4

Bournville School
NFLD/LBR B31 .... **167** E5

Bournville School of Art
BVILLE B30 .... **168** A4

Boydell Galleries
ERDW/CRVHL B23 .... **80** C6

Brackendale Shopping Centre
SHHTH WV12 .... **29** F3

Bradford Street Clinic
WSL WS1 .... **4** C4

Braidwood Day Special School
ERDW/CRVHL B23 .... **79** D5

Bramford CP School
DUDN DY1 .... **68** C5

Brandhall Clinic
LGLYGN/QTN B68 .... **143** D1

Brandon Way Industrial Estate
WBROM B70 .... **94** B2

Brasshouse Language Centre
LDYWD/EDGR B16 .... **123** D6

Brewery
WOLV WV1 .... **2** B4

Brickhouse Junior &
Infant School
BLKHTH/ROWR B65 .... **116** C4

Brickkiln Primary School
BDMR/CCFT WV3 .... **2** A5

Bridgeman Street Trading Estate
WSLW WS2............................ **4** A3

Bridge School
ERDW/CRVHL B23 .... **102** A1

The Bridge Trading Estate
SMTHWK B66 .... **121** D1

The Brierley Hill Health Centre
BRLYHL DY5.......................... **113** F4

Brierley Hill Leisure Centre
BRLYHL DY5.......................... **114** A5

Brierley Hill Primary School
BRLYHL DY5.......................... **114** A5

The Brier School
BRLYHL DY5.......................... **114** A4

Bristnall Hall High School
LGLYGN/QTN B68 .... **119** F4

Britannia High School
BLKHTH/ROWR B65 .... **117** F5

The Bristin School
HRBN B17 .... **121** E6

Broadcott Industrial Estate
CDYHTH B64 .... **116** C6

Broadmeadow Health Centre
BVILLE B30 .... **189** D3

Broad Street Gallery
WOLV WV1 .... **3** E3

Broadwalk Retail Park
WSL WS1 .... **51** F3

Broadway Medical Centre
DSYBK/YTR WS5 .... **52** B3

Broadway School
BFLD/HDSWWD B20................ **100** A3

Broadway Surgery
DSYBK/YTR WS5 .... **52** B3

Broadwell Industrial Park
OLDBY B69 .... **94** B4

Broadwyn Trading Estate
CDYHTH B64 .... **140** C1

Brockmoor Industrial Estate
BRLYHL DY5.......................... **112** C4

Brockmoor Primary School
BRLYHL DY5.......................... **113** E4

Bromford Junior Mixed School
CBROM B36........................... **103** F5

Bromford Road Industrial Estate
OLDBY B69 .... **94** C4

Bromley Hills Primary School
KGSWFD DY6 .... **112** B2

Bromley Primary School
BRLYHL DY5.......................... **113** D2

Brookfields Junior &
Infant School
WSNGN B18 .... **123** D3

Brooklands Hospital
CHWD/FDBR/MGN B37 .... **155** D1

Brook Park Industrial Estate
HAG/WOL DY9 .... **138** B4

The Brook Primary School
STRBR DY8 .... **112** B6

Brook Street Business Centre
TPTN/OCK DY4 .... **70** A5

Brookvale Primary School
ERDW/CRVHL B23 .... **101** D1

Brookvale Trading Estate
AST/WIT B6 .... **100** C2

Browning Street
Industrial Estate
LDYWD/EDGR B16 .... **123** D5

Brownmead Junior &
Infant School
BKDE/SHDE B34 .... **105** E6

Brunswick Park Trading Estate
DARL/WED WS10 .... **51** D5

Brymill Industrial Estate
TPTN/OCK DY4 .... **70** A4

BSA Business Park
SMHTH B10 .... **149** F3

BT Tower
CBHAMNW B3 .... **6** C3

Buckpool
Comprehensive School
STRBR DY8 .... **112** B4

Buddhist Fat Yue Temple
BRLYHL DY5 .... **114** A4

Bull Ring Shopping Centre
DIG/EDG B5 .... **7** E6

Bull Ring Trading Estate
BORD B9 .... **124** B6

Bull Street Industrial Estate
BRLYHL DY5 .... **113** D6

The Bungalow
Queensbury Day
Special School
ERDE/BCHGN B24 .... **102** B2

Burbidge Industrial Estate
BORD B9 .... **126** A4

Burman Infant School
SHLY B90 .... **192** C3

Burnt Tree CP School
OLDBY B69 .... **92** C3

Burnt Tree Industrial Estate
TPTN/OCK DY4 .... **93** D3

Burton Industrial Estate
CDYHTH B64 .... **140** A1

Bushbury Baths
WOLVN WV10 .... **12** A4

Bushbury Health Centre
WOLVN WV10 .... **12** A3

Bushbury Infant School
WOLVN WV10 .... **12** B4

Busill Jones JMI School
BLOX/PEL WS3 .... **16** B5

The Business Centre
YDLY B25 .... **150** B3

Butts Primary School
RUSH/SHEL WS4 .... **32** B4

Byng Kenrick Central School
STECH B33 .... **129** F4

CAB
CBHAMNE B4 .... **7** E4

Cadbury Sixth Form College
HWK/WKHTH B38 .... **188** B4

Cake Gallery
BVILLE B30 .... **188** C2

Calderfields Golf Club
RUSH/SHEL WS4 .... **33** E5

Caldmore Junior School
WSL WS1 .... **52** A1

Callowbrook First School
RBRY B45 .... **184** A5

Calshot Junior & Infant School
PBAR/PBCH B42 .... **76** C3

Calthorpe Special School
BHTH/HG B12 .... **148** C1

Camp Hill Industrial Estate
BHTH/HG B12 .... **148** C1

Camp Hill Old Edwardians Rugby
Football Club
SHLY B90 .... **193** D2

Canalside Industrial Estate
BRLYHL DY5 .... **113** E6

Canning Wharf
CBHAMNW B3 .... **6** B4

Cannon Business Park
BILS/COS WV14 .... **69** E2

Canterbury Cross Primary School
BFLD/HDSWWD B20 .... **99** F3

Canwell C of E Primary School
MGN/WHC B75 .... **41** D3

Cape Hill Medical Centre
SMTHWK B66 .... **121** E3

Cape Primary School
SMTHWK B66 .... **121** E3

Cardinal Newman
Secondary Modern
HRBN B17 .... **120** C5

Cardinal Wiseman RC School
KGSTG B44 .... **78** B1

Carlton Business Centre
VAUX/NECH B7 .... **125** E2

Carlyle Business Park
WBROM B70 .... **72** B6

Carters Green Medical Centre
WBROM B70 .... **95** E1

Cascades Swimming Baths
STECH B33 .... **128** A4

Caslon Primary School
HALE B63 .... **139** D5

Castle Bromwich Business Park
ERDE/BCHGN B24 .... **104** B4

Castle Bromwich Cricket Club
CBROM B36 .... **105** E5

Castle Bromwich Infant School
CBROM B36 .... **106** A5

Castle Bromwich Junior School
CBROM B36 .... **105** F6

Castlecroft Primary School
BDMR/CCFT WV3 .... **43** D1

Castle Meadows Surgery
SEDG DY3 .... **89** F3

Castle School
BLOX/PEL WS3 .... **17** D4

Castle Vale Health Centre
CVALE B35 .... **104** C2

Castle Vale Housing Action Trust
CVALE B35 .... **105** D1

Castle Vale Industrial Estate
WALM/CURD B76 .... **82** C5

Castle Vale School
CVALE B35 .... **105** D2

Castle Vale Shopping Centre
CVALE B35 .... **104** B2

Catherine De Barnes C of E
Junior & Infant School
SOLH B91 .... **177** D6

Catshill Village Surgery
BRGRVW B61 .... **198** C6

Causeway Green
Primary School
LGLYCN/QTN B68 .... **118** B4

Cavendish Surgery
WSNGN B18 .... **121** F3

Cedars Surgery
HIA/OLT B92 .... **174** A2

Central Industrial Estate
BKHL/PFLD WV2 .... **46** B1

Central Jamia
Mosque Ghamkolvia
SMHTH B10 .... **149** F2

Central Trading Estate
KGSWFD DY6 .... **88** B4

Centre Link Industrial Estate
VAUX/NECH B7 .... **125** D1

Century Industrial Estate
KGSTG B44 .... **56** A6

Chad Vale Primary School
HRBN B17 .... **145** F2

Chamber of Commerce
and Industry
BDMR/CCFT WV3 .... **24** C5

Chancel Industrial Estate
DARL/WED WS10 .... **49** F4

Chancel Industrial Estate
KGSWFD DY6 .... **88** A5

Chancel Industrial Estate
WLNHL WV13 .... **29** D5

Chancel Industrial Estate
WOLV WV1 .... **26** B6

Chancel Way Industrial Estate
PBAR/PBCH B42 .... **78** B6

Chandos Junior & Infant School
DIG/EDG B5 .... **148** A2

Chapel Fields Primary School
HIA/OLT B92 .... **152** B6

Chapelhouse Surgery
HALE B63 .... **139** D3

Chapel Street Industrial Estate
DUDS DY2 .... **115** F3

Charlemont Primary School
HHTH/SAND B71 .... **74** A3

Charles Street Industrial Estate
TPTN/OCK DY4 .... **72** A6

Charnwood Business Park
BILS/COS WV14 .... **47** E4

Cheapside Industrial Estate
BHTH/HG B12 .... **148** B1

Chelmsley Wood
Industrial Estate
CHWD/FDBR/MGN B37 .... **131** D2

Chelmsley Wood
Shopping Centre
CHWD/FDBR/MGN B37 .... **131** D5

Chelsea Trading Estate
AST/WIT B6 .... **124** C1

Cherry Oak School
SLYOAK B29 .... **168** A2

Cherry Orchard Primary School
BFLD/HDSWWD B20 .... **98** C2

Cherry Trees Special School
WMBN WV5 .... **64** B5

Cheston Industrial Estate
AST/WIT B6 .... **101** D6

Cheswick Green Junior &
Infant School
SHLY B90 .... **210** A2

Chilcote Junior School
HLGN/YWD B28 .... **192** B1

Child Health Centre
SCFLD/BOLD B73 .... **57** D5

Chillington Works
Industrial Estate
WOLV WV1 .... **26** B6

Chiropodist Surgery
KGSTG B44 .... **78** C4

The Chiropody Surgery
YDLY B25 .... **127** F6

Chivenor Junior &
Infant School
CVALE B35 .... **104** C3

Christ Church C of E
Infant School
DUNHL/THL/PER WV6 .... **23** D4

Christ Church C of E
Infant School
DUNHL/THL/PER WV6 .... **25** D3

Christ Church C of E
Primary School
BLOX/PEL WS3 .... **17** F6

Christ Church C of E
Primary School
OLDBY B69 .... **94** C5

Christ Church C of E School
SPARK B11 .... **149** D2

Christ Church School
DUNHL/THL/PER WV6 .... **23** E3

Chuckery Primary School
WSL WS1 .... **5** G4

Churchfields High School
HHTH/SAND B71 .... **74** A5

Church Lane Health Centre
STECH B33 .... **128** B4

Church of Christ the King School
KGSTG B44 .... **78** C3

Church of the Ascension C of E
Primary School
KGSWFD DY6 .... **87** E5

Cinema
DIG/EDG B5 .... **6** D6

City Estate
CDYHTH B64 .... **139** F1

City Hospital NHS Trust
WSNGN B18 .... **122** B3

City Plaza Shopping Centre
CBHAM B2 .... **6** D5

City Technology College
CHWD/FDBR/MGN B37 .... **130** C3

City Trading Estate
LDYWD/EDGR B16 .... **122** C4

Claregate Primary School
DUNHL/THL/PER WV6 .... **10** B6

Clarkes Industrial Estate
SCFLD/BOLD B73 .... **80** C1

Clent Parochial First School
HAG/WOL DY9 .... **180** B3

Cleton Street Business Park
TPTN/OCK DY4 .... **93** D2

Clifton Infant School
BHTH/HG B12 .... **148** C4

Clifton Junior School
BHTH/HG B12 .... **148** C4

Clifton Mosque
BHTH/HG B12 .... **148** B4

Clifton Road Industrial Estate
BHTH/HG B12 .... **148** B4

Clothier Street Primary School
WLNHL WV13 .... **28** C4

Club House
WOLVN WV10 .... **11** D6

CMT Industrial Estate
OLDBY B69 .... **94** C5

Coalpool Clinic
BLOX/PEL WS3 .... **32** B1

Cobham Business Centre
BORD B9 .... **125** F5

Cockshut Hill School
LGN/SDN/BHAMAIR B26 .... **152** C1

Cocks Moors Woods
Leisure Centre
ALE/KHTH/YWD B14 .... **190** B1

Codsall Clinic
CDSL WV8 .... **8** C2

Codsall County High School
 CDSL WV8 .... 8 C2
Codsall County Middle School
 CDSL WV8 .... 8 C2
Cofton Medical Centre
 NFLD/LBR B31 .... 186 C6
Cofton Primary School
 NFLD/LBR B31 .... 202 C1
Coldland Colts Football Club
 SOLH B91 .... 176 B5
Colebourne Primary School
 BKDE/SHDE B34 .... 128 A2
Colemore School
 ALE/KHTH/YWD B14 .... 169 F4
Coleshill Clinic
 CSHL/WTROR B46 .... 132 C1
Coleshill C of E Primary School
 CSHL/WTROR B46 .... 132 C1
Coleshill Heath Primary &
 Junior School
 CHWD/FDBR/MGN B37 .... 131 E6
Coleshill Industrial Estate
 CSHL/WTROR B46 .... 108 B3
Coleshill Leisure Centre
 CSHL/WTROR B46 .... 132 B1
Coleshill School
 CSHL/WTROR B46 .... 132 C4
Coleshill Town Council
 CSHL/WTROR B46 .... 132 C1
Coleshill Town Football Club
 CSHL/WTROR B46 .... 132 C4
College High School
 ERDW/GRVHL B23 .... 78 C5
College of Adult Education
 WOLV WV1 .... 3 E5
College of Food Tourism &
 Creative Studies
 CBHAMW B3 .... 6 B4
Colley Lane Health Clinic
 HALE B63 .... 139 E3
Colley Lane Primary School
 HALE B63 .... 139 E3
Collingwood Junior School
 WOLVN WV10 .... 12 A3
Colmers Farm Grant
 Maintained School
 RBRY B45 .... 185 D5
Colmers Farm Junior &
 Infant School
 RBRY B45 .... 185 D5
Colmore Junior & Infant School
 ALE/KHTH/YWD B14 .... 169 F4
Community Leisure Centre
 TPTN/OCK DY4 .... 69 F5
Conway Junior & Infant School
 SPARK B11 .... 149 D3
Coombswood & Hanne Surgery
 CDYHTH B64 .... 141 D2
Cooper & Jordan C of E
 Junior & Infant School
 ALDR WS9 .... 35 E1
Coppice County Junior School
 HIA/OLT B92 .... 176 A4
Coppice High School
 WNSFLD WV11 .... 14 C6
Coppice Junior & Infant School
 MGN/WHC B75 .... 39 E6
Corbett Hospital
 STRBR DY8 .... 136 C2
Corbett Infant School
 SMTHWK B66 .... 121 D2
Corbetts Industrial Estate
 DUDS DY2 .... 115 E1
Corngreaves Junior &
 Infant School
 CDYHTH B64 .... 115 F6
Cornwall Industrial Estate
 WASH/WDE B8 .... 125 E3
Cornwall Road Industrial Estate
 SMTHWK B66 .... 97 E6
Corpus Christi Primary School
 WNSFLD WV11 .... 14 C5
Corpus Christi RC School
 STECH B33 .... 127 F5
Coseley Medical Centre
 BILS/COS WV14 .... 69 E3
Coseley Secondary School
 BILS/COS WV14 .... 69 D2
Coseley Swimming Pool
 BILS/COS WV14 .... 69 E3
Cotteridge Junior & Infant School
 BVILLE B30 .... 168 C6
Cottesbrook Junior School
 ACGN B27 .... 151 E5

Cotwell End County
 Primary School
 SEDG DY3 .... 67 E4
County Bridge Primary School
 WSLW WS2 .... 30 A6
Court Farm Junior &
 Infant Schools
 ERDW/GRVHL B23 .... 80 A5
Crabtree Clinic
 CHWD/FDBR/MGN B37 .... 130 B5
Cradley C of E Primary School
 HALE B63 .... 139 E2
Cradley Heath
 Community
 Recreation Centre
 DUDS DY2 .... 116 A5
Cradley High School
 HALE B63 .... 139 D3
Cradley Town Football Club
 HALE B63 .... 139 E5
Craig Croft Child Health Clinic
 CHWD/FDBR/MGN B37 .... 131 E5
Craig Croft Medical Centre
 CHWD/FDBR/MGN B37 .... 131 E5
Cranmore County Infant School
 SOLH B91 .... 194 A4
Cranmore Industrial Estate
 SHLY B90 .... 194 A5
Crescent Industrial Park
 DUDS DY2 .... 91 D6
The Crescent Theatre
 CBHAMW B1 .... 123 D5
Crescent Works Industrial Park
 DARL/WED WS10 .... 29 F6
Crestwood Park Primary School
 KGSWFD DY6 .... 112 C2
Crestwood School
 KGSWFD DY6 .... 112 B2
Cricket Club
 GTB/HAM B43 .... 54 B5
Crocketts Lane Infant School
 SMTHWK B66 .... 121 D2
Croft Foundry Industrial Estate
 WLNHL WV13 .... 28 C5
Croft Infant School
 WSLW WS2 .... 31 F3
Cromwell Junior & Infant School
 VAUX/NECH B7 .... 125 D1
Cronehills Health Centre
 WBROM B70 .... 95 E2
Cronehills JMI School
 WBROM B70 .... 95 F1
Cronin Vet Surgery
 GTB/HAM B43 .... 75 E3
Crossings Industrial Estate
 BLOX/PEL WS3 .... 16 C5
Cross Quays Business Park
 OLDBY B69 .... 93 E3
Cross Street Health Centre
 DUDN DY1 .... 91 E4
Crown Meadow Primary School
 ALVE B48 .... 217 D3
Crystal Leisure Centre
 STRBR DY8 .... 136 C4
Culwell Industrial Park
 WOLVN WV10 .... 3 G2
Culwell Trading Estate
 WOLVN WV10 .... 26 A3
Curdworth Primary School
 WALM/CURD B76 .... 85 E5
Curu Nanak Sikh Temple
 WOLVN WV10 .... 26 A3
Dadsford Bridge
 Industrial Estate
 STRBR DY8 .... 112 A5
Dame Elizabeth Cadbury School
 BVILLE B30 .... 168 A4
Dame Ellen Pinsent School
 HRBN B17 .... 121 E5
Dame Ellen Pinsent School
 MOS/BIL B13 .... 170 C4
Damson Wood County
 Infant School
 HIA/OLT B92 .... 175 F4
Danesmore Park Primary School
 WNSFLD WV11 .... 14 B4
Darlaston Clinic
 DARL/WED WS10 .... 49 E3
Darlaston Community School
 DARL/WED WS10 .... 49 D3
Darlaston Football Club
 DARL/WED WS10 .... 49 F3

Dartmouth
 Comprehensive School
 GTB/HAM B43 .... 53 F6
Daw End School
 RUSH/SHEL WS4 .... 33 D1
Dawley Brook CP School
 KGSWFD DY6 .... 87 E6
Dawley Trading Estate
 KGSWFD DY6 .... 87 F5
Daylesford Hall Infant School
 HIA/OLT B92 .... 152 C6
Deanery C of E Junior School
 WALM/CURD B76 .... 82 B3
Deansfield High School
 WOLV WV1 .... 27 E5
Deeleys Industrial Estate
 WSLW WS2 .... 31 D1
Deepdale Industrial Estate
 DUDN DY1 .... 90 A2
Delph Industrial Estate
 BRLYHL DY5 .... 113 E6
Delves Junior & Infant School
 DSYBK/YTR WS5 .... 52 C4
Dental Health Centre
 KGSTG B44 .... 78 B1
Devonshire Road Junior School
 SMTHWKW B67 .... 120 B1
Deykin Avenue Junior &
 Infant School
 AST/WIT B6 .... 100 C3
Deyncourt CP School
 WNSFLD WV11 .... 13 D6
Dingle Primary School
 KGSWFD DY6 .... 112 C3
Doranda Way Industrial Park
 HHTH/SAND B71 .... 96 B4
The Dormston School
 SEDG DY3 .... 68 A3
Dormston Trading Estate
 DUDN DY1 .... 90 B1
Dorothy Pattison Hospital
 WSLW WS2 .... 31 D6
Dorothy Purcell Junior School
 BILS/COS WV14 .... 49 D6
Dorridge Cricket Club
 DOR/KN B93 .... 212 A6
Dorridge Gallery
 DOR/KN B93 .... 212 B4
Dorridge Junior & Infant School
 DOR/KN B93 .... 212 B4
Dorrington Junior &
 Infant School
 PBAR/PBCH B42 .... 76 C5
Doulton Trading Estate
 BLKHTH/ROWR B65 .... 116 B3
Dovecote Junior & Infant School
 CDSL WV8 .... 10 A4
The Dovecote Surgery
 LGLYGN/QTN B68 .... 143 F2
Downing Close Health Clinic
 DOR/KN B93 .... 212 C3
Dr Arora Surgery
 PBAR/PBCH B42 .... 77 F6
Dr Browns Surgery
 BORD B9 .... 126 C6
Dreamland Industrial Estate
 SPARK B11 .... 150 C3
Dr Gonzales Surgery
 KGSTG B44 .... 78 B3
Driffold Gallery
 SCFLD/BOLD B73 .... 59 D6
Dr Lewiss Surgery
 BORD B9 .... 126 C6
Droicon Industrial Estate
 BLKHTH/ROWR B65 .... 117 D3
Druids Heath Golf Club
 ALDR WS9 .... 21 E5
Dudley Central Trading Estate
 DUDS DY2 .... 91 E5
Dudley College
 DUDN DY1 .... 91 E3
Dudley College of Technology
 BRLYHL DY5 .... 113 F4
Dudley County Court
 BRLYHL DY5 .... 114 A3
Dudley Health Authority
 DUDN DY1 .... 90 C5
Dudley Kingswinford
 Rugby Football Club
 KGSWFD DY6 .... 86 C6
Dudley Leisure Centre
 DUDN DY1 .... 91 D4

Dudley Metropolitan
Borough Council
BRLYHL DY5...................................... **112** C5

Dudley Metropolitan
Borough Council
BRLYHL DY5...................................... **113** F5

Dudley Metropolitan
Borough Council
DUDN DY1.. **68** B6

Dudley Metropolitan
Borough Council
DUDN DY1.. **90** B6

Dudley Metropolitan
Borough Council
DUDN DY1.. **91** E3

Dudley Metropolitan
Borough Council
DUDN DY1.. **91** E4

Dudley Metropolitan
Borough Council
DUDS DY2.. **91** D5

Dudley Metropolitan
Borough Council
DUDS DY2.. **91** F6

Dudley Metropolitan
Borough Council
DUDS DY2.. **115** F3

Dudley Metropolitan
Borough Council
HAG/WOL DY9................................ **138** A5

Dudley Metropolitan
Borough Council
HALE B63.. **141** D6

Dudley Metropolitan
Borough Council
SEDG DY3.. **67** F2

Dudley Metropolitan
Borough Council
STRBR DY8...................................... **136** B4

Dudley Metropolitan
District Council
STRBR DY8...................................... **112** A5

Dudley Mosque &
Muslim Community Centre
DUDN DY1.. **91** F3

Dudley Priority Health
NHS Trust
DUDN DY1.. **90** A6

Dudley Priority Health
NHS Trust
KGSWFD DY6.................................... **112** A1

Dudley School
DUDN DY1.. **91** D3

Dudley Town Hall
DUDN DY1.. **91** E4

Dudley Water Sports Centre
DUDS DY2.. **115** D4

Dudley Wood Primary School
DUDS DY2.. **115** E5

Dudley Zoological Society
DUDN DY1.. **91** F3

Duncan Street Surgery
BKHL/PFLD WV2................................ **45** F2

Dunstall Hill Industrial Estate
DUNHL/THL/PER WV6........................ **25** C2

Dunton Trading Estate
VAUX/NECH B7................................ **101** F6

Durberville Road
Industrial Estate
BKHL/PFLD WV2................................ **46** B2

Eagle Industrial Estate
TPTN/OCK DY4................................ **71** F4

Eagle Industrial Estate
WBROM B70...................................... **72** A3

Eagle Trading Estate
HALE B63.. **140** C5

The Earls High School
HALE B63.. **141** D5

Earlswood Trading Estate
HOCK/TIA B94.................................. **221** E3

East Birmingham College
STETCH B33.................................... **153** D1

Eastbourne House School
ACGN B27.. **151** E5

Eastfield Junior & Infant School
WOLV WV1.. **26** B5

East Park Medical Practice
WOLV WV1.. **26** C5

East Park Primary School
WOLV WV1.. **47** D1

East Park Trading Estate
WOLV WV1.. **46** B1

Eastwood Industrial Estate
WSNGN B18...................................... **122** B3

Eaton Wood Medical Centre
ERDE/BCHGN B24............................ **103** F2

Eclipse Trading Estate
TPTN/OCK DY4................................ **70** A6

Edgar Stammers Junior &
Infant School
BLOX/PEL WS3.................................. **18** B6

Edgaston Shopping Centre
LDYWD/EDGR B16............................ **146** C1

Edgbaston C of E College for
Girls
EDG B15.. **146** C1

Edgbaston College
EDG B15.. **147** D4

Edgbaston Health Clinic
EDG B15.. **146** B4

Edgbaston Health Clinic
SOLH B91.. **174** B5

Edgbaston High School for Girls
EDG B15.. **146** B2

Edgewood Road Clinic
RBRY B45.. **201** D1

Edwards Street Day Hospital
WBROM B70...................................... **95** E2

Edward Street Hospital
WBROM B70...................................... **95** E2

The Ellowes Hall GM School
SEDG DY3.. **67** E6

Elmdon Trading Estate
CHWD/FDBR/MGN B37...................... **155** E4

Elmfield School
STRBR DY8...................................... **136** C6

Elmore Green Primary School
BLOX/PEL WS3.................................. **16** C4

Elms Farm Junior &
Infant School
LGN/SDN/BHAMAIR B26.................. **153** E2

Elms Health Centre
HALE B63.. **139** E3

Elm Street Infant School
WLNHL WV13.................................... **29** E4

Elm Terrace Clinic
OLDBY B69...................................... **93** D4

Elston Hall Primary School
WOLVN WV10.................................... **11** F1

Embassy Industrial Estate
HAG/WOL DY9.................................. **138** B4

Empire Industrial Park
ALDR WS9.. **20** B5

English Martyrs RC
Junior & Infant School
SPARK B11.. **149** E5

Enterprise Trading Estate
BRLYHL DY5...................................... **114** C4

Erdington Hall Primary School
ERDE/BCHGN B24............................ **102** B3

Erdington Industrial Park
ERDE/BCHGN B24............................ **104** B1

Erdington Medical Centre
ERDE/BCHGN B24............................ **102** A3

Essington Light Industrial Estate
WNSFLD WV11.................................. **14** B1

Ettingshall Lodge Surgery
BKHL/PFLD WV2................................ **46** F2

Ettingshall Primary School
BILS/COS WV14................................ **47** D3

European Business Park
OLDBY B69...................................... **94** A6

Eve Hill Medical Practice
DUDN DY1.. **91** D3

Eversfield Preparatory School
SOLH B91.. **195** D1

Express Way Industrial Estate
AST/WIT B6...................................... **124** A1

Eye Infirmary
BDMR/CCFT WV3.............................. **24** C5

Fairfax School
MGN/WHC B75.................................. **60** B4

Fairhaven Primary School
STRBR DY8...................................... **111** F4

Fair View Industrial Estate
WALM/CURD B76.............................. **85** D4

Fairway Primary School
HWK/WKHTH B38............................ **187** F3

Falcon Lodge Clinic
MGN/WHC B75.................................. **60** C4

Falcon Lodge Junior School
MGN/WHC B75.................................. **60** B4

Fallings Park Industrial Estate
WOLVN WV10.................................... **26** B2

Farndale Junior School
DUNHL/THL/PER WV6...................... **24** C3

Fazeley Industrial Estate
DIG/EDG B5...................................... **7** H5

Featherstone Junior &
Infant School
ERDW/GRVHL B23............................ **102** A1

Feldon Lane Clinic
RMSLY B62...................................... **142** A2

Fernbank Medical Centre
WASH/WDE B8.................................. **126** C3

Ferndale Primary School
GTB/HAM B43.................................. **76** A3

Fircroft College
SLYOAK B29.................................... **167** F3

Fire Station
CBHAMNE B4.................................... **7** F2

Firs Junior & Infant School
CBROM B36...................................... **104** A5

Fir Tree Junior & Infant School
DSYBK/YTR WS5................................ **52** C5

Fitzwarren School
TPTN/OCK DY4................................ **70** C5

Five Ways Shopping Centre
LDYWD/EDGR B16............................ **123** D6

The Foot Clinic
CBHAMNW B3.................................. **6** C4

Fordhouse Road Industrial Estate
WOLVN WV10.................................... **11** E5

Fordhouses Cricket Club
WOLVN WV10.................................... **11** F1

Forge Trading Estate
RMSLY B62...................................... **141** E4

Formans Trading Estate
SPARK B11.. **149** F6

Fort Industrial Park
ERDE/BCHGN B24............................ **104** B4

Foundry Road Junior &
Infant School
WSNGN B18...................................... **121** F1

Four Dwellings JMI School
RIDG/WDGT B32.............................. **143** D4

Four Oaks Junior & Infant School
FOAKS/STRLY B74............................ **38** A3

Four Oaks Medical Centre
MGN/WHC B75.................................. **39** D5

Four Oaks Saints Cricket Club
FOAKS/STRLY B74............................ **38** A2

Four Seasons Art Gallery
ERDE/BCHGN B24............................ **80** C6

The Fox Hollies Leisure Centre
ACGN B27.. **172** C2

Fox Hollies Special School
ACGN B27.. **172** C2

Fox Hollies Surgery
HLGN/YWD B28................................ **172** C2

Foxmill Estate
SPARK B11.. **171** F1

Foxyards County Primary School
TPTN/OCK DY4................................ **69** E6

Frank F Harrison
Community School
WSLW WS2.. **16** B6

Frankley Health Centre
RBRY B45.. **184** B4

Frankley Industrial Park
RBRY B45.. **185** D4

Frankley Middle School
RBRY B45.. **185** D3

Friar Park Clinic
DARL/WED WS10.............................. **51** F6

Gannow Middle School
RBRY B45.. **183** F6

Garratts Green Trading Estate
STETCH B33.................................... **129** D6

Gas Street Basin
CBHAMW B1.................................... **6** A6

Gate Lane Industrial Estate
SCFLD/BOLD B73.............................. **80** C1

Gate Medical Centre
WASH/WDE B8.................................. **125** F1

George Auden School
NFLD/LBR B31.................................. **166** B6

George Dixon Gm School
HRBN B17.. **121** E5

George Dixon Gm School Annexe
HRBN B17.. **121** E6

George Fentham Junior &
Infant School
HIA/OLT B92.................................... **178** C5

George Salter High School
WBROM B70...................................... **94** C1

Gibbons Industrial Park
KGSWFD DY6.................................... **88** C6

Gilberstone Primary School
LGN/SDN/BHAMAIR B26.................. **151** F4

G K Davies Industrial Estate
HAG/WOL DY9.................................. **138** C3

Glebefields Health Centre
TPTN/OCK DY4 .... **70** C3
Glebefields Junior & Infant School
TPTN/OCK DY4 .... **70** C2
Glenmead Junior & Infant School
PBAR/PBCH B42 .... **77** F3
Glynne Primary School
KGSWFD DY6 .... **111** E3
Golden Hillock
Community School
SPARK B11 .... **149** F4
Goldtel Industrial Estate
ETTPK/GDPK/PENN WV4 .... **46** C4
Goldthorne Medical Centre
ETTPK/GDPK/PENN WV4 .... **45** E3
Goldthorn Park Primary School
ETTPK/GDPK/PENN WV4 .... **45** F4
Good Hope Hospital
MGN/WHC B75 .... **59** F3
Good Hope NHS Trust
ERDW/GRVHL B23 .... **101** F1
Goscote Hospital
BLOX/PEL WS3 .... **18** B5
Goscote Industrial Estate
BLOX/PEL WS3 .... **18** A4
Gossey Lane Junior &
Infant School
STECH B33 .... **129** E5
Grace Mary CP School
OLDBY B69 .... **93** E6
Graiseley Primary School
BKHL/PFLD WV2 .... **45** E1
Granby Business Park
STECH B33 .... **129** F6
Grand Theatre
WOLV WV1 .... **3** E3
The Grange School
HAG/WOL DY9 .... **137** F5
Gravel Hill Surgery
WMBN WV5 .... **65** D5
Grazebrook Industrial Park
DUDS DY2 .... **115** D1
Great Barr Gm School
KGSTG B44 .... **77** F2
Great Barr Junior & Infant School
PBAR/PBCH B42 .... **77** E2
Great Bridge Industrial Estate
TPTN/OCK DY4 .... **71** E4
Great Bridge Junior &
Infant School
TPTN/OCK DY4 .... **71** E5
Great Western Industrial Estate
WSNGN B18.................................. **122** A1
Greenacres Junior &
Infant School
BILS/COS WV14.............................. **48** B3
Greenbank Surgery
HLGN/YWD B28 .... **172** A2
Greenfield Primary School
STRBR DY8 .... **136** B5
Greenfield Surgery
STRBR DY8 .... **136** B4
Greenhill Galleries
MOS/BIL B13................................ **170** C2
Greenholm Junior &
Infant School
KGSTG B44.................................... **78** A4
Green Meadow Junior &
Infant School
SLYOAK B29................................ **166** B4
Green Rock Junior &
Infant School
BLOX/PEL WS3 .... **18** A4
Greet Primary Infant &
Junior School
SPARK B11 .... **149** F5
Greets Green Road
Industrial Estate
WBROM B70 .... **94** B1
Gregston Industrial Estate
OLDBY B69 .... **95** D5
Grendon Junior & Infant School
ALE/KHTH/YWD B14 .... **190** C2
Grestone Junior & Infant School
BFLD/HDSWWD B20........................ **98** A1
Greswolde Gallery
DOR/KN B93 .... **213** D1
Greswold Junior & Infant School
SOLH B91 .... **175** D5
Griffin Industrial Estate
OLDBY B69 .... **118** B4
Griffins Brook Medical Centre
SLYOAK B29................................ **167** E4

Grove Lane Junior &
Infant School
HDSW B21 .... **98** B5
Grove Medical Centre
BKHL/PFLD WV2 .... **46** A1
Grove Surgery
SOLH B91 .... **175** E6
Grove Vale Primary School
GTB/HAM B43 .... **75** F2
Grypon Industrial Estate
BFLD/HDSWWD B20........................ **99** E3
Guardian Angels RC
Junior & Infant School
BKDE/SHDE B34 .... **130** A1
Gun Barrel Industrial Centre
CDYHTH B64 .... **140** C3
Guns Village Infant School
WBROM B70 .... **95** D1
Guns Village Junior School
WBROM B70 .... **94** C2
Gunter Primary School
ERDE/BCHGN B24 .... **104** A1
Gupta Trading Estate
OLDBY B69 .... **94** B4
Guru Nanak Sikh Temple
BDMR/CCFT WV3 .... **45** D1
Guru Nanak Sikh Temple
BKHL/PFLD WV2 .... **45** E2
Guy Motors Industrial Park
WOLVN WV10 .... **26** A2
G W S Trading Estate
TPTN/OCK DY4 .... **71** F2
Haden Hill Leisure Centre
CDYHTH B64 .... **140** B1
Haden Vale Surgery
CDYHTH B64 .... **140** A2
Hagley County Primary
Junior & Infant School
HAG/WOL DY9.............................. **159** D6
Hagley RC High School
STRBR DY8 .... **158** B6
Halas Industrial Estate
RMSLY B62 .... **141** E4
Halcyon Gallery
CBHAM B2 .... **6** D6
Haldon House Business Centre
BRLYHL DY5 .... **113** D6
Halesbury School
RMSLY B62 .... **142** A1
Halesowen C of E Primary School
HALE B63 .... **141** D5
Halesowen College
HALE B63 .... **140** C5
Halesowen College
HALE B63 .... **141** D4
Halesowen Cricket Club
HALE B63 .... **163** D1
Halesowen Harriers
Football Club
HALE B63 .... **139** D4
Halesowen Health Centre
HALE B63 .... **141** D6
Halesowen Industrial Park
RMSLY B62 .... **141** E3
Halesowen Leisure Centre
HALE B63 .... **141** D6
Halesowen Magistrates Court
HALE B63 .... **141** D6
Hale Trading Estate
TPTN/OCK DY4 .... **71** D6
Hall Green Infant &
Junior Schools
HLGN/YWD B28 .... **172** A3
Hall Green Little Theatre
ACGN B27 .... **172** C1
Hall Green Primary &
Infant School
HHTH/SAND B71 .... **73** E2
Hall Green School
HLGN/YWD B28 .... **172** A3
Hallmoor School
STECH B33.................................. **129** D4
Hall of Memory
CBHAMW B1 .... **6** B5
Hamd House School
BORD B9 .... **126** C5
Hamilton School
HDSW B21 .... **97** F5
Hampstead Clinic
GTB/HAM B43.............................. **75** F4
Hamstead Hall School
BFLD/HDSWWD B20........................ **76** A5
Hamstead Infant School
GTB/HAM B43.............................. **75** F4

Hamstead Junior School
GTB/HAM B43.............................. **75** F4
Hamstead Road Surgery
BFLD/HDSWWD B20........................ **98** C5
Handsworth College
HDSW B21 .... **98** C6
Handsworth Grammar
School for Boys
HDSW B21 .... **98** B5
Handsworth Leisure Centre
BFLD/HDSWWD B20........................ **98** B5
Handsworth Medical Practice
HDSW B21 .... **98** A5
Handsworth Mosque &
Islamic Centre
HDSW B21 .... **97** F5
Handsworth Rugby Club
DSYBK/YTR WS5 .... **53** F5
Handsworth Wood Girls
School & Sixth Form Centre
BFLD/HDSWWD B20........................ **98** B3
Hangley Hall
HAG/WOL DY9............................ **160** A5
Harborne Cycle Surgery
HRBN B17 .... **144** C3
Harborne Hill School
EDG B15...................................... **146** A3
Harborne Junior School
HRBN B17 .... **145** E3
Harborne Medical Practice
HRBN B17 .... **145** F3
Harborne Swimming Pool
HRBN B17 .... **145** D4
Harden Primary School
BLOX/PEL WS3 .... **18** A6
Harden Surgery
BLOX/PEL WS3 .... **18** A6
Hargate Junior & Infant School
HHTH/SAND B71.......................... **95** E1
Harry Mitchell Leisure Centre
SMTHWK B67 .... **120** B2
Harvey Road Health Centre
LGN/SDN/BHAMAIR B26 .... **152** A2
Harvey Works Industrial Estate
HALE B63 .... **140** B3
Harvills Hawthorn
Primary School
WBROM B70 .... **72** B4
Hasbury C of E School
HALE B63 .... **162** B1
Hasbury Primary School
HALE B63 .... **162** B1
Hatchford Brook Junior &
Infant School
HIA/OLT B92 .... **153** E6
Hatchford Gm Primary School
CHWD/FDBR/MGN B37 .... **130** B5
Hateley Heath Junior &
Infant School
HHTH/SAND B71.......................... **73** D4
Hatherton Lane Junior
Mixed & Infant School
WSLW WS2.................................... **30** B1
Hawbush Primary School
BRLYHL DY5................................ **113** D5
Hawkesley C of E Methodist
Junior School
HWK/WKHTH B38 .... **188** A6
Hawkesley Health Centre
HWK/WKHTH B38 .... **188** A6
Hawksmill Industrial Estate
BORD B9 .... **125** E6
Hawthorn Primary School
KGSTG B44.................................... **78** C4
Hawthorns Business Centre
SMTHWK B66 .... **96** C5
Hawthorns Industrial Estate
HDSW B21 .... **97** D8
Hawthorns Surgery
CSCFLD/WYGN B72........................ **81** D3
Haybridge High School
STRBR DY8 .... **158** B5
The Hayes Trading Estate
HAG/WOL DY9.............................. **138** C3
Hayley Green Hospital
HALE B63 .... **161** F3
Hayward Industrial Park
ALDR WS9 .... **20** C6
Heartlands High School
VAUX/NECH B7 .... **125** D3
Heathfield Gm High School
CDYHTH B64 .... **116** B5
Heathfield Primary School
LOZ/NWT B19 .... **99** E5

The Heathlands J I N C School
BKDE/SHDE B34 .... **104** B6

Heath Lane Hospital
HHTH/SAND B71 .... **73** F4

Heath Mount Primary School
BHTH/HG B12 .... **148** A3

Heath Park
Comprehensive School
WOLVN WV10 .... **26** C2

Heath Street Industrial Estate
SMTHWK B66 .... **121** F2

Heath Town Leisure Centre
WOLVN WV10 .... **26** B3

Hebrew Congregation
CBHAMW B1 .... **123** F6

High Arcal School
SEDG DY3 .... **68** B5

Highclare School
CSCFLD/WYGN B72 .... **81** E2

Highclare School
ERDW/GRVHL B23 .... **80** C6

Highcroft Hospital
ERDW/GRVHL B23 .... **101** F2

Highcroft Hospital
ERDW/GRVHL B23 .... **102** A1

Highfield Junior & Infant School
WASH/WDE B8 .... **126** A2

Highfields Junior &
Infant School
BLKHTH/ROWR B65 .... **141** E1

Highfields Primary School
BILS/COS WV14 .... **69** E1

Highfields School
ETTPK/GDPK/PENN WV4 ... **43** E4

Highgate Medical Centre
BHTH/HG B12 .... **148** B2

Highgate Primary School
DUDS DY2 .... **114** B1

Highgate Trading Estate
BHTH/HG B12 .... **148** C2

Highgate United Football Club
SHLY B90 .... **208** A1

High Street Surgery
ERDW/GRVHL B23 .... **80** C6

Highters Heath JMI School
ALE/KHTH/YWD B14 .... **191** D2

Hillary Infant School
WSLW WS2 .... **51** E2

Hill Avenue Primary School
ETTPK/GDPK/PENN WV4 ... **46** B6

Hillcrest Business Park
DUDS DY2 .... **91** E6

Hillcrest Industrial Estate
CDYHTH B64 .... **139** F1

Hillcrest School
RIDG/WDGT B32 .... **144** A6

The Hillcrest School &
Community College
DUDS DY2 .... **115** E2

Hillmeads Health Centre
HWK/WKHTH B38 .... **188** C4

Hillstone Junior & Infant
School House
BKDE/SHDE B34 .... **129** F2

Hillstone Primary School
BKDE/SHDE B34 .... **129** F2

Hill Top Industrial Estate
WBROM B70 .... **72** B3

Hilltop Medical Centre
LGLYGN/QTN B68 .... **119** E5

Hill West Junior & Infant School
FOAKS/STRLY B74 .... **38** B3

Hilton Trading Estate
ETTPK/GDPK/PENN WV4 ... **46** B5

Himley Hall
SEDG DY3 .... **87** F2

Hindu Temple
DARL/WED WS10 .... **50** B2

Hippodrome Theatre
DIG/EDG B5 .... **124** A6

Hive Industrial Centre
WSNGN B18 .... **122** B1

Hob Green Primary School
HAG/WOL DY9 .... **160** A1

Hobmoor Junior &
Infant School
YDLY B25 .... **151** F1

Hobs Moat Medical Centre
HIA/OLT B92 .... **174** C1

Hockley Brook Trading Estate
WSNGN B18 .... **122** C1

Hockley Hill Industrial Estate
WSNGN B18 .... **123** D2

Hockley Medical Practice
HDSW B21 .... **98** C6

Hodge Hill Girls School
CBROM B36 .... **103** E6

Hodge Hill School
CBROM B36 .... **103** E6

Holiday Wharf
CBHAMW B1 .... **123** E6

Holland House Infant School
CSCFLD/WYGN B72 .... **59** E5

The Hollies Clinic
LGLYGN/QTN B68 .... **119** D3

Hollies Industrial Estate
BKHL/PFLD WV2 .... **45** E1

Holloway Bank Trading Estate
DARL/WED WS10 .... **72** C2

Hollow Gallery
HIA/OLT B92 .... **173** F1

Holly Bush Medical Centre
RIDG/WDGT B32 .... **143** F2

Hollyfield Infant School
MGN/WHC B75 .... **60** B5

Holly Hall Clinic
DUDN DY1 .... **90** B6

Holly Hall Secondary School
DUDN DY1 .... **90** B5

Holly Hill Methodist C of E
First School
RBRY B45 .... **184** B3

Holly Lodge High School
SMTHWKW B67 .... **96** A6

Holly Park Industrial Estate
ERDE/BCHGN B24 .... **103** F3

Hollywood Junior &
Infant School
ALE/KHTH/YWD B14 .... **190** C4

Hollywood Primary School
ALE/KHTH/YWD B14 .... **190** C4

Holte School
LOZ/NWT B19 .... **99** F6

Holt Farm Primary School
RMSLY B62 .... **118** A6

Holy Child School
EDG B15 .... **147** D3

Holy Cross RC School
WALM/CURD B76 .... **60** C6

Holy Family RC School
SMHTH B10 .... **150** B2

Holyhead Primary School
DARL/WED WS10 .... **49** F6

Holyhead School
HDSW B21 .... **97** F5

Holy Name RC Primary School
GTB/HAM B43 .... **76** A2

Holy Rosary RC School
WOLV WV1 .... **26** C6

Holy Souls RC Primary School
ACGN B27 .... **151** E6

Holy Trinity C of E Junior &
Infant School
BFLD/HDSWWD B20 .... **99** E3

Holy Trinity Primary School
BILS/COS WV14 .... **48** A4

Holy Trinity Primary School
WBROM B70 .... **95** F4

Holy Trinity RC
Comprehensive School
SMHTH B10 .... **149** E1

Honeybourne School
HLGN/YWD B28 .... **172** B3

Horrell Road Health Centre
LGN/SDN/BHAMAIR B26 .... **152** C2

Horse Shoe Associated
Football Club
SHLY B90 .... **208** B1

Hospital
LDYWD/EDGR B16 .... **122** C6

Howley Grange
Primary School
RMSLY B62 .... **142** C4

Hrs Business Park
STETCH B33 .... **129** E6

Hrs Industrial Estate
STETCH B33 .... **129** E6

Hugh Meadow Infant School
CSHL/WTROR B46 .... **108** B5

Hulbert Industrial Estate
DUDS DY2 .... **115** D1

Hunters Hill School
BRGRVE B60 .... **214** B3

Huntingtree Primary School
HALE B63 .... **140** A5

Hurst Green Primary School
RMSLY B62 .... **142** A1

Hurst Street Primary School
BILS/COS WV14 .... **68** C3

Hussani Mosque
DUNHL/THL/PER WV6 .... **24** B3

Ikon Gallery
CBHAMW B1 .... **6** A6

Imex Business Estate
STETCH B33 .... **128** A2

Imex Business Park
BKHL/PFLD WV2 .... **45** D2

Imex Business Park
BORD B9 .... **125** F5

Imex Business Park
SPARK B11 .... **150** B3

Imex Business Park
TPTN/OCK DY4 .... **92** C2

Imex Industrial Estate
WSNGN B18 .... **122** C3

Indian High Commission
WSNGN B18 .... **6** A1

Indoor Market
DARL/WED WS10 .... **72** B1

Industrial Estate
BHAMNEC B40 .... **155** F5

Industrial Estate
SMTHWK B66 .... **97** E6

Industrial Estate
WASH/WDE B8 .... **125** F4

Infant Welfare Clinic
GTB/HAM B43 .... **75** F1

Inglenook School
SLYOAK B29 .... **147** D6

International Convention Centre
CBHAMW B1 .... **6** A5

Izons Industrial Estate
WBROM B70 .... **94** B3

Jack O Watton Industrial Estate
CSHL/WTROR B46 .... **107** F2

Jalalabad Mosque &
Islamic Centre
SLYOAK B29 .... **168** B1

Jalalabad Mosque & Madrassa
AST/WIT B6 .... **100** B5

James Watt Industrial Park
SMTHWK B66 .... **121** E1

James Watt Junior &
Infant School
HDSW B21 .... **98** A6

Jamia Mosque
DUNHL/THL/PER WV6 .... **24** C4

Jamia Mosque Mehr-ul-millat
SPARK B11 .... **149** E4

Jami Mosque & Islamic Centre
SMHTH B10 .... **149** F1

Jane Lane School
WSLW WS2 .... **30** B4

Janet Shaw Clinic
CHWD/FDBR/MGN B37 ..... **155** D1

Jerome Retail Park
WSL WS1 .... **4** B5

Jervoise Junior & Infant School
SLYOAK B29 .... **166** C2

Jockey Road Surgery
SCFLD/BOLD B73 .... **79** F2

John Black Day Hospital
CHWD/FDBR/MGN B37 ..... **155** D1

John Willmott School
WALM/CURD B76 .... **60** B5

Joseph Chamberlain College
BHTH/HG B12 .... **148** B3

Joseph Leckie School
DSYBK/YTR WS5 .... **52** A4

Joseph Turner Junior &
Infant School
TPTN/OCK DY4 .... **71** D4

Josiah Mason College
ERDW/GRVHL B23 .... **101** E1

Jubilee Park Primary School
TPTN/OCK DY4 .... **71** D3

Junction Industrial Estate
SMTHWK B66 .... **96** B5

Junction Two Industrial Estate
OLDBY B69 .... **118** B1

J W Green Swimming Pools
BDMR/CCFT WV3 .... **24** C6

Karis Medical Centre
LDYWD/EDGR B16 .... **122** B6

Kates Hill County
Primary School
DUDS DY2 .... **92** A5

Keelinge House Surgery
DUDN DY1 .... **90** B6

Kent Close CP School
HHTH/SAND B71 .... **73** E4

Key Business Park
ERDE/BCHGN B24 .... **104** A2

Key Industrial Park
WLNHL WV13 .... **27** F4

Keyway Retail Park
WLNHL WV13 .... **49** D1

Khalsa Industrial Estate
SMTHWK B66 .... **121** F3

Kineton Green Infant School
HIA/OLT B92 .... **173** F2

King Charles Primary School
WSLW WS2 .... **30** B5

King David Junior &
Infant School
MOS/BIL B13 .... **170** B1

King Edwards School
EDG B15 .... **146** C5

King Edwards VI Aston School
AST/WIT B6 .... **100** B5

King Edwards VI Camp Hill
School for Boys
ALE/KHTH/YWD B14 .... **169** E4

King Edward VI College
STRBR DY8 .... **136** C3

King Edward VI Five Ways School
RIDG/WDCT B32 .... **165** E3

King Edward VI
Handsworth School
HDSW B21 .... **98** C6

King Edward VI
High School for Girls
EDG B15 .... **146** C5

Kingfisher Industrial Estate
WBROM B70 .... **94** A1

King George V Primary School
HHTH/SAND B71 .... **96** A2

Kingsbury Business Park
WALM/CURD B76 .... **84** A6

Kingsbury Road School
ERDE/BCHGN B24 .... **102** C3

Kings Business Park
KGSTG B44 .... **55** F6

Kings Heath Junior School
ALE/KHTH/YWD B14 .... **170** A2

Kings Heath School
MOS/BIL B13 .... **170** C5

Kings Hill Business Park
DARL/WED WS10 .... **50** A5

Kings Hill Clinic
DARL/WED WS10 .... **50** A4

Kings Hill JMI School
DARL/WED WS10 .... **50** A4

Kingshurst Clinic
CHWD/FDBR/MGN B37 .... **130** C2

Kingshurst Infant School
CHWD/FDBR/MGN B37 .... **130** C1

Kingshurst Junior School
CHWD/FDBR/MGN B37 .... **130** C1

Kingshurst Parish Council
Playing Fields Pavilion
CHWD/FDBR/MGN B37 .... **131** D2

Kingsland JMI School
KGSTG B44 .... **56** B5

Kingsley Preparatory School
DOR/KN B93 .... **212** B3

Kings Norton Boys School
BVILLE B30 .... **188** A1

Kings Norton Girls School
BVILLE B30 .... **168** A6

Kings Norton High School
HWK/WKHTH B38 .... **188** B5

Kings Norton Primary School
BVILLE B30 .... **188** C2

Kingsrise Primary School
KGSTG B44 .... **79** D1

Kings Road Industrial Estate
YDLY B25 .... **150** B3

Kingstanding Leisure Centre
KGSTG B44 .... **79** D3

Kingstanding Special School
KGSTG B44 .... **78** A2

Kingsthorne Primary School
KGSTG B44 .... **78** C2

Kingston Industrial Estate
BORD B9 .... **124** C6

The Kingswinford Gm School
KGSWFD DY6 .... **87** F6

Kitchen Gallery
DOR/KN B93 .... **212** B4

Kitwell Primary School
RIDG/WDCT B32 .... **164** C4

Klaxon Tysley Industrial Estate
SPARK B11 .... **150** B5

Knowle C of E Junior & Infant School
DOR/KN B93 .... **213** E1

Knowle & Dorridge Cricket Club
DOR/KN B93 .... **212** C3

Knowle Football Club
DOR/KN B93 .... **197** E6

Knowle Village Cricket Club
DOR/KN B93 .... **197** E6

Krishna Temple
BKHL/PFLD WV2 .... **45** D2

Ladypool Junior & Infant School
SPARK B11 .... **149** D3

Ladywood Arts & Leisure Centre
LDYWD/EDGR B16 .... **122** C5

Ladywood Middleway
Health Centre
CBHAMW B1 .... **122** C4

Ladywood School
LDYWD/EDGR B16 .... **122** C5

La Galleria
CBHAMNW B3 .... **6** B5

Lakeside Medical Centre
DUNHL/THL/PER WV6 .... **22** A3

Lakey Lane Primary School
HLGN/YWD B28 .... **173** D3

Lane Green County First School
CDSL WV8 .... **9** D1

The Lane Medical Centre
BHTH/HG B12 .... **149** D4

Lanesfield Primary School
ETTPK/GDPK/PENN WV4 .... **46** C1

The Lanes Shopping Centre
SCFLD/BOLD B73 .... **81** D4

Langley High School
LGLYGN/QTN B68 .... **119** D3

Langley Junior & Infant School
HIA/OLT B92 .... **173** F5

Langley Primary School
OLDBY B69 .... **118** C2

Langley Public Baths
LGLYGN/QTN B68 .... **119** E3

Langley School
MGN/WHC B75 .... **60** C3

Langley Secondary School
HIA/OLT B92 .... **173** F4

Lansdowne Health Centre
WSNGN B18 .... **122** B3

Lapal Primary School
RMSLY B62 .... **142** B5

Lasercare Clinics
EDG B15 .... **147** D1

Laurie Pike Health Centre
AST/WIT B6 .... **99** F5

League of Friends Walsall
Hospitals
WSL WS1 .... **4** D4

Leamore Industrial Estate
WSLW WS2 .... **16** C6

Leamore Primary School
BLOX/PEL WS3 .... **17** E6

Lea Road Medical Practice
BDMR/CCFT WV3 .... **45** D1

Leasowes High School &
Community College
RMSLY B62 .... **142** A3

Leasowes Primary School
SMTHWK B66 .... **95** F6

Leaverstock Industrial Estate
STETCH B33 .... **129** E6

Lee Bank Business Centre
CBHAMW B1 .... **123** E6

Lee Bank Group Practice
EDG B15 .... **123** E6

Lee Bank Junior & Infant School
EDG B15 .... **147** E1

Leigh Junior & Infant School
WASH/WDE B8 .... **126** A1

Leighswood Infant &
Junior School
ALDR WS9 .... **21** D5

Leighswood Junior School
ALDR WS9 .... **21** D6

Lemar Industrial Estate
BVILLE B30 .... **169** E2

Lench Estate
BLKHTH/ROWR B65 .... **117** D5

Lennon Indoor Market
KGSTG B44 .... **56** C6

Leona Trading Estate
RMSLY B62 .... **117** F6

Lewisham Industrial Estate
SMTHWK B66 .... **96** C6

Leyhill Health Centre
NFLD/LBR B31 .... **166** A5

Ley Hill Junior & Infant School
NFLD/LBR B31 .... **165** F6

Ley Hill Primary School
MGN/WHC B75 .... **39** D5

Ley Hill Surgery
MGN/WHC B75 .... **39** D6

Lickey Primary & Middle School
RBRY B45 .... **200** B5

Lifford Trading Estate
BVILLE B30 .... **188** C1

Light Hall School
SHLY B90 .... **193** D5

Lightwoods Junior &
Infant Primary School
LGLYGN/QTN B68 .... **143** F1

Lindens JMI School
FOAKS/STRLY B74 .... **56** B3

Link One Industrial Park
WBROM B70 .... **72** A5

Linthurst First School
BRGRVE B60 .... **214** C3

Lion Industrial Park
ALDR WS9 .... **20** C4

Little Aston CP School
FOAKS/STRLY B74 .... **37** E1

Little London JMI School
WLNHL WV13 .... **28** C5

Little Sutton Junior &
Infant School
MGN/WHC B75 .... **39** F4

Locarno Junior & Infant School
TPTN/OCK DY4 .... **70** B5

The Lock Museum
WLNHL WV13 .... **28** B6

Lode Heath High School
SOLH B91 .... **175** E5

Lodgefarm Junior School
WSLW WS2 .... **30** A3

Lodge Forge Trading Estate
CDYHTH B64 .... **139** E2

Lodge Junior & Infant School
WBROM B70 .... **95** D2

Long Acre Trading Estate
VAUX/NECH B7 .... **101** E6

Long Knowle Primary School
WNSFLD WV11 .... **13** E5

Long Lane Industrial Estate
RMSLY B62 .... **117** F6

Long Lane Medical Centre
RMSLY B62 .... **117** F6

Long Ley Primary School
WOLVN WV10 .... **26** B4

Longmoor Day Special School
SCFLD/BOLD B73 .... **56** C6

Longwill Special School
NFLD/LBR B31 .... **166** C6

Lordswood Boys School
HRBN B17 .... **144** C1

Lordswood Girls School
HRBN B17 .... **144** C1

Lordswood Medical Practice
HRBN B17 .... **145** D3

Lower Farm JMI School
BLOX/PEL WS3 .... **17** E1

Lower Gornal Health Centre
SEDG DY3 .... **89** D3

Low Hill Medical Centre
WOLVN WV10 .... **12** A6

Loxdale Industrial Estate
BILS/COS WV14 .... **48** A5

Loxdale Primary School
BILS/COS WV14 .... **48** B5

Lozells Junior & Infant School
LOZ/NWT B19 .... **99** F6

Lugman Medical Centre
WSL WS1 .... **51** F2

Lutley Primary School
HALE B63 .... **161** F2

Lye Business Centre
HAG/WOL DY9 .... **138** B2

Lye CC
HAG/WOL DY9 .... **137** F4

Lye Mosque
HAG/WOL DY9 .... **138** A4

Lye Town Football Club
HAG/WOL DY9 .... **137** F4

Lyndon Green Junior School
LGN/SDN/BHAMAIR B26 .... **152** B3

Lyndon School
HIA/OLT B92 .... **152** C6

Lyng Primary School
WBROM B70 .... **95** E3

Magreal Industrial Estate
LDYWD/EDGR B16 .... **122** B4

Maidensbridge Primary School
KGSWFD DY6........................ 87 D4

Mainstream Industrial Park
VAUX/NECH B7 .... 125 E2

Malt Mill Industrial Estate
RMSLY B62 .... 141 F1

Mander Shopping Centre
WOLV WV1............................. 2 D4

Maney Hill Primary School
CSCFLD/WYGN B72.............. 81 F1

Manor Farm
Comprehensive School
RUSH/SHEL WS4.................. 33 D1

The Manor General Hospital
WSLW WS2........................... 31 E6

Manor High School
DARL/WED WS10 .... 51 F6

Manor Industrial Estate
WSLW WS2........................... 31 E6

Manor Park Junior &
Infant School
AST/WIT B6 .... 100 C5

Manor Practice
CSCFLD/WYGN B72.............. 59 E5

Manor Primary School
FOAKS/STRLY B74................ 36 C6

Manor Way Primary School
HALE B63 .... 141 E6

Maple Business Park
VAUX/NECH B7 .... 125 D1

Mapledene Junior &
Infant School
LGN/SDN/BHAMAIR B26 ...... 154 A3

Maple Leaf Industrial Estate
WSLW WS2........................... 31 D4

Marcus Galleries
ALE/KHTH/YWD B14 .... 170 A6

Market Street Surgery
KGSWFD DY6....................... 111 F2

Marlborough Junior &
Infant School
BORD B9 .... 126 A6

Marlow Estate
BLKHTH/ROWR B65 .... 117 D6

Marshalls Industrial Estate
BKHL/PFLD WV2.................. 45 E2

Marsh Hill Junior &
Infant Schools
ERDW/GRVHL B23............... 101 D1

Marston Green Clinic
CHWD/FDBR/MGN B37 .... 154 C2

Marston Green Infant School
CHWD/FDBR/MGN B37 .... 154 C2

Marston Green Junior School
CHWD/FDBR/MGN B37 .... 154 C2

Marston Road Industrial Estate
BKHL/PFLD WV2.................. 45 E2

Mary Elliot School
WSLW WS2........................... 32 A3

Maryvale RC Primary School
KGSTG B44.......................... 78 A1

Masjid E Noor Mosque
AST/WIT B6 .... 100 B6

Maternity Welfare Clinic
ETTPK/GDPK/PENN WV4...... 43 F3

Matthew Boulton
Technical College
DIG/EDG B5........................ 147 F1

Mayfield Preparatory School
WSL WS1.............................. 5 G6

Mayfield School
LOZ/NWT B19 .... 99 E5

Maypole Gallery
WMBN WV5.......................... 64 C4

Maypole Health Centre
ALE/KHTH/YWD B14 .... 190 B2

Meadow Green Primary School
HLYWD B47 .... 206 C4

Meadowside Surgery
HIA/OLT B92....................... 175 D1

Meadows Junior & Infant School
NFLD/LBR B31 .... 186 A3

Meadow View Junior &
Infant School
GTB/HAM B43...................... 55 F4

Meadwood Industrial Estate
BILS/COS WV14................... 47 F4

Medina Mosque
WSNGN B18......................... 98 C6

Megabowl
BRLYHL DY5........................ 113 F4

Megabowl
DIG/EDG B5........................ 124 A6

Menzies High School
HHTH/SAND B71 .... 73 E3

Merridale Primary School
BDMR/CCFT WV3.................. 24 C6

Merstone School
CHWD/FDBR/MGN B37 .... 130 C6

Mesty Croft Primary School
DARL/WED WS10 .... 50 C6

Middlemore Business Park
ALDR WS9 .... 34 A1

Middleway Industrial Estate
BHTH/HG B12...................... 148 B2

The Midland Bus &
Transport Museum
HLYWD B47 .... 206 A4

Midland House Dawley
Trading Estate
KGSWFD DY6....................... 87 F5

Midland Institute
CBHAMNW B3........................ 6 C4

Milking Bank Primary School
DUDN DY1........................... 90 A3

Millbuck Industrial Estate
WOLVN WV10........................ 11 F6

Millfield Day Special School
HHTH/SAND B71 .... 73 F3

Mill Lodge Primary School
SHLY B90 .... 192 A3

Minworth Junior & Infant School
WALM/CURD B76................... 83 F6

Mirfield Surgery
STECH B33......................... 129 E4

Moat Farm Junior &
Infant School
LGLYGN/QTN B68 .... 119 E4

Mobarak Health Centre
BHTH/HG B12...................... 148 A4

Molineux Youth & Sports Centre
WOLV WV1............................. 2 C2

Monarch Industrial Estate
SPARK B11......................... 150 C3

Monkspath Business Park
SHLY B90 .... 194 A4

Monkspath Business Park
SOLH B91 .... 194 B5

Monkspath Junior &
Infant School
SHLY B90 .... 211 D1

Monmore Park Industrial Estate
BKHL/PFLD WV2.................. 46 B2

Montgomery Junior &
Infant School
SPARK B11......................... 149 E2

Monway Industrial Estate
DARL/WED WS10 .... 49 F6

The Moore Group Business Centre
WSL WS1............................. 52 A1

Moor Green Football Club
HLGN/YWD B28 .... 172 A4

Moor Green JMI School
MOS/BIL B13....................... 169 E2

Moor Green Lane Medical Centre
MOS/BIL B13....................... 169 E2

Moor Hall Golf Club
MGN/WHC B75...................... 39 F6

Moor Hall Junior & Infant School
MGN/WHC B75...................... 39 F5

Moorlands Junior & Infant School
HHTH/SAND B71 .... 73 D3

Moor Lane Trading Estate
PBAR/PBCH B42.................. 100 B1

Moor Street Industrial Estate
BRLYHL DY5........................ 113 E4

Moreton Community School
WOLVN WV10........................ 12 B4

Moseley C of E Junior &
Infant School
MOS/BIL B13....................... 170 B1

Moseley Cricket Club
ALE/KHTH/YWD B14 .... 170 A5

Moseley Rugby Football Club
MOS/BIL B13....................... 170 A1

Moseley School
MOS/BIL B13....................... 171 F1

Mosque
SPARK B11......................... 149 D4

Mosque & Community Centre
RMSLY B62 .... 141 F1

Mosque Gamkol Sharif
SPARK B11......................... 149 D4

Mosque Ghousia
AST/WIT B6 .... 100 B6

Mosque Noor-ul-uloom
SMHTH B10 .... 150 A1

Mosque Taiyyibah
BDMR/CCFT WV3.................. 44 C1

Mosque & Teaching Centre
VAUX/NECH B7 .... 101 E6

Mossely Junior School
BLOX/PEL WS3..................... 16 B3

Moss Grove Surgery
KGSWFD DY6....................... 111 F1

Mossley Clinic
BLOX/PEL WS3..................... 16 C4

Mossley Primary School
BLOX/PEL WS3..................... 16 B3

Mount Pleasant Primary School
BRLYHL DY5........................ 114 A6

Moxley Industrial Centre
DARL/WED WS10 .... 49 E5

Moxley Medical Centre
DARL/WED WS10 .... 49 E3

Moxley Primary School
DARL/WED WS10 .... 49 D5

Mucklow Hill Industrial Estate
RMSLY B62 .... 141 E4

Mucklow Hill Trading Estate
RMSLY B62 .... 141 E4

Municipal Art Gallery
WOLV WV1............................. 2 D3

Museum & Art Gallery
CBHAMNW B3........................ 6 C5

Museum of the
Jewellery Quarter
WSNGN B18........................ 123 D2

Muslim Foundation Mosque
BFLD/HDSWWD B20............. 99 E4

Nanak Sar Sikh Temple
WSLW WS2........................... 51 D1

National Centre for
Cosmetic Surgery
OLDBY B69 .... 94 C6

National Indoor Arena
CBHAMW B1........................ 123 D5

National Motor Cycle Museum
HIA/OLT B92....................... 178 C1

The Natural Health Centre
BVILLE B30 .... 188 B3

Neachells Lane Industrial Estate
WLNHL WV13........................ 27 F3

Nechells Junior & Infant School
VAUX/NECH B7 .... 101 E5

Nelson Junior & Infant School
CBHAMW B1........................ 123 D5

Nelson Mandela Junior &
Infant School
BHTH/HG B12...................... 149 D4

Neptune Industrial Estate
WLNHL WV13........................ 49 E1

Netherbrook Primary School
DUDS DY2 .... 115 F5

Netherton Business Park
DUDS DY2 .... 115 F4

Netherton C of E Junior School
DUDS DY2 .... 115 E3

Netherton Cricket Club
DUDS DY2 .... 115 D3

Newbridge Doctors Surgery
DUNHL/THL/PER WV6 .... 24 B3

Newbridge Preparatory School
DUNHL/THL/PER WV6 .... 24 A3

New Cross Hospital
WOLVN WV10........................ 27 D2

New Cross Industrial Estate
WOLV WV1........................... 26 C4

Newfield Park Middle School
HALE B63 .... 140 C4

New Hall Junior & Infant School
MGN/WHC B75...................... 60 C4

Newhall Junior & Infant School
MGN/WHC B75...................... 61 E4

Newhampton Open Door Theatre
WOLV WV1............................. 2 B1

New Invention CP School
SHHTH WV12........................ 15 E6

Newman College
RIDG/WDGT B32.................. 165 E3

New Oscott Junior & Infant School
SCFLD/BOLD B73.................. 57 E6

Newton Industrial Estate
BORD B9 .... 125 F5

Newtown Health Centre
LOZ/NWT B19 .... 123 F1

Newtown Junior & Infant School
WBROM B70.......................... 93 F2

Newtown Swimming Pool
LOZ/NWT B19 .... 124 A1

Ninestiles School
ACGN B27 .... 173 D2
Nonsuch Primary School
RIDG/WDGT B32 .... 165 E1
Norfolk House School
EDG B15 .... 145 F1
North Birmingham College
PBAR/PBCH B42 .... 78 A4
North Birmingham
Health Authority
BORD B9 .... 126 C6
North Birmingham
Health Authority
ERDE/BCHGN B24 .... 102 C1
Northbrook Health Centre
SHLY B90 .... 173 E6
Northern Birmingham
Community NHS Trust
BORD B9 .... 127 D5
Northern Birmingham
Community NHS Trust
KGSTG B44 .... 78 C3
Northern Birmingham
Community NHS Trust
WALM/CURD B76 .... 82 B3
Northern Birmingham
Community NHS Trust
WSNGN B18 .... 122 B2
Northfield Health Centre
NFLD/LBR B31 .... 186 B2
Northfield Manor
Primary School
SLYOAK B29 .... 167 D4
Northfield Road Primary School
DUDS DY2 .... 115 F2
Northmoor Industrial Estate
BRLYHL DY5 .... 113 F4
Northside Business Park
WSNGN B18 .... 122 A2
North Solihull Sports Centre
CHWD/FDBR/MGN B37 .... 130 C4
North Walsall Junior &
Infant School
WSLW WS2 .... 32 A3
Northycote High School
WOLVN WV10 .... 12 A2
Norton Medical Practice
STRBR DY8 .... 136 A6
Oak Cottage Primary School
SOLH B91 .... 174 B5
Oakdale Trading Estate
KGSWFD DY6 .... 87 F4
Oakeswell Health Centre
DARL/WED WS10 .... 50 C6
Oakham Junior & Infant School
OLDBY B69 .... 93 D6
Oakham Surgery
OLDBY B69 .... 92 C5
Oaklands Academy of
Theatre Dance
BLOX/PEL WS3 .... 18 C1
Oaklands Primary School
ACGN B27 .... 173 E1
Oakleigh Trading Estate
BILS/COS WV14 .... 69 C3
Oakmeadow Junior School
WNSFLD WV11 .... 14 C6
Oak Street Trading Estate
BRLYHL DY5 .... 114 B6
Oakwood School
ALDR WS9 .... 20 C2
Ocker Hill Junior &
Infant School
TPTN/OCK DY4 .... 71 E3
Odeon Cinema
CBHAM B2 .... 7 E6
Odeon Cinema
CSCFLD/WYGN B72 .... 59 D6
Oldbury Green Retail Park
OLDBY B69 .... 94 B6
Oldbury Health Centre
OLDBY B69 .... 94 C6
Oldbury Jamia Mosque
SMTHWK B66 .... 95 F6
Oldbury Leisure Centre
OLDBY B69 .... 118 A1
Oldbury United Football Club
BLKHTH/ROWR B65 .... 118 A4
Old Bush Trading Estate
BRLYHL DY5 .... 114 A4
Old Church C of E JMI School
DARL/WED WS10 .... 49 E3
Old Edwardians Sports Club
HIA/OLT B92 .... 173 E6

Old Fallings Junior School
WOLVN WV10 .... 12 B4
Oldfields
CDYHTH B64 .... 139 F1
Old Forge Trading Estate
HAG/WOL DY9 .... 138 A3
Old Halesonians
Rugby Football Club
HAG/WOL DY9 .... 160 B1
Old Hall Industrial Estate
BLOX/PEL WS3 .... 17 E5
Old Hall School
WSLW WS2 .... 30 A2
Old Hill Cricket Club
CDYHTH B64 .... 140 B2
Old Hill Junior & Infant School
CDYHTH B64 .... 116 B6
Oldknow School
SMHTH B10 .... 150 A2
Old Limberlost Sports Club
BFLD/HDSWWD B20 .... 98 C2
Old Park Industrial Estate
DARL/WED WS10 .... 50 A5
Old Park Junior & Infant School
DARL/WED WS10 .... 50 A4
Old Park School
DUDN DY1 .... 90 B5
Oldswinford C of E
Primary School
STRBR DY8 .... 136 C6
Old Swinford Hospital School
STRBR DY8 .... 136 C5
Olive Hill School
RMSLY B62 .... 141 F2
One Stop Shopping Centre
PBAR/PBCH B42 .... 99 F2
Open market
BDMR/CCFT WV3 .... 2 C5
Open Market
CBHAMNE B4 .... 7 E4
Open Markets
DIG/EDG B5 .... 124 A6
The Open University
HRBN B17 .... 145 F3
Oratory RC Primary School
LDYWD/EDGR B16 .... 122 B5
Orchard Lane Clinic
HAG/WOL DY9 .... 138 A3
Orthodontists Surgery
ACGN B27 .... 150 C6
Osborne Junior & Infant School
ERDW/GRVHL B23 .... 80 C6
Oscott College
SCFLD/BOLD B73 .... 79 F2
Ounsdale High School
WMBN WV5 .... 64 B4
Ounsdale Sports Centre
WMBN WV5 .... 64 B4
Our Lady of Compassion
Primary School
HIA/OLT B92 .... 173 A4
Our Lady of Fatima RC
Parish School
HRBN B17 .... 144 B2
Our Lady of Lourdes RC
School & Church
MOS/BIL B13 .... 171 F5
Our Lady of St Kenelm RC
Primary School
HALE B63 .... 140 B5
Our Lady of the Wayside RC
Junior & Infant School
SHLY B90 .... 193 E5
Our Lady St Chads RC School
WOLVN WV10 .... 12 B5
Our Ladys RC Junior &
Infant School
STETCH B33 .... 129 F5
Owen Road Trading Estate
WLNHL WV13 .... 29 E6
Oxbarn Social & Sports Club
BDMR/CCFT WV3 .... 44 B2
Oxford Street Industrial Park
BILS/COS WV14 .... 48 B4
Paddys Wide Water
Industrial Estate
BRLYHL DY5 .... 113 E2
Paganel Junior & Infant School
SLYOAK B29 .... 166 C1
Paget Junior & Infant School
ERDE/BCHGN B24 .... 103 E1
Palfrey Infant School
WSL WS1 .... 51 F2

Palfrey Junior Mixed School
WSL WS1 .... 51 F2
Pallasades Shopping Centre
CBHAM B2 .... 6 D6
Palmers Cross Primary School
DUNHL/THL/PER WV6 .... 9 F5
Park Clinic
ERDW/GRVHL B23 .... 80 C6
Parkfield Clinic
BKHL/PFLD WV2 .... 45 F3
Parkfield High School
ETTPK/GDPK/PENN WV4 .... 46 A4
Parkfield Primary School
ETTPK/GDPK/PENN WV4 .... 46 A4
Parkfield Surgery
ETTPK/GDPK/PENN WV4 .... 45 F3
Park Hall Junior Gm School
DSYBK/YTR WS5 .... 53 E2
Park Hall Primary School
DSYBK/YTR WS5 .... 53 E2
Park Hall School
CBROM B36 .... 106 A4
Park Hill Primary School
DARL/WED WS10 .... 51 E5
Parkhill Primary School
MOS/BIL B13 .... 148 B5
Park Lane Industrial Estate
OLDBY B69 .... 94 C6
Park Lane Trading Estate
WOLVN WV10 .... 26 A2
Park Medical Centre
SMHTH B10 .... 150 A2
Parkrose Industrial Estate
SMTHWK B66 .... 97 D5
Parkside Industrial Estate
WOLV WV1 .... 26 B6
Parkside Junior School
SMTHWK B66 .... 121 D2
Park Trading Estate
WSNGN B18 .... 122 C1
Parkview Gallery
ALE/KHTH/YWD B14 .... 169 F4
Park View Lower School
WASH/WDE B8 .... 126 B2
Parkview Trading Estate
HWK/WKHTH B38 .... 188 B2
Parkway Industrial Estate
VAUX/NECH B7 .... 124 C3
Pavilions Shopping Centre
CBHAMNE B4 .... 7 F5
PDH Industrial Estate
DARL/WED WS10 .... 49 E5
PDH Industrial Estate
WLNHL WV13 .... 27 F4
Pedmore C of E Primary School
HAG/WOL DY9 .... 159 D2
Pedmore Road Industrial Estate
BRLYHL DY5 .... 114 B3
Pegasus Junior & Infant School
CVALE B35 .... 105 D1
Pelsall Clinic
BLOX/PEL WS3 .... 18 C1
Pelsall Comprehensive School
RUSH/SHEL WS4 .... 19 D4
Pelsall Village JMI School
BLOX/PEL WS3 .... 18 B1
Pendeford Business Park
COVEN WV9 .... 10 B2
Pendeford Health Centre
COVEN WV9 .... 10 C3
Pendene Complimentary
Medical Centre
WOLV WV1 .... 2 A3
Pennfields Health Centre
BDMR/CCFT WV3 .... 45 D1
Penn Hall Special School
ETTPK/GDPK/PENN WV4 .... 44 A6
Penn Hospital
ETTPK/GDPK/PENN WV4 .... 44 A5
Penn Industrial Estate
DUDS DY2 .... 115 F6
Penn Manor Medical Centre
ETTPK/GDPK/PENN WV4 .... 44 B5
Penns Primary School
CSCFLD/WYGN B72 .... 81 F5
Pens Meadow School
STRBR DY8 .... 112 B4
Pensnett School of Technology
BRLYHL DY5 .... 113 D2
Percy Business Park
OLDBY B69 .... 94 B6
Percy Shurmer Infant School
DIG/EDG B5 .... 148 A2

Percy Shurmer Junior School
BHTH/HG B12 .... **148** A2

Perry Beeches School
PBAR/PBCH B42 .... **77** E3

Perry Common Junior &
Infant School
ERDW/GRVHL B23 .... **79** D4

Perryfields High School
LGLYGN/QTN B68 .... **142** C1

Perryfields Junior &
Infants School
LGLYGN/QTN B68 .... **142** C2

Perry Hall Primary School
WNSFLD WV11 .... **28** B1

Personal & Child Health Centre
BVILLE B30 .... **168** C5

Perton Clinic
DUNHL/THL/PER WV6 .... **22** A3

Perton County First School
DUNHL/THL/PER WV6 .... **22** A2

Perton County Middle School
DUNHL/THL/PER WV6 .... **22** C3

Perton Parish Council
DUNHL/THL/PER WV6 .... **22** A3

Peterbrook Junior &
Infant School
SHLY B90 .... **191** F3

Peters Hill Primary School
BRLYHL DY5 .... **137** E2

Pheasey Clinic
GTB/HAM B43 .... **55** E6

Pheasey Park Farm
Primary School
GTB/HAM B43 .... **55** E5

Phillips Street Industrial Estate
AST/WIT B6 .... **124** B1

Phoenix Industrial Estate
BILS/COS WV14 .... **48** B5

Phoenix International
Industrial Estate
WBROM B70 .... **72** B6

Phoenix Road Industrial Estate
WLNHL WV13 .... **27** F4

Phoenix Works Industrial Estate
DARL/WED WS10 .... **50** A1

Picture Gallery
CBROM B36 .... **105** F6

The Picture Gallery
ERDW/GRVHL B23 .... **80** B5

The Picture House
STRBR DY8 .... **136** C5

The Picture House
WASH/WDE B8 .... **126** C2

The Picture House
WLNHL WV13 .... **27** F3

Pineapple Junior & Infant School
ALE/KHTH/YWD B14 .... **169** D6

Pines Day Special School
CBROM B36 .... **104** B5

Pinfold Industrial Estate
BLOX/PEL WS3 .... **17** E5

Pinfold Street JMI School
DARL/WED WS10 .... **49** E4

Planetary Industrial Estate
WLNHL WV13 .... **27** E3

Plantsbrook School
CSCFLD/WYGN B72 .... **59** E5

Plastic Surgery
SOLH B91 .... **175** E4

Pleck Business Park
WSLW WS2 .... **31** E6

Pleck Industrial Estate
WSLW WS2 .... **51** E1

Police Headquarters
CBHAMNE B4 .... **7** E3

Pool Hayes
Comprehensive School
SHHTH WV12 .... **29** D2

Pool Hayes Primary School
SHHTH WV12 .... **29** D1

Poplar Road Clinic
ALE/KHTH/YWD B14 .... **170** B2

Portway Road Industrial Estate
OLDBY B69 .... **118** A1

Pound Close Surgery
LGLYGN/QTN B68 .... **118** C4

Powke Lane Industrial Estate
CDYHTH B64 .... **116** C5

Premier Business Centre
HAG/WOL DY9 .... **138** C4

Premier Business Park
WSLW WS2 .... **4** A5

Premier Partnership Estate
KGSWFD DY6 .... **113** D3

Premier Trading Estate
VAUX/NECH B7 .... **124** B2

Priestley Smith Special School
ERDW/GRVHL B23 .... **79** D5

Primrose Hill Junior &
Infant School
HWK/WKHTH B38 .... **188** B5

Primrose Lane Health Centre
WOLVN WV10 .... **12** C5

Primrose Trading Estate
DUDS DY2 .... **115** F3

Prince Albert Junior &
Infant School
AST/WIT B6 .... **100** A5

Princes End Junior School
TPTN/OCK DY4 .... **70** A4

Princethorpe Junior &
Infant School
SLYOAK B29 .... **166** C2

Priory Clinic
DUDN DY1 .... **91** D2

Priory Courts
CBHAMNW B3 .... **7** E4

Priory Green Junior &
Infants School
COVEN WV9 .... **10** C3

Priory House Industrial Estate
WSNGN B18 .... **122** C2

Priory Junior Mixed &
Infants School
BLOX/PEL WS3 .... **17** D6

Priory New Way
Industrial Centre
AST/WIT B6 .... **124** A2

The Priory Primary School
DARL/WED WS10 .... **73** F1

The Priory Primary School
DUDN DY1 .... **91** D2

Prospect Trading Estate
CBHAMW B1 .... **6** A4

Providence Industrial Estate
HAG/WOL DY9 .... **138** B3

Pulse Business Centre
WSL WS1 .... **4** D5

Quarry Bank Infant School
BRLYHL DY5 .... **114** C6

Quarry Bank Primary School
BRLYHL DY5 .... **114** C6

Quarry Bank Surgery
BRLYHL DY5 .... **138** C1

Queen Elizabeth Hospital
EDG B15 .... **146** A5

Queen Elizabeth Law Courts
CBHAMNE B4 .... **7** F4

Queen Elizabeth
Psychiatric Hospital
EDG B15 .... **146** A5

Queen Marys Grammar School
WSL WS1 .... **5** H6

Queen Marys High School
RUSH/SHEL WS4 .... **5** F1

Queensbridge School
MOS/BIL B13 .... **170** A1

Queens College
EDG B15 .... **146** B4

Queens Court Trading Estate
WBROM B70 .... **94** B2

Queen Victoria Primary School
SEDG DY3 .... **67** F3

Quincey Rise Surgery
BRLYHL DY5 .... **137** E2

Quinton Junior & Infant School
RIDG/WDGT B32 .... **142** C3

Quinton Local Authority
RIDG/WDGT B32 .... **143** F4

Racecourse Road
Industrial Estate
DUNHL/THL/PER WV6 .... **24** C2

Raddlebarn Junior &
Infant School
SLYOAK B29 .... **168** C2

Radleys Primary School
RUSH/SHEL WS4 .... **19** E6

Radway Industrial Estate
SHLY B90 .... **194** A6

Rakegate Infant School
WOLVN WV10 .... **11** D4

Rakegate Junior School
WOLVN WV10 .... **11** D4

Raleigh Industrial Estate
HDSW B21 .... **97** D4

Ramgarhia Gurdwara Temple
SMHTH B10 .... **149** F2

Ramgarhia Sabha Sikh Temple
WOLV WV1 .... **2** B2

Ramgarhia Sikh Temple
CBHAMW B1 .... **6** A3

Reaside Clinic
RBRY B45 .... **185** D4

Reaside Middle School
RBRY B45 .... **184** A4

Redhall Junior & Infant School
SEDG DY3 .... **89** E2

Redhill Junior & Infant School
YDLY B25 .... **150** C3

Redhill School
STRBR DY8 .... **137** D4

Red Hill Street Clinic
WOLV WV1 .... **25** E3

Redhouse Industrial Estate
ALDR WS9 .... **34** A1

Redhouse Industrial Estate
ALDR WS9 .... **34** C1

Redhouse JMI School
ALDR WS9 .... **34** A2

Rednal Hill Junior &
Infant School
RBRY B45 .... **185** D6

Red Rooster Industrial Estate
ALDR WS9 .... **34** A1

Redwood Business Park
SMTHWK B66 .... **95** E6

Reflex Industrial Park
WLNHL WV13 .... **28** B4

Regent School
OLDBY B69 .... **92** C4

Regents Park Junior &
Infant School
SMHTH B10 .... **149** E1

Regional Health Authority
BKHL/PFLD WV2 .... **45** F2

Regis Comprehensive School
DUNHL/THL/PER WV6 .... **23** D2

Regis Medical Centre
BLKHTH/ROWR B65 .... **117** E6

Register Office
CBHAMW B1 .... **6** B6

Reliance Trading Estate
BILS/COS WV14 .... **47** D4

Reynalds Cross School
HIA/OLT B92 .... **173** F4

Ridgacre House Surgery
RIDG/WDGT B32 .... **143** F3

The Ridge Primary School
STRBR DY8 .... **135** E4

Ridgeway Surgery
SEDG DY3 .... **67** F4

Ridgewood High School
KINVER DY7 .... **135** E4

Ridpool Junior Mixed School
STECH B33 .... **129** D4

River Brook Medical Centre
BVILLE B30 .... **169** D3

R M W Business Centre
HAG/WOL DY9 .... **138** B4

Robbins Business Park
TPTN/OCK DY4 .... **72** A4

Robert Clinic
BVILLE B30 .... **168** A6

Roberts Infant School
SEDG DY3 .... **89** F2

Roberts Primary School
SEDG DY3 .... **90** A1

Robin Hood Junior &
Infant School
HLGN/YWD B28 .... **173** D5

Rocky Lane Trading Estate
VAUX/NECH B7 .... **124** C1

Rood End Primary School
LGLYGN/QTN B68 .... **119** E1

Rookery Road JMI Schools
HDSW B21 .... **98** A4

Rosedale C of E School
SHHTH WV12 .... **29** F2

Rosslyn School
HLGN/YWD B28 .... **172** C6

Rotton Park Medical Centre
LDYWD/EDGR B16 .... **121** F4

Rough Hay JMI School
DARL/WED WS10 .... **49** E2

Rounds Green Junior &
Infant School
OLDBY B69 .... **94** A6

Rovex Business Park
SPARK B11 .... **150** B4

Rowley Hall Junior &
Infant School
BLKHTH/ROWR B65 .... **117** E3

Rowley Regis College
BLKHTH/ROWR B65 .... **117** D4

Rowley Regis Hospital
BLKHTH/ROWR B65 .... **117** D5

Royal Brierley Trading Estate
BRLYHL DY5 .... **113** E5

Royal College of Nursing
EDG B15 .... **146** C1

Royal Orthopaedic Hospital
NFLD/LBR B31 .... **167** D6

Royal Society of Arts
CBHAM B2 .... **6** D5

Royal Theatre
CDYHTH B64 .... **115** F6

Royal Wolverhampton
Junior School
BDMR/CCFT WV3 .... **44** C2

The Royal Wolverhampton School
BKHL/PFLD WV2 .... **45** D2

Rubery Clinic
RBRY B45 .... **184** A6

Ruckleigh School
SOLH B91 .... **195** E1

Rufford Primary School
HAG/WOL DY9 .... **137** E4

Rushall Primary School
RUSH WS4 .... **19** D6

Russell Medical Centre
DARL/WED WS10 .... **72** B1

Russells Hall Hospital
BRLYHL DY5 .... **89** F6

Russells Hall Junior &
Infant School
DUDN DY1 .... **90** A4

Saab Surgery
SPARK B11 .... **150** B6

Sacred Heart Junior &
Infant School
TPTN/OCK DY4 .... **92** B1

Sacred Heart Junior Mixed School
BFLD/HDSWWD B20 .... **99** F4

Saddam Hussain Mosque
BFLD/HDSWWD B20 .... **99** F4

The Safe Harbour
Industrial Estate
AST/WIT B6 .... **78** B6

Sai Medical Centre
WSLW WS2 .... **31** E5

St Albans C of E Primary School
WNSFLD WV11 .... **15** D5

St Albans School
BHTH/HG B12 .... **148** B2

St Alpheges C of E Infant School
SOLH B91 .... **195** E3

St Alpheges Junior School
SOLH B91 .... **195** E3

St Ambrose Barlow RC
Primary School
HLGN/YWD B28 .... **172** C5

St Andrews C of E First School
RBRY B45 .... **215** F1

St Andrews C of E Infant School
DUNHL/THL/PER WV6 .... **24** B3

St Andrews Industrial Estate
BORD B9 .... **125** E5

St Andrews Junior & Infant School
BORD B9 .... **125** D5

St Annes RC Junior &
Infant School
HIA/OLT B92 .... **174** C1

St Annes Industrial Estate
WLNHL WV13 .... **29** D4

St Annes RC Junior &
Infant School
BHTH/HG B12 .... **148** C1

St Annes RC Junior &
Infant School
CHWD/FDBR/MGN B37 .... **130** C5

St Annes RC Primary School
FOAKS/STRLY B74 .... **56** A1

St Anthonys Junior & Infant School
WOLVN WV10 .... **11** F2

St Anthonys RC Junior &
Infant School
CHWD/FDBR/MGN B37 .... **130** C2

St Barnabas C of E
Primary School
ERDE/BCHGN B24 .... **102** C2

St Bartholomews
Primary School
ETTPK/GDPK/PENN WV4 .... **44** A6

St Benedict Biscop Primary School
WMBN WV5 .... **65** D4

St Benedicts Infant School
SMHTH B10 .... **150** B2

St Bernadette RC Junior &
Infant School
YDLY B25 .... **151** D1

St Bernadettes RC Primary School
WMBN WV5 .... **64** B5

St Bernards RC Junior &
Infant School
MOS/BIL B13 .... **171** E2

St Brigids RC Junior &
Infant School
NFLD/LBR B31 .... **186** B2

St Catherines RC Junior &
Infant School
EDG B15 .... **123** F6

St Chads Catholic Primary School
SEDG DY3 .... **67** F4

St Chads Junior & Infants School
LOZ/NWT B19 .... **123** F2

St Chad's RC Cathedral
CBHAMNE B4 .... **6** D2

St Christophers RC Primary School
CDSL WV8 .... **8** C1

St Clares Primary School
BFLD/HDSWWD B20 .... **99** D4

St Clements C of E Junior &
Infant School
VAUX/NECH B7 .... **101** D6

St Columbas RC Junior &
Infant School
RBRY B45 .... **185** F6

St Cuthberts RC School
WASH/WDE B8 .... **127** E3

St Dunstans RC Junior &
Infant School
ALE/KHTH/YWD B14 .... **170** A3

St Edmund Campion RC
Lower School
ERDE/BCHGN B24 .... **81** E5

St Edmund Campion RC School
ERDE/BCHGN B24 .... **81** D5

St Edmund & St John
Primary School
DUDS DY2 .... **92** A4

St Edmunds RC Primary School
WSNGN B18 .... **122** C3

St Edmunds RC School
DUNHL/THL/PER WV6 .... **24** A4

St Edwards RC Primary School
CSHL/WTROR B46 .... **132** C2

St Edwards RC Primary School
CSHL/WTROR B46 .... **132** C4

St Edwards RC School
SLYOAK B29 .... **168** C2

St Francis C of E Primary School
BVILLE B30 .... **167** F5

St Francis Junior & Infant School
RUSH/SHEL WS4 .... **19** E4

St Francis of Assisi RC
Comprehensive School
ALDR WS9 .... **35** E2

St Francis RC Junior &
Infant School
LOZ/NWT B19 .... **99** D6

St George & St Teresa RC
Junior & Infant School
DOR/KN B93 .... **212** C3

St Georges C of E Infants School
LOZ/NWT B19 .... **123** F2

St Georges C of E Primary School
LOZ/NWT B19 .... **123** F2

St Georges Junior Mixed School
LDYWD/EDGR B16 .... **122** B6

St Gerards Orthopaedic Hospital
CSHL/WTROR B46 .... **132** C2

St Giles C of E Junior School
WLNHL WV13 .... **29** D5

St Gregorys RC Primary School
SMTHWKW B67 .... **120** A5

St Huberts Primary School
LGLYGN/QTN B68 .... **119** E6

St James C of E Junior School
OLDBY B69 .... **117** F2

St James C of E Primary School
STRBR DY8 .... **135** F2

St James C of E School
HDSW B21 .... **97** E4

St James Medical Centre
HDSW B21 .... **97** F5

St James RC Junior & Infant School
RBRY B45 .... **184** C6

St James Road Museum &
Art Gallery
DUDN DY1 .... **91** E4

St John Bosco RC Primary School
HHTH/SAND B71 .... **73** D4

St John Fisher RC Junior &
Infant School
NFLD/LBR B31 .... **187** D6

St John & St Monica RC Junior &
Infant School
MOS/BIL B13 .... **148** A5

St Johns C E Primary School
WNSFLD WV11 .... **14** C1

St Johns C of E School
LDYWD/EDGR B16 .... **122** C6

St Johns C of E Junior &
Infant School
LDYWD/EDGR B16 .... **122** C5

St Johns C of E Primary School
DARL/WED WS10 .... **72** B1

St Johns Primary School
SEDG DY3 .... **86** B1

St John the Baptist RC Junior &
Infant School
CBROM B36 .... **107** D6

St John Wall RC School
HDSW B21 .... **97** E3

St Josephs Convent
Preparatory School
DUNHL/THL/PER WV6 .... **24** A1

St Josephs RC Junior &
Infant School
VAUX/NECH B7 .... **125** D1

St Josephs RC Primary School
STRBR DY8 .... **158** B1

St Josephs RC School
DARL/WED WS10 .... **49** E2

St Josephs RC School
MGN/WHC B75 .... **59** E2

St Josephs School
DUDS DY2 .... **92** A4

St Judes Junior & Infant School
DUNHL/THL/PER WV6 .... **24** B3

St Judes Junior School
BDMR/CCFT WV3 .... **24** B5

St Judes RC Junior &
Infant School
ALE/KHTH/YWD B14 .... **190** A3

St Kenelms C of E School
RMSLY B62 .... **182** C1

St Leonards C of E School
BILS/COS WV14 .... **47** D3

St Lukes C of E Junior &
Infant School
DIG/EDG B5 .... **147** F1

St Lukes Infant School
BKHL/PFLD WV2 .... **45** E2

St Lukes Junior School
BKHL/PFLD WV2 .... **45** D2

St Margaret Marys RC
Primary School
ERDW/CRVHL B23 .... **79** E5

St Margarets C of E Junior &
Infant School
HIA/OLT B92 .... **174** B1

St Margarets C of E School
GTB/HAM B43 .... **54** A5

St Margarets Hospital
DSYBK/YTR WS5 .... **54** A1

St Marks Primary School
BRLYHL DY5 .... **89** E6

St Marks RC Junior &
Infant School
PBAR/PBCH B42 .... **76** B4

St Martin de Porres RC Junior &
Infant School
MOS/BIL B13 .... **148** C6

St Martins C of E Primary School
BILS/COS WV14 .... **70** C1

St Martins C of E Primary School
TPTN/OCK DY4 .... **71** D6

St Martins Industrial Estate
OLDBY B69 .... **118** C1

St Mary & John R C J & I School
ERDE/BCHGN B24 .... **102** A3

St Mary Magdalene C of E
Junior & Infant School
HHTH/SAND B71 .... **73** F5

St Mary of the Angels RC School
ALDR WS9 .... **35** D2

St Mary & St Margarets C E
Junior & Infant School
CBROM B36 .... **105** D5

St Marys C of E Junior &
Infant School
SLYOAK B29 .... 167 F2
St Marys C of E Primary School
BFLD/HDSWWD B20 .... 98 C4
St Marys C of E Primary School
KGSWFD DY6 .... 87 F6
St Marys RC Primary School
DARL/WED WS10 .... 50 B5
St Marys RC Primary School
WSL WS1 .... 52 C1
St Marys RC School
BRLYHL DY5 .... 114 A5
St Marys RC School
HRBN B17 .... 145 E4
St Marys RC School
WOLVN WV10 .... 12 C6
St Marys & St Johns RC School
BKHL/PFLD WV2 .... 45 F1
St Matthews C of E Junior &
Infant School
VAUX/NECH B7 .... 124 C3
St Matthews C of E School
SMTHWK B66 .... 121 D2
St Michaels C of E Junior &
Infant School
RIDG/WDGT B32 .... 165 E3
St Michaels C of E School
BLOX/PEL WS3 .... 18 B3
St Michaels C of E
Secondary School
OLDBY B69 .... 117 F2
St Michaels School
WSNGN B18 .... 98 C3
St Nicholas RC School
SCFLD/BOLD B73 .... 80 B1
St Nicholas's C E First School
CDSL WV8 .... 8 B1
St Patricks C of E Junior &
Infant School
HOCK/TIA B94 .... 209 E5
St Patricks Junior Middle &
Infant RC School
WSLW WS2 .... 4 B1
St Patricks Primary School
WNSFLD WV11 .... 27 E2
St Patricks RC Junior &
Infant School
CHWD/FDBR/MGN B37 .... 131 E5
St Patricks RC School
WSNGN B18 .... 122 B3
St Pauls C of E Primary School
TPTN/OCK DY4 .... 70 B5
St Pauls RC Primary School
HWK/WKHTH B38 .... 188 C4
St Peter & Paul RC Primary School
ERDE/BCHGN B24 .... 103 E2
St Peters Collegiate School
DUNHL/THL/PER WV6 .... 24 A4
St Peters RC Junior &
Infant School
RIDG/WDGT B32 .... 165 E2
St Peters RC School
SOLH B91 .... 195 D3
St Peters Surgery
WSLW WS2 .... 31 F3
St Philips RC School
SMTHWK B66 .... 121 D1
St Philips Sixth Form College
LDYWD/EDGR B16 .... 122 B6
St Saviours Junior &
Infant School
WASH/WDE B8 .... 125 F2
St Stephens C of E
Primary School
WOLVN WV10 .... 26 A3
St Teresas RC Primary School
ETTPK/GDPK/PENN WV4 .... 46 A4
St Teresas RC School
BFLD/HDSWWD B20 .... 98 C3
St Thomas C of E School
WNSFLD WV11 .... 13 F6
St Thomas Community
High School
EDG B15 .... 147 E1
St Thomas More
Comprehensive RC School
BILS/COS WV14 .... 48 C2
St Thomas More
Comprehensive School
WLNHL WV13 .... 49 D1
St Thomas More RC
Primary School
LGN/SDN/BHAMAIR B26 .... 153 D4

St Thomas of Canterbury School
BLOX/PEL WS3 .... 32 B1
St Thomas RC Grammar School
HWK/WKHTH B38 .... 187 F2
St Thomas's C of E Junior &
Infant School
EDG B15 .... 147 F1
St Vincent De Paul RC School
VAUX/NECH B7 .... 125 D3
St Wilfrids RC Junior &
Infant School
CBROM B36 .... 104 B5
Salford Trading Estate
AST/WIT B6 .... 101 E5
Salim Mosque
WASH/WDE B8 .... 126 A1
Salisbury Place Industrial Estate
BDMR/CCFT WV3 .... 2 A6
Salisbury Primary School
DARL/WED WS10 .... 50 A2
Saltbrook Trading Estate
HALE B63 .... 138 C2
Saltley Business Park
VAUX/NECH B7 .... 125 F1
Saltley Health Centre
WASH/WDE B8 .... 126 A2
Saltley Industrial Centre
WASH/WDE B8 .... 125 E4
Saltley Leisure Centre
BORD B9 .... 126 C4
Saltley School
BORD B9 .... 126 C4
Salvation Army
CBHAMNE B4 .... 6 D2
Sandown County First School
DUNHL/THL/PER WV6 .... 22 B3
Sandwell Area Health Authority
SMTHWK B66 .... 96 A6
Sandwell Area Health Authority
SMTHWK B67 .... 120 C2
Sandwell Borough Football Club
OLDBY B69 .... 94 A6
Sandwell College
DARL/WED WS10 .... 72 C2
Sandwell College
SMTHWK B66 .... 120 C2
Sandwell College
WBROM B70 .... 95 E2
Sandwell District General Hospital
HHTH/SAND B71 .... 73 F6
Sandwell Health Authority
WBROM B70 .... 95 D1
Sandwell Health Authority Clinic
CDYHTH B64 .... 116 A6
Sandwell Metropolitan
Borough Council
BLKHTH/ROWR B65 .... 118 A3
Sandwell Metropolitan
Borough Council
CDYHTH B64 .... 140 B1
Sandwell Metropolitan
Borough Council
GTB/HAM B43 .... 75 F4
Sandwell Metropolitan
Borough Council
HHTH/SAND B71 .... 74 A3
Sandwell Metropolitan
Borough Council
LGLYGN/QTN B68 .... 119 E2
Sandwell Metropolitan
Borough Council
OLDBY B69 .... 94 A6
Sandwell Metropolitan
Borough Council
SMTHWK B66 .... 120 C1
Sandwell Metropolitan
Borough Council
TPTN/OCK DY4 .... 92 B2
Sandwell Park Industrial Estate
HHTH/SAND B71 .... 96 B4
Sandyhill Industrial Estate
SHLY B90 .... 192 C1
Sapcote Trading Centre
AST/WIT B6 .... 100 C2
Sapcote Trading Centre
CDYHTH B64 .... 116 B4
Sapcote Trading Centre
SMTHH B10 .... 150 A3
Sarehole Mill Museum
MOS/BIL B13 .... 171 F3
Sarehole Surgery
HLGN/YWD B28 .... 172 A3
Sarephed Medical Centre
SMTHWKW B67 .... 120 C2

Sargeant Turner Trading Estate
HAG/WOL DY9 .... 138 B3
Satellite Industrial Park
WLNHL WV13 .... 27 E3
School of Jewellery
CBHAMW B1 .... 123 D3
Scott Arms Shopping Centre
GTB/HAM B43 .... 76 A2
Sears Retail Park
SHLY B90 .... 193 F4
Selly Oak Health Centre
SLYOAK B29 .... 168 A2
Selly Oak Hospital
SLYOAK B29 .... 168 B2
Selly Oak Industrial Estate
SLYOAK B29 .... 168 A2
Selly Oak School
SLYOAK B29 .... 168 A3
Selly Park Girls School
SLYOAK B29 .... 169 D2
Selly Park Surgery
SLYOAK B29 .... 169 D1
Severne Junior & Infant School
ACGN B27 .... 173 E3
Shaftmoor Industrial Estate
HLGN/YWD B28 .... 172 B1
Shard End Surgery
BKDE/SHDE B34 .... 129 E1
Sharmans Cross Junior School
SOLH B91 .... 194 A1
Shaw Hill Junior & Infant School
WASH/WDE B8 .... 126 B3
Shawhurst Primary School
HLYWD B47 .... 206 C1
The Sheila Godfrey Clinic
DOR/KN B93 .... 212 B4
Sheldon Cricket Club
YDLY B25 .... 151 F1
Sheldon Heath School
STECH B33 .... 153 E1
Shelfield Clinic
RUSH/SHEL WS4 .... 19 E5
Shelfield Community School
RUSH/SHEL WS4 .... 19 E3
Shell Corner Industrial Estate
RMSLY B62 .... 141 F1
Shenley Lane Community
Association Sports Centre
SLYOAK B29 .... 166 C5
Shenstone Parish Council
FOAKS/STRLY B74 .... 37 F1
Shenstone Trading Estate
RMSLY B62 .... 141 E5
Shireland Hall Primary School
SMTHWK B66 .... 121 D4
Shireland High School
SMTHWK B67 .... 120 B3
Shirestone Primary School
STECH B33 .... 129 F5
Shiri Krishna Temple
DUDS DY2 .... 91 E5
Shirley Clinic
SHLY B90 .... 193 D2
Shirley Park Sports Club
SHLY B90 .... 210 C3
Shirley Road Health Clinic
ACGN B27 .... 173 D2
Shirley Temple
HLGN/YWD B28 .... 172 C6
Shopping Centre
LOZ/NWT B19 .... 123 E1
Short Heath Clinic
SHHTH WV12 .... 29 F1
Short Heath Junior &
Infant School
ERDW/GRVHL B23 .... 79 F5
Shorth Heath Junior School
SHHTH WV12 .... 29 F2
Showcase Cinemas
ERDE/BCHGN B24 .... 103 F3
Showcase Cinemas
WSLW WS2 .... 30 B6
Showell Green Surgery
SPARK B11 .... 149 E5
Showell Road Industrial Estate
WOLVN WV10 .... 25 F1
Shree Krishna Temple
HHTH/SAND B71 .... 73 D6
Shree Ram Mandir Hindu Temple
SPARK B11 .... 149 D3
Shri Guru Ravidass Temple
BKHL/PFLD WV2 .... 45 F2
Shri Guru Ravidass Temple
WLNHL WV13 .... 28 B6

Sikh Temple
  WLNHL WV13 .... **29** E5
Sikh Temple
  WNSFLD WV11 .... **27** F2
Sikh Temple
  WOLV WV1 .... **3** E3
Sikh Temple
  WSL WS1 .... **52** B2
Silver End Industrial Estate
  BRLYHL DY5 .... **113** D6
Singh Sabha Gurudwara Temple
  BFLD/HDSWWD B20 .... **98** A3
Sir Theodore Pritchett
  Junior & Infant School
  ALE/KHTH/YWD B14 .... **189** F3
Sir Wilfred Martineau School
  STECH B33 .... **129** F4
Sir Wilfrid Martineau School
  STECH B33 .... **129** F4
Sladefield Infants School
  WASH/WDE B8 .... **126** C2
Slade Junior & Infant N C School
  ERDW/GRVHL B23 .... **101** F3
Sledmere Primary School
  DUDS DY2 .... **115** F1
Small Heath Medical Centre
  BORD B9 .... **125** E6
Small Heath Business Park
  SMHTH B10 .... **150** B2
Small Heath Grant
  Maintained School
  SMHTH B10 .... **149** F2
Small Heath School &
  Community Centre
  SMHTH B10 .... **149** F1
Small Heath Trading Estate
  SPARK B11 .... **149** F3
Small Heath Trading Estate
  SPARK B11 .... **150** A3
Smethwick Medical Centre
  SMTHWK B66 .... **120** C1
Smethwick Swimming Centre
  SMTHWKW B67 .... **120** B5
Smiths Picture Gallery
  WBROM B70 .... **95** E3
Smiths Wood Parish Council
  CBROM B36 .... **106** C6
Smiths Wood Secondary School
  CBROM B36 .... **130** C1
Sneyd Community School
  BLOX/PEL WS3 .... **16** A3
Snow Hill Clinic
  BKHL/PFLD WV2 .... **3** E5
Soho Health Centre
  HDSW B21 .... **98** B6
Solihull College
  CHWD/FDBR/MGN B37 .... **131** E3
Solihull College
  SHLY B90 .... **193** F2
Solihull College
  SOLH B91 .... **194** C2
Solihull Football Club
  SOLH B91 .... **194** A1
Solihull Health Authority
  SHLY B90 .... **193** D3
Solihull Health Authority
  SOLH B91 .... **195** E1
Solihull Hospital
  SOLH B91 .... **195** F1
Solihull Ice Rink
  HIA/OLT B92 .... **153** D6
Solihull Magistrates Court
  SOLH B91 .... **195** E2
Solihull Metropolitan
  Borough Council
  SOLH B91 .... **195** E2
Solihull Rugby Union
  Football Club
  SOLH B91 .... **194** B1
Solihull School
  SOLH B91 .... **195** F1
Sommerville Primary School
  SMHTH B10 .... **150** A1
South Birmingham College
  BHTH/HG B12 .... **148** C4
South Birmingham College
  HLGN/YWD B28 .... **172** A3
South Birmingham
  College Technical Centre
  HLGN/YWD B28 .... **172** B2
South Birmingham
  Health Authority
  EDG B15 .... **146** C1

South Birmingham Health
  Authority
  SLYOAK B29 .... **168** A2
South Birmingham Mental
  Health NHS Trust
  BVILLE B30 .... **189** F2
Southern Birmingham
  Community Health NHS Trust
  BHTH/HG B12 .... **148** B4
Southern Birmingham
  Community Health NHS Trust
  MOS/BIL B13 .... **148** A6
Southside Business Centre
  BHTH/HG B12 .... **148** C4
South Staffordshire Council
  CDSL WV8 .... **8** C2
Sovereign Trading Estate
  STRBR DY8 .... **136** A4
Sparkbrook Health Centre
  SPARK B11 .... **149** D2
Sparkhill Swimming Pool &
  Fitness Centre
  SPARK B11 .... **149** E5
Spartan Industrial Centre
  WBROM B70 .... **72** A5
Speedwell Trading Estate
  YDLY B25 .... **150** C3
Spines Clinic
  WMBN WV5 .... **64** B5
Spon Lane Trading Estate
  WBROM B70 .... **95** E3
Sports Centre
  MOS/BIL B13 .... **169** E1
Springdale College
  SLYOAK B29 .... **167** E2
Springdale Primary School
  ETTPK/GDPK/PENN WV4 .... **43** E4
Springfield Industrial Estate
  OLDBY B69 .... **95** D6
Springfield Infant School
  BLKHTH/ROWR B65 .... **116** C3
Springfield Junior Mixed School
  MOS/BIL B13 .... **171** F1
Springfield Junior School
  BLKHTH/ROWR B65 .... **116** C3
Springfield Medical Practice
  SPARK B11 .... **149** F6
Springhill Business Park
  WSNGN B18 .... **122** C3
Spring Lane Industrial Estate
  SHHTH WV12 .... **29** E3
Spring Road Industrial Estate
  ETTPK/GDPK/PENN WV4 .... **46** C5
Sri Guru Ravidass Temple
  DARL/WED WS10 .... **49** F4
Stafford Road Sports Club
  BLOX/PEL WS3 .... **17** D3
Stag Industrial Estate
  BILS/COS WV14 .... **48** C5
Stambermill Industrial Estate
  HAG/WOL DY9 .... **137** F3
Stanhope Road Clinic
  SMTHWKW B67 .... **120** B4
Stanville Junior & Infant School
  LGN/SDN/BHAMAIR B26 .... **153** E3
Starbank Junior & Infant School
  SMHTH B10 .... **151** D1
Start Point Trading Estate
  SPARK B11 .... **149** F5
Station Road Industrial Estate
  BLKHTH/ROWR B65 .... **117** F5
Station Road Industrial Estate
  CSHL/WTROR B46 .... **108** B4
Stechford Health Centre
  STECH B33 .... **128** A5
Stechford Junior & Infant School
  STECH B33 .... **127** F5
Stechford Trading Estate
  STECH B33 .... **128** A3
Stephens Industrial Estate
  SPARK B11 .... **150** B5
Stepping Stones Medical Practice
  DUDN DY1 .... **91** D4
Steps to Health
  WOLVN WV10 .... **12** A6
Stevens Dental Health Centre
  STRBR DY8 .... **136** B5
Stirchley Junior & Infant School
  BVILLE B30 .... **168** C5
Stirchley Trading Estate
  BVILLE B30 .... **169** D5
Stock Exchange
  CBHAMNW B3 .... **6** C4

Stockland Clinic
  ERDW/GRVHL B23 .... **101** F1
Stockland Green Health Centre
  ERDW/GRVHL B23 .... **101** F1
Stockland Green
  Secondary School
  ERDW/GRVHL B23 .... **101** F1
Stone Cross Clinic
  HHTH/SAND B71 .... **74** A2
Stourbridge Clinic
  STRBR DY8 .... **137** D5
Stourbridge College
  STRBR DY8 .... **136** A4
Stourbridge College
  STRBR DY8 .... **136** C5
Stourbridge Cricket Club
  STRBR DY8 .... **136** B2
Stourbridge Football Club
  STRBR DY8 .... **136** B3
Stourbridge Galleries
  STRBR DY8 .... **136** B5
Stourbridge Industrial Estate
  STRBR DY8 .... **136** C3
Stourbridge Rugby Club
  KINVER DY7 .... **135** D3
Stourvale Trading Estate
  HALE B63 .... **139** F3
Stowheath Industrial Estate
  WOLV WV1 .... **46** C1
Stowheath Junior School
  WLNHL WV13 .... **27** F6
Stowlawn Primary School
  BILS/COS WV14 .... **47** E1
The Straits Primary School
  SEDG DY3 .... **66** C6
Stratford Road School Clinic
  SPARK B11 .... **171** F1
Strawberry Lane Industrial Estate
  WLNHL WV13 .... **27** E4
Streetly Clinic Infant
  Welfare Centre
  FOAKS/STRLY B74 .... **56** A1
Streetly Hockey & Cricket Club
  FOAKS/STRLY B74 .... **36** C6
Streetly Methodist
  Recreation Centre
  FOAKS/STRLY B74 .... **36** B5
Streetly Road Surgery
  ERDW/GRVHL B23 .... **79** F5
Streetly School
  FOAKS/STRLY B74 .... **56** B3
Streetsbrook Infant School
  SHLY B90 .... **193** E1
Summerfield Hospital
  WSNGN B18 .... **122** B3
Summerfield Junior &
  Infant School
  WSNGN B18 .... **122** A3
Summerfield School
  WSNGN B18 .... **122** A3
Summerhill Industrial Estate
  CBHAMW B1 .... **123** D4
Summerhill School
  KCSWFD DY6 .... **111** D1
Summit Crescent
  Industrial Estate
  SMTHWK B66 .... **96** A5
Sundridge CP School
  KGSTG B44 .... **56** A5
Sunrise Business Park
  STRBR DY8 .... **136** A2
Sunshine Infant School
  BLOX/PEL WS3 .... **17** E5
Superintendent Public Baths
  BVILLE B30 .... **168** B4
Superintendent Public Baths
  ERDW/GRVHL B23 .... **102** C1
Superintendent Public Baths
  SLYOAK B29 .... **168** B2
Superintendent Public Baths
  SPARK B11 .... **149** E6
Superintendent Public Baths
  VAUX/NECH B7 .... **101** E6
Sutton Arts Theatre
  CSCFLD/WYGN B72 .... **59** E5
Sutton Coldfield College of
  Further Education
  ERDE/BCHGN B24 .... **80** C6
Sutton Coldfield Girls School
  SCFLD/BOLD B73 .... **59** D6
Sutton Coldfield Hospital
  SCFLD/BOLD B73 .... **59** D5

Sutton Coldfield
  Magistrates Court
    FOAKS/STRLY B74.............. **59** D3
Sutton Coldfield Rugby Club
    WALM/CURD B76.............. **82** B2
Sutton Coldfield Town
  Football Club
    CSCFLD/WYGN B72.............. **59** E6
Sutton Coldfield Town Hall
    SCFLD/BOLD B73.............. **59** D3
Sutton College
    CSCFLD/WYGN B72.............. **59** E5
Sutton College
    FOAKS/STRLY B74.............. **59** E3
Sutton College
    SCFLD/BOLD B73.............. **59** E4
Sutton College of
  Further Education
    FOAKS/STRLY B74.............. **59** E3
Sutton Park Surgery
    SCFLD/BOLD B73.............. **56** C4
Sutton School
    DUDN DY1.............. **90** B5
Sutton Town Sports Club
    CSCFLD/WYGN B72.............. **59** E5
Sutton United FC
    MGN/WHC B75.............. **60** A4
The Swallows Industrial Estate
    SHLY B90.............. **193** F5
Swan Lane Industrial Estate
    WBROM B70.............. **72** C6
Swan Medical Centre
    YDLY B25.............. **151** F2
Swanpool Medical Centre
    TPTN/OCK DY4.............. **70** C3
Swanshurst School
    MOS/BIL B13.............. **170** C4
Swimming Baths
    WOLV WV1.............. **2** B3
Sycamore Green CP School
    DUDN DY1.............. **68** B6
Sycamore House Medical Centre
    WSL WS1.............. **52** C1
Talbots Lane Trading Estate
    BRLYHL DY5.............. **114** A6
Tamar Medical Centre
    DUNHL/THL/PER WV6.............. **22** A3
Tamebridge Industrial Estate
    PBAR/PBCH B42.............. **100** A1
Tameside Junior & Infant School
    DARL/WED WS10.............. **73** E1
Tame Valley Junior &
  Infant School
    CBROM B36.............. **103** F5
Tandon Medical Centre
    SEDG DY3.............. **68** A6
Telsen Industrial Centre
    AST/WIT B6.............. **124** B1
Temple Gallery
    CBHAMNW B3.............. **7** E4
Temple Meadow
  Primary School
    CDYHTH B64.............. **116** B6
The Temple
    BHTH/HG B12.............. **148** C2
Tettenhall College
    DUNHL/THL/PER WV6.............. **23** F3
Thorns Primary School
    BRLYHL DY5.............. **138** A1
The Thorns School
    BRLYHL DY5.............. **138** A1
Thornton Junior Mixed School
    WASH/WDE B8.............. **127** D2
Three Crowns Special School
    DSYBK/YTR WS5.............. **34** B6
Ticket Shop
    CBHAMNW B3.............. **6** D5
Tidbury Green Primary School
    SHLY B90.............. **208** A3
Tile Cross Trading Estate
    STETCH B33.............. **129** F6
Timberley Primary School
    BKDE/SHDE B34.............. **129** F1
Tindal Street Junior &
  Infant School
    BHTH/HG B12.............. **148** B4
Tipton Green Junior School
    TPTN/OCK DY4.............. **92** B1
Tipton Sports & Leisure Centre
    TPTN/OCK DY4.............. **71** D2
Tiverton Junior & Infant School
    SLYOAK B29.............. **168** B1
Tividale Business Park
    TPTN/OCK DY4.............. **93** D2

Tividale Comprehensive School
    OLDBY B69.............. **93** E4
Tividale FC
    OLDBY B69.............. **93** D4
Tividale Hall Junior &
  Infant School
    OLDBY B69.............. **92** C4
Tividale Junior & Infant School
    OLDBY B69.............. **93** D3
Tividale Medical Centre
    OLDBY B69.............. **93** F5
Topcliffe Primary School
    CVALE B35.............. **104** C2
Tower Hill Health Centre
    PBAR/PBCH B42.............. **76** C5
Tower Works Industrial Estate
    BDMR/CCFT WV3.............. **24** C6
Town Junior School
    CSCFLD/WYGN B72.............. **59** E5
T P Riley Comprehensive School
    BLOX/PEL WS3.............. **17** E3
Tractor Spares Industrial Estate
    WLNHL WV13.............. **27** F5
Trescott JMI School
    NFLD/LBR B31.............. **185** F2
Trevor Street Industrial Estate
    VAUX/NECH B7.............. **125** E1
Trinity C of E Junior School
    WOLVN WV10.............. **26** B3
Tromans Industrial Estate
    DUDS DY2.............. **115** F4
Tudor Grange School
    SOLH B91.............. **194** C3
Tudor Industrial Estate
    SPARK B11.............. **151** D4
Turves Green Boys School
    NFLD/LBR B31.............. **186** C5
Turves Green Girls School
    NFLD/LBR B31.............. **186** C4
Twickenham Primary School
    KGSTG B44.............. **79** E2
Two Gates Ragged School
    HALE B63.............. **139** E4
Tyburn Industrial Estate
    ERDE/BCHGN B24.............. **103** F3
Tyseley Industrial Estate
    SPARK B11.............. **150** A4
UCI Cinema
    BRLYHL DY5.............. **114** A5
UCI 8 Screens
    SHLY B90.............. **194** A6
Uffculme Clinic
    MOS/BIL B13.............. **170** A1
Uffculme Special School
    MOS/BIL B13.............. **170** A2
Ulverley Junior & Infant School
    HIA/OLT B92.............. **175** D3
Underhill Junior & Infant School
    WOLVN WV10.............. **13** D4
Underhill Primary School
    WOLVN WV10.............. **13** D4
Union Business Park
    WSLW WS2.............. **4** B4
Unisant Trading Estate
    CDYHTH B64.............. **116** B5
University Hospital NHS Trust
    SLYOAK B29.............. **168** A2
University of Aston In
  Birmingham
    CBHAMNE B7.............. **7** G2
University of Birmingham
    EDG B15.............. **146** A3
University of Birmingham
    EDG B15.............. **146** A4
University of Birmingham
    EDG B15.............. **146** B4
University of Birmingham
    EDG B15.............. **146** B5
University of Birmingham
    EDG B15.............. **146** C2
University of Birmingham
    EDG B15.............. **146** C3
University of Birmingham
    EDG B15.............. **146** C3
University of Birmingham
    EDG B15.............. **146** C6
University of Birmingham
    SLYOAK B29.............. **167** D4
University of Birmingham
    SLYOAK B29.............. **167** D5
University of Central England
    BFLD/HDSWWD B20.............. **98** A2
University of Central England
    CBHAMNE B4.............. **7** G1

University of Central England
    CBHAMNE B4.............. **7** G2
University of Central England
    CBHAMNW B3.............. **6** C5
University of Central England
    EDG B15.............. **146** B1
University of Central England
    PBAR/PBCH B42.............. **99** F2
University of Wolverhampton
    DUDN DY1.............. **91** D3
Uplands Junior & Infant School
    BDMR/CCFT WV3.............. **43** F1
Uplands Junior & Infant School
    SMTHWKW B67.............. **120** B4
U S A M Trading Estate
    WOLVN WV10.............. **11** F3
Valley Infant School
    HIA/OLT B92.............. **153** F6
Vaughan Trading Estate
    TPTN/OCK DY4.............. **93** D2
Vauxhall Trading Estate
    VAUX/NECH B7.............. **125** D3
Venkat Medical Centre
    STETCH B33.............. **130** A4
Vernon Trading Estate
    RMSLY B62.............. **141** E1
Vesey Gallery
    SCFLD/BOLD B73.............. **79** F2
Vets Surgery
    NFLD/LBR B31.............. **187** E1
Victoria Health Centre
    SMTHWK B66.............. **121** D3
Victoria Infant School
    TPTN/OCK DY4.............. **70** A6
Village Surgery
    SHLY B90.............. **209** F3
Villiers Primary School
    BILS/COS WV14.............. **47** F2
Villiers Trading Estate
    BKHL/PFLD WV2.............. **45** D2
Vulcan House Business Centre
    SOLH B91.............. **175** E5
Wake Green Football Club
    SHLY B90.............. **192** A5
Wake Green Surgery
    MOS/BIL B13.............. **148** C6
The Wallows Industrial Estate
    BRLYHL DY5.............. **113** F2
Walmley Ash First School
    WALM/CURD B76.............. **82** C4
Walmley Ash Middle School
    WALM/CURD B76.............. **82** C4
Walmley Cricket Club
    WALM/CURD B76.............. **82** A4
Walsall College of Arts &
  Technology
    WSL WS1.............. **4** C4
Walsall College of Technology
    WSLW WS2.............. **4** C2
Walsall Community Health Trust
    WSL WS1.............. **4** C6
Walsall Community Health Trust
    WSL WS1.............. **52** A1
Walsall Cricket Club
    WSL WS1.............. **52** C2
Walsall & District Doctors on Call
    BLOX/PEL WS3.............. **18** B5
Walsall Football Club
    WSL WS1.............. **51** F4
Walsall Health Authority
    WLNHL WV13.............. **28** B5
Walsall Health Authority
    WSL WS1.............. **5** E2
Walsall Health Authority
    WSLW WS2.............. **31** E6
Walsall Metropolitan
  Borough Council
    ALDR WS9.............. **20** B2
Walsall Metropolitan
  Borough Council
    WSL WS1.............. **4** D4
Walsall Metropolitan
  Borough Council
    WSL WS1.............. **4** D2
Walsall Rugby Club
    WSL WS1.............. **52** B3
Walsall Wood Junior &
  Infant School
    ALDR WS9.............. **20** C1
Ward End Junior & Infant School
    WASH/WDE B8.............. **126** C1
Ward End Junior & Infant School
    WASH/WDE B8.............. **127** D1

Ward End Medical Centre
WASH/WDE B8 .... **127** D2

Warley High School
LGLYGN/QTN B68 .... **118** C5

Warley Magistrates Court
OLDBY B69 .... **94** C6

Warren Farm Primary School
KGSTG B44 .... **79** B3

Warstones Primary School
ETTPK/GDPK/PENN WV4 .... **44** A3

Wartell Bank Industrial Estate
KGSWFD DY6 .... **87** F6

Warwick Road Surgery
SPARK B11 .... **149** E4

Warwick Road Trading Estate
SPARK B11 .... **149** F5

Warwickshire Constabulary
CSHL/WTROR B46 .... **132** B1

Warwickshire County Council
CHWD/FDBR/MGN B37 .... **130** C3

Warwickshire County Council
CSHL/WTROR B46 .... **132** B1

Warwickshire County
Cricket Club
DIG/EDG B5 .... **147** F4

Waseley Hills High School
RBRY B45 .... **183** F6

Washwood Heath School
WASH/WDE B8 .... **127** E2

Waterfront Business Park
BRLYHL DY5 .... **113** F3

Waterfront Business Park
BRLYHL DY5 .... **114** A4

Waterloo Industrial Estate
CBROM B36 .... **131** D2

Waterloo Road Jamia Mosque
DUNHL/THL/PER WV6 .... **25** E3

Water Mill Primary School
SLYOAK B29 .... **145** F6

Water Orton Cricket Club
CSHL/WTROR B46 .... **107** D2

Water Orton Primary School
CSHL/WTROR B46 .... **107** D3

Waterside Industrial Estate
BKHL/PFLD WV2 .... **46** C3

Waterside Industrial Estate
BLKHTH/ROWR B65 .... **116** B3

Watery Lane Industrial Estate
WLNHL WV13 .... **27** F4

Wattville Infant School
HDSW B21 .... **97** E6

Wattville Junior Mixed School
HDSW B21 .... **97** D5

Wattville Road Industrial Estate
SMTHWK B66 .... **97** D6

Waverley School
SMHTH B10 .... **150** C1

Webnor Industrial Estate
BKHL/PFLD WV2 .... **46** C3

Wednesbury Art Gallery
DARL/WED WS10 .... **72** B1

Wednesbury Chiropody Surgery
DARL/WED WS10 .... **50** B6

Wednesbury Cricket Club
DARL/WED WS10 .... **50** C5

Wednesbury Leisure Centre
DARL/WED WS10 .... **50** A6

Wednesbury Medical Centre
DARL/WED WS10 .... **72** A1

Wednesbury Oak Junior &
Infant School
TPTN/OCK DY4 .... **70** C2

Wednesbury Rugby Club
DARL/WED WS10 .... **72** B2

Wednesbury Town Hall
DARL/WED WS10 .... **72** B1

Wednesfield Football Club
WNSFLD WV11 .... **27** E1

Wednesfield High School
WNSFLD WV11 .... **28** A2

Wednesfield Village
Primary School
WNSFLD WV11 .... **27** F2

Welford School
BFLD/HDSWWD B20 .... **98** C5

Welsh House Farm Junior &
Infant School
RIDG/WDGT B32 .... **144** B5

Welsh Rugby Club
HIA/OLT B92 .... **177** E1

Weoley Castle Health Centre
SLYOAK B29 .... **166** C2

Weoley Castle Ruins & Museum
SLYOAK B29 .... **166** C1

Weoley Park Surgery
SLYOAK B29 .... **167** E2

Westacre Infant School
BDMR/CCFT WV3 .... **23** F6

West Birmingham
Community Health Council
CBHAMNW B3 .... **6** C3

West Bromwich Albion
Football Club
HHTH/SAND B71 .... **97** D4

West Bromwich Dartmouth
Cricket Club
HHTH/SAND B71 .... **96** B3

West Bromwich Magistrates Court
WBROM B70 .... **95** E2

Westcroft Special School
WOLVN WV10 .... **13** D3

West Cross Shopping Centre
SMTHWK B66 .... **95** F6

Western Business Park
RMSLY B62 .... **141** D2

Westfield County Primary School
WMBN WV5 .... **64** C4

Westgate Trading Estate
ALDR WS9 .... **34** A1

West Heath Hospital
HWK/WKHTH B38 .... **187** E5

West Heath Junior Mixed School
NFLD/LBR B31 .... **187** E4

Westhill College of Education
SLYOAK B29 .... **167** F2

Westhill College of Education
SLYOAK B29 .... **167** F3

West House School
EDG B15 .... **147** E1

West Midlands County Council
HALE B63 .... **141** D6

West Midlands Health Authority
LDYWD/EDGR B16 .... **122** A6

West Midlands Hospital
HALE B63 .... **139** F4

Westminster Industrial Estate
DUDS DY2 .... **115** F5

Westminster Junior School
BFLD/HDSWWD B20 .... **99** E4

Westminster Surgery
BFLD/HDSWWD B20 .... **99** E4

Weston Lane Industrial Estate
SPARK B11 .... **150** A5

West Park Hospital
WOLV WV1 .... **2** A3

West Park Hospital
WOLV WV1 .... **24** C5

West Park Infant School
WOLV WV1 .... **2** B2

West Park Junior School
WOLV WV1 .... **2** B1

Westwood Business Park
AST/WIT B6 .... **100** C4

Wharton Street
Industrial Estate
VAUX/NECH B7 .... **101** F5

Wheelers Lane Junior
Mixed School
ALE/KHTH/YWD B14 .... **170** B4

Wheelers Lane
Secondary School
ALE/KHTH/YWD B14 .... **170** B4

Whetstone Field Primary School
ALDR WS9 .... **35** D3

Whitecrest Primary School
GTB/HAM B43 .... **76** C1

Whitehall Industrial Park
TPTN/OCK DY4 .... **72** A6

Whitehall Infant School
WSL WS1 .... **52** A2

Whitehall Junior
Community School
WSL WS1 .... **52** B2

Whiteheath Clinic
OLDBY B69 .... **117** F2

Whitehouse Common
Junior & Infant School
MGN/WHC B75 .... **59** F2

Whitesmore Secondary School
CHWD/FDBR/MGN B37 .... **130** B6

Whitgreave Infant School
WOLVN WV10 .... **12** A5

Whitgreave Junior School
WOLVN WV10 .... **12** A5

Whitmore Medical Centre
WOLV WV1 .... **2** C1

Whitmore Reans Health Centre
DUNHL/THL/PER WV6 .... **24** C3

Whittington Oval Primary School
STETCH B33 .... **128** B5

Whittles Art Gallery
MOS/BIL B13 .... **148** B6

Wholesale Markets
DIG/EDG B5 .... **124** A6

Widney Junior School
SOLH B91 .... **194** B4

Wightwick Hall Special School
DUNHL/THL/PER WV6 .... **22** A5

Wilkes Green Junior &
Infant School
HDSW B21 .... **98** A4

Wilkinson Primary School
BILS/COS WV14 .... **48** B6

Willenhall Lane Industrial Estate
BLOX/PEL WS3 .... **16** C5

Willenhall Leisure Centre &
Public Baths
WLNHL WV13 .... **29** D6

Willenhall Town Football Club
WLNHL WV13 .... **28** B4

Willenhall Trading Estate
WLNHL WV13 .... **28** B6

William Cowper Primary School
LOZ/NWT B19 .... **124** A1

Willingsworth High School
TPTN/OCK DY4 .... **71** D1

Wilson Stuart School
ERDW/GRVHL B23 .... **79** E5

Windsor Gm High School
HALE B63 .... **140** B5

Windsor Industrial Estate
VAUX/NECH B7 .... **124** C2

Windward Way Industrial Estate
CBROM B36 .... **106** B5

Windy Arbor Junior School
CHWD/FDBR/MGN B37 .... **131** F5

Winster Grove Industrial Estate
KGSTG B44 .... **78** A1

Wishaw Cricket Club
WALM/CURD B76 .... **84** C1

Withymoor Primary School
BRLYHL DY5 .... **113** F6

Withy Road Industrial Estate
BILS/COS WV14 .... **47** E6

Witton Industrial Estate
AST/WIT B6 .... **100** C3

Witton Park Industrial Estate
AST/WIT B6 .... **100** C4

Woden Avenue Junior &
Infant School
WNSFLD WV11 .... **27** D1

Woden Junior School
WOLVN WV10 .... **26** A3

Wodensborough High School
DARL/WED WS10 .... **73** D1

Wollescote Business Park
HAG/WOL DY9 .... **138** B4

Wollescote Primary School
HAG/WOL DY9 .... **138** B5

Wolverhampton & Bilston
Athletic Club
DUNHL/THL/PER WV6 .... **24** B1

Wolverhampton Borough Council
WOLV WV1 .... **2** C4

Wolverhampton Borough Council
WOLV WV1 .... **2** D2

Wolverhampton Cricket Club
DUNHL/THL/PER WV6 .... **23** E1

Wolverhampton Grammar School
BDMR/CCFT WV3 .... **24** B5

Wolverhampton Healthcare
NHS Trust
WOLVN WV10 .... **27** D3

Wolverhampton Metropolitan
Borough Council
BDMR/CCFT WV3 .... **24** A6

Wolverhampton Metropolitan
Borough Council
WOLV WV1 .... **3** E2

Wolverhampton University
WOLVN WV10 .... **25** E1

Wolverhampton Wanderers
Football Club
WOLV WV1 .... **2** C1

Wombourne Cricket Tennis &
Bowling Club
WMBN WV5 .... **64** C4

Wombrook Industrial Estate
WMBN WV5 .... **64** A5

Woodacre Surgery
ERDE/BCHGN B24 .... **103** E2

Woodbourne Priory Hospital
HRBN B17 .... **121** E6
Woodcock Hill Junior & Infant School
NFLD/LBR B31 .... **166** A4
Woodcross Clinic
BILS/COS WV14.............................. **68** C1
Wood End Primary School
WNSFLD WV11 .... **13** F6
Woodgate Business Park
RIDG/WDGT B32 .... **165** D1
Woodgate Junior and Infant School
RIDG/WDGT B32 .... **165** D2
Woodgate Valley Health Centre
RIDG/WDGT B32 .... **165** E1
Wood Green High School
DARL/WED WS10 .... **51** D4
Wood Green Junior School
DARL/WED WS10 .... **50** B5
Woodlands Infant School
SHLY B90 .... **193** D5
Woodlands JMI School
SHHTH WV12................................ **29** F1
Woodlands Junior & Infant School
CBROM B36................................... **131** D1
Woodlands Road Mosque
SPARK B11 .... **171** E1
The Woodrush High School
HLYWD B47 .... **206** C1
Woodrush Rugby Club
HWK/WKHTH B38.......................... **205** D3
Woodsbank Trading Estate
DARL/WED WS10 .... **49** F5
The Woodsbank Trading Estate
DARL/WED WS10 .... **49** F5
The Woodsetton School
SEDG DY3 .... **68** B4
Woodside Industrial Estate
BRLYHL DY5.................................. **114** B2
Woodthorne Primary School
DUNHL/THL/PER WV6 .... **23** D3

Woodthorpe Primary School
ALE/KHTH/YWD B14 .... **170** A6
Woodthorpe Surgery
ALE/KHTH/YWD B14 .... **170** A6
Worcester Street Surgery
STRBR DY8 .... **136** B4
Wordsley Green Health Centre
STRBR DY8 .... **111** F5
Wordsley Hospital
STRBR DY8 .... **112** A4
Wrens Nest Junior School
DUDN DY1..................................... **90** C1
Wrens Nest Secondary School
DUDN DY1..................................... **69** D6
Wulfrun College
BDMR/CCFT WV3 .... **24** B5
Wulfrun College
WOLV WV1..................................... **2** C2
Wulfrun Shopping Centre
WOLV WV1..................................... **2** D5
Wulfrun Trading Estate
DUNHL/THL/PER WV6 .... **25** E2
Wychall Farm Infant School
NFLD/LBR B31 .... **187** E3
Wylde Green College
SCFLD/BOLD B73 .... **81** D2
Wylde Green Primary School
SCFLD/BOLD B73 .... **81** D4
Wyndcliffe Infant School
BORD B9 .... **125** E6
Wyndcliffe Junior School
BORD B9 .... **125** F6
Wyndley Leisure Centre
SCFLD/BOLD B73 .... **58** C4
Wyndley Swimming Baths
SCFLD/BOLD B73 .... **58** C5
Wynford Industrial Estate
YDLY B25...................................... **151** E4
Wythall Health Centre
HLYWD B47 .... **190** C6

Wythall Parish Council
HLYWD B47 .... **206** B2
Yardley Green Health Centre
BORD B9 .... **126** B6
Yardley Green Medical Centre
SMHTH B10................................... **149** E1
Yardley Junior School
LGN/SDN/BHAMAIR B26 .... **151** F2
Yardley Medical Centre
YDLY B25...................................... **151** D2
Yardleys Lower School
SPARK B11.................................... **150** A6
Yardleys School
SPARK B11.................................... **150** A6
Yardleys Upper School
SPARK B11.................................... **150** A5
Yardley Wood Health Centre
ALE/KHTH/YWD B14 .... **171** E6
Yardley Wood Junior Mixed School
ALE/KHTH/YWD B14 .... **191** F1
Yarnfield Junior & Infant School
HLGN/YWD B28 .... **150** C6
Yenton Infant School
ERDE/BCHGN B24 .... **81** D5
Yenton Junior Mixed School
ERDE/BCHGN B24 .... **81** E6
Yew Tree Hills Infant School
DUDS DY2 .... **115** D2
Yew Tree Primary School
DSYBK/YTR WS5 .... **53** D5
Yew Tree Primary School
SOLH B91...................................... **176** A6
Yorkmead Junior & Infant School
HLGN/YWD B28 .... **172** B1
Yorkswood Junior & Infant School
CHWD/FDBR/MGN B37 .... **130** B2
Zip Theatre
WOLV WV1...................................... **2** C1

Page 16

C3
1 Hollybank Cl
2 Kempthorne Gdns

Page 25

E5
1 Blossom's Fold
2 Corporation St
3 Darlington Yd
4 Mitre Fold
5 North St
6 Paternoster Rw
7 Queen Sq
8 Ring Road St
   Andrews
9 School St
10 Townwell Fold
11 Whitmore Hl

F5
1 Broad St
2 Castle Yd
3 Chubb St
4 Fryer St
5 Horseley Flds
6 Lichfield St
7 Little Park St
8 Long St
9 Market St
10 Princes Sq
11 Princess St
12 Railway St
13 Ring Road St Davids
14 St Mary's St
15 Short St
16 Westbury St
17 Wheeler's Fold
18 Whitmore St

F6
1 Bilston St
2 George's Pde
3 George St
4 Hospital St
5 Ring Road St
   Georges

Page 48

C4
1 Burns Pl
2 Horace Partridge Rd

Page 52

C5
1 Burford Cl
2 Camden Cl
3 Charnwood Rd
4 Plantation Rd

C6
1 Angelica Cl
2 Betony Cl
3 Bourton Cl
4 Burdock Cl
5 Buttercup Cl
6 Camomile Cl
7 Campion Cl
8 Germander Dr
9 Mallow Cl
10 Oxlip Cl
11 Rosehip Cl
12 Willowherb Cl
13 Woodstock Cl

Page 64

A5
1 Birch Coppice
2 Brookside Cl
3 Campion Cl
4 The Celandines
5 Clap Gate Gv
6 Deepdales
7 Forge Leys
8 The Hedges
9 Monks Cl
10 The Paddock
11 Rosebury Gv
12 Rushwater Cl

Page 70

B1
1 Masefield Cl

C3
1 Cranmore Cl
2 Eastfield Rd
3 Henn St
4 Kingsbury Rd
5 Kingsway Av
6 Mansell Rd
7 Mayhurst Cl
8 Palethorpe Rd
9 Stokes Av
10 Woodhall Cl
11 Wythwood Gv

C6
1 Cory Cft
2 Devine Cft
3 Edward Fisher Dr
4 Pepperbox Dr
5 Richmond Aston Dr
6 Simeon Bissell Cl
7 Stanton Gv

Page 71

E5
1 Broad Cft
2 Cinquefoil Leasow
3 Clover Piece
4 Coburg Cft
5 Cochrane Cl
6 Deeley Dr

Page 90

A2
1 Clearwell Gdns
2 Dinham Gdns
3 Dudmaston Wy
4 Hever Cl
5 Sedgefield Cl
6 Stokesay Ri
7 Winchcombe Cl

Page 91

F5
1 Bean Rd
2 Campbell St
3 Constitution Hl
4 Lloyd St
5 New Bond St
6 Oakeywell St
7 Rollason Rd
8 Shedden St
9 Spring Gdns

Page 92

C3
1 Barnett St
2 Beatrice Wk
3 Charlotte Cl
4 Crown Wk
5 Danks St
6 Elizabeth Ms
7 Lara Gv
8 Oakthorpe Gdns

Page 105

F4
1 Bowshot Cl
2 Foxford Cl
3 Hillhurst Gv
4 Kingsford Cl
5 Redliff Av
6 Springbrook Cl

Page 113

D2
1 Harriet Cl
2 Heydon Rd
3 Kingsford Nouveau
4 The Nook
5 Wesley Rd

Page 117

E6
1 Bassano Rd
2 Beet St
3 Ben Willetts Wk
4 Birmingham Rd
5 Cross St
6 Downing Cl
7 Frank Tommey Cl
8 The Heathlands
9 High St
10 Lench Cl
11 Marlow St
12 Payne St
13 Sturman Dr
14 Union St
15 Upper Ashley St
16 West St

Page 118

A1
1 Bristam Cl

A3
1 Canterbury Cl
2 Durham Rd
3 Ely Cl
4 Richards Cl
5 Truro Cl
6 Winchester Cl

Page 122

C5
1 Ashton Cft
2 Darnley Rd
3 Graston Cl
4 Sadlers Wk

Page 123

F5
1 Beak St
2 Bennett's Hl
3 Ethel St
4 John Bright St
5 Lower Severn St
6 Paradise St
7 Royal Mail St
8 Station St
9 Stephenson St
10 Swallow St
11 Temple Pas
12 Waterloo St

F6
1 Brownsea Dr
2 Chapmans Pas
3 Ellis St
4 Ernest St
5 Exeter Pas
6 Florence St
7 Hinckley St
8 John Bright St
9 Marshall St
10 St Jude's Pas
11 Severn St
12 Suffolk Pl
13 Upper Marshall St
14 Windmill St

Page 124

A6
1 Bath Pas
2 Claybrook St
3 Dean St
4 Gloucester St
5 Hurst St
6 Ladywell Wk
7 Skinner La
8 Smithfield Pas
9 Theatre Ap
10 Upper Dean St
11 Wrottesley St

C3
1 Adams St
2 Great Brook St
3 Newhaven Cl
4 Windsor St

C4
1 Forster St
2 Gopsal St
3 Lawford Cl
4 Northumberland St
5 Pitt St
6 St James' Pl

C5
1 Belmont Pas
2 Fawdry St
3 Little Edward St

C6
1 Bromley St
2 Clyde St
3 Hack St

Page 125

D5
1 Alport Cft
2 Farmacre
3 Hoff Beck Court Ct
4 Langdon St
5 Mease Cft
6 Mill Burn Wy
7 Quigley Av
8 Towpath Cl

F6
1 Bertram Rd
2 Eversley Rd
3 Hafton Gv
4 Holmwood Rd
5 Little Green La
6 North Warwick St

Page 126

C4
1 Bramble Dell
2 Newbank Gv

Page 127

F6
1 Bonham Gv
2 Laxton Gv
3 Linford Gv
4 Marlborough Gv
5 Rickyard Cl
6 Stuart's Dr

Page 128

C6
1 Fleetwood Gv
2 Fontley Cl
3 The Hays Kent's Moat
4 Somerland Rd

Page 129

D1
1 Ankermoor Cl
2 Appledorne Gdns
3 Camrose Cft
4 Copplestone Cl
5 Lingfield Gdns
6 Polesworth Gv
7 Ridgewood
8 Schoolacre Rd
9 Shepherds Standing

Page 136

A1
1 Aldridge Cl
2 Essington Cl
3 Harrop Wy
4 The Houx
5 The Junction
6 Zouche Cl

B4
1 Ballarat Wk
2 Enville Pl
3 Hemmings Cl
4 Hemplands Rd
5 Holly Gv
6 School St
7 Short St
8 Summer St

C5
1 Chapel St
2 College Rd
3 Prospect Gdns

C6
1 Craufurd Ct
2 Craufurd St
3 Farlands Dr
4 Foxfield Dr
5 Hall St
6 Heath La
7 Marlborough Dr
8 Oldfield Dr
9 Prospect Rw
10 Winchester Dr

Page 139

E4
1 Fatherless Barn Crs
2 Juniper Rl

Page 140

B1
1 Applewood Gv
2 Edgewood Cl
3 Meadow St
4 Penn St
5 Rowley Hill Vw
6 South Bank Rd
7 Woodcroft Cl
8 Woodland Rl

C5
1 High Leasowes
2 Queen St
3 Victoria St
4 Whitefriars Dr

C6
1 Bredon Ct
2 Broome Cl
3 Claremont Wy
4 Honeybourne Cl
5 Instone Rd
6 Pickersleigh Cl
7 Queensway
8 Wesson Gdns
9 Wychbury Ct

Page 141

F6
1 Carisbrooke Dr
2 County Park Av
3 Cricklewood Dr
4 Masefield Rl
5 Sandals Ri
6 Wentworth Rl

Page 148

A2
1 Barrow Wk
2 Berrington Wk
3 Clissold Cl
4 Cumberland Av
5 Horton Sq
6 Kinver Cft
7 Longmore St
8 Rathbone Cl
9 Rolling Mill Cl

A3
1 Cobden Gdns
2 Fitters Mill Cl
3 Four Stones Gv
4 Hampden Retreat
5 Hawkins Cl
6 Minivet Dr
7 Reaside Cft
8 Siskin Dr
9 Willmcote Cl

B3
1 Hollycot Gdns
2 Lapworth Gv
3 Royston Cft
4 Trevorne Cl
5 Upper Balsall Heath
   Rd
6 Vincent Cl

C4
1 Ash Av
2 Beech Av
3 Elm Av
4 Fir Av
5 Holly Av
6 Ivy Av
7 Laurel Av
8 Lilac Av
9 Malvern St
10 May Av
11 Myrtle Av
12 Oak Av
13 Sunny Av
14 Sycamore Av
15 Vine Av

Page 149

D1
1 Bassett Cft
2 Bolton Rd
3 Cooksey Rd
4 Gisborn Cl
5 Lawden Rd
6 Sandfields Av

D4
1 Ash Gv
2 Ash Wy
3 Beach Av
4 Beach Brook Cl
5 Chesterton Av
6 Colville Wk
7 Ivy Av
8 Swallow Cl
9 Trenville Av
10 Whitbourne Cl

E4
1 Inglewood Rd
2 Johnson Cl
3 Shakespeare St
4 Stratford St

Page 166

C4
1 Summerfield Dr
2 Tredington Cl
3 Trefoil Cl

Page 188

A5
1 Beech Hurst
2 Longdales Rd
3 Lydbrook Covert
4 Offenham Covert
5 Old Lime Gdns
6 Redbrook Covert
7 Sedgeberrow Covert
8 Tarrington Covert
9 Whitebeam Cft

Page 189

E3
1 Barnpark Covert
2 Cherhill Covert
3 Dorstone Covert
4 Drews Meadow Cl
5 Elkstone Covert
6 Goodrich Covert
7 Sherston Covert
8 Southwood Covert
9 Stapleford Cft
10 Swansbrook Gdns
11 Willsbridge Covert
12 Winterbourne Cft
13 Wynstead Covert

Page 194

B1
1 Sharmans Cross Rd

Notes

Notes